THIRD EDITION

ADVERTISING

PRINCIPLES AND PRACTICE

WILLIAM WELLS
University of Minnesota

JOHN BURNETT
University of Denver

SANDRA MORIARTY
University of Colorado

Prentice Hall, Englewood Cliffs, New Jersey 07632

THIRD EDITION

ADVERTISING

PRINCIPLES AND PRACTICE

Library of Congress Cataloging-in-Publication Data

Wells, William,
    Advertising : principles and practice / William Wells, John
Burnett, Sandra Moriarty. — 3rd ed.
        p.   cm.
    Includes bibliographical references and index.
    ISBN 0-13-722869-4
    1. Advertising.   I. Burnett, John.   II. Moriarty,
Sandra E. (Sandra Ernst)   III. Title.
HF5823.W455   1995
659.1—dc20   94-30364
                                              CIP

ADVERTISING: *Principles and Practice,* THIRD EDITION

Acquisition Editor: David Borkowsky

Editor-in-Chief for Development: Stephen Deitmer

Development Editors: Patricia Nealon and Robert Watrous

Production Editor: Esther S. Koehn

Managing Editor: Frances Russello

Interior/Cover Designer: B B & K Design, Inc.

Design Director: Patricia Wosczyk

Copy Editor: Donna Mulder

Proofreader: Anne Bosch

Permissions Editor/Ad Researcher: Mary Helen Fitzgerald

Photo Editor: Lorinda Morris-Nantz

Photo Researcher: Ilene Bellovin

Buyer: Marie McNamara

Supplements Package: Wendy Goldner and Melissa Steffens

Editorial Assistant: Cathi Profitko

Production Assistant: Renée Pelletier

Director of Marketing: Sandra Steiner

Marketing Manager: Patti Arneson

CHAPTER OPENING ILLUSTRATIONS: Chapter 1, adidas America; Chapter 2, Simona Cali Cocuzza/Black Star; Chapter 3, Charlie Cole/Sipa Press; Chapter 4, Oldsmobile Division of General Motors; Chapter 5, Procter & Gamble; Chapter 6, Copper Mountain Resort; Chapter 7, William Wrigley, Jr. Co.; Chapter 8, David Young-Wolff/PhotoEdit; Chapter 9, V & S Vin & Spirit AB; Chapter 10, Michael Newman/PhotoEdit; Chapter 11, W.B. Spunbarg/PhotoEdit; Chapter 12, Bob Daemmrich/Image Works; Chapter 13, PepsiCo., Inc.; Chapter 14, Joe Barahan/Stock Market; Chapter 15, Christopher Covatta; Chapter 16, Ceridian; Chapter 17, Mark Waki/Thiokol Corp.; Chapter 18, AP/Wide World Photos; Chapter 19, PepsiCo, Inc.; Chapter 20, Orlando/Orange County Convention & Visitors Bureau, Inc.; Chapter 21, Gamma Liaison; Chapter 22, Videocart, Inc.; Chapter 23, Del Mulkey/Photo Researchers and Hans Rudolph Jost.

 © 1995, 1992, 1989 by Prentice-Hall, Inc.
A Simon & Schuster Company
Englewood Cliffs, NJ 07632

Printed in the United States of America
10 9 8 7 6 5 4 3 2 1

ISBN 0-13-722869-4

Prentice-Hall International (UK) Limited, *London*
Prentice-Hall of Australia Pty. Limited, *Sydney*
Prentice-Hall Canada Inc, *Toronto*
Prentice-Hall Hispanoamericana, S.A., *Mexico*
Prentice-Hall of India Private Limited, *New Delhi*
Prentice-Hall of Japan, Inc., *Tokyo*
Prentice-Hall of Southeast Asia Pte. Ltd., *Singapore*
Editora Prentice-Hall do Brasil, Ltda., *Rio de Janeiro*

OVERVIEW

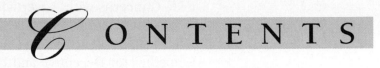

CONTENTS

$\mathcal{P}$ART II   ADVERTISING BACKGROUND, PLANNING, AND STRATEGY

5 The Consumer Audience   161

6 Strategic Research   207

12   Media Buying   395

$\mathcal{P}$ART V   ADVERTISING OPERATIONS

$\mathscr{P}$ART VI MISCELLANEOUS ADVERTISING

22 *Business-to-Business and Retail Advertising*   701

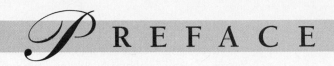

PREFACE

Advertising: Principles and Practice, Third Edition, is a comprehensive textbook and teaching package that brings advertising alive. This text's strengths are many. First, the voices of *real practitioners* are interwoven with the practical and theoretical lessons throughout the book. Second, today's *integrated marketing communications* approach has been incorporated in a meaningful way. Third, the book is *complete* and *current*. Fourth, content, organizations, and writing style offer students an appealing and thorough introduction to the field of advertising. Fifth, the teaching package provides the instructor with the tools needed to engage and hold student interest.

We have all heard the words and processed the images that advertising offers, from Just Do It to the Golden Arches. We know what appeals to us and entertains us. But what makes us buy? How does an advertising message convince us to make a purchase? How is that message built? How is it conveyed? How does that message fit into a business's strategy? In an introductory advertising course, students have only a few months to tackle these and other questions. *Advertising: Principles and Practice* provides the answers.

ADVERTISING AND THE REAL WORLD

Advertising professionals often question whether this field can be taught from a book. Although nothing compares with the experience of *being there*, it is a fact of life that all college students who want an introduction to advertising will not work in an advertising agency. How does this book help solve this problem?

PROFESSIONAL VOICES

To provide a real-life view of advertising for a student who wants an introduction to the field, we have consulted specialists from the different areas of advertising and brought their stories to life. Much of the narrative in this text reflects advertising as those working in the field see it—their theories, their styles and approaches, their rules of thumb, their hindsight and foresight, and their visions. Of course, not everyone in the field agrees with everyone else, so this book presents a variety of theories, styles, and approaches.

FOCUS ON EFFECTIVENESS

All the various professionals working in the field are important to getting the job done—artists, producers, performers, composers and arrangers, researchers, accountants, salespeople, and managers, to name a few. The focus of all their efforts, regardless of their area of expertise, is on the *most effective way to present a sales message to a potential consumer*. This is the focus of advertising departments and advertising agencies, of media sales departments and consumer behavior researchers, of huge global mega-agencies and small creative boutiques. All of these activities are ultimately directed at producing a message that sells something to someone, and that, too, is the focus of this book.

ART AND SCIENCE

Advertising is a combination of specialized skills and professions that incorporate a number of approaches and philosophies, including scientific, or numbers oriented; strategic, or problem/solution oriented; and artistic, or aesthetically oriented. An introduction to advertising is an introduction to all sides of the advertising field and to the processes—quantitative, strategic, and aesthetic—by which the sales message is planned and produced. This text covers both the art and the science of advertising.

REALISTIC SCOPE

Advertising includes a variety of disciplines and specialties, including research, media buying and planning, copy writing, art direction, print and broadcast production, media sales, sales promotion and product publicity, strategic planning, personnel management, budgeting, scheduling, negotiating, and even business presentations. Because advertising is a major element in a company's marketing plan, it works in conjunction with a firm's overall corporate marketing practices. As we will describe, this edition has been rewritten to reflect more effectively today's *integrated marketing communications approach*.

INTEGRATED MARKETING COMMUNICATION APPROACH

Advertising is a business, and advertising is part of business. Businesses whose goal is profit from the sales of products or services use the tool called advertising to carry a message to the consumer. Advertising is the voice, the expression of marketing. It is *communication*.

STRATEGY

The big picture in business includes a marketing strategy which begins with research, adds a thorough understanding of consumer behavior, runs realistic cost-benefit analyses, and emphasizes communication and problem solving. The advertising created and produced to support a firm's marketing strategy communicates through traditional print and broadcast advertising, sales promotion, and well-known media such as direct response, out-of-home and directory media, as well as—and increasingly—through alternative media such as interactive forms, advanced cable or telecommunications technology, or unique demand-based media. This book emphasizes how *new methods of communication are central to marketing communication*.

INFORMATION AND CHANGE

In turn, additional research and tight budgeting in today's economy provides the data and feedback that support the growth of marketing into new areas and away from other areas. In today's age of information, we have come to know this complete decision-making process as *integrated marketing communication (IMC)*. The incorporation of IMC into this text has broadened in this edition. *Advertising:*

Principles and Practice addresses this contemporary view as it applies to each specific area of advertising.

PROFESSIONALS AND BASIC PHILOSOPHIES

David Ogilvy, founder of Ogilvy & Mather and one of the true giants in the advertising world, opens his classic book *Ogilvy on Advertising* with a now well-known gem:

> I do not regard advertising as entertainment or an art form, but as a medium of information. When I write an advertisement, I don't want you to tell me that you find it 'creative.' I want you to find it so interesting that you *buy the product*. When Aeschines spoke, they said: 'How well he speaks.' But when Demosthenes spoke, they said, 'Let us march against Philip.'[1]

This is one of several basic philosophies that guided the direction of this book; not surprisingly, many of these philosophies touch on the same themes. For another example, the bottom line of advertising, according to Lou Hagopian, chairman of the N.W. Ayer agency, is *to sell more of something*. And according to John O'Toole, of the American Association of Advertising Agencies in New York, advertising is an important factor in our economic freedom of choice. In earlier editions of this book, this basic and practical sense of the business climate underlined the book's message that advertising is not only a business itself, but it is an important aspect of business in general. In this edition, this philosophy is furthered through the integrated marketing communications approach.

Bill Bernbach, a founder of Doyle, Dane, and Bernbach (now DDB Needham Worldwide) insisted that *what is said is only the beginning*. "How you say it makes people look and listen." When it is done well—and admittedly not all advertising is done well—advertising touches common chords in all of us with carefully composed messages. So, an important premise of this book is that although *what is said is important, how it is said is equally as important*. Insights into human behavior and respect for people are absolutely fundamental to good advertising. Unfortunately, not all advertising is good, and not all advertising respects the people it tries to reach, but that is still the goal of the true professionals in the business—and another premise of this book.

John O'Toole explains it best in his book *The Trouble with Advertising* when he says you have to respect the critical faculties of the contemporary consumer. He points to the fact that 66 percent of new products do not make it. They are purchased and evaluated by the public and not bought again, no matter how powerful the advertising may be. He calls the public "these formidable folks whose wrath is so fearful." He describes the implicit contract, or at least understanding, between the advertiser and the public that makes advertising work:

> I promise you this. My advertising won't lie to you, and it will not deliberately try to mislead you. It won't bore the hell out of you or treat you as though you were a fool or embarrass you or your family. But remember, it's a salesman. Its purpose

---

[1] David Ogilvy, *Ogilvy on Advertising*. (New York: Crown Publishers, Inc., 1983), 7.

is to persuade you to trade your hard-earned cash for my product or service.

So this is the real world of advertising—and this book is a medium of information to help the reader experience it in as lively and focused a fashion as possible.

Acknowledgments

Advertising: Principles and Practice, 3/E has benefited from an outstanding team of authors and contributors. We wish to acknowledge the assistance of many academics and professionals in bringing the real world of advertising into the text.

Various experts in the industry contributed to the development of the text and supplements package. We are indebted to Peter Turk of the University of Akron for lending his expertise to the media sections of the text. Norval Stephens of the Norval Stephens Company provided a wealth of experience in the areas of advertising agencies and international advertising, as well as gathering material for the Inside Advertising boxes. In addition, we extend our deepest gratitude to Charles Pearce for his insightful annotations and research. Special thanks to Lois J. Smith for preparing the Instructor's Manual, and to Robert Field for preparing the Study Guide and Test Item File. We would also like to thank John Murphy for his various contributions, including the Transparency Package, teaching notes, selection of the ABC video segments, and in-class exercises.

Numerous people assisted in the preparation of the case studies. The revised Honda case was provided by Joseph Shak of Rubin Postaer. The Lands' End case study was provided by Jill Palamountain of Lands' End. The Cancer Treatment Centers of America case study was provided by Roger O'Connor and Vicki Lorenz of Cancer Treatment Centers of America. The Repepping Diet Dr. Pepper case was provided by John T. Brien of Young & Rubicam. Danny Radcliff and Bob Moquin of the Orlando/Orange County Convention and Visitors Bureau were invaluable resources for the Orlando case in Chapter 20.

No text can be successfully developed without a supportive publisher. The team at Prentice Hall helped to develop both the text and the supplementary package. We express our gratitude to Stephen Deitmer, editor-in-chief for development for putting together the development team and smoothing rough spots; Sandy Steiner and Dave Borkowsky for overseeing the project; Esther Koehn for patience during the production process; Mary Helen Fitzgerald for researching ads and procuring text permissions; Lori Morris-Nantz and Ilene Bellovin for the photo research program; Wendy Goldner and Melissa Steffens for handling the supplements; and Sandy Steiner (wearing a new hat) and Patti Arneson for developing the promotional program.

Many reviewers provided helpful comments on the drafts of the chapters. Their time and thoughtful comments are appreciated.

Edd Applegate
Middle Tennessee State University

Richard Behrman
Elon College

Charles Armstrong
Kansas City Kansas Community
College

William Claypoole
Texas A&M University

Joel Davis
San Diego State University

Sue Anne Davis
University of California at Berkeley

George R. Franke
Virginia Polytechnic Institute &
State University

Vicki Griffis
University of South Florida

James B. Hunt
University of North Carolina at
Wilmington

Ronald B. Katz
Northwestern University

James M. Maskulka
Lehigh University

Mary Ann McGrath
Loyola University of Chicago

Anita M. Olson
North Hennepin Community
College

Stephen P. Phelps
Southern Illinois University at
Carbondale

James R. Smith
State University of New York at New
Paltz

John P. Thurin
University of Notre Dame

Donna Uchida
Colorado State University

D. Joel Whalen
DePaul University

Kurt Wildermuth
University of Missouri at Columbia

WILLIAM WELLS   One of the industry's leading market and research authorities, Bill Wells is Professor of Advertising at the University of Minnesota's School of Journalism and Mass Communication. Former Executive Vice President and Director of Marketing Services at DDB Needham Chicago, he is, in fact, the only representative of the advertising business elected to the Attitude Research Hall of Fame. He earned a Ph.D. from Stanford University and was formerly Professor of Psychology and Marketing at the University of Chicago. He joined Needham, Harper, Chicago as Director of Corporate Research. Author of the Needham Harper Lifestyle study as well as author of more than 60 books and articles, Dr. Wells also published *Planning for R.O.R.: Effective Advertising Strategy* (Prentice Hall, 1989).

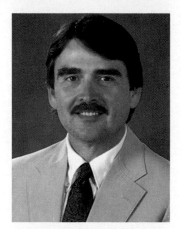

JOHN BURNETT   A Professor of Marketing at the University of Denver, he holds a D.B.A. degree in Marketing from the University of Kentucky. Dr. Burnett is author of *Promotion Management*, now in its third edition. In addition, he has had numerous articles and papers in a wide variety of professional and academic journals. In particular, his research has examined the effectivenees of emotional appeals in advertising and how various segments respond to such strategies. He is an active consultant in marketing and advertising and has served as a consultant for AT&T, the Dallas Mart, the AAFES organization, and Scott & White Hospitals. Dr. Burnett has won several teaching awards and serves as faculty advisor for student chapters of the American Marketing Association.

SANDRA MORIARTY   A Professor in the Integrated Marketing Program at the University of Colorado-Boulder, she holds a Ph.D. in instructional communication from Kansas State University. Before moving into full-time teaching, she owned her own public relations and advertising agency. In addition to the present text, Dr. Moriarty has written or co-written several books, including *Marketing, The Creative Package*, and *Creative Advertising*. She is also author of numerous professional articles and scholarly research reports. Her current research interests include the analysis of changing marketing practice and the development of new theoretical approaches in marketing communications.

NORVAL STEPHENS   This advertising professional provided assistance for the advertising agency and international chapters. His 40 years in marketing include management of the New York office and of the international division of a worldwide agency. He is a consultant and executive director of the International Federation of Advertising Agencies.

PETER B. TURK   Dr. Turk is a professor of marketing at the University of Akron. With ten years of professional experience in media research and strategic planning, he continues to write in this area, including two books. *Advertising Media Research Sourcebook* (NTC Books) and *Advertising Media, Strategy and Tactics* (William Brown), as well as an invited article on research developments for *Current Issues in Research and Advertising*, 1992.

"Bust
and
surviv

John

$\mathcal{I}$NTRODUCTION TO ADVERTISING

CHAPTER OBJECTIVES

When you have completed this chapter, you should be able to:

- Define advertising and discuss its component parts
- Understand the elements of great advertising
- Identify the eight types of advertising
- Explain the four roles of advertising
- Identify the four players in the advertising world
- Explain the impact on advertising of the invention of media forms such as print, radio, and television
- Relate key figures in the history of advertising to their contributions to the field
- Comprehend the future direction of advertising

# ADIDAS IS BACK

Its brand was the standard of athletic footwear in the 1970s, before the company lost its footing and was outpaced by rivals Nike and Reebok International. Now adidas AG, a German company, is poised to sprint toward a modest comeback. adidas (always spelled with a small "a") is showing signs of sales growth, although its growth is still minute compared with its big competitors. In 1993, adidas reported U.S. footwear sales of $190 million, up 3 percent from 1992, to rank it eighth in the industry.

adidas AG's strategy in the United States is to persuade young, urban consumers to buy the product with the familiar three stripes. "We're working on getting more shelf space, which will hopefully increase our sales, said CEO Robert Louis-Dreyfus. "Until then, we are going to go slowly with advertising."

The newest campaign for adidas started in March of 1994 in conjunction with the NCAA March Madness basketball championship tournament on CBS. The commercial from Team One Advertising, a subsidiary of Saatchi & Saatchi Advertising Worldwide, featured hyperactive ESPN analyst Dick Vitale as the "brain" of a teenage basketball player who is wearing adidas sneakers. Vitale shouts encouragement to the lad, who is walking off the court, shaking his head and trying to eliminate the incessant loud buzz. Besides that commercial, in New York City adidas also produced subway posters and two painted brick walls—one in Harlem, one in Brooklyn. Another television campaign featuring New York Knicks All-Star Guard John Starks is scheduled for 1995. "Nike and Reebok have become the Coke and Pepsi of athletic apparel," says a spokesperson at adidas America. "We need to communicate to customers in an entirely different way. Our advertising is trying to be an honest reflection of the athlete himself, and not trying to think of the next cute tagline." For instance, she says, phrases on the subway posters came directly from Starks while he was talking about playing basketball. "We're advertising shoes for the pure athlete, not someone who is just posing."

adidas sees an opportunity to get its foot in the door to reach the lucrative but fickle market of 12-to-17 year-olds. "There is a whole new generation of kids coming up who see their dads and grandfathers wearing Nike and Reebok," says Tom Cordner, Team One's cochairman and creative director. These young people "want their own identity." adidas may not have much choice in trying to tap them. Middle-aged consumers, who sigh nostalgically when reminiscing about their first pair of adidas sneakers, are not racing to purchase the brand's shoes and apparel these days.

Still, the beginning of a turnaround is evident. In 1993, adidas reported a pretax profit of 23 million marks, compared with a loss of 149 million marks in 1992. As for Louis-Dreyfus, he characteristically credits timing, rather than any business skills, for the start of the company's turnaround. "It's nice to have products selling again. As for my influence, it's better to be lucky than good."[1]

The situation facing adidas is indicative of the business climate of the 1990s. Growth industries, such as soft drinks, computer technology, and athletic ware, tend to be dominated by one or two companies—Coke and Pepsi, Apple and IBM, Nike and Reebok, respectively. Relatively minor players such as Diet Dr. Pepper, Compaq, and adidas, are faced with the unenviable task of attacking head on or pursuing a flanking strategy. adidas realizes that targeted advertising, in respect to both message and media, is the only way it can compete.

---

[1]Adapted from Kevin Goldman, "Adidas Tries to Fill Its Rivals' Big Shoes," *The Wall Street Journal*, (March 17, 1994):B5.

WHAT MAKES AN AD GREAT?

Is the "Always Coca-Cola" ad campaign great? Clearly, there are many critics in the industry who contend it is not great, it's not even good. Yet, defining what is great advertising is not easy. Experience has shown that greatness is definitely not based solely on a popularity contest. If that were true, Pepsi has produced great ads for many years (see Ad 1.1). Table 1.1 lists the television ads of 1992 deemed most popular with consumers. Pepsi's number-two position would seem to support this point. But note the product ahead of Pepsi. What do you think the current Little Caesar's ads have that make them more appealing than Pepsi's? Furthermore, as we mentioned earlier, do a product's sales necessarily follow the emergence of a great ad?

Clearly, the Coke ads produced in the 1960s were great. The "I'd like to buy the world a Coke" mountaintop ad is considered a classic. These ads won many industry awards and contributed significantly to brand awareness and increased sales. When did Coke ads stop being great? Some would argue that it began with the introduction of Diet Coke. The creative focus initiated by McCann-Erickson for Coke somehow was dissipated with the efforts of Lintas, the agency assigned to Diet Coke. Consumers couldn't discern if Coke was "it" or not. But others contend that many other factors in addition to advertising played a critical role in the relative success of the Coca-Cola franchise. Marketing decisions have been questioned. Was Diet Coke positioned too close to regular Coke, so that one product cannibalized the other? Did Coke interpret the changing demographics correctly? How about new and better competitors? Finally, the emphasis of price discounting as a way of life in the soft-drink industry dramatically changed the relative importance of advertising in the industry. Essentially, advertising—even the greatest advertising—cannot counter so many powerful factors. Still, what *is* great advertising?

Often the determination of great advertising is reduced simply to determining what people like best in advertisements. We all have our favorite ads. Which television commercials do you remember? Which radio commercials? Magazine ads? Why are they your favorites? If you are like most people, your favorite ads are either funny or have a clever execution. As we will see, the reasons why people like certain ads and the effectiveness, or greatness, of the ads are often based on the same qualities.

Several companies ask people questions that get to the "whys" of advertising preferences. *Advertising Age*, working with the SRI Research Center, conducts a monthly "Ad Watch" survey of advertising awareness. Video Storyboard Tests asks consumers to list the most outstanding print advertisements and television commercials. *Advertising Age* also regularly interviews top creative people to identify those ads that professionals think are most effective. The advertising industry evaluates its work through such award programs as the Clios, the EFFIES, and the Addy Awards. Just as achieving consumer recognition does not make an ad great, neither does winning industry prizes. Many agencies that have developed award-winning campaigns have been dropped by their clients because the ads did not increase sales for the company.

Although awards are still considered a necessary morale booster for creative staffs, a survey of advertising agencies shows that many agencies have pulled

"COME ALIVE" 1960   "PUPPIES"   "PONY"

"SKYWRITER"   "M.J. STREET"   "SOUND TRUCK"

"ARCHAEOLOGY"   "JOHNSON"   "APARTMENT 10 G"

"SWITCH"   "GLASNOST"   "PERFORMANCE"

"SHADY ACRES"   "COOL KIDS"   "CHILL OUT" 1991

Ad 1.1   This collection of Pepsi ads illustrates the creative philosophy of Pepsi-Cola over a 30-year period.

(Courtesy of BBDO)

Table 1.1

Most Popular Television
Commercials of 1992

1992 Rank	1991 Rank	Brand	Ad Agency
1	7	Little Caesar's Pizza	Cliff Freeman & Partners
2	1	Pepsi/Diet Pepsi	BBDO
3	4	Nike	Wieden & Kennedy
4	3	DuPont Stainmaster	BBDO
5	5	McDonald's	Leo Burnett/DDB Needham
6	2	Eveready Energizer	Chiat/Day
7	8	Budweiser	DMB&B
8	—	Reebok	Chiat/Day
9	6	Coca-Cola	McCann-Erickson
10	16	Taster's Choice	McCann-Erickson
11	—	Olympics promotions	CBS and NBC
12	17	Diet Coke	Lintas
13	10	Pizza Hut	BBDO
14	20	AT&T	Ayer/Ogilvy & Mather/Young & Rubicam/McCann-Erickson
15	19	Burger King	DMB&B/Saatchi & Saatchi
16	—	Lexus	Team One
17	13	Miller Lite	Leo Burnett
18	—	Jeep	CME KHBB
19	—	Michelin	DDB Needham
20	21	Bud Light	DDB Needham
21	23	Honda	Rubin Postaer
22	11	Coors Light	Foote Cone & Belding
23	—	Calvin Klein	In-house
24	—	Miller Genuine Draft	Backer Spielvogel Bates
25	—	Life Savers	FCB/Leber Katz

Source: Video Storyboard Tests Inc.
See Kevin Goldman, "Pizza Ads with Dash of Humor Top Pops," The Wall Street Journal (March 9, 1993):B1.

back from entering advertising competitions, reserving entries for those shows that have greater acclaim, such as the Clios, the New York Art Directors, the One Show, and the International Advertising Film Festival in Cannes, France. For example, BBDO, which annually enters 14 shows, is getting pickier about its choices. "The rising costs are outrageous and I don't think they're warranted," says creative administrator June Baloutine.

Agencies are not entering competitions for other reasons as well. In these days of awards proliferation, awards no longer seem to impress clients. Michael Lollis, executive vice president and executive creative director at J. Walter Thompson in Atlanta, states, "As there are more and more shows, they become less meaningful. If you enter often enough, you can win something someplace."[2]

Says Peter Sealey, "Whether or not Coke wins a Gold Lion at Cannes in 1993 is so immaterial as to be inconsequential to me."[3]

---

[2]Kathy Ruehle and Barbara Holsonback, "Some Agencies Deciding Awards Not Worth the Cost," Adweek (April 30, 1990):1, 10.

[3]Mark Landler, "Pepsi: Memorable Ads, Forgettable Sales," Business Week (October 21, 1991):36.

The situation was cogently summarized by David Ogilvy, interviewed at his Chateau Touffou in France: "If I could persuade the creative lunatics to give up their pursuit of awards, I would die happy. . . . Down with advertising that forgets to promise the consumer any benefit. Down with the creative show-offs. Too clever by half."[4]

So, if awards, popularity, and longevity are not reliable measures of great advertising, then what is?

CLASSICS

There are few ads that have stood the test of time. This chapter will discuss the objective and subjective criteria for greatness that these ads have consistently met. Certain ads are simply outstanding; they are classics. Some are from campaigns that have been running for a long time; others are single ads or campaigns that have been around for only a short time. What do all these ads have in common? Good ads work on two levels: *They engage the mind of the consumer and at the same time deliver a selling message.*

The California Raisins "I Heard It Through the Grapevine" commercials, for example, dominated the AdWatch awareness studies in the late 1980s (see Ad 1.2). The catchy music and the parody of a rhythm-and-blues singing group performing a 1960s hit have made this campaign a favorite of consumers and professionals alike.

The campaigns for Obsession, Nike, and Levi's 501 have each achieved a considerable level of success. Targeted primarily at young men, these ads reflect this group's interests and needs. Moreover, they have used a variety of techniques, such as humor, action, and sex, effectively enough to attract the attention of young males and keep it.

Spokespersons and celebrities have been an important part of many classic ads. Bill Cosby is a successful presenter for a number of companies, and his

[4]Noreen O'Leary, "Waiting for the Revolution," *Adweek* (June 15, 1992):30–34.

long-standing relationship with Jell-O has produced a number of winning ads. Ed and Frank, two invented but believable characters for Bartles and Jaymes Wine Coolers, became well-loved stars in their own continuing miniseries. Their "Baseball Tips" commercial, which ran for two weeks around the time of the 1988 World Series, reached and affected three times as many people as the average commercial.

Michael Jordan, the premier spokesperson of the 1990s, delivers believable commercials for Diet Coke, Wheaties, and Nike, to name but a few. His animated Coke ads, with a variety of cartoon characters, shown during the 1992 and 1993 Super Bowls produced awareness scores five times higher than the norm.[5]

These campaigns are widely remembered, not only because they are entertaining, but also because they involve viewers and make them wonder what the campaigns' creators will come up with next. The campaigns also use humor, ranging from soft and gentle to outrageous. Humor is an important part of some of the other all-time great ads, such as the Federal Express ad featuring the fast-talking executive. Underneath the funny characterizations, however, the Federal Express ads carry a hard-hitting message of dependability: "When it absolutely, positively has to be there overnight." The silly Little Caesars® Pizza! Pizza! character strikes our funny bone in a way that evokes a smile and he is easy to remember and associate with the product; he's effective—he can prompt a trip to Little Caesars for a purchase (Ad 1.3).

Great ads often touch emotions other than humor. The AT&T/Long-Distance Service "Reach Out and Touch Someone" campaign has been touching emotions since 1979. The messages are warm and sentimental, but more than that, they communicate the idea that it is easy and rewarding to call friends and family at any time.

Other outstanding ads have created memorable characters. Mikey, the finicky little boy who doesn't like anything, made viewers like Life cereal. The original commercial first ran in 1971 and was brought back in 1981. Even though the original Mikey is now grown up, the commercial has maintained its appeal for several generations of Life consumers.

Children, cats, and puppy dogs are lovable and give a product warm associations. The Oscar Mayer kids have been singing the product's theme song since 1973. The sing-along music contributes to the Oscar Mayer success story.

Often the characters are fictional, like Ed and Frank. Some of these characters, like Charlie the Tuna and the Jolly Green Giant, are total fantasy. But all of them capture the "inherent drama" of the product. Imagine yourself an advertiser who wants to position vegetables to make them acceptable to children. Why not use a cartoon character like a giant to promote them? But giants are fearsome, you think, so how do I make this character appealing to kids? Make him "Jolly." Leo Burnett, creative genius behind this campaign and others, such as Exxon's Tony the Tiger, had a real penchant for animal mascots, which have come to be called "critters" in the advertising industry. Burnett was able to take complex messages and embody them in a single cartoon character.

Drama is often an important aspect of successful advertising. One of the most dramatic advertisements ever produced was a commercial for the launch of the Apple Macintosh computer that took on Apple's most serious competitor, IBM. The stark images of the classic George Orwell novel *1984* (Ad 1.4) came alive in this commercial, which only ran once, on the 1984 Super Bowl before

---

[5]An *awareness* or *recall* score determines how well a consumer can remember all or parts of an advertisement. More will be said about awareness in Chapter 21.

100 million viewers. Not only was this ad a captivating drama, it also demonstrated the power of a timely media buy.

Significant images are another important part of advertising. Nike, with their "Just do it!" campaign has provided the intended audience—young athletic men and women, or athletic "wannabes"—with rewarding praise for the physically fit and consistent inspiration for the unfit to chuck their lethargy, to stop the tendency to accept the societal norm, and *just do it*. These images of men and women committed to "no pain—no gain," both inspire and challenge. This imagery is heightened through excellent photography, the use of celebrities, and dramatic situations. It is a type of advertising called, rather literally, *image advertising*.

Perhaps the most successful image advertising of all time, however, is the Marlboro campaign, which has been running since 1955. With overwhelming single-mindedness the campaign has focused on western imagery with cowboys, horses, and ranching. The cowboy myth is a strong and compelling image. This campaign has been successful both as communication and as a marketing effort. It has helped to make Marlboro the best-selling cigarette in the world. However, this seems to be changing (See Issues and Controversies box.)

CHARACTERISTICS OF GREAT ADS

What do you think makes an ad great? And what turns great ads into classics? What makes certain ads stand out in people's minds? And why do some ad campaigns continue to run for years, sometimes even for decades? From this discussion it should be clear that great advertising employs a variety of techniques: celebrities and spokespersons, fantasy characters, children and puppies, music, drama, significant imagery, and creative media buying. Advertising is the complex voice of marketing, and the rest of this book will try to explain how all of these factors are interwoven to create great advertising. The premise of this

The Marlboro Man: A Former Shadow of Himself

The consensus on Madison Avenue is that the most successful campaign in advertising history is the Marlboro Man. For over 40 years he has been riding the range, telling the world what a real man looks like—and smokes. It appears, however, that the ubiquitous cowboy is losing his effectiveness.

In an effort to freshen up the campaign, Philip Morris executives concede that they are moving away from using the classic image of the Marlboro Man on his horse. The new abstract interpretation of Marlboro Country is a vast departure from the traditional. A black-and-white graphic silhouette of the Marlboro Man's head is popping up on point-of-sales posters and bus shelters. The next wave of ads will begin integrating other new-fangled cowboys into its print campaign, including one that displays nothing but his blue-jeaned groin with a strategically positioned carton of Marlboros.

The radical change in the Marlboro campaign raises the question about how long an ad campaign can go before it begins to run out of steam. After all, advertising experts have always pointed to the Marlboro Man campaign, created by the Leo Burnett Agency, as one that could last forever. Dave Vaderha, president of Video Storyboard Tests, Inc., says the answer is simple: "The Marlboro Man's problem is old age. It's always the man, the horse, and the scenery—and it has remained unchanged for ten years."

David Dangoor, Philip Morris's senior vice president of marketing, insists the Marlboro campaign is "definitely" still going strong. He says the new cowboys are simply designed to "contemporize the look and create a more modern feel." Yet there is evidence that there may be serious problems in Marlboro Country. For one thing, sales have slipped, despite the fact that Marlboro is the most advertised cigarette brand, selling $240 million in 1992. Furthermore, likability surveys show that the Marlboro Man has taken a significant nosedive. Mr. Dangoor has an explanation for this drop: "All the negative propaganda against smoking has people not wanting to talk about the [Marlboro] campaign."

Some advertising experts indicate that another reason for the decline of Marlboro is the popularity of the Smokin' Joe Camel campaign. Although the Camel brand, produced by archrival R. J. Reynolds Tobacco, is relatively small—it holds 4.5 percent of the market compared with 25.5 percent for Marlboro—its success has been greatest with young males, who make up the crucial market for the cigarette industry. "Marlboro has done business as usual for too long," says Jackie Silver, a New York advertising consultant. "It's been badly upstaged by Camel's efforts." Even Mr. Dangoor concedes that Joe Camel is a "fun, great-looking, and very noticeable," campaign.

So, is the new Marlboro Man a response to Joe Camel or an attempt to revise a worn-out creative concept? The answer is probably both. Marlboro customers are aging and there is a clear need to woo younger smokers. The Marlboro groin shot could be a way of not only competing with Joe Camel's phallic vision, it also may give Marlboro the antiestablishment attitude it lacks. In addition, the pop-art graphic now on display in New York may appeal to younger smokers without raising the hackles of antismoking activists, who complain that Smokin' Joe is a cartoon that may appeal to children and the Marlboro Man seems to get younger in every ad. In fact, you can ascribe any age to the Marlboro graphic.

But Marlboro faces a fundamental dilemma: Its fortunes are so tied to the Marlboro Man that it can't afford to remake him too drastically for fear of alienating existing smokers. Notes one industry expert: "You really can't change the base campaign given the tremendous equity in the Marlboro Man. You have to be very careful about tampering with it."

Source: Susan L. Hwang, "New Marlboro Man is a Mere Shadow of His Former Self," *The Wall Street Journal* (September 14, 1992): B1, B5.

book, however, is that three broad dimensions characterize great advertising: strategy, creativity, and execution (See Ad 1.5). This book is built around these three dimensions.

Ally & Gargano

CLIENT: FEDERAL EXPRESS CORP.
PRODUCT: AIR FREIGHT
TITLE: "FAST PACED WORLD"
COMMERCIAL NO.: QFAS 1326 (:30)
DATE APPROVED: 7/14/81

1. MR. SPLEEN: (OC) Okay Eunice,travelplans,Ineedtobein NewYorkonMonday,LAon Tuesday,NewYorkon Wednesday,LAonThursday,

2. andNewYorkonFriday. Gotit? Soyouwanttoworkhere,well whatmakesyouthinkyoudeserve ajobhere?

3. GUY: Wellsirlthinkonmyfeet, I'mgoodwithfiguresandIhavea sharpmind.

4. SPLEEN: Excellent,canyou startMonday?

5. (OC): Andinconclusion,Jim, Bill,BobandTed,

6. businessisbusinesssolet'sgetto work. Thankyoufortakingthis meeting.

7. (OC): Peteryoudidabang-up job,I'mputtingyouinchargeof Pittsburgh.

8. PETER: (OC) Pittsburgh's perfect. SPLEEN: Iknowit's perfect,Peter,that'swhylpicked Pittsburgh. Pittsburgh'sperfect, Peter,MaylcallyouPete?

9. (OC): Congratulationson yourdealinDenverDavid.

10. I'mputtingyoudowntodealin Dallas. ANNCR: (VO) In this fast moving, high pressure, get-it-done yesterday world,

11. aren't you glad there's one company that can keep up with it all?

12. Federal Express. (SFX) When it absolutely, positively has to be there overnight.

Ad 1.5

The fast-talking executive ads for Federal Express are examples of great advertising.

(© 1981 Federal Express Corporation)

Strategy. Every great ad is strategically sound. In other words, it is carefully directed to a certain audience, it is driven by specific objectives, its message is crafted to speak to that audience's most important concerns, and it is run in media that will most effectively reach that audience. The measure of an ad's success is how well it achieves its goals, whether they be increased sales, memorability, attitude change, or brand awareness.

The crazy characters and situations in the Federal Express ads bring to life a very important selling premise about the essence of dependability. Mikey likes Life, so it must be good. See Concepts and Applications box for an example of how the Beef Industry Council repositioned its product for a new target segment.

Creativity. The *creative concept* is a central idea that gets your attention and sticks in your memory. Every one of the ads we've discussed has a Big Idea that is creative and original. Frank and Ed are unique characters, as is the Jolly Green Giant. Isuzu took the stereotype of the untrustworthy car salesman and created the unforgettable Joe Isuzu, who retired in 1993.

A concern for creative thinking drives the entire field of advertising. Planning the strategy calls for creative problem solving; the research efforts are creative; the buying and placing of ads in the media are creative. Advertising is an exciting field because of the constant demand for creative solutions to media and message problems.

Principle

Great ads are original, strategically sound, and perfectly executed.

Execution. Finally, every great ad is well executed. That means the craftsmanship is impressive. The details, the techniques, and the production values have all been fine-tuned. Many of these techniques are experimental, such as the Intel Computer commercial that uses ADOBE, a contemporary computer graphic software package. There is more to execution than technology, however. The warm touch in the AT&T commercials is a delicate emotional effect. It is sensitive without being overly sentimental or manipulative.

Good advertisers know that how you say it is just as important as what you say. *What you say* comes from strategy, whereas *how you say it* is a product of creativity and execution. The great ads, then, are ads that (1) are strategically sound, (2) have an original creative concept, and (3) use exactly the right execution for the message. Strategy, creativity, and execution—these are the qualities that turn great ads into classics.

$\mathcal{T}$HE WORLD OF ADVERTISING

DEFINING ADVERTISING

What is advertising? What are its important dimensions? The standard definition of advertising includes six elements. Advertising is a *paid form of communication*, although some forms of advertising, such as public service, use donated space and time. Not only is the message paid for, but the *sponsor is identified*. In some cases the point of the message is simply to make consumers aware of the product or company, although most advertising tries to *persuade or influence* the consumer to do something. The message is conveyed through many different kinds of *mass media* reaching a large *audience* of potential consumers. Because advertising is a form of mass communication, it is also *nonpersonal*. A definition of **advertising**, then, would include all six of those features.

advertising Paid nonpersonal communication from an identified sponsor using mass media to persuade or influence an audience.

> **Advertising** is *paid nonpersonal communication* from an identified *sponsor* using *mass media* to *persuade or influence* an audience.

In an ideal world every manufacturer would be able to talk one-on-one with every consumer about the product or service being offered for sale. Personal selling approaches that idea, but it is very expensive. Calls made by salespeople can cost well in excess of $150 per call.

Marketers who have products and services for sale avoid the enormous expense of personal contact by using mass media to convey their messages.

What's For Dinner?

The Beef Industry Council (BIC) is making a big push for beef with its new $42 million, 17-month campaign. These primary-appeal ads spotlight mouth-watering shots of beef in a variety of dishes that are more contemporary than traditional burgers and steaks. Color closeups of such sumptuous dishes as kabobs, stir fry, and unusual cuts are featured in the television ads with the tag "Beef. It's what's for dinner," narrated by actor Robert Mitchum and supported in the background by the music of several familiar American classics.

One thing for sure, if the campaign doesn't work it will not be because it wasn't based on a carefully crafted strategy. "It's what's for dinner," was the first campaign for BIC developed by Leo Burnett U.S.A. Unlike former ad efforts, the campaign shuns talk about nutrition and focuses instead on taste and different ways to prepare beef.

Research with consumers showed that when they were selecting foods and meats, "nutrition was not an issue," said Donna Schmidt, spokeswoman for Chicago-based BIC. "People are looking for variety and things that are easy to use," she said. "When we came right down to it, people wanted more information in ways to prepare beef."

Americans are gobbling up such leaner meats as chicken and turkey, whose consumption is on the rise. Although red meat is still the most popular meat in the United States, consumption levels fell 15 percent between 1986 and 1991, according to the U.S. Department of Agriculture.

Schmidt said ten years ago the taste gap between chicken and beef was very wide, with most people favoring beef. But because people are doing more creative things in preparing chicken, increasing numbers of consumers are favoring the taste of chicken. "Consumers still think of beef as steaks and burgers," she said.

In addition to TV spots, print ads featuring 30-minute recipes for preparing beef have appeared in several women's magazines and general-interest publications.

Past campaigns by BIC mainly targeted men using spokespeople with famous faces such as Cybill Shepherd and James Garner; the theme was "Real Food for Real People." But this new campaign mainly targets women 25 to 54 years old who have "commercial-oriented families." In the summer a separate set of ads runs, targeting men and their penchant for barbecuing.

"It's what's for dinner" is the most extensive marketing campaign BIC has done to promote beef consumption, according to Schmidt. In addition to print and TV ads, the campaign features in-store tie-ins with Lea and Perrins Steak Sauce and an 800 number people can call for recipe booklets or cooking tips.

Since this campaign represents a long-term commitment on the part of BIC, it is difficult to tell whether it is a success. We do know, however, that it is being guided by a carefully conceived strategy.

Source: Carrie Goerne, "Don't Blame the Cows, Beef Industry's Huge Campaign Hopes to Blunt Critics," *The Marketing News* (June 22, 1992): 1–2.

There the costs, for *time* in broadcast media and for *space* in print media, are spread over the tremendous number of people that these media reach. For example, $650,000 may sound like a lot of money for one ad on the Super Bowl, but when you consider that the advertisers are reaching over 100 million people, the cost is not extreme.

TYPES OF ADVERTISING

Advertising is complex because so many diverse advertisers try to reach so many different types of audiences. There are eight basic types of advertising.

Brand Advertising. The most visible type of advertising is *national consumer* *advertising*. Another name for this is *brand advertising*, which focuses on the development of a long-term brand identity and image. It tries to develop a distinctive brand image for a product.

Retail Advertising. In contrast, *retail advertising* is local and focuses on the store where a variety of products can be purchased or where a service is offered. The message announces products that are available locally, stimulates store traffic, and tries to create a distinctive image for the store. Retail advertising emphasizes price, availability, location, and hours of operation.

Political Advertising. *Political advertising* is used by politicians to persuade people to vote for them and therefore is an important part of the political process in the United States and other democratic countries that permit candidate advertising. Although it is an important source of communication for voters, critics are concerned that political advertising tends to focus more on image than on issues.

Directory Advertising. Another type of advertising is called directional because people refer to it to find out how to buy a product or service. The best-known form of *directory advertising* is the Yellow Pages, although there are many different kinds of directories that perform the same function.

Direct-Response Advertising. *Direct-response advertising* can use any advertising medium, including direct mail, but the message is different from that of national and retail advertising in that it tries to stimulate a sale directly. The consumer can respond by telephone or mail, and the product is delivered directly to the consumer by mail or some other carrier.

Business-to-Business Advertising. *Business-to-business advertising* includes messages directed at retailers, wholesalers, and distributors, as well as industrial purchasers and professionals such as lawyers and physicians. Business advertising tends to be concentrated in business publications or professional journals.

Institutional Advertising. *Institutional advertising* is also called *corporate advertising*. The focus of these messages is on establishing a corporate identity or on winning the public over to the organization's point of view.

Public Service Advertising. *Public service advertising* (PSA) communicates a message on behalf of some good cause, such as stopping drunk driving (MADD) or preventing child abuse. These advertisements are created for free by advertising professionals, and the space and time are donated by the media.

As you can see, there isn't just one kind of advertising; in fact, advertising is a large and varied industry. All of these areas demand creative, original messages that are strategically sound and well executed. In the chapters to come, all of these types of advertising will be discussed in more depth.

ROLES OF ADVERTISING

Advertising can also be explained in terms of the roles it plays in business and in society. Four different roles have been identified for advertising:

1. Marketing role
2. Communication role
3. Economic role
4. Societal role

The Marketing Role. Marketing is the strategic process a business uses to satisfy consumer needs and wants through goods and services. The particular consumers at whom the company directs its marketing effort constitute the *target market*. The tools available to marketing include the product, its price, and the means used to deliver the product, or the place. Marketing also includes a mechanism for communicating this information to the consumer, which is called *marketing communication*, or promotion. These four tools are collectively referred to as the *marketing mix* or the *4 Ps*. Marketing communication is further broken down into four related communication techniques: advertising, sales promotion, public relations, and personal selling. Thus advertising is only one element in a company's overall marketing communication program, although it is the most visible. The marketing role will be discussed in depth in Chapter 3.

The Communication Role. Advertising is a form of mass communication. It transmits different types of market information to match buyers and sellers in the marketplace. Advertising both informs and transforms the product by creating an image that goes beyond straightforward facts. Specific suggestions about how to accomplish these tasks will be discussed in later chapters on creating messages.

Principle

Advertising provides information that helps match buyers and sellers in the marketplace.

The Economic Role. The two major schools of thought concerning the effects of advertising on the economy are the market power school and the market competition school.[6] According to the market power school, advertising is a persuasive communication tool used by marketers to distract consumers' attention from the price of the product. In contrast, the market competition school sees advertising as a source of information that increases consumers' price sensitivity and stimulates competition.

Actually, little is known about the true nature of advertising in the economy. Charles Sandage, an advertising professor, provides a different perspective. He sees the economic role of advertising as "helping society to achieve abundance by informing and persuading members of society with respect to products, services, and ideals."[7] In addition, he argues that advertising assists in "the development of judgment on the part of consumers in their purchase practices."

The Societal Role. Advertising also has a number of social roles. It informs us about new and improved products and teaches us how to use these innovations. It helps us compare products and features and make informed consumer decisions. It mirrors fashion and design trends and contributes to our aesthetic sense.

Advertising tends to flourish in societies that enjoy some level of economic abundance, that is, in which supply exceeds demand. It is at this point that

---

[6]John M. Vernon, "Concentration, Promoting, and Market Share Stability in the Pharmaceutical Industry," *Journal of Industrial Economics* (July 1971):146–266.

[7]Charles H. Sandage, "Some Institutional Aspects of Advertising," Journal of Advertising *Vol. 1, No. 1* (1973):9.

advertising moves from being a simple informational service (telling consumers where they can find the product) to being a message designated to create a demand for a particular brand.

The question is: Does advertising follow trends or does it lead them? At what point does advertising cross the line between *reflecting* social values and *creating* social values? Critics argue that advertising has repeatedly crossed this line and has evolved into an instrument of social control. Although these concerns are not new, the increasing power of advertising, both in terms of money (we spend more annually educating consumers than we spend educating our children) and in terms of communication dominance (the mass media can no longer survive without advertising support), has made these concerns more prominent than ever.

Can advertising manipulate people? Some critics argue that advertising has the power to dictate how people behave. They believe that, even if an individual ad cannot control our behavior, the cumulative effects of nonstop television, radio, print, and outdoor ads can be overwhelming.

Although certain groups of people, such as young children, the less educated, and the elderly, might be more susceptible to certain kinds of advertising, it is hard to conclude that a particular ad or series of ads caused, tricked, or coerced anyone into making a particular buying decision. There is no solid evidence for the manipulative power of advertising because so many other factors contribute to the choices we make. Although advertising does attempt to persuade, most people are aware that advertisers are biased in favor of their own products and learn how to handle persuasive advertising in their daily lives. Manipulation and other ethical issues will be discussed in more detail in Chapter 2.

FUNCTIONS OF ADVERTISING

Not all advertising attempts to accomplish the same objectives. Although each ad or campaign tries to reach goals unique to its sponsor, there are two basic functions that advertising performs, along with several subfunctions.

Product advertising aims to inform or stimulate the market about the sponsor's product(s). The intent is clearly to sell a particular product, to the exclusion of competitors' products. Conversely, *institutional advertising* is designed to create a positive attitude toward the seller. The intent is to promote the sponsoring organization rather than the things it sells.

Direct Action versus Indirect Action. Product advertising may be either direct-action or indirect-action advertising. *Direct-action advertising* is intended to produce a quick response. Ads that include a coupon with an expiration date, or a sale with an expiration date, or an 800 number, or a mail-in order blank fall under this heading. *Indirect-action advertising* is designed to stimulate demand over a longer period of time. These advertisements inform customers that the product exists, indicate its benefits, state where it can be purchased, remind customers to repurchase, and reinforce this decision.

Primary versus Selective. Product advertising can also be primary or selective. *Primary advertising* aims to promote demand for a generic product. Thus ads by the Beef Industry Council promote beef; it really doesn't matter to the council which brand of beef you purchase. *Selective advertising* attempts to create demand for a particular brand. It typically follows primary advertising, which more or less sets the stage for selective advertising.

Commercial versus Noncommercial. Finally, product advertising can serve either a commercial or a noncommercial function. *Commercial advertising* promotes a product with the intent of making a profit. Most of the advertising you see in the mass media falls under this heading. In contrast, *noncommercial advertising* tends to be sponsored by organizations that are not in business to make money. Charities and nonprofit organizations such as museums produce this type of advertising. Although the goal may be to raise money for a particular cause, it could just as easily be the donation of time or ideas.

As noted, rather than selling a particular product, institutional advertising aims to establish a high level of goodwill. *Public relations institutional advertising* attempts to create a favorable image of the firm among employees, customers, stockholders, or the general public. Texaco Petroleum, for example, runs ads that highlight the company's attempts to protect the environment.

$\mathcal{T}$HE FOUR PLAYERS

In addition to the types of advertising and their various roles and functions, advertising can be defined in terms of those who play important roles in bringing ads to the consumer. The four primary players in the advertising world are:

1. The advertiser
2. The advertising agency
3. The media
4. The vendor

THE ADVERTISER

advertiser The individual or organization that initiates the advertising process.

Advertising begins with the **advertiser**—the individual or organization that usually initiates the advertising process. The advertiser also makes the final decisions about whom the advertising will be directed to, the media in which it will appear, the size of the advertising budget, and the duration of the campaign.

We can only estimate how much money is spent annually by advertisers. Even then, the estimates seem to be less accurate as the expenditure categories become more complicated. For example, Robert J. Coen, senior vice president/director of forecasting at McCann-Erickson Worldwide, who is considered the most reliable source of advertising expenditures, acknowledges that it's a guessing game.[8] Nonetheless, he reports that expenditures on U.S. advertising in 1992 were $131 billion, with an expected increase in 1993 of at least 6 percent, or a total of approximately $138 billion. In 1993, the growth in local advertising is expected to lead the way. This is primarily due to the fact that retailers are starting to experience positive effects from the gradually improving economy. The recovery in total advertising in 1992 was not as strong as expected because of the lack of a strong turnaround in local marketing activities.[9]

[8]Gary Levin, "Coen's Crystal Ball," *Advertising Age* (August 10, 1992):16.
[9]Robert J. Coen, "Ad Gains Exceed 6% This Year," *Advertising Age* (May 3, 1993):4.

Types of Advertisers. There are a number of different types of advertisers. Some manufacture the product or service; others sell manufacturers' products to the ultimate consumer; some use advertising to represent themselves and the services they provide; and others provide a service to the public. The various businesses that perform these tasks fall into four categories: manufacturers, resellers, individuals, and institutions.

Manufacturers *Manufacturers* actually make the product or service and distribute it to resellers or ultimate users for a profit. They usually build their advertising around a product brand name. Because so much advertising is sponsored by manufacturers, we are most familiar with this type of advertising.

Clearly, manufacturers spend more money on mass advertising than any other category. Note in Table 1.2 that only one nonmanufacturer, retailer Sears, Roebuck & Co., was in the top ten companies by ad spending in 1992.

Resellers *Resellers* are wholesalers and retailers who distribute the manufacturers' products to other resellers or to the ultimate user. Wholesalers promote their goods through personal selling and possess little expertise in advertising. Conversely, retailers advertise a great deal, either cooperatively with manufacturers or independently.

Individuals An *individual* advertiser is a private citizen who wishes to sell a personal product for a profit, to request a particular need, or to express a perspective or an idea. For example, a college student selling a motorcycle would place a classified ad in the school newspaper. This same student may advertise for collector baseball cards in a hobby magazine. Politicians often advertise to voters to express their position on certain issues.

Institutions The last group of advertisers includes *institutions, government agencies,* and *social groups.* They are distinguished from the other categories in that their primary objective is not to sell a product or generate profits but rather to raise issues, influence ideas, affect legislation, provide a social service, or alter behavior in ways that are seen as socially desirable. Examples are Mothers Against Drunk Drivers (MADD), the Southern Baptist Convention, the Metropolitan Museum of Art, a local school board, the U.S. Army, the Teamsters Union, and a government-sponsored campaign telling us to "get out and vote."

THE ADVERTISING AGENCY

The second key player in the advertising world is the advertising agency. Advertisers hire independent agencies to plan and implement part or all of their advertising effort. The agency-client partnership is the dominant organizational arrangement in advertising. There are approximately 10,000 advertising agencies in the United States.

Ongoing mergers and acquisitions are continually changing the rankings, but Young and Rubicam was the top agency worldwide in 1992, with worldwide gross income of $994 million, followed by McCann-Erickson Worldwide and BBDO Worldwide (see Table 1.3). Rankings change when you look at the agency "mega groups," which are actually holding companies that include the parent agency and all of its subsidiaries. As listed in Table 1.3, WPP Group was ranked first with 1992 worldwide gross income of $2.8 billion. The top 500 U.S. agen-

Top 10 companies by 1992 ad spending

Rank	Company	Total measured ad spending			Ad spending by brands in 200			Number of brands
		1992	1991	% chg	1992	1991	% chg	
1	Procter & Gamble Co.	$1,174.7	$1,166.5	0.7	$324.5	$310.6	4.5	6
2	Philip Morris Cos.	1,090.8	1,110.4	−1.8	665.4	679.3	−2.0	6
3	General Motors Corp.	947.9	1,056.5	−10.3	893.2	994.5	−10.2	8
4	Ford Motor Co.	601.8	517.7	16.2	570.1	490.0	16.3	3
5	Chrysler Corp.	567.3	414.8	36.8	521.3	386.4	34.9	4
6	PepsiCo	555.7	542.0	2.5	468.3	470.2	−0.4	4
7	Sears, Roebuck & Co.	546.0	462.3	18.1	467.6	440.0	6.3	2
8	Toyota Motor Corp.	440.1	442.5	−0.5	439.7	441.3	−0.3	2
9	General Mills	430.9	419.1	2.8	369.6	360.7	2.4	3
10	Unilever	420.9	371.4	13.3	92.7	72.0	28.7	2

Notes: Dollars are in millions. Source: LNA/Arbitron Multi-Media Service.

Top 10 categories among top 200 brands in 1992 spending

Rank	Category	Measured ad spending			Ad spending by media			Number of brands
		1992	1991	% chg	Print	Broadcast	Outdoor	
1	Automotive	$3,597.2	$3,407.6	5.6	$1,078.6	$2,512.2	$6.4	30
2	Retail	2,878.9	2,742.3	5.0	1,740.7	1,134.7	3.5	34
3	Food	1,780.1	1,629.2	9.3	221.8	1,556.6	1.7	18
4	Restaurants	1,334.6	1,246.5	7.1	10.7	1,303.0	20.8	12
5	Entertainment	1,065.2	926.9	14.9	337.1	720.9	7.2	11
6	Telephone	732.6	693.4	5.7	134.7	593.8	4.1	7
7	Financial	581.2	467.6	24.3	181.2	394.1	5.9	9
8	Beer & liquor	552.4	552.5	0.0	31.4	499.8	21.2	3
9	Personal care	536.8	432.0	24.3	178.2	358.6	0.0	11
10	Drugs & remedies	525.0	462.6	13.5	78.9	446.2	0.0	9

Notes: Dollars are in millions. Totals include only brands from within the Top 200. Source: LNA/Arbitron Multi-Media Service.

Measured media spending for 1992

Rank	Media	All measured brands			Top 200 brands		
		1992	1991	% chg	1992	1991	% chg
1	Newspaper*	$10,862.0	$10,641.3	2.1	$2,733.0	$2,617.3	4.4
2	Network TV	10,732.8	10,101.9	6.2	6,361.9	5,985.8	6.3
3	Spot TV	9,399.6	8,751.2	7.4	3,631.2	3,203.7	13.3
4	Magazine	7,104.8	6,515.2	9.1	2,278.6	1,946.9	17.0
5	Cable TV networks	1,590.5	1,412.5	12.6	648.2	496.7	30.5
6	Syndicated TV	1,306.4	1,204.7	8.4	550.0	511.9	7.4
7	Spot radio	1,092.4	1,141.6	−4.3	283.6	329.9	−14.0
8	Outdoor	655.0	684.0	−4.2	145.1	155.0	−6.4
9	Network radio	549.1	578.7	−5.1	215.6	251.5	−14.3
	Subtotal print media	17,966.9	17,156.5	4.7	5,011.6	4,564.3	9.8
	Subtotal broadcast media	24,121.6	22,611.9	6.4	11,690.4	10,779.5	8.5
	Total	43,292.5	41,031.0	5.5	16,847.1	15,498.8	8.7

Notes: Dollars are in millions. *includes newspaper-distributed Sunday magazines. Source: LNA/Arbitron Multi-Media Service.

Source: R. Craig Endicott, "Top Brands Record 8.7% Ad Hike." Reprinted with permission from Advertising Age (May 3, 1993): 38. Copyright, Crain Communications, Inc., 1993.

Table 1.3

Who's on Top in 1992 Gross
Income

Top 10 advertising organizations

Rank	Organization	Worldwide gross income	% chg
1	WPP Group	$2,813.5	5.7
2	Interpublic Group of Cos.	1,989.2	8.4
3	Omnicom Group	1,806.7	7.1
4	Saatchi & Saatchi Advertising	1,696.5	2.8
5	Dentsu, Inc.	1,387.6	−4.4
6	Young & Rubicam	1,072.3	1.4
7	Euro RSCG	951.2	−4.8
8	Grey Advertising	735.4	9.2
9	Foote, Cone & Belding	682.7	10.2
10	Hakuhodo	661.1	0.8

Top 10 U.S.-based consolidated agencies

Rank	Agency	Worldwide gross income	% chg
1	Young & Rubicam	$994.0	1.3
2	McCann-Erickson Worldwide	935.8	11.8
3	BBDO Worldwide	835.8	10.0
4	J. Walter Thompson Co.	815.4	12.0
5	Ogilvy & Mather Worldwide	789.1	4.2
6	Saatchi & Saatchi Advertising	783.6	3.4
7	DDB Needham	777.1	2.8
8	Lintas:Worldwide	763.0	4.8
9	Foote, Cone & Belding	682.7	10.2
10	Grey Advertising	673.8	9.6

Top 10 U.S. agency brands

Rank	Agency	U.S. gross income	% chg
1	Leo Burnett Co.	$313.8	4.9
2	J. Walter Thompson Co	268.8	14.9
3	Saatchi & Saatchi Advertising	268.2	−4.0
4	Grey Advertising	240.1	5.5
5	McCann-Erickson Worldwide	236.7	7.0
6	DDB Needham Worldwide	229.4	−6.1
7	Ogilvy & Mather Worldwide	215.7	2.0
8	BBDO Worldwide	215.7	2.0
9	Foote, Cone & Belding	214.1	4.5
10	D'Arcy Masius Benton & Bowles	198.6	−1.6

Notes: Dollars are in millions.
Source: R. Craig Endicott, "New York Regains Agency Crown." Reprinted with permission from Advertising Age (April 14, 1993): 1. Copyright, Crain Communications Inc., 1993.

cies and the nearly 1,000 foreign shops linked in the global networks of the 20 largest returned gross income of $14.5 billion, up 7.2 percent.[10]

An advertiser uses an outside agency because it believes the agency will be

[10] R. Craig Endicott, "New York Regains Agency Crown," *Advertising Age* (April 14, 1993):S-1.

more effective and efficient in creating an individual commercial or a complete campaign. The strength of an agency is its resources, primarily in the form of creative expertise, media knowledge, and advertising strategy. Chapter 4 will discuss agencies in more detail.

Large advertisers—either companies or organizations—are involved in the advertising process in one of two ways: (1) through their advertising department or (2) through their in-house agency.

The Advertising Department. The most common organizational arrangement in a large business is the *advertising department*. The primary corporate responsibility for advertising lies with the *advertising manager*, or *advertising director*, who usually reports to the *director of marketing*. In the typical multiple-brand, consumer-products company, responsibility is divided by brand, with each brand managed by a *brand manager*. The brand manager is the business leader for the brand and has the ultimate responsibility for sales, product development, budget, and profits, as well as for advertising and other promotions. The brand manager, or advertising director, along with the advertising agency, develops the advertising strategy.

The advertising is usually presented by the agency to the brand manager and the director of advertising. The director of advertising, a specialist in recognizing and supporting effective advertising, advises the brand manager. Frequently the advertising director is responsible for approving advertising before it undergoes preliminary testing with real consumers.

The advertising manager organizes and staffs the advertising department, selects the advertising agency, and coordinates efforts with other departments within the company and businesses outside the organization. The advertising manager is also in charge of advertising control, which involves checking on such things as: Have the ads been run? At the right time, the right size, and in the right place? Was the ad produced exactly the way the company wanted? Was the work done within the budget? Most importantly, did the advertisement reach its objectives?

Who performs these tasks varies within the industry and the size of the business. The small retailer, for example, might have one person (often the owner) laying out the ad, writing the copy, and selecting the media. Physical production of the ad may be farmed out to freelancers or to the local media. Large retailers have more complete advertising departments and may have specialists on staff to do much of the work in house. Manufacturers tend to rely more on ad agencies to perform these tasks, with the advertising manager acting as a liaison between the company and the agency.

The In-House Agency. Companies that need closer control over the advertising have their own in-house agencies. Large retailers, for example, find that doing their own advertising provides cost savings as well as the ability to make fast-breaking local deadlines. An **in-house agency** performs most, and sometimes all, of the functions of an outside advertising agency. According to the American Association of Advertising Agencies (AAAA), the percentage of total business handled by in-house agencies remained fairly constant in the late 1980s at about 5 percent.[11]

in-house agency An advertising department on the advertiser's staff that handles most, if not all, of the functions of an outside agency.

Most in-house agencies are found in retailing, for several reasons. First,

_____

[11]R. Craig Endicott, "Sales Surge 11% for Media Giants," *Advertising Age* (June 29, 1987):S-1.

retailers tend to operate under small profit margins and find they can save money by doing their own advertising. Second, retailers often receive a great many advertising materials either free or at a reduced cost from manufacturers and trade associations. Local media, for example, will provide creative and production assistance for free. Third, the timetable for retailing tends to be much tighter than that for national advertising. Retailers often create complete campaigns in hours, whereas advertising agencies may take weeks or months.

THE MEDIA

media The channels of communication used by advertisers.

The third player in the advertising world is the media used by advertisers. The **media** are the channels of communication that carry the messages from the advertiser to the audience. Media organizations are organized to sell space (in print media) and time (in broadcast media). A media representative meets with the agency media buyers to convince them that the medium is a good advertising vehicle for their client's message. The most frequently used advertising media are newspapers, television, radio, magazines, out-of-home media such as outdoor and transit, and direct response. The primary media used in advertising are shown in Table 1.4.

Principle

Media provide information necessary to match the medium with the message.

Media must deliver advertising messages in a way that is consistent with the creative effort. Media staffs gather relevant information about their audiences so the message can be matched with the medium. Media also need to sell the product to prospective advertisers. Media representatives negotiate directly with the advertiser or work through the agency and its media department. They usually initiate the selling effort and personally call on the decision makers.

VENDORS

vendors Institutions that provide certain expertise that advertisers and agencies cannot perform.

The final player in the world of advertising is the collective variety of service organizations that assist advertisers, advertising agencies, and the media— the **vendors**. Members of this group are also referred to as freelancers, consultants, and self-employed professionals. The list of possibilities is quite extensive and examples include freelance copywriters and graphic artists, photographers, music studios, computer service bureaus, printers, market researchers, direct-mail production houses, marketing consultants, telemarketers, and public relation consultants.

Why would one of the other advertising players hire a vendor? Common reasons might be that the advertisers have no expertise in that area, they're overloaded, or they wish to gain a fresh perspective. Often, vendors simply can do the job less expensively. Today the trend is clearly toward doing less in house or with agencies and more through freelancers. Several experts note that the main advantage to using freelancers over in-house departments or agencies is access to a broad range of specialized talent on an as-needed basis. The main idea is to utilize the talents and skills of individuals who are uniquely suited to particular projects.

Using freelancers provides broader, more flexible access to the best creative talent and a broader range of ideas than you can get either in house or through an agency. Discussion of vendors will be interlaced throughout the text.

Table 1.4

U.S. Advertising Volume

Medium	1991 Millions of dollars	1991 % of total	1992 Millions of dollars	1992 % of total	%chg
NEWSPAPERS					
National	3,685	2.9	3,602	2.7	–2.3
Local	26,724	21.2	27,135	20.7	1.5
Total	30,409	24.1	30,737	23.4	1.1
MAGAZINES					
Weeklies	2,670	2.1	2,739	2.1	2.6
Women's	1,671	1.3	1,853	1.4	10.9
Monthlies	2,183	1.8	2,408	1.8	10.3
Total	6,524	5.2	7,000	5.3	7.3
FARM PUBLICATIONS	215	0.2	231	0.2	7.4
TELEVISION					
Network	8,933	7.1	9,549	7.3	6.9
Cable (national)	1,521	1.2	1,685	1.3	10.8
Syndication	1,853	1.5	2,070	1.6	11.7
Spot (national)	7,110	5.6	7,551	5.8	6.2
Spot (local)	7,565	6.0	8,079	6.1	6.8
Cable (nonnetwork)	420	0.3	475	0.3	13.1
Total	27,402	21.7	29,409	22.4	7.3
RADIO					
Network	490	0.4	424	0.3	–13.5
Spot (national)	1,575	1.2	1,505	1.2	–4.4
Spot (local)	6,411	5.1	6,725	5.1	4.9
Total	8,476	6.7	8,654	6.6	2.1
YELLOW PAGES					
National	1,162	0.9	1,188	0.9	2.2
Local	8,020	6.3	8,132	6.2	1.4
Total	9,182	7.2	9,320	7.1	1.5
DIRECT MAIL	24,460	19.3	25,391	19.3	3.8
BUSINESS PAPERS	2,882	2.3	3,090	2.4	7.2
OUTDOOR					
National	637	0.5	610	0.5	–4.2
Local	440	0.3	421	0.3	–4.3
Total	1,077	0.8	1,031	0.8	–4.3
MISCELLANEOUS					
National	11,588	9.2	12,124	9.2	4.6
Local	4,185	3.3	4,303	3.3	2.8
Total	15,773	12.5	16,427	12.5	4.1
National total	72,635	57.5	76,020	57.9	4.7
Local total	53,765	42.5	55,270	42.1	2.8
GRAND TOTAL	126,400	100.0	131,290	100.0	3.9

Source: Robert J. Coen, "Ad Gains Could Exceed 6% This Year." Reprinted with permission from *Advertising Age* (May 3, 1993): 4. Copyright, Crain Communications Inc., 1993.
The McCann-Erickson U.S. advertising volume reports represent all expenditures by U.S. advertisers—national, local, private individuals, and so on. The expenditures, by medium, include all commissions as well as the art, mechanical and production expenses.

$\mathcal{T}$HE EVOLUTION OF ADVERTISING

Now that we have discussed the factors of great advertising and introduced the roles and functions of advertising, advertisers, agencies, and the media, let's look at how these roles and players developed historically.[12] The key players and events that influenced the development of advertising are listed in Figure 1.1.

THE ANCIENT PERIOD

Persuasive communication has been around since early times. Inscriptions on tablets, walls, and papyrus from ancient Babylonia, Egypt, and Greece carry messages listing available products and upcoming events and announcing rewards for the return of runaway slaves.

Because of widespread illiteracy before the age of print, most messages were actually delivered by *criers* who stood on street corners shouting the wares of the sponsor. Stores, and the merchandise they carried, were identified by signs. Information rather than persuasion was the objective of the early commercial messages.

THE AGE OF PRINT

The invention of movable type by Johannes Gutenberg around 1440 moved society toward a new level of communication—mass communication. No longer restricted by the time required by a scribe to hand-letter a single message, advertising could now be mass-produced. The availability of printed media to a greater number of people increased the level of literacy, which, in turn, encouraged more businesses to advertise. In terms of media, the early printed advertisements included posters, handbills, and classified advertisements in newspapers. Ad 1.6 is an example of an early print ad from the fifteenth century. The first printed advertisements in English appeared in London around 1472 tacked to church doors. The product advertised was a prayer book for sale.

The word *advertisement* first appeared around 1655. It was used in the Bible to indicate notification or warning. Book publishers, for example, headed most of their announcements with the term, and by 1660 it was generally used as a heading for commercial information, primarily by store owners. The messages continued to be simple and informative through the 1700s and into the 1800s.

The culmination of the age of print was the development of the newspaper. The very first U.S. newspaper was titled *Public Occurrences both Forreign and Domestick*; it appeared in 1690 and only lasted one issue. In 1704 the *Boston Newsletter* was the first paper to carry an ad, which offered a reward for the capture of a thief. James and Benjamin Franklin, early colonial printers, started the *New England Courant* in 1721. By the time of the American Revolution, there were over 30 newspapers in the United States. The first daily newspaper was *The Pennsylvania Evening Post and Daily Advertiser*, which appeared in 1783.

THE FORMATIVE YEARS

The mid-1800s marked the beginning of the development of the advertising industry in the United States. The emerging importance and growth of advertis-

---

[12]Much of this historical review was adapted from Stephen Fox, *The Mirror Makers* (New York: Vintage Books, 1985).

Figure 1.1

The evolution of advertising.

Period	People	Time	Events	People	Time	Events
Ancient Period			Signs	E.E. Calkins	1895	Image Copy
			Criers	John B. Kennedy	1904	Hard-Sell Copy
			Sequis	Claude Hopkins	1910	Reason-Why Copy
	Johannes Gutenberg	1441	Movable Type	Albert Lasker	1904 to 1944	Great Advertising Executive
	Wm. Claxton	1477	First Ad in English	Thoedore MacManus	1910	Atmosphere Advertising
		1625	First Ad in English Newspaper		1914	FTC Act Passed
		1655	Term Advertising Introduced		1917	Am. Assoc. of Advt. Formed
		1704	First U.S. Newspaper to Carry Ads	Stanley/Helen Resor	1920	Intro. Psych./Res.
Formative Period	Volney Palmer	1841	First Ad Sales Agent	Raymond Rubicam	1923	Y&R Formed
	George Rowell	1850	First Ad Wholesaler		1926	Commercial Radio
	Charles Bates	1871	First Formal Agency		1940	Selling Stratagems
	Francis Ayer	1875	Fixed Commission		1947	Commercial Television
	John Powers	1880	First Great Copywriter	Rosser Reeves Marion Harber	1950s	Mergers, Research and Hard-Sell
	E.C. Allen	1887	Magazine Advertising	Leo Burnett David Ogilvy	1960s	High Creativity
	J. Walter Thompson	1891	First Account Executive	William Bernbach	1970s	Back to the 50s
					1980s	Mergers and Creativity
					1990s	Accountability, Globalization, and Integrated Marketing Communications

The right-hand columns are under the heading **Modern Period**.

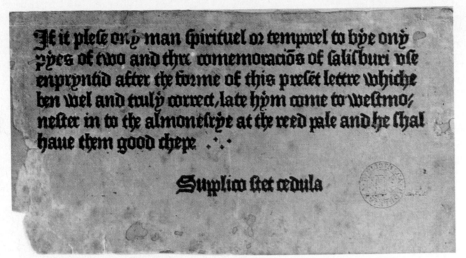

ing during this period resulted from a number of social and technological developments associated with the industrial revolution.

The Age of Mass Marketing. Because of inventions that increased productivity, such as the internal combustion engine and the cotton gin, manufacturers were able to mass-produce goods of uniform quality. The resulting excess production, however, could be profitable only if it attracted customers living beyond the local markets. Fortunately, the long-distance transportation network of rivers and canals was being replaced in mid-century by a much speedier system of roads and railroads.

All that remained for modern advertising to do was to devise an effective and efficient communication system that could reach a widely dispersed marketplace. National media developed as the country's transportation system grew. At about the same time a number of new technologies emerged that greatly facilitated mass marketing and mass communications. Most notably, the telegraph, the telephone, and the typewriter provided dramatic improvements in mass-message delivery. The early advertising experts, such as Volney Palmer, the first "adman," functioned strictly as *media brokers.* Palmer established himself as an "agent" in 1841 in Philadelphia, and opened a branch office in Boston in 1845 and New York in 1849, charging a commission for placing ads in newspapers. Thoroughly familiar with all the periodicals and their rates, these early media brokers had a keen ability to negotiate. They received their commissions out of the fees paid by publishers. The messages were prepared primarily by the advertisers or writers they hired directly and often featured exaggerated and outrageous claims.

By the late nineteenth century the advertising profession was more fully developed. Agencies had taken on the role of convincing manufactures to advertise their products. Ads had assumed a more complete informational and educational role. Copywriting had become a polished and reputable craft. Ad 1.7 is an example of an ad for an early advertising agency.

The Growth of the Retailer. In the late 1800s John Wanamaker revolutionized retailing. Before the Civil War there were no set prices for merchandise sold in retail outlets. As a result, store owners bartered and changed prices depending

on the perceived wealth of the customer being served or on their own need for cash that day. Wanamaker, who owned a dry-goods store in Philadelphia, changed this tradition by standardizing the prices on all the merchandise he sold. Furthermore, he established even greater credibility by offering a money-back guarantee. This strategy of honest dealings and straight talk was so successful that Wanamaker built two more outlets and the huge Philadelphia Grand Depot department store.

Wanamaker also hired the first well-known copywriter, John E. Powers. In 1880 Powers was hired to communicate Wanamaker's philosophy to the public. Powers "journalized" advertising by writing ads that were newsy and informationally accurate. He also made the ad more up to date with new copy every day. "My discovery," as Powers explained it, was to "print the news of the store."[13] With Powers's assistance, the sales volume in Wanamaker's stores doubled in just a few years.

The Advent of Magazines. During the 1800s most advertising was placed in newspapers or appeared on posters and handbills. Until the late 1880s magazines were a medium strictly for the wealthy and well educated, containing political commentaries, short stories, and discussions of art and fashion. This changed with the introduction of the *People's Literary Companion* by E.C. Allen,

---

[13]*Printer's Ink* (October 23, 1895).

Claude Hopkins, considered by some people to be the greatest copywriter of all times.

(Courtesy of FCB/Leber Katz Partners)

Copywriter John E. Kennedy explained that "Advertising is salesmanship in print."

(Courtesy of FCB/Leber Katz Partners)

Principle

"Advertising is salesmanship in print."

which appealed to a large group of general readers. Also, about this time Congress approved low postage rates for periodicals, which allowed magazines to be distributed economically by mail. The first magazine advertising appeared in July 1844 in the *Southern Messenger*, which was edited for a short time by Edgar Allan Poe.

Magazines offered a medium for longer, more complex messages. They also had enough lead time to permit the production of art such as engravings to illustrate articles and ads. As the production processes improved, photographs were introduced, and magazine advertisements became highly visual. Some of the earliest magazines to contain advertising are still around today, including *Cosmopolitan, Ladies' Home Journal*, and *Reader's Digest*.

MODERN ADVERTISING

By the beginning of the twentieth century the total volume of advertising had increased to $500 million from $50 million in 1870. The industry had become a major force in marketing and had achieved a significant level of respect and esteem.[14]

The Era of Professionalism

Calkens and Graphics The twentieth century also witnessed a revolution in advertising. Earnest Elmo Calkens of the Bates agency created a style of advertising that resembled original art and adapted beautifully to the medium of magazines. Calkens's ads not only attracted the viewer's attention but also increased the status and image of the advertiser. His work represented the first venture into image advertising.

Lord & Thomas Salesmanship Advertising took a dramatic detour when John E. Kennedy and Albert Lasker formed their historic partnership in 1905 at the powerful Lord & Thomas agency. Lasker was a partner in the firm and the managerial genius who made Lord & Thomas such a force in the advertising industry. Ads that sold the product were all that mattered to him. Because of Lasker's philosophy, the agency was able to make a profit when others were losing money. (See Ad 1.8.)

In 1905 Lasker was pondering the question: What is advertising? Like Powers, he had been approaching advertising as news. John E. Kennedy, who had worked for a variety of retailers and patent-medicine clients, responded with a note that said, "I can tell you what advertising is." When the two met, Kennedy explained, "Advertising is salesmanship in print."[15]

Thus was born the "sales" approach to advertising copy. Kennedy's style was simple and straightforward, based on the belief that advertising should present the same arguments a salesperson would use in person. This "reason-why" copy style became the hallmark of Lord & Thomas ads. Lasker, referring to his meeting with Kennedy in 1905, said, "The whole complexion of advertising for all America was changed from that day on."

Hopkins and Testing At the height of his career in the early 1930s Claude Hopkins was Lord & Thomas's best-known copywriter and made the unheard-

---

[14]*Printer's Ink* (October 23, 1953).

[15]Merrill DeVoe, *Effective Advertising Copy* (New York: Macmillan Co., 1956):21.

of-salary of $185,000. Sometimes called the greatest copywriter of all time, he
was also the most analytical.

Hopkins worked with direct mail and used that medium to test and refine
his techniques. In his 1923 book *Scientific Advertising*, he discussed the principles and laws he had discovered as a result of his constant copy testing: "One ad
is compared with another, one method with another. . . . No guesswork is permitted. One must know what is best. Thus mail-order advertising first established many of our basic laws."[16]

MacManus and Soft-Sell Theodore F. MacManus was a copywriter for the
young General Motors company, where he produced an image style of advertising resembling that of Calkens. He felt that a "soft-sell" rather than a "hard-sell"
copy style would better create the long-term relationship considered necessary
between a car manufacturer and its customers. Image was everything. The only
way to penetrate the subconscious of the reader was through a slow accumula-
tion of positive images.[17] The positive illusions created by MacManus for
Cadillac and Buick had much to do with their early successes.

War and Prosperity. With the outbreak of World War I, the advertising industry offered its services to the Council of National Defense. The Division of
Advertising of the Committee of Public Information was formed. This volunteer
agency created advertising to attract military recruits, sell Liberty Bonds, and
support the Red Cross and the war effort in general (see Ad 1.9). Thus was born
public service advertising that relied on volunteer professionals and donated
time and space.

J. Walter Thompson and the Postwar Boom After the war consumers were
desperate for goods and services. New products were emerging constantly (see
Ad 1.10). A great boom in advertising was led by the J. Walter Thompson agency

---

[16]DeVoe, *Effective Advertising Copy*, p. 22.

[17]*Printer's Ink* (January 31, 1918).

(JWT) through the innovative copy and management style of the husband-and-wife team Stanley and Helen Resor. Stanley administered the agency and developed the concept of account services.

The JWT agency was known for many innovations in advertising. The Resors coined the concepts of *brand names* to associate a unique identity with a particular product. They also developed the status appeal by which they persuaded nonwealthy people to imitate the habits of richer people. JWT advertising introduced modern marketing research to advertising. Stanley Resor also built a network of agencies, including some outside the United States.

Dealing with the Depression. Advertising diminished drastically after the October stock market crash and the onset of the Great Depression in 1929.

Advertising budgets were slashed in an attempt to cut costs, and advertisers and consumers alike began to question the value and legitimacy of advertising. Clients demanded more service and special deals. The Depression brought back the hard-sell, reason-why copy approach of Lasker and Hopkins and gave rise to the consumer movement and tighter government regulation. (See Ad 1.11.) The Federal Trade Commission (FTC), which was established in 1914 to prevent unfair or anticompetitive business practices, amended guidelines at this time to give the agency more consumer-oriented power. The Wheeler-Lea Amendment gave the FTC the power to curb "deceptive" or "unfair" advertising. The FTC was also given authority over false advertising of food, drugs, cosmetics, and therapeutic devices.

Principle

The value of an idea is measured by its originality.

Rubicam and Originality During and after the Depression Raymond Rubicam emerged as one of the giants of advertising. In the spring of 1923 he launched his own agency with John Orr Young, a Lord & Thomas copywriter. Young & Rubicam created unique ads with intriguing headlines. Rubicam emphasized fresh, original ideas. He also hired the researcher George Gallup and made research an essential part of the creative process. Research became an important part of advertising as research organizations founded by Daniel Starch, A.C. Nielsen, and George Gallup gave rise to the research industry.

Caples and Headlines John Caples, a vice president of Batten, Barton, Durstine and Osborn (BBDO), made a major contribution to the field in 1932 when he published *Tested Advertising Methods*. His theories about the "pulling power" of headlines were based on extensive mail-order and inquiry testing. Caples was also known for changing the style of advertising writing, which had been wordy and full of exaggerations. He used short words, short sentences, and short paragraphs.[18]

The Advent of Radio. Radio offered the Depression-weary consumer an inexpensive form of entertainment. The tremendous potential of radio created two serious problems for advertising, however. First, it meant that advertising agencies had to find or train staff employees who could write copy for the ear. The second problem was financial. In the early days of radio sponsors underwrote the programming, which involved a much greater financial commitment than a single ad. The growth of radio, however, was phenomenal. Twelve years after its first commercial broadcast, radio surpassed magazines as the leading advertising medium.

World War II. During World War II the advertising industry once again served as mass communicator for America. The War Advertising Council (WAC) used advertising to enlist recruits, sell war bonds, and encourage the planting of victory gardens and the sending of V-mail letters. Ad 1.12 is an example of a 1944 ad encouraging the purchase of war bonds. Over $1 billion was spent on the most extensive advertising campaign ever created. The effort was so successful that after the war, instead of disbanding, the WAC simply changed its name to the Advertising Council and has remained a very effective public service effort to this day.

---

[18]DeVoe, *Advertising Copy*, pp. 25–26.

John Mayner, Account Coordinator
Dally Advertising, Dallas

If you are interested in pursuing a career in advertising, the door is wide open for almost anyone from any background. Although I had no formal training in advertising, my eclectic background, education, and work experiences have served me well in this field.

As an undergraduate at the University of Texas at Austin, I had an extremely diverse and well-rounded liberal arts education—I was one or two classes short of a double major in history and English. While I was going to school, I worked at the state capitol as Assistant Sergeant-at-Arms in the House of Representatives. I worked for 3-1/2 years for a large corporate law firm, and I also worked as an au pair for an Austin family. After graduation, I landed a job as a kitchen assistant in a gourmet restaurant. After that, I proceeded to work in a Catholic lay apostolate that works with the poor, and then began a year-and-a-half stint as a legal assistant. While I was trying to figure out "what I wanted to be when I grew up," I took my GMAT, got accepted into Texas A&M University's MBA program, got a concentration in marketing, and began to get familiar with a lifestyle that is very similar to someone who works in the advertising field.

During my first semester in graduate school, I contacted Leo Burnett, asked if I could go to Austin for their presentation at the University of Texas, and it was there that I became hooked on the idea of working for an agency. I still remember listening to a gentleman named Bill Haljun, a senior vice president who had

Courtesy of John Mayner

worked at Burnett for over 20 years. He made it sound like the most exciting career imaginable. From that first campus visit with Leo Burnett, I decided that I was going to pursue a career in advertising in account services.

Even for those people who are lucky enough to find employment quickly, job searches are really stressful. I never would have imagined that it would take me ten months, 225 résumés and cover letters, and two trips to New York to land my first job in advertising.

Principle

For many products, differentiation is created by advertising.

Postwar Advertising. During the 1950s markets were inundated with "me too" products with similar features. "Keeping up with the Joneses" was the attitude among consumers, and many products stressing style, luxury, and social acceptance were forced to compete. The primary difference between many of these products was the image created by the advertising.

Rosser Reeves and the USP One person who was able to cut through this clutter of products was Rosser Reeves of the Ted Bates agency. Reeves proposed that an effective ad had to offer a "unique selling proposition" (USP) containing a benefit that was important to consumers and that no other competitor offered. "M&M's melt in your mouth, not in your hands" and "Double your pleasure, double your fun" are two USPs made famous by Reeves.

My first job was working as an assistant media planner at a large agency (Bloom FCA, with approximately $200 million in billings and 250 employees). Although I am grateful for the experience and the exposure that a larger agency was able to provide, the job itself was not a really good experience. The second-to-last pay period I was there I worked 212 hours in a two-week pay period (with no overtime or comp time) and was told by my planner when we left at 6:45 a.m. that we needed to be back at work by 9:00 a.m. to finish up our project. I soon began to reconsider what I was doing, and whether or not it was at all worthwhile.

It didn't take a genius to know that something was definitely wrong with my quality-of-life/professional outlook equation. I was making $14,000 a year, I rarely got to spend any time with my wife (we thought that nothing could be worse than graduate school, silly us), and my professional advancement opportunities were virtually nonexistent. In addition, work had become so oppressive that I started to get sick as I pulled into the parking garage each morning. That should be an obvious sign to anyone that something is definitely wrong or unhealthy with such a work environment.

In what proved to be the most wonderful solution to my predicament, on my last day of work at that big agency, I received a phone call from my brother-in-law saying that his agency, a much smaller creative shop in Fort Worth that I had interviewed with a year and a half earlier, had called him to see if I might still be interested. Not only did they have a job opening, but it was in account services. Six weeks later, I started working at Dally Advertising as an account coordinator.

Going to work for a much smaller agency has been a very positive experience for me personally. Due to the limitations of size, a smaller agency will force you to become a more well-rounded generalist, because you always pitch in on other accounts, new business prospects, and help out in other departments in a crunch. In my first week at Dally, I was able to help prepare for one of the largest pitches that our agency had ever been in on—that type of opportunity would never have been available to me at a much larger shop. In addition, when we had difficulty selling a very controversial public service campaign to one of our clients, I voiced my opinion that I thought we would have a much better opportunity selling that campaign to another group. I was then given the chance to "give away" my first campaign, less than six months into my job. Within 24 hours, I had my first appointment, and by the close of the week, I had sold my first campaign. That campaign went on to win Dally a National Addy Award, and I was able to be the account executive on that particular piece of business.

Although the hours are still long, and I still struggle from time to time with maintaining a balance between my personal and professional lives, I am much happier doing what I am now doing, and where I am doing it, than I was before. If you are patient and capable of measuring your success on your own terms and not on what others think it should be, then a career in advertising can offer you excitement, variety, and the strange pleasure that comes from knowing not any two days will ever be alike.

Bedell and Selling Strategems Like Caples, Clyde Bedell was a student and a master of mail-order copy. In a 1940 book *How to Write Advertising That Sells* he expressed his philosophy of advertising, which focused on the selling aspects. He developed a set of "31 Proved Selling Strategems" that defined the relationship between product features and selling points.[19]

The Advent of Television. In 1939 NBC became the first television network to initiate regular broadcasting. Not until the 1950s, however, did television become a major player in advertising. By the end of that decade television was the dominant advertising medium. Its total advertising revenues grew from

[19]DeVoe, *Advertising Copy*, p. 27.

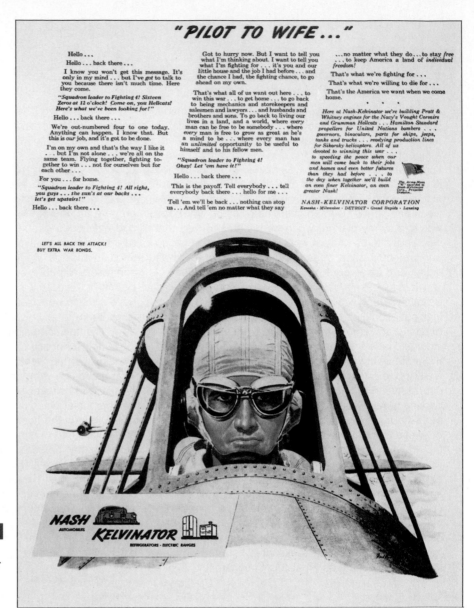

Ad 1.12

Many companies openly supported the World War II effort through their advertisements.

(Courtesy of William Heinemann)

$12.3 million in 1949 to $128 million in 1951.[20] Ad 1.13 is an example of a popular ad from the 1950s.

The Era of Creativity. The 1960s saw a resurgence of art, inspiration, and intuition in advertising. This revolution was inspired by three creative geniuses: Leo Burnett, David Ogilvy, and William Bernbach.

Burnett and Middle America Leo Burnett was the leader of the "Chicago School" of advertising. He believed in finding the "inherent drama" in every

---

[20]Stephen Fox, *The Mirror Makers: A History of American Advertising and Its Creators* (New York: Vintage Books, 1985):211.

product and then presenting it as believably as possible. The Leo Burnett agency created mythical characters who represented American values, such as the Jolly Green Giant, Tony the Tiger, Charlie the Tuna, and Morris the Cat. The most famous campaign, which was discussed in the Issues and Controversies box (p. 9) in this chapter, is the Marlboro Man, which has built the American cowboy into the symbol of the best-selling cigarette in the world. Burnett never apologized for his common-touch approach. He took pride in his ability to reach the average consumer.

Ogilvy: Discipline and Style David Ogilvy, founder of the Ogilvy & Mather agency, is a paradox because he represents both the "image" school of MacManus and Rubicam and "claim" school of Lasker and Hopkins. Although Ogilvy believed in research and mail-order copy with all of its testing, he had a tremendous sense of image and story appeal. He created enduring brands with campaign symbols like the eyepatch on the Hathaway man (see Ad 1.14). Among the other products he handled were Rolls-Royce, Pepperidge Farm, and Guinness.

The Art of Bernbach Doyle, Dane, and Bernbach opened in 1949. From the beginning, William Bernbach was the catalyst for the agency's success. A copy

Modess ... *because*

Hathaway turns its hand to seawear.

You see merely the tip of the iceberg. Just a sampling of a spanking new collection from Hathaway.

The shirts, like signal flags fluttering from halyards, make bright splashes of color; among them, such hues as orange and green and flaring yellow. Every shirt is the very plushest of cotton terry cloths.

In the matter of trousers and jackets, Hathaway has chosen to avoid the obvious fabrics. Instead, it has used a soft yet rugged canvas twill in a natural shade that contrasts with the vividness of the shirts.

The boat shorts are of canvas, too, double-pleated and cuffed and rigged with a flapped coin pocket.

The jacket is but one of three, each cut from bolts of pure cotton canvas twill. Not shown, a pullover jacket with a big kangaroo pocket in front. And another fitted with a snap-off hood.

This, then, is seawear. Casual things to wear while knocking around in boats or backyards. From those Yankee craftsmen at the C.F. Hathaway Co. up in Waterville, Maine.

Ad 1.15

This highly creative ad by Bill Bernbach reflects the 1960s.

(Courtesy of Dreyfus Fund Inc.)

Ad 1.16

The famous "Brother Dominic" campaign for Xerox was a true stimulus to sales.

(Courtesy of Xerox Corporation)

writer with an acute sense of design, he was considered by many to be the most innovative advertiser of his time. His advertising touched people by focusing on feelings and emotions. He explained: "There are a lot of great technicians in advertising. However, they forget that advertising is persuasion, and persuasion is not a science, but an art. Advertising is the art of persuasion."[21] (See the Dreyfus Lion, Ad 1.15)

The Era of Accountability The Vietnam War and the economic downturn of the 1970s led to a reemphasis on hard-sell advertising. Clients wanted results, and agencies hired MBAs who understood strategic planning and the elements of marketing. A great deal of advertising moved away from the 1950s "formula ads"—vignettes and slice-of-life commercials showing people enjoying the product. This is not to suggest, however, that this period was void of creative geniuses. On the contrary, Hal Riney, creator of the well-known Henry Weinhard's Private Reserve beer commercials, Bartles & Jaymes's Frank and Ed, and most recently, the award-winning Saturn commercials, has been at work since the early 1970s. Charlotte Beers was the creative genius behind the American

---

[21]*Printer's Ink* (January 2, 1953).

Express, "Cardholder since. . . . " campaign. Bill Backer is the man who created the legendary Coca-Cola hilltop singers commercial. He also came up with the "Tastes great, less filling" spots that turned Miller Lite beer into a major player. Finally, Jane Maas, who learned her craft from David Ogilvy, was the person responsible for the "I love New York" campaign, Prell shampoo, and Safeguard soap. Perhaps no campaign better reflects this era than the Xerox campaign featuring Brother Dominic (Ad 1.16). This is just a very small sample of the creative firepower that produced good advertising while running profitable businesses. It wasn't easy, yet 11 agencies, led by Y&R at $2.3 billion, had reached the billion-dollar mark by the end of the decade, compared to none in 1970.[22]

In response to the intense emphasis on performance and profit in the 1970s and 1980s, many consumer-product companies shifted their budgets from traditional media to *sales promotion*, which uses strategies such as coupons, rebates, and sweepstakes to generate short-term sales gains. Agencies either learned to create sales promotions or acquired firms that specialized in doing so.

The Future of Advertising. What advertising will be like in the 1990s and into the twenty-first century is still unclear. The advertising industry has come to realize just how vulnerable it is to the outside world, however. Many agencies closed when poor economic conditions in the late 1980s and early 1990s severely reduced advertising budgets.

A more important influence on the fate of advertising than economic conditions, however, is the changing demographics. The typical consumer will be older and wiser. Furthermore, these individuals will have a great acceptance of divergent views and lifestyles, increased acceptance of technology, and increased concern for social issues and for the environment. In addition, they will not accept trade-offs. Their view will be "Maximize. Don't compromise." For advertisers, this will mean a creative strategy that is more pointed and fact based, delivered at the moment when the consumer needs the information. The latter requirement will be provided by media technology, such as interactive cable, which allows the consumer to customize the advertising message. As we move closer to cable and satellite systems capable of delivering hundreds of choices, messages will become more and more customer specific.

Marketers are expecting a great deal more from advertising than they did a decade ago. Advertising must pay its own way—and quickly. Sales promotions, which directly affect sales, have replaced advertising in many cases. Moreover, clients are demanding more value-added services from agencies, at no extra charge. To cope with these new demands agencies have reduced staff size and carefully pruned services that are not cost-effective. They have also placed tremendous pressure on media companies to reduce their rates and to provide better measures of effectiveness. Thanks to ongoing technological advances, media will be able to report on how a particular ad affects actual purchase, brand switching, and customer retention. Accountability will be both expected and verifiable.

Undoubtedly the biggest trend in the 1990s is and will continue to be the continued growth in **integrated marketing communication.** According to Northwestern advertising professor Don E. Schultz, "The concept of integrated marketing communication (IMC) follows basically the concept of marketing: we start with the consumer needs and wants, and work back to the brand."[23] He

Integrated marketing communications The concept or philosophy or marketing that stresses bringing together all the variables of the marketing mix, all the media, all the actions with which a company reaches its publics, and integrating the company's strategy and programs.

[22]Fox, *Mirror Makers*, p. 262.

[23]Don E. Schultz, "Integration Helps You Plan Communication from Outside-In," *The Marketing News* (March 15, 1993):12.

contends this approach is now possible because of the tremendous improvements made in capturing data about who actually buys products. The assumption in the past was that the world was a mass market, and that standardized marketing communication was appropriate. The result was *inside-out planning*, where marketing and advertising planning was predetermined by the marketers. This strategy focuses on what the marketer wants to say, when the marketer wants to say it, about things the marketer believes are important about the brand, and in media forms the marketer wants to use.

Today, advertisers are able to do *outside-in planning*. Employing base amounts of data about customers and prospects, the advertiser can measure what customers have done over time, assess which promotional efforts customers responded to and those they did not, and determine when customers change their responses.

IMC means that the relationship between the advertisers and the agency will also change. Timm Crull, chairman-CEO of Nestlé USA, succinctly described this relationship in a recent speech at the American Association of Advertising Agencies annual meeting: "Agencies must help clients develop compelling advertising concepts that will serve as launching pads for the broad range of other marketing tools available. That list includes packaging, in-store promotions, direct mail, direct response, product 800 numbers, data base marketing, coupon redemption programs, cable programming—to name a few."[24]

Another trend that is sure to continue is the globalization of advertising. In the early 1990s the trade barriers throughout much of Europe came down, making it the largest contiguous market in the world. Eastern Europe, Russia, and China have at least partially opened their markets to Western businesses. Advertisers are moving into these markets, and ad agencies are forming huge multinational agencies with international research and media-buying capabilities. The advertising challenge, however, will not be global versus local. The objective will be to practice global and local advertising simultaneously. Standardizing ads or customizing ads will become a major strategic question.

Along with the trend toward globalization is a move toward tighter and tighter *niche marketing* to market segments and even to individuals. Mass advertising, as we know it, will change. New technologies will permit advertisers to reach select groups of consumers with selective media. Marketers will search for and implement media and marketing plans aimed at special selective markets. The direct-marketing chapter (Chapter 16) chronicles this move from mass marketing to individualized or personalized marketing.

Increasing trade concentration and increasing retailer sophistication will require a changing approach to advertising. Knowledge is power. The power is shifting from the marketer to the retailer, and the source of that power is information. In the future, the retailer will take a more active role in the communication effort. With increased concentration and sophistication, getting closer to the retailer will be critical. The advertiser and the ad agency must both play a more active role in local retail marketing.

The byword for advertising in the future will be *accountability*. Advertising will be forced to walk the precarious tightrope between creativity and profitability, and survival will go to the fittest.

---

[24]Timm Crull, "Nestlé to Agencies: 'Shake Mindset,'" *Advertising Age* (May 3, 1993):26.

UMMARY

- Classic ads that have stood the test of time work on two levels: they engage the mind of the consumer and at the same time deliver a selling message.

- The characteristics of a great ad are as follows: (1) It is strategically sound in that it is directed at a certain audience, driven by specific objectives, its message is crafted to speak to that audience's most important concerns, and it is placed in media that will most effectively reach that audience. (2) A great ad has a creative concept that gets the audience's attention and is remembered. (3) It employs the right execution for the message and the audience.

- The definition of advertising has six elements: (1) paid communication, (2) that is nonpersonal, (3) from an identified sponsor, (4) using mass media, (5) to persuade or influence (6) an audience.

- There are eight types of advertising, each appropriate for certain distinct strategies: (1) brand advertising, (2) retail advertising, (3) political advertising, (4) directory advertising, (5) direct-response advertising, (6) business-to-business advertising, (7) institutional advertising, and (8) public service advertising.

- Advertising fulfills (1) a marketing role, (2) a communication role, (3) an economic role, and (4) a societal role.

- Advertising has three basic functions: (1) advertising may be either direct-action or indirect-action advertising, (2) advertising can be primary or secondary, and (3) advertising can serve a commercial or noncommercial function.

- The four key players in the advertising industry are: (1) advertisers, (2) advertising agencies, (3) media, and (4) vendors.

- A firm's advertising can be handled either internally by an in-house agency or externally by an advertising agency. Companies often have advertising departments to either handle their own work or interface with an agency.

- The evolution of advertising has gone through many creative peaks and valleys, largely influenced by societal factors and the creative capabilities of the individuals working in advertising at the time.

- The future of advertising will be strongly affected by new organizational patterns both within the field itself and in the business community, globalization, and integrated marketing communication.

QUESTIONS

1. Critics charge that advertising seeks to manipulate its audience, whereas advertising's supporters claim that it merely seeks to persuade. Which interpretation do you agree with? Why?

2. "I'll tell you what great advertising means," Bill Slater said during a heated dorm discussion. "Great advertising is the ability to capture the imagination of the public—the stuff that sticks in the memory, like Dancing Raisins, or Levi's jeans commercials, or that rabbit with the drum—that's what great is," he says. "Bill, you missed the point," says Phil Graham, a marketing major. "Advertising is a promotional weapon. Greatness means commanding attention and persuading people to buy something. It's what David Leisure did for Isuzu. No frills, no cuteness—great advertising has to sell the public and keep them sold," he adds. How would you enter this argument? What is your interpretation of "great advertising?"

3. Walt Jameson has just joined the advertising department faculty in a university after a long professional career. In an informal talk with the campus advertising club, Jameson is put on the spot about career choices. The students want to know which is the best place to start in the

1990s—with an advertiser (a company) or with an advertising agency. How should Jameson respond? Should he base his answer on the current situation or on how he reads the future?

4 A strong debate continues at Telcom, a supplier of telephone communication systems for business. The issue is whether the company will do a better communication job with its budget of $15 million by using an in-house advertising agency or by assigning the business to an independent advertising agency. What are the major issues that Telcom should consider?

5 The chapter discussed a number of creative approaches that are honored in the history of advertising. When you think of Reeves, Burnett, Ogilvy, and Bernbach, do any of their styles seem suited to the 1990s? Do the years ahead seem to require hard-sell or soft-sell advertising strategies? Explain your reasons.

6 Identify five major figures in the history of advertising and explain their contributions to the field.

7 How did the advertising field change after the invention of movable type, radio, and television?

$\mathcal{S}$UGGESTED CLASS PROJECT

Form small groups of five or six students. Have a spokesperson contact one or two advertising agencies. Question one or more key individuals about the changes that have taken place in their agency and the industry during the last five years. (Prepare a list of questions ahead of time.) What kinds of changes do they expect in the next five years? Get together to write a report that is three to five pages long.

$\mathcal{F}$URTHER READINGS

AAKER, DAVID A., and JOHN G. MEYERS, *Advertising Management* (Englewood Cliffs, NJ: Prentice Hall, 1975).

BOGART, LEO, *Strategies in Advertising*, 2nd ed. (Lincolnwood, IL: NTC Business Books, 1990).

FOX, STEPHEN, *The Mirror Makers: A History of American Advertising and Its Creators* (New York: Vintage Books, 1985).

"How Advertising Is Reshaping Madison Avenue," *Business Week* (September 15, 1986):147.

JAFFE, ANDREW, "Entrepreneurs Fashion Lean, Mean Shops," *Adweek* (January 19, 1987):34.

OGILVY, DAVID, *Ogilvy on Advertising* (New York: Vintage Books, 1985).

ORNSTEIN, STANLEY I., *Industrial Concentration and Advertising* (Washington, DC: American Enterprise Institute, 1977).

ROTZELL, KIM B., and JAMES E. HAEFNER, *Advertising in Contemporary Society* (Cincinnati, OH: South-Western Publishing Co., 1986).

Secondary Uses: Avon's Skin So Soft

Whether by chance or by design, many firms' products have experienced significant sales increases as a result of "secondary" or "alternative uses." Secondary uses are simply any use of a product other than the one for which it was originally intended. Though most good marketing firms will perform extensive product research in an attempt to identify potential secondary uses for their products, many of the most noteworthy examples of secondary uses have been identified by consumers themselves and communicated via word-of-mouth.

Undoubtedly, the most widely known examples of multiple secondary uses are those for Arm and Hammer's Baking Soda. Originally sold as an ingredient essential to baking, Arm & Hammer's Baking Soda eventually found its way into million of refrigerators as a deodorant, into medicine cabinets as a tooth polish, and into washing machines as a laundry additive. As women increasingly joined the work force and, therefore, had less time for traditional baking, Arm & Hammer was glad to see alternative uses surface for its flagship product. In fact, the broadly held consumer belief in baking soda as a universal cleanser and deodorizer has led Arm & Hammer to develop a variety of baking soda-based cleaning and personal-hygiene products, including detergents, oven cleaners, litter-box deodorizers, and toothpastes and powders.

Generally, those products that have been on the market for the longest period of time have experienced the greatest incidences of alternative uses. Undoubtedly, this was a result of consumer necessity, as consumers were faced with a limited selection of brands of household cleaning products during the first half of this century. Consequently, those brands that were available at the time often served a variety of purposes.

With the broad range of specialized product choices facing today's consumers, it is rare for a relatively new product to have secondary uses at all, much less any that rival the product's original use. Consequently, Avon was pleasantly surprised when the company began receiving reports from consumers that one of its bath oils, Skin So Soft, was being broadly used in the Northeast as an insect repellent. Advertising for products that provide a medicinal or pesticidal benefit is closely regulated by the government, however, so Skin So Soft's secondary use as an insect repellent could not be advertised by Avon without expensive, lengthy testing and EPA approval. Thus, although Avon benefited from the media coverage of Skin So Soft's unique alternate use, they could not overtly promote the use.

Often companies faced with this situation find creative and legally acceptable methods of promoting their products' alternative uses without drawing the attention of state or federal regulators. Generally, this is achieved via public relations efforts. For example, a press release or, more subtly, a telephone call placed to a major newspaper or television station can stimulate free media coverage of the brand and its secondary use.

Whether or not Avon solicited media coverage of Skin So Soft's alternate use as an insect repellent may never be known because Avon has refused to respond to inquiries on the subject. Yet, in today's increasingly competitive consumer marketplace, any firm that is not actively researching secondary or alternative uses for its products either has very few potential end uses for its products or is not doing its job completely.

Source: ABC News *Business World*, #149 (September 3, 1989).

Questions

1. List five common household products that are frequently used for purposes other than their originally intended use. Provide both the originally intended use as well as the alternative or secondary use(s).

2. Besides the length, costly EPA testing required to register Skin So Soft as an insect repellent, what other reasons may have prompted Avon to avoid vigorously promoting Skin So Soft's use as an insect repellent?

3. Identify a situation in which a product's secondary use may have had a detrimental effect on demand for its primary use and explain why.

$\mathcal{A}$DVERTISING AND SOCIETY: ETHICS AND REGULATION

CHAPTER OUTLINE

- The Questionable Colors of Benetton
- Advertising Ethics
- Ethical Issues in Advertising
- Advertising and the Law

- The Federal Trade Commission
- FTC Concerns with Advertising
- Remedies for Deceptive and Unfair Advertising
- Self-Regulation

CHAPTER OBJECTIVES

When you have completed this chapter, you should be able to:

- Discuss the major issues that advertisers must address

- Explain the current judicial position concerning the First Amendment rights of advertisers

- Comprehend the role of the FTC in regulating advertising

- List and understand the characteristics of other federal agencies governing advertising

- Explain the remedies available to different groups when an ad is judged deceptive or offensive

- Discuss the self-regulatory opportunities available to advertisers and agencies

THE QUESTIONABLE COLORS OF BENETTON

Oliviero Toscani is undoubtedly the most controversial person in advertising, and he appears to enjoy the role immensely. The creative director of Benetton, Toscani will express his philosophy of advertising to anyone willing to listen: "Advertising agencies waste their client's huge budgets with stupid, look-alike ads. Research and account executives are useless and get in the way of executing new ideas. Ad agencies are obsolete. They don't know what's going on in the world. They create a false reality and want people to believe it. We show reality and we're criticized for it."

Toscani's willingness to take risks is well documented. In one campaign, Benetton placed ads in several U.S. magazines that were actual news photos, including striking shots of a dying AIDS patient, a terrorist car bombing, and Albanian refugees. When Toscani himself acts as the photographer, he manages to depict something that offends everyone: a Catholic nun and priest kissing, a bloody newborn baby with umbilical cord intact, pastel condom sheaths, a black woman breast-feeding a white baby.

A world-famous fashion photographer, Toscani came to Benetton in 1981 and was given free reign with the international retailer's creative efforts: "Advertising is not just about the selling of a product. It has an equal social obligation to do something more. Luciano Benetton really believes in the power of communication." Increasingly, so do other observers of Toscani's work. For example, American Express asked him to develop marketing concepts, which he put in the form of 15-second spots on the abstraction of wealth.

Critics, however, far outnumber supporters. "Sometimes I'm ashamed I'm in the advertising business category," says Arnie Arlow, executive vice president/creative director, TBWA Advertising. "To place a Benetton logo on the picture of [AIDS victim] David Kirby's deathbed is awful enough. To announce the availability of the new *Colors* magazine at Benetton stores is absolutely vulgar." Advertising critic Barbara Lippert takes exception to several Benetton ads. Her reaction to the print ad showing a boatload of refugees desperately swarming into the water is typical: "The way these award-winning shots are presented, there's no way to know, for example, that the image of desperate people fleeing a boat is in fact a photo of Albanians trying to get political asylum in Italy. The only accompanying text says that the spring/summer 1992 edition of *Colors Magazine* is available at Benetton stores and then offers an 800 number for a directory of store locations. It's almost pornographic to use such abstract suffering as a flag for a magazine offer."

Benetton has also been sued by several of its American retail outlets who believe that Toscani's provocative ads drive away customers. "What does a roll of toilet paper have to do with selling clothes?" asked Susan Oustalet, a former Benetton licensee in Biloxi, Mississippi. She blames Benetton's ads, in part, for causing her store to fail. "We've had people stick their heads in the door and say, 'We're not coming in here, you work for a sick company.'" Adds Debra Romano, a Florida-based retailer who has closed 12 of the 27 Benetton shops owned by her family: "We're talking about two different arenas here. If Benetton wanted to underwrite some cause, I'd be supportive. But we're trying to sell product. At this point everyone should know what Benetton is. But we still find a lot of people who know the name but don't know what we sell."

How has Benetton responded to its critics? Although the company fervently believes in its approach to advertising, the 1993 ads were slightly less provocative. Among the seven images are photos of an electric chair, an albino Zulu, and a poor child clutching a dirty white doll. Toscani says he will continue shooting ads with imagery as equally charged as these; "I don't think people are stupid. I think advertising people are stupid."[1] Still, given the fact that Benetton ads appear to have created more negative responses than positive ones, one would have to conclude that these ads are ineffective and the company would be better off without them.

Chapter 1 outlined some of the major social criticisms of advertising. Because advertising is so visible, it draws a great deal of attention from citizens and government. This chapter will examine in detail the ethical questions advertisers face as well as the regulations imposed by government and by the industry itself.

ADVERTISING ETHICS

Advertising is a dynamic public forum in which business interests, creativity, consumer needs, and government regulation meet. Advertising's high visibility makes it particularly vulnerable to criticism. In the case of Benetton, this visibility is both a vehicle for selling clothing and a platform for expressing opinions about social issues. As a consequence of mixing these perspectives, Benetton has appeared to pay a heavy price, at least in the United States. In 1992, the company's total number of stores dropped to around 300, down from a peak of about 700 in the 1980s. Even though worldwide revenue jumped 12 percent in 1991, Benetton lost $10 million in the United States.[2]

An annoyance with advertising in general is also expressed by the population at large. In one study conducted by Opinion Research Corporation, 59 percent of the 1,016 respondents indicated that the quality of advertising has improved "greatly" or "somewhat" since the mid-1980s. Yet 75 percent felt consumers are victims of advertising's hidden persuasions, which manipulate them into buying products they neither need nor can afford. And 32 percent found ads less believable than they were five years ago, against 24 percent who find them more trustworthy. In almost every case, women are more skeptical of advertising than men are. Overall, married consumers express more negative attitudes than their unmarried counterparts. Finally, the youngest of the respondents, aged 18 to 24, have the most positive reactions toward advertising.[3]

In a more recent survey, co-sponsored by *Advertising Age* and the Roper Organization, both consumers and marketing executives were queried about their attitudes toward advertising. The findings indicated that ad executives are getting fed up with the bad ads produced by their trade—and, importantly, that they're becoming more and more concerned about advertising clutter. "The quality of advertising is really lousy. [Marketing people] feel the bad stuff compromises their work," notes Allison Cohen, president of People Talk, a marketing consultancy in New York. On another note, a large number of consumers in the Roper poll said they "don't care one way or the other" about several types of advertising. Many research experts believe such ambivalence could be an indication of doom for the ad industry. "People care less because there is too much

[1]Adapted from Barbara Lippert, "Mixing Politics and Separates," *Adweek* (February 17, 1992):30; Noreen O'Leary, "Benetton's True Colors," *Adweek* (August 24, 1992):27–32; Elena Bowes, "Benetton Forges Ahead," *Advertising Age* (September 9, 1991):14.
[2]Elena Bowes, "Benetton Forges Ahead," *Advertising Age* (September 9, 1991):14.
[3]Debra Goldman, "And Now a Word From Our Viewers," *Adweek* (March 11, 1991):24–26.

advertising—they're just getting overwhelmed," People Talk's Cohen notes. "They are subject to so much that they tune it out." Perhaps most surprising was the fact that 42.5 percent of the people who work in advertising could not recall an ad seen during the past 24 hours. Only 17 percent of all consumers were able to recall a specific brand name.[4]

It is doubtful that negative attitudes toward advertising will ever disappear, so it is worthwhile to be aware of the social issues facing advertisers. Each of these issues is complex, and each involves the public welfare as well as freedom of speech. The collective advertising industry, including agencies, advertisers, and the media, has an important stake in how these social issues are viewed both by the public and by those in a position to pass legislation to regulate the industry.

ETHICAL CRITERIA

Although advertisers face extensive regulation, every issue is not covered by a clear, written rule. Many advertising-related issues are left to the discretion of the advertiser. Decisions may be based on a variety of considerations, including the objective of the advertising campaign, the attitudes of the target audience, the philosophies of the agency and the advertiser, and legal precedent. Many decisions are based on ethical concerns. Three issues are central to an ethical discussion of advertising: advocacy, accuracy, and acquisitiveness.[5]

Advocacy. The first issue is *advocacy*. Advertising, by its very nature, tries to persuade the audience to do something. Thus, it is not objective or neutral. This fact disturbs critics who think that advertising should be objective, informative, and neutral. They want advertising to provide information and to stop there. Most people, however, are aware that advertising tries to sell us something, whether it be a product, a service, or an idea.

Accuracy. The second issue is *accuracy*. Beyond the easily ascertainable claims in an advertising message (for example, does the advertised automobile have a sun roof and an AM/FM radio, and is it available in different colors?) are matters of perception. Will buying the automobile make me the envy of my neighbors? Will it make me more attractive to the opposite sex? Such messages may be implied by the situations pictured in the advertisements.

Ad 2.1 for Toyota's MR2, for example, has fun with this accuracy issue by including notes from the various people who would review it, commenting on important features overlooked in the preliminary version of the ad. This type of ad would appeal to a more upscale, intelligent consumer.

Most of us are realistic enough to know that buying a car or drinking a certain brand of scotch won't make us a new person, but innuendos in the messages we see cause concern among advertising critics. The subtle messages coming across are of special concern when they are aimed at particular groups with limited experiences, such as children and teenagers.

Acquisitiveness. The third issue is *acquisitiveness*. Some critics maintain that advertising is a symbol of our society's preoccupation with accumulating mater-

---

[4]Adrienne Ward Fawcett, "Even Ad Pros Hate Ad Clutter," *Advertising Age* (February 8, 1993):33.
[5]John Crichton, "Morals and Ethics in Advertising," in *Ethics, Morality & the Media*, Lee Thayer, ed. (New York: Hastings House, 1980):105–15.

Ad 2.1

Sometimes the accuracy issue can be turned into a humorous creative strategy.

(Courtesy of Toyota Motor Sales, U.S.A., Inc.)

ial objects. Because we are continually exposed to an array of changing, newer-and-better products, critics claim we are "corrupted" into thinking that we must have these products. The rebuttal of this criticism is that advertising allows a progressive society to see and choose among different products. Advertising gives us choices and incentives for which we continue to strive. For the most part, advertising simply tells consumers about goods and services that they implicitly demand. It is a part of the integrated marketing program that helps produce a satisfied, well-informed consumer.

Ultimately, it is the consumer who makes the final decision. If advertising for a product is perceived as violating ethical standards, consumers can exert pressure by refusing to buy the product or by complaining to the company and to a variety of regulatory bodies. However, decisions about advertising campaigns start with the advertiser.

"Advertising Principles of American Business" of the American Advertising Federation (AAF)

1. Truth—Advertising shall reveal the truth, and shall reveal significant facts, the omission of which would mislead the public.
2. Substantiation-Advertising claims shall be substantiated by evidence in possession of the advertiser and the advertising agency prior to making such claims.
3. Comparisons—Advertising shall refrain from making false, misleading, or unsubstantiated statements or claims about a competitor or its products or services.
4. Bait Advertising—Advertising shall not offer products or services for sale unless such offer constitutes a bona fide effort to sell the advertised products or services and is not a device to switch consumers to other goods or services, usually higher priced.
5. Guarantees and Warranties-Advertising of guarantees and warranties shall be explicit, with sufficient information to apprise consumers of their principal terms and limitations or, when space or time restrictions preclude such disclosures, the advertisement shall clearly reveal where the full text of the guarantee or warranty can be examined before purchase.
6. Price Claims—Advertising shall avoid price claims which are false or misleading, or savings claims which do not offer provable savings.
7. Testimonials—Advertising containing testimonials shall be limited to those of competent witnesses who are reflecting a real and honest opinion or experience.
8. Taste and Decency—Advertising shall be free of statements, illustrations, or implications which are offensive to good taste or public decency.

Source: Courtesy of the American Advertising Federation.

THE PROBLEM OF BEING ETHICAL

Although advertisers can seek help in making decisions about questionable advertising situations from such sources as codes of ethics (see the box entitled "Advertising Principles"), these codes provide only general guidance. When advertising decisions are not clearly covered by a code, a rule, or a regulation, someone must make an ethical decision. That person must weigh the pros and cons, the good and the bad, the healthy and harmful effects, and make a value judgment about an unfamiliar situation. These kinds of decisions are complex because there is no clear consensus about what constitutes ethical behavior and also because of the potential conflict between personal ethics and what might be good for the business. Even though it might increase sales of your product, do you use copy that has an offensive double meaning? Do you use illustrations that portray people in stereotypical situations? Do you stretch the truth when making a claim about the product? Do you malign the competitor's product even though you know it is basically the same as your own?

The complexity of ethical issues requires us to make a conscious effort to deal with each situation. We should develop personal standards of what is right and wrong so that we will be less likely to behave unethically. Remember, it is people who create the ethical atmosphere of the organization. Advertising people in particular must address the following questions:

- Who should, and should not, be advertised to?
- What should, and should not, be advertised?

- What should, and should not, be the content of the advertising message?
- What should, and should not, be the symbolic tone of the advertising message?
- What should, and should not, be the relationship between advertising and the mass media?
- What should, and should not, be advertising's conscious obligation to society?[6]

Unfortunately, answers to these questions are not always straightforward. Rather, the advertiser must consider a number of related factors, such as the nature of the company, mission, marketing objectives, reputation, available resources, and competition. Even then, what is or is not ethical is still a judgment call made by imperfect individuals. Mistakes are made, and some companies pay for them for a very long time.

ETHICAL ISSUES IN ADVERTISING

Advertising involves many ethical issues. The predominant issues concern puffery, taste, stereotyping, advertising to children, advertising controversial products, and subliminal advertising. Engaging in any of these techniques is always a matter of choice for the advertiser. Just because it is not illegal does not mean it is right. Moreover, concerned consumers may make choices for or against the products of one advertiser as opposed to another based on ethical issues.

PUFFERY

Because the federal government does not pursue cases involving obviously exaggerated, or "puffing," claims, the question of puffery has become an ethical issue rather than a legal one.

Virtually everyone is familiar with a variety of puffery claims made for different products. Sugar Frosted Flakes are "great," Burger King serves "the best darn burgers in the whole wide world," people buy Hallmark cards when they "want to send the very best," and so on. Such puffery claims are legally viewed as patently different from other advertising claims. The legal logic assumes that consumers expect exaggerations and inflated claims in advertising and therefore know that certain statements ("puffs") are not to be believed as literal facts.

puffery Advertising or other sales representation that praises the item to be sold using subjective opinions, superlatives, and similar mechanisms that are not based on specific fact.

Puffery is defined as "advertising or other sales representations which praise the item to be sold with subjective opinions, superlatives, or exaggerations, vaguely and generally, stating no specific facts."[7] Critics contend that puffery is misleading and should be regulated by the Federal Trade Commission (FTC). Defenders counter that reasonable people know puffery is just a way of showing enthusiasm for a product and consumers understand this aspect of selling.

Unfortunately, the empirical evidence supporting one position or the other

[6]Kim B. Rotzoll and James G. Haefner, "Advertising and Its Ethical Dimensions," in *Advertising in Contemporary Society* (Cincinnati, OH: South-Western Publishing Co., 1986):137–49
[7]"The Image of Advertising," *Editor and Publisher* (February 9, 1985).

is quite mixed. For example, studies supporting the critics found that audience members often draw inferences beyond the manifest content of an advertised statement, by reading the ad in terms of what the advertiser might have liked to have said. Rotfeld and Rotzoll produced results indicating that some consumers might in fact expect advertisers to be able to prove the truth of superlative claims.[8] Conversely, a study by Etzel and Knight found that inclusion of claim documentation did not influence consumers' response to particular ads.[9] Vanden Bergh and Reid found that the Starch recognition scores for ads and ad components were not significantly different when puffery was involved.[10] Finally, Rotfeld and Rotzoll concluded that consumers are no less likely to believe puffery claims than they are claims based on verifiable facts.[11]

TASTE AND ADVERTISING

We all have our own ideas as to what constitutes good taste. Unfortunately, because these ideas vary so much, creating general guidelines for good taste in advertising is difficult. Different things offend different people. What is in good taste to some people is objectionable to others. For example, there are a great many people who like the Benetton ads and find them tasteful. The same is true with another product category—designer jeans. Calvin Klein ads have become famous for their provocative appeals. In one *Vanity Fair* issue, there was a 116-page insert sponsored by Klein. It began with a photograph of a beautiful young male torso who is rubbing his soaking wet Calvins against his crotch. Altogether, we get four nudes of him under the water in the white-tiled stall. Although individuals in the 16–24 age group find such ads exciting and appealing, most older consumers view them with dismay.[12]

Product Categories and Taste. One dimension of the taste issue concerns the product itself. Television advertising for certain products, such as designer jeans, pantyhose, bras and girdles, laxatives, and feminine hygiene aids, produces higher levels of distaste than do ads for other product categories.[13] The fact that television has the ability to bring a spokesperson into our living rooms to "talk" to us about such "unmentionables" embarrasses many people, who then complain that the advertisements are distasteful. Although certain ads might be in bad taste in any circumstances, viewer reactions are affected by such factors as sensitivity to the product category, the time the message is received (for example, in the middle of dinner), and whether the person is alone or with others when viewing the message. There is also the issue of matching questionable ads with certain media or programs. Parents, for example, may object to a racy ad in *Sports Illustrated* or one that is seen by children in a prime-time family program.

In addition, taste changes over time. What is offensive today may not be

---

[8]Herbert J. Rotfeld and Kim B. Rotzoll, "Is Advertising Puffery Believed?" *Journal of Advertising*, 9, 3 (1980):16–20, 45.

[9]Michael J. Etzell and E. Leon Knight, Jr., "The Effect of Documented versus Undocumented Advertising Claims," *Journal of Consumer Affairs*, 10 (Winter 1976):233–38.

[10]Bruce B. Vanden Bergh and Leonard N. Reid, "Puffery and Magazine Ad Readership," *Journal of Marketing* 4, 4 (Spring 1980);78–81.

[11]Herbert J. Rotfeld and Kim B. Rotzoll, "Puffery vs Fact Claims—Really Different?" found in *Current Issues and Research in Advertising*, James H. Leigh and Claude R. Martin Jr., eds. (Ann Arbor, MI: University of Michigan Press, 1981):85–105.

[12]Barbara Lippert, "Calvin Klein, Masturbation and Jeans," *Adweek* (September 16, 1991):39.

[13]Bill Abrams, "Poll Suggests TV Advertisers Can't Ignore Matters of Taste," *The Wall Street Journal* (July 23, 1981):25.

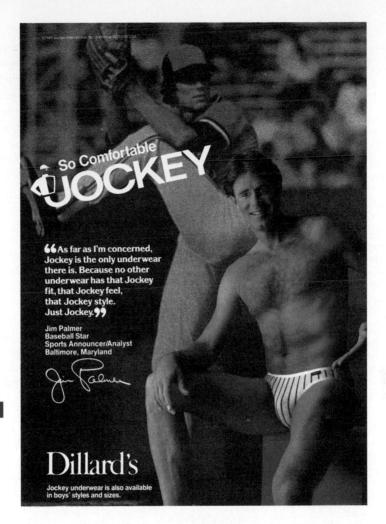

considered offensive in the future. In 1919 a *Ladies Home Journal* deodorant advertisement that asked the question, "Are you one of the many women who are troubled with excessive perspiration?" was so controversial that 200 readers immediately canceled their subscriptions.[14] By today's standards that advertisement seems pretty tame. Ad 2.2 is an example of a current ad that once would have been considered offensive.

Current Issues. Today's questions of taste center around the use of sexual innuendo, nudity, and violence. Although the use of sex in advertising is not new, the blatancy of its use is. The fashion industry has often been criticized for its liberal use of sex in advertising. There are experts in the fashion industry who feel that outrageous ads are necessary in order to appeal to the MTV generation. In response to the Calvin Klein insert discussed earlier, Larry Burstein, publisher of *Elle*, had the following to say: "Maybe it is a trend. I think people are trying very hard to come up with new ways of talking to their audiences...If people aren't getting what they want by doing things as usual, they're going to look for new

---

[14]Julian Lewis Watkins, *100 Greatest Advertisements. Who Wrote Them and What They Did* (New York: Moore Publishing Co., 1949):201.

and interesting ways to make things happen." Carl Portale, publisher of *Harper's Bazaar*, added, "What this does is force guys like me to try to think of alternative methods to get [fashion and cosmetic marketers] to stand out."[15] The fashion industry is also a leader in the use of *infomercials*, which are 30- or 60-minute ad programs. There are certainly consumers who find this program format objectionable as well, seeing it as an attempt to fool the consumer.

It is to the advantage of the advertiser to be aware of current standards of taste. The safest way to make sure that you are not overlooking some part of the message that could be offensive is to pretest the advertisement. Pretest feedback should minimize the chances of producing distasteful advertising.

STEREOTYPING IN ADVERTISING

stereotyping Presenting a group of people in an unvarying pattern that lacks individuality and often reflects popular misconceptions.

Principle

Debates about advertising ethics begin with the question: Does advertising shape society's values or simply mirror them?

Stereotyping involves presenting a group of people in an unvarying pattern that lacks individuality. Critics claim that many advertisers stereotype large segments of our population, particularly women, minorities, and the elderly. The issue of stereotyping is connected to the debate about whether advertising shapes society's values or simply mirrors them. Either way, the issue is very important. If you believe that advertising has the ability to shape our values and our view of the world, you will believe it essential that advertisers become aware of how they portray different groups. Conversely, if you believe that advertising mirrors society, you will think that advertisers have a responsibility to ensure that what is portrayed is accurate and representative. Advertisers struggle with this issue every time they use people in an ad.

Women in Advertisements. The portrayal of women in advertisements has received much attention over the years. Initially, critics complained that ads showed women as preoccupied with beauty, household duties, and motherhood. Advertising executives were accused of viewing women as zealous homemakers who were

> in endless pursuit of antiseptic cleanliness. Television ads for Lysol, Spic and Span, and Lemon Pledge, for example, show these ladies frantically spraying and polishing everything in sight—from refrigerator doors to dining-room tables to kitchen floors.[16]

Although there is still concern about this stereotype, more advertisers are recognizing the diversity of women's roles. However, with the effort to portray women as more than obsessive housewives came a different problem. Suddenly advertisements focused on briefcase-toting professional women (see Ad 2.3). Consider the commercial where a women discusses the benefits of serving her children a powdered breakfast drink. She is a NASA engineer. The image of "Supermom" has been displaced by the image of "Superwoman."[17]

In 1988 *Adweek* conducted a survey of 3,000 women that posed a number of questions about how women are depicted in advertising. Asked whether they agree that "The images of women in ads tend to be reasonable reflections of reality," less than 2 percent of respondents said they strongly agree whereas 32 per-

---

[15]Pat Sloan and Scott Donaton, "Klein 'Outsert': New Trend?" *Advertising Age* (September 9, 1991):12.
[16]William Miles, *The Image Makers* (Metuchen, NJ: Scarecrow Press, 1979).
[17]Jim Auchmutey, "Graphic Changes Charted in the Middle Class," Special Report: Marketing to Women, *Advertising Age* (September 12, 1985):15–17.

"You're checking into your hotel over the phone? Who do *you* know?"

"Hyatt."

Introducing **1-800-CHECK-IN,** an exclusive Hyatt service that allows you to actually check into your hotel room by telephone.
Simply dial 1-800-CHECK-IN and your Hyatt room will be ready and waiting when you arrive.
1-800-CHECK-IN is offered exclusively to members of the Hyatt Gold Passport frequent traveller program. If you are not yet a member, enroll free: 1-800-63-HYATT.
1-800-CHECK-IN, another Hyatt touch that's definitely worth checking into.

Feel The Hyatt Touch.

HYATT
HOTELS & RESORTS

Hyatt Regency San Francisco · Hyatt Regency Fort Worth · Hyatt Regency Long Beach · Hyatt Regency Dearborn · Hyatt on Capital Square (Columbus)
For reservations or more information about Hyatt Hotels and Resorts worldwide, call your travel planner or **1-800-233-1234.**
To enroll instantly, call the Hyatt Gold Passport desk at **1-800-63-HYATT,** or fax your name, address and daytime phone to **1-214-518-2571.**

Ad 2.3

This ad for Hyatt Hotels & Resorts portrays a more modern image of women in society.

(Courtesy of Hyatt Hotels & Resorts)

cent strongly disagreed. The survey also offered the statement "There are still too many dumb housewives in ads." Approximately 30 percent of respondents strongly agreed with this statement, whereas only 3 percent strongly disagreed. Finally, when asked whether "Working mothers in ads are too often portrayed as 'superwomen' with standards no one could live up to," 27.8 percent of the respondents strongly agreed.[18]

In early 1991 Maidenform introduced a new ad campaign featuring what some call "antiquated stereotypes" of women. After three years, the company has decided to drop its celebrity campaign, which featured male stars whispering about women and lingerie, and replace it with a new campaign that laments the negative stereotypes of women. Some critics charge that the news ads actually perpetuate these stereotypes. The ads criticize the stereotypes with a touch of humor in an attempt to confront them head on. In one ad, a female voice says, "Somewhere along the line, someone decided to refer to a woman as this," as images of a chick, a tomato, a fox, a cat, and a dog flash on the screen. The

---

[18]Thomas R. King, "Maidenform Ads Focus on Stereotypes," *The Wall Street Journal* (December 10, 1990).

The Problem at Michelob: Appealing to Women

Traditionally, women have played a minor role in beer ads targeted to men, an objectified role usually limited to leaning against a bar in a little spandex number or frolicking on the beach in some barely-there bikini. But Michelob has dared to break what some call the bimbo barrier.

In what industry insiders are hailing as the first of its kind, Michelob's new campaign gives women an equal share of the spotlight. And, amazingly enough, there doesn't seem to be an overwhelming amount of spandex in the spots. The women are shown in suits, overalls, normal dress. One of the print ads takes direct aim at women. The ad shows four professional-looking women at a restaurant drinking Michelob. The copy reads: "They used to call you the Sullivan sisters. Now? You're Sullivan, Williams, Nolan, and McGovern. But not tonight. Tonight, you're the Sullivan sisters." The ad ran in *Bon Appetit* as well as several women's magazines including *Vogue, Cosmopolitan*, and *Mademoiselle*.

The TV spots feature a mix of men and women in what Michelob calls "special occasions that make for a great day," for example, a men's hockey team celebrating a win, a victorious women's softball team, a new father hanging an "It's a boy" banner, and an older woman putting the finishing touches on a painting. One of the four ads features a female voice-over.

The response to this campaign has certainly been mixed. When critics cited Michelob for targeting women, the response from Jim Schumacker, senior brand manager for the Michelob family, was immediate. "Although the campaign definitely treats men and women equally, the company doesn't really see it as specifically addressing women. We think it transcends sex."

Perhaps the most serious concerns touched by the Michelob ads are health concerns, most notably the possibility of fetal alcohol syndrome, a condition of birth defects in babies born to mothers who drink heavily. Antialcohol activists are pointing to the latest liquor marketing efforts as further evidence of the need for legislation requiring warnings in all alcohol ads, includ-

ing one that would tell pregnant women not to drink at all. Beer marketers "are endangering the health of women," rails a spokesperson for the National Council on Alcoholism and Drug Dependence. "They're targeting woman of childbearing age. It's of great concern to us."

According to industry experts, the motivation for targeting women is pure economics. The beer market has been on a steady decline for several years, and women may be the only hope for turning that decline around. "The male market has been such an exploited market that there probably would be more opportunities with women," says Charlies Clagett, chief creative officer of the St. Loves office of ad agency D'Arcy Masuis Benton & Bowles, which handles Anheuser-Busch. "Beer marketers are seeing a niche that hasn't really been talked to before."

To consumer and health groups, that's an insidious strategy. The new marketing efforts, they say, are likely to appeal to lower-income, poorly educated young women—the same women who least understand the risk of drinking while pregnant. Too many pregnant women already think beer and wine aren't as bad as hard liquor. They contend that this advertising exacerbates an already serious problem.

Some beer executives are just plain baffled by the outcry. They figured they had appeased their critics by doing away with women as sex objects in their ads and treating women like actual consumers. "First we were criticized for ignoring the market," notes one individual, "and now we're criticized because we are advertising to women." Advertising industry expert Helen Berman sets them straight: "A lot of women are looking at beer advertising with a much more critical eye, particularly the professional, working women. If there's a change, it will be noticed."

Sources: Adapted from Joanne Lyman, "Beer Makers Brew Controversy with Ads Targeting Women," *The Wall Street Journal* (April 6, 1992):B1; Cyndee Miller, "Michelob Ads Feature Women—and They're Not Wearing Bikinis," *Marketing News* (March 2, 1992):2; Feinowitz, "Looking for Women," *Advertising Age* (March 16, 1992):2

announcer concludes by saying, "While these images are simple and obvious, women themselves rarely are. Just something we like to keep in mind when designing our lingerie."

Ad executives for the campaign claim that the ads are saying that

Ad 2.4

Although quite subtle, some critics might feel that this ad stereotypes the young male African-American.

(Courtesy of Fila Footwear USA)

Maidenform understands women, an approach more appropriate for the "back-to-basic" 1990s than the 1980s, which emphasized romance and glitz. The television ads will run in programs that portray women positively, such as *Murphy Brown* and *Designing Women*. The hope is that consumers will see the company as one that understands and stands behind women's concerns.[19] The Issues and Controversies box details the perils of another company that is having difficulty in their portrayal of women.

The challenge facing advertisers today is to portray woman realistically, in diverse roles, without alienating any segment of women. Experts agree that today's woman wants to see women portrayed with a new freedom, but also as mature, intelligent people with varied interests and abilities.[20]

Racial and Ethnic Stereotypes. Racial and ethnic groups also complain of stereotyping in advertising. The root of most complaints is that certain groups are shown in subservient, unflattering ways. Many times minorities are the basis of a joke or, alternatively, consigned to a spot in the background. There is also the suggestion that advertising perpetuates some of the myths associated with certain minorities. For example, does Ad 2.4 suggest that success in sports is a primary avenue to follow if African-American males are to succeed?

---

[19] Mark Dolliver, "The Sixth Annual Woman's Survey," *Adweek Special Report* (July 11, 1988):W4–W8.
[20] Lynn Folse, "Workers Labor to Raise Women's Status," Special Report: Marketing to Women, *Advertising Age* (September 12, 1985):36–38.

Other critics complain about underrepresentation of minorities in advertisements. A review of magazine and television advertising determined that blacks account for between 2 and 6 percent of models in print ads and about 13 percent in television advertisements. (Blacks constitute about 13 percent of the total U.S. population.)[21]

Senior Citizens. Another group frequently mentioned with regard to stereotyping is senior citizens, a growing segment of the population with increasing disposable income (see Chapter 5). Critics often object to the use of older people in roles that portray them as slow, senile, and full of afflictions. Although Clara Peller achieved success in the Wendy's hamburger commercials, some critics charged that these ads were too cutesy.[22] Others were offended by the shrill "Where's the beef?" and felt that the tone of the commercial portrayed older people as hard to get along with, obstinate, and unattractive.

In contrast, the Travelers ad (Ad 2.5) portrays senior citizens as a healthy, intelligent, forward-looking group in society.

Baby Boomers. Few groups in our society have been more extensively stereotyped than baby boomers. Born between 1946 and 1964, these 76 million people represent the largest of all markets. Of the original baby boomers,

---

[21]Lynette Unger and James M. Stearns, "The Frequency of Blacks in Magazine and Television Advertising: A Review and Additional Evidence," *Southern Marketing Association Proceedings*, Robert L. King, ed. (1986):9–13.

[22]Laurie Freeman and Nancy Giges, "Ads Giving Older Consumers Short Shrift," *Advertising Age* (November 3, 1986):92.

Ad 2.5

This ad provides a much more realistic picture of the elderly.

(Courtesy of Travelers Insurance Company)

(Courtesy of Bill Whitehead)

approximately 68 million are still alive, and they represent over one-fourth of the total population of the United States. Although the total bulk of the economic resources possessed by this group is impressive, the assumption that all baby boomers are wealthy and seek material possessions is inaccurate. Though nurtured through prosperous times, the baby boomers are considered an unlucky generation. Their unprecedented large numbers had to compete for college admission, interesting jobs, and housing. In a reversal of historic trends, boomers so far have experienced lower economic status than their parents.

Nevertheless, advertising has often been blamed for perpetuating the baby-boom myth of the "American Dream." The American Dream is to have it all; a beautiful car, a fancy home, a swimming pool, a beautiful body, and the money to travel and entertain. Clearly, it is a dream attainable for a very small percentage of baby boomers.

ADVERTISING TO CHILDREN

Advertising to children was one of the most controversial topics of the 1970s and led to a regulatory policy for the industry. In 1977 experts estimated that the average child watched more than 1,300 hours of television annually, which resulted in exposure to over 20,000 commercials.[23] Proponents of regulating

---

[23]National Science Foundation, *Research on the Effects of Television Advertising on Children* (1977):45.

Guidelines For Children's Advertising

The controversy surrounding the issue of children's advertising has encouraged the advertising industry to regulate this practice carefully. In the 1970s the industry issued written guidelines for children's advertising and established the Children's Advertising Review Unit within the Council of Better Business Bureaus to oversee the self-regulatory process. The Unit revised the written guidelines in 1977 and again in 1983. The following are the five basic principles on which guidelines for advertising directed at children are based.

1. Advertisers should always take into account the level of knowledge, sophistication, and maturity of the audience to which their message is primarily directed. Younger children have a limited capability for evaluating the credibility of what they watch. Advertisers, therefore, have a special responsibility to protect children from their own susceptibilities.

2. Realizing that children are imaginative and that make-believe play constitutes an important part of the growing up process, advertisers should exercise care not to exploit that imaginative quality of children. Unreasonable expectations of product quality or performance should not be stimulated either directly or indirectly by advertising.

3. Recognizing that advertising may play an important part in educating the child, information should be communicated in a truthful and accurate manner with full recognition by the advertiser that the child may learn practices from advertising which can affect his or her health and well-being.

4. Advertisers are urged to capitalize on the potential of advertising to influence social behavior by developing advertising that, wherever possible, addresses itself to social standards generally regarded as positive and beneficial, such as friendship, kindness, honesty, justice, generosity, and respect for others.

5. Although many influences affect a child's personal and social development, it remains the prime responsibility of the parents to provide guidance for children. Advertisers should contribute to this parent-child relationship in a constructive manner.

Source: "Self-Regulatory Guidelines for Children's Advertising," 3rd ed. Children's Advertising Review Unit, National Advertising Division, Council of Better Business Bureaus, Inc. (1983);4–5.

children's advertising were concerned that children did not possess the skills necessary to evaluate advertising messages and to make purchase decisions. They also thought that certain advertising techniques and strategies appropriate for adults were confusing or misleading to children. Two groups in particular, Action for Children's Television (ACT) and the Center for Science in the Public Interest (CSPI), petitioned the FTC to evaluate the situation.

In 1978 the FTC initiated proceedings to study possible regulation of children's television. Several regulations were suggested, including the banning of some types of advertising directed at children. Opponents of the proposed regulations argued that many self-regulatory mechanisms were already in place and that, ultimately, the proper place for restricting advertising to children was in the home.[24]

After years of debate over the issue, the proposed FTC regulations were abandoned. This did not mean, however, that advertisers to children had unlimited freedom. Advertising to children was carefully monitored by self-regulation. The National Advertising Division (NAD) of the Council of Better Business Bureaus, Inc., set up a group charged with helping advertisers deal with children's advertising in a manner sensitive to children's special needs. (The NAD is discussed in more detail later in the chapter.) The Children's Advertising Review Unit (CARU) was established in 1974 to review and evaluate advertising directed at children under the age of 12.

Then, on October 2, 1990, the House of Representatives and the Senate approved the Children's Television Advertising Practice Act, which restored 10.5-minute-per-hour ceilings for commercials in weekend children's television programming and 12-minute-per-hour limits for weekday programs. The act also restored rules requiring that commercial breaks be clearly distinguished from programming and barring "host selling," tie-ins, and other practices that involve the use of program characters to promote products.

ADVERTISING CONTROVERSIAL PRODUCTS

Alcohol and Tobacco. One of the most heated advertising issues in recent years is the proposed restrictions on advertising such product categories as alcohol and tobacco. Restrictions on products thought to be unhealthy or unsafe are not new. Cigarette advertising on television and radio has been banned since January 1, 1971. In 1987 the issue was the advisability of a total ban of every form of media advertising of tobacco and alcohol products. A 1986 Tobacco-Free Young American Project poll of 1,025 Americans—70 percent nonsmokers and 30 percent smokers—found that most respondents favored tougher restrictions on public smoking and tobacco-related promotional activities.[25]

Proponents of such a ban argued that advertising tobacco or alcohol products might result in sickness, injury, or death for the user and possibly others. Restricting advertising of those products would result in fewer sales of the products and consequently would reduce their unhealthy effects.

Opponents of an advertising ban countered that banning truthful, nondeceptive advertising for a legal product is unconstitutional. As attorney and First Amendment authority Floyd Abrams pointed out, "Censorship is contagious and habit-forming . . . even for commercial speech. . . . What we need is more speech, not less. There would be a precedential effect for all other lawful products . . . that are said to do harm." Opponents also cited statistics demonstrating

---

[24]"The Positive Case for Marketing Children's Products to Children," Comments by the Association of National Advertisers, Inc., American Association of Advertising Agencies and the American Advertising Federation Before the Federal Trade Commission (November 24, 1978).
[25]Joe Agnew, "Trade Groups Align to Counter Public, Government Ban Efforts," *Marketing News* (January 30, 1987):1, 18.

that similar bans in other countries had proved unsuccessful in reducing sales of tobacco and alcohol.[26]

The tobacco and alcohol industries have maintained that their intent is to advertise only to those who have already decided to use their products and not to persuade nonusers to try them. Adolph Coors Company sponsored a "Gimme the Keys" television commercial intended to remind people to be responsible drinkers. They also developed a public service campaign using the movie character "E.T." to deliver the message, "If you go beyond your limit, please don't drive. Phone home." More recently, Coors ran a television commercial for Coors' Light that used the tag line "right beer now—but not now" to depict safe times for drinking, such as a social gathering, and unsafe times, such as before getting into a car.

Still, the negative publicity seems to supersede the positive. Joe Camel, an advertising spokesanimal for R. J. Reynolds, has clearly caused the greatest controversy. It all began with a series of studies reported in the *Journal of the American Medical Association*. In the first study, involving 229 preschool children, researchers determined that, by age six, children recognize Joe Camel as readily as they do Mickey Mouse. By high school, according to the second study, nearly half the students think Joe "is cool." The third study looked at 5,040 California teenagers, ages 12 to 17, and found that Camel's increasing popularity with the 131 smokers among them paralleled the buildup of the Joe Camel campaign. The authors allege that illegal sales of Camels to minors have skyrocketed from $6 million to $476 million a year, since the inception of the campaign.[27] Although R. J. Reynolds has vehemently rejected these findings, it appears the damage to Joe and the industry has been done.

The outcome of the proposed advertising bans has far-reaching implications for advertisers, advertising agencies, and the general public. For example, magazine publishers could be financially devastated if print tobacco ads were banned (see Table 2.1). According to one report, as many as 165 magazines would fold without tobacco advertising.[28]

Condoms. Another topic of controversy is whether condoms should be advertised and, if so, in what media. Magazines have been more receptive to condom ads than television. Even though the National Association of Broadcasters repealed its ban on the broadcast of contraceptive ads in 1982, the major networks have hesitated to accept condom ads because of the sensitive nature of the product. Supporters of such advertising contend that the growing number of sexually transmitted diseases, including AIDS, makes such advertising necessary. They further argue that such messages can be done in good taste and at appropriate times, so that few groups would be offended. This issue raises difficult questions that will not be easily resolved.

SUBLIMINAL ADVERTISING

Generally when we think of messages we consider symbols that are consciously seen and heard. However, it is possible to transmit symbols in a manner that puts them below the threshold of normal perception. These kinds of messages

---

[26]Steven W. Colford, "Tobacco Ad Foes Press Fight," *Advertising Age* (February 23, 1987):12; and "Strict Ad Bans Not Effective," *Advertising Age* (August 8, 1986).
[27]"Camels for Kids," *Time* (December 23, 1991):52.
[28]Scott Donaton, "Publishers Bracing for Smoke-Free Pages," *Advertising Age* (March 12, 1990):3.

Magazine	Tobacco advertising (in millions)	Tobacco advertising as a % of overall ad revenue
Star	$6.7	43.4
Penthouse	5.1	25.3
Field & Stream	5.9	15.9
Life	6.2	12.7
McCall's	7.0	11.2
Sports Illustrated	35.0	10.8
TV Guide	30.5	10.8
Redbook	7.0	10.2
Popular Science	2.0	9.3
People	27.5	9.0
Playboy	7.7	8.9
Ladies' Home Journal	7.0	8.4
Glamour	6.2	7.1
Cosmopolitan	7.9	6.9
Newsweek	16.6	6.9
U.S. News & World Report	8.6	6.7
Better Homes & Gardens	10.1	6.6
Time	22.9	6.5
Family Circle	8.3	6.2
Woman's Day	6.9	6.0
Southern Living	3.1	5.0

Note: Four magazines in the top 25 do not accept tobacco advertising.
Source: 1990 Leadership Council on Advertising Issues.

subliminal message A message transmitted below the threshold of normal perception so that the receiver is not consciously aware of having viewed it.

are termed *subliminal* A **subliminal message** is one that is transmitted in such a way that the receiver is not consciously aware of receiving it. This usually means that the symbols are too faint or too brief to be clearly recognized. The furor over subliminal perception began with a 1958 study by James Vicary in a movie theater in Fort Lee, New Jersey, where the words "Drink Coke" and "Eat Popcorn" were flashed on the screen, allegedly resulting in increased sales of popcorn and Coke. More is said about this early history in the Concepts and Applications box.

The issue was further publicized by Vance Packard in his book *The Hidden Persuaders*, and more recently, Wilson Bryan Key discussed the subject in his books *Subliminal Seduction* and *Media Sexploitation*. Key maintains that subliminal "embeds" are placed in ads to manipulate purchase behavior, most frequently through appeals to sexuality. For example, he suggests that 99 percent of ads for alcoholic beverages employ subliminal embeds. Key contends that the messages are buried so skillfully that the average person does not notice them unless they are pointed out. He believes the subliminal embeds are the work of airbrush touch-up artists.[29] Ad 2.6, sponsored by the American Association of Adver-

---

[29]Walter Weir, "Another Look at Subliminal Facts," *Advertising Age* (October 15, 1984):46.

Concepts & APPLICATIONS

Vicary: Below Consciousness

(Since so much controversy has surrounded the initial studies reported by James M. Vicary, we thought it might be revealing to get a first-hand report from someone who witnessed the historical event).

In September 1957, I began what to me was a serious study of contemporary applied psychology at Hofstra College in Hempstead, Long Island. At exactly the same time, in nearby New York City, an unemployed market researcher named James M. Vicary made a startling announcement based on research in high-speed photography later popularized by Eastman Kodak Company.

Some time before, a device had been developed that could emit a flash of white light at a speed of one sixty-thousandth of a second. It was called the tachistoscope. The light impulse of the tachistoscope was so fast that it was imperceptible to human consciousness—what I was learning as a psychology student to call *subliminal* because it was below (*sub*) the threshold (*limen*) of human perception.

Armed with the scientific sound of *tachistoscope*, Vicary invented a sparkling new pseudoscience, and proceeded to contact the CEOs, marketing directors, and advertising managers of multimillion-dollar operations headquartered in New York City. Basically, he offered to serve them on retainer as a motivational research consultant while he developed the process he called *subliminal advertising*. His persuasive sales pitch was that consumers would comprehend information projected at one sixty-thousandth of a second, although they could not literally "see" the flash. And he sent a news release to the major media announcing his "discovery" without any scientific validation whatsoever. His media relations program in full swing by November, Vicary invited 50 reporters to a film studio in New York where he projected some motion-picture footage and claimed that he had also projected a subliminal message. He then handed out another of his well-written news releases claiming that he had actually conducted major research on how an invisible image could cause people to buy something even if they didn't want to.

The release said that in an unidentified motion-picture theater a "scientific test" had been conducted in which 45,699 persons unknowingly had been exposed to two advertising messages projected subliminally on alternate nights. One message, the release claimed, had advised the moviegoers to "Eat Popcorn" while the other read "Drink Coca-Cola." Vicary swore that the invisible advertising had increased sales of popcorn an average of 57.5 percent, and increased the sales of Coca-Cola an average of 18.1 percent. No explanation was offered for the difference in size of the percentages, no allowance was made for variations in attendance, and no other details were provided as to how or under what conditions the purported tests had been conducted.

When I learned of Vicary's claim, I made the short drive to Fort Lee, New Jersey to learn firsthand about his clearly remarkable experiment. The size of that small-town theater suggested it should have taken considerably longer than six weeks to complete a test of nearly 50,000 movie patrons. But even more perplexing was the response of the theater manager to my eager questioning. He declared that no such test had ever been conducted at his theater.

During the next several months Vicary backed off many of his initial claims. By spring he stated that subliminal advertising would only work as what he called "reminder advertising"…with "a level of affect similar to that of a billboard seen out of the corner of the eye from a speeding car."

Despite this back-pedaling on the potential power and influence of his purported discovery, by the middle of 1958, James Vicary had reportedly signed contracts with many of America's largest advertisers totaling some $4.5 million. Then, sometime in June 1958, Mr. Vicary disappeared from the New York marketing scene, reportedly leaving no bank accounts, no clothes in his closet, and no hint as to where he might have gone. The big advertisers, apparently ashamed of having been foiled by such an obvious scam, have said nothing since about subliminal advertising.

Source: Stuart Rogers, "How a Publicity Blitz Created the Myth of Subliminal Advertising," *Public Relations Quarterly* (Winter, 1993).

tising Industries, reflects the industry's opinion of the subliminal advertising theory.

Whether subliminal stimuli can cause some types of minor reactions has

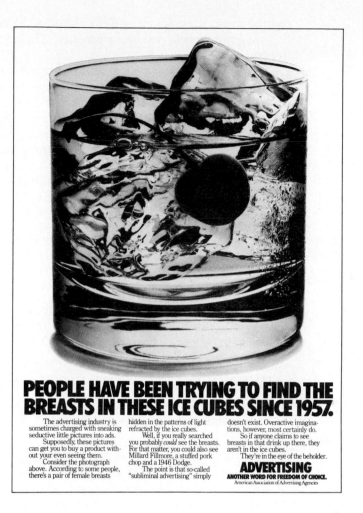

PEOPLE HAVE BEEN TRYING TO FIND THE BREASTS IN THESE ICE CUBES SINCE 1957.

The advertising industry is sometimes charged with sneaking seductive little pictures into ads.

Supposedly, these pictures can get you to buy a product with-out your even seeing them.

Consider the photograph above. According to some people, there's a pair of female breasts

hidden in the patterns of light refracted by the ice cubes.

Well, if you really searched you probably *could* see the breasts. For that matter, you could also see Millard Fillmore, a stuffed pork chop and a 1946 Dodge.

The point is that so-called "subliminal advertising" simply

doesn't exist. Overactive imagina-tions, however, most certainly do.

So if anyone claims to see breasts in that drink up there, they aren't in the ice cubes.

They're in the eye of the beholder.

ADVERTISING
ANOTHER WORD FOR FREEDOM OF CHOICE.
American Association of Advertising Agencies

never been the advertising issue. In tightly controlled laboratory settings sub-liminal stimuli have been shown to produce some reactions, such as a "like/dis-like" response. The advertising issue is whether a subliminal message is capable of affecting the public's *buying behavior*.

Research in this field has uncovered several practical difficulties with the theory that subliminal embeds can be used to influence buying behavior. To begin with, perceptual thresholds vary from person to person and from moment to moment. Symbols that are subliminal to one person might be consciously per-ceived by another. A message guaranteed to be subliminal to an entire audience would probably be so weak that any effect would be limited. Another problem is the lack of control that the advertiser would have over the distance and posi-tion of the message receiver from the message. Differences in distances and posi-tion could affect when the stimulus is subliminal and when it is recognizable. The third problem comes from the effect of recognizable (supraliminal) mater-ial, such as the movie or commercial, used in conjunction with the subliminal message. The supraliminal stimulus might overpower the subliminal material.

Besides the physiological limitations that make it questionable that sublim-inal messages can cause certain behaviors, there are several pragmatic issues. Most importantly, consumers normally will not buy products they don't need or can't afford to purchase, regardless of the advertising message and whether it is presented subliminally or directly. There will always be freedom of choice.

Furthermore, there are many factors besides the advertising message itself that induce consumers to purchase a product. (These influences will be discussed in more detail in Chapter 5.)

Nonetheless, many people still believe subliminal advertising is used frequently, widely, and successfully. Little evidence exists to support this belief, however. A survey of advertising agency art directors found that over 90 percent claimed no personal knowledge of the use of subliminal advertising. Timothy Moore concluded after his overview of the subliminal area, "In general, the literature on subliminal perception shows that the most clearly documented effects are obtained in only highly contrived and artificial situations. These effects, when present, are brief and of small magnitude. . . . These processes have no apparent relevance to the goals of advertising."[30]

ADVERTISING AND THE LAW

Few elements of business have been more heavily legislated than advertising. This section discusses the most important federal legislation as well as advertisers' attempts at self-regulation (see Figure 2.1).

ADVERTISING AND THE FIRST AMENDMENT

Freedom of expression in the United States is protected from government control by the Bill of Rights to the Constitution. In particular, the First Amendment states that Congress shall make no law "abridging the freedom of speech, or of the press; or the right of people peaceably to assemble, and to petition the Government for a redress of grievances." Initially, the Court ruled that freedom of expression is not absolute, although only the most compelling circumstances justify prior restraint on the spread of information. Specifically the Court held that the First Amendment applied to most media, including newspapers, books, magazines, broadcasting, and film. However, since Congress adopted the amendment in 1791, the Supreme Court has continued to reinterpret it as it applies to different situations. Table 2.2 lists some of the important First Amendment legislation.

The First Amendment has been used to strike down many statutes prohibiting commercial expression. For example, as a result of the *Virginia Pharmacy* ruling, states no longer can bar attorneys from advertising the prices of "routine" legal services, home owners from advertising their houses by placing "For Sale" signs in their yards, drugstores from advertising contraceptives, or utilities from promoting the use of electricity.[31]

Can advertisers now assume they are free from government regulation? Hardly. Essentially, the Court has ruled that the scope of the commercial-speech guarantee is limited. Only truthful and not misleading or deceptive commercial speech is protected. By contrast, the Court secures both false and misleading news reports if published without malice, that is, with no intention to deceive

---

[30]Timothy Moore, "Subliminal Advertising: What You See Is What You Get," *Journal of Marketing* (Spring 1982):38–47.
[31]Ivan L. Preston, "A Review of the Literature on Advertising Regulation," in *Current Issues and Research in Advertising* (1983), James H. Leigh and Claude L. Martin, eds. (Ann Arbor: University of Michigan Press, 1983):2–37.

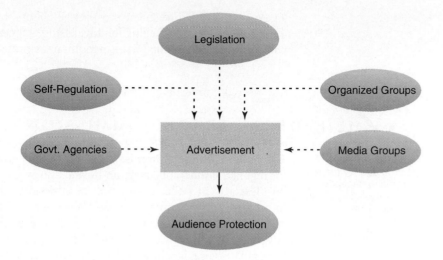

Figure 2.1

Regulatory factors affecting advertising.

and not made recklessly. In fact, until two critical rulings in 1993, there was considerable question about how strong First Amendment protection for advertising was. In the first case, *Cincinnati* v. *Discovery Network*, the city had revoked the permits issued to companies that publish magazines consisting principally of advertising to place 62 free-standing newsracks on public property. In the Cincinnati case, the Court decided the fit between the newsrack ban and the enforcement of safety and appearance (the reasons for the ban) was not tight enough to justify the city's action. In the second case, the Court ruled that Fane,

Table 2.2

First Amendment Legislation

Valentine v. *Christensen (1942)*
First Amendment does not protect purely commercial advertising because that type of advertising does not contribute to decision making in a democracy.

Virginia State Board of Pharmacy v. *Virginia Citizens Consumer Council (1976)*
States cannot prohibit pharmacists from advertising prices of prescription drugs because the free flow of information is indispensible.

Central Hudson Gas & Electric Corporation v. *Public Service Commission of New York (1980)*
Public Service Commission's prohibition of promotional advertising by utilities is found to be unconstitutional, placing limitations on government regulation of unlawful, nondeceptive advertising.

Posadas de Puerto Rico Associates v. *Tourism Company of Puerto Rico (1986)*
Puerto Rican law banned advertising of gambling casinos to residents of Puerto Rico.

Cincinnati v. *Discovery Network (1993)*
Court ruled that the Cincinnati City Council violated the First Amendment's protection of commercial speech when it banned newsracks of advertising brochures from city streets for aesthetic and safety reasons, while permitting newspaper vending machines.

Edenfield v. *Fane (1993)*
Court ruled that Florida's prohibition of telephone solicitation by accountants to be unconstitutional.

a CPA, was entitled to solicit prospective clients through telemarketing.[32] Both these rulings are encouraging for advertising, suggesting that the Supreme Court will continue to view the First Amendment as protection for commercial speech.

THE FEDERAL TRADE COMMISSION

Federal Trade Commission (FTC) A federal agency responsible for interpreting deceptive advertising and regulating unfair methods of competition.

The **Federal Trade Commission (FTC)** is the government agency responsible for regulating much of American business. It was established in 1914 to prevent business activities that were unfair or anticompetitive. Its original mission was to protect business rather than the consumer, and its enabling act contained no statement about advertising. In 1922, a Supreme Court ruling placed deceptive advertising within the scope of the FTC's authority, giving the agency the right to regulate false labeling and advertising as unfair methods of competition. Figure 2.2 shows the organization of the Federal Trade Commission.

The Wheeler-Lea Amendment, passed in 1938, extended the FTC's powers, and the agency became more consumer oriented. This amendment added "deceptive acts and practices" to the list of "unfair methods of competition." In addition, the Wheeler-Lea Amendment gave the FTC authority to (1) initiate investigations against companies without waiting for complaints, (2) issue cease-and-desist orders, and (3) fine companies for not complying with cease-and-desist orders. The FTC was also given jurisdiction over false advertising of foods, drugs, cosmetics, and therapeutic devices. False advertising was defined as "any false representation, including failure to reveal material facts."[33]

The FTC acquired increased authority during the late 1960s and mid-1970s through a series of important acts, which are listed in Table 2.3, along with other advertising legislation. An issue of high concern to the advertising industry was winning congressional reauthorization of the FTC, a feat last accomplished in 1982. The U.S. Senate passed the reauthorization bill in 1989. In addition to appropriating a substantial budget increase, the Senate also commissioned a study identifying those areas under the FTC's jurisdiction that might be appropriate for state enforcement and eliminate the agency's ability to make new rules regulating commercial advertising on the basis of unfairness. Unfortunately, the House and Senate have been unable to reconcile differences over the FTC's ability to use unfairness as the basis for rule-making, and as of early 1993, there was still debate about a reauthorization bill.

In addition, the laissez-faire political climate of the 1980s resulted in new appointees to the FTC who were less aggressive in regulating advertising. The Reagan administration's position was that regulation was justifiable only if it produced economic benefits that outweigh the costs. However, when George Bush succeeded Reagan as president in 1989, the FTC once again became more rigorous in enforcing business trade regulations. The FTC of the Bush administration was especially aggressive in enforcing regulation on advertising, including health claims or promotions for alcohol and tobacco products.[34]

Some people think that the end of the Reagan era signaled a change in the

[32]Alan Pell Crawford, "Getting an Edge," *Adweek* (May 10, 1993):24; Bernard H. Seegan, "High Court Revives 1st Amendment for Ads," *Advertising Age* (April 26, 1993):22.
[33]*Bates v. State Bar of Arizona*, 433 U.S. 350 (1977); *Linmark Associates, Inc. v. Township of Willingboro*, 431 U.S. 85 (1977); *Carey v. Population Services International*, 431 U.S. 678 (1977); *Central Hudson v. Public Services Commission*, 6 Med. L. Reptr. 1497 (U.S. 1980).
[34]Steven W. Colford, "Bush FTC May Clamp Down on Ads," *Advertising Age* (April 17, 1989):63.

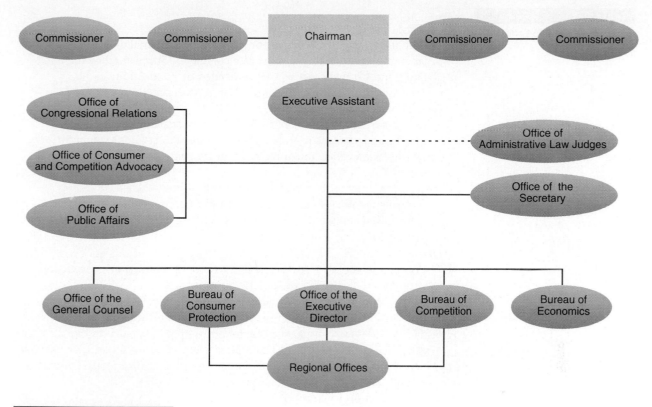

Figure 2.2

Organization of the Federal Trade Commission.

(Source: Office of the Federal Register National Archives and Records Administration, *The United States Government Manual 1989/90*)

hands-off attitude that insulated marketers from regulation. In her coming-out speech in 1990, FTC Chairman Janet Steiger warned agencies that they will be held accountable for ads or practices deemed unfair or deceptive. The response of one advertising executive was typical of the industry: "We haven't heard that from the FTC for years, and I think a lot of agencies don't understand their liability."

With the election of Bill Clinton, there was a great deal of speculation about the direction the FTC would take and whether he would replace Janet Steiger. With respect to the FTC, John Kamp, vice president of the American Association of Advertising Agencies, is sure that President Clinton will increase regulations, especially in the area of TV advertising to children.[35] As for Commissioner Steiger, both liberals and conservatives agree that she has done an exceptional job, and as of early 1994 she has neither offered her resignation nor has it been requested.

Another outcome of the soft FTC years was the development of the National Association of Attorneys General, an organization determined to regulate advertising at the state level. Members of this organization have been successfully bringing suits in their respective states against such advertising giants as Coca-Cola, Kraft, and Campbell Soup.[36]

---

[35]Steven W. Colford, "Clinton Win Raises Fear of Tougher FTC, FCC," *Advertising Age* (October 26, 1992):6.

[36]Steven W. Colford, "FTC Warns Agencies; Eyes Tobacco, Cable," *Advertising Age* (March 12, 1990):6; "Attorney General's Office Investigates Advertising Claims," *Marketing News* (February 29, 1988):16.

Table 2.3

Important Advertising Legislation

Pure Food and Drug Act (1906)

Forbids the manufacture, sale, or transport of adulterated or fraudulently labeled foods and drugs in interstate commerce. Supplanted by the Food, Drug, and Cosmetic Act of 1938; amended by Food Additives Amendment in 1958 and Kefauver-Harris Amendment in 1962.

Federal Trade Commission Act (1914)

Establishes the commission, a body of specialists with broad powers to investigate and to issue cease-and-desist orders to enforce Section 5, which declares that "unfair methods of competition in commerce are unlawful."

Wheeler-Lea Amendment (1938)

Prohibits unfair and deceptive acts and practices regardless of whether competition is injured; places advertising of foods and drugs under FTC jurisdiction.

Lanham Act (1947)

Provides protection for trademarks (slogans and brand names) from competitors and also encompasses false advertising.

Magnuson-Moss Warranty/FTC Improvement Act (1975)

Authorizes the FTC to determine rules concerning consumer warranties and provides for consumer access to means of redress, such as the "class action" suit. Also expands FTC regulatory powers over unfair or deceptive acts or practices and allows it to require restitution for deceptively written warranties costing the consumer more than $5.

FTC Improvement Act (1980)

Provides the House of Representatives and Senate jointly with veto power over FTC regulation rules. Enacted to limit FTC's powers to regulate "unfairness" issues in designing trade regulation rules on advertising.

THE FTC AND ADVERTISERS

Regardless of the philosophy of a given administration, the very existence of a regulatory agency like the FTC influences the behavior of advertisers.

Although most cases never reach the FTC, advertisers prefer not to run the risk of a long legal involvement with the agency. Advertisers, are also conscious that competitors, with a lot of consumer dollars at stake, may be quick to complain to an appropriate agency about a questionable advertisement. As was suggested in an editorial in *Advertising Age*:

> We've long since agreed that lies, deception, and fraud are beyond debate. No, ethics in advertising goes far beyond that. To the study of fine-linesmanship of what constitutes "weasel-wording" and what constitutes the whole truth. . . . If the copy stretches the truth even by a hair, or can be misinterpreted by anyone exposed to it, find another way. Chances are you'll end up with a stronger, more believable, more persuasive product presentation. And isn't that what good advertising is all about anyway?[37]

Ultimately, most advertisers want their customers to remain happy and

---

[37]Win Roll, "A Valuable Lesson in Integrity," *Advertising Age* (May 25, 1987):18.

pleased with their products and advertising, so they take every precaution to make sure their messages are not deceptive.

FTC CONCERNS WITH ADVERTISING

DECEPTION

Principle

Data must be on file to substantiate claims made by advertisers.

Deceptive advertising is a major focus of the FTC. Some of the activities that the commission has identified as deceptive are deceptive pricing, false criticisms of competing products, deceptive guarantees, ambiguous statements, and false testimonials. Until recently, the legal standard of deceptiveness involved judging only that an advertisement had the *capacity* to deceive consumers, not that it had actually done so. In 1983 the FTC changed the standard used to determine deception. The current policy contains three basic elements:

1. Where there is representation, omission, or practice, there must be a high probability that it will mislead the consumer.

2. The perspective of the "reasonable consumer" is used to judge deception. The FTC tests "reasonableness" by looking at whether the consumer's interpretation or reaction to an advertisement is reasonable.

3. The deception must lead to material injury. In other words, the deception must influence consumers' decision making about products and services.[38]

This new policy makes deception more difficult to prove. It also creates uncertainty for advertisers, who must wait for congressional hearings and court cases to discover what the FTC will permit.

In March 1993, The Federal Trade Commission announced that it was beginning an investigation of five leading diet-program marketers for false and misleading advertising claims. This concern about the weight-loss industry began in earnest with a series of hearings chaired by Representative Ron Wyden (D-Ore) in 1990. In this instance, the committee suggested that "before and after" ads should be banned, implying that they unrealistically suggest large weight losses for everyone. They also called for more monitoring of dieters with obesity-related illnesses, and for boosting the standards for diet-program administrators.[39] In the present situation, the FTC seeks to develop industrywide advertising rules instead of investigating companies on a case-by-case basis. The five marketers under investigation are Physicians Weight Loss Centers of America, Weight Watchers International, Jenny Craig, Inc., Diet Center, and Nutri/System.

The FTC has been investigating the diet industry for several years, focusing much of its attention on ad claims that the low-calorie diet programs were safe and effective. The FTC contends such claims were misleading because they failed to disclose that monitoring by a physician was required to minimize potential health risks. In addition, claims that weight loss will be maintained must be tempered with a statement based on National Institutes of Health Research that weight loss is temporary for most dieters.[40]

---

[38]"Letter to Congress Explaining FTC's New Deception Policy," *Advertising Compliance Service* (Westport, CN: Meckler Publishing, November 21, 1983) and Ivan Preston, "A Review of the Literature":2–37.

[39]Joseph Weber, "The Diet Business Takes It on the Chin," *Business Week* (April 16, 1990):86–87.

[40]Steven W. Colford, "FTC Probes Claims of 5 Diet Programs," *Advertising Age* (March 29, 1993):2.

REASONABLE BASIS FOR MAKING A CLAIM

The advertiser should have a reasonable basis for making a claim about product performance. This involves having data on file to substantiate any claims made in the advertising.

Determining the reasonableness of a claim is done on a case-by-case basis. The FTC has suggested that the following factors be examined:

1. Type and specificity of claim made
2. Type of product
3. Possible consequences of the false claim
4. Degree of reliance by consumers on the claims
5. The type and accessibility of evidence available for making the claim[41]

RICO SUITS

One of the most serious legal issues facing advertisers has been the recent application of the Racketeer Influenced and Corrupt Organizations Act (RICO) to false advertising lawsuits. Originally designed in 1970 to help curb fraud and organized crime, the broadly worded statute became an increasingly attractive legal weapon against advertisers in late 1989 after it was used in a false advertising suit against Ralston-Purina. Because losing a RICO suit means triple damages, legal costs, and the stigma of being labeled a "mobster," Ralston-Purina agreed to settle.

In early 1991 there were at least six RICO suits pending against companies. Coors was charged with falsely advertising Coors beer as being made from Rocky Mountain spring water, and CPC International was charged with false claims that Mazola corn oil products could lower serum cholesterol. Mobil Corporation was charged with false package labeling, advertising and promoting Hefty trash bags as biodegradable, and using sales proceeds to continue a faulty marketing campaign. The charge was dismissed, as was the claim that the relationship between Mobil and its ad agency Wells, Rich, Greene, New York (WRG) was unlawful. According to the RICO criterion, it is unlawful for someone employed or associated with an enterprise affecting interstate commerce to participate in the enterprise's affairs through racketeering activity. Mobil's relationship with WRG did not satisfy the definition of an enterprise.

RICO was enacted to prevent organized crime from taking illegal money and putting it into a legal enterprise and the taking of control of an innocent enterprise by racketeers. The Mobil ruling may be an indication that the proliferation of such suits may be decreasing. The concern over RICO suits is that they may reduce advertisers' inclination to settle regulatory disputes with federal or state agencies through consent decrees. Advertisers fear that the terms and admissions from these settlements will be used against them in subsequent RICO suits. Congress has attempted to stem the use of RICO suits with legislation, based on the shakiness of the argument that the ads in question, and only the ads, caused the consumers to purchase the product or service.[42] Legislation to reduce the application of RICO was introduced by Representative William J. Hughes in

[41]*Federal Trade Commission v. Raladam Company*, 283 U.S. 643 (1931).
[42]Steven W. Colford, "Mobil's RICO Victory Bolsters Ad Industry," *Advertising Age* (December 10, 1990);1, 59; Steven W. Colford and Ira Teinwitz, "Coors, CPC to Fight RICO Ad Charges," *Advertising Age* (October 22, 1990); and Barbara Hobsonback, "RICO Suit Looms: Volvo Probes Slow," *Adweek* (December 3, 1990):21.

1991. Critics were concerned, however, that reducing the power of RICO in any way would also reduce its ability to affect organized crime. The bill did not pass.[43]

COMPARATIVE ADVERTISING

The FTC supports comparative advertising as a way of providing more information to consumers. A substantial percentage of all television commercials use a comparative strategy. The commission requires that comparative claims, like other claims, be substantiated by the advertiser (see Ad 2.7). Comparative advertising is considered deceptive unless the comparisons are based on fact, the differences advertised are statistically significant, the comparisons involve meaningful issues, and the comparisons are to meaningful competitors (see Table 2.4).

ENDORSEMENTS

A popular advertising strategy involves the use of a spokesperson who endorses the brand (see Chapter 8). Because consumers often rely on these endorsements when making purchase decisions, the FTC has concentrated on commercials that use this approach. Endorsers must be qualified by experience or training to make judgments, and they must actually use the product. If endorsers are comparing competing brands, they must have tried those brands as well. Those who endorse a product improperly may be liable if the FTC determines there is a deception. Determining whether the endorsement is authentic is not easy. Is Michael Jordan a regular Coke drinker? Does Shaquille O'Neill really crave Pepsi? Are either qualified to judge the quality of the product? There is also the problem of implicit endorsement when a celebrity does a voice-over for a TV commercial. Tom Selleck is the voice behind AT&T, Demi Moore speaks for Keds shoes, and Jack Lemmon represents Honda.

DEMONSTRATIONS

Product demonstrations in television advertising must not mislead consumers. A claim that is demonstrated must be accurately shown. This mandate is especially difficult for advertisements containing food products because such factors as hot studio lights and the length of time needed to shoot the commercial can make the product look quite unappetizing. For example, because milk looks gray on television, advertisers often substitute a mixture of glue and water. The question is whether the demonstration falsely upgrades the consumer's perception of the advertised brand. The FTC evaluates this kind of deception on a case-by-case basis.

One technique some advertisers use to sidestep restrictions on demonstrations is to insert disclaimers or supers, verbal or written words that appear in the ad that indicate exceptions to the claim being made. One recent example is a 30-second spot for Chrysler's Jeep Cherokee that starts out cleanly and concisely, with bold shots of the vehicle and music swelling in the background. Suddenly the message is less clear; for several seconds five different, often lengthy disclaimers flash on the screen in tiny, eyestraining type, including "See

---

[43]Jonathan M. Moses, "Guiliani Works Other Side of RICO Street," *The Wall Street Journal* (September 16, 1992):B8.

Ad 2.7

This comparison ad appears to meet all the criteria of a fair comparison.

(Courtesy of National Dairy Board)

When your potassium comes with dairy calcium, you don't need a bunch.

An 8-ounce glass of milk has about as much potassium as the average banana. And an 8-ounce cup of yogurt has even more. Dairy foods can be an excellent source of potassium. And many other essential nutrients as well. Including, of course, calcium.

Milk and yogurt, like all dairy foods, also come in a variety of lower fat alternatives. So build your family's diet on a firm foundation of dairy foods. It's the perfect way to avoid nutritional slip-ups.

Dairy Foods. The Basics of Good Nutrition.

©1990 N.D.B.
National Dairy Board
America's Dairy Farmers

dealers for details and guaranteed claim form" and "Deductibles and restrictions apply."[44]

REMEDIES FOR DECEPTIVE AND UNFAIR ADVERTISING

The most common sources of complaints concerning deceptive or unfair advertising practices are competitors, the public, and the FTC's own monitors. If a complaint is found to be justified, the commission can follow several courses of action. Until 1970 cease-and-desist orders and fines were the FTC's major

---

[44]Thomas R. King, "More Fine Print Clouds Message of Commercials," *The Wall Street Journal* (July 12, 1990):B1.

1. The intent and connotation of the ad should be to inform and never to discredit or unfairly attack competitors, competing products, or services
2. When a competitive product is named, it should be one that exists in the marketplace as significant competition.
3. The competition should be fairly and properly identified but never in a manner or tone of voice that degrades the competitive product or service.
4. The advertising should compare related or similar properties or ingredients of the product, dimension to dimension, feature to feature.
5. The identification should be for honest comparison purposes and not simply to upgrade by association.
6. If a competitive test is conducted, it should be done by an objective testing service.
7. In all cases the test should be supportive of all claims made in the advertising that are based on the test.
8. The advertising should never use partial results or stress insignificant differences to cause the consumer to draw an improper conclusion.
9. The property being compared should be significant in terms of value or usefulness of the product to the consumer.
10. Comparisons delivered through the use of testimonials should not imply that the testimonial is more than one individual's thought unless that individual represents a sample of the majority viewpoint.

Source: James B. Astrachan, "When to Name a Competitor," Adweek (May 23, 1988):24.

weapons against deception, but the commission has developed alternative remedies since then, including corrective advertising, substantiation of advertising claims, and consumer redress.

CONSENT DECREES

consent decree An order given by the FTC and signed by an advertiser, agreeing to stop running a deceptive ad.

A **consent decree** represents the first step in the regulation process after the FTC determines that an ad is deceptive. The FTC simply notifies the advertiser of its finding and asks the advertiser to sign a consent decree agreeing to stop the deceptive practice. Most advertisers do sign the decree, thereby avoiding the bad publicity and the possible fine of $10,000 per day for refusing to do so.

CEASE-AND-DESIST ORDERS

cease-and-desist order A legal order requiring an advertiser to stop its unlawful practices.

When the advertiser refuses to sign the consent decree and the FTC determines that the deception is substantial, a **cease-and-desist order** will be issued. The process leading to an issuance of a cease-and-desist order is similar to a court trial. An administrative law judge presides, FTC staff attorneys represent the commission, and the accused parties are entitled to representation by their lawyers. If the administrative judge decides in favor of the FTC, an order is issued requiring the respondents to "cease-and-desist" their unlawful practices. The order can be appealed to the full five-member commission.

Deborah K. Johnson, *Senior Vice President/ Marketing Director, Ackerman McQueen, Oklahoma City*

As marketing director of Ackerman McQueen, Debby gets involved with clients from all four Ackerman offices as well as managing her own accounts.

5:00–6:30 A.M. Write Prizm presentation for Remington Park racetrack and review agency recommendation for Homeland (regional supermarket chain).

7:00 A.M. Wake rest of the family and get kids ready for school.

8:15 A.M. While driving kids to school, get call on cellular phone from an agency producer. Need to confirm we can use footage from Department of Commerce for a Fred Jones Manufacturing video. Call client and get approval. Remind producer to follow up with talent payment information.

8:30 A.M. Arrive at office. Find out regular Monday morning meeting with Homeland is postponed until Tuesday. Hooray. Some extra time.

8:40 A.M. Creative director stops by to ask if I have reviewed PSC videotape for the Southwestern Bell Mobile Systems' client over the weekend. I did. She asks if I can get approval from the client. Call client who will review it one more time and call me back.

Courtesy of Deborah K. Johnson

9:00 A.M. Meet with the management supervisor on Oklahoma Tourism to be sure we are in agreement over topics for brainstorming meeting scheduled for 2 p.m. today.

9:30 A.M. Call NRA board member to check on telemarketing test we are conducting. Still have some problems with telemarketing firm; call company to fix them.

10:00 A.M. Conference call with management supervisor in our Tulsa office and public relations person in our Washington, DC office to go over the NRA test plan.

CORRECTIVE ADVERTISING

corrective advertising A remedy required by the FTC in which an advertiser who produced misleading messages is required to issue factual information to offset these messages.

Principle

Corrective advertising is required when the FTC determines that an ad has created lasting false impressions.

Corrective advertising is required by the FTC when consumer research determines that lasting false beliefs have been perpetuated by an advertising campaign. Under this remedy, the offending firm is ordered to produce messages that correct any deceptive impressions created in the consumer's mind. The purpose of corrective advertising is not to punish a firm but to prevent that firm from continuing to deceive consumers. The FTC may require a firm to run corrective advertising even if the campaign in question has been discontinued.

The landmark case involving corrective advertising was *Warner-Lambert* versus *FTC* in 1977. According to the FTC, Warner-Lambert's 50-year-old campaign for Listerine mouthwash had been deceiving customers into thinking that Listerine was able to prevent sore throats and colds or to lessen their severity. The company was ordered to run a corrective advertising campaign, mostly on

Good news! *The Wall Street Journal* is going to run a feature on it tomorrow and *USA Today* is interested, too.

10:15 A.M.	SBMS client calls and gives approval for video.
10:30 A.M.	Presbyterian Health Foundation client calls with changes to the press release for meeting tomorrow.
10:45 A.M.	Review final printed economic impact brochure for the Presbyterian Health Foundation. Looks great. Authorize delivery to the client.
11:00 A.M.	Meet with AE to discuss changes to PHF press release and marketing plan needs for Louisiana Downs (racetrack).
Noon	Meet with account supervisor on OG&E (electric utility) to discuss changes for cogeneration slide presentation. Also discuss upcoming new safety campaign and ads for the Heat Pump Association.
12:30 P.M.	Media director calls to discuss my suggested changes to the Homeland presentation and to ask if I have written my section yet for a new business presentation for our Dallas office. Promise I will have it tomorrow.
1:15 P.M.	Get back from lunch. OG&E client calls to say they want to have a conference call with Lippincott & Margulies in New York tomorrow afternoon to discuss corporate identity program. Discuss agenda and confirm I am available.
1:30 P.M.	NRA client asks if I can go to Dallas and meet with telemarketing firm in person tomorrow. Leave voice mail for OG&E client asking to change conference call. Ask my assistant to get plane tickets for me.
2:00–5:30 P.M.	Participate in brainstorming session for Oklahoma Tourism with clients, media director, management supervisor, and creative director. Outline recommendations for five-year plan.
5:40 P.M.	Talk to OG&E client; decide to do conference call from Dallas tomorrow.
6:00 P.M.	Head of our Dallas office calls to fill me in on some other new business activity.
6:15 P.M.	Pack up scripts and other things I will need for telemarketing discussion and head for home.
6:30 P.M.	Get home and the phone rings. Account executive fills me in on potential media scheduling problems for the Southwestern Bell Telephone print campaign. Tell her how they can be fixed.
6:45 P.M.	Greet my kids and start my other job as mom to Dan (9), Rachel (7), and Ben (5), not to mention, my husband, Joe (age undisclosed.)

television, for 16 months at a cost of $10 million. Interestingly, even after the corrective campaign ran its course, 42 percent of Listerine users continued to believe the mouthwash was being advertised as a remedy for sore throats and colds, and 57 percent of users rated cold and sore throat effectiveness as a key reason for purchasing the brand.[45] These results raised doubts about the effectiveness of corrective advertising, as consumers may continue to remember earlier advertising claims without integrating the "details" corrective advertising may supply. However, the *Warner-Lambert* case remains significant because for the first time the FTC was given the power to apply retrospective remedies and to attempt to restrict future deceptions. In addition, the Supreme Court rejected

---

[45]William Wilke, Dennis L. McNeil, and Michael B. Mazis, "Marketing's 'Scarlett Letter': The Theory and Practice of Corrective Advertising," *Journal of Marketing* (Spring 1984):26.

the argument that corrective advertising violates the advertiser's First Amendment rights.

 TC HINTS

It should be obvious by now that creating ads that are FTC-proof is not easy. In 1993 the FTC published a bulletin titled "Law Enforcement Achievements and Ongoing Projects." It represents a compilation of ads that prompted action by the commission during the period from October 1, 1989 through March 31, 1993. Among the FTC's targets: an antibaldness product employing the impressive-sounding "Helsinki Formula"; another company claiming to have cures for baldness and cellulite; yet another firm proffering cures for baldness and impotence; a marketer of bulletproof vests claiming certification under government standards; a grapefruit marketer making health claims for the fruit; and weight-loss claims for bee pollen.[46]

THE LEGAL RESPONSIBILITY OF THE AGENCY

With the resurgence of the FTC has come a new solution for deception—making the ad agency liable. To quote FTC Chairman Janet Steiger, "An agency that is involved in advertising and promoting a product is not free from responsibility for the content of the claims, whether they are express or implied. You will find the commission staff looking more closely at the extent of advertising agency involvement."[47] Essentially an agency is liable for deceptive advertising along with the advertiser when the agency was an active participant in the preparation of the ad and knew or had reason to know that it was false or deceptive.

Three recent examples point to the extent to which the FTC has taken this warning seriously. In 1990 the FTC slapped sanctions on Lewis Galoob Toys and its agency for ads that the FTC said showed toys doing things they really couldn't do. Under terms of the consent agreement, Galoob and its agency, Towne, Silverstein, Rotter, of New York, are prohibited from misrepresenting a toy's ability to move without human assistance. In addition, future ads must disclose that assembly is required when such a toy is shown fully assembled in a commercial.[48]

In 1991 a group of state attorney generals reached a settlement with Pfizer and ad agency Ally & Gargano. Pfizer and Ally agreed to stop making a number of deceptive claims in their advertising about the plaque-reducing qualities of Pfizer's Plax mouthwash, and Pfizer agreed to pay the states a total of $70,000 in investigative costs.[49]

In 1992 Judge Kimba Wood found that Wilkinson, the maker of the Ultra Glide shaving system, intended to make misleading claims and enjoined the campaign. The court awarded Gillette damages of nearly $1 million, and then it assessed matching damages against Wilkinson's agency Friedman Benjamin.[50]

---

[46]"How to Get Yourself on the Wrong Side of the FTC," *Adweek* (May 10, 1993):18.
[47]Steven W. Colford, "FTC Warns Agencies; Eyes Tobacco, Cable," *Advertising Age* (March 12, 1990):6.
[48]Steven W. Colford, "FTC Hits Galoob, Agency for Ads," *Advertising Age* (December 10, 1990):62.
[49]"Ally in Plax Settlement," *The Wall Street Journal* (February 12, 1991):B4.
[50]Stephen P. Durchslag, "Agency Liability Extends to False Advertising Claims," *Promo* (October 1992):17.

The following is a list of tips to avoid legal pitfalls in advertising that one law firm offers agencies:

1. Early in the creative process, get written permission from the appropriate people if an ad carries the potential to violate copyright and/or privacy laws.

2. During production, make sure no one hires a person to sound like, look like, or otherwise represent a celebrity.

3. Before the shoot, get the producers' affidavit signed to substantiate that demonstrations are not mockups.

4. Have regular seminars with a lawyer to update staff on specifically how to stay within the limits of advertising law.[51]

SUBSTANTIATING ADVERTISING CLAIMS

In 1971 the FTC initiated a policy that required advertisers to validate any claims when requested by the commission. Advertisers must have a "reasonable basis" for making a claim. It is the responsibility of the advertiser to show the reasonableness of claim; it is *not* up to the FTC to disprove a claim's validity. Documentation may be based on a variety of sources, including scientific research and the opinions of experts.

CONSUMER REDRESS

The Magnuson-Moss Warranty-FTC Improvement Act of 1975 empowers the FTC to obtain consumer redress in cases where a person or a firm engages in deceptive practices. The commission can order any of the following: cancellation or reformation of contracts; refund of money or return of property; payment of damages; and public notification.

FOOD AND DRUG ADMINISTRATION

Food and Drug Administration (FDA) A federal regulatory agency that oversees package labeling and ingredient listings for food and drugs.

Two other major government agencies deal with advertising-related concerns: the **Food and Drug Administration (FDA)** and the **Federal Communications Commission (FCC)**. The FDA is the regulatory division of the Department of Health and Human Services. It oversees package labeling and ingredient listings for food and drugs and determines the safety and purity of foods and cosmetics. Although not directly involved with advertising, the FDA provides advice to the FTC and has a major impact on the overall marketing of food, cosmetics, and drugs.

FEDERAL COMMUNICATIONS COMMISSION

Federal Communications Commission (FCC) A federal agency that regulates broadcast media and has the power to eliminate messages, including ads, that are deceptive or in poor taste.

The FCC was formed in 1934 to protect the public interest with regard to broadcast communication. It has limited control over broadcast advertising through its authority to issue and revoke licenses to broadcasting stations. The FCC is concerned with radio and television stations and networks, and it has the power to eliminate messages, including ads, that are deceptive or in poor taste. The

---

[51]Barbara Holsomback, "Ad Agencies Feel Piercing Glare of Watchdogs," *Adweek* (December 3, 1990):18.

agency monitors only those advertisements that have been the subject of complaints and works closely with the FTC with regard to false and deceptive advertising. The FCC takes actions against the media, whereas the FTC is concerned with advertisers and agencies.

OTHER FEDERAL AGENCIES

Other federal agencies are involved in the regulation of advertising, although most are limited by the type of advertising, product, or medium. For example, the Postal Service regulates direct-mail and magazine advertising and has control over the areas of obscenity, lottery, and fraud. Consumers who receive advertisements in the mail that they consider sexually offensive can request that no more mail be delivered from that sender. The postmaster general also has the power to withhold mail that promotes a lottery. Fraud can include any number of activities that are questionable, such as implausible get-rich-quick schemes.

The Bureau of Alcohol, Tobacco, and Firearms within the Treasury Department both regulates deception in advertising and establishes labeling requirements for the liquor industry. This agency's power comes from its authority to issue and revoke annual operating permits for distillers, wine merchants, and brewers. Because there is a danger that public pressure could result in banning all advertisements for alcoholic beverages, the liquor industry strives to maintain relatively tight control on its advertising.

The Patent Office, under the Lanham Trade-Mark Act of 1947, oversees registration of trademarks, which include both brand names and corporate or store names as well as their identifying symbols. This registration process protects unique trademarks from infringement by competitors. Because trademarks are critical communication devices for products and services, they are important in advertising.

Finally, the Library of Congress provides controls for copyright protection. Legal copyrights give creators a monopoly on their creations for a certain time. Advertising is a competitive business where "me too" ads abound. Copyrighting of coined words, illustrations, characters, and photographs can offer some measure of protection from other advertisers who borrow too heavily from their competitors.

Certain state laws also regulate unfair and deceptive business practices. These laws are important supplements to federal laws because of the sometimes limited resources and jurisdiction of the FTC and the Justice Department. Because these laws are so numerous and diverse, we cannot begin to examine them in this chapter.

$\mathscr{S}$ELF-REGULATION

societal marketing concept
A concept that requires balancing the company, consumer, and public interest.

Based on the discussion thus far, it would appear that all advertising and advertisers must be carefully governed because without that control all ads would be full of lies. Nothing could be further from the truth, however. For the great majority of advertisers, a societal marketing approach is followed. Philip Kotler defines the **societal marketing concept** as follows: The organization's task is to determine the needs, wants, and interests of target markets and to deliver the desired satisfactions more effectively and efficiently than its competitors in a way that preserves or enhances the consumer's and society's well-being. This requires a careful balance between company profits, consumer-want satisfaction, and public interest.[52]

Principle

Self-regulation encourages voluntary withdrawal of deceptive advertising.

Admittedly, this is not an easy balance to maintain. Yet, advertisers realize that everything they do is carefully scrutinized by millions of consumers and a host of agencies. Therefore, it has become necessary for advertisers to regulate themselves even more stringently than do the government agencies discussed earlier. Using this system of self-regulation ensures that societal marketing is more likely to become a reality.

J.J. Boddewyn offers a classification for different levels of self-regulation: (1) self-discipline—norms are developed, used, and enforced by the firm itself, (2) pure self-regulation—norms are developed, used, and enforced by the industry itself, (3) co-opted self-regulation—the industry, on its own volition, involves nonindustry people (for example, consumer and government representatives, independent members of the public, experts) on the development, application, and enforcement of norms, and (4) negotiated self-regulation—the industry voluntarily negotiates the development, use, and enforcement of norms with some outside body (for example, government department or a consumer association).[53] We will discuss examples of the first two categories.

SELF-DISCIPLINE

Virtually all major advertisers and advertising agencies have in-house mechanisms to review ads for both ethical and legal problems. A number of U.S. advertisers (Colgate-Palmolive, General Foods, AT&T) have developed their own codes of behavior and criteria for the acceptance of advertisements. This practice is accepted internationally as well. In the Netherlands, industry has encouraged the appointment in all agencies, advertisers, and media of an "ethical officer" responsible for overseeing the application of the Dutch Advertising Code as well as general principles of ethical behavior. In Swedish advertising agencies, an executive trained and experienced in marketing law and known as the "responsible editor" reviews for acceptability all the advertisements and other materials produced.

At a minimum, advertisers and agencies will have every element of a proposed ad evaluated by an in-house committee, or lawyers, or both. When one considers how closely every word, picture, and intonation is critiqued, it is somewhat amazing that any ads still get in trouble.

NATIONAL AGENCIES

In the case of both advertisers and advertising agencies, the most effective attempts at self-regulation have come through the Advertising Review Council and the Better Business Bureau. In 1971 the National Advertising Review Council was established by several professional advertising associations in conjunction with the Council of Better Business Bureaus. The main purpose of the council is to negotiate voluntary withdrawal of national advertising that professionals consider to be deceptive. The National Advertising Division (NAD) of the

---

[52]Philip Kotler, *Marketing Management: Analysis, Planning, Implementation, and Control*, 7th ed. (Englewood Cliffs, NJ: Prentice Hall, Inc. 1991):25–26.
[53]J.J. Boddewyn, "Advertising Self-Regulation: Private Government and Agent of Public Policy," *Journal of Public Policy and Marketing* (1985):129–141.

Council of Better Business Bureaus and the National Advertising Review Board (NARB) are the two operating arms of the National Advertising Review Council.

NAD The NAD is a full-time agency made up of people from the field of advertising. It evaluates complaints that are submitted by consumers, consumer groups, industrial organizations, and advertising firms. The NAD also does its own monitoring. After a complaint is received, the NAD may ask the advertiser in question to substantiate claims made in the advertisement. If such substantiation is deemed inadequate, the advertiser is requested either to change or to withdraw the offending ad. When a satisfactory resolution cannot be found, the case is referred to the NARB.

Principle

Media can refuse to accept advertising that violates standards of truth or good taste.

NARB The NARB is a 50-member regulatory group that represents national advertisers, advertising agencies, and other professional fields. When a case is appealed to the NARB, a five-person panel is formed that consists of three advertisers, one agency person, and one public representative. This panel reviews the complaint and the NAD staff findings and holds hearings to let the advertiser present its case. If the case remains unresolved after the process, the NARB can (1) publicly identify the advertiser and the facts about the case and (2) refer the complaint to the appropriate government agency (usually the FTC). Although neither the NAD nor the NARB has any real power other than threatening to invite governmental intervention, these groups have been relatively effective in controlling cases of deception and misleading advertising.

LOCAL REGULATION: BBB

At the local level self-regulation has been supported by the Better Business Bureau (BBB). The BBB functions much like the national regulatory agencies, and in addition provides local businesses with advice concerning the legal aspects of advertising. The origin of the bureau can be traced to the truth-in-advertising campaign sponsored by the American Advertising Federation in 1911. Since that time more than 240 local and national bureaus, made up of advertisers, agencies, and media, have screened hundreds of thousands of advertisements for possible violation of truth and accuracy. Although the BBB has no legal power, it does receive and investigate complaints and maintain files on violators. It also assists local law enforcement officials in prosecuting violators.

MEDIA REGULATION AND ADVERTISING

The media attempt to regulate advertising by screening and rejecting ads that violate their standards of truth and good taste. For example, *Reader's Digest* does not accept tobacco and liquor ads, and many magazines and television stations will not show condom ads. Each individual medium has the discretion to accept or reject a particular ad. In the case of the major televisions networks, the ARC's advertising standards and guidelines serve as the primary standard.

A FINAL THOUGHT

It is clear that advertising, as a high-profile industry, will remain extremely susceptible to controlling legislation and the criticisms of the general public. Rather than lamenting such scrutiny and becoming defensive, advertisers would be wise to take the initiative and establish individual ethical parameters that anticipate and even go beyond the complaints. Such a proactive stance will facilitate the creative process and avoid the kind of disasters that result from violating the law or offending certain publics.

In addition, as advertisers, agencies, and media become more and more global, it will be imperative that the players understand the ethical standards and laws in which they operate. For example, in Hungary tobacco ads have been banned since the Communist occupation and are still on the books. Advertisers who violate the code of conduct in Brazil can be fined up to $500,000 or given up to a five-year prison sentence. This would certainly prompt an advertiser to be very careful. The smart advertiser follows the advice given by David Ogilvy, founder of Ogilvy & Mather: Never run an advertisement you would not want your family to see.

*S*UMMARY

- In general, the public and many advertisers feel advertising is unethical and hold a low opinion of advertising.

- Ethical questions about advertising revolve around three criteria: advocacy, accuracy, and acquisitiveness.

- The primary ethical issues facing advertising are: puffery, taste, stereotyping (of women, racial and ethnic groups, senior citizens, and baby boomers), communicating with children, controversial products, and subliminal advertising.

- The primary legal protection available to advertising is the First Amendment, and the level of protection has varied over time.

- The Federal Trade Commission is the most important government agency affecting advertising.

- The Federal Trade Commission deals with the following advertising legal issues: deception, reasonable basis for making a claim, RICO suits,

comparative advertising, endorsements, and demonstrations.

- The FTC can initiate the following remedies for deceptive and unfair advertising: consent decrees, cease-and-desist orders, and corrective advertising.

- An ad agency can be held legally liable if the agency was an active participant in the preparation of the ad and knew or had reason to know that it was false or deceptive.

- A number of other government agencies influence advertising, including: The Food and Drug Administration, Federal Communications Commission, The Postal Service, The Bureau of Alcohol, Tobacco, and Firearms, and others.

- Advertising engages in a great deal of self-regulation, and at various levels: self-discipline, pure self-regulation, co-opted self-regulation, and negotiated self-regulation.

*Q*UESTIONS

1. Two local agencies are in fierce contention for a major client in Hillsboro. The final presentations are three days away when Sue Geners, an account executive for the Adcom Group, learns from her sister-in-law that the creative director for the rival agency has serious personal prob-

lems. His son has entered a drug rehabilitation program and his wife has filed for a divorce. Because this information comes from inside the clinic, Sue knows it's very unlikely that anyone in the business side of Hillsboro has any knowledge of this. Should she inform Adcom management?

If she does, should Adcom warn the prospective client that a key person in the rival's agency's plans will be seriously limited for months to come?

2 Sue Geners, our account executive from the last question also has a quandary of her own. Adcom keeps very strict hourly records on its accounts for billing and cost accounting purposes. Sue has an old friend with an Adcom client that needs some strong promotional strategy. The client, however, is very small and cannot afford the hours that Sue would have to charge. Should Sue do the work and charge those hours to one of her large clients? Should she turn down her friend? What should she do?

3 Zack Wilson is the advertising manager for the campus newspaper. He is looking over a layout for a promotion for a spring break vacation package. The headline says "Absolutely the Finest Deal Available This Spring—You'll Have The Best Time Ever If You'll Join Us in Boca." The newspaper has a solid reputation for not running advertising with questionable claims and promises. Should Zack accept or reject this ad?

4 The Dimento Game Company has a new video game on basketball. To promote it, "Slammer" Aston, an NBA star is signed to do the commercial. In it Aston is shown with the game controls as he speaks these lines: "This is the most challenging court game you've ever tried. It's all here—zones, man-to-man, pick and roll, even the alley oop. For me, this is the best game off-the-court." Is Aston's presentation an endorsement or is he a spokesperson? Should the FTC consider a complaint if Dimento uses this strategy?

5 What are the central issues in ethical decision making? Write a short evaluation of a current ad campaign utilizing three ethical criteria.

6 Think of an ad you have found deceptive or offensive. What bothered you about the ad? Should the media have carried it? Is it proper for the government or the advertising industry to act in cases like this? Why or why not?

7 There is a great deal of controversy surrounding subliminal advertising. Do you think subliminal advertising exists? If so, what do you believe are risks associated with this technique?

𝒮UGGESTED CLASS PROJECT

Select three print ads that you feel contain one or more of the ethical issues discussed in this chapter. Ask five people (making sure they vary by gender, age, or background) how they feel about the ads. Conduct a mini-interview with each of your subjects; it would be helpful to have a list of questions prepared. Write a report on these opinions that follows the format of your questionnaire. Don't be afraid to draw your own conclusions. What differences or similarities do you see across the different target groups?

𝒡URTHER READINGS

ARMSTRONG, GARY M., AND JUDITH L. OSANNE, "An Evaluation of NAD/NARB: Purpose and Performance," *Journal of Advertising*, 12(1983):15–26.

BUCHANAN, BRUCE, AND DORON GOLDMAN, "U.S. vs. Them: The Mindfold of Comparative Ads,"

Harvard Business Review (June 1989):38–50.

ROTZELL, KIM G., AND JAMES E. HAEFNER, *Advertising in Contemporary Society* (Cincinnati, OH: South-Western Publishing, 1990).

SCHUDSON, MICHAEL, *Advertising: The Uneasy Persuasion* (New York: Basic Books, 1984).

$\mathscr{V}$IDEO $\mathscr{C}$ASE

Water Rescue

When the top management of DDB Needham Worldwide decided to adopt a cause against which the creative energies of the agency's worldwide network could be mobilized, the first task was to select an appropriate cause among the many worthy possibilities. Through consultation with environmentalists, scientists, and conservationists, the agency discovered that water conservation and purification are major problems in every country where DDB Needham has offices, and that safe, abundant water is a universally compelling issue.

Realizing that water problems are to some extent unique to every locality, DDB Needham management asked each local DDB Needham office to undertake a communication project intended to address conservation and restoration problems in conjunction with local clients, local environmental organizations, local governmental units, and other interested parties.

The DDB Needham San Francisco office "adopted" the Monterey Bay Aquarium and produced a television spot that dramatized the aquarium's conservation activities. In cooperation with the Government Information Service and the Water Supplies Department of Hong Kong, the Hong Kong office of DDB Needham produced a series of public service announcements that recalled the Hong Kong water shortages of 1962–1963 and 1966, and drove home the point that those shortages can recur if water is not treasured.

Working with the Water Board of Perth, Australia, the agency produced a series of spots that warned against the consequences of excessive lawn sprinkling. In Canada, DDB Needham Toronto undertook a campaign that advocates reclamation of the Don River Valley. With the National Wildlife Federation, the Detroit office produced newspaper advertisements listing 25 ways to "make the Great Lakes great again," and a television commercial in support of the federation's work. With the Lake Michigan Federation, the Chicago office produced a series of newspaper and magazine advertisements carrying headlines like, "Not even the frugal gourmet has a recipe like this," and "This isn't something out of Jules Verne; it's a trout out of Lake Michigan."

For New York City, the agency developed a self-liquidating campaign based on the logo, H_2OPE. This campaign is self-financing, through sales of T-shirts, water bottles, stickers, and associated items.

Because water consumption and water reclamation both depend upon large numbers of complex factors and because an assortment of overlapping and mutually reinforcing communications occur simultaneously, it is extremely difficult to trace the individual effects of any one campaign. However, every reinforcement counts, and there have been many reinforcements. All the environmental and government agencies involved regard these contributions from the private sector as valuable additions to their ongoing efforts.

Source: Adapted from Keith L. Reinhard, "Project Water Rescue," *Advertising Age* Dinner, June 17, 1992, Chicago, Illinois.

Questions

1. Do you feel there are any potential ethical or legal problems with advertising such as this?

2. Provide examples of copy or illustrations that would reflect puffery or deception.

$\mathcal{A}$DVERTISING AND THE MARKETING PROCESS

CHAPTER OBJECTIVES

When you have completed this chapter, you should be able to:

- Understand the concept of marketing, and the role of advertising within the marketing strategy

- Appreciate the concept of the market and the four types of markets

- Explain the marketing concept and its evolution

- Explain and define the 4Ps of marketing and how they interface with advertising

HOGS AROUND THE WORLD

Katsumi Abe fell in love with Harley-Davidson motorcycles just after World War II, when as a small boy he was awed by the American soldiers powering their big bikes through Tokyo's rubble. Today, at 53, he heads a Harley riders' club that goes out touring once a month in military-style formation.

Middle-aged nostalgics or Hell's Angels wannabes, Japanese Harley fans aren't alone. Across the Australian outback, on roads winding through Germany's Black Forest, on Mexico City's crowded streets, scores of riders are discovering the thrill of hopping a Harley. Harley-Davidson Inc.'s bike sales abroad are expected to hit $285 million in 1993, or 24 percent of the company's $1.2 billion total, up from $115 million and 14 percent of sales in 1989.

Much of this success began in the United States when Harley-Davidson was able to win tariff protection against heavyweight bike imports. Then the company overhauled its marketing program. The strategy: Package a lifestyle, complete with Harley Owners' Groups (HOGS), magazines, clothing, and biker rallies. It also entailed a complete reengineering of the once-famous "hog." Sure enough, the company attracted aging baby boomers trying to feel young. By 1989, its U.S. market share hit 63 percent.

The comeback complete, Harley began to focus on overseas markets. However, the company did not have a dealer organization overseas, and its marketing effort consisted of translating U.S. ads word for word into another language. In the late 1980s, Harley-Davidson began to recruit more dealers in Japan and Europe. More important, it decided to customize its U.S. marketing package for different cultures. "As the saying goes, we needed to think global but act local," says Harley's vice president for worldwide marketing, Jerry G. Wilke. This meant publishing Harley magazines in foreign languages and staging beer-and-band rallies. But it also meant changing ads and tweaking its tried-and-true methods of building customer loyalty.

Take Japan. Based on the long-standing tendency of the Japanese to desire anything American, the hog seemed to be a sure bet. Until 1992, corporate headquarters had insisted the Japanese division use the U.S. print-ad campaign. But, Toshyiumi Okui, president of the Japanese unit, worried that desolate scenes and the tag line "one steady constant in an increasingly screwed-up world" wouldn't win over Japanese riders. In 1992, he got permission to run a separate ad campaign juxtaposing American images with traditional Japanese ones: American riders passing a geisha in a rickshaw, Japanese ponies nibbling at a Harley motorcycle. It's too soon to pinpoint the new campaign's effect on sales. But waiting lists for Harleys in Japan are as long as six months.

Wilke believes the marketing program and customer ties Harley is building will ensure long-term growth overseas.[1]

THE CONCEPT OF MARKETING

The international rekindling of the Harley hog points to the potential power of marketing. It also suggests two other important ideas. First, advertising is just a

[1]Adapted from Kevin Kelly, "The Rumble Heard 'Round the World: Harleys," *Business Week* (May 24, 1993):58–59; Junu Bryan Kim "Advertising Age Marketing 100," *Advertising Age* (July 5, 1993): S-1, S-16; Ken Wells, "Global Ad Campaigns, After Many Missteps, Finally Pay Dividends," *The Wall Street Journal* (August 27, 1992): B3; and John K. Johansson, " The Sense of 'Nonsense': Japanese TV Advertising," *Journal of Advertising* (March 1994): 17–26.

part of the total marketing effort. Second, marketing strategies, including advertising, are not easily transferred from one culture to another. The purpose of this chapter is to provide a perspective on the marketing function and how it influences the advertising effort. This relationship underlies at a basic level the integrated marketing communication strategy introduced in Chapter 1. It also serves as a foundation for the rest of this book.

The American Marketing Association defines **marketing** as "the process of planning and executing the conception, pricing, promotion, and distribution of ideas, goods, and services to create exchanges that satisfy individual (customer) and organizational objectives."[2] Marketing can also be defined in terms of its ultimate business objectives; that is, marketing is a process intended to find, satisfy, and retain customers, while the business makes a profit. Although the exchange itself is the focus of the effort, marketing is a complicated process operating in a complex business environment. There are general principles that suggest how to best perform a marketing task, but every business customizes marketing to fit its particular situation.

The success of a given marketing effort depends on whether a *competitive advantage* for a product can be established in the minds of consumers. A competitive advantage is attributed to a product when a consumer makes the judgment that the product comes closer to satisfying his or her needs than does a competitor's product. A human need is a state of felt deprivation, such as hunger, shelter, a need for affection, knowledge, or self-expression. These needs can be rational or irrational. Harley-Davidson sells a great many motorcycles in Japan because of the irrational need of many Japanese to own any product made in the United States. Sometimes the consumer decides that none of the choices provided by marketers is acceptable and so makes no purchase. Often you go to a mall looking for a particular style of clothing and come home empty-handed. At other times, one choice is perceived to be superior, and the consumer does make a purchase. That's what happened when you selected the college you are currently attending. This is referred to as an **exchange**—the act of obtaining a desired object from someone by offering something of value in return. The process began with a simple barter system, when a farmer exchanged corn for salt, for example, and continues today when we purchase shoes in exchange for a credit card payment (a promise to pay). Today, more than ever, the process of creating an exchange is not random, and it requires a great deal of marketing effort—in other words, for the marketer the process revolves around a marketing plan.

As we will discuss in Chapter 7, a *marketing plan* involves different stages: a research stage, during which the marketing environment, including the consumer, is analyzed; a strategic stage, during which objectives are developed, along with the enduring strategy for achieving them; an implementation stage, which involves the coordination of the marketing strategy with actual marketing activities; and the evaluation stage, when it is determined to what extent the objectives were achieved. Figure 3.1 is a sample marketing plan. Figure 3.2 illustrates advertising's place in the marketing plan.

Marketing is a part of the overall business plan, and advertising is an integral but relatively small part of the marketing plan. Recall how Harley-Davidson had to resolve tariff issues before it could even begin to think about marketing. Traditionally, the hierarchy of strategies employed by businesses starts with the marketing mix, which involves activities such as designing the product, includ-

marketing Business activities that direct the exchange of goods and services between producers and consumers.

exchange The process whereby two or more parties give up a desired resource to one another.

---

[2] "AMA Board Approves New Marketing Definition," *Marketing News* (March 1, 1985):1.

Mission

To become the premiere source of residential and commercial services and products to consumers in the United States and selected international markets. These services and products will be ones that improve the quality of life and assist the consumers in maintaining their property and surrounding.

Objectives

1. To develop the [Company] Quality Service Network, which will be made up of several service companies, each being specialists in their own field, which the consumer can access through one source.
2. To build market share in each of the operating units.
3. To maintain a minimum of X% annual increase in both revenues and profits.

The operational objectives are:

1. To make available the entire range of consumer services in a profitable and timely manner in all major markets in the United States.
2. To establish and enforce quality standards among all the operating units.
3. To introduce some of the services into selected foreign markets.

The major marketing objectives of the [Company] Quality Service Network are:

1. Cross sell to existing customers of one [Company] operating unit the services of the other operating units.
2. Expand the customer base of the [Company] Network to include customers who have no services with any operating unit.
3. Increase customer loyalty and retention.
4. Expand the number of services available through the [Company] Quality Service Network.

Strategy

1. Each operating unit will continue to build brand awareness for its own service or product. [X], [Y], and [Z] will be promoted under their respective brand names.
2. All the different services and products will be linked together by the 1-800-XXX-XXXX number and the Partners Logo Block.
3. Channels of distribution will be increased by expansion of the services into all markets. Certain segments of the business may be more suitable to franchising while others should be company owned.
4. Foreign markets will be pursued with a minimum investment strategy. A foreign partner will be selected to license the know-how from [Company]. [X] will be the entering brand in the [foreign] markets.
5. The *Partners Pledge* will represent the minimum standards by which all operating units are measured. All [Company] service centers must agree to abide by the pledge before they will be certified to operate under the [Company] Quality Service Network umbrella. This Partners Pledge will be the network's guarantee to the customer that service will be delivered on time and that the job will be done right.

Summary of Mission and Objectives by Operating Units

[Company] currently provides the following services:

Residential and commercial cleaning of carpets, upholstery, and drapes; residential disaster restoration; contract cleaning services; residential home cleaning service, lawn care service; termite and pest control; home system care; and consumer products.

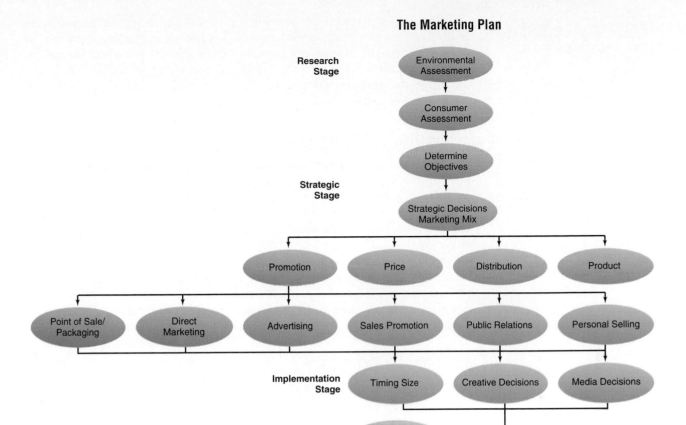

The Marketing Plan

Research Stage
- Environmental Assessment
- Consumer Assessment
- Determine Objectives

Strategic Stage
- Strategic Decisions Marketing Mix
  - Promotion
  - Price
  - Distribution
  - Product

- Point of Sale/Packaging
- Direct Marketing
- Advertising
- Sales Promotion
- Public Relations
- Personal Selling

Implementation Stage
- Timing Size
- Creative Decisions
- Media Decisions

Evaluation Stage
- Creative Evaluation Response Evaluation

Figure 3.2

The place of advertising in the marketing plan.

ing its package; pricing of the product, as well as terms of sale; distribution of the product, including placing it in outlets accessible to customers; and promoting or communicating about the product. This last element, promotion or marketing communication, is the home base for advertising, along with public relations, sales promotion, personal selling, packaging/point of sale, and direct marketing. Each of these promotional techniques has its own set of capabilities, some of which complement one another, some of which duplicate each other's efforts. For example, advertising is capable of reaching a mass audience simultaneously and repeatedly. It is also an excellent device for informing customers about new products or important changes in existing products. Reminding customers to buy and reinforcing past purchases are two other strengths of advertising. Finally, advertising can persuade customers to change their attitudes, beliefs, or behavior. Public relations possesses several of these same strengths. Sales promotion, personal selling, and direct marketing are all similar in that they prompt behavior in a timely manner.

Superior advertising cannot save an inferior marketing plan or rescue a bad product—at least not for long—but inferior advertising can destroy an excellent plan or product. (This is illustrated in the Issues and Controversies box.) Therefore, it is as important for the advertising director to have a thorough understanding of marketing and all its facets as it is for the marketing manager to understand how advertising works. This mutual awareness and understanding is the underlying premise of integrated marketing communication.

This chapter provides only a simple overview of marketing. In the real world of advertising a much deeper understanding of the entire marketing process, as well as of the specific marketing strategy employed by the client, would be required. (Readers who wish to understand marketing at a deeper level are referred to the reading list at the end of this chapter.) The starting point for our overview is the market itself.

THE IDEA OF A MARKET

market An area of the country, a group of people, or the overall demand for a product.

The word *market* originally meant the place where the exchange between seller and buyer took place. The term has taken on several additional meanings. Today we speak of a **market** as either a region where goods are sold and bought or a particular type of buyer.

The term implies that the buyer and seller are not paired at random but rather are engaged in negotiation, because each has evaluated the likelihood that the other will be able to satisfy his or her needs and wants. How is this accomplished? Businesses are able to locate the best market for an existing or potential product through experience and market research. Likewise, customers rely on experience, market information, and many other factors (including advertising) to identify markets where they believe they will find the best value.

TYPE OF MARKETS

When marketing strategists speak of markets they are generally referring to groups of people or organizations. The four primary types of markets are (1) consumer, (2) business-to-business (industrial), (3) institutional, and (4) reseller (see Figure 3.3).

Consumer. Consumer markets consist of people who buy products and services for their own personal use or for the use of others in the household. As a student, you are considered a member of the market for companies that sell jeans, sweatshirts, pizza, textbooks, backpacks, and bicycles, along with a multitude of other products.

Business-to-Business (Industrial). Industrial markets consist of companies that buy products or services to use in their own businesses or in making other prod-

Figure 3.3
The four principal types of markets.

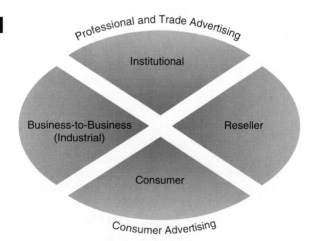

Another Advertising Marriage Gets Rocky

John Rock epitomizes the phrase "shoot from the hip." Rock hadn't expected to be playing the gunslinger at age 56. He was planning to take early retirement from General Motors and settle back on his ranch. But as GM's woes mounted and its management upheavals began in the spring of 1992, Rock got the call to fix Oldsmobile. One of the first things he did was to tell Leo Burnett, the agency that created the Marlboro Man, that it had to hit the trail. Burnett, which prides itself on maintaining long-term accounts with a blue-chip roster of clients, was stunned at its dismissal, as was the rest of the advertising world. By the fall of 1992 the boardroom drama that had begun in April concluded with the ouster of GM chairman Robert Stempel. With a massive shakeup at the country's biggest company under way, nothing was certain anymore.

Although agencies of record for other GM cars appeared at this writing to be unworried, certain facts have suggested they should be. First, although some GM divisions show rising sales, the company has been losing overall market share because of a shortage of new "home run" products. Oldsmobile has been by far the biggest offender, having slumped from sales of 1.1 million cars in the mid-1980s to about 450,000 in 1991. All divisions were put on notice to protect their franchises and start turning profits—or else. Second, GM's management restructuring has led to the creation of a post that will coordinate sales and brand advertising across all divisions for the first time. Finally, while some GM agencies may have escaped the criticism that stung Burnett's work for Olds, passable ads are no longer a security blanket.

Observers are split as to who is to blame for this "divorce." Some critics say the agency's account team had grown complacent. Others say any complacency is understandable, given a client that had no idea where it was going. Even general marketing manager Knox Ramsey admits, "Olds has not been the best of clients for some time, and we know that." But Ramsey doesn't hesitate to demand accountability: "Certainly our ad agency played a role in what has gone wrong." However each side views the past, there is little disagreement that the clock began ticking when the agency introduced "The New Generation of Olds" tagline and the "This is not your father's Oldsmobile" theme in 1988. Olds sales had dropped precipitously in 1987, falling 40 percent even as the consumer economy was humming along. The old tagline, "Olds Quality, Feel It," was getting stale and anemic, and GM loyalists were defecting in droves to the midsize imports. "The New Generation of Olds" line made sense because several new and different vehicles, such as a redesigned Cutlass Supreme that had escaped notice, the Silhouette minivan, and the Bravada sport utility were coming on line. But the theme violated a basic tenet of copywriting by telling consumers what an Oldsmobile is *not* without telling them what it *is*. Because all Olds seemed to mean to most consumers was "old," the thinking was the sleek new products would speak for themselves when customers went to showrooms.

Heading into the 1989 model year, Olds and Burnett appeared as if they had gotten it right. Upon reviewing the new work, dealers actually stood and cheered. But a funny thing happened as the ads started to appear in the fall of 1988. The new vehicles didn't. The dramatically designed Silhouette minivan, the Bravada sport utility, and the Cutlass Supreme convertible were late getting to market. As the new advertising spurred showroom traffic, car buyers were greeted by salespeople polishing up Cutlass Cieras and Delta 88s, two models that looked to have been designed by Frigidaire.

In 1990, Michael Losh was moved over from Pontiac to take over Olds. Trained in finance and engineering and known to dislike the marketing side of the business, Losh killed half of the "New Generation" TV spots his first year. In his second year he scrapped the campaign in favor of "The Power of Intelligent Engineering," a theme GM execs say is grounded in Oldsmobile's history of spearheading new technology, such as the Rocket 88 engine. John Smale, former CEO of Proctor & Gamble and new president of GM, knows that "if blame is to be placed on one side or the other for the lack of focus at Oldsmobile, it belongs more on the shoulders of the GM general managers and former sales and marketing managers than on Burnett."

In the end, the anguish Burnett has gone through may prove beneficial—as a form of shock therapy! (More will be said in Chapter 4 about the Oldsmobile situation, and how it impacted upon the agencies involved.)

Adapted from John Kascht, "Panic in Detroit," *Adweek* (January 11, 1993):19–23

ucts. General Electric, for example, buys computers to use in billing and inventory control, steel and wiring to use in the manufacture of its products, and cleaning supplies to use in maintaining its buildings.

Institutional. Institutional markets include a wide variety of profit and nonprofit organizations, such as hospitals, government agencies, and schools, which provide goods and services for the benefit of society at large. Universities, for example, are in the market for furniture, cleaning supplies, computers, office supplies, groceries and food products, audio-visual materials, and tissue and toilet paper, to name just a few.

Reseller. The reseller market includes what we often call "the middlemen." These are wholesalers, retailers, and distributors who buy finished or semifinished products and resell them for a profit. Resellers are considered a market by companies that sell such products and services as trucks, cartons, crates, and transportation services (airlines, cruise ships, and rental car agencies).

Of the four markets, the consumer market is probably the largest in terms of dollars spent on advertising. Marketing to this group is generally done through mass media such as radio, television, newspapers, general consumer magazines, and direct-response advertising media. The other three markets—industrial, institutional, and reseller—are reached through trade and professional advertising in specialized media such as trade journals, professional magazines, and direct mail.

THE MARKETING CONCEPT

Principle

Integrated marketing communication requires a thorough understanding of all the components of marketing, including the facets that must be communicated to consumers.

The historical evolution of marketing is not only interesting; it also provides important insights as to why marketing is the way it is in the decade of the 1990s. Although a simplification, from the industrial revolution in the 1860s until the 1950s, marketing emphasized two activities: mass production and efficient product delivery. The heroes of the 1800s were larger-than-life financiers and empire builders, such as Morgan, Rockefeller, and Carnegie, who built enormous factories to make new products and transportation networks to deliver these products. This was followed in the 1900s by geniuses such as Ford and Watson, who opened the door to mass production with new technologies. The Roaring Twenties were followed by the Great Depression, a time of significant suffering and deprivation; there was very little cause for marketing. World War II converted U.S. factories to war production: tanks and jeeps, artillery and ammunition, and fighters and bombers. Following the war, there was a greater demand for products after four years of ration coupons and sacrifice. The economy picked up as soldiers went to work, married, and had children. Marketing had not been formalized as a concept, and with the increased demand for goods sales efforts were not as important. Getting the product out to consumers was paramount, making efficient manufacturing the most important function of the decade.

By the late 1950s, the initial surge of demand had been satisfied and the economy had begun to shift, yet production-oriented companies sought to maintain profitability by either taking cash out of the manufacturing process or selling more product. Mass marketing was invented to sell standardized, mass-produced products to a similarly standardized, undifferentiated mass of consumers. The role of marketing was to sell. The role of advertising was to reflect the stereotypical values and mores that were in the popular culture (through television and other media) and to create formula-driven ads, over and over again. During the 1960s, the term *marketing concept* was introduced. It suggested that everything started with the needs and wants of the customer. Although it was a noble sentiment, it was mostly lip service, and business went on as usual. There is a handful of businesses, such as L.L. Bean and United Parcel Service (UPS), who appeared to adopt this perspective, but they are the exception.

Many business historians posit that it was not until the late 1980s that the marketing concept was truly embraced by business. More than likely, business had no choice. Consumers are now better educated, wiser, and empowered with opinions and dollars. World trade barriers have come down and we are introduced to a global society, with new competitors and more and better choices. Me-too products, although very profitable, are no longer always acceptable to most consumers. There is no homogeneous American culture, and people are not buying products exclusively to "keep up" with others. Today, marketers know that in order to compete effectively, they must focus on consumer problems and try to develop products to solve them. Performing this task well promises the ultimate competitive advantage. The marketing concept states: First determine what the customer needs and wants, and then develop, manufacture, market, and service the goods and services that fill those particular needs and wants.

Adopting the marketing concept affects advertising as well. Primarily, advertising is employed as a mechanism for delivering information. Through research, the marketer understands how the consumer makes decisions most efficiently and satisfactorily. This information is then incorporated within advertising messages. The intent is for advertising to facilitate decision making. More importantly, the goal is to create advertising that is honest, useful, and matches the needs of the customer so that the customer is satisfied with the choices made. When advertising is guided by the marketing concept, there is a central goal—satisfying the customer—that helps coordinate advertising with the other marketing functions and increases the likelihood that a particular advertisement will be successful.

This is exactly the philosophy that has made Honda so successful in the American market. When consumers wanted fuel efficiency, Honda was there with the Civic. When they wanted roominess, comfort, and performance, Honda was ready with the Accord. Ad 3.1 shows how Honda has maintained this high level of quality and integrity.

$\mathscr{T}$HE 4PS OF MARKETING

In his book *Basic Marketing* Jerome McCarthy popularized the classification of the various marketing elements into four categories that have since been known in the marketing industry as the "4Ps"[3] (see Figure 3.4). They are:

---

[3]E. Jerome McCarthy and William D. Perreault, Jr., *Basic Marketing* (Homewood, IL: Irwin, 1987):37.

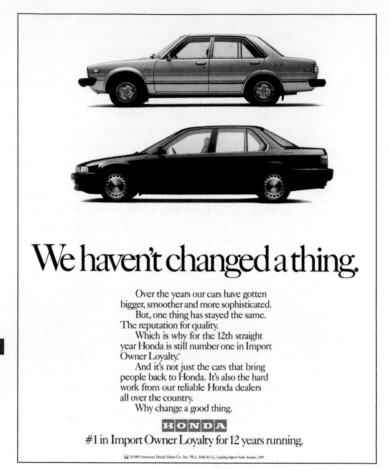

We haven't changed a thing.

Over the years our cars have gotten bigger, smoother and more sophisticated. But, one thing has stayed the same. The reputation for quality.

Which is why for the 12th straight year Honda is still number one in Import Owner Loyalty.*

And it's not just the cars that bring people back to Honda. It's also the hard work from our reliable Honda dealers all over the country.

Why change a good thing.

HONDA

#1 in Import Owner Loyalty for 12 years running.

© 1989 American Honda Motor Co., Inc. *R.L. Polk & Co., Leading Import Sales Analysis, 1991.

1. *Product*: Includes product design and development, branding, and packaging.
2. *Place* (or Distribution): Includes the channels used in moving the product from the manufacturer to the buyer.
3. *Price*: Includes the price at which the product or service is offered for sale and establishes the level of profitability.
4. *Promotion* (or Marketing Communication): Includes personal selling, advertising, public relations, sales promotion, direct marketing, and point-of-sales/packaging.

It is the job of the marketing or product manager to manipulate these elements to create the most efficient and effective *marketing mix*.

PRODUCT

The product is both the object of the advertising and the reason for marketing. Marketing begins by asking a set of questions about the product offered. These questions should always be asked from the consumer's perspective: What product attributes and benefits are important? How is the product perceived relative to competitive offerings? How important is servicing? How long do they expect the product to last?

Product

• Design and
  Development
• Branding
• Packaging

Place

• Distribution Channels
• Market Coverage

Price

• Price Copy
• Psychological Pricing
• Price Lining

Promotion

• Personal Selling
• Advertising
• Sale Promotion
• Direct Marketing
• Public Relations
  and Publicity
• Point of Sale /
  Packaging

Customers view products as "bundles of satisfaction" rather than just physical things. For example, in the United States, some car buyers perceive automobiles made in Germany and Japan as offering superior quality, better gas mileage, and less costly service and maintenance than American cars. At the luxury level, cars such as Porsche, BMW, Audi, and the Mazda RX-7 now offer the status and prestige once associated with Cadillac and Lincoln (see Ad 3.2). Thus, the intangible, symbolic attributes foreign-made automobiles now possess over

Ad 3.2

The copy in this ad for the Porsche 911 Turbo describes the commitment to quality that makes it a luxury car.

(Courtesy of Porsche)

The ultimate Porsche.
(Isn't that redundant?)

Let us put it even more directly: The Porsche 911 Turbo is the Porsche of Porsches. A sportscar built not to the standards of a sportscar, but to the impossibly high standards of a race car.

A combination of 315 thoroughbred horses and massive ABS-fortified brakes not only propel it from 0 to 60 in a mere 4.25 seconds, but also stop it faster than any other production car in the world. (Not surprisingly, it effortlessly defeated the world's other premier sportscars to win the inaugural IMSA Bridgestone Potenza Supercar Championship.)

Yet match that brawn to the dramatically-improved new transmission, steering, suspension, and creature comforts of the new generation of Carrera, and you have a beast that is remarkably well-mannered.

But we are becoming redundant. Test drive the new generation of 911 Turbo and you will agree it is not just the world's ultimate sportscar. It is the ultimate Porsche. **The Porsche 911 Turbo.**

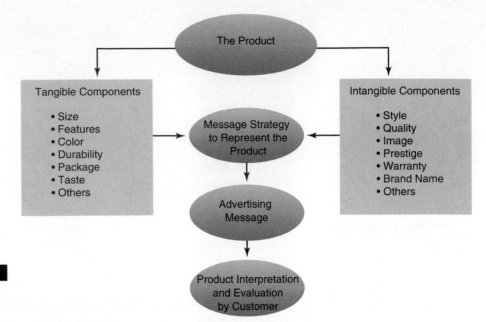

Figure 3.5

Tangible and intangible characteristics of a product.

and above the tangible ones perform psychological and social functions for the buyer. Figure 3.5 portrays both tangible and intangible product characteristics.

To have a practical impact on consumers, managers must translate these product characteristics into concrete attributes with demonstrable benefits. In other words, they must develop message strategy. Consider packaged cookies. The physical ingredients might include sugar, flour, chocolate, and baking powder. The intangible features might be an implied return policy and a reputable brand name. However, these characteristics are too far removed from the real attributes or benefits customers perceive. A customer looks for descriptive phrases such as "tastes like homemade" or "a great afternoon snack," so these are the real pieces of information the marketer desires to communicate. Stressing the most important attributes is the key to influencing customer choices and serves as the foundation for much of advertising.

Product Life Cycle. The concept of *product life cycle* was introduced by Theodore Levitt in an article in the *Harvard Business Review* in 1965.[4] It is based on a metaphor that treats products as people and assumes they are born (introduced), develop (grow), age (mature), and die (decline).

A newly developed product is first presented to its market during the introductory stage. Operations are characterized by high costs, low sales volume, and limited distribution. If the product is a true innovation (that is, unknown to the consumer group), marketing communication must stimulate *primary demand* rather than *secondary demand*. That is, the type of product rather than the seller's brand is emphasized. The role of advertising might be to educate or carry sales promotion inducements such as coupons or samples.

The second stage of the product life cycle is the growth stage. By this stage, the product has received a general acceptance, previous purchasers continue

---

[4]Theodore Levitt, "Exploit the Product Life Cycle," *Harvard Business Review* (November–December 1965):81–94.

Concepts & APPLICATIONS

Trying to Save Spam

Move aside, Big Mac. Out of the way, Whopper. America had better brace its belly for something new, something different. The Spamburger. Yum! That's right, Spam, the product you either "love" or "wouldn't touch with a ten-foot pole," is trying to make a comeback. Actually, this "mystery meat" is closing in on the sale of the five-billionth can. So you can hardly label it a marketing failure. Yet, Geo. A. Hormell & Co. is spending $12 million to command new respect for Spam, to make Spam hip, to cook up a new Spam specialty.

Beginning in May 1993, Omnicom Group's BBDO presented spots showing Spam as never before: decked with Cajun spices; grilled on a barbecue by smiling youngsters on a California beach; shrouded in neon on a giant, computerized billboard of New York's Times Square. Creating this transition hasn't been easy. Spam's main claim to fame is its status as a cultural comedy icon, the grist for countless comedy monologues and the subject of a devastating Monty Python bit. It conjures up everything unappealing about canned, processed food from the fat-laden 1950s. Even Hormel and BBDO seem to have had a tough time in their effort. In one ad that was used in test markets in the South and the West, an actor playing Joe Average looks puzzled and tells the camera: "Spam was made from ham, right? So, really, this is a hamburger." He sounds as if he is trying to convince himself.

The market position of Spam is quite respectable. Sales in 1992 were just shy of $100 million, or an 82 percent share of the market that IRI defines for canned luncheon meat. "It has a broad appeal in every age category," says Harry Balzer, vice president of NPD Group, a Chicago firm that tracks Americans' eating habits. (Although, he adds, it tends to "skew" to lower-income households and is not popular in homes of the college-educated and professional.) The company likes to note that some 60 million people eat 3.8 cans per second. Despite Spam holding its own, however, there is a need to give the brand a contemporary appeal and show consumers alternative uses, says Joe Johnson, Hormel's president and chief operating officer. The company has even trademarked the Spamburger name. "We had to expand the user base," says Jon Firestone, president and chief executive officer at BBDO's Minneapolis office. "The whole country is aware of the brand, but there are a lot of nontryers. We needed to get them to try it, and to get those users to do so more often."

Will this new campaign reposition Spam? Can you change a product, when people like David Letterman are proposing "Spam-on-a-rope," for people who get hungry in the shower? It seems unlikely.

Adapted from Kevin Goldman, "BBDO Spices Up New Ways to Serve Spam," *The Wall Street Journal* (May 3, 1993):B10.

their purchasing, and new buyers enter in large numbers. The success of the new product attracts competitors. The aim of advertising often shifts from building brand awareness to creating a clear brand position and illiciting conviction and purchase. Advertising expenditures are based on those of competitors. Premium athletic shoe marketers such as Nike, Inc. and Reebok find themselves currently in this position.

In maturity, the company shares the market with successful and rigorous competitors. This stage is characterized by continued sales increases, but the rate of increase continually moderates and toward the end of the period becomes almost negligible. Marginal producers are forced to drop out of the market, and price competition becomes increasingly severe. Advertising often becomes more image based, attempting to protect and reinforce the equity the brand holds. (See Ad 3.3.) Also, advertising may become more a responsibility shared with intermediaries, especially retailers through cooperative advertising programs. With cooperative advertising, the cost of advertising is shared by the advertisers

and the intermediaries. Soft-drink marketers, as well as beer manufacturers and fast-food retailers, find themselves at this stage.

Finally, many products face a period of obsolescence when they no longer sell as well as they previously did. Example of products in decline include wine coolers, window air conditioners, push lawn mowers, and typewriters. During this stage of decline, advertising may be reduced or eliminated altogether. Not all products have to decline, however; a product may be reformulated or turned around, and the product life cycle begins again. This tactic, called *take-off strategy*, is exactly what Harley-Davidson used to recoup its sales.

branding The process of creating an identity for a product using a distinctive name or symbol.

Branding. When you think of bread, what product name comes to mind? When you think of facial tissues, what product name occurs to you? What product name comes to mind when you picture a copy machine? Do you think of a product name when you think of salt?

Wonder Bread, Kleenex, Xerox, and Morton's have been extensively advertised over many years. **Branding** makes a product distinctive in the marketplace, just as your name makes you unique in the society in which you live. However, there are subtle differences. A *brand* is the name, term, design, symbol, or any other feature that identifies the goods, service, institution, or idea sold by a marketer. The *brand name* is that part of a brand that can be spoken, such as words, letters, or numbers. Hershey's is a brand name, as is K2R. The *brand mark*, also known as the *logo*, is that part of the brand that cannot be spoken. It can be a symbol, picture, design, distinctive lettering, or color combination. The

Travelers red umbrella is found on all their ads (see Ad 3.4). When a brand name or brand mark is legally protected through registration with the Patent and Trademark Office of the Department of Commerce, it becomes a *trademark*.

The importance of the brand cannot be overestimated. When we talk about *brand equity*, we are referring to the reputation that name or symbol connotes. It is on every important message and becomes synonymous with the company. Losing brand equity, through excessive discounting, producing substandard products, or poor service has proven disastrous for many companies.

Packaging.   The package is another important communication device. In today's marketing environment a package is much more than a container. The self-service retailing phenomenon means that the consumer in the typical grocery store or drugstore is faced with an endless array of products. In such a situation the package is the message. When the package works in tandem with consumer advertising, it catches attention, presents a familiar brand image, and communicates critical information. Many purchase decisions are made on the basis of how the product looks on the shelf.

An article in *Advertising Age* explained the importance of the package as a communication medium: "Even if you can't afford a big advertising budget, you've got a fighting chance if your product projects a compelling image from

Ad 3.4

Travelers brand equity is maintained partially through the awareness of its red umbrella logo.

(Courtesy of The Travelers Insurance Company)

When you choose a Managed Care and Employee Benefits program it affects more than your company's bottom line. It affects the lives of your employees and their families. Which is why The Travelers is committed to providing both savings and quality for the people you trust and the people they love.

We offer your employees the caring and expertise of over 100,000 health professionals in more than 130 major metropolitan areas, as well as a nationally recognized wellness and counseling program that is preventing illness through innovation.

And our Managed Care System can be customized to provide your company with the flexibility to make the most of your benefit dollars. In fact, we've actually *reduced* the rise in health care costs for our customers by over 30%.

With one of America's largest managed care networks, we understand the importance of taking care of one another.

But most importantly, we offer a program that recognizes one truth for employer and employee alike — the greatest wealth of all has little to do with money.

© 1993 The Travelers Insurance Company and its Affiliates, Hartford, CT 06183.

The**Travelers**ʃ
AMERICA'S UMBRELLA℠

the shelf."[5] For products that are advertised nationally, the package reflects the brand image developed in the advertising. It serves as a very important reminder at that critical moment when the consumer is choosing among several competing brands. As an advertising medium, the package has to be an eye-catcher as well as an identifier. Most of us carry around in our minds some kind of visual image of our most familiar products. That image is usually the package.

In sum, packaging is an important part of the advertising strategy. It is the constant communicator. Packages that are colorful, cleverly designed, functional, and complementary to the product enhance the advertising effort. Such a package facilitates the association between the package and the brand name. Finally, the package is an effective device for carrying advertising messages.

PLACE (THE CHANNEL OF DISTRIBUTION)

It does little good to manufacture a fantastic product that will meet the needs of the consumer unless there is a mechanism for delivering and servicing the product and receiving payment. Those individuals and institutions involved in moving products from producers to customers make up the **channel of distribution.** Resellers, or intermediaries, are primary members of the channel who may actually take ownership of the product and participate in its marketing. Wholesalers, retailers, and modes of transportation are typical channel members. Each is capable of influencing and delivering advertising messages.

For example, the primary strength of wholesalers is personal selling. Wholesalers do not advertise often. There are, however, instances when special types of advertising strategies are employed. For instance, regional wholesalers are apt to use direct mail, trade papers, or catalogs. Local wholesalers may use newspapers or local radio. The copy tends to be simple and straightforward with few pictures or illustrations. Conversely, retailers are quite good at advertising, especially local advertising. The retailers' main concern is that the advertising be directed at their own customers. The media used, the copy employed, and the size and frequency of ads, and so on will vary from one retailer to another. The ad for the Tenafly Department Store is a typical retail ad. (See Ad 3.5.)

Other channel-related decisions influence advertising as well. Part of the channel nomenclature includes the idea of a "channel captain," or the dominant member in a channel of distribution. Historically, the channel captain tended to be the manufacturer. This pattern has been reversed during the last two decades, and today retailers such as Wal-Mart and Mervyns tend to dominate. Consequently, the leverage possessed by the channel captain often extends into the realm of advertising. For example, Sears may strongly influence the advertising strategy of its product suppliers, for example, General Electric and Texas Instruments. General Electric may have similar power over a small appliance chain.

Is the channel direct or indirect? Companies that distribute their products without the use of a reseller engage in *direct marketing.* Companies such as Lands' End, Spiegel, and Burpee Seeds all use direct-marketing channels. In place of stores or personal salespeople, direct marketing relies on advertising media to inform and stimulate customer purchase responses. Direct marketing will be discussed in more detail in Chapter 16.

In *indirect marketing* the product is distributed through a channel structure that includes one or more resellers. A key decision in indirect marketing con-

[5]Lori Kesler, "Shopping Around for a Design," *Advertising Age* (December 28, 1981):2–4, 2–8.

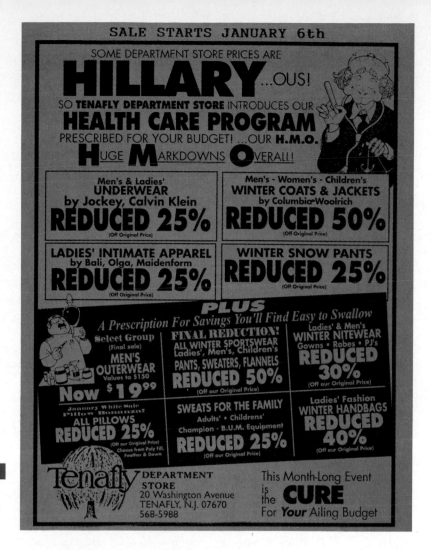

cooperative advertising A form of advertising in which the manufacturer reimburses the retailer for part or all of the retailer's advertising expenditures.

cerns resellers' involvement in advertising. Wholesalers and especially retailers are often expected to participate in the advertising programs offered by producers. Through **cooperative advertising** allowances the producer and reseller share the cost of placing the advertisement. This activity not only saves money (because local advertising rates are less expensive than national rates); it also creates an important tie-in with local retailers, who often have a much greater following than the producer's brand does.

Wholesalers and retailers also initiate their own advertising campaigns, which often highlight the items of various manufacturers. Few manufacturers can match the advertising impact of retailers such as Sears, J.C. Penney, or Federated Stores. Rather, manufacturers attempt to penetrate these outlets in order to take advantage of their advertising strength.

Another channel-related factor that may influence advertising is whether a push or a pull strategy is being employed. A *pull strategy* directs marketing efforts to the ultimate consumer and attempts to "pull" the product through the channel; the process is fueled by consumer demand. There is usually a large emphasis on consumer advertising, along with incentives to buy such as coupons, rebates, free samples, or sweepstakes. Little is expected from resellers other than to stock the product. In contrast, a *push strategy* directs marketing efforts at resellers, and success depends greatly on the ability of intermediaries

Lauren Berger
Senior Vice President/Management Supervisor
DDB Needham Worldwide

Time/Place	Attendees	Issues
8:30-9:00 A.M. Office	—	Organize for the day.
9:00-9:15 A.M. Office	Two Account Supervisors	Meet to discuss important issues of the day that may need my involvement.
9:15-9:45 A.M. AMD's Office	Associate Media Director (AMD) Senior Planner Account Supervisor	Review Metroliner Service media plan for special promotion period.
9:45-10:30 A.M. CD's office	SVP Creative Director Creative Team Account Supervisor	Review roughcut of two commercials and address client comments.
10:30-11:00 A.M. BUD's office	Business Unit Director (BUD)	Brief Business Unit Director on creative meeting and other key issues.
11:00-11;45 P.M. Office	Director of Career Development	Discuss agency training programs designed for Account Management personnel.
11:45-12:30 P.M. Office	As needed	Return phone calls, review mail, meet with account people as needed.
12:30-2:00 P.M. Local Restaurant	Strategic Planning Supervisor (DDBN-Chicago)	Discuss Amtrak's use of integrated marketing as input for agency's integrated marketing planning program.
2:00-3:30 P.M. 10th floor Conference Room	Task Force (Account Management, Research, Creative, Media Groups)	Business review of Auto Train and discussion of agency point of view on new competitive airline pricing strategies.
3:30-3:45 P.M. via phone	Client	Brief agency on new service introduction between Boston and New York, which will require special program.
3:45-4:15 P.M. Office	Research Planning Director	Discuss recommended changes to Amtrak's tracking study based on new advertising strategies.
4:15-5:00 P.M. Office	Account Group	Follow up on client direction on new service, discuss responsibilities, timetables.
5:00-5:15 P.M. Office	—	Return phone calls.
5:15-6:00 P.M. Office	As needed.	Write memos, meet with account people *re*: personnel issues, client projects, internal issues, etc.

to market the product, including the use of advertising. Thus, advertising may be first targeted at resellers in order to gain their acceptance; then it is targeted at ultimate users through joint manufacturer-reseller advertising.

A final channel-related decision influencing advertising concerns the *market coverage* desired. Three strategies are possible: exclusive distribution, selective distribution, and intensive distribution. With *exclusive distribution*, only one distributor is allowed to sell the brand in a particular market. Two examples of companies that employ exclusive distribution are Rolls-Royce and Ethan Allen Furniture. The retailer is expected to provide a strong personal selling effort, effective merchandising, and heavy participation in cooperative (co-op) advertising. *Selective distribution* expands the number of outlets but restricts participation to those outlets that prove most profitable to the manufacturer. Florsheim Shoes, Farrah Fashions, and Timex all engage in selective distribution. The role of advertising is quite varied under this arrangement, but normally the manufacturer does some mass advertising and offers co-op possibilities. *Intensive distribution* involves placing the product in every possible outlet (including vending machines) in order to attain total market coverage. Intensive distribution is used to market soft drinks, candy, and cigarettes. Advertising is paramount in this situation. Because little personal selling can be expected from the retailer, it is up to mass advertising to create brand awareness and preference.

Market coverage also dictates the geographic distribution of the product. This may influence both the creative strategy and the media strategy. In the case of the former, an ad for a product distributed in the Pacific Northwest and Florida (for example, rain gear) may require significant changes in copy and illustration. In terms of media, the selection of media is clearly a function of a product's geography. An ad placed in *The New York Times* makes no sense for a product sold only in Utah. Of course, there also are instances when national marketers change their copy or illustration for different parts of the country. Ford has done this with its truck advertising. Healthy Choice also modifies its copy depending upon geographic location.

PRICING

The price a seller sets for a product is based not only on the cost of making and marketing the product but also on the seller's expected level of profit. Certain psychological factors also affect the price. For example, it has long been assumed that price suggests quality in the consumer's mind.

Ultimately, the price charged is simply based on what the traffic will bear, given what the competition is doing, the economic well-being of the consumer, the relative value of the product, and the ability of the consumer to gauge that value.

With the exception of price information delivered at the point of sale, advertising is the primary vehicle for telling the consumer about the price and associated conditions of a particular product. The term *price copy* has been coined to designate advertising copy devoted primarily to this information.

In turn, there are a number of pricing strategies that influence the specific creative strategy employed in a particular ad. For example, *customary* or *expected* pricing involves the use of a single well-known price for a long period of time. Movie theaters, the U.S. Post Office, and manufacturers of candy and other products sold through vending machines use this pricing strategy. Only price changes would be made explicit in advertising. As shown in Ad 3.6, the airline industry has become known for its emphasis on price reductions.

Sensational Savings To Europe.

Hurry! Sale Ends Soon.

Fares are each way based on round-trip purchase.

JFK or Boston To:	SUMMER	FALL
Brussels	$359	$309
London	$280	$235
Manchester	$280	$235
Paris	$384	$334
Zurich	$359	$309

San Francisco, San Jose or San Diego To:	SUMMER	FALL
Brussels	$459	$409
Frankfurt	$484	$434
Munich	$484	$434
Paris	$484	$434
Stockholm	$449	$399

Miami To:	SUMMER	FALL
Brussels	$384	$334
Madrid	$384	$334
Manchester	$335	$285
Munich	$409	$359
Stockholm	$409	$359

Washington, D.C. To:	SUMMER	FALL
Berlin	$384	$334
London	$315	$265
Manchester	$315	$265
Paris	$384	$334
Zurich	$359	$309

Chicago To:	SUMMER	FALL
Frankfurt	$434	$384
Madrid	$409	$359
Manchester	$399	$349
Paris	$434	$384
Zurich	$409	$359

Los Angeles To:	SUMMER	FALL
Berlin	$484	$434
Duesseldorf	$484	$434
Glasgow	$385	$320
Milan	$459	$409
Zurich	$459	$409

Dallas Fort Worth To:	SUMMER	FALL
Brussels	$409	$359
London	$399	$349
Milan	$409	$359
Paris	$434	$384
Stockholm	$424	$374

These are some examples of our low fares to Europe. Call for information about fares from your city.

Act now and get a great deal on travel to American Airlines cities throughout Europe. Just purchase your tickets by midnight, June 30, 1993, and enjoy savings to all of the popular cities listed above. This limited-time offer is good for summer or fall travel. Seats with these special low fares are limited and advance purchase is required. So hurry and act now. For reservations or more information, call your Travel Agent or American Airlines at **1-800-624-6262.** *Consulte a su agente de viajes o llame gratis a American Airlines al 1-800-633-3711 en español.*

 Super Savings On Our Fly AAway Vacations℠ Packages.

Combine our low air fares with these or any of our other Fly AAway Vacations packages. Call your Travel Agent or American at 1-800-832-8383.

FLY/DRIVE EUROPE
$99 *per night, double occupancy.*

Novotel Hotels And Hertz® Rent A Car Bonuses.

Fly AAway Vacations, Novotel Hotels and Hertz® Rent A Car are giving you a great deal! Novotel Europe A La Carte Fly/Drive hotels start as low as $99*† per night with your 11th night free after booking 10 nights. Hertz rental cars start at just $18 per day§ with your 11th day free after booking 10 days. Call today for details and our new Novotel Europe A La Carte Fly/Drive brochure.

LONDON ON YOUR OWN
$295 *7 Days/6 Nights per person, double occupancy.*

Land only. Air fare not included.

This outstanding offer includes six nights accommodations, continental breakfast daily, hotel service charges and taxes. Other hotels available. Call for information.

Harewood or Earls Court Park Inn	$295
White House ... *Best Value, Best Buy!*	$409
Copthorne Tara	$415

PARIS ON YOUR OWN
$295 *7 Days/6 Nights per person, double occupancy.*

Land only. Air fare not included.

This outstanding offer includes six nights accommodations, continental breakfast daily, hotel service charges and taxes. Other hotels available. Call for information.

Lorette	$295
Adagio	$399
Concorde St. Lazare ... *Best Value, Best Buy!*	$499

AmericanAirlines®
Something special to Europe.

RESTRICTIONS: Fares are each way based on round-trip purchase for Economy travel Monday through Thursday and are nonrefundable. Travel other days available at additional cost. Seats are limited. Fares may not be available on all flights and are subject to change without notice. Fares are subject to government approval. For all travel, up to $32 per round trip in local airport charges may be collected in addition to the advertised price. Government taxes and fees of $28 to $38, varying by destination, are not included. Cancellation/change penalties apply. Other restrictions may apply. **For Destinations Except The U.K.:** Summer fares are for departures through 8/31/93 and fall fares are for departures 9/1/93-10/28/93. Saturday night minimum stay and 60-day maximum stay requirements apply. Tickets must be purchased within 72 hours of making reservations but no later than 6/30/93. **For The U.K.:** Summer fares are for departures through 9/15/93 and fall fares are for departures 9/16/93-10/14/93. Seven-day minimum stay and 45-day maximum stay requirements apply. Tickets must be purchased 21 days in advance of travel. *Prices are per person, double occupancy. Package prices valid only with the purchase of round-trip transatlantic travel on American Airlines. Travel days, minimum/maximum stay requirements and prices/effective dates vary by package/hotel for travel 6/10/93-10/31/93. Other dates and hotels/tours are available at additional cost. Prices are subject to change and to hotel/tour availability. Cancellation/change penalties and other significant restrictions may apply. †Basic hotel rate. Supplement may apply. Call for details. §Car-only prices quoted on a per-day basis in Belgium with a minimum rental period of seven days. Rental car for six days or less available at additional cost. Gas, refueling charges and optional insurance not included. Cars may not be taken into Ireland. Cars must be picked up and returned in the same country.

Ad 3.6

The airline industry has spent the last decade emphasizing price reductions.

(Courtesy of American Airlines)

Psychological pricing techniques are intended to manipulate the judgment process employed by the customer. A very high price—for example, prestige pricing, where a high price is set to make the product seem worthy or valuable— would be accompanied by photographs of an exceptional product or a copy platform consisting of logical reasons for this high price. Conversely, a dramatic or temporary price reduction is translated through terms such as "sale," "special," and "today only."

Finally, *price lining* involves offering a number of variations of a particular product and pricing them accordingly. Sears Roebuck, for example, offers many of their products on a "good," "better," and "best" basis. Price lining requires that the ad show the various products so that consumers can assess the relative differences.

It is important that advertising clearly and consistently reflects the product's pricing strategy. For many consumers, this ad-price tandem represents the initial decision to purchase.

PROMOTION

Advertising, personal selling, sales promotion, public relations, direct marketing, and point-of-sales/packaging represent the primary techniques available to the marketer for communicating with target markets. These combined techniques are referred to as **promotion** or **marketing communication**. Marketing promotion is defined as "persuasive communication designed to send marketing-related messages to a selected target audience." With the refocusing of commerce from product-centered to consumer-centered strategies, the revolution in marketing brought together a group of activities that had existed on the fringe of the manufacturing process. Bogart explains that "when American business was reorganized in the postwar years, marketing emerged as a major function" that coordinated previously separate specialities—such as product development, sales promotion, merchandising, advertising, and market research; "great emphasis was placed on the integrated marketing plan."[6]

The idea of coordination suggests that there are a number of elements involved in the marketing process, including the product, the distribution channel, the sales force, and the marketing communication program. These elements can also be viewed as *activities*, such as product design and development, branding, packaging, pricing, distribution, personal selling, advertising, sales promotion, and public relations. Combining these four communication devices in a way that produces a coordinated message structure is called the **promotion mix**. The basic elements of the promotion mix—personal selling, advertising, sales promotion, public relations, direct marketing, and point-of-sales/packaging—appear in most marketing plans. These elements differ in terms of their intended effect, the type of customer contact, and the time element of response. (See Figure 3.6.)

Personal Selling. *Personal selling* is face-to-face contact between the marketer and a prospective customer. The intention is to create both immediate sales and repeat sales. There are several different types of personal selling, including sales calls at the place of business by a field representative (field sales), assistance at an outlet by a sales clerk (retail selling), and calls by a representative who goes to consumers' homes (door-to-door selling). Personal selling is most important for companies that sell products requiring explanation, demonstration, and service. Such products tend to be higher priced.

Advertising. *Advertising* has already been defined in Chapter 1, and several of

promotion That element in the marketing mix that communicates the key marketing messages to target audiences. Also called **marketing communication**.

promotion mix The combination of personal selling, advertising, sales promotion, and public relations to produce a coordinated message structure.

Principle

Advertising helps the salesperson by laying the groundwork and preselling the product.

---

[6]Leo Bogart, *Strategy in Advertising*, 2nd. Ed. (NTC Business Books; Lincolnwood, IL, 1990):3.

Promotion Type	Intended Effect	Customer Contact	Timing
Personal Selling	Sales	Direct	Short
Advertising	Attitude Change Behavior Change	Indirect	Moderate-Low
Sales Promotion	Sales	Semidirect	Short
Direct Marketing	Behavior Change	Semidirect	Short
Public Relations	Attitude Change	Semidirect	Long
Point of Sale/ Packaging	Behavior Change	Direct	Short

Figure 3.6

Promotional-mix comparison.

its key characteristics were discussed at the beginning of this chapter. It differs from the other promotional elements in several ways. Although advertising has a greater ability to reach a larger number of people simultaneously than do the other elements, it has less ability to prompt an immediate behavioral change. Furthermore, the contact between the advertiser and the audience is indirect, and it takes a longer period of time to deliver information, change attitudes, and create a rapport or trust between the two parties.

Sales Promotion. *Sales promotion* includes a number of communication devices offered for a limited period of time in order to generate immediate sales. Simply stated, sales promotion is an extra incentive to buy *now*. Examples are price discounts, coupons, product sampling, contests or sweepstakes, and rebates. Sales promotion will be discussed in greater detail in Chapter 18.

Advertising is used to promote sales promotion activities such as sweepstakes and contests. Sales promotions can also be used in support of advertising campaigns. Advertising and sales promotion can work together to create a *synergy* in which each makes the other more effective.

Public Relations. *Public relations* encompasses a set of activities intended to enhance the image of the marketer in order to create goodwill. Public relations includes publicity (stories in the mass media with significant news value), news conferences, company-sponsored events, open houses, plant tours, donations, and other special events.

Rather than attempt to sell the product, public relations seeks to influence people's attitudes about the company or product. In most cases the lag effect associated with public relations is quite long, making any relationship between promotion and sales difficult to determine.

Advertising interacts with public relations in several ways. A public relations event or message can serve as part of an advertising campaign. Product publicity can also be used in support of an advertising campaign. For example, Kingsford charcoal sponsors a Ribfest cooking contest in Chicago that includes giving free charcoal to all contestants. This event reinforces the association between Kingsford and outdoor activities. Public relations is discussed in greater detail in Chapter 19.

Direct Marketing Direct marketing is a rapidly changing field and its definition is evolving. However, it does have some basic characteristics: (1) it is an interactive system that allows two-way communication; (2) it provides a mechanism for the prospect to respond; (3) it can occur at any location; (4) it provides a measurable response; and (5) it requires a database of consumer information. Direct marketing is the fastest growing element in marketing because it provides the consumer with the three things he or she wants most—convenience, efficiency, and compression of decision-making time.[7] For example, when a consumer buys shirts from Lands' End, every step of the process is smoothly executed, from the toll-free conversation with the order taker to prompt delivery of well-made, fully guaranteed shirts, billed to a Visa card at a cost lower than many retail stores charge. Unfortunately, not all direct-marketing techniques are viewed as viable product sources for consumers. A great deal is still viewed as junk mail; especially in disfavor is unsolicited material that advertises cheap merchandise or implies high risks.

Messages delivered for direct-marketing products are usually called *direct-response advertising*. It is designed to motivate customers to make some sort of response, either an order or an inquiry. Direct-response advertising is directed to target groups through vehicles such as direct mail, telemarketing, print, broadcast, catalogs, and point-of-purchase displays. More will be said about this topic in Chapter 16.

Point-of-Sale/Packaging Point-of-sale (POS) and packaging encompass all the communication devices and marketing messages found at the place where the product is sold. The message-delivery capabilities of the package discussed earlier come into play here. POS materials include signage, posters, displays, and a variety of other materials designed to influence buying decisions at the point of purchase. Estimates vary, depending upon the product category, that from 30 percent to 70 percent of our purchases are unplanned. This marketing material is intended to take advantage of that fact, along with fulfilling other basic communication objectives, such as product identification, product information, and product comparisons.

The role advertising plays in this context may vary as well. Often the POS materials are an extension of the ad. Michael Jordan posters and cut-outs are found in every store that sells a product sponsored by Michael Jordan. Seasonal events, such as Fourth of July or Christmas, may produce matching ads and posters.

ADVERTISING AND THE MARKETING MIX

Having examined the elements that make up the marketing mix, you are now better prepared to understand how advertising and marketing interact. As noted at the beginning of this chapter, advertising is a subset of marketing that relies on the evaluation and coordination of product-centered and consumer-centered strategies. The product must come first. Its characteristics, its strengths and weaknesses, and its position in the marketplace all dictate the rest of the marketing mix. Advertising must account for all these factors as well as reflect the price of the product and the way it is distributed. For a highly technical prod-

---

[7]John J. Burnett, *Promotion Management* (Boston: Houghton Mifflin Company, 1993):652–53.

uct, advertising will probably take a backseat to personal selling and support services. Such advertising would tend to be laden with facts and restricted to trade magazines targeted at a very well-defined audience. For a product such as Peter Pan peanut butter, it is critical to create brand awareness and provide basic product information through mass advertising; advertising would play a much more important role. A wide range of media would be used. Advertising copy would attempt to instill an emotional appeal for a product that is inherently unexciting. Because price is important to consumers who buy peanut butter, print ads would probably carry coupons.

Even products that have a similar marketing mix may use very different advertising strategies. A case in point is found in the computer industry. When Apple Computer entered the market, they realized that they faced a serious competitive disadvantage. They attacked IBM through their product innovations and breakthrough advertising. IBM and Apple followed very different creative strategies to achieve comparable objectives. Both were driven by their own unique marketing mix.

SUMMARY

- Understanding how marketing works and the role advertising plays within the marketing strategy is mandatory for successful advertising.

- The success of marketing is dependent upon whether a business can create a competitive advantage that results in an exchange.

- Exchange takes place within a market; there are four types of markets: (1) consumer, (2) business-to-business (industrial), (3) institutional, and (4) reseller.

- The marketing concept focuses on the needs of the consumer rather than the predetermined goals of the marketer.

- The marketing mix identifies the most effective combination of the four primary marketing functions: product, price, place (or distribution), and promotion (or marketing communication).

- The product consists of a bundle of tangible and intangible components that satisfies the needs of the customer.

- It is assumed that a product goes through a predictable life cycle (i.e., introduction, growth, maturity, and decline) and that advertising plays a different role at each stage.

- A product also has a branding strategy that makes the product distinctive in the marketplace.

- An effective package not only holds the product but is an important communication device.

- A channel of distribution is the basic mechanism for delivering the product to the customer, receiving payment, and servicing the product.

- The two primary types of channel institutions are wholesalers and retailers, each of which employ advertising in a unique manner.

- Several other channel-related factors influence advertising: Who is the channel captain? Is the channel direct or indirect? Is a push or pull strategy being followed? Is the market coverage exclusive, selective, or intensive?

- Price includes the cost, profit, and value expectations. Factors that influence advertising include the need for price copy, the customary or expected price, psychological pricing, and price lining.

- Promotion or mass communication includes advertising, sales promotion, public relations, personal selling, point-of-sale packaging, and direct marketing; together these are called the promotion mix.

- Each element of the promotional mix contributes to the ability of the company to communicate in a special way.

QUESTIONS

1 Find examples of three advertisements that demonstrate the marketing concept. What elements of these ads reflect this approach?

2 How would you advertise a toothpaste at the four different stages in its life cycle?

3 Imagine you are starting a company to manufacture fudge. Consider the following decisions:

a. Describe the marketing mix you think would be most effective for this company.

b. Describe the promotion mix you would recommend for this company.

c. How would you determine the advertising budget for your new fudge company?

d. Develop a plan for a brand image for this fudge.

4 Professor Baker tells his advertising class that advertising's relationship to marketing is like the tip of an iceberg. As the class looks puzzled he explains that most (80 percent) of the iceberg cannot be seen. "It's the same with consumer's perception of how much of marketing is advertising-related," Baker explains. What is Baker trying to illustrate with the iceberg analogy?

5 In the 1980s marketers began to look for short-run marketing strategies. This often meant investment in activities other than advertising. Advertising professionals warned companies about ignoring the need for long-run investment through advertising. What activities would marketers use for short-run results? What is the connection between advertising and long-run marketing objectives?

6 The chapter stressed integration of advertising with other components of the marketing mix. If you were in marketing management for Kellogg cereals how would you see advertising supporting product, price, and place? Could advertising improve each of these functions for Kellogg? Explain your answer.

7 Angie Todd, an account assistant at a local advertising agency, is upset at the comments of a marketing consultant during a media reception. The consultant is telling listeners that consumer advertising has lost its edge and does not have credibility. He claims consumers pay no attention to glitter or glitz (advertising); they just want a deal on price. "I'll bet none of you can name even two consumer products last year with ad campaigns that made any difference to the target consumer," he challenged. If you were Angie how would you respond?

SUGGESTED CLASS PROJECT

Interview the manager of a large retail outlet store in your area, such as Target, K-Mart, or Wal-Mart. Assess how the various elements of the promotion mix are used. Study a few diverse products such as food items, blue jeans, and small appliances. You might even talk to the automotive service department. Write a report, making conclusions about how advertising comes into play.

FURTHER READINGS

AAKER, DAVID A., RAJEEV BATRA, and JOHN L. MYERS, *Advertising Management* 3rd ed. (Englewood Cliffs, NJ: Prentice Hall, Inc., 1992).

BLY, ROBERT, *Advertising Manager's Handbook*, (Englewood Cliffs, NJ: Prentice Hall, 1993).

HARDY, KENNETH G., and ALLAN J. MAGRATH, *Marketing Channel Management* (Glenview, IL: Scott, Foresman, 1988).

LODISH, LEONARD M., *The Advertising and Promotion Challenge* (New York: Oxford University Press, 1986).

MONROE, KENT B., *Pricing: Making Profitable Decisions* (NEW YORK: MCGRAW-HILL, 1979).

SHIMP, TERENCE, *Promotion Management and Marketing Communications* (Chicago: Dryden, 1993).

WIND, YORAM J., *Product Policy: Concepts, Methods, and Strategy* (Reading, MA: Addison-Wesley, 1982).

On the Wrong Scent: BiC Parfum

Long known in the United States primarily for its low-cost disposable pens, the BiC Corporation began to branch out into other product areas in the 1970s. BiC's newfound aggressiveness in the marketplace increased the company's strengths in low-cost plastic production to bring consumers the convenience of disposability and affordability.

BiC's first successful new-product venture was the Clic, a disposable plastic lighter that retailed for under 1 dollar. The Clic made fumbling with matches and the messy refilling of fluid-fuel lighters a thing of the past by providing a reliable, adjustable butane gas flame. As the popularity of Clic expanded, other manufacturers began producing attractive sleeves and holders to make the lighter suitable for almost any social occasion.

Buoyed by the success of the Clic, BiC caught Gillette, Schick, and Wilkinson off guard by introducing its next new product—the disposable plastic razor. The old adage of "give them the razor and sell them the blades" had served the industry well until BiC began selling the razor *and* the blades for the price of the other manufacturers' blades alone. The industry has never been quite the same since the disposable razor made its appearance. Some manufacturers, such as Gillette and Schick, responded by rushing to develop their own disposable razors, while investing heavily in new technology to make their replacement blade cartridges more effective and more competitive against the disposables. Other manufacturers, like Wilkinson and its Sword blades, have yet to regain the market share they enjoyed before disposable razors were introduced.

The late 1980s and early 1990s were not as good for BiC as the early years. The media reported incidents of burn injuries resulting from leaking and exploding Clic lighters, culminating in a story on *60 Minutes*. Although BiC denied any problems with the Clic, the persistent media coverage nonetheless had a significant effect on sales of the disposable lighter. Sales of BiC's disposable razors suffered as well as the competition gained market share at BiC's expense. Meanwhile, Gillette readied its long-awaited Sensor razor and blades, which offered a new innovation in shaving that disposable razors could not match. Schick was rumored to be developing a similar product.

Perhaps most concerning of all for BiC was increased environmental consciousness emerging among consumers in the late 1980s. This "green consumerism" emphasized reusability and recyclability, threatening to give disposability, BiC's original strength, a bad name. It was therefore no surprise when BiC announced the introduction of yet another new product, this one providing the affordability that was the company's hallmark but deemphasizing disposability: BiC parfum (perfume). BiC reportedly chose to target the fragrance category because the industry lacked a quality, affordable product. Because quality and price had always been synonymous in the fragrance industry, BiC earmarked $20 million in advertising and promotional support for Parfum to help change existing consumer perceptions. Deemphasizing disposability did take some of the pressure off of BiC to price the product at a minimum, so BiC Parfum was introduced at $5 a bottle, a bold price by the company's usual standards. Although other manufacturers, such as Avon, had been offering low-cost perfumes for several years, BiC became the most notable recent case of a firm with a reputation for low-cost products entering the fragrance industry.

Despite BiC's extensive marketing efforts, however, Parfum failed, forcing the company to drop the product within 2 years of its introduction.

Source: "BiC Markets New Perfume," *Business World* #125 (March 5, 1989).

Questions

1 Explain the factors you think contributed to the failure of BiC Parfum.

2 What does the following statement by Charles Revson say about the intangible nature of cosmetics: "In the factory we make cosmetics; in the store we sell hope"? How did BiC's failure to consider it doom Parfum?

3 What parallels can be drawn between consumer perceptions in the fragrance industry and the wine industry?

Too bad you're addicted to impor

Demand Better. Eighty

ADVERTISING AGENCIES

CHAPTER OBJECTIVES

When you have completed this chapter, you should be able to:

- Understand the functions of an advertising agency
- Explain how an agency is organized
- Recognize the pressures for change in the business
- Understand how agencies are paid
- Comprehend the impact of technology in this sector as in other business sectors

113

THE ONE THAT DIDN'T GET AWAY

A client switching an account from one agency to another is advertising news that makes the daily press as well as advertising trade journals. This is the story of one time when a client reviewed its agency assignment and decided to stay (and this happens in roughly 20 percent of cases). It is the story of how the Leo Burnett Company retained General Motors' Oldsmobile account in a category (automobiles) that has seen a great deal of turmoil in the 1990s. (See Table 4.1.)

Account switches are news because they happen. In the period from 1987 to 1992, 67 percent of the clients of the 50 largest agencies moved some or all of their business to another agency. The agency that fared best during this period was Leo Burnett, which had a loss rate of 24 percent, or six out of 25 clients listed in 1987.[1]

In September 1992, after years of declining sales and market share, the Oldsmobile Division of General Motors announced that it was putting its advertising business up for review. A team of Oldsmobile executives and dealers reviewed a long list of agencies, visited more than a dozen, and asked for presentations from a short list of finalists.

In the midst of this review, other market factors intruded. As often happens, a change of management at Oldsmobile triggered the advertising review. But as General Motors suffered a string of quarterly losses, the business press began to suggest that Oldsmobile would be discontinued. Division management faced the now exacerbated problem of selling cars to a public beginning to wonder if Oldsmobile would soon be extinct.

---

[1]Adapted from Joanne Lipman, "Study Shows Clients Jump Ship Quickly," *The Wall Street Journal* (May 21, 1992):B8.

Table 4.1 — Fallout in Automotive Accounts Since 1991

Marketer	Billings	Original Agency	Review Announced	Status
Volvo	$40 million	Scali, McCabe, Sloves	Feb. 1991	Messner Vetere Berger McNamee Schmetterer/Euro RSCG
Subaru	$60 million	Levine, Huntley, Vick & Beaver	June 1991	Wieden & Kennedy
Isuzu	$95 million	Della Femina, McNamee	Aug. 1991	Goodby, Berlin & Silverstein
Peugeot	$10 million	Lord, Dentsu & Partners	Aug. 1991	Left market
Sterling	$20 million	Grace & Rothschild	Aug. 1991	Left market
Mercedes-Benz	$130 million	McCaffrey & McCall	Feb. 1992	Scali, McCabe, Sloves
Daihatsu	$10 million	Kresser/Craig	Feb. 1992	Left market
Jaguar	$20 million	Geer, DuBois	July 1992	Ogilvy & Mather
Oldsmobile	$140 million	Leo Burnett USA	Sept. 1992	Stayed at Burnett
Mazda's Amati	$60 million	Lord, Dentsu & Partners	Oct. 1992	Canceled launch
BMW	$65 million	Ammirati & Puris	Oct. 1992	Mullen

Source: Reprinted with permission from Advertising Age (November 2, 1992):1. Copyright, Crain Communications, Inc., 1992.

This called for drastic and radical action. A crisis team including Oldsmobile and Burnett personnel was established at Oldsmobile to guide the marketing effort, to focus on the strengths of Oldsmobile, to get dealer morale up, and to get sales moving. Instead of offering more rebates, the decision was made to select one or two best-selling models, load them with options, and "value price" them to sell.

The market crisis and the urgent need to get a strong program into the market forced client and agency management to take personal charge of the rescue effort. And that made the difference.

Meanwhile, agency chairman Richard (Rick) Fizdale took personal control of the Oldsmobile account. Marketing strategy direction moved from the Burnett office in Detroit to Burnett headquarters in Chicago.

When Oldsmobile announced in mid-1993 that it was retaining Burnett, both sides agreed that the grueling hours spent together, objectively facing the problems each had with the other, showed them that they could work together under pressure. Oldsmobile was convinced that Burnett was the right agency.

Since the decision, Burnett closed its Detroit office, opened a small service office in Lansing, and is doing all the planning and execution in Chicago.

The marketing program has been substantially integrated and local agencies handling Oldsmobile regional dealer business are increasingly adopting the Demand Better campaign from Burnett. Today, talk of the imminent death of Oldsmobile has changed to reviews of its new models and its new aggressiveness.

ESSENCE OF THE BUSINESS: VALUE-ADDING IDEAS

This chapter will deal with the organization of an advertising agency. Before understanding what an advertising agency does, let's consider why agencies exist. Advertisements can be written for clients by individuals outside of agencies and even sometimes by the clients themselves. Media can be bought through media-buying companies or by clients directly, and research projects can be carried out by research companies. So what does the advertising agency do that has caused this type of organization to dominate the industry worldwide?

When functioning at their best, advertising agencies create value for their clients in ways lawyers and accountants simply do not. When an agency clearly interprets to its client what customers want and expect and then communicates information about the client's product or service so meaningfully, so uniquely, or so consistently that customers reward that brand or product or service with their loyalty, then the value of the agency comes most sharply into focus.

But basic marketing wisdom and business intuition tell us that, to do this effectively, communication (not just advertising) must do more than merely transmit data. Rather it must "tailor the product story to a potential customer . . . ."[2] Communication at this level converts data into perceptions. Perceptions themselves become key facts in differentiating between products.

The *perceived value* of a brand was raised to new heights when British companies and then others began to recognize on their balance sheets the value, presumably the market value or value to another corporate buyer, of brands that

---

[2] *The Value Side of Productivity*. Committee on the Value of Advertising, American Association of Advertising Agencies (1989).

they owned. These brand values were largely due to the contribution of advertising created by advertising agencies.

The essence of the agency business, the goal each agency strives to achieve, is to add **perceived value** to the product or service of its client. This is done by giving the product a personality, by communicating in a manner that shapes the basic understanding of the product, by creating an image or memorable picture of the product, and by setting the product apart from its competitors. Transamerica has achieved this kind of value by using its distinctive headquarters building as a symbol and trademark. (See Ad 4.1.)

Whether the advertising agency business is enduring mergers, buyouts, consolidations, retrenching, whether it is adding services or not, the essence and purpose of the advertising agency is to create and direct communication about a product or service so that the product or service is perceived to have a unique value. In this way the advertising becomes part of the product or service.

What follows is the story of how an advertising agency organizes to accomplish the goal of adding value to brands. Although the agency may not always succeed, the goal of every advertising agency is to fulfill their clients' hopes of adding value to their products or services.

As Edwin L. Artzt, chairman-CEO of Procter & Gamble put it:

> "We believe in advertising. We believe it is our most effective marketing tool—the very lifeblood of our brands."[3]

---

[3]Edwin L. Artzt, "The Lifeblood of Brands," *Advertising Age* (November 4, 1991):32.

perceived value The value that a customer or buyer intrinsically or subjectively attaches to a brand or service. It is the image or personality that differentiates one product from a virtually identical competitor.

Ad 4.1

Transamerica has consistently used its advertising to build brand awareness by featuring the visual of its headquarters pyramid building.

(Courtesy of Transamerica Corporation)

Table 4.2   Top 25 Brands in 1992

Rank		Brand, product, service & parent company	Total measured ad spending		
'92	'91		1992	1991	% chg
1	2	McDonald's restaurants, McDonald's Corp.	$413,469.0	$387,326.5	6.7
2	*	Sears stores, Sears, Roebuck & Co.	409,222.7	391,335.9	4.6
3	3	Ford cars, trucks & vans, Ford Motor Co.	404,935.2	371,448.2	9.0
4	4	Kellogg breakfast foods, Kellogg Co.	379,880.4	351,109.1	8.2
5	1	AT&T telephone svcs, AT&T Co.	376,892.7	389,901.3	−3.3
6	6	Toyota cars, trucks, & vans, Toyota Motor Corp.	324,133.2	315,274.4	2.8
7	8	General Mills cereals, General Mills	250,941.0	253,977.8	−1.2
8	*	J.C. Penney's stores, J.C. Penney's Co.	236,037.1	157,526.7	49.8
9	*	Circuit City stores, Circuit City Stores	235,037.1	238,956.0	−1.6
10	7	Chevrolet cars, trucks & vans, General Motors Corp.	232,559.8	262,939.3	−11.6
11	10	Budweiser beer, Anheuser-Busch Cos.	226,943.6	212,145.6	7.0
12	9	Miller beer, Philip Morris Cos.	222,286.0	233,719.4	−4.9
13	11	Dodge cars, trucks & vans, Chrysler Corp.	208,064.5	174,601.4	19.2
14	12	Nissan cars, trucks & vans, Nissan Motor Co.	204,611.0	163,937.0	24.8
15	22	Columbia movies & recordings, Sony Corp.	194,931.3	139,595.2	39.6
16	16	Disney cable, parks, shows, videos, Walt Disney Co.	183,599.2	149,997.8	22.4
17	*	Kmart stores, Kmart Corp.	180,267.2	201,139.5	−10.4
18	18	Coca-Cola & Diet Coke beverages, Coca-Cola Co.	172,739.5	148,374.3	16.4
19	26	American Express financial svcs, American Express Co.	167,341.4	131,912.1	26.9
20	*	Macy's stores, R.H. Macy & Co.	165,849.9	180,145.5	−7.9
21	24	Burger King restaurants, Grand Metropolitan	161,507.4	133,589.1	20.9
22	21	Honda cars, Honda Motor Co.	155,676.5	142,152.0	9.5
23	14	Mazda cars & trucks, Mazda Motor Corp.	152,887.9	156,773.9	−2.5
24	*	Montgomery Ward stores, Montgomery Ward & Co.	152,613.4	125,364.2	21.7
25	17	Kraft foods, Philip Morris Cos.	150,354.5	149,486.5	0.6

Notes: Dollars in thousands. *1991 rankings omitted because newspaper spending data was restated.
Source: LNA/Arbitron Multi-Media Service (Reprinted with permission from Advertising Age, May 31, 1993, 38). Copyright, Crain Communications, Inc., 1993.

The spending for the leading brands in the United States is shown for 1992 in Table 4.2.

INTEGRATED MARKETING COMMUNICATION

The advertising agency business, as well as advertising as an industry, is periodically subject to short-term fads and long-term trends. It is difficult in the early stage to distinguish what may be a passing fancy and what may be a significant change in the way business is conducted.

The stable procedure during the period from the late 1950s until the middle to late 1980s was the marketing plan concept. Developed out of the packaged-goods category, this was a system based on identifying a target market or audience, stating a clear and measurable objective, developing a strategy on how to achieve that objective, and finally crafting specific plans to carry out that strategy.

Beginning in London in the late 1970s, Boase Massini Pollett (now BMP DDB Needham) refined this system by adding an account planner. The account planner is a person or department responsible for gathering all available intelligence on the market and the consumer and preparing a comprehensive recommendation centering on the consumer. At the same time, the computer was expanding the ability to collect, collate, and analyze data. The available media were multiplying in number, specificity, and type.

The issue became how to integrate the planning with the disparate elements of a company's contact with its publics in the business world, including its own departments. The investor relations department might be explaining a severe downsizing, public relations might be promoting the qualifications of the chief executive, while the marketing department was launching a line extension with advertising telling about the latest price or value-pack promotion. Did the parts work together? Was there a complementary impact? Not likely.

From this condition arose the concept of *integrated marketing communications, (IMC)*, which was introduced in Chapter 1. Professor Don Schultz of the Medill School of Journalism at Northwestern University, a former copywriter, recognized the lack of integration of marketing efforts and was a pioneer in enunciating the principles of IMC. Even at Northwestern, public relations and copywriting were taught at Medill, while marketing and advertising strategy were offered at the Kellogg School of Management, a few hundred unconnected yards away. Dr. Schultz established the department of integrated marketing communications and organized a curriculum around the IMC concept.

Problem solved? Hardly. Not only was IMC difficult to install at client organizations because of what Dr. Schultz called "functional silos," really turf wars among departments, but client managements did not understand how the advertising agency fitted into the integrated marketing plan. According to a study commissioned by the Promotion Marketing Association of America among 100 senior-level marketing executives, 60 percent rated IMC as the most important strategy factor in the next three to five years (see Table 4.3), but meeting IMC needs via an advertising agency was hard to envision. As few as 10 percent believed that their company would find its IMC needs met by an advertising agency. The pressure to integrate increases as options proliferate. As Professor Schultz put it:

Table 4.3

Factors Influencing Marketing Strategies

Factor	Importance Rank (%)
Integrated marketing communications	60
Consumer lifestyle changes	55
Economic trends	45
Everyday low-pricing strategies	32
New retail formats	29
Integration of consumer/trade promotion	27
Globalization	26

Source: NPO Group. Reprinted with permission from Advertising Age (March 22, 1993):3. Copyright, Crain Communications, Inc., 1993.

Technology is what makes IMC possible, and the more rapidly technology diffuses, the faster IMC grows and matures. Because technology drives and supports IMC, it is not just another passing marketing fad or hot communications topic that will fade and die.

Instead, IMC is likely the future of all marketing communications.[4]

In the advertising agency field, several agencies and agency groups developed their own approach to integrated marketing. Young & Rubicam touted the "whole egg" concept. Ogilvy & Mather, highly regarded for its rigorous internal training, educated its employees on integrating client efforts. While chairman of the American Association of Advertising Agency (4As), DDB Needham chairman Keith Reinhard tried to lead the industry to adopt IMC. Saatchi & Saatchi group acquired several specialty companies in an array of fields from public relations to sales promotion to product design as it strove to satisfy perceived or anticipated client needs—only to sell off many of these new divisions to avoid bankruptcy in the early 1990s.

Many large advertising agencies with subsidiary companies in several marketing areas used the profit center organization. It was often the case that one profit center, even a department within the agency, was reluctant to let a client get away to another agency subsidiary. Leo Burnett company, a monolithic agency that never bought subsidiaries in other categories, led the way in integrating services within the agency. Leo Burnett retained Professor Schultz to educate its staff on IMC. Another agency, Price/McNabb in Asheville, North Carolina, having heard Schultz at an International Federation of Advertising Agencies' seminar, also adopted IMC using Schultz as a consultant. Price/McNabb, cited by *PR Magazine* as one of the five best integrated advertising agencies, abolished profit centers by department and by city among its four offices and sold its planning, advertising, and public relations strengths as one agency.

What of the client opinion that integrated marketing is probably not a service to be bought from an advertising agency? One contributing factor was the experience that an agency might be strong in advertising but weak in direct marketing. The Interpublic Group sought to overcome this by adopting a "general contractor" approach. For a fee of 1.5 percent of billing, presumably 10 percent of revenue (.015 divided by the typical commission of 15 percent equals 10 percent), an Interpublic agency would develop the overall strategy and retain the requisite agency or company to carry out the plan, be it advertising, public relations, direct-response marketing, event marketing, database marketing, or design development—either within the IPG agency group or outside of it, as appropriate. (Commissions and fees are discussed in detail later in this chapter.)

Smaller agencies or agencies without the resources of giants like Interpublic, Omnicom, and WPP, or the huge international agencies such as Young & Rubicam, Grey, and Leo Burnett could compete for IMC business through strategic alliances. Strategic alliances are agreements between firms of different marketing specialties to complement each others' services and provide referrals. Basically, a strategic alliance is a plan to cooperate, not compete.

Experience at Price/McNabb with strategic alliances to augment the agency's ability to work in integrated marketing has taught Charles R. Price, Jr., chairman, "that we need to have established relationships with more than one specialist

---

[4]Don E. Schultz, *Marketing News* (February 15, 1993):20.

Inside ADVERTISING

Sara Schmid, Traffic Coordinator, Colle & McVoy, Inc., Minneapolis

I graduated with a journalism degree from the University of Missouri and began working at Colle & McVoy the following summer. As traffic coordinator I'm responsible for taking a project from creative conception to the printing and production stages. It's my responsibility to see that an ad meets all the internal deadlines in order to reach the print or broadcast media by the scheduled issue or air date. What I like about my position is the chance to work with all parts of the agency including creative, account service, media, and production. It's a great way to learn about agency business.

8:30 A.M. I arrive at work and check my phone and electronic mail messages. I read over my status sheet which describes all my current account projects and make a list of the day's top priorities.

9:00 A.M. Check the work logs in the keylining and Mac graphics areas to see how much work they anticipate for the day. The graphic coordinator hands me a layout for a GE Capital job that was done last night and I run it back to the proofreader.

9:30 A.M. Call the post office in Omaha, Nebraska, to check the postal permit code and verify a zip+4 number for a direct-mail project. Next I call three trade publications to get the most current information on print dates, extension deadlines, and production size specifications.

9:45 A.M. Meet with the copywriter and account executive on the United Way account to review the creative blueprint for the upcoming holiday radio campaign. We review the communication objectives and target audience of the campaign and establish copy and approval deadlines based on a December 15 air date.

10:45 A.M. Collect concepts for a Cliff's Study Ware packaging project. I'll review the concepts with the art director, make color copies, and have a mock-up done in keylining so the concepts can go out to the client via overnight FedEx.

11:00 A.M. Meet with the creative team, production manager, and account executives on the SmithKline Beecham Animal Health account to discuss changes for a print ad which will run in January publications. Because materials are due to the publications at least 15 days before the issue

company in a field." Price/McNabb has found strategic partners in research and database marketing but finds sales promotion agencies still look upon themselves as complete purveyors of service and often don't understand the long-range principle of brand building through IMC.

As the 1990s unfold, we are seeing that the trends in the business toward merging, heightened competition, and integrated marketing have changed the entire field. The proportion of client marketing budgets declined from over 60 percent in advertising in the 1970s to less than 35 percent in 1992.[5] The recession from 1991 to 1992 even saw total advertising spending decrease in 1991, the first time this phenomenon had occurred in three decades. Agencies restructured, closed branch offices, expanded by acquiring agencies in nearby markets to secure a client and achieve economies of scale, dropped departments (usually research and even media) and replaced them with strategic partners, and even closed their doors.

---

[5]Joe Cappo, "Agencies: Change or Die," *Advertising Age* (December 7, 1992):26.

date, this ad needs to be completely produced by mid-December. The client has asked that some of the creative elements change but still wants to run in January books. The timeline will be tight but if all goes well, we should make the deadline.

12:00 P.M. Once a week the traffic group meets during lunch. Today we meet the new production manager and talk about our different accounts. And the agency pays for our pizza so even in advertising there is such a thing as a free lunch.

1:00 P.M. The account executive for Cliff's tells me that we need to make a black plate change on an existing ad and hands me a copy of the revisions. I pull the galley from the previous ad and take it back to the Mac graphics department. The galley is the tag at the top of the Mac printout that tells the graphic designer what the previous number and code was so they can revise the ad based on existing information.

1:30 P.M. Make a traffic schedule for the SmithKline Beecham Animal Health job opened that morning. The schedule is really a calendar that notes all the important deadlines in order for a job to meet the end date (in this case, the publication's closing deadline). Every calendar should schedule time for concepts, client approval, typesetting, photo shoot and photo processing, keylining or electronic keylines from the Mac, production, and shipping.

2:15 P.M. Pull samples of previously produced ads and fill out a materials order with the production secretary to have slides made for a client's sales meeting.

2:30–5:00 P.M. Sprint through the agency, following up on jobs in progress (usually between six to eight a day), routing radio scripts for approval, photocopying TV storyboards, routing proofs in the final stage of production, distributing job jackets, closing out old jobs with the accounting department, verifying publication shipping addresses, and bringing jobs to and from Mac graphics.

After 5:00 P.M. Restore some semblance of order to my office since I have been tearing in and out of it all day. At the end of the day I try to file jobs that are completed. This keeps my office neater and helps me find things even after a job is finished. Before leaving, I make a list of tomorrow's priorities so I won't lose my sanity when I come back the next morning. Sanity is important in a career that moves at an insanely fast pace.

Two defining events occurred in the early 1990s that reflect the client thrust for greater efficiency and new sources for critical services: (1) the appointment of Creative Artists Agency (CAA) by Coca-Cola and (2) the formation of Pentacom by BBDO, an agency of the Omnicom Group, to buy all the media for all agencies serving the Chrysler Corporation.

CAA is a talent service. As described in Chapter 1, its entrepreneurial president, Mike Ovitz, convinced Coca-Cola, which was reported to be having difficulty keeping the basic Coca-Cola campaign fresh, that CAA could use its stable of movie and television stars, film directors, and writers to deliver breakthrough concepts. The results were mixed: Coke awareness grew due to increased media spending behind the new commercials while at the same time research indicted low persuasion. But the die was cast.[6] Here was a major new source of creative ideas and their production, especially in television commercials. McCann-Erickson, the appointed and continuing agency for Coca-Cola Classic, has been

[6]Adrienne Ward Fawcett, "CAA Coke Ads Fall Flat on Persuasion," *Advertising Age* (May 10, 1993):4.

struggling to maintain its position. Its parent, Interpublic Group (IPG), has seen Coca-Cola transfer business to other IPG agencies and add new agencies for special assignments.[7]

The other sharp departure from tradition was the outcome of a request to agencies serving the Chrysler Corporation to recommend a means of achieving lower unit costs or greater impact from the media expenditures divided among three agencies. Chrysler adopted the proposal by BBDO to form a separate media-buying company, which became an independent subsidiary of BBDO functioning exclusively as the media management for Chrysler and the media department for each agency.[8] From the time this plan was announced in 1993, no company spending $100 million or more in media could confidently believe it had found the most effective way of planning and buying media if it had not examined the Chrysler model—or asked its agencies for a similarly unique solution. By the end of the year, General Motors, after a review, consolidated $800 million in media buying in a new media operation to be formed as a subsidiary of Lintas within the Interpublic Group.[9]

What are the implications of these two radical developments amid the other trends in the business? In the past, clients had gone to outside suppliers for research projects and not used agency research departments, or they had used both outside and agency research. Clients had used media-buying services but had never established their own. Clients had used creative boutiques or other agencies for creative concepts in competition with the appointed agency but had never gone to a talent agency for an entire campaign.

To bring this discussion back to the essence of the business—value-adding ideas—advertising agencies are responding to these many new challenges by becoming generalists in strategy while developing and recommending tactics in specific areas of expertise, especially creative execution. If an agency is competitive in media, research, sales promotion, public relations, or other areas related to the business, the agency will offer these services as part of a complete plan. Through IMC, the agency will seek to guide strategy and coordinate execution, using its own departments or strategic partners.

WHY HIRE AN AGENCY?

Agencies are retained to plan and execute client advertising efforts, whether as part of IMC or in fulfilling the communication strategy. But, as mentioned, each segment of these plans can be purchased separately. Why should an advertiser sign a long-term contract with a full-service agency? What extra benefit comes from hiring such an agency? What comfort level does a client achieve by appointing an agency? Does it cost more or less to use an agency than to buy services separately? Some thoughts appear in the Concepts and Applications box, p. 123.

The answers vary from client to client and from agency to agency, but generally the agency-client relationship is carefully established and maintained. Although the trade press reports the comings and goings of notable clients from

---

[7]Melanie Wells, "Coke's New View of Shops Prompts Gallo Comparisons," *Advertising Age* (October 18, 1993):4.
[8]Richard Brunelli, "Chrysler Sets Up Agency Buying Unit," *Brandweek* (May 10, 1993):5.
[9]"GM Merging Media Buying at Interpublic," *The Wall Street Journal* (December 8, 1993):B5.

What Companies Expect from Their Advertising Agency

Several high-ranking representatives of well known firms responded to a request from a marketing consultant. They were asked to define the essence of the client-agency relationship—from their own points of view. There were some lofty thoughts—but no one seemed to forget the details.

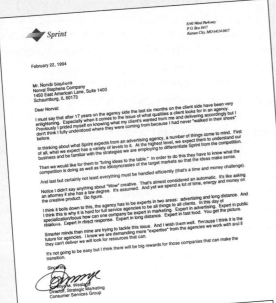

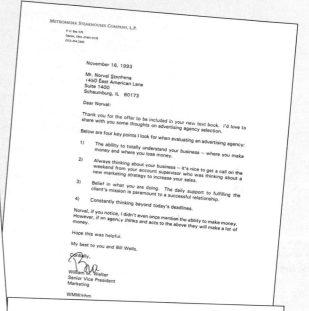

one agency to another, the fact is that the average tenure of a client with an agency is between seven and ten years. Some have lasted 50 years. The following is a discussion of the reasons why advertisers establish long-term relationships with agencies.

EXPERTISE, OBJECTIVITY, AND DEDICATION

An established agency has gained expertise through years of experience and can offer objective advice to its clients. Agencies are committed to solving problems for and delivering service to their clients.

Professional Expertise. An agency acquires experience by working with a variety of clients; agency professionals can apply lessons learned with one client to another. Applying a broad perspective through the varied backgrounds and skills of employees often is the key to solving difficult advertising problems. This perspective is often lacking in smaller in-house agencies or limited departments. Just as a company may hire an outside law firm even if it has an attorney on staff, so too a company may hire an agency to work for its advertising department in order to benefit from the agency's professional expertise.

Objectivity. Clients expect an agency to tell them when they are misreading the market or are out of step with consumers. Agency objectivity is a necessary part of the relationship. Someone from outside the client company is more likely to speak up and is better able to maintain an independent and detached view of the marketplace and the consumer. Advertising people are experts in their field, whereas few clients feel competent to approve, as well as create, advertisements. They depend on the agency for professional judgment. Wieden & Kennedy brought this kind of judgment to Nike by finding new ways to show the benefits of exercise, as illustrated in Ad 4.2.

Dedication and Commitment. Clients, especially those who nurture the relationship, receive dedication and commitment from their agencies. The agency becomes very much a part of the client team. This client-agency relationship serves as an incentive for the agency to produce an extra effort, an interest in

Ad 4.2

Wieden & Kennedy's campaign for Nike has been successful in establishing a brand name with an image consumers are not likely to forget.

(Courtesy of Nike and Wieden & Kennedy)

every aspect of the client's business, and a drive never to be satisfied with "good enough." The commitment to a client's business and the need to remain objective can produce some of the most difficult decisions in the business. Agencies that hold fast to their point of view may lose a client but not their own self-respect.

STAFFING AND MANAGEMENT

Agencies provide the human resources and management skills necessary to the task.

Specialists. Even the largest clients might have need for a statistician, a network negotiator, a television producer, or a special-events coordinator only once a year. Only large agencies that have multiple accounts needing these kinds of services can afford to employ these specialists full time.

Managing Creative People. Those who work for advertising agencies may not be at all like the employees of a corporation. Artists, writers, and television producers might not fit easily into the culture of the corporate environment. Stated work hours, dress codes, and limitations on overtime would be difficult to enforce among the creative "free spirits" who tend to work in advertising. Pay scales may vary widely: It might be difficult to explain why a brilliant writer who has odd work habits is paid more than a department head. Advertising agencies provide a friendly environment for these people. Agencies can organize skills, maintain morale, and build spirit more effectively among creative people than corporations can.

Flexibility in Staffing. Client advertising budgets go up and down, and as the budget level increases or decreases, so does the employment level. Because agencies handle a number of clients, they are better able to adjust the comings and goings of clients. Clients might find it difficult to accommodate their staffing levels to the condition of the marketplace. A company with a commitment to employee loyalty (or a very liberal termination policy) might find it difficult to deal with hiring and firing employees whose positions depend on the advertising budget. Clients have decided it is better to let the agency deal with staffing, spreading the effects among a roster of clients and building personnel policies that adjust to and compensate for these risks.

The size of agency staffs has been declining in recent years. Between October 1992 and October 1993, advertising-related jobs with the top 16 U.S. agencies decreased by 3.1 percent. These top 16 agencies employ 22 percent of all agency workers. Total U.S. employment in agencies for the same period was down by 0.8 percent to 152,700, but off 3.9 percent from 1990. Total U.S. advertising spending began a slow recovery after 1991, but at a rate only matching inflation (see Table 4.4).[10] This downward trend is expected to continue. According to the American Association of Advertising Agencies, the average number of people per million dollars in billings continued its long decline by dropping from 2.37 in 1984 to 1.57 in 1992. The reasons for this decrease in advertising staffing in the large agencies are due to increased pressures from clients on compensation paid to agencies and a desire by the agencies for greater efficiency and productivity by reducing corporate overhead and support staffs.

---

[10]Melanie Wells, "Burnett, Others Feed Staff-Cutting Trend," *Advertising Age* (December 6, 1993):5–8.

Table 4.4   Full-Time Staffing Levels of Top 16 Agency Employers

Rank		Agency	Primary Office			Total		
1993	**1992**		**Oct. '93**	**Oct. '92**	**% chg.**	**Oct. '93**	**Oct. '92**	**% chg.**
1	1	Leo Burnett Co., Chicago	2,263	2,405	–5.9%	2,263	2,405	–5.9%
2	3	Foote, Cone & Belding, Chicago	2,018	2,010	0.4	2,462	2,488	–1.0
3	2	DDB Needham Worldwide, New York	1,952	2,098	–7.0	2,606	2,754	–5.4
4	4	Young & Rubicam, New York	1,899	1,945	–2.4	4,000	4,254	–6.0
5	6	J. Walter Thompson USA, New York	1,870	1,873*	–0.2	2,277	2,310	–1.4
6	5	D'Arcy Masius Benton & Bowles, NY	1,844	8,894	–2.6	2,343	2,462	–4.4
7	7	McCann-Erickson Worldwide, NY	1,625	1,624	0.1	1,720	1,714	0.4
8	8	Grey Advertising, New York	1,558	1,581	–1.5	2,353	2,353	0.0
9	9	BBDO Worldwide, New York	1,414	1,525	–7.3	4,107	4,171	–1.5
10	10	Saatchi & Saatchi Advertising, NY	1,411	1,464	–3.6	1,670	1,758	–5.0
11	11	Ogilvy & Mather, New York	1,190	1,260	–5.6	1,832	1,872	–2.1
12	12	Ketchum Communications, Pittsburgh	1,145	1,113	2.9	1,206	1,243	–3.0
13	14	CME KHBB, Minneapolis	1,083	1,062	2.0	1,083	1,062	2.0
14	15	Bozell, New York	1,021	1,029	–0.8	1,739	1,772	–1.9
15	13	Backer Spielvogel Bates Worldwide, NY	1,080	1,075	–7.0	1,333	1,410	–5.5
16	16	Lintas: Worldwide, New York	999	991	0.8	1,828	1,900	–3.8
		Top 16 agency total	24,292	24,949	–2.6	34,832	35,928	–3.1
		U.S. agency total**				152,700	153,900	–0.8
		Top 16 as % of U.S. agency employees				22	23	

Source: Reprinted with permission from Advertising Age (December 6, 1993):34. Copyright, Crain Communications, Inc., 1993.

The reason total employment in the industry has dropped less is reflected in the trend for small and medium agencies to add services in public relations, database management, direct response, Yellow Pages, recruitment advertising, and in taking over the production of newsletters, annual reports, and employee communications.

Testing the Water Agencies are more flexible in staffing and in dealing with changing employment levels, as noted. This provides clients with the option of trying out a staff position, perhaps in a new sector of business or a new marketing discipline, by asking the agency for a fee to establish and define a job. Since freelance specialists or others with agency experience may want to pioneer an area of potential growth with the promise of long-term future employment, the agency may be better able to explore the new position with less disruption if it fails than the client would.

$\mathcal{T}$HE AGENCY WORLD

Advertising agencies range in size from small shops to giant businesses that employ thousands. The smallest agencies usually have up to a dozen employees and bill up to $10,000,000. Medium-sized agencies bill $10,000,000 to $100,000,000. These boundaries are subjective and are used in describing U.S.

agencies. In smaller markets these small agencies tend to offer a range of services for specialized markets. For example, Lewis Advertising in Mobile, Alabama, has its own public relations department, a collateral production unit, and a department that specializes in hospital and health care advertising. To deal with special situations, employees develop special skills. Hood, Light & Geise agency in Harrisburg, Pennsylvania, billing less than $5 million, has three divisions: advertising, public relations, and association management. In larger markets, agencies usually specialize either in a type of service, such as creative work or collateral (brochures, reports, newsletters), or in a particular type of market, such as health care, agribusiness, or the upscale market. Marketing Resources of America near Kansas City focuses on strategic marketing for clients and then bundles the skills needed for a client; these skills include advertising but also could include in-store promotions and dealer training.

The forms, services provided, and types of agencies are in constant change. Entry to the business is virtually unimpeded. Terminated employees often perform free-lance service if they cannot find full-time jobs. People working at home are an increasing source of specialized skills, whether part-time or full-time. The business appeals to entrepreneurs who have a skill in a rapidly developing industry sector. The boundaries defining one type or service are not fixed. The following types, while not an exhaustive list, are described to show the variety found in the advertising agency business.

FULL-SERVICE AGENCY

In advertising, a full-service agency is one that has on staff the four major staff functions—account management, creative services, media planning and buying, and research. A full-service advertising agency will also have its own accounting department, a traffic department to handle internal tracking on completion of projects, departments for broadcast and print production (usually organized within the creative department), and a human resources department. Two key distinctions are whether the agency's personnel are full-time, as they would be in a full service agency, and the extent of the services. The boundary of what is included is restricted by what is affordable within the revenue the agency receives; conversely, services are expanded to the extent an agency can negotiate a fee for special service.

Typically, an agreement between a full-service agency and a client will determine that the agency, for the commission received on media and production services or for an agreed fee, will analyze market data, propose a strategy, prepare a recommendation, produce the advertising, place it in approved media, verify the advertising's appearance as ordered, invoice the client against the approved budget, collect funds from the client, and disburse those funds to media and suppliers. Normally, not included in the basic agreement and not covered by the revenue the agency receives are public relations work, research projects, direct marketing, event marketing and sales promotion, for example. Some agencies offer these services to clients through departments or subsidiaries that render the specific service, or clients may use specialty agencies for these activities. The largest full-service agencies are shown in Table 4.5.

CREATIVE BOUTIQUES

Creative boutiques are organizations, usually relatively small agencies (two or three people to a dozen or more), that concentrate entirely on preparing the

Table 4.5   Top 25 U.S. Advertising Agencies

Rank		Agency, headquarters	U.S. gross income		U.S. billings
1992	1991		1992	% chg	1992
1	1	Leo Burnett Co., Chicago	$313.8	4.9	$2,104.1
2	4	J. Walter Thompson Co., New York	268.8	14.9	1,892.2
3	2	Saatchi & Saatchi Advertising, New York	268.2	−4.0	1,849.7
4	5	Grey Advertising, New York	240.1	5.5	1,595.5
5	6	McCann-Erickson Worldwide, New York	236.7	7.0	1,578.7
6	3	DDB Needham Worldwide, New York	229.4	−6.1	1,910.7
7	7	Ogilvy & Mather Worldwide, New York	215.70	2.0	1,443.7
8	8	BBDO Worldwide, New York	215.68	2.0	1,646.9
9	9	Foote, Cone & Belding Commun., Chicago	214.1	4.5	2,154.6
10	10	D'Arcy Masius Benton & Bowles, New York	198.6	−1.6	2,016.8
11	11	Young & Rubicam, New York	194.8	−1.7	1,835.5
12	12	Backer Spielvogel Bates Worldwide, NY	146.4	−9.5	976.0
13	13	CME KHBB, Minneapolis	136.0	2.8	1,008.5
14	14	Lintas: Worldwide, New York	124.6	2.4	830.3
15	17	Ketchum Communications, Pittsburgh	107.7	4.6	833.7
16	16	Bozell, New York	106.3	3.0	850.0
17	15	Wells, Rich Greene BDDP, New York	99.0	−5.7	919.0
18	20	Chiat/Day, Venice, California	98.8	33.7	760.6
19	19	N W Ayer, New York	88.0	13.8	848.0
20	18	Ross Roy Advertising, Bloomfield Hills, MI	81.4	1.0	542.3
21	22	Lintas:Marketing Communications, New York	76.4	26.2	509.4
22	21	TMP Worldwide, New York	75.1	22.4	500.8
23	33	Alcone Sims O'Brien, Irvine, California	68.5	64.3	316.4
24	23	Wunderman Cato Johnson Worldwide, NY	65.6	9.2	483.6
25	25	DIMAC Direct, Bridgeton, MO	57.7	10.0	163.5

Source: Reprinted with permission from Advertising Age (April 14, 1993):16. Copyright Crain Communications, Inc., 1993.

creative execution of client communications. A freelance creative person differs from a creative boutique chiefly by the nature of employment and extent of service. A freelance creative writer may work with a freelance artist. Together, they might present their creative recommendation to a client. But they are each individual practitioners. A creative boutique will have one or more writers and artists on staff. The organization typically is capable of preparing advertising to run in print media, outdoor, radio, and television. The focus of the organization is entirely on the idea, the creative product. There is no staff for media, research, strategic planning, or annual plan writing. Creative boutiques usually are hired by clients but are sometimes retained by an advertising agency when it is "stuck" or has an overload of work.

Creative boutiques are not as long-lived as full-service agencies. They depend on a small group of individuals, frequently organized as a partnership. If a key individual leaves, the creative boutique may disband. Some of the most successful boutiques, on the other hand, have become full-service agencies. Grace and Rothchild in New York started as a creative service and has grown to over $75 million in capitalized billing—hardly a boutique any more.

Medical Agencies. This is a type of agency that concentrates on advertising for pharmaceutical companies such as Abbott, Merck, Pfizer, Hoffman-LaRoche, and Upjohn. Medical agencies require staff members with detailed knowledge of chemistry and pharmacology as well as an understanding of medical practices and laws relating to health care advertising. People with advanced scientific degrees are often hired or retained by these agencies as consultants. This type of agency carries out most of the functions a full-service agency performs but concentrates in the medical field. Seminars, symposia, and the writing and publication of technical papers relating to the business are often planned and managed by pharmaceutical agencies. These agencies may be small such as Durot, Donahoe & Purohit of Rosemont, Illinois, with 12 employees, or large, such as Kallir Phillips Ross, Sudler & Hennessey, and Medicus Intercom of New York City, each with well over 100 employees.

These agencies have been growing more rapidly than the total industry, as prescription drugs have been released for over-the-counter sale as part of a government effort to reduce health care costs. Many full-service agencies and holding companies have responded by buying medical agencies. Eight of the top ten medical shops are now owned by full-line agencies.[11] It is difficult to predict how changing America's health care system will affect these agencies, but managed competition and drug-buying cooperatives will probably reduce the market for medical agencies.

Minority Agencies. Agencies that focus on one ethnic group, or minority agencies, grew substantially in the 1980s as marketers realized that African-Americans and Hispanic-Americans, the two largest minorities, had different preferences and buying patterns from the general market. These agencies are organized much the same as full-service agencies, but they are specialists in reaching and communicating with their market.

Burrell Advertising in Chicago is one of the largest and most successful of the African-American agencies. Tom Burrell worked for several general-market agencies before starting his agency. With over 100 employees, Burrell Advertising represents such clients as Brown Forman Beverage Co., Ford Motor Company, McDonald's, Polaroid, Procter & Gamble, Coca-Cola, Stroh's Brewery, and Sony Corporation.

Conill Advertising founded in 1968 is representative of Hispanic agencies. Conill handles national accounts and is minority-managed. This New York agency is now owned by Saatchi & Saatchi and has 45 employees. Clients include Helene Curtis, Procter & Gamble, and Toyota.

The market for Hispanic advertising has attracted agencies from outside the continental United States. Noble & Asociados of Mexico City (now owned by DMB&B) opened an office in Irving, California, and is billing over $20 million. Premier Maldonado, the leading independent agency in San Juan, Puerto Rico, opened an office in Miami in the late 1980s to capitalize on its Hispanic marketing experience to serve its clients in the "upper 48."

The 1990 U.S. Census counted more than 24 million foreign language households, many of which are bilingual. The largest foreign language group is Hispanic, 71 percent of the total, at 17.3 million households, followed by German, 1.5 million, Italian 1.3 million, and Chinese at 1.2 million.

Targeting minorities is not without problems. African-American groups in

---

[11]Adweek's *Marketing Week* (March 12, 1990):RC27.

Inside ADVERTISING

Sharon M. McCafferty, Account Coordinator, Wolf Blumberg Krody, Cincinnati

7:30 A.M. Cup of coffee while I make out my schedule for the day. I have a photo shoot for United Way that should take most of the morning. I am able to work pretty close to the United Way projects in writing the focus sheets and maintaining our client-agency relationship. I also attempt to roughly sketch out my afternoon plans.

8:00 A.M. Arrive at the site. Our project is to take a picture of a woman standing outside "her" home. We have a model scheduled to arrive at 10:00. Our model is actually a recipient of the services United Way offers. Since I was also the vehicle used to find our volunteer model, it is important that I am here to assure she understands all the goings-on of the shoot.

8:15 A.M. Discussion with Diana, the art director, about what color jacket our model should wear. Because the shoot is taking place outdoors, Diana wants to make sure she has something that will stand out. I brought a few orange and red jackets and sweaters for possible options. We decided to wait for our model to arrive.

8:30 A.M. Help photographer set up. Although he does all the cameras, I offer help moving the plants and other props to balance the shot and in general offer any friendly assistance he may require.

9:30 A.M. Our model is early! After briefly explaining the layout and concept, I bring her inside while Todd, our photographer, and his assistant Alex, finish preparing the lighting. Inside, Grace (our model) and I talk about various things, ranging from weather to city news to the new sweater she's wearing.

10:00 A.M. After what started out to be a cloudy morning, the sun comes out and Todd has to change the lighting. Just a few minutes delay . . .

10:20 A.M. We begin shooting. Todd tries to direct Grace, who follows directions really well. I make a mental note to check with the production manager to see how our printing sources are going. We're running close to the deadline and I need to make sure that the wrinkles are smoothed out before we send out for final art.

11:00 A.M. Go to the office. Check messages and respond in kind.

11:15 A.M. Meet with creative team for Rockwell. I need to answer questions for the focus sheet I just wrote for a new Rockwell brochure to be developed. The questions are simple but I need to call the product manager with one point. I take this time to inform her of some other printing dates she inquired about last time we spoke. I then write a job update, answering the question for the creative department

New York and Chicago have tried to remove billboards advertising alcohol and cigarettes from their neighborhoods. R.J. Reynolds was forced by public pressure, touched off by criticism from Health and Human Services Secretary Louis Sullivan, to withdraw Uptown cigarettes from test. The brand was aimed at African-Americans. Operation PUSH boycotted Nike shoes in 1990 when the organization felt Nike was presumably marketing to the African-American community but not returning enough of its revenue to that community. Nike had used African-American athletes extensively in its advertising but did not use a minority advertising agency. It has since appointed one.

African-American and Hispanic advertising agencies have been vocal in criticizing the infringement of free speech implied by the attempted removal of

	in writing and briefly sketch out a conference report outlining my conversation with the product manager from Rockwell.	3:45 P.M.	Receive job requiring immediate attention: I need to call some newspapers and magazines to find out their closing dates. I quickly make calls, write up the memo, and distribute.
12:00 P.M.	Lunch with my coworkers in account service. Catch up on a few updates I missed this morning and my supervisor gives me a couple tips on the Rockwell budget summary I'm developing.	4:15 P.M.	Grab yogurt and a bagel. While eating, I run through mail and file appropriate updates in their job bags. Take notes on changes and write scheduling into my personal planner.
1:00 P.M.	Once a week, I answer phones during the receptionist's lunch break. It's not a job to be taken lightly; I am, for some people, the first impression of Wolf Blumberg Krody.	4:30 P.M.	Minor corrections to status report. Complete changes, make copies, distribute.
2:00 P.M.	Status meeting. Once a week, the Rockwell team (including client service, creative, and production) meets for an hour to discuss all the jobs in progress. At this time, scheduling for new job deadlines is performed and updates are given. Not only do I have input on my jobs, but I also keep track of progress of the entire Rockwell account and by the end of day I should have a new job status report ready. Meeting breaks.	4:45 P.M.	Type up Church Organ Systems spec sheets for production artist to format. Dump onto a disk and pass to traffic coordinator, who will pass to production artist.
		5:00 P.M.	Finish Rockwell budget summary. This summary is sent monthly with billing and charts showing how much money was spent per job and how that compares to the estimate. Not an easy task when there are approximately eight pages worth of job listings. Complete, run by supervisor for final okay.
3:00 P.M.	Check voice mail and e-mail.		
3:15 P.M.	Status report. Weekly I update progress of jobs for my accounts (Rockwell, King's Daughters' Medical Center, and Church Organ Systems) and distribute this information in the form of a written report. This report is distributed internally as well as to the client. Once completed, I give it to my supervisor for final okay.	6:00 P.M.	Change clothes, clean up desk, get ready to run home. I run home from work (8 miles) about once a week depending on the weather and my workload. I run with one of the vice presidents in the design division, who usually runs me into the ground. An exhaustive finish to a busy day.

advertising material from ethnic neighborhoods while maintaining the wisdom and the right of the advertisers to segment markets.[12] The ethical side of the issue is that so-called sin products, alcohol and tobacco, which can lead to addiction and health problems, are more heavily advertised in their neighborhoods than to the population in general. Advertising follows usage patterns. Activists argue this focus is leading to greater usage of the products. Marketers counter that they are putting their marketing efforts where their customers are.

Agencies have not taken a separate route to serve the largest minority,

---

[12]*Business Week* (April 30, 1990):72.

women. There have been several attempts, but in all agencies, including African-American and Hispanic agencies, women comprise a major proportion of staff (frequently 60 percent) and most agencies have been adept in advertising to women.

IN-HOUSE AGENCIES

In-house agencies are advertising agencies owned and supervised by the companies who advertise. They are organized like independent agencies but can take a variety of forms. The advertising director of the company is usually the chief executive officer of the agency. The director supervises account managers responsible for brands or business groups. The in-house agency has writers and artists as needed, traffic personnel, media specialists, all of whose functions will be explained later in this chapter. If the company has a research department, this specialty will probably not be duplicated in the in-house unit. The in-house agency may do its own billing, paying, and collecting, but it is more likely to use the company's accounting department. Why use an in-house agency? Here are the reasons:

- *Savings.* To the extent that the agency duplicates the staffing of a client or has counterparts in the client's firms, this expense can be eliminated. Probably the most appealing reason is that every agency seeks to make a profit on a client's business, and by taking the work inhouse that profit can be saved. A failure to realize this profit is the reason many return to the use of an outside agency.

- *Specialization.* Clients in a highly technical field often find it difficult to get scientifically correct copywriting from an agency. They watch a copywriter master the field and then get promoted or transferred to another account. Better to have someone who knows the business on staff in the in-house agency. The disadvantage to this solution is the burn-out a copywriter may experience working in one field without variety.

- *Priority Service.* Clearly the in-house agency works only for the client and is available immediately for high-priority projects. There are no conflicts with other clients for the use of key personnel or the time of agency management.

- *Minimum Staffing.* The in-house agency attempts to staff for minimum requirements and engages freelance staff to handle peak workloads. Freelance operators may not always be available and may not possess the requisite knowledge, although management of freelance services is a function built into the in-house agency's role, and problems certainly can be controlled with good planning. The need for flexibility cuts both ways. When problems arise, as noted in the previous section, some clients may again employ ad agencies so that the peaks and valleys of workloads may be spread out.

MEDIA-BUYING SERVICES

media-buying service A company that offers to buy media directly for advertisers and performs basically only this service.

Media-buying services first flowered in the 1970s, as media experts in advertising agencies felt they could make more money on their own than in an agency. They were probably correct, and media salaries have increased substantially since the late 1970s. Media services called on advertisers to propose buying media at rates as low as 1 percent of spending for network television, 2 percent to 3 percent for national magazines, and somewhat more for local newspapers and radio on a nationwide basis.

The relative popularity of the creative boutique, especially in New York and Chicago at the same time, augmented the breakup of services normally provided by full-service agencies. As mentioned, a creative boutique does not plan or buy media. The client might turn that assignment over to a media-buying service or plan the media internally and pay a buying service to execute the plan.

As media became more and more complex with additional media choices, the growth of cable, the segmentation of magazines, and the wide variety of radio stations, the cost to maintain a competent media department caused some smaller agencies to use media-buying services. Clients, introduced to media-buying services either on their own or through agencies that had dropped media, found the services competent, professional, and often possessing substantial buying power. Media buyers with these services, often buying in more markets or in greater quantities than some advertising agencies, delivered media at greater efficiency. Although the media-buying services seldom can beat the top 25 agencies in buying clout, they can usually better small and medium agencies, especially in spot television and spot radio buying in markets with which the smaller agencies are not familiar.

Western International Media Corporation, with more than $900 million in annual media buying, is the largest of the group. It opened in 1970 in Los Angeles after an earlier attempt by its founder, Dennis Holt, in New York and now has offices in more than 20 cities in the United States and Canada. Western Media works almost exclusively for advertising agencies and services only one advertiser directly. It has expanded its services to agencies by offering market research; print, outdoor, Yellow Pages, television, and radio production; Hispanic media and marketing; premiums and employee incentives; syndication and promotional broadcast placement.

CPM, founded by Norman Goldring in 1969 in Chicago, is typical of the media-buying services that work for agencies and for advertisers. Clients include Walgreen, Ralston, Kinko, and Turtle Wax. CPM employs 55 people and handles more than $100 million in media annually. In 1993 it split off its direct-response unit, CPO (for cost per order), into a separate company. Its clients include NordicTrack, Montgomery Ward, and Cancer Treatment Centers of America.

HOW AGENCIES ARE ORGANIZED

As the agency grows larger, a division of labor occurs. Most full-service agencies offer specific functions handled by specialists. Smaller agencies offer the same basic functions, but they employ a smaller number of people who are less specialized and may perform more than one function. For the purpose of giving a full explanation, the following description of agency organization is based on larger agencies. Figure 4.1 offers a humorous look into the inner workings of an advertising agency.

Because employment at large agencies has not been growing, there are more entry-level employment opportunities in smaller agencies or in smaller markets. For that reason, profiles of the workday for employees of small as well as large agencies will be included in this chapter.

business unit A cluster of related products or services that functions as if it were a company within a larger corporation.

Major corporations are focused on one or a cluster of product lines, brands, or services called **business units**. Advertising agencies use a similar structure

Figure 4.1

The Ad Game.

(Source: Advertising Age, December 21, 1987: 18. Copyright Crain Communications, Inc.)

but have a variety of clients and product lines. The agency's products, however, are ideas rather than goods. These ideas are manifested in advertisements and plans for campaigns and media programs.

Rather than organizing around a business unit, an agency organizes around a client's account. Because clients come and go and account needs change, agencies must be adaptable. The agency must encourage new ideas and protect them as they are refined. Openness and flexibility are more important than organizational structure in most agencies. Furthermore, agencies must organize internally to function as a business as well as externally to work with their clients.

Unlike corporations, agencies often change structure to accommodate the needs of new clients or the talents of their people. For example, an agency might have one client that advertises a leading brand on a national basis using primarily television and national magazines. For this client, the emphasis in staffing might be in the creative and research departments. Another client in the fast-service restaurant field, which has local cooperatives of owner-operators or franchisees in major markets, would need field service account executives to work with the co-ops and the franchisees. There are, however, standard functions around which most large and small agencies organize. The following are the four primary functions of most agencies:

1. Account management
2. Creative services
3. Media services
4. Research

In addition to these major functional areas, most agencies offer support services, such as traffic, print production, financial services, personnel, and, increasingly, direct marketing. Figure 4.2 illustrates the organization of a large advertising agency. For comparison, Figure 4.3 describes a small agency.

ACCOUNT MANAGEMENT

account management The function within an advertising agency that maintains liaison with the client, supervises day-to-day work and development of recommendations and plans.

The role of **account management** is to serve as a liaison between the client and the agency in order to ensure that the agency focuses its resources on the needs of the client. At the same time, the agency also develops its own point of view, which is presented to the client. Once the client (or the client and the agency together) establishes the general guidelines for a campaign or even one advertisement, the account management department supervises the day-to-day development of recommendations within these guidelines. These guidelines answer the following questions:

Figure 4.2

Organization chart for a large agency: Elkman Advertising and Public Relations handles $50 million in billings annually.

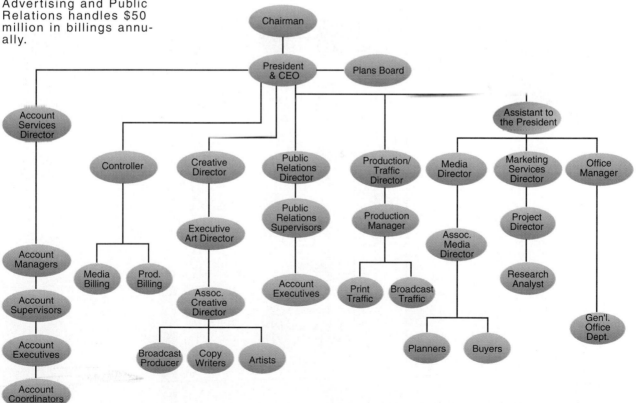

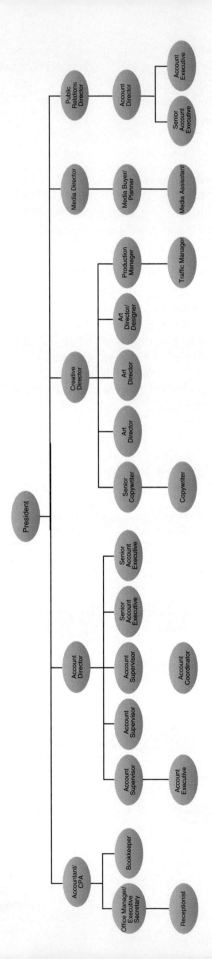

Figure 4.3 Organization chart for a small agency: The Morrison Agency handles $15 million in billings annually.

1. What is the purpose of the advertising?
2. Who is the target audience?
3. What promise does the advertising make?
4. What is the support for this promise? Are there secondary support points for specific target audiences or models of the product?
5. What media will deliver the message?
6. What is the tone or personality of the advertising?
7. Are there unique opportunities in terms of timing, competitive weaknesses, technological leadership, customer loyalties, or brand equities that must be considered?

Chapter 3 discusses brand names and their dominance in product marketing. A company's brand is assigned to a brand manager. The brand manager at the client firm is typically the contact for the account manager from the agency. This person is responsible for supervising all aspects of the brand's marketing: manufacturing, packaging, distribution, improvements, changes occasioned by environmental or safety laws, trade relations, promotions, public relations, profits, and advertising. This person is variously boss, God, tyrant, friend, partner, and guardian of the relationship with the agency.

Providing service to the brand manager and the client in general can be a difficult role for the account manager. Deadlines can sometimes be missed. An ad may not produce anticipated results. Agency profitability requirements may cause conflicts in levels of staffing a client may want. The agency recommendation may be unusually blunt or even critical. But the agency must maintain its independence and an honest point of view. Paul Harper, chairman emeritus of DDB Needham, put the role in perspective this way in a *Memorandum to All Our Account Executives*:

> Most good clients have strong views of their own. You will win client respect for yourself and the agency mainly for two things: (1) for forthrightness and thoroughness in presenting the agency's views, and (2) for respectful knowledge of the problems the client faces as he makes his own often difficult decisions. When his answer is "No," as it will sometimes be, this may be a professional defeat. But it will never be a moral defeat if the agency's position has been well presented and stoutly defended.

Account management in a major agency typically has four levels: management representative or supervisor, account supervisor, account executive, and assistant account executives. Sometimes a fifth level may exist, the account director, who is above the account supervisor. A smaller agency will combine some of these levels and probably have only two or at most three levels.

Management Supervisor. The *management supervisor* reports to the upper management of the agency. This person provides leadership on strategic issues, looks for new business opportunities, helps guide personnel growth and development within the account team, keeps agency management informed, and ensures that the agency is making a realistic profit on the account. The position normally carries the title of senior vice president and is offered to someone who has been working in account management for 10 to 15 years.

Account Supervisor. The *account supervisor* usually is the key working executive on the client's business and the primary liaison between the client and the agency. This person directs the preparation of strategic plans, assigns priorities, reviews and approves all recommendations before they are taken to the client, supervises the presentation of annual plans and other major recommendations to the client, and ensures agency adherence to deadlines and schedules. Account supervisors usually carry the title of vice president.

Account Executive. The *account executive* is responsible for day-to-day activities that include keeping the agency team on schedule and delivering the services as promised to the client. Other functions include seeing that all assignments are completed on time and within budget, maintaining the operating records of the account, preparing status and progress reports, supervising the production of materials, and securing legal or network approval of all advertising before production begins.

Assistant Account Executive. The *assistant account executive* is normally in the entry-level position in the agency's account management department. The focus is on learning the business and helping the account executive with records and schedules. Computer literacy is now required at least through account supervisor level in most agencies because records are stored and reports written on computers and shared within the account group or even the entire agency. Some agencies are so computerized that computer literacy is required to function within the agency.

CREATIVE DEVELOPMENT AND PRODUCTION

To some people *creative organization* is an oxymoron—they believe that creativity can only occur in an unstructured environment. In an agency, however, management must take into consideration how people work together and what assignments are flowing through the agency. The wisest agency managers are flexible in terms of organization but strict in terms of quality and deadline control. Young & Rubicam stated its creative point of view in Ad 4.3.

    The creative members of the agency typically hold one of the following positions: creative director, creative department manager, copywriter, art director, or producer. In addition to these positions, the broadcast production department and the studio are two other areas where creative personnel can apply their skills.

Principle

Creative management is flexible in organization but is strict in quality and deadline control.

Creative Director. Most agencies have one senior executive called the *creative director*, or executive creative director, who serves as the agency's creative conscience. Other comparable titles include executive creative director or director of creative services This person stimulates the department to improve its creative work and approves all ideas before they are presented outside the department. Because of the importance of the creative product, the creative director may be a member of the agency's board of directors or senior management group.

Creative Department Manager. Another person may oversee the internal management process, the administrative activities needed to keep the department running. Referred to as the *creative department manager*, this person handles budgeting, salary administration, office assignments, hiring and supervising secretarial and support staff, recruiting professional staff, and internal accounting. Practitioners may refer to the creative department manager as "house mother," "warden," "priest," "rabbi," "confessor," "crying towel," or "punching bag,"

You can really fly
once you know where you're going.

We believe the sharpest advertising strategies provide the greatest creative freedom. Only when you know exactly where you're going can the imagination soar free, without fear or formulas.
YOUNG & RUBICAM INC.

acknowledging the parental and instructive nature of the job. Creative directors can survive the loss of a senior staff member more easily than the loss of the creative department manager.

The Creative Group. Two types of people are generally found within the creative department. One is the brilliant, and sometimes eccentric, creator who conceives, writes, and produces innovative advertising. A staff is often built around this person as an extension of his or her skills. The second type is the coach, who delegates assignments, works with the staff to find an idea, and then molds, improves, nurtures, and inspires the staff. Agencies organize teams around these people, who may be called creative group heads or associate creative directors. Both the creator and the coach can coexist within the creative department. In fact, many people possess characteristics of both types, but the coach typically supervises the larger team of people.

A *creative group* includes people who write (*copywriters*), people who draw ideas for print ads or television commercials (*art directors*), and people who translate these ideas into television or radio commercials (*producers*). In many agencies an art director and copywriter who work well together are teamed, and a support group is built around them. Art directors and copywriters are discussed in more detail in Chapter 13.

Broadcast Production. In some cases the broadcast production department is a separate department (as the print production department usually is), but more often it will be a part of the creative department. Because the execution of the

An agency art director.
(Laima Druskis)

tone and action of broadcast advertising is so central to its success, the creative team usually works with a broadcast producer, who is directly involved in the filming or videotaping and editing of a commercial.

The Studio. An art studio is another part of the creative department. The studio includes artists who specialize in presentation pieces, lettering, and paste-up. (Presentation pieces are discussed in more detail in Chapter 14.) Beginning art directors often start in an agency studio. The computer is increasingly doing the work once done in the studio and in some agencies has replaced the studio and some of the print production functions.

The Computer. Graphics capabilities of today's computers, particularly the Apple Macintosh, have brought them into everyday use in creative departments. The computer commonly is used for fast rough layouts, quick changes on storyboards, and even finished production for some black-and-white newspaper ads. In broadcast, computer applications are increasingly promising with the advent of CD-ROM and sound capabilities. The Concepts and Applications box entitled "Charging Practices and the Computer" discusses some benefits and problems of using computers in advertising.

MARKETING SERVICES

Some agencies have combined media and research under one executive and called the resulting function *marketing services*. Market research is an important component of any media decision. Central to that decision is a clear understanding of the target audience. The same profile of the target audience is needed by the creative department. The practice of combining management of media and research is not universal. For clarity of understanding, the functions will be dealt with separately in the text. How they are organized in each agency is a management decision. We begin with media.

Media Planning and Buying. The media department performs one of the most complex functions in an advertising agency. It must recommend the most effi-

Charging Practices and the Computer

Introducing the computer into the production stream of agencies has had an unexpected effect and elicited a variety of reactions. Assembling a mechanical, or a paste-up, of all the elements of an advertisement was once the work of the studio artists or an art director who was particularly adept at this skill. The studio might charge $75 per hour and the exacting effort might require more than one hour of work for each different size or variation of the advertisement.

Enter the computer, with all the elements scanned into memory. The first mechanical might take 20 to 30 minutes. Each successive variation, while a completely separate mechanical, might take only a few minutes. Agencies continuing to charge $75 per hour for studio work found themselves losing money. In response, they switched to flat rates for completed work. These rates typically were lower in total than the hourly fee and almost always delivered a higher profit margin even after amortizing the cost of the computer, which could be priced as much as $75,000. In the end, the client benefited from lower costs, and the agency increased its profits and sometimes formed a new prof-it center by doing mechanical work for other clients or smaller agencies.

Because agency personnel turnover usually exceeds 30 percent per year, higher in clerical and hourly paid positions and lower at management level, the computer did not cause layoffs. What it did was enable agencies to train employees for more skilled tasks and not replace those who left. Layoffs are not the result of computerization as much as they are of client losses and budget reductions.

The look of media departments is changing as computer terminals are replacing the printed schedules and rate cards used for buying media time. Computer printers initially inundated media departments with paper. Many media departments now are turning to computers that store schedules, rates, changes, and pre- and post-buy analyses. This information is shared interactively with clients on computer screens instead of paper printouts and then approved by keystroke. The printed version is commanded only if needed. Other members of the agency and the client firm can be alerted to changes through the computer.

cient means of delivering the message to the target audience. Most media departments basically break down into three functions: planning, buying, and research. These functions will be outlined here and discussed in more detail in Chapters 9 and 12.

The Media Planner Developing a media plan is a creative skill that involves determining which medium or media to use, when, for what length of time, and at what cost. The *media planner* must be involved in the overall strategy and creative development of the advertising campaign. Most media and creative plans are prepared concurrently so the message and the medium will work together.

The Media Buyer The *media buyer* determines what media coverage is likely to be available at what costs. Buying involves ordering media on behalf of the client according to the plan approved by the client. Once the client approves the plan, the media buyer acts quickly to place orders. There is no point in recommending a plan calling for advertising on specific network television programs if those programs are already sold. Chapter 9 details the media-buying process.

Rapid changes in market conditions triggered by timely research (from scanners in retail outlets or daily inventory control by computer) have caused frequent adjustments in media plans and schedules. Without computers and laser printers these changes would have been difficult to plan and track and very expensive in terms of agency time. The computer has not only made rapid response possible, its capabilities have driven change.

Media Research In addition to planning and buying, most media departments have a media research section that gathers and evaluates media data. The department's forecasts of future prices, ratings of television programs, and audience composition are prepared by the media research manager. Media research often provides entry-level positions in clerical and data gathering for computer-literate newcomers.

RESEARCH DEPARTMENT

Full-service agencies in the United States usually have a separate department specifically devoted to research. The emphasis in agency research is on assisting the development of the advertising message. Most major agencies conduct research before the advertising is prepared to make the advertising more focused and appropriate to the target audience. They also purchase research from companies that specialize in this area. The leading research firms in each country work on projects both for clients and agencies. The leading U.S. firms are shown in Table 4.6.

Table 4.6 Top Research Companies by U.S. Research Revenues

Rank		Company, headquarters	Gross U.S. research revenues			Total research revenue		U.S. offices	U.S. full-time employee
1992	1991		1992	1991	% chg	1992	% chg		
1	1	A.C. Nielsen Co.*, Northbrook, Ill.	$515.0	$492.0	4.7	$1,305.0	8.8	NA	NA
2	3	Information Resources Inc., Chicago	241.6	198.7	21.6	276.4	24.1	11	2,930
3	4	IMS International*, Cham, Switzerland	195.0	165.0	18.2	586.0	15.1	NA	NA
4	2	Arbitron Co., New York	178.3	201.7	−11.6	178.3	−11.6	NA	2,200
5	5	VNU Business Information Services, New York	145.0	128.0	13.3	145.0	13.3	NA	1,950
6	6	Westat, Rockville, Md.	113.7	87.2	30.4	113.7	30.4	2	NA
7	7	Maritz Marketing Research, Fenton, Mo.	69.7	59.6	16.9	69.7	16.9	6	540
8	9	Abt Associates, Cambridge, Mass.	62.7	55.3	13.5	62.7	13.5	3	560
9	12	Walsh International, Phoenix	55.0	44.0	25.0	87.0	26.1	25	1,350
10	8	M/A/R/C Group, Irving, Texas	52.8	55.9	−5.5	53.9	−3.9	9	540
11	13	Gallup Organization, Princeton, N.J.	49.9	42.4	17.9	58.4	19.6	12	550
12	10	NFO Research, Greenwich, Conn.	47.1	44.8	5.1	47.1	5.1	11	386
13	11	Elrick & Lavidge, Atlanta	46.8	44.0	6.4	46.8	6.4	5	275
14	16	NPD Group, Port Washington, N.Y.	44.0	36.0	22.2	57.0	18.8	12	475
15	14	Market Facts, Arlington Heights, Ill.	41.0	40.0	2.5	41.0	2.5	4	530
16	17	Walker Group, Indianapolis	38.1	30.9	23.2	38.7	18.9	NA	343
17	15	MRB Group, London	36.1	37.3	−3.3	100.8	4.5	11	800
18	18	Intersearch, Horsham, Pa.	29.1	27.7	5.1	30.1	6.7	2	180
19	22	BASES Group, Covington, Ky.	26.9	21.7	24.0	28.0	23.3	5	191
20	24	Millward Brown, Naperville, Ill.	24.7	19.7	25.2	70.2	17.0	4	274
21	21	National Research Group, Los Angeles	24.1	22.7	6.3	27.0	7.1	NA	NA
22	19	Burke Marketing Research, Cincinnati	24.0	23.5	2.1	24.4	1.2	10	213
23	20	Chilton Research Services, Radnor, Pa.	23.8	23.5	1.3	23.8	1.3	1	163
24	23	Research International, London	22.9	21.2	8.0	145.5	17.8	15	976
25	25	Roper Starch Worldwide, Mamaroneck, N.Y.	21.3	19.7	8.2	22.8	8.1	2	196

Notes: Dollars are in millions.
*Indicates *Advertising Age* estimate.
Source: Reprinted with permission from Advertising Age (October 18, 1993):S–2. Copyright Crain Communications, Inc., 1993.

Most European advertising agencies either do not have a research department or have only a research director, who is responsible for commissioning outside research projects and interpreting the results for the agency. This European pattern is becoming more common in North America.

Whether composed of a single person in a small agency or teams of professionals in a large agency, the research department has a number of duties besides helping creative development. It ensures that the agency has reliable information, screens all new research findings to determine if they change the body of information about a brand, company, industry, or market, and provides the agency with accurate information about consumer behavior. When conducting original research, the agency almost always concentrates on consumer attitudes and behavior. Advertising research will be discussed in more detail in Chapters 6 and 21.

An important philosophical consideration is how the research function is positioned in the agency. It should not be the judge of creative. It should be the scout, the eyes and ears of the agency. By concentrating on precreative research and on evaluating consumer reaction to creative alternatives, the research department contributes to the development of new ways to think about the consumer. Most agencies ask clients to conduct postresearch studies to evaluate the advertising after it has made its contribution.

Principle

Research should be a partner with the creative side in the development of great advertising, not a scorekeeper or judge of the creative department.

INTERNAL SERVICES

The departments in an agency that serve the very important "backroom" operations are called internal service departments. They get the work produced, get it to the media, handle the finances, and manage relationships with employees. These include the traffic department, print production, financial services, human resources or personnel, and the direct-marketing department.

Traffic Department. The traffic department is responsible for internal control and tracking of projects to meet deadlines. The account executive works closely with the assigned traffic coordinator or traffic manager to review deadlines and monitor progress. The traffic department is the lifeline of the agency, and its personnel keep track of everything that is happening in the agency.

Trafficking requires diligence, tact, and great attention to detail. Diligence is needed to keep track of the progress of elements of a campaign as they come together to ensure that the key jobs, the ones upon which other departments depend to meet deadlines, are not allowed to slip. Tact is needed to negotiate with creative people who complain they never have enough time, have too many jobs to complete, but appreciate a traffic manager who pushes the critical assignments and buys a day or two on ones with a cushion in the schedule. Attention to detail is needed because it is the task of the traffic coordinator to get the job finished, assemble all the bills and charges, and deliver the proper signatures to financial services for billing to the client. Although computers now can help trace and program projects (and have reduced the size of traffic departments), nothing can replace the persistent traffic coordinator who has heard every excuse for delay.

Principle

The traffic department is the life-line of the agency.

Print Production. Taking a layout, a photograph or an illustration, and a page of copy and turning these elements into a four-color magazine page or a full-page newspaper advertisement is the work of the print production department.

Because of the technical nature of making the printing plates, adjusting and matching color, and achieving reproduction, print production is not handled within the creative department. In contrast, television and radio production usually are part of creative development. In print productions the art director on the account normally supervises the illustrator or photographer and approves the work but does not supervise the production of the material sent to the publication. The use of computers and the increasing power and definition of computer graphics are moving some print production to the art director's computer terminal, but most production for four-color ads and brochures is still done in the print production department.

Financial Services Whether large or small, the agency must send its invoices out on time, pay its bills on time, control its costs, ensure that expenses incurred on behalf of a client are properly invoiced to that client, meet its payroll, pay its taxes, and make a profit within its budget. The chief financial officer manages these functions. In a large agency the treasurer is responsible for cash management, seeing that funds are invested until needed, bills are paid just before they are due, cash discounts are taken, and cash reserves are available for peak billing periods. The comptroller is charged with internal procedures, for example, conducting internal audits to prevent misuse of agency resources, making sure that money is not spent without authority, large checks are countersigned, and invoices are not paid unless approved.

Human Resources An operation of any size requires keeping personnel files and records. The larger the agency, the more likely it will have a professional human resources or personnel staff. These people handle the hiring and firing of clerical, secretarial, and support staff. Recruitment of professional staff, although conducted by the head of the department in which the person will work, is normally coordinated by the human resources department. Frequently this department is responsible for ensuring that equal opportunity guidelines are met. Both the financial services and human resource departments of advertising agencies function the same way as do comparable departments in corporations.

Direct-Marketing Department The increase in the use of direct marketing (covered in Chapter 16) and clients' requests for consulting services in direct marketing have led to the development of direct-marketing departments and direct-marketing subsidiaries. An agency's direct-marketing department is responsible for creating advertising that is designed to stimulate the target audience to send in a coupon, call a telephone number, or mail in an order. Information about the people who reply are maintained on computer lists. Direct mail often is used to send offers or promotions to lists of users or prospective users.

How Agencies Are Paid

Agencies derive their revenues and, therefore, their profits from two main sources—commissions and fees. To understand these processes, we must first understand the word *agent*. An agent is someone who acts for another. In this case, an advertising agency acts for a client in creating advertising.

THE COMMISSION SYSTEM

Early advertising agents acted on behalf of the medium rather than on behalf of the client. Well into the nineteenth century advertising agents acted as representatives for newspapers, magazines, and handbill printers. If the agent brought advertising to the publisher, the publisher paid the agent a **commission**, which was justified by the work the agent did in bringing the publisher the business and preparing the advertisement for publication. The agent might write the copy, prepare the layout, set the type, and arrange for any drawings or plates that were part of the advertisement. These efforts saved the publisher time and work.

As advertising grew in importance, advertisers began to work with fewer and fewer agents and eventually signed with one agent exclusively. In 1901, Clarence Curtis of Curtis Publishing granted a 15 percent commission to advertising agencies—10 percent for preparation of material and 5 percent for prompt payment. This practice changed the entire advertising industry. Instead of representing one medium to many advertisers, the agent now acted on behalf of one client and placed ads with many media. The commission system remains, however, as a legacy of the early years of advertising.

commission A form of payment in which an agent or agency receives a certain percentage (historically 15 percent) of media charges.

HOW THE COMMISSION SYSTEM WORKS

A 15 percent commission long has been considered standard even though it is now observed more in the breach (see Table 4.7). As Timm Crull, chairman-CEO of Nestlé USA, pointed out, the battle is more fierce now because of:

1. Intense and increasing competition
2. Rapidly changing demographics
3. An explosion of new media

Crull stated, "If advertising is to continue to serve as the anchor in the overall marketing plan, agencies must come up with more than clever messages....I believe that major advertising agencies are understandably reluctant to abandon the lucrative comfort of traditional broadcast media to explore the full range of media alternatives."[13]

It is standard in the sense that most media allow agencies a 15 percent commission. (Outdoor is 16.67 percent.) For example, if it costs $100,000 to run a

[13]Timm Crull, "Nestlé to Agencies: 'Shake Mindset,'" *Advertising Age* (May 3, 1993):26.

Table 4.7

How Clients Compensate Agencies

Account Size	Standard 15% Commission	Sliding-scale or Lower Commission	Labor-Based Fee
Percentage of advertisers choosing each option, by account size			
Under $10 million	36	4	47
$10 million - $49 million	31	28	35
$50 million+	29	50	13
All advertisers	33%	26%	32%

All figures may not add up to 100 percent because some advertisers gave other responses or no answer
Source: Association of National Advertisers. Reprinted with permission from Advertising Age (May 11, 1992):26. Copyright, Crain Communications, Inc., 1992.

television commercial, the agency commission at 15 percent is $15,000. Stated another way, the agency bills the client $100,000 but pays the station $85,000.

In the 1980s, starting first in Great Britain, clients began to squeeze the 15 percent commission in an attempt to reduce expenses. When advertising accounts were opened for presentation, the client might indicate it intended to pay, say, 12 percent commission. When agencies accepted that commission, it undercut the 15 percent commission standard. Negotiated commission rates, especially for the largest budgets of $10,000,000 and up, are common. Confidential sources indicate that the largest agencies averaged about 12 percent commission in 1992 on commission clients.

Although the 15 percent commission system is common, it is not universal. In New Zealand, for example, the commission allowed by media is 20 percent. The argument for this higher rate is that New Zealand is a small country and its agencies have to do as much work to prepare a campaign to reach 3.5 million New Zealanders as would, say, a U.S. agency to reach a much larger audience. In Australia, five times as populous, the commission allowed by media is 16 percent. Throughout the world, while the commission rate allowed by media is most commonly 15 percent, clients are increasingly negotiating to get some of that commission back. Very large clients frequently negotiate sliding scales on commission: for example, 15 percent up to $10 million, 12 percent from $10 million to $25 million, and 10 percent above that.

Table 4.8 shows how the commission system works and how agencies derive their profits. In this example, 15 percent will be used, but the principle will be the same regardless of the percent commission used.

The percentages shown are within a range the industry considers typical. In the late 1980s, the rate of profit of the publicly held agencies was slightly below 6 percent. In 1992, the six largest public agencies (Foote, Cone & Belding; Grey;

Table 4.8

Commission System Components

		Percentage of Billing	Percentage of Revenue
Billings placed in media	$5,000,000	100%	
15% commission (agency revenue)	750,000	15.0	100%
Expenses			
Direct salaries*	250,000	5.0	33.3
Indirect salaries**	165,000	3.3	22.0
Social security, health benefits	125,000	2.5	16.7
Rent	45,000	0.9	6.0
Travel	10,000	0.2	1.3
Telephone, postage, etc.	10,000	0.2	1.3
Supplies	10,000	0.2	1.3
All other	20,000	0.4	2.7
Profit sharing	50,000	1.0	6.7
Gross profit	65,000	1.3	8.6
Tax	20,000	0.4	2.7
Net profit after tax	45,000	0.9	6.0

*Direct salaries apply to people who work directly on client business.
**Indirect salaries apply to people who do not work directly on client business: senior management, accounting, telephone operators, studio, mailroom, receptionist.

Table 4.9

Public Agency Results (1992 Fiscal Year)

Agency	Revenue ($million)	Net Income ($millions)	After-Tax Profits (%)
Foote, Cone & Belding	353.3	21.7	6.1
Grey Advertising	564.5	16.5	2.9
Interpublic Group	1,856.0	111.9	6.0
Omnicom Group	1,356.0	65.5	4.7
Saatchi & Saatchi	1,120.2	(18.9)	(1.7)
WPP Group	1,927.9	(23.3)	(1.2)

Source: Annual Reports

Interpublic; Omnicom; Saatchi, and WPP) had combined after-tax profits of 2.4 percent, with a high of 6.1 percent for FCB and 6.0 percent for Interpublic but losses of under 2 percent on revenue for WPP and Saatchi (see Table 4.9).[14]

What happens when the commission is lower than 15 percent and how is the rate set? The rate is negotiated between client and agency. What work will be done by the agency and what will be charged for separately are included in the negotiation. Here are examples:

Included	**Sometimes Included**	**Charged Separately from the Commission**
Analysis of client research	Layouts	Advertising production
Preparation of overall strategy	Telephone	TV production
Creation of advertising	Duplicating	Travel not related to client contact
Media planning	Test market plans	Shipping
Media buying	Travel directly related to client contact	Postage
Payment of suppliers	Alternate campaigns	Delivery charges
Billing to client		Market research
Research in support of recommendation		Direct marketing
Discounts for prompt payment		Public relations
Syndicated media services		Interest for late payment

Advertising agencies are asking clients to pay for services that can be said to be *intangible*. Marketing strategies, for instance, are costly services when provided by marketing consultancies. Martin Sorrell, chief executive of WPP Group, argues agencies should charge for them.[15]

If the agency agrees to a commission of 10 percent, here is how that works:

Billing placed in media	$5,000,000
15 percent commission from media	750,000
10 percent commission rate	500,000
Rebated to client	250,000

---

[14] From the agencies' annual reports.
[15] Martin Sorrell, *Advertising Age* (March 19, 1990):1.

The media accepts the order for $5,000,000 and bills the agency $4,250,000. The agency charges the client $4,750,000 instead of $5,000,000 and makes a commission of 10 percent on the theoretical $5,000,000 budget. A full 15 percent commission as shown in Table 4.7 is the practice in only one-third of the cases.

To the degree that the agency does not charge for items in the sometimes included column or for items usually charged separately from commission, the agency effectively lowers its rate of commission.

Some media and most production houses—those that make printing plates or produce television commercials—do not allow agency commissions. The agency then will gross up the outside charge to reflect the commission. Here is how that works:

		Net	**Grossed Up**
Media cost	$100,000		
15% commission	15,000		
Net cost to agency	85,000	85%	100%
Equivalent commission	15,000		17.65%

If the $85,000 cost of service to the agency has no commission allowance, and a 15 percent commission is agreed upon with the client, the agency adds $15,000 (17.65 percent) to the $85,000 when billing the client. If the agreed-upon commission is 10 percent, the $85,000 represents 90 percent of what the agency charges the client. The agency adds $9,444 (11.1 percent) to gross up the amount so that its final charge to the client ($94,444) contains a 10 percent ($9,444) commission.

THE FEE SYSTEM

The alternative form of compensation is the fee system. This system is comparable to the means by which advertisers pay their lawyers and accountants. The client and agency agree on an hourly **fee**, or charge. This fee can vary according to department or levels of salary within a department. In other cases, a flat hourly fee for all work is agreed upon regardless of the salary level of the person doing the work. Charges are also included for out-of-pocket expenses, travel, and the items normally charged separately under a commission system. These are charged net, without any markup or commission. All media are billed to the client net of any commission.

Trust is the critical element in a fee system. The client must believe that each person in the agency is keeping track of his or her time accurately and charging that time correctly to a particular brand or project. In addition, the client must believe that the agency's hourly charge for salary, overhead, and profit is fair.

How is the agency fee calculated? The agency assigns costs for salary, rent, telephone, postage, internal operations, equipment rentals, taxes, and other expenses, and then determines what hourly charge will recover all of these costs and also provide the agency with a profit. A common rule of thumb in setting a fee is to charge three times the person's annual salary divided by the number of hours that person worked.

Here is how the agency profit and loss statement might look compared to the commission system. In this example, there is equivalent billing of $5,000,000 and 1.7 people per million dollars of billing working on the business. The client, therefore, has the services of 8.5 people, approximately five of whom would work directly on the account. Since the agency using the fee system would be seeking substantially the same revenue ($750,000) and is charging only for the five people who work on the business (direct salaries), the fee would be three times the direct salaries ($750,000 ÷ $250,000). Assme an 1800-hour work year and an average of $50,000 per year for those working on the account:

Average salary	$50,000
Divided by 1800 hours, direct cost per hour	$27.77
Multiplied by 3, fee charge per hour	$83.33
9,000 hours times $83.33 per hour	$750,000

If the other costs remain the same, the agency will achieve a profit after tax of $45,000. With the 15 percent commission system now being regularly discounted, agencies are under pressure to reduce operating costs and waste. No matter what the level of commission or fee is, the agency seeks to achieve a profit of approximately 6 percent of revenue received by the agency from each client.

An interesting difference appears between the commission and fee systems when a client decides to cut the advertising budget. Under the commission system, when the client cancels advertising to save money, whatever is canceled is saved. Under the fee system, the client saves the amount of the schedule that is canceled but will have to pay the agency for the hours and expense required to contact the media, revise the media plan, and redo the billing.

The fee system has many supporters within the field. Those who favor it over the commission system believe that an agency's payments should not be based on the price a medium charges. The commission system has survived, however, because it is simple, easy to understand, and puts pressure on an agency to keep its costs down.

A variation on the fee system is incentive-based agency compensation. Under this system, details of which are not generally made public, the agency performance is judged by a combination of objective and subjective standards. Seldom does even outstanding performance produce much more than the equivalent of 15 percent of billings, and acceptable performance will often pay less than 15 percent. If media buying is removed from the agency, the base commission will almost certainly be in a range of 10 percent to 13 percent, with a bonus of 1 percent to 2 percent for high performance.

The agencies have not just supinely accepted reductions in commissions and fees. In 1993, Margeotes, Fertitta & Weise fired Remy Martin. "More and more ad agencies are walking away from low-margin accounts, rather than struggle to stick by them."[16]

THE FUTURE OF ADVERTISING AGENCIES

Is the advertising agency an endangered species? Seldom in its less than 200-year history (although one Japanese agency claims to be 400 years old) has the advertising agency been in such turmoil as in these last years of the twentieth

---

[16]Kevin Goldman, "Poor Payoffs Push Agencies to Drop Clients," *The Wall Street Journal* (November 17, 1993):B1.

Issues & CONTROVERSIES

Conflicts and Loyalty

The standard industry contract states that the agency agrees not to handle different products or companies in the same category or industry. For example, an agency that represents Coca-Cola will not represent Pepsi. In contrast to lawyers or accountants, who may specialize in a sector or an industry and handle a number of clients in the same field, advertising agencies agree not to work for a competing product or company because this would cause a conflict of interest. ("How can you work for a competitor and assure me I am getting your best ideas and the best media buys?") In theory, the conflict clause is simple. In practice, it has become one of the major controversies in the industry for several reasons: mergers of clients, internationalization of agencies, and the megamergers of agencies.

As clients merged, agencies and clients were confronted with new complexities. A client might acquire a new division and want the agency to take on the new assignment—but the agency already might be representing the leading product in the category from another very important client. Either way, the agency would risk offending one client. In a worst-case scenario, both clients insist that the agency resign the other company because only one of the company's many divisions compete with the client. Usually, goodwill and loyalty resolve these problems of how conflict is interpreted. Clients often will agree that the agency can handle divisions of competing companies as long as the agency keeps the people working for one multidivision client from working on any division of another multidivision client. For example, the 1987 merger of Doyle Dane Bernbach, the agency for Weight Watchers International, with Needham Harper Worldwide, the agency for the Mrs. Paul product line, created a potential conflict because both companies produced frozen fish. However, the Campbell Soup Company, which owns the Mrs. Paul line, did not ask the new agency to drop either product. (Later, DDB Needham lost the business in a product alignment among Campbell agencies.)

Loyalty is important. Agencies develop loyalties to clients and vice versa. The conflicting policies of each client are subject to interpretation. Client nationalities even come into play. One case involved a Japanese client's U.S. division and a U.S. company. Inquiring about the Japanese client's reaction to the agency soliciting a U.S. company would be taken by the Japanese company as a lack of loyalty, even though the U.S. company was comfortable that the inquiry be made. Out of loyalty to a client, an agency might keep itself free of direct conflicts (product-to-product) anywhere in the world and avoid indirect conflicts (where two companies have similar divisions but the agency avoids the second company altogether). Companies rewarded this loyalty by avoiding agencies serving their competitors anywhere. This was especially true with soap and detergent products (Procter & Gamble, Colgate, Lever, and Henkel); automobiles (General Motors, Ford, Chrysler, Toyota, and Nissan); beer (Anheuser-Busch, Miller, and Stroh's); and is increasing in food (Nestlé, Kraft General Foods, RJR Nabisco, and Mars). Agencies that have one client in each of these categories will not accept, or be cleared to accept, another client in this category.

Internationalization creates a second problem. Suppose a client has no European distribution nor plans to enter Europe. Could its U.S. agency safely take a competitive product in its client's category in Germany? Usually the answer is yes, but in one recent instance the U.S. client was bought by a European company, and the agency found itself with an unanticipated conflict problem in Europe. Mergers in the United States and continuing acquisition of companies by the large global corporations have created a need for agencies and clients to maintain communication on what the policy is and how it will be interpreted. This requires a central clearing mechanism at agency headquarters which includes new product assignments. These are particularly nettlesome problems. What if two clients the agency has successfully kept separate decide the same week to ask the agency to begin work in the same new product area? The agency suddenly is in possession of a valuable piece of competitive intelligence. The best solution is to keep the decision at the highest level and make an informed judgment quickly.

century. Traditional means of payment, organization, services, competition, and market segmentation are changing. Agency staffs have been reduced and revenues are down. Due to a decade of mergers and consolidation, client-agency conflicts have arisen, as the Issues and Controversies box on page 150 describes.

In addition to the emergence of these difficulties, advertising is undergoing structural change brought about by the advances of technology in production, programming, databases, specialty printing, desktop publishing, proliferation of television channels, CD-ROM capabilities of home computers, and now interactive media. The organizational structure of agencies, methods of payment, and even reasons for hiring agencies are all subject to review. In times of stress an organization's structures and innovations are put to the test. The agency's response to such tensions will either renew the life of the organization or signal its demise. The most successful advertising agencies are those that have been willing to be flexible and to adjust to the times, and they are likely to remain successful. Agency managers tend to be younger than corporate managers, even in the largest agencies, and typically are more willing to try new things and to organize quickly for opportunities.

The 1960s and 1970s were times of growth for the big agencies. The 1980s saw megamergers, acquisitions, and the growth of the mega-agencies and holding companies. The 1990s are becoming a time of testing economies of scale, contributions of service, and ways to build client trust and reliance. An endangered species? Without necessary adaptations, it certainly is at risk. The creativity that is such an essential product of an advertising agency, however, will almost certainly serve the best agencies well as they face these new challenges. The creativity characteristic of the field may also generate innovations in structure, in means of payment, and in relations with clients. Agencies that had reorganized and developed innovative approaches to client service and concept development were reporting record years in the early 1990s. These included Colle & McVoy in Minneapolis, which closed three branches and concentrated its resources in the Twin Cities, and Larkin, Meeder & Schweidel in Dallas, which has aggressively provided full marketing strategic advice. The advertising agency, even if in modified form, will continue to be an exciting place to work.

SUMMARY

- When functioning at their best, advertising agencies develop campaigns that enhance the value of the brands they handle.

- Agencies usually have four basic functions: account management, creative development and production, media planning and buying, and research.

- Support departments typically include traffic, print production, financial services, and human resources. Many agencies also develop other services as sources of profit.

- The account management function acts as the primary liaison between the agency and the client.

- Computerization has had a significant effect on the advertising agency business since the 1980s.

- Agencies typically have received a 15 percent commission from media placed, although this rate is increasingly being negotiated and will vary from country to country. Under the fee system, agencies' charges are computed on the basis of actual time and services provided.

- The economic climate of the late 1980s and early 1990s provoked many changes in the world of advertising agencies, including megamergers and increased competition.

QUESTIONS

1 What is the central reason an advertising agency exists?

2 What impact has integrated marketing communications had on advertising agencies?

3 Why does the organizational chart for an agency remain flexible?

4 What is the symbiotic relationship between creative boutiques and media-buying services?

5 Why has the 15 percent commission system weakened as the industry standard? Why do many agencies prefer the fee system to the commission system?

6 Why has the growth of ethnic agencies and media targeting of minorities brought these two into conflict with activists?

7 How do agencies separate the internal management function from the creative process in the creative department?

8 Why are agencies under such pressure that their structure and form may change?

9 State two essential differences between the commission and the fee systems of compensation.

10 Name two events that reflect major change in the agency business.

11 Why do clients sometimes create in-house agencies?

12 Why has employment decreased in the largest agencies and grown in the rest in recent years?

13 Has the percentage of advertising in client marketing budgets grown or decreased in recent years? Why?

14 Give examples of how technology has had an impact on the agency business.

SUGGESTED CLASS PROJECTS

1 Advertising is a discipline. Creation of advertising requires background information, often unavailable to a class. But advertising as a business practice can be understood by reversing the process. Divide the class into groups of four or five. Collect one or two print advertisements or tape one or two commercials for the same brand or company. Then work back to formulate the creative platform:

a. What is the purpose of the advertising?

b. Who is the target audience? Be as specific as possible in terms of age, income, occupation, habits, and attitudes.

c. What is the promise of the advertising? Is is a claim from the advertiser or a benefit to the user?

d. What is the support for the promise?

e. What media were used and why?

f. What is the tone being used and the personality being conveyed?

2 Form three or four "agencies" within the classroom. Form one smaller "client" group. (Drawing names might be best.) Each group needs to structure itself for job responsibilities. The client group provides an assignment (the same) for everyone to "produce," by gathering the elements of a current campaign. Candidates could include a car brand (for which material would be available at a local dealership), a fast-food outlet, or a brand of clothes (Levis, Dockers, J. Crew, Gap). The agencies would be given a copy platform and samples of the existing campaign, asked to critique the campaign, and to suggest new executions and a new slogan within the deadline. How would each agency delegate work responsibilities to complete the campaign? For fairness, each agency receives the same fee, and each has the same resources or access to the same resources, including comput-

ers. The client group decides which agency best meets the objective.

3. All advertising assignments can be reduced to a simple question: "How do we sell this thing?" Imagine this "thing" is an extra goat you have around, and the job is to sell it.

The following is a progression of ten headline ideas from ten copywriters, each with a different approach.

a. *Goat for Sale*. This is pure, simple marketing. An announcement of the availability of a product.

b. *Buy a Goat*. This adds urgency with a call to action.

c. *Buy a Great Goat*. Some hard sell, introducing the idea that all members of this product category may not be alike.

d. *Buy a Goat Instead of a Sheep*. Breaking out of the envelope, expanding the potential category. Sowing the seeds of discontent among sheep users, hoping to raise the category development index of goats.

e. *Save on a Goat*. A nice retail feel to this one.

f. *Goat. Guaranteed*. There may be some buyers out there who lack confidence in their ability to know a good goat when they see one. This should ease their concerns.

g. *Buy a Cheap Labor-Saving Device*. Aha! The Theodore Levitt school: You aren't buying a product, you're buying the solution to a problem. The rational benefit to the buyer is spelled out.

h. *Buy an Affectionate Labor-Saving Device*. Even better: an emotional benefit. You can't wait to read the body copy.

i. *Give a Goat a Home*. The ultimate cop-out, a shameless appeal to guilt. But it could work, depending on the illustration.

j. *Don't Let Someone Else Get Your Goat*. A cutesy pun with no meaning, but the approach most favored by lazy writers.

Rank each of these approaches, in descending order of expected effectiveness. The criterion is which will sell the goat, not which will win an award or make you feel good. You might suggest alternatives, but don't give it away, as in, "Free Goat."

Class project 3 was suggested by George Lemmond, Lemmond Associates, Roswell, Georgia.

FURTHER READINGS

DUBOFF, ROBERT S., "Can Research and Creative Coexist?" *Advertising Age* (March 17, 1986):18, 22.

"U.S. Advertising Agency Profiles: 1988 Edition," *Advertising Age* (March 30, 1988). (Special edition.)

MAYER, MARTIN, *Whatever Happened to Madison Avenue?* (Little Brown & Co., 1991).

Chiat/Day

Founded in 1968 by Jay Chiat and Guy Day, Chiat/Day has been responsible for some of the most memorable advertising ever produced by a domestic agency. Yet, as the agency rose, it faced many of the painful challenges currently facing the industry as a whole.

Chiat/Day started out as a small boutique operation and quickly began producing notable work for increasingly larger clients. In the early '80s, Chiat/Day began to gain attention with its visible work for Apple, California Coolers, Nike, and others. Then in the late '80s, Chiat/Day lost virtually all of its most visible accounts while successfully winning what was then the largest single account move in the history of U.S. advertising: Nissan Motor Corporation.

As the agency struggled to absorb the Nissan account, which more than doubled Chiat/Day's billings overnight, it also pursued an aggressive acquisitions and expansion program. In addition to opening new offices and acquiring packaging, graphics, public relations, and direct-mail firms, Chiat/Day merged with an Australian agency and became Chiat/Day/Mojo. The agency's formula for success was actually fairly simple: Hungry, talented, young creative people working at below-average pay levels for the opportunity to be part of a "hot creative shop."

Chiat/Day/Mojo operates using account planning, which emphasizes frequent informal contact with customers in focus groups conducted by the account planners themselves. The agency believes that this concept has helped it to produce its breakthrough work.

Chiat/Day's merger with the Australian agency Mojo turned out to be a financial disaster. One motive for the merger was the opportunity to obtain a larger share of Nissan's worldwide advertising by becoming Nissan's agency in Australia. But this was not to be. Furthermore, the merger precipitated conflicts between two quite different and geographically separated agency cultures, and it was finally doomed by a sharp economic downturn that put severe strains on all Australian advertising agencies. The merger ended with the sale of what was left of Mojo.

Chiat/Day's other expansions were equally inauspicious. Purchases of and alliances with European agencies lead to the loss of key executives and key clients. The New York office, anchored by the American Express account, was devastated when that account returned to Ogilvy & Mather after little more than a year at Chiat. Ogilvy & Mather, working with a consultant to American Express, developed the highly visual format (shown in the accompanying ad) that restored the successful but discontinued "Do You Know Me?" campaign to win back the account.

From its classic "1984" spot for Apple's Macintosh to the work for Nissan and Energizer, Chiat/Day has manifested two characteristics that separate it from the pack: It communicates a clear selling message, and it always entertains.

Sources: Courtesy of Chiat/Day and *Chiat/Day: The First Twenty Years* (Kessler); Rizzoli, 1990.

Questions

1. Chiat/Day has produced some of the most memorable advertising created in the United States,—some of the most noteworthy advertising bombs, such as the indecipherable Reebok U.B.U. campaign and the cloyingly yuppie Nissan Built for the Human Race efforts. Why do you think it is possible for an agency to produce both brilliant work and work that flops?

2. Is it more difficult for the creative process to thrive in a bureaucratic environment? Why?

3. Many of the hottest creative agencies in the country did not exist 20 years ago. Why would the age of an agency influence its creative ability?

The Honda Way

In the fall of 1969 Honda produced the top-selling motor-cycle in America. Honda automobiles, however, had not yet appeared in this country. Over 7,000 miles away at Honda corporate headquarters in Tokyo, plans were being made to change that.

The plans were successful. By the 1980s Honda cars were some of the most popular in the United States, and in 1989 the Honda Accord was the number-one selling car in America. What took the company from zero to 717,000 cars a year in record time? It was a combination of engineering prowess, technological inno-vation, commitment, and good timing, all driven by a company philosophy known as "The Honda Way." This philosophy included a consistent, yet flexible, marketing and advertising strategy.

From the beginning, Honda's marketing philosophy stressed supplying high-efficiency products at a reason-able price. The company has continually emphasized customer satisfaction. Honda Associates were encour-aged to be ambitious and daring, to develop fresh ideas, to embrace challenges, and to respond quickly to unforeseen changes and opportunities. In 1969 Honda engineers set the ambitious goal of developing a "world car." This project took them to the center of a profoundly changing automotive marketplace.

At that time over 88 percent of all automobiles sold in the United States came from Detroit. Moreover, the majority of imported cars were European, not Japanese. Toyota was the leading Japanese import followed by Datsun (now Nissan). Mazda and Subaru were just mak-ing plans to enter the U.S. market.

The popularity of the Volkswagon Beetle convinced Honda executives that a market for a quality small car existed in the United States. In 1970 Honda introduced its first car to America—the N600. Sales were modest. Only a few thousand were sold. Then, in 1973, the com-pany introduced its "world car," the innovative Honda Civic. The Civic was nearly 8 inches longer than the 600 model, and it featured an advanced 4-cylinder engine and front-wheel drive. Available in both a 2-door sedan and a 3-door hatchback, it was priced at only $2,150.

Although the Civic was well-received by the auto-motive press and the American public, it was still con-sidered too small. At that point, however, international politics intervened. In October 1973 the Arab oil-produc-ing countries banned oil imports to the West. As gaso-line lines grew and prices skyrocketed, Detroit's large engines—some delivering under 12 miles per gallon—began to lose their appeal. Sales of small, fuel-efficient

automobiles like the Honda Civic grew rapidly. By the end of 1974 Civic sales had climbed to over 43,000.

Meanwhile, the OPEC embargo produced tough new federal fuel economy regulations. The Environ-mental Protection Agency (EPA) issued strict new emis-sions standards. As Detroit carmakers scrambled to meet the new regulations, Honda engineers had already developed their next big idea: the 1975 Civic CVCC. With its fuel-efficient new engine, the Civic not only met the EPA clean air standards, it also ran on any grade of fuel. At 42 miles per gallon, the Civic was promoted as both the most fuel-efficient and the lowest-priced car in America. The advertising campaign for the Civic posi-tioned the car in the foremost of the move toward eco-nomical transportation. The Honda advertising slogan, "What the World Is Coming To," stressed the innovative philosophy behind the Civic. More than 100,000 Civics were sold.

Then Honda's research indicated that the market was about to change once again. As both fuel shortages and gasoline prices eased somewhat, car buyers began to favor values like quality, roominess, performance, and comfort. Honda developed a car to meet this need and in June 1976 launched what would become its most popular model—the Accord.

Honda advertising emphasized the roominess and lively performance of the Accord. The automotive press praised its clean design and advanced engineering. The public reception was remarkable: By the end of 1978 Honda sales had climbed to over 274,000 cars.

During this time, car buying had become more com-plex. There was a growing number of manufacturers and car models. Financing was more complicated, and Detroit was offering an expanded array of optional equipment. Amid this confusion, Honda's marketing approach was clear and simple: Honda builds quality cars that are simple to drive simple to park, simple to understand, and simple to own. The message was summed up in Honda's slogan, used in print ads, brochures, on television and even on shopping bags, "We Make It Simple" (see Exhibit A). It was The Honda Way—and it worked.

By the end of 1978 Hondas was number three in import car sales, behind Toyota and Nissan. Over the next few years, the company increased its momentum by refining and expanding its product line. Honda's third series, the Prelude, was introduced in 1979. In 1980, the second generation Civic was named *Motor Trend* maga-zine's "Import Car of the Year." Annual sales were now

Why we make it simple.

Honda set out to design one car that suited the basic transportation needs of the entire world.

So to help us discover that basic design we studied and analyzed data from 91 different countries. We collected information on everything from road conditions in Morocco to rainfall in Denmark to the dimensions of the average motorist in the United States.

In time the answer became clear. If Honda was to fill a universal need, we would have to build a simple car.

Simple to drive, simple to park, simple to understand, simple to own.

Today we offer three simple cars. The Honda Civic 1200, the Honda Civic CVCC, and the Honda Accord.

Consider for a moment how simplicity can help minimize just one of today's many automotive problems: the cost of gasoline.

All Hondas meet emissions requirements without a catalytic converter. So all Hondas run on regular as well as unleaded gasoline.

But don't be misled. A simple design is often the most difficult. For all their simplicity, Hondas are among the most sophisticated cars in their price range.

There is, of course, another reason why we make simple cars. The reason is you. We know that choosing a new car can be a complex problem.

It's a problem, however, that we can solve quite easily by giving you your choice of just three cars.

There. Now haven't we made your life simple?

HONDA
We make it simple.

well over 375,000. In 1984 Honda launched it's newest idea—the CRX. Conceived as a sporty commuter car with high gas mileage, it too was named *Motor Trend's* "Import Car of the Year." In addition, the Honda Prelude and Civic Hatchback captured the first and second runner-up sports, making it the first time ever that a single manufacturer had won the top three spots in the long history of this prestigious competition.

Honda was now selling 12 different models in the United States, at the rate of over half a million cars per year. For the first time, Honda advertising began to focus on the particular personality of each model instead of using a unifying corporate slogan. Honda portrayed its luxury Accord as the benchmark in its class and the Prelude Sports Coupe as "a sports car for adults." Its second generation Civics were marketed as being larger and more stylish than their predecessors while still keeping earlier fuel economy and value. Ironically, "We Make It Simple" was no longer the way to advertise an increasingly sophisticated product line, which now appealed to a wide variety of buyers.

Customer satisfaction has always been emphasized as part of The Honda Way. In 1986 Honda outperformed Mercedes-Benz to become number one in overall customer satisfaction, based on owners' ratings of both the quality of their cars and of the dealerships that service them. Honda spotlighted this success by announcing in print advertising, "We're Happy You're Happy."

When it came time for *Motor Trend's* 1988 "Import Car of the Year" competition, Honda once again captured the top three spots. The redesigned CRX Si won the top honors, followed by the Prelude Si with 4-wheel steering and the Civic 4-door sedan. In typical Honda fashion, advertisements announcing the award stated simply, "Who says it's lonely at the top?" (see Exhibit B).

One reason for Honda's consistently strong performance in customer satisfaction is its dealer network. Honda works closely with its dealers to insure that their operations—sales, service, parts, and accessories—reflect the quality of the cars themselves. Honda provides its dealers with support materials, from sales training and service manuals to full-line product brochures and videos.

Part of Honda's corporate philosophy is to be a good corporate citizen. In this spirit, Honda began another important campaign: saving lives. For 3 consecutive years—long before it became fashionable to do so—Honda sponsored a multimillion-dollar advertising effort to persuade drivers to use their seat belts. The company placed ads designed to convince drivers of the importance of seat belts in saving lives on television and in print media.

Responsible corporate citizenship took another form as well. By 1980, with the desire to manufacture products in the market in which they are sold, Honda began work on a new automobile plant in Marysville, Ohio. The decision posed both problems and opportunities. Research indicated that prospective buyers might perceive an Ohio-built Honda as inferior to one made in Japan. However, many Americans who felt uncomfortable buying an imported car would now consider buying an Accord built in the United States.

Honda decided to use advertising and marketing campaigns to help sell the idea of its Ohio-made cars. These campaigns described the contribution that Honda

was making to the U.S. economy (see Exhibit C). The company also ran a series of ads in key business publications, such as *The Wall Street Journal*, emphasizing the quality of Ohio-built Accords.

When the Marysville plant opened in November 1982, the Honda state of mind had been successfully imported to Ohio. Impartial road tests gave the American-built Accord and the imported Accord equal marks on fit, finish, and overall quality. Moreover, Honda began to implement a new five-part strategy for the future of Honda's operations in the United States, which called for Honda's total manufacturing involvement in this country to reach $1.7 billion. The recently completed manufacturing plant in nearby East Liberty, Ohio, is now producing Civic 4-door sedans at a rate of 150,000 per year. Other facets of the strategy called for an increase of research and developmental activities, the expansion of production engineering, the increase of domestic content in American made Hondas to 75 percent, and the export of U.S.-built Honda products.

By the end of the 1990 many of these goals had been reached. The Marysville plant was operating ahead of capacity, producing over 360,000 cars per year, and Honda was selling more American-built cars than imported cars in the United States. The Anna, Ohio engine facility had produced its one-millionth Honda engine. In December 1990, building off of the success of their number-one selling Accord model, Honda introduced the Accord Wagon. This vehicle was the first Honda completely designed, engineered, and manufactured in the United States.

Before the introduction of the Accord Wagon, the Accord Coupe, first introduced in 1988, had been the first Honda to be manufactured exclusively in the United States. A special edition of this Accord became the first Japanese nameplate ever exported back to Japan where it immediately became a much sought-after status symbol among the upwardly-mobile Japanese. In 1991 Honda planned to export 70,000 automobiles to Japan and other countries. The new Accord Wagon was the first U.S. built Japanese car to be exported to Europe, where Honda sold about 5,000 units in 1991.

The automotive market of the '90s has changed dramatically. The selling environment for automobiles has become increasingly difficult. There has been a proliferation of the number of car models that compete within Honda's core volume segments. American manufacturers are producing automobiles that are now approaching the quality levels of the Japanese brands. In this new, dynamic sales environment, Honda's advertising effort has quietly evolved to respond to the demands of the '90s marketplace.

The role of Honda national advertising is to continue to maintain the positive image of the brand. To make Honda brand advertising efforts more effective, Rubin Postaer and Associates, Los Angeles now includes planning in its development process to glean additional insight to the consumer. This insight is used to help develop ad programs that are extremely effective in talking to the consumer. This has helped make successful introductory campaigns for new Honda products such as the all-new 1994 Accord and the sport/utility vehicle, the Passport (see Exhibit D).

On the retail level, Honda consolidated its dealer association advertising, formerly done by 51 separate regional agencies, with RPA in a new agency named *RP alpha*. This unified effort helps Honda provide a consistent retail image while continuing to support its overall brand/model image strategies. With this new organiza-tion, Honda regional dealer advertising works in concert with the Honda national image effort. This move effectively focuses Honda's advertising effort on breaking through the clutter and boosting overall image and sales with a single voice.

From the beginning, perhaps the key factor in Honda's success has been consistency. Honda products have consistently been of the highest quality and value, and they have continued to evolve in terms of engineering innovations, performance, styling, and comfort. Throughout the years Honda has also maintained a consistent image through its advertising and marketing. Honda advertising has always appealed to the intelligence and common sense of its customers. Consistently clever and subtle, often lighthearted and whimsical, but always honest and confident, Honda's advertising treats the buying public with respect by presenting a message that allows consumers to think for themselves and draw their own conclusions.

Exhibit D

Introducing the Passport from Honda. It's the one with a 175-horsepower V-6 engine. It's the one with four-wheel drive. It's the one on top.

The Passport HONDA

Honda's advertising created by Rubin Postaer and Associates, has received high praise from industry authorities. A commercial for the 1990 Accord called "Art Gallery" (see Exhibit E) emulated the engineering magic that allowed Fred Astaire to dance on the ceiling in the movie *Royal Wedding*. In this sport, a new Accord is driven off the wall of a museum with the line, "You have to drive it to believe it," as the only copy. *Adweek* advertising critic Barbara Lippert stated, "Rubin Postaer endows Honda with another masterpiece." She went on to say that, "Since 1980 few things have been as consistently engaging as Honda commercials. Honda spots are thinking people's car commercials; they're clever, beautifully shot, and never obvious."

This praise was, perhaps, best summed up by automotive expert Chris Cedergren, who said, "Honda's strength is in the fact that they don't radically change their advertising every 6 months like others do. Honda definitely won't tamper with success."

Sources: Adapted from "The Honda Way: The Marketing of Honda Automobiles in America." (Courtesy of Sanford Edelstein, Rubin Postaer and Associates.)

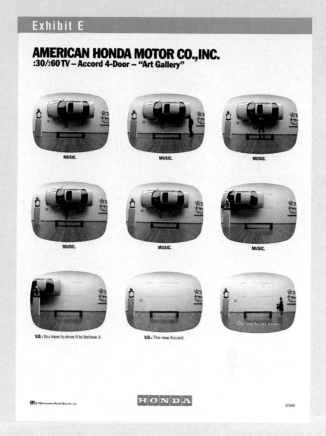

Exhibit E

AMERICAN HONDA MOTOR CO.,INC.
:30/:60 TV – Accord 4-Door – "Art Gallery"

Questions for Discussion

1. What themes in Honda's advertising and marketing reflect what you know of social needs and issues in the 1990s?

2. What advertising strategy could be used to position Honda cars in a more competitive market during the 1990s? How can Honda reach the desired audience for these cars?

$\mathcal{T}$HE CONSUMER AUDIENCE

CHAPTER OBJECTIVES

When you have completed this chapter, you should be able to:

- Understand the different factors that affect the responses of consumers to advertisements

- Define the concept of culture and subculture as it applies to advertising and consumers

- Distinguish between psychographics and demographics and explain how advertisers use each

- Relate such concepts as family, reference groups, race, and VALS to the practice of advertising

FINDING THE RIGHT MAN

The macho man, like the sexy blond, is nearing extinction on the advertising landscape. But even after being sensitized to sexual stereotypes, Madison Avenue hasn't quite decided who should replace him.

Lately advertisers seem to fire more random shots than ever as they struggle with what kind of man to depict in trying to appeal to regular guys. A peculiar set of fellows is turning up in commercials: from hypernurturing single dads to goofy, tongue-tied bachelors to even artistic "animals."

Hulk Hogan, the huge and well-sculpted professional wrestler, was captured painting a sunset at the beach in a spot for Right Guard antiperspirant. Such an oddball creative tactic may be comic inspiration—but it also crystallizes the confusion. Pat Cunningham, creative director of Ayer New York, which created the ad, says the Right Guard campaign, called "Animals," casts well-known tough guys in uncharacteristic poses to reach a "rough-and-tumble audience" of men. "Even animals have to go out in polite society," he says. "We wanted to show that even Hulk Hogan is a sensitive human being underneath."

Some marketing experts say one problem is trying to divide the male population into just two extremes—the sensitive, enlightened nonsexist nice guy and the girl-watching, sports-talking Joe Sixpack. Another dilemma: Women still buy many of the products used by men, and so the main message must appeal to them as well.

And so advertisers must tiptoe along a tightrope. For example, Bain de Soleil and Coppertone have introduced sport lotions, another attempt to woo men and broaden the appeal of their products beyond sunbathers. Coppertone's ads feature a muscular man riding a bicycle, believing that traditional male beefcake is the way to go. Another industry that is following this same approach is the men's underwear market. The singer Marky Mark is to underwear sales what actress/model Brooke Shields once was to jeans sales. Flexing his muscles or grabbing his crotch, Marky Mark is featured both alone and with nubile model Kate Moss.

At the other extreme, even venerable Old Spice after-shave is changing. In the old ads, "Mariner Man" cruises through port, whistling a familiar jingle and attracting stares from lovely lasses. As he escorts one away, he tosses an Old Spice bottle to an envious nerd. The new ad kept the basic plot intact, set the scene at the beach—and got rid of the nerd. The woman supposedly is attracted to the man for who he is, not some magic potion.

Simon Silvestor, an agency account director, made the following observation about the "Man or Caveman" controversy. "During research men will spout all kinds of stuff. When a woman leads an automobile focus group, men talk about wanting safety features and leg room. But when a man leads the discussion, it's 'I just want something I can accelerate at traffic lights.' A lot of men are going in for this New Man image, but deep down they're all alike."[1]

---

[1] Adapted from Laura Bird, "Madison Avenue Stalks Today's Archetypal Male," *The Wall Street Journal* (March 5, 1992):B1, B7; Pat Sloan, "Underwear Wants to be Outgoing," *Advertising Age* (February 8, 1993):6; Kathleen Deveny, "Seeking Sunnier Sales, Lotion Makers Play on Fears, Target Teens and Men," *The Wall Street Journal* (May 24, 1991):B1, B3.

CONSUMER BEHAVIOR

The confusion around the man of the 1990s is not unique. Marketers are confused about women, children, the elderly, and minorities, to name but a few. Old Spice and Right Guard are no more sure of their depiction than Delta Airlines is of their portrayal of "supermom." Understanding the behavior of customers to the best of your ability is the goal of any successful business.

The goal of advertising is to persuade the consumer to do something, usually to purchase a product. If advertising is to attract and communicate to audiences in a way that produces this desired result, advertisers must first understand their audiences. They must acquaint themselves with consumers' ways of thinking, with those factors that motivate them, and with the environment in which they live.

This difficult task is further complicated by the fact that the elements advertisers must take into account are constantly changing. Information that is appropriate to consumers today is often invalid tomorrow. Furthermore, advertisers must appeal to a complex consumer audience that is affected by many factors. In other words, the breadth of coverage is challenging. Advertisers must draw on input available from fields such as psychology, anthropology, and sociology to learn all they need to know about people.

Furthermore, there will be exceptions to every pattern or behavior. It is important to be prepared for these exceptions but not to assume that they negate the observed pattern. Finally, as target markets get larger and businesses move into other countries, finding general patterns of consumer behavior will become more difficult because each culture must be assessed separately.

In this chapter we will restrict our coverage to the specific behaviors people engage in as consumers. At the same time, we recognize that a great deal of what a person does outside the role of consumer is also relevant to advertising.

THE CONSUMER AUDIENCE

consumers People who buy or use products.

Consumers are people who buy or use products in order to satisfy needs and wants. There are actually two types of consumers: those who shop for and purchase the product, and those who actually use the product. This distinction is important because the two groups can have different needs and wants. In the case of children's cereals, for example, parents (the purchasers) look for nutritional value, whereas children (the users) look for a sweet taste and a game on the back of the package. Have you ever noticed that many cereals are advertised as *both* fun and "low sugar"? Because of the consumer orientation in marketing, consumer behavior is a very important field. Companies need to understand how consumers think and make decisions about products. In order to do this they conduct sophisticated research into consumer behavior. Companies must know who their consumers are, why they buy, what they buy, and how they go about buying certain products. (Consumer research will be discussed in Chapter 6.)

Principle

Marketers look at people as consumers who buy products; advertisers look at people as an audience for messages.

Figure 5.1 depicts a general model of consumer behavior, including the most relevant components and the relationship between these variables. It serves as the framework for this chapter.

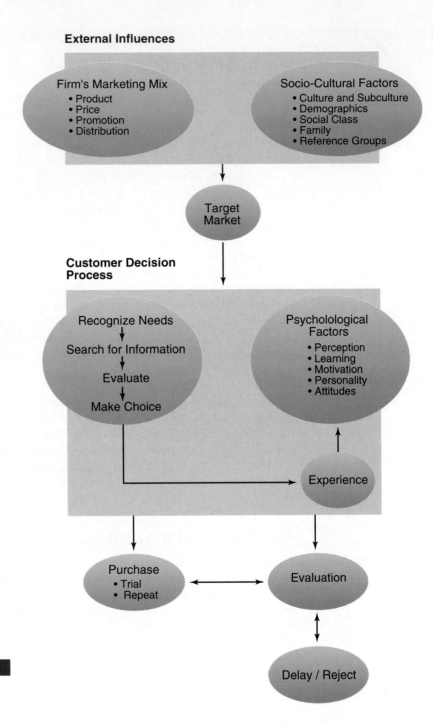

External Influences

Firm's Marketing Mix
• Product
• Price
• Promotion
• Distribution

Socio-Cultural Factors
• Culture and Subculture
• Demographics
• Social Class
• Family
• Reference Groups

Target Market

Customer Decision Process

Recognize Needs
↓
Search for Information
↓
Evaluate
↓
Make Choice

Psycholological Factors
• Perception
• Learning
• Motivation
• Personality
• Attitudes

Experience

Purchase
• Trial
• Repeat

Evaluation

Delay / Reject

Figure 5.1

A model of consumer decision making.

MARKET SEGMENTATION/TARGET MARKETING

The advertising manager is responsible for answering many questions about the consumer or industrial customer. This would be an insurmountable task without the framework provided by market segmentation. Kotler and Armstrong define *market segmentation* as the process of dividing a market into distinct groups of buyers who might require separate products or marketing mixes.[2] Market segmentation divides potential consumers of a particular product into several submarkets or segments, each of which tends to share one or more significant characteristics.

For example, a 1993 study commissioned by MasterCard International identified five different primary shopping types:

- Price Hounds (22 percent), who are constantly searching for the lowest price
- Low-Interest Shoppers (22 percent), who typically do not find shopping exciting
- Brand Bargain Hunters (20 percent), who still cling to the status of brand names of the 1980s, but also seek out good buys
- Quality Service Enthusiasts (19 percent), who expect high levels of service
- Disenchanted Shoppers (17 percent), who have largely given up on finding shopping an enjoyable experience, while admitting that making shopping facilities more comfortable would help.[3]

As this example illustrates, segmentation enables organizations to design a marketing strategy that matches the market's needs and wants. Advertising, in particular, can be more focused. However, most firms do not have the capabilities to market their product effectively to all viable segments, so they select one or more target markets from the available market segments. The *target market* is a group of people (segment) who are most likely to respond favorably to what the marketer has to offer.

Market segments and target market(s) are based on the consumer characteristics and behaviors discussed in this chapter. (A more complete list of characteristics and behaviors is shown in Table 5.1.) A market segment can be based on geography (domestic versus foreign), usage level of the product (heavy versus light), brand loyalty (disloyal versus highly loyal), and type of customer (ultimate user versus business user or industrial user). There are a great many characteristics that can be used to separate people into segments and target markets.

The segmentation process begins after the advertiser understands how and why the consumer generally thinks, feels, and behaves in a particular manner. Only then can the advertiser design a campaign that will effectively reach the fade-resistant laundry detergent market, the premium ice cream market, or the frequent business traveler market.

$\mathscr{I}$NFLUENCES ON YOU AS A CONSUMER

Your responses to an advertising message are affected by many factors. Study yourself. You are going to be the subject of our field research for this chapter.

---

[2]Philip Kotler and Gary Armstrong, *Marketing: An Introduction*, 2nd ed. (Englewood Cliffs, NJ: Prentice Hall, 1990):203.
[3]"Shopping Still a 'Favorite' Pastime," *Promo* (February 1993):52.

Table 5.1

Major Segmentation Variables for
Consumer Markets

Variable	Typical Breakdowns
Geographic	
Region	Pacific, Mountain, West North Central, West South Central, East North Central, East South Central, South Atlantic, Middle Atlantic, New England
County size	A, B, C, D
City size	Under 5,000; 5,000–20,000; 20,000–50,000; 50,000–100,000; 100,000–250,000; 250,000–500,000; 500,000–1,000,000; 1,000,000–4,000,000; 4,000,000 or over
Density	Urban, suburban, rural
Climate	Northern, southern
Demographic	
Age	Under 6, 6–11, 12–19, 20–34, 35–49, 50–64, 65+
Sex	Male, Female
Family size	1–2, 3–4, 5+
Family life cycle	Young, single; young, married, no children; young, married, youngest child under 6; young married, youngest child 6 or over; older, married, with children; older, married, no children under 18; older, single; other
Income	Under $10,000; $10,000–$15,000; $15,000–20,000; $20,000–30,000; $30,000–$50,000; $50,000 and over
Occupation	Professional and technical; managers, officials, and proprietors; clerical, sales; craftsmen, foremen; operatives; farmers; retired; students; homemakers; unemployed
Education	Grade school or less; some high school; high school graduate; some college; college graduate
Religion	Catholic, Protestant, Jewish, other
Race	White, black, Asian, Hispanic
Nationality	American, British, French, German, Scandinavian, Italian, Latin American, Middle Eastern, Japanese
Psychographic	
Social class	Lower lowers, upper lowers, working class, middle class, upper middles, lower uppers, upper uppers
Lifestyle	Belongers, achievers, integrateds
Personality	Compulsive, gregarious, authoritarian, ambitious
Behavioristic	
Purchase occasion	Regular occasion, special occasion
Benefits sought	Quality, service, economy
User status	Nonuser, ex-user, potential user, first-time user, regular user
User rate	Light user, medium user, heavy user
Loyalty status	None, medium, strong, absolute
Readiness stage	Unaware, aware, informed, interested, desirous, intending to buy
Attitude toward product	Enthusiastic, positive, indifferent, negative, hostile

Source: Philip Kotler and Gary Armstrong, Marketing: An Introduction, 3rd ed. (Englewood Cliffs, NJ: Prentice Hall, 1993):191.

You are a product of the culture and the society in which you were raised. Many of your values and opinions were shaped by your social environment. Likewise, you are a product of the family in which you were raised, and many of your habits and biases were developed within the family environment.

You are also an individual. As you matured and began to think for yourself, you developed your own individual way of looking at the world, based on such factors as your age, income, sex, education, occupation, and race. Deep within you are factors that influence every decision you make—such things as how you perceive events and other people, how you learn from experience, your basic set of attitudes and opinions, your internal drive and motivation, and the whole bundle of characteristics called your "personality."

CULTURAL AND SOCIAL INFLUENCES

cultural and social influences The forces that other people exert on your behavior.

culture The complex whole of tangible items, intangible concepts, and social behaviors that define a group of people or a way of life.

norms Simple rules for behavior that are established by cultures.

values The source for norms, which are not tied to specific objects or behaviors.

The forces that other people exert on your behavior are called **cultural and social influences.** They can be grouped into four major areas: (1) culture, (2) social class, (3) reference groups, and (4) family.

Culture. **Culture** is defined as a complex of tangible items (art, literature, buildings, furniture, clothing, and music) called *material culture*, along with intangible concepts (knowledge, laws, morals, and customs) that together define a group of people or a way of life. The concepts, values, and behaviors that make up a culture are learned and passed on from one generation to the next. The boundaries each culture establishes for behavior are called **norms**. Norms are simple rules that we learn through social interaction that specify or prohibit certain behaviors.

Customs are overt modes of behavior that constitute culturally approved ways of behaving in specific situations. For example, taking one's mother out for dinner and buying her presents on Mother's Day is an American custom that Hallmark and other card companies support enthusiastically. However, customs do vary from region to region and from country to country. For example, a weekend getaway (see Ad 5.1) is a custom adopted by many American couples who have the income to escape.

The source for norms is our **values**. An example of a value is personal security. Possible norms expressing this value range from bars on the window and double-locked doors in Brooklyn, New York, to unlocked cars and homes in Eau Claire, Wisconsin. Values are few in number and are not tied to specific objects or situations. For several decades researchers have attempted to identify *core values* that characterize an entire culture. One simplified list consists of nine core values: (1) a sense of belonging, (2) excitement, (3) fun and enjoyment in life, (4) warm relationships, (5) self-fulfillment, (6) respect from others, (7) a sense of accomplishment, (8) security, and (9) self-respect. Advertisers often refer to core values when selecting their primary appeals. Because values are so closely tied to human behavior, private research firms attempt to monitor values and look for groupings of values and behavioral patterns. Values are discussed in more detail later in the chapter. Ad 5.2 reports on a research study sponsored by *Good Housekeeping* magazine, titled "Family Values in the '90s."

Cultural influences have broad effects on buying behavior. For example, the busy working mother of today is not as devoted to meal preparation and household cleaning as was the full-time homemaker of the past. Food marketers have changed their promotional strategies to reach these women, and we now see more advertising for fast foods, convenience foods, and restaurants.

To see what a weekend at Residence Inn can do for the average couple, fold here.

Our Weekend Getaway rates will bring the two of you closer together. Because Residence Inn by Marriott has everything you need. Free continental breakfast, a full kitchen, even a fireplace in some rooms.

A cultural trend prevalent in the United States for the last decade or so has been eating low-calorie, low-fat foods in order to be slim or for good health. As noted in the Concepts and Applications box on page 170, this pattern seems to be changing.

How does culture affect you as a consumer? Can you think of any cultural factors that influence your behavior? How about patriotism and sacrificing for the good of others? Can you see yourself signing up for the Peace Corps? How about materialism? How do you feel about acquiring possessions and making money?

Subcultures A culture can be divided into *subcultures* on the basis of geographic regions or human characteristics such as age, values, or ethnic background. More specific criteria have also been suggested: (1) an economic system, or the way in which benefits are distributed; (2) social institutions, or participation in an identified institution; (3) belief systems, which include religious and political affiliations; (4) aesthetics, or art, music, dance, drama, and folklore; and (5) language, including dialects, accents, and vocabulary.

In the United States, for example, we have many different subcultures: teenagers, college students, retirees, southerners, Texans, blacks, Hispanics,

THE NEW TRADITIONALIST FAMILY.

ITS STRUCTURE MAY BE CHANGING,
BUT ITS STRENGTH IS NOT.

Here's the traditional family portrait–circa 1993. Sandra Manzke, a single mother and successful business woman, and six boys between 12 and 16. Two are her own. Four were added when Sandra became engaged to their father, who recently died. They're still close. They still spend weekends with her and her boys.

It may sound confusing, but anyone who has seen them ski together, play together, or just hang around the house together will never doubt that this is "family" in every sense of the word.

They're living proof that family values are as strong as ever, even though the family "structure" is changing.

We found overwhelming evidence of that fact in the latest Good Housekeeping/Roper survey: "Family Values in the '90s." We asked over 1,500 parents and children about their life, their family, their values.

The study reveals the highest level of optimism about the family and family values that we have seen in ten years. Obviously that's good news for Good Housekeeping. For four generations, Good Housekeeping – the Magazine, the Institute, and the Seal – have been dedicated to the values of the American family.

For a copy of Good Housekeeping's "Family Values in the '90s" study – contact your Good Housekeeping account manager.

AMERICA BELIEVES IN GOOD HOUSEKEEPING

Ad 5.2

This ad addresses the change in traditional American families.

(Courtesy of Good Housekeeping)

athletes, musicians, and working single mothers, to list just a few. Within subcultures there are similarities in people's attitudes and secondary values.

What subcultures do you belong to? Look at your activities. Do you do anything on a regular basis that might identify you as a member of a distinctive subculture?

social class A way to categorize people on the basis of their values, attitudes, lifestyles, and behavior.

Social Class. A **social class** is the position that you and your family occupy within your society. Social class is determined by such factors as income, wealth, education, occupation, family prestige, value of home, and neighborhood.

Every society has some social class structure. In a rigid society you are not allowed to move out of the class into which you were born. In the United States we like to think we have a classless society because it is possible for us to move into a different class regardless of what social class our parents belonged to. However, even in the United States we speak of an upper class, a middle class, and a lower class.

Marketers assume that people in one class buy different goods from different outlets and for different reasons than people in other classes. Advertisers can

Fat Is Fun

If you are tired of going to the supermarket and seeing hundreds of processed foods labeled "light," "healthy," "low fat," and "sodium free," take heart and check out some of the newer offerings. Many sport lite-free names such as Chocolate Macadamia, Cookie Dough Dynamo, or Roasted Honey Nut. Health claims? Forget it. Examine the ingredients of Häagen-Daz Co.'s new Triple Brownie Overload ice cream, and you find a catalog of everything that makes life worth living: fresh cream, sugar, chocolate liquor, butter, pecans, egg yolks. Oh, yes—there's skim milk, too.

Is fat back? Ever cagey, marketers aren't openly urging consumers to pig out anew. But in ads and labels, words such as "real" and "rich" are popping up more often. Says Lawrena K. Hathaway, president of the Best Foods grocery-products division at CPC International Inc., "There is definitely a trend toward the full-flavored foods." Full flavor often means plenty of salt, sugar, and fat. CPC's new Roasted Honey Nut Skippy peanut butter has more than 4 percent of the market. The six rich new ice creams launched in Häagen-Daz's "Exträas" line have increased the company's dollar share of the ice cream market from 5.9 percent to 7.9 percent. Overall, Häagen-Daz's ice creams outsell its better-for-you frozen yogurt 13 to 1.

So why is fat regaining favor? Call it a sign of nervous times. "In a period of increasing stress, consumers are placing emphasis on comfort foods," says Judith Langer, president of Judith Langer Associates, a New York market research firm. The sight of President Clinton chowing down at McDonald's probably helps, too. And after a decade of grimly gnawing at health foods, many are yearning for the real thing. "If I eat something I can't enjoy, like all this light stuff, then why eat anything at all?" says Stephen Bookspan, 23-year-old owner of Cartoon Saloon, a Manhattan bar.

True, marketers are hardly abandoning low-fat or low-cholesterol foods. After all, the market is now worth an estimated $12 billion, according to Packaged Facts, Inc., a New York research firm. But more and more companies are busy stocking the larder with richer fare to lure the shoppers who have seen the "lite"— and didn't like it.

Source: Adapted from Sunita Wadekar Bhargava, "Gimme a Double Shake and a Lard on White," *Business Week* (March 11, 1993):59; Kathy Tyrer, "Weight-Loss Marketers Go on Spending Binge," *Adweek*, (January 10, 1994):8; Johny E. Calfee, "FTC's Hidden Weight-Loss Ad Agenda," *Advertising Age*, (Oct. 25, 1993):29.

get a feel for the social class of a target market by using marketing research or available census data.

In what class do you see yourself? Does social class affect what you buy and how you respond to advertising? Do you know people you would consider to be upper- or lower-class? Do they buy different products than you do? Do they look at products differently in terms of price or quality?

REFERENCE GROUPS

reference group A group of people that a person uses as a guide for behavior in specific situations.

A **reference group** is a collection of people that you use as a guide for behavior in specific situations. General examples of reference groups are political parties, religious groups, racial or ethnic organizations, clubs based on hobbies, and informal affiliations such as fellow workers or students.

For consumers, reference groups have three functions: (1) they provide information; (2) they serve as a means of comparison; and (3) they offer guidance. Sometimes the group norms have the *power* to require the purchase or use of certain products (uniforms, safety equipment). The reference group members may be so *similar* to you that you believe that any product or service the group members use is right for you too. Ads that feature typical users in fun or pleasant surroundings are using a reference-group strategy. You also may be *attracted* to a particular reference group and wish to be like the members of that group

The proliferation of fast-food restaurants is an example of the influence of culture on consumer behavior.

(Courtesy of Dennie Cody/FPG)

family Two or more people who are related by blood, marriage, or adoption and live in the same household.

household All those people who occupy one living unit, whether or not they are related.

lifestyle The pattern of living that reflects how people allocate their time, energy, and money.

out of respect or admiration. Advertisers use celebrity endorsements to tap into this desire.

Think about all the groups you belong to, both formal and informal. Why do you belong to these groups? How do other members influence you or keep you informed? Have you ever bought anything specifically because it was required by a group you belonged to?

Family. A **family** consists of two or more people who are related by blood, marriage, or adoption and live in the same household. A **household** differs from a family in that it consists of all those who occupy a living unit, whether they are related or not.

Your family is critical to how you develop as an individual. It provides two kinds of resources for members: *economic*, such as money and possessions; and *emotional*, such as empathy, love, and companionship. The family is also responsible for raising and training children and establishing a lifestyle for family members. Your **lifestyle** determines how you spend your time and money and the kinds of activities you value.

It is important for advertisers to understand the structure and workings of the family. For example, the U.S. family structure is changing because of an increase in divorces, later marriages, one-parent and two-family households, and other alternative family systems. (These changing family structures are discussed in more detail later in the chapter.) Advertisers must create messages that appeal to the needs and lifestyles of these consumers. A family's purchase and consumption patterns offer some interesting challenges as well. For instance, most families have members, such as parents, who screen and evaluate product information. Other members, such as children, strongly influence which product or brand is purchased, although they are not necessarily the actual decision makers. The family is our most important reference group because of its longevity and intensity. Other reference groups, such as peers, coworkers, and neighbors, tend to change as we age and switch occupations or residency. Advertisers respond to the family in various ways. As reflected in Anheuser-Busch's advertisement (Ad 5.3), manufacturers—whose products are sometimes abused—should advertise their products in a careful and sensitive manner.

WHEN IT COMES TO TEACHING YOUR CHILDREN ABOUT RESPONSIBLE DRINKING, YOU ARE THE LEADING AUTHORITY.

Parents are the most influential teachers children have. Through their guidance, love and encouragement, parents have a powerful impact on the lives of their kids.

At Anheuser-Busch, we believe the sooner parents begin to teach the responsibilities of drinking, the more likely it is that kids will decide not to drink before they're of legal age—and to drink wisely, if they choose to drink, when they become adults.

With this in mind, we've developed an educational program called Family Talk About Drinking.

It features a series of informative guides written with help from prominent authorities on children, family counseling, and alcohol research.

The guides cover everything from peer pressure and recognizing teenage drinking problems to drinking and driving and the community resources available to you and your kids. For free copies, just call 1-800-359-TALK.

And start giving your children the guidance that only you can give.

LET'S STOP UNDERAGE DRINKING BEFORE IT STARTS.

Anheuser-Busch, Inc.
©1992 ANHEUSER-BUSCH·ST. LOUIS, MO

Ad 5.3

Anheuser-Busch advertises its products in a careful and sensitive manner.

(Courtesy of Anheuser-Busch, Inc.)

How has your family influenced you in your choice of schooling, lifestyle, and the way you spend your time and money? Now think about your best friend. Are the two of you different in any ways that can be traced to family differences?

PERSONAL INFLUENCES

Every consumer is a product of culture and society, social class, and family. Ultimately, however, a consumer is an individual. Individual characteristics strongly influence the way you think, decide, and behave as a consumer. These characteristics can be divided into two categories: demographic variables and psychographic variables. *Demographics* are the statistical representations of social and economic characteristics of people, including age, sex, income, occupation, and family size. In contrast, *psychographics* refer to people's psychological variables, such as attitudes, lifestyles, opinions, and personality traits.

DEMOGRAPHICS

demography The study of social and economic factors that influence human behavior.

Demography is the study of those social and economic factors that influence how you behave as an individual consumer. These factors serve as the basis for much of the advertising strategy. Knowing the age, sex, occupation, and race of the members of the target audience assists advertisers in message design and media selection.

Age. People in different stages of life have different needs. An advertising message must be understandable to the age group to which the product or service is targeted and should be delivered through a medium used by members of that group. How old are you? What products did you use five or ten years ago that you don't use now? Look ahead five or ten years—what products will you be in the market for then? What products do your parents buy that you don't? Do you read different publications and watch different programs than your parents do? If you were in the market for a car, would you look at the same features that your parents look at? In the United States several trends with respect to age have a direct bearing on advertising.

As noted in Figure 5.2, the U.S. population will continue to age, with the 65 and over age group representing our largest age group by 2030.

Baby Boomers The baby boom includes all U.S. citizens born between 1946 and 1964. During that period 76.4 million people were born in the United States of whom approximately 68 million are still alive.[4] We have already described some of the characteristics of the baby boomers in Chapter 2. Recall that the majority of baby boomers are in blue-collar occupations, and they have fallen short of reaching the American Dream. Despite having a better education, higher-paying jobs, and more family members in the work force, baby boomers are experiencing a crisis of expectations due to increasing costs and excessive competition for higher-paying jobs. Younger baby boomers (ages 29 to 37), however, are enjoying the hard work of the older members of the group. This younger

---

[4]"Growing Pains at 40," *Time* (May 19, 1986):22–41.

Age

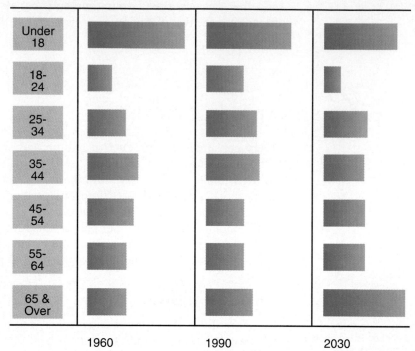

| | 1960 | 1990 | 2030 |

Figure 5.2

This bar graph shows that the percentage of people 65 and older is increasing in the United States.

Source: U.S. Census Bureau, 1990

group is somewhat smaller and has found career opportunities and job advancement to be much easier and more readily available because the older boomers have expanded the size of the job market. It is this group that has been able to obtain many of the material possessions associated with the American Dream.[5]

Other predictions about the characteristics of baby boomers in the 1990s are found in Table 5.2.

The Elderly As the baby boomers become more frustrated, the elderly market is growing in size and importance. By the turn of the century one person in eight will be 65 or older.

The importance of senior citizens to the advertiser, however, is not just the tremendous growth in their numbers. Rather, the opportunities offered by seniors are found in their differences. For instance, the "young old"—those who chose early retirement and those in their seventies—are healthier and wealthier than those who formerly filled this slot. Marketers have responded to the new elderly population by introducing a host of products that appeal to affluent, healthy people who have free time. Advertisers often portray the elderly as attractive and active. Even products difficult to advertise, such as adult diapers, have been positively portrayed through testimonials by former movie star June Allyson. In addition, several new media that are directed to the elderly have emerged. Examples are the Silver Pages directory, telemarketing, and magazines such as *Modern Maturity, New Choices,* and *Extended Vacations.*

Gender. Gender, or sex, is an obvious basis for differences in marketing advertising. When we talk about gender differences, we consider both primary and

---

[5]Alan L. Otten, "Baby Boomer People Make Less But Make Do," *The Wall Street Journal* (July 5, 1990):B1.

Table 5.2

Boomers in the 1990s

Category	Characteristics
Parents	Nearly 90 percent of Americans will have children at some time during their lives. For a huge segment of society, that time is now.
Fathers	As the new baby boomlet begins to walk, talk, and struggle with homework assignments, fathers will become more important.
The Fit	At age 40, Mark Spitz was training to swim in the 1992 Olympics. He's not alone. While most baby boomers won't try out for the Olympics, they will join him in a passionate battle against aging.
The Un-Fit	Beyond age 40, serious health problems become much more common. The number of people with chronic diseases should increase sharply with the aging of the baby boom in the 1990s.
Downscale	The pendulum of public concern is swinging back in favor of helping the poor and near-poor. We may even see a redefinition of poverty, which increases the size of the downscale segment.
Upscale	With the baby-boom generation entering its peak earning years, the number of affluent households will grow. But they won't necessarily feel rich or spend lavishly, because most Americans identify with the middle class no matter how upscale their income.
Workers	At 66 percent, the share of the population in the paid labor force is greater today than ever before in our history. Businesses can profit by helping workers balance work and home life.
Entrepreneurs	There are too many baby boomers for the few top spots in America's companies. The consequence will be new businesses started by frustrated employees, more self-employment, more moonlighting (already at a record high), more home offices, and a blurring of work and home life.
Women in charge	Over half the women who work full-time think of their work as a career rather than just a job. As career-minded baby-boom women gain in job experience, the number who control the bottom line will grow rapidly.
Housewives	Markets have fragmented, but traditional markets still exist—they've become segmented markets just like all the rest. According to recent studies, the attitudes of housewives are diverging from those of working women. These growing differences will make it easier to target the women who opt for this lifestyle.

Source: American Demographics (August 1990):2.

secondary differences. *Primary* gender differences are physical or psychological traits that are inherent to males or females. The ability to bear children is a primary female trait. *Secondary* gender traits tend to be primarily associated with one sex more than the other. Wearing perfume and shaving legs are secondary traits associated with women. The primary gender characteristics of men and women create demands for products and services directly associated with a person's sex. In the past there were many taboos regarding the marketing of such products. For example, marketers of tampons or sanitary pads were once restricted to advertising in media and retail outlets devoted strictly to women; and condoms, purchased almost exclusively by men, were behind-the-counter (or perhaps under-the-counter) items. Today these barriers have all but vanished, and primary female and male products are marketed in similar ways and in comparable media.

Marketing products related to secondary sexual characteristics has become more complicated. For example, hair, skin, and body type have long provided reliable clues to marketers. Skin-care products were the exclusive domain of women, and erotic magazines were restricted to men. Now skin-care products for men represent a $60 million market and *Playgirl* magazine is popular with women. Ad 5.4 illustrates this point.

As prevalent as this crossover effect appears, many consumers will consider certain brands masculine or feminine. It is unlikely that men would use a brand of after-shave called White Shoulders. The Gillette Company found that women would not purchase Gillette razor blades, so they introduced new brands with feminine names such as "Daisy" and "Lady Gillette." Marketers of products formerly associated with one sex who want to sell them to both sexes find it necessary to offer "his and her" brands or even different product names for the same basic goods. What products do you buy that are unisex? What products do you use that are specifically targeted to your sex?

Ad 5.4

An example of a crossover ad of a traditionally female product targeted to male consumers

(Courtesy of Clairol, Inc.)

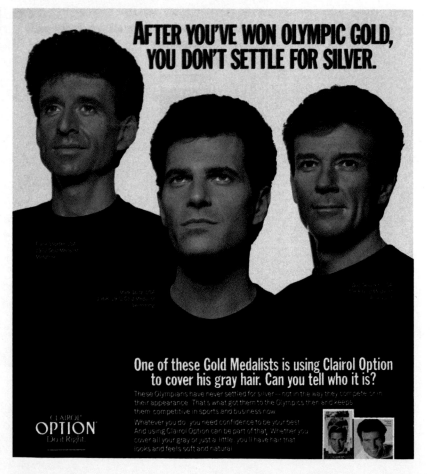

Family Status. Your purchasing patterns are affected by your family situation. People living alone buy different products, in different sizes, than do people living in families. Has your family's spending patterns changed since you went to college? Unless your parents were able to start a college fund when you were born, they have probably had to reduce their purchases of luxury items, vacations, and new cars to help send you to school.

Although the most common arrangement among U.S. families remains two parents with children, a number of alternative family arrangements have become more common. The prevalence of divorce—the number of divorces granted each year more than doubled from 1977 to 1990, although most divorces are followed by remarriage—has enlarged three other family categories: divorced with no children, single parent with children, and the blended family, or "his, hers, and ours" family with children from different marriages living together in the same home with remarried parents. Each family system has its unique problems and offers special marketing opportunities.[6] Table 5.3 depicts an interesting bit of information about people who divorce, that is, who they are most likely to remarry.

In addition, not everyone wishes to get married. According to experts, one-half of all U.S. households in 1990 included single men and women living alone.[7] However, generalizing about singles would be a mistake because they are a diverse group who experience a wide range of economic well-being and display varied spending patterns. Single people who have never married, for example, have a great deal of personal freedom and spend heavily on themselves. In contrast, divorced women with children often struggle financially and many of them represent a new poverty group. Unmarried couples who share a household (cohabitation) represent another alternative. This group, although estimated to be only 2 percent of the population, exhibits some interesting purchasing patterns. Uncertain how long their relationship will last, they are reluctant to purchase shared items and instead have duplicates of many household items (stereos, furniture, and small appliances).[8]

[6]Thomas Exter, "Look Ma, No Spouse," *American Demographics* (March 1990):63.
[7]Thomas Exter, "Alone at Home," *American Demographics* (April 1990):55.
[8]Judith Waldrop, "Living in Sin," *American Demographics* (April 1990):12.

Table 5.3

Who Remarries Whom: The most common type of remarriage unites two divorced people.*

		Brides			
		Never Married	**Divorced**	**Widowed**	**Total**
Grooms	**Never Married**	None	261,600	12,000	273,600
	Divorced	257,100	455,600	32,500	745,200
	Widowed	8,700	30,800	32,100	71,600
	Total	265,800	748,000	76,600	1,090,400

*Marriages involving at least one previously married partner, by previous marital status of each partner, 1988.
Source: Barbara Foley Wilson and Sally Cunningham Clark, "Remarriages: A Demographic Profile," Journal of Family Issues (June 1992).

The final factor strongly affecting the American family is the increase in the number of women in the work force. More than half of all women between the ages of 15 and 64 now work outside the home, and women comprise one-third of the world's work force.[9] The two-income couple has caused a substantial realignment of family spending and role responsibilities. Families with two wage earners eat out more often, own more expensive cars, take more expensive vacations, and wear more expensive clothes. Men in many of these families participate in child care, housecleaning, food shopping and preparation, and laundry responsibilities. Do both of your parents work? Do you have friends whose families are headed by only one wage earner? Do you see a difference in your lifestyles? How have your parents divided the family responsibilities?

Education. The level of education you have attained also influences your behavior as a consumer. Advertisers know they must market products differently to better-educated consumers than to the less-educated. Consumers with higher educations are often more responsive to technical-scientific appeals, prefer informative ads, and are better able to judge the relationship between the price and quality of a product. The trend toward a better-educated consumer is expected to continue through the 1990s. By the year 2000 nearly 30 percent of all Americans over age twenty-five, male and female, will have a college degree.[10]

Occupation. Most people identify themselves by what they do. Even non-wage earners such as homemakers and students identify themselves this way. There has been a gradual movement from blue-collar occupations to white-collar occupations during the last three decades. There have also been shifts within white-collar work from sales to other areas, such as professional specialty, technical, and administrative positions. Furthermore, the number of service-related jobs is expected to increase, especially in the health-care, education, and legal and business-service sectors. Much of this transition is a direct result of advanced computer technologies, which have eliminated many labor-intensive blue-collar occupations.[11] This shift has affected advertising in a number of ways. Most notably, blue-collar jobs are seldom portrayed in advertisements anymore, and ad copy tends to be more technical. Also, women are being depicted increasingly in professional roles.

You belong to the student occupational category, but you are also in training for some other profession. Why did you choose that career objective? Obviously, your decision to go to college was affected by occupational considerations, as well as by the geographical area in which you live. What other decisions have you made on the basis of your occupation or profession—either past, present, or intended?

Income. You are only meaningful to a marketer if you have the resources to buy the product advertised. That means you must possess money and credit. It also means you must have some **discretionary income**, the money available to a household after taxes and basic necessities such as food and shelter are paid for. As your total income increases, the proportion that is considered discretionary income grows at a much faster rate. Some 26 million American households are

discretionary income The money available for spending after taxes and necessities are covered.

---

[9]William B. Johnston, "Global Work Force 2000: The New World Labor Market," *Harvard Business Review* (March–April 1991):117.
[10]Judith Waldrop and Thomas Exter, "What the 1990 Census Will Show," *American Demographics* (January 1990):30.
[11]Walter Kiechel III, "How Will We Work in the Year 2000?" *Fortune* (May 17, 1993):38–52.

thought to have significant discretionary income. Although this group represents only 29 percent of all households, it receives 53 percent of all consumer income before taxes.[12]

The distribution of income among the population has a great impact on marketers. Essentially, the middle class, which represented 60 percent of U.S. households in the 1950s, is expected to decrease in the coming years. By the year 2000 only 30 percent of U.S. households will be middle class. The affluent will represent another 30 percent (compared to 10 percent in 1950), and the working class will account for the remaining 40 percent, with 20 percent of these households below the poverty level (compared to 30 percent of households in the working class in 1950, 8 percent of which were below the poverty level).[13] Clearly, the rich are getting richer and the poor are getting poorer. Thus, the bulk of demand in the 1990s will be for both premium products and low-end, no-frills items.[14]

Can you think of any product that you wanted to buy recently but could not afford? Do you have a "wish list" of purchases you would like to make "someday"?

Race and Ethnicity. The United States has long been considered the "melting pot" of the world—an image implying that the diverse peoples who have settled here have adopted the same basic values and norms. This idea is probably less true than most people imagine. Race and ethnic background might not influence the consumer behavior of most white Anglo-Saxon Americans, simply because such considerations are not very important in their daily lives. However, there is evidence that this group actually has a strong tendency to adopt the tastes of others. Witness the tremendous growth in the consumption of ethnic foods, especially Mexican, Chinese, Thai, Indian, and Vietnamese cuisines.

According to the 1990 Census, blacks remain the largest minority group, representing 12 percent of the population, the same percentage as in 1980. Hispanics represent 8 percent, a 3 percent increase since 1980, and their numbers are expected to grow even faster during the 1990s. Asians and other races represent only 3 percent of the total population, but this is a 65 percent increase since 1980. (See Table 5.4.)

A consumer survey conducted by Impact Resources of Columbus, Ohio, compared Asian consumers in four metropolitan areas in California with American consumers in general. The results showed that 54 percent of Asian Americans shop as a leisure activity compared with 50 percent of the general population. Asians also rank quality higher than price in choosing a store. Moreover, the survey indicated that Asian Americans are more comfortable with technology than is the general population. They are more likely to use automated teller machines and to own VCRs, CD players, microwave ovens, home computers, and telephone answering machines.[15]

Racial and ethnic identities affect both self-image and consumer behavior of nonwhites and people with strong ethnic backgrounds. This is a complex area, however, because race and ethnicity are difficult to separate from such factors as family, language, and reference groups. For example, although in the United States we use the label "Hispanic" to identify members of many different ethnic groups, members of these groups do not identify with this umbrella term, but

[12]Bickley Townsend, "This Is Fun Money," *American Demographics* (October 1989):39–41.
[13]Betsy Sharkey, "The Chameleon Decade" *Adweek*: Marketing to the Year 2000 (September 11, 1989):32.
[14]The government's definition of poverty, as of 1990, is an income of $13,359 or less for a family of four.

Table 5.4

A Population Shift

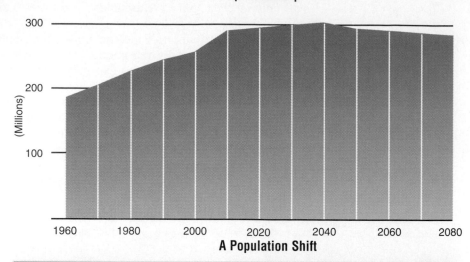

A Population Dip

A Population Shift

Group	1990	2040	2080
		(Percent of Total Population)	
White*	84.1	76.9	72.6
Black	12.4	15.3	16.3
Other†	3.5	7.8	11.1
Over 65	12.6	22.6	24.5
Under 35	53.5	40.8	39.2

* Includes Hispanics, currently 7.5 percent of all whites.
† Mainly Asian, Pacific Islanders, and American Indians.
Source: U.S. Census Bureau.

differentiate themselves as distinct cultures. Using the same ad in the Cuban community in Miami, the Puerto Rican community in New York, and the Mexican-American community in San Antonio could therefore prove disastrous for an advertiser. A similar confusion exists for the African-American market (see Issues and Controversies box).

GEOGRAPHIC LOCATION

Knowing where people live is important to advertisers. Marketers study the sales patterns in different regions of the country to discover variations in the purchase behavior of consumers. People residing in different regions of the country have different needs for certain products or services. Someone living in the Midwest or Northeast is more likely to purchase products for removing snow and ice, for example, whereas a Floridian would be more apt to buy suntan lotion or beach attire. There are also differences between urban areas and suburban or rural areas. Swimming pools that sell well in a residential suburban neighborhood would not be very much in demand in an urban neighborhood filled with apartment buildings.

In addition, marketers analyze different markets by population and growth rates. The population of different states and regions of the country will affect the weight of advertising placed in specific areas. For example, according to the

Issues & CONTROVERSIES

Black Is Black, Or Is It?

In an effort to increase black consumer advertising, black advertising executives struggle against several misconceptions about black consumers. The two most noted are: (1) *blacks and whites can be reached in the same way*, and (2) *using an all-black cast offends white audiences.*

In 1988, Robert Pits, marketing professor at DePaul University, and his colleagues conducted a value-based study among black and white consumers. A mixed group was shown four commercials (for Ford, Crest, McDonald's, and Coca-Cola) featuring all-black casts and produced by Burrell Advertising, a black-owned firm. Overall, the research revealed: *Blacks see more* and *whites see less.*

According to the study, "What whites fail to see (is) very evident to the black audience…whites fail to realize certain social, respect, and accomplishment values present in some advertising. An important aspect of the black experience (is the) struggle for fulfillment, belonging, accomplishment and respect in a white-dominated culture."

The study also suggests that whites are not offended by all-black presentation. Whites reacted almost as positively toward the tested advertising as blacks—only the "takeaway" was different.

Pepper Miller, president of P. Hunter & Associates, a Chicago-based market research company, provides the following observations about blacks and whites:

- Blacks receive advertising more literally than white consumers.

- Blacks want copy and visuals that correspond exactly.

The Greyhound Bus Co. decided to reach out to blacks by running commercials on black radio stations. But instead of tailoring its messages to black consumers, it used the same commercials aired on other radio stations. These commercials had a country-western sound track, which is the least favored music genre among blacks.

- Blacks and whites have different preferences in taste, too. Although blacks drink less coffee than the national average, they are much more likely than other Americans to lace their coffee with large amounts of sugar, cream, or nondairy creamer. Candy, cookies, and desserts are an important part of the black diet—most people want something sweet with their meals. This is also reflected in their beverage choices, and it explains why Kool-Aid is a heavy favorite among blacks of all ages.

- Blacks want to see equal representation of themselves, particularly in health and beauty product advertising.

- Black consumers generally see themselves as having more fashion flair than white consumers.

Eugene Morris, president of E. Morris Ltd, posits that effectively advertising to blacks means embracing the values held by the black community. He notes several such factors. Language can be quite important. For example, there is an ongoing debate about the use of the terms *African-American* and *black*. While *African-American* is becoming increasingly common as a way to express ethnic pride, *black* is still used extensively and few are offended by it.

In sum, advertisers who want to maintain or strengthen sales in black markets must make a special effort to reach this market. When they succeed, the rewards will be substantial.

Sources: Adapted from Eugene Morris, "The Difference in Black and White," *American Demographics* (January 1993):44–48; Persephone Miller, "Black Viewers See More," *Advertising Age* (April 30, 1990):29.

1990 Census, the Northeast had become the least populous region of the country, whereas the South, with 87 million people, had the highest population.[16]

The 1990 Census also showed that states in the South and West accounted for nearly 90 percent of the nation's ten-year population gain. Although the Midwest was the slowest-growing region, it was still the second most populous

[16]Waldrop and Exter, "What the 1990 Census Will Show," p. 24

Table 5.5

Population and Change in
Population by Region,
1980–1990

	1990 population	1980 population	change	percent change
				1980–90
United States	249,870	226,546	23,324	10.3%
Northeast	50,911	49,135	1,776	3.6%
Midwest	59,939	58,866	1,073	1.8%
South	87,012	75,372	11,640	15.4%
West	52,008	43,172	8,836	20.5%

Source: Adapted from American Demographics (January 1990):24.

area in the nation. California gained more people than any other state—over 5 million since 1980. Texas and Florida gained more than 3 million residents each year during the 1980s, and Georgia gained over 1 million. In contrast, the populations of West Virginia, Iowa, and the District of Columbia decreased.[17] This kind of information is valuable to an advertiser in deciding where and to whom to target specific advertising messages. Table 5.5 illustrates the changes in the U.S. population from 1980 to 1990.

PSYCHOGRAPHICS

We have analyzed you as a member of social and reference groups and have looked at your personal characteristics. Now let's look at the internal elements that make you an individual. The variables that shape your inner self are referred to as your *psychological makeup.*

psychographics All the psychological variables that combine to shape our inner selves, including activities, interests, opinions, needs, values, attitudes, personality traits, decision processes, and buying behavior.

Advertisers use the term **psychographics** to refer to all the psychological variables that combine to shape our inner selves. Psychographics goes beyond demographics in attempting to explain complex behavior patterns. For example, why does one mother with a newborn infant use disposable diapers whereas another mother chooses reusable cloth diapers? And why does she use Pampers when others use generic brands or the brand for which they have a coupon? Why does one person drive a brand-new BMW, whereas a neighbor in the identical condo next door drives an old Ford?

To explain these "true" motivations for behavior, advertisers look at a variety of dimensions, including activities, interests and hobbies, opinions, needs, values, attitudes, and personality traits. Taken together, these elements give a much broader picture of a person than do demographic data.

Although hundreds of different dimensions are encompassed under *psychographics*, the areas with the most relevance to advertising are: perception, learning, motives, attitudes, personality, lifestyles, and buying behavior.

perception The process by which we receive information through our five senses and acknowledge and assign meaning to this information.

Perception. Each day you are bombarded by stimuli—faces, conversations, buildings, advertisements, news announcements—yet you actually see or hear only a small fraction. Why? The answer is perception. **Perception** is the process by which we receive information through our five senses and assign meaning to it. Perceptions are shaped by three sets of influences: the physical characteristics of the stimuli, the relation of the stimuli to their surroundings, and conditions within the individual. It is this last set of influences that makes perception a per-

[17]Ibid., p. 24.

sonal trait. Each individual perceives a given stimulus within a personal frame of reference. Factors that influence this frame of reference include learning experiences, attitudes, personality, and self-image. The process is further complicated by the fact that we are exposed to a great number of stimuli. Some of these stimuli are perceived completely, and some partially, some correctly, and some incorrectly. Ultimately, we select some stimuli and ignore others because we do not have the ability to be conscious of all incoming information at one time.

Selective Perception The process of screening out information that does not interest us and retaining information that does is called **selective perception**. Think about the route you take when driving to school every day. How many stimuli do you perceive? If you're like most people, you perceive traffic signals, what's going on in your car, other traffic, and pedestrians crossing in front of you. This is selective perception. This same process is repeated when we watch television or read a magazine. It also occurs when we look at an ad and perceive only the headline, a photograph, or a famous spokesperson. In addition to our tendency to select stimuli that are of interest to us, we also perceive stimuli in a manner that coincides with our reality. That is, your world includes your own set of experiences, values, biases, and attitudes. It is virtually impossible to separate these inherent factors from the way you perceive. For example, we naturally tend to seek out messages that are pleasant or sympathetic with our views and to avoid those that are painful or threatening. This is called **selective exposure**. Consumers tend to selectively expose themselves to advertisements that reassure them of the wisdom of their purchase decisions. Similarly, when we are exposed to a message that is different from what we believe, we engage in **selective distortion**. For example, a consumer may "hear" that an automobile gets good gas mileage, even though the salesperson has clearly indicated this is not so, because the consumer perceives other features of the car as perfect and therefore wants very much to buy it. (See Ad 5.5.)

Advertisers are interested in these selective processes because they affect whether consumers will perceive an ad and, if so, whether they will remember it. Selective perception is also strongly influenced by our attitudes toward the person, situation, and idea. If we hold a strong positive attitude toward safety, for example, we will tend to perceive messages that deal with this subject. In turn, we will tend to remember details about the message, such as product features and the brand name, when perception is intense. More will be said about attitudes later in the chapter.

Our response to a stimulus has a direct bearing on advertising. A large part of what the brain processes is lost after only an instant. Even when we try very hard to retain information, we are unable to save a lot of it. **Selective retention** describes the process we go through in trying to "save" information for future use. Advertising can facilitate this process by using repetition, easily remembered brand or product names, jingles, high-profile spokespeople, music, and so forth. Its ability to stimulate and assist the consumer in selective retention often determines the success of an individual ad. For instance, Table 5.6 shows that the way we perceive a simple communication device, such as typeface in a product's logo, can influence our opinions about quality, value, and so on.

Cognitive Dissonance Another possible response to selective perception is a feeling of dissatisfaction or doubt. Seldom does a purchase produce all the expected positive results. According to the theory of **cognitive dissonance**, we tend to compensate or justify the small or large discrepancy between what we

selective perception The process of screening out information that does not interest us and retaining information that does.

selective exposure The ability to process only certain information and avoid other stimuli.

selective distortion The interpretation of information in a way that is consistent with the person's existing opinion.

selective retention The process of remembering only a small portion of what a person is exposed to.

cognitive dissonance A tendency to justify the discrepancy between what a person receives relative to what he or she expected to receive.

Perception.

Reality.

To a new generation of Rolling Stone readers, pigs live on farms. You'll find the cops living in Beverly Hills or on Hill Street, now heralded instead of hated. If you're looking for an 18 to 34 year old market that is taking active part instead of active protest, you'll have a riot in the pages of Rolling Stone.

Ad 5.5

This classic ad for *Rolling Stone* illustrates our tendency to distort.

(Courtesy of Rolling Stone)

Principle

An ad will be perceived only if it is relevant to the consumer.

actually received and what we perceived we would receive. Research on this phenomenon has shown that people engage in a variety of activities to reduce dissonance.[18] Most notably, they seek out information that supports their decision and they ignore or distort information that does not. Advertising can play a central role in reducing dissonance. For example, car manufacturers anticipate where dissonance is likely to occur and provide supportive information, IBM uses testimonials by satisfied customers, and restaurants include discount coupons with their print ads.

The next time you watch television, study yourself as you view the ads. What do you select to pay attention to? Why? When do you "tune out"? Why? Did you find yourself disagreeing with a message or arguing with it? Can you see how your own selection processes influence your attention and response to advertising?

Learning. Perception leads to learning—that is, we cannot learn something unless we have accurately perceived the information and attached some meaning to it. Because people often associate attempts at learning with formal education, they tend to think of it as a conscious, deliberate, tedious, and painful process. In fact, learning is typically an unconscious activity; consumers don't usually even know when it's happening. It does happen, however, starting early in life and continuing throughout. If advertisers understand how learning takes place, they can design ads to optimize the learning of the key elements in the ad, such as brand name, location, product features, price, and so forth. Understanding how learning takes place is important for other reasons as well.

---

[18]Leon Festinger, *A Theory of Cognitive Dissonance* (Evanston, IL: Row, Peterson, 1957):83.

Table 5.6

Meanings Conveyed by Type
Style

	Highest Quality	Best for Recording Music	Poorest Value	Preference
A. MEMOREX	1st	2nd	5th	2nd
B. Memorex	5th	5th	3rd	5th
C. **MEMOREX**	3rd	3rd	1st	3rd
D. *Memorex*	4th	4th	2nd	4th
E. memorex	2nd	1st	4th	1st

*Source: D.L. Masten, "Logo's Power Depends on How Well It Communicates with Target Market,"
Marketing News (December 5, 1988):20.*

Most notably, we can learn different attitudes, beliefs, preferences, values, and standards, all of which may lead to changes in purchase behavior. As you might recall from our discussion on corrective advertising in Chapter 2, occasionally we learn something so well, such as "Listerine prevents colds," that we cannot unlearn it.

Cognitive Learning Various theories have been developed to explain different aspects of learning. Typically, two schools of learning are considered. The first is called the *cognitive* school. Cognitive interpretations emphasize the discovery of patterns and insight. Cognitive theorists stress the importance of perception, problem-solving, and insight. They contend that most learning occurs not as a result of trial-and-error or practice but of discovering meaningful patterns that enable people to solve problems. These meaningful patterns are called "gestalts," and cognitive theories of learning rely heavily on the process of insight to explain the development of gestalts. This is comparable to the "ah ha" effect that occurs when we finally figured out how calculus worked.

When confronted with a problem, we sometimes see the solution instantly. More often we need to search for information, carefully evaluate what we learn, and make a decision. Cognitive learning characterizes people as problem solvers who go through a complex process of mentally processing information. Advertisers employing this perspective concentrate on the role of motivation in decision making and the mental processing consumers do when making decisions.

Connectionists The second school of learning, the connectionists, argues that people learn connections between stimuli and responses. The connectionists school is further divided into classical conditioning and instrumental conditioning. Essentially, *classical conditioning* pairs one stimulus with another that already elicits a given response. Classical conditioning is often associated with experiments of Ivan Pavlov, in which a dog was taught to salivate at the sound of a bell.

Instrumental or *operant* conditioning depends on the voluntary occurrence of behaviors that are then rewarded, punished, or ignored. The greatest practical development of instrumental conditioning is attributed to B. F. Skinner and his followers. According to Skinner, most learning takes place in an effort to control the environment—that is, to obtain favorable outcomes. Control is gained by means of a trial-and-error process during which one behavior results in a more favorable response than do other behaviors. The reward received is instrumental in teaching the person about a specific behavior that provides more control. For advertisers, this process requires emphasizing repetition and discrimination in order to convince consumers that their brand provides greater rewards than do other brands.

For example, learning would include a stimulus such as needing a new pair of shoes. This stimulus—worn-out shoes—is called a *need*. Next, a cue addresses that particular need, such as a local department store that is having a shoe sale. You may respond to this cue in a positive way because you have purchased shoes there before and have been very satisfied. Finally, *reinforcement* of learning occurs when the response is followed by satisfaction. Positive reinforcement strengthens the relationship between the cue and the response and therefore increases the probability that the response will be repeated.

Habit When we have repeated a process many times and continue to be satisfied with the outcome, we reach a point called *habit*. Habit is a limitation on or total absence of information seeking and evaluation of alternative choices. Purchasing by habit provides two important benefits to the consumer: (1) it reduces risk; and (2) it facilitates decision making. Buying the same brand time and again reduces the risk of product failure and financial loss for important purchases. Habit also simplifies decision making by minimizing the need for information search. Obviously, advertisers would like consumers to be habitual users of their product. Achieving that requires a powerful message backed by a superior product. American automakers learned a hard lesson when they assumed that American consumers would continue habitually to purchase cars built in the United States even though they were inferior to Japanese cars. Once a habit is formed, the role of advertising is to reinforce that habit through reminder messages, messages of appreciation, and actual rewards, such as coupons, premiums, and rebates. Breaking a consumer's habit is very difficult. Attacking a well-entrenched competitor may only make consumers defensive and reinforce their habit. Offering the consumer new relevant information about yourself or your competition is one successful approach. Providing an extra incentive to change, such as coupons, or free samples, has also proved effective. Certainly consumers who are price sensitive tend to habitually purchase items of the lowest cost. This deal-prone individual has a habit that is difficult to break.

Advertisers use a number of techniques to improve learning. Music and jingles improve learning because they intensify the repetition. Creating positive associations with a brand also enhances learning. Testimonials by well-liked celebrities and scenes of attractive people in attractive settings are used to intensify positive associations. Humor is employed because it gives the audience some reward for paying attention. Ad 5.6 is an example of advertising that creates a positive association with a product.

motive An unobservable inner force that stimulates and compels a behavioral response.

Motivation and Needs. A **motive** is an internal force that stimulates you to behave in a particular manner. This driving force is produced by the state of tension that results from an unfulfilled need. People strive—both consciously and subconsciously—to reduce this tension through behavior they anticipate will fulfill their needs and thus relieve the stress they feel.

At any given point you are probably being affected by a number of different motives, some of which may be contradictory. Some motives are stronger than others, but even this pattern changes from time to time. For example, your motivation to buy a new suit will be much higher when you start going out on job interviews.

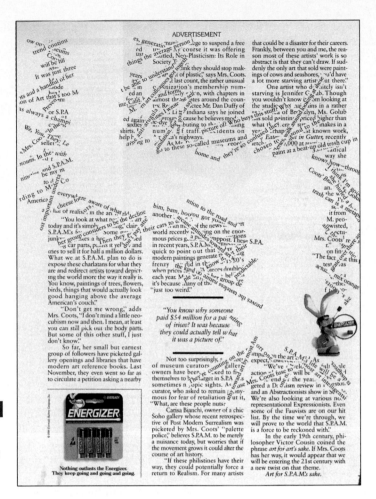

What are your buying motives? Think back over all your purchases during the past week. Did you have a reason for buying those products that you might tell your mother or an interviewer, but also a hidden reason that you will keep to yourself? You can see how important the concept of buying motives is to an understanding of consumer behavior.

needs *Basic forces that motivate you to do or to want something.*

Needs are the basic forces that motivate you to do something. Each person has his or her own set of unique needs; some are innate; others are acquired. *Innate needs* are physiological and include the needs for food, water, air, shelter, and sex. Because satisfying these needs is necessary to maintaining life, they are referred to as *primary needs. Acquired needs* are those we learn in response to our culture or environment. These may include needs for esteem, prestige, affection, power, and learning. Because acquired needs are not necessary to our physical survival, they are considered *secondary needs* or motives. Abraham Maslow noted that needs exist in a hierarchy, and that we tend to satisfy our primary needs before our secondary needs. He identified five different need categories that can be arranged vertically, with the most primary at the bottom: (1) physical or biological needs, (2) safety and security needs, (3) love and affiliation needs, (4) prestige and esteem needs, and (5) self-fulfillment needs. Although it's very useful to examine this hierarchy, looking at needs from a cross-sectional point of view is also helpful. From a cross-sectional perspective, no one category of needs consistently takes precedence over the others. A list of general consumer needs is shown in Table 5.7.

Attitudes. An **attitude** is a learned predisposition, a feeling that you hold toward an object, a person, or an idea that leads to a particular behavior. An attitude focuses on some topic that provides a focal point for your beliefs and feelings. Attitudes also tend to be enduring. You can hold an attitude for months or even years.

We develop and learn attitudes, we are not born with them. Because attitudes are learned, we can change them, unlearn them, or replace them with new ones. Attitudes also vary in direction and in strength. That is, an attitude can be *positive* or *negative,* reflecting like or dislike.

Attitudes are important to advertisers because they influence how consumers evaluate products. A strong positive attitude might be turned into brand preference and loyalty. For example, most American consumers over the age of 50 know that test pilot Chuck Yeager is one of our national heroes. An ad such as the one shown hopes that the readers will transfer their positive attitude toward such a hero to the sponsoring product—Rolex. (See Ad 5.7.) A weak attitude, even if it is positive, might not be enough to convince you to act. Changing an attitude is not impossible, but it is difficult.

Attitudes also reflect consumers' values. They tell the world what we stand for and identify the things and ideas we consider important. They also track our positive and negative reactions to things in our life. Opinion research is used to check how people feel about other people, products, brands, appeals, and contemporary trends. One of the most important areas for opinion research in advertising is product and brand perception. It is important to know how the consumer sees the product before developing an advertising strategy. Furthermore, advertisers must be aware of the factors with which the product is associated in the consumer's mind.

The results of a survey conducted by Roper College Track might prove a point about attitudes. Essentially, the survey wanted to determine what college students buy with their food money. In other words, how do their attitudes about food and meals translate into specific behavior? Quick and easy meals are most attractive to students, so the microwave is an appliance that plays a major role in student lives. Cereal is a staple; there are some college students who regularly stock three different kinds of cereals, one for each meal. Far and away, the most popular food is pizza, followed by hamburgers. Other highly regarded items were subs, chicken wings, fried mozzarella sticks, onion rings, French fries, Oreos and Chips Ahoy!, Cool Ranch Doritos, Twinkies, Mountain Dew, and Jolt! Any of this ring a bell?[19]

Personality. All of these personal and psychological factors interact to create your own unique personality. A **personality** is a collection of traits that makes a person distinctive. How you look at the world, how you perceive and interpret what is happening around you, how you respond intellectually and emotionally, and how you form your opinions and attitudes are all reflected in your personality. Your personality is what makes you an individual.

Self-Concept Self-concept refers to how we look at ourselves. Our self-image reflects how we see our own personality and our individual pattern of strengths

---

[19]Susannah Baker, "College Cuisine Makes Mother Cringe," *American Demographics* (September 1991):10–11.

Table 5.7

Consumer Needs

Achievement

The need to accomplish difficult feats; to perform arduous tasks; to exercise your skills, abilities, or talents.

Exhibition

The need to display yourself, to be visible to others; to reveal personal identity; to show off or win the attention and interest of others; to gain notice.

Dominance

The need to have power or to exert your will on others; to hold a position of authority or influence; to direct or supervise the efforts of others; to show strength or prowess by winning over adversaries.

Diversion

The need to play; to have fun; to be entertained; to break from the routine; to relax and abandon your cares; to be amused.

Understanding

The need to learn and comprehend; to recognize connections; to assign causality; to make ideas fit the circumstances; to teach, instruct, or impress others with your expertise; to follow intellectual pursuits.

Nurturance

The need to give care, comfort, and support to others; to see living things grow and thrive; to help the progress and development of others; to protect your charges from harm or injury.

Sexuality

The need to establish your sexual identity and attractiveness; to enjoy sexual contact; to *receive* and to *provide* sexual satisfaction; to maintain sexual alternatives without exercising them; to avoid condemnation for sexual appetites.

Security

The need to be free from threat of harm; to be safe; to protect self, family, and property; to have a supply of what you need; to save and acquire assets; to be invulnerable to attack; to avoid accidents or mishaps.

Independence

The need to be autonomous, to be free from the direction or influence of others; to have options and alternatives; to make your own choices and decisions; to be different.

Recognition

The need for *positive* notice by others; to show your superiority or excellence; to be acclaimed or held up as exemplary; to receive social rewards or notoriety.

Stimulation

The need to experience events and activities that stimulate the senses or exercise perception; to move and act freely and vigorously; to engage in rapid or forceful activity; to saturate the palate with flavor; to engage the environment in new or unusual modes of interaction.

Novelty

The need for change and diversity; to experience the unusual; to do new tasks or activities; to learn new skills; to be in a new setting or environment; to find unique objects of interest; to be amazed or mystified.

Affiliation

The need for association with others; to belong or win acceptance; to enjoy satisfying and mutually helpful relationships.

Succorance

The need to *receive* help, support, comfort, encouragement, or reassurance from others; to be the *recipient* of nurturant efforts.

Consistency

The need for order, cleanliness, or logical connection; to control the environment; to avoid ambiguity and uncertainty; to predict accurately; to have things happen as you expect.

Source: Adapted from Robert B. Settle and Pamela L. Alreck, Why They Buy (New York: John Wiley & Sons, 1986):26–28.

"If you want to grow old as a pilot, you've got to know when to push it, and when to back off." *Chuck Yeager*

Throughout his remarkable career, Chuck Yeager has shown an uncanny talent for what pilots call "pushing the edge of the envelope." At 21, only three years after boarding his first plane, Yeager was leading a squadron of fighter pilots in World War II. And at the age of 24, he became the first person to fly faster than the speed of sound.

Attempting such dangerous feats is one thing. Living to describe them to your grandchildren is another. Displaying the enormous courage, skill and cool judgment needed to do both has made General Chuck Yeager an authentic American hero.

Although retired from the military, Yeager remains a man on the move. He's an avid sportsman with a lifelong love of the outdoors, a lecturer and a consulting test pilot who still loves to fly. "Maybe I don't jump off 15-foot fences anymore," said Yeager, "but I can still pull 8 or 9 G's in a high-performance aircraft." And in all his exploits, Yeager depends on a rugged and reliable timepiece. "I wore a Rolex 40 years ago when I broke the sound barrier and I still do today," says Yeager matter-of-factly. "A pilot has to believe in his equipment. That's why I wear a Rolex."

ROLEX

Rolex GMT-Master II in stainless steel and 18kt gold with matching Jubilee bracelet.
Write for brochure. Rolex Watch U.S.A., Inc., Dept. 663, Rolex Building, 665 Fifth Avenue, New York, N.Y. 10022
© 1991 Rolex Watch U.S.A., Inc. Rolex, GMT-Master and Jubilee are trademarks.

Ad 5.7

Older consumers hold strong positive attitudes toward Chuck Yeager—and hopefully any product he recommends.

(Courtesy of Rolex Watch U.S.A., Inc.)

and weaknesses. Take a minute to think of the traits that best describe you. What do they tell you about your own self-concept? Are they basically positive or negative? Do you have high or low self-esteem? What image of yourself do you see?

Now consider yourself as a consumer. Explain how these same characteristics affect your response to different products, to advertising, and to your behavior as a consumer. Can you see how understanding personality is important in developing a relevant message?

Lifestyles. Lifestyle factors are often considered the mainstay of psychographic research. Essentially, lifestyle research looks at the ways people allocate time, energy, and money. Marketers conduct research to measure and compare people's activities, interests, and opinions—in other words, what they usually do or how they behave, what intrigues or fascinates them, and what they believe or assume about the world around them.

Value and Lifestyle Systems (VALS) Classification systems that categorize people by values for the purpose of predicting effective advertising strategies.

VALS The firm of SRI International is famous for its **Values and Lifestyles Systems (VALS)** conceptual models that categorize people according to their values and then identify the consumer behaviors associated with those values. VALS systems are used to show clients how consumer groups are changing and how these changes will affect the client's advertising strategy. The first model, VALS 1, was introduced in 1978 and contained nine categories that divided the American population along a hierarchy of needs. At the bottom of the hierarchy were the survivors and sustainers; at the top were the integrateds. Two separate paths led from the bottom to the top. One was outer-directed and included belongers, emulators, and achievers, who took their cues from the world around them. The other path was inner-directed, the I-am-me's, experimentals, and societally conscious, who tended to make their own rules. The problem with using these segments is that they reflected a population of people who were in their twenties and thirties in the 1970s, and this population changed quite a bit in the 1980s. Moreover, businesses found it difficult to use these segments to predict buying behavior or to target consumers.

For these reasons SRI developed a new system in 1989. The firm dropped values and lifestyles as the basis for its psychographic segmentations scheme, having determined that the link between values and lifestyles and purchasing choices was less strong than it had once seemed. The new system—VALS 2—is based on a questionnaire that reveals unchanging psychological stances rather than shifting values and lifestyles, and is considered the superior system (see Figure 5.3). The psychographic groups in VALS 2 are arranged in a rectangle. They are stacked vertically by resources (minimal to abundant) and horizontally by self-orientation (principle-, status-, or action-oriented). Resources include income, education, self-confidence, health, eagerness to buy, intelligence, and energy level.

Figure 5.3

Values and Lifestyle Systems (VALS 1 and VALS 2).

Source: American Demographics (July 1989):26.

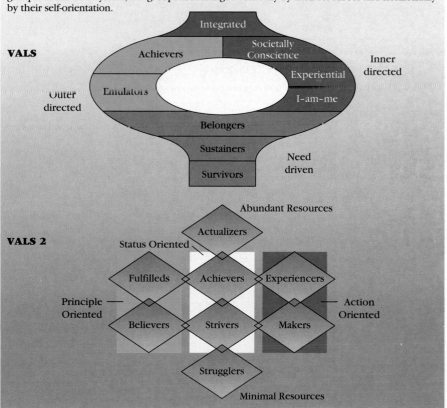

Old and New

The nine original VALS psychographic segments have been replaced by eight new psychographic groups. In the new system, the groups are arranged vertically by their resources and horizontally by their self-orientation.

A person's position along the resource/self-orientation axis determines which of eight classifications he or she falls into; actualizers, fulfilled, achievers, experiencers, believers, strivers, makers, or strugglers. Members of each group hold different values and maintain different lifestyles. Actualizers, for example, are located above the rectangle and have the highest incomes and such high self-esteem and abundant resources that they can indulge in any or all self-orientations. Image is important to these people. Because of their wide range of interests and openness to change, actualizers' purchases are directed at "the finer things in life."[20] Obviously, knowing the psychographic orientation of consumers is a valuable asset to an advertiser in deciding to whom messages should be targeted.

Even more important, however, is that these VALS 2 categories correspond to consumer behaviors that are useful to the advertiser. This relationship is illustrated in Table 5.8, where the eight categories correspond with the frequency of certain activities.

BUYING BEHAVIOR

The information we have discussed thus far is used by advertisers to understand how the consumer decision-making process works—in other words, how the consumer goes about buying the product. Although at first it sounds like an individual process that cannot be generalized across consumers, there is evidence that most people engage in a similar decision process. Our understanding is also enhanced if we view decision making as either a low-involvement or high-involvement process.

---

[20]Martha Farnsworth Riche, "Psychographics for the 1990s," *American Demographics* (July 1989):25 26, 30–32.

TABLE 5.8 VALS 2 Segment Activities

Item	Actualizer	Fulfilled	Believer	Achiever	Striver	Experiencer	Maker	Struggler
Buy hand tools	148	65	105	63	59	137	170	57
Barbecue outdoors	125	93	82	118	111	109	123	50
Do gardening	155	129	118	109	68	54	104	80
Do gourmet cooking	217	117	96	103	53	133	86	47
Drink coffee daily	120	119	126	88	87	55	91	116
Drink domestic beer	141	88	73	101	87	157	123	50
Drink herbal tea	171	125	89	117	71	115	81	68
Drink imported beer	238	93	41	130	58	216	88	12
Do activities with kids	155	129	57	141	112	89	116	32
Play team sports	114	73	69	104	110	172	135	34
Do cultural activities	293	63	67	96	45	154	63	14
Exercise	145	114	69	123	94	143	102	39
Do home repairs	161	113	85	82	53	88	171	58
Camp or hike	131	88	68	95	84	156	158	33
Do risky sports	190	48	36	52	59	283	171	7
Socialize weekly	109	64	73	90	96	231	94	62

Note: Figures under each segment are the index for each segment (100 = Base rate usage).
Source: SRI International

high-involvement decision process Decisions that require an involved purchase process with information search and product comparison.

low-involvement decision process Decisions that require limited deliberation; sometimes purchases are even made on impulse.

Low- and High-Involvement Decision Making When we think about the thought process we go through in making product decisions, it is fairly safe to say that for the more expensive, personal, or emotion-laden products (such as automobiles, medical care, clothes, and vacations), we expend a great deal of effort, whereas for the inexpensive, less-exciting products that are purchased regularly, such as those found at supermarket checkout counters, we exert very little thought and effort. The former is called a complex, **high-involvement decision process**, whereas the latter is labeled a simple, **low-involvement decision process**. Table 5.9 shows how this involvement level and the decision-making process relate to one another.

This concept of involvement originated in the research conducted on hemispheral lateralization, that is, right-brain–left-brain functioning. The left hemisphere of the brain specializes in cognitive activities, such as reading and speaking. People who are exposed to verbal information cognitively analyze the information through left-brain processing and form mental images. Conversely, the right hemisphere of the brain is concerned with nonverbal, timeless, and pictorial information. This scheme can be applied to product decision making. Product decisions that have high personal relevance and contain a high perceived risk are called high-involvement purchases, and they necessitate complex decision making. Products at the opposite end of the relevance/risk continuum are low-involvement purchases that require simple decision making. Simple decision making requires very little information and virtually no evaluation. We discuss complex decision making next.

Decision Process. The process consumers go through in making a purchase varies considerably between low-involvement and high-involvement situations. There are some generally recognized stages, however, and these are highlighted in Figure 5.4. The stages are (1) need recognition, (2) information search, (3) evaluation and comparison, (4) outlet selection, (5) purchase decision, and (6) postpurchase evaluation.

Table 5.9

Consumer Decision Process for High- and Low-Involvement Purchase Decisions

	Low-Involvement Purchase Decisions	High-Involvement Purchase Decisions
Problem recognition	Trivial to minor	Important and personally meaningful
Information search	Internal to limited external search	Extensive search
Alternative evaluation	Few alternatives evaluated on few performance criteria	Many alternatives considered using many performance criteria
Store choice, purchase	One-stop shopping where substitution is very possible	Multiple store visits with substitution less likely
Postpurchase activities	Simple evaluation of performance	Extensive performance evaluation, use, and disposal

Source: D. Hawkins, R. Best, and K. Coney, Consumer Behavior, 5th ed. (Homewood, IL: Irwin, 1992):21.

Figure 5.4

The major stages of the consumer purchase process.

Courtesy of Marty Horn, Associate Director of the Delta Group, DDB Needham Worldwide.

Need Recognition The first stage, *need recognition*, occurs when the consumer recognizes a need for a product. This need can vary in terms of seriousness or importance. The goal of advertising at this stage is to activate or stimulate this need. For example, the Burger King "Aren't you hungry?" campaign appeals to people's appetites and nutritional needs.

Information Search The second stage is the *information search*. This search can be casual, such as reading ads and articles that happen to catch your attention, or formal, such as searching for information in publications like *Consumer Reports*. Another type of informal search is recalling information you have seen previously. Advertising helps the search process by providing information in the advertisement itself.

Evaluation and Comparison The third stage is *evaluation and comparison*. Here we begin to compare various products and features and reduce the list of options to a manageable number. We select certain features that are important and use them to judge our alternatives. Advertising is important in this evaluation process because it helps sort out products on the basis of features.

Outlet Selection and Purchase Decision The fourth stage is *outlet selection*. Is this product available at a grocery store, a discount store, a hardware store, a boutique, a department store, or a specialty store? Will the consumer select the brand first and then try to find a store that carries it, or will he or she select a store first and then consider the available brands? Instore promotions such as packaging, point-of-purchase displays, price reductions, banners and signs, and coupon displays affect these choices. (Sales promotion techniques will be discussed in more detail in Chapter 18). The outlet is the site of the fifth stage, which is the actual *purchase*.

Postpurchase Evaluation The last step in the process is the point where we begin to reconsider and justify our purchase to ourselves. As soon as we purchase a product, particularly a major one, we begin to engage in postpurchase evaluation. Is the product acceptable? Is its performance satisfactory? Does it live up to our expectations? This experience determines whether we will repurchase the product or even return it to the store.

Even before you open the package or use the product, you may experience doubt or worry about the wisdom of the purchase. This doubt is called *postpurchase dissonance*. Many consumers continue to read information even after the purchase in order to justify their decision to themselves. Advertising, such as copy on package inserts, helps reduce postpurchase dissonance by restating the features and confirming the popularity of the brand or product.

THE KEY TO EFFECTIVE ADVERTISING: UNDERSTANDING THE AUDIENCE

Once a year, DDB Needham Worldwide mails questionnaires to a sample of 4,000 U.S. adults, covering various lifestyle topics from eating habits to attitudes toward neatness. The data are used to create in-depth profiles of client's target consumers. Betty Crocker wants to know who buys cake mixes, Wrigley's would be interested to know that 40 percent of Americans think people shouldn't chew gum in public, and Listerine and Scope want to know what percentage of the population thinks people should use mouthwash to ameliorate bad breath.

The detailed profiles DDB Needham compiles are passed on to the creative people working on the specific accounts. A person responsible for the National Dairy Board campaign, for example, needs to know who are the heavy users of cheese. These Lifestyle studies provide data on demographics, attitudes, beliefs, habits, needs, and opinions on all sorts of topics, from religion, family, and morals to the economy, law enforcement, and volunteerism—all the information necessary for developing and appropriately targeting campaigns.

Some of the questions asked may seem irrelevant, such as asking respondents to agree or disagree with the statement, "I like the look of a large lamp in a picture window," or "I would do better than average in a fistfight." These responses are valuable, however, and help to determine whether a person has traditional values, how he or she feels about sex roles, and help round out the profiles.

The Lifestyle studies also help to disprove some of the popular myths of so-called "trends" that seem to be appearing. For example, although it is believed that families don't eat together anymore, the Lifestyle data show that 75 percent of respondents say their whole family usually eats dinner together.[21]

Although it is impossible for us to know everything about the people with whom we communicate, the more we do know, the more likely our message will be understood. This same assumption is true for advertisers, although at a much broader level. Fortunately, advertisers have the resources to conduct extensive research that taps this information. Such research must not only be accurate, it must also be conducted constantly because people are always changing.

In this chapter we identified several key audience traits and behaviors that are relevant to the advertiser. There are more traits and behaviors that we have not discussed. Furthermore, those involved in the design and implementation of an advertisement may interpret these traits differently. We all have our own perceptions of things. The key to successful advertising is staying sensitive to the consumer. If all you know about your audience is what the computer printout tells you, you are unlikely to be an effective communicator. Creative advertising

---

[21]Joseph M. Winski, "Lifestyle Study: Who We Are, How We Live, What We Think," *Advertising Age* (September 24, 1990):25.

requires both basic awareness and empathy. In the next chapter we will turn to the specific research and planning strategies involved in achieving this kind of consumer awareness.

𝒮UMMARY

- The social and cultural influences on consumers include society and subcultures, social class, reference groups, and family.

- Personal influences on consumers include age, gender, family status, education, occupation, income, and race.

- Psychological influences on the individual as a consumer include perception, learning, motivation, attitudes, personality, and self-concept.

- Advertisers identify audiences in terms of demographics and psychographics.

- Demographic profiles of consumers include information on population size, age, gender,

education, family situation, occupation, income, and race.

- Psychographic profiles on consumers include information on attitudes, lifestyles, buying behavior, and decision processes.

- Your personality reflects how you look at the world, how you perceive and interpret what is happening, how you respond, and how you form opinions and attitudes.

- The decision process involves six stages: need recognition, information search, evaluation and comparison, outlet selection, purchase decision, and postpurchase evaluation.

𝒬UESTIONS

1 How must advertisers adjust to the elderly? Do you think different adjustments will be required when the baby boomers enter this group? What kind?

2 Choose four VALS categories and find one or more print advertisements that appear to be targeted to individuals in each category. Explain why you think the ad addresses that audience.

3 What are the six stages in the consumer decision process? Give examples of how advertising can influence each stage. Find an ad that addresses the concern of consumers in each stage.

4 Sean McDonnell is the creative director for Chatham-Boothe, an advertising agency that has just signed a contract with Trans-Central Airlines (TCA). TCA has a solid portfolio of consumer research and has offered to let the agency use it. McDonnell needs to decide whether demographic, psychographic, or attitude/motive studies are best for developing the creative profile of the TCA target audience. If the choice were yours,

which body of research would you base a creative strategy on? Explore the strengths and weaknesses of each.

5 Look at the social class segments illustrated in Table 5.1. State which two class segments would be most receptive to these product marketing situations:

a. Full line of frozen family-style meals (for microwaving) that feature superior nutritional balances.

b. Dairy product company (milk, cheese, ice cream) offering an exclusive packaging design that uses fully degradable containers.

6 If the projected U.S. age shifts forecasted for the next 20 years happen, what impact would these changes have on our current advertising practices (creative and media selection influences)?

7 Avon Products has established an admirable reputation for residence-to-residence personal selling. Now the corporation has seriously modified its marketing approach. What changes in consumer lifestyles have happened to prompt Avon's shift? How can Avon change with the times without giving up personal salesmanship?

✐UGGESTED CLASS PROJECT

Posing as a customer, visit one or more stores that sell stereo systems. Report on the sales techniques used (check on advertising, point-of-purchase displays, store design, and so forth). What beliefs concerning consumer behavior appear to underlie these strategies?

✐URTHER READINGS

BARD, B., "The Eighties Are Over," *Newsweek* (January 4, 1988):40–45.

MULLEN, BRIAN, AND CRAIG JOHNSON, *The Psychology of Consumer Behavior* (Hillsdale, NJ: Lawrence Erlbaum Associates, 1990).

POPCORN, FAITH, *The Popcorn Report* (New York: Currency and Doubleday, 1991).

PRUS, ROBERT C., *Pursuing Customers: An Ethnography of Marketing Activities* (New York: Sage Publications, 1989).

ROBERTSON, THOMAS S., AND HAROLD H. KASSARJIAN, *Handbook of Consumer Behavior* (Englewood Cliffs, NJ: Prentice Hall, 1991).

SCHIFFMAN, LEON G., AND LESLIE LAZAR KANUK, *Consumer Behavior* (Englewood Cliffs, NJ: Prentice Hall, 1987).

SETTLE, ROBERT B., AND PAMELA L. ALBECK, *Why They Buy: American Consumers Inside and Out* (New York: John Wiley & Sons, 1986).

Cinnamon Toast Crunch

The extremely competitive ready-to-eat cereal category includes more than 216 brands, of which roughly one third are consumed primarily by children. Although most purchasers of children's cereals purchase them regularly, they seek variety. They are not brand loyal in any strict sense.

Cinnamon Toast Crunch enjoyed a reputation as one of the leading children's cereal brands. However, distribution had peaked, and competition was growing. It was, therefore, in danger of losing market share.

The advertising task was to sustain and strengthen Cinnamon Toast Crunch's position within the presweetened cereal category. Research had indicated that children ages 6 to 12 have greater influence on the purchase of Cinnamon Toast Crunch than on the purchase of other cereal brands. This age group was designated as the target audience for the advertising.

Research had also indicated that children ages 6 to 12 will not accept a cereal that does not have exceptional taste appeal, that they are especially visually oriented, and that they are more likely to be persuaded by visual proof than by verbal claims. Accordingly, the campaign called The Taste You Can See, focused on the cinnamon sugar that consumers can see on every piece.

The advertising, developed by CME•KHBB, General Mills' advertising agency, portrayed children as "in the know"—able to see what adults cannot. In the spots, children reversed roles with stereotypical adult authority figures (teachers and parents) and taught the adults why they prefer Cinnamon Toast Crunch.

The media plan featured broad-reaching national television—network spots and cable—all on programs favored by children. Promotional support included direct mail and freestanding insert coupons, in-store sampling, in-pack cross-couponing, and periodic discounts offered to the trade.

During the first month of the Taste You Can See campaign, Cinnamon Toast Crunch enjoyed a 20 percent weekly pound share increase, despite the fact that no other major marketing efforts were then underway. With the additional promotional support, Cinnamon Toast Crunch continues to sustain its gains and remains the only one of the top six brands in its category that has not experienced a sales decline.

Questions

1 Develop a decision-making model that depicts how a 6-to-12 year-old would process a decision to purchase a cereal.

2 How would this model be useful in creating ads?

3 What other characteristics of children would be important to understand before starting the creative process? the media plan?

$\mathscr{S}$TUDYING CONSUMER TRENDS

$\mathscr{U}$SING SOCIAL TRENDS FOR ADVERTISING DECISIONS

Ad 5A.1

The Betty Crocker "Sweet Talker" campaign.

(Courtesy of DDB Needham Worldwide)

Several years ago, Betty Crocker adopted the "Sweet Talker" advertising campaign to provide a fresher, more contemporary, less traditional image to its line of baked goods. This image "makeover" was necessary in order to reflect the current lifestyle of Betty Crocker's target audience more accurately.

When long-term trends indicated that time-pressed consumers couldn't afford the time to get their houses neat and clean, Rubbermaid designed an advertising campaign around a line of new products that were durable and highly effective in easing the burden and drudgery of housework.

As these two examples suggest, major decisions about manufacturing, marketing, and advertising products to American consumers are based in part on assumptions about how consumers' attitudes, beliefs, and behaviors are changing. In other words, business decisions are often predicated on assumptions about *trends* in American values and lifestyles.

SPOTTING TRENDS

Advertisers spot trends in values in at least four ways:

1. *Personal Observation.* Some advertising executives believe that spotting trends is simply a matter of observing what others are doing. They ask friends, neighbors, and acquaintances what they think, buy, read, watch, and listen to. In addition, they comb the popular press, books, and other literature to see what others say is happening.

2. *Qualitative Research.* Qualitative research, such as focus group discussions and in-depth interviews with "real people," is an extremely popular way that businesses monitor what's going on in society.

3. *Trend Experts.* Another approach is to let trend experts identify trends. These "gurus" often use personal observation and qualitative research for much of their "expertise."

4. *Periodic Measurement.* The fourth approach is to survey large and representative samples of the population over time. These surveys typically include a lengthy battery of questions about people's attitudes, interests, and behavior on a wide range of subjects.

Ad 5A.2

The Rubbermaid "Workout" campaign.

(Courtesy of DDB Needham)

One such survey is the Lifestyle Study conducted by the advertising agency DDB Needham Worldwide. This survey, conducted annually since 1975, has a sample of 4,000 men and women nationwide.

Respondents are asked over 1,000 questions on their attitudes and opinions on diverse topics, the activities in which they participate, the kinds of products and services they use, their media habits, and demographics.

REAL TRENDS, IMAGINARY TRENDS

Courtesy of Marty Horm, Associate
Director of the Delta Group, DDB
Needham Worldwide

The first three approaches to spotting trends—personal observation, qualitative research, and trend experts or gurus—have one important element in common. All three depend on *stories*. Trend spotters who employ their own personal observations depend on stories they tell to themselves. Moderators of focus groups and in-depth interviews, as well as trend gurus, depend mostly on stories others have told to them.

The benefit of stories is that they produce fascinating ideas and hypotheses that are easy to believe. For example, here's a brief excerpt from a *Newsweek* (December 19, 1988) story about the Midwest:

> Kathy and Jack Ellis were not thrilled about moving to the Midwest from suburban New Jersey three years ago. Besides being separated from family and friends, there was the culture shock to consider. "My image was bib overalls," says Kathy, "that sort of thing."
>
> Now, Kathy and Jack can hardly say a bad word about Kansas City. When Jack returns home from a business trip back East, he feels as if he were going on vacation. "I take a big breath. I make a big sigh. It's just so wonderful to be back home."

On the basis of this and other stories, *Newsweek* concluded that the

HEARTLAND IS HOT!

This type of coherent detail makes us believe that the story must be true. We may even know people like Kathy and Jack. We are ready to believe that there is a trend toward people moving to the Midwest and embracing heartland values and lifestyles.

The trouble with relying solely on stories to spot trends, however, whether from personal observation, qualitative research, or trend gurus, is that such stories often cannot distinguish real trends from imaginary trends. As convincing as the story is of Kathy's and Jack's love of Kansas City, it hardly constitutes a trend toward Midwest migration. A careful and systematic analysis of population changes conducted by the U.S. Census indicates that at the time the story was written metropolitan areas were growing everywhere *except* in the Midwest! Thus, the news magazine provided an excellent example of what might be called an imaginary trend.

Stories cannot help us distinguish real trends from imaginary trends because the samples are small and unrepresentative, and there is no reliable history to compare with current findings. Sometimes an observation which appears to be a trend is just a unique and impressive case. Other times, the trend has been present all along but has gone unnoticed.

Compared to stories, periodic measurement has one unquestionable benefit: *accuracy*. Trends reported from periodic measurement rely on *data* drawn from large, representative samples of the population. Unfortunately, data with tables of percentages and clinical-looking trend lines are less exciting and memorable than a well-told story. Nevertheless, it is periodic measurement that provides the degree of accuracy advertising decision makers need.

Here are some other examples of trends generated from stories and posited

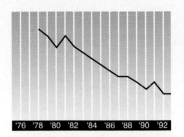

Graph 1

Our whole family usually eats dinner together.

by trend experts. Some of them are supported by periodic measurement; some are not.

Many trend experts have said that today's family is so abuzz with activity that, as one trend expert put it, "it is nearly impossible for families to sit down together for dinner." Accordingly, some advertisers have portrayed family dinners as hit-and-miss affairs and have positioned their products as catering to this on-the-go lifestyle.

Unfortunately, such advertising and product positioning may miss the mark.

According to the DDB Needham Lifestyle Study, 74 percent of married Americans currently say their family "usually eats dinner together." Similar results have been obtained from surveys conducted by *The New York Times/CBS News* and *The Los Angeles Times*. While this percentage has declined since 1975, the descent has not been as dramatic, nor is the level as low, as some trend experts would have us believe.

Another supposedly widespread trend is "grazing," that is, eating small, quick meals on the run. Often, these meals consist of foods normally thought of as snacks or appetizers. Sometimes grazing means skipping meals altogether and simply snacking during odd moments of the day. Many products positioned in advertising as "meals-on-the-run" for the time-pressed consumer are attempting to cash in on this trend. But can advertisers take this trend to the bank? Perhaps not.

First, the percentage of people who regularly eat breakfast, lunch, and dinner is pretty much the same today as it was in the early and mid-1980s.

Looking more closely at lunch, a time when grazing is said to be quite popular, the percentage of people who say they often skip lunch or just have a light snack at noon is not increasing sharply. In fact, it is not increasing at all; it is *declining*.

No doubt some people are grazing. Some people may even graze a lot. But grazing hardly appears to be as large a social phenomenon as we may have heard.

Finally, only about one person out of three admits to eating mini-meals made up of snacks and appetizers—a percentage that is flat for women and declining for men.

Advertising strategy and advertising copy based on assumptions about trends can easily go wrong. Inaccurate estimates of the magnitude and direction

Graph 2

I eat breakfast/lunch/dinner every day.

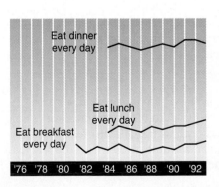

Graph 3

At noontime, I often skip lunch or just have a light snack.

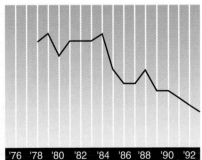

Graph 4

I find myself eating meals made up of foods I would normally consider to be snacks and appetizers.

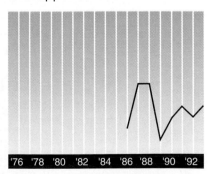

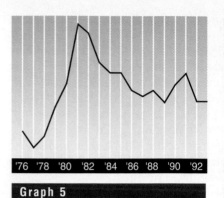

Graph 5

No matter how fast our income goes up, we never seem to get ahead.

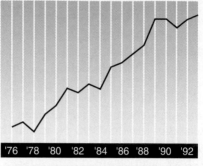

Graph 6

Meal preparation should take as little time as possible (women only).

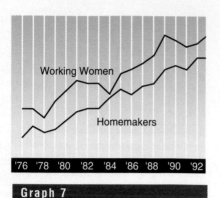

Graph 7

Meal preparation should take as little time as possible (working women vs. home-makers).

of a trend can produce advertising campaigns that don't "ring true" to the target customer. Conversely, accurate estimates of the magnitude and direction of trends can greatly improve the chances of a successful advertising campaign.

DETAILS, DETAILS

The preceding cases do not mean that all trends reported by the news media or offered up by trend gurus are imaginary. Many are real. For example, the news media and many trend experts have frequently highlighted the effects of inflation on consumer attitudes. In the DDB Needham Lifestyle Study, this effect also is easy to see.

As inflation grew in the late 1970s and early 1980s, people expressed deep concern about making ends meet. As inflation cooled during the remainder of the 1980s, so too did people's worries about losing their nest egg.

When trends are relatively easy to detect, periodic measurement can add important details on exactly how and among whom they are at work. For example, many media discussions of working women have remarked on how employment has affected the time available to prepare meals at home. The DDB Needham Lifestyle Study also has uncovered this trend, as shown by the steady increase among women in agreement with the statement "Meal preparation should take as little time as possible."

Much of the media focus of this subject assumes that the increase in this sentiment is due solely to the increase in the number of working women who must meet the demands of both their families and their jobs.

Yet, when we separate working women from homemakers, we see that sharply increasing proportions of women in *both* segments are seeking to reduce the amount of time spent on preparing meals.

THE UNNOTICED TREND

Possibly the most important contribution of periodic measurement is revealing a trend that was previously unnoticed but is both important and real. An advertiser that discovers such a trend has a decided advantage over the competition.

Let's put ourselves in the shoes of an advertising agency executive in charge

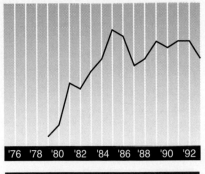

Graph 8

I try to avoid foods with a high salt content.

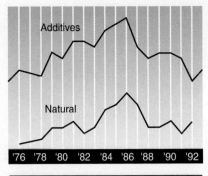

Graph 9

I try to avoid foods that have additives in them; I try to eat natural foods most of the time.

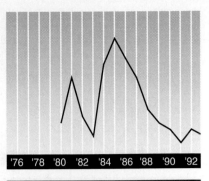

Graph 10

I try to select foods that are fortified with vitamins, minerals, and protein.

of advertising a client's new line of healthy, microwavable entrées. We know that during the 1970s and 1980s, consumer concern about food and its relationship to health grew dramatically. As such, we are developing an advertising campaign that emphasizes the line's all natural, vitamin-rich, protein-rich, low-sodium food.

However, an unnoticed but real trend we may have missed is that some of the food concerns that were growing dramatically are now temporarily on hold or, in some instances, in reverse.

The proportion of people who say they try to avoid foods with a high salt content reached its peak in the mid 1980s and has declined somewhat since.

Natural and additive-free foods have lost some of their appeal. Furthermore, the proportion of people who try to select foods that are fortified with vitamins, minerals, and protein has decreased throughout the second half of the 1980s.

Therefore, an advertising campaign based on the assumption that concerns about salt, additives, and vitamins would continue to increase would not reflect what is really going on.

All this is not to say that health and nutrition are no longer important issues for Americans. They are. Concern about cholesterol is growing. People are avoiding fat.

A high-fiber diet continues to be an important issue for many Americans.

These trends provide valuable knowledge about the environment in which advertising for nutritious products will appear. For example, an advertiser may decide to shift the emphasis from "all natural and low in sodium" to "low in fat and cholesterol," areas of increasing interest to consumers. (Of course, this strategy assumes that the advertiser's product can deliver the low-fat, low-cholesterol attributes.)

Or the advertiser may decide to take a different route. Advertising copy can still refer to the all natural, low-sodium attributes of the product line. In light of consumer trends in these two areas, however, the advertising may place greater emphasis on some other appropriate product characteristic, such as "superb taste."

These various advertising strategies might also change the advertiser's competition. The competition for a product that emphasizes its low-fat, low-cholesterol benefits may be other "diet" meals. With a strategy that focuses primarily on taste, the competition may be premium-priced, "nondiet" meals. Likewise,

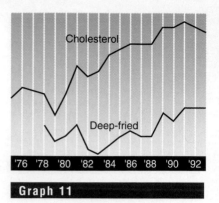

Graph 11

I try to avoid foods that are high in cholesterol; I try to avoid prepared deep-fried foods.

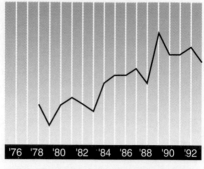

Graph 12

I make a special effort to get enough fiber (bran) in my diet.

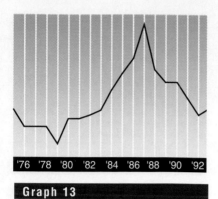

Graph 13

Television is my primary form of entertainment.

different strategies would call for different target audiences for the advertising. A "nutrition" advertising strategy might focus on older consumers who are concerned by their intake of fat and cholesterol. A taste strategy might be aimed at middle-aged consumers who are fussy about the taste of microwavable entrées.

BEWARE OF PITFALLS

It is important to emphasize that trend watching is not a solution for all advertising problems. Even when the trend data being analyzed are drawn from periodic measurement, which is the preferred choice, the marketer must beware of certain pitfalls.

First, the advertiser must realize that *attitudes can be put into action in many different ways*. Specific behaviors, such as buying a particular product, do not always follow general attitudes or values. For example, even though a large majority of Lifestyle respondents say they "like to buy new and different things," new-product success rates are only about 10 percent. Simply being new isn't enough; the product has to satisfy a real consumer need.

A second point to which the advertiser must be sensitive is that *many things can come between an attitude and behavior*. The growing consumer interest in dietary fiber has not translated into huge market shares for those cereals that are *very* high in fiber. Although possessing the specific property that consumers seem to want, in this case, a lot of fiber, many high-fiber cereals simply do not taste as good as lower-fiber, sweeter cereals. Thus, "taste" has come between the attitude (a desire for high-fiber foods) and the behavior (the purchase of high-fiber cereals).

Finally, the advertiser should be aware that *trends can reverse at any time*. We have already seen a reversal of major trends in diet and nutrition. Yesterday's trends are no guarantees of tomorrow's product triumphs.

Another example of a reversing trend is interest in television. From 1975 to 1987, the percentage of Americans who said "television is my primary form of entertainment" grew steadily. Since then, that percentage has plummeted.

Will the impending explosion from current programming to hundreds of available channels with "something for everyone" and interactive offerings that will allow consumers to choose from a variety of advertising options reverse this decline? Systems such as Time Warner's Full Service Network are now being tested to learn the answer.

If specific behaviors do not always follow trends in attitudes, or if social trends do not always parallel business trends, why do advertisers think it still is important to monitor trends?

The reason is simple. The savvy advertiser knows how to avoid, or at least be sensitive to, the pitfalls listed previously. Having solid trend information at one's disposal, even with its limitations, is a much more desirable alternative to having no trend information. Even worse is having trend "information" that is largely or even partly wrong.

Almost all facets of marketing—including advertising, promotion, packaging, and price—are a form of communicating to a target consumer. The better the advertisers know their targets, the more effectively they can communicate with them. Trend information about consumers' values and lifestyles provides advertisers with a much more detailed and thorough understanding of the target market than unaided judgment could provide. And that knowledge can greatly increase the chances for campaigns that speak directly to what is on consumers' minds.

TEAR

Sink your
mountain are
Colorado. 76 tra
best in North A
of your time on
Because we ha
high-speed quad
minutes from De
are available t
vacation
*For reservatio
or 8*

⊄⊅ COPPER

$\mathscr{S}$TRATEGIC RESEARCH

CHAPTER OBJECTIVES

When you have completed this chapter, you should be able to:

- Explain the difference between qualitative and quantitative research

- Identify sources of exploratory research in government departments, trade associations, secondary and primary research suppliers, and advertisers' and agencies' research departments

- Develop a research program using the five parts of a strategy document

- Distinguish between primary and secondary research

- Understand how and when to use the six basic research methods: surveys, experiments, observation, content analysis, in-depth interviews, and focus groups

- Understand how research is used in the development of the creative message

COPPER MOUNTAIN'S RESEARCH ODYSSEY

During the 1986 ski season Copper Mountain Resort near Denver, Colorado, experienced a sharp decline in its number of front-range day skiers—skiers who came for the day from Colorado Springs, Boulder, and Denver. One possible reason for the decline was that skiing in general was losing out to other forms of outdoor recreation, not only at Copper Mountain, but everywhere. In that case, the managers of Copper Mountain might have wanted to join industry programs intended to lure people back to skiing; they did not have the resources to solve a problem of this size alone.

Another possibility was that Copper Mountain was losing share of the Denver-area ski business to Keystone and Breckenridge, Copper Mountain's closest neighbors. In that case, Copper Mountain's managers would have wanted to identify the reasons for the defections and see what they could do to regain the lost business.

Still another possibility was that the whole Denver ski area was losing skiers to Vail or Steamboat or to new resorts in Utah or California. If so, Copper Mountain would have wanted to know whether the problem was centered in Vail or Steamboat, or in Utah or California, or possibly in some combination of all four. If so, they would have wanted to join Keystone and Breckenridge in efforts to persuade skiers to ski near Denver.

Copper Mountain's managers had a lot of information available to guide their planning. Government surveys and forecasting studies and surveys and studies sponsored by the ski industry provided trend data on number and destinations of ski trips, attitudes toward skiing, and comparisons among skiing and other major forms of outdoor recreation. These surveys and studies could provide clues as to whether skiing was declining in popularity and what activities were replacing it. The surveys would also help identify the geographic, psychographic, and demographic groups among whom the declines were most precipitous, as well as provide some provisional assessment of the reasons why.

To supplement this very useful information, Copper Mountain had findings from its own research program, which included an annual mail survey among past and potential customers. This survey asked questions about skiing practices and preferences, about skiing conditions and facilities at Copper Mountain and its principal competitors, and about reasons for choosing one skiing destination over another. In conjunction with the surveys by government and industry sources, this information could help Copper Mountain's managers determine where and why they were losing business.

Copper Mountain also conducted between 2,000 and 3,000 "chairlift" interviews each year—that is, interviewers rode the chairlift asking about skiing habits and preferences, about whether customers were skiing more or less this year than in previous years and why, about the skiing conditions, facilities, and personnel at Copper Mountain and its major competitors, and about awareness of and reaction to Copper Mountain's advertising and marketing programs. Finally, Copper Mountain sponsored periodic focus-group discussions with local skiers. These free-ranging in-depth interviews covered topics as specific as individual Copper Mountain advertisements and as general as the emotional reactions evoked by the skiing experience. They were also an important source for generating and testing campaign themes.

Taken together, the data collected from these surveys and interviews provided much food for thought. First, and most importantly, the findings supported management's belief that the decline in business was greatest among front-range day skiers and that front-range day skiers were but one of three important segments of the business; the other two were those skiers who spent a week or more at the resort and those who came to Copper Mountain from Keystone or Breckenridge in search of new skiing experiences.

The Copper Mountain surveys did point to one potentially solvable problem close to home. Many skiers, especially front-range day skiers, said that although Copper Mountain was well know as a "skier's mountain," it was perceived as lacking the night life of its nearby competitors. At Copper Mountain the skiing was great, but there wasn't much to do after sundown. The surveys also indicated that cost was becoming an increasingly important factor.

Finally, Copper Mountain's surveys showed that although Keystone and Breckenridge did take shares of Copper Mountain's business, they also *contributed* to that business because many of Copper Mountain's day skiers came from Keystone or Breckenridge. More importantly, the surveys disclosed that the variety offered by the three different resorts attracted a significant number of highly profitable customers who might otherwise have gone to Utah or California.

This information was used in developing new advertising. The resort's previous campaign, called Share Our Secret, had focused on Copper Mountain's already high reputation as a skier's mountain. The new campaign was called White Hot and featured plenty of downhill powder, but also provided for a shift in emphasis depending on the advertisement's intended audience.

When the White Hot and Share Our Secret concepts were both presented to focus groups, the vote went to Share Our Secret because the campaign focused more single-mindedly on the skiing experience. When the White Hot concept was paired with a vivid illustration of a downhill skier, however, respondents said, "Oh, look at all that powder! I won't be disappointed if I go to ski there." Further, when references to night life were increased, responses became even more enthusiastic.

With the introduction of the White Hot campaign, Copper Mountain's ongoing research program showed high awareness of the advertising and increases in the number of both front-range day skiers and longer-term visitors—all during a period when business in other areas was down dramatically.[1] Later in this chapter, we will complete the story of Copper Mountain's strategic campaign.

One of the ads from Copper Mountain's White Hot campaign.

(Courtesy of Copper Mountain Resort)

$\mathcal{R}$ESEARCH: THE QUEST FOR INTELLIGENCE

Principle

Understanding can come from research as well as from experience.

If an advertising agency were a factory, the products coming out the back door would be advertisements and media purchases. The raw material going in the front door would be information. Information is the basic ingredient from which all advertisements and all media purchases are made.

This information comes from two major sources. The first and most important source is the collective business and personal experience of the advertiser and the advertising agency. In the Copper Mountain case, for example, all of Copper Mountain's top executives had previous experience in the ski business. They also spent a great deal of their own time talking to managers of other resorts, including resorts such as cruise lines and amusement parks, reading about skiing and ski resorts, talking to customers, and communicating with their employees and with one another about management and planning problems. Many of Copper Mountain's managers were skiers themselves.

[1] Adapted from Joseph Hydholm, "Retaining Heat: Research and a Strong Marketing Program Keep Copper Mountain's Business Hot," *Quirk's Marketing Research Review* (March 1991):6–7, 40–41.

Every advertising campaign has similar personal input. For example, Shirley Polykoff, the copywriter who created the classic, award-winning Does she or doesn't she? campaign for Clairol hair coloring, recounted this experience:

> In 1933, just before I was married, my husband had taken me to meet the woman who would become my mother-in-law. When we got in the car after dinner, I asked him, "How'd I do? Did your mother like me?" and he told me his mother had said, "She paints her hair, doesn't she?" He asked me, "Well do you?" It became a joke between my husband and me; anytime we saw someone who was stunning or attractive we'd say, "Does she or doesn't she?" Twenty years later, I was walking down Park Avenue talking out loud to myself, because I have to hear what I write. The phrase came into my mind again. Suddenly I realized, "That's it. That's the campaign."[2]

The second source of information is formal research—surveys, in-depth interviews; **focus groups**, which are like in-depth interviews but involve a group rather than individuals, and all types of primary and secondary data. **Marketing research** is used to identify consumer needs, develop new products, evaluate pricing levels, assess distribution methods, and test the effectiveness of various promotional strategies. One type of marketing research, called **market research**, is much more specific and is used to gather information about a particular market. Although information of this sort plays a major role in every major advertising campaign, it is always assimilated into, combined with, altered by, and sometimes even overwhelmed by the professional and personal experiences of the writers, producers, and art directors who create the advertising and by the business and personal experiences of the marketing executives who approve that advertising. Advertising is never the product of personal experience alone, however. Even as brilliant an inspiration as Shirley Polykoff's recollection of a 20-year-old experience was no doubt checked against the experiences of others and subjected to various forms of testing before it ever appeared in a magazine. All advertising campaigns are complex blends of fact and fiction, judgment, experience, inspiration, speculation, science, magic, and art.

EXPLORATORY RESEARCH

Exploratory research is informal intelligence gathering. When advertising people get new accounts or new assignments, they start by reading everything that is available on the product, company, and industry: sales reports, annual reports, complaint letters, and trade articles about the industry. What they are looking for with exploratory research is a new insight, an insight that ultimately might demand more formal research and, perhaps, the development of a new strategy.

In an advertising agency the end users of exploratory research are the writers, art directors, and producers who create the advertisements and the media planners and buyers who select the media through which those advertisements reach the public. Before these end users begin their tasks, however, a great many other professionals play important roles in gathering, editing, and organizing research information. Among the most important of these professionals are researchers who work for government departments, trade associations, sec-

---

[2]Paula Champa, "The Moment of Creation," *Agency* (May–June 1991):31–37.

ondary research suppliers, primary research suppliers, and the research departments of advertisers and advertising agencies.

Government Organizations. Through its various departments the U.S. government provides an astonishing array of statistics that can be of great importance in making advertising and marketing decisions. Those statistics include census records and estimates of the U.S. population's size and geographical distribution, as well as highly detailed data on the population's age, income, occupational, educational, and ethnic segments. Demographic information of this kind is fundamental to decision making about advertising targets and market segmentation. An advertiser cannot aim its advertising at a target audience without knowing that audience's size and major dimensions.

In addition to basic population statistics, the U.S. government issues thousands of reports on topics of great interest to advertisers. For instance, the government publishes reports on food labeling and advertising, regulation of alcohol and tobacco marketing, auto safety, and sales and marketing of farm products and financial services. Figure 6.1 offers a sampling of reports that can be obtained from the U.S. government.

Many state governments issue reports on the status of in-state business as well as trend data on business development, construction, tourism, education, retailing, and medical services. These reports, which would include information on tourism, ski resorts, and recreational facilities, would help Copper Mountain measure its performance against the performance of its competitors.

Foreign governments provide information roughly parallel to the information issued by the U.S. government. In other countries that information is just as useful as it is in the United States and is essential in planning and executing multinational advertising.

Figure 6.1

U.S. Government reports of interest to advertisers

Survey of Current Business: Basic operational statistics on U.S. business. (Bureau of Economic Analysis of the U.S. Department of Commerce)
Requirements of Laws and Regulation Enforced by the U.S. Food and Drug Administration: Laws and regulations affecting food and beverage advertising. (U.S. Department of Health and Human Services, Food and Drug Administration)
Economic Issues: How Should Health Claims for Foods Be Regulated? Regulation of health claims in food advertising. (Bureau of Economics, Federal Trade Commission)
Children's Information Processing of Television Advertising: How children react to television commercials. (National Technical Information Service, U.S. Department of Commerce)
Food Consumption: Households in the United States, Seasons and Year 1977–78, released in 1983: Detailed data on consumption of a wide range of foods. (Human Nutrition Information Service, U.S. Department of Agriculture)
Guidelines for Relating Children's Ages to Toy Characteristics: Rules that govern toy advertising. (U.S. Consumer Product Safety Commission)
Vital and Health Statistics: Smoking and Other Tobacco Use: Consumption of tobacco products. (U.S. Department of Health and Human Services, National Center for Health Statistics)
Franchising in the Economy: Statistical review of franchised businesses. (U.S. Department of Commerce International Trade Administration)

Trade Associations. Many industries support trade associations that gather and distribute information of interest to association members. For instance, the American Association of Advertising Agencies (AAAA) issues reports on *The Advertising Agency of the Future, Patterns of Agency Compensation, Case Studies in Effective Advertising, Managing Your Agency for Profit, Executive Compensation and Employee Benefits, Analysis of Agency Costs,* and *Types of Insurance Carried by Agencies.* The major consumers of such reports are advertising agencies themselves, which use them in making salary and staffing decisions, monitoring their own performance, and keeping tabs on competitors. However, much of this information would also be useful to research suppliers, personnel recruiters, advertising media companies, and anyone else to whom advertising agencies are important customers. In a direct-marketing program designed to sell a service to agency executives, for example, basic knowledge of the industry would guide selection of the executives to be addressed, the pricing and design of the service itself, and even the choice of words used to describe the offer.

As background for its own advertising and marketing decisions, Copper Mountain had access to a series of reports entitled *Sports Participation,* issued by the National Sporting Goods Association, *American Teenagers and Sports Participation,* issued by the Athletic Footwear Associations, and *Cost of Doing Business Survey for Ski Shops,* issued by the National Ski Retailers Association.

Other major trade associations include the Radio Advertising Bureau, which publishes *Radio Facts,* an overview of the commercial radio industry in the United States; the Association of Home Appliance Manufacturers, which conducts research and reports industry statistics; the American Meat Institute, which publishes *Meat Facts,* an annual statistical review of the industry; the American Paper Institute, which gathers, compiles, and disseminates current information on the paper industry; and the National Soft Drink Association, which publishes *NSDA News* every month, covering legislative issues affecting soft-drink bottlers and suppliers to the soft-drink industry.

Secondary Research Suppliers. Considering the overwhelming amount of information available from government reports, trade associations, and other sources of marketing data, it is not surprising that a mini-industry has sprung up to gather and organize this information around specific topic areas. Because this information was originally collected by some other organization (and usually for some other purpose), the research is called **secondary research**, and the firms that collect and organize the information are called *secondary research suppliers.* The two most important secondary research suppliers are FIND/SVP and Off-The-Shelf Publications, Inc.

In addition to firms that provide written reports, a new breed of secondary research supplier now provides information via computer terminal. Among the most important of these on-line vendors are Dialog Information Services, Inc., Lexis/Nexis, Dow Jones News/Retrieval, and Market Analysis and Information Database, Inc. With a connection to Dialog Information Service, Copper Mountain's managers could have used Dialog's Marketing and Advertising Information Service to access information on competitors' sales, market shares, and marketing activities. They could have used the Donnelley Demographics database to retrieve mobility, housing, education, income, population, and household information for the local area and for other areas that might be sources of customers. The Prompt database could have been used to identify hot trends in the leisure market in general and in the skiing industry in particular.

secondary research
Information that has been compiled and published.

primary research Information that is collected from original sources.

Principle

Secondary research is information that has already been compiled for you; primary research is information you find out yourself.

Primary Research Suppliers. Much of the information that ultimately appears in the form of advertisements or media purchases is gathered by research firms that specialize in interviewing, observing, and recording the behavior of those who purchase, or influence the purchase of, industrial and consumer goods and services. Firms that collect and analyze this kind of **primary research** are called *primary research suppliers.*

The primary research supplier industry is extremely diverse. The companies range from A.C. Nielsen, which employs more than 45,000 workers in the United States alone, to several thousand one-person entrepreneurs who conduct focus groups and individual interviews, prepare reports, and provide advice on specific advertising and marketing problems. The most comprehensive listing of primary research suppliers is the *International Directory of Marketing Research Companies and Services*, published by the American Marketing Association (AMA). Copper Mountain has relied heavily on primary research, information that is proprietary. Most of this research is conducted by an independent research firm specializing in the ski and leisure-time industry and is directed by a market research manager.

Many advertising agencies subscribe to very large-scale surveys conducted by the Simmons Market Research Bureau (SMRB) or by Mediamark Research, Inc. (MRI). The surveys conducted by these two organizations employ large samples of American consumers (approximately 30,000 for each survey) and include questions on consumption or possession of a very wide range of products and services and usage of all the major advertising media. The products and services covered in the MRI survey range from toothbrushes and dental floss to diet colas and bottled water to camping equipment and theme parks.

Strictly speaking, both SMRB and MRI are secondary data sources; they are primarily intended to be used in media planning, which will be discussed in detail in Chapter 9. Because these surveys are so comprehensive, however, they can be mined for consumer information. Through a computer program called Golddigger, for example, an MRI subscriber can select a consumer target and ask the computer to find all the other products and services and all the media that members of the target segment use more than do consumers in general. The resulting profile provides a vivid and detailed description of the target as a person—just the information agency creatives need to help them envision their audiences.

Advertisers' Research Departments. Almost all large advertisers maintain marketing research departments of their own. These departments collect and disseminate secondary research data and conduct concept tests, product tests, test markets, package and pricing tests, and attitude and usage studies—all types of large- and small-scale consumer explorations. The immediate "clients" of advertisers' marketing research departments are the top offices of their respective companies and the line-product managers who are responsible for the pricing promotion, advertising, distribution, sales, and profit of their brands. As we will discuss later in this chapter, much of this information ultimately finds its way into advertising.

The marketing research department of the Oscar Mayer Foods Corporation provides a good example. Oscar Mayer's marketing research department is divided into two groups: brand research and marketing systems analysis. The brand research group conducts primary and secondary consumer research and sales analysis, serves as a marketing consultant to product managers, reports and interprets broad consumer trends, and works on projects intended to improve marketing research methods. The marketing systems analysis group performs sales analyses based on shipment and store scanner data, supports computer users within the marketing and sales departments, and manages Oscar Mayer's marketing information center.[3]

The product's performance, the performance and marketing activities of competing products, and the needs, wants, values, and attitudes of consumers are essential input to the strategy document described later in this chapter. For many advertising campaigns, the advertiser's marketing research department is the key source of such intelligence. Often this department is also responsible for one other activity that directly affects the marketer's advertising: It either conducts or supervises the testing procedures that determine whether an advertising campaign should run. These testing procedures, often called *copy tests*, are discussed in detail in Chapter 21. Copy tests are of great importance to the advertiser because they determine which advertising messages do and do not reach the public. They are therefore directly responsible for the success or failure of the advertising program.

Copy tests are possibly even more important to the advertising agency. In the course of developing a campaign an agency will create many alternatives, some or all of which may be tested by the advertiser's testing system. If that system rejects much of the work submitted, the account can require so much extra work that the agency cannot make a profit on it. Even more importantly, the agency's creative reputation (and the careers of its writers, art directors, and producers) depends on the ads that get through the testing system. Any system that persistently rejects the agency's "best" creative efforts is certain to become an object of bitter controversy.

The Inside Advertising box recounts a day in the life of professional researcher Jack Stratton, director of Consumer Research Services at General Mills. In this account we see persistent concerns about the methods used in various types of consumer research and attempts to make sure that General Mills' Consumer Research Department is serving the information needs of other departments in the company. At the end of this particular day, a 2-hour discussion took place, which centered on the never-ending uncertainties surrounding evaluative copy research: Are the research methods now in use serving the purposes for which they were designed? Or are they being misused in ways that might do more harm than good? These are very important questions to both the advertiser and the agency.

Even when an advertiser is not large enough to support a marketing research department of its own, the information generated in the course of marketing activities can play an important part in determining how that firm will communicate with the public. For example, while revising the marketing program for its line of plant containers, the Weathashade division of the Gale Group—a manufacturer of outdoor lawn and garden supplies based in Apopka, Florida—conducted focus groups with potential customers, in-store observations of plant container purchasers, and both in-person and telephone interviews with retailers and distributors. This research led to the following recommendations:

- Integrate the indoor and outdoor offering under one umbrella, but develop a brand, name, and merchandising system in which either brand can stand alone.

---

[3]Charlie Etmekjian and John Grede, "Marketing Research in a Team-Oriented Business: The Oscar Mayer Approach," *Marketing Research: A Magazine of Management Applications*, 2, no. 4 (December 1990):6–12.

Inside ADVERTISING

Jack Stratton, Director, Consumer Research Services, General Mills, Inc.

8:15 A.M. It snowed last night and the roads are slippery. I arrive at the CRS Building later than normal. My first meeting is with the Manager of Product Guidance Research at Research and Development (R&D). His group's research precedes the large-scale product tests my group fields. He cites recent progress in getting R&D developers to test several variables simultaneously in designed experiments. We both see our biggest challenge as convincing the marketing divisions to move from their one-variable-at-a-time mentality.

9:30 A.M. Make phone calls.

10:00 A.M. Meet with my client service reps for the breakfast cereal division. We discuss client feedback on recent projects. Seems each of the business units in the division wants its research results in a different format. Whatever happened to standardization?

10:30 A.M. I walk through the building, stopping to talk with employees I don't see regularly, especially those in data processing.

11:30 A.M. At my request, a quantitative analyst takes me through some data tables she presented yesterday at a meeting I missed.

12:00 NOON Lunch with my Manager of Stimulus Testing. We walk next door to the R&D cafeteria.

1:00 P.M. Review progress on annual objectives with the Manager of Quantitative Analysis. We agree to repackage one of our product-testing techniques and market it more aggressively.

2:00 P.M. An outside supplier presents a new concept-testing method. It has advantages

Source: Courtesy of Jack Stratton.

over what we can offer, but the price is steep. We are noncommittal about whether we will steer some business their way.

3:00 P.M. Read through in-basket.

3:30 P.M. The Vice President of Marketing Services (my boss) and the Director of Advertising come to CRS for an update on our copy-testing methods. We explain the mechanics of the adult and kid methods. The discussion quickly shifts to very fundamental issues. Are we "slavishly" following a system without understanding how the advertising really works? Is persuasion more important than recall? The session runs an hour late. Our visitors gain a better sense of how we test. We learn of recent examples where our findings have been interpreted too rigidly by divisional marketing researchers.

5:30 P.M. I leave to pick up my son from basketball practice.

- Take advantage of the planned purchase behavior and develop emotional appeals to both the novice and the expert gardener.
- Emphasize size, durability, and fade resistance in the outdoor offering. Emphasize size, color, style, value, and quality in the indoor offering. Emphasize lifestyle and performance convenience for both lines.

- Because of the potential opportunity, Weathashade should be the first company to create major brand recognition in this product category.

- The packaging and merchandising system will increase sales by creating excitement, attracting attention, stimulating interest with product ideas, and suggesting lifestyles. Information should be provided to maintain interest and aid purchase but this information should avoid being highly technical.

- The system should create a selling environment to take advantage of space through efficient stacking, to display the product, and to increase brand presence and awareness. A small on-product label denoting pot size and usage should be explored to reinforce brand awareness in the absence of the full merchandising system. Unique free-standing merchandisers could be incorporated into the design. The merchandising system must be flexible enough to allow use of one component, of multiple components, or of any combination.[4]

When these recommendations were followed, sales increased over 200 percent, surpassing even the most optimistic expectations. Thus strategic research, translated into effective communication, produced impressive results even in the absence of a budget that could support advertising in national magazines or on network television.

Advertising Agency Research Departments. In the 1950s all the major advertising agencies featured large, well-funded, highly professional research departments. Agencies highlighted their research power in new-business presentations, and had a list been made of the most respected leaders in the advertising research field at that time, many oi the names on that list would have been found on agency research department payrolls.

One of the reasons for this prominence was that profit margins in the 1950s allowed the agencies to provide expensive and impressive advertising and marketing research at no extra cost to their clients. Another was that many advertisers' own marketing research departments were relatively underdeveloped. In some cases, such as the Maxwell House Division of General Foods, the advertising agency research department supplied *all* the research used by the client.

In the 1960s both of these conditions began to change. Agency profit margins shrank to the level where agencies found it increasingly difficult to provide research at no extra cost. At the same time, partly as a result of agencies' declining research role, advertisers' own marketing research departments began to grow. By the end of the decade most major advertisers had developed effective research departments that bore primary responsibility for marketing research. In most cases, they took over the evaluative testing of advertisements as well.

Those trends continue today. Although some of the largest agencies, including Young and Rubicam, Grey Advertising, and the Leo Burnett Company, still invest heavily in their own research departments, others have sharply curtailed internal research activities and some have turned the research function over to account managers. Smaller agencies, which never had large research departments to begin with, now hire outside research suppliers on a case-by-case basis.

In those agencies that still have internal research departments, efforts now focus on projects that contribute directly to the development of advertising.

---

[4]"Growing Indoors: Research Helps Makers Of Gardening Containers Expand," *Quirk's Marketing Research Review* (October 1990):6–7, 33–35.

These projects may range from two or three group interviews intended to show how consumers talk about a product or a brand, through small- or medium-scale surveys of consumers' opinions and attitudes concerning a specific product or service category, to relatively large-scale surveys, like the annual DDB Needham Lifestyle Study, intended to identify and measure activities, interests, and opinions within segments of the consumer population.

Those agencies that are too small to sustain internal research departments usually employ outside research suppliers when they need help. In some cases, these agency-supplier relationships become so productive that the supplier fulfills most of the roles of an internal research department.

Information Centers. All large advertising agencies, and even some relatively small ones, maintain specialized libraries (often called *information centers*) that provide access to reference volumes, such as dictionaries, encyclopedias, atlases, cookbooks, books of famous quotations, and trade and general newspapers and magazines. Writers, art directors, and producers use these sources when they need more information about a client, a product, or a brand, and when they are browsing in search of creative ideas. The information center is one of the most important features of the advertising agency research department. Even agencies that are not large enough to support a full-fledged research department usually have an information center of some kind. For a sample of the questions that come in to an information center, see Figure 6.2.

Many information centers also maintain subject and picture files. Subject files contain clippings from magazines, newspapers, and government and trade reports, all classified by subject matter. The subjects may range from "advertisers," "airlines," "animal food," "auto care," and "baby market" to "video," "watch industry," "water softeners," "wine," and "women." Picture files may include "Americana," "amusements," "animals," "architecture," "art," "water," "waterfalls," "witches," "X-rays," and "zodiacs." The subject files provide quick synopses of subjects that may suddenly become important. The picture files provide images that jog creative work. Some of the pictures spark creative ideas and eventually inspire other pictures that finally appear in ads.

Many information centers are wired into Lexis, the Dow Jones Retrieval Service, and other computerized utilities that provide instant access to information in the general and trade press. To take just one example, a Lexis search on key words "Visa" and "Olympics Sponsorship" might produce seven pages abstracting current articles on those related topics from *Mediaweek, Adweek's Marketing Week, Advertising Age, Euromarketing, ABA Banking Journal, Campaign, Bank Advertising News*, and *Tour and Travel News*. This file would give anyone interested in Visa's role in the Olympics a quick and current rundown on what is being written on the topic.

WHO ORGANIZES THE FACTS?

A typical advertising campaign might be influenced, directly or indirectly, by information from many sources, including the advertiser's marketing research department, one or more of the primary or secondary outside research suppliers, and the agency's research department itself. Surprisingly, the problem usually is not too little information, but too much. Someone must sift through the **qualitative data**, which seek to understand how and why consumers behave as they do, and the **quantitative data**—the numerical data such as exposures to ads, purchases, and other market-related events—that are available. This person

qualitative data Research that seeks to understand how and why people think and behave as they do.

quantitative data Research that uses statistics to describe consumers.

- Compile trends of the 1990s as they relate to diet and salt and the impact of salt on the environment.
- We plan to shoot in Sydney and northern Australia. What is the average temperature and rainfall there for mid-July? What are the famous places and landmarks?
- What information regarding the Fourth of July is available at the Information Center? I need both historic and fun ideas.
- I need pictures of birds flying in a flock, teens walking on a sandy beach, a close-up of shells on the beach, a close-up of a red rose, sand dunes with dramatic effect, and pictures of brightly dressed ladies—right away.
- Who are the leading marketers of frozen dinners and entrees? I need sales and market shares.
- Give me the number of families with children under 5 years old, the number of households with heads 25 to 45 years old, and the number of households with incomes over $25,000.
- What was the average Dow Jones Industrial Average in 1993?
- How much did Michael Jordan get for the Nike and Wheaties commercials? What was the package deal?
- Are people concerned about cholesterol in pancakes? Are people aware that pancakes have cholesterol?
- How many breakfast foods containing oats were introduced during the last 5 years?
- What is the weight of a hockey puck?
- How big is the foot-powder market?
- We need pictures of Simon and Garfunkel, the cast of *The Mary Tyler Moore Show*, President Jimmy Carter and his family, and the 1980 U.S. National Hockey Team. We also need their bios.
- We need pictures of brand characters—the original look and the revised ones. Examples: Betty Crocker, the Campbell Soup children, and the Morton Salt girl.

Figure 6.2

A sample of questions answered by a typical advertising agency information center.

must also separate the potentially relevant from the irrelevant material and put the outcome into a format that decision makers and creatives can use.

In advertising agencies with internal research departments that task usually falls to the research department staff. Indeed, the ability to organize huge amounts of information and to deliver that information in a useful form is one of the most important skills members of an advertising agency research department can have. In agencies without research departments the task of collecting and organizing information usually falls to members of the account group. Even in agencies with research departments members of the account group are likely to be highly involved in the final decisions as to what information will be passed on to those who will create the campaign. An account manager who is doing his or her job effectively will play a major role in every facet of the agency's work on his or her brand.

account planner The person responsible for the creation, implementation, and modification of the strategy on which creative work is based.

Account Planning. As mentioned in Chapter 4, Boase Massimi Pollitt (BMP), an advertising agency in London, England, originated the concept of the **account planner**, a new way of thinking about the role of research within an advertising agency. Partly because of the consistently high recognition accorded to BMP's creative work, this concept has spread to other London agencies as well as to agencies in Europe, Asia, and the United States.

Charles Cannon, director of Studies at the Institute of Practitioners in Advertising, in London, defined account planning this way:

The account planner is responsible for the creation, implementation, and modification of the strategy on which creative work is based. The planner will therefore be responsible for the generation, selection, and interposition of the research evidence at each stage of the advertising process, namely, in strategy development (such as the creation of the strategy), and in creative development (such as the implementation of the strategy), and in market evaluation (such as the assessment of effectiveness in the marketplace with a view to the maintenance or modification of the strategy for future work).

He went on to elaborate:

(a) The core craft skill of planning is the translation of research evidence into advertising judgment.

(b) In this sense, account planning is the integration of the research function into the account team.

(c) Research relevant to advertising almost never speaks for itself and almost always requires interpretation which must be based on knowing about research *and* knowing about advertising, not one or the other on its own.[5]

When confronted with definitions of this kind, members of research departments of U.S. advertising agencies usually say, "That's what we've been doing all the time!" Indeed, if an advertising agency research department has not been performing many of these functions, it has probably ceased to exist.

Whether the information providers are called researchers, planners, or members of the account group, the most effective agency research parallels the planner model. Under one name or another, account planning is here to stay. The person who can pick out the most useful information from the suffocatingly large amount of data available, and who can make that information instantly relevant to the problem at hand, will always have an important role in the creative process.

THE STRATEGY DOCUMENT

The outcome of strategic research usually reaches agency creative departments in the form of a *strategy document* or *creative brief*. Although the exact form of this document differs from agency to agency and from advertiser to advertiser, most have five major parts: the marketing objective, the product, the target audience, the promise, and the brand personality.

MARKETING OBJECTIVE

The section of the document that presents the marketing objective reviews the competitive situation and establishes a goal for the campaign. It includes both

---

[5]Charles Cannon, "The Role Of The Account Planner," paper presented at the Conference of the Institute of Canadian Advertising, London, England (June 1986).

past and present sales figures; market shares of the brand and of its major competitors; competitors' advertising and promotional resources, tactics, and practices; and any other information about the brand that may lead to a prediction of early success or risk of failure. Although advertisers and agencies are acutely aware that marketing success depends on many factors besides advertising, advertisers do expect advertising to help them meet their marketing goals. It is therefore important that everyone involved in the development of the campaign understand exactly what those goals are. If the advertiser has an unspecified but totally unreasonable marketing objective, and the agency, through ignorance, implicitly agrees to meet that objective, the agency has unknowingly put itself in an extremely vulnerable position. In the strategy document the marketing objective should be specific; it should be agreed to at the outset.

THE PRODUCT

The product section of the strategy document includes the results of product tests, consumers' perceptions of the brand and its major competitors, and tests of or reactions to the brand's and its competitors' advertisements, promotions, retail displays, and packaging. In other words, any facts, opinions, perceptions, or reactions to the product that might fuel an advertising campaign are presented in this section of the strategy document.

THE TARGET AUDIENCE

The next section of the document provides a demographic and psychographic description of the campaign's target audience. The demographic data come from secondary sources or from surveys that reveal the age, income, education, gender, and geographical distribution of the consumers who might be persuaded to adopt the brand. The psychographic information comes from attitude and opinion surveys, individual in-depth interviews, or focus groups, all of which help paint a portrait of the target as a person. The Lifestyle box examines how an advertiser uses research to attract a specific target audience. Ad 6.1 for MTV is an example of an ad that is targeted at a specific audience.

Both the creative team, who must create communication, and the media planners, who must decide how and when to contact targets most efficiently, need to know as much as they can, in as much depth and detail as possible, about the people they are trying to reach.

PROMISE AND SUPPORT

Advertising always promises some sort of reward the customer can obtain by buying or using the advertised product or service. The promise section of the strategy document tells writers and art directors which reward, out of many possibilities, the advertising should promise. The support section of the strategy document indicates which facts about the product and its users are likely to make that promise most acceptable. Such insights into consumer motivations and purchasing decisions help solve the often difficult puzzle of selecting the most motivating promise and deciding how that promise will be supported.

BRAND PERSONALITY

Brands, like people, have personalities. When a brand has a winning personality, its advertising should perpetuate and reinforce that personality. When a brand

Every day millions eat us up and come back for more.

Which will it be tonight? Slice, pound, simmer and stir? Or unwrap, unpack and zap? You'll try just about everything once. Because of all the things in life you don't want to miss, tops on the list is a good dinner.

How do you get in the face of a generation that crams in so much? With MTV.

Two-thirds of MTV's audience is 18 to 34. The age group that's crashing down the aisles, making their own brand choices, putting food on the table—and still hooked on MTV.

Does it surprise you to learn that besides our strong teen base, so many MTV viewers are 18 to 34? Look at it this way—what does a better job of feeding their interest?

Call up and chew the fat with our Sr. VP/Ad Sales, Harvey Ganot, at (212) 258-8181.

MTV 18→34's
THEY CAN'T OUTGROW IT.
IT'S JUST TOO ENORMOUS.

Principle

Know your product intimately.

has a less-than-desirable personality, advertising should work to remedy the problem. Research that asks potential customers what the brand and its competitors would be like if they were people supplies the information needed to specify the brand's present personality and identifies the kind of improvements that are needed.

STRATEGY STATEMENT

A strategy document is usually prefaced by a brief *strategy statement* that distills the document's main points. Following the strategy statement, the document itself presents the highlights of the most relevant research. Figure 6.3 is an example of a typical strategy statement.

Although formats vary considerably from advertiser to advertiser and from agency to agency, some way of conveying in writing what is known about the product, the brand, the competitive situation, and the prospective customer is as essential to an advertising campaign as a blueprint is to a construction project.

MESSAGE DEVELOPMENT RESEARCH

For the sake of orderly exposition, it is convenient to speak as though research contributes to advertising in a logical, systematic, and linear way. Someone in the

LIFESTYLE

Research Reveals: Mothers Have Changed

How should a baby-food company modify its products and its advertising to attract today's young mothers? Or should it make any changes at all? One company commissioned a mail survey of women typical of Middle America; the study was designed to compare responses from a 1980 survey with those of 1989. Each participant in the research had at least one child 2 years of age or younger.

One major factor in the preferences of the 1989 respondents was the craze for healthy eating. These mothers felt that it's never too early to begin to eat healthy foods. They were quite receptive to buying baby foods that contain natural ingredients and are low in salt and cholesterol. Equally important, these respondents were willing to pay more for these products if necessary, even though they felt rather pinched for funds.

In contrast to the 1980 respondents, the 1989 mothers did not feel that their family income was sufficient to satisfy most of their important desires. In fact, one half of these mothers asserted that their families were already too heavily in debt. Fortunately, the newer mothers were optimistic that their family finances would improve markedly within five years.

Although the newer mothers didn't say that children are the most important element in a marriage, they did assert that in making family decisions, the children's needs should come first. This was a distinct difference from mothers in the prior decade. Compared to the mothers of 1980, the newer mothers weren't such fervent cooks and preferred that meal preparation require as little time as possible. The mothers themselves seemed to have healthier eating patterns than did the women in the earlier study. They were less likely to skip lunch, for example, or to feel they overate.

In general, the mothers of 1989 were seeking interesting, even adventurous, personal lives. Over the nine-year time span the more recent mothers were more likely to see themselves as people who would "try anything once." They bought on impulse and relished the fun of purchasing new products or different things for themselves and their families. However, they were just as concerned as the earlier mothers about checking on prices, shopping for specials, and making shopping lists before they set out. The newer mothers were also far less partial to store brands and instead tried to stick to well-known brand names. Unlike the earlier mothers, they did not feel that advertising insults the purchaser's intelligence, although both the 1980 and the 1989 mothers thought that advertising provides information that shapes better buying decisions.

The mothers of 1989 were more concerned with creating a distinctive appearance than were the earlier set of mothers, and they definitely wanted to feel attractive to males.

The women in the later survey were also more apt to feel that they worked hard and operated under a good deal of pressure. They didn't find much spare time in their days, and they were less likely to establish neighborhood friendships. Perhaps this was because a majority expected to be moving at least once within the next five years. All in all, they were not entirely content with their lives and would do things differently, given the chance.

Exercise: Now that you know something about how recent consumers, as compared to those of a decade earlier, feel about their lives, what kinds of research do you think might help you sharpen your advertising message?

Source: DDB Needham Worldwide, *Lifestyle Profile: Changes In Mothers Of Children 2 Years And Younger, 1980 vs. 1989* (July 1989).

---

agency research department or the account group collects and organizes a vast array of facts, distills those facts into a strategy document, and hands that document over to previously uninformed writers and art directors, who then go off and create some advertising.

That impression is almost entirely wrong. Although facts do indeed play an important role in many advertising campaigns, they are always filtered through and evaluated against a system of ideas, experiences, prejudices, memories of past successes and failures, hierarchical relationships, and tastes and preferences within the advertiser's own company and within the advertising agency. Decisions as to what facts find their way into advertisements are never cut and dried.

1. Marketing Objective

Increase consumption of milk by members of the target audience by 10 percent.

2. The Product

Although milk is considered to be among the healthiest of beverages, milk drinking drops off sharply in the teenage years. Part of the problem is concern about fat and calories, part has to do with taste, and part has to do with milk's childish and unexciting image. Advertising can have its most direct effect on the image problem.

3. The Target Audience

Males and females 16 to 30 years old. Milk is a beverage they had to drink as children, and although they are still drinking it, they are choosing more often to drink other beverages. Milk has become less relevant to their lifestyle. They believe milk doesn't go as well with foods they like, such as pizza, Mexican cooking, and Oriental dishes. Females in particular are concerned about the calories and fat in milk.

Other beverages, such as soft drinks, are of greater interest to this group. Soft drinks are an exciting, versatile, and socially acceptable alternative to milk, which is practical, unexciting, and conservative.

These people are active and energetic. They want very much to be popular with their peers, to be attractive, and to look and feel fit.

4. Promise and Support

Today's milk can help you become the attractive, fun, dynamic person you want to be (promise). Milk has the nutrition your body needs to look and feel terrific. Today's most attractive and dynamic people drink milk. Ice-cold milk tastes great (support).

5. Brand Personality

Personality now: childish, practical, conservative. Needed personality: exuberant, contemporary, young adult.

Furthermore, as writers and art directors begin working on a specific creative project, they almost always conduct at least some informal research of their own. They may talk to friends—or even strangers—who might be in the target audience. They may visit retail stores, talk to salespeople, and watch people buy. They may visit the information center, browse through reference books, and borrow subject and picture files. They will conjure up old memories, as Shirley Polykoff did when thinking about the Clairol campaign. They will look at previous advertising (especially the competition's) to see what others have done, and in their heart of hearts they will become absolutely convinced that they are able to create something better than, and different from, anything that has been done before. This informal, personal research has a powerful influence on what happens later on.

DIAGNOSTIC RESEARCH AND EARLY FEEDBACK

diagnostic research Research used to identify the best approach from among a set of alternatives.

early feedback Preliminary reactions to alternative creative strategies.

Diagnostic research is used to choose the best approach from among a set of alternatives. As creative ideas being to take shape, writers and art directors bounce their ideas off each other and discuss them with their supervisors in the creative group. At this point, they may request some feedback from consumers, just to help them decide whether they are on the right track. **Early feedback** is the target audience's evaluation of alternative creative strategies. This feedback usually takes the form of loose, unstructured conversations with members of the target audience, either in individual interviews or in focus groups. Sometimes the people working on the advertising participate in these conversations; sometimes they only watch.

When advertising begins to approach a more finished form, diagnostic research becomes more clearly defined. Creative concepts are translated into rough comprehensives and storyboards—presentation pieces that show the artwork and print to be used in the final ad. Ideas begin to look more like print ads and television commercials. Consumers now have something specific to look at, and their reactions and evaluations to the concepts presented are taken more seriously.

Consumers aren't the only source of input at this stage, however. Supervisors within the creative department react favorably or unfavorably to early versions. Creative directors—the executives who are ultimately responsible for the agency's creative product—exercise editorial control. Creative review boards—groups of senior executives—might have the final word concerning what may and may not be submitted to the client.

In most cases, the advertiser also plays a part. Brand managers or their assistants review and comment on rough executions of the ad. They might request major changes. They might also pass the advertisement up the line so that higher-level executives can make contributions.

Whether from the agency or the client, these evaluations are all based on guesses about how consumers ultimately will react to the advertising. This is where diagnostic research can help. Instead of *guessing* how prospects will interpret an advertisement, the agency and the advertiser can *hear* what real consumers think.

Contact Methods. Message development research may use any combination of methods to contact customers. The contact can be in person, by telephone, or by mail. In a personal interview the researcher asks questions of the respondent directly. The questions can be either tightly structured in a questionnaire or they can be presented in an open-ended format. These interviews often are conducted in malls or downtown areas.

A telephone survey is used when the questions are relatively simple and the questionnaire is short. It is efficient and, depending on the number of interviewers, can reach many people quickly and easily. A mail survey can be longer and more in-depth than a telephone survey; however, it has to be absolutely clear because no interviewer is present to explain procedure or ambiguous questions.

Primary research data can be reported *quantitatively* in tables of numbers. For example, a survey might find out how many people prefer two-ply toilet paper. The results would be expressed quantitatively as a number and as a percentage of the total. If the survey also reported spontaneous comments, or **verbatims**, it would include *qualitative* data.

verbatims Spontaneous comments by people who are being surveyed.

Survey Research. Several types of quantitative research are important in marketing and advertising. **Survey research** uses structured interview forms to ask large numbers of people the same questions. The questions can deal with personal characteristics, such as age, income, behavior, or attitudes. The people can be from an entire group, or **population**, or they can be a representative **sample** of a much larger group. Sampling uses a smaller number of people to represent the entire population.

survey research Research using structured interview forms that ask large numbers of people exactly the same questions.

population Everyone included in a designated group.

sample A selection of people who are identified as representative of the larger population.

experiments A research method that manipulates a set of variables to test hypotheses.

Experimental Research. In **experiments** researchers attempt to manipulate one (and sometimes more than one) important variable while controlling all the other variables that might affect the outcome. For example, an agency might want to know which of two strategies works better for a particular audience. People who represent that audience would be divided into equivalent groups, and the first group would be shown a verbal execution of one strategy, while the second group would be shown the other. Both groups would then be questioned about whether they understood, liked, or were moved by the message. Differences in response could be used to estimate which of the two strategies is likely to be more effective.

Direct Observation. Direct observation is a type of field research that takes researchers into natural settings where they record the behavior of consumers. Researchers might, for example, conduct an *aisle study* in a supermarket. The assignment would be to note how people buy a particular product or brand. Do they deliberate or just grab a product and run? Do they compare prices? Do they read the labels? How long do they spend making the decision?

A pioneering study of the direct-observation technique concluded that "direct observation has the advantage of revealing what people actually do, as distinguished from what people say [they do]. It can yield the correct answer when faulty memory, desire to impress the interviewer, or simple inattention to details would cause an interview answer to be wrong."[6] The biggest drawback to direct observation is that it shows *what* is happening, but not *why*. The results of direct observation are, therefore, often combined with the results of personal interviews to provide a more complete and more understandable picture of attitudes, motives, and behavior.

Content Analysis. In preparation for a new campaign, agency researchers or account executives often conduct systematic audits of competitors' advertisements. These audits might include only informal summaries of the slogans, appeals, and images used most often, or they might include more formal and systematic tabulation of competitors' approaches and strategies. The basic question always is: "What are competitors doing, and how can we do it better?" By disclosing competitors' strategies and tactics, analysis of the content of competitive advertisements provides clues to how competitors are thinking, and suggests ways to develop new and more effective campaigns to argue against and possibly even overcome their efforts.

In-Depth Interviews. A common type of qualitative research is the in-depth one-on-one interview. This technique is used to probe feelings, attitudes, and behaviors such as decision making. The insights can be instructive about how typical members of the target audience respond to the product, to competitors' products, to the advertiser's marketing efforts, and to competitors' advertising and marketing activities.

Focus Groups. A *focus group* is another method used to structure qualitative research. As we mentioned earlier, the focus group is like an in-depth interview, except that it involves a group rather than an individual. The objective is to stimulate people to talk candidly about some topic with one another. The interviewer sets up a general topic and then lets conversation develop as group interaction takes over. (See the following Concepts and Applications box.)

Perils of Qualitative Diagnosis. Although in-depth interviews and focus groups provide valuable feedback at early stages in the creative process, they are not

---

[6]William D. Wells and Leonard A. Lo Sciuto, "Direct Observation of Purchasing Behavior," *Journal of Marketing Research* (August 1966):227–33.

Focus groups have become increasingly important within the creative process.

without problems. The samples of consumers are usually very small, and they may not be truly representative of the whole audience. In the Copper Mountain case, for example, respondents living in the Denver area might underestimate many of the factors that encourage out-of-state skiers to choose Copper Mountain instead of California or Utah resorts.

Because the advertising ideas submitted to early qualitative evaluation are usually in very rough form, they might omit some important element that would make them work very well in the context of a full campaign. In the Copper Mountain focus groups, the "White Hot" idea was poorly received at first, until it was coupled with spectacular illustrations of snow.

A third problem specific to focus groups is that sometimes a small minority of respondents dominates the group, imposing their opinions on everyone else. Although a skilled interviewer can moderate this kind of behavior, the loudest and most authoritative respondents often contribute more than their fair share. Furthermore, when interested parties witness qualitative interviews, they cannot help but single out and remember comments that support their special points of view. With a few off-hand remarks from a small sample of respondents, a copy-writer, an art director, an account director, or a brand manager can become

Focus Groups

In a typical focus group, members of the target audience are invited to attend a group discussion at a central interviewing location.

When the group has been assembled and seated around a conference table, the "moderator" introduces the group members to one another and tries to make them feel at home. The moderator then leads the group through a preset list of topics, encouraging responses and attempting to make sure that all members of the group have opportunities to express what they think and how they feel.

Most focus group facilities provide a viewing room where observers can watch and listen to the discussion from behind a "one-way" mirror. Although respondents are told about the observers, they soon forget that they are there.

Focus groups are valuable because they bring decision makers into direct contact with consumers. Most marketing executives, and most members of advertising agency creative departments, live so differently from their customers that they have little direct day-to-day contact with how consumers think.

The outcome of a focus group depends heavily on the skill of the moderator. The moderator's responsibilities are to make sure that the most significant points are adequately covered and to follow up the most potentially useful ideas by asking insightful, probing questions. That task requires the ability to think quickly in a complex and rapidly changing interview. It requires sensitivity and good judgment, and it demands an understanding of what the client needs to know. Moderators with those skills are scarce and are therefore in constant demand.

After the interview the moderator usually meets with the observers to discuss and evaluate what has gone on. In this discussion the moderator might contribute observations derived from other interviews or from other research in which the problem was somewhat the same.

The moderator may prepare a report that summarizes and evaluates the results obtained from a series of groups. Often such reports contain extensive quotations from the group interactions so that readers who were not in attendance can get some feel for how consumers reacted and for the language they used to express their thoughts. Such information can prove extremely helpful to writers who must understand the thoughts and feelings of their audience.

Focus groups provide direct contact with consumers. Compared with many other research methods, they are more intimate and more personal, and they can be fast and cheap. Although focus groups have many obvious limitations, they are becoming more and more popular.

absolutely convinced that he or she had been on the right track all along. Sometimes even when better evidence presents itself at a later time these convictions can be very hard to alter.

In spite of the inevitable perils, however, the assets of diagnostic research outweigh its liabilities, and both individual in-depth interviews (sometimes called *one-on-ones*) and focus groups are widely used today. For a more detailed description of how focus groups are set up, conducted, and evaluated, see the Concepts and Applications box.

COMMUNICATION TESTS

The drawbacks of qualitative diagnosis have led many advertisers to use communication tests instead. These are one-on-one interviews, usually conducted in shopping malls that supply central interviewing facilities. Shoppers are recruited to fill out questionnaires on their age, sex, income, and product usage. They are asked to participate in a "study of consumers' opinions," and they are sometimes offered a small fee for their cooperation.

In the interviewing room respondents are shown advertisements one at a time and asked a standard list of questions such as:

- As you looked at the commercial, what thoughts or ideas went through your mind and what feelings did you have?

- In your own words, please describe what went on and what was said in the commercial.

- Besides trying to sell the product, what was the main point of the commercial?

- What was the name of the product advertised?

- Was there anything in this commercial that you found confusing or hard to understand?

- What, if anything, did you like or dislike about this commercial?

As the respondents answer the questions, the interviewer writes down the answers verbatim. The answers are later analyzed to determine how well respondents understood the message and how they reacted to the way the message was presented.

The verbatim comments are coded into categories such as:

- Main-point playback
- Spontaneous-claim recall
- Name recall
- Positive feelings
- Negative feelings
- Reactions to characters
- Believability
- Likes
- Dislikes

Communication-test samples are generally larger and usually somewhat more representative of the target audience than are the samples typically used for individual in-depth interviews or focus groups. Furthermore, although the coding of verbatim responses always requires a certain amount of judgment, it is not as casual and subjective as the interpretation of the more qualitative forms of diagnostic research.

Many communication tests also include a set of scales intended to capture a wide range of reactions. These scales, designed to include most of the ways consumers can respond to advertisements, supplement the answers to the open-ended questions. They also help less articulate respondents express their opinions, and they sometimes suggest ideas that respondents have not thought to mention.

Even though the communication test has some obvious limitations, it can usually provide answers to three fundamental questions:

1. Did the advertisement convey the message it was intended to convey?

2. Did the advertisement convey any messages it was not intended to convey?

3. How did consumers react to the characters, the setting, the message, and the tone of the advertising?

The answers to these questions are valuable because they come at a time when it is still relatively easy to make changes. Changes will be much more difficult and expensive to make later in the advertising development process. Early feedback is especially important, for example, in catching and weeding out plot lines that may involve stereotyping and other negative portrayals of some groups. It is much better not to have developed an advertisement fully than to have to pull it later—with apologies.

Although not all communication-test results are that clear-cut, these tests can reveal that an advertisement is failing to deliver the message it was intended to deliver, or that it is succeeding in delivering a message never intended. Such findings can avoid a lot of problems later on.

HOW RESEARCH IS USED: BACK TO COPPER MOUNTAIN

Advertising campaigns evolve continuously, and sale results are never final. Now that we know the details of strategic research, let's see how successful Copper Mountain's campaign has been recently. As a result of the White Hot campaign and Copper Mountain's other marketing efforts, Copper Mountain's 1990–1991 ski season was the best ever, measured in number of skier visits. However, the season was not so good when measured in terms of total resort revenue. To counter deep discounts offered by competitors, Copper Mountain had discounted lift tickets and these discounts had led to a decrease in income. Visits up; revenue down: a condition that had to be corrected.

An additional problem surfaced in 1991–1992. In an effort to restore revenue, Copper Mountain modified its discount program and became less price competitive in a time of economic recession. Furthermore, several of Copper Mountain's immediate competitors completed substantial, visible, and effectively advertised upgrades in physical facilities. These changes led to decreases in visits to Copper Mountain and further decreases in revenue.

Therefore, Copper Mountain's objective for the 1992–1993 ski season became "increase visits without sacrificing revenue to deep discount offers," in the face of an economic recession and stronger competitors. At this point, research reentered the strategic picture. Copper Mountain's research had consistently shown that the physical nature of the mountain itself was one of Copper Mountain's most important and most enduring advantages. Unlike other ski mountains, Copper Mountain naturally divided into three areas: one most appropriate for beginners, one most appropriate for intermediate skiers, and one most appropriate for advanced skiers. In describing this natural feature before the Copper Mountain resort was constructed, a report from the U.S. Forest Service had said, "If a mountain was ever created for skiing, it is Copper Mountain."

Copper Mountain's natural three-way separation is an important competitive advantage because it provides an opportunity to segment ski activities in such a way that paths used by beginners, intermediate, and advanced skiers did not intermingle and interfere with each other. Focus groups and chairlift inter-

WHAT A LITTLE TEMPORARY INSANITY CAN DO FOR YOUR STATE OF MIND.

Let loose for some therapy. At Copper Mountain. 76 trails, four bowls and 20 lifts – including two high-speed quads. And we're just 75 minutes from Denver. We have packages that will help you save like crazy, too. *For reservations, call your travel agent or 800-458-8386.*

COPPER MOUNTAIN® RESORT
COLORADO

views had consistently shown that, as might be expected, natural traffic control improved the skiing experience for skiers at all skill levels.

Consequently, the White Hot campaign yielded to a new campaign that was itself segmented to take maximum advantage of this unique terrain configuration. One segment of the campaign, placed in ski magazines during September and October, appealed to expert skiers. One advertisement in this segment showed an obviously challenging ski path down an untouched segment of the mountain. The headline was, "Tear This Up." (See page 206.) Another advertisement in this segment also pictured an obviously challenging path for experts. It said, "What a little temporary insanity can do for your state of mind" (see Ad 6.2).

A second segment of the campaign addressed less aggressive "destination" skiers. Inspired by a survey finding that consumers in general were feeling increasingly hassled by world and national events, especially the downturn in the economy, it said, "Life is an uphill battle. Reverse the trend for a week or two" (Ad 6.3). The copy focused less on challenging terrain, and more on Copper Mountain's resort amenities.

A third segment of the campaign addressed front-range day skiers. Based on findings from chairlift surveys, this segment drove home the point that, due to

Copper Mountain's segmented terrain, waiting lines were shorter at Copper Mountain than at local competitors. To illustrate this competitive advantage, the campaign employed television—a medium that would have been prohibitively expensive for the national coverage required by the other segments.

Under the new theme line of Colorado's Perfect Mountain, the segmented campaign contributed to a new record season. Revenue increased, and visits increased among all types of skiers. Note the qualification "contributed to." One of the factors that contributed mightily to the success of the Colorado's Perfect Mountain campaign was a *great snow year*. In the 1992–1993 ski season, Colorado received more snow than it had at any time in recent history. The snow was especially heavy late in the season, when skiing would normally have become much softer.

As the history of the White Hot campaign demonstrates, successful advertising cannot continue to produce sales increases on its own. By itself, advertising cannot overcome competitors' advantages, and it cannot compensate for sharp downturns in the economy. Advertising must evolve along with other segments of the marketing mix to adjust to competitors' activities and to other changes in the marketing environment. This evolution is greatly aided by a continuing flow of information as to what is going on, especially fresh information about how customers and potential customers are feeling, thinking, and reacting. This information makes reasoned adjustments possible and contributes greatly to the sales results of advertising. No doubt things will change again for Copper Mountain, and no doubt further adjustments based on additional infor-

Ad 6.3

This ad is addressed to destination skiers.

(Courtesy of Copper Mountain Resort)

LIFE IS AN UPHILL BATTLE.
REVERSE THE TREND FOR A WEEK OR TWO.

Something about a downhill run exhilarates and liberates. At Copper Mountain, you can make those runs on 76 trails and four bowls rated the best in America. Our ski-in/ski-out alpine village offers a variety of shopping, restaurants and nightlife. Vacation packages start at just $52,* including AAA Four-Diamond lodging, lift tickets and access to our $3 million Racquet and Athletic Club.
Call your travel agent or 800-458-8386, Ext. 1.

COPPER MOUNTAIN® RESORT
COLORADO

*Rates per person, per night based on double occupancy and subject to space availability. Rate available through 12/12/91. Certain restrictions apply.

mation will be needed. For an advertiser like Copper Mountain, the advertising task is never finished, and the marketing game is never over.

As we noted early in this chapter, information is the raw material out of which advertising campaigns are made. Although much of this information comes from the professional and personal experiences of those who are responsible for creating and approving the advertising, a great deal of it comes from research of one type or another. In the end, these sources of information are intricately and untracably mixed. Examples like, "Does she or doesn't she?" and those in which one specific research finding led directly and unambiguously to one particular illustration or theme line are rare. And, even in those cases, many other considerations play important parts in the development of the campaign. In one way or another, research plays an important role in most advertising campaigns. Still, research is only *one source* of creative inspiration, as following chapters show.

UMMARY

- Information is the basic ingredient from which all advertisements and all media purchases are made.

- A very important part of advertising information comes from the personal and professional experiences of the men and women who are responsible for developing and evaluating the advertising. Another part of this information comes from formal research. In the development of any campaign these two information sources interact in complex ways.

- Formal research is provided by government departments, trade associations, secondary research suppliers, primary research suppliers, and the research departments of advertisers and advertising agencies.

- In the development of an advertising campaign the problem is seldom too little information but too much. Someone must identify, collect, and organize the most useful information and present it in a useful form. That task usually falls to members of the advertising agency research department, or, in the absence of a research department, to the account group.

- The most important research information usual-

ly goes into a strategy document that is, in a rough sense, a plan for the campaign.

- The difficult decisions as to just what information should go into the strategy document and how that information should be interpreted call for interactive judgments on the part of the advertiser and its agency. Within the agency, these judgments involve all those responsible for making sure that the communication works. These judgments are never automatic or obvious, nor are they cut and dried.

- Once creative work has started, the developing advertising ideas may be checked for effectiveness with the intended audience through relatively qualitative and informal diagnostic research.

- Although diagnostic research provides exposure to real consumers, it also opens the possibility that potentially excellent ideas may be rejected or that previous prejudices may be confirmed. Despite these risks, diagnostic research provides a valuable safeguard against the possibility that the finished advertising will fail to convey the intended message or that it will contain some message it was not intended to convey.

QUESTIONS

1. Every year Copper Mountain must decide how much emphasis to put on front-range day skiers versus skiers from the Denver market who stay overnight versus skiers from outside Copper Mountain's geographic area. What research information would help Copper Mountain's managers make those decisions? Where would they get that information?

2. Suppose you had the opportunity to develop a research program for a new bookstore serving your college or university. What kind of exploratory research would you recommend? Would you propose both qualitative and quantitative studies? What specific steps would you take?

3. The research director for Angelis Advertising always introduces her department's service to new agency clients by comparing research to a road map. What do maps and research studies have in common? How does the analogy of a map also indicate the limitations of research for resolving an advertising problem?

4. Judging from the chapter discussions, would you expect the following databases to be developed from primary or secondary resources:

   a. national television ratings

   b. consumer brand's ad awareness scores

   c. household penetration levels for VCRs

5. Research professionals recommend using focus groups to help develop a campaign strategy or theme, but many are opposed to using focus groups to choose finished ads for the campaign. Is this contradictory? Why or why not?

6. A new radio station is moving into your community. Management is not sure how to position the station in this market and has asked you to develop a study with this decision.

   a. What are the key research questions that need to be asked?

   b. Outline a research program to answer those questions that uses as many of the research methods discussed in this chapter as you can incorporate.

7. In the course of diagnostic research, a few focus group respondents contradict an opinion based on years of professional and personal experience. Suppose that opinion is held by your client's top management. If you are a researcher, what do you do? Suppose that opinion is held by the creative director of your agency. What do you do? Suppose it is your opinion. What then?

SUGGESTED CLASS PROJECT

Run a focus group. Brainstorm to come up with something the class would like to advertise, for example, new audio equipment. Divide into researchers and the consumer group (you can run two groups and trade roles, if you like). Meet to decide on questions and format. Make assignments for note taking, facilitating, and collecting and organizing feedback. Write a report.

FURTHER READINGS

DAY, GEORGE S., *Market-Driven Strategy: Processes for Creating Value* (New York: The Free Press, 1990).

EMORY, C. WILLIAM, *Business Research Methods*, 3rd ed. (Homewood, IL: Irwin, 1985).

FLETCHER, ALAN, AND THOMAS BOWERS, *Fundamentals of Advertising Research*, 3rd ed. (Belmont, CA: Wadsworth, 1988).

GREEN, PAUL E., DONALD S. TULL, AND GERALD ALBAUM, *Research for Marketing Decisions*, 5th ed. (Englewood Cliffs, NJ: Prentice Hall, 1988).

KERIN, ROGER A., VIJAY MAHAJAN, AND RAJAN VARADARAJAN, *Contemporary Perspectives on Strategic Market Planning* (Needham Heights, MA: Allyn and Bacon, 1989).

WEIERS, RONALD M., *Marketing Research*, 2nd ed. (Englewood Cliffs, NJ: Prentice Hall, 1988).

VIDEO CASE

ConAgra's Second Healthy Choice

Following its successful introduction of Healthy Choice premium frozen dinners and entrées, ConAgra decided to expand this franchise by extending the brand name to a new line of Healthy Choice cold cuts.

While other marketers had previously introduced "light" cold cuts to appeal to calorie-conscious consumers, no major competitor had addressed health directly. Healthy Choice recognized the opportunity for creating a health segment in that category, with a brand that offered the multidimensional benefits of quality, taste, variety, and health. Healthy Choice capitalized on this opportunity by introducing a full line of popular cold cut varieties especially formulated to be lower than other cold cuts in fat, cholesterol, and sodium.

The target for Healthy Choice Cold Cuts was defined demographically as "upscale women, 25–54." More importantly, the target was defined psychographically as "intelligent, health-conscious consumers who lead busy, active lives and are driven by the need for convenience-oriented products that offer the optimal balance of taste and nutrition." The psychographic definition was especially important because it influenced the creative strategy.

The creative strategy, developed and executed by CME•KHBB, ConAgra's advertising agency, was to generate awareness among health-interested consumers that Healthy Choice Cold Cuts offered an opportunity to eat healthfully, while still providing the taste benefits of their favorite cold cuts. This strategy was based on the research finding that while consumers buy cold cuts primarily for convenience, taste and variety, they are aware that many varieties of standard cold cuts contain undesirably large amounts of fat, cholesterol, and sodium.

The strategy was to communicate that *now* consumers had another choice, and this choice was a healthier choice.

The introductory television commercials employed elements of the successful Healthy Choice frozen dinner and frozen entrée campaigns: celebrity spokespersons, conversational format, and a straightforward presentation of the brand story. The print capitalized on the opportunity to provide nutritional details, and to link the brand with Dorothy Hamill's healthy image.

The media strategy was designed to generate awareness and trial of Healthy Choice Cold Cuts through a continuous presence at "impact levels" for the six-month introductory period. The largest media investment was in national spot and daytime television. A smaller investment in prime-time television enhanced the introduction. Print included large-reach women's service magazines, and health-oriented publications such as *Health, Cooking Light*, and *Prevention*.

Supplemental marketing programs included national in-store couponing, on-pack couponing, and cross-couponing with other Healthy Choice products. In addition, press releases generated editorial coverage of the new Healthy Choice Cold Cuts, and merchandising programs, conducted in concert with the print media, offered free cookbooks and other incentives.

Despite higher spending by Healthy Favorites, a competing line of cold cuts introduced by Oscar Mayer almost simultaneously, Healthy Choice Cold Cuts achieved a leadership position in this new category. The brand exceeded dollar share goals by 45 to 135 percent during the introductory and sustaining periods.

Questions

1 The creative format for the Healthy Choice campaign included celebrity spokespersons, conversational delivery of the message, and straightforward presentation of the brand story. Suppose that the advertiser had decided to take a more emotional approach. How would that decision have affected the promise and support section of the strategy document?

2 What are the arguments for and against such a change?

3 If this change were made, how would it affect the media strategy?

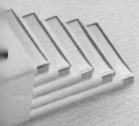

$\mathscr{S}$TRATEGY AND PLANNING

7

CHAPTER OUTLINE

- Wrigley Keeps the World Chewing
- Strategy and Planning
- The Marketing Plan
- The Advertising Plan
- The Creative Plan and Copy Strategy

CHAPTER OBJECTIVES

When you have completed this chapter, you should be able to:

- Identify the key elements of a marketing plan and an advertising plan
- Understand how marketers allocate funds among advertising and other marketing functions
- Explain the difference between product-centered and prospect-centered strategies
- List the key elements of a creative platform

37

WRIGLEY KEEPS THE WORLD CHEWING

Each year, the Wm. Wrigley Jr. Company manufactures more than 14,000 tons of chewing gum which is sold in over 121 countries and territories worldwide.

Chewing gum is a lucrative business—Wrigely's only business. Indeed, Wrigley dominates the world of chewing gum more thoroughly than the Coca-Cola Company looms over soft drinks. Wrigley has a 48 percent share of a $2.4 billion U.S. retail market, nearly twice that of Warner-Lambert Co., the biggest competitor, which makes Trident and Dentyne. And it soundly beats the competitive threat from consumer-goods powerhouse RJR Nabisco, Inc., maker of Beech-Nut and Care Free.

Wrigley's success is a true mystery. In selling gum, Wrigley is a throwback to the time before micromarketing. It continues to run television advertising campaigns with themes that have been around since Eisenhower. It seldom resorts to sweepstakes or other gimmicks to promote its brands. Even so, Wrigley's Doublemint remains paramount among gum buyers worldwide, while Juicy Fruit, Wrigley's Spearmint, Extra, Freedent, and Big Red are holding their own.

"The advertising community bad-mouths Wrigley," says Al Reis, a marketing consultant. "But what Wrigley does is very successful." Atypically, Wrigley almost always maintains or increases ad spending in tough times because gum is such an impulse purchase Wrigley figures it can't afford to become less visible. In 1990 it spent about $158 million on advertising, up from $134 million in 1989.

Historically, Wrigley always plays to win. It has been a fierce competitor ever since founder William Wrigley Jr. refused to join the so-called chewing gum trust—a merger of the industry's six largest companies in 1899—and decided to compete on his own. The company was one of the first to offer premiums such as razors and lamps to merchants as an inducement to sell Wrigley's gum. In 1915, it mailed a stick of gum to everyone listed in U.S. phone books.

Wrigley hit a bad patch in the late 1970s, when its market share declined to 35 percent over a four-year period as competitors began promoting sugar-free gums; but it made a comeback in 1984 with Extra and pushed extra hard. "We had a very late start, and the key was formulating what we felt was a superior product," says Ronald Cox, Wrigley's group vice president of marketing. The more than $30 million Wrigley spent launching Extra was the most it had ever spent on a new brand. By 1989, Extra had become the industry's best-selling sugarfree gum.

Wrigley has also prospered from making something of a science of the relationship between retail price and the number of sticks in a pack. Its Plen T Pak of 17 sticks makes up the bulk of Wrigley sales, but little things mean a lot. After 25-cent packages of five sticks were reintroduced in 1987 (following two years of study and 15 years of not offering a single, or a five-stick pack), Wrigley's single-pack sales increased, and market share rose about 4 percent.

Wrigley also has the industry's most effective distribution network, capable of shipping more than a million pounds of chewing gum a day. And, to stay in touch, Wrigley has its telephone salespeople contact most wholesalers at least once a week. That way, nobody ever runs out of Wrigley brands.

Leo Shapiro, a Chicago-based marketing consultant, sums up the mystique of Wrigley as follows: "The truth is they don't have all that much to sell. . . . The key to their advertising is to refresh their name in the mind of consumers without saying anything."[1]

---

[1] Adapted from Brett Pulley, "Wrigley is Thriving, Despite the Recession, in a Resilient Business," *The Wall Street Journal* (May 29, 1991):A1, A8.

Advertising is both an art and a science. The art comes from writing, designing, and producing exciting messages. The science comes from strategic thinking. Advertising is a disciplined art, and achieving the disciplined side of advertising is the focus of this chapter. Advertising messages aren't created by whimsy or a sudden flash of inspiration. Messages are formulated to accomplish specific objectives, and then strategies are developed specifically to achieve those objectives. This is all done through a process called *planning*.

STRATEGIC PLANNING: MAKING INTELLIGENT DECISIONS

Strategic planning is the process of determining *objectives* (what you want to accomplish), deciding on *strategies* (how to accomplish the objectives), and implementing the *tactics* (which make the plan come to life). All of this occurs within a specified time frame. Marketing and advertising strategies are chosen from an array of possible alternatives. Intelligent decision making means weighing these alternatives and sorting out the best approach. Often there is no *right* way, but there may be a *best* way to accomplish your objectives.

Wrigley's Chewing Gum, as indicated in the opening of this chapter, has apparently found the right way to market its product line. Despite a very conservative advertising program, Wrigley knows exactly what it wants advertising to do. It may seldom win awards, but the company is achieving its goals. The program is carefully planned, every detail is checked, and research scrutinizes every element.

It is sometimes difficult even for those experienced in advertising to tell the difference between an objective and a strategy. Both are important to the development of successful marketing and advertising plans; they are related to each other, but they are also different and serve different purposes. An objective is a *goal* or *task* to be accomplished. A strategy is the *means* by which the goal is accomplished.

Principle

Strategic thinking means weighing the alternatives and identifying the best approach.

For example, if the goal is to reinforce brand loyalty for the product, then any number of strategies could be employed to accomplish that task. Suppose, though, that the advertiser wants to create brand loyalty by emphasizing that the brand delivers more of the benefit than do competing brands. The number of tactics that could be used with that strategy is almost infinite. For instance, the brand could be compared with its leading competitor. Other possible tactics to carry out the strategy are a demonstration, a testimonial, an emotional or funny story, or a straightforward fact-based approach. Naturally, decisions related to media would be intertwined at both the strategic and tactical levels. Engaging in comparison advertising is only relevant if the message reaches the target audience at the right time and the medium reinforces the necessary credibility.

business strategic plan An overriding business plan that deals with the broadest decisions made by the organization.

function plans Plans that relate to specific business functions.

Planning Documents. Planning is usually a three-tiered operation beginning with the **business strategic plan,** moving on to **functional plans,** such as a *marketing plan* or a *financial plan,* and ending with specific plans for each element under that function, such as a *product plan* or an *advertising plan.* Naturally, each ensuing plan is dependent upon the plan that preceded it. It is possible, for example, that the business strategic plan for a particular business suggests that advertising is not necessary. Note how many products in your supermarket have no advertising support, for example, specialty items such as spices and ethic foods. There are probably good business reasons for this situation.

The intent of this chapter is to provide you with a basic understanding of the advertising planning process. In order to do this, however, a brief overview of the business plan and the marketing plan is given. Note that many of the components of the marketing plan were introduced in Chapter 3 and will not be reexamined here.

THE BUSINESS PLAN

Typically, the business plan relates to a specific division of the company or a strategic business unit (SBU). These divisions or SBUs share a common set of problems and factors that can be identified. Strategic planning centering around these units is the most efficient way to plan and optimize the chances for success. Although there are many ways of looking at this planning process, Figure 7.1 depicts a highly regarded model. It begins with a *business mission* statement. Such a statement is derived from the broader corporate mission and includes the broad goals and policies of the business unit, as the next step away from overall corporate goals and policies. Does this business unit want to pursue long-term growth, short-term profits, or technological leadership? How does it feel about its customers, its employees, its stockholders?

The business next would examine its external environment as it relates to the SBU. Environmental factors are normally outside the control of the business and must be monitored for possible opportunities or possible threats. An *opportunity* is viewed as an area for the company's marketing process to move into where the company would enjoy a competitive advantage. Numerous mergers have occurred during the 1990s between related high-tech communication companies (for example, TCI and U.S. West), whose managers felt that combining resources would allow the new company to take advantage of important opportunities. A *threat* is a trend or development in the environment that will erode the business position of the company unless purposeful marketing action is taken. Competition is a common threat, and international competition is increasingly a factor. U.S. automakers are just beginning to meet the threat of Japanese imports. When a business carefully prioritizes its opportunities and the threats against it, it arrives at a much better position for success.

There is also a need for the business to assess its internal competencies. What are the company's major *strengths* and *weaknesses*? Either of these could revolve around financial conditions, personnel issues, and technical expertise, to name but a few. One wonders: Will Chrysler Motors survive without Lee Iaccoca? Companies that are very production-oriented often find they make

Figure 7.1

The business planning process.

Source: Philip Kotler, Marketing Management: Analysis, Planning, Implementation, and Control, 8th ed. (Englewood Cliffs, NJ: Prentice Hall, 1993):79.

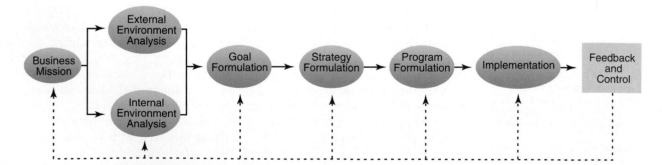

great products but have nobody to buy them, or sell them, for that matter. The company may need to develop its consumer base and hire a sales force. Based on this assessment the company weighs the relative importance of these internal strengths and weaknesses and the external threats and opportunities and prioritizes them, a procedure called a SWOT (strengths, weaknesses, opportunities, threats) analysis.

After the business unit managers have defined the SBU's mission and examined its external and internal environment, they can proceed to develop specific objectives and goals for the planning period. Most businesses pursue several goals at the same time, for instance, sales growth, higher return on investment, higher quality, and market-share improvement. These goals should be prioritized; they should be stated quantitatively; they should be realistic; and they should be consistent.

strategy formulation Specifies how the business expects to reach stated objectives.

Strategy formulation states how the business expects to reach its goals. That is, specific programs are outlined that relate to each goal. For example, many corporations throughout the late 1980s and early 1990s viewed cost leadership as the best strategy regardless of the goal. CEOs were selected strictly based on their reputation for ruthless cost cutting. Prominent examples are IBM and General Motors, fervent proponents of this strategy. Other companies, such as Microsoft, believe that technological innovation is the way to go, regardless of the costs. Still other companies, such as ConAgra, maker of Healthy Choice, have decided to focus on one market—the health conscious in this example. (It should be noted that ConAgra's decision to put all its strategic emphasis on the health-conscious niche may be a risky one, since there is emerging evidence that the baby boomers are going back to a less healthy lifestyle.)

Once the business has developed its principal strategies for attaining its goals, it must work out supporting programs for carrying out these strategies. Thus, if the business has decided to attain technological leadership, it must run programs to strengthen its research and development (R&D) department, gather intelligence on the newest technologies that might affect the business, and so forth.

Even the best plans run the risk of failure if there is poor implementation. Some businesses are wonderful planners but simply cannot handle the hundreds of decisions that are required to implement that plan. Perhaps the company might not have a skilled workforce or it simply may be understaffed. Or perhaps employee motivation is not strong enough. A successful company often promotes enough shared values among its personnel that people are willing to work harder for a common goal.

Assuming that a new plan is implemented, the business needs to track the results and monitor late developments in the environment. Depending upon these findings, the company must determine what, if any, adjustments are necessary.

THE MARKETING PLAN

marketing plan Document that proposes strategies for employing the various elements of the marketing mix to achieve marketing objectives.

A **marketing plan** is a written document that proposes strategies for employing the various elements of the marketing mix to achieve marketing objectives. It analyzes the marketing situation, identifies the problems, outlines the marketing opportunities, sets the objectives, and proposes strategies and tactics to solve

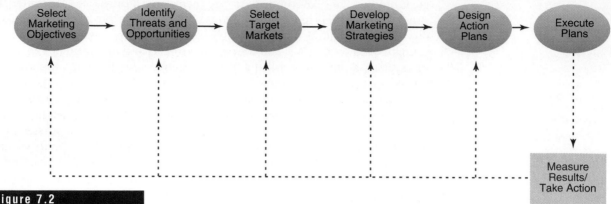

Figure 7.2

Steps in the marketing plan.

these problems and meet objectives. A marketing plan is developed and evaluated annually, although sections dealing with long-run goals might operate for a number of years. Some companies are finding that the marketplace changes so rapidly today that plans have to be updated more frequently than once a year—perhaps even quarterly.

To a large extent, the marketing plan parallels the business strategic plan and contains many of the same components. This is shown in Figure 7.2. For advertising managers, the most important part of the marketing plan is the marketing strategy. It links the overall strategic business plan with specific marketing programs, including advertising. Also, the marketing plan is able to draw on much of the necessary preliminary research that the business plan has already supplied. Therefore, the marketing plan can start cleanly with a statement of objectives. Assessment of the external and internal environments is done on an as-needed basis.

MARKETING OBJECTIVES

As indicated, the marketing planning process often begins with a selection of objectives. The objective may refer to a percentage of market share, unit sales, store traffic, or profit. In some companies the marketing planning process generates the company's corporate objectives; in others, marketing objectives are derived from the company's overall corporate objectives. In most successful companies, corporate objectives and marketing objectives influence each other.

Guided by the marketing objectives and market research, the marketer must then identify and evaluate market opportunities. Finding the cure for AIDS, for example, is a market opportunity for hundreds of pharmaceutical and research firms. Sometimes opportunities are identified by customers' complaints or suggestions. In the case of high-tech companies, opportunities are often little more than a new product looking for a problem. It took the marketing people at 3M over four years to find a profitable use for the adhesive that led to Post-it Notes. In either case, companies must have a mechanism for collecting information, examining trends, and assessing possible opportunities.

PROBLEMS AND OPPORTUNITIES

The heart of strategic planning is analysis—the process of figuring out what all the information and data mean. After you have studied what sometimes seems to be a mountain of information, the problems and opportunities begin to emerge. Spotting the key problem is often very difficult. It takes experience, marketing sophistication, an analytical mind, and a unique way of looking at things. It has been said that a well-defined problem is more than half of the solution. Obversely, an ill-defined problem may not be capable of being solved.

It has also been said that a problem is merely an opportunity in disguise. Some problems that are identified can be solved or overcome. Some have to be circumvented. Others can be turned into opportunities by those with creative minds.

SELECTING TARGET MARKETS

As we know, a *market segment* (the topic of Chapter 5) is a group of consumers having one or more similar characteristics. The dog food market, for example, is segmented according to age of the dog, its weight or breed, and activity level. Dog-owning consumers make choices among brands in these three of four segments. A company selects market segments that can be best served from a competitive point of view. (See Ad 7.1.) The segments selected are the *target markets*.

MARKETING STRATEGIES

An important part of planning is identifying the key strategic decisions that will give the product or firm a competitive advantage in the marketplace. Strategy selection begins with several assumptions that the marketer makes about the market. These assumptions determine the relative emphasis to be given to each of the marketing mix components and lead to the next stage of the planning process.

The initial assumption deals with how the marketer views the composition and ensuing behavior of the marketplace. Two choices are evident. Either the marketer treats the market as *homogeneous*—that is, as a single, large unit—or as *heterogeneous*, as a group of separate, smaller parts known as segments. The former results in a market aggregation strategy, which calls for creating a single product supported by a single marketing program designed to reach as many customers as possible. Originally, Coke followed this single-product approach, until it was forced to consider segmentation. An assumption that the market contains much diversity, or is heterogeneous, results in a market segmentation strategy, which divides the market into several segments. Each segment tends to be homogeneous within itself in all significant aspects, and from these segments the marketer identifies, evaluates, and selects target markets. A company that uses this segmented approach aims to design products that match market demands and design advertising messages specifically aimed toward one or more target markets.

Regardless of whether the market is assumed to be homogeneous or heterogeneous, assumptions must be made about how to best differentiate the product. *Product differentiation* is twofold; it is a *process*, which consists of a series of strategic decisions, and it is a state or marketplace *position* in which the product offering is perceived by the consumer to differ from the competition. A product's perceived differences can be either physical or nonphysical product characteristics, including price. For many years, Miller Lite beer differentiated itself on two basic traits: "tastes great and less filling." Jell-O differentiates itself on the "fun" dimension. As a result, Jell-O also owns the "fun dessert" position in the minds of kids—it is perceived to be fun to eat.

Stated simply, positioning is how the marketer wants the consumer to view its product relative to the competition. Although product differentiation plays a role in creating a product position, product differences account for only part of a product's position. A positioning strategy also includes the manner in which a product's factors are combined, how they are communicated, and who communicates them. Lexus creates a position for its automobiles with elegant showrooms, knowledgeable salespeople, exceptional service, print ads in upscale media, and little talk of price. A product's desired position is the last set of assumptions the planner must make before moving on to the next set of decisions. Ads 7.2 and 7.3 show companies that have established clear positions in the customer's mind.

DESIGNING ACTION PLANS

In order to develop specific action plans, each element of the marketing strategy must be dissected. Typically, at this stage, marketers specify plans for each aspect of the marketing mix. Simply using different proportions of these mix variables makes dramatic differences in marketing action programs possible. The goal is to design a marketing mix that will appeal to the target market and prove

profitable, given the limitations imposed by available resources and the requirements of the marketing strategy.

EXECUTING PLANS

Implementing the typical marketing plan requires a great number of decisions. Making sure the product reaches the warehouse at the right time, that ads are run on schedule, and that salespeople receive the right support material represent just a sample of the details that must be tracked day by day, or even minute by minute. Poor execution has been the downfall of many excellent marketing plans. A case in point is Stouffer Foods Corporation's Right Course frozen dinner entrées. Relying heavily on its reputation for high quality, Stouffer decided to introduce an upscale, exotic set of offerings such as Chicken with Peanut Sauce and Fiesta Beef with Corn Pasta. These choices were made without any input from retailers. In addition, the advertising campaign didn't appear until four weeks after the products were introduced. The products did not sell well.

EVALUATING PLANS

Every marketing plan must include a control component that compares actual performance with planned performance. In most modern businesses, computerization allows access to several performance indicators that management can monitor daily or at any interval they choose. Usually, an annual review is a minimum. In addition to collecting performance data, managers must assess why these particular results have occurred. Finally, if the marketer determines that the gap between objectives and performance is significant enough, corrective action must be taken.

$\mathcal{T}$HE ADVERTISING PLAN

Advertising planning, which must dovetail with marketing planning, can occur at three levels. A firm may operate with an annual advertising plan. In addition to or instead of an annual advertising plan, a firm may develop a *campaign plan* that is more tightly focused on solving a particular marketing communication problem. Finally, a company may put together a copy strategy for an individual ad that runs independent of a campaign. The advertising plan and the campaign plan are similar in outline and in structure. The following discussion focuses on the elements of an advertising plan or a campaign plan.

An **advertising plan** matches the right audience to the right message and presents it in the right medium to reach that audience. In other words, three basic elements summarize the heart of advertising strategy:

advertising plan A plan that proposes strategies for targeting the audience, presenting the advertising message, and implementing media.

- *Targeting the audience*: Who are you trying to reach?
- *Message strategy*: What do you want to say to them?
- *Media strategy*: When and where will you reach them?

The outline that guides the development of an annual or campaign advertising plan is similar in some ways to that for a marketing plan. There is a situation analysis section and objectives and strategies are identified, for example, in both marketing and advertising plans. The most important differences are found in the sections that focus on message and media strategies. A typical advertising or campaign plan can be outlined as follows:

- Situation Analysis:

    The advertising problem

    Advertising opportunities

- Key Strategy Decisions:

    Advertising objectives

    Target audience

    Competitive product advantage

    Product image and personality

    Product position

- The Creative Plan
- The Media Plan
- The Promotion Plan

    Sales promotion

    Public relations

- Implementation and Evaluation
- Budget

SITUATION ANALYSIS

The first step in developing an advertising plan (as well as a marketing plan) is not planning but *backgrounding*—in other words, researching and reviewing the current state of the business in terms of its communication implications. This section details the search for and analysis of important information and trends affecting the marketplace, the competition, consumer behavior, the company itself, and the product or brand. The key word in the title of this section is *analysis*, and that means making sense of all the data collected and figuring out what it means for the future success of the product or brand.

Problems and Opportunities One way to analyze the situation is in terms of the problems that can be identified and the opportunities that can be created or maximized. Advertising exists to solve some kind of communication problem that affects the successful marketing of a product. Analyzing the situation and identifying the problem that can be solved with an advertising message are at the heart of strategic planning.

Different agencies employ different strategies. For example, BBDO uses a process called "Problem Detection" as the basis of its strategy building.[2] Problem Detection takes the question directly to consumers to find out what bothers them about the product or product category.

DDB Needham searches for "Barriers to Purchase."[3] These barriers are reasons why people are not buying any or enough of a product. The American Dairy Association asked DDB Needham to find out why the consumption of cheese was declining. A study identified the major barriers to increased consumption and eventually directed the agency toward the *one* barrier that was most easily correctable through advertising: the absence of *simple* cheese recipes for homemakers.[4]

Flowers Direct is a long-distance floral delivery service that competes with FTD and 1-800-FLOWERS, both of whom, it was discovered, have a major weakness that Flowers Direct can exploit. Flowers Direct connects the caller with a florist in the area where the customer is sending the flowers rather than placing the order with a neighborhood florist who then handles the communication. The advertising challenge was to explain this problem to the consumer and then capitalize on Flower Direct's opportunity to create a competitive advantage.

Advertising can only solve message-related problems such as image, attitude, perception, and knowledge or information. It cannot solve problems related to the price of the product or its availability. A message can speak, however, to the perception that the price is too high. It can also portray a product with limited distribution as exclusive. In other words, although advertising does not determine the actual price or availability of a product, it can affect the way price and availability are perceived by consumers.

ADVERTISING STRATEGY DECISIONS

There is a group of key decisions that is crucial to the development of advertising strategy: setting objectives and identifying the target audience, competitive advantage, product position, and establishing a brand image and brand personality.

Advertising Objectives The statement of advertising objectives evolves directly from the problem and opportunity analysis and answers the questions: What

---

[2]E.E. Norris, "Seek Out the Consumer's Problem," *Advertising Age* (March 17, 1975):43–44.
[3]*Research for R.O.I.:1987 Communications Workshop*, DDB Needham, Chicago (April 10, 1987).
[4]"In-Home Consumption of Natural Cheese," Chicago, unpublished report by DDB Needham Worldwide (1987).

does this advertising message need to accomplish? What effect does it need to have on its audience? Basically advertising seeks to establish, modify, or reinforce attitudes, causing consumers to try a new product, buy more of it, or switch brands. Brand advertising seeks to create an image or personality for a product and carve out a unique position for it.

Models of effects help analyze message impact and structure objectives as a series of steps called a **hierarchy of effects**.[5] One classic approach, the AIDA model, describes the impact on consumers as beginning with *attention*, then moving to *interest*, then *desire*, and finally *action*. A variation is a model developed by Colley, called the DAGMAR model (Defining Advertising Goals for Measured Advertising Results), which begins with *awareness*, moves to *comprehension*, then *conviction*, and ends with *action*.[6] It works like this: If you have skin allergies and Procter & Gamble advertises a new detergent for people with sensitive skin, the ad will probably catch your attention—you are aware of a possible desire for the product. If you are the person who buys detergent for your household, then you may find yourself interested in the idea of this new formulation—you have comprehended its value. You may want to try it and, therefore, when you receive a coupon in the mail, you may respond by picking up a trial package when you are at the store; in other words, you are spurred to action.

As Figure 7.3 demonstrates, simpler effects, such as awareness, are relatively easy to create and get high levels of response. The more complex the effect, the lower the level of response. In other words, a lot of people may be aware of the product, but far fewer will actually try it. The hierarchy model illustrates the relative impact of these various effects with the simplest, but broadest, impact at the bottom and the most complex, but smallest impact, at the top.

Michael Ray developed the *think-feel-do* model of message effects, which

hierarchy of effects A set of consumer responses that moves from the least serious, involved, or complex up through the most serious, involved, or complex.

---

[5]John D. Leckenby, "Conceptual Foundations for Copytesting Research," *Advertising Working Papers*, no. 2 (February 1976).
[6]Russell Colley, *Defining Advertising Goals for Measured Advertising Results* (New York: Association of National Advertisers, 1961).

Figure 7.3

Setting objectives using a Hierarchy-of-Effects model.

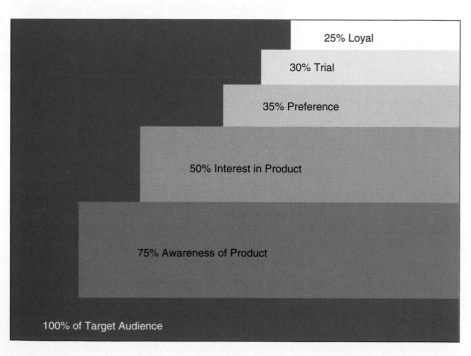

25% Loyal

30% Trial

35% Preference

50% Interest in Product

75% Awareness of Product

100% of Target Audience

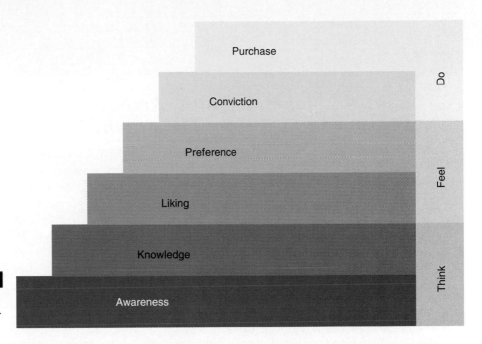

presumes that we approach a purchase situation using a sequence of responses.[7] In other words, we (*think*) about something, then we form an opinion or attitude about it (*feel*), and finally we take action and try it or buy it (*do*). This model identifies three categories of effects called *cognitive* (mental or rational), *affective* (emotional), and *conative* (decision or action). Robert C. Lavidge and Gary A. Steiner associate these categories with the hierarchy of effects in the model depicted in Figure 7.4.[8]

The think-feel-do model is also called the *high-involvement* model because it depicts a series of standard responses typically found with consumers who are active participants in the process of gathering information and making a decision; they are "active" thinkers. This standard hierarchy is likely to be found with product categories and situations where there is a need for information, such as high-priced or major purchases, or where there is a lot of product differentiation, as in industrial products and consumer durables. This type of advertising usually provides many product details and is very informative.

In contrast, the *low-involvement* model changes the order of responses to *think-do-feel*, with the idea that consumers learn about a product, try it, and then form an opinion. This situation occurs when there is little interest in the product or when there is minimal difference between the products, requiring little decision making. It also describes impulse purchasing. A third variation is the *do-feel-think* model, which explains how people try something and learn from the experience. It is called a *rationalization model* because consumers typically select from several alternatives and then rationalize their decision by developing strong positive feelings about the product.

target audience People who can be reached with a certain advertising medium and a particular message.

Targeting the Audience. Advertising identifies a **target audience**, people who can be reached with a certain advertising medium and a particular message. The

[7]Michael L. Ray, "Communication and the Hierarchy of Effects," in *New Models for Mass Communication Research*, P. Clarke, ed. (Beverly Hills, CA: Sage Publications, 1973):147–75.
[8]Robert C. Lavidge and Gary A. Steiner, "A Model for Predictive Measurements of Advertising Effectiveness," *Journal of Marketing*, (October 1961):59–62.

John McGrath, Account Manager, J. Walter Thompson, Chicago

In my 10 years as an ad agency account management person, the question I'm asked most often is, "what exactly do you *do*?" The question is so common that I find myself routinely answering it during student interviews, at cocktail parties, and even during college football games. As a result, I've distilled the answer down to a simple analogy: account management is like the hub of a wheel.

To illustrate the wheel analogy, I explain that ad agencies really aren't like the rigid, linear organizations common to many industries. Rather, agencies tend to be structured into circles of experts who work on resolving client problems. At JWT, these circles are called Core Teams and consist of experts in the fields of Research, Creative, and Media. Also included in the circle are other disciplines such as Legal and Ad Services (the people who work with TV stations and magazines to make sure the right ads run at the right time).

At the center of this circle, like the hub of a wheel, lies the Account Management group, including account supervisors, account executives (known as account representatives at JWT), and assistant account representatives (the entry level account management position at JWT). This group, or "hub," exists to serve two purposes: to keep the "wheel" together, and to keep it moving in the right direction.

The visual below demonstrates how the wheel works for one of my primary accounts, Northwestern Mutual Life Insurance (NML). JWT's relationship with NML dates back nearly 50 years, an unusually long record of service for the advertising industry. Over the years, JWT has earned NML's trust, and in return, we have helped build its image as "The Quiet Company." It is the Account Management group's responsibility to ensure that this relationship remains strong, and that NML's advertising objectives are fully addressed by all the resources JWT can muster.

Courtesy of John McGrath.

The figure illustrates how the Account Management group interacts with other NML Core Team members. The lines linking the center of the diagram with the perimeter represent the number of times in an average week that Account Management communicates with each of the other experts in NML's Core Team. These linkages are like spokes connecting the hub to the rim of a wheel; they keep the wheel tightly focused on NML's business.

The figure also demonstrates the way Account Management helps to keep the wheel moving. First, for example, I work closely with two Core Team members from JWT's Research Department to review the advertising objectives suggested to us by NML. Before any new advertising is created or any media plan prepared, we discuss whether the objectives are clear and sound. Specifically, we review data to identify NML's most promising potential sales prospects, and consider the unique consumer benefit which will make these people consider NML as their life insurer.

Next, Core Team members from the Creative Department become involved. Typically this includes a Creative Director and two or three teams of writers and art directors. My role is to help these Creative experts "wrap their heads around" the target audience and the

target audience can be equivalent to a target market, but it often includes people other than prospects, such as those who influence the purchase. For example, the target audience for an over-the-counter diet program might include doctors, pharmacists, dietitians, and government agencies concerned with health and nutrition, as well as consumers.

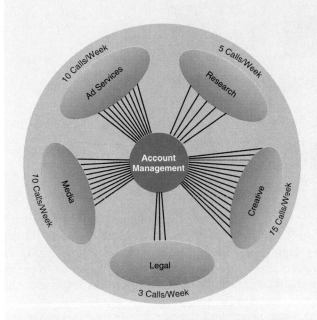

10 Calls/Week — Ad Services

5 Calls/Week — Research

Account Management

Media — 10 Calls/Week

Creative — 15 Calls/Week

Legal — 3 Calls/Week

Creative and Legal team members to agree on acceptable layouts and copy for the ad.

While all this Creative and Legal activity is still hot, I am simultaneously working with JWT's Media Department to determine the best place and time for NML advertising to appear. Typically, I deal with a Media Director, a supervisor, and one or two planners. My job is to make sure they too are comfortable with NML's advertising objectives. I also share the advertising idea with them because there are many occasions when Media team members suggest a unique ad format or size that the Creatives never dreamed of. In the final analysis, they come up with a media plan which maximizes the exposure of the new advertising to NML's target audience. Because of the sophisticated nature of NML's target, this plan usually employs news- and financial-oriented magazines as well as special TV events like the Winter Olympic Games.

Meanwhile, I am also working with the two Ad Services coordinators assigned to NML. They are constantly examining the sizes and formats of all the proposed new advertising and working out schedules for everything to be shot and produced in time to make the insertions outlined in the media plan. Their skill helps to ensure that the advertising that the Core Team has worked so hard to develop will run in the right place at the right time.

It's amazing how complex the "wheel" of an account can be. But if the account is managed properly, the wheel functions very smoothly. It's subjected to a lot of pressure, but it holds together and keeps moving in the direction that's right for the client. Through experience, I've found that this happens when all the experts on the Core Team work together as equals—just like the hub and the rim of a wheel are useless without one another.

So there you have it; a two minute explanation of Account Management. Now, on to the fourth quarter…

consumer benefit we want the advertising to convey. They probe, joke, think, and question. Sometimes they play "devil's advocate" and challenge me to defend the NML's advertising objectives. It's not unusual for Creatives to ask me: "are these really the people we should be talking to?" or "do we think consumers really care about that?" By the end of the process, my job is to ensure the Core Team feels confident enough about the project to begin brain-storming ideas which will become NML's new advertising.

Once the new advertising idea is born, I turn to our Legal Department to ensure that it will be able to pass regulatory hurdles. It's not uncommon for one of NML's ads to be challenged on the grounds that "the network will never accept it," or "you better be prepared for the competition to challenge you." Many meetings and phone calls later, I am usually able to get my

Target audiences are described in terms of their *demographic categories*. Because these categories often overlap, the process of describing an audience is also the process of narrowing the targeting. For example, you might use such descriptors as women 25 to 35 and suburban mall shoppers. These two categories would overlap because a certain percentage of women 25 to 35 are also in the suburban mall shopper category. Each time you add a descriptor, the tar-

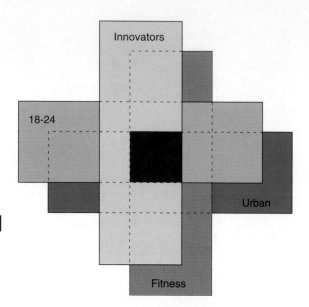

Figure 7.5

Targeting involves the use of overlapping descriptors to identify the most receptive audience.

geted audience gets smaller because the group is more tightly defined. This kind of analysis lets the advertising planner pinpoint the target and zero in on the most responsive audience. Figure 7.5 illustrates how these descriptors zero in on a target. Demographic descriptions like these are particularly important to media planners who are comparing the characteristics of a targeted audience with the characteristics of the viewers, listeners, or readers of a particular medium.

Audiences are also profiled in terms of the personality and lifestyle of the typical audience member. The attempt here is to identify a real person and make that person come to life for the creative people, who then try to write believable messages that will appeal to this person. For this reason, advertising planners usually redefine the target as a **profile** of a typical user of the product. Writers then associate that general profile with someone they know. Creatives have a hard time writing moving messages to a pile of statistics. They can write much more easily and believably to someone they know who fits the description.

profile A composite description of a target audience employing personality and lifestyle characteristics.

Product Features and Competitive Advantage. An important step in figuring out competitive advantage is to analyze your product in comparison to your competitors' products. **Feature analysis** is an easy way to structure this analysis. First make a chart for your product and competitors' products listing each product's relevant features. For example, taste is important for sodas, horsepower and mileage are important for cars, and trendiness is important for fashion watches. Next evaluate the lists in terms of how important each feature is to the target audience (based on primary research) and then evaluate how well the products perform on that feature. Your competitive advantage, as illustrated in Table 7.1, lies in that area where you have a strong feature that is important to the target and where at the same point your competition is weak.

feature analysis A comparison of your product's features against the features of competing products.

Principle

Competitive advantage means you are strong in some area that matters to the target and your competitors are weak in that *area.*

Brand Personality Creating a brand personality for a potato might sound like an impossible challenge, but that actually has been accomplished by Idaho Potatoes. The Idaho Potato Commission has been so successful that, while most people are aware of Idaho Potatoes and associate them with the highest quality,

Table 7.1

Feature Analysis

Feature	Importance to Prospect	Yours	Product Performance		
			X	Y	Z
Price	1	+	−	−	+
Quality	4	−	+	−	+
Style	2	+	−	+	−
Availability	3	−	+	−	−
Durability	5	−	+	+	+

the Idaho Potato has almost gone generic. That is, most people refer to russet potatoes as Idaho Potatoes, regardless of what state they are grown in. However, the Idaho ® Potato name is a federal registered trademark of the Idaho Potato Commission. In an award-winning campaign, the Commission has taught consumers that Idaho Potatoes are unique and to look for the "Grown in Idaho" seal to ensure they are getting genuine Idaho Potatoes. (See Ad 7.4.)

Product Positioning The way in which a product is perceived by consumers relative to its competition is called **positioning**. The concept of positioning was developed by Jack Trout and Al Ries in a 1972 article that pointed to an advertising classic, the We try harder campaign for Avis. The ad positioned the car-rental company as an underdog that would serve its customers better because it had to work harder to compete with the number-one company, Hertz.

Midwest Express Airlines, a national airline offering jet service to over 20 major business destinations from its bases of operations in Milwaukee and Omaha, has used a business strategy that offers comfort and luxury—two-across, wide leather seats, gourmet food, and truly friendly service—at a time when other airlines are cutting back on service and crowding in passengers. However, this "best care in the air" theme did not position the airline completely, and research found that consumers thought the airline was more expensive at a time when the recession made travelers more price sensitive. A new theme, "Best Care. Same Fare." (Ad 7.5) was implemented in the early 1990s in an Effie-award-winning campaign that extended the old position to include value as well as quality service.

Establishing and moving positions requires a tremendous advertising effort. Both Marlboro cigarettes and Miller beer were originally sold to women at one time. Both were later repositioned as "macho" products through extensive and costly advertising campaigns, although recently the audience for beer is being widened to once again include women.

Perceptual Maps Positioning research begins with the feature analysis described previously. From this research you should be able to describe the most relevant attributes of your product. You can then create a *map of the marketplace* that locates the position of your product relative to the positions of all the competitors. A sample two-dimensional (using two attributes) **perceptual map** based on the preceding feature analysis appears in Figure 7.6.

Strategically, the first step is to identify the current position of the product, if one exists, using some form of perceptual mapping. For a new product, and

positioning The way in which a product is perceived in the marketplace by consumers.

perceptual map A map that shows where consumers locate various products in the category in terms of several important features.

YOUNG & RUBICAM SAN FRANCISCO

CLIENT: IDAHO POTATO COMMISSION
PRODUCT: CORPORATE
TITLE: "JUST A SPUD"

LENGTH: :30 TV
COMM'L NO.: ZYRD 1173
DATE: 9/24/91

GROWER: For years now we've been trying to get folks to look for our Grown in Idaho seal

to certify they're getting great quality potatoes.

And we've had some suggestions

like this,

or this,

or, for heaven sakes, even this.

SINGING POTATO: HEY HO, I'M FROM IDAHO.

GROWER: But I think we ought to stick to growing potatoes

and leave looking for the seal up to you.

Just keep an eye peeled,

it's on every bag.

And remember, if it's not from Idaho, it's just a spud.

EFFIE AWARD WINNER

for some existing ones, a position must be established. For ongoing product lines, the decision is either to reinforce a current position or to move it.

IMPLEMENTATION AND EVALUATION

The last section of an advertising plan contains details of the implementation strategy, including scheduling and determining the budget, as well as techniques for evaluating the success of the advertising plan. We will talk in more detail about schedules in the media-planning and media-buying chapters (Chapters 9 and 12). Evaluation is based on how well the plan meets its objectives; a variety of research techniques can be used to monitor effectiveness. One specific type of control is copy testing, a scientific evaluation of the effectiveness of an advertisement. Copy testing is discussed in more detail in Chapter 21.

Ad 7.5

Midwest Express has clearly positioned themselves as the best value in air travel.

(Courtesy of Midwest Express Lines, Inc.)

THE ADVERTISING BUDGET

The advertising budget is established by the company and is usually broken out from the overall marketing communication budget in the marketing plan. In other words, a certain percentage of the *marketing budget* is allocated to *market-*

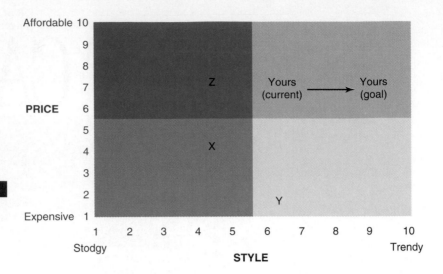

ing communication, and within that budget a certain percentage is allocated to *advertising*. Budget decisions are based on the emphasis given to marketing communication within the marketing mix and to advertising within the marketing communication program.

The budget level is important in terms of an advertising or campaign plan because it determines how much advertising the company can afford. In other words, a $50,000 budget will only stretch so far and will probably not be enough in most markets to cover the costs of television advertising. In addition to television costs, the budget level also determines how many targets and multiple campaign plans a company or brand can support. McDonald's, for example, can easily carry on multiple campaigns designed to reach different target audiences. Certain types of advertisers—industrial and business-to-business, for example—typically operate on smaller advertising budgets than do consumer package-goods companies. Their media choices and narrow targeting strategies reflect their budget and these companies often rely more on direct mail, trade publications, and telemarketing for their advertising.

The big question at each of these levels (marketing mix, marketing communication mix) is: How much should we spend?[9]

Historical Method History is the source for a very common budgeting method. For example, a budget may simply be based on last year's budget with a percentage increase for inflation or some other marketplace factor.

task-objective method A budgeting method that builds a budget by asking what it will cost to achieve the stated objectives.

Task-Objective Method The **task-objective method** is probably the most common method for determining the budget level. This method looks at the objectives set for each activity and determines the cost of accomplishing each objective; what will it cost to make 50 percent of the people in your market aware of this product? How many people do you have to reach and how many times? What would be the necessary media levels and expenses?

percent-of-sales method A technique for computing the budget level that is based on the relationship between cost of advertising and total sales.

Percent-of-Sales Method The **percent-of-sales method** compares the total sales with the total advertising (or promotion) budget during the previous year or the

[9]John J. Burnett, *Promotion Management*, 2nd ed. (St. Paul, MN: West Publishing, 1988).

average of several years to compute a percentage. This technique can also be used across an industry to compare the expenditures of different product categories on advertising.

For example, if a company had sales figures of $5 million last year and an advertising budget of $1 million, then the ratio of advertising to sales would be 20 percent. If the marketing manager predicts sales of $6 million for next year, then the ad budget would be $1.2 million. The following explains how the percent of sales is computed and applied to a budget.

$$\text{Step 1:} \quad \frac{\text{Past advertising dollars}}{\text{Past sales}} = \text{\% of sales}$$

$$\text{Step 2:} \quad \text{\% of sales} \times \begin{array}{l} \text{Next} \\ \text{year's} \\ \text{sales} \\ \text{forecast} \end{array} = \begin{array}{l} \text{New} \\ \text{advertising} \\ \text{budget} \end{array}$$

Competitive Methods Budgeting often takes into account the competitive situation and uses competitors' budgets as benchmarks. *Competitive parity* budgeting relates the amount invested in advertising to the product's share of market. In order to understand this method, you need to understand the *share-of-mind* concept, which suggests that the advertiser's share of advertising—that is, the advertiser's media presence—affects the share of attention the brand will receive, and that, in turn, affects the share of market the brand can obtain.[10] The relationship can be depicted as follows:

$$\frac{\text{Share of}}{\text{media voice}} = \frac{\text{Share of}}{\text{consumer mind}} = \frac{\text{Share of}}{\text{market}}$$

You should keep in mind, however, that the relationships depicted here are used only as a rule of thumb. The actual relationship between share of media voice—an indication of advertising expenditures—and share of mind or share of market depends to a great extent on factors such as the creativity of the message and the amount of clutter in the marketplace. In other words, a simple increase in the share of voice does not guarantee an equal increase in share of market.

For example, Jolly Rancher is David taking on Goliath in the hard candy segment, where Life Savers has 85 percent of the market and a 99 percent share of voice. In other words it has done more than dominate the market, it has owned the media. In an early 1990s campaign that also won an Effie award, Jolly Rancher set out to overtake Life Savers in the rolled candy business (Ad 7.6). In one year, from 1990 to 1991, it moved its share of voice from 1 percent to 21 percent and gained a 39 percent market share increase as a result.

THE CREATIVE PLAN AND COPY STRATEGY

So far we've been discussing advertising planning in terms of an annual plan or a campaign plan, but planning goes on at another level, too. A copy strategy can

---

[10]Ibid.

Ad 7.6

Sometimes it is impossible to spend as much as a competitor. Jolly Rancher successfully uses creativity to make up for their financial limitations.

(Courtesy of Leaf, Inc.)

creative platform A document that outlines the message strategy decisions behind an individual ad.

also be developed for an individual advertisement, and this document focuses directly on the message and the logic behind its development.

These plans go by various names—*creative* or *copy platform*, *creative work plan*, or *creative blueprint*. Not all agencies use such a document, but all copywriters work from some kind of systematic analysis of the problem to be solved. A **creative platform** is simply a way to structure this kind of analysis. It also serves as a guide to others involved in developing the advertisement so that everyone is working with the same understanding of the message strategy.

Most creative platforms combine the basic advertising decisions—problems, objectives, and target markets—with the critical elements of the sales message strategy, which include the selling premise, or main idea, and details about how the idea will be executed. Although outlines differ from agency to agency, the creative platform will include some or all of the following strategic decisions.

Creative Platform	
Advertising Strategy	**Message Strategy**
1. Problems and opportunities	1. Selling premise (claim, benefit, promise, reason why, or USP)
2. Objectives	2. Execution:
3. Target audience	Creative concept
4. Competitive advantage	Personality, tone, feel, or "look" of
5. Brand image and personality	the ad
6. Product position	

MESSAGE STRATEGIES

Advertisements can sell the product in a generic way, a strategy which works only when the product dominates the market, or they can sell the *brand*, a strategy which is usually considered to be more effective. Goodyear, for example, moved from its generic Take Me Home campaign to one that more aggressively set the brand apart from others. The ads end with a slogan that focuses on brand identification: "Nobody Fits You Like Goodyear."

Another message option considers the information content of the advertisement relative to its associational or emotional import. Information advertising is usually straightforward, fact filled, and often focused on news. This approach works for high-involvement products, or in a case where consumers are searching for information to make a decision. That situation, however, is not as common as the low-involvement situation in which consumers are making decisions about products that need minimal information and spend much less time in decision making. In those situations, advertising is more likely to focus on establishing an image or touching an emotion.

SELLING PREMISES

Every salesperson has his or her own idea of how to approach the prospect. Different people and different situations require different strategies, and salespeople are generally more comfortable with certain approaches than with others. The same is true in advertising. The various approaches to the logic of the sales message are called **selling premises.** The most common premises are categorized as either product-centered or prospect-centered.

selling premises The sales logic behind an advertising message.

Product and Prospect Strategies *Product-centered strategies* refer to advertisements that focus on the product itself. These ads look at the attributes, also called *features*, of the product and build a selling message around them; an example is the Jolly Rancher ad that dramatizes the candies' flavors. A **claim** is a statement about performance: how long the product lasts, how much it cleans, how little energy it uses. Torture tests, competitive tests, and before-and-after demonstrations can generate particularly strong claims. Often a scientifically conducted test provides support for the claim.

claim A statement about the product's performance.

Probably the least effective message strategy is one that focuses on the company and emphasizes the company's point of view, goals, and pronouncements with an overuse of the pronoun *we*. This kind of copy is boastful and egotistical.

When you see copy with pompous headlines like "We're #1," "We've been in business for 50 years," or "We're reaching out in new directions," you know you are reading *brag-and-boast* advertising.

Prospect-centered strategies are very much in tune with the consumer-oriented marketing concept, which focuses on needs and wants rather than on what the company can produce. A number of message strategies are built on prospect-centered messages such as benefits, promises, reasons why, and unique selling propositions (USPs).

Benefits In benefit strategies, the product is promoted on the basis of what it can do for the consumers. The Midwest Express ad demonstrate how the airline's unique features are translated into comfort for the traveler. To develop a benefit strategy, you must be able to turn an attribute into a **benefit.** Take a common product, like the shoe you're wearing. Ask yourself what each feature of that shoe does. Look at the sole—besides keeping your feet off the ground, what else does it do for you? Composition leather, for example, means it is durable and long-wearing; textured rubber may mean nonslip; different types of soles have shock-absorption features built in to help diminish the punishment of jogging or aerobics.

The following formula can be used to develop a benefit. First identify a feature, and then tell what it means to you. Fill in the blanks and you will have developed a benefit statement.

The _____ feature is important because it will do _____ for me.

Note that the benefit is strictly in the mind of the consumer, not in the product. It is subjective. Some sample benefit statements are:

- Crest's stannous fluoride means you don't have to worry about cavities.
- Du Pont's cordura nylon means backpacks can be light and yet tough.
- Noxzema's Clear Pink formula brings deep cleaning to sensitive skin; its Clear Green formula brings deep cleaning to oily skin.
- Hampton shoe's Bio Glide provides extra foot stability in each phase of the walking motion.

Promises A benefit statement that looks to the future is called a *promise*. It says something will happen if you use the advertised product. For example, if you use a certain type of toothpaste, then your breath will smell better, or your teeth will be whiter, or you will have extra cavity protection. Hershey's used a promise strategy to reinvigorate sales for its cocoa, which had picked up the image of being high in fat and bad for you.

To develop a promise, use the following formula. First specify how you use the product, and then follow with a statement of what it *will* do for you.

When I use   product , I will get   what benefit .

As you can see from the formula, what you promise is a benefit, so the two are related. Following are several examples of promises:

When I use Dial deodorant soap, I will feel more confident than when I use other brands.
When I take Amtrak, I will be more comfortable, better treated, and more valued (than when I take a plane).

benefits Statements about what the product can do for the user.

Principle

Focus on benefits, not features. Explain what the product can do for the prospect.

When I take Excedrin for my headache, I will be better able
to cope with the stresses in my life.
When I stay at Ramada, I will have fewer hassles than when I
stay at other hotels.

reason why A statement that explains why the feature will benefit the user.

Reason Why A **reason why** you should buy something is another form of a benefit statement. It differs from a promise in that it clearly states a reason for the benefit gained. In many benefit strategies this reason is unstated, implied, or assumed. A reason-why statement is based on logic and reasoning. The development of this form is highly rational. A reason-why statement usually begins with a benefit statement, then follows with a "because" statement that provides the "proof" or "support."

Ad 7.7 for Neutrogena Shampoo is an example of a reason-why ad. Even the headline begins with the word "why." The copy then goes on to provide all the reasons set up in the headline. To provide even more of an impression that the ad is fact-based, it is designed to appear like the editorial matter in the women's magazines in which it appears. The following are some sample reason-why state-

Ad 7.7

Neutrogena gives reasons for using their shampoo in this reason-why ad.

(Courtesy of Neutrogena Corporation/Dailey & Associates/Photo/Bybee S.F.)

ments. Notice how the "because" statement is used to give support to the argument in the examples.[11]

- When I take Amtrak from New York to Washington, I will feel more comfortable, better treated, and more valued than when I take a plane *because* Amtrak is a more civilized and less dehumanizing way to travel.

- When I use Dial deodorant soap, I will be more confident than when I use another brand *because* Dial has twice as much deodorant ingredient as the next-best-selling brand.

unique selling proposition A benefit statement about a feature that is both unique to the product and important to the user.

Unique Selling Proposition The concept of a **unique selling proposition**, or USP, is based on a benefit statement that is both unique to the product and important to the user. The heart of a USP is a *proposition*, which is a promise that states a specific and unique benefit you will get from using the product. If the product has a special formula, design, or feature, particularly if protected by a patent or copyright, then you are assured that it is truly unique. This is why a USP is frequently marked by the use of an "only" statement, either outright or implied. For example, the following is a USP taken from the ad copy for a camera:

> USP: This camera is the only one that lets you automatically zoom in and out to follow the action of the central figure.

Support Regardless of which selling premise an advertiser uses, you should be able to analyze the logic behind the premise. Most selling premises demand facts, proof, or explanations to support the claim, benefit, reason, or promise. Support may be more important than any other part of the message strategy because it lends credibility to the premise. If the message is to be believable or have impact, it must have support. An example of a USP and its support is this excerpt from the strategy statement for Hubba Bubba bubble gum:

> USP: Hubba Bubba is the only chewing gum that lets you blow great big bubbles that won't stick to your face.
> Support: Hubba Bubba uses a unique and exclusive nonstick formula.

EXECUTION DETAILS

Execution of the strategy is the heart of the creative process in advertising. Developing the execution involves coming up with a creative idea variously called the *Big Idea*, or the *theme*, or the *creative concept*. This is where the creative people take the bare bones of a strategy statement and express that strategy in a way that is captivating and exciting. The execution is the creative team's "imaginative leap" that produces outstanding advertising that is both attention-getting and memorable. Creativity is discussed in detail in Chapter 13.

The details of the execution—how the advertisement looks and "feels"—are discussed in chapters on creating ads for various types of media (Chapters 14 through 17). What we are talking about here is the tone of the ad—is it serious, funny, concerned, or sympathetic?

---

[11]William D. Wells, *Planning for R.O.I.* (Chicago: DDB Needham Worldwide, 1987).

Before you can begin to understand how this creative process works, however, you must know how *advertising* works, which is the subject of the next chapter.

SUMMARY

- Advertising messages are formulated to accomplish specific objectives, and then strategies are developed specifically to achieve these objectives. This is accomplished through strategic planning.
- Strategic planning is the process of determining objectives, deciding on strategies, and implementing tactics.
- Planning is usually a three-tiered operation containing interrelated operations: the business strategic plan, functional plans, and advertising plans.
- The business plan relates to a particular company division or strategic business unit. It begins with the mission statement and is followed by an analysis of the external and internal environment, goal formulation, strategy formulation, and program formulation.
- A marketing plan (functional level) proposes strategies for employing the various elements of the marketing mix to achieve marketing objectives. It parallels the business plan. Its parts include: selection of marketing objectives, identification of threats/opportunities, selection of target markets, development of marketing strategies, design of action plans, and evaluation of results.
- An advertising plan matches the right audience to the right message and presents the message in the right medium to reach the audience.
- A typical advertising plan includes the following components: situation analysis (problems/opportunities); key strategic decisions (objectives, target audience, competitive advantage, product image, product position); the creative plan; the media plan; the promotion plan; implementation and evaluation; and budgeting.
- The creative plan includes copy strategies that are used for individual ads.
- Message strategies determine what is going to be said about the product and how. This is reflected by the selling premise (sales logic). Possible premises include: benefit, promise, reason why, and unique selling proposition.

QUESTIONS

1. What do advertisers mean by *strategy*? What are the key considerations in an advertising strategy?

2. Think of a product you have purchased recently. How was it advertised? Which strategies can you discern in the advertising? Did the advertising help to convince you to purchase the product? Why or why not?

3. Day-Flo products sold 400,000 units in 1993. The total category sales (all competitors) for 1993 was 3.5 million units. What was Day-Flo's share of sales in 1993? In 1994 Day-Flo's objective is to increase unit sales by 15 percent; projections for total category sales are estimated at 10 percent. If these projections prove to be correct, what would Day-Flo's share of the market be at the end of 1994?

4. Advertising strategies are particularly sensitive to marketers who follow benefit-segmentation targeting. If you were marketing a new line of denim jeans for women, what are some of the logical benefit segments that consumer research would identify? How would advertising creative strategy shift according to segment priorities? Be as specific as possible.

5. The following is a brief excerpt from Luna Pizza's situation analysis for 1993. Luna is a regional

producer of frozen pizza. Its only major competitor is Brutus Bros.

	Actual 1993	Est. 1994
Units Sold	120,000	185,000
$ sales	420,000	580,000
Brutus $ sales	630,000	830,000

Estimate the 1994 advertising budgets for Luna under each of the following circumstances:

a. Luna follows a historical method by spending 40 cents per unit sold in advertising with a 5 percent increase for inflation.

b. Luna follows a fixed-percentage-of-projected-sales-dollars method, using 7.0 percent.

c. Luna follows a share-of-voice method. Brutus is expected to use 6 percent of sales for its advertising budget in 1994.

6 A key to marketing-advertising strategy is the ability to convert attributes into customer-oriented benefits. Look at these attributes for an automobile for the future and change them to benefit statements.

a. The "V" car computer-directed braking system that senses the exact pedal pressure needed for every road surface condition.

b. The "V" has a special battery with a separate section that is climate insulated against any temperature extreme.

c. The "V" has a programmed memory for the driver's seat that automatically positions height, distance from pedals, and steering wheel for each user.

𝒮UGGESTED CLASS PROJECT

Select two print ads—one for a consumer product and one business-to-business. Working from the ad, determine the selling premise, the product position, the product image, the competitive advantage, and the specific target audience. What were the objectives? Were they achieved? Determine where the strategy was clear and where it was unclear.

𝐹URTHER READINGS

AAKER, DAVID, RAJEEV BATRA, AND JOHN G. MYERS, *Advertising Management*, 4th ed. (Englewood Cliffs, NJ: Prentice Hall, 1992).

BELCH, GEORGE E., AND MICHAEL A. BELCH, *Introduction to Advertising and Promotion Management* (Homewood, IL: Irwin, 1990).

BURNETT, JOHN J., *Promotion Management* (Boston: Houghton Mifflin Company, 1993).

ENGEL, JAMES F., MARTIN R. WARSHAW, AND THOMAS C. KINNEAR, *Promotional Strategy*, 8th ed. (Homewood, IL: Irwin, 1993).

ROSSITER, JOHN R., AND LARRY PERCY, *Advertising and Promotion Management* (New York: McGraw-Hill, 1987).

SCHULTZ, DON E., AND STANLEY I. TANNENBAUM, *Essentials of Advertising Strategy*, 2nd ed. (Lincolnwood, IL: NTC Business Books, 1988).

SHIMP, TERENCE, *Promotion Management and Marketing Communications*, 3rd ed. (Chicago: Dryden, 1992).

Teenage Angst: The Jordache Basics Campaign

The blue-jean and denim-apparel industry had been dominated by Levi Strauss and Company until the late 1970s. As the 1980s approached and Levi's recovered from a disastrous attempt to break into the high end of the men's fashion industry with suits, sports coats, and slacks under the Levi's brand name, several new and old apparel manufacturers took on Levi's flagship blue-jean product with their own jeans brands. As Levi's held on tightly to the traditional men's and women's jeans market, Calvin Klein, Jordache, and others took jeans uptown with different cuts, colors, and styles. While Levi's hurried to duplicate some of the less radical jeans transformations of its competitors, Wrangler was lining up famous rodeo stars to try to pick away at Levi's traditional source of strength as America's original jeans from the wild west.

As fashion began to win out over functionality in the jeans category, apparel makers that could carve out the most unique image for their products in their advertising experienced significant increases in sales. From the famous Brooke Shields "nothing comes between me and my Calvins" ads for Calvin Klein jeans to the ambiguous Guess? jeans campaign, image advertising has played a dominant role in the marketing of jeans and denim fashion products over the last decade.

Jordache initially jumped into the fray with the Jordache Look campaign. The campaign was the most primitive and obvious of the various image-oriented jeans campaigns of its time. The ads were dominated by closeups of tight-fitting Jordache jeans while the lyrics of the repetitive jingle stated, "It's the Jordache look." The message seemed to work particularly well among teenagers because form-fitting jeans were an integral part of the junior-high, high school, and college dating scene at the time. As Calvin Klein and others made jeans fashionable for adults to wear, Jordache built on its base strength among teenagers.

As the sophistication level of 1980s' teenagers was elevated by years of MTV and "brat pack" Hollywood feature films targeted to teens, Jordache could no longer rely on the relatively crude approach taken with the "Jordache Look" campaign. Learning from their more artful competition, Jordache developed the Jordache Basics campaign, which featured a variety of post-yuppie model/actors discussing contemporary teen issues. Part way through the campaign, the superimposed tag line "Jordache Basics" was joined by a superimposed subheadline "because life…is not." Prior to the superimposed tag lines at the end of the spots, the presence of Jordache products was only subtly conveyed by the actors and actresses donning Jordache apparel.

Subtle product identification is common in advertising in the fashion and cosmetics industries. However, advertising media levels must be large enough for viewers to be aware of the product's identity from prior viewings. In this way, subsequent viewings of ads in the campaign are attributed to the correct product. Yet, even with a very focused media placement strategy on a single, very targeted station, such as MTV, the extreme subtlety of the Jordache product identification and the obtuse image message conveyed by the Jordache Basics campaign probably reduced effectiveness.

Advertising considered controversial by the target audience can actually have a negative impact on product sales. Undoubtedly, several of the Jordache Basics campaign spots could have been considered controversial, at least by parents if not by the teenage target audience itself. In one spot an attractive teenage girl claims she hates her mother because she believes her mother is more attractive than she is.

The Jordache Basics campaign raises the issue of form over substance, which often plagues image-oriented advertising. In this case, parent bashing is used as an attempt to position Jordache jeans and denim apparel as hip and antiestablishment.

The Jordache Basics campaign was somewhat groundbreaking, both in its use of an extremely subtle image-based message as well as in its subsequent self-parody. However, because the effectiveness of image-based advertising to generate product sales is often difficult to quantify, Jordache and its competitors may never know with certainty if the creative breakthroughs in the Jordache Basics campaign were a move forward in fashion advertising or a costly mistake.

Questions

1. Based on the "Jordache Basics* advertising, recreate what you think Jordache used as the copy platform for the campaign and justify your answer.

2. Because advertising media frequency is critical to an advertising campaign with a subtle selling message, what television dayparts, stations, or specific programs would you recommend to Jordache? Justify your answer.

$\mathcal{H}$OW ADVERTISING WORKS

8

CHAPTER OBJECTIVES

When you have completed this chapter, you should be able to:

- Understand the barriers that an effective advertisement must overcome

- Be familiar with the different levels on which a viewer or reader will react to an ad

- Explain the different functions of an ad

- Explain what "breakthrough advertising" is and how it works

ZAPPROOFING THE ADS

When people don't care for a commercial, they have a weapon to express their dislike—the remote control. Ever since its arrival in viewers' homes, this simple piece of technology has enabled viewers to avoid advertisements they dislike by pushing one button. Readers have been flipping past print ads for years by turning pages; with the remote control, viewers can just as easily flip past television commercials. Moreover, because the new viewing environment with more networks, independents, and cable channels offers so many attractive alternatives, viewers are zapping more frequently than ever before.

Zapping is one type of avoidance; another is *zipping*, which means fast-forwarding past the commercials on prerecorded videotapes. A related behavior is *grazing*, which means flipping around the channels, stopping now and then to look briefly at something, and then moving on. A person adept at grazing knows when a commercial break is about to begin and can time the cycle to return to the original program just as the break ends.

The Pretesting Company of Englewood, New Jersey, analyzes commercials to determine where in a commercial audience members are likely to zap it. By knowing when and what turns people off, the company can tell which commercials stand a better chance of not being zapped. For example, Pretesting found that the word *period* in commercials for sanitary pads and tampons was embarrassing for women viewers. In laboratory studies some 60 percent of the women viewers, upon hearing that word, zapped the commercial before it was complete.

The Pretesting Company has found that comparative ads and ads that leave out the brand name until the end are prone to zapping, as are parodies of other commercials, especially if people don't like the originals. A number of agencies are using this service to isolate problems and to develop ads that will capture and hold viewers' attention. The key to zapproofing is to develop ads with "stopping power." Of course, once the ad arrests viewers' attention, it must continue to hold attention by addressing needs that are relevant to viewers' interests.[1]

ADVERTISING IMPACT

Keith Reinhard, president of DDB Needham, has said, "Today, more than ever, if advertising is not relevant, it has no purpose. If it is not original, it will attract no attention. If it does not strike with impact, it will make no lasting impression."[2] Relevance, originality, and impact—ROI—are key elements of effective advertising. Advertising that is relevant speaks to you about things you care about; advertising that is original catches your attention by its creativity; and advertising that has impact arouses your emotions and makes a lasting impression.

---

[1] Adapted from Jon Berry, "Zap Attack: How Audience Research Is Shaping Ads." *Adweek* (July 9, 1990):1; Carrie Heeter and Bradley S. Greenberg, *CableViewing* (Norwood, NJ: Ablex, 1988); and Sandra Moriarty, "Explorations into the Commercial Encounter," American Academy of Advertising Annual Conference, Reno, NV (April 1991).

[2] William D. Wells, *Planning for R.O.I.* (Englewood Cliffs, NJ: Prentice Hall, 1989):x–xi.

In order to understand the importance of these ingredients and the environment within which they are created, this chapter will focus on the psychology behind advertising. It is important for you to know how advertising works—and doesn't work—in order to understand how advertising is created. First, let's discuss the environment in which advertising operates, and the audience's interaction with the advertisement.

THE ADVERTISING ENVIRONMENT

The advertising environment is extremely cluttered. Some 40,000 magazines and journals are published in the United States every year, and more than 10,000 radio stations crowd the airwaves. Seventy percent of American homes are now wired for cable television, and the average household can view 35 channels. Tied to the explosion in media outlets is the monumental increase in the number of commercial messages. Since 1965, for example, the number of network television commercials has tripled from approximately 1,800 to nearly 5,400 per year. Networks often run five or six commercials in a row; during prime time commercials average 10.5 minutes per hour.[3]

As you can see, advertisers compete fiercely for people's attention. Advertisements occur within a glut of information-laden messages. Other media, other ads, news stories, outside distractions, and random thoughts get in the way of advertisers' very expensive and carefully constructed commercial messages.

THE AUDIENCE

Given this cluttered environment, most people give advertising only *divided attention*. A few ads may break through and receive total concentration, but not many. At best an ad gets half the mind and one eye. Advertisers are also up against a *short attention span*. Human concentration happens in quick bursts. The actual information that gets attended to is often nothing more than a quick impression or a message fragment.

Information Processing. Besides problems with attention, viewers have problems making sense out of the mass of information that assaults them. Media messages become entangled in other thoughts and memories. Our minds are not tidy, and the approach we take to making sense of information is not predictable or thorough. For example, most people reading a newspaper or magazine look at both editorial information and advertisements. They browse, scan, jump back and forth, and find snippets of useful information in both categories. Ads and editorials are scanned or ignored; the information derived from both may well be fragmentary.

Similarly, every time you watch a television commercial, you decide whether to attend to it or not. The decision is always yours, even though you may not be aware you are making it. If you make a commitment, the commitment lasts only as long as the message maintains your interest. When you lose interest, your attention shifts and you move on to your own thoughts or to some outside distraction.

---

[3] Peter F. Eder, "Advertising and Mass Marketing," *The Futurist*, (May–June 1990):38–40.

Avoidance. We have already mentioned that most people are very good at avoiding information that doesn't interest them. Bombarded with a huge number of commercials on television, you have no doubt become very good at avoidance. If you are like most people, you will either change the channel, mute the sound, leave the room, or turn your attention elsewhere. Typical viewers may note the first commercial in a cluster, then, depending on whether it catches their attention, they may or may not stick around for the remaining message.[4] Actually, very few people watch all the way through a commercial break.

Furthermore, many consumers are scornful of advertising. A national survey found that 60 percent of consumers agreed that "advertising insults my intelligence," and over 70 percent said they "don't believe a company's products."[5] Disbelief, dislike, and irritation are important aspects of the consumer response to advertising. The Issues and Controversies box entitled "The Irritation Factor" takes a closer look at these aspects.

BREAKTHROUGH ADVERTISING

This discussion dramatizes how few advertisements actually get read or watched. You may scan the stories and ads in the newspaper, but with limited concentration. Less than half of all ads actually are noticed on a "thinking" level. Perhaps 20 percent are read a little, and very few are read thoroughly.

Advertising that makes any impact at all breaks through this inattention and mindless scanning; it helps consumers sort out and remember what they see and hear; and it overcomes avoidance and scorn. Such advertising is called *breakthrough advertising*. It is relevant and original; and it has impact. It speaks to the concerns of its audience on a personal level without being patronizing or phony.

*T*HE PSYCHOLOGY OF ADVERTISING

How does advertising work? This is a very complex question. One thing we do know is that advertising may communicate a number of messages in a number of areas simultaneously. For example, at the same time you are understanding a copy point, you may also be forming a favorable or an unfavorable opinion of the product being advertised. The message's impact on both knowledge and liking can happen simultaneously.[6]

The following discussion will analyze how advertising works in terms of four basic psychological categories: *perception, awareness, understanding,* and *persuasion.*

PERCEPTION: CREATING STOPPING POWER

When something has been perceived, the message has registered. One of the biggest challenges for advertisers is simply to get consumers to notice their mes-

---

[4] Sandra E. Moriarty, "The Commercial Encounter."
[5] Stephen J. Hoch and Young-Won Ha, "Consumer Learning: Advertising and the Ambiguity of Product Experience," *Journal of Consumer Research* (September 1986):221–33.
[6] Sandra E. Moriarty, "Beyond the Hierarchy of Effects: A Conceptual Model," in *Current Issues and Research in Advertising*, James H. Leigh and Claude R. Martin, Jr., eds. (Ann Arbor: University of Michigan Graduate School of Business, 1983):45–56.

The Irritation Factor

Why do people like some commercials and despise others? Irritating ads are defined as those that cause displeasure and momentary impatience. The response is more negative than simple *dislike*.

Research has found that disliked advertising might work anyway because it generates high levels of attention and recall. Even if consumers dislike these commercials, when they get to the store they remember the product name and forget their irritation at the ad. Still, it makes sense to assume that viewers' negative perceptions of the message usually do carry over to the product itself. One wonders if those irritating commercials are successful *in spite* of the message strategy rather than because of it.

Research into irritating advertising has found that a major source of irritation is the product itself; for example, feminine-hygiene products, underwear, laxatives, and hemorrhoid treatments. Regarding message strategy, irritation levels are higher when the situation is contrived, phony, unbelievable, or overdramatized. In the case of a sensitive product, the ads are more irritating when the product and its use are emphasized; indirect approaches seem to work better. Viewers also don't like to see people "put down" or forced into stereotypical roles. Neither do they like to see important relationships threatened, such as mother-daughter or husband-wife.

What do you think about the irritation factor in advertising? Can you remember any ads that you particularly disliked? Can you remember some that you liked? Why did you react that way? Are there products and situations where it isn't important for the commercial to be liked? If a particular commercial is irritating and unpopular but the product sells well, should that commercial be considered a success? Why or why not?

Source: David A. Aaker and Donald E. Bruzzone, "Causes of Irritation in Advertising," *Journal of Marketing* (Spring 1985):47–57.

---

sages. This is harder than it appears. Not only do consumers miss more than half the messages directed at them, other messages continuously compete for their attention. As an outdoor ad for the Los Angeles fire department, Ad 8.1 has stopping power.

Exposure. The first step in perception is simple *exposure*. Exposure is primarily a media-buying problem. First the message has to be placed in a medium that your target sees, reads, watches, or listens to. Exposure is, therefore, the minimum requirement to perception. If your target never sees or hears the advertisement, or if your target skips the page or changes the channel, then no matter how great the message is, it will *not* be perceived.

Attention. Once the audience has been exposed to the message, the next step is to keep their attention. Attention means the mind is engaged; it is focusing on something. Attention is aroused by a *trigger*, something that "catches" the target's interest. The trigger can be something in the message or something within the reader or viewer that makes him or her "lock onto" a particular message. In print it may be a sale price in large type, a startling illustration, or a strong headline. On television the trigger may be sound effects, music, a scene that is action oriented or visually interesting, or a captivating idea.

Getting attention involves more than just attracting the notice of the viewer or reader, however. When you are in the scanning mode, your attention is wandering. Nailing down attention requires some kind of *stopping power*. Ads that stop the scanning are usually high in intrusiveness, originality, or relevance.

TH OF JULY.

THERE'S NOTHING COOL ABOUT FIREWORKS.
L.A. CITY FIRE DEPT.

Intrusiveness. Advertisements are designed to be attention getting. That means they sometimes have to be intrusive—in other words, they demand attention. Intrusiveness is particularly important for products that have a small "share of mind"—those that are either not very well known or not very involving or interesting. In many cases there is little difference between competing brands, so the product interest is created solely by the advertising message.

What can you do to create this kind of impact? Many intrusive ads use loud, bold effects to attract viewer attention—they work by shouting. Others use captivating ideas or mesmerizing visuals. For print ads, for example, research has found that *contrast* can attract viewer attention. If every other ad in the medium is big and bold, then be small, quiet, and simple—use a lot of white space. If everything is tiny and gray (like type), then be bold and black or use color. If everything is colorful, then use black and white. Identify the characteristics of the medium environment and then do something different.

Originality. Creative advertising is unique, novel, or original. The function of originality is to capture attention. People will notice something that is new, novel, or surprising. Original advertising breaks through the old patterns of seeing and saying without being irrelevant or bizarre. The unexpectedness of the new idea is what creates stopping power.

Advertising agencies go to great lengths to create intrusive advertising. An article in *The New York Times* described an effort at the Young & Rubicam (Y&R) agency to push its creative people to take more risks to make their ads more distinctive. For an Irish Spring ad the agency used a fully clothed man with a bar of soap in his hand. By all appearances, he is about to launch into a standard pitch. Suddenly the ad turns slapstick. He loses control of the soap. It squirts him in the face and lathers up in his pocket. Such unorthodox ideas are being used successfully by Y&R to sell things like toothpaste, coffee, and ice cream.

To encourage this kind of freewheeling thinking Y&R set up a program called the Risk Lab that allows copywriters and art directors to have their ideas informally tested by researchers in the early stages of concept development. The director of creative research, Dr. Stephanie Kugelman, took the title "Dr. Risk" and moved to the creative floors to work closely with the creative people.

AWARENESS: MAKING AN IMPRESSION

Once a message has been perceived and has caught your attention, your perceptual process can move on to the next step, which is awareness of the message and the product. Awareness implies that the message has made an impression on the viewer or reader, who can subsequently identify the advertiser. Note that although awareness of the advertising comes first, awareness of the advertising is not the ultimate objective. As far as the advertiser is concerned, the ultimate objective is awareness of the product, not the advertisement.

Attention is a message-design problem. The advertising message can, and must, compete with other messages in the same medium. Within a news medium, the advertising has to be able to compete with the intrinsically interesting nature of the news. In an entertainment medium like television, the advertising has to compete with the mesmerizing entertainment values of programming. Radio is almost always a background medium, and outdoor advertising is directed toward an audience whose attention, by definition, is directed elsewhere. Not only does outdoor advertising have to compete for attention, it also has to be able to win out over distractions such as other signs along the road, the car radio or tape deck, and conversations among passengers.

Relatively low levels of attention can create a minimal level of awareness. If the objective is simply brand or product reminder, then the attention level doesn't need to be as high as it does when the objective calls for the understanding of a copy point.

Relevance. Most people want to hear or read about themselves and the things they care about. They want to know how to improve their skills, look better, live longer, make more money, or save themselves time and expense. People will pay attention to advertising only if it's worth their while to do so. They make a deal with the advertiser: "Make it worth my time and I'll pay attention to your message as long as it doesn't bore me."

Selective perception, which we discussed in Chapter 5, is driven by relevance. We pay attention to ads that speak to our wants and needs by providing information about such things as work, hobbies, roles, and relationships. Selection—being interested in one thing and not in something else—is also driven by changing conditions. When we are hungry or thirsty, for example, we pay more attention to food and drink ads.

Product Interest There are many types of relevance. You might be interested in the product advertised or in some element in the ad itself—the model or star, the promise made in the headline or by the announcer, or an unusual graphic or production technique. Different topics, product categories, and products have different levels of *built-in interest.* Some products are just inherently more interesting than others. Food and vacations, for example, are more interesting to most people than are toilet cleaners. Some products are of interest to specific groups of people. A man might look at an ad for tires but avoid an ad for hair spray.

Personal Relevance Interest is usually created by one of two things—personal involvement or curiosity. You have some predispositions that affect what interests you—getting through school, hobbies, a trip you want to take, or a career goal. If a message applies to any of these elements in your list, then it affects you personally and the message has personal relevance. Most people also respond to general "human-interest" items—a topic that strikes some universal chord, such as babies, kittens, and puppies, as well as tragedies and success stories.

Curiosity provides the "cognitive nudge" that engages your mind. Whenever you are confronted with something new, there is a period of curiosity, usually accompanied by doubt or some kind of questioning. New information is often greeted by phrases like "Can you believe it?" This confrontation of curiosity with doubt means you have entered the *interested* state. You are interested because the message *might* be personally relevant.

Advertisers who are trying to develop a message that stimulates interest will speak to the personal interests of their target audience as well as do something to elicit curiosity. Ads that open with questions or dubious statements are designed to build interest and create curiosity. For example, Ad 8.2 for Charles David Footwear uses a provocative headline to pull readers into the ad. We discussed getting attention as the *stopping power* of an advertisement; keeping attention is the *pulling power* of an ad—it keeps pulling the reader or viewer through to the end of the message.

Maintaining Interest. Interest is a momentary thing; it dies easily as attention shifts. A major challenge to advertisers is to maintain interest until the point of the message is reached. Because of the scanning and browsing behavior of many readers and viewers, maintaining interest is more difficult than arousing it.

If you are worried about maintaining interest in an advertisement, then you must consider the pulling power of your message. This is in part a sequencing problem: Does your copy pull the reader or viewer through to the end? How does the message develop? For example, if you start with a question, then the

Ad 8.2

This ad for footwear attracts attention with a bold headline, large type, and the savvy message that while the product offers status, the purchaser is innocent of snobbery.

(Courtesy of Charles David Footwear)

Lisa Bugman, Marketing Research Manager, Star Tribune

6:30–6:50 A.M. Take a brief look at the international, national, and local headlines.

7:30–9:00 A.M. Attend a panel discussion on developing and maintaining positive vendor relationships sponsored by the Advertising Federation.

9:15–11:30 A.M. Attend a brand image research study kick-off meeting with steering committee members. Specifically, outline the project flow, milestones, timeline, and responsibilities. Outcome of this research will help us to understand reader and nonreader perceptions of the newspaper as well as characteristics that readers and nonreaders attribute to the paper and our competition.

11:30–12:15 P.M. Clear voice mail...eleven messages—another busy day! Personally return five messages, voice mail information back to three, and plan to act on information given to me by the remaining three messages I received.

12:15–1:00 P.M. Work out for a brief time in the fitness center located in the building. Grab a quick lunch.

1:00–2:00 P.M. Work on issues raised in the kick-off meeting held earlier today. Gather and send organizational background information to the vendor who will actually conduct the focus groups and phone survey work.

2:00–2:30 P.M. Discuss reorganization issues and concerns with colleagues.

2:30–3:30 P.M. Meet with the internal communication council to discuss how to measure the effectiveness of internal communication vehicles. About one year ago a survey was administered to determine the effectiveness of the communication pieces employees use to obtain company information. Based on study results, changes were made to the communication vehicles. This council is now interested in a "postsurvey" measure of effectiveness for vehicles that were modified and a baseline measure for vehicles created in the past year. For comparison purposes we will most likely modify the survey conducted a year ago.

3:30–4:30 P.M. Read a document distributed in a marketer database meeting two days ago. Take notes from document to prepare for next meeting.

4:30–5:30 P.M. Sort in-basket and clear voice mail. Take necessary action on items and put the rest on next day's "Things To Do" list.

6:30–7:30 P.M. Ride bikes with my husband along the Mississippi River...a great way to relax after work.

8:00–8:45 P.M. Read the complete newspaper.

reader has to continue through the ad to find the answer. Storytelling is a good technique to hold the audience. Most people want to know how a story comes out. Suspense, drama, and narrative are good literary tools for maintaining interest.

Television has built-in sequencing because of the moving image. If skillfully used, the motion and action of a video message are hard to ignore. A layout in a print ad can do the same thing. A layout can be designed with strong direction or movement cues that keep the eye of the reader engaged.

involvement   The intensity of the consumer's interest in a product.

Involvement. Relevance is a key factor in the concept of **involvement** which refers to the intensity of the consumer's interest in a product, medium, or message. *High involvement* means that a product—or information about it—is important and personally relevant. *Low involvement* means that the product or information is perceived as unimportant. Typically, people in a high-involvement situation—as when purchasing a new car, home, or European vacation—will be searching for information and critically evaluating it. Advertising for high-involvement products usually provides a lot of information about the product. In contrast, low-involvement purchases, such as chewing gum, toothpaste, and paper towels, are made without much searching and with little effort to think critically about the decision. Advertising for this type of product often focuses on simple slogans or images.

The word *involvement* is also used to describe an advertising technique that tries to get the audience to participate in how the message develops and evolves. Compelling readers or viewers to get involved in the message either physically or mentally is a strong persuasive technique. For example, some ads start with a question in order to draw people into constructing the answer. An oil company advertisement displays a big picture of a beautiful forest and asks the reader to find the oil well hidden somewhere among the trees to dramatize the point that oil drilling can be respectful of nature. The more involved viewers or readers are in developing the message, the more impact the message has.

UNDERSTANDING: MAKING IT CLEAR

Being aware of the message is not enough. The message must be understood as well. *Understanding* refers to a conscious mental effort to make sense of the information being presented. That is how we learn things. Whereas attention can be a relatively passive response, understanding demands an active response from the reader or viewer. It is an important part of the process of dealing with information. First we find ourselves interested, then we learn something about the subject of our interest, then we file it away in our memories. That is called *knowing.*

Informational advertising Advertising that presents a large amount of information about the product.

Understanding is particularly important for ads that present a lot of information—brand, price, size, how the product works, when and where to use it, and so on. When product differences exist, the features and how they translate into selling points are also important pieces of information to understand. An important requirement of **informational advertising** is that the explanation be clear and relevant to the prospect. Consumers have little patience with ads that are confusing, vague, or unfocused. The reader or viewer must be able to follow the logic, make discriminations, compare and contrast points of view, comprehend reasons and arguments, synthesize and organize facts, and, in general, make sense of things. If you are designing an advertising message where understanding is an objective, your ad must present the facts in a way that makes it easy for people to assimilate the information. Clarity is important.

Teaching and Knowing. Teaching is an important aspect of advertising because most advertisers want people to know something after they have read, watched, or heard the message. Knowledge means the facts have been acquired through experience or study. In the case of new products, ads must bridge the gap in people's experience by teaching them how to recognize and use the product.

The literary tools of a message designed to stimulate understanding include definition, explanation, demonstration, comparison, and contrast. Definition and explanation are primarily verbal concepts, but demonstration, comparison, and contrast are often communicated in visuals. Any visual, whether print or video, can be used to compare two products or to show before-and-after scenarios. Television is particularly good for demonstration because it can show a sequence of operations.

Association. Another way to "know" something is to make a connection in your mind. When you link up two concepts—fall and football, or Coca-Cola and refreshment, for example—you have learned something. Association is used in advertising to build images. Advertisements that use association try to get you to know something by linking the product with something you aspire to, respect, value, or appreciate—like a pleasant experience or an envied lifestyle or person.

A metaphoric use of association appears in a campaign for the printer language called PostScript. This is a difficult concept to sell, so the creators of the advertising used a cherry to represent "the best part" of the computer system (see Ad 8.3).

PERSUASION: MAKING MOVING MESSAGES

In addition to providing information, advertisements must persuade people to believe or do something. A persuasive message will try to establish, reinforce or change an attitude, build an argument, touch an emotion, or anchor a conviction firmly in the prospect's belief structure.

Believability is an extremely important concept in advertising. Do con-

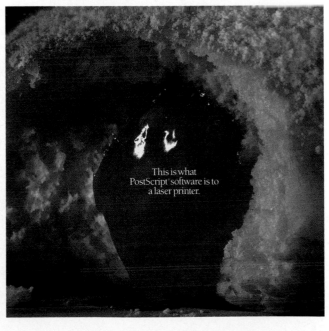

A persuasive message will shape attitudes, build a logical argument, touch emotions, and make the prospect believe something about the product.

sumers believe the messages? Are the claims believable? Do spokespersons, particularly authority figures, have credibility? Consumers say they do not believe in advertising claims, but at the same time they find advertising helpful in making better decisions. Recent research has found that although consumers want proof of the validity of advertisers' claims, they do not require very convincing evidence to accept these claims.[7]

In Chapter 6 you learned that support is an important element in the message strategy. Remember, support refers to everything in the message that lends credibility to the promise. If you want your message to be believable or to have impact, you must provide support, such as facts, convincing argument, or conclusive demonstrations.

appeal Something that moves people

Appeals. Persuasion in advertising rests on the psychological appeal to the consumer. An **appeal** is something that makes the product particularly attractive or interesting to the consumer. Common appeals are security, esteem, fear, sex, and sensory pleasure. Appeals generally pinpoint the anticipated response of the prospect to the product and message.

Advertisers also use the word *appeal* to describe a general creative emphasis. For example, if the price is emphasized in the ad, then the appeal is value, economy, or savings. If the product saves time or effort, then the appeal is convenience. A message that focuses on a mother or father making something for a child—like cookies or a rocker—might elicit an appeal of family love and concern. A *status appeal* is used to establish something as a quality, expensive product. *Appetite appeal* using mouth-watering visuals is used in food advertising.

Attitudes and Opinions. Beliefs, attitudes, and values structure our opinions, which in turn reflect how negatively or positively we feel about something. This is how we *evaluate* the information we receive.

People's opinions are built on a complex structure of attitudes. Every person has a different attitude structure based on individual experiences. Advertising that seeks to affect this complex structure of attitudes will usually attempt to accomplish one of three things:

1. Establish a new opinion where none has existed before
2. Reinforce an existing opinion
3. Change an existing opinion

New opinions need to be created when a new product is introduced. Consumer opinion concerning the product or service, of course, will be modified or confirmed as the product is used. No matter how strong your advertising, a bad experience with a new product will negate all of the positive attitudes your message has implanted.

The Saturn automobile advertisement is an example of advertising that is trying to change an attitude (see Ad 8.4). Its message is trying to rebuild consumer confidence in American automobile manufacturing by focusing on the people who make the cars and their enthusiastic participation in the building process.

Likability. Likability is an important indicator of positive attitudes toward a product or a message. An advertiser will try to build positive attitudes for new

---

[7] Hoch and Ha, "Consumer Learning," pp. 221–33.

Ad 8.4

By showing the dedicated employees who make the Saturn automobile, the company hopes to change the negative attitude that has developed about American automobile quality.

(Reprinted with permission of Saturn Corporation)

brand loyalty Existing positive opinions held by consumers about the product or service.

products and maintain existing positive attitudes for successful mature products. When a product is liked well enough by consumers to generate repeat sales, that is called **brand loyalty.**

It is more unusual, and much harder, to try to change negative attitudes. If your product has a negative image—perhaps because the initial product or marketing strategy was faulty—then a major objective is to turn that consumer attitude around.

Amtrak, for example, once suffered from an extremely negative image. Travelers assumed that long-distance trains would be late, that on-board service would be poor, and that equipment would be outdated and in bad condition. After these problems were corrected, Amtrak advertising focused on the task of persuading travelers to give Amtrak another try. While many travelers did return to Amtrak, and some routes became so popular that travelers must reserve space well in advance, some of the old impressions linger.[8] Once established, negative attitudes are extremely difficult to cure.

Twizzlers, a licorice candy, had a category problem. It had to compete against such big names as Tootsie Roll in the "chewy candy" subcategory of the candy market. DDB Needham took on the challenge and created a strikingly visual campaign based on "singing mouths" that sang into a Twizzler micro-

---

[8] "Amtrak Case Study," unpublished document by DDB Needham, New York (1991).

phone. Because the ads were so effective, sales increased by 30 percent during the first year of the campaign. The licorice category grew at a rate of 7 percent, most of which represented Twizzler's growth.[9]

It is important to remember that advertising alone cannot repair a faulty product. If lack of brand loyalty is due to bad experience with the product itself, or with packaging, pricing, or some other element of the marketing program, advertising that persuades consumers to buy the product will only make matters worse. A product problem is a product problem, not an advertising problem. The power of advertising is not unlimited.

Arguments. Persuasive messages deal with more than basic attitude structure. People are persuaded by argument or reasoning. Reasons are based on logic and the development of an argument. Argument in this sense refers not to a disagreement, but to a line of reasoning where one point follows from another, leading up to a conclusion. Your ad must focus on logic and proof when you are dealing with reasons. That is why the "reason-why" selling premise is a very common message strategy used in advertising. It is also why the support section of the creative strategy is so important.

Emotions. Persuasion is not only a logical process; it is also concerned with emotions. How someone "feels" about your product, service, brand, or company may be just as important as what that person knows about it. *Feeling* in this sense refers to an attitude, but it is an attitude surrounded by emotions. The intensity of the response—the impact—comes from the emotions. If you touch someone's emotions with your message, he or she is more likely to remember the message. The telephone and greeting-card companies have been very successful with emotional campaigns because, after all, they are selling sentiment—warm feelings, love, missing someone, nostalgia, and so on. Ad 8.5 expresses the emotion behind a phone call.

Many of our buying decisions are emotional ones. We buy shoes because we don't want to go barefoot, but we buy a closetful of shoes for other reasons: different styles for different occasions and different moods. We often use "logical" surface reasons to justify emotional decisions that we don't acknowledge, even to ourselves.

Principle

People buy products because they find the advertisement convincing, not because they find it amusing.

conviction A particularly strong belief that has been anchored firmly in the attitude structure.

Conviction. Attitudes, reasons, logic, and emotion are all part of the persuasive package. What they lead to is belief. We believe something about every product we purchase; if we didn't, we wouldn't buy it. We believe it is good for us, it will make us look better or live better, or it will make us richer or healthier. Even low-involvement products like chewing gum involve some belief system. I buy this brand of gum rather than another one because I believe this gum will taste better, freshen my breath, or do less damage to my teeth.

A **conviction** is a particularly strong belief that has been anchored firmly in the attitude structure. It is often built of strong rational arguments that use such techniques as test results, before-and-after visuals, and demonstrations to prove something. Opinions based on convictions are very hard to change. An advertiser who can build conviction in the target audience achieves a strong competitive advantage.

Conviction may be based on convincing argument. It may be based on

---

[9] "Twizzler Case Study," unpublished documents by DDB Needham, New York (1993).

I got this brother. He used to crack me up. When we were kids, he'd make up these jokes. Most of 'em didn't make much sense. But he'd always break out laughin', which made me laugh, and pretty soon we're both rollin' on the floor in tears. I called him today. Just to say hi. And you know what? That son of a gun did it again...

When you're far apart, long distance is the easiest way to let someone know how you feel. Just pick up the phone and dial 1+. And a little of you will go a long, long way.

The one to call on.

🔔 **Southwestern Bell Telephone**

demonstration. According to the old adage, seeing is believing. Product performance that can be demonstrated tends to remove doubt and increase belief in the sales message.

LOCKING POWER: MAKING IT MEMORABLE

Whereas perception and attention are necessary for stopping power, and maintaining awareness is necessary for pulling power, ads that work effectively also have *locking power*—that is, they lock their messages into the mind. If you can't remember seeing the ad, or if you can remember the ad but not the brand, then you might as well not have seen it as far as the advertiser is concerned. When you go to the supermarket, it is important that you remember that soft drinks are on sale. It is also important that you remember the sale was for a certain brand. How does that process happen?

Our memories are like filing cabinets. You watch a commercial, extract those parts of it that interest you, and then find a category in your mental filing cabinet where you can store that fragment of information. The fragment, incidentally, may not look much like the original information as it was presented because your mind will change it to make it fit into your own system of concerns, preoccupations, and preconceptions.

A week later you may not remember that you have a fragment labeled "soft drink" filed away, or you may not be able to find it in the file. Most of us have messy mental filing systems. You have probably found yourself trying to remember something that you know. You can concentrate until your head hurts, and the thought just won't come to the surface. It does come back when it is cued, however. Maybe you remember the party you have planned for the weekend and that *reminds* you about the soft drink sale. That is how the *cueing* process works to pull things out of the file and back onto the top of our minds. A pink bunny reminds you that you need batteries and that they should be the Energizer brand.

Advertising research focuses on two types of memory—**recognition** and **recall**. Recognition means you can remember having seen something before; in other words, it has achieved *top-of-mind awareness*. Recall is more complex. It means you can remember the information content of the message. These concepts and research methods are discussed in more detail in Chapter 21.

Vampire Creativity. One of the greatest challenges in the advertising world is to create memorability. However, it is easier to create a memorable advertisement than it is to create an advertisement that makes the product memorable. Testing has proved time and again that people often remember the commercial, but not the product. This problem, called **vampire creativity**, occurs primarily with advertisements that are *too* original, *too* entertaining, or *too* involving. The story of the commercial can be so mesmerizing that it gets in the way of the product. Celebrity advertising can have this problem. When major rock stars appear in song-and-dance extravagances for soft drinks, many viewers cannot remember which star is associated with which product. It is essential that the commercial establish a strong link between the message and the product so that remembering the advertisement also means remembering the brand.

Repetition. You can do several things to ensure the memorability of your message. One technique is *repetition*. Psychologists maintain that you need to hear or see something a minimum of three times before it crosses the threshold of perception and enters into memory. **Jingles** are valuable memorability devices because the music allows the advertiser to repeat a phrase or product name without boring the audience.

Clever phrases are also useful not only because they catch attention, but also because they can be repeated to intensify memorability. Advertisements use **slogans** for brands and campaigns (a series of ads run under an umbrella theme). How many slogans can you identify in the Slogan Test box? **Taglines** are used at the end of an ad to summarize the point of the ad's message in a highly memorable way such as: "Nothing outlasts the Energizer. They keep going and going and going." Both slogans and taglines are written to be highly memorable, often using *mnemonic* devices (techniques for improving memory) such as rhyme, rhythmic beats, and repeating sounds.

Key Visuals. In addition to verbal memorability devices, many print ads and most television commercials feature a **key visual**. This is a vivid image that the advertiser hopes will remain in the mind of the viewer. Remember that the memory's filing system usually stores fragments of information. Television is primarily a visual medium, and an effective commercial is built on some dominant scene or piece of action that conveys the essence of the message and can be easily remembered.

recognition An ability to remember having seen something before.

recall The ability to remember specific information content.

vampire creativity An advertising problem in which an ad is so creative or entertaining that it overwhelms the product.

Principle

An advertising message should make the product, not the advertisement, memorable.

jingles Commercials with a message that is presented musically.

slogans Frequently repeated phrases that provide continuity to an advertising campaign.

taglines Clever phrases used at the end of an advertisement to summarize the ad's message.

key visual A dominant image around which the commercial's message is planned.

logo Logotype; a distinctive mark that identifies the product, company, or brand.

signature The name of the company or product written in a distinctive type style.

superimpose A television technique where one image is added to another that is already on the screen.

Memorability also has a structural dimension. Just as the beginning of an advertising message is the most important part for attracting attention, the end or closing of a message is the most important part for memorability. If you want someone to remember the product name, repeat it at the end of the commercial. Most print ads end with a **logo** (a distinctive mark that identifies the product or company) or a **signature** (the name of the company or brand written in a distinctive type style). Television commercials often conclude with a memorable tagline and **superimpose** the product name on the last visual, accompanied by the announcer repeating the brand name.

ℋOW BRAND IMAGES WORK

Brand personalities and brand images create a feeling of familiarity with a known product. Because this product is known, the consumer is reassured that it is appropriate to buy it again. That is the secret behind the phenomenal success of McDonald's over the years. The fast-food chain has a familiar and comfortable image, and consumers know from experience that it offers cleanliness, service, and dependable quality at reasonable prices. Branding creates memorability, but it also establishes preferences, habits, and loyalties. In other words, it creates a platform on which a relationship is built between a brand and its user.

Branding is particularly important for *parity products*—those products for which there are few, if any, major differences in features. The products are *undifferentiated* in the marketplace, but through the development of a brand image, they are differentiated in the minds of their users. Soaps are relatively indistinguishable. What enhances the difference between one soap and another is advertising. In such cases the *distinction* may be minor, but the *difference* is not—because the difference lies in the perceived image and personality of the product. Product personalities were discussed in Chapter 7. Personality is important both in positioning a brand and in developing a brand image.

BRAND IMAGE

brand image A mental image that reflects the way a brand is perceived, including all the identification elements, the product personality, and the emotions and associations evoked in the mind of the consumer.

A brand identifies and represents a particular product, but it is much more than just a name. It is an image in customers' minds that reflects what they think and feel about a product—how they value it. A **brand image** is a mental image that reflects the way a brand is perceived, including all the identification elements, the product personality, and the emotions and associations evoked in the mind of the consumer. *Product personality*—the idea that a product takes on familiar human characteristics, such as friendliness, trustworthiness, or snobbery—is an important part of an image.

A brand, then, has both a physical and a psychological dimension. The physical dimension is made up of the physical characteristics of the product itself and the design of the package or logo—the letters, shapes, art, and colors that are used to define the graphics of the image. In contrast, the psychological side includes the emotions, beliefs, values, and personalities that people ascribe to the product. For example, when you talk about the *brand image* of Hershey's, you are talking about the chocolate itself, and also about the distinctive brown

Slogan Test

Here is a list of well-known slogans. How many can you identify? What does this test tell you about the role of slogans in establishing product memorability? How do slogans contribute to brand equity?

1.	Somethin' for nothin.'	a.	Met Life
2.	Most loved cars in the world.	b.	Oldsmobile
3.	Just do it.	c.	Busch
4.	Once you pop you just can't stop.	d.	Chevy trucks
5.	Get ___. It pays.	e.	Allstate
6.	Smart. Very smart.	f.	Visine
7.	Head for the mountains.	g.	Master Card
8.	Don't leave home without it.	h.	Prudential
9.	Like a rock.	i.	Domino's
10.	Gets the red out.	j.	Mazda
11.	Breakfast of champions.	k.	Ford
12.	Smart money.	l.	Nike
13.	Let the good times roll.	m.	RCA
14.	You're in good hands.	n.	Miller Lite
15.	Changing Entertainment. Again.	o.	Toyota
16.	Tastes great. Less filling.	p.	Volkswagen
17.	It's your money. Demand better.	q.	American Express
18.	Quality is Job 1.	r.	Wheaties
19.	Own a piece of the rock.	s.	Magnavox
20.	It just feels right.	t.	U. S. Army
		u.	Kawasaki
		v.	Pringles

(Answers, 1-i, 2-p, 3-l, 4-v, 5-a, 6-s, 7-c, 8-q, 9-d, 10-f, 11-r, 12-g, 13-u, 14-e, 15-m, 16-n, 17-b, 18-k, 19-h, 20-j)

package, the lettering of the name, and the multitude of impressions and values conveyed by its slogan "the all-American candy bar."

Promise. A brand is also a promise of value. Because it seeks to establish a familiar image, a brand also creates an expectation level. Green Giant, for example, has built its franchise on the personality of the friendly giant who watches over his valley and makes sure that Green Giant vegetables are fresh, tasty, and nutritious. The name Green Giant on the package means there are no unexpected and unwanted surprises when you buy a Green Giant product. An accumulated reservoir of goodwill and good impressions is called **brand equity**.

brand equity The use of a respected brand name to add value to a product.

BUILDING A BRAND

Brand Equity. *Brand equity* is an increasingly important concept in the 1990s. The idea that a respected brand name adds value to a product goes back to the dawn of modern marketing and poses many questions: How much value is added? Can that value be enhanced? Can it be transferred? Castle & Cook, Inc., for example, extensively researched its well-known Dole brand and discovered

Cheerios maintains a very strong brand image—even among its different flavors of cereals.

that the Dole name stood for much more than pineapple. As a result, Castle & Cooke launched Dole Fruit & Juice bars and other frozen desserts. Cheerios has expanded to embrace a variety of Cheerios cereals, including Apple Cinnamon, Honey Nut, and Multi-Grain Cheerios. In contrast, Walt Disney Company discovered that any Disney film would be perceived as targeted to a young audience. Instead of looking for a way to extend the Disney name to films targeted at an adult audience, Disney launched Touchstone Films.

Branding is a way to assist the consumer's memory process. It identifies a product and also makes it possible to position the product relative to other brands. The tools used to lock brands into the memory include distinctive names, slogans, graphics, and characters.

Brand Names. Names have both denotative and connotative meanings. Denotative aspects tell what the brand is or does, like Head and Shoulders and Intensive Care. The connotative meaning contains a suggestion or association—a meaning that is supposed to carry over to the product, such as Bounce or Mustang. Some brand names don't say much, like Breck or Sony. Names like these take on meaning only through extensive advertising and the familiarity that comes from product use. Slogans work the same way, although they can carry more content than a simple name. Xerox, whose name has become practically synonymous with the copier product category, is repositioning itself with a new slogan: "the document company." It is broadening its image beyond that of copy machines.

Research into names considers linguistics as well as associations. How does the name sound? What does it sound like, and what does it remind you of? Manufacturers must also be certain that the name does not convey any unintended meanings. When Esso renamed itself Exxon, it conducted years of study to find a distinctive name that did not have any unwanted meanings.

Interbrand, a linguistics company that charges as much as $100,000 per name, came up with Polaroid's Spectra and the analgesic Nuprin. The San Francisco-based company Namelab takes a linguistic approach, building words from a table of 6,200 one-syllable sounds. Other namesmiths rely more on outside focus groups, which might include consumers, professional writers, or even Scrabble fanatics. Many firms also have computers that coin words by the bucketful or catalog millions of previous rejects.[10]

Graphic Elements. The brand's personality is displayed in distinctive graphics used in packaging and other forms of communication. A *logo* is a characteristic mark that identifies the maker. The graphic elements in the logo and the package design that define the graphic image include distinctive type, colors, and art.

A **trademark** is a distinctive visual brand that identifies a company's products. For example, distinctive detailing easily separates the bucking bronco used by Ford's Bronco from the prancing horse used be Ferrari (see Ad 8.6). Trademarks are an important part of the brand image.

Symbolic characters are used both to help identify a product and to associate it with a personality. The Marlboro cowboy and the Charlie woman and classic examples of symbols that represent an attitude with which the audience might want to identify. The Pillsbury Doughboy is a lovable character that associates warm, positive feelings with the company and its products. Mr.

trademark Sign or design, often with distinctive lettering, that symbolizes the brand.

---

[10] B. G. Yovovich, "What Is Your Brand Really Worth?" *Adweek* (August 8, 1988).

Ferrari and Ford use a variation on the same symbol—the horse.

(Courtesy of Ferrari North America and Ford Motor Company)

transformation advertising
Image advertising that changes the experience of buying and using a product.

Goodwrench is the kind of friendly, helpful repairman you can trust. His image counters the stereotype of the auto repairman as a swindler. The Maytag repairman is not only friendly, he's lonely because Maytag washing machines are so dependable that he never gets to see customers. All these symbols convey subtle, yet complex, meanings about the product's values and benefits, in addition to serving as an identity cue.

Because the effects of image advertising build up over time, consistency is critical to this process. You can't say one thing today and something different tomorrow. David Ogilvy, founder of Ogilvy and Mather, believed strongly in brand-image advertising. He said that every ad should contribute to the image. The message should focus on what that image is supposed to be, and should be ruthlessly consistent.[11]

TRANSFORMATION ADVERTISING

Although most brands of jeans are physically very much alike, advertising has transformed Levi's 501s beyond the basic requirements of the category. Levi's has been endowed by advertising with the capacity to provide an experience different from the experience that comes from wearing any old pair of jeans. Advertising does more than tell consumers about product attributes. It actually transforms the consumer's experience when the consumer uses the product.

Experiences based on transformation advertising are very real. The experience of smoking a Marlboro is different from the experience of smoking a Pall Mall. The experience of using Coast is different from the experience of using Irish Spring or a generic bar of soap. If you doubt the reality of such differences, try giving your mother a watch for her birthday in a box that comes from K mart as opposed to giving the same watch in a box that comes from Tiffany. No doubt, you'll find the experiences of buying, giving, and wearing the watch are quite different.

Advertising provides information and at the same time transforms the experience of buying and using the product. Transformation is the secret to building a product personality and image. It is an expensive objective. In addition to consistency, one of the requirements for **transformation advertising** is frequent exposure. The process takes time because the effect is cumulative.

For transformation advertising to be effective in selling a product it should be *positive*. Its function is to make the experience richer, warmer, and more enjoyable. Wearers of Levi's jeans truly enjoy wearing Levi's more than they enjoy wearing jeans without the Levi's symbol (see Ad 8.7).

Transformation is not equally appropriate for every product. Upbeat advertising messages might not work for products related to drudgery or unpleasant experience because such a message would sound phony. It may not be possible to turn cleaning the oven, scrubbing the floor, or taking a laxative into a joyous occasion. When advertisements try to do this, they stretch credibility and sacrifice effectiveness.

However, it is possible to use transformation advertising to turn around perceived negatives. For example, the campaign for the financial company HFC, "People use our money to make the most out of life," has taken some of the threat out of applying for a loan. The State Farm "agent" series, "Like a good

---

[11] David Ogilvy, *Confessions of an Advertising Man* (New York: Dell, 1964).

The Levi 501 campaign is an example of transformational advertising.

(Courtesy of Levi Strauss & Company)

neighbor, State Farm is there," helped generate trust in a potentially brittle relationship. "The Friendly Skies of United" has, over the years, taken some of the anxiety out of flying.

Another requirement for transformation advertising is that it "ring true." Because transformation advertising deals with images, it may not be technically verifiable in a literal sense, but it must *feel true*. The characters must act as the real people in that situation would act, and they must use the product as people would use it in real life.

A final requirement for transformation advertising is that it must link the brand so tightly to the experience that people cannot remember it without remembering the brand. One example where this did *not* occur involved a series of ads for a soap company that said:

"New blouse?"	"No, new bleach."
"New dress?"	"No, new bleach."
"New shirt?"	"No, new bleach."

That campaign created a strong link between the experience and the *product category*, but not the brand. Almost everyone remembered the line. Almost no one remembered the advertiser.[12]

We know that most advertisements just "wash over" their audiences without any effect. Effective advertisements, in contrast, strike a responsive chord. In other words, they have impact, which means they overcome audience indiffer-

---

[12]Wells, *Planning for R. O. I.*

ence and focus attention on the message. Furthermore, they catch attention without being irritating, and they keep attention while penetrating the mind. Advertisements that deliver impact have stopping power, pulling power, and lock the message into the mind of the target audience.

$\mathcal{S}$UMMARY

- An advertisement must compete with other advertisements, with surrounding editorial and entertainment stimuli, and with hundreds of other possible distractions for viewers' and readers' attention. To be effective, an advertisement must attract attention and hold it.

- The first step in attracting and holding attention is to *stop* the viewer or reader. Advertisements that are *intrusive*—that demand attention—have the most stopping power. Intrusiveness comes from the physical characteristics of the ad itself—its loudness, size, length, contrast, or color, for instance. More importantly, intrusiveness comes from the originality of the ad's design and the personal relevance of the ad's subject matter.

- In addition to *stopping power,* advertisements must have *pulling power*—they must hold as well as attract attention. Pulling power is achieved through inviting design, and through the personal relevance of the message.

- Information advertisements must be clear and factual. They work by providing information about the benefits of the brands they advertise. This information may change attitudes and opinions. It may also associate pleasant feelings and experiences with the brand, thereby making the brand more likable.

- When an informational advertisement works, it facilitates conviction—a firm belief that the brand is superior to its competitors. This belief, which is also influenced by ongoing personal experience with the brand, is known as *brand equity*. Brand equity is one of a marketer's most valuable and hardest-won achievements. It is the key factor in brand loyalty.

- Emotional associations with the brand also contribute to brand equity. Brand equity is not solely due to information, reason, and logic. It is in part a general, hard-to-pin-down, undifferentiated favorable disposition.

- In addition to attracting and holding attention, effective advertisements have *locking power*—they lock enduring impressions into memory. These impressions are strongest and most durable when the advertisement is original and personally relevant. They are strengthened by vivid, creative design, and by frequent repetition.

- The sum of these impressions, combined with other experiences with the brand, constitutes the brand's image. A strong, favorable image is the most important property a brand can have. An unfavorable image is a handicap that must be overcome if the brand is to survive in free-market competition.

- Advertising is one—but only one—of the factors that can help a marketer overcome an unfavorable image. If the unfavorable image is due to a defect in the product, or to a defect in a nonadvertising aspect of the marketing program, advertising alone cannot repair it.

- *Transformation advertising* transforms the consumer's experience of using the brand. It makes this experience warmer, richer, and more enjoyable than the experience would have been without the advertising. Transformation advertising can be and often is an important contributor to the brand's image.

- To be effective, transformation advertising must be consistent, and it must be frequent, because the transformation process is cumulative. Furthermore, even though transformation advertising may not be technically verifiable in a literal sense, it must *feel* right. Transformation cannot take place when the feeling conveyed by the advertising and the experience of using the brand are incompatible.

- Effective advertisements strike a responsive chord. They overcome indifference and focus attention on the advertiser's message. They catch and hold attention without being irritating, and leave a lasting favorable impression. This impression may be factual, it may be emotional, or it may be a subtle combination of factual and emotional.

- Effective advertisements have stopping power, pulling power, and locking power. They attract and hold attention, and they make lasting impressions. They make significant contributions to the brand's equity by producing essential, favorable changes in the individual consumer's view of the brand's reputation.

QUESTIONS

1 What is meant by breakthrough advertising? How is this accomplished?

2 What are some common methods of attracting and maintaining consumer interest?

3 How does the construct of perception-awareness-understanding-persuasion relate to advertising? What types of ads are appropriate at each level?

4 Mary Proctor is an associate creative director in an agency that handles a liquid detergent brand that competes with Lever's Wisk. Mary is reviewing a history of the Wisk theme "ring around the collar." It is one of the longest-running themes on television, and Wisk's sales share indicates that it has been successful. What is confusing to Mary is that the Wisk history includes numerous consumer surveys that all show consumers find "ring around the collar" a boring, silly, and altogether irritating advertising theme. Can you explain why Wisk is such a popular brand even though its advertising campaign is so disliked?

5 The chapter identifies four major operations in advertising creative strategy: perception, awareness, understanding, and persuasion. Emotional tactics are discussed under "persuasion," but emotion figures in the other operations as well. Identify how the creative use of emotion can enhance each operation. To bolster your position, select a current advertising campaign that supports your analysis.

6 Bill Thomas and Beth Bennett are a copywriter/art director creative team who often amuse themselves by arguing about famous ad campaigns. Their current subject is the Energizer bunny commercials. Bill says this is a perfect example of *vampire creativity*. Beth disagrees, stressing the theme's strength through "interest" and "ambiguity." Who is right? Why?

SUGGESTED CLASS PROJECT

From current magazines, identify five advertisements that have exceptionally high stopping power, five that have exceptionally high pulling power, and five that have exceptionally high locking power. Which of these advertisements are primarily informational, and which are primarily transformational? How do the informational advertisements differ from the transformational advertisements in use of illustrations, headlines, body copy, and type style?

FURTHER READINGS

AAKER, DAVID A., and ALEXANDER L. BIEZ, *Brand Equity and Advertising*, (Hillsdale, NJ: Lawrence Erlbaum, 1993), Chapters 5, 8, 11.

BOGART, LEO, *Strategy in Advertising: Matching Media and Messages to Markets and Motivation*, 2nd ed. (Chicago: Crain Books, 1984).

BURTON, PHILIP WARD, and SCOTT C. PURVIS, *Which Ad Pulled Best?* 7th ed. (Lincolnwood, IL: NTC Business Books, 1993).

OGLIVY, DAVID, *Confessions of an Advertising Man* (New York: Atheneum, 1980).

PATTI, CHARLES H., and SANDRA E. MORIARTY, *The Making of Effective Advertising* (Englewood Cliffs, NJ: Prentice Hall, 1990).

RAYMOND, MINER, *Advertising That Sells: A Primer for Product Managers* (Cincinnati, OH: Black Rose, 1990).

REEVES, ROSSER, *Reality in Advertising* (New York: Alfred A. Knopf, 1963).

WELLS, WILLIAM D., *Planning for R.O.I.* (Englewood Cliffs, NJ: Prentice Hall, 1989).

Integrated State Marketing

Every state attempts to position itself as an attractive tourist destination. In campaigns of this kind, the key questions always are, which of the state's advantages should be featured? And how should those features be translated into appealing communications? The state of Oklahoma asked its advertising agency, Ackerman McQueen, to develop an integrated advertising and marketing campaign to attract tourists to Oklahoma. The first step was to review every other state's tourism programs.

Once Ackerman McQueen and Oklahoma tourism officials had identified ways to portray the state's features, the next step was to conduct telephone interviews with potential vacationers. The sample included respondents in Oklahoma City, Tulsa, and smaller Oklahoma cities and in Dallas, Houston, Wichita, and St. Louis. The object of the interviews was to assess reactions to positioning alternatives and to measure impressions of Oklahoma as a place to take a vacation.

The interviews showed that Oklahoma did not have a bad image; it had *no* image. Less than 20 percent of the out-of-state respondents could name any Oklahoma attraction that interested them. Although Oklahoma City respondents had taken advantage of some of the recreational facilities in their home town, few had made the two-hour trip to Tulsa, and few Tulsans had even considered Oklahoma City. Worse yet, 82 percent of Oklahomans planned to vacation, or take a week-end trip, out of state rather than in state.

Based on this research, the planning team set three communication goals: (1) fill the image vacuum, (2) promote a variety of attractions, and (3) do a better job of holding in-state visitors. They also saw opportunities to target North Texas and Wichita, Kansas.

The campaign positioned Oklahoma as "Oklahoma Native America"—American in its native state. This theme called attention to Oklahoma's American Indian culture (Oklahoma has more American Indians than any other state); its Native Waters (the state's splendid lakes and waterfalls); its Native Speed (Oklahoma is the horse capital of the world); its Native Music (music festivals); and its Native Buffalo.

The television portion of the campaign included six commercials. All used the same original music track featuring American Indian drums and flute, and quick cuts of "native" attractions throughout the state. Outdoor and print portions of the campaign also ran.

Collateral materials reinforced the mass-media campaign. Oklahoma's Vacation Guide, which potential visitors could request via an 800 number, featured the campaign theme, as did state highway maps, the state highway brochure, and even license plates and drivers' licenses. The Native America logo and American Indian iconography also appeared on T-shirts, sweatshirts, and wall posters.

Other Oklahoma tourism groups embraced Native America in their advertising. When a group of Oklahoma Indians danced at a major tourism conference in Germany, the event received international coverage.

A post-campaign awareness and attitude study showed that awareness of Oklahoma's television advertisements had increased 27 percent, that Oklahoma's image as a tourist destination had become clearer and more favorable, and that intentions to vacation in Oklahoma had increased significantly. Most important of all, a separate study of 2,000 people who had requested vacation information found that "conversion"—the proportion of inquirers who actually followed through by taking a vacation in Oklahoma—increased from 33 percent to 36 percent. Although an increase of three percentage points may seem small, it represents a large increase in tourist spending within the state, amounting to about a one-third increase in the state's return on its investment in advertising.

Questions

1. Given what you know of Oklahoma's assets and liabilities as a tourist destination, what do you think of the planning team's decision to focus on Native America? What other opportunities would have been available? How would you go about deciding among these alternatives?

2. In its efforts to integrate advertising with other forms of marketing communication, Oklahoma appears to have covered all the bases. Can you think of any missed opportunities?

3. Of the various ways Oklahoma used to evaluate the effectiveness of its advertising, which are most convincing? Why?

Where Credit Is Due

In the days before computers, the back rooms of banks were filled with clerks and bookkeepers who entered, added, and subtracted endless streams of numbers that recorded the deposits and withdrawals made in person or by check by the bank's customers. In those days, banks closed at 3 p.m. to give their clerical armies time to record and reconcile the day's activities.

As computers began to take over large portions of this careful and arduous labor, systems analysts began to realize that electronic records could replace paper records. This realization soon led to confident predictions that the United States would become a "checkless, cashless society."

Although the United States has not yet become a checkless, cashless society, plastic credit cards with electronic sensors have indeed replaced checks and cash at least in part for many consumers. This replacement—partial though it still is—has generated a large and still-growing segment of the financial services industry.

Until the 1980s the credit card business was dominated by American Express, Master Card, and Visa. American Express differed from Visa and Master Card in that American Express required that card users repay the entire debit balance within a few weeks of the end of each monthly credit cycle. Visa and Master Card allowed and in fact encouraged their cardholders to maintain a limited debit balance, on which Visa and Master Card charged above-market interest. The opportunity to carry a credit balance segmented credit card users into "transactors" and "revolvers." "Transactors" paid their balances monthly, regardless of the card's requirements. "Revolvers" carried credit balances. Interest on those balances provided important income to the Visa and Master Card systems.

Another difference between American Express and Visa and Master Card was that American Express maintained more exclusive entrance requirements. American Express required higher income and more accumulated capital before an applicant could become an American Express cardholder. This difference meant that, compared with holders of Visa and Master Card, American Express cardholders were, on the average, more affluent.

In addition to yearly fees collected from cardholders, American Express, Visa, and Master Card all collected service charges from retailers each time a card was used. On the premise that American Express cardholders were more affluent and therefore more desirable customers, American Express demanded higher service charges. Although retailers objected to these higher charges, many (but far from all) retailers agreed to pay them because they were afraid of alienating American Express customers.

Advertising entered this picture in several ways. First, by informing consumers of the availability and advantages of credit cards, advertising by all three of the major credit card systems created millions of credit card users. This user base, along with other advantages (such as fewer uncollectible checks) encouraged large numbers of retailers to accept credit card payment.

Second, because American Express "members" were on the average more affluent, American Express was able to differentiate itself from its competitors by implying in its advertising that American Express card users were somehow more distinguished. As this advertising campaign took hold, prestige became an increasingly important motive for using (and accepting) American Express instead of Master Card or Visa.

Thus, advertising played two important and quite different roles in the early stages of the credit card business. It helped create demand for credit cards in general, and it helped differentiate competitors' offerings. Note that neither of these achievements would have been possible with advertising alone. Credit cards did indeed provide financial services that large numbers of consumers found useful. American Express cardholders were indeed somewhat more affluent and, therefore, in some sense better customers (i.e., better credit risks) than the holders of cards issued by competitors.

As might be expected, some consumers overused their credit cards and found themselves in serious financial trouble. Credit card marketers were criticized for encouraging this overuse, and much of the blame was laid at the door of credit card advertising. As in other product and service categories, advertising was criticized, not entirely unreasonably, for contributing to a negative side effect that advertisers had certainly not intended.

In the 1980s, Sears introduced the Discover card, offering "no annual fee" and a substantially lower interest rate on unpaid balances. This lower interest rate made the Discover card especially attractive to "revolvers." Sears made heavy use of advertising to inform consumers of these two important advantages. Television and print advertising and a heavy direct-mail campaign targeted at the most desirable potential customers persuaded millions of Americans to add the Discover card to the credit cards already in their wallets. This outcome, in turn, persuaded many retailers to accept the Discover card along with all the others.

Meanwhile, American Express introduced a Gold card, in an effort to leverage the prestige motive even further. Although the Gold card obtained a viable segment of prestige-oriented credit card users, part of this segment came from American Express Green card users. Furthermore, the Gold card idea was relatively easy to copy, and both Visa and Master Card promptly followed. These moves, countermoves, and their consequences, demonstrate that advertisers are not all-powerful. Even the most artful advertising and the most carefully planned market segmentation have limits.

In the 1990s, additional competitors entered the already crowded and segmented credit card market. In conjunction with Master Card and Visa, General Motors and other automobile manufacturers offered credit of up to 5 percent of credit card charges toward future automobile purchases, an extension of similar offers of "frequent flier miles" by major airlines. General Electric offered credit toward purchase of General Electric products, and AT&T offered a Universal card (a Master Card) that can be used to make both telephone calls and retail purchases.

The history and development of credit cards provide excellent illustrations of the complex roles that advertising can and often does play in the marketing of products and services. First of all, the entire credit card industry is based on a significant technological achievement. Credit cards are more useful and more convenient than checks for many purposes, and represent a meaningful improvement in the financial system. But before this technological achievement could come into widespread use, both consumers and retailers had to understand and appreciate its benefits. Advertising helped create consumer awareness of and interest in the credit card as a generic product. While this awareness and

Exhibit A

interest was critically important, it was not created by advertising alone. The product itself had a valuable service to offer.

With the growth of consumer demand, retailers responded by making credit card use increasingly routine and convenient. Advertising accelerated this change, both by influencing retailers directly and indirectly through requests from consumers.

As use of credit cards grew, unintended side effects appeared among vulnerable segments of consumers. Because advertising's role in the growth of credit card use was so obvious, advertising received a share of the blame for these serious but unintended consequences.

As the credit card category developed, the major competitors used advertising to develop future category growth, to segment the market, and to differentiate themselves from their competitors. New competitors, offering new advantages, employed media advertising in combination with direct marketing and various forms of sales promotion to identify and differentiate their offerings and to convey the benefits of those offerings to potential customers. All of these developments, in one form or another, are likely to be found in advertising's complex and varied roles in the marketing of any service or any product.

Questions

1. The small differences that now separate one credit card brand from another are known as *marginal differentiation*. In what other major product or service categories is marginal differentiation common?

2. How do advertising strategies in product or service categories characterized by marginal differentiation differ from advertising strategies where differences among brands are larger? (Advertising strategies are discussed in Chapter 6.)

3. Select a leading brand in a product or service category characterized by marginal differentiation and a leading brand in a product or service category where differences among brands are larger, and write advertising strategies for both.

4. Write advertising strategies for those two brands' principal competitors.

ABSOLUT L.A.

ABSOLUT BI

MEDIA STRATEGY AND PLANNING

CHAPTER OUTLINE

- Working Together: Designing Ads for Specific Media

- The Function of Media Planning in Advertising

- The Aperture Concept in Media Planning

- Media Planning Operations: Information Sources and Analysis

- Media Planning Operations: Setting Objectives

- Media Planning Operations: Developing Strategies

- Media Planning Operations: Media Selection Procedures

- Media Planning Operations: Staging a Media Plan

CHAPTER OBJECTIVES

When you have completed this chapter, you should be able to:

- Understand the central position of media planning in campaign development and how this function utilizes information from numerous sources, including product sales performance, competitor surveillance, and message creative strategy, to form the campaign design

- Understand the organization and purpose of the media plan, and see how each decision on selection and scheduling is coordinated with the client's sales objectives

- Explain how planners use communication aperture to give direction to media planning strategy

- Explain how the media's qualitative features (atmosphere and environment) are blended with their quantitative dimensions (reach, frequency, and efficiency) to provide the needed profile for selection

WORKING TOGETHER: DESIGNING ADS FOR SPECIFIC MEDIA

What used to be a wall of misunderstanding and professional indifference between the media planners and those responsible for creating the advertising is now becoming a gateway to shared ideas. This revolution in cooperative spirit is all the more impressive when you consider the vocational distance between these major players in advertising. Media planners, known by some as "the bean counters" of advertising, deal in dollars and research probabilities, whereas the creative team, called "hippie dreamers" by some, concoct visual and verbal imagery. Unlikely collaborators, for sure, but many advertising agencies have been able to shove these personality differences aside in the quest for successful campaigns. The classic illustrations of role reversal depict media analysts proposing creative approaches to media use and writers and art directors recommending where the ads should appear.

Nowhere was this cooperation more apparent than in the work of TBWA, a New York-based agency, for Vin & Spirit Absolut Vodka. The Absolut media strategy concentrates in business and consumer magazines. With as many as 100 magazines involved in the campaign, the creative demand was enormous. Much of the burden was lessened, however, because the agency's media and creative departments worked together on magazine selection and tailored advertising to each magazine's readership. The following are some examples of this innovative partnership.

The media department suggested that the creative team design theater programs (playbills), to be followed up with a compatible theme. Agency creatives developed "Absolut Bravo," a photo of the Absolut bottle surrounded by roses.

Playboy was not on the media department's list of magazines until TBWA creatives dreamed up "Absolut Centerfold," a hilarious takeoff on the magazine's "Playmate of the Month" feature. The Absolut ad included a profile of the "centerfold model," complete with "Measurements" (11" X 11" X 11"), "Favorite Books or Plays" (*The Iceman Cometh* and *Soul on Ice*), and even a unique version of "Ambitions" ("To Always Be Cool, With or Without Ice").

Ads placed in Los Angeles-area magazines featured an LA-style swimming pool in the shape of the Absolut bottle. Similarly, for New York City-area readers, the advertisement showed a photo of the Brooklyn Bridge, with the supporting stonework assuming a new distinctive outline: the Absolut bottle.

Even trade publications were given unique treatment. When media planners recommended advertising in *Advertising Age* magazine, the Absolut art director responded with "Absolut Subliminal," with a glass filled with suspiciously encoded ice cubes.

When asked to discuss this creative mastery of a medium, Richard Costello, TBWA's president and chief executive officer, cited the force behind the cooperation between his media and creative staffs: "What . . . (this) has done for us is give us a more open mind and put more demand on all departments to be creative in their ideas than what otherwise would be the case."

In a period of soaring media costs, tighter budgets, and cluttered communication channels, the synergy provided by the new harmony between media and creative is a refreshing and needed change.[1]

---

[1] Adapted from Gary Levin, "Meddling in Creative More Welcome," *Advertising Age* (April 9, 1990):S–4, S–8.

THE FUNCTION OF MEDIA PLANNING IN ADVERTISING

media planning A decision process leading to the use of advertising time and space to assist in the achievement of marketing objectives.

Media planning is a problem-solving process that translates marketing objectives into a series of strategic decisions. The ultimate goal is to place the advertising message before a target audience. The planning decisions involved include: which audiences to reach, where (geographic emphasis), when (timing), for how long (campaign length), and how intense (frequent) the exposure should be. Media planning is a blend of marketing skills and familiarity with mass communication. Because it deals with the most significant portion of the advertiser's budget (cost for space and time), it is a crucial element in contemporary advertising.

Media planning was not always the sophisticated process it is today. In fact, it has undergone a substantial evolution in the last 25 years. What was once a clerical function of choosing media positions and contracting for them is now a central element in marketing strategy. Media department employees who once worked silently "behind the scenes" are now in the forefront directing marketing strategy.

This chapter is an introduction to media planning, with particular emphasis on its integral role in merging the science of marketing with the art of advertising. As you will see, the planner's role is twofold: He or she must act as both a marketing analyst and an expert appraiser of media channel effectiveness.

THE APERTURE CONCEPT IN MEDIA PLANNING

Each customer or prospect for a product or service has an ideal point in time and place at which he or she can be reached with an advertising message. This point can be when the consumer is in the "search corridor"—the purchasing mode—or it can occur when the consumer is seeking more information before entering the corridor. The goal of the media planner is to expose consumer prospects to the advertiser's message at these critical points.

aperture The ideal moment for exposing consumers to an advertising message.

This ideal opening is called an **aperture.** The most effective advertisement should expose the consumer to the product when interest and attention are high. Aperture can be thought of as the home-run swing in baseball: The ball meets the bat at the right spot and at the precise instant for maximum distance.

Locating the aperture opportunity is a major responsibility of the media planner. The planner must study the marketing position of the advertiser to determine which media opportunities will do the best job of message placement. This is a complex and difficult assignment. Success depends on accurate marketing research, appreciation of the message concept, and a sensitive understanding of the channels of mass communication.

$\mathcal{M}$EDIA PLANNING OPERATIONS: INFORMATION SOURCES AND ANALYSIS

Media department people often believe they are the "hub" in the advertising wheel, the central point where each campaign element (spoke) is joined. In part, this belief is based on the amount of data and information that must be gathered, sorted, and analyzed before media decision making can begin. Figure 9.1 illustrates the sources of the required information. This chapter will explore how this information is used at subsequent stages in media planning.

MARKETING SOURCES

Media analysis is described as the crucial bridge between product marketing and advertising strategy because so much of the activity in the marketplace has a direct bearing on media decisions.

Area Sales Patterns. Virtually no company that sells products or services in multiple markets has balanced or equal sales across all territories. The sales activity and sales rank often are different for each area. Because a major role of advertising is to support sales activity, media plans usually vary the amount of advertising designated to each sales territory. As a consequence, each market's sales reports are used to determine geographic dollar allocations.

Month-by-Month Sales Patterns. The timing of the advertising schedules is a vital strategy in media planning. Most sales for consumer products fluctuate. Media timing (when to start and stop a campaign) should reflect the sales calendar or seasonality for each advertiser. To do this accurately, planners carefully follow the consumer demand trends apparent from the monthly sales report.

Distribution Patterns. The success of most brands is heavily dependent on how many of each market's retailers carry (stock) the product. Marketers with poor or just-developing distribution may be unable to exploit even good market

Figure 9.1

Sources of information in media planning.

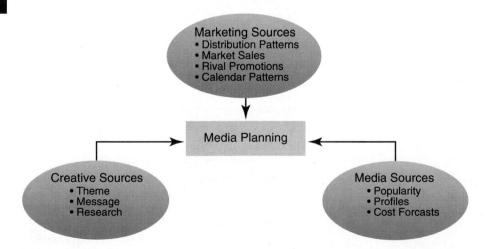

potentials until they improve their distribution. Marketing people alert media planners to unsatisfactory distribution patterns so that ad spending can be modified accordingly.

Competitor's Advertising Patterns. Rival companies may compete heavily for certain markets or regions, whereas other markets may only be lightly considered. A study of recent advertising history will give the planner some idea of how much advertising to expect from the competition. Heavy concentrations of competitive advertising may change a brand's spending strategy for a region or market. For more on this subject, see the "share of voice" (SOV) discussion later in this chapter.

CREATIVE SOURCES

Close cooperation between media planners and those responsible for the creative decisions can produce sales results. Sharing information influences a number of media strategies, including the choice of the creative theme, the media vehicle, and consumer research.

Theme Characteristics. The recommended creative solution (what to say and how to say it) to an advertising challenge usually influences where the message should be placed. For example, complicated copy platforms, such as those for high-involvement products (running shoes or sports cars), might require the use of print media. Media planners must pay close attention to the thinking of the creative department.

Message Characteristics. Creative tactics can also affect media vehicle choices. The tone of the message may indicate that one television program type is right and another one wrong for this creative approach. Media environments are discussed in more detail later in the chapter.

Creative Performance Research. Companies often monitor audience reaction to the advertising message (see Chapter 21). Although copy testing is primarily a measure of creative impact, media planners can use the data to make a number of decisions, including the number of messages to be used and the continuity pattern of the advertising.

MEDIA SOURCES

The eventual selection of a medium (a single form of communication, such as television) and specific media vehicles (a single program, radio station, magazine title, and so on) depends on the availability of media research and information supplied to media planners and buyers on the size and profile of the audience and the media costs for space or time.

Media Popularity. Two obvious criteria for media selection are the size of the audience available for each media vehicle and how well the vehicle's audience matches the characteristics of the target market. Media planners and buyers have access to syndicated media audience research that estimates numbers of readers, viewers, and listeners from current audience studies. These data enable planners to forecast the popularity of most of the mass media. More important than the size of the audience are the social and economic profiles of audience members, including demographics, interests and lifestyles, purchasing patterns, and other characteristics that describe potential consumers.

Media Cost Forecasting. Because media plans are developed long before the campaign begins, a careful and accurate estimate of what the advertiser will pay for space and time is vital to successful planning.

Media Characteristics. Information on the media is not all numbers, such as audience size. Planners also need to know about the qualities of the media. How influential are they with the audience? How believable? Do they involve the audience beyond entertainment or information? These and questions about media atmosphere are characteristics of each medium. The answers help planners estimate the impact the advertisement might have on the target audience.

MEDIA PLANNING OPERATIONS: SETTING OBJECTIVES

Each media plan has a series of objectives that reflect some basic questions, the answers to which comprise a strategic plan of action.

The basic questions that direct media strategy are whom to advertise to, which geographic areas to cover, when to advertise, and what the duration of the campaign should be.

FINDING TARGET AUDIENCES IN MEDIA OPPORTUNITIES

There are two major challenges facing media planners today in searching the media for target audience opportunities. Both of these challenges involve the type of research available to the media planner.

Marketers' profiles of valued customers and prospects are provided by company research. These profiles often contain descriptions of peoples' interests, activities, and attitudinal concerns—in all, a valuable insight into the company's target audience. The problem for media planners is that these profiles are not used by the mass media in describing *their* audiences. The result forces planners into translating the marketing research into a context that fits surveys of the mass media. This is not an easy job. Suppose the marketer was looking for prospects with strong ecological feelings. With no media measurement, the planner would have to find another indicator of environmental concerns.

Another challenge is the lack of compatible audience research for the many new and often unique media for advertising and sales promotion. New traditional media (e.g., magazines or cable networks) must wait some time before research companies can supply audience estimates. For innovative media (e.g., store-based advertising, special-event promotions), the existing research firms do not have compatible measurements available. While these opportunities have marketing value, it is very hard to judge their impact without research.

The following are the most common media audience measurements available to media planners. They are discussed in an order based upon availability.

Concepts & APPLICATIONS

Orion Innovates Media Strategies

In November 1990 Orion Pictures released the film *Dances with Wolves*, starring and directed by Kevin Costner. The film is about a young soldier torn between his loyalties to the Union Army and the Sioux Indian tribe. In marketing *Dances with Wolves*, Orion joined the growing group of movie studios that target their advertising to more specific audiences. The company showed film trailers of *Dances with Wolves* on college campuses, in video stores, and on television screens in consumer electronics stores.

Universal Pictures' executive vice president of worldwide marketing, Simon Korblit, explained why movie studios have become attracted to media considered nontraditional for the film industry: "Just [like] the way you want to be different with creative, now we're trying to be different with media." The studios' objective is to differentiate themselves and their films from other movie studios. The hope is that using different targeted media will attract more moviegoers.

Orion Pictures faced two challenges in marketing *Dances with Wolves*. The first was the movie's three-hour length, and the second was its subject matter. The company's response was to target the film at those moviegoers who were already interested in the subject matter and to get them to spread the word to others. As part of Orion's $8 million to $10 million budgeted media plan, Foote, Cone & Belding, the agency representing the studio, bought 60-second radio spots, which aired on November 9, 1990, on six American Indian stations. The commercial was written in English and then translated into American Indian languages appropriate for each station's audience. The strategy also included a very large network television buy. Many of the ads emphasized both Kevin Costner's starring role and the environmental issues the film invokes.

Media strategies targeted at upscale, well-educated adults included a sweepstakes promotion for the movie aired on cable's Discovery Channel and a special screening of the film to benefit the Nature Conservancy, a conservation group, that was advertised by public service announcements featuring Kevin Costner.

Orion also bought into Preview Tech, a company that distributes laser discs of film trailers to be aired on the 200 television monitors in each of the 165 con-

Orion Pictures utilized various media strategies in advertising their 1990 film *Dances with Wolves*, starring Kevin Costner. (Photofest)

sumer electronic outlets in Circuit City Stores. Each film distributed by Preview Tech runs for one month in this fashion. Universal's Simon Korblit explained the reason for such a media investment: "Whenever we can gain exposure for a trailer outside the traditional arena, we want to do that."

Orion is not the only movie studio to realize the value of targeted media planning. Warner Bros. used direct mail to promote *Memphis Belle*, its movie about World War II bomber pilots, to veterans, pilots, and readers of Time-Life Books' series on World War II. Mirimax Films created a campaign targeted at the handicapped to advertise its 1989 Oscar-winning movie *My Left Foot*. The trade-off for this kind of innovative media advertising is that funds are diverted from more standard television and newspaper advertising. As John Jacobs, vice president of media at Warner Bros., states: "As a studio, you can only [afford to] get involved with one or two of these things."

So far, the trend is going strong, but only time will tell if this new approach to targeting movie audiences will prove profitable.

Source: Adapted from Marcy Magiera, "*Dances* Joins Film Efforts to Target Ads," *Advertising Age* (November 5, 1990):1, 67.

Demographics. Demographics represents the most common "name tags" given to people. People are described by their age, income (personal and household), education, occupation, marital status, family size, and several other tags. Ad 9.1 for *The Sporting News*, for example, is targeted at men and is very gender-specific. For a more detailed discussion of demographics, refer to Chapter 5.

Product-Use Segmentation. Audiences can also be classified according to their consumption habits (usage). Media planners obtain information on which products readers, viewers, or listeners buy and how often they use or consume these products.

Psychographics Psychographics looks for more sensitive measures of motivation and behavior. It attempts to classify people according to how they feel and act. For example, the lifestyle profile, one form of psychographic research, describes people by the way they view their careers and leisure recreation pur-

MAMA NEVER SAID THERE'D BE DAYS LIKE THIS.

Today, mama's got a lot more cooking than dinner. That's why she reads Family Circle? The magazine that's not written for old fashioned housewives, it's written for the newest, hottest mamas ever. Or at least 23,000,000 of them.

FamilyCircle

FOR THE WOMEN OF TODAY RAISING THE GENERATION OF TOMORROW.

Ad 9.2

This advertisement for *Family Circle* magazine emphasizes the nontraditional lifestyle of its female readers.

(Courtesy of The Family Circle, Inc.)

suits (see Ad 9.2). A lifestyle profile provides perspective on people's *chosen* social and cultural environment. Preferences for products, services, and entertainment are identified from these consumer self-evaluations.

SALES GEOGRAPHY: WHERE TO ADVERTISE?

Sales geography is an important aspect of many advertising plans. As we mentioned earlier, although companies may distribute goods and services in many cities and states, sales are seldom consistent across areas. Even the most popular brands in sales leadership positions are not that way in every market. Differences affect which markets are used in the campaign and the dollars allocated. For the media planner a system is needed to accurately and fairly distribute the advertising dollars.

TIMING: WHEN TO ADVERTISE?

When is the best time to place the message before the target audience? The concept of aperture suggests advertising is most effective when people are exposed at a time when they are most receptive to the product information. This is easier said than done. Media planners might have to juggle a number of variables to make correct timing decisions: how often the product is bought, if it is used more in some months than others, and how heavily it is advertised by competitors month to month. Each combination of influences makes the timing strategy unique to each company and brand.

Seasonal Timing. Much of consumer demand for products and services is influenced by weather patterns. Recreation equipment, agricultural products, beverages, and foods all will reflect changes in season. Aperture exists when the target audience considers their calendar needs.

The strategic challenge for planners is locating the beginning aperture point and estimating how long the campaign should run to cover the demand. Because weather forecasting can be chaotic, media plans must have built-in flexibility.

Holiday Timing. The timing of advertising schedules can also be coordinated with holidays and other national celebrations. Just as with seasonal planning, media planners must exercise careful judgment regarding when to use advertising to take advantage of the consumer's interest. Nowhere is this judgment more critical than in advertising children's toys and gifts.

Holiday toys and gifts for children pose a fairly tricky problem for media planners. There are two target audiences involved—the child (user) and the adult (buyer). Are both targets making a brand decision at the same time? If not (which is often the case), the planner must decide which target takes priority.

Day-of-the Week Timing. Retail advertisers know their customers' shopping patterns first-hand. Shopping patterns are dictated by needs, work schedules, and payroll calendars; each day of the week is not equal in shopping traffic. Retail advertising is often used to create traffic during the normally slower times. For example, stores often advertise price specials during the midweek, when shopping is slower, rather than on Friday or Saturday, when it is already heavier.

Hour-of-the-Day Timing. Aperture is dictated by peoples' needs in the day. Advertising in selected media should be scheduled when product need is high.

Hour-of-the-day timing is used by companies that target special consumer groups, such as children and teens (after-school hours and Saturday mornings), or senior citizens (early morning rather than evening positions).

DURATION: HOW LONG TO ADVERTISE?

How many weeks of the sales year should the advertising run? If there is a need to cover most of the weeks, the advertising will be spread rather thin. If the amount of time to cover is limited, advertising can be more heavily concentrated. The selection of pattern depends on a number of factors, including the advertising budget, consumer use cycles, and competitive strategies.

The Advertising Budget. If their advertising allocations were unlimited, most companies would advertise every day. Not even the largest advertisers are in this position, as all advertising budgets are limited. Shorter schedules with stronger levels of advertising must be used instead.

Consumer-Use Cycles. Continuity should match consumer-use cycles (the time between purchase and repurchase), especially for products and services that demand high usage rates, such as soft drinks, toothpaste, candy and gum, fast-food restaurants, and movies. The marketer views these cycles as the number of times customers can be gained or lost.

Competitive Advertising. In crowded product categories (household products, food, and durable goods) few advertisers are willing to ignore the advertising activity of competitors. In such situations scheduling decisions are made in response to the amount of competitive "traffic." The objective is to find media where the advertiser's voice is not suppressed by the voices of competitors. This concept, often called **share of voice** (percent of total advertising messages in a medium used by one advertiser), might mean scheduling to avoid the heavy clutter of competing advertising.

share of voice The percentage of advertising messages in a medium by one brand among all messages for that product or service.

*M*EDIA PLANNING OPERATIONS: DEVELOPING STRATEGIES

To achieve the key plan objectives of who (target), where (location), when (time frame), and how long (duration), media planners use a selection process of choosing the best alternatives and methods to satisfy the plan's needs. The following section discusses some of the strategies used to meet company objectives.

TARGET AUDIENCE STRATEGIES: NEW TECHNOLOGY OF MEASUREMENT

Although media planners are captives of the audience research used in the mass media, there are valuable developments in the near future that may meet the challenges.

Retail Scanners. With the expansion of scanning at cashier stations and checkouts, marketing research is gaining much more knowledge about the individual consumer's purchasing behavior. Efforts are underway to match buyer activity with specific media preferences; a single source matching product and media likes and dislikes.

Database Developments. The computer has revolutionized the old-fashioned customer list. An individual's product preference can be stored by name and address. In logic it is only a small step to also store media choices on what individuals watch, hear, and read.

These person-specific sources of data could eventually make much of the industry's use of demographics and psychographics unnecessary and obsolete.

GEOGRAPHIC STRATEGIES: ALLOCATING MEDIA WEIGHT

When a regional or national marketer's sales patterns are uneven, it is often the media planner's task to balance sales with advertising investment market by market.

The formula used to allocate advertising dollars may use any or all of the following market statistics: target population, distribution strength, and media

Tom Jonas, Manager of Strategy Development, CME•KHBB, Minneapolis

8:15–9:00 A.M. Arrive at office, check E-mail, voice-mail, and real mail for urgent messages and changes to the day's schedule. Return phone calls. Write list of what needs to be done today: Begin writing a presentation outlining the results of a strategy development case, meet with client and account executive to determine a new-products development plan, meet with new business coordinator to check on slide production and slide format, prepare for and attend a meeting on the repositioning of a cereal that is not achieving its sales objectives.

9:00–9:30 A.M. Meet with Sharon Guerre in her office to review different slide layouts and colors for the presentation of a strategy development case to about 150 people. Review alternatives, decide on three that she should develop a bit more, and agree to meet later in the day.

9:30–11:00 A.M. Have a conference call in my office with our snack-cakes client and the account executive about developing a strategic plan and planning process to determine where the snack-cake market is headed, how the overall business is changing, and ways in which the client can exploit those anticipated changes.

Reach agreement on the steps we want to take, discuss how the client is going to need to sell-in the approach to her top management. We're in agreement as to the steps and what needs to be done. The account executive will summarize our conversation, write up what we've discussed, give it to me to review, and then forward to the client sometime late next week. We've agreed that we'll meet in two weeks to determine where to go from here, since there are immediate planning issues that our client needs to address in the meantime.

11:00–11:45 A.M. Work with management supervisor, account executive, and research supervisor to refine an outline for a new business presentation. Focus specifically on research findings from consumers and retailers to determine possible positioning opportunities for the brand, who the most critical target audiences are, and what some of the key positioning criteria should be.

11:45–12:15 A.M. Make "rounds" of creative and account floors to check on how people are coming with key assignments and see where I may be needed.

Talk with the creative team that's working with me on a new-product introduction for an "enthusiasm

costs, in addition to company sales results. In Chapter 7, a marketing system called brand and category development was described. This is a popular method for low-involvement convenience product allocations.

The planner's ideal advertising allocation to a market will provide enough of the budget to fulfill each area's sales objectives. Heavy allocations in weak sales areas are not made unless there are strong marketing reasons to expect significant growth. Conversely, strong sales markets may not receive proportional increases in advertising unless there is clear evidence that company sales can go

check" and see if they have any questions about the background of the assignment they've been given and any suggestions as I begin drafting positioning alternatives.

The account supervisor on cereals wants to talk to me about some changes in the creative blueprints that occurred while she was out of the office and with which she is not sure she is in agreement. Review whether the revisions are appropriate and really focus attention on what consumers apparently believe to be most compelling before a final recommendation is made to the client. In the end, we agree that the changes that have been made are consistent with the initial direction and have focused on the most important factors that are likely to motivate the consumer.

12:15–1:30 P.M. Go to the health club to do some aerobics and Cybex circuit. Grab lunch.

1:30–2:30 P.M. Learn that a meeting scheduled for 3:00 to 5:00 P.M. has been canceled! Review a memo my assistant just prepared, revise a fee estimate for a strategy development proposal.

The management supervisor on a new business assignment stops by to discuss what role he would like me to play, and check my schedule between now and the presentation in two months. We agree which steps will be critical, block out some time on my calendar and agree that he'll get me the briefing materials as soon as possible.

Place a call to a client regarding revised strategy development fee, leave a message.

2:30–3:00 P.M. Review latest slide formats and colors with Sharon Guerre for the strategic presentation.

3:00–3:30 P.M. Talk with others in the office about the implications of recently announced top-management changes and the reorganization of account services.

3:30–3:45 P.M. Take a phone call from the office president and update him on the status of a strategy development and creative assignment we've been given for a new-product introduction.

3:45–5:00 P.M. Review research on a new-product introduction we have been assigned. Begin outlining issues, targets, and possible positioning opportunities, which will lead to a presentation and creative blueprint. Determine if additional consumer research is likely to be required.

5:00–5:30 P.M. Check messages, return phone calls, review calendar for tomorrow, and check that I'm either prepared or can wing it.

5:30 P.M. Depart.

much higher. Allocation strategy needs the combined efforts of the media planner and marketing (sales) management to be successful.

TIMING/DURATION STRATEGIES: CONTINUITY PATTERNS

When to advertise can mean seasons, months, or parts of the day, but it all fits into the aperture concept. The strategy to accomplish these objectives involves

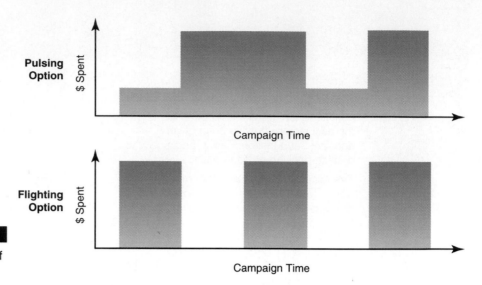

Figure 9.2

The continuity tactics of pulsing and flighting.

continuity The strategy and tactics used to schedule advertising over the time span of the advertising campaign.

a balancing of the advertising dollars available with the length of the campaign. A **continuity** strategy is a compromise to spread the advertising without sacrificing impact. Planners who cannot afford or do not want continuous scheduling have two other methods to consider: pulse patterns and flight patterns. (See Figure 9.2.)

pulsing An advertising scheduling pattern in which time and space are scheduled on a continuous but uneven basis; lower levels are followed by bursts or peak periods of intensified activity.

Pulse (Wave) Patterns. **Pulsing** is a popular alternative to continuous advertising. It is designed to intensify advertising prior to an open aperture, and then to reduce advertising to much lighter levels until the aperture opens again. The pulse pattern has peaks and valleys.

Fast-food companies like McDonald's and Burger King use pulsing patterns. Although the competition for daily customers demands continuous advertising, they will greatly intensify activity to accommodate special events such as new menu items, merchandise premiums, and contests. Pulsed schedules cover most of the year, but still provide periodic intensity.

flighting An advertising scheduling pattern characterized by a period of intensified activity called a *flight*, followed by periods of no advertising, called a *hiatus*.

carry-over effect A measure of residual effect (awareness or recall) of the advertising message some time after the advertising period has ended.

Flight Patterns. The **flighting** strategy is the most severe form of continuity adjustment. It is characterized by alternating periods of intense advertising activity and periods of no advertising (hiatus). This on-and-off schedule allows for a longer campaign without making the advertising schedule too light. The hope in using nonadvertising periods is that consumers will remember the brand and its advertising for some time after the ads have stopped. Figure 9.3 illustrates this awareness change. The line represents the rise and fall of consumer awareness of the brand. If the flight strategy works, there will be a **carry-over effect** of the past advertising that will sustain memory of the product until the next advertising period begins. The advertiser will then have fewer worries about low share-of-voice conditions.

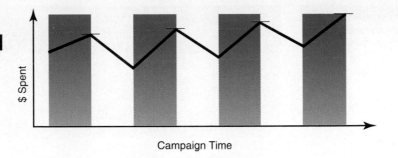

Figure 9.3

Flighting tactics are supported by awareness research that proves recall does not disappear once advertising stops. Awareness is shown by the single line.

$ Spent

Campaign Time

MEDIA PLANNING OPERATIONS: MEDIA SELECTION PROCEDURES

Setting objectives and recommending strategies help to focus the media plan, but other factors must be considered in selecting the advertising media and the specific vehicles that will carry the message. These "yardsticks" measure the number of different people exposed to the message (reach), the degree of exposure repetition (frequency), and the efficiency (cost per thousand or CPM) of the selected vehicles. Each of these major dimensions of media planning will be examined in detail. In order to understand their contribution, however, you must first be familiar with the basic audience terms planners use to measure media impact.

AUDIENCE MEASURES USED IN MEDIA PLANNING

In the same way that a carpenter uses feet and inches and a printer uses points and picas, the media planner uses special terms to evaluate a media plan.

Gross Impressions. Impression represents one person's opportunity to be exposed to a program, newspaper, or a magazine, or outdoor location. Impressions, then, measure the size of the audience either for one media vehicle (one announcement or one insertion) or for a combination of vehicles as estimated by media research.

If *Late Night with David Letterman* has an audience of 100,000 viewers, then each time the advertiser uses that program to advertise a product, the value in impressions is 100,000. If the advertiser used an announcement in each of four consecutive broadcasts, the total viewer impressions would be 100,000 times 4, or 400,000. In practice, planners discuss **gross impressions**—the sum of the audiences of all the media vehicles used in a certain time spot—when dealing with multiple vehicles in a schedule. The summary figure is called *gross* because the planner has made no attempt to calculate how many *different* people viewed each show. Gross values simply refers to the number of people viewing, regardless of whether each viewer saw one, two, or all of the shows. All the planner

gross impressions The sum of the audiences of all the media vehicles used within a designated time span.

Table 9.1

National Target Audience Impressions, September 1993

Media Vehicle	Target Impressions	Number of Messages	Total Target Impressions
Jeopardy	3,270,000	4	13,080,000
People Magazine	8,620,000	2	17,240,000
U.S.A. Today	1,700,000	2	3,400,000
			33,720,000

needs to do is find the audience figure for each vehicle used, multiply that figure by the times the vehicle was used, and add the vehicle figures to get the sum of "gross impressions." See Table 9.1 for an example of impressions.

Gross Rating Points. Gross impression figures become very large and difficult to remember. The rating (percentage of exposure) is an easier method of measuring the intensity of schedules because it converts the raw figure to a percentage. The sum of the total exposure potential expressed as a percentage of the audience population is called **gross rating points**.

gross rating points (GRP) The sum of the total exposure potential of a series of media vehicles expressed as a percentage of the audience population.

To demonstrate, in the previous example, *David Letterman* had 100,000 viewer impressions. Suppose there were a total of 500,000 possible viewers (total number of households with televisions, whether the sets are on or off) at that hour. The 100,000 viewers watching *Letterman* out of the possible 500,000 would represent 20 percent of viewers, or a 20.0 rating. The gross rating point total on four telecasts would be 80 (20 rating times 4 telecasts).

Total rating values are calculated just as total impressions are. The sum of rating points can be used to calculate the total of gross rating points for any schedule, whether actual or proposed. In Table 9.2 the impressions schedule is changed to gross rating points.

REACH AND MEDIA PLANNING

An important aspect of an advertising campaign is how many *different members of the target audience* can be exposed to the message in a particular time frame. Different, or unduplicated, audiences are those that have at least *one* chance for message exposure. Most advertisers realize a campaign's success is due, in part, to its ability to reach as many prospects as possible.

reach The percentage of different homes or people exposed to a media vehicle or vehicles at least once during a specific period of time. It is the percentage of unduplicated audience.

Reach is the percentage of the target population exposed at least once to the advertiser's message within a predetermined time frame. The reach of a schedule

Table 9.2

National Target Audience Gross Rating Points, September 1993

Media Vehicle	Target Rating	Number of Messages	Total Gross Rating Points
Jeopardy	3.5	4	14.0
People Magazine	9.1	2	18.2
U.S.A. Today	2.0	2	4.0
			36.2

Table 9.3

Viewing Homes/Week for *Late Night With David Letterman*

Home	Week 1	Week 2	Week 3	Week 4	Total Viewings
1	📺	—	📺	📺	3
2	—	📺	—	📺	2
3	📺	—	—	—	1
4	—	📺	—	—	1
5	—	📺	📺	📺	3
6	—	—	—	—	0
7				📺	1
8	📺	📺	📺	—	3
9	📺	—	📺	—	2
10	—	—	—	—	0
Viewing/Week	4	4	4	4	16

is produced according to research estimates that forecast the unduplicated audience. Most of the mass media are measured in this way, although for some media the estimate is only a statistical probability. This means the reach is not based on actual data but is calculated from the laws of chance. Reach can only be calculated when the planner has access to media audience research or projections from statistical models. It is not guesswork.

To see how the reach calculation could work in television activity, we use a very simplified situation. Our fictional television market of Hometown, U.S.A., has a total of only ten television households. Table 9.3 is a television survey that shows home viewing for *David Letterman* using a frequency analysis. The viewing survey is for four weeks during which the commercial ran once each week.

Each week four homes viewed *Late Night With David Letterman*. Because there are ten homes in Hometown, the average program rating per week was four of ten or 40.0. This viewing was done by all homes except home 6 and home 10. To be counted as "reached," the household only has to view *one* episode, and eight of the ten homes did that. The reach is then eight of ten, or 80 percent.

This reach calculation can also be made in newspapers and magazines if the readership research can show the overlap or duplicated readers between two or more publications. If a planner wanted to figure the target reach between *Time* and *Newsweek* magazines, he or she needs the sole readers (i.e., reads only) of each publication along with the total readers for each one. The addition of the sole readers for each divided by total target population will calculate the reach.

FREQUENCY AND MEDIA PLANNING

As important as the percentage of people exposed (reach) is the number of times they are exposed. This rate of exposure is called **frequency**. Whereas the reach estimate is based on only a single exposure, frequency estimates the number of times the exposure is expected to happen.

To measure the frequency of a schedule, planners use two methods: a "shorthand" summary called *average frequency* or the preferred frequency

frequency The number of times an audience has an opportunity to be exposed to a media vehicle or vehicles in a specified time span.

Magazine	Reader/Issue	Rating (GRP)	Unduplicated Readers
Today's Happiness	50,000	50.0	30,000
News Round-Up	40,000	40.0	15,000
Yuppie Life	18,000	18.0	11,000
Totals	108,000	108.0	56,000

Target Population: 100,000
Total Gross Impressions: 108,000
Gross Rating Points: 108.0
Unduplicated Readers: 56,000
Reach: 56.0 (56,000/100,000)
Average Frequency: 1.9 issues seen (108,000÷56,000 = 1.9)
or (108 GRP÷56 Reach = 1.9)

method that shows the percent of audience reached at each level of repetition (exposed once, twice, and so on). Both methods are illustrated next.

Average Frequency. To figure the "average" frequency you need only two numbers: the gross rating points (GRP) of a schedule and the reach estimate. The average frequency can also be calculated from the gross impressions and the unduplicated impressions if ratings are not available. Table 9.4 illustrates a situation involving a purchase of space in three magazines. For demonstration, the schedule is summarized in rating and impression values.

The schedule involves three magazines: *Today's Happiness, News Round-Up,* and *Yuppie Life.* Each magazine is listed by its total readership, readers expressed as a percent (rating), and the number of unduplicated readers (those who do not read either of the other two magazines). Note the formula calculations at the bottom of the table. Average frequency is calculated as follows:

$$\text{Average frequency} = \frac{\text{Gross rating points}}{\text{Reach(\%)}}$$

or

$$\text{Average frequency} = \frac{\text{Gross audience impressions}}{\text{Unduplicated impressions}}$$

Frequency Distribution. Average frequency, however, can give the planner a distorted idea of the plan's performance. Suppose you had a schedule that could be seen a maximum of 20 times. If we figured the average from one person who saw 18 and another who saw 2 exposures, the average would be 10. But 10 exposures isn't close to the experience of either audience member. Planners who consider frequency in a functional way will choose to calculate *frequency distribution* whenever possible. The distribution will show the number of target audience members.

Table 9.5 demonstrates the principle for a magazine schedule of three news magazines: *Time, Newsweek,* and *U.S. News & World Report.* Each publication is to receive two insertions for a total of six advertising placements. The minimum exposure would be one insertion, and the maximum would be six.

Issues Read	Readers	Target Population (Percentage)
0	44,000	44.0
1	7,000	7.0
2	6,500	6.5
3	20,000	20.0
4	10,600	10.6
5	8,200	8.2
6	3,700	3.7
Totals	100,000	100.0

56,000 read at least one issue. Reach = 56.0

The planner evaluating this distribution might consider changing this schedule. First, 44 percent of the target audience would *not* be exposed. Then, only 23 (22.5) percent of the target would read more than half the scheduled issues (e.g., four, five, or six).

The frequency distribution method is more revealing, and thus more valuable, than the average frequency method of reporting repetition. However, frequency distribution data are only available from special research tabulations or from sophisticated math models, and this special research may be expensive.

COMBINING REACH AND FREQUENCY GOALS: EFFECTIVE FREQUENCY

As we have just seen, the reach of an audience alone is not a sufficient measure of an advertising schedule's strength. Many media planners now feel that there should be a threshold or minimum level of frequency before any audience segment can be considered "exposed to the advertising message." In other words for anyone to be considered part of the "reached" audience, he or she must have been exposed *more than once*. This theory essentially combines the reach and the frequency elements into one. This combination is known as **effective frequency**.

What is this level of repetition? There is no single standard in media planning today, and it is doubtful there will ever be one. True, some observers say that two or three is the minimum, but to prove an ideal level, all the brand's communication variables must be known (aperture, message content, consumer interest, and competitor intensity).

Even without all the answers, planners can use their knowledge and experience to determine a probable range of effective frequency. The theory and technique behind these determinations is complex. Although the understanding of these questions is not complete, many planners are convinced that effective frequency is the essential planning dimension.

COST EFFICIENCY AS A PLANNING DIMENSION

The media plan is not only evaluated in terms of audience impressions. As we mentioned earlier, the cost of time and space determines the number of message units that can be placed. These costs also influence the selection of media or of media vehicles. Inherent in media planning is the notion that media should be selected according to their ability to expose the largest target audience for the lowest possible cost. The key to this notion is the *target* audience because the advertiser wants prospects and not just readers, viewers, or listeners. The *target audience* is that proportion of a media audience that best fits the desired aperture. Therefore, the cost of each media vehicle proposed should be evaluated in relation to the medium's delivered target audience. The process of measuring the target audience size against the cost of that audience is called *efficiency*—or more popularly, **cost per thousand** (CPM) and **cost per rating** (CPR).

cost per thousand (CPM) The cost of exposing each 1,000 members of the target audience to the advertising message.

cost per rating (CRP) A method of comparing media vehicles by relating the cost of the message unit to the audience rating.

Cost per Thousand. The CPM analysis is best used to compare vehicles within a medium (one magazine with another or one television program with another). It is also more valuable to base it only on that portion of the audience that has the target characteristics. To calculate the CPM you need only two figures: the cost of the unit (page or 30 seconds) and the estimated target audience. The target audience's gross impressions are divided into the cost of the unit to determine the advertising dollars needed to expose 1,000 members of the target.

$$\text{CPM} = \frac{\text{Cost of message unit}}{\text{Gross impressions}} \times 1,000$$

Here are some examples from print and broadcast vehicles to illustrate the formulas used in CPM analysis.

Magazines An issue of *You* magazine has 10,460,000 readers who could be considered a target audience. The advertising unit is a four-color page and its rate is $42,000. The CPM is:

$$\text{CPM} = \frac{\text{Cost of page or fractional page unit}}{\text{Target audience readers}} \times 1,000$$

$$\frac{\$42,000 \times 1,000}{10,460,000} = .004015 = \$4.02$$

Television The show *Inside Gossip* has 92,000 target viewers. The cost of a 30-second announcement during the show is $850.

$$\text{CPM} = \frac{\$850}{92,000} \times 1,000 = \$9.24$$

Cost per Rating. Some planners prefer to compare media on the basis of rating points (ratings) instead of impressions. The calculation is parallel, with the exception that the divisor in CPR is the rating percentage rather than the total impressions used in CPM.

$$\text{CPR} = \frac{\text{Cost of message unit}}{\text{Program or issue rating}}$$

(*Note:* Because this is not on a per-thousand basis, the multiplication by 1,000 is not necessary.)

If the target audience rating for the program *Inside Gossip* were 12.0 and the cost were still $850, the CPR would be 850÷12, or $70.83.

Although both efficiency calculations are used, the CPR is favored by planners for its simplicity. Both the CPM and the CPR are relative values. The absolute numbers mean very little unless there are similar values to compare. A planner would not know if *Newsweek's* CPM of $27.89 for the target audience were good or bad unless he or she had comparable figures for *Time* and *U.S. News & World Report*.

Although these efficiency analyses can be used across media (comparing one medium to another), such comparisons should be made with caution. When comparing the CPMs for radio and television, for example, you are comparing very different audience experiences, and if the experience is totally different, it is difficult to say that one medium is more efficient than the other. CPM and CPR are more valid when used to compare alternatives *within* a medium.

SELECTING ACCEPTABLE MEDIA ENVIRONMENTS

Success in media planning depends on more than knowledge of the audience size, reach, and cost per thousand. Success also involves some intangibles that can influence the target consumer's reception of the advertising message. Intangibles include both positive and negative communication conditions. To many readers, viewers, or listeners, the advertising message is seldom a desired intrusion. Although audiences only tolerate advertising (with the exception of shopping ads in newspapers), it is still risky for a company to run its advertising in an "alien" environment (a position of weaker communication potential). Three environmental areas deserve particular discussion: media content-product compatibility, media-created moods or atmospheres, and media clutter.

Media Content-Product Compatibility. Media content is said to be compatible with the product when the advertiser can find programming or editorial material that complements the message. Think of the sport and recreation magazines that are filled with advertisements for clothing and equipment. Think of televised golf and tennis matches, financial reports, hunting and fishing shows, cartoon adventures, and cooking shows. All offer advertisers a ready-made focus. One attraction of the opportunities is audience characteristics. The other attraction is the special communication between the customer and the content. When this environment is right, advertising becomes enjoyable rather than intrusive. Ad 9.3 for *Sassy* magazine is an example of compatibility between product and content.

Media-Created Moods. Moods or atmospheres are created by the programming or editorial content of the media vehicle. Audience members react to content moods, and their emotional reaction is either good or bad for the advertising message that follows. Television situation comedies such as *Murphy Brown* and *Home Improvement* and *Wings* are designed to produce laughter. Other programs create tension or anxiety (*L.A. Law*, and made-for-television movies). Companies sensitive to these variations in atmosphere demand that their commercials be run in atmospheres that will support brand and advertising acceptance by the audience. For example, General Foods (Jell-O Products) will not allow its commercials to run during programming that is not fully suitable for family audiences. Other firms are very cautious about advertising on programs that deal with controversial subjects or social issues.

We're so impressed with our readers, we're giving them our jobs.

I want you to know I have greatly enjoyed your magazine for the past two years of my life. I read it right before I practice my triangle. My goldfish, Ed, also very much enjoys your magazine. I read it to him every day. I long for the day Ed and I can work on the *Sassy* staff. I know it will be a tough job, but we can handle it.

J.J. and Ed, Elkhorn, WI*

We're not sure what we can do for Ed, but this young lady is being offered a job on our staff. In fact, we're going to let a whole group of SASSY readers publish our December, 1990 issue. Pick the subject matter, write the articles, conduct the interviews...everything.

Why are we doing this? Well, we keep claiming we're the one voice of all the young women's magazines that speaks the language of our audience. The December issue will be proof of that claim.

It's also a publishing first—an event people everywhere will be watching. And it will benefit any advertiser to be a part of it. Even if you're above the age of 21, read this issue. And please let us know if you think any of our jobs are in jeopardy.

Sassy

There are five years in a woman's life when she really needs a best friend.

* This is an excerpt from one of the 451,944 letters SASSY received in 1989.

CIN 2

Media Clutter. Most of the mass media allow too many promotional messages to compete for audience attention. Media planners cannot avoid all cluttered conditions, but they can reduce or limit the effect of clutter by isolating their messages from those of competitors and by advising against the use of the most cluttered media.

Judging medium clutter is a subjective process. Some people believe the commercial pod (a string of continuous broadcast messages run during program interruptions) is a severe form of clutter. Others feel that magazines that designate 50 percent of their pages to advertisements are cluttered. Every advertising media format is capable of becoming overcrowded to the point where communication is negatively affected.

MEDIA PLANNING OPERATIONS: STAGING A MEDIA PLAN

Principle

Media plans are interwoven with all other areas of advertising: the budget, the target audience, the advertising objectives, and the message demands.

To control the flow of information to the plan and to ensure that each component makes a logical contribution to strategy, the planner uses a sequence of decision stages to form the media plan. The plan is a written document that summarizes the recommended objectives, strategies, and tactics pertinent to the placement of a company's advertising messages. Plans do not have a universal form, but there is a similar (and logical) pattern to the decision stages. To illustrate a style of presentation in a real-life setting, we use an actual media plan (excerpted) from the National Dairy Board. The National Dairy Board's mission is to strengthen the dairy industry's position in domestic and foreign marketplaces. The example used relates specifically to the cheese portion of the National Dairy Board's challenge.

A systematic direction of media plans would begin with the general and work down to the more specific questions. Similarly, it would begin with the most important decisions and work down to those of lesser priority. The following section offers a brief description of each stage.

BACKGROUND/SITUATION ANALYSIS

The background/situation analysis is the marketing perspective discussed in the beginning of the chapter. The National Dairy Board summarized overview includes consumer target profiles, geographic considerations, and seasonality (see Figure 9.4).

MEDIA OBJECTIVES/APERTURE OPPORTUNITIES

A media objective is a goal or task to be accomplished by the plan. Objectives are pertinent to the brand's strategy, specifically detailed, and capable of being measured within a given time frame. The objectives listed in the media portion should be limited to goals that can be accomplished specifically from media directions (see Figure 9.5). Measurable media objectives usually focus on reach

Figure 9.4

National Dairy Board overview.

(Courtesy of DDB Needham Worldwide)

Brand: National Dairy Board—Cheese	**Media Budget: 18,700M**
Marketing Objective:	To increase in-home consumption of domestic cheeses.
Demographic Target:	Women Age 25–54
	3+ Household Size
	Household Income of $30,000+
Target Universe:	22,710.0 (27% of all women)
Psychographics:	Middle class, sticks to basic foods, busy, active, family-oriented
Geographic Skew:	None
Seasonality:	Relatively flat, with increased sales in the November/December period.
Creative Executions:	Television: 15's
	Print Page 4/C Bleed

Figure 9.5

National Dairy Board
media objectives.

*(Courtesy of DDB Needham
Worldwide)*

MEDIA OBJECTIVES

Target advertising to medium/light cheese users, demographically defined as:
  Women Age 25-54
  3+ Household Size
  $30,000+ Household Income
Provide national advertising support
Schedule 12 months of support recognizing greater consumption during the
  November/December period
Achieve comparable monthly W25-54 GRP levels vs. year ago

Aperture being sought

Every-week support
  • Complements branded advertising activity
  • Recognizes every-week usage and purchase opportunities
Emphasize biweekly pay periods
  • Greater cheese sales opportunities due to increase in discretionary income
Best Food Day concentration
  • Complements the higher incidence of grocery shopping

and frequency projections. Similarly, aperture guidance (though less specific) details the best opportunities of exposing the National Dairy Board's message. Observe that the objectives concentrate on target profile, geographic priorities, and scheduling requirements. Note the aperture importance of scheduling cheese advertising when consumers are most likely to grocery shop.

STRATEGY: SELECTION OF MEDIA

This section of the media plan explains why a single medium or set of media are appropriate for the campaign objectives. A sound strategy should be able to anchor each dimension to the recommendation.

Because planning occurs usually months before the campaign actually begins, some detail is omitted. For the television portion of the National Dairy Board campaign (Figure 9.6), the planner cannot be assured of the program availability or specific pricing in television. In such situations the recommendation must deal with the overall characteristics without identifying specific locations. This isn't guesswork, as the anticipated performance of the television activity is shown in detail.

THE FLOW CHART: SCHEDULING AND BUDGETING ALLOCATION

The graphic document depicted in Figure 9.7 on page 320 is designed to illustrate most of the media recommendations. It shows the month-by-month placement of messages, details the anticipated impact through forecasted levels of GRPs, and illustrates how the campaign budget is allocated by medium

Audience Delivery

# Weeks:	52 weeks of television
Geography:	National, with emphasis in cable homes due to higher incidence of cheese usage and advertising cost efficiencies
Television:	40% Daytime
Daypart Mix:	25% Primetime
	20% Early Fringe
	15% Weekend

W25-54 GRPs

Television:	7500
Print:	1800
Total:	9300

Average Monthly Audience Delivery (W25-54)

	Cable Households	Non-Cable Households
Reach/Avg. Freq.	98/10.1	89/4.3
Reach at 4+:	83%	42%

Media Buying Tactics

Daytime
  Minimum of 70% of weight in above average rated programs
  Minimum of 75% of weight is soap opera programming.
  Not more than one commercial in a single program.
Early Fringe Syndication
  Emphasis on talk, sit-com, and entertainment type programs vs. court shows.
  A large mix of programs purchased on a weekly basis to maximize reach.
Primetime
  Drama and news programming is the priority to complement greater audience attentiveness.
Cable
  A large mix of networks purchased to maximize reach. Program sponsorships and billboards are highly desirable.
Magazines
  Position advertising on the right hand page in the food section opposite 100% recipe edit.

and by month. In a concise fashion a flow chart is the "blueprint" of the media plan.

The media plan is a recommendation and must be accepted before any further steps are taken. In fact, planning is only the first stage in the advertising media operations. Once the plan directions are set, the actual selection, negotiation, and contracting must be done for time and space. These duties, known as media buying, are the subject of Chapter 12, which examines how buyers convert objectives and strategies into tactical decisions. Before the role of buyer is examined, however, you need to learn more about the advertising media. Chapters 10 and 11 will provide the foundation for a better understanding of the "seller" side of the media business.

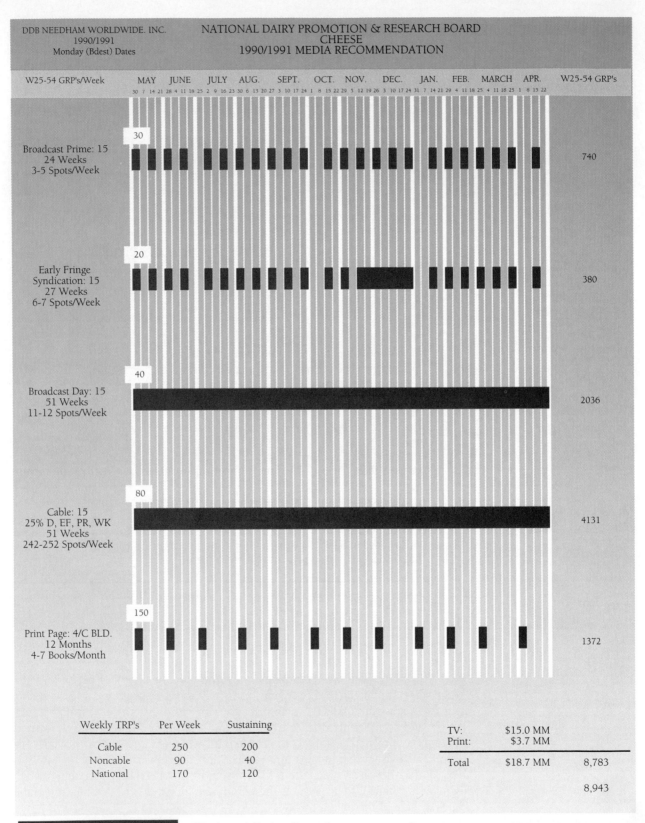

Figure 9.7 National Dairy Board consumer plan. *(Courtesy of DDB Needham Worldwide)*

SUMMARY

- Media planning utilizes the company's full marketing intelligence to decide on the placement of advertising messages.

- The media planner's ultimate goal is known as *aperture*, placing a message before target consumers at the point when their purchase interest is high.

- Media planning objectives are directed by a series of key questions including: who (target), where (location), when (time frame), and how long (duration).

- The selection of media for the campaign is based on a number of factors including target size (impressions/reach), repeated exposure opportunities (message frequency), cost efficiency (CPM/CPR), and important qualitative features such as content moods and other compatible message environments.

- Media-related decisions are presented in a systematically organized document called a media plan. Plans are directed by media goals to be accomplished and the strategies and tactics needed to achieve each goal.

QUESTIONS

1. Why is the media planning function considered the bridge between sales marketing and the creative function of advertising?

2. Allan Johnson is a graduating senior from a mideastern journalism program. He is seeking some career advice from one of his professors. Allan has an interest in advertising, and wants to know what an advertising journalism major with a business minor in marketing has prepared him for. In addition to account management positions, the professor urges Allan to consider media planning as a logical entry-level position. Why does the professor advise this? Why is marketing study so important for media planners?

3. Susan Ellet has just begun a new job as senior media planner for a relatively new automobile model from General Motors. Facing a planning sequence that will begin in 4 months, Susan's media director asks her what data and information she needs for her preparation. What sources should Susan request? How will she use each of these sources in the planning function?

4. If the marketing management of McDonald's restaurants asked you to analyze the aperture opportunity for its breakfast entrees, what kind of analysis would you present to management?

5. The Pioneer account has accepted your recommendation for ten one-page insertions (ten issues) in a magazine known as the *Illustrated Press*. The magazine reaches an estimated 3,000,000 target readers per month, or a 10 percent rating per issue. The cost per page of the publication is $20,000. What are the total gross rating points delivered by this schedule? What is the cost per rating point and the CPM target readers?

6. If you were doing a frequency analysis composed of two magazines, a radio network schedule, and a national newspaper, would you rather use the average frequency procedure or a frequency distribution analysis? Defend your choice.

7. Explain why media planners try to *balance* reach, frequency, and continuity of proposed media schedules. What considerations go into this decision?

SUGGESTED CLASS PROJECT

In performing an aperture analysis, consider these products: video games (e.g., Nintendo), man's cologne (e.g., Obsession), computer software (e.g., Lotus), and athletic shoes for aerobics (e.g., Reebok). For each of the preceding products, find the answers to these questions:

1. Which media should be used to maximize aperture leverage?
2. How does aperture work in each of your recommendations?
3. Explain how timing and the duration of the advertising improves the aperture opportunity.

FURTHER READINGS

BARBAN, ARNOLD M., STEVEN M. CRISTOL, AND FRANK J. KOPECK, *Essentials of Media Planning: A Marketing Approach*, 2nd. ed. (Lincolnwood, IL: NTC Business Books, 1987).

BRUVIC, ALLEN, *What Every Account Executive Should Know About Media* (New York: American Association of Advertising Agencies, 1989).

JUGENHEIMER, DONALD W., PETER B. TURK, AND ARNOLD M. BARBAN, *Advertising Media Strategy and Tactics* (Dubuque, IA: Brown and Bookmark, 1992).

SISSORS, JACK, AND LINCOLN BUMBA, *Advertising Media Planning*, 3rd ed. (Chicago: NTC Business Books, 1989).

$\mathscr{V}$ I D E O $\mathscr{C}$ A S E

Call Waiting

Since 1986 U S West had not supported its call-waiting service with advertising, nor had the company aggressively marketed this service to its customers. Consequently, in 1991, U S West's call-waiting service had the second-lowest household penetration of all the Regional Bell Operating Companies.

Research indicated that awareness of call waiting was high among U S West's customers. More than eight out of ten were familiar with the service. Research also indicated that the majority of U S West's nonsubscribers believed that the service was unnecessary. The problem, therefore, was to educate customers about the benefits of call waiting and to persuade customers to try it.

The target was middle-aged adults (18–54) with high incoming-call volumes. The consumers live in busy households within U S West's 14-state region.

The creative strategy focused on building awareness of the benefits of call waiting and building desire to try the service by positioning it as an effective way to avoid missing important phone calls. Using realistic, everyday scenarios, the advertising developed by

CME•KHBB, U S West's advertising agency, portrayed situations in which typical consumers missed important calls while they were already on the phone.

The media strategy was designed to increase awareness through high levels of spot television, supported by newspaper and radio. Introductory six-week flights kicked off the campaign in 23 markets, and were followed by four-week flights designed to reduce the number of disconnections among customers who had agreed to try the service during the introductory period.

The introductory campaign included a 30-day free trial offer delivered via newspaper, free-standing inserts, direct mail, and tags on radio and television commercials. This promotion included a program that offered bonuses for call-waiting sales to U S West service representatives.

This integrated combination of advertising, consumer promotion, and sales promotion exceeded its goal. By the time the campaign concluded, it had added more than 300,000 new U S West call-waiting customers.

Questions

1. Comment on how the media strategy for the U S West campaign supported the firm's advertising objective.

2. How was the target market reached?

3. Is there any aspect of the campaign that could have been omitted and the same result achieved?

$\mathcal{P}$RINT MEDIA

CHAPTER OBJECTIVES

When you have completed this chapter, you should be able to:

- Understand the similarities and differences between newspapers and magazines

- Explain the advantages and disadvantages of newspaper, magazine, and other forms of media advertising

- Explain the major trends in print advertisements

$\mathscr{K}$IDS WHO READ

Children are an audience worth targeting in hundreds of consumer markets. But reaching them with television commercials is rapidly growing more expensive and less efficient. Advertisers are looking for better ways to deliver messages to American youth. Increasingly, they are turning to magazines and newspapers.

Children's versions of *Sports Illustrated*, *National Geographic*, *Field and Stream*, and *Consumer Reports* are already being thumbed by little hands. The numbers of periodicals for youngsters almost doubled between 1986 and 1991, with 81 new titles. Fifty-seven percent of children read magazines. That is more than the share of children who read comic books. Children who read magazines are slightly more likely to be boys than girls, and they are also more likely than nonreaders to live in high-income households. Compared with the audience for children's TV, the readers are a smaller and more select group.

The demographics convincingly show that many established children's TV shows are now crossing over to print. The list of crossover publications includes *Sesame Street Magazine*, the monthly *Nickelodeon*, Fox's *Kid Club* magazine, and Disney's *Duck Tales*. *Sesame Street Magazine*, like its parent television show, has a strong educational emphasis. Yet the magazine's parents' guide section carried almost 200 pages of advertising in 1990.

Sports Illustrated for Kids is successful because it offers advertisers a mix of flexibility and precision in reaching children. One advertiser, General Mills' Wheaties, offered a free subscription on cereal boxes; another advertiser, McDonald's, coproduced a nutrition and fitness guide for teachers' use.

Newspapers are not overlooking children, either. More than two-thirds of teenagers read at least one daily newspaper a week, according to Simmons Market Research Bureau. Not surprisingly, readership increases with age; half of teenagers (ages 12 to 17) read both daily and Sunday editions of a newspaper. The demographics of teenage newspaper readers are similar to those of adults. White teenagers are more likely to read than blacks, for example, and Sunday readership is higher than weekday readership. Teens who live in the Northeast are most likely to read a newspaper, while those who live in the South and in rural areas are least likely. Dozens of newspapers now print special sections for children. The national leader may be a weekly children's section in the *Fort Worth Star-Telegram* called "Class Acts." The material in the 12-page supplement is syndicated to about 20 other papers. Article topics range from what it means to be adopted to getting a fair shake at allowance time. The target audience is young ages 8 to 14, but editor Sharon Cox says her 300 to 500 pieces of weekly mail also include letters from kindergartners and high school students.

Several weekly pages and sections in the *Chicago Tribune* are aimed at children, including "Spots," in the Sunday funnies; "In-Style," a fashion spotlight; "Preps Plus," a Friday feature on school sports; and "Take 2," which includes a panel of high school movie reviewers. A special section completely devoted to a young audience, "Kid News," appears on Thursdays. "Newspapers have an aging audience," says *Tribune* comics editor John Lux, so they must try to develop the daily habit among younger groups.

Children influence billions of dollars a year in consumer spending. As long as children remain a choice market segment, print media options for them should grow more plentiful, more sophisticated, and more focused.[1]

PRINT MEDIA

Throughout most of the history of mass communication, print was the only readily accessible means of storing information and retrieving it at will. Print is the keeper of records, the vault of great literature, the storehouse of historic accomplishments. In advertising, it differs from broadcast media in several ways. For example, print media deliver messages one topic at a time and one thought at a time, whereas television and electronic media use a simultaneous approach, delivering a great deal of information in a rapid-fire manner. Furthermore, print advertising has a history and credibility unmatched by broadcast advertising. These differences have important consequences for advertisers and media planners to consider.

Advertisers benefit from the selective targeting print media provide as well. For example, those wishing to capture a college-age audience may be inclined to advertise in *U.* or one of the other popular college newspapers or magazines. For an advertiser trying to target college students, print is preferable because it utilizes a very structured information-processing style. Essentially, college students are constantly reading and absorbing information with intensity and credibility. Can we assume that this concentration carries over to print media? Probably. Can we assume that people tend to trust print more than broadcast and absorb it more carefully? Definitely.[2] In a 1986 study sponsored by *Audits and Surveys*, both men and women indicated a higher attention-level score for magazines than for television. Reasons given revolved around the fact that reading requires a more intensive involvement, whereas television can be taken in more passively.[3] In another study Jacoby, Hoyer, and Zimmer found that print was better *comprehended* than either television or audio presentations of the same material[4]

Finally, in a study sponsored by *The Atlantic* and conducted by the Roper Organization, influential consumers (defined as those with a high level of community or political involvement) found print advertising more effective than did the average American, but they are less swayed by TV advertising.[5]

Nevertheless, print media makers have had to recognize that their appeal is not universal. In general, we have become a broadcast-oriented society. Print does not work with all people, Consequently, it is not relevant to all advertisers. However, it is a viable alternative for certain advertisers under certain conditions. These conditions, along with the history, structure, and advantages and disadvantages of newspapers and magazines, will be the focus of this chapter. Table 10.1 summarizes the dollars spent on advertising for all the primary mass media. It is a useful reference device for this chapter and the one that follows.

---

[1]Adapted from S. K. List, "The Right Place to Find Children," *American Demographics* (February, 1992):44–48.
[2]Edward Jay Whetmore, *Mediamerica*, 4th ed. (Belmont, CA: Wadsworth Publishing Co., 1989):20.
[3]"Study of Media Involvement," *Audits and Surveys* (November 1986).
[4]Jacob Jacoby, Wayne D. Hoyer, and Mary R. Zimmer, "To Read, View or Listen? A Cross-Media Comparison of Comprehension," in *Current Issues & Research in Advertising*, James H. Leigh and Claude R. Martin, Jr., eds. (Ann Arbor: The University of Michigan, 1983):201–18.
[5]Julie Liesse, "Print Ads Top TV in Reaching 'Influentials'," *Advertising Age* (September 14, 1992):44.

Table 10.1 Total U.S. Ad Spending by Category and Media

Category	Year	Total Ad spending	Consumer magazine	Sunday magazine	Local newspaper	National newspaper	Outdoor	Network TV	Spot TV	Syndicated TV	Cable TV networks	Network radio	National radio
Retail	1992	$7,696.7	$180.3	$127.5	$4,906.6	$11.7	$81.5	$441.5	$1,552.0	$27.4	$64.2	$71.3	$232.7
	1991	5,123.0	194.6	88.2	2,492.7	13.0	63.1	359.8	1,524.2	25.5	42.4	92.1	227.2
Automotive	1992	5,913.5	1,036.6	29.7	910.7	110.1	47.5	1,578.8	1,851.0	50.0	146.8	50.9	101.2
	1991	5,359.6	940.3	38.3	746.0	103.1	52.1	1,632.9	1,481.9	44.9	117.4	71.2	131.6
Business, consumer services	1992	4675.8	500.6	33.8	1,353.9	291.2	82.4	851.3	1,106.1	56.5	145.4	78.5	176.1
	1991	3,823.6	442.7	29.2	1,205.9	245.1	62.7	624.6	810.7	43.3	112.5	77.2	169.7
Food	1992	3,511.8	461.3	51.3	29.4	1.4	10.5	1,483.2	879.3	305.4	182.1	34.4	73.5
	1991	3,556.3	433.4	29.1	36.5	4.1	9.2	1,495.4	974.3	294.6	141.0	41.9	96.7
Entertainment	1992	3,141.0	63.3	37.3	407.3	9.3	62.8	1,035.5	1,236.0	84.6	105.8	15.1	84.2
	1991	2,919.6	58.5	35.8	387.0	6.8	53.1	916.6	1,196.0	81.8	83.0	15.6	85.4
Toiletries & cosmetics	1992	2,427.2	719.3	27.7	7.8	3.5	1.8	1,110.3	273.5	119.3	143.1	7.0	13.8
	1991	2,250.3	631.4	21.8	6.8	1.3	2.3	1,048.6	293.3	125.6	92.5	8.2	18.6
Travel, hotels & resorts	1992	2,240.7	332.5	51.0	1,097.1	110.4	38.8	199.1	247.6	7.7	51.6	35.9	68.9
	1991	2,228.5	335.4	49.0	1,063.0	106.9	48.6	213.3	233.6	8.0	49.1	33.4	88.1
Drugs & remedies	1992	2,087.4	276.2	26.6	80.3	5.6	12.6	935.4	370.8	154.1	108.3	95.2	22.4
	1991	1,810.9	165.0	19.5	78.3	3.0	12.6	900.7	341.4	122.0	80.1	56.3	32.0
Direct response cos.	1992	1,402.2	616.3	377.6	99.2	46.3	1.1	72.9	89.6	26.6	32.0	36.7	3.8
	1991	1,219.8	553.9	300.7	64.9	27.7	1.7	42.3	76.8	31.0	53.5	62.1	5.1
Candy, snacks & soft drinks	1992	1,234.2	64.5	4.0	13.2	3.0	7.1	566.7	299.1	113.2	89.6	30.5	43.2
	1991	1,147.6	55.2	2.4	13.5	1.3	7.0	513.4	318.5	106.0	72.2	20.5	37.6
Apparel	1992	1,065.8	493.1	27.7	12.1	5.7	5.3	399.7	78.8	27.2	55.3	8.9	12.0
	1991	922.6	421.9	27.8	6.9	5.2	11.3	272.9	86.9	26.9	41.5	7.5	13.8
Insurance & real estate	1992	979.7	135.6	11.3	403.9	50.2	22.4	167.3	119.3	7.1	22.9	15.5	24.1
	1991	795.1	142.4	13.1	215.5	50.6	23.2	176.3	107.8	8.0	19.6	19.1	19.3
Sporting goods, toys	1992	885.6	169.6	3.4	6.3	2.3	0.2	241.8	259.6	107.4	91.9	0.7	2.3
	1991	698.7	145.7	2.3	5.1	4.3	0.5	182.3	206.8	95.3	51.5	1.8	3.0
Beer & wine	1992	850.8	63.5	5.1	12.3	1.9	36.0	365.6	203.5	27.5	53.9	7.2	74.3
	1991	843.7	51.6	5.4	12.8	4.0	32.2	381.0	209.2	26.1	43.5	1.5	76.2
Publishing & media	1992	804.2	203.3	14.7	237.9	14.5	33.6	39.2	162.7	7.3	25.1	22.2	44.7
	1991	712.8	195.8	11.8	195.7	10.6	34.6	47.8	137.9	4.6	18.9	21.9	33.4
Computers, office equipment	1992	732.9	347.6	3.9	50.2	135.5	2.8	125.2	21.9	6.7	21.6	1.5	16.2
	1991	649.0	286.4	9.7	44.7	121.0	3.4	119.0	16.8	6.4	19.1	12.9	9.6
Household equipment	1992	670.1	160.9	14.8	18.1	2.2	0.4	286.6	93.2	41.1	45.7	3.3	3.8
	1991	614.0	113.8	10.6	21.0	2.7	1.1	283.8	96.1	46.8	28.7	6.9	2.4
Soaps & cleansers	1992	601.8	71.4	5.1	3.0	0.3	0.3	298.4	108.9	54.3	49.1	6.4	4.8
	1991	603.4	71.5	2.6	3.0	0.2	2.1	283.1	160.9	48.6	25.2	0.9	5.2

Table 10.1 (cont.)

Category	Year	Total Ad spending	Consumer magazine	Sunday magazine	Local newspaper	National newspaper	Outdoor	Network TV	Spot TV	Syndicated TV	Cable TV networks	Network radio	National radio
Electronic entertainment	1992	413.0	112.5	4.1	34.2	4.8	0.7	116.9	68.5	23.1	34.8	8.3	5.1
	1991	374.7	91.8	1.8	15.2	7.1	1.5	126.4	68.8	19.6	31.4	9.1	1.9
Cigarettes	1992	382.3	224.0	26.9	6.6	0.8	123.5	0.0	0.1	0.0	0.0	0.4	0.1
	1991	496.3	265.7	29.0	12.8	1.5	184.9	0.0	0.2	0.0	0.1	2.1	0.0
Building materials	1992	344.5	83.5	8.1	50.2	1.8	0.9	87.5	67.2	6.4	27.4	2.8	8.7
	1991	301.5	79.3	7.1	36.8	2.0	3.1	72.2	63.6	4.9	21.6	0.5	10.5
Jewelry, optical	1992	341.4	155.1	9.1	6.9	7.8	2.1	109.6	18.7	7.1	20.6	1.3	2.0
	1991	350.8	157.6	11.6	6.1	4.0	2.4	114.8	23.4	10.3	16.5	2.3	1.8
Gasoline & lubricants	1992	304.0	17.9	0.9	9.5	3.6	6.9	70.7	135.0	4.5	16.7	0.6	37.8
	1991	308.1	27.8	0.5	15.2	4.8	6.1	48.9	152.3	1.4	8.9	0.0	42.3
Household furnishings	1992	260.2	124.9	11.1	42.3	1.2	0.1	37.8	27.6	6.6	4.6	0.0	4.1
	1991	243.5	116.0	11.0	28.3	0.6	0.6	41.2	38.7	2.9	2.8	0.0	1.4
Liquor	1992	236.3	185.4	8.8	8.4	5.8	21.2	0.0	2.1	0.0	0.0	1.4	3.2
	1991	286.6	228.9	8.2	7.7	3.1	29.3	0.0	5.0	0.7	0.3	1.4	2.0
Horticulture & farming	1992	214.8	19.4	14.0	48.4	1.3	0.4	27.0	52.2	2.7	18.4	8.0	23.2
	1991	206.4	21.0	8.9	48.5	1.5	0.5	30.1	50.1	2.0	12.6	9.1	22.0
Pets & pet foods	1992	170.3	34.0	1.8	6.1	0.1	0.0	68.8	27.5	12.2	16.8	1.8	1.1
	1991	199.1	39.0	4.5	6.5	0.1	0.5	83.8	28.4	17.1	14.6	2.9	1.7
Freight, industrial	1992	152.1	34.8	0.0	6.3	14.2	0.5	54.4	32.5	0.0	4.8	0.2	4.3
	1991	162.6	42.8	0.2	6.6	10.4	0.1	61.7	34.3	0.0	4.1	0.2	2.2
Industrial materials	1992	121.3	45.6	0.1	7.7	8.7	1.3	40.4	10.6	0.3	4.5	1.8	0.2
	1991	115.1	57.5	0.5	6.0	8.3	1.2	27.5	10.0	0.0	3.8	0.0	0.3
Business propositions	1992	39.5	26.9	0.6	1.8	7.2	0.7	0.0	1.6	0.0	0.1	0.2	0.3
	1991	39.0	27.6	0.6	2.9	4.1	0.2	1.3	1.2	0.0	0.6	0.0	0.6
Airplanes (not travel)	1992	21.9	12.3	0.0	2.7	5.2	0.1	0.0	0.5	0.0	1.0	0.0	0.6
	1991	19.6	10.1	0.0	1.5	6.9	0.2	0.1	0.7	0.0	0.1	0.0	0.1
Miscellaneous	1992	333.8	132.6	4.0	39.6	96.3	49.7	0.5	2.9	0.5	6.6	1.0	0.0
	1991	301.1	110.3	12.5	44.1	97.5	32.7	0.0	1.2	0.2	2.4	0.1	0.0
Total	1992	44,256.7	7,105.1	941.9	9,920.1	963.7	655.0	10,752.5	9,399.7	1,286.6	1,590.5	549.1	1,092.4
	1991	38,683.0	6,515.2	794.0	6,837.3	862.9	684.0	10,101.9	8,751.2	1,204.7	1,211.6	578.7	1,141.6

Dollars are in millions.
Source: 100 Leading National Advertisers, Reprinted with permission from Advertising Age (September 29, 1993): 8 Copyright, Crain Communications, Inc., 1993.

NEWSPAPERS

Newspapers were once the nation's medium of choice. Today they compete with a wide range of media for audience share and advertising dollars. Advertisers can now choose between newspapers, point-of-purchase advertising, electronic media, and direct mail, to name but a few apart from broadcast. Audiences can get the news faster by turning on their television and radio; they can get the news in depth by watching all-news cable channels such as CNN. A new generation has grown up with this wider range of media options, and this generation is not in the habit of reading a daily newspaper. The consequences are evident. A century ago, there were 18 daily newspapers (dailies) published in New York City alone. As of 1990, only five existed; one was in Spanish, and three were tabloids that were fighting among themselves. Most U.S. cities are surviving now with only one daily paper.

The initial response of the newspaper industry to this fierce competition was to develop new technologies to alleviate the most glaring deficiencies of the medium, which were poor reproduction and lack of sound, movement, and color. Examples are the move from hot metal to cold, or computerized, type, text editing, offset printing, on-line circulation information systems, electronic libraries, data-base publishing, and, most recently, satellite transmission and computerization. There have also been attempts to match the advantages offered by magazines and radio (market selectivity) and television (total market coverage). Examples of market selectivity are free-standing inserts and special-interest newspapers. The latter strategy is reflected in nationally distributed newspapers such as *The Wall Street Journal* and *USA Today*. Finally, the high cost of competition, combined with the increased costs of newspaper production, has resulted in a general consolidation in the newspaper industry. The major owners have become publishing empires, such as Gannett, Knight-Ridder, and Times-Mirror. Other newspaper conglomerates are Newhouse Newspapers, the Tribune Company, and the New York Times Company.

Statistics for 1990 indicated that total morning, evening, and Sunday circulation was 41.3 million, 21 million, and 62.4 million, respectively, compared to equivalent figures of 29.4 million, 32.7 million, and 54.6 million in 1980.[6] Tables 10.2 and 10.3 provide additional facts related to newspapers. Note that the top advertisers tend to be retailers.

THE STRUCTURE OF NEWSPAPERS

Newspapers can be classified by three factors: frequency of publication, size, and circulation.

Frequency of Publication Newspapers are published either daily or weekly. There are approximately 1,650 dailies and 8,000 weeklies in the United States.[7] Daily newspapers are usually found in cities and larger towns.

Dailies have morning editions, evening editions, or all-day editions. Daily papers printed in the morning deliver a relatively complete record of the previous day's events, including detailed reports on local and national news as well as

---

[6]1970–1989, *Editor & Publisher International Yearbook*, 1990:17.
[7]Jon Berry, "These Are the Good Old Days," *Adweek Supplement* (April 23, 1990):6–9.

Table 10.2

Top 25 National Newspaper
Advertisers

Rank	Advertiser	National newspaper spending		
		1992	1991	%chg
1	Fidelity Investment Cos.	$29.7	$22.0	35.0
2	General Motors Corp.	28.7	25.6	12.2
3	Dreyfus Corp.	18.1	13.2	37.2
4	IBM Corp.	17.6	10.3	71.0
5	AT&T Co.	16.9	20.3	−16.9
6	American Express Co.	15.0	14.2	5.9
7	Ford Motor Co.	14.7	10.0	46.7
8	Dow Jones & Co.	14.6	13.1	12.1
9	Toyota Motor Corp.	14.5	11.8	23.1
10	Hewlett-Packard Co.	13.2	12.8	3.0
11	Compaq Computer Corp.	11.9	8.7	37.3
12	Merrill Lynch & Co.	11.7	9.2	27.5
13	Damark International	10.6	8.8	21.1
14	Marriott Corp.	10.3	9.3	10.6
15	Chrylser Corp.	9.8	8.8	11.0
16	Apple Computer	8.9	5.6	59.2
17	Daimler-Benz AG	8.1	4.5	80.3
18	Franklin Distributors	8.0	8.2	−1.4
19	Chemical Banking Corp.	7.7	3.2	139.5
20	BMW AG	7.3	14.3	−48.9
21	AMR Corp.	6.7	6.7	0.8
22	ITT Corp.	6.6	4.4	50.6
23	U.S. Government	6.5	5.1	28.4
24	Delta Air Lines	6.2	5.3	16.8
25	Sprint Corp.	6.0	2.5	136.9

Dollars are in millions.
Source: 100 Leading National Advertisers, Reprinted with permission from Advertising Age (September 29, 1993) 36. Copyright, Crain Communications Inc., 1993.

on business, financial, and sports events. Evening papers follow up the news of the day and provide early reports of the events of the following day. Evening papers also tend to depend more on entertainment and information features than do morning papers. The *San Francisco Examiner* is an example of a daily evening paper. Approximately 30 percent of the dailies and a few of the weeklies also publish a Sunday edition. The *Chicago Sun-Times* is a daily paper that publishes both a morning and a Sunday edition. In 1990 there were 834 Sunday papers in circulation, nearly twice as many as had existed 50 years earlier.[8] Sunday newspapers are usually much thicker and contain a great deal of news, advertising, and special features. The circulation of Sunday papers is usually greater than that of dailies because they contain more information and because they appear on a day when readers have more leisure time to spend reading a paper.

Weekly papers appear in towns, suburbs, and smaller cities where the volume of hard news and advertising is not sufficient to support a daily newspaper.

---

[8]Berry, "These Are the Good Old Days," pp. 6–9.

Table 10.3

Top 25 Local Newspaper Advertisers

Rank	Advertiser	Local newspaper spending		
		1992	1991	%chg
1	May Department Stores Co.	$303.5	$155.2	95.6
2	Circuit City Stores	186.9	73.3	155.0
3	Federated Department Stores	175.7	92.4	90.3
4	R.H. Macy & Co.	171.3	139.2	23.1
5	Sears, Roebuck & Co.	165.9	88.5	87.5
6	Kmart Corp.	129.0	49.7	159.7
7	Dayton Hudson Corp.	120.2	46.0	161.2
8	Dillard Department Stores	117.0	22.6	417.2
9	Montgomery Ward & Co.	107.6	44.1	144.1
10	Carter Hawley Hale Stores	106.4	70.5	51.0
11	J.C. Penney Co.	95.2	33.6	183.4
12	Mercantile Store Co.	73.7	20.5	259.0
13	American Stores Co.	70.7	57.2	23.7
14	Tandy Corp.	59.7	24.3	146.0
15	AMR Corp.	55.0	68.7	−19.9
16	Sony Corp.	53.7	30.7	74.6
17	Woodward & Lothrop	45.1	1.7	2574.2
18	Time Warner	45.0	33.1	36.1
19	Delta Air Lines	40.5	53.6	−24.5
20	Ford Motor Co.	38.1	27.2	40.3
21	Kroger Co.	37.6	10.9	245.1
22	Continental Holdings	36.3	30.2	20.2
23	Melville Corp.	35.6	19.5	82.6
24	AT&T Co.	33.8	28.3	19.3
25	Dixons Group	33.6	18.2	84.1

Dollars are in millions.
Source: 100 Leading National Advertisers, Reprinted with permission from Advertisers Age (September 29, 1993): 34. Copyright, Crain Communications, Inc. 1993.

These papers emphasize the news of a relatively restricted area; they report local news in depth but tend to ignore national news, sports, and similar subjects. Weeklies are often shunned by national advertisers because they are relatively high in cost, duplicate the circulation of daily or Sunday papers, and generate an administrative headache because ads must be placed separately for each newspaper. *Beverly Review* is an example of a weekly circulated in a Chicago neighborhood.

Size. Newspapers are typically available in two sizes. The first, referred to as the **tabloid**, consists of five or six columns, each about 2 inches wide, and a total length of approximately 14 inches. This form makes tabloids look similar to an unbound magazine. The *Chicago Sun Times* employs this size, as does the New York *Daily News*, the *National Enquirer*, and *The Star*. The *standard size*, or **broadsheet**, newspaper is twice as large as the tabloid size, usually eight columns wide and 300 lines deep, or 22 inches deep by 14 inches wide. For both pragmatic and aesthetic reasons, however, many standard-sized newspapers have recently reduced their layouts to six columns wide. More than 90 percent of all newspa-

tabloid   A newspaper with a page size five to six columns wide and 14 inches deep.

broadsheet   A newspaper with a size of eight columns wide and 22 inches deep.

pers use standard size. *The New York Times* is an example of a standard-size newspaper.

The newspaper format is not fixed and frozen. The success of *USA Today* indicates that newspapers can and will adjust to changing consumer tastes. *USA Today* stories are brief and breezy, dressed up with splashy graphics and full color in every section, and include an array of charts and graphs to simplify the day's events for the reader. Ad 10.1 is an example of a newspaper with a novel format, influenced by the success of *USA Today*, and designed to attract young readers.

Advertisers' major criticism of the newspaper industry has not been as much about the lack of standardization of news format as about the standardization of advertisement format. Historically, national advertisers were discouraged from using newspapers because each paper had its own size guidelines for ads, making it impossible to prepare one ad that would fit every newspaper. This problem was resolved in 1981 with the introduction of the Standard Advertising Unit

Ad 10.1

The Chicago Tribune newspaper has varied its format in recent years.

Figure 10.1

The expanded Standard Advertising Unit system.

(Source: Guide to Quality Newspaper Reproduction, joint publication of the American Newspaper Publishers Association and Newspaper Advertising Bureau, 1986)

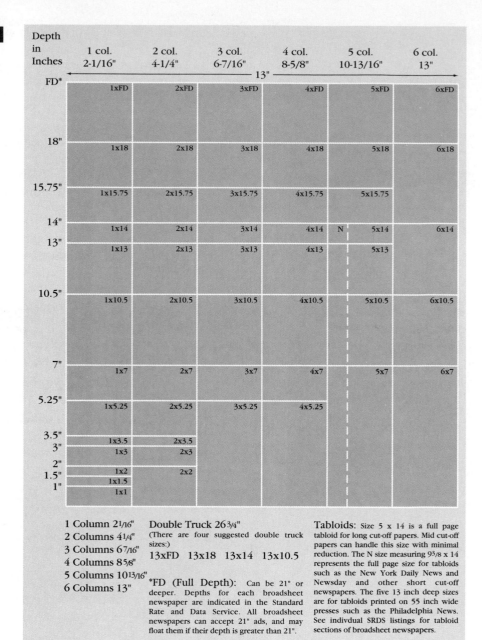

Depth in Inches	1 col. 2-1/16"	2 col. 4-1/4"	3 col. 6-7/16"	4 col. 8-5/8"	5 col. 10-13/16"	6 col. 13"
FD*	1xFD	2xFD	3xFD	4xFD	5xFD	6xFD
18"	1x18	2x18	3x18	4x18	5x18	6x18
15.75"	1x15.75	2x15.75	3x15.75	4x15.75	5x15.75	
14"	1x14	2x14	3x14	4x14	N 5x14	6x14
13"	1x13	2x13	3x13	4x13	5x13	
10.5"	1x10.5	2x10.5	3x10.5	4x10.5	5x10.5	6x10.5
7"	1x7	2x7	3x7	4x7	5x7	6x7
5.25"	1x5.25	2x5.25	3x5.25	4x5.25		
3.5"	1x3.5	2x3.5				
3"	1x3	2x3				
2"	1x2	2x2				
1.5"	1x1.5					
1"	1x1					

1 Column 2 1/16"
2 Columns 4 1/4"
3 Columns 6 7/16"
4 Columns 8 5/8"
5 Columns 10 13/16"
6 Columns 13"

Double Truck 26 3/4"
(There are four suggested double truck sizes:)

13xFD   13x18   13x14   13x10.5

*FD (Full Depth): Can be 21" or deeper. Depths for each broadsheet newspaper are indicated in the Standard Rate and Data Service. All broadsheet newspapers can accept 21" ads, and may float them if their depth is greater than 21".

Tabloids: Size 5 x 14 is a full page tabloid for long cut-off papers. Mid cut-off papers can handle this size with minimal reduction. The N size measuring 9 3/8 x 14 represents the full page size for tabloids such as the New York Daily News and Newsday and other short cut-off newspapers. The five 13 inch deep sizes are for tabloids printed on 55 inch wide presses such as the Philadelphia News. See indivdual SRDS listings for tabloid sections of broadsheet newspapers.

(SAU) system designed by the American Newspaper Publishers Association and the Newspaper Advertising Bureau. The present version was introduced in 1984 and is shown in Figure 10.1. It is now possible for an advertiser to select one of the 56 standard ad sizes and be assured this ad will work in every newspaper in the country.

Circulation. For the most, part, newspapers are a mass medium, attempting to reach either a regional or a national audience. Industry people use the word **circulation** to refer to the number of newspapers sold. A few newspapers have a *national* circulation, such as the *London Times* and *USA Today*; a far greater number are restricted to a *regional* circulation. Some newspapers, however, have attempted to reach certain target audiences in other ways. Most common among

circulation A measure of the number of copies sold.

these are newspapers directed at specific ethnic or foreign-language groups, such as *El Nuevo Herald*, a Spanish daily published in Miami (see Ad 10.2). Over 200 newspapers in the United States are aimed primarily at black Americans. In New York City alone papers are printed in Chinese, Spanish, Russian, Yiddish, German, and Vietnamese.

AT&T uses black, Asian, and Hispanic papers to tout local corporate events; Honda, Canon, and Ricoh advertise in Japanese papers; and Carnation and GTE run ads in Hispanic papers in California and other regions. As is the case with mainstream newspapers, most advertisers are local retailers, especially ethnic restaurants, travel agents, banks, and stores.[9]

Special newspapers also exist for special-interest groups, religious denominations, political affiliations, labor unions, and professional and fraternal organizations. For example, *Stars and Stripes* is the newspaper read by millions of military personnel.

[9]Christine Larson, "Ethnic Issues," *Adweek* (May 6, 1991):N.3.

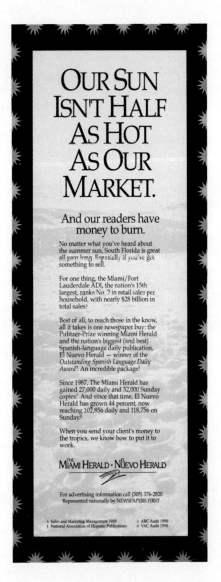

THE READERS OF NEWSPAPERS

Newspaper readers encompass all income brackets, educational levels, age groups, and ethnic backgrounds. They live in cities, suburbs, towns, resorts, and rural areas. By all demographic standards, the newspaper is a solid mass-market medium.

In 1992, the average weekday readership of newspapers increased to 115 million adults, a slight rise from 1991. Now representing about 68 percent of the adult population, newspapers once had a much broader base of support, as high as 80 percent in the 1960s[10] Frequent readers of daily newspapers tend to be the most regular readers of the Sunday paper. Nearly half of all adults receive home delivery of a Sunday or weekend newspaper; delivery levels are highest in middle-size cities and lowest in rural locations and the largest metropolitan areas.

Two-thirds of adults read the newspaper on an average Sunday. Over four Sundays, adult newspaper readership increases to 88 percent. The average reader spends 62 minutes reading the Sunday edition, compared with an average of 45 minutes on the weekday paper. Gender differences also exist. Men tend to read the "hard news" section of the Sunday paper, which includes the political, financial, and front-page sections. They also tend to read the sports section, whereas women do not have a particular preference (see Figure 10.2). There are age differences as well. Those 35 and older are more likely than young readers to read news sections; those under 35 regularly read the comics, television booklet, entertainment and fashion sections, and inserts.[11]

Newspaper readership increases with age and with educational attainment. People aged 18 to 24 are 37 percent less likely than the average adult to be heavy newspaper readers (*heavy reading* is 25 or more papers in four weeks, or slightly more than one paper a day). Adults aged 25 to 34 are 17 percent less likely than average to be heavy readers, but those aged 35 to 44 are 17 percent more likely. The most faithful readers are aged 45 to 54, who are 24 percent more likely, and those aged 55 to 64, who are 22 percent more likely than average to be heavy newspaper readers. Probably the best single indicator of newspaper readership is education. College graduates are 65 percent more likely than the average adult to regularly read a newspaper, and those with postgraduate degrees are 87 percent more likely than the average adult to regularly read a newspaper.[12]

MEASURING THE NEWSPAPER AUDIENCE

The most useful way to assess newspaper readers is in terms of how they use the newspaper. In 1993 the Newspaper Association of America compiled a report from Simmons Market Research Bureau's Media & Markets studies of adults in 22,400 households. Of the readers surveyed, 65 percent scanned the entire paper in 1983, but only 54 percent scanned the entire paper in 1992. General news remained by far the most popular section of the newspaper among all types of readers. General news was looked at by 92 percent of all readers in 1992, down only slightly from 1979.[13]

The Audit Bureau of Circulations. Statements regarding newspaper circulation are verified by the Audit Bureau of Circulations (ABC), an independent auditing

[10]Kim Long, *The American Forecaster Almanac*, 1993 Business Edition.
[11]"The Sunday Newspaper and Its Readers," *Newspaper Advertising Bureau* (October 1988).
[12]Joe Schwartz and Thomas Exter, "The News from Here," *American Demographics* (June 1991):50–54.
[13]Christy Fisher, "Newspaper Readers Get Choosier," *Advertising Age* (July 26, 1993):5–21.

Figure 10.2

Each section of the newspaper appeals differently to men and to women.

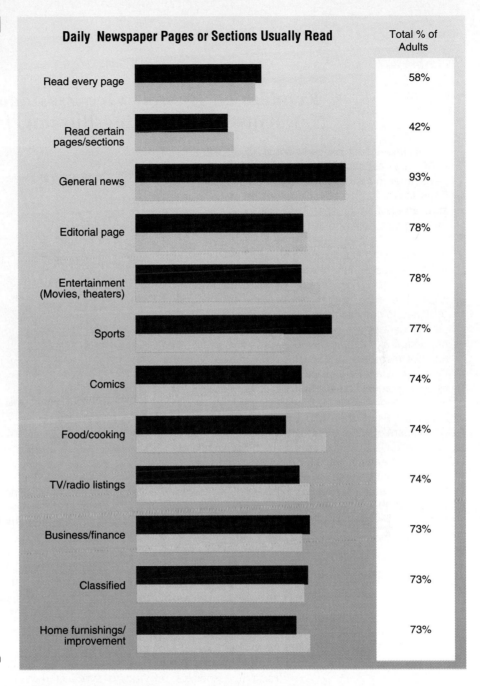

Daily Newspaper Pages or Sections Usually Read

	Total % of Adults
Read every page	58%
Read certain pages/sections	42%
General news	93%
Editorial page	78%
Entertainment (Movies, theaters)	78%
Sports	77%
Comics	74%
Food/cooking	74%
TV/radio listings	74%
Business/finance	73%
Classified	73%
Home furnishings/improvement	73%

■ Men
▨ Women

group that represents advertisers, agencies, and publishers. Members of the ABC include only paid-circulation newspapers and magazines. The ABC reports have nothing to do with setting the rates that a newspaper charges. They simply verify the newspaper's circulation statistics and provide a detailed analysis of the newspaper by state, town, and county. The newspaper can charge whatever it desires. Advertisers may decline to pay, however, if the rate is out of line with the paper's relative circulation figures as reported by ABC. Other companies, such as the Advertising Checking Bureau, provide newspaper research data and information on competitive advertising.

Kenneth O. Hustel, Vice President, Newspaper Advertising Bureau, Inc.

Organizations such as the National Advertising Bureau (NAB) are responsible for the economic health of the newspaper industry. As noted in this box, people like Kenn Hustel spend a very active life trying to make sure newspapers prosper. The following is a look at the morning schedule of a vice president of NAB.

Prior to the Thanksgiving holiday, I must meet with my newspaper Future of Advertising (FOA) teammates in Minneapolis—next Tuesday or Wednesday would be ideal. The FOA project is a team-selling project designed to convince a major advertiser to plan a sustaining newspaper program in a broad list of daily newspapers. The team involves a member of the NAB and two members of a specific newspaper—generally the senior marketing executive and the national advertising manager. The Bureau provides marketing services support, and in the event creative work is required, either the NAB or the creative services department of the member newspaper will be involved. Preparation of the advertising plan, presentation, et al. are in the hands of the three-person sales team.

Our category is ready-to-eat cereals (R-T-E). Following a thorough marketing review of this business we determined the category leader as our target account. The analysis includes not only secondary

Courtesy of Kenneth O. Hustel.

data sources, but also personal fact-finding sessions with appropriate advertising principles at each company and each of their agencies.

Newspapers that do not belong to an auditing organization must provide either a "publisher's statement" or a "Post Office statement" to prospective advertisers. The former is a sworn affidavit, and the latter is an annual statement given to the Post Office.

Simmons-Scarborough. The research firm Simmons-Scarborough Syndicated Research Associates provides a syndicated newspaper readership study that annually measures readership profiles in approximately 70 of the nation's largest cities. The study covers readership of a single issue as well as the estimated unduplicated readers for a series of issues. Scarborough is the only consistent measurement of popular audiences in individual markets.

ADVERTISING IN NEWSPAPERS

Although newspapers are not formally classified by the type of advertising they carry, this is a useful way of thinking about newspapers. There are three general types of newspaper advertising: classified, display, and supplements.

In our second presentation we encountered some resistance from the advertising agency, who suggested we target our effort toward the promotional budget rather than the consumer media budget. This means we need to see the client, since they control the promotional funds.

We have been persistently trying to schedule a meeting with the client's director of marketing services. We carefully explained our purpose and agenda as we requested a short 45 minutes of time. This morning we were "officially" advised that she has no interest in reviewing our concepts and ideas. I find this appalling. I always thought companies would be highly interested in learning of proposals/ideas that could conceivably move their business ahead. Most companies subscribe to this principle, but not all. I suppose we could go a level or two higher to force a meeting, but to what avail? That would only guarantee a hostile atmosphere and a negative response to our recommendation. Not to worry. We have another target that will be far more receptive.

I must remember to call the other major Chicago-based agency on the client's cereal business to review our complete proposal. These people provided us with helpful information during a fact-finding session, so it is appropriate for us to share the program with them. I'll try to schedule for mid-December. This also provides us with an opportunity to show the strong thinking and comprehensive program we can apply to other accounts controlled by the agency. You never know where business might emanate from, so it's important to take advantage of all opportunities.

Next week in the Twin Cities, our sales team will review our strategic sales plan for our new target. Because some time has elapsed since out initial fact-finding session with the client, we might well reexamine the status and direction of the client's cereal advertising program. If the client dictates, we will be prepared to visit with the New York-based ad agency responsible for the R-T-E cereal business within 2 weeks. Following those sessions, we will write the plan developing creative strategy, have NAB-NY prepare some conceptual creative units, and try to get back to the client in early January 1991.

As the R-T-E cereal project rolls ahead, I need to push ahead on a similar project for an Indianapolis-based major household cleaner/food protection company. The ad director of the consumer-products division listened to our target account proposal and quickly accepted our challenge. Since her company is under a mandate to search and examine media alternatives (to network television), our proposal struck a positive chord.

Our project has now reached the point where we are prepared to discuss it in detail with both agencies. I will call company ad director tomorrow to advise of our plans to meet with both agencies late the first week of December. I'll write the letters in Columbus and fax to my office for processing.

---

classified advertising
Commercial messages arranged in the newspaper according to the interests of readers.

Classified. Historically, **classified advertising** was the first type of advertising found in newspapers. Classified ads generally consist of all types of commercial messages arranged according to their interest to readers, such as "Help Wanted," "Real Estate for Sale," and "Cars for Sale." Classified ads represent approximately 40 percent of total advertising revenue. *Regular classified* ads are usually listed under a major heading with little embellishment or white space. *Display classified* ads use borders, larger type, white space, photos, and occasionally, color. Often newspapers will include legal notices, political and government reports, and personals in the classified section.

display advertising Sponsored messages that can be of any size and location within the newspaper, with the exception of the editorial page.

Display. **Display advertising** is the dominant form of newspaper advertising. Display ads can be of any size and are found anywhere within the newspaper, with the exception of the editorial page. Display advertising is further divided into two subcategories—local (retail) and national (general) display advertising.

Local display advertising is placed by local businesses, organizations, or individuals who pay the lower, local advertising rate. The difference between what is charged for local display advertising and national display advertising is referred to as the *rate differential*. In a study conducted by the American Association of Advertising Agencies, it was determined that a national advertiser would be charged an average of 75 percent more than a local retailer for 1,000 inches of newspaper advertising, and 95 percent more for advertising in dailies having circulations of more than 250,000. That 75 percent differential is up 13 percentage points from a similar 1989 study; it marked the largest national/local rate differential since 1933.[14] National ads represent only 13 percent of the $30.4 billion in advertising placed in newspapers in 1991, as opposed to 52 percent for retail and 35 percent for classified. Approximately 85 percent of all display advertising is local, placed by local businesses.

This higher cost is justified by several factors. First, newspapers contend that national advertisers ask for more assistance from newspapers, especially with special promotions, such as coupons and free-standing inserts. Second, they argue that national advertisers are less reliable than local advertisers, often placing no ads for weeks or months at a time. Finally, newspapers believe that the national advertiser is unlikely to change the number of ads placed in a given newspaper regardless of whether the rate goes up or down.

As a result of these higher rates, national advertisers have been reluctant to use newspapers or have looked for ways to get around the rate differential. One alternative that allows the national advertiser to pay the local rate is cooperative (co-op) advertising with a local retailer. *Co-op advertising* refers to an arrangement between the advertiser and the retailer whereby both parties share the cost of placing the ad. The exact share is negotiated between the two parties. Co-op advertising is discussed in more detail in Chapter 22. Some newspapers have created "hybrid" rates that are offered to regular national advertisers, such as airlines, car-rental companies, and hotels. Some newspapers discount for frequency or as an incentive to attract certain categories of advertising.

National display advertising is run by national and international businesses, organizations, and celebrities to maintain brand recognition or to supplement the efforts of local retailers or other promotional efforts.

supplements Syndicated or local full-color advertising inserts that appear in newspapers throughout the week.

Supplements. Both national and local advertising can be carried in newspaper supplements. **Supplements** refer to syndicated or local full-color advertising inserts that appear throughout the week and especially in the Sunday edition of newspapers. One very popular type is the magazine supplement, of which there are two kinds—syndicated and local.

Syndicated supplements are published by independent publishers and distributed to newspapers throughout the country. The logo for the publisher and the local paper appear on the masthead. The best-known syndicated supplements are *Parade* and *USA Weekend*. *Local supplements* are produced by either one newspaper or a group of newspapers in the same area. Whether syndicated or locally edited, magazine supplements resemble magazines more than newspapers in content and format.

free-standing insert advertisements Preprinted advertisements that are placed loosely within the newspaper.

Another type of newspaper supplement is the **free-standing insert advertisement** (FSIA), or "loose insert." These preprinted advertisements range in size from a single page to over 30 pages and may be in black and white or full color. This material is printed elsewhere and then delivered to the newspaper. Newspapers charge the advertiser a fee for inserting the material plus a special rate for carrying the ad in a particular issue. This form of newspaper advertising

---

[14]Christy Fisher and Joe Mandese, "4 A's Hits Newspapers' National Rates," *Advertising Age* (June 1, 1992):40.

is growing in popularity with retail advertisers for two reasons: (1) It allows greater control over the reproduction quality of the advertisement; and (2) the multipage FSIA is an excellent coupon carrier. Newspapers are not necessarily happy about the growth of free-standing inserts because they make less revenue from this form of advertising.

THE ADVANTAGES OF NEWSPAPERS

There are numerous advantages to advertising in newspapers. These include market coverage, comparison shopping, positive consumer attitudes, flexibility, and interaction of national advertising and local retailers.

Market Coverage. Undoubtedly the most obvious asset is the extensive market coverage provided by newspapers. When an advertiser wishes to reach a local or regional market, newspapers offer an extremely cost-efficient way to do so. Even special-interest groups and racial and ethnic groups can be reached through newspapers.

Comparison Shopping. Consumers consider newspapers valuable shopping vehicles. Many use newspapers for comparison shopping. Consumers can also control when and how they read the paper, as well as which papers they choose in the first place. As a result, they view newspaper ads very positively.

Positive Consumer Attitudes. Consumers maintain positive attitudes toward newspapers in general. Readers generally perceive newspapers—including the advertisements—to be very immediate and current, as well as highly credible sources of information.

Flexibility. Flexibility is a major strength of newspapers. Newspapers offer great geographic flexibility. Advertisers using them can choose to advertise in some markets and not in others. Newspapers are often flexible in the actual production of the ads as well. Unusual ad sizes, full-color ads, free-standing inserts, different prices in different areas, and supplements are all options for a newspaper advertiser.

Newspapers are even willing to carry product samples. For example, Procter & Gamble recently delivered millions of sample sizes of either Vidal Sassoon Ultra Care Shampoo, Conditioner, or Finishing Rinse through Sunday newspapers in New England and the Midwest. The packet was either affixed to an advertising insert card or a sealed plastic bag. Papers charged 19 cents per sample delivered.[15]

Introduction of National and Local. Finally, newspapers provide an excellent bridge between the national advertiser and the local retailer. A local retailer can easily tie in with a national campaign by utilizing a similar advertisement in the local daily. In addition, quick-action programs, such as sales and coupons, are easily implemented through local newspapers.

Charlotte Weisinberger, J. Walter Thompson's media director, summarizes the benefits of advertising in newspapers: "There are a number of things—from representing a local retailer, to breaking a last-minute campaign, to couponing,

---

[15]Lorne Manly, "P&G Says Bag This," *Mediaweek* (July 22, 1993):1, 4.

Jennifer Zwief, Account Executive, Cramer-Krasselt, Milwaukee

8:15 A.M. It's Wednesday. I'm meeting a colleague before attending a client meeting. We need approval of a radio commercial which was recorded on Monday and finished on Tuesday. The commercial must be at Seattle radio stations tomorrow. We really need approval.

8:30 A.M. We play the radio commercial for client #1. Everyone listens attentively. The client approves the commercial with one minor change. The creative director and I are relieved and happy.

We discuss another project about to be produced, a direct-mail piece. It needs one addition to the copy. We promise new copy will be available tomorrow. I hope we can keep that promise.

10:00 A.M. I'm back at the office. My chair is full of mail, and my telephone is flashing with messages. I listen to voice mail messages first, amazed by how long that takes. Client #2 confirms meeting for next week. Traffic lets me know they need insertion instructions. Media has some new information. Pretty much routine business. I follow up by phone or in person.

10:30 A.M. Time to begin reviewing a document summarizing budgets for this year, as well as next year for client #2. Right now, we make sure we're on target with this year's budget. We also finalize plans and budgets for next year. There is no room for mistakes on a budget document. I go over every number twice, some three times. We'll be presenting this budget to the client early next week.

I talk with the media director about our status on preliminary media negotiations for next year. Since this affects budgeting, we'll want to review this information during next week's meeting. To date, the bottom line of our media negotiations totals less than what we budgeted. Good news.

11:40 A.M. We have an internal meeting with the account team for client #2. We review creative concepts for two print ads which will be presented to the client on Friday. We have multiple executions for each of the two ads; the client likes choices. The concepts meet the objectives and effectively communicate the product benefits and features. The layouts and copy are next.

to telling a detailed story that won't fit in a 30-second spot—that newspapers simply do better than any other medium."[16]

THE DISADVANTAGES OF NEWSPAPERS

Like every other advertising medium, newspapers also have their disadvantages. The issues that are most problematic in newspaper advertising are a short life span, clutter, limited reach of certain groups, product criteria, and poor reproduction.

Short Life Span. Although a great many people do read newspapers, they read them quickly and they read them only once. The average life span of a daily newspaper is only 24 hours.

Clutter. High clutter is a serious problem with most newspapers. This is partic-

---

[16]Warren Berger, "What Have You Done for Me Lately?" *Adweek* (April 23, 1990):13.

	The creatives have a day and a half to do this, which isn't much time for them.
Noon	It's the annual pumpkin-carving contest at Cramer-Krasselt—a record number of entries this year. Everyone gathers in the breakroom for the judging. It is hard to decide which is funnier—the entries or the awards. I hope the creative department didn't waste all its creative energy on pumpkins.
1:00 P.M.	I write a creative work plan for a project that is needed next year for client #2. This project includes two ads, a direct-mail piece and a response card. The work plan details the background information, objectives, target audience, product benefits and features, and any other mandatories. After the management supervisor approves the work plan, it will be circulated to the entire account team and traffic will schedule a meeting to review the work plan. We need creative concepts in five weeks.
2:00 P.M.	I have a couple of client phone calls. We discuss several upcoming projects and finalize some details.
2:30 p.m.	It's time for production billing for client #1. Our new cost-control system at the agency makes this easier. I must review

each project to make sure its description is accurate, that all invoices are correct and assigned to the appropriate category, and that the invoice total matches the production estimate. After review, these jobs go to accounting. The accounting department processes the actual invoice. Now it's time to write a cover memo to be sent with the invoices.

4:00 P.M.	The research director, management supervisor, and I have a meeting to decide how to best answer client #2's follow-up question from a benchmark research study we completed a month ago. We agree to the next steps and set a due date.
4:30 P.M.	The management supervisor sits down to discuss the day's events. We need this time together to gather thoughts and make sure everything on today's agenda did get finished today. Then we prioritize what needs to be done before the end of the week.
4:45 P.M.	I write a couple of memos and make a few more phone calls before attending a "going away" party for one of the art directors.

ularly true on supermarket advertising days and on Sundays, when information overload reduces the impact of any single advertisement.

Limited Coverage of Certain Groups. Although newspapers have wide market coverage, certain market groups are not frequent readers. For example, newspapers traditionally have not reached a large part of the under-20 age group. The same is true of the elderly and those speaking a foreign language who do not live in a large city.

Because of the rate differential and the difficulty of making thousands of buys, newspapers often are not able to provide total market coverage for national advertisers. Recently, in an attempt to rectify this situation, newspapers in three states worked together to form a one-order/one-bill network tailored and priced to appeal to the national automobile dealer associations. The network is tailored to cover an association's trading area and does not include unwanted circulation.[17]

---

[17]Christy Fisher, "Newspapers Link to Attract Auto Groups," *Advertising Age* (November 30, 1992):36.

Product Criteria. Newspapers suffer the same limitations shared by all print media. Certain products should not be advertised in newspapers. Products that require demonstration would have a difficult time making an impact in the newspaper format. Similarly, products that consumers do not expect to find advertised in newspapers, such as professional services (doctors, lawyers) and tradespeople (plumbers, electricians), might easily be overlooked.

Poor Reproduction. With the exception of special printing techniques and preprinted inserts, the reproduction quality of newspapers is comparatively poor and limiting, especially for color advertisements, although color reproduction has improved thanks to the popularity of *USA Today*. Color reproduction is an expensive alternative to black and white, so advertisers want their money's worth. In addition, the speed necessary to compose a daily newspaper prevents the detailed preparation and care in production that is possible when time pressures are not so great.

THE FUTURE OF NEWSPAPERS

Tomorrow's newspapers will be different from today's newspapers. Some people predict newspapers will be read on a flat, tabloid-size hand-held screen. Others say color pages will evolve into faxed pages through high-speed machines. Still others think ink-on-paper will long remain the medium of choice for newspapers, although technology—such as audiotext, videotext, and fax—will provide ways to supplement the daily news product.

Though it is unclear exactly what the newspaper of the future will be, it is certain that newspapers will change to keep up with the needs of readers and advertisers and to retain a competitive edge against other forms of delivery and entertainment.

A few examples will demonstrate what newspapers have done to date. The Media Laboratory at the Massachusetts Institute of Technology is doing research on user modeling, a project which will allow for creation of *The Daily Me*, a paper tailored to an individual's interests. This newspaper could be available in various forms, such as on a personal computer screen, as a printout, on the TV screen, or by audio. Knight-Ridder is working on making general-interest newspapers, with individually requested supplemental news items, available via a portable, tabloid-sized screen. This system will allow the reader to turn pages, clip and save articles, and call up background information, all with a touch of an electronic pen.

For some papers, such as *The New York Times* and the *Los Angeles Times*, the object today is to use technology to repackage information the newspaper already offers and provide products to support core advertisers. The *Los Angeles Times* has user-paid audiotext lines and offers Financial Faxs, a service which tracks 10 to 15 requested stocks. It also sends a fax version of the paper to Moscow five days a week. *The New York Times* has TimesFax, a daily fax product offered to subscribers in Japan, hotels in Europe, and cruise ships.[18] (More is said about audiotext in the Concepts and Applications box).

Whatever technology newspapers employ in the future, it is clear that advertising must have a major input.

---

[18]Christy Fisher, "Newspapers of Future Look to Go High-Tech as Experiments Abound," *Advertising Age* (October 5, 1992):S–3, S–8.

Concepts & APPLICATIONS

Papers Worth Listening To

Imagine this: You're an advertiser seeking suitable prospects. A day after running an ad in the local paper you get a list of candidates, all of whom indicate a desire to buy your products. Or this: You're a reader and have questions on an article or want more information. You can place a free call to hear a live excerpt from the event, an updated report, or more details along with a short ad.

Several newspapers already are tapping into this technology, using a media called *audiotext* in ways that go beyond traditional lines among newspapers, broadcast media, and in some cases direct-response advertising. Audiotext is a phone-in service that provides to the caller information that is usually related to an advertised product or service. This is most often accomplished through the familiar 800- and 900-numbers system; the choice depends of course on who pays for the service. The biggest issue in newspapers these days is no longer if or when audiotext will be implemented, but how. Some examples follow. *The Washington Post* recently used the computer capabilities of the "Post Haste" audiotext system to compute effects of the Clinton tax plan for individuals who punched in their income and deductions. *The Hartford Courant's* audiotext lines don't include ad messages but are used as a value-added lure to attract print advertising. The paper says it raised its print revenues by $450,000 by offering advertisers customized audio-

text programs that aren't easily duplicated by other media. *Courant's* advertisers, both large and small, are allowed access to the paper's sophisticated audiotext system and may use it as their own without any mention of the paper. For example, in return for Vermont Ski & Tour Association running a $130,000 campaign, the paper used its system to provide Vermont ski conditions, entry to a contest and, if the caller wanted, instant switchover to reservations numbers for individual Vermont resorts.

The Wall Street Journal, which has an extensive 800 and 900 lineup of financial audiotext lines, isn't using advertising on lines directly tied to the paper. "Those who want the kind of information we offer don't want ad messages interfering with content," says Tom Pace, executive director of Dow Jones Voice Information Systems. The paper also is offering phone numbers to advertisers in a program under testing with Bell South.

While most papers are getting into audiotext, some express caution about its prospects. "My problem with audiotext is that it doesn't really work for the kind of information usually offered," says Henry Scott, director of new-product development for *The New York Times*. "Audiotext isn't a passive medium. You are limited by what else you can do."

Adapted from Ira Teinowetz, "Good Listeners for Audiotext," *Advertising Age* (April 25, 1993):5–8, S–9.

MAGAZINES

The earliest American magazines were local journals of political opinion. Most were monthly and did not circulate far beyond their geographic origins. Andrew Bradford's *American Magazine* was the first to appear in the colonies in 1741, arriving three days earlier than Benjamin Franklin's *General Magazine and Historical Chronicle*. Both publications folded within six months. Since that time, magazines have come and gone. All have been aimed at specific audiences; most sell advertising and are published monthly.[19] Figure 10.3 offers a pictorial view of the evolution of magazines throughout history. Despite the high risks associ-

---

[19]John McDonough, "In Step with History," *Advertising Age* (May 24, 1989):23.

In 1930, Henry Luce launched Fortune, which weighed three pounds and cost the then-staggering price of $1.

When Time magazine burst forth in 1923, it had no correspondents, no bureaus. But it had "attitude."

Like its mass audience brethren, Collier's had a huge circulation before its demise, while The New Yorker flourished on a much smaller base.

The Ladies' Home Journal, founded in 1883, was among the earliest magazines to accept advertising and make it work for them.

One of the great post-World War II magazine success stories, Playboy embodied the dilemmas of its age, praising intelligent women in its "philosophy" while stressing other attributes in its photographs.

Figure 10.3

The evolution of magazines from 1883 through 1990.

(Reprinted with permission from Advertising Age, May 24, 1989. Copyright 1989, Crain Communications, Inc. 1989)

ated with the magazine business, there appears to be no decline in the number of new magazines.

New magazine launches peaked in 1989, when 605 titles were introduced, more than double the number of titles launched in 1985. In 1991, the number of new magazines dropped to 541, with 1992 slightly higher.[20] Historically, over 50 percent of new titles fail. This is illustrated in Table 10.4. In addition, publishers are investing more money than ever in existing titles. Individual magazines have become bigger and brighter. Heavy paper stocks, lush photographs, and sophisticated graphics are used to create beautiful, eyecatching editorial environments that entice both readers and advertisers.

Upscale magazines seem to have an edge over mass consumer magazines in attracting advertisers. Upscale advertisers don't look to promotion spending as an alternative to advertising. Instead, they tend to turn to the image advertising that upscale magazines provide. For example, magazines such as *Gourmet*, *Architectural Digest*, and *Condé Nast Traveler* all have increased their ad pages since 1990. Steve Forbes, president and CEO of *Forbes* magazine, attributes this increase to gains in the "luxury category" of advertising, such as Rémy Martin Amérique, Cadillac, and Jaguar. *Elle* senior vice president/publisher Anne Sutherland Fuchs says that her magazine's "strong push to shore up [its] position with upscale advertisers has helped it buck the tide of ad page decline facing many women's magazines."[21] However, as noted in the Issues and Controversies box, upscale magazines don't necessarily carry upscale ads.

The magazine industry has entered the "age of skimming," a time when readers acquire 80 percent of their information from the story titles, subheadings, captions, and pictures rather than from the editorial content. Although magazine advertising revenue in 1992 was $7.1 billion, magazines are still unsure of which format to adopt and which audiences to target.[22] This is a medium that advertisers tend to view cautiously. Table 10.5 lists the 1992 rankings of the top 25 magazines by advertising revenue. Table 10.6 shows the top 25 magazine advertisers for the same year.

THE STRUCTURE OF MAGAZINES

The Standard Rate and Data Service classifies magazines according to their frequency of publication and their audience. The magazine industry also classifies magazines by *geographic coverage*, *demographics*, and *editorial diversity*.

---

[20]Laura Loro, "Heavy Hitters Gamble on Launches," *Advertising Age* (October 19, 1992):S–13.
[21]Iris Cohen Selenger, "Mags with Upscale Ads Show Gains," *Adweek* (November 12, 1990):19.
[22]Jon Berry, "Trade Magazines," *Adweek Supplement* (September 1, 1989):196.

Table 10.4

A Selective Lst of Magazines that Were Introduced or Failed in 1992

Introduced	Failed
Cigar Aficionado	American Film
Dirt	Connoisseur
Future Sex	European Travel & Life
Men's Journal	M
Prison Life	National Lampoon
Smart Money	New York Woman
Vibe	Quayle Quarterly
Wired	Philip Morris Magazine
Worth	Punch
Young Executive	Regardie's

Source: Adweek (March 1, 1993): CM4.

Table 10.5

Top 25 Magazines in Advertising Revenue

Rank	Title	1992 Revenues (millions)	% Change vs. 1991
1	People Weekly	368.2	6.7
2	Time	342.8	5.0
3	Sports Illustrated	314.1	−2.8
4	TV Guide	276.2	−1.1
5	Newsweek	258.4	10.4
6	Business Week	211.1	−4.1
7	U.S. News & World Report	195.8	14.1
8	Good Housekeeping	193.8	17.1
9	Better Homes & Gardens	188.5	17.8
10	Forbes	173.4	11.0
11	Family Circle	158.4	21.9
12	Cosmopolitan	135.7	6.4
13	Fortune	133.8	−12.7
14	Woman's Day	130.9	30.5
15	Reader's Digest	120.4	24.5
16	Ladies' Home Journal	117.2	4.3
17	Vogue	106.7	3.7
18	Glamour	101.1	10.5
19	Money	94.9	8.0
20	McCall's	93.6	10.5
21	Golf Digest	79.8	12.0
22	Southern Living	78.7	24.2
23	Redbook	77.7	7.8
24	Rolling Stone	74.2	2.3
25	Parents	71.5	14.9

Source: PIB survey of consumer magazines; adapted from Adweek (March 1, 1993): CM 23.

Audience. Three types of magazines are categorized by the audiences they serve. The first category, *consumer magazines*, is directed at consumers who buy products for their own consumption. These magazines are distributed through the mail, newsstands, or stores. Examples are *Reader's Digest*, *Lear's*, *Time*, and

Table 10.6

Top 25 Magazine Advertisers

Rank	Advertiser	Magazine spending 1992	1991	%chg
1	General Motors Corp.	$238.3	$250.4	−4.8
2	Philip Morris Cos.	219.2	213.6	2.6
3	Procter & Gamble Co.	164.7	143.1	15.1
4	Ford Motor Co.	161.7	149.6	8.1
5	Chrylser Corp.	151.5	107.6	40.8
6	Nestlé SA	118.3	77.4	52.9
7	Toyota Motor Corp.	107.6	105.4	2.2
8	Unilever	86.4	81.0	6.6
9	Nissan Motor Co.	76.3	30.0	154.1
10	Johnson & Johnson	68.2	56.3	21.1
11	Sony Corp.	65.9	55.5	18.8
12	Grand Metropolitan	65.2	83.0	−21.5
13	American Brands	64.4	64.4	−0.1
14	Mazda Motor Corp.	59.3	46.4	27.7
15	Time Warner	59.0	66.9	−11.8
16	Honda Motor Co.	58.4	58.1	0.5
17	Ralston Purina Co.	45.7	24.2	88.6
18	IBM Corp.	45.5	15.9	186.4
19	Bradford Exchange	44.8	45.3	−1.2
20	AT&T Co.	41.4	48.8	−15.2
21	Dow Chemical Co.	40.9	18.1	126.2
22	Roll International	40.5	33.8	20.0
23	American Express Co.	40.3	21.4	88.2
24	Nike Inc.	39.5	31.4	25.5
25	RJR Nabisco	39.1	61.2	−36.1

Note: Dollars are in millions.
Source: 100 Leading National Advertisers, Reprinted with permission from Advertising Age (September 29, 1993): 40. Copyright, Crain Communications, Inc. 1993.

People. The second category is *business magazines.* These magazines are directed at business readers and are further divided into *trade papers* (read by retailers, wholesalers, and other distributors; for example, *Chain Store Age*), *industrial magazines* (read by manufacturers; for example, *Concrete Construction*), and *professional magazines* (read by physicians, lawyers, and others; for example, *National Law Review*). Business magazines are also classified as being vertical or horizontal publications. A *vertical publication* presents stories and information about an entire industry. *Women's Wear Daily*, for example, discusses the production, marketing, and distribution of women's fashion. A *horizontal publication* deals with a business function that cuts across industries, such as *Direct Marketing. Farm magazines* represent a third category. They go to farmers and those engaged in farm-related activities. *Peanut Farmer* is an example of a farm magazine.

Geography. Magazines generally cover certain sections or regions of the country. The area covered may be as small as a city (*Los Angeles Magazine* and *Boston Magazine*) or as large as several contiguous states (the southwestern edition of

Southern Living Magazine). Geographic editions help encourage local retail support by listing the names of local distributors in the advertisement.

Demographics. Demographic editions group subscribers according to age, income, occupation, and other classifications. *McCall's*, for example, publishes a ZIP edition to upper-income homes. A ZIP edition is a special version of the magazine which is sent to subscribers who live in a specific zip code. A zip code presumably tells something about the people living in an area. They typically share common demographic traits, such as income. *Newsweek* offers a college edition, and *Time* sends special editions to students, business executives, doctors, and business managers.

Editorial Content. Various magazines emphasize certain types of editorial content. The most widely used categories are: general editorial (*Reader's Digest*), women's service (*Family Circle*), shelter (*House Beautiful*), business (*Forbes*), and special interest (*Ski*).

Physical Characteristics. The structure of the magazine industry is also reflected in the terminology used to describe the physical characteristics of a magazine. The most common magazine page sizes are $8^1/_2 \times 11$ inches and 6×9 inches.

Distribution and Circulation. The method used to distribute a magazine partly reflects its structure. **Traditional delivery** is either through *newsstand purchase* or *home delivery* via the U.S. Postal Service. **Nontraditional delivery** systems include hanging bagged copies on doorknobs, delivery within newspapers, and delivery through professionals. Magazines distributed through nontraditional delivery systems are provided free. This is referred to as *controlled circulation* as opposed to *paid circulation*. Rodale Press, located in Pennsylvania, is one of the most active publishing houses in developing controlled circulation. Two Rodale Magazines, *Prevention* and *Men's Health*, are often placed in doctors' waiting rooms.

traditional delivery   Delivery of magazines to readers through newsstands or home delivery.

nontraditional delivery   Delivery of magazines to readers through such methods as door hangers or newspapers.

THE READERS OF MAGAZINES

Approximately 92 percent of all adults read at least one magazine per month. This is true of both males and females. On average, adults read nine different issues of magazines per month. The average magazine is read over a period of two days, for 54 minutes in total reading time, by an average of four adults per copy.[23] It is therefore safe to conclude that the American public has a voracious appetite for magazines and the unique and specialized information they provide. *Sports Illustrated* is an example of a magazine that is targeted at a specific audience.

Readers also appear to have a positive attitude toward magazine advertising. Approximately 79 percent of adults consider magazine advertising "helpful as a buying guide." Roughly 75 percent express positive attitudes toward various aspects of magazine advertising, including the amount of information carried, the use of color, and the provision of coupons. Women tend to have slightly more positive attitudes than men do. In general, people pay relatively more attention to magazine advertising than to television advertising.[24]

---

[23]Mediamark Research Inc., *Doublebase 1988 Study:*19.
[24]"Study of Media Involvement," *Audits & Surveys* (March 1988).

Issues & CONTROVERSIES

Magazines Appeal to the Masses

Magazines are proving worthy competitors to the neighborhood garage sale with the increasing appearance of advertising for knick-knacks. Innocent as they may seem, collectibles from such companies as Franklin Mint and Bradford Exchange are burgeoning. Sources estimate sales of collectibles total over $1.5 billion, up about 30 percent from five years ago. Ad spending is growing too. The industry spent about $500 million on advertising in 1992, sources say, up about 15 percent from 1991.

The category has been a godsend to many women's magazines during the recent recession. Instead of cutting back, as so many magazine advertisers did in recent years, collectible marketers started investing more. Magazine ad spending by American Protection Industries, parent of Franklin Mint, grew 19 percent in 1992, making it the twentieth largest magazine advertiser. In Sunday magazines, Franklin Mint is the second-largest advertiser.

Just who buys these products? The target is middle America, mostly female, ages 30 to 50. But the male target is growing. Sculptures, mugs, steins, and model cars are becoming hot in the industry, addressing more of a male audience. "Given the volume they are running in women's service books, with a median age of 41 and 42, the audience may be the median and up. New products are probably aiming for the median and down," says Barbara Litrell, senior vice president/publisher of *McCalls.* Traditionally, the collector has been the 40-plus person, but that may be changing. "People are returning to the home and returning to nesting. They are doing home decorating that does involve more collecting," she notes. The most successful products pull an emotional heartstring. Dolls and plates are really hot.

Marketers are trying different advertising strategies to woo consumers. Franklin Mint has run ads, created inhouse, that feature celebrities such as race car driver Danny Sullivan, supermodel Paulina Porzikova, media maven Ted Turner, Philadelphia Eagles quarterback Randal Cunningham and former Supreme Court Chief Justice Warren Burger. The marketer also offers an upscale collector's edition of Parker Brothers' Monopoly and a Remington Chess set. There have also been Loony Toons and Jetsons and Flintstones Chess sets, targeted to a younger, more hip crowd. Lenox, whose advertising is assigned to FCB/Leber Katz Partners, New York, is offering a limited edition Bill of Rights Eagle along with the Smithsonian Institute. Part of each purchase benefits the Smithsonian.

While there are creative marketing attempts, some publishing executives worry that collectibles ads aren't aesthetically appealing and give the magazines that carry them a "dowdy" image. In fact, some other advertisers request being positioned six pages away from them. They feel their own upscale image will be lessened by close proximity to a collectible ad.

Excerpted from: Laura Lovo, "Magazines Make for Impressive Collections," *Advertising Age* (October 19, 1992): S–3.

MEASURING MAGAZINE READERSHIP

Magazine rates are based on the number of readers, which correlates with the circulation that a publisher promises to provide—that is, the *guaranteed circulation.* Table 10.7 lists the 25 largest magazines by circulation. As with newspapers, the ABC is responsible for collecting and evaluating these data to ensure that guaranteed circulation was obtained. The ABC audits subscriptions as well as newsstand sales. It also checks the number of delinquent subscribers and rates of renewal.

Magazine circulation refers to the number of copies of an issue sold, not to the readership of the publication. A single copy of a magazine might be read by one person or by several people, depending on its content.

The Simmons Market Research Bureau (SMRB) goes one step further by relating readership patterns to purchasing habits. The Bureau provides data on

Rank	Magazine	Average Total Paid 1992	% change vs. 1991
1	Modern Maturity	22,879,886	1.9
2	Reader's Digest	16,258,476	−0.1
3	TV Guide	14,498,341	−3.7
4	National Geographic	9,708,254	−1.0
5	Better Homes & Gardens	8,002,585	0.0
6	The Cable Guide	5,889,947	15.3
7	Family Circle	5,283,660	4.3
8	Good Housekeeping	5,139,355	−1.0
9	Ladies' Home Journal	5,041,143	−0.5
10	Woman's Day	4,810,445	4.1
11	McCall's	4,704,772	−7.2
12	Time	4,203,991	3.2
13	People Weekly	3,506,816	3.7
14	Sports Illustrated	3,432,044	4.1
15	Playboy	3,402,630	−4.1
16	National Enquirer	3,401,263	−9.5
17	Redbook	3,395,029	−12.1
18	Newsweek	3,240,131	0.5
19	Prevention	3,234,901	1.0
20	AAA World	3,107,468	11.0
21	American Legion	2,953,941	0.6
22	Star	2,931,305	−5.5
23	Cosmopolitan	2,705,224	−1.3
24	Auto Club News	2,540,275	2.7
25	Southern Living	2,374,530	0.6

Note: Figures are averages for six months ended December 31, 1992.
Source: Audit Bureau of Circulations, BPA International; adapted from Adweek (March 1, 1993) CM 22.

who reads which magazines and which products these readers buy and consume. Most advertisers and agencies depend greatly on SMRB estimates of magazine audiences. Other research companies, such as Starch and Gallup and Robinson, provide comparable information about magazine audience size and behavior. More is said about these research firms in Chapters 11 and 12.

MRI. A company known as MediaMark provides a service called MRI that measures readership for most popular national and regional magazines (along with other media). Reports are issued twice a year and cover readership by demographics, psychographics, and product usage.

ADVERTISING IN MAGAZINES

Magazines are a valuable medium for reaching many demographic groups. By their nature, magazines must fill a niche with unique editorial content in order to satisfy specific groups of readers. As a result, they are extremely diverse in terms of their characteristics, readers, and reader interaction. In evaluating a magazine, it is important for advertisers to examine the full range of characteristics that distinguish one magazine from all others.

Technology. New technologies have enable magazines to distinguish themselves from one another. For example, *selective binding*, and *ink-jet imaging* allow publishers to construct and personalize issues for individual subscribers one signature or insert at a time. Selective binding combines information on subscribers kept in a data base with a computer program to produce a magazine that includes special sections for subscribers based on their demographic profiles. Ink-jet printing permits a magazine such as *U.S. News & World Report* to personalize its renewal form so that each issue contains a renewal card already filled out with the subscriber's name, address, and so on. Personalized messages can be printed directly on run-of-book ads (the technology that is used for the entire magazine) or on inserts.

Desktop publishing is another mainline technology used by many magazines. This method, when combined with satellite transmission, allows magazines to close pages just hours before presstime—eliminating the long lead time that has traditionally been a serious drawback of magazine advertising. A final technology that has improved the advertising effectiveness of magazines is the adoption of sophisticated data-base management. This lets publishers combine the information available from exact subscriber lists with other public and private lists to create complete consumer profiles for their advertisers.

As is the case with newspapers, magazines are also moving away from paper toward the computer. Experts predict that 20 percent of publications will be available via computer by 2000, either as replacements or supplements to print versions.[25]

Format. Each magazine or magazine category uses its own terminology to describe its format. Nevertheless, all magazines share some characteristics. For example, the front cover of a magazine is called its *first cover page*. The inside of the front cover is called the *second cover page*, the inside of the back cover the *third cover page*, and the back cover the *fourth cover page*. Normally the double-page spread is the largest unit of ad space sold by magazines. The two pages face each other. When a double-page ad is designed, it is critical that the *gutter* (the white space between the pages running along the inside edge of the page) be bridged or jumped—meaning that no headline words run through the gutter and that all body text is on one side or the other. A page without outside margins, in which the color extends to the edge of the page, is called a *bleed page*. Magazines can sometimes offer more than two connected pages (four is the most common number). This is referred to as a *gatefold*. Armstrong Floors has used a five-sided gatefold in the inside front cover of *Better Homes & Gardens* magazine for several years. The use of multiple pages that provide photo essays is really an extension of the gatefold concept. As noted in Chapter 2, Calvin Klein has employed this format. Photo essays also are becoming more common in magazines such as *Fortune* and *Business Week*; these magazines may present a 20-page ad for business in a foreign country, such as Japan or South Korea. Finally, a single page or double page can be broken into a variety of units called *fractional page space* (for example, vertical half-page, horizontal half-page, double horizontal half-page, half-page double spread, and checkerboard).

---

[25]Adrienne Ward, "Plugging Along," *Advertising Age* (October 6, 1991):S–1.

THE ADVANTAGES OF MAGAZINES

The benefits of magazine advertising include the ability to reach specialized audiences, audience receptivity, a long life span, visual quality, and the distribution of sales promotion devices.

Target Audiences. The overriding advantage of magazines in the 1940s and 1950s was their ability to reach a wide, general audience. This is no longer true. As noted, the greatest areas of growth are expected to be in special-interest magazines and special editions of existing publications. The ability to reach specialized audiences has become a primary advantage. For example, a set of magazines published by the Hearst Corporation is referred to as the Seven Sisters and is clearly targeted to contemporary American women. These seven include *Better Homes and Gardens, Ladies' Home Journal, Family Circle, Redbook, Woman's Day, McCalls,* and *Good Housekeeping.*

Audience Receptivity. The second advantage of magazines is their high level of audience receptivity. The editorial environment of a magazine lends authority and credibility to the advertising. Many magazines claim that advertising in their publication gives a product prestige. Clearly an ad in *Fortune* would impress business audiences, just as an ad in *Seventeen* would impress teenagers.

Long Life Span. Magazines have the longest life span of all the media. Some magazines, such as *National Geographic* or *Consumer Reports*, are used as ongoing references and might never be discarded. Other publications, such as *TV Guide*, are intended to be used frequently during a given period of time. In addition, magazines have very high reach potential because of a large *pass-along*, or secondary, audience of family, friends, customers, and colleagues.

Finally, people tend to read magazines at a relatively slow rate, typically over a couple of days. Therefore, magazines offer an opportunity to use long copy. The magazine format also allows more creative variety through multiple pages, inserts, and other features.

Visual Quality. The visual quality of magazines tend to be excellent because they are printed on high-quality paper stock that provides superior photo reproduction in both black and white and color. This production quality often reflects the superior editorial content. Feature stories are frequently written by well-respected writers.

Sales Promotions. Magazines are an effective medium through which to distribute various sales promotion devices, such as coupons, product samples, and information cards. A 1987 Post Office ruling allowed magazines to carry loose editorial and advertising supplements as part of the publication provided the magazine is enclosed in an envelope or wrapper[26] Ad 10.3 illustrates a sales promotion in a magazine.

THE DISADVANTAGES OF MAGAZINES

Magazines are limited by certain factors. The most prominent disadvantages are limited flexibility, high cost, and difficult distribution.

---

[26]DDB Needham, *Media Trends* (1987):55.

Introducing Prego Frozen Italian Entrees.

Prego™

Homemade taste. It's in there!™

Limited Flexibility Although magazines offer many benefits to advertisers, long lead time and lack of flexibility and immediacy are two of their drawbacks. Ads must be submitted well in advance of the publication date. For example, advertisers must have engravings for full-color advertisements at the printer more than two months before the cover date of a monthly publication. As noted earlier, however, magazines that have adopted desktop publishing and satellite transmission are able to avoid this limitation and can close just hours before presstime. Magazines are also inflexible in respect to available positions. Prime locations, such as the back cover or inside front cover, may be sold months in advance. Some readers do not look at an issue of a magazine until long after it has reached their homes; therefore, impact builds slowly.

High Cost. The second disadvantage associated with magazines is their relatively high cost. In 1993 the cost for a full-page four-color ad in *Newsweek* magazine's national edition was $120,835. For a general-audience magazine such as *Newsweek*, the cost per thousand (CPM) is quite high, and magazines of this type do not compare favorably with other media on this score. However, magazines with carefully segmented audiences, such as *Byte*, can be very cost-efficient because a tightly targeted audience is more expensive to reach than a mass audience.

Distribution. The final disadvantage associated with magazines is the difficulty of distribution. Many magazines, such as *Woman's Day* and *People*, are purchased primarily through newsstands. Yet there is no way that 2,500 different magazines can all appear on store racks. Some magazines are simply not available to all members of all possible target audiences.

Summary

- Print media are static and visual. They are superior to broadcast media in respectability, permanence, and credibility.

- Newspapers, which are still the leading local medium, have improved their technology owing to increased competition from broadcast and direct mail, but they are diminishing in number.

- The structure of newspapers is determined by frequency of publication, size, and circulation.

- Newspaper readers encompass all income brackets, educational levels, age groups, and ethnic backgrounds. However, readership varies by gender, age, and interests.

- Newspaper audiences are measured through two independent agencies: The Audit Bureau of Circulation (ABC) and Simmons-Scarborough.

- There are three general types of newspaper advertising: classified, display, and supplements.

- The greatest advantage of advertising in newspapers is extensive market coverage. The biggest disadvantages are a short life span, clutter, and poor reproduction.

- Magazines have the greatest ability to reach preselected or tightly targeted audiences. This selectivity is exhibited through the elaborate structure found in the industry.

- Magazines are categorized by audience, geography, demographics, and editorial content.

- Approximately 92 percent of all adults read at least one magazine per month. There are several other features that characterize magazine readers as well.

- Magazine readership is measured by the ABC, Simmons Market Research Bureau (SMRB), and MediaMark.

- Advertising in magazines does have drawbacks, including limited flexibility, high costs, and difficult distribution.

Questions

1. Discuss the various characteristics of newspaper readers. What are the implications for an advertiser considering newspapers?

2. You are the head media planner for a small chain of upscale furniture outlets in a top 50 market that concentrates most of its advertising in the Sunday magazine supplement of the local newspaper. The client also schedules display ads in the daily editions for special sales. Six months ago a new high-style, metropolitan magazine approached you about advertising for your client. You deferred a decision by saying you'd see what reader acceptance would be. Now the magazine has shown some steady increases (its circulation is now about one quarter of the newspaper's). If you were to include the magazine on the ad schedule, you'd have to reduce the newspaper linage. What would be your recommendations to the furniture store?

3. Many magazines have editorial environments that are well suited to certain products and services (home service, entertainment, sports, recreation, and financial magazines). Compatibility between the advertising and the reader's editorial interest is a plus. However, editorial "compatibility" will attract your competitors' ads too. Would having a number of competitors' ads in an issue where your ad appeared cause you to

consider less compatible publications? Explain your reasons.

4 Discuss the advantages and disadvantages of advertising in newspapers and magazines from the viewpoint of the advertising directed for GE small appliances.

5 Peter Wilcox, a display salesman for the *Daily Globe*, thought he had heard all the possible excuses for not buying newspaper space until he called on the manager of a compact disc store that sold new and preowned discs. "I've heard about newspaper reader studies that prove how wrong the audience is for me. Readership is too adult—mostly above 35 years of age," he said. "And besides, readers of newspapers are families with higher incomes—the wrong market for our used disc business," he continued. If the Globe is a typical metropolitan daily, could the store manager be correct? In any event, how should Wilcox try to counter the manager's views?

6 A terrific debate is going on in Professor Morrison's retail advertising class. The question is: "Why do national advertisers refuse to seriously consider newspapers in media plans?" The advertising manager for a home products company argues that despite newspaper's creative limitations, more firms would buy newspaper space if the medium did not practice rate discrimination against national companies. The sales manager for a small chain of newspapers admits the price difference, but says it is justified by the extra attention, and commissions (sales rep and agency) newspapers have to pay for each national order. The sales manager also claims the price issue is a "smokescreen" for advertisers to hide their continuing "love affair" with television. Which position would you accept? Is price difference an issue large enough to restrict marketer's interest? How does cooperative advertising figure into the debate?

$\mathscr{S}$UGGESTED CLASS PROJECT

Contact a medium-to-large newspaper and magazine. Think of yourself as a potential advertiser. What do you need to know? Collect all the relevant information and services provided to advertisers. Ask as many questions as you need to. Compare the types of information and services available. Was the customer service helpful? Is this the right choice of media for your "company"? Analyze the results in a brief report: begin by stating your product and your advertising goals; then state what you might or might not accomplish by advertising in the publication. Make a decision.

$\mathscr{F}$URTHER READING

ALSON, AMY, "The Search for National Ad Dollars," *Marketing & Media Decisions* (February 1989): 29–30.

ANGELO, JEAN MARIE, "One Out of Four Mags Goes Off Rate Card," *Inside Print* (December 1988):21.

DAMIANO, STEVE, "For Women, Business and Pleasure," *Marketing & Media Decisions* (April 1990):14.

HUHN, MARY, "Breaking the Black-and-White Habit," *Adweek Special Report—1988* (April 26, 1988):27.

MATOVELLI, JOHN, "Toward an Age of Customized Magazines," *Adweek Special Report—Magazine World 1989* (February 13, 1989):36–37.

PERRY, DAVID, "Performance Advertisers Practice What They Preach," *Business Marketing* (March 1988):86

STRAUSS, STEVE, *Moving Images: The Transportation Poster in America* (New York: Fullcourt Press, 1984).

Video Case

Infomercials

With the advent of numerous alternatives to traditional network television programming, such as cable, television stations across the country have been forced to use less orthodox techniques to generate acceptable revenues. One of the most notable examples of this trend is the increased use of "infomercials."

Infomercials are, in theory, informational videos featuring and sponsored by branded products or services. For example, Clorox produced an infomercial in the mid-1980s, which showed how its cleaning products could be used to clean up smoke damage after a fire. Originally conceived by advertisers as an acceptable way to slip product messages into a commercial-free environment of public television, infomercials have evolved to the point where they are now often merely 30- to 60-minute ads for products. However, for those viewers who tune in late or slip out of the room during the brief disclaimer that differentiates infomercials from true entertainment-based programming, infomercials can be mistaken for "normal" programs. Whether because of this confusion or because of the inherent effectiveness of infomercials as a marketing technique, they have been extremely successful.

Unfortunately for the unwary consumer, infomercials lack even the types of cursory guidelines and regulations that limit traditional advertising's use of false or deceptive claims. Nonetheless, the advertising community has thus far failed to single out infomercials for increased regulation.

Independent and network television also stand to lose in the long run if infomercials continue to proliferate. Just as advertisers fear that infomercials that make false claims could damage the credibility of advertising as a whole, television station owners must address the issue of whether infomercials that look like entertainment-based programming could damage the credibility of their regular programs. Television stations can profit from this type of advertising, however, because they can simply sell the entire 30- to 60-minute time period in which the infomercial runs to the infomercial producers rather than buying regular programming and trying to sell commercial space. Although this has obvious short-term benefits, if the credibility and authenticity of regular entertainment-based programming is questioned by the public, viewership will drop as will the price that stations can charge for commercial time.

The issue is more complex for advertisers. Anything that negatively affects the credibility of advertising can jeopardize that technique's long-term ability to sell products. However, the competitive nature of most industries is such that any new marketing tool that has proven itself effective cannot be summarily dismissed.

The infomercial format is well adapted for direct address to small market segments. Managers of vacation destinations, and marketers of automobiles and exercise equipment—among others—have found that videotaped infomercials mailed directly to prospective purchasers is an especially effective communication medium. In some cases prospective purchasers identify themselves by calling an 800 number or mailing a coupon for more information. In other cases marketers identify prospects from lists of previous purchasers, or lists of owners of related products.

Once the marketer has identified prime prospects, the marketer can develop an infomercial designed to appeal especially to that segment and can mail the videotape directly to members of the intended audience. Infomercials on videotape have all the motion and sound advantages of infomercials on television. In addition, consumers who receive videotapes pay closer attention to them than they do to infomercials on television, and many consumers who receive tapes give or lend them to others who have similar interests.

Although most consumers who receive infomercials on videotape find them interesting and useful, this method of communication is especially open to abuse, largely because the standing government and industry regulations that police truth in advertising are difficult to enforce. Thus, as infomercials on videotape become more common, advertisers can expect to be required to comply with new forms of regulation.

Source: "It's Really a Commercial," *20/20* (September 18, 1990).

Questions

1. Explain how infomercials can actually be good for consumers.

2. As advertising costs have increased, advertisers have responded by producing shorter and shorter commercials. Given this trend, how can infomercials actually benefit advertisers?

3. a. Explain how and why infomercials should be regulated.
   b. Explain why infomercials should not be regulated.

357

BROADCAST MEDIA

CHAPTER OBJECTIVES

When you have completed this chapter, you should be able to:

- Understand the basic nature of both radio and television

- Describe the audience for each medium and explain how that audience is measured

- List the advantages and disadvantages of using radio and television commercials

So Long to Television

As competition tightens, distribution changes, and pricing strategies shift, watch for marketers to take a different approach to auto advertising. That was the message delivered by Graham Phillips, Ogilvy & Mather vice chairman. Automobile design is already far too indistinguishable from one model to the next. Quality has become the price of entry, and soon there will be supermarkets where competing nameplates sit side by side on the showroom floor like so many stereos at Circuit City.

With that kind of parity, marketers must find ways to deliver complex information that won't fit in a 30-second commercial. "Advertising is probably seen as less important today by clients that it was some years ago," Phillips noted. What will lure customers will depend more on issues like after-sales service and the ownership experience. Even price, with the advent of the no-dicker sticker and leasing, which Phillips said will soon extend to all models, will become less critical in the mix. Lease arrangements with an emphasis on monthly payments will lessen the importance of price as a purchase factor.

With car marketers more dependent than ever on existing customers, Phillips expects a greater focus on direct-marketing programs and building databases to support those efforts. Keeping customers loyal to an automobile brand when they reenter the marketplace will become critical to success. Car buyers rate television and print advertisements much lower as a source of information than information supplied by factory brochures or even information dealers deliver verbally, according to Phillips. That means marketers will need to find ways to deliver brochures before the customer even gets to the automobile showroom. Already automobile brands including Acura, Infiniti, and Volvo have begun mailing product brochures to targeted lists of potential car customers.

Should this trend away from television continue, the consequences to this medium would be dire. Perhaps some of the technological changes discussed in this chapter will once again unite television and the automobile.[1]

Broadcast media, the process of transmitting sounds or images, includes both radio and television. Advertising experts contend that creating commercials for broadcast media is quite different from creating advertisements for print media. Certainly broadcast media tap into different human senses: sight (through movement and imagery) and sound.

Print is a *space* medium that allows the reader to digest information and images at his or her own speed. Broadcast is a *time* medium that affects the viewer's emotions for a few seconds and then disappears.

Chapter 10 introduced print media and its place in advertising. This chapter will explore broadcast media. The overview contained in these chapters will provide the necessary background for Chapter 12, Media Buying.

---

[1]Adapted from Shelly Garcia, "Auto Advertising Is Shifting Gears," *Adweek* (February 22, 1993):2.

$\mathcal{T}$HE STRUCTURE OF TELEVISION

A great deal of change has taken place in the technical aspects of television. As a result, several different types of television systems are now available to advertisers for delivery of their messages to audiences.

WIRED NETWORK TELEVISION

Whenever two or more stations are able to broadcast the same program, which originates from a single source, a network exists. Networks can be "over-the-air" or cable.

Currently there are four national over-the-air television networks—the American Broadcasting Company (ABC), the Columbia Broadcasting System (CBS), the National Broadcasting Company (NBC), and Fox Broadcasting Company. The first three own 15 regional stations, and the remaining 600 regional stations are privately owned **affiliates** (each network has about 200 affiliates). An affiliate station signs a contract with the national network (ABC, CBS, NBC, or Fox) whereby it agrees to carry network-originated programming during a certain part of its schedule. For example, WDIV-TV is NBC's Detroit affiliate. These major networks originate their own programs and are compensated at a rate of 30 percent of the fee charged for programs in a local market. In turn, affiliates receive a percentage of the advertising revenue (12 to 25 percent) paid to the national network and have the option to sell some advertising time during network programs and between programs. This is the primary source of affiliate revenues.

In over-the-air *network scheduling* the advertiser contracts with either a national or a regional network to show commercials on a number of affiliated stations. Sometimes an advertiser purchases only a portion of the network coverage, known as a *regional leg*. This is common with sports programming where different games are shown in different parts of the country.

UNWIRED NETWORK TELEVISION

In contrast to the wired networks like ABC, NBC, CBS, and Fox, which do business directly with their affiliates in terms of programming, the unwired network station has nothing to do with programming and everything to do with advertising sales. Unwired networks are basically sales representative organizations that represent large market stations on a commission basis (15 percent). They simplify the buying process for the agency by designating one person at a network to handle the total buy. They also assist the client in media planning.[2]

PUBLIC TELEVISION: THE FIFTH NETWORK

Although many people still consider public television to be "commercial free," in 1984 the Federal Communications Commission (FCC) liberalized the rules,

affiliate A station that is contracted with a national network to carry network-originated programming during part of its schedule.

---

[2]Cara S. Trager, "Unwired Networks Work to Unplug Rivals' Shares," *Advertising Age* (April 14, 1986): S-8.

allowing the 341 PBS stations to interpret the line between underwriting and outright sponsorship that once seemed so absolute. The FCC says messages should not make a call to action or make price or quality comparisons. Public television lobbied for advertising to compensate for the cutback in federal funding that first occurred during the Nixon administration and to compete more effectively with cable television. PBS is an attractive medium for advertisers because it attracts a large upscale audience and because it adopted a much more consistent programming schedule beginning in the 1980s.

Current FCC guidelines allow ads to appear on public television only during the local 2.5-minute program breaks. Each station maintains its own acceptability guidelines. Some PBS stations accept the same ads that appear on paid programming. A DeBeers Diamonds ad, showing a man presenting a diamond anniversary band to his wife, ran a lengthy schedule on eight public stations, including WLIW KERA in Dallas and WTTW in Chicago. Most of the spots that run on public television, however, are created specifically for public stations.[3]

Other PBS stations will not accept any commercial corporate advertising, only noncommercial ads that are "value-neutral." Such messages may include nonpromotional corporate and product logos and slogans, business locations and telephone numbers that are not used for direct-response selling, and brand names, service marks, and logos. In other words, there is no attempt to "sell" anything through these ads. Sponsors of PBS programming usually also are advertisers, but in a quite subtle fashion. For example, the Chubb Group of Insurance Companies, which spends more than $1 million to underwrite *American Playhouse,* chooses to simply show their name and the statement, "Brought to you by the Chubb Group of Insurance Companies."

In sum, PBS reaches affluent, educated households as well as minority and lower-end consumers. According to Nielsen data, during a typical week, 54 percent of U.S. households tune in to PBS sometime during the day. In addition, PBS still has a refined image and advertisers are viewed as good corporate citizens.[4]

CABLE AND SUBSCRIPTION TELEVISION

cable television A form of subscription television in which the signals are carried to households by a cable.

The initial purpose of **cable television** was to improve reception in certain areas of the country, particularly mountainous regions and large cities. However, alternative programming, with an emphasis on entertainment and information, has been primarily responsible for the rapid growth of cable systems.

According to the Cable Advertising Bureau (CAB), cable network ad revenues were $230 million in 1982. By the end of 1992 they reached $3.6 billion, and are expected to be $5.2 billion by the end of 1995. Cable penetration reached 65 percent in 1992 and is expected to climb to 70 percent by 1994, and to 90 percent by the year 2000.[5] Table 11.1 lists the top cable network advertisers in 1992.

Some of these cable systems develop and air their own programs as well as pass along programs initiated by VHF stations, the 12 channels (2-13) located on the very high frequency band on the wavelength spectrum, or UHF (ultra-high frequency) stations, such as WTBS. "Pay programming" is an option avail-

---

[3]Keith Dunnawant, "PBS: Dynamo or Dinosaur?," *Adweek* (February 24, 1992):18–26.
[4]Carrie Goerne, "Funding Losses, Competition Force PBS to Pitch Itself as a Marketing Company," *Marketing News* (May 11, 1992):1, 16.
[5]Carrie Goerne, "Some See Cable TV Law as Threat to Ad Growth," *Marketing News* (November 9, 1992):1–2.

Table 11.1

Top 25 Cable Television Network
Advertisers

Rank	Advertiser	1992	1991	%chg
1	Procter & Gamble Co.	$112.0	$67.8	65.2
2	General Motors Corp.	41.9	32.4	29.6
3	Anheuser-Busch Cos.	37.7	31.4	19.9
4	Philip Morris Cos.	36.9	25.0	47.8
5	General Mills	33.5	31.8	5.2
6	Hasbro	29.6	15.6	90.5
7	American Home Products Corp.	25.8	19.1	35.0
8	AT&T Co.	25.0	19.3	29.4
9	Mars Inc.	21.9	16.6	32.3
10	Eastman Kodak Co.	21.7	19.1	13.5
11	McDonald's Corp.	20.3	16.2	25.3
12	Sears, Roebuck & Co.	19.7	20.3	−3.3
13	Chrysler Corp.	19.3	13.4	44.5
14	Time Warner	18.4	29.3	−37.0
15	Kellogg Co.	17.7	9.5	85.9
16	PepsiCo	16.9	15.1	11.7
17	Levi Strauss & Co.	16.1	12.5	29.3
18	Grand Metropolitan	15.8	11.6	36.0
19	Wm. Wrigley Jr. Co.	15.1	13.9	8.7
20	Clorox Co.	14.8	9.0	65.0
21	Nestle SA	13.9	10.4	34.0
22	Ford Motor Co.	13.4	14.0	−4.3
23	Nintendo Co.	13.1	8.9	46.8
24	American Express Co.	12.9	5.5	134.9
25	Ralston Purina Co.	12.8	10.7	19.6

Note: Dollars are in millions.
Reprinted with permission from Advertising Age (September 29, 1993):50. Copyright, Crain Communications, Inc., 1993.

able to subscribers for an additional monthly fee. Pay programming normally consists of movies, specials, and sports under such plans as Home Box Office, Showtime, and The Movie Channel. In 1990, 12 million American homes were wired for pay cable.[6] Pay networks do not currently sell advertising time. Homes that do not subscribe to cable may purchase "subscription television" that is broadcast over the air with an electronically scrambled signal. Subscribers own a device that unscrambles the signal.

Origins of Cable Programs. Most of the programming shown on cable television is provided by independent cable networks such as Cable News Network (CNN). the Disney Channel, the Nashville Network, Music Television (MTV), the Entertainment and Sports Programming Network (ESPN), and a group of independent superstations whose programs are carried by satellite to cable operators (for example, WTBS-ATLANTA, WGN-CHICAGO, and WWOR-NEW YORK). Although approximately 80 percent of cable programming is provided through these systems, the cable operators themselves are originating more of their own programs.

[6]Sarah Polster, "Cable Gains 17.9%: Growth Pace Slows, Pay Cable Is Struggling." *Advertising Age* (June 25, 1990):36.

Cable Scheduling. *Cable scheduling* is divided into two categories: network and local. The system is the same as for the noncable systems. Network cable systems show commercials across the entire subscriber group simultaneously. Local advertisers are able to show their commercials to highly restricted geographic audiences through **interconnects,** a special cable technology that allows local or regional advertisers to run their commercials in small geographical areas through the interconnection of a number of cable systems. Interconnects are either "hard," in which different ads are distributed electronically by cable or microwave, or "soft," in which the same commercials are simply scheduled at the same time. Either way, they offer small advertisers an affordable way to reach certain local audiences through television.

Mergers. Once considered a high-risk industry with little potential for profit, the cable industry is now in the maturity stage of its life cycle. Even small cable operations have been quite profitable, and it is apparent that cable television is here to stay. Even though the cable industry is still quite fragmented (see Figure 11.1), there is evidence that recent mergers and acquisitions will change this configuration by the year 2000. In essence, the battle is between the $183 billion telecommunications industry and the $20 billion cable industry. The battleground is the emerging technology: the next generation of televisions will be digital. Digitization—the transfer of analog pictures, text, and video into a series of ones and zeros—will allow information to flow into households just like electricity does today. As a result, tomorrow's viewers will see only what they want to see.

The question then becomes which industry, telecommunications or cable, is better able to deliver this new technology. The best alternative appears to be coaxial cable which is already used by cable television providers. Coaxial cable can carry much more information than the copper wires used by most telephone systems.

Undoubtedly the premier player in this battle to date is John Malone, CEO of Tele-Communications Inc., the largest cable system. Currently, TCI has a 25

interconects A special cable technology that allows local advertisers to run their commercials in small geographical areas through the interconnection of a number of cable systems.

Figure 11.1

The cable industry is highly fragmented.

(Source: Adapted from Andrew Kupper, "The No. 1 in Cable TV Has Big Plans," Fortune, June 28, 1993:97.)

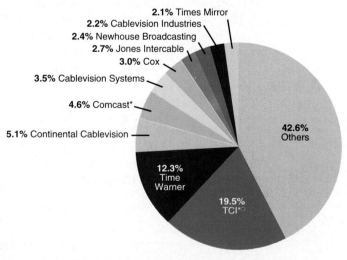

Share of Subscriber Households

2.1% Times Mirror
2.2% Cablevision Industries
2.4% Newhouse Broadcasting
2.7% Jones Intercable
3.0% Cox
3.5% Cablevision Systems
4.6% Comcast*
5.1% Continental Cablevision
12.3% Time Warner
19.5% TCI*
42.6% Others

* TCI and Comcast recently purchased by Storer Communications Cable Systems.

percent stake in TBS and CNN as well as 49 percent of the Discovery Channel. He has invested $2 billion in fiber-optic cable and other new technologies that have added hundreds of channels to his cable system to let viewers watch movies whenever they wish. He also has joint ventures with QVC home shopping network, Rupert Murdoch's News Corp., Caroles Films, CAA, AT&T, McCaw Cable, and Microsoft.[7]

Cable seems to be partly responsible for a downward trend in the share ratings of the three major networks. In November 1990 the total network share for the Big Three was 63, down from 67 in 1989, 69 in 1988, and 71 in 1987. Various other factors have contributed to the Big Three's decline in viewership, including the spread of the direct-broadcasting satellite business and the growth of the Fox Television Broadcasting Network. It is changes in the cable industry, however, that have been largely responsible for the decrease in network shares. Although some people maintain that the higher caliber of network programming will allow the networks to stay well ahead of cable, the networks need to be wary of federal changes in cable regulation and the increasing growth of the cable industry.

Some experts argue that cable's rise is certain to slow dramatically. Competition from new channels, fragmentation of the existing audience, a wave of new technology, and the threat of unfriendly legislation will all test cable's mettle over the next several years. Some of the difficulties cable faces are the industry's own making. For instance, video compression and fiber optics will enable cable systems to offer more channels and subject national cable networks to greater competition from within. A study by the brokerage firm Moran & Associates says 90 percent of all cable subscribers will have an average of 75 channels by 1997. The leading edge of that growth is already here. Time Warner Inc. is testing a 150-channel system in Queens, NY, and phone companies U S West and AT&T are trying out pay-per-view systems that will allow customers to choose from a vast array of movies at any time.[8] Another issue facing the cable industry is customer pirating. (See Issues and Controversy box.)

LOCAL TELEVISION

Local television stations are affiliated with a network and carry both network programming and their own programs. Costs for local advertising differ, depending on the size of the market and the demand for the programs carried. For example, KHIO in Houston charges local advertisers $1,950 for a 30-second spot during prime time. This same time slot may cost $150 in a small town.

The local television market is substantially more varied than the national market. Most advertisers are local retailers, primarily department stores or discount stores, financial institutions, automobile dealers, restaurants, and supermarkets. Advertisers must buy time on a station-by-station basis. Although this arrangement makes sense for a local retailer, it is not an efficient strategy for a national or regional advertiser, who would have to deal individually with a large number of stations.

SPECIALTY TELEVISION

Several alternative delivery systems have appeared recently. These systems attempt to reach certain audiences with television messages in a way that is more

Principle

Network advertising schedules are dominated by large national advertisers.

---

[7]Andrew Erdman, "The No. 1 in Cable TV Has Big Plans," *Fortune* (June 28, 1993):92–98.
[8]Stephen Battaglio, "The Rise and Fall," *Adweek* (April 6, 1992):10–16.

Pirates: Alive and Well

When fight fans in Maryland tuned in to the much-touted pay-per-view match between Mike Tyson and Razor Ruddock, hundreds of viewers were sucker-punched at the opening bell. That's when the picture on their screens went wavy. The local cable system had suddenly scrambled signals in a way that obliterated the picture on television sets that had illegal converter boxes.

In the first hour, the cable company received more than 200 complaints from disgruntled viewers—all of whom had expected to get the event without paying for it. A day later scores more called. When pressed for answers about their service, most hung up.

But it was only brief relief for a company that loses $12 million a year in pirated pay services. And this cable system is not the only one hurting. Federal investigators have uncovered a number of illegal cable distributors whose vast networks display an unprecedented sophistication and financial scope. The illegal distributors sell from warehouses instead of car trunks now, and national advertising, direct-mail campaigns, and 800 numbers have helped them build multimillion-dollar operations. They even accept credit cards. In a recent raid in New York, investigators seized 50,000 illegal decoders from a company with an estimated $10 million in annual revenue.

"Cable piracy is pervasive, it's growing and there is no quick cure for the problem," says Jim Allen, director of the National Cable Television Associations's cable theft office. Cable system operators argue that the same people who steal cable would never dream of walking into a 7-Eleven and swiping a Twinkie. "People don't think stealing cable is a real crime. They don't take it seriously," says Kent Walker, an assistant U.S. attorney in California who is negotiating a plea bargain with a distributor who was arrested with 40,000 illegal descramblers.

Revenue lost from cable theft—or piracy as the industry likes to call it—has doubled in five years to more than $3 billion, according to the National Cable Television Association. Cable piracy is particularly painful for the industry now because the torrid growth of years past is all but over. The electronic theft is especially damaging to the pay-television business. Most pirates subscribe to the cheapest cable service and buy illegal decoders to heist monthly pay services costing $30 to $70 a month.

Cable operators are struggling to fight back, doggedly pursuing pirates with private detectives, amnesty programs, ad campaigns, and new high-tech countermeasures. With the aid of new scrambling, or "encryption," technology some cable operators are firing "electronic bullets" into pirates' homes—streams of data that render the illegal descramblers useless—but the research is still costly and requires sophisticated equipment. Cable systems are also pursuing criminal convictions and are increasingly squeezing distributors and pirates in civil court.

Source: Adapted from Mark Roluchaux, "Cable TV Pirates Become More Brazen, Forcing Industry to Seek New Remedies," *The Wall Street Journal* (May 7, 1992):B1, B8.

effective or efficient than network, cable, or local television. For example, low-power television (LPTV) was licensed by the FCC to provide television outlets to minorities and communities that are underserved by full-power stations or have signals that cover a radius of 15 miles, as opposed to full-power stations, whose signals can reach viewers in a 70-mile radius. The system can be picked up by homes through personal antennas and carries advertising for local retailers and businesses. Multipoint distribution systems (MDS) and subscription television (STV) both deliver limited programming without incurring the cost of cable installation. The former is used by hotels and restaurants to give guests access to special movies and other entertainment. The latter offers one-channel capabilities of pay-cable-type programming transmitted to individual homes through a signal decoder. Advertisers who use STV typically sell products related to the audience watching the STV program. All these specialty systems can carry advertisements.

INTERACTIVE TELEVISION

After several false starts, interactive television may finally come of age by the end of the 1990s. *Interactivity* or *viewer control* can take one of three forms. The first type is video-on-demand (VOD), where viewers control what and when they watch. Pay-per-view (PPV) is a limited version of VOD that allows viewers to choose programs at predetermined two-hour intervals. The second type of interactivity is a system that stores information at the television set and allows viewers to choose programs with a box in the home, in much the same way VCRs and videotapes function today. The third type of interactivity is the *simulcast,* which transmits digital information in conjunction with an actual broadcast. Simulcast viewers can control the programming itself. By punching in their choices on a keypad, viewers can second-guess NFL quarterbacks or order more information during a documentary.[9]

An example of interactive television is Interactive MTV. If someone is watching Interactive MTV, he or she can use the remote control to see the lyrics of the video playing on the screen, change the camera angle, or even buy the album directly through the television set. Interactive viewers can also "talk back" to MTV by voting on what videos they like and dislike, or entering promotional contests.[10]

As for the implications for advertising, according to McCann-Erickson's media director Gordon Link, "It doesn't take a brain surgeon to realize that interactive television systems are going to change advertising. The world we are going into will establish new relationships between the marketer, the consumer, and the media."[11]

TELEVISION SYNDICATION

syndication Television or radio shows that are reruns or original programs purchased by local stations to fill in during open hours.

The **syndication** boom has been fueled mainly by the growth of independent stations that require programming. Syndicated shows are television or radio programs that are purchased by local stations to fill in open hours. Today both networks and independents have been forced to bid on these shows, referred to as *strips* (like a comic strip, a syndicated strip is a show that appears daily at the same time) to fill the many open hours in the morning, late afternoon, early evening, and late night. This open time is the result of the prime-time access rule (PTAR), which forbids network affiliates in the 50 major U.S. television markets from broadcasting more than three hours of prime-time programming in any one four-hour slot.

Every winter hundreds of station directors attend the National Association of Television Program Executives (NATPE) meeting in order to bid on the many shows available for syndication. The top five syndicated shows in 1992 were *Wheel of Fortune, Star Trek, Jeopardy, Oprah Winfrey,* and *Entertainment Tonight.* The top 25 syndicated advertisers are listed in Table 11.2.

Off-Network Syndication. There are two primary types of syndicated programming. The first is *off-network syndication,* which includes reruns of network shows. Examples are *M*A*S*H, The Bob Newhart Show, Star Trek,* and *Remington*

---

[9]Rebecca Piirto, "Taming the TV Beast," *American Demographics* (May 1993):34–40.
[10]Carrie Goerne, "Interactive Channel Among MTV's Plans to Reach Narrower Markets," *Marketing News* (November 9, 1992):6.
[11]John Mandese, "McCann's Bet," *Marketing & Media Decisions* (February 1990):27–29.

Table 11.2

Top 25 Syndicated Television
Advertisers

Rank	Advertiser	1992	1991	%chg
1	Philip Morris Cos.	$133.8	$109.0	22.8
2	Procter & Gamble Co.	94.1	103.6	−9.1
3	Kellogg Co.	52.5	51.5	2.0
4	Unilever	44.1	36.9	19.4
5	Warner-Lambert Co.	28.3	30.3	-6.8
6	Hasbro	27.5	25.3	9.0
7	Mattel	25.1	19.0	32.1
8	Mars Inc.	20.6	24.4	−15.6
9	Wm. Wrigley Jr. Co.	20.5	15.1	35.4
10	Johnson & Johnson	20.1	20.5	−2.2
11	Nestlé SA	19.8	21.4	−7.8
12	Grand Metropolitan	19.4	27.6	−29.5
13	Sears, Roebuck & Co.	18.9	17.9	5.6
14	McDonald's Corp.	18.9	17.7	6.7
15	RJR Nabisco	18.3	20.5	−10.6
16	Hershey Foods Corp.	17.7	12.3	44.5
17	Nintendo Co.	17.4	16.1	8.0
18	Sara Lee Corp.	16.0	8.5	88.0
19	SmithKline Beecham	15.1	12.1	24.6
20	Eastman Kodak Co.	15.0	18.7	−19.8
21	Bristol-Myers Squibb Co.	13.8	11.6	18.7
22	General Motors Corp.	13.5	15.2	−11.6
23	Time Warner	13.1	25.0	−47.4
24	Bayer AG	13.0	13.1	−0.8
25	Quaker Oats Co.	12.0	10.1	19.3

Note: Dollars are in millions.
Reprinted with permission from Advertising Age (September 29, 1993):48. Copyright, Crain Communications, Inc., 1993.

Steele. The FCC imposes several restrictions on such shows. Most important, a network show must produce 65 episodes before it can be syndicated. The prime-time access rule prohibits large network affiliates from airing these shows from 7:30 P.M. to 8:00 P.M. Eastern time. These shows are often used as lead-ins to the local or network news.

The most expensive off-network show to date has been *The Cosby Show,* the most popular program in television history. Syndicator Viacom Enterprises did not have much difficulty selling the show to 174 stations for an estimated $500 million to $600 million for rerun rights covering four years. In return, each station received 11 30-second spots to sell in each episode.

First Run Syndication. Sometimes network shows that did not meet the minimal number of episodes, such as *Too Close for Comfort, It's a Living,* and *What's Happening!!!,* are purchased from the networks and moved into syndication even as they continue to produce new episodes. This is referred to as "first-run" syndication. Such shows are now produced strictly for syndication, an arrangement that allows them to avoid the FCC's primetime access rule. Syndicators also produce their own original shows. Recent examples include *Kung Fu: The Legend Continues* and *Time Trax.* In 1993, 87 syndicated shows were offered. This included 22 new shows, including 13 daily (strip) series.

In negotiating the price a station will pay for a show, the syndicator can deal in cash, barter, or a combination of the two. A cash deal is simple: The syndicator grants the station the right to run a show for a specified period in return for a cash license fee. Cash syndication was once the only, and is still the largest, part of the $3.5 billion syndication industry: Station license fees are estimated at $1.8 billion to $2.0 billion annually. However, it is not growing very fast because stations have been relatively short of cash in recent years.

Beginning about 1980, faced with competition that was driving program prices up and revenues down, stations began paying for programming by giving back to the syndicator a portion of the commercial time in the show instead of cash. The syndicator then sold this time, packaged as national units, to national advertisers. This is the system known as advertiser-supported or *barter syndication.*

Trading programs for commercial time, rather than cash, is not a new idea: It is the way network television has always operated. But because syndicators generally back less commercial time in a show than the networks, the stations have more local time to sell and hence can make more money. For example, a half-hour show in syndication typically carries six commercial minutes. In a "full-barter" deal, the syndicator will give the local station half the time, 3 minutes, to sell to spot advertisers. He will keep the remaining 3 minutes to sell to national advertisers. In a "cash/barter" deal (standard for many daily series), the syndicator takes back a smaller amount of time but charges a cash license fee as well.

There are several problems with bartering. One is that advertisers expect the syndicated show to be sold to enough stations to cover at least 70 percent of the market, with a preferred rate of 80 to 85 percent. New shows often don't reach this level. Also, guaranteed ratings are not always met. Furthermore, because of the tremendous competition, a 2-3 share is not uncommon, meaning the syndicated program is only delivering 2 to 3 percent of the audience watching television during that time period. Finally, contracts with some stations stipulate that the national commercials—the barter spots—must run in the more desirable time slots, even if the show itself no longer is carried in that time period.

Finally, the excessive supply of new shows offered for syndication during the next three to five years may mean that shows such as *The Wonder Years* and *Evening Shade* will not receive the huge cash prices that *Cosby* and *Cheers* once did. Consequently, syndicators will be forced to either accept barter deals or not sell the shows (see Table 11.3). This heavy reliance on barter and old shows may have dire consequences to the syndication industry.[12]

$\mathcal{T}$ELEVISION ADVERTISING

Like television programing, television ads can be aired through a number of different arrangements. Television advertisers can run their commercials through

---

[12]Kevin Goldman, "Sitcom Syndicators are Laughing Less," *The Wall Street Journal* (January 24, 1992):B1.

Table 11.3   Trends in Reruns of Situation Comedies

Sept. '92 Show (Network/ Distributor)	Number Of Stations Buying Show	Sept. '93 Show (Network/ Distributor)	Number Of Stations Buying Show	Sept. '94 Show (Network/ Distribution)	Number Of Stations Buying Show
Dear John (NBC/Paramount)	75	*Coach* (ABC/MCA)	62	*Evening Shade* (CBS/MTM)	—
Designing Women (CBS/Columbia)	175	*Empty Nest* (NBC/Buena Vista)	48	*Fresh Prince of Bel Air* (NBC/Warner Bros.)	—
Murphy Brown (CBS/Warner Bros.)	102	*Doogie Howser, M.D.* (ABC/20th Century Fox)	2	*The Simpsons* (Fox/20th Century Fox)	—
Roseanne (ABC/Viacom)	100	*Family Matters* (ABC/Warner Bros.)	58		
The Wonder Years (ABC/Turner Program- ming Services)	62	*Major Dad* (CBS/MCA)	—		

Source: —"Sitcom Syndicators are Laughing Less," *The Wall Street Journal* (January 29, 1992):B1.

over-the-air network scheduling, local scheduling, cable scheduling, or unwired networks.

FORMS OF TELEVISION ADVERTISING

The actual form of a television commercial varies depending on whether a network, local, or cable schedule is employed (see Figure 11.2). Networks allow either *sponsorships* or *participations,* and local affiliates allow *spot announcements* and *local sponsorships.*

sponsorship An arrangement in which the advertiser produces both a television program and the accompanying commercials.

Sponsorships. In **sponsorships**, which characterized most early television advertising, the advertiser assumes the total financial responsibility for producing the program and providing the accompanying commercials. Examples of early sponsored programs are *Bonanza* (sponsored by Chevrolet), *The Hallmark Hall of Fame,* and *The Kraft Music Hour.* Sponsorship has a powerful impact on the viewing public, especially because the advertiser can control the content and quality of the program as well as the placement and length of commercials. However, the costs of producing and sponsoring a 30- and 60-minute program make this option too expensive for most advertisers today. An alternative is for several advertisers to produce a program jointly. This plan is quite common with sporting events, where each sponsor receives a 15-minute segment.

Although not strictly a sponsorship, *infomercials* have come onto the scene during the last decade and have many of the same characteristics of a sponsorship. More is said about infomercials in the Concepts and Applications box.

participations An arrangement in which a television advertiser buys commercial time from a network.

Participations. Sponsorships represent less than 10 percent of network advertising. The rest is sold as **participations** in which advertisers pay for 15, 30, or 60 seconds of commercial time during one or more programs. The advertiser can buy any time that is available on a regular or irregular basis. This approach not

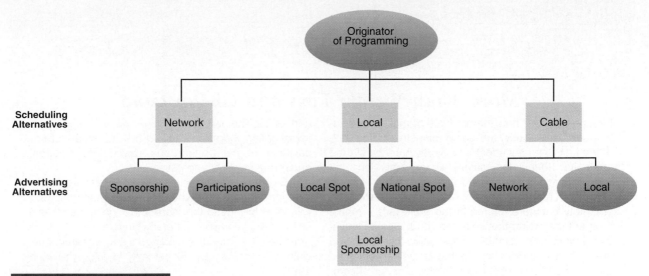

Figure 11.2

This figure illustrates the choices that face a television advertiser.

only reduces the risks and costs associated with sponsorships but also provides a great deal more flexibility in respect to market coverage, target audiences, scheduling, and budgeting. Participations do not create the same high impact as sponsorships, however, and the advertiser does not have any control over the content of the program. Finally, the "time avails" (available time slots) for the most popular programs are often bought up by the largest advertisers, leaving fewer good time slots for the small advertisers. For example, in October 1990 Coca-Cola Company and General Mills, Inc., each agreed to pay NBC more than $40 million for commercial time on the 1992 Summer Olympics. Coca-Cola's deal was said to be worth between $42 million and $44 million, and General Mill's deal was closer to $40 million. As of late 1990, NBC projected a prime-time average Nielsen rating of 16.9 for advertisers, and the average household cost per thousand worked out to be approximately $17. (Nielsen ratings are discussed in more detail in the next section.) Furthermore, NBC offered its advertisers a 90 percent guarantee on its ratings projections.[13]

spot announcements Ads shown during the breaks between programs.

Principle

Spot buys are dominated by local advertising.

Spot Announcements. The third form a television commercial can take is the **spot announcement**. (Note that the word *spot* is also used in conjunction with a time frame such as a "30-second spot," and this usage should not be confused with spot announcements.) Spot announcements refer to the breaks between programs, which local affiliates sell to advertisers who want to show their ads locally. Commercials of 10, 20, 30, and 60 seconds are sold on a station-by-station basis to local, regional, and national advertisers. The local buyers clearly dominate spot television. The leading advertisers of spot announcements are listed in Table 11.4.

The breaks between programs are not always optimal time slots for advertisers because there is a great deal of clutter from competing commercials, station breaks, public service announcements, and other distractions. Program breaks also tend to be time when viewers take a break from their television sets.

---

[13]John McManus and Wayne Walley, "Coke, GM Plan $40M Deals for NBC's Olympics," *Advertising Age* (October 29, 1990):, 62.

More Than Weight Loss and Cheap Land

Infomercials, until now the province of makers of gadgets and beauty aids, are going mainstream. In 1992, on the first Saturday after Volvo North America started airing its 30-minutes safety infomercials on Los Angeles stations, area Volvo dealers set up 145 test drives from among 800-number callers requesting the car-safety brochure offered in the ad. That's a robust number for a maker that sold only 12,021 cars in all of California in 1991. "Dealers made sales they attributed directly to the infomercials, so they're feeling very good about the ad," said Bob Austin, Volvo director of communications. Because of the success in Los Angeles, the automaker is leaning toward using this format to help introduce its new front wheel drive 850 sports sedan, as well as continuing to air the current safety ads.

As a mainstream advertiser, Volvo's foray into what's euphemistically termed *paid commercial programming* represents something of a watershed in the infomercial business. In 1992, infomercials commanded over $200 million in television placements and sold over $600 million worth of products, mostly in low-cost late-night or early morning slots. Volvo's experiment, according to industry experts, has been widely watched, as is the sales surge of upscale Nordic Trak and Soloflex equipment advertised on infomercials, and appears to be motivating other major corporations to consider long-form ads as an adjunct to mainstream media placements. Among major marketers looking into airing new long-form ads is General Motors' Saturn Division, whose so-called *documercial* about its Spring Hill, Tennessee, plant by ad shop Hal Riney & Partners made a splash when it aired in 1990. Others believed to be looking into infomercials include AT&T

and GTE. The latter telephonic giant is said to be investigating long-form ads to sell its "smart phone" package of call-waiting and forwarding, electronic answering service, and caller ID.

By 1995, media billings for corporate use of the long-form format on prime time and daytime television will equal billings in the more traditional entrepreneurial infomercial market generally aired late at night. It is projected that media spending for traditional infomercials will increase by 20 percent, to $250 million by 1995.

Other mass marketers, however, harbor doubts about the longer paid format. Gerry Perry, national ad manager at Toyota Motor Sales, U.S.A., expressed skepticism about ads that would spoonfeed viewers heavy doses of Toyota data. "That's what our dealers are for," he said, adding that he believes two-way interchanges are more credible than passive, one-sided presentations. Many large advertisers simply don't like the idea of jumping into a marketing arena long dominated by gimmicky products like the Great Wok of China. After making one infomercial in 1992, Club Med has abandoned the format to return to 30-second spots. The failure rate for infomercials is staggeringly high: By some estimates, only one in ten hits the jackpot. Even with plugs from Farrah Fawcett, Hulk Hogan, and Vanna White, a spate of recent infomercials has bombed.

Source: adapted from David J. Jefferson and Thomas R. King, "Infomercials Fill Up Air Time on Cable, Aim for Prime Time," *The Wall Street Journal* (October 22, 1992):A1, A7; Pat Hinsberg, "Infomercials Shift Onto Mainstream Airwaves," *Adweek* (March 30, 1992):2; Elaine Underwood, "Cable's Home Shopping: Too Legit to Quit?" *Adweek* (March 22, 1993):9.

THE TELEVISION AUDIENCE

With an estimated $28 billion in advertising revenues in 1992, television is big business.[14] Television has become a mainstay of American society. Nearly 33 million new television sets were sold in 1988, an all-time record. Thirteen million VCRs were sold in the same year, 300,000 less than the record-setting level of 1987. In 1989, 70 percent of U.S. homes had remote control tuning capabil-

[14]Television Bureau of Advertising, Inc. (New York, 1993).

Table 11.4

Top 25 Spot Television
Advertisers

Rank	Advertiser	1992	1991	%chg
1	Procter & Gamble Co.	$236.4	$283.7	−16.6
2	PepsiCo	223.4	261.4	−14.5
3	General Mills	222.8	201.0	10.8
4	Philip Morris Cos.	185.1	206.8	−10.5
5	Chrysler Corp.	171.6	68.2	151.5
6	Toyota Motor Corp.	151.9	123.9	22.6
7	General Motors Corp.	132.7	109.9	20.7
8	McDonald's Corp.	132.3	149.1	−11.2
9	Ford Motor Co.	120.6	78.9	52.9
10	Nissan Motor Co.	111.7	85.2	31.1
11	Time Warner	98.0	80.8	21.3
12	Anheuser-Busch Cos.	92.2	92.4	−0.3
13	Walt Disney Co.	85.9	71.9	19.6
14	Kellogg Co.	83.0	71.4	16.2
15	American Home Products Corp.	69.6	67.7	2.9
16	Hasbro	64.8	52.5	23.5
17	AT&T Co.	63.9	61.7	3.5
18	Grand Metropolitan	63.3	65.1	−2.8
19	Nestlé SA	59.1	73.6	−19.7
20	American Stores Co.	58.1	56.2	3.3
21	Honda Motor Co.	57.6	35.2	63.9
22	Coca-Cola Co.	57.1	61.6	−7.3
23	Unilever	55.8	84.3	−33.8
24	Imasco	54.1	52.3	3.5
25	Dayton Hudson Corp.	52.1	52.5	−0.8

Note: Dollars are in millions.
Reprinted with permission from Advertising Age (September 29, 1993):46. Copyright, Crain Communications, Inc., 1993.

ity.[15] In 1990 over 82 percent of U.S. households had a television set in the living room, over 65 percent had one in the bedroom, and over 20 percent kept a television in the family room.[16] People gather around the set day after day, night after night, to find a source of entertainment, an escape from reality. This dependency explains why a great number of advertisers consider television their primary medium. What do we really know about how audiences watch television? Are we a generation of zombielike television addicts? Or do we carefully and intelligently select what we watch on television?

A great deal of information describing the characteristics of television viewers has been gathered. For example, the total hours of viewing television per week in 1992 was 41.6 hours for households without cable and 56.2 hours for households with cable.[17] Furthermore, adults spend more time with television than with all other major media combined. Television is also perceived as the source of most news as well as the most credible news source.[18]

---

[15]Alice K. Sylvester, "Controlling Remote," *Marketing & Media Decisions* (February 1990):54.
[16]*Adweek* (November 12, 1990):19.
[17]"Who's Watching Cable?" *Adweek* (April 6, 1992):30.
[18]"The Power of Spot TV," *Advertising Age,* (September 23, 1992):T-15.

The viewers' love-hate relationship with television has also been well documented. In one Gallup study, just 31 percent of adults said they watched too much television in the late 1970s, compared with 42 percent in 1991. Despite their guilt, however, nearly 60 percent say that watching television is a good use of their time. Nearly 40 percent say they would read more books if they didn't have a television set, but 72 percent of the respondents said they don't plan to change their viewing habits.[19] Viewer ambivalence was noted in a *TV Guide* survey as well. Just 37 percent of viewers say they prefer to watch programs in their entirety, 32 percent don't hesitate to change channels during a program, and another 28 percent change channels only during commercials. Yet, one-quarter of Americans say they wouldn't live without television, not even for a million dollars. Another one in five wouldn't give it up for a penny less.[20]

HOW PEOPLE WATCH TELEVISION

Further insights into the question of how people watch television were provided by a five-month study done by Peter Collett, research psychologist at the University of Oxford in England. Collett used a video camera to examine the viewing behavior of 20 families. After studying 400 hours of videotape, Collett concluded that viewers often do anything but view. They read, talk, knit, vacuum, blow-dry their hair, and sometimes fight over the remote control. The study found two major responses to commercials: A large segment (approximately 45 percent) watched less than 10 percent of a given commercial, and another segment (approximately 15 percent) watched more than 90 percent of a spot. Why this disparity? Collett believes it has to do with the following:

- The nature of the commercial, the way in which it is structured, or the nature of the product advertised.
- The makeup of the audience. Some viewers tend not to watch commercials at all; others are "commercial consumers."
- The positioning of commercials: What time of day they run, where spots fall in the commercial break.
- Viewer attention, perhaps related to the presence of others in the room. For example, the more people present, the fewer the commercials that are watched.
- The programming environment. If a break follows a popular, engaging program, viewers spend more time watching the commercial messages.

This study suggests that most people are not true television addicts. Actually, most people seldom give their full attention to the set. These facts must be kept in mind when considering television as an advertising medium.[21]

MEASURING THE TELEVISION AUDIENCE

Many of us have had our favorite television show taken off the air because of "poor ratings." Although we may have had some idea of how these ratings were derived, the "Nielsen family" and the rating process remain a mystery to most people.

Actually, the derivation of television ratings is a relatively simple process. Several independent rating firms periodically sample a portion of the television

[19]Judith Waldrop, "Who's Hooked on TV?" *American Demographics* (August 1991):21.
[20]Claudia Montague, "How Viewers Feel About TV," *American Demographics* (March 1993):18–19.
[21]Mary Connors, "Catching TV Viewers in the Act of Being Themselves," *Adweek* (March 9, 1987):30.

viewing audience, assess the size and characteristics of the audiences watching specific shows, and then make these data available to subscribing companies and agencies, which use them in their media planning. Currently, A.C. Nielsen dominates this industry and provides the most frequently used measure of national and local television audiences. Table 11.5 offers an example of the statistics Nielsen provides.

Nielsen Indexes. Nielsen measures television audiences at two levels: network (Nielsen Television Index, NTI) and spot (Nielsen Station Index, NSI). For local measurement, two measuring devices are used. The most famous is the Nielsen Storage Instantaneous Audimeter, or audimeter for short. The audimeter can record when the set is used and which station it is tuned to, but it cannot identify who is watching the program. Data on who is watching are provided by diaries mailed each week during survey months to sample homes in each of the 211 television markets—that amounts to approximately one million diaries a year.

People Meters Nielsen began to measure not only what is being watched but who is watching in the fall of 1987. People meters provide information on what television shows are being watched, the number of households that are watch-

Table 11.5 — Ratings and Share for Nielsen's Top Programs

Rank	Program	Telecast Date	Network	Duration Minutes	Average Audience (%)	Share	Average Audience (000)
1	M*A*S*H Special	Feb. 28, 1983	CBS	150	60.2	77	50,150
2	Dallas	Nov. 21, 1980	CBS	60	53.3	76	41,470
3	Roots Pt. VIII	Jan. 30, 1977	ABC	115	51.1	71	36,380
4	Super Bowl XVI Game	Jan. 24, 1982	CBS	213	49.1	73	40,020
5	Super Bowl XVII Game	Jan. 30, 1983	NBC	204	48.6	69	40,100
6	XVII Winter Olympics—Wed-2	Feb. 23, 1994	CBS	180	48.5	64	45,690
7	Super Bowl XX Game	Jan. 26, 1986	NBC	231	48.3	70	41,490
8	Gone With The Wind-Pt. 1 (Big Event-Pt 1)	Nov. 7, 1976	NBC	179	47.7	65	33,960
9	Gone With The Wind-Pt. 2 (NBC Mon. Mov.)	Nov. 8, 1976	NBC	119	47.4	64	33,750
10	Super Bowl XII Game	Jan. 15, 1978	CBS	218	47.2	67	34,410
11	Super Bowl XIII Game	Jan. 21, 1979	NBC	230	47.1	74	35,090
12	Bob Hope Christmas Show	Jan. 15, 1970	NBC	90	46.6	64	27,260
13	Super Bowl XVIII Game	Jan. 22, 1984	CBS	218	46.4	71	38,800
13	Super Bowl XIX Game	Jan. 20, 1985	ABC	218	46.4	63	39,390
15	Super Bowl XIV Game	Jan. 20, 1980	CBS	178	46.3	67	35,330
16	ABC Theater (The Day After)	Nov. 20, 1983	ABC	144	46.0	62	38,550
17	Roots Pt. VI	Jan. 28, 1977	ABC	120	45.9	66	32,680
17	The Fugitive	Aug. 29, 1967	ABC	60	45.9	72	25,700
19	Super Bowl XXI Game	Jan. 25, 1987	CBS	206	45.8	66	40,030
20	Roots Pt. V	Jan. 27, 1977	ABC	60	45.7	71	32,540

Note:
— Average Audience % rankings based on NTI Pocketpiece Reports—January 1961 through February 27, 1994.
—Above data represent sponsored programs, telecast on individual networks, i.e., no unsponsored or joint network telecasts are reflected in the above listings.
— Programs under 30 minutes scheduled duration are excluded.
Source: Nielsen Media Research, Copyright 1994. Used with permission.

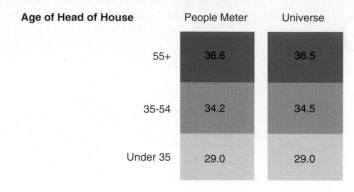

Figure 11.3

A description of the sample characteristics measured by the people meter.

(Source: "Nielsen Putting It All Together," Nielsen Newscast No. 4 [1985]:6. Courtesy of Nielsen Newscast)

Sample Characteristics

Age of Head of House	People Meter	Universe
55+	36.6	36.5
35-54	34.2	34.5
Under 35	29.0	29.0

Education of Head of House

	People Meter	Universe
4+ Years of College	31.3	20.9
1+ Years of College	22.2	16.2
4 Years of High School	30.9	36.0
1+ Years of High School	8.8	12.2
1-8 Years of Grade School	6.9	14.3

ing, and which family members are watching. In the fall of 1987 Nielsen replaced its Audimeter and diary system with *people meters* that provide information on what television shows are being watched, the number of households that are watching, and which family members are viewing. The type of activity is recorded automatically; household members merely have to indicate their presence by pressing a button. People meters have become the primary method for measuring national television audiences. For an illustration of the characteristics of the people-meter subjects, see Figure 11.3.

People meters are quite controversial, however. Criticism of the people meter was heard in the fall of 1990, when ABC, CBS, and NBC all refused to renew their contracts with Nielsen Media Research (ultimately, all three contracts were renewed). The reason was a big unexplained drop in reported television usage during the first quarter of 1990 and the ensuing ratings shortfall that forced the networks to give away an estimated $150-million worth of advertising time to advertisers. The networks blamed Nielsen, alleging faulty methodology in compiling ratings. Nielsen replied that an internal investigation found nothing was amiss with its system, and that the decline in the national ratings was supported by a decline in the local measurements.

ClusterPLUS A. C. Nielsen is always looking for an opportunity to offer their subscribers something extra. Nielsen now provides data for the 47 ClusterPLUS geodemographic groupings developed by Donnelley Marketing Information Services. According to Nielsen, *geodemographic clusters* are distinct types of neighborhoods. Each of the nation's 250,000 census block groups is assigned to one of 47 cluster groups based upon its demographic and socioeconomic makeup. Cluster 1, the Established Wealthy, is composed of the most elite, affluent neighborhoods in places like Greenwich and Beverly Hills. Residents of Cluster 47, Lowest-Income Black Female-Headed Families, live in poverty-stricken areas such as the South Bronx or Watts.

One packaged-goods manufacturer used the ClusterPLUS Nielsen connection to market an ingredient used in baking cakes and cookies. The goal was to buy television commercials only for programs whose audience has a large proportion of consumers who regularly bake from scratch. By merging the ten highest-ranking clusters that fit the audience profile into one target group, the packaged-goods marketer got a detailed look at the product's best prospects. He decided to zero in on older, rural, and blue-collar viewers in the South and Midwest.[22]

Nielsen's audience measurement service covers every television market at least four times each year. These ratings periods, when all 211 markets are surveyed, are known as "sweeps." In all markets Nielsen uses diaries to measure viewing. In 32 markets the service uses both household meters and diaries to measure TV set usage and audience identity.

Nielsen publishes its findings between four and seven times per year in a descriptive format called the Viewers in Profile (VIP) report. A **television market** is an unduplicated geographical area to which a county is assigned on the basis of market size. One county is always placed in just one television market to avoid overlap. Nielsen refers to its television markets in which local stations receive the majority of the viewing hours as Designated Market Areas (DMAs).

television market An unduplicated geographical area to which a county is assigned on the basis of the highest share of the viewing of television stations.

ADVANTAGES AND DISADVANTAGES OF TELEVISION

ADVANTAGES

Advertisers would not invest large sums of money in television commercials unless these ads were effective. The major strength of television that make it appealing as an advertising medium are cost efficiency, impact, and influence.

Cost Efficiency. Many advertisers view television as the most effective way to deliver a commercial message. The major advantage of television is its wide reach. Millions of people watch some television regularly. Television not only reaches a large percentage of the population, it also reaches people who are not effectively reached by print media. For example, NBC's *Today* show would average approximately $18,500 for a 30-second spot, and the household CMP would be $4.50. This mass coverage, in turn, is extremely cost-efficient. For an advertiser attempting to reach an undifferentiated market, a 30-second spot on a top-rated show may cost a penny or less for each person reached.

Principle

Television advertising reaches mass audiences and is very cost-efficient.

Impact. Another advantage of television is the strong impact created by the interaction of sight and sound. This feature induces a level of consumer involvement that often approximates the shopping experience, including encountering

---

[22]Jonathan Marks, "ClusterPLUS Nielsen Equals Efficient Marketing," *American Demographics* (September 1991):16.

a persuasive salesperson. Television also allows a great deal of creative flexibility because of the many possible combinations of sight, sound, color, motion, and drama. Television has tremendous dramatic capacity; it can make mundane products appear important, exciting, and interesting. In other words, television can create a positive association with the sponsor if the advertisement is "likable."

Influence. The final advantage of television is that it has become a primary facet of our culture. For most Americans television is a critical source of news, entertainment, and education. It is so much a part of us that we are more likely to believe companies that advertise on television, especially sponsors of drama and educational programs such as IBM, Xerox, and Hallmark Cards, than we are to believe those that don't. Sometimes this influence comes from a tie-in with a popular celebrity, such as Tommy Lasorda for Ultra Slim-Fast (see Ad 11.1).

DISADVANTAGES

Despite the effectiveness of television advertising, problems do exist, including expense, clutter, nonselective targeting, and inflexibility.

Expense. The most serious limitation of television advertising is the extremely high *absolute* cost of producing and running commercials. Although the cost per person reached is low, the absolute cost can be restrictive, especially for smaller and even mid-sized companies. Production costs include filming the commercial (several hundred to several hundred thousand dollars) and the costs of talent. For celebrities such as Bill Cosby, Bo Jackson, Candice Bergen, and Michael Jordan, the price tag can be millions of dollars (see Ad 11.2). The prices charged for network time are simply a result of supply and demand. Programs that draw

the largest audiences can charge more for their advertising space. A 30-second prime-time spot averages about $185,000. Special shows, such as the Super Bowl, World Series, or Academy Awards, charge much more. Some experts estimate that only 50 U.S. companies can afford a comprehensive television media schedule at these costs. It has been said that television advertising is very cheap if you can afford it. (See Table 11.6)

Clutter. Television suffers from a very high level of commercial clutter. The number of network television commercials increased by 35 percent from 1981 to 1989.[23] In the past, the National Association of Broadcasters (NAB) restricted the amount of allowable commercial time per hour to approximately 6 minutes. In 1982 the Justice Department found this restriction illegal. Although the networks now continue to honor the NAB guidelines, this could change as their needs for revenue increase. The Justice Department ruling could eventually increase the number of 30-second commercials, station-break announcements, credits, and public service announcements, which in turn would diminish the visibility and persuasiveness of television advertising. Although in recent years the growth of the 15-second spot (:15) has been responsible for much of the clutter in television advertising, 1990 marked the beginning of the decline of

---

[23]*Media Trends*, DDB Needham Worldwide (February 1991): 29.

Table 11.6

Most Expensive TV Shows

Program	Cost of 30-Second Spot
Murphy Brown (CBS)	$310,000
Cheers (NBC)	300,000
Roseanne (ABC)	290,000
Coach (ABC)	280,000
Monday Night Football (ABC)	265,000

Source: Reprinted with permission from Advertising Age (September 7, 1992):3. Copyright, Crain Communications, Inc., 1992.

Shiro Kurosai, Radio/Television Department
Nihon Keizai Advertising, Tokyo

Shiro Kurosai is positioned in Nihon Keizai Advertising's Media Headquarters Radio/Television Department and is in charge of television media planning and buying. He is a graduate of Rikkyo University in Tokyo and is in his fifth year at the agency.

8:40 A.M.	As usual, I board the train for the commute to work. I'm not much of a morning person so I listen to music on my Walkman to gradually wake myself up. Of my hobbies, music takes up the greatest part of my attention. And performing on weekends in a rock band with friends from my school days is the thing I enjoy most.
9:30–10:00 A.M.	The first thing to do at work is to look over yesterday's memos and confirm today's schedule. After that I am overrun with calls from each client's account manager. Because most of the workday is spent out of the office, every morning and evening is a constant exchange of phone calls. As this is the time for presentations for the November–December television spot campaigns, we talk briefly about the data that have been gathered. Several of the clients who have already had presentations are scheduled to give a decision this evening. So I relay a progress report to the people in charge at the television stations.
10:00–11:30 A.M.	We hold a meeting with section managers, department manager, and head office manager to examine plans for new television programs to start in April of next year in the commercial broadcast time slots our company presently holds. The program now being shown in that slot is a golf tournament; its reviews are fair, but it is in its seventh year and has lost its central sponsor. There are about 20 possibilities for replacement, and there is hardly time to go through each one's features and problems.
11:30–1:00 P.M.	Mr. Hanamoto, TV Osaka Tokyo Branch's agency sales manager, payed me a visit. After briefly confirming the important areas with regard to a sponsoring client's television publicity during a program scheduled for next week, we go out to a nearby steak house for lunch together. During lunch we avoid discussing business as much as possible and enjoy a light private discussion. A relaxed meal tastes better than a so-called "power lunch."
1:00–1:30 P.M.	Mr. Kabashima, my section chief, Mr. Asakoshi, a client account manager, and I board the subway to head for TV Tokyo. On the subway I run my eyes across several hanging ads for the latest issues of magazines. This is the easiest way to quickly pick up on what the current topics are.
1:30–3:00 P.M.	At TV Tokyo we attended a meeting about a one-time golf program that will be broadcast at the end of

these shorter commercials since their introduction in 1983. Finally, much of the clutter is also a result of the many network and local stations promoting their own programming. The extent of network clutter is illustrated in Table 11.7.

Nonselective Audience. Despite the introduction of various technologies that better target consumers, television remains nonselective. Network television still

the year. Those participating were program producer Mr. Wachi and the directors from Cross TV who will undertake production, Mr. Koseki and Mr. Yamamoto. This program will be recorded on a golf course managed by the main client, a tourist/leisure-related company, and the world renowned golfer Gary Player will be participating. Recording will take place in mid-November, but the broadcast will be at the start of the year-end vacation on December 30, during which time the crucial audience, Japan's businessmen, will most likely be at home glued to their televisions. Meeting time is spent mainly discussing what is to be anticipated on the day of recording. What is decided today will be announced to the client in a presentation next week.

3:00–4:30 P.M.	After the meeting we walk over to TV Tokyo's business section. First we confirm next week's presentation schedule with the manager. By maintaining a cooperative relationship with the television station, as opposed to proceeding independently, we can work with a much higher level of certainty. After we have finished conferring about that program we move on to meet with the spot CM manager's desk. It is also important to exchange information about client trends, and so on, in facing the latest spot CM demand period.
4:30–5:00 P.M.	We board the subway to return to the office.
5:00–5:30 P.M.	I return to my desk and return calls

from the memos that came while I was out. From the information confirmed this morning, two good reports have come in. However, one other decision we had been waiting for was put off until after tomorrow. I immediately put in calls to the television station's respective account managers to inform them of the news.

5:30–6:30 P.M.	An automobile goods manufacturer who has already decided on a television spot campaign has expressed dissatisfaction with the time-slot proposal we had submitted, so the account manager and I meet for a discussion on the matter. If we don't resolve the differences in opinion we have between ourselves, it will be very difficult to convince our client of anything.
6:30–7:30 P.M.	It has been a rigorous day, but now I begin preparing the materials for a presentation to a client tomorrow. The commercial time slots have already been decided on so I neatly put it in chart form on the word processor. I proofread it twice and, as there are no errors, today's work is done!
7:30 P.M.	The other workers who have stayed late too head to a bar nearby, but I get on the train to go home. I pull out my Walkman again and this time listen to the tape my band recorded on the weekend. I've got to practice for next weekend. But this is ultimately a relaxed and enjoyable moment. In either case, it's something I can feel good about—that I accomplished something during a difficult day.

Principle

Television should be used as a primary medium when the objective is to reach a mass audience simultaneously with a visual impact.

attracts about 75 percent of the U.S. audience. Although the networks attempt to profile viewers, their descriptions are quite general, offering the advertiser little assurance that appropriate people are viewing the message. Thus television advertising includes a great deal of *waste coverage*—that is, communication directed at an unresponsive (and often uninterested) audience that may not fit the advertiser's target market characteristics.

Table 11.7

Broadcast Clutter Has Increased in Three of the Four Networks: 1990 to 1991

Network	Commercial Minutes per Prime-Time Hour	
	November 1990	March 1991
ABC	10:14	10:16
CBS	10:46	11:06
NBC	10:40	11:00
FOX	12:23	12:03

Source: "Commercial Clutter Up on Big Three Networks," The New York Times (October 4, 1991):C-1.

Inflexibility. Television also suffers from a lack of flexibility in scheduling. Most network television is bought in the spring and early summer for the next fall season. If an advertiser is unable to make this up-front buy, only limited time-slot alternatives will remain available. Also, it is difficult to make last-minute adjustments in terms of scheduling, copy, or visuals.

THE STRUCTURE OF RADIO

signals A series of electrical impulses that compose radio and television broadcasting.

frequency The number of radio waves produced by a transmitter in 1 second.

Radio can be classified according to transmission and power. The actual range of the station depends on the height of the antenna, the quality of the equipment, and so forth. Radio is a series of electrical impulses called **signals** that are transmitted by *electromagnetic waves*. Radio signals have a height (amplitude) and a width. The width dictates the frequency of the radio signal. A **frequency** is the number of radio waves a transmitter produces each second. The wider the signal, the lower the frequency, and the narrower the wave, the higher the frequency. Frequency is measured in terms of thousands of cycles per second (kilohertz) or millions of cycles per second (megahertz). Thus a radio station assigned a frequency of 930,000 cycles per second would be found at 93 on your radio dial. The Federal Communications Commission (FCC) assigns these frequencies to ensure that station signals do not interfere with one another.

AM RADIO

Radio stations are designated either AM or FM. An AM, or *amplitude modulation,* station has the flexibility to vary the height of its electromagnetic signal so that during the daytime it produces waves, called *ground waves,* that follow the contour of the earth. At night the station transmits waves into the sky, called *sky waves,* that bounce back to earth and are picked up by receivers far beyond the range of the station's ground waves.

The actual power or strength of an AM signal depends on the power allowed by the FCC. Stations with a broadcast range of approximately 25 miles are considered *local stations.* Most local stations are allowed 100 to 250 watts of power. In contrast, *regional stations* may cover an entire state or several states. The most powerful stations are called *clear channel stations* and may use up to 50,000 watts (KMOX in St. Louis is an example). The relative power of each type of station will vary, depending on the frequency assigned. Generally, the lower the frequency, the farther the signal will travel.

FM RADIO

An FM, or *frequency modulation,* station differs from AM in that the band width (frequency) is adjusted rather than the height (amplitude), which remains constant. Because the signal put out by an FM station follows the line of sight, the distance of the signal depends on the height of the antenna. Typically, 50 miles is the maximum signal distance. However, the tonal quality of an FM signal is superior to that of AM.

AM radio revenue is growing at approximately 1 percent annually, but the growth on FM stations exceeds 7 percent. In 1989 FM stations accounted for 76 percent of all radio listeners and 60 percent of all radio advertising revenue.[24] The loss of AM listenership, due to the perception that FM offers better sound quality, is likely to put more AM stations out of business.

As radio's importance as a local medium increases, more of its programming will be satellite-delivered from radio network. Aaron Daniels, president of ABC Radio Networks, predicts that 30 percent of the country's 10,000 stations will use satellite-delivered programming by the middle of the 1990s. In addition, more stations will use satellite networks to reduce their programming costs.[25]

CABLE AND DAB RADIO

In addition to the dominant AM and FM radio delivery systems, cable radio was launched in 1990. The technology uses cable television receivers to deliver static-free music via wires plugged into cable subscribers' stereos. The thinking behind cable radio is that cable television needs new revenue and consumers are fed up with commercials on radio. The service typically is commercial-free and costs $7 to $12. An example is Digital Music Express, which offers CD sound in 30 formats around the clock.

DAB, or digital audio broadcast, exists in Europe and is expected to be introduced in the United States by 1995. DAB is essentially perfect quality audio delivery. Potentially, it offers the capability for listeners to listen to the same station all the way across the country. It means better sound, less interference, and possible audience extension. In effect, it's a defense against other technologies, such as CDs.[26]

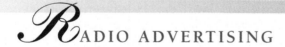

$\mathcal{R}$ADIO ADVERTISING

network radio A group of local affiliates providing simultaneous programming via connection to one or more of the national networks through AT&T telephone wires.

Radio advertising is available on national networks and on local markets. **Network radio** refers to a group of local affiliates connected to one or more of the national networks through telephone wires and satellites. The network provides simultaneous network programming, which is quite limited compared with network television programming. Therefore many local or regional stations belong to more than one network, with each network providing specialized programming to complete a station's schedule. Ad 11.3 is an example of a radio net-

---

[24]Stephen Battaglio, "Radio," *Adweek* (September 11, 1989):184.
[25]Ibid,:185.
[26]Melanie Rigney, "New Technology Brings Radio to Cutting Edge," *Advertising Age* (September 9, 1991):S1, S6.

work print ad. Each station then sends out the network's signal through its own antenna. There are also regional networks (for example, Intermountain Network and the Groskin Group) that tend to serve a particular state or audience segment, such as farmers.

NETWORK RADIO

Complete market coverage combined with quality programming has increased the popularity of network radio. Over 20 national radio networks program concerts, talk shows, sports events, and dramas. Satellite transmission has produced important technological improvements. Satellites not only provide a better sound but also allow the transmission of multiple programs with different formats. Network radio is viewed as a viable national advertising medium, especially for advertiser of food, automobiles, and over-the-counter drugs.

In the 1980s network radio went through a period of consolidation that produced four major radio networks: Westwood One, CBS, ABC, and Unistar (see Ad 11.4). The Radio Advertising Bureau reported revenues of $424 million for network radio in 1989. Over $1.5 billion was spent on national spot advertising out of a total of $8.4 billion in advertising revenues. The growth of network radio is also attributed to the increase in syndicated radio shows and unwired networks.[27]

Syndication. As the number of affiliates has boomed, so has the number of news syndicated radio shows, creating more advertising opportunities for companies

---

[27]Stephen Battaglio, "Radio," *Adweek* (October 30, 1989):M.O.44.

eager to reach new markets. In fact, syndication and network radio have practically become interchangeable terms. Syndication has been beneficial to network radio because it offers advertisers a variety of high-quality specialized programs. Both networks and private firms offer syndication. Essentially a syndication offers a complete catalog of programming to the local affiliate. For example, Transtar Radio Network, located in Colorado Springs, claims about 600 affiliates. Its only direct competitor is Satellite Music Network, Dallas, which claims 800 affiliates. Both networks offer 24-hour programming daily, which could provide a station with all its programming needs. With this kind of arrangement a broadcaster needs nothing but a satellite dish and a sales staff. The station remains, but much of the operating costs disappear.

Unwired Networks. The final reason for the growth of network radio is the emergence of unwired networks. Network radio has always been at a disadvantage because of the difficulty of dealing with the many stations and rate structures available in large markets. This system was discussed earlier in connection with unwired television networks.

SPOT RADIO

spot radio advertising A form of advertising in which an ad is placed with an individual station rather than through a network.

In **spot radio advertising** an advertiser places an advertisement with an individual station rather than through a network. Although networks provide prerecorded national advertisements, they also allow local affiliates open time to sell spot advertisements. Table 11.8 lists the leading spot radio advertisers. Spot radio advertising represents nearly 80 percent of all radio advertising. Its popularity is a result of the flexibility if offers the advertiser. With over 8,000 stations

Rank	Advertiser	1992	1991	%chg
1	Philip Morris Co.	$24.9	$40.6	−38.7
2	Anheuser-Busch Cos.	18.7	19.2	−2.9
3	News Corp.	15.8	13.3	19.5
4	Kmart Corp.	15.6	10.8	44.4
5	General Motors Corp.	15.2	22.3	−31.8
6	Southland Corp.	14.8	21.6	−31.3
7	PepsiCo	13.9	15.2	−8.3
8	American Stores Co.	11.6	12.7	−8.7
9	Grand Metropolitan	10.5	8.2	28.7
10	BellSouth Corp.	10.3	8.8	17.2
11	Bell Atlantic Corp.	10.0	7.4	34.4
12	Delta Air Lines	9.6	12.9	−25.5
13	GTE Corp.	9.5	10.1	−5.4
14	AT&T Co.	9.3	6.8	35.4
15	Coca-Cola Co.	9.1	7.4	23.9
16	Montgomery Ward & Co.	8.3	5.5	50.5
17	Melville Corp.	8.1	5.0	62.3
18	Sears, Roebuck & Co.	7.9	10.4	−24.3
19	U.S. West	7.5	6.6	15.0
20	Dayton Hudson Corp.	7.2	6.8	5.3
21	Amoco Corp.	6.9	5.7	21.2
22	Pacific Telesis Group	6.7	9.9	−31.7
23	Texaco	6.7	8.7	−22.5
24	Mobil Corp.	6.7	5.6	19.2
25	Van Munching & Co.	6.6	3.2	104.7

Note: Dollars are in millions.
Reprinted with permission from Advertising Age (September 29, 1993):38. Copyright, Crain Communications, Inc., 1993.

Principle

Spot advertising dominates radio scheduling.

available, messages can be tailored for particular audiences. In large cities such as New York, Chicago, or Los Angeles, 40 or more radio stations are available. Local stations also offer flexibility through their willingness to run unusual ads, allow last-minute changes, and negotiate rates. Buying spot radio and coping with its nonstandardized rate structures can be very cumbersome, however.

Radio advertising revenue is divided into three categories: network, spot, and local. Network revenues are by far the smallest category, accounting for approximately 5 percent of total radio revenues. National spot advertising makes up the remaining 5 percent.

THE RADIO AUDIENCE

Principle

Radio is a highly segmented medium.

Radio is a highly segmented medium. Program formats offered in a typical market include hard rock, gospel, country and western, "Top 40" hits, and sex advice. Virtually every household in the United States (99 percent) has a radio set (527 million radios in total, with an average 5.6 sets per household), and most of these sets are tuned in to a vast array of programs.[28]

Market researcher Michael Hedges separates radio listeners into four segments: station fans, radio fans, music fans, and news fans. Station fans make up the largest segment of radio listeners, at 46 percent. They have a clear preference for one or two stations and spend up to 8 hours or more each day listening to their favorite. Most station fans are women between the ages of 25 and 44. Radio fans represent 34 percent of the population. They may listen to four to five different stations per week, and they show no preference for one particular station. Most are under 35 years of age, though many women aged 55 and older are radio fans. Only 11 percent of the population are music fans—people who listen exclusively for the music being played. Men between the ages of 25 and 45 are most likely to be music fans, although many elderly adults also fit the profile. Finally, a percentage of radio listeners choose their station based on a need for news and information. They have one or two favorite stations, listen in short segments, and are almost exclusively aged 35 or older.[29]

A traditional radio audience that seems to have gone through quite a transition lately is the teen audience. In the case of network radio, for example, audience levels for young adults aged 12 to 34 were down approximately 5.6 percent, or 400,000 listeners, according to RADAR data below. Part of this decline is due to the fact that several network systems have abandoned the youngest segment of this market in favor of the 25- to 54-year-old format and the Oldies format[30] Like many other markets, radio has followed the Baby Boomers. Portable tape and CD players with headsets have also played a part.

MEASURING THE RADIO AUDIENCE

Advertisers considering radio are most concerned with the number of people listening to a particular station at a given time. The radio industry and independent research firms provide several measures considered useful to the advertiser.

The most basic measure is the station's *coverage*. This is simply the geographical area (which includes a given number of homes) that can pick up the station clearly, whether or not they are actually tuned in. A better measure is *circulation,* which measures the number of homes that are actually tuned in to the particular station. This figure is influenced by such factors as the competing programs, the type of program, and the time of day or night.

Arbitron. Several major audience rating services operate in the advertising industry. One, the Arbitron Ratings Company, estimates the size of radio audiences for over 250 markets in the United States. The primary method used by Arbitron is a seven-day self-administered diary that the person returns to Arbitron at the end of the week. Editors check that each diary has entries for every day and that the postmark shows the diary wasn't mailed before the week was over.

Radar. A second radio rating service is Radio's All-Dimension Audience Research (RADAR). This service deals with local and network radio. For RADAR,

[28]J. Thomas Russell and Ronald Lane, *Kleppner's Advertising Procedure,* 11th ed. (Englewood Cliffs, NJ: Prentice Hall, 1990):208.
[29]"Radio Days," *American Demographics* (November 1988):18.
[30]Stephen Battaglio, "Where Have All the Young Radio Listeners Gone?" *Adweek* (February 25, 1991):26.

Statistical Research calls 12,000 respondents for seven consecutive days and asks about network radio listening done the day before. The company contacts respondents before beginning data collection, so they can pay better attention to their listening habits. Final reports are based on data collected over 48 weeks.

Birch/Scarborough-VNU. Birch conducts 100,000 random phone interviews a month for its 273 markets, asking listeners aged 12 and older what they listened to yesterday and the day before yesterday. It also collects extensive demographic and product usage information for the Scarborough Report, an annual lifestyle report of the top 55 markets. The frequency of these reports varies according to the size of the market.

ADVANTAGES AND DISADVANTAGES OF RADIO

Radio is not for every advertiser, and it is important to understand the relative strengths and weaknesses of this medium.

ADVANTAGES

Target Audiences. The most important advantage offered by radio is that it reaches specific types of audiences by offering specialized programming. In addition it can be adapted to different parts of the country and can reach people at different times of the day. Radio, for example, is the ideal means of reaching people driving to and from work. Known as *drive time,* these radio time slots provide the best audience for many advertisers.

Speed and Flexibility. The *speed and flexibility* of radio have been noted already. Of all the media, radio has the shortest *closing period,* in that copy can be submitted up to airtime. This flexibility allows advertisers to adjust to local market conditions, current news events, and even the weather. For example, a local hardware store can quickly implement a snow shovel promotion the morning after a snowstorm.

Principle

Radio offers high reach at low cost.

The flexibility of radio is also evident in its willingness to participate in promotional tie-ins. An example is the "Maalox Moments" that have successfully united a packaged-goods marketer, retailers, and radio stations ("Stuck in traffic? The dog ate the notes you left out for the big presentation at 8:00 A.M.? Your kid did *what,* and you have to leave work early and see the principal?")[31].

Costs. Radio may be the least expensive of all media. Because airtime costs are relatively low, extensive repetition is possible. In addition, the cost of producing a radio commercial can be low, particularly if the message is read by a local station announcer. Radio's low cost and high reach of selected target groups make it an excellent supporting medium. In fact, the most appropriate role for most radio advertising is a supportive one.

Mental Imagery. An important advantage of radio is the scope it allows for the listener's imagination. Radio uses words, sound effects, music, and tonality to

---

[31]Howard Schlossberg, "Local Radio Tie-Ins Break Through Promotional Clutter," *Marketing News* (May 11, 1992).

enable listeners to create their own picture of what is happening. For this reason radio is sometimes referred to as the "theater of the mind." The script for John Moore Plumbing (Figure 11.4) demonstrates how radio effectively creates mental pictures.

High Levels of Acceptance. The final advantage of radio is its high acceptance at the local level. Partly because of its passive nature, radio normally is not perceived as an irritant. People have their favorite radio stations and radio personalities, which they listen to regularly. Messages delivered by these are more likely to be accepted and retained. More is said about the power of radio personalities in the Issues and Controversies box.

DISADVANTAGES

Inattentiveness. Radio is not without its drawbacks. Because radio is strictly a listening medium, radio messages are fleeting and commercials may be missed or forgotten. Many listeners perceive radio as pleasant background and do not listen to it carefully.

Lack of Visuals. The restrictions of sound may also hamper the creative process. Clearly, products that must be demonstrated or seen to be appreciated are inap-

Figure 11.4

This radio script illustrates the use of humor in creating a memorable scene without the use of visuals.

	John Moore Plumbing
	(*A telephone rings twice. A man groggily answers:*)
He:	John Moore Plumbing.
She:	It's 2 A.M. and I'm not asleep . . .
He:	I'm not either.
She:	Are you having insomnia too?
He:	No, I'm having a phone conversation.
She:	When I can't sleep I read the Yellow Pages. Do you ever do that?
He:	No.
She:	Anyway, I saw that John Moore Plumbing is open 24 hours a day. So I thought I'd call . . .
He:	Well, John Moore Plumbing has a 24-hour emergency service. Do you have an emergency?
She:	Well, I'm desperate. Does desperate count?
He:	Are you desperate about plumbing?
She:	Sometimes.
He:	How 'bout tonight?
She:	Sorry, I have plans for tonight.
He:	No, no. I mean do you have leaking pipes or a backed-up toilet or something?
She:	Hold on a second, I'll check.
Announcer:	When you have a plumbing emergency in the middle of the night or middle of the day, call John Moore. Call 590-5555. 24 hours a day. And you'll always get prompt service when you call John Moore Plumbing. Even at 2 A.M.
She:	Toilets are fine. I can't see the pipes.
He:	Why not?
She:	They're underwater.
He:	I'll be right over.
She:	I'll set a place for you . . .
Announcer:	John Moore Plumbing. 590-5555. Call John. And get more.

Better to Be Heard and Not Seen?

The February 8, 1993 issue of *Newsweek* carried a front-cover warning to America's political and media elites. Talk radio, the magazine intoned, has remade American politics and is poised—for better or worse—to remake the way the country is governed. The five-page story was the most visible in a seemingly endless string of recent print and television reports detailing the arrival of talk radio as a major sociopolitical force.

Since discovering talk radio, the media also seems to have accepted the curious notion, fostered by talk hosts and hostesses themselves, that the format is a two-way Radio-Free Europe. It has been portrayed as a place where harried, fretful Americans—isolated from their leaders, Big Media, and each other—go to speak their minds and hear what their fellow citizens really think. Local television stations race to the local talk-radio station for "public reaction" stories on major events, the prestigious daily papers write articles detailing what talk-show callers around the country are saying about the issue-of-the-moment, suggesting what the mood of the people will be.

But it doesn't. What emerges is the mood of a statistically minuscule group of people who are hardly representative of the public—and whose thoughts have often been filtered and massaged every bit as much as a letter to the editor or a man-on-the-street interview. The typical talk station attracts roughly 2 percent to 5 percent of the local radio audience. According to one recent study, over one-third of those listeners are 65-plus, and just over half are 55 or older. People between the ages of 18 and 34, by contrast, account for just 14 percent of the audience. A widely accepted industry rule of thumb says just 1 percent of those listeners, a majority of them men, ever phone in to express their opinions. And, just who are these callers? Well, they are obviously folks with the motivation, time, and ability to hang on the phone in the middle of a workday—retirees, homemakers whose kids are at school, the unemployed, the self-employed, shift workers, college kids, and increasingly in recent years, people with cellular car phones.

So what are the implications for advertisers? According to the Simmons Market Research Bureau, the talk-radio audience indexes well above the general population in number of college graduates, professional managers, and households with incomes over $100,000. There is also a widely held perception that by virtue of its maturity, the talk audience has more disposable income than fans of other radio formats.

Properly done, the format can be informative, thought-provoking, and absolutely captivating. It can reveal what a few of your more outspoken fellow citizens think about the issues, and may even help shape your opinions on those matters. And, it can certainly help an advertiser move product.

Adapted from Randall Bloomquist, "The Powers That Would Be," *Adweek* (May 3, 1993):36–39.

Principle

Radio should be used as a support medium when the target audience is clearly defined and visualization of the product is not critical.

propriate for radio advertising. Creating radio ads that encourage the listener to see the product is a difficult challenge. Experts believe that the use of humor, music, and sound effects may be the most effective way to do this.

Clutter. The proliferation of competing radio stations, combined with the opportunity to engage in heavy repetition, has created a tremendous amount of clutter in radio advertising. Coupled with the fact that radio listeners tend to divide their attention among various activities, this clutter greatly reduces the likelihood that a message will be heard or understood.

Scheduling and Buying Difficulties. The final disadvantage of radio is the complexity of scheduling and buying radio time. The need to buy time on several stations makes scheduling and following up on ads very complicated. The bookkeeping involved in checking nonstandardized rates, approving bills for payment, and billing clients can be a staggering task. Fortunately, computers and large-station representatives have helped alleviate much of this chaos.

UMMARY

- Broadcast media include both radio and television. Whereas print media are bound by space, broadcast media convey transient messages and are bound by time.

- Among the different television systems that an advertiser can use are network, cable, subscription, local, specialty, and public television. Network television is still the dominant form.

- The size of the television audience is measured in a number of ways, including the use of diaries and people meters.

- Television offers advertisers cost efficiency, impact, and influence.

- Advertisers have a choice of scheduling their commercials on a network, local, or cable scheduling basis.

- Television commercials can take the form of sponsorships, participations, or spot announcements.

- Radio is classified as either AM or FM according to transmission and power.

- The audience for radio can be measured in terms of a station's coverage or its circulation.

- The advantages of radio include specialized programming, speed and flexibility, low cost, the use of mental imagery, and high levels of acceptance. Its disadvantages include inattentiveness, lack of visuals, clutter, and scheduling and buying difficulties.

QUESTIONS

1. What are the major differences between broadcast and print media? How are the two media similar?

2. Describe television syndication. Contrast off-network syndication with first-run syndication. What is barter syndication? How does syndication affect the advertiser?

3. What are the primary advantages and disadvantages offered to advertisers by cable television? How do interconnects affect the decision to advertise on cable?

4. You are a major agency media director who has just finished a presentation to a prospective client in convenience food marketing. During the Q and A period a client representative asks you this question, "We know that television's viewer loyalty is nothing like it was ten or even five years ago with cable and VCRs. There are smaller audiences per program each year, yet television time-costs continue to rise. Do you still believe we should consider commercial television as a primary medium for our company's advertising?" How would you answer?

5. Local market radio audiences are primarily measured by the diary (Arbitron) and the telephone interview (BIRCH). If you, as a media sales director for a radio station, had to choose one service to measure station popularity, which one would you subscribe to? Assume that the cost of each service is roughly the same.

6. Message clutter affects both radio and television advertising. Advertisers fear audiences react to long commercial pods by using the remote control for the television set or the push button on the radio. Some have proposed that advertisers should absorb higher time costs to reduce the frequency and length of commercial interruptions. Others argue that broadcasting should reduce the number of commercials sold and also reduce program advertising even if it means less profit for broadcasters. Which of these remedies would be the best to take in the 1990s?

7. One of the interesting ways to combine the assets of radio and television is to use the sound track of television commercials for the radio creative. Why would an advertiser consider this media/creative strategy? What limitations would you mention?

$\mathscr{S}$UGGESTED CLASS PROJECT

As a group, make a chart for five radio stations, of the type of station (easy listening, top 40, classical, and so on), the products commonly advertised, and the probable target markets for these products. Note the time of the day these products are advertised. Try to get three or four times as many products as there are people in your group. Now put all of the products in a hat and have everyone draw one. Each student now is responsible for advertising his or her product. He or she needs to allocate a budget of $2,500 among the five stations for a week's worth of programming. It costs $250 for 30 seconds of air time.

$\mathscr{F}$URTHER READINGS

Broadcasting/Cable Yearbook 1992 (Washington, DC: Broadcast Publications, Inc.)

KALISH, DAVID, "Bad Reception," *Marketing & Media Decisions,* August 1988, pp. 63–65.

Television: The Critical View, 4th ed. (New York: Oxford University Press, 1987).

WHETMORE, EDWARD J. *Mediamerica,* 4th ed. (Belmont, CA: Wadsworth Publishing Co., 1989).

WILLIAM, MARTIN, *TV: The Casual Art* (New York: Oxford University Press, 1982).

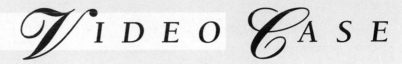

Mining an Untapped Market

The dream of every business is to find an untapped market of consumers with pent-up demand and few places to shop. In women's apparel, the last untapped market may be large-size women's clothing, designed especially for women size 14 and up.

For years, the only clothing available to plus-size women were polyester muumuus that resembled movable pup tents. Specialty chain Lane Bryant was one of the few retailers to cater to this market; others steered clear, fearing that large-size women would spoil their chic image. Reluctant retailers were convinced that large-size women were inclined to spend little on their wardrobes. While one out of three women in the United States wears large sizes, these items account for only 15 percent of women's apparel purchases. What mainstream retailers failed to realize is that poor selection and quality were responsible for poor sales.

Designers, manufacturers, and retailers alike see the financial potential of this neglected market. While approximately 20 million American women wear large sizes today, that number is expected to increase in the years ahead. "Unfortunately, as you get older, you also tend to get heavier," explained Paine Webber financial analyst Anita Wager. Indeed, among the 40-plus group, four out of ten women wear larger sizes.

Thanks to retailers like Memphis-based Catherines Stores and manufacturers like Liz Claiborne, larger women finally have something to shop for and stores that cater to their needs. The result is an avalanche of consumer dollars unequaled in any other apparel line. While 1982 large-size apparel sales totaled less than $6 billion, 1991 sales reached $10 billion. Not surprisingly, high-priced items grew faster than any other market segment and now account for some $2 billion in sales.

Catherines Stores alone racked up approximately $250 million in sales in 1993, up from only $171 million a year earlier. These stores, which operate under the names Catherine's, PS...Plus Sizes, Plus Savings, Added Dimensions, and The Answer, use direct-mail and newspaper advertising to reach customers. According to Melanie Anderson, director of advertising, the stores often run newspaper ads in conjunction with direct-mail pieces. These ads promote specific lines, collections, and clearance sales, especially during the month of January. Catherines also runs cooperative newspaper ads along with such manufacturers as Levi's, Koret, and Playtex.

The typical ad, says Anderson, is about 14 to 16 inches—two columns by 7 inches—and is run in local-area newspapers with large circulations as well as community papers. The newspaper chosen is the one that can best reach targeted customers. Catherines expands its use of newspaper ad space to promote new-store openings. In this case, it relies on 55-inch ads—five columns by 11 inches—used in conjunction with radio, television, and billboards, to communicate its message. Catherines operates 352 outlets in 37 states.

Although Catherines has been approached by women's specialty magazines, including *Redbook,* Anderson has not yet decided to move to this medium. "We've talked about using an infomercial format," she said, "but we've made no final decisions."

Advertising for large-size women's apparel is likely to grow in the years ahead along with the market itself as companies realize that the time to strike is now. "These customers have had empty closets for a long time," said Bruce Nelson, manager of special sizes of Dayton Hudson's department store chain. "Now they're making large multiple purchases while the rest of the world just needs to update their wardrobes."

Sources: Melanie Anderson, Advertising Director, Catherines Stores, telephone interview, February 1, 1994; Catherines Stores Corporation, *1992 Annual Report;* Jennifer Corsi, Public Relations Coordinator, Liz Claiborne, correspondence and press releases, January 31, 1994; Amy Feldman, "Hello, Oprah, Good-Bye, Iman," *Forbes,* March 16, 1992, pp. 116–117; "This Specialty Retailer Sees Big Things Ahead," *Money,* September 1993, p. 66.

Questions

1. Why do you think Catherines Stores considers newspapers a more attractive advertising medium than magazines?

2. What is the attraction of cooperative advertising for Catherines?

3. If you were the advertising director of a large-size apparel manufacturer, what media would you use to reach the largest number of potential customers?

MEDIA BUYING

12

CHAPTER OBJECTIVES

When you have completed this chapter, you should be able to:

- Explain how media buying is different from media planning and how it complements media planning

- Understand the major duties of media buyer: research analyst, expert evaluator, negotiator, and troubleshooter

- Explain how buyers translate media plan objectives into target-directed advertising schedules

- Understand why negotiation skills are more important today to advertising strategies than ever before.

AN ADVERTISER'S DILEMMA: REACHING THE TWENTYSOMETHINGS

Late in 1992, Karen Richie, an advertising media executive, issued a wake-up call to the advertising world about a new generation of consumers: "Face it. Boomers (the baby boomer generation) are getting old." Ms. Richie warned the media to develop advertising vehicles for a group ready and able to overtake boomers as the primary market for nearly every product category. Call them "busters," "generation X," or "twentysomethings," these 46 million 18- to 29-year-olds are not in the shadows of marketing any longer. They are a viable and lucrative consumer opportunity that must be served by print and broadcast media.

Some advertisers have been savvy to the market, but the media buyers are finding a scarcity of media to reach them. The traditional media are still preoccupied with baby boomer audiences. Still, smart media buyers can identify a small but growing list of ways to expose these young adults. The opportunities are a combination of old (those willing to change direction) and new (dedicated to the twentysomethings).

Magazines are a good illustration where the changeover includes old and new titles. Both *Entertainment Weekly* and *Rolling Stone* have been dominant with boomers but now are expanding editorial direction to appeal to younger readers. *Entertainment Weekly* uses popular culture interests to crossover generations. It claims 38 percent of its readers are 18 to 29, while 41 percent are 30 to 44 years old. In a similar fashion, *Rolling Stone* is attempting to appeal to twentysomethings without losing its boomer readers. "It is definitely a balancing act," says Dana Fields, a *Rolling Stone* publisher. She points to the cover celebrities used on issues as evidence where youth-oriented "grunge bands" such as Nirvana and Spin Doctors alternate with Eric Clapton and Neil Young. The magazine's sales promotion to media buyers also reflects this balancing. Look closely at the list of "mental" topics displayed in the *Rolling Stone* advertisement (see Ad 12.1 on page 397) and notice both boomers and busters are represented.

Some new magazines do not try balancing readers interests—they are dedicated to this new market. Titles such as *Details, Spin*, and hip-hops like *Vibe* (see Ad 12.2 on page 398) and *The Source* are carefully designed for what twentysomethings are "about."

Over-the-air television, thus far, has only one sincere outlet for twentysomethings—Fox Network. It claims 38 percent of its adult viewers age 18 to 29. That is about twice the average of NBC, CBS, and ABC. Fox does this with programs like *The Simpsons, In Living Color*, and *Beverly Hills 90210*. Why are the regular networks behind and often weak with attempts?

According to a *TV Guide* critic, Jeff Jarvis, the reason is the wrong people are making the decisions. "It's a bunch of 50-year-olds trying to figure out what a bunch of 20-year-olds wants to watch," says Jarvis.

The most hopeful sources for video programming appear to be coming from cable television networks. From the leader MTV (See Ad. 12.3 on page 400) through newer options E! and Comedy Central, cable television seems more inclined to portray younger lifestyles.

Many observers would guess that radio is an obvious buyer's choice but it isn't that simple. As Ms. Richie explains: "(This) is still a medium dominated by baby boomers." She backs this up by observing that metropolitan radio dials are cluttered with stations offering classic rock and other "oldie" formats. Media buyers looking for station opportunities must be very sensitive to music preferences of the twentysomething group.

As for the near future, some good advice for media buyers comes from Jack Kennard, a marketing director for Brown-Foreman beverage company: "(Anyone) seriously pursuing a twentysomething target has got to adopt specific criteria that may be different from traditional . . . experiment and look for alternatives. . ."[1]

MEDIA-BUYING FUNCTIONS

A media buyer has a number of distinct responsibilities and duties, which we will describe here in an operational sequence. We will discuss some of the most important buyer functions in more detail later in the chapter.

PROVIDING INSIDE INFORMATION TO THE MEDIA PLANNER

Media buyers are close enough to day-to-day changes in media popularity and pricing to be a constant source of inside information to media planners. For example, a newspaper buyer discovers that a key newspaper's delivery staff is going on strike, a radio-time buyer learns a top disk jockey is leaving a radio station, or a magazine buyer's source reveals that the new editor of a publication is going to seriously change the editorial focus. All of these things can influence the strategy and tactics of current and future advertising plans.

[1]Scott Donaton, "The Media Wakes Up to Generation X," *Advertising Age* (February 1, 1993): 16–17.

Ad 12.1

This *Rolling Stone* ad emphasizes a wide audience appeal.
(Courtesy of Rolling Stone)

Tonight *SHE'LL SLEEP WITH LL COOL J—shower with Yo-Yo and study with Run DMC.*

all color ONE **VIBE.**

Principle

Media buyers must know everything there is to know about media vehicles and their performance.

MEDIA VEHICLE SELECTION

One essential part of buying is choosing the best media vehicles to fit the target audience's aperture. The media planner lays out the direction, but the buyer is responsible for choosing the specific vehicles. Armed with the media plan directives, the buyer seeks answers to a number of difficult questions. Does the vehicle have the right audience profile? Will the program's current popularity increase, stabilize, or decline? How well does the magazine's editorial format fit the brand? Does the radio station's choice of music offer the correct atmosphere for the creative theme? How well does the newspaper's circulation pattern fit the advertiser's distribution? The answers to those questions bear directly on the campaign's success.

NEGOTIATING MEDIA PRICES

Aside from finding aperture-related target audiences, nothing is considered more crucial in media buying than securing the lowest possible price for placements. Time and space charges make up the largest portion of the advertising budget so there is continuing pressure to keep costs as low as possible. To accomplish this, buyers operate in a world of transaction or negotiation.

MONITORING VEHICLE PERFORMANCE

In an ideal world every vehicle on the campaign schedule would perform at or above expectations. Likewise, every advertisement, commercial, and posting would run exactly as planned. In reality, underperformance and schedule problems are facts of life. The buyer's response to these problems must be swift and decisive. Poorly performing vehicles must be replaced or costs must be modified. Production and schedule difficulties must be rectified. Delayed response could hurt the brand's sales.

POSTCAMPAIGN ANALYSIS

Once a campaign is completed, the buyer's duty is to review the plan's expectations and forecasts against what actually happened. Did the plan actually achieve GRP, reach, frequency, and CPM objectives? Did the newspaper and magazine placements run in the positions expected? Such analysis is instrumental in providing the guidance for future media plans. For a full discussion of postcampaign research see Chapter 21.

These five tasks provide highlights of media buying. For a better understanding of buying operations, however, we need to look at some of these duties in closer detail.

SPECIAL SKILLS: EXPERT KNOWLEDGE OF MEDIA OPPORTUNITIES

If you were to ask media buyers what they need to know in order to do their jobs, they would probably say "Everything I can." Buying media has a great many dimensions. Network and local television stations are constantly changing and rearranging programs. Radio stations alter their music formats. Media audiences change their habits. Media prices are fluid and increase or decrease at different times.

Knowledge means keeping up with changes. Media buyers need experience to anticipate how changes will affect the advertiser's plans. Many media buyers concentrate on a single medium. For example, television buyers do nothing but buy television time. Whereas media planners work with a broad range of opportunities, media buyers develop narrow but deep expertise in one medium.

MEDIA CONTENT

As we emphasized in Chapter 9, media placement strategy is more than a popularity contest of choosing the media vehicles with the largest target audience. Often the buyer must also judge the message environment. Does it have the right mood or style for the advertiser's message? Is the media vehicle overcrowded with other ads or commercials? Is it careful in its production of messages? The answers to these questions cannot be found in reader surveys or broadcast ratings. Buyers monitor sample copies of publications, listen to off-the-air tapes, and study analyses of media content.

The ad shows:

EVER HEAR
ANYONE REFER TO THE
NBC GENERATION?

MTV is not a TV channel. It's a cultural force. People don't watch it. They live it. MTV has affected the way an entire generation thinks, talks and buys. No other network can say that. MTV is their channel. The music, news and shows are for them. So, what's in it for you? Your message is for them, too. When they see your message on MTV, it's like you're joining their club. Suddenly you're one of them. You know what they love. You know what they hate. You know what they need. And they know that you know. You know?

MTV MUSIC TELEVISION

AUDIENCE HABITS

People's media preferences are neither stable nor consistent. Audiences are fickle about how they spend their leisure time. Their interests change with the seasons. They grow tired of one entertainment mode and shift to another. Buyers cannot afford to wait until the shift is obvious; they must sense it coming and select accordingly. Fresh and interested media options provide the best opportunities for aperture. Buyers who can judge where media audiences are headed will be waiting. In Ad 12.4 *Good Housekeeping* is stressing reader loyalty and trust. What products would particularly value this?

RESEARCH EVALUATION

Besides their constant exposure to standard audience research (such as Arbitron and SMRB), media buyers are inundated with research and special analyses by

Ad 12.4

In this ad *Good Housekeeping* stresses the value of believability in advertising.
(Courtesy of Good Housekeeping)

media salespeople. This information may be special interpretations of standard research, or it may be a special research study ordered by the station or publication. Because such research is less than objective, buyers must carefully judge it. Did it follow sound statistical guidelines? Was the sample size adequate? Buyers are responsible for deciding if sales-presented research is valuable to the client.

SPECIAL SKILLS: KNOWLEDGE OF MEDIA PRICING

Marketers bear many costs in the advertising campaign. They pay for the talent that develops the message, the production to create the message, and the media costs to place the message before the target audience. With few exceptions, media costs are the largest area of advertising investment.

MEDIA COST RESPONSIBILITIES

Media buyers should be experts in all aspects of media pricing, not only in price negotiations but also for gathering historical price experience.

The buyer's cost training begins with an understanding that the advertiser and the media are adversaries. Marketers want the lowest possible price, and the media try to charge as much as they can. As the marketer's representatives, the buyers are expected to use all skills and leverage to secure the lowest prices. They must not, however sacrifice target audience profiles or reach objectives. The price paid must be balanced against the size and quality of the audience delivered.

Media buyers must develop skills in three costs areas: charting media cost trends, learning to use media rate cards, and balancing audience to price (CPM). The following discussion describes each of these areas in more detail.

cost trends A history of changes in the average unit (per message) prices for each medium that is used in cost forecasting.

Average Cost Trends. The prices paid for advertising in the recent past are carefully monitored. These are called **cost trends.** Cost changes can be compiled in a number of ways including: national averages for each medium, for particular media vehicles (i.e., sports events), and for individual markets. In Table 12.1 there is an excerpt of network television changes between 1992 and 1993. Notice the significant changes month-to-month; this is partially due to the open-pricing system. This also emphasizes the value of cost trend analysis.

Media Price Formats (Rate Cards). Each media company has its own way of charging for its advertising positions. Some, such as national cable and network television, prefer not to use set pricing at all. They allow complete negotiation with each advertiser to determine the price. (Open pricing will be discussed in more detail later in the chapter.) Others present price schedules through a published format called a *rate card*, which includes the price for each message unit (size or length), the types of incentive discounts available, and scheduling and production requirements.

Although rate cards follow general formats, there is no standard for prices or discounts. Each rate card is unique. The variety of rate cards and formats may seem overwhelming to beginners. Through steady experience, however, the buyer learns to master each approach. To give you some idea of how the rate cards are organized, here are two illustrations—one for magazines and one for television.

Table 12.1

Network Television Cost Trends: 1992 vs. 1993

Cost Change	Jan. %	Feb. %	Mar. %	Apr. %	May %	Jun. %
Daypart:						
Daytime	−1.0	−34.0	12.0	6.0	5.0	10.0
PrimeEvening	−7.0	−5.0	3.0	−10.0	3.0	−4.0
News (M-Sun)	0.0	16.0	31.0	11.0	−21.0	22.0

*Based on average costs for a 30 second position.
Source: Adweek's Marketer's Guide to Media, Fall/Winter (1993-94): 14–15.

Figure 12.1

Magazine Rate Card
(frequency discount)

BLACK/WHITE RATES				4-COLOR RATES				
	1 ti	3 ti	6 ti	12 ti		1 ti	3 ti	6 ti	12 ti
1 Page 21,000	20,400	19,175	18,025	1 Page 32,000	31,050	30,120	28,915
1/2 Page 13,000	12,610	12,230	11,850	1/2 Page 19,200	18,625	18,060	17,340
1/4 Page 7,800	7,600	7,400	7,180	1/4 Page 11,500	11,270	11,045	10,715
Spread 43,000	40,850	38,810	37,250	Spread 67,000	64,320	61,100	58,660

Consumer Magazines. Figure 12.1 illustrates a common style of rate card that offers discounts based upon the number of insertions used within the contract year. The more insertions (an ad in an issue) used per publication the lower the cost for each insertion. To illustrate, the excerpt in Figure 12.1 shows a one-time "4-Color" cost for a page advertisement as $32,000. If the marketer was to contract for 12 one-page units, the individual price for each one would drop to $28,915 (a 10 percent discount).

Advertisers can receive these discounts in advance (before they run the full schedule) or as a lump sum at the end of the schedule contract (a *rebate*). If discounts are taken in advance and the advertiser does *not* complete the schedule, the advertiser has to pay the difference between the discount taken and the discount earned (called a *short rate*).

Local Television. Television station sales departments would have a very hard time trying to publish an individual price for each television program, or for spots between programs. Each program has a different size and type of audience, and each month there are program changes that affect popularity.

The stations' solution to this problem of finding a fair price for each position is illustrated in Figure 12.2. Notice that rates are defined for hours of the day (dayparts). Each day segment offers four different prices (F to P3). The F is the highest rate an advertiser can pay. It also means the position belongs to the advertiser as long as the advertiser wants it. The P rate means it is *preemptible*, meaning movable. If another advertiser is willing to pay a higher rate for the advertiser's position, the station will take the position away from the company paying the lower price. The numbers P1-P3 refer to how much notice you have before preemption. The price selected by the buyer should reflect how needed that position is. The risk is clear; clients can save money by using lower rates but risk losing a valuable audience. Buyer experience pays off with these rates cards because they can balance the risk with the cost saving.

Cost-per-Thousand Patterns (CPM). Experienced buyers keep a careful record of the **CPM trends** for local media in each market. Changes in CPM trends may signal shifts in media popularity or shifts in advertising demand. This information prepares buyers beginning negotiation. It also helps media allocations market-to-market.

CPM trends Longitudinal (long-term) history of average cost-per-thousand tendencies of advertising media that is used to assist in forecasting future CPM levels.

SPECIAL SKILLS: MEDIA VEHICLE SELECTION AND NEGOTIATION

Principle

Negotiation involves getting the best schedule at the best price.

A buyer's knowledge and expert preparation are tested when he or she represents the client in the media marketplace. It is here that execution of the plan takes place. The key questions are: Can the desired vehicles be located, and can a satisfactory schedule be negotiated?

THE BOUNDARIES: WORKING WITHIN PLAN REQUIREMENTS

The boundaries of media negotiation are usually set by the advertising plan (Chapter 7). How many dollars are available? Who is the target audience? When does the advertising run? What atmosphere is desired? What is the duration of scheduling? Question after question must be answered to construct the advertiser's schedule. The following paragraphs detail some of the critical considerations.

Dollar Allocations. The budget in an advertising campaign limits the dollars available to achieve plan objectives. **Allocations** include all the other money decisions concerning how to divide the budget. Allocations of dollars will determine how much money each medium will receive, how much will be spent per month or per week, how many dollars each geographic area will receive, and so on. Media buyers follow the allocation recommendations as closely as possible.

Target Audiences. The media plan will try to give the buyer a clear profile, with media-sensitive characteristics, of the target prospect. Research services, such as Simmons, offer data on particular audience markets, such as the media preferences of children (see Ad 12.5). If multiple targets are specified by the plan, the plan should also specify a weight or priority for each characteristic.

Airline advertising offers a good illustration. Suppose an airline profiled a

allocations Division or proportions of advertising dollars among the various media.

Figure 12.2

Local Television Rate Card

DAYPART	F	P1	P2	P3
Day 6 AM–3 PM....	65	60	55	40
Evening 5–8 PM ...	110	100	90	75
News	230	220	200	185
Prime 8–11 PM	250	200	170	145
Late Evening	85	70	60	45

key prospect as an adult traveler, between 25 and 54 years old, with a sales/managerial occupation. This profile specifies two elements: age and occupation. But which dimension is more important?

Target audience research from the media plan will often reveal the *relative* importance of each profile characteristic. If the audience research for the airline indicated that although both the age and the occupation of prospects were important, occupation (professional or managerial) was twice as important as age, the buyer would assign these audience priorities as value weights. For each media vehicle evaluated, the portion of the media audience having the goal occupation would be doubled (X2), whereas the age segment would be used as it appears (X1). Once the **weighted audience values** are calculated, they would be added together to determine the highest audience score. Table 12.2 demonstrates this process for two television shows, *60 Minutes* and *Nightline*.

weighted audience values
Numerical values assigned to different audience characteristics that help advertisers assign priorities when devising media plans.

Timing and Continuity. Many schedules must work within a tight time frame. Buyers are expected to follow any flight or pulse pattern required by the media plan (see Chapter 9). The buyer must adjust the number of message placements to reflect the desired campaign calendar. The greater the changes in intensity and in advertising periods, the more difficult the scheduling is for the buyer.

Gross Rating Point Levels. Many plans dictate weighting messages according to goals based on desired repetition (frequency) or exposure (reach). Often the rating point levels are used primarily for budget guidance. These levels are then translated by the buyer into insertion frequencies (print) or into announcement frequencies (broadcast). The buyer's task is to use the GRP guides (with the dollar allocation) to develop schedules that can also match frequency and reach objectives.

For example, imagine this situation for a clothing retailer. The plan calls for a special month-long schedule for October. The buyer's instruction might look like this:

- Desired GRP Level: 460/month

- Medium: Spot Television

- Dayparts: 25 percent of GRP in Evening-Fringe (5–7:30 P.M.) and

- 75 percent in Prime Evening (8:00–11:00 P.M.)

The buyer for each market would negotiate schedules for 4 weeks at an average target GRP of 115 per week (4 weeks × 115 AVG. GRP = 460). The placements must follow the dayparts and the proportions. Evening fringe should have 115 (25 percent of 460). Prime evening should have 345 (75 percent of 460 GRP).

Daniel J. Cahill, Media Buyer/Planner, Wolf Blumberg Krody, Cincinnati

8:00–9:00 A.M. Breakfast meeting with a sales representative from *Ladies' Home Journal*. The magazine has come to us with a proposal for White-Westinghouse. We take some time to go over our corporate discount and some merchandising opportunities. It's a great deal, but we can't commit until we square budgets with the client.

9:00–10:15 A.M. My morning meeting has put me slightly behind. I need to finish a media plan for a campaign in Ashland, Kentucky for King's Daughters' Medical Center. The client has decided to extend their schedule until the end of the year, and I have to crunch numbers and prepare flowcharts for an 11:00 A.M. meeting. As I'm printing out a rough draft of the schedule, the account supervisor tells me the campaign has been put on hold.

10:15–11:45 A.M. I need to check up on some work we've been coordinating with Kohler's distributors. I make follow up phone calls to the distributors to make sure they have all necessary materials for their upcoming promotions. The production manager and I find some problems with one of a distributor's materials, and we need to put a rush on the creative. I call to let the distributor know where we stand.

11:45 A.M.–12:30 P.M. Luncheon at the Advertising Club of Cincinnati reviewing local television stations and their importance to the market I run into some old friends from an agency where I used to work.

1:30–2:00 P.M. Quick meeting with an account executive on the White Westinghouse team to review changes for a trade plan proposal.

2:00–2:30 P.M. Phone calls from media sales representatives have piled up and need to be returned. Many of the reps want to know the state of the plan for King's Daughters'. Also, there are some makegoods from the current flight. Others are interested in White-Westinghouse's plans for fourth quarter.

2:30–3:00 P.M. We are working on a pro bono project for Juvenile Diabetes, and they need some suggestions for cheap, alternative media opportunities.

3:00–4:30 P.M. The agency has a new business opportunity resulting from a pitch made earlier in the week. Management briefs me on goals, budgets, and so on and tells me they would like to see a media plan late tomorrow morning. I make phone calls and leave messages with reps so I can get the information I will need in the morning. I will be in here early tomorrow.

4:30–5:30 P.M. Kohler has asked for some big ideas for an upcoming promotion. We organize a group to come up with incentive programs for distributors and contractors. We come up with some good ideas, but everyone is a little braindead so we decide to regroup tomorrow morning around 8:00 A.M.

5:30–6:00 P.M. Fax over some proofs to a Kohler distributor in Colorado for approval. We talk about the changes, and I get them to the production manager as she is leaving.

6:00–6:45 P.M. Get a jump on the new business media plan due tomorrow morning. I crunch as many numbers as possible to get ahead before tomorrow. Record my hours for the day and try to get out of the office for an 8:00 softball game.

NEGOTIATION: THE ART OF A BUYER

Just as a labor union transacts with management for pay raises, security, and work conditions, so does a media buyer pursue special advantages for clients. The following are some of the key areas of negotiation.

Vehicle Performance. Selection through negotiation is especially important when the medium offers many options and when the buyers might need to use forecasted audience levels. One serious example is network television.

Nighttime programming is particularly fluid or changeable. Because of the dollars at risk, networks are very quick to rearrange programs, to cancel them and replace them with new ones, and to make other sorts of shifts. Buyers of time in network television are usually faced with selecting programs that (1) are new, (2) are not new but have been scheduled on a different night, or (3) have new lead-in programs. Under these conditions, little, if anything, stays the same. Selection must be made with little or no guarantee of audience popularity. Buyers deal with these uncertainties through careful research on the type of program (action, situation comedy), the rating history of the time slot, the audience flow patterns of competing programs, and other factors.

Unit Costs. Getting a low price has always been a goal for media buyers, but today it is mandatory. The published price is no longer acceptable to advertisers. **Open pricing**, in which each buyer or buying group negotiates a separate price for each vehicle, is gaining favor. Open pricing makes buyer negotiation both important and risky. The balance or trade-off between price and audience objectives must be fully understood before an all-out pursuit of open pricing is attempted. Some media experts fear that pricing will replace all other values, and media will eventually be treated like a bag of grain or a barrel of oil. These experts know that there is a very important balance to maintain between cost and value. No matter what pressure the buyer is under for low prices, he or she must balance a vehicle's quality with its cost.

open pricing A method of media pricing in which prices are negotiated on a contract-by-contract basis for each unit of media space or time.

Preferred Positions. In magazines there are assumed readership advantages in having the advertising message placed next to well-read pages or in special editorial sections. These placements are known as **preferred positions**. Imagine the value to a food advertiser of having its message located in a special recipe section that can be detached from the magazine for permanent use by the homemaker. How many additional exposures might that ad get? An ideal position in newspapers might be opposite the editorial page or a location in the food, financial, or sports section. With so many competing "voices," buyers are very anxious to find the most widely read sections.

preferred positions Sections or pages of magazine and newspaper issues that are in high demand by advertisers because they have a special appeal to the target audience.

Because they are so visible, preferred positions often carry a premium surcharge, usually 10 to 15 percent above standard space rates. In these days of negotiation space buyers are not hesitant about requesting that such charges be waived. Buyers will offer publications a higher number of insertions if the special positions are guaranteed without extra cost.

Extra Support Offers. In this time of strong emphasis on all sorts of promotional emphasis besides advertising, buyers are not shy about demanding additional assistance from the media beside space and time. These activities,

A WORLD OF MEREDITH MERCHANDISING/SALES SUPPORT OPPORTUNITIES

We can also help create a customized merchandising/sales support program that maximizes the effectiveness of your advertising with your sales staff, distributors and dealers. Some of the many possibilities:

▲ Producing special videos for promotional use.
▲ Using consumer direct mail lists (35 million names in all) for specialized direct marketing.
▲ Creating special publications to maintain contact with your customers or with your distribution network.
▲ Using Meredith books as consumer premiums or in sales incentive programs.
▲ Conducting quantitative or attitudinal marketing research.
▲ Using our real estate network to reach homebuyers.

These and other programs can be used individually or in combination.

Ad 12.6

In addition to providing advertising space and time, the media must offer merchandising and sales support to advertisers.

(© Copyright by Meredith Corporation 1988. All rights reserved.)

sometimes called *value-added* services, can take on any number of forms including: contests, special events, merchandising space at stores, displays, and trade-directed newsletters. The "extra" depends on what facilities each media vehicle has, and how hard the buyer can bargain with the dollars available.

Some media companies have decided to actively solicit marketers' budgets by integrating or packaging multimedia activities. At this time when integrated marketing communication programs are being favored, these plans are receiving serious consideration by marketing managements and media buyers alike. In Ad 12.6 the Meredith Company promotes a number of their available operations.

Marie Netolicky, National Television Buyer, DDB Needham, Chicago

I'm running late this morning—late enough so that I must phone in a "hold" to ABC before I leave home. A "hold" on two :30 units in *The American Comedy Awards* will reserve it at the negotiated price until I can get an order from the client. This was unexpected. We recommended a two-night sponsorship in the mini-series *The Bourne Identity*, based on the Robert Ludlum novel. Can you believe it? The ratings projection is good, but the client will not purchase it because they "don't like the leading man and woman." When will professional people learn to keep their personal feelings out of a sound business decision? Anyway, the last thing the client said last night was they *definitely* wanted two :30's in the awards show.

With that phoned in, I proceed to the office. When I get in, there are already five messages waiting for me. As I grab a cup of tea and look through my morning mail, the network calls me back to inform me that only one :30 unit is left in the awards show. They are holding that one :30 for me, but this changes everything. I now must go back to the drawing board and reconstruct another recommendation, because one :30 will not achieve the media plan goals.

While I try to rethink and rework, my two associates—planners on our accounts—pop in and out of my office with questions, problems, solutions, and jokes for comic relief. I could use them! Meanwhile I try to reach the media supervisor to discuss the changes to the recommendation, and we keep playing phone tag. My boss steps into my office to tell me he would like to meet with me and a few other supervisors in our group to discuss long-term national cable TV negotiations. The agency purchases all the following year's cable TV for all our clients in order to leverage the combined dollars for an efficient corporate rate. These negotiations can take months when you have as many as 15 cable networks with which to negotiate. I finally reach the media supervisor on the changes and we discuss the alternatives. She asks if I am available for a conference call with the client and, of course, I am. I wait until 12:40 P.M. to get a call back from her saying that I will not be needed for the conference call. Her boss is sending her over to the client to speak to them directly and to sell the new alternative recommendation.

By now it is 2:00 P.M. and I have to deal with the traffic problem. I speak to the associate media director

(Courtesy of Marie Netolicky)

on this account and we decide which of the other brands will cover the spots for the unfinished creative. I call a meeting with the broadcast traffic manager and the planner, and we agree on what is to be done. I really feel for the planner because his job is to change all the brand codes against the spots so that traffic can reschedule. Network and syndication are not bad, but the cable television changes involve several hundred units.

Finally, I receive the phone call I have been waiting for —the media supervisor calls and tells me that the alternative recommendation sold and that the client was happy. All that is left now is to get some promotional posters ordered with the client's logo imprinted on them.

It's getting near the end of the day, and I go through the rest of my mail. And the mail is endless...trade magazines to read, client correspondence that outlines new projects, contracts that must be checked and filed, and interoffice memos that need to be acted upon. And it starts all over again tomorrow.

SPECIAL SKILLS: MAINTAINING PLAN PERFORMANCE

Today a media buyer's responsibility to a campaign does not end with the signing of space and time contracts. Buys are made in advance on *forecasted* audience levels—the expectation that the audience for a vehicle will be at a certain level. What if vehicles underperform? What happens if unforeseen events affect scheduling? What if newspapers go on strike, if magazines fold, if a television show is canceled? Buyers must fix these problems.

MONITORING AUDIENCE RESEARCH

When campaigns begin, the forecasts in the media plan are checked against actual performance. Whenever possible, buyers check each incoming research report to determine whether the vehicle is performing as promised.

Broadcast Research. Change is the foundation of broadcast buying. Forecasting future popularity or target audience interest is full of risk. Once the schedule is running, buyers make every attempt to get current audience research. It is the only way to assure that schedules are performing according to the forecast.

Publication Research. Newspaper and magazine readership reports are produced less frequently than broadcast ratings, but print buyers are still concerned over changes in circulation. If a circulation audit shows a drop, it may indicate serious readership problems. Furthermore, buyers also check the publication issues to verify if advertisements have been correctly placed.

Out-of-Home Media Checking. Major users of outdoor advertising understand it is necessary to visually check sign and billboard positions. The condition of the ad, the presence of obstructions (buildings or trees), and any other situation that would reduce the expected audience exposure must be checked.

SCHEDULE AND TECHNICAL PROBLEMS

Temporary snags in scheduling and in the reproduction of the advertising message are usually unavoidable. For missed positions or errors in handling the message presentation, buyers must be alert to make the needed changes to reconcile difficulties. Most adjustments involve either replacement positions at no cost or money refunds. This policy of various forms of substitution is called *making good on the contract* The units of compensation are known as **makegoods**. Here are some examples.

Program Preemptions. Special programs or news events often interrupt regular programming. When this happens, the commercial schedule is also interrupted. **Program preemptions** occur nationally and locally. In the case of long-term interruptions—for example, congressional hearings or war coverage—buyers may have difficulty finding suitable replacements before the schedule ends.

Missed Closings. Magazines and newspapers have clearly set production dead-

makegoods Compensation given by the media to advertisers in the form of additional message units that are commonly used in situations involving production errors by the media and preemption of the advertiser's programming.

program preemptions Interruptions in local or network programming caused by special events.

lines, called *closings*, for each issue. Sometimes the advertising materials do not arrive in time. If the publication is responsible, it will make some sort of restitution. If the fault lies with the client or the agency, there is no restitution by the publication.

Technical Problems. Technical difficulties are responsible for the numerous "goofs," "gliches," and "foul-ups" that haunt the advertiser's schedule. In a classic example the buyer for a major airline received a call from the sales representative of the *Washington News*. The makeup staff at the newspaper had missed the intended position for the airline's ad and had run it instead on the *obituary page*. Damage done, makegood was forthcoming. In an extreme case the buyer for a new consumer brand learned that someone at a television station had inserted a "super" (an optical phrase superimposed on the film or tape) informing viewers that the product was *only* available in two small area towns. In truth, those towns accounted for less than 10 percent of the brand's distribution. The damage was serious, and the station did more than make good. It settled out of court.

Most technical problems are not quite so disastrous. "Bleed-throughs" and out-of-register colors for newspapers, torn billboard posters, broken film, and tapes out of alignment are more typical of the problems that plague media schedules.

$\mathscr{S}$UMMARY

- Media buying involves a serious of duties and functions that are separate from media planning.

- Media buyers are responsible for executing the media plan recommendations. To do this they must find and select the media vehicles that best fulfill the advertiser's needs.

- The media buyer must observe activity in the media marketplace, analyze audience research, negotiate for positions and price, and monitor schedule performance.

- Price negotiation has become more important as media have shifted from fixed to flexible pricing. Buyers are under strong pressure to get the lowest possible rates without sacrificing desired audience values.

- Buyers are also responsible for maintaining the performance standards established by the media plan throughout the campaign. Changes that lower the value of the message placements must be rectified quickly and efficiently.

$\mathscr{Q}$UESTIONS

1 Explain the job-related differences between media planning and media buying. Which job do you feel would be more challenging and satisfying? Assume that both positions offer equal compensation.

2 Mavis Cord is the senior buyer-negotiator for network television for her agency. Through

"insider" production contracts she has learned that a key program in the upcoming Willow Foods campaign is having serious production problems (star-director conflict). The start of the schedule is still two months away. Because this new program is projected to be one of the hits of the fall season, Willow management has been very excited about merchandising opportunities using the show's star. What should Mavis do, if anything, about this situation? How should she use her confidential information?

3 Your client is a major distributor of movie videotapes. Its yearly plan for magazines has been settled and you are in negotiation when you learn that a top publishing company is about to launch a new magazine dedicated to movie fans and video collectors. Although the editorial direction is perfect, there is no valid clue as to how the magazine will be accepted by the public. Worse, there won't be solid research on readership for at least a year. The sales representative offers a low charter page rate if the advertiser agrees to appear in each of the first year's issues (monthly). There is no money to add the publication to the existing list. To use it you will have to remove one of the established magazines from your list. Is the risk worthwhile? Should the client be bothered with this information considering that the plan is already set? What are your recommendations?

4 Bob Maples is the head buyer on the Killer Cola account. One portion of the soft drink's media plan involves a news programming buy in Columbus for radio advertising. The plan's primary goal is to develop frequent exposure against the target audience. Below are the highlights of two competing proposals. Only one can be selected. Which station should Bob recommend and why?

Station	Monthly Cost ($)	Announcements per Month	Target Impressions per Month
WOOK	2000	50	307,000
KLOD	1992	83	285,000

5 *Environmental Weekly* is one of the fastest-growing publications in the consumer sector. It has just announced that it will adopt an open-pricing program for space rates. The sales manager of EW has warned, however, that each magazine buy will be negotiated separately (if one of the agency clients gains a low page rate, it will not set a standard for others). As the head of the magazine buying group, what problem(s) does this approach suggest to you? What will you recommend to the department's director?

6 Discuss the difference between open and fixed media pricing. How does the use of these price policies affect the buying process?

$\mathcal{S}$UGGESTED CLASS PROJECT

Identify the best media buys that are *locally* available to expose a twentysomething audience. Set them in priority and discuss ranking. Specifics, such as newspaper name, station call letters, and cable channel are necessary.

$\mathcal{F}$URTHER READINGS

ARNOLD, M., DONALD W. JUGENHEIMER, and PETER B. TURK, *Media Research Sourcebook and Workbook* (Lincolnwood, IL: NTC Business Books, 1989).

WALL, ROBERT W., *Media Math: Basic Techniques of Media Evaluation* (Lincolnwood, IL: NTC Business Books, 1987).

Cosmetic Companies Discover Women of Color

The 1990 U.S. Census sounded an alarm to consumer products manufacturers that they could no longer afford to ignore the African-American, Asian, and Hispanic markets. The census told these companies that minorities now represented one out of every four Americans and that the Asian and Hispanic populations were increasing at more than ten times the rate of the white population. Marketers also learned that the African-American community, the nation's largest minority group, was growing at more than twice the rate of whites and that, as a whole, minorities were becoming richer. In the past 20 years, for example, the annual income of African-Americans grew sixfold to $270 billion.

Arguably, the census's message was heard most loudly in the corporate offices of cosmetics companies—firms whose stock in trade is covering the complexions of American women. Indeed, since skin tone is the most obvious difference between whites and people of color, cosmetics companies are responding to these demographic shifts more quickly than other consumer manufacturers. Encouraging their responsiveness is the buying power of minority consumers. Black women spend about three times as much on cosmetics as white women for a total of about $600 million a year.

The first mainstream cosmetics manufacturer to recognize the enormous potential in ethnic cosmetics was Maybelline, which introduced its Shades of You line in 1990. Estée Lauder followed a year later with All Skins, 115 foundation shades in its Prescriptives line that promised to satisfy the cosmetic needs of *all* women of color. Since then such cosmetics giants as Revlon, Clinique, Cover Girl, and Clarion have added their own lines of makeup for darker skins.

As cosmetics companies place greater emphasis on the "coloring of America," they have had to devise advertising strategies to reach minority markets. Ken Smikle, president of the African-American Marketing and Media Association, explains: "Marketing to African-Americans is a competitive imperative. It's not a question of *if* firms should market to blacks, but *how*."

In the not too distant past, the approach acknowledged minorities with a few black models. However, an increasing awareness of the unique cultural preferences and values of minority consumers is changing the way advertisers reach out.

A study conducted at De Paul University found that blacks respond best to ads that portray a range of images from the black community and prefer products that acknowledge the unique background of African-Americans. Tom Burrell, chairman and CEO of Chicago-based Burrell Communications Group, agrees. "Blacks are significantly different in terms of approach—our history, how we came here, how we developed as citizens," said Burrell. "There is a significant difference in behavior, and that manifests itself all the way to the marketplace."

Cosmetic companies are learning that these markets are not monolithic and that the differences in consumer behavior between blacks, Hispanics, and Asians often require different advertising strategies. For example, minority media may be needed to target a specific group. This approach has been used most successfully with Hispanic consumers. Nancy Tellet, senior vice president and director of media services for Conill Advertising, explains: Hispanics "are holding on to their mother tongue. . . . To advertise to them and get them to buy your products, you have to be able to communicate effectively." The Asian market represents a greater challenge since it is splintered among different communities, including Chinese-Americans, Japanese-Americans, and others.

As multiculturalism takes hold through the sheer force of numbers, cosmetic companies will be looking for more and better ways to reach minority consumers.

Sources: Sharon Barman, "Drawing Color Lines," *Working Woman*, August 1993, p. 50; Elizabeth Brous, "Multicultural Beauty," *Vogue*, June 1993, pp. 128 and 130; Christy Fisher, "Ethnics Gain Market Clout," *Advertising Age*, August 5, 1991, pp. 1 and 12; Maria Mallory, "Waking Up to a Major Market," *Business Week*, March 23, 1992, pp. 70–73; Gretchen Morgenson, "Where Can I Buy Some?" *Forbes*, June 24, 1991, pp. 82–84; Eugene Morris, "The Difference in Black and White," *American Demographics*, January 1993, pp. 44–49; Janice C. Simpson, "Business Buying Black," *Time*, August 31, 1992, pp. 52–53; Pat Sloan, "New Maybelline Line Targets Blacks," *Advertising Age*, December 17, 1990, pp. 1 and 36.

Questions

1. Why is knowledge of the unique cultures of the African-American, Hispanic, and Asian communities important to media buyers?

2. What specific steps would you take to determine the best media buys to reach minority consumers of women's cosmetics?

3. List five ads that were specifically targeted at minority consumers and assess the effectiveness of the chosen media.

Interactive Media and Marketing

One of the most important technological developments of the 1990s is the growing interactivity of communication media from newspapers to television. The new interactive technology provides consumers with the capacity to "talk back" to the media in many ways. Television viewers, while enjoying a dramatic increase in the number of television channels available, will be able to ask for specific programs, to request more special-interest information, to zap uninteresting programs or advertisements, and to order products and services from the easy chair. Newspapers, too, are finding ways to become interactive, such as the *Star Tribune* Fonahome service. These changes are of great interest to advertisers and advertising agencies alike.

Take, for example, how newspaper classified advertisements for homes and apartments for rent have changed in the *Star Tribune*. From the earliest days of newspapers, advertisements of homes and apartments for rent have been important sources of information to the public and important sources of revenue to newspaper publishers. The format of the "Rental Real Estate Classified" section has remained unchanged for many years: multiple listings of brief, abbreviated descriptions of rental properties. However, the *Star Tribune* Fonahome service has changed the section completely, to the benefit of both renters and newspaper publishers. Now, if Sue Jones wants to rent an apartment that offers certain amenities, allows pets, is in a particular price range, and is located in a certain part of town, she can call the *Star Tribune* Fonahome service and talk to a licensed real estate agent. The agent will check Sue's specifications against a database of listings and send her a rental information packet containing photographs, floor plans, videotapes, and directions to properties that meet her profile. This packet is free of charge and will allow Sue to review options in the comfort of her home. She can save time and effort by looking through the detailed descriptions before making appointments to visit properties she wants to consider.

Before Fonahome was acquired by the *Star Tribune*, it was an independent business. From the *Star Tribune's* point of view, Fonahome represents a service to its readers and an innovative improvement on traditional classified real estate advertising. From Fonahome's point of view, the *Star Tribune* represents an established and trusted "parent," a much-expanded base of potential customers, and an ideal vehicle for advertising and promotion of its specialized services. The acquisition of

Fonahome benefited both the newspaper and the service, and set the stage for promoting Fonahome to a much larger segment of potential renters.

When Fonahome joined the *Star Tribune*, it discontinued advertising in other media and doubled its *Star Tribune* allocation. It increased the number and size of its ads, included color photographs in some of them, and advertised in the Business, Sports, and Variety sections as well as in the Rental section of the newspaper. In the first three months of this new campaign, the number of *Star Tribune* rental inquiries approximately doubled. As a result, property owners gained access to a larger and better-informed audience of potential renters, while renters saved time and effort and were able to make better-informed choices.

This example demonstrates how effective interactive advertising can be. Instead of providing one-way messages—as traditional classified advertising always has— *Star Tribune* Fonahome provides an opportunity for two-way interaction. *Star Tribune* Fonahome representatives talk to each renter individually and assemble packages of information that each caller will find particularly useful. In this sense, *Star Tribune* Fonahome is

Exhibit A

OUR CLASSIFIEDS NOW TALK BACK.

Apartment information is now just a phone call away. Call us with your specifications. We'll send photos, floor plans and detailed information on apartments that match. It's fast. It's free. And it's how to find the right apartment right now.

673-8888

both a personal and a mass medium. This new development shows how effective interactive advertising can be and how beneficial and effective advertising can be when it conveys genuinely useful information.

Furthermore, the new world of interactive media and marketing will have far-reaching effects on advertising agencies and how they operate. Here is how Keith Reinhard, CEO of DDB Needham Worldwide, sees the probable changes ahead for his industry.[1]

Let's begin our discussion of the future of marketing by going back to 1887. In that year, Americans were provided with an unprecedented opportunity to "interact" with a merchant without being present at the store: the Sears catalog. Once the "technology"—that is, the catalog—was in the home, the customer, not the advertiser, decided when the communication would take place, and the customer, not the advertiser, decided which department would be shopped and how much time would be spent in each section—be it farm machinery, undergarments, even automobiles. The customer, not the advertiser, decided how much information to absorb, to review, or to avoid.

Assuming that the catalog designers had done a decent job of consumer research, there would invariably be an item or two of interest to the shopper. In this event, an order form was completed and mailed, and in a few weeks' time, the product was delivered. This was an early, low-tech example of remote, interactive selling. It is this basic process that the new interactive media technologies will enhance and expedite.

In contrast with the Sears catalog, and with personal selling, television evolved as radio with picture. Now the advertiser, not the customer, was in complete control. With radio, at least the listener could wander around the kitchen or the living room and still hear the program. With television, the viewer had to sit down when the program started and stay sitting there. The viewer only received and did not send. There was no interactivity at all. The viewer was told what to watch and when to watch it. Thus, television interrupted the interactivity of marketing by requiring that the customer sit silently inactive, captive to the medium and therefore to the seller. The new interactive media bring us back to where the customer, not the advertiser, chooses the time of the appointment.

I am not suggesting that a simplistic back-to-the basics approach will lead marketers to success with the new and infinitely more complicated interactive media, but I have become convinced that brushing up on the fundamentals of selling is a necessary first step, and that some of those fundamentals have gotten lost on the one-way streets of conventional television.

My checklist of the fundamentals of selling goes

[1]Excerpts from Keith K. Reinhard, "How to Sell Along the Information Highway," *Business Week* Symposium (September 22, 1993).

Exhibit B

GET THE UNABBREVIATED VERSION.

Get the whole story on your next apartment. Call us with your specifications. We'll send photos, floor plans and detailed information on apartments that match. It's fast. It's free. And it's how to find the right apartment right now.

Star Tribune
FONAHOME
673-8888

something like this: Know, honor, and love the customer. Offer the right merchandise. Present products in an inviting way. Spell out features and benefits clearly. Make it easy to buy.

The task we face in the new world of interactive media and marketing is nothing less than learning how to apply these fundamentals in the fractionated and computerized marketplace of the future.

In the new media marketplace we will be able to get a much better fix on the information that will reach the customer. Advertisers will know precisely who is seeing the message and be able to track their buying and viewing habits. Gross reach and frequency numbers will give way to cost-per-sale or cost-per-inquiry measurements.

Even as we become more knowledgeable about our customers, it will be easier for viewers to avoid traditional types of commercials. For instance, it will become possible to watch *60 Minutes* with or without commercials—at two different prices of course. This means that we will have to honor our customers. We will have to attract and hold them.

With so many audience fragments, offering the right merchandise at the right time will be easier from a technical standpoint but much more complicated to plan. Better strategic planning and much more precise targeting will be required. We will also see a return to advertiser-sponsored and/or produced programs appealing to homogeneous interest groups, and more coventures between media companies, marketers, and advertising agencies. A coventure between a ski-channel, a ski-

equipment manufacturer, and an advertising agency might be an example. Or a maker of scuba gear might invite viewers to learn more about Jacques Cousteau's equipment, then order it.

Because marketers will be speaking to smaller, more narrow target groups, an advertiser such as Ford could put an Escort commercial in two neighborhoods of a city while at the same time running a spot for a Lincoln Town Car in another.

The challenge of selecting the right merchandise for each of the many reachable groups will give rise to a whole new era of strategic research and planning. We must keep reminding ourselves that the new order of things will center on the fact that advertising messages will be chosen by the consumer. This spells doom for ads which insult the intelligence or offend sensibilities. Advertisers will need to aim not only to be inviting, but irresistible.

The old Sears catalog did a reasonably good job of spelling out features and benefits, and many of the best advertising writers got their start by learning to write catalog copy. Features and benefits will be important to a customer who will once again control the process. Many customers already access such information through computer sources such as Prodigy.

Conventional advertising told the customers what the advertiser wanted them to know. In the age of interactive media and marketing, the advertiser must tell customers what they want to know. We envision automobile channels, for example, which will allow the new car buyer to compare the models he or she is considering feature for feature, side by side, at the touch of a key. However information is provided, capacity and demand for more information about products can only benefit the consumer and lead to greater quality and value in more product categories.

Interactive media will make it much easier to buy goods and services from a wide range of categories. Macy's has already started a shopping channel. A service called Peapod is being tested by Jewel stores through 1,500 homes in the Chicago area. Customers can shop these food stores at home, aisle by aisle, or product by product, or by creating their own list.

On-site electronic media and interactive kiosks in malls and stores will add to the ease of buying for those who still prefer a trip to the mall—and people will indeed continue to visit the mall. In fact, there may be new stores in the mall—retail outlets for advertisers on the electronic highway. Think of J. Crew catalog which led to J. Crew stores.

The thought of customers shopping aisles of supermarkets from home, however, underscores what may turn out to be the toughest challenge of all for marketers in the new interactive multimedia world. Building strong national brands was relatively easy in the simpler, mass-marketing world of network television. How we advise clients to build brands in the new marketplace is the subject that occupies more of our time these days than perhaps any other. We know for certain the task will require the skillful orchestration of all media voices into one chorus of brand symbols and values.

This development will require advertising agencies to transform themselves from mass-media specialists to multimedia specialists. Trademarks will have to become trustmarks, and marketers will need to devote extensive efforts to what is referred to as relationship marketing—maintaining the bond between brand and customer. More and more, in an interactive world, brand loyalty will be earned as much by what a company stands for as by what a company makes.

We're anxious to get started on this electronic trip to the future and follow the road wherever it takes us—all the way to virtual reality, where we'll be able to let people test drive a car, tour a house, and sample a cruise or a new high-speed train.

In that connection, I'm reminded of a woman named Brenda Laurel, who lives in Banff, Canada, and is creating virtual-reality environments for people who will never be able to go there. "The whole course of human development," she says, "has been a march toward finding better ways to share the contents of our imaginations with each other. In the VR field, there's a kind of naive belief that once we're able to do that better…we'll suddenly be a whole lot better at understanding each other."

Questions for Discussion

1 What benefits accrue to each of the following in the acquisition of Fonahome by the *Star Tribune:* (a) Fonahome, (b) the *Star Tribune*, (c) rental property owners, and (d) renters?

2 Why must advertising agencies transform themselves from mass-media specialists to multimedia specialists, according to Keith Reinhard?

3 How will interactive media and marketing shift the focus of advertising from the advertiser to the customer?

$\mathcal{T}$HE CREATIVE SIDE OF ADVERTISING

13

CHAPTER OBJECTIVES

When you have completed this chapter, you should be able to:

- List various characteristics of creative people

- Explain what advertisers mean by a creative concept

- Describe the various stages involved in creating an advertisement

- Understand how the various elements in an advertisement work together to create impact

- Distinguish between effective copywriting and adese

HOW IDEAS EVOLVE: PEPSI'S GENERATION WITH AN ATTITUDE

How are ads created? Let's look at the process that has evolved at BBDO for Pepsi, one of its most important clients. Pretend it's a Monday in October and you are in Los Angeles for the shoot for the Pepsi commercials that will break in the Super Bowl, the blockbuster event that has television's biggest audience watching.[1]

The pressure is on. Not only are there only a few weeks left before the ads run at the corporate meeting, the commercials that appear in this annual Super Bowl of Advertising receive almost as much hype as the game itself. Add to that BBDO's mission to make the Pepsi commercials some of the most popular ads on television. Then ratchet up the pressure a few notches with Pepsi president Craig Weatherup's declaration that "We are our advertising." Does that give you some idea what is at stake?

Although most aspects of the campaign had been laid out long before the BBDO creative team got to Sound Stage 8 at Culver Studio a few miles from Venice Beach, no idea is static, even for a huge client like Pepsi. In contrast to some agencies (and clients) that want a final script carved in stone before moving into the expensive production stage, ideas are treated like amoebas at BBDO—they are expected to keep dividing and mutating as they develop. "We never stop trying to take it to a different level," says Ted Sann, BBDO executive creative director who, along with Don Schneider, senior vice president/creative director, created the Pepsi ads.

On this Monday in October, shooting this new package of three Pepsi-Cola ads, things are running behind schedule, nothing quite clicks, and tension keeps the air electric. Legendary director Joe Pytka is framing his shots interrupted by emotional explosions. At 6'5" with his unruly mane of long blond hair, a sometimes caustic temperament, and a strong personal artistic vision, Pytka is a presence not easily tampered with. That's how these shoots always begin, says one of the BBDO staff as he chews on nails already bitten to the quick.

The campaign tries to move Pepsi back to its roots—to its youthful association. But this isn't just a replay of old lines like "the Pepsi generation" that sounded good several years ago. It's an attempt to get in touch with the new generation, and this is a generation with an attitude. What BBDO wants to capture in these shots is this attitude. The BBDO team along with Pytka spent downtime on the set going through tape after tape of teenagers. "We're looking for our version of what's young, cool and hip," says Sann. "That doesn't have to do with being good looking but with having some character and an attitude." There are hundreds of Polaroids of kids tacked up on a series of bulletin boards. About 60 were told to show up at Venice Beach for the shoot the next day.

A quick synopsis of the three ads and how they are evolving:

"Smiling": A sociologist muses about youth in the serious nineties. As he spins out theories of introspection, moderation, and the return to "quiet elegance," the camera grabs kids in various states of excess proving that every wacky thing that has been said about generation X is true.

"How You Spend Your Life": The spot takes a numbers approach, with an "old" professor type narrating how the average person spends his or her life, among other things: 24.5 years sleeping, 2.4 years in the bathroom, 3.2 years listening to boring lectures. During the first days of the shoot, a kid had been cast to handle the narra-

---

[1]Adapted from Betsy Sharkey, "Super Angst," *Adweek* (January 25, 1993): 24–33.

tive. "Just for the hell of it, we also decided to have an older, boring person read," says Schneider. "Casting starts to bring a script to life. We loved the kid, but we see other things coming out with the older guy." Although the general consensus is that they'll use the older actor, Pytka shoots it both ways. By the time the shoot wraps, the agency creatives have come full circle, opting to use the kid instead. Such decisions come down to how something finally plays on the screen.

"That's Life": This spot visually tracks a kid through his adult life as he imagines it, including "wife, kids, barbeque with the in-laws, bowl on Wednesdays, kiss a little butt at the office, make middle management, retire to Miami, buy some white shoes and pants that come up to my chest and complain about the government full-time." The main sight gag is that while everyone around him ages, our hero remains a curly-haired 13-year-old with a baseball cap. Hours are spent trying to milk the visual impact of each scene. For example, to go along with the line "kiss a little butt at the office," a number of scenarios are tried, but having the kid say, "Nice tie, sir," as he passes his boss plays best.

Now it's just 12 days before the Super Bowl and the BBDO creative directors are in the editing room still massaging the ads. Only two weeks before, they added an entirely new twist to the "Smiling" spot, taking what had been just a voice-over and casting a professor type to give the voice a visual context. Initially, the ad was conceived as visuals of kids doing their thing with the sociologist relegated to a voice-over, using BBDO chairperson/CEO Phil Dusenberry's voice. But in the editing process, the creative team became convinced there had to be a visual to go with the voice. New footage was shot and Dusenberry's voice was dropped from what had been a finished ad only three weeks earlier. They rushed to film the newly recruited actor, then intercut his scenes throughout the spot.

The point is that creative ideas don't tend to leap into the script fully shaped and ready for production. Creative development is an evolving process with lots of tinkering and revising. We'll continue talking about how this campaign evolved as we discuss the process of creating ads in this chapter.

THE CREATIVE CONCEPT

creative concept A "big idea" that is original and dramatizes the selling point.

Behind every good advertisement is a **creative concept**, a Big Idea that makes the message distinctive, attention-getting, and memorable. In the Pepsi campaign, the Big Idea is the irreverent attitude of today's youth toward the adult world. It's a classic story line except instead of focusing on rebellion, BBDO touches on the funny side of the generation battle as it is played out in teenagers who would just as soon not grow older.

Finding the brilliant creative concept involves what advertising giant Otto Kleppner called the creative leap.[2] To come up with the Big Idea, you have to move beyond the safety of the *strategy* statement and leap into the creative unknown. The creative team's mission is to find a novel and unexpected way to showcase a sales point. In its business language the idea might sound like a dull statement of strategy, but in an advertisement this same idea is expressed in a way that grabs the audience's mind. The creative leap dramatizes the strategy

[2]Thomas Russell and Glenn Verrill, *Otto Kleppner's Advertising Procedure*, 11th ed. (Englewood Cliffs, NJ: Prentice Hall, 1990):457.

behind the message, captures attention, and makes the advertisement memorable.

The springboard for the leap is the strategy. Advertising has to be creative, but it also has to be strategic. However, there is a big difference between the *creative brief*, usually written in marketing language, and the creative concept which is another term for the Big Idea. The difference represents the "leap," which is "not merely a step away from that which existed before, but miles away."

The creative concept then becomes the springboard for the **execution** of the advertisement and that also must be handled creatively. The word *execution* refers to all the details and decisions involved in production of the advertisement. The hours spent on casting in the Pepsi campaign and working out the lines and the lighting and the fast-cut pacing are all part of the execution and contribute to the successful development of the idea.

Roles. All agencies have *copywriters* and *art directors* who are responsible for dreaming up the creative concept and crafting the execution. They frequently work in teams of two, are sometimes hired and fired as a team, and may successfully work together for a number of years. The *creative director* manages the creative process and plays an important role in focusing the strategy of ads and making sure the creative concept is strategically on target.

Usually both members of the creative team come up with concept ideas as well as word and picture ideas. Their writing or design specialties come into play more in the crafting of the idea once it is agreed upon.

The concept may come to mind as a visual, a phrase, or a thought that uses both visual and verbal expression. If it begins as a phrase, the next step is to try to visualize what the concept looks like. If it begins as an image, the next step is to come up with words that express what the visual is saying. Words and pictures reinforce one another as in the American Cancer Society's Fry Now ad, Ad 13.1.

WHAT MAKES AN IDEA CREATIVE?

Creative ideas aren't limited to advertising. People such as Henry Ford, who created and then advertised his Model T, and Steven Jobs, the co-founder of Apple Computer, are highly creative. They are idea people, creative problem solvers, and highly original thinkers. Creative people are found in business, in science, in engineering, as well as in advertising.

ROI. The creative philosophy of DDB Needham Worldwide is summarized in a play on the bottom-line concerns of business as ROI: relevance, originality, and impact. These three characteristics help describe what makes ideas creative in advertising.

Advertising is a disciplined, goal-oriented field that tries to deliver the right message to the right person at the right time. The goal is persuasion that results in either a change of opinion or a sale. Ideas have to mean something important to the audience. In other words, they must have **relevance**.

Advertising is directed at convincing people to do something. Unlike a painting, a building, or a technological breakthrough, creativity in advertising requires empathy, a keen awareness of the audience: how they think and feel, what they value, and what makes them take notice. A creative idea has to speak to the right audience with the right sales message. The purpose of advertising is

first and foremost to sell the product, service, or idea. No matter how much the creative people or the client or the account executive may like an idea, if it doesn't communicate the right message or the right product personality to the right audience, then it won't work. Liking the idea simply isn't enough.

An advertising idea is considered creative when it is novel, fresh, unexpected, and unusual. **Original** means one of a kind. Any idea can seem creative to you if you have never thought of it before, but the essence of a *creative* idea is that no one else has thought of it either.

original One of a kind; unusual and unexpected.

In classes on creative thinking, a teacher will typically ask students to come up with ideas about, for example, what you can build with ten bricks. Some ideas—such as a wall—will appear on many people's lists. Those are obvious and expected ideas. The original ideas are those that only one person thinks of.

An unexpected idea can be one with a twist, an unexpected association, or catchy phrasing. A familiar phrase can become the raw material of a new idea if it is presented in some unusual or unexpected situation. An ad for Bailey's Irish Cream, for example, shows the product being poured into a wine glass over ice cubes. The twist is in the headline that reads: "Holiday on Ice." A play on words is also a good way to develop something unexpected. The American Cancer Society used the headline "Fry Now, Pay Later" for its safe-tanning message (see Ad 13.1)

cliché A trite expression, an overused idea.

Unoriginal advertising is not novel or fresh; it is the common or obvious idea. Look-alike advertising copies somebody else's great idea. Unfortunately, a great idea is only great the first time around. When it gets copied and overused, it becomes a **cliché**. Even though professionals continually disparage copycat advertising, it remains a dominant advertising form. Although everyone is searching for a great idea, not everyone is lucky or talented enough to find one.

One of the most copied advertising ideas in history is the Perception/Reality campaign for *Rolling Stone* magazine created by the Fallon McElligott agency. The campaign, which began running in 1985, pairs people's "perceptions" of the magazine as a publication for hippies with the reality of who the early hippie readers of *Rolling Stone* have become, using visual and verbal puns. The campaign has become so popular within the advertising community that every time a creative team has an assignment that asks them to change a perception, they are tempted to create a copycat ad. An example of the *Rolling Stone* campaign is shown in Chapter 5.

impact The effect that a message has on the audience.

To be creative, the ideas must also have **impact**. Most advertisements just "wash over" the audience. A commercial with impact can break through the screen of indifference and focus the audience's attention on the message and the product. An idea with impact helps people see themselves or the world in a new way. The classic campaign for V-8 vegetable juice demonstrates the impact of a creative idea when the various characters hit themselves on the forehead in the familiar gesture that says "Why didn't I think of that" while saying aloud, "I could have had a V-8." That ad expresses the impact and power of a relevant, new idea.

An ad with impact has the stopping power that comes from an intriguing idea—something you have never thought about before. An example of how a startling thought can stop you and make you think is equating driving with playing in the mud as in the Effie award-winning Isuzu ad, Ad 13.2, with how a child develops personality traits.

Strategy and Creativity. Let's look at the relationship between strategy and the creative concept. To be creative, an idea must be both different (novel, unexpected) and right for the product and target. Good advertising is both original and strategically sound—it is both an art and a disciplined solution to a communication problem. Creative people in advertising must answer to both masters, and this makes creative advertising extremely difficult to do. Cleverness is not enough. Jim Osterman, *Adweek* editor, explained in his column, "I get ample opportunity to see the work students are doing. It's fresh and has attitude, but some of it wouldn't sell because it's not strategic. That doesn't mean it's bad work, but it does mean that just being clever is not enough. To me, great creative has to be targeted creative as well."[3]

Positioning is as important as targeting. The Pepsi advertising has evolved strategically over time. The "Gotta Have It" line, which had been Pepsi's slogan

---

[3]Jim Osterman, "Whatever's Clever Is Never Enough," *Adweek* (October 25, 1993):54.

Mike Shine proudly displaying his homemade "mud pie" circa 1968.

THEY SAY ONLY

PERSONALITY

TRAITS

ARE DEFINED AT AN

EARLY AGE.

Mike Shine proudly displaying his 4 WD, 3.1 liter, V6 Rodeo circa 1992.

IF YOU WERE THE KIND OF KID WHO COULD / INTRODUCE YOU TO THE RODEO. A RUGGED 4WD / AND THE RODEO COMES WITH AN INCREDIBLY / YOU'RE ALREADY AN OLDER GUY, THAT'S

GO OUT OF THE HOUSE WEARING WHITE, AND / SPORT UTILITY VEHICLE THAT CAN GO THROUGH / LOW PRICE TAG. WHICH MEANS YOU DON'T / ALRIGHT TOO. LIKE WE ALWAYS SAY, IT'S

COME BACK WEARING WHITE, READ NO FURTHER. / MOST ANYTHING YOU'LL EVER ENCOUNTER, / HAVE TO WAIT UNTIL YOU'RE REALLY OLD / NEVER TOO LATE TO HAVE

IF YOU WERE THE OTHER KIND, WE'D LIKE TO / (or in your case, go looking for). / TO BE ABLE TO AFFORD ONE. OF COURSE, IF / A HAPPY CHILDHOOD.

ISUZU

Practically/Amazing

Ad 13.2

Isuzu targets people who live unconventional lives and drive unconventional cars.

before the Pepsi attitude campaign, was a statistical success—consumers rated Pepsi advertising as one of their Top 10 favorites. But that slogan, which replaced the "Choice of a New Generation" theme that had worked so well since Michael Jackson and the Pepsi Generation began in the early 1980s, moved away from Pepsi's long-held position as owning the "young and hip" franchise. The client wanted to get that position back. For the new campaign, the "Gotta Have It" line was supported with a tagline that reaffirms the Pepsi attitude: "Be Young. Have Fun. Drink Pepsi."

The Leo Burnett agency has developed an approach to analyzing the message design that keeps both strategy and creativity in perspective. Called *structural analysis*, it first looks at the power of the narrative or story line and then evaluates the strength of the product claim. Finally, it looks at how well the two aspects are integrated—that is, how the story line brings the claim to life. The creative team checks to see if the narrative level is so high that it overpowers the claim or if the claim is strong but there is no memorable story. Ideally, these two elements will be so seamless that it is hard to tell whether the impact derives from the power of the story or strength of the claim.

CREATIVE THINKING

How do you get creative ideas? One of the myths of the advertising business is that only certain people are creative. Actually, creativity is a special form of problem solving, and everyone is born with talent in that area.

Furthermore, creativity is not limited in advertising to the "creative side."

Advertising is a very creative business that demands imagination and problem-solving abilities in all areas. Media planners and researchers, for example, are just as creative as copywriters and art directors in searching for innovative solutions to the problems they face.

An idea, according to James Webb Young, a legendary advertising executive, is "a new combination" of thoughts. In his classic book *A Technique for Producing Ideas*, Young claimed that "the ability to make new combinations is heightened by an ability to see relationships."[4] An idea is a thought that is stimulated by placing two previously unrelated concepts together. The juxtaposition sets up new patterns and new relationships and creates a new way of looking at things. This phenomenon has been described as making the familiar strange and the strange familiar. A creative idea involves a "mind-shift." Instead of seeing the obvious, a creative idea looks at something in a different way, from a different angle as in Ad 13.3, which associates a package of gum with carry-on luggage.

free association An exercise in which you describe everything that comes into your mind when you think of a word or an image.

Creative thinking uses a technique called **free association**. Young's definition of a new idea calls for the juxtaposition of two seemingly unrelated thoughts. That is what happens in associative thinking. In free association you think of a word and then describe everything that comes into your mind when you imagine that word. Associative thinking can be visual or verbal—you can start with a picture or a word. Likewise, you can associate by thinking of either pictures or words.

An example of how free association works is the campaign for the state of Texas by GSDM advertising agency. The agency's famous Don't Mess with Texas antilitter campaign is a takeoff on a common pseudo-macho phrase, but it has a twist because of the double meaning of the word *mess*.

Actually researchers say there are two basic approaches to getting ideas: *creative* approaches using techniques such as brainstorming and free association and *analytical* approaches based on techniques such as market analysis and consumer research. Creative techniques tend to generate more new-product ideas compared with the analytical, but both are needed for effective creativity.[5]

---

[4]James Webb Young, *A Technique for Producing Ideas*, 3rd ed. (Chicago: Crain Books, 1975).
[5]Trevor Sowrey, "Idea Generation: Identifying the Most Useful Techniques," *European Journal of Marketing*, 24 (5): 20–29.

Divergent Thinking. Creative thinking is different from the way you think when you try to balance your checkbook or develop an outline for an essay in English class. Most of the thinking that students do in classrooms is rational and is based on a linear logic whereby one point follows from another, either inductively or deductively.

Creative thinking uses an entirely different process. J. P. Guilford, a well-known cognitive psychologist, distinguished between convergent thinking and divergent thinking.[6] **Convergent thinking** uses linear logic to arrive at the "right" conclusion. **Divergent thinking** which is the heart of creative thinking, uses associative thinking to search for all possible alternatives.

Right and Left Brain. In current neurophysiology these two types of thinking have been associated with different hemispheres of the brain. Left-brain thinking is logical and controls speech and writing; right-brain thinking is intuitive, nonverbal, and emotional. Most people use both sides of their brains, depending on the task. An artist is generally more oriented to right-brain thinking, whereas an accountant is more left-brained. A person who is left-brain dominant is presumed to be logical, orderly, and verbal. In contrast, a person who is right-brain dominant deals in expressive visual images, emotion, intuition, and complex interrelated ideas that must be understood as a whole rather than as pieces.[7]

THE CREATIVE PROCESS

There is a tendency to think of a creative person as someone who sits around waiting for an idea to strike. In comic books that is the point where the light bulb comes on above the character's head. In reality, most people who are good at thinking up new ideas will tell you that it is hard work. They read, they study, they analyze, they test and retest, they sweat and curse and worry, and sometimes they give up. Major breakthroughs in science or medicine may take years, decades, even generations. The unusual, unexpected, novel idea doesn't come easily

Certainly any individual is capable of coming up with an idea or two, but in reality, as Osterman pointed out, many of those ideas are either lacking in potential, impractical to produce, or outside the product's strategy. This is especially true of the ideas that arise without the aid of disciplined procedures. Random ideas come mainly by chance but in a disciplined systematic approach, such as that diagrammed in Figure 13.1, ideas are generated through an organized procedure. Rarely do the ideas just come from "out of the blue."

Despite differences in terms and emphasis, there is a great deal of agreement among the different descriptions of the creative process. The creative process is usually portrayed as following sequential steps. As long ago as 1926 an English sociologist named Graham Wallas first put names to the steps in the creative process. He called them: *preparation, incubation, illumination,* and *verification.*[8]

A more comprehensive process is suggested by Alex Osborn, the former head of the BBDO agency, who established the Creative Education Foundation, which runs workshops and publishes a journal on creativity:

convergent thinking   Thinking that uses logic to arrive at the "right" answer.

divergent thinking   Thinking that uses free association to uncover all possible alternatives.

---

[6]J. P. Guilford, "Traits of Personality," in *Creativity and Its Cultivation,* H. H. Anderson, ed. (New York: Harper & Brothers, 1959).
[7]Betty Edwards, *Drawing on the Right Side of the Brain* (Los Angeles: Tarcher, 1979).
[8]Graham Wallas, *The Art of Thought* (New York: Harcourt, Brace & World, Inc., 1926).

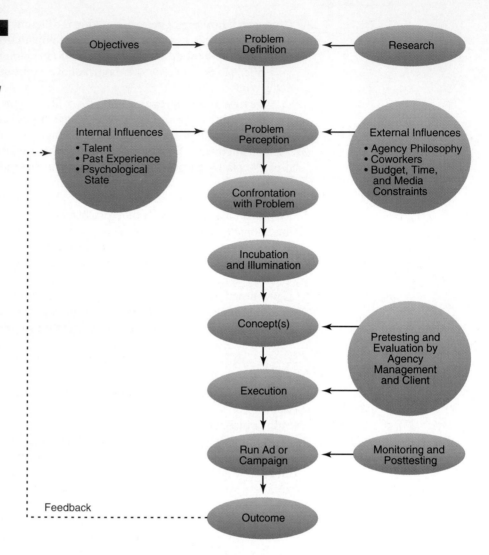

Figure 13.1

The creative process in advertising.

(Source: Reprinted from Marketing News, *March 18, 1983:22, published by the American Marketing Association. Bruce Vanden Bergh, "Take this 10-Lesson Course on Managing Creatives Creatively.")*

1. Orientation: pointing up the problem
2. Preparation: gathering pertinent data
3. Analysis: breaking down the relevant material
4. Ideation: piling up alternative ideas
5. Incubation: letting up, inviting illumination
6. Synthesis: putting the pieces together
7. Evaluation: judging the resulting ideas[9]

Although the steps vary somewhat and the names differ, all creative strategies seem to share several key points. Researchers consistently have found that ideas come after the person has immersed himself or herself in the problem and worked at it to the point of giving up. *Preparation* and *analysis* is that essential period of hard work when you read, research, investigate, and learn everything you can about the problem.

---

[9]Alex F. Osborn, *Applied Imagination*, 3rd ed. (New York: Scribners, 1963).

Next comes ideation, a time of playing with the material, of turning the problem over and looking at it from every angle. This is also a period of teasing out ideas and bringing them to the surface. Most creative people develop a physical technique for generating ideas, such as doodling, taking a walk, jogging, riding up and down on the elevator, going to a movie, or eating certain foods. It is a highly personal technique used to "get in the mood," to start the wheels turning. The objective of this stage is to generate as many alternatives as possible. The more ideas that are generated, the better the final concepts.[10]

The processes of analysis, juxtaposition, and association are mentally fatiguing for most people. You may hit a blank wall and find yourself giving up. This is the point that Young describes as "brainfag." It is a necessary part of the process.

Incubation is the most interesting part of the process. This is the point where you put your conscious mind to rest and let your subconscious take over the problem-solving effort. In other words, when you find yourself frustrated and exasperated because the ideas just won't come, try getting away from the problem. Go for a walk, go to a movie, do anything that lets you put the problem "out of your mind," because that is when the subconscious will take over.

Illumination is that unexpected moment when the idea comes. Typically, the solution to the problem appears at the least expected time: not when you are sitting at the desk straining your brain, but later that evening just before you drop off to sleep or in the morning when you wake up. At an unexpected moment the pieces fit together, the pattern is obvious, and the solution jumps out at you.

Principle

Ideas come at the most unexpected times—but only after hard work.

One of the most important steps is the *verification* or evaluation stage, where you step back and look at the great idea objectively. Is it really all that creative? Is it understandable? Most of all, does it accomplish the strategy? Most people working on the creative side of advertising will admit that many of their best creative ideas just didn't work. They may have been great ideas, but they didn't solve the problem or accomplish the right objective. Copywriters will also admit that sometimes the idea they initially thought was wonderful does not project any excitement a day or week later.

Part of evaluation involves the personal go/no go decision which every creative person has to be able to make. Craig Weatherup, Pepsi president/CEO explained, "You must have a clear vision...and have the nerve to pull the trigger." Weatherup is willing to pull the trigger on ideas for Pepsi advertising strategies, as is BBDO's Dusenberry. "On Pepsi, the kill rate is high," Dusenberry says. "For every spot we go to the client with, we've probably killed nine other spots."

brainstorming A creative-thinking technique using free association in a group environment to stimulate inspiration.

Principle

In brainstorming, seek quantity but defer judgment.

Brainstorming. **Brainstorming** is a technique developed in the early 1950s by Alex Osborn.[11] Brainstorming uses associative thinking in a group context. Osborn would get a group of six to ten people together in his agency and ask them to come up with ideas. One person's ideas would stimulate someone else, and the combined power of the group associations stimulated far more ideas than any one person could think of alone. The secret to brainstorming is to remain positive. The rule is to defer judgment. Negative thinking during a brainstorming session can destroy the informal atmosphere necessary to achieve a novel idea.

Another type of divergent thinking uses such comparisons as analogies and

---

[10]Bruce G. Vanden Bergh, Leonard N. Reid, and Gerald A. Schorin, "How Many Creative Alternatives to Generate," *Journal of Advertising, 12* (1983):4.
[11]W. J. J. Gordon, *The Metaphorical Way of Learning and Knowing* (Cambridge: Penguin Books, 1971).

metaphors, as in the Wrigley's ad (Ad 13.3). Young's definition of an idea also called for the ability to see new patterns or relationships. This is what happens when you think in analogies. You are saying that one pattern is like or similar to another totally unrelated pattern. William J. J. Gordon, a researcher in the area of creative thinking, discovered in his research that new ideas were often expressed as analogies. He has developed a program called *Synectics* that trains people to approach problem solving by applying analogies.[12]

THE CREATIVE PERSON

Is creativity a personality trait we are born with or a skill we can develop? Geneticists studying the issue contend that we are all born with creative potential—the ability to solve problems by combining complex and sometimes unrelated ideas. Some people have more natural skills than others—people like Joe Pytka who is featured in the Inside Advertising box. You probably know people in your school and circle of friends who are just naturally zany, coming up with crazy off-the wall ideas. In terms of being creative, these people start off with a little advantage. But that's all it is. And it may be a disadvantage if they can't tame their craziness to fit into an office environment or the world at large.

As a matter of fact, a lot of the traits that lead to creative thinking—being nonconforming and unconventional, for example—are smothered in the educational process, which is more concerned with teaching children to be "well behaved." Both education and society can punish children for being different and that, of course, is the springboard for creative thinking.

Research by the Center for Studies in Creativity and the Creative Education Foundation, both in Buffalo, New York, has found that most people can sharpen their skills and develop their creative potential, just as most people can learn to play the piano. But first you need to know what makes a creative person creative and then you can work on developing those skills.

Personal Characteristics. Although everyone has some problem-solving abilities, certain traits seem to be typical of creative problem solvers. The first is that they soak up experiences like sponges. They have a huge personal reservoir of material: things they have read, watched, or listened to, places they have been and worked, and people they have known.

Research has found that creative people tend to be independent, self-assertive, self-sufficient, persistent, and self-disciplined, with a high tolerance for ambiguity. They are risk takers, and they have powerful egos. In other words, they are *internally driven*. They don't care much about group standards and opinions. They are less conventional than are noncreative people and have less interest in interpersonal relationships.

Creative people typically have an inborn skepticism and very curious minds. They are alert, watchful, and observant, and reach conclusions through intuition rather than through logic. They also have a mental playfulness that allows them to make novel associations. They find inspiration in daydreams and fantasies, and they have a good sense of humor.

In general, creative people tend to perform difficult tasks in an effortless manner and are unhappy and depressed when they are not being creative. In

---

[12]Ibid.

addition to having many positive characteristics, however, they have also been described as abrasive, hard to deal with, and withdrawn.

What characteristics do creative thinkers *not* exhibit? They are into dogmatic (although they can be stubborn), and they have little patience with authoritarian people. These people don't follow the crowd, and they like being alone. They aren't timid, and they don't care much about what other people think.

Visualization Skills. Most copywriters have a good visual imagination as well as excellent writing skills. Art directors, of course, are good visualizers, but they can also be quite verbal. Stephen Baker, in his book *A Systematic Approach to Advertising Creativity*, describes "writers who doodle and designers who scribble" as the heart of the advertising concept team.[13]

Writers as well as designers must be able to visualize. Good writers paint pictures with words; they describe what something looks like, sounds like, smells like, and tastes like. They use words to transmit these sensory impressions. Most of the information we accumulate comes through sight, so the ability to manipulate visual images is very important for good writers. In addition to seeing products, people, and scenes in their "mind's eye," good writers are able to visualize a mental picture of the finished ad while it is still in the talking, or idea, state.

Visualization, the ability to imagine how the ad or commercial will look, is critical to people on the creative side of advertising. For example imagine you are creating an advertisement for Alaska Airlines and come up with the idea of attributing a personality to the airline. How would you turn that idea into a visual? Ad 13.4 shows how Alaska Airlines' creative people accomplished that mission.

---

[13]Stephen Baker, *A Systematic Approach to Advertising Creativity* (New York: McGraw-Hill Book Co., 1979).

Ad 13.4

How would you create the idea visually that an airline has a bland personality? The Alaska Airlines ad used a common symbol to represent the generic quality of most airline companies.

(Courtesy of Alaska Airlines)

Creative advertising people are zany, weird, off the wall, and unconventional but they are not eccentric. In other words, they are still very centered on doing effective advertising. Some try to be eccentric in style and appearance and wear it as a badge to announce their creativity. But advertising is a business and businesspeople, however creative, still have to be in touch with the forms and style of business. If you are so eccentric that your agency is afraid to let you make the presentation of your ideas to the client, then your style gets in the way of your productivity and that can damage a career as well as kill a campaign presentation.

Creative people in advertising also have to live with deadlines—a factor that separates the fine artist from the advertising creative. You have to be able to push ideas together when you are under pressure and tired. Some creative people say it's the pressure that makes them perform; the more pressure, the better their work.

Advertising is a tough, problem-solving field where you don't have the luxury of waiting for a creative concept to appear. According to former advertising executive Gordon White, "It is creativity on demand, so to speak. Creating within strict parameters. Creativity with a deadline."[14]

In order to force group creativity against a deadline, some agencies have special rooms and processes for brainstorming—rooms, for example, with no distractions and interruptions, such as telephones, and walls that can be papered over with tissues covered with ideas. Other agencies rent a suite in a hotel and send the creative team there to immerse themselves in the problem, again without distractions from the office. When GSDM, for example, was defending its prized Southwest Airlines account, president Roy Spence ordered a 28-day "war room" death march that had staffers working around the clock, wearing Rambo-style camouflage, and piling all their trash inside the building to keep any outsiders from rummaging around for clues to their pitch[15]

Personal Development. For many years conventional wisdom was that, like Einstein, you were either born creative or you were not. Today research demonstrates that almost anyone can learn to develop his or her innate creativity.[16] Creativity is not a talent, it is a way of operating, a mode of behavior. Learning how to operate more creatively, then, is possible for anyone. People who are successful in the creative world have learned how to get into the mood and how to proceed. That is, they have developed a *way of operating* that stimulates their innate creative abilities. Sometimes it's ritualized: One writer may ride the elevator up and down or take a walk along a certain route as a mental signal to the creative mode; another writer may sharpen pencils as a way to jumpstart the creative process.

Attitude is a big part of it.[17] Research into the personalities of creative people has found that the primary personality difference between those who are creative and those who are not is that creative people *believe* they are creative. So, for someone who wants to be more creative, understanding the importance of that basic mind-shift is the first step in unleashing creative potential.

[14]Gordon E. White, "Creativity: The X Factor in Advertising Theory," in *Strategic Advertising Decisions: Selected Readings*, Ronald D. Michman and Donald W. Jugenheimer, eds. (Columbus, OH: Grid, Inc., 1976):212.
[15]Noreen O'Leary, "Roy Spence's Perpetual Campaign," *Adweek* (November 29, 1993):24–28.
[16]Scott G. Isaksen, Gerard J. Puccio, and Donald J. Treffinger, "An Ecological Approach to Creative Problem Solving," *Journal of Creative Behavior*, 27 (3), 1993: 149–170.
[17]Michael Michalko, *Tinkertoys* (Berkeley, CA: Ten Speed Press, 1991).

Leonardo da Vinci, Albert Einstein, and Georgia O'Keefe excelled in different fields, but all three qualify as creative geniuses.

(Leonardo da Vinci, Albert Einstein, and Georgia O'Keefe, courtesy of The Bettmann Archives.)

The opposite of that principle is that negative thinking is the single most destructive factor for a creative person. Being in a bad mood, depressed, or unconfident almost always sets you up for a bad creative day. Professionals, of course, sometimes get depressed and have bad moods, so how do they continue to be productive? They develop ways to put the bad mood aside when they move into their creative mode. They do it instinctively because most of them realize that their job responsibilities rise above the daily difficulties of life. When they are on the job, the other stuff gets filed in a back compartment of the mind.

Research also shows that wide *experience* is a prerequisite to creativity. Creative people need mental fodder to work with, a lot of material stewing in the mind's melting pot. Anything you can do to build up your reservoir of life experiences helps. Working, particularly in an environment foreign to your upbringing, such as picking peas in the fields during summer vacation or working in a cannery when you grew up in an upper-middle-class suburban home, brings you in touch with people whose lives and concerns are different from yours. Being around people who see the world differently, which also comes from travel, always broadens the experiences of open minded people.

Likewise, reading and staying in touch with a variety of mass media such as publications and programs aimed at different audiences adds to your reservoir. Every advertising creative person interviewed for a study on how they work mentioned their voracious reading habits and compulsive need to know everything on television, in the movies, and on the radio.[18] Being tuned in, plugged in, and in touch with popular culture is very important.

Understanding how the creative process works is the biggest step in learning to be more creative. Most people who think they aren't creative simply don't work at it hard enough. The mental digestion process takes time and effort. Develop your own getting-started techniques like doodling with words and pictures. Creative people often fill pads with what seems to be aimless doodling. They even sleep with notepads by their beds. In fact, these half-sketched ideas and phrases are the raw materials of ideas. This stage often leads to what seems to be a blind wall. Don't give up too easily; take a walk instead. Too many people give up too soon.

---

[18] Carl Walston, unpublished study of creative thinking, University of Colorado, 1991.

A Working Relationship with Joe Pytka

Joe Pytka is one of advertising's most award-winning directors. But Pytka is not the easiest director to work with. The creative team on the Pepsi shoot mentioned at the beginning of the chapter has watched him give a caustic assessment of the relative IQs of BBDO creative directors Ted Sann and Don Schneider; scream about how cheap the agency is; storm off the set in the middle of shooting a scene to work out his frustrations on a makeshift basketball court; patently refuse to shoot other shots; and deliver absolutely exquisite film at the end of the day that has everyone excited.

For Pytka the brief emotional thunderstorms are part of his creative process. In the midst of what seems a cross between iconoclastic rage and sheer indifference, he takes the problem of the moment, dissects it, then finds a way to shoot it that will give the agency what it wants, and more. "You have a story to tell," says Pytka, "and you have to understand the vocabulary of the process. Most stories stripped down to the basics aren't that interesting. Your vocabulary is the actor, the sets."

Sann is a quiet force on the set, an understated counterpoint to Pytka. He and Schneider spend the days moving between the monitor and Pytka in a frame-by-frame analysis. Their dialog sounds a lot like the bizarre discussions Jerry and George have each week on the television show *Seinfeld*. One second they'll be debating whether the food used for particular scene looks more like road-kill in a blanket (Schneider's assessment) or, as Sann supposes, possum tarts. The next minute they're evaluating whether the narrator of one spot should be a kid or an old, Pat Paulsen, type.

Over the years, Sann and Pytka have developed a rhythm to their relationship that is played out hour after hour on the shoot. Sann has essentially learned to make room for Pytka's style. Pytka's excesses, in everything from temper to experimentation with endlessly different technical systems, has been an integral part of Pepsi's commercial success from the early days with Michael Jackson to the recent Ray Charles series. It's relationships like this that make the creative process work for both Pepsi and Pytka.

Source: Betsy Sharkey, "Super Angst," Adweek *(January 25, 1993):24–33.*

Another way to become more creative is to develop your associative thinking skills. You can practice free association by yourself. Just look around the room, pick out an object, relax, open your mind, and see what thoughts come into it. The more often you do this, the more comfortable you will be with the process. You will find that the number and variety of associations increase. Strive for the funniest, silliest, craziest associations you can think of—that is how you develop the ability to come up with original associations.

Analogies are also useful exercises. Look around the room and pick out something. Ask yourself what that item is like—what it resembles either physically or functionally. Functional analogies compare processes such as how something works or how something is used. A vacuum cleaner is like…an anteater, the tentacles of an octopus, a swimmer gasping for air. Keep playing with the images—once again, the crazier the better. The creative mind is a muscle that can be strengthened through exercises like making associations and analogies, but it takes practice.

MANAGING THE CREATIVE PROCESS

Management styles and the agency atmosphere are both very important factors in nurturing creativity and they vary tremendously across agencies. Some are rule-by-fear shops with threats of firing, barracuda like colleagues swimming on your flanks, and screaming bosses who try to terrorize you into brilliant thinking. Needless to say, that approach doesn't work very well. Some agencies are businesslike, with endless rules and rigid work procedures. While that may impress clients, rigid procedures don't add much to the creative process either.

As described in the Concepts and Applications box, many agencies are experimenting with new ways to manage the creative process, encouraging whatever it takes to develop ideas and yet keep the work on schedule and on target. Chiat-Day is recreating itself as a "virtual office," which means an office that can be anywhere. The creative people can work wherever they want to work—at home, on a mountaintop, in the middle of a busy city. As long as they are attached to the office by a fax machine and phone line, they can do their work however and wherever they work best.

BBDO's experiments with small independent creative teams is one way to break down the anonymity and bureaucracy of a big agency and bring the creative people to the front line of the business. The Pepsi campaign is a testimony to the system institutionalized by BBDO chairperson/CEO Phil Dusenberry to ensure that creativity does not get lost in the corridors of the giant agency. Dusenberry has devised a remarkably fluid mechanism for sculpting advertising.[19] Essentially, the agency is constructed as if there were ten or so separate, small advertising shops instead of just one large one. The arrangement allows for radical changes in direction, for on-the-spot invention, and for what Dusenberry calls "terrific accidents."

The creative system at BBDO, refined over time, is designed to protect the fragile creative process, although not fragile egos. Rejection, Dusenberry says, is part of the game. Intense competition among the small, mobile creative teams is blended with an almost complete lack of bureaucracy within the agency. Creative and strategic review boards no longer exist, dropped by Dusenberry to help eliminate the mediocrity that plagued BBDO's work in the 1970s. A direct link between creative teams and the client is nurtured. Pepsi's director of advertising, Marina Hahn, spends the better part of her time in liaison with the agency. And top management at Pepsi talks with top management at BBDO. Because the work is not shrouded in mystery and clients are made a part of the process, they seem to trust the agency. That translates into a latitude to experiment.

THE CREATIVE EXECUTION

We have mentioned that there are two dimensions to the creative side of an advertisement: the creative concept and its execution. We have discussed the creative concept and how creative ideas are born; now let's move on to the execution factors that also contribute to the relevance, originality, and impact of the advertising.

MESSAGE STRATEGIES

What is said in an advertisement is determined by a strategic platform called a *creative brief*, work plan, or blueprint. This document presents and explains the logic behind the ad message, the creative concept, and the executional details

---

[19]Betsy Sharkey, "Super Angst," *Adweek* (January 25, 1993):24–33.

that bring the idea to life. Since effective advertising is built on strategy, it is important to understand how different strategies affect the creative options.

It is also important to understand how strategy can get in the way of creative thinking. There is a real danger in focusing too heavily on the marketing objectives and ignoring the need for original, novel ideas. *Strategy hypnosis*, an extreme concentration on strategy, can stifle creative thinking. The environment can also block creative thinking. Bureaucracy, specialization, and time clocks can all hinder the spirit of exploration and playfulness necessary for creative thinking.

Different types of strategies take different types of *message design*—figuring out what to say and how to say it. The strategy is first of all a reflection of the product and its product category. Some kinds of products such as clothes, jewelry, and cosmetics are fashion items, and their advertising often makes its own fashion statement. Other kinds of advertising are for products used in the home (cleansers, light bulbs), for personal care (toothpaste, toilet paper and tissue, laxatives, cold remedies), or for sustenance (food of all kinds including snacks and soft drinks). In Europe these are described as *fast-moving consumer goods (fmcg)*; in the United States they are called *packaged goods*. Advertising for these products can range from the basic problem solution (ring around the collar, toilet bowl, or sink) to fun (the Pepsi Generation and the Pillsbury Doughboy).

In explaining the difference that the product category makes in the type of advertising used—and in defense of the Chicago School of advertising with its "family values" approach—Ralph Rydholm, chairperson/CEO of Tatham Euro RSCG, said, "Seventy percent of what we advertise in Chicago, we put in our mouths. You want warm wholesome images for things you put in your mouth, not cold, angular, sharp, fast images for things you put in your mouth."[20]

By "things you put in your mouth," Rydholm means food. Other "in your mouth" categories include beverages, beer, fast food, vitamins, over-the-counter medicines, cigarettes, and toothpaste. The Chicago-based Leo Burnett agency is a good example of an agency that handles both product categories and "family value" creative ideas. It has created the Jolly Green Giant, the Pillsbury Doughboy, Tony the Tiger, and Charlie the Tuna as well as that giant icon of Americana, the Marlboro cowboy. "We don't have a lot of clients in the categories that look for the cutting edge work—travel, high tech, fashion, and automotive," Rydholm explained. "We work for leading companies that make things for everybody and we write ads for people, not just for people in the ad business."

Some packaged-goods advertising is considered dull because it delivers a message about a product that isn't very exciting, but Marshall Ross, executive creative director CME-KHBB, explains that is what makes a creative challenge and that's where the Chicago School is strong. "When you see a spot that's well done for a can of peas—and some agencies are doing good work here for those kinds of products—you realize it can be done, and that's what we need to strive for as an agency community."

Public service advertising and pro bono ads involve a different, more emotional or punchier style. *Pro bono* ads are done for free or for a very small fee for nonprofit groups and firms too small to have much of an advertising budget. Agencies like such clients because they will usually let the agency be as free and creative as it can be, unfettered by the restrictions of strategy statements and budget approvals. These ads are showcased in award shows. Some agencies, like

---

[20]Beth Heitzman, "For Chicago Advertising: School's Out," *Adweek* (November 1, 1993):18–20.

The Fun of It

In terms of creative atmosphere, one agency that is making headlines is Los Angeles-based Stein Robaire Helm, whose founders specifically set out to create a worker-friendly environment—both humanistic and creative—that balances strategic thinking with innovation. It allows creative autonomy while it makes strong demands. The irreverence and stream-of-consciousness style of this agency comes from people who don't seem to realize the ad industry has been in the throes of a seemingly endless recession.

In a business and at a time when people are frequently running on a short fuse and in general working more and enjoying it less, these people are having fun. The irreverent tone of the Ikea work is an example. One spot features a bruiser of a guy, face pressed against the inside of your television set, eyeing your room, and then grunting a single line in your direction: "You need new furniture." Another print ad promoting a plant sale at the store reads, "If you manage to kill it, we'll replace it. If you manage to kill two, don't ever consider buying a hamster."

"Nothing trickles down faster than fear," says art director Kirk Souder in explaining what makes SRH different. Most of the people at SRH have experienced management by terror at some point in their careers. At SRH, an idea may be rejected, but the person will not be. No one is cut off at the knees in the name of building a creative fire. The agency looks for people who have a "nice" streak. It is critical to the agency culture to find people who have the right chemistry. It's called the "Missouri factor," since two of the partners are from Missouri and insist on that sort of midwestern decency.

The almost complete lack of a formal structure and the flow of ideas and energy produce an atmosphere, an oxygen, that spawns commercial after commercial that is completely fearless, pushed to the edge. Doors rarely close and most of the staff of 37 walk in and out of open workspaces that float like inner tubes in unstructured space. Foosball games and Nerf football are used to work off the pressure of deadlines and ideas that won't come.

There are moments, long ones, when work is done at *warp speed* given the volume of work that the SRH staff handle. "With a creative department this small, it's a glass menagerie," says art director Mike Rosen who left New York to work at SRH. "There is nowhere to hide." The standards are as tough as the time demands. Ikea is typical: 50 to 60 ads will have to be completed within little more than a month. Each one is expected to be out of the ordinary and to work for the client.

At Ikea, store traffic levels and sales provide a quick measure of what works and what does not. *Accountability* is as critical a pillar of the agency as is creative, although there is a strong belief that one does not have to be sacrificed to attain the other.

Betsy Sharkey, "Welcome to the Fun," *Adweek* (October 26, 1992):22–30.

Fallon-McElligott in Minneapolis, have built their creative credentials on such work. The agency is very frank in admitting it originally set out to win as many awards as possible in order to get the attention of major advertisers outside of Minneapolis. The strategy worked and the agency has helped build the reputation of Minneapolis as a center for creative advertising.

Not all public service advertising is for small clients and many times the creative ideas, given the heart-tugging message platform, are very strong. One campaign that won all kinds of creative awards in 1993 (The One Show, the Art Directors Club, and Cannes, among others) for the New York Homeless Coalition showed homeless people on the streets of New York singing lines from "I Love New York." The gutsy people in their mean surroundings framed by the familiar music created a powerful irony.

Hard and Soft Sell. In addition to the product category, there are other message design decisions that affect how the execution is shaped.

Advertisements are designed to touch either the head or the heart. These two approaches are also called *hard sell* and *soft sell*. A **hard sell** is a rational, informational message that is designed to touch the mind and create a response based on logic. The approach is direct and emphasizes tangible product features and benefits. Hard-sell messages try to convince the consumer to buy because the product is very good, better, or best.[21] An example of this approach is a commercial for Cheer laundry detergent, which shows a mother and her teenage son arguing about the laundry. The son concedes to his mother when he sees how All-Temperature Cheer removes the dirt from his shirts of different colors and different fabrics.

Soft sell uses an emotional message and is designed around an image intended to touch the heart and create a response based on feelings and attitudes. The subtle, intriguing, and ambiguous commercials Jordache, Calvin Klein, and Guess jeans produce illustrate how advertisers sell moods and dreams more than product features.

A soft sell can be used for hard products. For example, if you were designing an ad for an auto-parts store, you might be inclined to take a rational, informative approach. However, NAPA auto parts ran an emotional ad that showed a dog sitting at a railroad-track crossing, forcing a truck to break hard to avoid hitting him as a train bears down on the scene. The slogan puts the heart-stopping visual story into perspective: "NAPA because there are no unimportant parts."

The research firm McCollum/Spielman has found that although the emphasis today is on soft-sell advertising, hard-sell messages have not become extinct. In a random two-hour viewing of afternoon soap operas, researchers counted 36 hard-sell commercials out of a total of approximately 42 commercials run during the period. In a different study the company found that although hard-sell commercials might be less arresting than soft-sell, nearly two-thirds of those studied enjoy acceptable levels of brand awareness. They also discovered that hard sell was clearly more persuasive than soft sell.

Lectures and Dramas. Most advertising messages use a combination of two basic literary techniques: lecture and drama. A **lecture** is a serious structured instruction given verbally by a teacher. A **drama** is a story or play built around characters in some situation. Both techniques are used in advertising.

Lectures are a form of direct address. Stylistically, the speaker addresses the audience from the television or written page. The audience receives the message "at a distance." The speaker presents evidence (broadly speaking) and employs such techniques as an argument to persuade the audience. Some lectures work by borrowing expertise from authority figures or experts in certain technical areas, such as Michael Jordan for Nike, and Chuck Yaeger (a former test pilot) for Delco automobile parts. Compared with unknown presenters, such "authorities" are more likely to attract audience respect and attention.

Because advertising lectures work by presenting facts, they face the same kinds of problems schoolteachers face. The audience often becomes distracted by other matters, discounts part or all of the evidence, makes fun of the source, or disputes every point. In many cases these responses dilute or even cancel the message the advertiser wants to convey. Lectures do not have to be dull, however.

One advantage of lectures is that they cost less to produce. Another is that

---

[21]"The Hard Sell: How Is It Doing?" *Topline (August 1986).*

they are more compact and efficient. A lecture can deliver a dozen selling points in seconds, if need be. Because the current trend is toward shorter commercials, lectures may become more common because they are so efficient—it takes time to set up a dramatic scene and introduce characters. A third advantage of lectures is that they get right to the point. A lecture can be perfectly explicit, whereas drama relies on the viewer to make inferences.

A drama is a form of indirect address, like a movie or a play. In a drama the characters speak to each other, not to the audience. In fact, they usually behave as though the audience were not there. Members of the audience observe and sometimes even participate vicariously in the events unfolding in the story. They are "eavesdroppers."

Like fairy tales, movies, novels, parables, and myths, advertising dramas are essentially stories about how the world works. Viewers learn from these commercial dramas by inferring lessons from them and by applying those lessons to their everyday lives.

A commercial drama can be very powerful. The source of the power is the viewer's involvement in the story development. When a drama rings true, the viewer "joins" in it, draws conclusions from it, and applies those conclusions to his or her own life. From the viewer's perspective, conclusions drawn from dramas are "mine," whereas conclusions urged in lectures are "ideas that other people are trying to impose on me."

One important thing to remember is that the drama should be inherent to the product. In other words, don't tell a cute or funny story just to be entertaining. There is a drama in every product, and the product must be central to the drama. The tendency in using drama is to forget or downplay the point of the ad. Even with dramatic forms, you still need a solid selling premise.

Principle

Stress the inherent drama of the product.

Many television commercials combine lecture and drama. One common format begins as a drama, which is then interrupted by a short lecture from the announcer, after which the drama concludes. An example of this is the classic Charlie the Tuna ads. Charlie is a cartoon character who is always being placed in some situation where he aspires to "good taste." The commercials then turn to real-life product shots of tuna fish being used in meals while the announcer explains the quality of Starkist tuna. The commercials close with Charlie once again realizing he is not good enough for Starkist, but vowing to keep trying.

FORMAT FORMULAS

In addition to these basic approaches, advertisers use a number of common format formulas for advertising messages. These include straightforward and factual messages, demonstrations, comparisons, humor, problem-solution, slice of life, and spokesperson.

In a *straightforward factual* message, the advertisement usually conveys information without using any gimmicks or embellishments. Such ads are rational rather than emotional. Cigarette advertisements that make claims about low tar, for example, are usually presented in a straightforward manner. Business-to-business advertising also is generally factual in tone.

Volvo, BMW, and Saab use straightforward factual copy for their cars. For example, in one BMW ad, the headline simply reads: "How purists tell a future classic from a contemporary antique." In contrast, other car companies use beauty shots of their cars against pretty backgrounds such as mountains, deserts, or beaches.

Two other types of message formats that are usually straightforward and rational in tone are *demonstrations* and *comparisons*. The demonstration focuses on how to use the product or what it can do for you. The product's strengths take center stage. In demonstration seeing is believing, so conviction is the objective. Demonstration can be a very persuasive technique.

A comparison contrasts two or more products and usually finds the advertiser's brand to be superior. The comparison can be direct, in which a competitor is mentioned, or indirect, with just a reference to "other leading brands." Advertising experts debate the wisdom of mentioning another product in comparative advertising, particularly if it is a category leader. A direct comparison has to be handled carefully, or you may find your expensively purchased time or space is simply increasing your competition's awareness level.

In the *problem-solution*, also known as the *product-as-hero* technique, the message begins with some problem, and the product is presented as the solution to that problem. This is a common technique used with cleansers and additives that make things run smoother. Automotive products often use problem-solution. The Wrigley's ad (Ad 13.3) highlights a problem for smokers on airplanes—smoking is prohibited—and proposes a solution: Chew gum instead. A variation is the *problem-avoidance* message where the problem is avoided because of product use. This is a form of threat appeal. It is often used to advertise insurance and personal-care products.

The **slice of life** is an elaborate version of a problem-solution message presented in the form of a little drama. It uses some commonplace situation with "typical people" talking about the problem. Procter & Gamble (P&G) is particularly well known for its reliance on the slice-of-life technique. The P&G version puts the audience in the position of overhearing a discussion wherein the problem is stated and resolved. There is something very compelling about listening in on a conversation and picking up some "tip." The tip, of course, is a P&G product.

Using a person to speak on behalf of the product is another popular message technique. *Spokespersons* and *endorsers* are thought to build credibility. They are either celebrities we admire, experts we respect, or someone "just like us" whose advice we might seek out. One of the problems with a spokesperson strategy is that the person may be so glamorous or so attractive that the message gets lost. Although anyone can be a spokesperson, endorsers usually fall into one of four categories:

1. A created character like the Pillsbury Doughboy or Madge the manicurist
2. A celebrity like Ray Charles for Diet Pepsi or Bill Cosby for Jell-O
3. An authority figure like a doctor for an over-the-counter drug product
4. A typical user who represents as closely as possible the targeted audience

The box entitled "The Jolly Green Spokesgiant" takes a closer look at the use of a created character to advertise a product.

A **testimonial** is a variation of the spokesperson message format. The difference is that people who give testimonials are talking about their own personal experiences with the product. Their comments are based on personal use, which has to be verifiable or the message will be challenged as deceptive.

The Jolly Green Spokesgiant

In 1926 a drawing of a giant appeared on the label of the Minnesota Valley Canning Company's extra-large sweet peas. Two years later the giant was colored green, and when Leo Burnett opened his ad agency, with Minnesota Valley Canning as his first client, he added the word "jolly." Thus was born the Jolly Green Giant, the spokesperson for Pillsbury's Green Giant vegetables for over 65 years.

The Green Giant first appeared in print ads in the 1930s and was finally taken to television in the early 1960s. A man of few words, all the giant has ever uttered is the widely known phrase "Ho Ho Ho." To balance the Giant's silence, the Little Green Sprout was created, "chatting up a storm" and imparting his inside knowledge of the Green Giant products to consumers. The Sprout communicates the necessary product knowledge, allowing the Giant to retain his status as the strong, silent overseer of the valley. The giant is always in the background of the ads, his features obscured, and he moves and speaks very little. This portrayal is consistent across foreign markets, where the Giant receives the same positive response from consumers.

According to Gary Klengl, president of Green Giant Company in Minneapolis, "The giant gives consumers a reason to believe." The character is "bigger than life" and is able to connect with people's emotions, touching "the child within the consumer." The character also has years of consistency on his side and continues to stand for high quality and reasonable prices.

A 1991 study of food-product characters, however, indicates that the Giant's Q ratings (measures of overall appeal) are not as high as they could be. Of those consumers surveyed, 91 percent said they were familiar with the Green Giant, but the character's Q rating was 19. (Little Sprout had a Q rating of 29). This rating is average—the average food-product character had a familiarity rating of 72 percent and a Q score of 19—indicating that the Giant is a good fit for the product line but he doesn't generate a lot of enthusiasm. Higher Q scores went to Poppin' Fresh (36), the California Raisins (37), Tony the Tiger (28), and the Domino's Pizza Noid (23).

Some suggest that the company needs to do something to make the Green Giant more modern, humanistic, authoritative, or educational. Greg Lincoln, director of advertising services at Pillsbury, disagrees. He feels the character's consistency is what appeals to consumers: "It's a known entity." The company is expanding on the Green Giant concept, however. In newer ads for Green Giant mushrooms, for example, Sprout is seen outside of the valley, and the Giant is absent altogether. But he'll be back, and the company does not intend to introduce any new characters. As Huntley Baldwin, executive vice president of creative services at Leo Burnett, says, the campaign has been so durable because "the advertising has been characterized by an innocent charm that has made it fun to watch." The Green Giant has successfully stood for freshness, quality, and consistency for over 65 years and continues to offer consumers an emotional connection with the company and its products.

Source: Adapted from Cyndee Miller, "The Green Giant: An Enduring Figure Lives Happily Ever After," *Marketing News* (April 15, 1991):2. *(Courtesy of Green Giant.)*

TONE

Because it is written as if it were a conversation, advertising copy can also be described in terms of *tone of voice*. In developing a statement of message strategy, copywriters are often asked to describe the tone of the ad. Most ads are written as if some anonymous announcer were speaking. Even with anonymity, however, there may be an identifiable tone of voice. Some ads are angry, some are pushy, some are friendly, others are warm or excited.

Message tone, like tone of voice when you speak to someone, reflects the emotion or attitude behind the ad. Ads can be funny, serious, sad, fearful. Recently *attitude* has become a synonym for a style of advertising that is *in your face*, or even abrasive. The Pepsi attitude commercials described in the opening story are examples of this type of approach. Another is Ad 13.5 which is a house ad for an advertising agency that is trying to sell its attitude. The attitude is its passion for the business, but the graphic presentation is very much in keeping with iconoclastic approaches more typical of MTV and Generation X. Analyze what this ad says about the type of creative people working at Harris-Drury-Cohen.

Although most of the 1980s and early 1990s were fairly serious and stimulated generally conservative and inoffensive advertising, that seems to be changing in the mid-1990s, when attitude is creeping into advertising in a backlash against the self-righteous enforcers of correct thinking. The in-your-face style of Rush Limbaugh and Howard Stern have opened the door for freer expression on some previously taboo—politically incorrect—topics.[22]

Advertising is usually slow to pick up on such cultural trends, but an ad for Rib Ticklers barbecue sauce by Seattle-based Cole & Weber is sure to offend both the animal rights movement and vegetarians. With a children's choir singing in the background, the commercial begins with an ode to barnyard animals—the cow, the chicken, the lamb. Then a barbecue grill appears silhouetted against a brilliant blue sky and the announcer says, "Let's eat them."

The copy strategy behind using humor is the hope that people will transfer the warm feelings they have as they are being entertained to the product. Humor is hard to handle, however. Although everyone appreciates a good joke, not everyone finds the same joke funny. Some advertising experts advise against using humor because of the danger it will overpower the brand identification—people will remember the punch line and forget the product name. This was the long-time philosophy of David Ogilvy, founder of the Ogilvy and Mather agency, although he has changed his opinion in recent years and is now saying some humor, if deftly handled, is acceptable.

Principle

Humor should focus attention on the selling point.

For a humorous ad to be effective, the selling premise must center around the point of the humor. Humor should *never* be used to poke fun at the product or its users. One campaign character who consistently scores well with the public is the Energizer bunny who shows up in the middle of other television spots, parody programs, and vintage movies.

WORDS AND PICTURES

Two of the most important factors in the execution are the words and the pictures—and that's true in both print and broadcast advertising. Even radio can evoke mental pictures through suggestive or descriptive language and sound effects. Typically advertising planners and researchers focus on the words when they consider the effectiveness of advertising (through copy testing), and yet there is substantial evidence that the vast majority of all advertising communication received occurs nonverbally. An increasing number of advertising effectiveness studies focus on the visual imagery in the advertising.

Principle

Words and pictures work in combination to create a concept.

Research has proven that well-integrated advertising where the words and pictures work together to present the creative concept is most effective. But within the frame of the creative concept, keep in mind that words and pictures also do different things.

Visuals are thought to be better at getting attention, although words can be strong if they are bold and don't have to compete with the visual. Pictures also communicate faster than words. A picture is seen instantaneously, but verbal communication must be deciphered word by word, sentence by sentence, line by line.

Visuals are thought to be easier to remember, although some verbal phrases can make a long-term impression, such as "Where's the beef?"—which is why slogans are so important. Many people remember messages as visual fragments.

---

[22]Joshua Levine, "In Your Face," *Forbes* (November 22, 1993):164–167.

Diane Bednarik, Account Executive, Elkman Advertising and Public Relations, Bala Cynwyd, PA

As an account executive for Pennsylvania Tourism, Diane Bednarik is responsible for implementing advertising campaigns promoting Pennsylvania as a tourist destination. At the same time, Bednarik also oversees the internship program for the agency which involves as many as ten interns per semester.

7:45 A.M.   My day starts out with a one hour drive into the office. It's a very scenic, relaxing drive which gives me time to think about my agenda for that day. I usually stop once in the morning for a soda and a Philly soft pretzel to give me energy for the morning commute.

8:45–9:15 A.M.   As soon as I get into my office, I switch on my computer and log in for the day. I check my mail bin to see what is hot for the day and review any internal correspondence. I respond to messages and return phone calls from the previous day.

9:15–10:30 A.M.   Client just called with a hot assignment—a four color ad that will run in Germany. This means the ad will need to be translated into German. The turnaround time on this project seems impossible to meet—three weeks. I discuss assignment with my account manager and agree on action steps. I open up a new job number and fill out paperwork with the details needed to begin concept development.

10:30–11:30 A.M.   Called meeting with creative department to discuss assignment. Creative director expressed his concern about the deadline date and asked for an extension. We discussed the objective of the ad and what it needs to say.

11:30–12:30 P.M.   Called IFAA contact in Germany to discuss translation assignment. Agency agreed to have copy translation completed by the following week. Finally got through to publishing company in Germany to ask for an extension. Extension was granted but only by a couple of days. Ran back to creative department to inform them of the absolute deadline. Needless to say, I did not make their day.

12:30–1:00 P.M.   Reviewed resumes for intern positions. Set up intern interviews for the following week.

1:30–2:00 P.M.   Lunch! Sat back in my office and caught up on account activity in *Advertising Age*.

2:00–3:00 P.M.   Reviewed media plan with account manager and media director on an upcoming cooperative program with the Pocono Mountains Vacation Bureau. Faxed media plan to partner and was given approval to place buy in the recommended publications.

3:00–3:30 P.M.   Meeting with creative department to discuss objective of the ad for the cooperative program. We agreed that the focal point of the ad is that the Poconos is the perfect destination for golf vacation for the whole family. The creative team feels good about the assignment and will have a concept developed by next week.

3:30–4:30 P.M.   Reviewed notes from client meeting the previous day. Wrote client conference report recapping the issues discussed at meeting and the action steps agreed upon.

4:30–5:00 P.M.   Updated account manager on key issues and the status of hot projects.

5:00–5:30 P.M.   Cleared up my desk and made notes for tomorrow.

5:31 P.M.   Back in the car for another hour commute. Now to think about dinner. On second thought, I'll talk hubby into taking me out to dinner.

These are key images that they lock into their minds. You probably remember the word *home* in terms of the image of a specific house in which you have lived. Most of us remember a print ad in terms of how it looked. A television commercial is remembered for some key visual image that is just a section or fragment of the entire commercial. It is the power of this visual image that makes an ad easy to remember and creates effective impact.

Before deciding whether to emphasize words or pictures, a creative team has to consider the underlying strategy for the ad. For example, if the message is complicated, if the purchase is deliberate and well considered, or if the ad is for a high-involvement product, then the more information the better, and that means using words. If you are doing reminder advertising or trying to establish a brand image, then you may want to put less emphasis on words and more on the visual impression. Undifferentiated products with low inherent interest are often presented with an emphasis on the visual message.

The Power of the Visual. An ad for Saab demonstrates the power of the visual by deliberately avoiding nearly all copy. The picture is taken from inside a car on a winding highway, looking over the driver's hands. The headline reads: "What we could tell you about the Saab 900 in the space below is no substitute for ten minutes in the space above." The "space below" where the body copy would normally be found was left blank in the layout.

The Benetton ads are great examples of strong visuals that make a lasting impression as well as an editorial statement. Benetton has used a controversial campaign that features a picture of a white man's hand and a black man's hand handcuffed together as well as a nun and a priest kissing, and a dying AIDS patient surrounded by his family.

The global marketer is known for using strong visuals to draw symbolic parallels between its multicolor and multicultural apparel and larger world issues, such as racial harmony. These parallels are confirmed through the company's slogan, "United Colors of Benetton." In the early 1990s Benetton toned down the campaign with a series of ads that promoted brotherhood. The campaign used more subtle and safe imagery, such as cute black and white children and a white dog paw-in-paw with a black cat. Later that year Benetton ads became less subtle, however. One ad showed test tubes filled with blood, labeled with the names of world leaders, to show that all people are the same. Benetton's more recent campaigns have moved back into other issue-oriented areas such as AIDS and overpopulation, as the company continues to make a statement about being socially conscious.

Different people respond to words and pictures in different ways. When you think of a car, do you think of an image or a word? Some people are highly visual and automatically think and remember in images; others are more verbal and would respond with a word like Ford or Ferrari.

Research involving print advertising has found that more than twice as many magazine readers are captured by a picture in an ad as by the headline. Furthermore, the bigger the illustration, the higher the attention-getting power of the advertisement. Ads with pictures are noticed more than are ads composed entirely of type. Ads with pictures also tend to pull more readers into the body copy. In other words, the initial attention is more likely to turn to interest with a strong visual. Similar research with television has found that the pictorial elements of a television commercial are better remembered than are the words.

Art Direction. The person who is primarily responsible for the graphic image of

Principle

What you show can speak more effectively than what you say.

Artistic creativity is essential to successful advertising.

(Courtesy of Stock/Boston)

art director The person who is primarily responsible for the visual image of the advertisement.

the advertisement is the **art director**. The art director "composes" the visuals in both print and video and "lays out" the ad elements in print. Artists may do the specific illustrations or renderings, but the art director is the chief arranger of these elements. He or she is responsible for the visual "look" of the message.

One of the primary decisions made by an art director is whether to use photography or artwork (animation in television). Photography is the mainstay of the advertising business because it is "real" and adds credibility to the message. Seeing is believing, after all. Probably three-fourths of all advertising visuals are photographic. Of the photographs, around 80 percent are realistic. Illustrations in print and animation on television are used for fashion, fantasy, and exaggerated effects.

If the decision is to use photography, then there are different styles of images to choose from. A reportorial style uses dramatic black-and-white images to try to imitate photojournalism. Documentary style also uses black and white or sepia (a brown tone), but the style is more stark. Most products and product scenes, however, are shot in realistic full color, either in a studio, on a set, or on location.

Different photographers specialize in different types of shots. Some are great with fashion, others shoot buildings, some are good at landscapes, others know all the difficulties of shooting food, and still others specialize in photographing babies or animals. Each area demands specialized knowledge of how to handle lighting, staging, props, and models.

If the layout calls for illustrations, the art director must decide which artist to use. Every artist has a personal style, although most good artists are able to shift styles somewhat to reflect the nature of the message. There is a big difference between a *loose* style, which is somewhat rough, primitive, or casual in appearance, and a *tight* style, which is detailed, perhaps even technical. Some artists are good at realistic effects, whereas others are better at abstract or highly stylized effects, as in fashion advertising. Some are good cartoonists.

copywriter The person who writes the text for an ad.

Copywriting. Advertising writing is called *copy*, and the person who shapes and sculpts the words in an advertisement is called a **copywriter**. Copywriters are preoccupied with language. They listen to how people talk. They read everything they can get their hands on, from technical documents to comic books. They are tuned in to current expressions and fads.

Versatility is the most common characteristic of copywriters. They can move from toilet paper to Mack trucks and shift their writing style to match the product and the language of their target. Copywriters don't have a style of their own because the style they use has to match the message and the product. Some veteran copywriters specialize in certain types of writing, but beginners find themselves advertising all types of products. Except in a few rare cases, advertising copy is anonymous, so people who crave a by-line generally would not be very happy as copywriters.

There is good writing and there is bad writing in advertising, just as there is in every other area of expression. Some of the characteristics discussed here are features of good advertising writing, although all ads are not written this way.

Advertising has to win its audience, and usually it is in competition with some other form of programming or editorial matter. For that reason, the copy should be as easy to understand as possible. Unless the rewards are exceptional, most people will shun advertising copy that taxes them. Simple ads avoid being gimmicky or too cute. They don't try too hard or reach too far to make a point. The Soloflex campaign is a good example of a simple concept simply expressed. The visual is of a well-built man taking off his shirt. There is no headline, but the short body copy is set in large type and serves as a long headline. The copy reads: "To unlock your body's potential, we proudly offer Soloflex." The short slogan is a play on words: "Body by Soloflex."

Advertising copy uses short, familiar words and short sentences. You will probably notice in print advertising that some of the paragraphs are only one sentence long. Every attempt is made to produce copy that looks or sounds easy to understand. Long blocks of copy in print, which are too "gray" or intimidating for the average reader, are broken up into short paragraphs with many subheads. The equivalent of a long copy block in television advertising is a long speech by the announcer. Television monologues can be broken up by visual changes, such as shots of the product. Sound effects can also be used to break up the heaviness of the monologue.

Advertising copy is very tight. Every word counts because both space and time are expensive. There is no time or room for ineffective words. Copywriters will go over the copy a hundred times trying to make it as concise as possible. The tighter the copy is, the easier it is to understand and the greater its impact will be.

The more specific the message, the more attention-getting and memorable it is. The better ads won't say "cost less" but will spell out exactly how much less the product costs. There isn't a lot of time to waste on generalities.

The best advertising copy sounds natural, like two friends talking to one another. It is not forced; it is not full of generalities and superlatives; it does not brag or boast. Conversational copy is written the way people talk. It uses incomplete sentences, fragments of thoughts, and contractions.

In order to get the right tone of voice, copywriters usually move away from the target audience description and concentrate on the typical user. If they know someone who fits that description, then they write to that person. If they don't, then they may go through a photo file, select a picture of the person they think fits the description, and develop a profile of that personality. They may even hang that picture above their desk while they write the copy.

One way that advertising differs from other writing is in the use of direct

Principle

Keep it simple.

Principle

Write to someone you know and match the tone of voice to the situation.

address. It is perfectly acceptable in copywriting to use "you" in direct address. In fact, a conscious attempt to use "you" will force copywriters to be more natural and less affected in their writing. It also forces them to think about the product in terms of the prospect and benefits.

"We" copy is advertising that is written from the company's point of view. It tends to be more formal, even pompous. It is also called **brag-and-boast copy**. Research has consistently found that this is the weakest of all forms of ad writing. "I" copy is used occasionally in testimonials or in dramas such as slice of life where a leading character speaks about a personal experience.

Unfortunately, advertising does have a style that is so well known that it is parodied by comedians. It is a form of formula writing, called **adese**, that violates all the preceding guidelines. Adese is full of clichés, superlatives, stock phrases, and vague generalities. For example, imagine saying things like this to a friend: "Now we offer the quality that you've been waiting for—at a price you can afford." "Buy now and save." Can you hear yourself saying that aloud?

An ad by Buick for its Somerset line is full of adese. The headline starts with the stock opening: "Introducing Buick on the move." The body copy includes superlatives and generalities such as:

"Nothing less than the expression of a new philosophy."

"It strikes a new balance between luxury and performance; a balance which has been put to the test."

"Manufactured with a degree of precision that is in itself a break-through."

The problem with adese is that it looks and sounds like what everyone thinks advertising should look and sound like. Because people are so conditioned to screen out advertising, messages that use this predictable style are the ones that are the easiest to notice and avoid.

EFFECTIVE CREATIVITY

Advertising also has to be effective, in other words, the creative ideas are used in support of the strategy and the selling message. Advertising can be considered effective only after it has been evaluated in some way. The McCollum Spielman research firm has determined the characteristics of effective creative messages based on 25 years of research. (see Table 13.1). The Magazine Publishers of America has been running a series of ads under the headline "I wish I'd done that ad," which reflects the highest compliment one creative person can say about another's work. Ad 13.6 is an example of an ad that has received this kind of praise.

Evaluating the effectiveness of their work is a problem for some creatives in advertising who may lack an understanding of strategy and an ad's objectives. They are frequently at a loss for words when asked how well their advertising fared in the marketplace.[23] They are more interested in winning awards than in achieving sales objectives. The legendary Bill Bernbach reminds the creative person to make the product—not the author—shine:

---

[23]Carl F. Walston, "The Aesthetic Dimension of Advertising," unpublished master's thesis, University of Colorado, 1991.

Table 13.1

Twelve Creative Hot Buttons

What is good creative? Here are the 12 recurring qualities found in the most sales-effective advertising McCollum Spielman has measured, 25 years and some 25,000 copy tests later.

1 Brand rewards/benefits are highly visible through demonstration, dramatization, lifestyle, feelings, or analogy.

2 The brand is the major player in the experience (the brand makes the good times better).

3 The linkage between brand and execution is clear (scenario revolves around and highlights the brand).

4 The execution has a focus (there's a limit to how many images and vignettes the consumer can process).

5 Feelings (emotional connectives) are anchored to the needs and aspirations of the targeted consumer.

6 Striking, dramatic imagery is characteristic of many successful executions, enhancing their ability to break out of clutter.

7 An original, creative signature or mystique exists in many of the best commercials, to bond the consumer to the brand and give it a unique personality.

8 In food and beverage advertising, high taste appeal is almost always essential.

9 The best creative ideas for mature brands frequently employ fresh new ways of revitalizing the message.

10 Music (memorable, bonded tunes and lyrics) is often integral to successful executions for many brands.

11 When humor is used, it is relevant, with clear product purpose.

12 When celebrities are employed, they are well matched to brands, have credibility as users/endorsers and their delivery is believably enthusiastic.

Source: McCollum Spielman Worldwide, Topline (October 1993):2.

Merely to let your imagination run riot, to dream unrelated dreams, to indulge in graphic acrobatics and verbal gymnastics is *not* being creative. The creative person has harnessed his imagination. He has disciplined it so that every thought, every idea, every word he puts down, every line he draws, every light and shadow in every photograph makes more vivid, more believable, more persuasive the product advantage.[24]

One problem is the risk-adverse nature of many large organizations—both agencies and clients. It is difficult to evaluate a new idea because you don't have any benchmarks; it is easier to evaluate ideas that have been used before because you know how they were received. Consequently, a manager will use a proven formula for an ad, knowing that the approach is safe and the ad probably won't fail, even though it may not be highly successful either. A new approach is always a gamble. The creative person who tries a new idea may be dismissed as lucky if the ad is successful or incompetent if it fails. In such an environment

---

[24]Bill Bernbach, *Bill Bernbach Said* (New York: Doyle Dane Bernbach International).

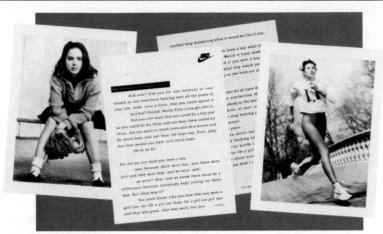

creative people often choose to play it safe when working with a multimillion-dollar investment.

Another problem in evaluating the contribution of the creative dimension is the attitude of some managers who scorn the use of the word *creative* because they feel it deflects people's attention away from the purpose of the advertising, which is to persuade and sell. Most copy testing, which reflects this viewpoint, is focused on persuasiveness and recall (awareness) measures. A hint that there might be another factor appeared in a study by the Advertising Research Foundation.[25] It was found that *liking* may be just as important, if not more so,

---

[25]Russell I. Haley, "The ARF Copy Research Validity Project," *Journal of Adverting Research* (April/May 1991):11–32; Cyndee Miller, "Study Says 'Likability' Surfaces as Measure of TV Ad Success," *AMA Newsletter* (January 1, 1991):6.

than persuasion and recall. This finding has been treated as heresy by the hard-nosed persuade-and-sell managers. It did open the door, however, to a broader view of what makes an advertisement effective and makes it possible to do a more thorough evaluation of what the creative dimension really contributes to advertising effectiveness.

Good creative people know that every advertising message is up against a cluttered environment and a generally indifferent audience. The only way to break through is to express the selling message in an original, fresh way. In other words, dull advertising can be persuasive but it will rarely get the attention of the audience. Breakthrough advertising, to be effective, has to be both persuasive and creative.

*S*UMMARY

- The Big Idea is the creative concept around which the entire advertising campaign revolves and behind the creative concept is the execution of the idea, which also has to be handled creatively.

- A creative concept must have relevance, originality, and impact.

- All people are born with creative skills.

- Creative people tend to be right-brain, rather than left-brain, dominant. These differences correspond roughly to divergent versus convergent thinking.

- The two basic sales approaches used in advertising are "hard sell" and "soft sell."

- The two basic literary techniques used in advertisements are lectures and dramas. Some ads use a combination of the two.

- Common advertising formats include humor, problem-solution, slice of life, spokesperson, straightforward factual, and comparisons and demonstrations.

- Effective copywriting is informal, personal, conversational, and concise. Forced, unnatural writing is referred to as *adese*.

- Advertising has to be effective. That means creativity is used to enhance the strategy of the message.

*Q*UESTIONS

1. What are some of the major traits of creative people? Which characteristics of the advertising world do you think enhance creativity? Which discourage it?

2. Find a newspaper or magazine advertisement that you think is bland and unexciting. Rewrite it, first to demonstrate a hard-sell approach, and then to demonstrate a soft-sell approach.

3. One of the challenges for creative ad designers is to demonstrate a product whose main feature cannot be seen by the consumer. Suppose you are an art director on an account that sells shower and bath mats with a patented system that ensures the mat will not slide (the mat's underside is covered with tiny suction cups that grip the tub's surface). Brainstorm for some ways to demonstrate this feature in a television commercial. Find a way that will satisfy the demands of originality, relevance, and impact.

4. In the past Diet Pepsi ran a commercial involving the famous blind musician and vocalist Ray Charles, in which, as a practical joke, someone

switched Diet Coke for the sponsored drink. The joke was reversed when Ray Charles immediately discovered the switch once he tasted Pepsi's competitor. Was Mr. Charles's role in that commercial one as a spokesperson or a testimonial? Was there a symbolic idea behind the strategy? Which of the formats and formulas discussed in the chapter best fits this Diet Pepsi commercial?

5 Peter Madison, a sophomore in advertising, is speaking informally with a copywriter from a local advertising agency following the writer's class presentation. Peter states his strong determination to be some sort of creative professional once he gets his degree. "My problem is that I'm a bit shy and reserved. I'm interested in all sorts of stuff, but I'm not really quick in expressing ideas and feelings. I'm not sure my personality is suited for being an advertising creative. How do I know if I've picked the right career direction?" What advice should that writer give Peter?

6 Some time ago a copywriting analyst warned writers that they should be aware of the "ignorance distance" between the writer and the audience. He meant avoiding copy that is either over the heads of the audience or well below the audience's knowledge of the product. What are the copy dangers in speaking above the audience's frame of reference? What are the dangers of underestimating the audience's knowledge? Which of the elements discussed in the "copywriting" section of the chapter would reduce these threats of "ignorance distance"?

$\mathcal{S}$UGGESTED CLASS PROJECT: BRAINSTORMING

Divide the class into groups of eight to ten. Each group should find an area to work apart from other groups. Here's the problem: Your community wants to encourage people to get out of their cars and use alternative forms of transportation. How many different creative concepts can your team come up with to express that idea in an advertisement? Brainstorm for 15 minutes as a group, accumulating every possible idea regardless of how crazy or dumb it might initially sound. Have one member be the recorder and list all the ideas as they are mentioned. Then go back through the list as a group and put an asterisk next to the ideas that seem to have the most promise. When all the groups reconvene in class, each recorder should list his or her group's ideas on the blackboard. Cover the board with all the ideas from all the groups. As a class, pick out the three ideas that seem to have the most potential. Analyze the experience of participating in a brainstorming group and compare the experiences of the different teams.

$\mathcal{F}$URTHER READINGS

BAKER STEPHEN, *A Systematic Approach to Advertising Creativity* (New York: McGraw-Hill Book Co., 1979).

DE BONO, EDWARD, *Lateral Thinking: Creativity Step by Step* (New York: Harper and Row, 1970).

GORDON, W. W. J., *The Metaphorical Way of Learning and Knowing* (Cambridge, MA: Penguin Books, 1971).

MARRA, JAMES L., *Advertising Creativity: Techniques for Generating Ideas* (Englewood Cliffs, NJ: Prentice Hall, 1990).

MICHALKO, MICHAEL, *Tinkertoys*, (Berkeley, CA: Ten Speed Press, 1991).

MORIARTY, SANDRA, *Creative Advertising*, 2nd ed. (Englewood Cliffs, NJ: Prentice Hall, 1990).

YOUNG, JAMES WEBB, *Technique for Producing Ideas*, 3rd ed. (Chicago, Crain Books, 1975).

$\mathscr{V}\text{IDEO } \mathscr{C}\text{ASE}$

Garbage

Every advertiser knows that consumers respond to vivid images. In the environmental arena, one of the most vivid images of the late 1980s was that of a gigantic, ominous garbage barge traveling up and down the East Coast of the United States seeking a place to disgorge its unwanted cargo. The garbage barge's odyssey, covered every evening on the network news, drove home the size of America's solid waste problem.

The image of the homeless barge helped convince Americans that solid waste disposal is a critical, immediate national issue—more critical and immediate than litter, for example. This rearrangement of national priorities prompted Keep America Beautiful, a nonprofit environmental organization, to reconsider the creative content of its public service announcements. Through the 1970s and 1980s, these announcements had featured Iron Eyes Cody, a Native American. Few could forget the tear running down his cheek as he surveyed once-beautiful lands defiled by litter.

Keep America Beautiful's communication problem was to evoke an image that would be as relevant as the garbage barge and as powerful as Iron Eyes Cody. To help define this new image, Rotando, Lerch & Iafelice, Keep America Beautiful's volunteer advertising agency, commissioned a series of individual, in-depth interviews with a cross section of Americans from a variety of backgrounds. The interviews sought respondents' views on environmental issues, especially the solid waste problem, and their reactions to environmental messages.

The interviews disclosed that, while many Americans were keenly aware of environmental degradation, many felt helpless as individuals. One common reaction was, "Yes, these problems are immediate and serious, but they are overwhelming. I'm just one person. What can I do about them?"

Another common reaction, often from the same respondents, was a peculiar sort of complacency. The reaction was, "Someone else is taking care of it," or "I'm recycling. What more can I do?"

The interviews reinforced the premise that a new, powerful image was needed. The interviews also suggested that while the new image must elicit strong emotional reaction, it must not be totally negative. It must not promote hopelessness or cynicism, but rather offer a ray of hope for the future. Finally, the interviews indicated that concerned citizens wanted specific detailed information. They wanted to know what more they as individuals can do to protect the environment.

The need to convey a powerful but positive image and the need to convey more information than can be covered in a 30-second television commercial led Rotando, Lerch & Iafelice to create a public service announcement that combines a powerful, future-oriented image with an invitation to call or write for action-oriented information. The announcement opens on a closeup of an attractive, happy baby. As the camera pulls back to show that the baby is surrounded by trash, the narration, read by actor Michael Douglas, says, "For future generations, our country is leaving behind our knowledge, our technologies, our values . . . and 190 million tons of garbage every year. Recycling alone just can't do it. Keep America Beautiful is an organization that can do something. We have solutions that have worked in cities and towns across the country. What can you do? More than you think!" The announcement concludes with an invitation to write to Keep America Beautiful or call an 800 number to request a free booklet that explains how individuals can help solve the problem it portrays so graphically.

Adapted from Joseph Rydholm, "Here's Looking At You, Kid," *Quirk's Marketing Research Review*, 7, No. 3 (March 1993):6–7, 28–29.

Questions

1. One creative option would have been to continue to use Iron Eyes Cody. What are the arguments for and against extending this vivid and familiar image?
2. Another option would have been to use the wandering garbage barge. What are the arguments for and against this possible solution?
3. What do you think of Rotando, Lerch & Iafelice's answer to the image question? Can you think of a better way to address these complex issues?
4. Suppose Keep America Beautiful were to consider Iron Eyes Cody, the garbage barge, the baby, and your idea. How would they be able to tell which was the most effective?

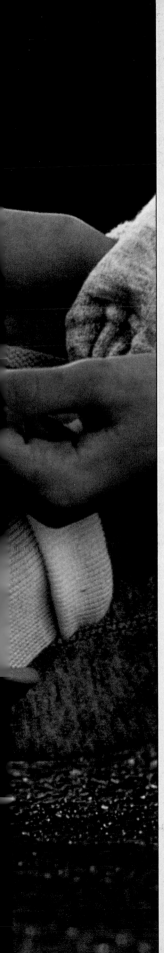

CREATING PRINT ADVERTISING 14

CHAPTER OBJECTIVES

When you have completed this chapter, you should be able to:

- Distinguish between the key features of newspaper and magazine advertising
- List the various elements of a print ad and their function
- Understand the process by which print ads are created
- Distinguish between letterpress, offset, gravure, and silk-screen printing

HOW DO YOU WRITE TO WOMEN IN THIS DAY AND AGE?

Hannah the Housewife has largely disappeared from the images in advertising, unless it's a spoof. The executive superwoman is also a fading image. Most advertisers realize that women are multidimensional and such stereotypes are irritating, if not counterproductive. But what is an advertiser to do to write ads that are sensitive rather than stereotyping for a women's market?

This is a particular problem for athletic shoe advertisers who use women's magazines to reach their audience. As Barbara Lippert, *Adweek's* advertising critic, has pointed out, the whole area of women's fitness has become entirely cliché-ridden—from the high-powered executive on the run in the 1970s to the running woman in sports bra and Lycra in the 1980s.[1] Of course, so have the men's shoe ads with their superhuman jocks pumping up their egos.

The Nike's women's campaign has been evolving for several years under the guidance of creatives Charlotte Moore and Janet Champ at Portland-based Weiden and Kennedy. It's moved from taking on the world to self-conquest, self-direction, and self-acceptance. The copy has moved back and forth from mildly aggressive feminism ("You were born a daughter" and "A woman is often measured by the things she cannot control") to instructive ("You must decide") to personal reflection ("Did you ever wish you were a boy?") to poetry ("How could you not move?").

Nike isn't the only shoemaker searching for a tone of voice that reaches women. Avia has used advertising with an attitude much more pronounced than Nike's. One headline announces, "Screw the laws of gravity." The copy begins, "I've never been the type to let anyone tell me what I can and can't do."

The Nike 1990s campaign, however, has been proclaimed for its sense of self. As Mary Moore, VP and chief creative officer at Wells Rich Greene BDDP, observed in the Wish I'd Done that Ad campaign about "Wish you were a boy?" (see Chapter 13): "It's a pleasure to feel that shock of recognition. To have somebody out there express a thought I wasn't sure anyone else had." She explains why this campaign works for many women: "You'd swear it's talking to you alone but it's reaching thousands of others who share the same feeling and are affected the same way."

Whether you are male or female, do you think the Nike approach works to sell athletic shoes? If you worked on a men's shoe account that didn't have Nike's budget for expensive celebrity athletes, would you consider such an approach? How would it work for men?

This chapter will introduce you to print advertising, which actually covers a variety of forms of advertising—everything from matchbooks to catalogs. In order to focus on the principles of print, however, we concentrate on newspaper and magazine advertising. First we will look at how the type of print medium interacts with the creative message, as well as the limitations each medium creates.

---

[1]Adapted from Barbara Lippert, "Defining Women," *Adweek* (March 1, 1993):p. 28.

ℙRINT ADVERTISING

The foundation of modern advertising message strategy and design lies in the early print formats. The earliest mass-produced commercial messages either appeared in newspapers or as handbills. Thus many advertising guidelines originated with print, and print techniques, such as headline writing, are still considered basic concepts. Many things have changed over the years. Television has had a tremendous impact on advertising. Visuals, which were limited in the early press to infrequent woodcuts, are now as important as words. Print advertising continues to be important, however, and still serves as a foundation in that its techniques are the easiest to understand and analyze. We will therefore begin our discussion of media and their creative characteristics with newspapers and magazines.

The key elements of print advertising are divided between copy and art. The **copy** elements include headlines, underlines and overlines, subheads, body copy, captions, slogans, and taglines. **Art** refers to the visual elements, which include illustrations or photography, the type, logotypes (logos) and signatures, and the *layout* itself, which is the arrangement of all the elements.

copy The written elements in an ad, including headlines, underlines and overlines, subheads, body copy, captions, slogans, and taglines.

art The visual elements in an ad, including illustrations, photos, type, logos and signatures, and the layout.

NEWSPAPER ADVERTISEMENTS

Most people see newspaper advertising as a form of news. In fact, when newspapers have gone on strike, what people say they miss the most are the ads—they have other sources of news—but newspapers are the primary source of local advertising. Newspaper advertising is one of the few forms of advertising that is not considered intrusive. People consult the paper as much to see what is on sale as to find out what is happening in City Hall. For this reason, newspaper advertisements do not have to work as hard as other kinds of advertising to catch the attention of an indifferent audience.

In addition, because the editorial environment of a newspaper is generally more serious than entertaining, newspaper advertisements don't have to compete as entertainment, as television ads do. Therefore, most newspaper advertising is straightforward and newslike. Local retail advertising announces what merchandise is available, what is on sale, how much it costs, and where you can get it.

The serious editorial tone also can carry over to advertising, as is demonstrated in Ad 14.1, which is an advocacy ad on behalf of the advertising industry that runs in such publications as *The New York Times* and *The Wall Street Journal*.

Principle

Advertising is news too.

Production Characteristics. Daily newspapers are printed at high speed on an inexpensive, rough-surfaced, spongy paper, called **newsprint**, that absorbs ink on contact. The demands of speed and low cost have traditionally made newspaper reproduction rather low-quality printing.

Newsprint is not a great surface for reproducing fine details, especially photographs and delicate typefaces. Most papers offer color to advertisers, but

newsprint An inexpensive, tough paper with a rough surface, used for printing newspapers.

"Does advertising work? You have our word on it."

Russell L. Hanlin, President and CEO, Sunkist Growers, Inc.

"An orange...is an orange...is an orange. Unless, of course, that orange happens to be a Sunkist.

Indeed, a Sunkist® orange is considered something quite special. And this is due, in great part, to our consistent commitment since the day we began advertising in 1908, to creating a brand image.

Today, after nearly a century of advertising, we have a name eighty percent of consumers know and trust.

It is a name synonymous with excellence and quality. A name recognized as one of the top brand names around the world. And a name to be proud of.

We're also quite proud to have the longest, one-brand client/agency relationship in the advertising industry.

Now, what have advertising and Sunkist done besides sell oranges, lemons, grapefruit and tangerines?

I'd like to think that we've had an impact on America's attitudes towards health. I look back to a 1916 print ad titled, 'Drink an Orange' that introduced the idea of orange juice to America. Sunkist was also the first national advertiser to emphasize the importance of vitamin C to the American public.

At Sunkist we're very proud of the role we've played in bringing our particular brand of sunshine to the world. And we're also very aware of the essential role advertising has played in that endeavor. You have our word on it."

American Association of Advertising Agencies

If you would like to learn more about the power of advertising, please write to Department D, AAAA, 666 Third Avenue, New York, New York 10017, enclosing a check for five dollars. You will receive our booklet, *It Works! How Investment Spending in Advertising Pays Off*. Please allow 4 to 6 weeks for delivery. This advertisement was prepared by Foote, Cone & Belding, Los Angeles.

---

in register A precise matching of colors in images.

Principle

Illustrations reproduce better than photos in newspapers.

because of the limitations of the printing process, the color may or may not be **in register** (aligned exactly with the image).

We are accustomed to seeing news photographs that are somewhat "muddy," but most of us expect better quality in advertising. Although photographs are used in newspaper advertising, illustrations generally reproduce better. Illustrations in newspaper advertisements are bold, simple, and specifically designed to reproduce well within the limitations of the printing process.

Most newspapers subscribe to an artwork service, called a *mat service* that sends general and seasonal illustrations directly to the advertising department.

This generic art satisfies the needs of most local advertisers. Larger newspapers may have their own graphic artists who are available to local advertisers. Some major advertisers have their own art services through their trade associations, such as banks and savings and loan associations. Large department stores often have an in-house advertising staff that includes artists. Stores also hire **freelance artists**, who provide original art for the store's ads.

This scene is changing, however. *USA Today* has pioneered much better quality reproduction for daily newspapers. Because the paper itself is of better quality, photographs and color reproduction are considerably better than are those found in most newspapers. Significant use of color is an important part of the *USA Today* formula. Many newspapers are upgrading their technology to catch up with *USA Today,* so quality color is more easily available to advertisers today.

Even fancy printing techniques are now possible. Some newspaper advertisements include decals and logos that have been printed with a special heat-transfer ink. These can be cut out of the paper and then ironed onto T-shirts. These techniques will be discussed in more detail later in the chapter.

MAGAZINE ADVERTISEMENTS

Advertising that ties in closely with the magazine's special interest may be valued as much as the articles. For example, skiers read the ads in the ski magazines to learn about new equipment, new technology, and new fashions. Readers of professional publications may cut out and file ads away as part of their professional reference library. For this reason magazine ads are often more informative and carry longer copy than do newspaper ads. Still, despite this built-in interest, ads must catch the attention of the reader who may be more absorbed in an article on the opposite page. To do that, magazine advertising tends to be more creative than newspaper advertising, using beautiful photography and graphics with strong impact (see Ad 14.2). Magazines are also particularly useful for image advertising, as noted in the opening story on Nike's women's shoe campaign.

Production Characteristics. Magazines have traditionally led the way in graph-

We brake for fish.

Can you spot the Range Rover in this picture?

The British have always driven on the wrong side of the road.

ic improvements. The paper is better than newsprint; it is slick, coated, and heavier. Excellent photographic reproduction is the big difference between newspapers and magazines. Magazines do use illustrations, but they employ them to add another dimension, such as fantasy, to the visual message.

Magazine advertisements are also turning to more creative, attention-getting devices such as pop-up visuals, scent strips, and computer chips that play melodies when the pages are opened up.

WRITING FOR PRINT

In Chapter 13 we talked in general about advertising copywriting. In this chapter we will examine the specific demands of print advertising, both words and pictures. There are two categories of copy: display and body copy, or text. **Display copy** includes all those elements that the reader sees in his or her initial scanning. These elements, usually set in larger type sizes, are designed to get attention and to stop the viewer's scanning. **Body copy**, the text of the message, includes the elements that are designed to be read and absorbed.

display copy Type set in larger sizes that is used to attract the reader's attention.

body copy The text of the message.

HEADLINES

Most experts on print advertising agree that the headline is the most important display element. The **headline** works with the visual to get attention and communicate the creative concept. This Big Idea is usually best communicated through a picture and words working together. For example, the ads for Range Rover (Ad 14.2) only work if you put the words and pictures together. The headline "We brake for fish" makes no sense unless you understand the picture of the vehicle fording the stream. The same is true for "Can you spot . . . ?" and ". . . wrong side of the road."

headline The title of an ad; it is set in large type to get the reader's attention.

The headline, however, is a very important element in print advertising because it pulls the concept together and in most ads carries the responsibility for helping people make sense of the message and get the point of the ad. It's important for another reason. For people who are scanning, they may read nothing more, so the point has to be clear from the headline or the combination of headline and visual. Researchers estimate that only 20 percent of those who read the headline go on to read the body copy.[2] Because headlines are so important, there are some general guidelines for their development and particular functions that they serve. A headline must *select* the right prospect, *stop* the reader, *identify* the product and brand, and *start* the sale by luring the readers into the body copy.

Principle

Tell as much of the story in the headline as possible.

The Headline's Function. Ideally, a good headline will attract only those who are prospects; there is no sense attracting people who are not in the market for the product. A good headline *selects out target audience members* by speaking to their interests. An old advertising axiom is: "Use a rifle, not a shotgun."

An example of signaling that the Nike target is women is found in headlines that begin, "A woman is often measured, . . . " or "You were born a daughter."

---

[2] Philip Ward Burton, *Which Ad Pulled Best?* (Chicago: Crain, 1981).

Once the prospects have been selected, stopping and grabbing their attention is critical. As discussed in Chapter 8, this responsibility, shared with the visual, is a measure of the strength of the creative concept. An advertisement by General Motors that focused on its automotive testing used a picture of a car driving on rough cobblestones. The headline was unexpected. It read: "One way or another we will destroy this car."

One way to stop and grab readers is to involve them in completing the message. *Involvement techniques* can have tremendous impact. Questions can be puzzling, make you think, and invite you to participate in the development of the message. Furthermore, you feel compelled to read on to find out the answer. The Nike ad that asks, "How can you not move in shoes like these?" uses direct address and a question to intensify the reader's involvement. If you actually get the reader to complete the question, then you are using *closure,* a psychological principle in which the reader participates by completing the message.

Product and brand identification is very important. At the very least, the headline should make the product category clear to the reader. The headline should answer the question: "What kind of product is this?" The more the brand is tied into the concept, the more likely you are to leave some minimal identification with the 80 percent of the audience who look at the ad, read the headline, and then move on.

The "Does advertising work?" headline, even though it is an advocacy ad, clearly identifies the subject.

Another function of a good headline is to *introduce the selling premise.* If the strategy calls for a benefit, a claim, a unique selling proposition (USP), a promise, or a reason why, that message should be telegraphed in the headline. If you have a strong sales point, lead with it. For example, even though the execution for the Alpo ad (Ad 14.3) uses soft humor, the headline is still focused solidly on the research behind the product.

Finally, a good headline *will lead the reader* into the body copy. In order for that to happen, the reader has to stop scanning and start concentrating. This need to change the perceptual mode—the "mind set"—is the reason only 20 percent of scanners become readers.

In contrast, an ad for Trojans condoms by Backer Spielvogel Bates/NY makes a very pointed argument on a very touchy subject for its young, single-person target audience by combining headline with body copy:

> *"I didn't use one because I didn't have one with me."*

Get Real

If you don't have a parachute, don't jump, genius.

Types of Headlines. Headlines can be grouped into two general categories: direct and indirect action. *Direct headlines* are straightforward and informative, such as the Tylenol headline about "The Power to Stop Pain." They select the audience with a strong benefit, promise, or reason why. They identify the product category, and they link the brand with the benefit. Direct headlines are highly targeted, but they may fail to lead the reader into the message if they are not captivating enough.

Action techniques include news announcements, assertions, and commands. News headlines obviously are used with new-product introductions, but

New ALPO Cat Food is the product of exhaustive research.

Several years ago, ALPO asked six leading veterinary and nutritional authorities to pool their intellectual resources on the subject of cat care.

The first product of that effort is called "Feline Nutrition and Feeding Management," and is perhaps the definitive document on the topic.

The second is called ALPO Cat Food.

PROTEIN VARIETY (IN ELEVEN FLAVOR VARIETIES).

Working from the principles outlined in the monograph, ALPO has developed both canned and dry formulations that combine high-quality, highly digestible proteins from seven food sources. Each ALPO product therefore offers an ideal amino acid balance for maintaining overall body condition and enzyme systems in both adult and growing animals.

FUS AND TAURINE: DEFUSING THE FEAR.

In an effort to reduce the risk of FUS, some manufacturers have lowered ash content, thereby potentially compromising necessary levels of minerals such as calcium. But published research now indicates that dietary acidification can reduce urine pH to minimize formation of struvites. the most common cause of FUS. ALPO Dry Cat Food has been acidified to produce a mildly acid urinary pH while still assuring an adequate mineral balance.

Taurine, an essential amino acid whose deficiency has been associated with some commercial canned cat foods in the past, has also been carefully considered in the ALPO development process. Consequently, feeding studies conducted at the ALPO Pet Center have proven that cats maintain normal plasma taurine levels when fed the ALPO formulations.

PALATABILITY: THE LAST WORD IN PET FOOD.

To comply with AAFCO standards, our foods are fed to—and proven nutritious for cats of all kinds. To comply with ALPO standards, they must also be enjoyed.

Every ALPO product is the product of extensive taste testing at our cattery. Because even after all the nutritional requirements and all the clinical studies, the highest standards ALPO Cat Food will ever have to satisfy are those of your clients' cats.

For a free copy of "Feline Nutrition and Feeding Management," write us at:
ALPO Feline Nutrition
P.O. Box 4000
Lehigh Valley, PA 18001

Ad 14.3

Alpo uses a funny headline that also makes an important product statement.

(Courtesy of Alpo Petfoods, Inc. Copyright 1990)

---

also with changes, reformulations, new styles, and new uses. An assertion is used to state a claim or a promise. A command headline politely tells the reader to do something. The headline used in an ad for Nike starts out "The body you have is the body you inherited, but YOU MUST DECIDE WHAT TO DO WITH IT." It's an unusual graphic technique since the headline, as indicated by the capital letters, actually falls at the end of the sentence, but it's a good example of a command headline.

Indirect headlines are not as selective and may not provide as much information, but they may be better at luring the reader into the message. They are provocative and intriguing, and they compel people to read on to find out the point of the message. Indirect headlines, like those in the Range Rover ads (Ad 14.2), use curiosity and ambiguity to get attention and build interest.

Techniques for indirect headlines include questions, how-to statements, challenges, and puzzlements. Challenges and puzzling statements are used strictly for their provocative power. All these techniques require the reader to examine the body copy to get the answer or explanation. Sometimes these indirect headlines are referred to as "blind" because they give so little information. A blind headline is a gamble. If it is not informative or intriguing enough, the reader may move on without absorbing any product name information.

Headline Writing. Writing a headline is tremendously challenging. Writers will cover notepads with hundreds of headlines and spend days worrying about the wording. Headlines are also carefully tested to make sure they can be understood at a glance and that they communicate exactly the right idea. *Split-run tests* (two versions of the same ad) in direct mail have shown that changing the wording of the headline, while keeping all other elements constant, can double, triple, or quadruple consumer response. That is why the experts, such as David Ogilvy, state that the headline is the most important element in the advertisement.[3]

OTHER DISPLAY COPY

In addition to headlines, copywriters also craft the subheads and captions that continue to help lure the reader into the body copy. These are considered display copy in that they are usually larger and set in different type (bold or italic) than the body copy. Subheads are sectional headlines and are also used to break up a mass of "gray" type (or type that tends to blur together when one glances at it) in a large block of copy. Captions are very useful in explaining what's happening in photos, since people often find such visuals confusing. Captions also have very high readership.

Slogans and taglines are used for memorability. Product and campaign slogans are repeated from ad to ad. A *tagline* is a particularly memorable phrase that is used at the end of the ad to wrap up the idea.

Copywriters employ a number of literary techniques to enhance the memorability of slogans and taglines. Some slogans use a startling or unexpected phrase; others use rhyme, rhythm, alliteration (repetition of sounds), or parallel construction (repetition of the structure of a sentence or phrase). This repetition of structure and sounds contributes to memorability. Notice the use of these techniques in the following slogans:

- BMW: "The Ultimate Driving Machine"
- Army: "Be all that you can be"
- *The Wall Street Journal*: "The daily diary of the American dream"

BODY COPY

The body copy is the text of the ad, the paragraphs of small type. The content develops the sales message and provides support, states the proof, and gives the explanation. This is the persuasive heart of the message. You excite consumer interest with the display elements, but you win them over with the argument presented in the body copy. The *Copy Checklist* compiles a number of suggestions for writing display as well as body copy.

Principle

The headline catches their eye, but the copy wins their heart.

The relationship between the headline and the body copy is important and determines how effective the ad is in arousing interest and stopping the reader's scanning. Ad 14.4 demonstrates how important it can be to read the body copy—even though in this ad the body copy is just one line set in very small type—in order to get the full impact of the ad's message.

Types of Body Copy. There are as many different kinds of writing styles as there are copywriters and product personalities. Some body copy is *straightforward* and written in the words of an unknown or unacknowledged source. A *narrative* style may be used to tell a story, which may be either in the first person or the third person. A *dialogue* style lets the reader "listen in" on a conversation.

---

[3]David Ogilvy, *Ogilvy on Advertising* (New York: Vintage Books, 1985).

One of the most difficult writing style challenges involves translating technical information, like that written for the high-technology and medical industries, into understandable language. The Issues and Controversies box addresses this problem.

Like poetry, body copy is very well crafted. Copywriters will spend hours, even days, on one paragraph. They will write a first draft, revise it, then tighten and shorten it. After many revisions the copy gets read by others, who critique it. It then goes back to the writer, who continues to fine-tune it. Body copy for most major ads is revised over and over again.

Notice the craftsmanship in the "You were born a daughter" ad from Nike's women's campaign, which reads as if it were a poem. As you read it, notice the use of natural language, personal address, parallel structure, and alliteration and the familiar tagline at the end that ties it back in to Nike's other campaigns:

Sooner or later, you start taking yourself seriously.
You know when you need a break. You know
when you need a rest. You know what to get worked
up about, and what to get rid of.
And you know when it's time to take care
of yourself, for yourself. To do something that makes
you stronger, faster, more complete.
Because you know it's never too late to have a life.
And never too late to change one.

Just do it.

Read poetry. Make peace with all except the motor car.

Schwinns' are red, Schwinns are blue. Schwinns are light and agile too. Cars suck. The end.

Established 1895. Re-established 1994.

Ad 14.4

The anticar message builds in this ad by Schwinn until it explodes at the end of the body copy.

(Courtesy of Schwinn Cycling & Fitness Inc.)

Structure of Body Copy. Two paragraphs get special attention in body copy: the *lead-in* and the *close*. The first paragraph of the body copy is another point where people test the message to see if they want to read it. Magazine article writers are particularly adept at writing lead paragraphs that pull the reader into the rest of the copy.

Closing paragraphs in body copy are difficult to write because they have to do so many things. Usually the last paragraph refers back to the creative concept and wraps up the Big Idea (see Chapter 13). Often the closing will use some kind of "twist," an unexpected tie-in with the concept. In addition, direct-action messages include some kind of *call to action* with instructions on how to respond. Even indirect-action advertisements, such as brand-reminder ads in magazines, may use some kind of call to action, perhaps a reminder of where the product can be found.

*D*ESIGNING FOR PRINT

Architects design buildings in their minds and then translate the details of the structure onto paper in a form known as a *blueprint*. The blueprint guides the

More Than You Ever Wanted to Know

Have you noticed those pharmaceutical ads in magazines followed by a page full of medical gobbledegook? Have you ever wondered why it's there? Why any company in its right mind would spend good advertising dollars to run technical medical information in tiny type? The answer, of course, is that the government requires it.

Here's the situation. The Food and Drug Administration requires that all prescription drug advertising must give a precise list of a drug's risks, benefits, and uses. Developed for drug ads in physicians' professional journals, the FDA has just transferred the same rules over to consumer advertising. The problem didn't exist until drug makers started spending some $200 million to advertise about a dozen prescription products to consumers.

But why would they want to do that? There are certain prescription categories where pitching the product directly to the consumer rather than indirectly through the doctor seems to work. Such advertising has helped turn the nicotine patch, for example, into an $800 million category. Other advertising includes Ortho Pharmaceutical's birth-control pill, Wyeth-Ayerst Labs Norplant contraceptive, and Merck's ads reminding men to ask their doctors about prostate disease. And then there's Rogaine, the product that Upjohn promotes as a treatment for baldness.

The FDA believes the page of "medicalese" is necessary to make sure that important information about the product's dangers and side effects is available. Drug makers say it is a waste of time, space, and money since consumers won't read it. Consumer groups are critical for a different reason; they feel drug makers could bury vital information that needs emphasizing in the sea of small type.

Who is right? What is the right way to handle this technical but important information in advertisements? Or should it even be in the ads, since consumers can't buy the product without a doctor's prescription? What do you think?

"Drug Ads: A Prescription for Controversy," *Business Week* (January 18, 1993):p. 58.

construction of a building. It tells the builder what size everything is and what goes where.

The same things happens in advertising. The art director takes the creative concept that has been developed with the copywriter and visualizes in his or her mind how the final ad will look. This visual inventiveness is characteristic of good designers.

Art directors manipulate the elements on paper to produce a **layout**, which is a plan that imposes order and at the same time creates an arrangement that is aesthetically pleasing. A layout is a map, the art director's equivalent of a blueprint. The art director positions and sizes the elements. These include the visual or visuals, the headline and other supplemental display copy, copy blocks, captions, signatures, logos, and other details such as boxes, rules, and coupons.

A layout has several roles. First, it is a communication tool that translates the visual concept for others so that the idea can be discussed and revised before any money is spent on production. After it has been approved, the layout serves as a guide for the production people who will eventually handle the typesetting, finished art, photography, and pasteup. In some cases the layout acts as a guide for the copywriter who writes copy to fit the space. It is also used for cost estimating. Figures 14.1A through 14.1D on pages 468 and 469 demonstrate some of the major steps involved in creating a print ad.

layout A drawing that shows where all the elements in the ad are to be positioned.

LAYOUT STYLES

The most common layout format is one with a single dominant visual that occupies about 60 to 70 percent of the area. Underneath it is a headline and a copy block. The logo or signature signs off the message at the bottom. A variation on that format has a dominant visual and several smaller visuals in a cluster. A panel or grid layout uses a number of visuals of certain sizes.

Less frequently you will see layouts that emphasize the type rather than art. Occasionally you will see an all-copy advertisement where the headline is treated as type art. A copy-dominant ad may have art, but it is either embedded in the copy or positioned at the bottom of the layout.

The truth is there are many ways to lay out an ad and different layouts can create an entirely different feeling about the product. For example, look at two different ads for work boots on page 470 and the way they are designed. The Timberland ad is part of a campaign that features what Barbara Lippert, in her critique of this campaign in *Adweek,* calls Big Mama Weather—snow, ice, water, and mud (which is illustrated in Ad 14.5A). In another ad in that campaign, the shot of what looks like a woman's eyes peering between a leather and fur hat and a snowcaked muffler is explained by the headline in a turn-of-the-century typeface, "In the Iditarod, the idea that there are only snowmen is abominable." Also appealing to explorers who master Mother Nature is an ad showing clumps of ice floating at the end of a melting glacier somewhere in the Antarctic headlined, "How to Survive a Meltdown."

Contrast that ad with the Dunham boot ad (Ad 14.5B), which looks like a work of fine art. The reflective attitude of the serene outdoor scenes say this boot is for people who appreciate the beauty of nature. Likewise, a picture of a steel-driving man balanced on a crosspiece of girders, which is depicted in another ad in the campaign, is an artful arrangement. Even the copy is poetic. But the difference clearly lies with the visual impact that comes from the picture, the type, and the ads' layouts.

Developing Layouts. There are several steps in the normal development of a print layout and they are depicted in the series showing the development of a Maybelline ad, Figure 14.1. Most art directors—and sometimes copywriters at this stage—work with a form known as **thumbnail sketches**. These are quick miniature versions of the ad, preliminary sketches (more like doodles) that are used for developing the concept and judging the positioning of the elements. In

thumbnail sketches Small preliminary sketches of various layout ideas.

Figure 14.1A

Thumbnails. The artist tries different ways to lay out the elements in an ad. This is an artist's conception of an artist's conception.

Figure 14.1B

A rough layout. The rough contains little detail (note the nonsense type) and is used for size and placement.

Figure 14.1C

The mechanical (on opposite page). Used in offset printing, the mechanical is a photoready original with all of the elements properly placed. Various instructions are printed on transparent overlays.

Figure 14.1D

The final proof (on opposite page.

(Courtesy of Maybelline USA.)

semicomp A layout drawn to size that depicts the art and display type; body copy is simply ruled in.

the early stages of development an art director may fill page after page with these thumbnail sketches, trying to decide what the ad will look like and where the elements will be positioned.

The second step is a *rough layout*. Roughs are done to size but not with any great attention to how they look. Once again, a rough layout is for the art director's use in working out size and placement decisions. It is sometimes called a *visualization*. In newspaper ads the "rough" may be the only step before the layout goes to production.

In order to show the idea to someone or test various concepts, the art director will usually move to the next step, which is a **semicomp** ("comp" is short for comprehensive). A semicomp is done to the exact size of the ad, and all the elements are exactly sized and positioned. It is done by hand, but because it is going to be presented to others, extra care is taken to make it look good.

In a semicomp the art is sketched in, usually with felt-tip markers. Color is added where appropriate. Shading for black and white is done with various gray markers to indicate tonal variations. The display type is lettered in to resemble the style of type in the final ad. The body copy is indicated by ruling in parallel lines that indicate the size of the body type and the space it will fill. Most advertising layouts are presented in either the rough layout or semicomp stage. The semicomp is used for most routine presentations.

comprehensive A layout that looks as much like the final printed ad as possible.

On special occasions a full-blown **comprehensive** may be developed. This is an impressive presentation piece. Type may be set, particularly for the display copy. Body copy is often just nonsense type (also called *Greeking* type), either commercially available or cut out of another publication. It is supposed to be the right size and resemble the actual typeface specified for the ad. The art may be a rendering by an artist who specializes in realistic art for comps, or it may be cut out of another publication. The idea is to make the comp look as much as possible like the finished piece. It is used for presentations to people who cannot visualize what a finished ad will look like from a semicomp. It is also used in important situations like new business presentations and agency reviews.

The last stage in the production process is the development of **mechanicals**, also called **keylines**. These are extremely carefully prepared pasteups intended for the printer. They are strictly for production use. Mechanicals are disappearing as more agencies and printers move to electronic publishing. With computer composition and layout, everything is done on the screen and the computer prints out an electronically assembled image—or sometimes a page negative that is one step closer to printing plates.

DESIGN PRINCIPLES

A layout begins with a collection of miscellaneous elements, usually a headline and other display copy, one or more pieces of art, maybe some accompanying captions, body copy complete with subheads, a brand or store signature, and perhaps a trademark, a slogan, or a tagline. Local retail advertising will also include reminder information such as address, hours, telephone number, and credit cards accepted. Arranging all of these elements so that they make sense and attract attention is a challenge. These decisions are both functional and aesthetic. The functional side of a layout makes the message easy to perceive; the aesthetic side makes it attractive and pleasing to the eye.

There are a number of design principles that help structure the way elements are arranged in a layout. The first is organization. We know from research into perception that organized visual images are easier to recognize, perceive, and remember than are visual images without any order.[4] By order, we mean *organization*—imposing some pattern on the placement of the elements. If you take a piece of tracing paper as we have done here with the Mustang ad, Figure 14.2, and convert the major elements of any good ad to geometric shapes, a pattern will emerge. A layout without any order lacks visual coordination of the elements.

The next thing you will notice when you study the tracing paper is that your eye follows some kind of *visual path,* or *direction,* when it scans the elements. This path is determined by the ordering of the elements. In Western countries most readers scan from top to bottom and from left to right, a process tagged the **Gütenberg Diagonal** by graphics expert Edmund Arnold. The tissue paper on the Mustang ad in Figure 14.2 illustrates with the red line how the eye progresses from the upper left to the lower right. Most layouts try to work with these natural eye movements, although directional cues can be manipulated in a layout to cause the eye to follow an unexpected path. The biggest problem occurs when the visual path is unclear.

Most good layouts have a starting point, called the *dominant element.* Within the design process, someone must determine the relative importance of the various elements in order to decide which one should be dominant. Normally the dominant element is a visual as in the Everlast ads (Ad 14.6). But it can be a headline if the type is sufficiently big and bold to overpower the other elements. By definition there can be only one dominant element; everything else must be

---

mechanicals (keylines)   A finished pasteup, with every element perfectly positioned, that is photographed to make printing plates for offset printing.

Principle

The layout imposes structure on chaos.

Gütenberg diagonal   A visual path that flows from the upper left corner to the lower right.

---

[4]Gerald Murch, *Visual and Auditory Perception* (Indianapolis: Bobbs-Merrill Co., 1973).

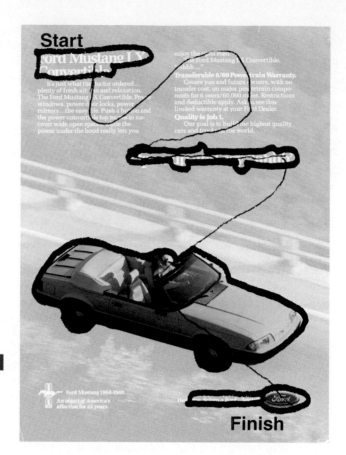

Figure 14.2

Even without the highlighting, you can trace the eyeflow of this Ford ad.

(Courtesy of Ford Motor Company)

focal point The first element in a layout that the eye sees.

subordinate. This element is the **focal point** of the ad; it is the first thing you see.

A layout begins with a collection of discrete elements and colminates in a design with *unity*. All the elements fuse into one coherent image: The pieces become a whole. On a visual level the content of the message must fuse with the form of the presentation. The ad's appearance should match its message. You wouldn't use delicate letters for an ad about Mack trucks, nor would you use fanciful art for an ad targeted to truck drivers. Using one typeface rather than several is a good technique for creating unity, particularly for display copy. If there is a dominant artistic style, stick to it. Ultramodern type doesn't fit with an illustration that looks Victorian.

Neighboring elements that touch and align are another important aspect of unity. An old axiom states the importance of *grouping* things: "Keep things together that go together." Captions need to adjoin the pictures to which they refer. Headlines lead into the text, so the headline should be over the body copy. Pictures providing a different view of the same thing should be grouped.

White space is not simply an area where nothing happens. It can be massed and used as a design element. It works in one of two ways: It either frames an element, as in the Everlast shorts ad (Ad 14.6A), which gives it importance; or it separates elements that don't belong together. Because it sets things apart, white space is used as a prestigious cue in layouts for upscale stores and products.

Contrast indicates the importance of the various elements. Contrast makes one element stand out because it is different. People notice opposites, the unex-

Principle

Think unity. Keep things together that go together.

Principle

If everything is bold, then nothing is bold.

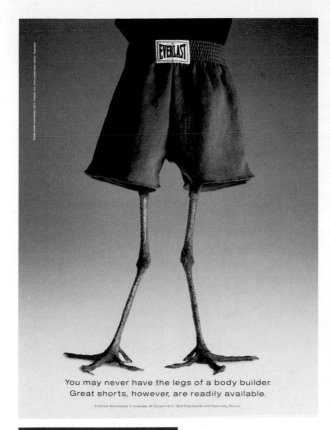

Ad 14.6A

Ad 14.6B

The ads in the Everlast campaign use strong, dominant visuals as the focal point of the layout.

(Courtesy of Everlast Sportswear, USA Classic Inc.)

pected. Contrast is also used to separate an ad from its surroundings. Because the newspaper environment is mostly black and white, an ad that uses color will stand out in contrast. In magazines, where most of the ads and editorial materials use color, a black-and-white ad might stand out. Black-and-white ads, by definition, are high in contrast. They can create dramatic, high-contrast images. A small ad or illustration can dominate if it contrasts effectively with its surrounding. Size is important in establishing contrast. The difference between the shirt and the type in the Everlast ad (Ad 14.6B) is a good example of how contrast contributes to impact.

When an artist decides where to place an element, he or she is manipulating *balance*. A layout that is not in a state of visual equilibrium seems to be heavier on one side than the other. A layout that is out of balance looks like a mistake. There are two types of balance—formal and informal. *Formal balance* is symmetrical, left to right. Everything is centered. Formal balance is conservative and suggests stability. *Informal balance* is asymmetrical and creates a more visually exciting or dynamic layout. Informal balance is much harder to achieve because it requires manipulating and counterbalancing visual weights around an imaginary **optical center**. Counterbalancing uses the teeter-totter principle: Larger figures are positioned closer to the fulcrum than are smaller figures.

Proportion is both an aesthetic and a mathematical principle that concen-

optical center A point slightly above the mathematical center of a page.

trates on the relative sizes of the elements. The basic idea is that equal proportions are visually uninteresting because they are monotonous. Two visuals of the same size fight with one another for attention, and neither provides a point of visual interest. Copy and art, for example, should be proportionately different. Usually the art dominates and covers two-thirds to three-fifths of the page area.

The architect's axiom applies to *simplicity*: Less is more. The more elements that are crowded into a layout, the more the impact is fragmented. Don't overload the layout. The fewer the elements, the stronger the impact. *Clutter* is the opposite of simplicity. It comes from having too many elements and too little unity.

COLOR

Color is used in advertising to *attract attention, provide realism, establish moods*, and *build broad identity*. Research has consistently shown that ads with color get more attention than do ads without color. In newspapers, where color reproduction may not be very accurate, *spot color*, in which a second accent color is used to highlight important elements, has proved to be highly attention-getting. Realism is important for certain message strategies where full-color photographs may be essential. Some things just don't look right in black and white: pizza, flower gardens, beef stroganoff, and rainbows, for example. Color is needed to do justice to the content.

Color has a psychological language that speaks to moods and symbolic meanings. Warm colors, such as red, yellow, and orange, are bright and happy. Pastels are soft and friendly. Earth tones are natural and no-nonsense. Cool colors, such as blue and green, are aloof, calm, serene, reflective, and intellectual. An award-winning campaign for Levi Strauss Co.'s Dockers was built on the mood value of different colors. Ad 14.7 shows the "brown" ad; other ads featured gray, tan, blue, and black.

Yellow and red have the most attention-getting power. Red is used to sym-

Ad 14.7

The Dockers campaign for its men's products used the mood association of various colors as its theme.

(Courtesy of Levi Strauss & Co.)

bolize alarm and danger, as well as warmth. Yellow combined with black is not only attention-getting but also dramatic because of the stark contrast in values between the two colors. Black is used for high drama and can express power and elegance.

Color association can be an important part of a brand image. Johnnie Walker Red has built a long-running campaign on all the warm associations we have with red, such as sunrises and sunsets, a fireplace, even an Irish setter. Kool cigarettes has used the color green so extensively that you can recognize the ad even when the product image is obliterated. IBM uses the color blue so extensively that the company is referred to as "Big Blue."

*P*RINT PRODUCTION

Getting a print ad produced involves a bit of knowledge of the graphic arts industry. Courses are available to help you learn more about that industry, however, we will briefly review some aspects of production that you may need to be able to discuss or manage.

TYPOGRAPHY

Words in a print ad are presented as either hand-drawn letters or handwriting or the characters are officially typeset by computer or photocomposition equipment.

Most people don't even notice the letters in an ad, which is the way it should be. Good typesetting doesn't call attention to itself because its primary role is functional—to convey the words of the message. As George Lois, chairman and creative director at Lois Pitts Gershon Pon/GGK, stated: "It's important the typography doesn't get in the way of an idea."[5] Type also has an aesthetic role, however, and the type selection can, in a subtle way, contribute to the impact and mood of the message.

font A complete set of letters in one size and face.

Typeface Selection. The basic set of typeface letters is called a **font**. A type font contains the alphabet for one typeface in one size plus the numerals and punctuation (see Figure 14.3). The alphabet includes both capital letters, called *uppercase,* and small letters, called *lowercase*. You may want to specify *all caps,* which means every letter is a capital, or *U&lc* (upper and lower case), which means the first letter is capitalized and the others are lowercase.

Most people don't realize that designers must choose among thousands of typefaces to find the right face for the message. Within each category of type are

---

[5]Noreen O'Leary, "Legibility Lost," *Adweek,* (October 5, 1987): D7.

14 pt

ABCDEFGHIJKLMNOPQRSTUV
abcdefghijklmnopqrstuvwxyz
1234567890

ABCDEFGHIJKLMNOPQRSTUVWXYZ ABCD

ABCDEFGHIJKLMNOPQRSTUVWXYZ   ABCD

Figure 14.4

The top line is printed in serif letters; the bottom line in sans-serif.

Principle

Type faces have distinctive personalities.

serif A typeface with a finishing stroke on the main strokes of the letters.

sans serif A typeface that does not have the serif detail.

italic A type variation that uses letters that slant to the right.

point A unit used to measure the height of type; there are 72 points in an inch.

type families, which are made up of typefaces of similar design. Two of the major categories are serif and sans serif. The **serif** is the little flourish that finishes off the end of the stroke. "Sans" means "without" in French, which is how **sans serif** letters are identified: They are missing the serif. Most of the sans serif typefaces are clean, blocky, and more contemporary in appearance (see Figure 14.4).

The posture, weight, and width of a typeface also vary, as shown in Figure 14.5. Posture can vary from the normal upright letters to a version that leans to the right, called **italic**. The weight of the typeface can vary depending on how heavy the strokes are. Most typefaces are available in *boldface* or *light*, in addition to the normal weight. Variation in width occurs when the typeface is spread out horizontally or squeezed together. These variations are called *extended* or *condensed*.

Printers' Measures. To understand type sizes, you must understand the printers' measuring system. Type is measured in **points**, which are the smallest unit available (see Figure 14.6). There are 72 points in an inch.

Most designers consider type set in 14 points or larger to be display copy

14.5

Common typeface variations.

This is set in a light typeface
This is set in a normal weight
This is set in a boldface.
This is set in italic.
This is set in an expanded typeface.
This is set in a condensed typeface.

Figure 14.6

Examples of different sizes available for Times Roman typeface.

6 POINT

ABCDEFGHIJKLMNOPQRSTUVWXYZABCDEFGHIJKLMNOPQRSTUVWXYZABCDEFGHIJKLMNOPQRSTUVWXYZAB
abcdefghijklmnopqrstuvwxyzabcdefghijklmnopqrstuvwxyzabcdefghijklmnopqrstuvwxyzabcdefghijklmnopqrstuvwx   1234567890

12 POINT

ABCDEFGHIJKLMNOPQRSTUVWXYZ ABCDEFGHIJKLMN
abcdefghijklmnopqrstuvwxyz abcdefghijklmnopqrstu 1234567890

18 POINT

ABCDEFGHIJKLMNOPQRSTUVWXYZ

abcdefghijklmnopqrstuvwxyz   abcdefghijkl

1234567890

pica   A unit of type measurement used to measure width and depth of columns; there are 12 points in a pica and 6 picas in an inch.

justified   A form of typeset copy in which the edges of the lines in a column of type are forced to align by adding space between words in the line.

and type set 12 points or smaller to be body copy. The width of columns, also called *line length,* is measured in **picas**. The pica is a bigger unit of measurement than the point. There are 6 picas in an inch and 12 points in a pica. So 12-point type is exactly 1 pica high, or one-sixth of an inch.

Justification.   One characteristic of typeset copy as opposed to typewriter copy is the forced alignment of the column edges. With **justified** copy, such as you are reading here, every line ends at exactly the same point. Other options are available to advertisers. One variation is to let the right line endings fall where they will. This is called *ragged right* as our definitions in the margin illustrate. You can also specify the opposite, *ragged left,* although that is a very unusual way to set type. If you want to specify that either edge be justified, then the phrase *flush left* or *flush right* is used. Another option is to set everything *centered,* which means neither the right nor the left edges align, but instead everything is centered around a vertical mid-point axis.

Legibility.   As previously mentioned, type selection is primarily functional. The objective of *legibility* is to convey the words as clearly as possible. Because reading is such a complex activity, the type should make the perceptual process as easy as possible. If the type is difficult to read, most people will turn the page. Research has discovered a number of type practices that can hinder the reading process.[6] All capital letters, for example, can create legibility problems, as can reverse type (white or light-colored letters against a black or darker background), unusual typefaces, and surprinting the type over a photo or some kind of patterned background.

THE ART

The word *art* refers to the graphics, whether an illustration or a photograph. Although art directors lay out the ad, they rarely do finished art. If an illustration is needed, then an artist is hired, usually freelance. Fashion illustration is different from cartooning, for example. If a photo is needed, then a photographer is hired. Both artists and photographers tend to have personal styles or specialties, and the right person has to be found for the visual.

line art   Art in which all elements are solid with no intermediate shades or tones.

Art Reproduction   There are two general types of images that are reproduced in print. A simple drawing is called **line art** because the image is just solid black lines on a white page. Photographs, however, are much more complicated because they have a range, or shades, of gray tones between the black and white. The phrase *continuous tone* is used to refer to images with this range of gray values.

halftones   Images with a continuous range of shades from light to dark.

Because printing is done with a limited number of inks, printers must be able to create the illusion of a range of grays. Continuous-tone art and photos must be converted to **halftones** in order to be printed. In the *halftone process,* the original photograph is shot through a fine screen (see Figure 14.7). Areas on the original that are dark will create large dots that fill the space; if the original is light, then a tiny dot will be surrounded by empty white space. The image, in other words, is converted to a pattern of dots that gives the illusion of shades of gray. If you look at a photograph in most newspapers, you may be able to see the dot pattern with your naked eye.

The quality of the image depends on how fine the screen is that is used to

---

[6]Rolf Rehe, *Typography: How to Make It Most Legible* (Indianapolis: Design Research Publications, 1974).

Figure 14.7

This figure contrasts the same image reproduced as line art (left) and a halftone (right).

convert the original picture to a dot pattern. Because of the roughness of newsprint, newspapers use a relatively coarse screen, usually 65 lines per inch. (This is referred to as 65-line screen.) Magazines use fine screens, which may be 90, 110, 120, and on up to 200 lines per inch. The higher the number, the finer the screen and the better the quality of the reproduction.

Screens are also used to create various *tint blocks*, which can either be shades of gray in black-and-white printing or shades of color. A block of color can be printed solid or it can be *screened back* to create a shade. These shades are referred to as a range of percentages such as 100 percent (solid) down to 10 percent (very faint). Examples of screens are found in Figure 14.8.

COLOR REPRODUCTION

Besides reproducing halftones, the other major problem for printers is the reproduction of full color. When you look at a slide, you see a full range of colors and shades. It would be impossible to set up a printing press with a separate

Figure 14.8

These spectra show the different screens for black and for a color.

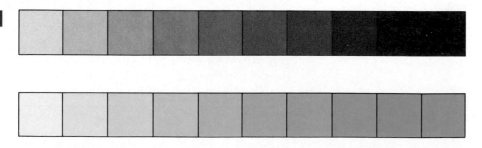

ink roller for every possible hue and value. How, then, are these colors reproduced?

The solution to this problem is to use a limited number of base colors and mix them to create the rest of the spectrum. Full-color images are reproduced using four distinctive shades of ink called **process colors**. They are magenta (a shade of pinkish red), cyan (a shade of bright blue), yellow, and black.

Printing inks are transparent, so when one ink overlaps another, a third color is created. Red and blue create purple, yellow and blue create green, yellow and red create orange. The black is used for type and, in *four-color printing*, adds depth to the shadows and dark tones in an image.

The process used to reduce the original color image to four halftone negatives is called **color separation**. The negatives replicate the red, yellow, blue, and dark areas of the original. The separation is done photographically, beginning with original full-color images on slides. (Slides, or transparencies, produce the most accurate and grain-free images.) Color filters are used to screen out everything but the desired hue. A separate color filter is used for each of the four process colors. Lasers are now used to scan the image and make the separations. Figure 14.9 illustrates the process of color separation.

New technologies have made it possible for a color piece to go directly from computer to film. Some agencies don't create mechanicals at all anymore.

process colors   Four basic inks—magenta, cyan, yellow, and black—that are mixed to produce a full range of colors found in four-color printing.

color separation   The process of splitting a color image into four images recorded on negatives; each negative represents one of the four process colors.

Figure 14.9C

Yellow and red plates.

Figure 14.9D

Blue (cyan) plate.

Instead, ads are created on the computer and transmitted to a service bureau or color separation house by modem or floppy disks. There they can go directly to film.

Using computers for illustrations is creatively simple. The difficulty is in photography. In theory, a transparency can be scanned into a traditional high-end prepress system, then data can be sent to a Macintosh, for example, and assembled into an ad and then returned to the system for output on film. In reality, such files use up huge amounts of memory and time, and color calibration is not yet sophisticated enough to guarantee that what you see is what you get. What actually happens is that art directors work with low-resolution scans for positioning purposes only. The prepress operators then assemble the ad electronically, replacing the position-only scans they've made from transparencies in the traditional way.

As these methods are perfected, the time-consuming, labor-intensive assembling of ad pieces will be replaced with desktop color imaging. Color matching can be expensive, but it can also save companies money in stripping

Figure 14.9E

Black plate.

Figure 14.9F

The finished ad with all four process colors.

(Courtesy of Redbook)

costs and typesetting, and the industry is optimistic about the continuing refinement of computerized color graphics.[7]

PRINTING PROCESS

There are a number of printing processes used in advertising such as *letterpress*, which is used for numbering and specialty printing effects; *offset lithography* which is the most popular type of printing for newspapers and most magazines; *rotogravure*, which is used for long print runs with quality photographic reproduction; *flexography*, which prints on unusual surfaces; and *silk screen*, which is used to print posters, T-shirts, and point-of-sale materials.

If an ad is going to run in a number of publications, there has to be some way to distribute a reproducible form of the ad to all of them. For letterpress, a

---

[7]Cathy Madison, "Ads Brought To You In Computerized Color" *Adweek* (January 14, 1991):24

Ashley Patterson, Senior Account Executive, The Morrison Agency, Atlanta

8:35–9:10 A.M. Coffee, bagel, and the first paperwork of the day. I try to spend the first half hour of my mornings cleaning out my "In" box (where invoices to be approved, interoffice correspondence, and other administrative things tend to pile up).

9:10–9:30 A.M. Meet with our traffic manager to review the status of my clients' jobs in production. Everything seems to be in order. I make a note to track down a missing insertion order and push to get an approval this afternoon on a trade ad that has a fast-approaching deadline.

9:30–10:00 A.M. Review random color separations for the Lovable catalog with our production manager. We double check each photo to make sure that there are no wrinkles or imperfections in the bras. We decide that the bras look fine, but a couple of the models look unnaturally tan. We circle the color corrections to be made and send them back with our vendor. We also proof the type on the mechanical boards for the catalog one last time before I take them to the client. This is very tedious since it includes prices and detailed style information on every bra.

10:00–10:20 A.M. Brief meeting with our media director regarding some research I need his help with on competitive spending.

10:30–11:00 A.M. Review the alternate translations of three Lovable consumer ads that we wanted to run in a Spanish magazine network. The publication has a copywriter on staff who has submitted translations of our ads. One of our headlines—"It's the Icing on Your Birthday Suit"—translates in Spanish to "It's the Fig Leaf on Eve's Suit." I'm not happy with this, but it is the third attempt so far at a translation so I call the client to discuss. We agree that we will run the other two ads and skip this one. I submit the approved ads to the production department to begin typesetting.

11:00–11:30 A.M. Prepare a job order and a creative strategy document for a sales video that Lovable wants to do for a select audience of buyers and vendors.

11:30–11:45 A.M. Talk to the editor of *Body Fashions/Intimate Apparel*, whom I recently met at a Lovable function. We discuss an upcoming article that she wants us to be interviewed for. I prepare a list of questions per

mat made from a kind of papier-mâché is sent, along with a *proof* made from the original engraving. For gravure printing, film positives are sent to the publications. The duplicate material for offset printing is a "slick" proof of the original mechanical. These proofs are called *photoprints* or *photostats*, which are relatively cheap images. *Veloxes*, or *C-Prints* are better-quality prints.

A number of special printing effects are created at the end of the production process. These are mechanical techniques that embellish the image using such methods as embossing or foil stamping. The last step in production is the *binding*, where the pages of a publication are assembled.

our discussion and submit them to our public relations department so we may schedule an interview.

12:00–1:00 P.M. Lunch at the mall with a friend. We swing by Macy's on the way out so I can take some Polaroids of an especially effective point-of-purchase concept in the foundations department, which embarrasses my friend a little.

1:00–1:45 P.M. Return phone calls and sift through my mail.

1:45–2:00 P.M. One of my calls was from the client, approving the trade ad with some minor changes. I write a change-it form and submit it to the production manager, who breathes a sigh of relief.

2:00–3:15 P.M. Meet with the supervisor and account team from our public relations department to review the status of a Breast Health Awareness program the agency is producing in conjunction with Lovable. One of the components of this campaign will include a special hang-tag that includes a message on Breast Health Awareness and a phone number for the American Cancer Society. We discuss logistics and pricing on the program, and how we

will work in tandem to produce the point-of-purchase.

3:30–4:45 P.M. Initial team meeting with our creative director, account supervisor, and writer/art director team on a naming/repositioning assignment for one of Lovable's new lines. Our goal is to develop a name and a campaign which will help Lovable move into the better department store category. We discuss timing, budgets, and initial creative strategy. The next step is to get production estimates for the assignment by job so that we may get client approval on the overall budget. The creative team is chomping at the bit on this one!

4:45–5:30 P.M. More "In" box clean-up. It's amazing how fast the pile builds up!

5:30–6:00 P.M. Make my "To Do" list for tomorrow, confirm a couple of appointments by phone, and then head home.

7:45 P.M. At home, I read my new *Glamour, Allure*, and *Bridal Guide*, clipping two relevant articles. One of the perks of having a fashion account is a comp subscription list that includes about 20 of my favorite magazines. This and free lingerie—what more could I want?

tip-ins Preprinted ads that are provided by the advertiser to be glued into the binding of a magazine.

Newspapers are folded, and the fold holds the sheets together. Magazines are folded, stapled or sewn, and trimmed. Sometimes a separate cover is glued on. During this binding process separate preprinted ads provided by the advertiser can be glued in. Such ads are called **tip-ins**. They are used when an advertiser wants particularly fine printing or wishes to include something that can't be accommodated in the normal printing process. Most perfume manufacturers, for example, are tipping in perfume samples that are either scratch-and-sniff or scented strips that release their fragrance when pulled apart.

NEW TECHNOLOGY

A new technology, based on computers and transmission by phone line using fiber optics or by satellite, has generated a revolution in print media. Computerized typesetting now makes it easy to transmit type electronically. Art can be *digitized* (broken into tiny grids, each one coded electronically for tone or color) and then transmitted. Fiber optics can send type, art, or even complete pages across a city for local editions of newspapers. Satellites make national page transmission possible for regional editions of magazines and newspapers such as *U.S.A. Today*.

Printing by personal computer, utilizing easy-to-use software, is taking over the low end of the typesetting function. In addition to typesetting, page layouts as well as advertising layouts can be done on a personal computer. This new approach to typesetting and layout is called *desktop publishing*. Graphics that can be drawn and modified on computers are now being used in many newspapers.

At the higher end of the typesetting function, many quality typesetting systems use some kind of computer-based *pagination* equipment that combines sophisticated computer typesetting with page layout capabilities.

Inkjet printing, which is a type of printing directed by computer, is becoming more common. It can speed up the entire printing process by eliminating many of the technical steps in printing, such as negatives and plate-making. It will soon be possible to go directly from the computer to a printed publication. This may make it feasible to customize the content of a publication, advertising as well as articles, to the interest of the reader, thus creating a new world of one-on-one publishing and, eventually, personalized target marketing. *Time* magazine used this to print subscribers' names on each cover.

SUMMARY

- The key elements of a print ad are divided between copy—the headlines, text, and other verbal elements—and art, which refers to the visual elements including illustrations, photographs, type, and layout. In an effective advertisement, all these elements work together to create impact.

- While newspapers are focused on news, the ads they carry usually also announce something and provide useful information to the paper's readers. Magazines are usually more tightly targeted than newspapers to readers' special interests and have better-quality reproduction, which means the advertisements can use better color, more finely detailed photographs, and more detailed artwork.

- Headlines target the prospect, stop the reader,

identify the product, start the sale, and lure the reader into the body copy. Body copy provides the persuasive details such as support for claims, proof, and reasons.

- A layout arranges all the elements to provide a visual order that helps the reader to process the information in the ad; at the same time it is aesthetically pleasing and makes a visual statement for the brand. Layouts are built in stages starting with thumbnails and moving through rough comprehensives and full comprehensives to the production stage where they are turned into mechanicals.

- Color is used in advertising to attract attention, provide realism, establish mood, and build brand identity. Color is reproduced in print using a process that photographically separates full nature color into four negatives than can be reproduced in four colors of ink. These will overlap to create the illusion of full color.

- The most common printing process for newspapers and most magazines is offset lithography. Other types of printing occasionally used in advertising include letterpress, rotogravure, flexography, and silk screen.

QUESTIONS

1. What are the major features of a print ad? What is the purpose of each one?

2. Collect a group of ads for department and discount stores. Compare their layouts. What does the layout "say" about the type of store and the merchandise it carries?

3. Think of ads you have seen in newspapers and magazines over the past ten years. What trends, if any, do you notice? How do you account for these trends?

4. We read from left to right and top to bottom. This pattern forms the natural "Z" shape. What does the chapter call this pattern of direction? Now look at some advertising in a favorite magazine. Do any of the ads *not* follow this pattern? Trace the visual direction used. What shape does it take? Why would the designer choose this direction pattern?

5. A student struggles with a layout assignment involving informal balance. She has a dominant vertical illustration element placed at the right side of her page. Her difficulty is finding some other element (copy block or small illustration) to balance the size and strength of the key visual. When she asks her instructor for help, he tells her, "You've forgotten one of the simplest principles of equilibrium: You don't always need other copy and design pieces to balance the dominant object." What does he mean?

6. Search your area newspapers for ads for clothing stores. Sort these into expensive stores and those that feature lower-priced apparel. Now compare the design aspects of each type of store. How many differences do you see in design, art, type, and other elements? Do any of these differences produce a store personality or image? Identify those print concepts in the ad that provide a special "signature" for the store.

SUGGESTED CLASS PROJECT

If you are making a pitch to get an athletic shoe account, what approach would you consider? What is there left to do? This is the problem McCann Erickson faced when it won the estimated $4 million Brooks Sports' athletic shoe account. That's a relatively small budget compared to the huge Nike budgets. The assignment is to name, position, and launch the new brand. The advertising is mostly print and will run in both men's and women's magazines as well as fitness and trade publications. You are part of the art director/copywriter team. Develop the "spec" work (speculative) for the presentation. Develop an idea for the campaign and rough out two sample ads.

ℱURTHER READINGS

ADLER, KEITH, *Advertising Resource Handbook* (East Lansing, MI: Advertising Resources, Inc., 1989).

BAIRD, RUSSELL N., DUNCAN MCDONALD, RONALD H. PITTMAN, and ARTHUR T. TURNBULL, *The Graphics of Communication*, 6th ed. (New York: Harcourt, Brace, Jovanovich, 1993).

BENDINGER, BRUCE, *The Copy Workshop,* 2nd ed. (Chicago: The Copy Workshop, 1993).

BURTON, PHILIP WARD, *Which Ad Pulled Best?* (Chicago: Crain, 1981).

KEDING, ANN, and THOMAS H. BIVINS, *How to Produce Creative Advertising* (Lincolnwood, IL: NTC, 1991).

MORIARTY, SANDRA E., *Creative Advertising,* 2nd ed. (Englewood Cliffs, NJ: Prentice Hall, 1991).

NELSON, ROY PAUL, *The Design of Advertising,* 7th ed. (Madison, WI: Brown & Benchmark, 1994).

REHE, ROLF, *Typography: How to Make It Most Legible* (Indianapolis: Design Research Publications, 1974).

The Gap: Creating Print Advertising for a Changing Market

For years The Gap was a retailing steam engine that no one could stop. With casual attire the uniform-of-choice of baby boomers, their parents, and children, sales of The Gap's denim jeans, khaki pants, all-cotton shirts and sweats, and wool sweaters catapulted the earnings of the San Francisco-based retailer into the financial stratosphere. By the end of 1991, sales had reached $2.5 billion, up 30 percent from the year before.

The Gap's strategy was to sell "good style, good quality, good value"—a mission it undertook with the help of a unique, magazine-based advertising campaign that communicated the primacy of consumer taste. In 1988, The Gap launched its "Individuals of Style" campaign—a series of dramatic black-and-white photos, featuring such well-known celebrities as Spike Lee, Kim Basinger, and Miles Davis. Each celebrity wore a single item of basic Gap apparel as well as clothes from his or her personal wardrobe. The visual message of classic simplicity combined with individual style helped convince consumers that Gap clothes were cool. Not wanting to overdo a good thing, The Gap eventually discontinued the ads, at least for a while.

Buoyed by the campaign's success, The Gap seemed invincible for about six years. Its concept of selling well-made, moderately priced basics in an attractive, trendy setting was the right merchandising approach for the times. However, The Gap's success was due only in part to its merchandising genius. The inability of competitors to produce comparable apparel at lower costs than The Gap gave the retailer a near monopoly on the kinds of clothes Americans wanted to wear.

This changed when the economic recession forced consumers to look for bargains and when companies such as J. C. Penney and K mart began selling back-to-basics apparel at prices consumers could not ignore. Adding to The Gap's problems was the discontent of female customers who began to tire of the no-frills look. As a result of competitive pressure and changing tastes, The Gap's profits declined in 1992, the first time since 1984.

Recognizing the need to revise its merchandising strategy, The Gap introduced more fashionable, higher-priced items in the fall of 1993. Along with denim jeans and rugby shirts, shoppers also found stretch pants and leather vests. Persuading consumers that The Gap had a wider variety of merchandise was the challenge of the company's new print advertising campaign. Not surprisingly, the campaign featured more than just the basics. In a series of magazine ads, waiflike model Kate Moss wore Gap form-fitting sleeveless turtlenecks, a far cry from the Individuals of Style campaign.

Does this mean that the Gap's Individuals of Style campaign and back-to-basics look are dead? Certainly not. The Gap just reincarnated them in another form. In the fall of 1993, the retailer unveiled a six-week print campaign, running in three national magazines, to sell its casual, khaki pants to a larger, somewhat older audience. The campaign featured archival photos of 13 celebrities wearing their own khakis. At the bottom right-hand corner of the black-and-white photos is The Gap logo. Each photo is also accompanied by copy likening khakis sold by The Gap to those worn by "legendary writers, actors, adventurers with style." Featured celebrities include Humphrey Bogart, Marilyn Monroe, and Pablo Picasso.

After the first Individuals of Style campaign ended, Maggie Gross, The Gap's senior vice president for advertising and marketing, made the prediction that the campaign would be back "when the time is right" but with a different slant. An appeal to the nostalgia of older baby boomers seems to be the strategy of the 1990s, combined, of course, with a second set of ads that tells consumers that the basics look is only part of the picture.

Sources: Christina Duff, "Gap's New Line Goes Beyond the Basics," *The Wall Street Journal*, (August 12, 1993):B1; "Gap Ads to Feature Celebrities in Khakis," *The New York Times* (August 18, 1993):D17; Michael Janofsky, "Advertising: Imitation May Be Flattery, But Conehead Ad Is Alien to The Gap," *The New York Times* (July 15, 1993):D21; Russell Mitchell, "A Bit of a Rut at The Gap," *Business Week* (November 30, 1992):100; Russell Mitchell, "How the Gap's Ads Got So-o-o Cool," *Business Week* (March 9, 1992):64; Russell Mitchell, "A Humbler Neighborhood for The Gap," *Business Week* (August 16, 1993):29; Russell Mitchell, "The Gap: Can the Nation's Hottest Retailer Stay on Top?" *Business Week* (March 9, 1992)58–64.

Questions

1. How would you assess the effectiveness of The Gap's dual ad campaigns—one featuring Kate Moss and the other looking at adventurers who wore khakis—to communicate the retailer's broadened variety of merchandise?

2. The Gap uses black-and-white photos in many of its print campaigns. How effective is this technique in selling the product?

3. In what ways are The Gap's newest print ads right for the times?

$\mathscr{C}$REATING BROADCAST ADVERTISING

CHAPTER OBJECTIVES

When you have completed this chapter, you should be able to:

- Understand the roles of the various people associated with television commercials, including the producer, director, and editor

- List the various stages in the production of a television commercial

- Identify the critical elements in radio and television commercials

- Read and understand a radio script and a television script

- Compare and contrast radio ads and television commercials

$\mathcal{M}$ASTERING TELEVISION COMMERCIALS

The making of the newest Mastercard commercials has not been nearly as exciting as, say, the making of Michael Jackson's *Thriller* video. We don't have any dancing beer bottles or talking fingers or animatronic sheep. What we do have is a campaign that tries to differentiate a product in a category that doesn't have what you would call a gaping chasm of difference. But it seems enough people have noticed the campaign, considering supermarket use of Mastercard jumped about $200 million in the first quarter of 1993.

To start, making a Mastercard company commercial requires the following ingredients:

1. One copywriter
2. One art director
3. Two creative directors
4. Several account people.

You will also need assorted meetings, presentations, focus groups, and frantic late-night phone calls. You also need a strategy. Credit cards have been sold for so long as passports to an absurdly fantastic "good life" where you jaunt off at lunch for Tahiti and say, "Forget the luggage, we'll just charge a whole new wardrobe when we get there!" We took the premise that a credit card is nothing but a piece of plastic that people use to buy things and do things and basically just deal with things. It's a tool. So it follows that people ought to choose a credit card the way they would choose any tool. You should pick a credit card based on how well it does credit card things.

Starting from that point, we went through all the post-1980s imaginations about honesty—just coming out and saying that a credit card won't make you prettier or smarter or more popular. And then it occurred to us that if you used it right, maybe it would do those things, after all. Mastercard is accepted at 62 cajillion places around the world, so if you used it to get a new haircut or a chemical peel or a makeover or liposuction, it could make you better looking.

In any case, once you've got the strategy, the idea, and a minivan full of scripts, you need a voice-over that can carry it off. We went with Rob Morrow, *Northern Exposure*'s Dr. Joel Fleischman. Rob really understood the attitude. In fact, he delivers the scripts so naturally that people are always asking us how much involvement he has in the spots. He reads them. That's it. So while Rob Morrow is the perfect voice and an excellent actor and a nice guy to boot, he doesn't have any creative input.

Once we get through testing and making the necessary revisions, it's time to produce. So it's off to the Four Seasons hotel in Los Angeles, America's advertising dormitory, for about a month.

Take all of this, toss it into stage five on Raleigh studios, shake well, and you've got a good idea of how to make our Mastercard commercials. When you see them, we hope you like them. At the very least, we hope you don't get that look on your face that you get when you bite into a piece of candy out of a Whitman's Sampler and you think it's caramel but it turns out to be creamed coconut and you hold it in your mouth trying to keep it from touching your taste buds while you look for a napkin or something to spit it out in.[1]

---

[1]Adapted from Brent Bouchez and Adam Goldstein, "The Plastic Universe," *Adweek* (September 6, 1993):28–30.

THE TELEVISION ENVIRONMENT

Brent Bouchez and Adam Goldstein, pictured front and left respectively in our chapter-opening photo, the creative minds behind the Mastercard campaign, appear to be minimizing the tremendous effort that goes into creating an effective television commercial. In fact, a 30-second spot that flies by you as you watch your favorite television show represents hundreds of hours of careful planning and execution. In earlier chapters we discussed the pros and cons of broadcast media. In this chapter we present an overview of how television and radio commercials are developed and produced.

Like most Americans, you probably have a love-hate relationship with television commercials. On the one hand, you may have a favorite commercial or campaign. The Bartles and Jaymes wine cooler commercials by the Hal Riney Agency have been amazingly successful using two elderly men to sell wine coolers to an audience composed primarily of young women—because the characters are so captivating. On the other hand, you can probably identify a dozen commercials that you resent so much you turn the channel or leave the room the minute they appear. You might hate the product or see the characters in the commercial as stupid and the message as insulting. Your reaction may be personal—different people like different things; strategic—you are not in the target for that particular product and the message isn't addressed to you; or factual—there are, after all, a number of dreadful commercials on television.

CHARACTERISTICS OF TELEVISION COMMERCIALS

Television commercials are characterized in two ways: They can achieve audience acceptance if they are well done, and they can minimize viewers' patterns of avoidance if they are intriguing as well as intrusive.

Acceptance. People do like to watch commercials if the ads are well done. They watch excerpts from the annual Clio awards given for television advertising when they appear as an item on news broadcasts. Television shows on famous ads and advertising bloopers consistently get high ratings. Lines from commercials can even take on a life of their own, such as "Do you know me?" from the American Express campaign and "Thanks, I needed that" from a Mennen Skin Bracer commercial. The Wendy's line "Where's the beef?" went from an immensely popular commercial to a catch phrase used by one political candidate, Walter Mondale, against another, Gary Hart, in the 1984 presidential primaries.

Principle

Television commercials should be intriguing as well as intrusive.

Intrusiveness. Most people pay more attention to television than they do to radio programming. People watching a program they enjoy are frequently absorbed in it. Their absorption is only slightly less than that experienced by people watching a movie in a darkened theater. Advertising is considered an unwelcome interruption because it disrupts concentration. This intrusiveness can be disconcerting and can cause the viewer to be even less receptive to the commercial message.

Another problem confronting television advertisers is the tendency of viewers to switch channels or leave the room during commercial breaks. Because of television viewers' strong patterns of avoidance, commercials have to be intriguing as well as intrusive.

Angela Turner, Account Executive, SMW Advertising, Toronto

As an account executive for SMW Advertising, Angela manages the accounts of the CTV Television Network, Nikon Canada, Outward Bound, and Lands' End.

8:30–9:00 A.M.
As the morning begins with my ritual cup of coffee, I tune in to CTV on my office television; although time won't permit watching the programs my client has to offer, I may catch new on-air promotions. I scan the new copy of *Marketing* magazine to check for any current affairs on my clients' business and notice an article on *NYPD Blue*, the newly acquired show on CTV which is receiving a lot of press due to its controversial program content. I then take a few moments to listen to messages which may have come in on my voice-mail and prioritize my agenda for the day.

9:00–9:45 A.M.
Sign off on production billing dockets for one of my clients, Lands' End, and put them aside to be taken to the accounting department. While finishing this off, I place a call to the client requesting final information for an ad to be placed in an upcoming issue of *Harrowsmith* for which the material deadline is quickly approaching. With the revisions in hand, the action of my day begins as I head to the traffic department.

9:45–10:45 A.M.
As I return to my desk, I am approached by my supervisor on CTV who has received an urgent message from the client. Creative will be required for an upcoming issue of the *Hollywood Reporter* congratulating ABC on their fortieth anniversary. As we discuss the creative strategy we realize that, with the given material closing date, concept presentation will be required the next day. On that note I place a quick call to set up the creative team and forewarn them about the urgency of the job.

10:45 A.M.–12:30 P.M.
While finishing up with media for the booking of the ad, traffic notifies me that the CTV creative team has been lined up for the job. I head down to brief the team and discuss different angles which the ad could take. Before leaving them to it, I confirm creative requirements for the movie ad *Bullitt* to appear in an upcoming issue of *TV Guide*. With confidence I head back to my office to set up a presentation time the following day for the ABC ad.

12:30–1:30 P.M.
While sharing my lunch with *The Shirley Show*, a CTV daytime talk show, I notice a new CTV Big Event on-air promotion and make a mental note to

*T*HE NATURE OF COMMERCIALS

MESSAGE STRATEGY

Every advertising medium is different, and copywriters are adept at writing messages that take advantage of each medium's particular set of strengths. Television

	mention it to the client. I take a final look at the calculations I had previously prepared for CTV billing and make necessary notes to discuss with the director of client services before the final figures are sent out.
1:30–2:30 P.M.	Traffic delivers final press proofs of the Outward Bound Winter Experience poster and pamphlet produced last week; I write a quick note to the client to notify her that the final printed pieces will be delivered the next day and send the proofs out by courier. With this done, I make a few calls to request the final revised production estimates to forward to the client.
2:30–2:45 P.M.	Touch base with traffic and the creative team to ensure all is well with creative development for the required CTV ads and confirm deadlines.
2:45–3:45 P.M.	Meet with Nikon supervisor to discuss the installation of the Mediacom outdoor billboard at its new location; apparently the handpainting of the new creative will be completed as scheduled. However, our media department was notified by Mediacom that the new board may not be ready. This prompts a brief meeting to discuss our available options. Also touch base on a required letter to Nikon to accompany production estimates for Christmas Gift

	Guide creative and material revisions.
3:45–4:30 P.M.	Listen and respond to several messages on my voice-mail and am notified that the CTV reprints I had requested of the four-color TV Book ads we produced are ready. Have a brief meeting with CTV media planner on the budget control report we are currently developing. We finalize the most current production and media dollars spent to date and make final revisions. It should now be ready to take to the client for discussion.
4:30–5:00 P.M.	Call traffic to discuss the status of various jobs and confirm due dates. Package the reprints of CTV color ads we did for TV Books and request they be prepared for courier the next morning.
5:00–5:30 P.M.	Finish off a contract report documenting the CTV activities of the day and hand it over to my secretary for distribution. Organize things on my agenda that will have to carry over to the next day and make final phone calls. I then head to the research department to begin an extracurricular evening of attending a focus group for one of our clients that is taking place in house; don't finish up until 10:15 P.M.—an unusually long day.

is unlike radio or print in many ways—in the most important way, it is a medium of moving images.

Principle

Television uses motion and action to create impact.

Action and Motion. Television is a visual medium, and the message is dominated by the impact of visual effects. But, you might observe, newspapers and magazines also use visuals. So what makes the difference in impact between television and print visuals? It is the moving image, the action, that makes television so much more mesmerizing than print. When you watch television you are watching a walking, talking, moving world that even gives the illusion of being three-dimensional. Good television advertising uses the impact of action and motion to attract attention and sustain interest.

Principle

Television uses stories to entertain and to make a point.

Storytelling. Stories can be riveting if they are well told, and television is our society's master storyteller. Most of the programming on television is storytelling. But stories do more than just entertain—they express values, teach behavior, and show us how to deal with our daily problems. Television shows such as *Roseanne, Blossom*, and *Northern Exposure* all include discussions of ethics, morals, or personal values.

Effective television advertisements also use storytelling, both for entertainment value and to make a point. These little stories can be funny, warm, silly, or heart-rending, just as in real life. *Slice of life* advertising is simply instruction in a soap opera format. Emotion is best expressed in a narrative form. In Ad 15.1 Judy Collins sings ". . . My father always promised us that we would live in France . . ." while a homeless woman tries to comfort a child.

Emotion. More than any other advertising medium, television has the ability to touch emotions, to encourage people to feel things. This ability to touch the feelings of the viewer makes television commercials entertaining, diverting, amusing, and absorbing. Real-life situations with all their humor, anger, fear, pride, jealousy, and love come alive on the screen. Humor, in particular, works well on television. The Wendy's classic Russian fashion show ad used comical characters and situations to get attention.

These emotions are pulled from natural situations that everyone can identify with. Hallmark has produced some real tear-jerker commercials about those times of our lives that we remember by the cards we get and save. Kodak and Polaroid have used a similar strategy for precious moments that are remembered in photographs.

The copy for a commercial by Miller Lite illustrates the use of two types of emotions: humor and friendship. Two years after abandoning its 17-year-long Tastes Great, Less Filling campaign, Miller returned to humor with a fresh approach. Notes Dick Strup, Miller senior vice president, marketing, "We wanted a campaign that clearly leveraged the brand equity of 'Great taste, less filling,' the humor and camaraderies. This executional device has all three. It beats what is on the air currently, and it offers opportunities to leverage in other areas of the marketplace."[2] Miller Lite's campaign combines gourmet cooking with wrestling, golf with football, calf roping with courtroom drama to make its point.

Principle

Demonstrations are persuasive on television because we believe what we see.

Demonstration. Demonstration was discussed in Chapter 7 as an important message strategy. If you have a strong sales message that lends itself to demonstration, then television is the ideal medium for that message. Its realism makes the demonstration persuasive. Believability and credibility are high because we believe where we see with our own eyes.

Sight and Sound. Television is an audiovisual medium—that is, it uses both

---

[2]Ira Teinowitz, "Reviewing Miller Lite: Can New Ads Do This?" *Advertising Age* (June 14, 1993):3.

United Way provides a narrative through song in order to tell its story.

(Courtesy of United Way)

Principle

Sight and sound should reinforce one another.

sight and sound—and an effective television commercial fuses the audio and visual elements. One of the strengths of television is its ability to reinforce verbal messages with visuals or visual messages with verbal.

Hooper White, who has been making television commercials since the 1950s, says in his book *How to Produce an Effective TV Commercial* that "The idea behind a television commercial is unique in advertising." He explains that it is a combination of sight and sound: "The TV commercial consists of pictures that move to impart fact or evoke emotion and selling words that are not read but heard." He concludes: "The perfect combination of sight and sound can be an extremely potent selling tool."[3]

The point of audio-visual fusion is that words and pictures must work together or else commercials will show one thing and say something else. Researchers have found that people have trouble listening and watching at the same time unless the audio and visual messages are identical

ELEMENTS

Various elements work together to create the visual impact of television commercials. Audiovisual elements do not stand alone. They must be put into the right setting and surrounded by appropriate props. The right talent must be chosen, and appropriate lighting and pacing are critical, along with other elements.

Video. The visual dominates the perception of the message in television, so copywriters use it as the primary carrier of the concept. The *video* elements include everything that is seen on the screen. Copywriters use visuals, the silent speech of film, to convey as much of the message as possible. Emotion is expressed most convincingly in facial expressions, gestures, and other body language. Good television writers try not to bury the impact of the visual under a lot of unnecessary words.

[3]Hooper White, *How to Produce an Effective TV Commercial* (Chicago: Crain Books, 1981).

A tremendous number of visual elements must be coordinated in successful television ads. Because television is theatrical, many of the elements, such as characters, costumes, sets and locations, props, lighting, optical and computerized special effects, and on-screen graphics, are similar to those you would use in a play, television show, or movie. Because of the number of video and audio elements, a television commercial is the most complex of all advertising forms.

Audio. The audio dimensions of television and radio ads are the same—music, voices, and sound effects—but they are used differently in television commercials because they are related to a visual image. An announcer, for example, may speak directly to the viewer or engage in a dialogue with another person who may or may not be on-camera. A common manipulation of the camera-announcer relationship is the **voice-over**, in which some kind of action on the screen is described by the voice of an announcer who is not visible. Sometimes a voice is heard *off-camera*, which means it is coming from either side, from behind, or from above.

voice-over A technique used in commercials in which an off-camera announcer talks about the on-camera scene.

Talent. A television commercial has all the ingredients of a play. The most important element is people, who can be announcers (either on- or offstage), presenters, spokespersons, "spokesthings" (like talking butter dishes), character types (old woman, baby, skin diver, policeman), or celebrities, such as Michael Jordan, who despite his retirement from the NBA can still support the products that he endorses.[4] People in commercials are called **talent**. Some commercials use just parts of people, such as hands, feet, or the back of the head.

talent People who appear in television commercials.

Depending on what kind of people are being used, *costumes* and *makeup* can be very important. Historical stories, of course, need period costumes, but modern scenes may also require special clothing such as ski outfits, swim suits, or cowboy boots. The script should specify which costumes are essential to the story. Makeup may be important if you need to create a skin problem or to change a character from young to old.

Props. In most commercials the most important *prop* is the product. The ad should reflect the essential properties of the product. Does it come in a package? Does it have a distinctive logo? How should it be depicted? Can you show it in use? What other props are necessary to make the story come together? Sometimes props are critical to the action, like a tennis racket in a tennis scene. Sometimes they are used just to set the scene, like the patio table and tray of drinks in the background behind the tennis players. The script should identify every important element in the scene.

Principle

The most important prop is the product.

Setting. The setting is where the action takes place. It can be something in the studio—from a simple table top to a constructed **set** that represents a storefront. Commercials shot outside the studio are said to be filmed *on location*. In these cases the entire crew and cast are transported somewhere. The location could be an alley or a garage down the street, or it could be some exotic place like New Zealand.

set A constructed setting where the action in a commercial takes place.

Lighting. Lighting is another critical element that is usually manipulated by the

---

[4]Jeff Jensen, "Air Jordans Still Standing Tall Even After Retirement of Their Namesake," *Advertising Age* (November 1, 1993):3.

director. Special lighting effects need to be specified in the script. For example, you might read "Low lighting as in a bar," or "Intense bright light as though reflected from snow," or "Light flickering on people's faces as if it were reflecting from a television screen."

Graphics. There are several types of visuals that are filmed from a flat card or generated electronically on the screen by a computer. Words and still photos are shot from a card. Words can also be computer-generated right on the screen. The **crawl** is computer-generated letters that appear to be moving across the bottom of the screen.

Stock footage is a previously recorded image, either video, still slides, or moving film, that is used for scenes that aren't accessible to normal shooting. Examples are shots from a satellite or rocket, historical scenes such as World War II scenes, or a car crash.

Pacing. The speed of the action is another important factor in a television commercial. Pacing describes how fast or how slow the action progresses. Some messages are best developed at a languid pace; others work better when presented at an upbeat and fast pace. If the pacing is an important part of the message, then it needs to be explained in the script.

FILMING AND TAPING

Producing a major national commercial may take the work of hundreds of people and cost as much as half a million dollars. The "1984" commercial for Apple Computer that ran only once during the 1985 Super Bowl used a cast of 200 and is estimated to have cost half a million dollars.[5] Since that time even more expensive commercials have been produced. The expense only makes sense if the ads will reach large numbers of people.

There are a number of ways to produce a message for a television commercial. It can be filmed live or it can be prerecorded using film or videotape. It can also be shot frame by frame using animation techniques.

Live. In the early days of television most commercials were shot live. The history of advertising includes numerous stories about refrigerator doors that wouldn't open and dogs that refused to eat the dog food. These traumatic experiences explain why most advertisers prefer to prerecord a commercial rather than gamble on doing it live.

Even in cases where an activity is live, such as a sporting event, a three- to seven-second delay is built into the televising process. This allows a commercial delivered by a sports announcer, for instance, to be stopped before it goes on the air if there was an error. Thus, there are very few instances when a commercial is actually live.

Film. Today most television commercials are shot on 16 mm or 35 mm film. The film is shot as a negative and processed, after which the image is transferred to videotape. This transferring technique is called *film-to-tape transfer.*

Film consists of a series of frames on celluloid that, for advertising, is usually 35 mm wide. Actually, each frame is a still shot. The film passes through a

[5]David Carey, "Advertising in the '80s: A Roaring Comeback," *Financial World* (March 20, 1985):8–9.

projector, and the small changes from frame to frame create the illusion of motion. Film is shot at 24 frames per second. In film-to-tape transfer the film has to be converted to videotape that uses 30 frames per second.

Editing on film is done by cutting between two frames and either eliminating a segment or attaching a new segment of film. The term **cut**, which comes from this editing procedure, is used to describe an abrupt transition from one view of a scene to another.

cut An abrupt transition from one shot to another.

Videotape. Until the 1980s **videotape** was thought of as an inferior alternative to film. It was used primarily by the news side of the television industry because it records sound and images instantly, without a delay for film processing, and the videotape can be replayed immediately, Videotape's "cheap cousin" image has changed dramatically in the last decade. First of all, the quality of videotape has improved. The film-to-tape transfer has seen significant improvements. Also, a number of innovations in editing have made the process more precise and faster; computer editing has improved accuracy and made special effects possible. Thus, a director can look at one version of a television ad (including editing) minutes after it is shot and make immediate modifications.

videotape A type of recording medium that electronically records sound and images simultaneously.

Animation. **Animation**, which uses film rather than videotape, records drawn images one at a time, frame by frame. Cartoon figures, for example, are sketched and then resketched with a slight change to indicate a small progression in the movement of an arm or a leg or a facial expression (see Ad 15.2). Animation is traditionally shot at 12 or 16 drawings per second. Low-budget animation uses fewer drawings, and consequently the motion looks jerky.

Because of all the hand work, animation is labor-intensive and expensive. It takes a long time to create an animated commercial because of the drawing time, though the introduction of computers is speeding up the process. Now illustrators need draw only the beginning and the end of the action sequence; the computer plots out the frames in between.

animation A type of recording medium in which objects are sketched and then filmed one frame at a time.

A variation on animation is called **stop motion**, a technique used to film inanimate objects like the Pillsbury Doughboy, which is a puppet. The little character is moved a bit at a time and filmed frame by frame. The same technique is used with **claymation**, which involves creating characters from clay and then photographing them. The dancing raisins in the "Heard It Through the Grapevine" commercial by the California Raisin Advisory Board are the product of the claymation technique.

stop motion A technique in which inanimate objects are filmed one frame at a time, creating the illusion of movement.

claymation A technique that uses figures sculpted from clay and filmed one frame at a time.

$\mathscr{P}$LANNING AND PRODUCING COMMERCIALS

PLANNING TELEVISION COMMERCIALS

In planning a television commercial, there are many considerations. The producers of the Mastercard commercial we discussed at the beginning of the chapter had to plan how long the commercial would be, what shots would appear in each scene, what the key visual would be, and where to shoot the commercial.

Lengths. As we discussed in Chapter 11, the most common length for a commercial on broadcast television today is 30 seconds. Because of the increasing

DDB NEEDHAM WORLDWIDE, INC.
CLIENT: FRITO-LAY, INC.
PRODUCT: CHEE-TOS® BRAND CHEESE
          FLAVORED SNACKS

Frito Lay

TITLE: "C.C. RIDER"
LENGTH: 30 Seconds
COMM'L NO.: PECH-9023

(Music under) CHESTER: Chester Cheetah here,

scoutin' out the Chee-tos delivery route. Man, those other cheese puffs

ain't nothin' but fluff

to this Chee-tos buff.

(SFX: CRUNCH!)

(SFX)

I'm the polka-dot pursuiter

on my bad motor scooter.

After the one, and only

Chee-tos !

(SFX: CRUNCH!!)

It's not easy bein' Cheesy.

!EIEIEIEIEIE!

AVO: Chee-tos, the cheese that goes...

(SFX) ...Crunch!

costs of air time, 60-second commercials are becoming rare. Some network commercials now run in 20-second and 15-second formats. An advertiser may buy a 30-second spot and split it in half for two related products in the line. If the two messages are interdependent, the strategy is called *piggybacking*. An example of piggybacking is a 15-second cake mix ad sharing a 30-second spot with a 15-second frosting ad.

Scenes. A commercial is planned in scenes. These are segments of action that occur in a single location. Within each scene there may be a number of shots from different angles. A 30-second commercial is usually planned with four to six scenes, though a fast-paced commercial may have many more.

Key Frames. The writer and art director begin the planning together. The television equivalent of a thumbnail sketch is called a **key frame**. Because television is a visual medium, the message is developed from a key visual that contains the heart of the concept. The last frame in the Mastercard commercial, which shows the company logo, is the key frame. The various concepts are devised, tested, and revised as key visuals. When a concept seems promising, the writer and art director move to a rough *script* and *storyboard*, which we will discuss later.

Local Productions. Most local retail commercials are simple, relatively inexpensive, and are shot at the local station or production facility on videotape. The sales representative for the station may work with the advertiser to write the script, and the station's director handles the filming of the commercial. These commercials may not have extravagant production techniques, but they can be just as effective as any big-budget production.

DETERMINING A POINT OF VIEW

A commercial's message is best delivered with various degrees of viewer involvement, depending upon the situation. The camera can take one of two *points of view* to accomplish this. An *objective* point of view connotes that the camera will make an impersonal recording of the action. In this instance, the camera records the action from the viewpoint of an observer who is uninvolved in the action taking place. In this framework, people on camera tend to not look into the lens, and a high angle or overhead shot might be the best way to shoot this type of commercial.

The *subjective* point of view takes a very different approach. Subjective camera includes the viewer as part of the action. The camera will often represent you, the viewer, as part of the scene and the actors often will look into the lens. Consequently, eye-level camera angles often are employed, suggesting that an observer is watching the action at a natural height.

SCRIPTS AND STORYBOARDS

A print advertisement is created in two pieces: a copy sheet and a layout. Commercials are planned with two similar documents. A script is the written version with all the words, dialogue, lyrics, instructions, and description; the storyboard shows the number of scenes, the composition of the shots, and the progression of the action.

Television Scripts. A television **script** is a detailed document. It includes the visual plan of the commercial plus all the descriptions necessary to assist the director or producer in finding the location or building the set, the talent agency in casting the talent, the composer/arranger in creating the music, and the producer in budgeting and scheduling the entire project.

The script is written in two columns with the audio on the right and the video on the left. Ad 15.3 for State Farm Insurance is an example of a television script with key frames from the commercial. The key to the structure of a television script is the relationship between the audio and the video. The video is typed opposite the corresponding audio. Sometimes these are numbered to correspond to the frames on the storyboard.

Storyboards. The **storyboard** is the visual plan, the layout, of the commercial. It uses selected frames to communicate how the story line will develop. It depicts the composition of the shots as well as the progression of action and the interaction of the audio with the video. A 30-second commercial will be planned with six to eight frames. These frames, of course, are stills. They don't show action; they can only suggest it by a pictorial progression. The art director must determine which visuals convey the most information. Underneath the frame will be a short version of the audio, just enough to locate the dialogue in relation to the video. The storyboard is a very important tool for showing the basic concept of the commercial to the client and other agency members.

Animatics and Photoboards. As the concept is revised and finalized, the script becomes more detailed and the storyboard art more finished. A finished story-

STATE FARM INSURANCE
9/18/89
RURAL
:30 TV

   "Hoffrogge/Rural"

VIDEO		AUDIO
OPEN ON RURAL MINNESOTA FARM.- DAWN	AGENT:	I grew up on a farm just down the road. I know 'most everybody in town, and handle the insurance for quite a few.
CUT TO SCENES OF AGENT WITH: LOCAL RESIDENTS, FAMILIES TOWN SHOPKEEPERS INTERCUT WITH SCENES OF: FAMILY LIFE CHILDREN PLAYING LEAF RAKING ETC.		I'm their State Farm agent... Dennis Hoffrogge. My job is to help my neighbors. To help 'em protect their families, and the things they've worked for. It's a job I take seriously. Every State Farm agent does.
CUT TO DENNIS IN HIS OFFICE, CU AT DESK		Y'know, State Farm started out in small towns just like this.... people trying to help their neighbors. We're <u>still</u> helpin'.
CUT TO WIDE SHOT OF TOWN FROM EXTREME HIGH ANGLE	SING:	LIKE A GOOD NEIGHBOR, STATE FARM IS THERE.

I'm their State Farm Agent . . .

SOLO SINGER (VO): AND LIKE A GOOD NEIGHBOR,

STATE FARM IS THERE.

animatic A preliminary version of a commercial with the storyboard frames recorded on videotape along with a rough sound track.

photoboard A type of rough commercial, similar to an animatic except that the frames are actual photos instead of sketches.

board is equivalent to a comprehensive in print. To make the storyboard even more realistic, the frames may be shot on slides for presentation to the client. If the frames are recorded on videotape along with a rough sound track, the storyboard is called an **animatic**. Animatics are frequently used for client presentations and market research sessions. If frames are actual photographs of the action, which are more realistic, they are called **photoboards**. You have been looking at photoboards in many of the ads depicted throughout this book.

THE TEAM

A locally produced commercial uses the station's personnel for most of the production roles. In addition to a lot of time and a great deal of money, however, producing a major national advertisement requires a number of people with specialized skills. The agency crew usually includes the copywriter, art director, and producer. The outside people include a production house, a director and shooting crew, a talent agency, a music arranger/director plus musicians, and a film or video editor. The client's advertising manager is also involved throughout the planning and production.

The copywriter, art director, and possibly a creative director and producer work together to develop the idea and translate it into a script and a storyboard. The copywriter writes the actual script, whether it involves dialogue, narrative, lyrics, announcement, or descriptive copy. The art director develops the storyboard and establishes the "look" of the commercial, whether realistic, stylized, or fanciful.

producer The person who supervises and coordinates all of the elements that go into the creation of a television commercial.

The **producer**, usually an agency staff member, is in charge of the production. He or she handles the bidding and all of the arrangements, finds the specialists, arranges for casting the talent, and makes sure the budget and the bids all come in together.

The production house usually coordinates the entire shoot, working closely with the agency staff. The production house normally provides the director, but may choose to use a freelance director instead, particularly if that director's special "look" is desired for the commercial. The production house provides most of the technical expertise and equipment needed to produce the commercial.

director The person in charge of the actual filming or taping of the commercial.

The **director** is in charge of the actual filming or taping: the look of the set and lighting; how long the scenes and pieces of action are; who does what and moves where; and how the lines are spoken and the characters played. The director manages the flow of action and determines how it is seen and recorded by the camera.

composer The person who writes the music.

arranger The person who orchestrates the music, arranging it for the various instruments, voices, and scenes.

The music **composer** writes original music; the music **arranger** orchestrates that music for the various instruments and voices to make it fit a scene or copy line. The copywriter usually writes the lyrics or at least gives some idea of what the words should say. A composer who does a lot of commercials, such as Barry Manilow, might write the lyrics along with the music. Musicians are hired as needed, from a complete orchestra to a marching band to a vocalist.

editor The person who assembles the best shots to create scenes and who synchronizes the audio track with the images.

In a film production the **editor** becomes involved toward the end of the process and puts everything together. Film is shot from a number of different cameras, each representing a different angle. The audio is recorded on multiple tracks. The editor's job is to decide which are the best shots, how to assemble the scenes, and how the audio tracks work best with the assembled video.

PRODUCING A TELEVISION COMMERCIAL

Commercials for local stores are relatively inexpensive to produce because they use the facilities and staff of the local station. The production process for a major national television commercial, however, is long and expensive. It is also involved and complex. The script and storyboard are reviewed and approved by the client and become the basis for the production planning. The producer and staff first develop a set of *production notes*, describing in detail every aspect of the production. These are important for finding talent and locations, building sets, and getting bids and estimates from the specialists.

Preproduction. Before the commercial can be filmed or taped, a number of arrangements need to be handled. Once the bids have been approved, a preproduction meeting of the creative team and the producer, director, and other key players is held. The meeting attempts to outline every step of the production process and anticipate every problem that may come up. A detailed schedule is also finalized and agreed to by all parties.

The talent agency is in charge of casting, which is accomplished through a series of auditions. A location has to be found and arrangements made with owners, police, and other officials to use the site. If sets are needed, then they have to be built. Finding the props is a test of ingenuity, and the prop person may wind up visiting hardware stores, second-hand stores, and maybe even the local dump. Costumes may have to be made.

The Shoot. Although the actual filming takes a rather short time, the setup and

Television Terminology

Distance (camera to image): Long shot (LS), full shot (FS), medium shot (MS), wide shot (WS), close-up (CU), extreme close-up (ECU or XCU)

Camera Movement
- Zoom in or out: The lens on the camera manipulates the change in distance. As you zoom in, the image seems to come closer and get larger; as you zoom back, it seems to move farther away and get smaller.
- Dolly in and out: The camera itself is wheeled forward or backward.
- Pan right or left: The camera is stationary but swings to follow the action.
- Truck right or left: The camera itself moves right or left with the action.
- Boom crane shoot: Camera mechanism moves over a scene.

Transitions
- Cut: An abrupt, instantaneous change from one shot to another.
- Dissolve: A soft transition where one image fades to black while another image fades on.

- Lap dissolve: A slow dissolve with a short period in which the two images overlap.
- Superimposition: Two images held in the middle of a dissolve so they are both on-screen at the same time.
- Wipe: One image crawls across the screen and replaces another.

Action
- Freeze frame: Stops the scene in midaction.
- Stop motion: Shots are taken one at a time over a long period. Used to record animation, claymation, or something that happens over a long period of time, like a flower blooming.
- Slow motion: Suspends the normal speed of things by increasing the number of frames used to record the movement.
- Speeded-up motion: Increases the normal speed by reducing the number of frames used to record the movement.
- Reverse motion: The film is run backward through the projector.

Shooting a television commercial is an expensive and complicated process.

(Courtesy of DDB Needham Worldwide)

rehearsal can take incredible amounts of time. It may seem as though nothing is happening when actually everyone is busy setting up and checking specialized responsibilities.

The film crew includes a number of technicians, all of whom have to know what is happening and what they are supposed to do. Everyone reports to the director. If the sound is being recorded at the time of shooting, the recording is handled by a *mixer*, who operates the recording equipment, and a *mic* or *boom* person, who sets up the microphones. For both film and video recording, the camera operators are the key technicians.

Other technicians include the *gaffer*, who is the chief electrician, and the *grip*, who moves things such as the sets. The grip also lays track for the dolly on which the camera is mounted and pushes the camera on the dolly along the track at the required speed. The *script clerk* checks the dialogue and other script details and times the scenes. All of the technicians are supported by their own crew of assistants. A set is a very busy, crowded place. The box entitled "Television Terminology" on page 503 offers a concise definition of terms commonly used in television commercial production.

The commercial is shot scene by scene, but not necessarily in the order set down in the script. Each scene is shot and reshot until all the elements come together. If the commercial is filmed in videotape, the director plays it back immediately to determine what needs correcting. Film, however, has to be processed before the director can review it. These processed scenes are called *dailies*.

rushes Rough versions of the commercial assembled from unedited footage.

Rushes are rough versions of the commercial assembled from cuts of the raw film footage. They are viewed immediately after the filming to make sure everything necessary has been filmed.

synchronize Matching the audio to the video in a commercial.

If the audio is to be recorded separately in a sound studio, it is often recorded after the film is shot to **synchronize** (sync) the dialogue to the footage. Directors frequently wait to see exactly how the action appears before they write and record the audio track. If the action occurs to music, then the music may be recorded prior to the shoot and the filming done to the music.

Postproduction. For film, much of the work happens after the shoot. That is when the commercial begins to emerge from the hands and mind of the editor. Editing can condense time, extend time, and jumble time. Condensing time

Television Ain't What It Used To Be

Everyone knows that commercial clutter is up and retention is down. What may surprise you, however, is how much the styles and techniques used in television commercials have changed during the 15 years that Video Storyboard Tests has been tracking viewers' responses to current advertising. Here are the ten most radical changes on consumers' perceptions of television advertising.

- Musicals are a thing of the past. A lot of popular commercials in the late 1970s and early 1980s included original scores and extremely sophisticated staging with elaborate choreography. In recent years advertisers are no longer competing with all the other music that's out there but are adapting already well-known music to their needs.

- Kids, yes; pets, maybe. Kids and pets are cute and sincere. Pets appeal to pet owners; kids appeal to parents. Correct that. Kids appeal to grandparents. Today, the animals are done and kids rule the roost.

- Comparative pricing comes to television. Until recently, network television was considered too dignified a medium for product price wars. Taco Bell really burst the bubble in 1989 with its execution plugging a 39-cent taco. All the fast-food outlets were in the price/value fray by 1991.

- The role of celebrities improves. Celebrities come in two types: those who were celebrities before the commercials and those who became celebrities because of the commercials. There has been a decline in the latter. Celebrities approval rating, which had slipped to 17 percent in 1987, climbed back to 27 percent in 1992. Athletes have gained over show business personalities in recent years, and women showbiz celebrities also have gained favor.

- Humorous commercials fade. Of the ten different types of commercials tracked for persuasion, humorous commercials have always been at the top. However, although 64 percent of viewers considered them to be persuasive in 1990, only 55 percent thought so in 1992.

- Best commercials: Where the girls are. All of the beer brands except for Budweiser had the same theme in 1992: Boy meets girl through beer. Continuing this look-alike pattern not only draws charges of mindless sexism but also reduces the product category to a commodity.

- Serials can work. The first successful serial began in 1990 with the Taster's Choice couple. The campaign's first three installments finished No. 16 in 1991; the campaign moved up to No. 10 in 1992.

- Parody replaces intrigue. Commercials that don't look like commercials—intriguing spots that don't deliver a message or brand name until the very end—were quite popular a decade ago. But "bait and wait" is also extremely risky. Ever since Joe Isuzu, the more popular antiadvertising technique has been parody.

- Visual techniques keep coming. As technology improves, more and more commercials—23 percent in 1992 as opposed to 15 percent in 1988—rely on visual techniques, including Disney-type animation to dazzling high-tech effects.

- The death of tearjerkers and heartgrabbers. During the first ten years of this research, 13 percent of the most popular commercials tugged heavily on the heartstrings. In recent years, the figure has been about 5 percent. Emotional spots suffer from the same problem that musical ones do: Viewers feel the emotion but do not readily translate it to a message to buy.

Adapted from Dave Vadehra, "My, How TV Spots Have Changed," *Advertising Age* (August 16, 1993):16.

might show a man getting off from work, cut to the man showering, then cut to the man approaching the bar. Extending time is the train approaching the stalled car on the tracks. By cutting to various angles it may seem the train is taking forever to reach the car. To jumble time, you might cut from the present to a flash-back of a remembered past event or flash forward to an imagined scene in the future.

In film a **rough cut** is a preliminary edited version of the story. The editor chooses the best shots and assembles them to create a scene. The scenes are then joined together. After the revision and reediting is completed, an **interlock** is made. The audio and film are separate, but they are timed, and they can be listened to simultaneously. The final version with the sound and film mixed together is called an **answer print**.

In order for the commercial to run at hundreds of stations around the country, duplicate copies have to be made. This process is called **dubbing**, and the copies are called **release prints**. Release prints are distributed on 16 mm film or videotape. Because the industry now uses the film-to-tape transfer process, most production is done on videotape, thereby avoiding much of the film-laboratory work.

rough cut A preliminary rough edited version of the commercial.

interlock A version of the commercial with the audio and video timed together, although the two are still recorded separately.

answer print The final finished version of the commercial with the audio and video recorded together.

dubbing The process of making duplicate copies of a videotape.

release prints Duplicate copies of a commercial that are ready for distribution.

RULES OF THUMB FOR PRODUCING TELEVISION COMMERCIALS

A great many questions must be answered in creating a television spot. How much product should there be in your commercial? Should the action be fast or slow? Is it wise to defy tradition and do unusual ads that create controversy? Every producer and director will respond to these questions differently depending on his or her personal preferences. Nevertheless, there are a few general principles that correspond to all successful television commercials:

1. Gain the interest of your viewer at the beginning—the first three seconds are critical.

2. Look for a key visual—a scene that encapsulates your entire selling message into one neat package.

3. Be single-minded. Tell one important story per commercial. Tell it clearly, tell it memorably, and involve your viewer.

4. Observe the rules of good editing. Make it easy for the viewer to get into the idea for the commercial.

5. Always try to show the product in close up at the end.[6]

The Concepts and Applications box on page 505 describes the results of a recent study that delineates other possible guidelines for creating television.

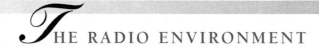

THE RADIO ENVIRONMENT

Principle

Radio creates images in the imagination of the listener.

Imagine you are writing a musical play. This particular play will be performed before an audience whose eyes are closed. You have all the theatrical tools of casting, voices, sound effects, and music available to you, but no visuals. Imagine having to create all the visual elements—the scene, the cast, the costumes, the facial expressions—in the imagination of your audience. Could you do it?

[6]A. Jerome Jewler, *Creative Strategy in Advertising*, 4th ed. (Belmont, CA: Wadsworth Publishing, 1992):264–265.

This is how radio works. It is a theater of the mind in which the story is created in the imagination of the listener. The listeners are active participants in the construction of the message. How the characters look and where the scene is set come out of their personal experience. Radio is the most personal of all media.

CHARACTERISTICS OF THE RADIO ENVIRONMENT

Of all advertising media, radio is the one that relies most heavily on the special talents of the copywriter. Production budgets tend to be comparatively low; there is no need to choose type styles or layout formats. Radio urges the copywriter to reach into the depths of imagination and cunning to create an idea that rouses the apathetic listener. The radio writer cannot hide behind props and techniques. Radio forces the writer to write better, to revise, to take more time with his or her craft. In radio, you are alone with your imagination. This is why radio is a good showcase for talent.

Writing for radio is fun, but it is also very challenging because of the need to create an imaginary visual. Successful radio writers and producers have excellent visualization skills and a great theatrical sense. In addition, radio has some unique characteristics that make it a challenging medium for advertisers.

Personal. Radio is the most intimate of all media. It functions as a good friend in our culture, particularly for teenagers. Radio has one wonderful advantage over print media and that is the human voice, whether it is a newscaster's, a sportscaster's, a talk-show announcer's, or a singer's. The "boombox" on the shoulder or the earphones on a jogger reflect this intimate relationship.

Programming is oriented toward the tastes of particular groups of people. In that sense radio is a very specialized type of medium.

Principle

Like a friend, radio speaks to us one on one.

Most people who are listening to the radio are doing something else at the same time.

(Courtesy of J.F. Kainz/The Stock Option)

Inattention. There is one serious problem, however. Although radio is pervasive, it is seldom the listener's center of attention. Most people who are listening to the radio are doing something else at the same time, like jogging or driving. The listener's attention can focus on radio, particularly during programming that demands concentration like news and weather, but generally radio is a background medium.

Even though most people listen to radio with divided attention, strategists in radio advertising have employed three tactics that usually heighten the listener's attention level. The first is to engage in heavy repetition. During a 30-minute drive home, a driver can listen to the same jewelry store ad four times. Almost unconsciously, the listener becomes aware of the three facts detailed in the ad. A second tactic is to present the radio copy in the context of music or humor. Both are consistent attention getters, and they inspire memory as well. Finally, timing the radio ad to correspond to an immediate need works quite well. Restaurant ads played while the listener drives home and special weekend-event announcements on Friday evenings and Saturday mornings are two examples. Ultimately, radio advertisers must intrude upon the inattention of the listener yet not be so intrusive as to anger the listener. More will be said about these tactics in the next section.

MESSAGE STRATEGY

The radio message is ephemeral—it is here one moment and gone the next. You cannot tune in to the middle of an ad and then go back to the headline, as you can with print. You cannot reread a radio message. The key to the success of radio advertising is to evoke visual images based on what the listener hears. Writers creating ads for radio need to capitalize on its intimacy and the imagination of the listener. For example, one award-winning radio ad is titled "Hubble Telescope," sponsored by Nike Flight basketball shoes. It begins with the dead-pan delivery of a basketball player in a sports arena. He thumps the ball on the floor a few times and then says his shoes are propelling him upward. His words begin to echo as he nears a ventilation duct, then his voice takes on the quality of one communicating from space as he leaves the confines of the arena. When he spots the Hubble Telescope in space, he says, "Nike, it's so beautiful, pal."

Creating vivid images is what makes radio copywriting so challenging. Peter Hockstein of Ogilvy & Mather offers these ten rules for making better radio commercials:[7]

1. Identify your sound effects. Tell listeners what they're hearing, and they'll be more likely to hear it.

2. Use music as a sound effect.

3. Build your commercial around a sound: the sound of a crisp new cracker, for example, or thunder to represent the power of a solid bank account.

4. Give yourself time. Fight for 60-second spots. It is often impossible to establish your sound effects in 30 seconds and still relate them to product benefits.

5. Consider using no sound effects. A distinctive voice or a powerful

---

[7] Peter Hochstein, "Ten Rules for Making Better Radio Commercials," Ogilvy & Mather's *Viewpoint* (1981).

message straightforwardly spoken can be more effective than noises from the tape library.

6. Beware of comedy. It's rare when you can sit down at your computer and match the skill of the best comedians. On the other hand, well-written and relevant humor can be a powerful advertising technique.

7. If you insist on being funny, begin with an outrageous premise: Lake Michigan will be drained of water and refilled with whipped cream. A man puts on his wife's nightgown at 4 a.m. and goes out to purchase *Time* magazine—and the cops catch him.

8. Keep it simple. Radio is a wonderful medium for building brand awareness. It's a poor medium for registering long lists of copy points or making complex arguments. What one thing is most important about your product?

9. Tailor your commercial to time, place, and specific audience. If it is running in Milwaukee, you can tailor it for Milwaukee. You can talk in the lingo of the people who will be listening and to the time of day in which your commercial will be broadcast. Talk about breakfast at the breakfast hour or offer a commuter taxi service during rush hour.

10. Present your commercial to your client on tape, if possible. Most radio scripts look boring on paper. Acting, timing, vocal quirks, and sound effects make them come alive.

There is one element this list does not address—the problem of retention. Because radio is a transitory medium, the ability of the listener to remember facts, such as the name of the advertiser, along with the address and phone number, is constantly challenged. To help the listener remember what you are selling, you must mention the name of the product emphatically. An average of three mentions in a 30-second commercial and five mentions in a 60-second commercial may not be too frequent, as long as the repetition is not done in a forced and annoying manner. And since the last thing listeners hear is what they tend to remember longest, you will certainly want to mention the key selling idea and the brand name at the close of the commercial.

WRITING FOR AUDIO

Writing radio copy requires a particular style and certain tools. Like television scripts, radio copy is written for a certain time frame and according to a particular form and code.

STYLE

vernacular Language that reflects the speech patterns of a particular group of people.

Radio copywriters write in a conversational style using **vernacular** language. Spoken language is different from written language. We talk in short sentences, often in sentence fragments and run-ons. We seldom use complex sentences in speech. We use contractions that would drive an English teacher crazy. Spoken language is not polished prose, as demonstrated in the Nynex Yellow Pages spot. See Ad 15.4.

Nynex Yellow Pages 'Genealogist'

Announcer: As they say, you can find anything in the Nynex Yellow Pages, and today under the heading of Genealogists we found Dr. Ian Hadley.

Dr. Hadley: Michael.

Announcer: Dr. Hadley, you trace family roots, I guess.

Dr. Hadley: Yes, as a matter of fact, we traced your family roots as far back as the Battle of Hastings.

Announcer: Well, that's interesting.

Dr. Hadley: Your ancestor Ethelred the Fleet led the retreat from the battle to the forest.

Announcer: Probably just regrouping.

Dr. Hadley: They spent the next several hundred years living as vassals and indentured servants. And they reappear, interestingly, at the time of the American Revolution. The Battle of Lexington was fought on their land.

Announcer: Minutemen, fighting for the young country.

Dr. Hadley: Well, no, they had left a week earlier to, ah, disappear into the forest.

Announcer: To fight on as guerrillas.

Dr. Hadley: That's speculation.

Announcer: I guess this is the family coat of arms?

Dr. Hadley: Yes, this is your family crest.

Announcer: Mighty oak tree, spreading its limbs.

Dr. Hadley: Yes, and if you look carefully, you'll notice a small man cowering behind the mighty oak tree.

Announcer: Well . . . If it's out there, it's in your Nynex Yellow Pages. [Aside] We can't vouch for the accuracy of all these services, of course . . .

Dr. Hadley: And the Latin inscription, *Festina ad silva* . . .

Announcer: Why would anyone need another?

Dr. Hadley: Or . . . "Make haste to the woods."

Word choice should reflect the speech of the target audience. Slang can be hard to handle and sound phony, but copy that picks up the nuances of people's speech can sound natural when carefully written. Each group has its own way of speaking, its own phrasing. Teenagers don't talk like 8-year-olds or 80-year-olds. A good radio copywriter has an ear for the distinctive patterns of speech that identify social groups.

TOOLS

Radio uses three primary tools to develop messages: *voice, music,* and *sound effects.* These can be manipulated to create a variety of different effects.

Voice. Voice is probably the most important element. Voices are heard in jingles, in spoken dialogue, and in straight announcements. Most commercials have an announcer, if not as the central voice, at least at the closing to wrap up the product identification. Dialogue uses character voices to convey an image of the speaker—a child, an old man, an executive, a Little League baseball player, or an opera singer. The absence of pictures demands that the voices you choose help listeners "see" the characters in your commercial.

Music. Music is another important element of radio. Don Wilde of SSC&B said at a symposium that "Music has been found to be more effective in persuasiveness than celebrity endorsements, product demos, or hidden camera techniques." He explained: "It falls just a little under humor or kids. If you write a humorous jingle on kids, you've got it made."[8]

So-called "jingle houses" are companies that specialize in writing and producing jingles for radio and television. The people who work in this side of the music industry prefer the term "commercial music." A custom-made jingle—one that is created for a single advertiser under strict specifications—can cost $10,000 or more. In contrast, many jingle houses create "syndicated" jingles made up of a piece of music that can be applied to different lyrics and sold to several different advertisers in different markets around the country. These jingles may only cost around $1,000 or $2,000.

In Chapter 8 we mentioned the use of jingles—catchy songs about a product that carry the theme and product identification. These finger-snapping, toe-tapping songs have tremendous power because they are so memorable. Jingles are good for product identification and reminder messages, but they do not effectively convey complex thoughts and copy points.

Jingles can be used by themselves as a musical commercial, or they can be added to any other type of commercial as a product identification. A straight announcer commercial, for example, might end with a jingle. Musical forms can be easily adapted to the station's programming. Most major campaigns that use radio produce a number of different versions of the jingle, each one arranged to match the type of music featured in the programming, whether it is country and western, rock, reggae, or easy listening.

Music can also be used behind the dialogue to create mood and establish the setting. Any mood, from that of a circus to that of a candle-lit dinner, can be conveyed through music. Music can be composed for the commercial or it can be borrowed from an already recorded song. There are also a number of music libraries that sell stock music. This music is not copyrighted, however, so there is no guarantee that other ads will not use the same music.

Sound Effects. **Sound effects (SFX)** are also used to convey a setting. The sound of sea gulls and the crash of waves, the clicking of typewriter keys, and the cheers of fans at a stadium all create images in our minds. Sound effects can be original, but more often they are taken from records. As with anything else, restraint is a good rule of thumb with sound effects. Use only those you need unless the genuine purpose is to bombard the listeners with sounds.

SCRIPTING

Timing. As we discussed in Chapter 11, radio commercials are written for a limited time frame. The common lengths are 10, 20, 30, and 60 seconds. The 10-second and 20-second commercials are used for reminders and product or station identification. More elaborate messages are usually 30 or 60 seconds. The 60-second spot is quite common in radio, although it has almost disappeared in television, where the more common length is 30 seconds.

As a rule of thumb, you can estimate that about two words a second is average for a well-paced commercial. You can go as high as 135 words in a 30-second commercial. If you exceed these limits, chances are your speaker will have to rush through the copy with little or no time for those pauses and special inflections that add color and dimension to the spoken word.

---

[8]Aliza Laufer, "Agency Panel Mulls the Impact of :15s on Jingle Biz at SAMPAC Symposium," *Back Stage* (February 7, 1986):1.

Principle

The simpler the jingle, the higher the memorability.

sound effects (SFX) Lifelike imitations of sounds.

Forms. Like television scripts, radio scripts use a common form and code. The scripts are typed double-spaced with two columns. The narrow column on the left describes the source of the sound, and the wider column on the right gives the actual content of the message, either words or a description of the sound and music.

The typing style is important because typed cues tell the producer and announcer instantly what is happening. For example, anything that isn't spoken is typed in capital letters. This includes the source identification in the left column and all instructions and descriptions that appear in the right column. Underlining is used to call attention to music and sound effects in the right column so the announcer can see instantly that those instructions are not to be read over the microphone as if they were copy. If you write radio scripts often, you will probably use a preprinted form that sets up the columns and the identification information for the commercial at the top. Ad 15.5 is an example of a radio script.

DDB NEEDHAM WORLDWIDE

Project Help   11/17/87   DR/jks
"No Place Like Home"
:60 Radio
"INTRUSION ALARM"

ANNCR: There's someone walking around right next to me.

                You probably don't hear him. That's the way he likes

                it. Because he's an intruder. And an intruder in

                your home steals much more than just your valuables...

                He steals your privacy. Your security. Your sense

                of home.

                And no insurance check can begin to replace that.

SFX: ALARM

ANNCR: Now you definitely hear this.

                This is the sound of the new Eversafe Intrusion Alarm.

                It mounts easily on a door or a window. To keep

                intruders out. And what you value in.

                The Eversafe Intrusion Alarm is part of a full-line

                of home safety and security products that you'll

                find at the Eversafe Center. One place with all

                the elements you need to create an entire security

                system. To protect your home. From intruders, fire,

                or even power blackouts.

                So visit your Eversafe Center. You'll find it at

                _____. And protect what's yours. With

                Eversafe.

                Cause there's no place like home.

DDB Needham Worldwide Inc. 303 East Wacker Drive, Chicago, Illinois 60601-5282 Telephone (312) 861-0200 Telex: 211614   Adelaide
Amsterdam · Auckland · Baltimore · Bangkok · Barcelona · Brisbane · Brussels · Chicago · Denver · Detroit · Dunedin · Düsseldorf · Hamburg
Hong Kong · Honolulu · Kuala Lumpur · Lisbon · London · Los Angeles · Madrid · Melbourne · Mexico City · Milan · Montreal · Munich · New
York · Paris · Perth · San Francisco · Singapore · Stockholm · Sydney · Taipei · Tokyo · Toronto · Vienna · Washington, D.C. · Wellington · Zurich

PRODUCING A RADIO COMMERCIAL

Radio commercials are produced in one of two ways. They are either taped and duplicated for distribution, or they are recorded live. The more common form is the taped radio commercial.

TAPED COMMERCIALS

mixing Combining different tracks of music, voices, and sound effects to create the final ad.

The radio *producer* is in charge of getting the commercial casted, recorded, mixed, and duplicated. All the sound elements are recorded separately or *laid down* in stages. Voices can be double- and triple-tracked to create richer sounds. There may be as many as 24 separate tracks for an ad. **Mixing** occurs when the tracks are combined, with appropriate adjustments made in volume and tone levels.

National radio commercials are produced by an advertising agency, and duplicate copies of the tape are distributed to local stations around the country. Commercials for local advertisers might be produced by local stations, with the station's staff providing the creative and production expertise. The recording is done in house using the station's studio.

Many such commercials are designed to run five seconds short of the time purchased to give the local announcer time to add a *live local tag* (where to buy the product, sales dates, and so on). Copy for the tag is included with the produced tape.

LIVE SPOTS

By their nature, live spots are usually composed of straight announcer copy. The inclusion of sound effects, music, or additional speaking parts would require studio production. The live script is advantageous to the local retailer who must get a message on the air in a matter of hours.

An unusual experiment in live radio was conducted in Chicago in 1987, when the *Chicago Tribune* hired two of the city's top radio personalities to ad-lib commercials while they bantered on the air. The approach was the idea of Hal Riney & Partners. Media columnists criticized the ads for not sounding like ads. The "extemporaneous ad-lib announcement" involved reading an item—whether personal ad, column, or news story—from the *Tribune* and mentioning the paper's name. The ads were paid for and listed as 60-second commercials in the station's program log.[9]

MESSAGE TRENDS

What does the future have in store for broadcast advertising? Cable and videocassettes are having a tremendous impact on television commercials. The nature of the advertising message has changed dramatically, and the percentage of the

---

[9]Julie Liesse Erickson, "Riney, *Tribune* Spark Interest in Radio Ad(Lib)," *Advertising Age* (November 9, 1987):3.

audience that watches and listens to the commercials has diminished. Clutter on the networks, the increasing costs of commercials, and smaller audiences have forced television commercials to become more competitive than ever before.

LENGTH AND CONTENT

Infomercial A long commercial that provides extensive product information.

There are two observable trends in the length of television messages. As previously explained, network commercials are getting shorter, with 15-second spots becoming more and more common. In alternative media such as cable, videocassettes, and movie theaters, advertising messages are getting longer—often lasting 2 to 5 minutes. **Infomercials**, as we discussed in Chapter 1, are even longer commercials—some lasting 30 or 60 minutes—that provide extensive product information.

The informative commercials playing on cable and videotext and in theaters allow room for the development of longer messages. At the same time, the creative demands of the shorter commercials on network television call for simpler messages that are as concise and pointed as the messages on outdoor boards. Reminder ads with to-the-point brand imagery seem to work best in these short formats. The trends in message design, then, are to be more informative in the alternative media and more concise on traditional network television.

ZAPPROOFING

As we discussed in Chapter 8, the threat of zapping commercials, or editing out ads when recording on VCR, makes the creative side of the message even more important. To survive in this new era when control over the message is in the hands of a viewer holding a remote-control device requires an "awesome creative effort" that will make "the commercials even better than the programs."[10] Len Sugarman, executive vice president and creative director at Foote, Cone & Belding, says that zapproofing calls for "advertising that is more intriguing up front. . . more intriguing and beautiful."[11]

---

[10]Richard Christian, "Can Advertising Survive Split 30s, Zapping, Globalization, High Tech, Million Dollar Minutes, Narrowcasting, and Even More Accountability?" *Back Stage* (May 31, 1985): 12, 24.
[11]"Can Ad Agency Creativity Combat Zapping, Zipping?" *Television/Radio Age* (November 11, 1985):63–65.

The VCR Voice Programmer can zap through commercials on command.

Beware the Zapper

Coming soon to a home theater near you, the machine that zapped Madison Avenue. No, not a Japanese monster movie, but rather a modest hand-held remote control that will tell a VCR to tape a program, then will "zap" the commercials, all using voice commands.

From Canoga Park, California, Voice Powered Technology markets the VCR Voice Programmer for about $149.95. The remote control, which interacts with a VCR, can respond to four different voices and automatically starts recording a program on a programmed date, time, and channel. During replay, the VCR will fast-forward through a commercial at the command "zap it."

By way of introduction, several infomercials were aired on selected network affiliates and independent stations in various forms as different pricing and ordering formats were tested. "The [initial] results have been very good, but what we're doing is still fine-tuning because we think it will be huge," said Tim O'Leary, vice president and cocreative of Tybee Productions, which wrote and produced the infomercials.

Voice Powered Technology is also experimenting with different infomercials pitches, as well as with other products, such as a tape rewinder or VCR head cleaner, offered when a consumer places an order via an 800 number. The marketing maven for VCR Voice Programmer is Robert Grossman, a former executive with Foote, Cone & Belding and DDB Needham Worldwide in Los Angeles. Despite his agency background, Mr. Grossman offered no apologies for promoting a machine that stamps out commercials. "Any marketer has one loyalty, and that's to his customers. This is a feature that consumers want. It's not for us to say that we'll limit its marketability because of its effect on media."

Next up for Voice Powered Technology is the Voice Reminder, which will "tell the consumer what he wants to remember when he wants to remember it," Mr. Grossman said. "It will buzz, then tell the consumer in his own voice, 'Call Bill Tuesday 4 p.m.' It replaces the string around your finger."

Adapted from Steven W. Colford, "Admen Beware, Zapper Is Here," *Advertising Age* (February 8, 1993):12.

Arthur Meranus, executive vice president and creative director at Cunningham & Walsh, separates ads into those that use a traditional tell it up front approach, sometimes referred to as the P&G (Procter & Gamble) approach, and those that use "some sort of likability in the beginning." The traditional commercials start by telling the viewer what the product is and what it promises. Meranus feels, however, that the trend is toward commercials that start with likability devices, such as the Bud Light sight gags.[12] *Zapproofing* commercials means designing them to be entertaining—dramatic, funny, puzzling, or emotional.

Another threat to television advertising, which has been a characteristic of radio listening for many years, is called *grazing*. Combine the many choices offered by cable systems with the television remote control and you have grazing. Men are particularly guilty of constantly switching channels, often when the commercial comes on. Grazing is much easier than zapping and may prove to be a more serious problem. However, as noted in the Issues and Controversies box, the ease of zapping is improving.

EMBEDS

Another technique used to beat the zipping and zapping is to embed the commercial message in some kind of programming. For example, during the Texas

---

[12]Ibid.

Sesquicentennial, Media Drop In Productions produced a series of true tales about Texas featuring Willie Nelson. Included within the 45 vignettes were commercials for Wrangler jeans. In this instance Willie Nelson delivered the stories to the audience, while a voice-over delivered the advertising messages. However, it is not unusual for an actor to deliver the ad message. This was quite common in the early days of network television when advertisers sponsored an entire program, such as *The Dinah Shore Chevrolet Show*.

IMAGE MANIPULATION

Sophisticated computer graphic systems, such as those used to create the *Star Wars* special effects, have pioneered the making of fantastic original art on computers. At the same time, MTV has generated some of the most exciting video techniques to be seen anywhere on television. The messages are filled with action, unexpected visuals, and, most of all, imaginative special effects.

In the new computer-animated world, television images are changing dramatically. Already the Quantel Paint Box system is being used by computer graphics specialists to create and manipulate video images. Eventually, as costs decrease, these systems will find their way into the art director's office and will expand the graphic capabilities of the agency and production houses—both for print and for video.

Computer graphics artists brag that they can do anything with an image using a computerized "paintbox"—they can make Mel Gibson look 80 or Ronald Reagan look 30. They can look at any object from any angle or even from the inside out. Photographs of real objects can be seen on television as they change into art or animation and then return to life.

An example of computer graphics is a commercial by the computer production company Charlex for Pringles potato chips that shows six children munching on Pringles that appear to come out of their computers. The set is a collection of real elements, including desks, chairs, computers, students, and bookcases, but the scene is "perfectly colorized, cloned, and totally paintboxed, right down to shadows and lighting effects." The wide-angle pan reveals six children plucking Pringles from their computer screens. However, two of those youngsters were created via paintbox. Likewise only three computers actually existed in the original scene; the rest were cloned by paintbox.[13]

INTERACTIVE MEDIA

Another technological change that may affect the way broadcast ads are created in the future is interactive media. Recall from our discussion in Chapter 11 that interactive media will allow the consumer to select from a myriad of choices within a commercial. In the case of an auto manufacturer, for example, the company may dispatch a sales representative to a viewer's home to offer a test drive after the viewer simply presses a button. Or a catalog could be sent electronically to a printer placed beside a television set in the viewer's living room. Want more information on a Ford vehicle? Push a button and a videotape could be mailed to your house.

[13]*Television Radio Age* (November 11, 1985).

Interactive advertising also may involve activities that attempt to draw consumers' attention to a specific commercial. Viewers may be asked to respond to elements in a spot in order to receive, say, a $2 coupon. For example, a viewer may be asked to hit a button as soon as he or she understands the message in a commercial so that the viewer can get the coupon.

How will interactive media influence broadcast advertising? The keynotes of the new era are sponsorship, embeds, and target marketing. There likely will be many more *full sponsorships*; this means that the viewer won't be able to take advantage of a service without sitting through an ad. Consequently, there will be times when viewers won't be able to tell the difference between the advertising and the programming. With embedded advertising the ad becomes part of the program, or vice versa. As media companies learn more about viewers, interactive ads will become more and more targeted. Add the interactive component, and the problem becomes designing commercials that contain (on demand) all the components that might interest all the viewers.

*S*UMMARY

- A television commercial is characterized as acceptable if it is well done, intrusive, and if it can gain the attention of the viewer without annoying.

- The most common message strategies employed in television commercials are: combining action and motion, storytelling, the use of emotion, demonstration, and combining sight and sound.

- There are several possible elements in a typical television commercial: video, audio, talent, props, setting, lighting, graphics, and pacing.

- A number of ways to produce a message for a television commercial exist: live film, prerecorded film or videotape, or animation techniques that include shooting frame by frame.

- Planning and producing television commercials require a number of decisions involving: the length, the number of scenes, key frames, whether to use local production, the appropriate point of view, and the creation of scripts and storyboards.

- Producing a television commercial usually includes a team consisting of a director, producer, composer, and editor. Production goes through a variety of stages: preproduction, the shoot, rushes, and postproduction.

- A radio commercial relies heavily on the special talents of the copywriter; it is characterized as being more personal but requiring less listener attention.

- Like television scripts, radio copy is written for a certain time frame and according to a particular form and code. The style tends to be vernacular. The primary creative tools are the proper voice, music, and appropriate sound effects.

- Radio commercials can be live or taped.

- There are several trends that will affect the creation of broadcast commercials in the future: Commercials will get shorter, but infomercials will provide lengthy commercials; commercials that reduce zapproofing and grazing will be produced; and commercials will be embedded into programming, especially in the case of interactive media.

*Q*UESTIONS

1 Think of an effective television commercial you have seen recently. Why was it effective? What types of creative efforts do you think went into producing this commercial? How long do you

think it took to produce? How much do you think it cost?

2. How has the emergence of cable television and VCRs affected the nature of commercials? How might they affect advertising in the future?

3. What are the major characteristics of radio ads? How do these characteristics reflect the use of voice, music, and sound effects?

4. Professor Strong has set up a lively debate between the advertising sales director of the campus newspaper and the manager of the campus radio station, which is a commercial operation. During the discussion the newspaper representative says that most radio commercials sound like newspaper ads, but are harder to follow. The radio manager responds by claiming that radio creativity works with "the theater of the mind," something that no newspaper ad can do. Can you explain what these creative positions mean? Do you agree with either one?

5. Jingles are a popular creative form in radio advertising. Even so, there are probably more jingles that you don't want to hear again than ones that you do. Identify several short musical bits that you really dislike. Consider the reasons why you do not like them. Do they reflect on the advertiser? Write some descriptive statements on why these jingles don't work in your case.

6. Rough ideas for television commercials are often tested on selected members of the target audience. Sometimes tests use key visuals or storyboards; other times they use photoboards or even animatics. If you were deciding which testing style to use, would the type of product help you decide? Give some examples of products that would be better tested with animatics than with storyboards.

7. Television is primarily a visual medium. However, very few television commercials are designed without a vocal element (actors or announcers). Even the many commercials that visually demonstrate products in action use an off-screen voice to provide information. Why is there a need to use the voice to provide continuity and information?

SUGGESTED CLASS PROJECT

Select a product that is exclusively advertised through print. Examples of such products are alcohol, cigarettes, many industrial products, school supplies, and several canned food items. Develop a 30-second television spot for this product, providing a complete schedule of activities beginning with the creative component and ending with a completed ad. (You can stop with the storyboard). Include all the key decisions a producer and director would make.

FURTHER READINGS

BALDWIN, HUNTLEY, *Creating Effective TV Commercials* (Chicago: Crain Books, 1972).

HEIGHTON, ELIZABETH J., AND DON R. CUNNINGHAM, *Advertising in the Broadcast Media* (Belmont, CA: Wadsworth Publishing Co., 1976).

ORLIK, PETER B., *Broadcast Copywriting* (Boston: Allyn and Bacon, 1982).

TERRELL, NEIL, *The Power Technique of Radio-TV Copywriting* (Blue Ridge Summit, PA: Tab Books, 1971).

WHITE, HOOPER, *How to Produce an Effective TV Commercial* (Chicago: Crain Books, 1981).

ZEIGLER, SHERILYN K., AND HERBERT H. HOWARD, *Broadcast Advertising* (Columbus, OH: Grid, 1978).

VIDEO CASE

Nature Valley Granola Bars and Bites

Prior to March 1992, Nature Valley Granola Bars had experienced consistent growth within the granola category, a category which had grown more than 20 percent over the past two years. However, key competitors were dramatically outpacing category growth and the Nature Valley brand. The increase in both the category size and the number of new-product entries encouraged Nature Valley to develop a two-pronged strategy for increasing its share position in this highly competitive category.

Research indicated that consumers were trying to balance the need to eat better against a desire for good taste. As a result, the strategy for the franchise was to inform consumers in an interesting and engaging way that Nature Valley Granola Bars and Nature Valley Granola Bites are both wholesome and good tasting.

For Nature Valley Granola Bars, the target was "adults, 25–54, who are aware of Nature Valley Granola Bars but not currently purchasing the product." For Nature Valley Granola Bites, the target was "women, 25–54, who are purchasers of wholesome snacks for their families." These target designations, based on known purchasing patterns, influenced both the creative strategy and the media strategy.

The creative strategy for Bars was intended to remind nonpurchasers of what purchasers already know: that Nature Valley Granola Bars are a unique combination of wholesome, good-tasting ingredients one can feel good about eating. The creative strategy for Bites focused on introducing this new product to moth-

ers, as a means of expanding the franchise. Both Bars and Bites were to be advertised with a similar look and feel: contemporary, honest, and sincere, without sacrificing the fun aspects of the category.

The campaign, developed by CME•KHBB, Nature Valley's advertising agency, used a white backdrop and minimalistic graphics to emphasize the wholesomeness of Nature Valley products. The spot for Bars depicted the product growing up from the ground, while the more family-oriented spot for Bites depicted the product falling from a tree. Both spots used the theme line, "The Candy Bar Nature Intended," to underline the product's wholesome message.

Broadcast media included daytime network television to reach the Bites target and broader-reach syndicated television to reach the Bars target. Print media included women's service and general-interest magazines.

Within seven months, Nature Valley Granola Bites achieved nearly 50 percent brand awareness, contributing to a 200 percent increase in overall awareness of Nature Valley. This awareness level established a 20-year record high for the franchise.

More important, the new product, Granola Bites, achieved a substantial share of the granola category without cutting into Granola Bar purchases. Instead, Bites' gains occurred at the expense of Nature Valley's former number-one and number-three granola competitors.

Questions

1. What alternative creative strategies could be employed for these two products?

2. Are there any risks in using the current approach? What are they?

CREATING DIRECT-RESPONSE ADVERTISING

CHAPTER OBJECTIVES

When you have completed this chapter, you should be able to:

- Define direct-response advertising

- Distinguish between direct-response advertising, direct marketing, and mail order

- Evaluate the various media that direct-response advertising can utilize

- Explain how today's technology has transformed the nature of direct response

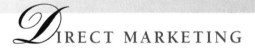

CERIDIAN SPRINGS INTO ACTION

Changing a company's payroll system can be a wrenching decision for many financial officers and that's what ADP, the leading payroll processing company, was banking on when it snapped up Bank of America's payroll processing business. Unchallenged, most of Bank of America's customers might have allowed management of their payroll services to be renewed by ADP. But Ceridian Employer Services, an ADP competitor, saw an opportunity to turn its database of ADP customers into a marketing tool for stealing share.

Ceridian, formerly Control Data Corporation, markets automated payroll processing and information management services as a small, flexible, service-oriented supplier. To get that message out to the thousands of financial decision makers about to set up with ADP, Ceridian used direct marketing to quickly cut through the clutter and tell them Ceridian was an alternative. Created by St. Paul-based Kramstra Communications, the campaign strategy was to educate current Bank of America customers about the value and flexibility of Ceridian's services and reach people before they made the decision to stay or switch. The company launched a three-part program in September that began with a postcard asking "Would You Have Chosen ADP If You Were Given a Choice?" Next came a cardboard box, delivered via first-class mail, that teased recipients with "Don't Let ADP Box You In" printed on the outside. Inside was a triangle-shaped desktop lucite box with Ceridian's triangular logo on its lid. The third and final effort featured a similar box, asking "Is Your Payroll System Too Rigid?", inside of which was a gold-plated Slinky. The mailings were sent to a list of 7,500 ADP customers, which Ceridian's sales force had been building.

"We've been using direct for some time, but this was our first attempt at a dimensional mailing," commented Maureen McDonough, Ceridian's manager of communications. "The Slinky campaign tied in nicely with our message of flexibility, and the mailings were obtrusive enough to get noticed." Ceridian has charted $1.3 million in sales from this program and is planning a similar campaign in other markets later this year.[1]

DIRECT MARKETING

Principle

Traditional advertising targets groups of people; database advertising targets the individual.

databases Lists of consumers with information that helps target and segment those who are highly likely to be in the market for a certain product.

A revolution is taking place in marketing and advertising as marketers are moving to more direct forms of communication with their customers. In the past marketing communication was a monolog, with advertisers talking to anonymous consumers through the mass media. Now communication is becoming a one-on-one dialog through computers, the mail, video, and the touch-tone telephone.

With the advent of computers and the development of extensive **databases**—files of information that include names, addresses, telephone numbers, and demographic and psychographic data—it is becoming possible for an advertiser to develop one-on-one communication with those most likely to be in the market for a certain product. This is the ultimate in "tight" targeting, because the information allows advertisers to understand consumers more thoroughly and

---

[1]Adapted from Kerry J. Smith, "Innovative Mailing Puts Spring in Ceridian's Sales," *Promo* (March 2, 1993):33.

zero in on primary prospects. In other words, although traditional advertising targets groups of people, database advertising targets the individual.

According to the Direct Marketing Association, **direct marketing** "is an interactive system of marketing which uses one or more advertising media to effect a measurable response and/or transaction at any location."[2] Pete Hoke, Jr., publisher of *Direct Marketing* magazine, adds one element to this definition: "In direct marketing, a database—a customer file—must exist." Embedded in this definition are five components.

First, direct marketing is an *interactive system;* that is, the prospective customer and the marketer engage in two-way communication. This allows for a much more precise feedback, typically a behavior on the part of the consumer—compared to the surrogate or more vague measures of effectiveness available for image advertising.

A second characteristic of direct marketing is that a *mechanism for the consumer to respond* to the offer is always made available. Making a measurable response available suggests that the characteristics of respondents and nonrespondents can be assessed.

A third characteristic of direct marketing is that the *exchange between the buyer and the seller is not bound by a retail store or salesperson.* Location is not an issue—the order can be made at any time of the day or night and product delivery can be made to the consumer's home.

A fourth trait and the element that suggests the primary strategic advantage offered by direct marketing is that the *response is measurable.* That is, direct marketing allows the marketer to calculate precisely the costs of producing the communication effort and the resulting income. Some posit that the ability for a type of marketing to be held accountable is the reason for the tremendous growth of direct marketing.

The final element of direct marketing is the necessity for a *database of consumer information.* Through the information in databases, the direct marketer can target communications to an individual consumer or a specific business customer who has been identified as a viable prospect. To marketers, direct marketing offers the ability to reach appropriate target audiences with the right benefits.

If this discussion still seems diffuse, let's look at a few primary, easily identified divisions within direct marketing: direct mail, telemarketing, and electronic-response media. The differences among these three lie in *how* the message is transmitted from the marketer to the consumer—and, ideally, back again. In the case of direct mail, generally the U.S. Postal Service transmits the message; in telemarketing, it's the telephone, and with electronic media, the television and radio usually predominate. These divisions are not clean, however, because one single direct-marketing project may use one or even all of the ones just mentioned. For example, you receive a catalog from Land's End in the mail. That's direct marketing. You decide to order items from the catalog by completing the order blank and returning it via mail. That's direct marketing. Or, say you decide to take advantage of the company's 800 number to place your order. That, too, is direct marketing.

The general benefits direct marketing offers to consumers are: convenience, efficiency, and compression of decision-making time. One can see how these benefits are derived when a consumer purchases a product through one of the video shopping systems such as QVC. Mrs. Smith calmly sits in front of her tele-

[2]*Direct Marketing* (October 1990):22.

direct marketing A type of marketing that uses media to contact a prospect directly and elicit a response without the intervention of a retailer or personal sales.

vision and watches the various merchandise explained, demonstrated, and modeled. She notes an items she likes, places an order via the toll-free number, pays with her Visa card, and receives delivery in 48 hours. The item costs considerably less than retail, has a money-back guarantee, and she never left home.

TYPES OF DIRECT MARKETING

Direct marketing takes many different forms, although three basic categories exist: the one-step process, the two-step process, and the negative option. The *one-step process* allows the consumer to respond to an ad in a media vehicle and receive the product by mail. Often, the consumer will receive a *bounce-back* brochure promoting related merchandise with the order. The *two-step process* requires that the consumer must first be qualified before ordering the product. This might mean a required physical exam in the case of an insurance company, or a credit check before the purchase of an expensive piece of jewelry. Several catalog companies will charge a nominal fee for the catalog and apply the fee to the purchase price. Finally, the *negative option* requires that the consumer joins a plan, such as those offered by video or book clubs, that automatically sends unrequested merchandise unless the consumer mails a response card by a specific date. As an incentive to join, the initial merchandise is often offered with a free gift, extra merchandise, or a discount price.

$\mathcal{T}$HE DIRECT-RESPONSE INDUSTRY

Direct-response has been an important advertising area for over a century. The first major venture by an important national company into mail order was the publication of the Montgomery Ward catalog in 1872.[3] The Direct Mail/Advertising Association was founded in 1917. Currently known as the Direct Marketing Association (DMA), it has long been active in industry research and professional training programs. One of DMA's most successful programs is a seminar for college students sponsored by its Direct Marketing Educational Foundation.

Direct response has been a fast-growing segment of the advertising industry in recent years. In the early 1980s annual growth averaged 30 percent. Total 1990 U.S. direct-response volume rose 18.3 percent. The current state of the industry is depicted in Figure 16.1 As indicated, direct-response includes a wide spectrum of categories.[4]

Direct marketing is one of the selling methods applied in virtually every consumer and business-to-business category. For example, direct marketing is used by IBM, Digital Equipment, Xerox, and other manufacturers selling office products. It is used by almost every bank and insurance company. It is used by airlines, hotels, and cruise lines, as well as by resorts and government tourist agencies. It is used by packaged-goods marketers, such as General Foods, Colgate, and Bristol Myers; by household product marketers, such as Black and Decker; and by automotive companies, such as Ford, Buick, and Cadillac. Direct marketing is also employed for membership drives, fund raising, and solicitation

---

[3]Kenneth C. Otis II, "Introduction to Direct Marketing," DMMA Manual Release 100.1 (April 1979):1.
[4]"Direct Marketing—An Aspect of Total Marketing," *Direct Marketing* (September 1993):4.

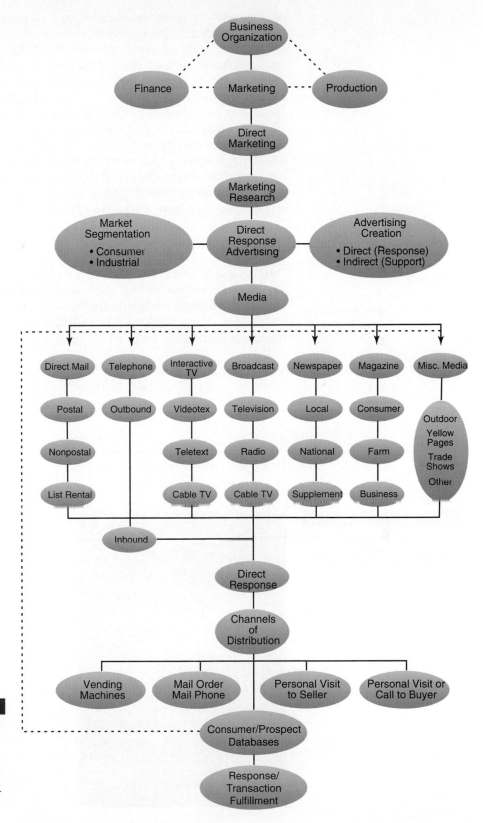

of donations by nonprofit organizations such as the Sierra Club, Audubon Society, and political associations.

An example of a company that has invested heavily in integrated marketing communication vis-à-vis direct marketing is Apple Computer. At Apple, the Direct Marketing Group (DMG) has found in direct mail the power of a targeted communications tool that has a role in selling as well as a role in moving customers toward the sale with information and education. The department, which supports Apple's direct-sales business, works with Apple's marketing groups to develop direct-mail campaigns to raise awareness, shift attitudes, generate leads, fill seminars, support retail sales, and build stronger, more involved relationships between Apple, its prospects, and its customers. Apple corporate database delivers access to information that helps every part of the company understand and access through the mail a group of Apple users and prospects.[5]

REASONS FOR GROWTH

Direct-response advertising is growing for both social and technological reasons. The influx of women into the work force in recent decades and the rise in the number of single-parent homes are two societal factors. Furthermore, both men and women are very busy today and find shopping a nuisance. They would rather not spend their precious leisure time looking for a place to park at the mall.

Technological advances have made direct response more efficient for marketers and more beneficial for shoppers. Zip codes and toll-free numbers have made it easier for consumers to respond (see Ad 16.1). Another major factor has been the credit card. With an automated billing system, a customer can call in

---

[5]Catherine Nunes and Lin Andrews, "Apple Mail Targets Corporate PC Users," *Advertising Age* (September 27, 1993):7.

Ad 16.1

This direct-response ad includes a toll-free number that makes it easy for customers to order the product if there is no nearby store that carries it.

(Courtesy of Godiva Chocolatier)

Which Came First?

an order and give a number for billing. The order is filled immediately; the company does not have to wait for a check to be mailed and cleared by the bank. These technological improvements have created the "armchair shopper" who would just as soon shop from the easy chair at home as drive to a store.

The Computer. The technology that has had the biggest impact on direct marketing is the computer. Advertisers use the computer to manage lists of names, sort prospects by important characteristics such as zip code or previous ordering patterns, handle addressing, and feed personalized addresses into the printing process. Consumers are also beginning to use their personal computers at home to reach marketers through computerized home-shopping services.

Computers and their programs are getting smarter. On-line services, such as Prodigy, run by Sears, not only provide the user with on-line buying services but also remember purchases and, over time, build a purchase profile of each user. This kind of information is very valuable to marketers, resellers, and their agencies. Already some grocery stores have computerized their grocery carts with displays that show advertised specials as the customer moves from one aisle to another. Customers at a few of these stores have been issued bank cards to use in making purchases at these particular stores. When a customer makes a purchase using the card, the store's computer provides an item-by-item list of that customer's purchases and adds this to the demographic and income information on the customer's card application. The banks are so interested in this information that they are willing to waive the usual fees and charges to the store in trade for the data.

Personalized advertising in a variety of media may become the norm in the near future. Smart computers, used with videotext systems and cable broadcast facilities, will be able to tailor messages precisely to each of us as individuals. Imagine hitting a milestone birthday or obtaining a new job and finding that all of the advertisements you now receive are tailored to these new characteristics about yourself.

On another front, AT&T and Ford Motor Company's Lincoln-Mercury division signed on for the launch of *Newsweek Interactive*, a CD-ROM version of the newsweekly being rolled out in June in an IBM-compatible format. And Active Card Networks, a division of Paris-based Adventure SA, is helping to roll out in the United States an interactive device that allows consumers to play along with television games and earn points that can be redeemed at participating retailers. The situation is cogently summarized by Ellen Oppenheim, senior vice president/media director at FCB/Leber Katz Partners. "We believe that interactive media will fundamentally change how people will use their televisions and think it's important that our clients have an opportunity to understand this at an early stage of its development."[6]

INTEGRATED DIRECT MARKETING

Throughout this text we have been extolling the benefits of integrated marketing as a managerial approach. Historically, direct marketing is the first area of

---

[6]Scott Donaton, "Interactive Ventures Sign First Ad Deals," *Advertising Age* (May 24, 1993):4.

marketing communication that has adopted this philosophy. In fact, it would be appropriate to rename direct marketing as *integrated direct marketing*. To be concise, instead of treating each medium separately, integrated direct marketing seeks to achieve precise, synchronized use of the right medium at the right time, with a measurable return on dollars spent. Here's an example: Say you do a direct-mail campaign, which commonly generates a 2 percent response, a percentage long viewed as a good or average return. If you include a toll-free 800 number in your mailing as another option to the standard mail-in reply—with well-trained, knowledgable, tightly scripted individuals handling those incoming calls—you will achieve a response of 50 percent to 100 percent over and above the base return of 2 percent. You will go to a 3 percent to 4 percent response rate.

If you follow up your mailing with a phone call—within 24 to 72 hours after your prospect receives the mailing—you can generate a response 100 percent to 700 percent higher than the base rate. So, by adding your 800 number, you bring the rate from a 2 percent response to 3 percent or 5 percent. By following up with phone calls, you add another 2 percent to 14 percent, bringing your response rate as high as 5 percent to 18 percent. This example has integrated only two marketing channels, direct mail and telemarketing.

The principle behind integration is that not all people respond the same way to direct mail. One person may sit down and very carefully fill out the order form. Someone else may immediately reach for the phone to call the 800 number. Most people, however, if an ad has grabbed them at all, tend to think to themselves, "Looks interesting, but I'm not sure it's for me. Let me put it in my pending pile." That pile grows and grows—and then goes into the garbage at the end of the month. The phone call, however, may get them off the fence and take a suggested action.

Hewlett-Packard, AT&T, Citibank, and IBM have all used integrated direct marketing to improve their response rates dramatically. In this economy, with markets shrinking because of competition and market budgets flat, integration is the smartest option.

PROBLEMS WITH DIRECT MARKETING

Tremendous growth and poor early management have created serious problems in the direct-marketing industry. Many of the troubles are symptoms of managerial nearsightedness, a failure to consider long-term goals, and the organization as a whole.

One initial problem stems from the trade-off between short-term versus long-term strategies. Several direct-marketing techniques are characterized as "one-shot" strategies. Examples of the short-term approach crop up daily in consumer mailboxes: mailings that look like telegrams, air-express packages, legal communications, or government documents. Short-term direct marketing does get a response—for a while, until customers become wary. Telemarketing techniques have proven to be even a greater irritant to consumers. Calls that disturb meals or an evening of relaxation, or play a voice recognition recording, prompt 2 to 7 percent of consumers to buy. But at what price? This type of direct market consists of short-term, disloyal customers who were really fooled or coerced into responding. It also reinforces the "junk messages" image that many consumers hold of direct marketing.

A second problem with direct marketing is its tendency not to mesh well with a company's operations, its distribution systems, communications, research, overall strategy, or even culture. For example, direct marketers have been part of programs that have failed because they are so successful: catalog companies have run out of inventories, costing them not only short-term sales but long-term goodwill; financial firms have generated too many leads for their salespeople to follow up. Another common failure in integration involves direct marketing and advertising. Direct-marketing messages and advertising messages often do not reinforce each other because, organizationally, the people who do direct-response advertising usually are not integrated with people who do advertising. Nor is the advertising agency integrated with the direct-marketing agency or in-house group. This is changing, however.

A final problem with direct marketing is its relatively high cost per thousand. Although it is hard to accurately document a general figure, experts posit that direct-response advertising has a higher CPM than image advertising. A direct-mail campaign, for example, still can cost between $200 and $500 per thousand households. The cash differential will likely continue to rise as the costs of both postage and paper increase. Bulk mailing, although cheaper than first class, offers no guarantees on time of delivery, and delays are common. Thus, sale mailers by retailers may arrive after the sale is over.

DIRECT-RESPONSE ADVERTISING

No doubt, creative approaches and placement strategies in direct-response advertising are far different for each type of product or service for sale. The one common thread that seems to run through all types of direct-response advertising is that of action. That is, **direct-response advertising** seeks to achieve an action-oriented objective—such as an inquiry, a visit to a showroom, an answer to a questionnaire, or the purchase of a product—as a result of the advertising message and without the intervention of a sales representative.

Ad 16.2 for Amtrak, for example, looks like a traditional advertisement

direct-response advertising A type of marketing communication that achieves an action-oriented objective as a result of the advertising message.

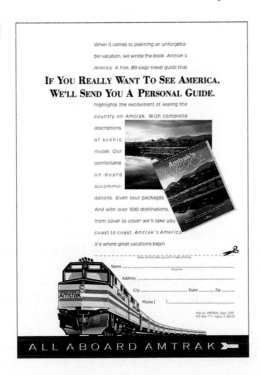

except that it is promoting a coupon to encourage inquiry. Direct-response advertising can use any medium—magazines, newspapers, radio, television, or direct mail. The focus on the objective contrasts with *brand or image advertising*, where the desired response to the advertising message is typically awareness, a favorable attitude, or a change of opinion. With brand or image advertising, the actual sale is made by a retailer in a store or a sales representative who calls at the office or home.

Obviously direct response can be a very efficient form of sales communication because it eliminates that second sales step. Historically, however, it has been seen as less efficient because it didn't reach as many people as did mass-media advertising or, if it did, the cost of reaching them individually was very high. Today this argument is being reconsidered. Direct response is now seen as reaching a prime audience—people who are more likely than the average person, for some reasons related to their demographics or lifestyles, to be interested in the product. In other words, although it costs more per impression, direct-response advertising has less waste than mass-media advertising. It is better targeted. Furthermore, although it lacks personal contact, which is an important element in closing some types of sales, the newer forms of interactive media are beginning to solve that problem as well.

DATABASE MARKETING

As we mentioned earlier, the growth of extensive databases has contributed to more targeted communication with consumers. CCX, for example, is a database program that stores more than 1 billion names and allows list users to mix and match information. Stan Rapp explains that nearly 90 percent of major airlines, car rental companies, hotels, resorts, retailers, and marketers of financial services, package goods, agricultural equipment, and cars have or are developing databases to derive their communication programs.[7] This new development is also referred to as *database marketing, relationship marketing*, or *"MaxiMarketing."*[8] More and more marketers are moving to this new form of direct marketing as a way to develop a deeper and longer-lasting relationship with their customers. Auto companies, for example, are using database marketing systems to link national marketing, service, and dealer organizations with customers. Databases allow companies to call new customers within 30 days of delivery of their cars to get their impressions of the product and to take care of any problems. Such systems can also be used to profile customers and research their purchasing behaviors.

List brokers have thousands of lists tied to demographic, psychographic, and geographic breakdowns. They have classified their data on America's households down to the carrier routes. For instance, one company has identified 160 zip codes it calls "Black Enterprise" clusters, inhabited by "upscale, white-collar, black families" in major urban fringe areas. If you want to target older women in New England who play tennis, most major firms would be able to put together a list for you by combining lists, called **merging**, and deleting the repeated names, called **purging**.

Nintendo has a 2-million-name database it uses when it introduces more powerful versions of its video game system. The names and addresses were gathered from a list of subscribers to its magazine, *Nintendo Power*. The company

merging The process of combining two or more lists of prospects.

purging The process of deleting repeated names when two or more lists are combined.

---

[7]Lauro Loro, "Databases Seen as 'Driving Force,'" *Advertising Age* (March 18, 1991):39.
[8]Stan Rapp and Tom Collins, *MaxiMarketing* (New York: McGraw-Hill Book Co., 1987).

believes that many of its current customers will want to "trade up" and this direct communication will make it possible for Nintendo to speak directly to its most important target market about new systems as they become available. Nintendo began its database in 1988 and credits database marketing with helping it to maintain its huge share of the $4.7 billion video game market.

As discussed in the Issues and Controversies box, the evolution of massive databases is not without its problems. The "right to privacy" alarm has been sounded since shows like *60 Minutes* and *48 Hours* have featured the sharing and selling of databases.

Interactive Technology. The new interactive technology, however, is what makes this area of direct marketing so exciting. Interactive means the consumer can respond back to the message. The telephone is the prime example of a media vehicle that both delivers and receives messages. For example, Pepsi planned a call-in sweepstakes for the 1991 Super Bowl but postponed the effort because it feared the nation's telecommunication capacity could not handle the response. Interactive technology is being developed, possibly using toll-free 800 numbers or 900 pay-for-call numbers, that will be able to generate 30,000 simultaneous calls and take detailed messages, like answers to a trivia quiz or a credit card order. Such systems will be capable of handling up to 300,000 phone calls in 30 minutes. At present, this system still envisions using a bank of clerks to transcribe names and addresses spoken by callers, but computer voice recognition will eliminate that need when that technology becomes available.

The secret to the success of database marketing is the power of the computer to manage the incredible wealth of descriptive data that are now being accumulated along with prospect lists. Most list brokers have standard lists for sale, but in addition they can sort, merge, and purge lists to custom-design one to fit a particular prospect profile.

$\mathcal{M}$ANAGING DIRECT MARKETING

Direct marketing employs the same general planning framework suggested for advertising earlier in this text. It is unique, however, because of certain elements considered crucial to its success. For example, direct marketing is dependent on the quality of its database. It also uses special media to deliver messages. Many of these components have been covered in earlier chapters. The discussion that follows highlights elements unique to direct marketing. We begin with a brief description of the key players in direct marketing.

Three main players are involved in direct-response marketing: *advertisers* who use direct response to sell products or services by phone or mail; certain *agencies* that specialize in direct-response advertising; and *consumers* who are the recipients of direct-mail and phone solicitations.

THE ADVERTISERS

There are more than 12,000 firms engaged in direct-response marketing whose primary business is selling products and services by mail or telephone.[9] This

---

[9]Mary Lou Roberts and Paul D. Berger, *Direct Marketing Management* (Englewood Cliffs, NJ: Prentice Hall, 1989).

They Know Who You Are!

The privacy issue is going public as consumers complain and direct marketers fight for their right to conduct business. Many industry insiders expect the issue to get more attention from the Clinton administration. Consumers' privacy problems with direct marketers involve two key issues. The first is fairly basic: Some consumers simply feel they shouldn't have to deal with pitches flooding their mailboxes and telephones. The second issue is far more complex. It involves sophisticated databases and other wonders of modern technology that allow marketers to mine a wealth of information about consumers: everything from the names and ages of their children to what kind of socks they prefer.

That type of information is invaluable to direct marketers, allowing them to zero in on prime targets for their products and services. But increasing numbers of consumers are voicing concern that there's too much personal information floating around in those databases, and they want to know how it got in there. In a Harris-Equifax Consumer Privacy Survey conducted in late 1992, 78 percent of the respondents said they were concerned about threats to their personal privacy. More than half of the respondents said they felt that information about consumers will become less protected by 2000. The majority of the more than 1,200 survey respondents believed it was acceptable for companies to check public-record information on consumers applying for credit, auto insurance, or jobs. However, most objected if the consumer hadn't initiated a transaction.

In 1992, more than 1,000 bills on privacy issues were presented in state legislatures. At least ten bills made an appearance at the federal level. Consumer advocates are also pushing for protection of the consumer's right to privacy. The American Civil Liberties Union has said that while direct marketing can be valuable to marketers and consumers, there's a need for a watchdog group to protect personal privacy rights.

The direct-marketing industry has effectively argued that there is no need for legislation and that self-regulation is working. As proof, it points to the Direct Marketing Association's Mail Preference Service (MPS) and Telephone Preference Service. Consumers who do not wish to be contacted by direct marketers can register with one or both of the services. The DMA puts these names into a file and makes them available to direct marketers four times a year.

"It's a very complicated issue. Privacy means a lot of different things to different people. Mere mention of the word privacy and you have a reaction," said Steve Cone, chairman of Epsilon, a database marketing subsidiary of American Express. "My read on the American public is that it's not a top-of-the-mind issue," said Cone. "People say they get too much mail, but when you ask them if they want all mail stopped, they say 'no, but why can't people send things I want?' which is why we have databases." What concerns consumers is that companies trade personal information, he said, but what much of the public doesn't understand is that when a company buys a list, it only has one-time use of names and addresses. "Believe it or not, companies are not in business to irritate the consumer by doing bad or improper things with the data," he said.

Adapted from Cyndee Miller, "Privacy vs. Direct Marketing," *Marketing News* (March 1, 1993):1, 14, 15; Gary Levin, "DMA Speakers Caution Use of Databases," *Advertising Age* (April 5, 1993):37.

---

number does not include the many retail stores that use direct marketing as a supplemental marketing program. Traditionally, the product categories that have made the greatest use of direct marketing have been book and record clubs, publishers, insurance, collectibles, packaged foods, and gardening firms. A study sponsored by the DMA identified the most common users of direct-response advertising.[10]

Direct-response consumer categories include:

1. Apparel (including jewelry)
2. Home furnishings

---

[10]Neil Doppelt, "Measuring Direct Marketing: DMA's Industry Statistics Survey," *DMA Focus* (January–February 1987):7.

A woman ordering mer-
chandise directly from a
catalog.

(Teri Stratford)

3. Periodicals

4. Appliances

5. Books

6. Records

7. Gardening

Direct-response business categories include:

1. Computer technology

2. Books

3. Office supplies

4. Computer supplies

Some of the largest direct-marketing firms are well known because they are major retail firms that use national advertising, but others are not as familiar because they only engage in direct marketing. Among the largest U.S. direct marketers are Sears, J.C. Penney, Time-Warner, and the American Automobile Association.[11]

THE AGENCIES

Three types of firms are involved in direct-response advertising: advertising agencies, independent direct marketing agencies, and service firms.

---

[11]Arnold Fishman, "The 1986 Mail Order Guide," *Direct Marketing* (July 1987):40.

Advertising Agencies. First are the *advertising agencies*, whose primary business is general media advertising. These agencies either have a department that specializes in direct response or they might own a separate direct-response company. Many major advertising agencies that want to provide integrated, full-service promotional programs for their clients are buying direct-response companies because this is such an important part of the corporate promotional program.

The ability of traditional advertising agencies to integrate direct marketing into their operation has proven very challenging for many. Apparently, the differences between direct and traditional advertising are greater than first envisioned.

Independent Agencies. The second category is the *independent, full-service, direct-marketing agency*. These companies specialize in direct response, and many of them are quite large. Table 16.1 lists the top ten direct-market agencies. The largest direct-marketing agencies include some firms that specialize only in direct response and others that are affiliated with major agencies.

Service Firms. The third category is made up of the *service firms* that specialize in supplying such services as printing, mailing, and list brokering.

A type of service firm that is vital to the success of many direct-marketing strategies is the *fulfillment house*. Essentially these businesses are responsible for making sure consumers receive whatever they request in a timely manner, be it a catalog, additional information, or the product itself.

THE CONSUMERS

Most people have a love-hate relationship with direct-response advertising. They complain about the "junk mail" that clutters their mailbox. They hate to get telephone calls at dinnertime asking for donations, no matter how good the cause. They ridicule the salesperson on television who is demonstrating a new screwdriver. However, they respond. They buy through direct-mail letters and catalogs, they listen to the personal sales pitch over the telephone, and they call in orders after watching television ad pitches.

New Shoppers. Although people might dislike the intrusiveness of direct-response advertising, they appreciate the convenience. Former Postmaster General Preston Tisch observed that it is "a method of purchasing goods in a society that is finding itself with more disposable income but with less time to spend it."[12]

Stan Rapp described this new consumer in his speech to the annual DMA conference a few years ago as "a new generation of consumers armed with push-button phones and a pocket full of credit cards getting instant gratification by shopping and doing financial transactions from the den or living room." He pointed to the tremendous success of Domino's Pizza, with its home-delivery service, as the fastest-growing sector of the $12 billion pizza market.[13]

Relative to merchandising history, the push-button shopper is a new breed. It takes some daring to order a product you can't see, touch, feel, or try out. It is not like shopping at a retail store. This new breed of consumer is self-confident and willing to take a chance but doesn't like to be disappointed.

Principle

The push-button shopper is self-confident and willing to take chances on a product that can't be seen, touched, or tried on.

---

[12]"Outlook '87," *Target Marketing* (January 1987):25–28.
[13]"Looking into the Future of Direct Marketing," *Direct Marketing* (May 1987):144–145, 153.

TABLE 16.1   Top Direct-Response Agencies by U.S. Volume

Rank 1992	Rank 1991	Agency, headquarters	U.S. direct response volume 1992	1991	% chg	Total U.S. volume 1992	% chg
1	1	**Ogilvy & Mather Direct**, New York	$390.0	$344.1	13.3	$390.0	13.3
2	3	**Wunderman Cato Johnson**, New York	330.8	241.4	37.0	483.6	20.6
3	4	**Bronner Slosberg Humphrey**, Boston	301.0	223.4	34.7	301.0	34.7
4	2	**Rapp Collins Marcoa**, New York	297.2	253.0	17.5	333.2	19.5
5	6	**Lintas:Marketing Communications**, Warren, Mich.	266.5	173.9	53.2	509.4	26.2
6	5	**FCB Direct/U.S.**, Chicago	198.8	201.0	–1.1	198.8	–1.1
7	7	**Kobs&Draft Worldwide**, Chicago	174.2	155.9	11.7	174.2	11.7
8	8	**DIMAC Direct**, Bridgeton, Mo.	163.5	138.8	17.8	163.5	17.8
9	13	**Chapman Direct Advertising**, New York	153.3	113.2	35.3	153.3	35.3
10	10	**Barry Blau & Partners**, Fairfield, Conn.	151.4	127.0	19.2	151.4	19.2
11	12	**Customer Development Corp.**, Peoria, Ill.	146.0	122.0	19.7	146.0	19.7
12	11	**Grey Direct International**, New York	135.0	125.0	8.0	135.0	8.0
13	9	**Direct Marketing Group**, New York	130.1	131.9	–1.4	130.1	–1.4
14	15	**Devon Direct Marketing & Advertising**, Berwyn, Pa.	122.3	99.1	23.4	122.3	23.4
15	14	**Cohn & Wells**, San Francisco, Calif.	105.4	108.7	–3.0	105.4	–3.0
16	19	**Ross Roy Communications**, . Bloomfield Hills, Mich	80.0	70.0	14.3	281.0	7.3
17	16	**Inter/Media Advertising**, Encino, Calif.	79.4	77.6	2.4	85.8	3.2
18	18	**A.Eicoff & Co.**, Chicago	78.0	75.0	4.0	103.9	4.0
19	17	**Russ Reid Company**, Pasadena, Calif.	71.0	77.1	–7.8	71.0	–7.8
20	29	**Brierley & Partners**, Dallas	64.4	45.8	40.8	64.4	40.8
21	26	**GSP Marketing**, Chicago	62.6	51.7	21.1	62.6	21.1
22	34	**Gillespie**, Princeton, N.J.	61.6	35.7	72.4	93.0	4.5
23	21	**McCann Direct**, New York	60.0	59.0	1.7	60.0	1.7
24	25	**Lowe Direct**, New York	57.2	53.3	7.3	57.2	7.3
25	45	**Holland Mark Martin**, Burlington, Mass.	55.9	28.2	98.2	55.9	98.2

Note: Dollars are in millions.
Source: Reprinted with permission from Advertising Age (July 12, 1993):S–1. Copyright, Crain Communications, 1993.

Creating Loyalty. One of the historical truths about the direct-marketing industry was that merchandisers tended to view the relationship with the consumer as a short-term one, with the assumption that losing one unhappy consumer is not a disaster since another sucker is right around the corner. While there are some direct marketers that still employ this philosophy, most have realized that maintaining a long-term relationship with the consumer is crucial.

Changing the attitude of the consumer toward direct marketing has not been easy. The question is: How do you create consumer loyalty? Several attempts are evident. Fleet Financial Group has a customer loyalty program that offers cardholders a 20 percent discount on merchandise ordered from a selection of 14 catalog merchants. Unlike single-use catalog discount certificates, Fleet's program uses an access number that awards discounts to cardholders each time they place an order via the catalog's 800 number and charge the transaction to their Fleet credit card.[14] Similarly, Saks Fifth Avenue identified a group of customers who accounted for half of all sales and offered the group exclusive benefits through a program called Saks First. The benefits include fashion newsletters and first crack at all sales.

Perhaps the most ambitious attempt to create consumer loyalty is through a concept called *lifetime customer value* (LCV). LCV is simply a measure, over time, of how much purchase volume you can expect to get from the various purchase segments. To put it scientifically, LCV is "the over-time volume/financial contribution of an individual customer or customer segment, based on known consumption habits plus future consumption expectations, where contribution is defined as return on investment, i.e., revenue gains as a function of marketing costs."[15] In simple terms, by knowing a consumer's past behavior, you can decide how much you want to spend to get him or her to buy your product—and you can track your investment by measuring the response.

ℳANAGING THE DATABASE

As noted earlier, the database is the very essence of direct marketing. According to the Direct Marketing Association, a marketing database has four primary objectives:[16]

1. To record names of customers, expires (names no longer valid), and prospects;

2. To provide a vehicle for storing and then measuring results of advertising (usually direct-response advertising);

3. To provide a vehicle for storing and then measuring purchasing performance; and

4. To provide a vehicle for continuing direct communication by mail or phone.

Managing this process is extremely difficult, and it is growing in complexity along with improved technology. The initial decision a company must make is whether it will gather data from internal sources, external sources, or both. Internal, or in-house, databases are derived from customer receipts, credit card information, or personal information cards completed by customers. The internal approach is cost-effective as long as the company has the expertise and resources. If either expertise or resources are lacking, a company can obtain commercial databases from firms whose sole purpose is to collect, analyze, categorize, and market an enormous variety of detail about the American consumer. Companies such as National Decision Systems, Persoft, and Donnelly Marketing Information Systems are only a few of these firms. For example, Donnelly recently took the wraps off Hispanic Portraits, a database of households that segments the U.S. Hispanic population into 18 cluster groups.[17]

---

[14]Dennis Chase, "Customer Loyalty Targeted," *Advertising Age* (November 2, 1992):15.
[15]Barbara Jack, "There's No Rocket Science to 'Lifetime Customer Value'," *Promo* (October 1992):27.
[16]Fred R. McFadden and Jeffrey A. Hoffer, *Data Base Management* (Menlo Park, CA: Benjamin/Cummings, 1985):3.
[17]Glenn Heitsmith, "New Hispanic Marketing Tools Announced," *Promo* (March 1993):33.

DESIGNING A DIRECT-MARKETING PIECE

Although there are differences depending on the medium used, all direct-marketing pieces have five equal components. Moreover, there are certain sound principles of design and strategy that apply. The five elements are: (1) the offer, (2) the medium, (3) the message, (4) timing and sequencing, and (5) customer service.

The *offer* constitutes all the variables that together are intended to satisfy the needs of the consumer. Because of the unique benefits provided through direct marketing, the offer may contain the following elements—a price, the cost of shipping and handling, optional features, future obligations, availability of credit, extra incentives, time and quantity limits, and guarantees or warranties.

Selecting the *medium* and the *message* are decisions that go hand-in-hand with direct marketing. The message strategies discussed in earlier chapters are equally applicable to direct marketing. The media used in direct marketing have been specially developed to accommodate the unique advantages of direct marketing and will be discussed later in this chapter.

There is a great deal of similarity between the *timing* and *sequencing* of direct marketing and of advertising. The direct marketer must consider questions about repetition, seasonality, flighting versus pulsing, and one-shot programs versus campaigns. One difference, however, is the greater emphasis placed on the strategic aspect of direct marketing. In advertising, creative execution receives most of the attention; the key to the success of direct marketing, however, is reaching the right person at the right time.

Direct marketing owes its evolution from junk-mail status to credibility to the introduction of *customer service*. The types of customer service offered, such as toll-free telephone numbers, free limited-time trial, and acceptance of several credit cards, for example, are important techniques for overcoming customer resistance to buying through direct-response media. The Concepts and Applications box demonstrates how one company has successfully implemented a direct-marketing plan.

THE MEDIA OF DIRECT RESPONSE

Direct response is a multimedia field. All conventional advertising mass media can be used, as well as others that you might not think of as advertising media, such as the telephone and the postal service. Sometimes media are used in combination. A mail offer, for example, may be followed up with a telephone call. Advertising are allocating increasing sums of money to direct-response media.

Telemarketing is clearly the growth area in direct response. It includes both incoming and outgoing calls—in other words, any telephone call related to direct marketing comes under this category, including offers, orders, inquiries, and service calls. The calls placing orders may be in response to ads in any of the media. Direct mail through television is expensive because of the costs of production and airtime.

Concepts & APPLICATIONS

MCI Reaches Us Direct

MCI Communications says it combined database wizardry with fully integrated marketing to create Friends & Family, its successful discount calling plan. With the plan—unique in the long-distance industry—MCI has created a new database of existing, new, and potential customers, one closely linked with media advertising, aggressive telemarketing, and direct-mail efforts.

Friends & Family, launched in March 1991, offers a 20 percent discount on frequently called numbers, as long as the people at the other end of the line are also participants in the program. Each customer is allowed up to 12 domestic telephone numbers in a "calling circle," which he or she creates by furnishing MCI with the names of frequently called numbers. MCI then contacts those parties—or the customers can make the contacts themselves—to enlist their participation.

For competitive reasons, MCI won't detail the types of computer or data management systems it uses to execute Friends & Family, but company executives say the program has enhanced its marketing capabilities dramatically by teaching MCI a great deal about *relationship marketing*. Carol Herod, vice president/product management, says what made Friends & Family tick is a "seamless integration" of marketing elements—all tied to its new database. Those elements unfolded in the following way:

- To pique consumer interest about a new product, MCI broke network television "teaser" commercials in February.

- On March 1, network television, print, and outdoor advertising began describing Friends & Family, with ads providing a toll-free telephone number for consumers.

- A heavy telemarketing campaign, linked to the growing new database of enrollees and their calling-circle nominees, was launched once responses began coming in.

- An intensive three-step direct-mail campaign was undertaken. It began with an initial solicitation explaining the product and asking for calling-circle nominees from existing and prospective customers.

- A mail update followed within two weeks of customer sign-up—regardless of whether customers enrolled via direct response, telemarketing outreach, or direct mail—giving customers the initial status of their calling circle.

- Eight weeks after sign-up, another update was mailed listing final calling-circle status and asking customers for assistance in contacting people who hadn't enrolled. MCI offered customers five free minutes of long-distance calling per nominee to help enroll those people.

The program was not only successful in increasing market share by 2 percentage points, it also proved to be a less expensive way to increase business than other methods, Ms. Herod says. "The database we've gathered allows us to create a dialog with our customers, so we're constantly in touch with them about who's in their calling circle as they add or subtract names. Whether they call us for service or for a question about their bill, we can talk to our customers about relevant, personal issues when we update their list of frequently called numbers," she says.

Adapted from Kate Fitzgerald, "Circle of 'Friends' Rounds Out MCI Base," *Advertising Age* (January 13, 1992):26, 28.

DIRECT MAIL

Direct mail provides the historical foundation for the direct-response industry. A direct-mail piece is a complex, self-standing advertising message for a single product or service. It may be as simple as a single-page letter or as complex as a package consisting of a multiple letter, a brochure, supplemental flyers, and an order card with a return envelope.

Direct mail continues to be the main medium of direct-response messages.

It accounted for nearly 66 percent, or $1.4 billion, of total direct response media spending in 1990.[18] Direct mail spending grew by 4 percent in 1992.

Most direct mail is sent using the third-class bulk mail permit, which requires a minimum of 200 identical pieces. Third class is cheaper than first class, but it takes much longer to be delivered. Estimates of nondelivery of third-class mail run as high as 6 to 8 percent.

Characteristics. Direct mail, more than any other medium, demonstrates how a message can sell a product without the help of a salesperson. Because direct mail is a self-contained sales message, it has to deliver all the information and all the incentives necessary to make a sale. If it didn't work, it wouldn't have been used all these decades. Response rates for direct mail are generally higher than those for any other medium used in direct marketing.[19]

There are a number of advantages associated with direct mail as compared to traditional mass media. First, the medium offers a variety of formats and provides enough space to tell a complete sales story. Second, since direct mail has little competition when received, it can actually engage the reader's attention. Third, it is now possible to personalize direct mail across a number of characteristics, such as name, product usage, and income. Fourth, direct mail is particularly conducive to marketing research and can be modified until the package matches the desired target audience. Finally, direct mail allows the marketer to reach audiences who are inaccessible by other media.

The primary drawback of using direct mail is the widespread perception that it is junk mail. According to the 1991 Harris-Equifax Consumer Privacy Survey, about 46 percent of the public still sees direct-mail offers as a nuisance, and 90 percent considers them an intrusion of privacy.[20] A second disadvantage of direct mail is the high cost per prospect reached. A great deal of this high cost is a result of postage. In fact, a technique that some direct-mail organizations use to cut postage costs is called *remailing*. Simply, direct marketers send their materials to the United States from foreign countries. Remailers typically ship prepared mailings in bulk to a Central American country such as Panama or Honduras, where postal rates to U.S. addresses are much lower than in the United States.[21] The postal service is attempting to stop this practice. A final disadvantage of direct mail is the heavy reliance on the quality of the mailing list.

Message Format. Direct mail can be anything and look like anything, but most pieces follow a fairly conventional format. The packaging usually includes an outer envelope, a letter, a brochure, supplemental flyers or folders, and a reply card with a return envelope.

The Outer Envelope One of the most important elements in direct mail is the outer envelope. The critical decision by the target is whether to read the mailing or throw it out, and that decision is made on the basis of the outer envelope. Actually, the industry estimates that three-fourths of the pieces do get read. Ad 16.3 gives examples of outer envelopes.

Advertisers use a number of techniques to get people to open the envelope. One is to state the offer on the outside: "Save $50 on a set of china." If an incen-

Principle

The critical decision whether to read or toss is made on the basis of the outer envelope.

---

[18]Wylie, "Recession Felt, But Direct Shops Gain," p. 32.
[19]Katzenstein and Sachs, Direct Marketing, p. 118.
[20]Carrie Goerne, "Direct Mail Spending Rises, But Success May Be Overblown," Marketing News (March 2, 1992):6.
[21]Ibid.

Ad 16.3

Examples of direct-mail envelopes. What characteristics of these envelopes would encourage recipients to examine the contents?

(Courtesy of Time-Life Music, Reader's Digest Association, and Crest Fruit.)

Principle

Direct-response letters have to do the work of hundreds of people.

tive is part of the offer, then that might be used: "Order now and get a free telephone." An envelope that looks very much like it contains a check is another type. A *teaser* statement or question might be used to spark curiosity: "What is missing from every room in your house?" A "peek-through window" may be used to show part of the product; a "show-through envelope" can call attention to the message design of the brochure and the quality and colorfulness of its graphics. Teaser copy is especially valuable when advertisers are mailing third class to a new or unknown list.

The Letter The letter is second in importance because it is the next thing seen after the envelope. The letter highlights and dramatizes the selling premise and explains the details of the offer. Most letters are two to four pages long, although many are longer. Research has found that people with any interest in the product will read everything in the letter. The letter has to carry the full weight of the marketing, advertising, and sales effort.

Bill Jayme, one of the best copywriters in direct-response advertising, has commented that people "often ask why we in direct marketing are so verbose. Letters that can run to eight pages. Brochures the size of a bedsheet." He explains why: "Because a single mailing package must in one fell swoop do the work, in more conventional selling, of many hundreds of people."[22]

The style of the letter is personal. It usually begins with a personal salutation that includes the target's name. The tone is a little different from that of traditional media advertising. It points out things about the offer as a friend might. The first paragraph works like a headline to convince the reader to stay with the message all the way through. It may dramatize the selling premise, spark curiosity, or make some incredible statement as a way to build interest. Often the first paragraph will also introduce a task, such as finding a personalized sticker, that will provide the consumer with additional benefits or prizes.

The body of the letter provides support, explanation, proof, documentation, and details. This is serious hard-sell copy. One critical part of the letter is the postscript (P.S.). Because the postscript is highly attention-getting, most writers use it to wrap up or restate the offer.

The Brochure Accompanying the letter may be a brochure that features the product in glowing color. The letter uses words; the brochure uses graphics to create impact. The product is displayed in as many attractive settings as possible. Demonstrations and how-to-use visuals are included, if appropriate. These can be one-page flyers, multipanel folders, multipage brochures, or spectacular

---

[22]John Francis Tighe, "Complete Creative Checklist for Copywriters," *Advertising Age* (February 9, 1987):24, 69.

broadsheets Large brochures that unfold like a map.

broadsheets that fold out like maps to cover the top of a table. Smaller, supplemental pieces may also be used as postscripts or for additional details or incentive offers (see Ad 16.4).

The Response Device The response device is the order form, often including a toll-free phone number. It should summarize the primary selling points and be simple to read and fill out. Finally, since the order form is a legal document, it is important that the firm's legal department clear all wording.

The Return Device The return device is any mechanism that allows the consumer to return the necessary information. It can be an information request form, an order form, or a payment. Typically, a response envelope is provided unless a card is used as a response device. The envelope serves as an incentive and is convenient, especially if the postage is prepaid.

Message Functions. The functions of a direct-mail message are similar to the steps in the sales process. The mailing plays many roles. First it has to get the attention of the targeted prospect. Then it has to create a need for the product, show what it looks like, and demonstrate how it is used. Furthermore it has to be able to answer questions like a good salesperson and reassure the buyer. It might have to provide critical information about product use. It must inspire confidence, minimize risk, and establish that the company is reputable. Finally, it has to make the sale, which involves explaining how to buy, how to order, where to call, and how to pay or charge the purchase. There may even be an incentive to encourage a fast response.

The List. Direct-mail advertising can only be effective if the mailing list targets the appropriate customers. If the prospects are not in the market for the product, then even the best direct-mail package will be thrown away. The biggest problem with computer-generated lists is accuracy. Updating mailing addresses is a constant problem in a mobile society. Other errors include addressing a woman as a man (and vice versa) and misspelling names.

The mailing list is really a segmentation tool. The list is usually categorized in terms of certain consumer characteristics, such as demographics (young mothers), professions (accountants, hair stylists, engineering professors), inter-

ests (sailing, jogging, cat or dog owner), or buying behavior (buys from upscale catalogs). As with all other forms of advertising, the more selective and upscale the list, the more it will cost.

Lists can be purchased or rented from *list managers*, people who work for companies that offer lists of group memberships that they want to market, or from list brokers. A *list broker* handles a variety of lists from many different sources and can act as a consultant to help you find a list or compile your own list from several different sources.

There are three types of lists: house lists, response lists, and compiled lists. *House lists* are lists of customers maintained by a company, store, or association. Most retailers know that their most important target audience is their own customers, so it is important to identify these people and keep in touch with them. Stores offer their own credit plans in order to maintain this link. They also offer things like service plans, special sale announcements, and contests that require customers to sign up. Some stores fill in the customer's name and address at the cash register on the sales slip, and the carbon copy becomes a source of names for the list. This is probably the most valuable list available to a store or company.

A *response list* is derived from people who respond to something such as a direct-mail offer or solicitation from a group whose members are similar to the advertiser's target audience. For example, if you sell dog food, you might like a list of people who have responded to a magazine ad for a pet identification collar. These lists are usually available for rent from the original direct-mail marketer. This type of list is very important because it indicates a willingness to buy by direct mail.

A *compiled list* is one that is rented from a direct-mail list broker who represents a company that has a house list for sale or who works for a direct-mail company that is in the business of building lists. These are usually lists of some specific category, such as sports car owners, new home buyers, graduating seniors, new mothers, association members, or subscribers to a magazine, book club, or record club.

Lists can be further combined using a computer that has the ability to merge several lists and purge the duplicate names. For example, you may want to develop a list of people who are in the market for upscale fine furniture in your city. You could buy a list of new home buyers and combine that with a list of people who live in a desirable census tract. These two lists together would let you find people who have bought new homes in upscale neighborhoods. The merge/purge capability is very important to avoid using several lists that have the same names, in which case people may receive multiple copies of the same mailing. This is annoying to the recipient and expensive to the mailer.

THE CATALOG MARKETPLACE

A catalog is a multipage direct-mail publication that shows a variety of merchandise. The big books are those produced by such retail giants as Sears Roebuck, Montgomery Ward, and J.C. Penney. The Spiegel company is a major catalog merchandiser that doesn't have a retail outlet. Saks Fifth Avenue, Neiman-Marcus, and Bloomingdale's are major retailers that support their in-store sales with expensive catalogs.

The catalog business went through a decade of explosive growth, increasing 25 to 30 percent in the mid-1980s, but the industry has settled down in the

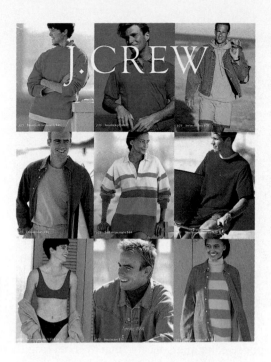

1990s and is coming to grips with saturated markets. The postal rate increase in 1991 was one factor in the slowdown. A slowing economy is another. Catalog experts estimate that sales in 1990 totaled $30 billion to $35 billion and are now growing only at a rate of 8 to 12 percent a year.

Specialty Catalogs. The real growth in this field is in the area of specialty catalogs. There are catalogs for every hobby, as well as for more general interests, such as men's and women's fashions, sporting goods, housewares, gardening, office supplies, and electronics. There are catalogs specifically for purses, rings, cheese and hams, stained-glass supplies, garden benches, and computer accessories—to name just a few. For example, Balducci's fruit and vegetable store in Greenwich Village, New York City, produces a catalog promising overnight delivery of precooked gourmet meals.

Some of these retailers have their own stores, such as L.L. Bean, Williams-Sonoma, and Banana Republic. Others, such as Hanover House and FBS, offer their merchandise only through catalogs or other retailers. Levi's, for example, has always depended on other retailers to distribute its products, but it is now planning a catalog that will make the entire Levi's line available to its customers. Some of the merchandise is relatively inexpensive, like the Hanover line, which is usually $10 or less. Others are much more upscale.

Even corporate giant IBM has gotten into the specialty catalog business. In 1993 IBM mailed more than 1 million four-color catalogs that for the first time will carry the full range of IBM personal computer lines along with numerous non-IBM accessories and software (see Ad 16.6.).[23] The direct-mail catalog category now accounts for 20 percent of all sales of personal computers.

Catalogs are the chief beneficiaries of the social changes that are making armchair shopping so popular. In fact, catalogs are so popular that direct-

---

[23]Gerry Khormouch, "IBM Readers Major Direct Mail Effort," *Adweek* (May 31, 1993):10.

response consumers receive mailings offering them lists of catalogs available for a charge. People pay for catalogs the way they pay for magazines: An increasing number of catalogs can now be purchased at newsstands.

Designing the Catalog Message. The most important part of the catalog message is the graphics. Products are displayed in attractive settings showing as many details and features as possible. People scan through a catalog, looking at the pictures. Only after they have been stopped by the visual do they read the copy block. Thus copy is usually at a minimum and provides such details as composition, fabric, color, sizes, and pricing.

Some catalogs are low-budget, particularly those in special-interest areas such as hobbies and professional supplies. A catalog for woodworkers or plumbers might be printed on cheap paper in black and white. Most general-interest catalogs, however, are moving to quality reproduction with slick paper and full-color printing. The fashion catalogs are often shot at exotic locations, and the reproduction values are excellent.

Some catalogs are designed to create an image, such as the Banana Republic and Caswell-Massey catalogs, which come in unusual sizes and use distinctive illustrative styles. Caswell-Massey is an apothecary that dates back to Colonial days and carries an unusual assortment of soaps, brushes, after-shave lotions, and colognes. Banana Republic specializes in the "jungle look" in fashion, and each of its catalogs features a story about some expedition to an exotic location. Ad 16.7 is an example of two specialty catalogs.

Electronic Catalogs. Catalogs are becoming available in videocassette and computer disk formats. Buick developed an "electronic catalog" on computer disk. The message is interactive and features animated illustrations. It presents graphic descriptions and detailed text on the Buick line, including complete specifications, and lets you custom-design your dream car.[24] The electronic catalog has been marketed to readers of computer magazines.

Video catalogs are being considered by a number of advertisers. Video offers

---

[24]"Software Beats Hard Sell at Buick," *Advertising Age* (November 24, 1986):59.

a dynamic live presentation of the product, its benefits, and its uses. With more than half of American homes owning VCRs, this medium is becoming increasingly important. Cadillac developed a video brochure for Allante, its new luxury car. Air France and Soloflex have also investigated videos for in-home promotions.

PRINT MEDIA

Ads in the mass media are less directly targeted than are direct mail and catalogs. However, they can still provide the opportunity for a direct response. Ads in newspapers and magazines can carry a coupon, an order form, an address, or a telephone number of customers to respond to. The response may be either to purchase something or to ask for more information. In many cases the desired response is an inquiry that becomes a sales lead for field representatives.

One of the most interesting experiments with personal targeting using magazines was *Time* magazine's cover in 1990 that incorporated each reader's name into its cover design. The covers read, "Hey (subscriber's name here) don't miss our really interesting story on the junk mail explosion" (see Ad 16.8). Newsstand copies read: "Hey, you at the newsstand." The article, incidentally, noted that 92 million Americans responded to direct-marketing in 1989, a 60 percent increase in six years.

In *MaxiMarketing* Rapp and Collins discuss the power of *double-duty advertising* that combines brand-reinforcement messages with a direct-response campaign to promote a premium, a sample, or a coupon. Giorgio perfume, Cuisinart, and Ford all use multifunctional advertising in magazines that works two or more ways, including direct response.[25]

American Express is using this double-duty concept in its attempt to combine magazine and direct marketing. The company has launched *Your Company*, a quarterly mailed to more than 1 million American Express corporate card members who own small businesses. *Your Company* was launched by four sponsors—IBM, United Parcel Service, Cigna Small Business Insurance, and American Express Small Business Services. American Express also mails a mag-

[25]Rapp and Collins, *MaxiMarketing*, p. 171.

azine, *Connections*, to college students. Such efforts combine the editorial direction of a magazine with direct advertising's ability to target a narrow audience based on demographics and lifestyle. Magazines have been trying to do this with demographic editions and selective bindings as well.

Reply Cards. In magazines the response cards may be either *bind-ins* or *blow-ins*. These are free-standing cards that are separate from the ad. Bind-in cards are stapled or glued right into the binding of the magazine adjoining the ad. They have to be torn out to be used. Blow-in cards are blown into the magazine after it is printed by special machinery that "puffs" open the pages. These cards are loose and may fall out in distribution, so they are less reliable.

BROADCAST MEDIA

Television and radio have also become involved in direct-marketing advertising.

Television. Television is a major medium for direct marketers who are advertising a broadly targeted product and who have the budget to afford the ever-increasing costs of television advertising. Direct-response advertising on television used to be the province of the late-night hard sell with pitches for vegematics and screwdrivers guaranteed to last a lifetime. As more national marketers such as Time-Warner move into the medium, the direct-response commercial is becoming more general in appeal.

In a departure from its traditional reliance on magazine ads and its door-to-door sales force, Avon aired a series of television commercials in 1992 encouraging women to buy its products via a toll-free number. One 30-second commercial featured a woman using Anew, a skin product Avon is touting for wrinkles. So far, sales are up 13 percent and sales leads have increased by 33 percent.[26]

Cable Television Cable television lends itself to direct-response commercials because the medium is more tightly targeted to particular interests. For example, ads on MTV for products targeted to the teenage audience can generate a tremendous response. Sales are soaring on the Home Shopping Network (HSN), a cable network that displays merchandise in living color. The QVC network, a home-shopping channel, and HSN reported more than 57 million subscribers in 1990.

J.C. Penney is the first major retailer to go on air via a cable hookup. The company invested $40 million in its new interactive home-shopping service called Teleaction. Through this "video catalog" service, customers can order the merchandise on screen by using their push-button phones.[27]

Radio. Radio has not been a dynamic medium for direct-response advertising because most experts believe the radio audience is too preoccupied with other things to record an address or a telephone number. Home listeners, however, are able to make a note and place a call, and local marketers have had some success selling merchandise this way.

Radio's big advantage is its targeted audience. Teenagers, for example, are easy to reach through radio. There has even been some success selling products such as cellular phones and paging systems specifically to a mobile audience.

TELEMARKETING

telemarketing A type of marketing that uses the telephone to make a personal sales contact.

The telephone system is a massive network linking almost every home and business in the country. More direct-marketing dollars are spent on telephone ads using **telemarketing** than on any other medium. The telephone combines personal contact with mass marketing, which is an important factor in relationship marketing.

COSTS

Personal sales calls are very expensive but very persuasive. Telemarketing is almost as persuasive, but a lot less expensive. A personal sales call may cost anywhere from $50 to $100 when you consider time, materials, and transportation. A telephone solicitation may range from $2 to $5 per call. That is still expensive, though, if you compare the cost of a telephone campaign to the cost per thousand of an advertisement placed in any one of the mass media. Telemarketing is four to five times as expensive as direct mail.[28]

If this medium is so expensive, why would anyone use it? The answer is that the returns are much higher than those generated by mass advertising.

---

[26]Jeffrey A. Trachtenberg, "Avon's New TV Campaign says, 'Call Us,'" *The Wall Street Journal* (December 28, 1992):B1.

[27]"Penney Says Teleaction to Start by September," *Advertising Age* (June 8, 1987):82.

[28]Katzenstein and Sachs, *Direct Marketing*.

Telemarketing has to be efficient to be justifiable. The revenue has to justify the bottom-line costs.

CHARACTERISTICS

Telemarketing is personal; that is its primary advantage. The human voice is the most persuasive of all communication tools. Although many people regard a telephone solicitation as an interruption, there are still large numbers who like to talk on the telephone. Some people are flattered by receiving a telephone call, even if it is just a sales pitch.

Two-way. Telephone conversations are also two-way. There is a conversation in which the prospect can ask questions and give responses. This conversation can be tailored to individual interests. Furthermore, if the person isn't a prospect, the caller can find out immediately and end the call.

There are two types of telemarketing: inbound and outbound. An *inbound* or incoming telemarketing call originates with the customer. Calls originating with the firm are outgoing or *outbound*.

Inbound calls are customer responses to a marketer's stimulus, whether a direct-mail piece, a direct-marketing broadcast, a catalog, or a published toll-free number. Since it is almost impossible to schedule customer calls, every effort must be made to ensure that the lines are not blocked. Although most inbound telemarketing occurs via toll-free 800 numbers, the 1-900 number has also grown in popularity. The popularity is a result of the interactive capacity of 1-900 numbers, which enables callers to respond to questions and leave information via touch-tone phones.

Outbound telemarketing is used by direct marketers whenever they take the initiative for a call—for opening new accounts, qualifying, selling, scheduling, servicing, or profiling consumers. Wide Area Telephone Service (WATS) is often used as an economic long-distance vehicle.

Telemarketing Firms. Most companies that use telemarketing hire a specialized company to handle the solicitations and order taking. They do this because most of the activity occurs in bunches. If a company advertises a product on television, for example, the switchboard will be flooded with calls for the next 10 minutes. Companies that do occasional direct-response advertising don't have the facilities to handle a mass response. A service bureau that handles a number of accounts is more capable of coping with the bursts of activity that follow promotional activities.

THE MESSAGE

The most important thing to remember about telemarketing solicitations is that the message has to be simple enough to be delivered over the telephone. If the product requires a demonstration or a complicated explanation, then the message might be better delivered by direct mail.

The message also needs to be compelling. People resent intrusive telephone calls, so there must be a strong initial benefit or reason-why statement to convince prospects to continue listening. The message also needs to be short; most people won't stay on the telephone longer than 2 to 3 minutes for a sales call. That, of course, is still a lot longer than a 30-second commercial.

THE FUTURE OF DIRECT MARKETING

It is clear that the relationship between advertising and direct marketing will become more intense. It is not a coincidence that a medium offering measurable levels of response has grown while others have shriveled. Direct mail, and the proliferation of infomercials with toll-free numbers, are clear signals for the future of advertising. Successful marketers are investing more creativity in ads that create a response instead of just conjuring an image. Moreover, these responses can be swift, measured, and catalogued for future use. Unlike most traditional brand advertising, direct-response advertising actually builds an infrastructure from a customer database.

Direct-response advertising inherently understands that wallet share and purse share is just as important as mind share. The implications of an advertising industry built around direct response are profound.

SUMMARY

- Direct marketing always involves a one-on-one relationship with the prospect. It is personal and interactive.

- The growth in direct-response advertising has been stimulated by technologies such as computers, zip codes, toll-free numbers, and credit cards.

- Direct-response advertising can use any advertising medium, but it has to provide some type of response or reply device.

- Direct-response advertising has benefited from the development and maintenance of a database of customer names, addresses, telephone numbers, and demographic and psychographic characteristics.

- The new push-button consumer is busy and appreciates the convenience of shopping at home or at the office.

- A direct-mail advertising piece is a complex package using an outer envelope to get attention, a cover letter, a brochure, an order card, and a return envelope.

- Catalogs are so popular that some consumers will pay to get their names on the mailing lists.

- Telemarketing is the biggest direct-response area; it combines the personal contact of a sales call with mass marketing.

QUESTIONS

1. What are the major advantages of direct response compared to other forms of advertising? The major disadvantages?

2. What types of firms produce direct-response advertising?

3. Hildy Johnson, a recent university graduate, is interviewing with a large garden-products firm that relies on television for its direct-response advertising. "Your portfolio looks very good. I'm sure you can write," the interviewer says, "but let me ask you a serious question. What is it about our copy that makes it more important than copy written for Ford, or Pepsi, or Pampers?" How should Hildy answer that question? What can she say that would help convince the interview-

er she understands the special demands of direct-response writing?

4 We know that copy and illustration are vital parts of a successful direct-mail campaign, but there must be some priorities. Review the Chapter 13 section on "What Makes an Idea Creative." All of the components are important, but which one is the first consideration for direct-response creativity? Defend your choice.

5 One of the smaller privately owned bookstores on campus is considering a direct-response service to cut down on its severe in-store traffic problems at the beginning of each semester. What ideas do you have for setting up some type of direct-response system to decrease "traffic overload"?

6 Suppose you are the marketing director for a campus service organization dedicated to assisting needy people and families in the immediate area. What are your ideas for developing a telemarketing program to promote campus fund raising? Would it be better to solicit money directly or indirectly by having people attend specially designed events? Your primary targets are students, faculty, and staff.

SUGGESTED CLASS PROJECT

1 Select a consumer product that is not normally sold through direct marketing. Create a direct-marketing campaign for this product. Be sure to specify your objectives and indicate the parts of the offer as well as the medium and the message.

2 Notice what sort of direct-mail advertising you and your family receive. Extrapolate what sort of database you are likely to be part of. Refer to Chapter 7 to get a precise characterization of the groups and subgroups to which you might belong. Keep in mind age, geography, past buying habits, and so on. Evaluate your reactions: Do you mind being on such lists? Why or why not? Are you likely to order products as a result of receiving a direct-mail advertisement? If so, how frequently? Write a brief report.

FURTHER READINGS

KATZENSTEIN, HERBERT, AND WILLIAM S. SACHS, *Direct Marketing* (Columbus, OH: Merrill Publishing Co., 1986).

"Looking into the Future of Direct Marketing," *Direct Marketing*, May 1987, pp, 144–45, 153.

RAPP, STAN, AND TOM COLLINS, *MaxiMarketing* (New York: McGraw-Hill Book Co., 1987).

RAPP, STAN, AND TOM COLLINS, *The Great Marketing Turnaround* (Englewood Cliffs, NJ: Prentice Hall, 1990).

ROBERTS, MARY LOU, AND PAUL D. BERGER, *Direct Marketing Management: Text and Cases* (Englewood Cliffs, NJ: Prentice Hall, 1989).

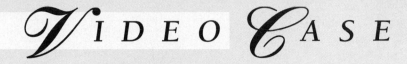

We've Seen the Future and It's Home Shopping

At a troubled time in retailing, analysts are watching the phenomenon of home shopping become a glimmer of hope—a savior of sorts—to fix industry ills. Still in its infancy, home shopping has grown from a base of zero in 1986 to over $2 billion in 1992, and sales are expected to keep growing by at least 20 percent a year. At the heart of this explosion are the QVC and Home Shopping Networks, both of which advertise an array of products, ranging from clothing to gold jewelry, from cosmetics to throw pillows, and make sales when consumers order merchandise via toll-free phone lines.

Although, according to *Business Week*, home shopping's image is now so lowbrow that it conjures up thoughts of "selling tacky figurines to the more woebegone denizens of trailer parks," its horizons are expanding rapidly into classier territory. Here are some examples of home shopping's new world:

- In just 90 minutes, socialite designer Diane Von Furstenberg sold $1.2 million in dresses on QVC and also plans to market her jewelry, fragrance, and home furnishings collections in the same way. One of the advantages of home shopping, said Von Furstenberg, is that "when you sell on TV, you do the selling and the advertising all at once."

- Tony Fifth Avenue retailer Saks Fifth Avenue has also adopted the home shopping approach to advertising. When the retailer ran its first one-hour show on QVC in 1993, it sold $570,000 worth of merchandise in its Real Clothes Collection. When designer Arnold Scaasi aired his clothing on QVC, he had a similar response. "I was just thrilled that I was reaching a consumer who doesn't have anywhere to shop," said Scaasi. "People call in saying there are no stores in their area that have this kind of clothes—better clothes selling for $135 to $225 with more styling."

Upscale retailers such as Nordstrom, Williams-Sonoma, Bloomingdale's, Spiegel, and Sharper Image are attracted to what home shopping will become as the number of cable channels approaches 500, thereby allowing marketers to target specific consumers. "The expansion of the number of cable channels will be the critical difference for a lot of specialty retailers like Sharper Image and Brooks Brothers," said Richard Thalheimer, Sharper Image's chairperson.

Using electronic superhighways, consumers will be able to take personal shopping trips via cable television. The industry envisions shoppers choosing the store, department, or type of product they want to purchase via interactive menus on their television screens.

Shrinking leisure time is largely responsible for home shopping's phenomenal growth. Working women no longer have time to spend hours browsing at the mall and prefer the convenience of shopping at home. The home shopping networks also plan to target frequent catalog shoppers who are already in the habit of shopping from home. Realizing the move from print catalogs to cable television may leave them behind, cataloguers like Spiegel Inc. are turning to the tube themselves. "We're in the retail business to provide consumers with a convenient way to shop," said Debbie Koopman, a Spiegel spokesperson.

Despite the sophistication of the technology, retailers still need a solid advertising approach to reach home shoppers and elicit orders. Experience has taught home shopping pioneers that there are key elements in a successful home shopping pitch. Among these are:

- An air of exclusivity; consumers want merchandise they perceive as limited or hard to get

- "Bargain" prices to make up for hefty shipping and handling costs

- Celebrity spokespersons who glamorize inexpensive merchandise

Analysts believe that retailers who master these techniques and learn to travel the right roads on the electronic superhighway have a strong future in home shopping. As for consumers, they're just waiting for the chance to forget the mall.

Sources: Scott Donaton, "Home Shopping Networks Bring Retailers on Board," Advertising Age (April 19, 1993):98; Annetta Miller and Seema Nayyar, "Highbrow Goes Lowbrow," Newsweek (April 5, 1993):48–49; Pat Sloan and Kate Fitzgerald, "Macy's Rings Up Home Shopping," Advertising Age (June 7, 1993):8; Laura Zinn, "Retailing Will Never Be the Same," Business Week (July 26, 1993):54–60.

Questions

1. What did Diane Von Furstenberg mean when she said, "When you sell on TV, you do the selling and the advertising all at once"?

2. Why is increasing the number of cable channels to 500 important to specialty retailers?

3. Do you envision home shopping working in conjunction with other forms of direct-response advertising, including direct mail and catalogs?

CREATING DIRECTORY AND OUT-OF-HOME ADVERTISING

17

CHAPTER OBJECTIVES

When you have completed this chapter, you should be able to:

- Understand how consumers use the Yellow Pages to search for information about stores, products, and services

- Describe the characteristics of a well-written and well-designed Yellow Pages ad

- Understand the effect of a moving audience on the design of a billboard

- Explain the difference between interior and exterior transit advertisements

- Identify innovative media to use to deliver sales, reminder, and action messages

Advertisers looking for an attention-grabbing way to smash through clutter have a new medium to consider—outer space. For about $500,000, a marketer with an eye to the heavens can buy 58 feet of prime ad space on the hull of a Conestoga 1620 expendable rocket scheduled for launch from NASA facilities at Wallops Island, Virginia.

The unprecedented attempt to attract ad dollars to help offset the launch's cost is part of a NASA program called Comet, or Commercial Experiment Transporter. The program will also allow companies to conduct in-flight experiments during the 30-day orbit of the 1,000-pound satellite and service module. Upjohn, Eli Lilly, Du Pont, and Motorola are among the companies that have bought space on the launch for in-flight experiments, virtually all of a highly scientific nature.

But the challenge of turning the Conestoga into a glorified Goodyear blimp is up to Space Marketing, a Roswell, Georgia, company that first targeted soft-drink and fast-food advertisers for the ads. Selling the space "is certainly doable," said Andes Hoyt, NASA's public relations coordinator for the Comet program. "NASA provided the seed money for this program, but not enough companies put their own into the program, so there was a decision to allow them to sell the [rocket] space."

Space Marketing president Mike Lawson said he hopes to finalize a deal with a single sponsor soon. Besides the chance to flash its logo across the exterior of the rocket, the marketer will benefit from related promotions, including a 900 number for people to leave messages that will be beamed back from space and nationwide tours of shuttle mock-ups. "We are looking for an aggressive and imaginative partner who is interested in the 'high' visibility of being part of this dramatic space launch and its associated promotional programs," Mr. Lawson said. "Not only will our advertising partner have billboard space on the exterior of the 58-foot Conestoga rocket, but we would want them to be included in our national campaign to select a young boy and girl who will actually push the button that sends the rocket into space."

There are some potential drawbacks—like crashing on launch or being totally ignored by a national and global audience inured to space launches. But Mr. Lawson believes the novelty will guarantee a sizable audience for the 30 to 60 seconds of launch time in which the rocket and logo will be visible. Film of the liftoff of a rocket bearing a product's logo "would make a heck of a commercial for anyone interested," said Mr. Lawson. But he did acknowledge that advertisers contacted about the launch have been skeptical so far.[1]

One might conclude that advertisers who would consider placing their ad on the side of a spaceship have really gone off the deep end. Imagine paying $500,000 for a billboard that will last 30 to 60 seconds, then be dropped into the ocean, never to be seen again. Yet advertisers have been willing to pay much more for a spot on the Super Bowl or the final episode of *Cheers*. Selecting media that will maximize aperture is still the goal—whether it is network television or spaceships. This chapter is about two types of media that do not have the high visibility of television or magazines but still play an important role in a given media strategy—directories and out-of-home media.

---

[1] Adapted from Steven W. Colford, "NASA to Sell Ads in Space," *Advertising Age* (January 11, 1993):1, 40.

$\mathscr{D}$IRECTORY ADVERTISING

Directories are books that list the names of people or companies, their phone numbers, and their addresses. In addition to this information, many directories publish advertising from marketers who want to reach the people who use the directory. The most common directories are produced by a community's local phone service. Of course, the Yellow Pages is also a major advertising vehicle, particularly for local retailers. The Yellow Pages revenues for 1992 were $11 billion, making it the fourth-largest advertising medium.[2]

But that is just the beginning of the directory business. There are an estimated 7,500 directories available, and they cover all types of professional areas and interest groups. In advertising, for example, the *Standard Directory of Advertisers and Advertising Agencies* (known as the red books) take advertising targeted at potential advertisers, as does *The Creative Black Book*, which takes ads for photographers, illustrators, typographers, and art suppliers. Similar publications are available in cities that have large advertising communities.

The ads in trade and professional directories are usually more detailed than those in consumer directories because they address specific professional concerns, such as qualifications and scope of services provided. Trade directories also use supplemental media such as inserts and tipped-in cards (glued into the spine) that can be detached and filed. Although many different kinds of directories take advertising, this chapter will focus on Yellow Pages advertising.

Yellow Pages advertising is described as **directional advertising** because it tells people where to go to get the product or service they are looking for. There is one important difference between this kind of advertising and brand-image advertising, which attempts to create a desire to buy: Directory advertising reaches prospects—people who already know they have a need for the product or service. If you are going to move across town and you want to rent a truck, you will consult the Yellow Pages. Directory advertising is the primary media form that is actively consulted by prospects who need or want to buy something and have decided to buy.

YELLOW PAGES ADVERTISING

The Yellow Pages directory lists all local and regional businesses that have a telephone number. In addition to the phone number listing, retailers can also buy display space and run a larger ad. The industry's core advertisers are service providers—restaurants, travel agents, beauty parlors, and florists, for example—rather than retailers, which have been hard hit by the economic slowdown of the late 1980s and early 1990s. For some small businesses, the Yellow Pages is the only medium of advertising. Approximately 88 percent of Yellow Pages advertising is generated from local businesses.

Principle

Yellow Pages advertising is not intrusive because the audience is looking for the information in the ad.

Although there has always been a certain amount of competition among businesses in the same category listings, the competition has become more intense and complex since the breakup of AT&T in 1984. With deregulation, the local Bell companies and their directories are faced with competition from many

---

[2]Dave Martin, "Lunch with Dave Martin," *Mediaweek* (January 6, 1992):10.

independent sources. Most major cities now have a number of alternative and competing local directories.

Some 200 publishers produce more than 6,500 Yellow Pages directories. And because AT&T never copyrighted the term *Yellow Pages*, any publisher can use the term. In many cities, there are competing directories, giving advertisers a choice and an opportunity to target their messages. (In fact, there are so many competing directories in some areas that publishers of Yellow Pages have taken to advertising to build customer loyalty.)

Many of these are aimed at general consumers, but there are also books that specialize by providing listings for certain regions or neighborhoods or by targeting certain consumer groups, such as the Silver Pages for senior citizens or Spanish-language books for Hispanics.

Some coastal areas have their own boater's directories. There's even a commercial marine directory. In addition to telephone numbers and advertisements for every imaginable product and service relating to pleasure boating and commercial shipping, these directories contain information on tides, harbor descriptions, U.S. Coast Guard regulations, and other important boating information.

The Yellow Pages industry has made many important changes in order to make themselves a more viable media alternative. For example, audiotext combined with Yellow Pages is now available in approximately 175 cities in the United States and Canada. After referring to the appropriate section of the Yellow Pages directory, the consumer dials an access number and a code for the individual advertiser and listens to a message about business hours, special services, special promotions, or other helpful information. The Talking Yellow Pages also offers news, sports, weather, and financial information. Yellow Pages publishers have also begun offering a variety of merchandising services. Many carry coupon pages and samples. Telephone subscribers in Orange County, California received with their Yellow Pages a 16-page set of discount coupons for Pizza Hut pizza, Reese's Pieces, Peter Pan peanut butter, and other food and nonfood items.

THE AUDIENCE

The behavior of consumers using the Yellow Pages is considerably different from that of consumers using other forms of mass-media advertising. For this reason directory advertisements are designed differently than other ads. As stated earlier, the Yellow Pages are consulted by consumers who are interested in buying something. They know what they want, they just don't know where to find it. Almost 90 percent of those who consult the Yellow Pages follow up with some kind of action.[3] Because a Yellow Pages ad is the last step in the search for a product or service by a committed consumer, the ads are not intrusive.

A study conducted by *SMRB Research* showed that the heaviest consumer user of the Yellow Pages continues to be a person who is young to middle-aged, well educated, professional or managerial, living in a metropolitan suburban area, and enjoying a relatively high income. The heavy user reads magazines and newspapers, is exposed to outdoor advertising, and listens to the radio. Television viewing is relatively low.[4]

According to a survey by the Gallup organization for *Advertising Age*, the Yellow Pages are used primarily for comparison shopping. Of the consumers

---

[3]"How to Write an Ad for the Yellow Pages," ad by Southwestern Bell Telephone that ran in local community newspapers.
[4]"Simmons 1990 Study of Media and Markets," *SMRB Research* (1991).

surveyed, 40 percent said they use the Yellow Pages to compare different stores and suppliers. Another 32 percent use the directory to find the business closest to their residence, 10 percent use it to check store hours, and 6 percent use it for local maps.[5] Of the more affluent consumers, 47 percent said that the larger display advertisements are most useful to them.

When thinking about the audience for Yellow Pages ads, industry experts suggest that there are two basic categories.[6]

Those who know you:	Those looking for what you offer:
■ Current and former customers	■ Customers new to the market
■ Recommended customers	■ Emergency buyers
■ Those who have seen your ads	■ Those dissatisfied with your competitors
■ Passersby	■ Infrequent buyers
■ Credit card customers	■ Competitive shoppers
	■ Transients (browsers)

As noted in the Concepts and Applications box, the characteristics of the audience for Yellow Pages changes in foreign countries.

CREATING THE YELLOW PAGES AD

As noted in the chronology displayed in Ad 17.1, the design of Yellow Pages ads has changed during the last 60 years. Yet there are basic principles that have withstood the test of time. Although unlike other forms of advertising that have to attract the attention of an indifferent audience, Yellow Pages ads still have to stand out in a cluttered environment.

Once they locate the category, most consumers tend to "browse" through the listings. The decision about which store to call or visit will be based on certain criteria, the first being the size of the ad. Larger ads typically get more attention than smaller ads.

Another decision factor is convenience, especially location and hours. Most people prefer to shop at the nearest store. Large directories in major metropolitan areas often group businesses by geographical area. Other factors that affect the consumer's decision are the scope of the services or product lines available and the reputation or image of the store.

Finally, when a consumer is unfamiliar with a product category or they have no particular selection criteria in mind, the business listed first alphabetically may get the call.

Index and Headings. The most important feature of Yellow Pages advertising is the category system. Because consumers must be able to find the product, store, or service in the directory, category headings are extremely important.

NYNEX used a sweepstakes promotion to anchor these headings in its consumers' memories. Cash prizes were given to residents who knew both the advertised "heading of the day" and its corresponding page number in the Yellow Pages. NYNEX also won awards for its creative commercials that featured visual puns built on headings such as "Civil Engineers." The commercial showed a

---

[5]Williams, "Shielded from Recession," S–1.
[6]Alan D. Fletcher, "Target Marketing Through the Yellow Pages," *Yellow Pages Publishers Association* (1991):24.

The Yellow Pages Turn East

Yellow Pages publishers have turned to the east as they eye uncharted territories for directories and future growth. The virgin regions of Eastern Europe and the new Commonwealth of Independent States are in many ways easier to tackle than the locked-up markets of Western Europe, where several governments grant exclusive publishing contracts.

German, Austrian, and U.S. companies have won Yellow Pages publishing contracts in Czechoslovakia, Hungary, and Moscow during the last 18 months. And they and other publishers still are scouring the area for available deals. "If you have a lot of money and good nerves, Eastern Europe is a very interesting market," says Rolf Schimmel, Budapest-based general manager of Hungary and Austria for Mueller Verlag, Germany's largest directory publisher.

Companies such as Marvol are actively entering Eastern Europe and Russia.

REACH MOSCOW'S DECISION MAKERS
EASY AD PLACEMENT
UP TO 34.5% COMMISSIONS
CLOSE DATE: 2/ 15/ 92

FOR MORE DETAILS AND A MEDIA KIT OR TO PURCHASE
A COPY OF THE DIRECTORY PLEASE CONTACT:
Alan Shaw · **MARVOL**USA
Vice President
1925 Century Park East • Tenth Floor • Los Angeles, CA 90067
(310) 553-6100 or toll free at (800)-4-MARVOL• fax (310) 553-9340

"Building business in undeveloped markets makes a lot of sense," says Don Mackenzie, president-CEO of NYNEX Information Resources in Middleton, Massachusetts. "Look at Central and Eastern Europe; these economies are becoming market economies and have plans to [build their] transportation infrastructure. NYNEX was awarded a 10-year contract to publish the Prague Yellow Pages and also has won the bid to publish Yellow Pages for the Czech region of Czechoslovakia. NYNEX will publish 500,000 copies of its first Prague book, which will be distributed free from post offices."

U.S. advertisers include Honeywell, Citibank, and Xerox. Others are from Germany, France, and Taiwan. "The directory is sorely needed here," says Len Taubman, president of Mediatel, Nynex's Czech subsidiary. "There is nothing [people] can use other than the white pages," he says, which are published by the telephone company. Those are hard to follow, he says: "It's really a hybrid [white pages and Yellow Pages] and it's very difficult to use." The directories NYNEX will publish will look similar to the company's U.S. books, says Mr. Taubman, although the headings will be specific to the Czech market and in both English and Czech.

While publishers agree Eastern Europe holds plenty of opportunity, when it comes to making profits they say companies need more patience than entrepreneurial spirit. Most Western directory companies present in Eastern Europe don't expect to break even until 1995 at the earliest.

Real patience is required in other ways, since the concept behind the Yellow Pages is foreign to Eastern Europeans. "You have to spend a lot more time selling advertisers because they have to understand the benefits of the book," notes Mackenzie. "In addition, you have to teach salespeople how to sell, a skill unnecessary in the old regime, where demand always exceeded supply."

Adapted from Elena Bowes, "East Europe Entices Publishers," *Advertising Age* (March 16, 1992):S–6, S–7, S–9.

group of railroad engineers in overalls with caps and bandanas sitting in a parlor setting and having tea. The NYNEX ad in Ad 17.2 uses that same concept to attract advertisers.

If there is any doubt about where people would be likely to look, then the

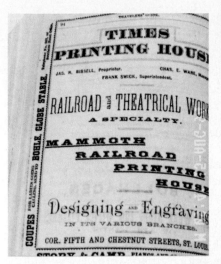

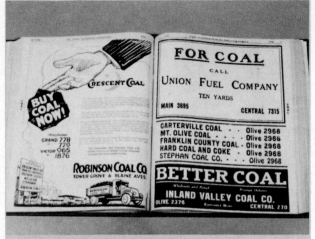

This series of Yellow Pages ads shows the changes over the years. Clockwise from upper left: 1882, 1920s; 1930s; 1940s.

(Courtesy of Link magazine.)

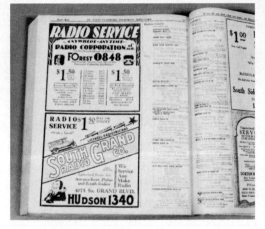

best practice for an advertiser is to use multiple ads that cover all possible headings. For example, a store selling radios may be listed under "Appliances" or even under "Television." It is critical for an advertiser to know how people search

NYNEX ads used a series of puns in their headings.

(Courtesy of Yellow Pages Association)

for the store or service and to make sure information is found under every possible heading that they might use.

Critical Information. Certain pieces of information are critical to a Yellow Pages ad. In addition to location and hours of operation, the telephone number of course must be included. The Yellow Pages, after all, is a directory of phone numbers, and many consumers will call to see if the product is available before making a trip. Note the multiple telephone numbers listed in Ad 17.3 for IBM.

Principle

The headings are the key to searching for something in the Yellow Pages.

Writing. Yellow Pages specialists advise using a real headline that focuses on the service or store personality rather than a label headline that just states the name of the store. The ad should describe the store or the services it provides, unless the store's name is a descriptive phrase like "Overnight Auto Service" and "The Computer Exchange." In Ad 17.4, because "Great Bear" gives no clue to the product, the advertiser uses descriptive phrases and a drawing.

Complicated explanations and demonstrations don't work very well in the Yellow Pages. Any information that is timely or changeable can become a problem because the directory is only published once a year.

Within the Yellow Pages industry and among sales representatives, basic copy factors for Yellow Pages ads are summarized by the term *RASCIL*. This acronym suggests that, depending on the company, ads might stress:[7]

- *R*eliability: years in business, references, connection with well-known firms or associations and safety.
- *A*uthorized Sales and Service: national brand names.
- *S*pecial Features: credit cards and 24-hour service.
- *C*ompleteness of Lines or Services: range and variety, special type and quality.
- *I*llustrations: emblems and slogans.
- *L*ocation/Large, Clear, Easy-to-Read Phone Number: maps, landmarks, and major intersections.

The Design. Among the key design elements of Yellow Pages ads are size, image, and graphics.

Size When people browse through the ads in a category, their choice of a company or product is often influenced by the size of the ad. One study reported that the larger the ad, the more favorable the consumer perception.[8]

Nevertheless, deciding on the best sizes and format can be difficult. The advertiser should begin by reviewing competitors' advertisements that may appear under different headings in the same directory. Depending on the nature of an advertiser's business and sales objectives, the best ad size and format can range from a simple, one-line listing up to one a size larger than the largest ad under a heading.

Image People make decisions based on the reputation and image of the store. This unique personality should be reflected in the design of the ad. Is it a high-quality, upscale, expensive store? Is it nostalgic or classy or exclusive? When you

---

[7]Fletcher, "Target Marketing Through the Yellow Pages," p. 25.
[8]Dennis Hinde and Gary Scofield, "Is Bigger Better in Yellow Pages Ads?" *Journalism Quarterly* (Spring 1984):185–87.

Ad 17.3

This ad for IBM contains a great deal of valuable information, including several telephone numbers for various services.

(Courtesy of IBM)

Ad 17.4

This ad develops a strong brand image.

(Courtesy of Great Bear Spring Co.)

Ad 17.5

This ad for a chain of retail florist shops used stylized flowers and a tasteful layout to create a visually attractive ad.

(Courtesy of Conroy's Flowers)

look through the Yellow Pages for restaurants, women's clothing stores, or hair stylists, can you tell something about the personality of the store from the ad? This personality is communicated through the headline, the illustration, the layout, and the use of type (see Ad 17.5).

Graphics In addition to communicating a store image, the design performs several other functions. In a competitive market, design helps an ad stand out. An illustration, for example, can make an ad more visible. The attention-getting elements should also be big and bold. Spot color, which is becoming available at an additional cost, contributes tremendously to the impact of the ad.

Simplicity is very important. Specialists advise advertisers to keep the number of elements to a minimum. If you must use a lot of pieces, then organize the layout carefully so that the visual path is clear and things that belong together are grouped together. A fanciful display type may be used for the headline to communicate an image, but try to avoid using a variety of faces in a variety of sizes. Use a list with *bullets* (a series of dots) rather than an extended block of body copy to list important points.

Photographs don't reproduce well in phone books, given the quality of the paper and printing. Line drawings work better, although a high-contrast photo may be acceptable. Avoid any graphic that has a lot of detail. Full-color art also does not reproduce well. Maps are very important, but they need to be simplified to show only major streets in the immediate neighborhood.

ELECTRONIC DIRECTORIES

A recent development in directories is the electronic Yellow Pages, a database accessed by computer. These databases are used primarily in business-to-business communication, although the idea is becoming popular among consumers who have computers hooked up to telephone modems and who subscribe to such on-line services as Prodigy. We mentioned Prodigy, the joint venture

Pat Cafferata, President and CEO, Young & Rubicam, Chicago

As chief executive officer of the advertising firm of Young & Rubicam Chicago, Pat Cafferata becomes involved in various advertising activities with clients throughout the country. Here she describes a typically hectic day in the world of advertising.

5:15 A.M. Arose. Picked up *Chicago Tribune* on way to Evanston Athletic Club. Did workout, and, while riding LifeCycle, read the *Tribune*'s business section first, paying special attention to George Lazarus's column which reports up-to-the-minute happenings in advertising and marketing. Returned home to get ready for work.

7:15 A.M. Received call from an account director from Y&R's office in Tokyo. He needed help producing a beer commercial that would use "western" imagery to sell beer in Japan.

8:00 A.M. Arrived at my office. Made calls to Y&R corporate office in New York regarding a fund-raising event being chaired by a client. Also made call to Y&R board member requesting executive vice president title for executive creative directors in my office.

8:30 A.M. Reviewed roughcuts of five television commercials for Icehouse beer. Planned revisions to be made before client presentation tomorrow.

9:15 A.M. Listened to report of focus groups conducted in Boston and Buffalo on new campaign for Molson Golden and Light beers. Planned client meeting to be held day after tomorrow.

10:15 A.M. Met with executive creative directors to discuss staff additions to creative department. Also discussed need for updated computer graphics programs for each art director. Our information resources manager attended that part of the meeting.

---

between IBM and Sears, in the previous chapter as a form of direct marketing; however, it also carries electronic directories.

The concept of electronic directories was pioneered in France by Minitel, which provides consumers there with access to telephone listings, news, and sports through a network of 5 million small video terminals located throughout the country. As of spring 1991, the regional Bell companies were prohibited from entering into this type of electronic publishing. The U.S. government maintains that a dominant carrier of information (technical transmission) should not also be the source of information because that would give it too much control (although this is changing). These services therefore were primarily provided by independent publishers who were actively exploring the possibilities for this new type of information and advertising.

10:45 A.M. Returned phone calls from Y&R's action marketing company, Wunderman Cato Johnson, discussing integrated marketing program for Y&R Chicago client, Navistar, which manufactures and sells International trucks.

11:00 A.M. Reviewed television and print creative for Hunter Fans client, evaluating rough boards for strong branding and leadership cues for Hunter's high-quality fans.

12:15 P.M. Reviewed office real estate situation and new floor plan for housing new staff members being hired to handle recent new business successes. Ate carry-in box lunches.

1:30 P.M. Conducted interview with Kellogg MBA student wanting to get a summer internship at Y&R Chicago.

2:15 P.M. Returned four phone calls. Reached only one person but resolved two other issues by leaving voice mail messages.

2:45 P.M. Met with KGF account director to discuss client's evaluation of Y&R's work over past year.

3:15 P.M. Called client at Miller Brewing Company and Y&R's legal counsel to discuss a legal issue on a Miller print ad. Walked over to Y&R account executive's office to discuss next steps for solving the legal issue.

3:40 P.M. While returning to my office, I was asked by a management supervisor to review

two new Navistar print concepts before he left for the client's office in a half hour.

4:00 P.M. Discussed week's travel schedule with my assistant. Approved five expense accounts and two salary increases. Approved hiring a freelance print producer to cover peak workload on Sears.

4:30 P.M. Read day's mail. Wrote memo to my boss in New York updating him on activities on Miller Brewing account. Called account planner at Y&R New York to discuss upcoming strategy review for Molson. Called media director at Y&R New York to discuss staff needs in our media department.

5:30 P.M. Reviewed radio scripts for Leinenkugel's radio advertising. Discussed changes to scripts since they are being recorded by Jake Leinenkugel tomorrow.

6:15 P.M. Walked a few blocks to meeting of the Illinois Nature Conservancy. Helped fundraising committee develop strategies for corporate sponsorships from Illinois-based businesses.

7:15 P.M. Drove home. Ate dinner with my husband (whatever we could prepare quickly) and watched *Murphy Brown* and *Dave's World* (which had been videotaped, knowing we might not be home in time to watch them at broadcast times).

OUT-OF-HOME ADVERTISING

out-of-home advertising
Advertising that embraces all advertising that is displayed outside the home—from billboards, to blimps, to in-store aisle displays.

Not so very long ago, a media planner would base a schedule around newspaper, radio, television, and outdoor advertising. The outdoor portion was easy—there were 8- and 30-sheet posters and painted bulletins. Not so any more. Even the name of the medium has changed. It is no longer outdoor advertising, it is **out-of-home advertising**. There are still 8- and 30-sheet poster panels and wonderful, giant painted bulletins, but now add bus exteriors, both bus cards and fully painted buses, painted walls, telephone kiosks, truck displays, taxi signs, transit/rail platforms, airport/bus terminal displays, bus shelter displays, bus benches, shopping mall displays, and in-store clock and aisle displays. And don't forget blimps and airplanes towing messages over Yankee Stadium and the scoreboard inside.

Out-of-home advertising has taken giant steps to target specific people with specific messages at a time when they are most susceptible to its impact. A sign at the telephone kiosk reminds you to call for reservations at your favorite restaurant, a sign on the rail platform suggests you enjoy a candy bar while riding the train, and a bus card reminds you to listen to the news on a particular radio station.

Yet these steps are really history repeating itself. Public communication has fulfilled a human need from the Stone Age onward, and humans have communicated visual ideas openly for others to admire. Over 5,000 years ago, hieroglyphics on obelisks directed travelers and Egyptian merchants chiseled sales messages into stone tablets and placed them along public roads. By the fifteenth century, bill posting was an accepted practice in Europe. In the mid-1880s, outdoor advertising became a serious art form.

There are many success stories from the early outdoor advertising days, but the most notable was a little company that tried giving product away on approval and hoped the consumer would pay for it. When this didn't work, the managers tried a series of signs that took 18 seconds to read at 35 miles per hour. *He played The Sax/Had no B.O./But His Whiskers Scratched/So She Let Him Go/Burma Shave.* This worked so well that for nearly 40 years, from 1925 to 1963, almost 7,000 sets of 40,000 individual tiny signs dotted the roads from Maine to Texas. Today total spending on outdoor media is estimated to be over $1.5 billion.

Out-of-home advertising has enjoyed great success during the decade of the 1990s. Yet this has not been without change, opposition, and self-discipline. As much as 50 percent of poster panel and painted bulletin space used to be filled with cigarette and liquor advertising. Social pressure and lifestyle changes have decreased these categories to less than 20 percent, forcing the outdoor companies to find new sources of revenue. Entertainment and amusements, travel, media, health care, and apparel have taken up most of the slack. The other major shift has been from predominantly national advertisers to local companies and national companies with a local message.

BILLBOARDS

There are two kinds of standardized billboards: poster panels and painted bulletins.

Posters. Posters are lithographed or silkscreened by a printer and shipped to an outdoor advertising company. They are then prepasted and applied in sections to the poster panel's face on location. Table 17.1 shows the top outdoor advertisers.

Early posters and signs were primarily pictorial or symbolic because most of the population couldn't read. A sculptured wooden shoe over the door indicated a shoemaker; a sign of a lady with a crown indicated the Queens Crown pub. Graphics remain central to the design of posters as well as other forms of outdoor advertising. Even if a poster is predominantly type, the type will be designed artistically for maximum impact. The key to most posters, however, is a dominant visual with minimal copy.

TABLE 17.1

Top 25 Outdoor Advertisers

Rank	Advertiser	Outdoor spending		% chg
		1992	1991	
1	Philip Morris Cos.	$59.9	$70.1	−14.5
2	RJR Nabisco	29.1	51.7	−43.7
3	Loews Corp.	26.4	35.0	−24.7
4	McDonald's Corp.	12.5	6.9	79.8
5	American Brands	11.7	12.5	−6.1
6	Anheuser-Busch Cos.	10.9	11.6	−6.2
7	B.A.T. Industries	10.5	24.3	−57.0
8	Grand Metropolitan	5.7	7.7	−26.0
9	Seagram Co.	5.2	7.7	−32.2
10	BankAmerica Corp.	5.1	5.7	−9.8
11	Brown-Forman Corp.	4.5	4.4	4.1
12	S&P Corp.	4.1	2.0	103.4
13	PepsiCo	3.8	2.9	30.9
14	General Motors Corp.	3.7	6.4	−42.7
15	Brooke Group	3.2	2.1	51.7
16	CBS Inc.	3.0	2.2	36.0
17	Bass PLC	3.0	3.3	−10.0
18	Hospitality Franchise Systems	2.8	3.5	−20.0
19	Matsushita Electric Industrial Co.	2.8	3.3	−15.7
20	Adolph Coors Co.	2.7	3.2	−13.8
21	Delta Air Lines	2.5	2.2	13.8
22	Walt Disney Co.	2.5	0.4	593.1
23	Guinness PLC	2.4	5.9	−59.0
24	Wendy's International	2.3	1.9	21.5
25	Imasco	2.2	2.0	6.6

Notes: Dollars are in millions. Source: Competitive Media Reporting
Source: Reprinted with permission from Advertising Age (September 29, 1993):54. Copyright, Crain Communications, Inc., 1993.

The design for an outdoor board is supplied by the advertiser or agency. For poster panels, the art is printed on a set of large sheets of paper. Thousands of copies can be printed and distributed around the country. The sheets are then pasted like wallpaper on existing boards by the local outdoor advertising companies that own the boards. The standard sizes of poster boards are the *30-sheet poster*, with a printed area 9 feet 7 inches by 21 feet 7 inches surrounded by margins of blank paper; and the *bleed poster*, with a printed area 10 feet 5 inches by 22 feet 8 inches that extends all the way to the frame. Smaller eight-sheet posters are 5 feet high and 11 feet wide. These "junior posters" are used by groceries and local advertisers and are generally placed for exposure to pedestrian traffic as well as vehicular traffic.

In Europe and on university campuses special structures called **kiosks** are designed for public posting of notices and advertisements. Some of these locations are places where people walk by; others are places where people wait. The location has a lot to do with the design of the message. Kiosks are appearing in more U.S. locations, and there are also some out-of-home media that serve the

kiosks Multisided bulletin board structures designed for public posting of messages.

same function as the kiosk, such as the ad-carrying bus shelter and the sign subway riders encounter coming up the exit stairs.

If people are moving, then the design needs to be simple and easy to read instantly. If people are waiting, then the advertiser has a captive audience, and the poster can present a more complicated message.

The format of all out-of-home advertising has a tremendous impact on its message design. The format is extremely big and extremely horizontal, and visuals and layouts are forced to accommodate to these dimensions. Television screens are slightly horizontal, and magazine and newspaper pages are vertical. A design for a magazine or newspaper page doesn't transfer very well to a billboard because of the elongated horizontal dimension.

Extensions can be added to painted billboards to expand the scale and break away from the limits of the long rectangle. The extensions are limited to 5 feet 6 inches at the top and 2 feet at the sides and bottom. These embellishments are sometimes called **cutouts** because they present an irregular shape that reflects something like a mountain range or a skyscraper.

As part of a campaign against drunk driving, a billboard was created using the remnants of an actual car a family of four was killed in by a drunk driver (see Ad 17.6). This billboard is distinctive and memorable both because of its message and because of the way it is communicated outside the confines of the flat surface of the billboard. Table 17.2 shows the top ten categories in billboard advertising in 1992.

Painted Bulletins. Painted bulletins are prepared by artists working for the local outdoor advertising company. They are hand-painted either on location or in the shop on removable panels that can be hoisted up and attached to the billboard frame. All three of the standardized poster panel sizes maintain a basic 2-1/4:1 proportion. The painted bulletin used for local advertising is even more horizontal than poster panels; the proportion is 3-1/2:1.

The standard size of painted bulletins is 14 feet by 48 feet. Some use a *rotary plan* and are moved to different places every 30, 60, or 90 days for greater exposure. Others are *permanent* and remain at one location.

Painting a large-scale image takes an unusual eye because the details are so much larger than life. Up close the work looks like an impressionistic painting because the colors, contrasts, and shading patterns are so exaggerated. From a

SOMETIMES IT TAKES A FAMILY OF FOUR TO STOP A DRUNK DRIVER.

PAID FOR BY MSI INSURANCE FOUNDATION AND GOLDEN VALLEY HEALTH CENTER.

MADD

NAEGELE

Table 17.2

Top 10 Out-of-Home Ad
Categories, 1992

Rank	Category	Spending ($ millions)	Change from '91
1	Cigarettes, tobacco & accessories	$123	−34%
2	Business & consumer services	84	+30%
3	Retail	82	+28%
4	Entertainment & amusements	64	+17%
5	Miscellaneous/general retail	50	+51%
6	Automotive, auto accessories	47	−7%
7	Travel—hotels & resorts	39	−20%
8	Beer & wine	36	+12%
9	Publishing & media	34	−3%
10	Insurance & real estate	23	−5%

Source: Leading National Advertisers Outdoor Advertising Service. Reprinted with permission from Advertising Age (March 15, 1993):8. Copyright, Crain Communications, Inc., 1993.

distance the details blend together to create a recognizable image. For advertisers who maintain a more stable message and image, the painted bulletin is more impressive and is less likely to be affected by weather, vandalism, and so on. As to cost effectiveness, this seems to be a function of the objectives of the advertiser. Table 17.3 lists the advantages and disadvantages an outdoor advertiser should consider.

MESSAGE DESIGN

Outdoor messages differ from other advertising messages. Some of the key elements are discussed below.

Concept. Effective outdoor advertising is built on a strong *creative concept* that can be instantly understood. The idea needs to be creative because the message has to get attention and be memorable. Most of all, it has to make the point quickly. For example, a billboard for a doughnut store announcing that it now sells cookies featured a huge, one-word headline filling the entire board that

Principle

Effective outdoor advertising is built on a strong creative concept that can be understood instantly.

Table 17.3

Advantages and Disadvantages of Outdoor Advertising

Advantages	Disadvantages
■ *Impact*: Outdoor is big, colorful, hard to ignore, and larger than life.	■ *Message*: Because the message must be simple and brief, you can't develop an involved story or copy points.
■ *Strategy*: An excellent reminder medium, outdoor can also be used to trigger an impulse.	■ *Exposure*: The average driver is exposed to an outdoor message for only a few seconds.
■ *Message*: Outdoor can showcase a creative concept.	■ *Criticism*: Some critics feel outdoor advertising is visual pollution.
■ *Cost*: Outdoor is the least expensive of all major advertising media based on CPMs.	■ *Availability*: Because of criticism of outdoor advertising, some areas restrict or ban billboards.
■ *Long Life*: Outdoor is good for messages that need to be repeated.	

read: "Goody." The two O's in the middle were both round cookies. The underline read: "Winchell's has gone cookies." The concept was expressed in both words and visuals.

Copywriting. The copy on a billboard is minimal. Usually there is one line that serves both as a headline and as some kind of product identification. The most important characteristic is *brevity*. The words are short, the phrases are short, and there are no wasted words. Some books suggest that no more than six to seven words be used. The headline is usually a phrase, not a sentence. There is nothing equivalent to the body found in a print ad. The best copy for outdoor is a short, catchy phrase. It needs to catch attention, but it also needs to be captivating in order to be memorable. Often the phrase will be a play on words or a twist on a common phrase. For example, a billboard for Orkin pest control showed a package wrapped up with the word "Orkin" on the tag. The headline read: "A little something for your ant." A billboard for Best Food mayonnaise showed a butcher block with tomatoes, lettuce, cheese, and rye bread sitting next to the mayonnaise bottle. The headline read: "Best on the block."

The Design. Because billboards must make a quick and lasting impression, design is critical to their effectiveness.

Layout The integration of art and headline is critical for the development of a strong concept. The layout is compact, with a very simple visual path, usually beginning with a strong graphic, followed by a catchy headline, and ending with some kind of product identification. The relationships should be so clear and so integrated that the elements are perceived as one whole concept. Ad 17.7 for "Erase Illiteracy" is an example of a good layout.

Graphics The most important feature of billboard design is high visibility. *Visibility* means that a billboard is conspicuous; it is noticeable; it bursts into view. The illustration should be an eye-stopper.

What makes something visible? Size is one factor. It offers a grand scale,

Ad 17.7

This billboard uses words and visuals together in a very effective manner.

much larger than life, and therefore can create tremendous impact. You can depict a 25-foot-long pencil or a pointing finger that is 48 feet long. The product or the brand label can be hundreds of times larger than life. Most elements on a billboard are big and bold—the type as well as the illustrations.

Bold, bright color is another characteristic of impact. The outdoor industry has done significant research on color and color combinations. It has found that the greatest impact is created by maximum contrast between two colors. The strongest contrast, for example, comes from dark colors against white or yellow. Yellow adds tremendous impact as well as contrast. Other bright colors also add impact. The visibility problem is compounded by the fact that outdoor boards are seen at all times of the day and night under all kinds of lighting conditions. The most visible billboards use bright, contrasting colors.

Another aspect of visibility is the clarity of the relationship between foreground and background. In outdoor advertising the best practice is to make this distinction as obvious as possible. A picture of a soft drink against a jungle background will be very hard to perceive when viewed from a moving vehicle at a distance. The background should never compete with the subject.

Typography. Type demands unusually sensitive handling. It has to be easy to read at a distance by an audience in motion. The outdoor industry has researched type legibility on billboards. Among its conclusions is to avoid all-capital letters because that is the hardest typographical form to read. Ornamental letters, depending on how fanciful they are, can also be hard to read, as can script and cursive letters. Anything that is unusual can create legibility problems. Experts in outdoor advertising advise using simple, clean, and uncluttered type.[9]

Distance. Planning for reading at a distance is an important aspect of billboard design. The Institute for Outdoor Advertising has developed a poster distance scale viewer that designers use in planning the layout. Designers realize that a layout on a desk has a very different impact than a billboard by the side of a highway. The viewer lets them evaluate the design as it would be seen at a distance from a moving car.

Product Identification. Product identification is another important aspect of the design of outdoor advertising. Most billboards focus attention on the product. The distinctive label on a cold, dripping Perrier bottle filled the entire space on one billboard. Underneath was the headline: "It's only natural." The red Smirnoff label with its distinctive typeface appeared on another board next to an olive and a lemon peel. The headline was a play on words: "Olive 'R Twist." The Marlboro billboard in Ad 17.8 is a good example of strong product identification.

PRODUCTION OF OUTDOOR ADVERTISING

As a result of modern technology, outdoor ads can now utilize a number of special effects.

Lighting. Lighting is a very important aspect of outdoor advertising. Illuminated billboards against a nighttime sky can create a compelling visual. In urban areas illuminated billboards may be combined with special lighting effects that blink and change colors. Neon may even be added. These displays are called

---

[9]*A Creative Guide to Outdoor Advertising* (New York: OAAA Marketing).

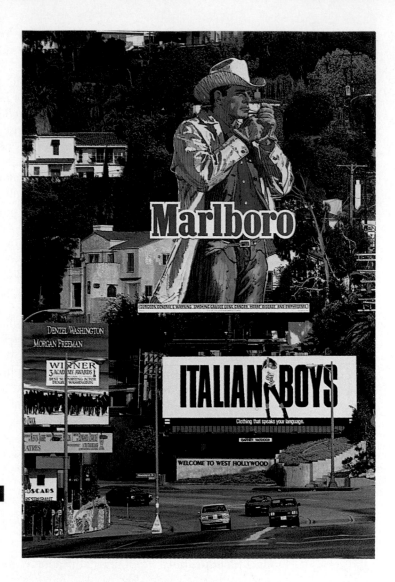

spectaculars Billboards with
unusual lighting effects.

holography A technique that
produces a projected three-
dimensional image.

spectaculars. Las Vegas and Times Square in New York display many examples
of lighted spectaculars.

A new *backlighting* technique used for nighttime showings appears to make
the background of the board disappear so that the image pops out against the
black sky. Another experiment involves the use of an internally illuminated
transparent polyvinyl that gives the appearance of a luminous image projected
onto a screen. Some advertisers are experimenting with **holography**, which can
project a three-dimensional image from a board or onto a board.

Shape. Designers have been searching for decades for techniques to break away
from the rectangular frame of most boards. Extensions help, but advertisers are
also experimenting with designs that create the illusion of 3-D effects by playing
with horizons, vanishing lines, and dimensional boxes.

Inflatables are even closer to 3-D. Giant inflatable liquor bottles and cigarette
packs made of a heavyweight stitched nylon inflated by a small electric fan have
been added to outdoor boards. An especially impressive billboard for

Times Square in New York offers many examples of the elaborate outdoor ads known as spectaculars.

(Courtesy of Comstock)

kinetic boards Outdoor advertising that uses moving elements.

Marineland shows a 3-D creation of Orca, Marineland's killer whale, bursting through the board.

Motion. Revolving panels, called **kinetic boards**, are used for messages that change. These two-, three-, or four-sided panels can contain different messages for different products or they can be used to develop a message that evolves. Two- or three-sided stationary panels can be used to create a message that changes as the viewer passes by—different angles giving different versions of the message.

Motors can be added to boards to make pieces and parts move. Disk-like wheels and glittery things that flicker in the wind have all been used to create the appearance of motion and color change. Special effects include techniques to make images squeeze, wave, or pour.

BUYING OUTDOOR SPACE

During the last decade, the outdoor industry has taken steps to increase its professional standards—and thereby be more competitive with other media. The industry has adopted a system based on the gross rating points (GRPs); it has gathered more data on audience segments; and organizations such as Out-of-Home Media Services (OHMS) have emerged. OHMS conducts research on the industry and provides a national buying service for outdoor and transit advertising.

The GRP system provides a quantifiable measurement for exposure by defining a standardized unit for space sales. If an advertiser purchases 100 GRPs daily, the basic standardized unit is the number of poster panels required in each market to produce a daily effective circulation equal to 100 percent of the population of the market. (*Note*: This formally was called a 100-showing). As used by the outdoor industry, a rating point is 1 percent of the population one time. GRPs are based on the daily duplicated audience as a percentage of a market. If three posters in a community of 100,000 people achieve a daily exposure to 75,000 people, the result is 75 GRPs.

Advertisers can purchase any number of units, although 75, 50, or 25 GRPs daily are common. The number of panels required for 100 GRPs varies from city to city. Posters are rented for 30-day periods. Painted bulletins and spectaculars are bought on an individual basis, usually for one, two, or three years.

THE AUDIENCE

As one would expect, accurately measuring the mobile audience for outdoor advertising is very difficult. Media that cannot verify their audience size or composition usually have a slim chance of being selected by advertisers. In the case of outdoor advertising, this assessment process is still under revision. Currently, however, the audience reach-frequency of outdoor advertising is reported nationally by Simmons Market Research Bureau (SMRB) and locally by Audience Measurement by Market of Outdoor (AMMO). It all begins with a series of local market surveys that the outdoor industry conducts periodically in specific U.S. markets. These are called *calibration surveys*. Purposes are (1) to measure respondents' actual frequencies of exposure and (2) to relate these frequencies to respondents' demographic characteristics and travel behavior. Frequency of exposure to a 100-GRP advertisement, in a week, is measured by the *map recall* method in which the respondent recalls each trip out of home in the past seven days and physically draws his or her travel route on a separate map for each trip. In the home office, a transparent sheet is laid over each map, showing the location of panels in a 100 GRP, and trained office coders tally the number of exposures (if any) for each respondent trip. Although a bit more complicated, this information is sampled and verified by SMRB at the national level and by AMMO at the local level. As noted earlier, there are flaws in this mechanism that are being rectified. One problem is accounting for all the people and possible travel patterns. This issue is discussed in a somewhat different context in the Issues and Controversies box.

TRANSIT ADVERTISING

Transit advertising is primarily an urban advertising form that uses vehicles to carry the message to people. The message is on wheels, and it circulates through the community. Occasionally you might see trucks on the highway that carry messages. Many semitrailer trucks carry graphics to identify the company that owns them. Some of these graphics are striking, such as the designs on the sides of the Mayflower Moving trucks and the Steelcase trucks. In addition to this corporate identification, the sides of trucks may also be rented out for more general national advertising messages. Trucks are becoming moving billboards on our nation's highways.

The Out-of-Home Dilemma

One of the problems facing media experts is how to count people who are experiencing media away from home. People read magazines at the doctor's office, listen to the radio while shopping at the mall, and watch television at their favorite bar. It is in the category of television where the controversy looms largest.

In a series of meetings in New York, Chicago, and Los Angeles, Nielsen Market Research asked its advertising and television clients for input on developing a plan to integrate out-of-home viewing into regular syndicated ratings reports. But the request brought an outcry from agency executives concerned that the networks may use out-of-home data to inflate the price of advertising. Out-of-home estimates would increase network television ratings by 25 percent overall, adding about 20 million viewers each week to the Big 3's share figures.

Traditionally, Nielsen has counted only viewing inside television sample households. Viewers in such venues as bars, hotels, offices, and on college campuses have historically been considered an implicit part of television buys. But in recent years, the Big 3 have sought to make the value of out-of-home viewing a key part of their negotiations. Nielsen has already conducted three customized studies for the Big 3 to measure out-of-home viewing via personal diaries that viewers use whenever they watch television. The first

two studies, in 1989 and 1991, showed overall television viewing levels are about 2 percent higher than current estimates, and as much as 25 percent higher for specific TV shows and dayparts. The third study, conducted in 1992, shows that, on average, network television audiences are 4 percent higher than those reported in Nielsen's regular syndicated ratings reports when out-of-homes are included. The study found a wide range of out-of-home viewership among adults depending on the show. For example, *Love and War* had no statistically measurable out-of-home viewers among adults, while *Letterman* had a nearly 10 percent boost in its audience size from people viewing outside the home, and *Nightline* had a boost of 16 percent. Overall, Nielsen found that 28 million adults watch television in out-of-home locations each week and that 23 percent of their viewing exceeds five hours each week.

Ultimately, nobody disputes that there are out-of-home viewers who are currently not being measured. The real question, however, is not how to measure them, but whether to measure them, who to measure, and how it will impact the buying and selling of television time.

Adapted from Joe Mandese, "Out-of-Home TV: Does It Count?" *Advertising Age* (January 18, 1993):53; Joe Mandese, "What People Watch Away from Home," *Advertising Age* (March 20, 1003):13.

Transit advertising also includes the posters seen in bus shelters and train, airport, and subway stations. They are targeted at commuters and travelers. Most of these posters must be designed for quick impressions, although posters on subway platforms or bus shelters are often studied by people who are waiting and thus may present a more involved or complicated message.

Transit advertising is reminder advertising; in other words, it is a high-frequency medium that lets advertisers get their name in front of a local audience at critical times such as rush hour and drive time. Frito-Lay used a transit campaign to promote its Smartfoods, the white cheddar cheese popcorn. The campaign's objective was to demonstrate that Smartfood is everywhere and to make the image a powerful presence in a local market. Other companies are making more and more use of this type of advertising as well.

THE AUDIENCE

There are two types of transit advertising—interior and exterior. **Interior transit advertising** is seen by people riding inside buses, subway cars, and some

interior transit advertising
Advertising on posters that are mounted inside vehicles such as buses, subway cars, and taxis.

exterior transit advertising
Advertising posters that are mounted on the sides, rear, and top of vehicles.

taxis. **Exterior transit advertising** is mounted on the sides, rear, and top of these vehicles, and it is seen by pedestrians and people in nearby cars.

Targeting. Transit messages can be targeted to specific audiences if the vehicles follow a regular route. Buses that are assigned to a university route will expose a higher proportion of college students, whereas buses that go to and from a shopping mall will expose a higher population of shoppers.

MESSAGE DESIGN

Interior Transit. Interior advertising in buses and subways uses a format called **car cards**. These cards are mounted in racks above the windows and in panels at the front and back of the vehicle. The car cards are horizontal, usually 11 inches high by either 28, 42, or 56 inches wide.

car cards Small advertisements that are mounted in racks inside a vehicle.

Interior advertising is radically different from exterior transit advertising. People sitting in a bus or subway car are a captive audience. Their ride averages 20 to 30 minutes. Some read books or newspapers, but most watch other riders, look out the window, and read and reread the ads. In addition, most people who commute on mass transit ride both ways, so the messages get studied twice.

As a result, car cards can have longer and more complex messages than outdoor or exterior panels. The only problem with length is visibility. The messages are read from a distance and frequently at an angle. The type must be big enough to be legible given this seating problem.

Principle

Interior transit advertising uses longer and more complex messages because it can be studied.

Car cards offer other opportunities for extending the message. Many cards come with *tear-offs* and *take-ones*. Tear-offs are pads of coupons or other information that are glued to the car card. Take-ones are pockets filled with flyers or leaflets. Both can be used for coupons, recipes, or just to provide more in-depth information.

Exterior Transit. Exterior advertising panels are very similar to outdoor boards and the same guidelines are used in their design. The only difference is that the vehicle carrying the message, as well as the reader, may be in motion. This makes the perception of the message even more difficult. Exterior panels are designed like small billboards: simple, bold, catchy, and legible.

Principle

Exterior transit advertising is designed like small billboards with simple, bold, and catchy messages.

Station Posters These mini-billboards are located at bus, railroad, subway, and air terminals. The most common units are the two-sheet poster (46 inches by 60 inches) and the one-sheet poster (46 inches by 30 inches).

$\mathcal{M}$OVIE ADVERTISING

trailers Advertisements that precede the feature film in a movie theater.

Most movie theaters will accept filmed commercials to run before the feature. Called **trailers**, these advertisements are similar to television commercials but are generally longer and better produced. Theater messages are usually 45 seconds or 1 minute in length. This gives more time for message development than the typical 30-second television spot. There is even talk of 2-minute mini-films for theater showings.

THE AUDIENCE

Principle

Theater advertising is the most compelling form of advertising because of the impact of larger-than-life images in the dark on the big screen.

There may be some limited targeting of these messages in terms of location and the type of audience attracted by various kinds of movies. The important audience factor, however, is the attention and concentration generated by the theater environment. The projection of larger-than-life images in a darkened theater is totally unlike the experience of watching television. The impact of the large screen makes for a compelling image that commands total attention. It is very difficult for the audience to turn off or tune out whatever is happening on that screen.

MESSAGE DESIGN

The critical feature of theater advertising is that it must function as entertainment. People in theaters have a low tolerance for hard-sell messages. Dramas and MTV techniques, with their music and intense imagery, have been particularly effective with theater advertising.

THE CONTROVERSY

Movie advertising isn't universally appreciated. Moviegoers have been known to picket outside movie theaters to express their displeasure that advertisements are being shown before the feature movies. Walt Disney refuses to let its movies be shown in movie houses that run commercials before the films. People have also been known to boo and hiss in the theater when these commercials come on. Most people who resent these ads explain that they have paid money to attend the movie and therefore they shouldn't be subjected to commercials.

The decision to run ads is usually not up to the individual theater but is made by the motion picture companies and the distributors who handle the films. Theaters typically limit the commercials to no more than three per film. Ads will be run for everything from cars to credit cards to the Marine Corps, but the mix usually depends on the type of audience perceived as watching that particular film. Movies though to appeal to teenagers, for example, will often open with MTV-like advertisements. As with most advertising, some theater ads are irritating and some are entertaining.

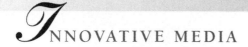

INNOVATIVE MEDIA

SALES MESSAGES

New and novel media are constantly being utilized as vehicles for advertising messages. Pay telephones are beginning to carry advertising space. This can be a highly targeted medium. If you want mall shoppers, then you can reach them at telephone booths in malls; if you want travelers, use the airport telephones; if you want college students, advertise on campus pay telephones.

indicia The postage label printed by a postage meter.

Companies that have their own postage meters use the **indicia** for printed messages on the envelopes of the correspondence. Some people have even suggested that the government sell space on postage stamps for advertising messages.

Even garbage and trash cans on the city streets are being used for short messages. These advertisements can carry short copy lines and product symbols. Bus-stop benches are also available for short copy such as slogans, although visuals don't work well on benches.

REMINDER MESSAGES

Blimps have been around for decades and, of course, the Goodyear Blimp is a classic example of *brand-reminder advertising*. Planes pulling banners have been used over major outdoor events such as fairs and football games. More recently, hot air balloons have carried commercial messages.

Athletic competition makes heroes, and heroes are good message endorsers. Consequently, almost every sports event is a display for special-interest advertising. All the tennis, skiing, swimming, and golf equipment manufacturers prominently display their brands on the course or on the athletes' clothing.

Other sponsors, such as beer companies, simply like to affiliate with an attention-getting event such as the Indy 500 or the Super Bowl. The Indy cars are covered with decals for the sponsors who underwrite the cost of getting the car into the race and onto the track.

ACTION MESSAGES

Grocery carts now have placard space that can be rented. These are reminder messages, but they function like point-of-purchase advertising (see Chapter 18). They confront the shopper at the moment when he or she is ready to make a purchase.

Coupons are being printed on the back of tickets to major events like college football games. Coupons are also showing up on the back of grocery store receipts.

There are even advertisers who are producing their own video cassettes. Two Buick regional ad groups provide personalized videocassette messages about the dealerships' cars to prospects who call a toll-free number. Each video includes a 2-minute talk by a local dealer as well as an on-screen video letter addressed to the consumer, inviting him or her to call the dealership with questions.

Blimps offer a creative way to advertise.

(David Wells/The Image Works)

SUMMARY

- The Yellow Pages is the most universal advertising medium.
- Yellow Pages ads focus on the service offered or the store personality.
- Posters are the oldest form of advertising.
- Posters are graphic, and the focus of the message is the visual.
- Outdoor advertising delivers messages to moving audiences using "quick-impact" techniques such as strong graphics and short, catchy phrases.
- A billboard is the largest advertising medium.
- National billboards are distributed as preprinted posters; local billboards are original, hand-painted art.
- Interior transit messages can be studied; exterior messages must be seen in a glance.
- Theater advertising is the most compelling form of advertising because of the impact of larger-than-life images on the big screen; it is controversial, however.
- Innovative media include a wide variety of techniques that either deliver a sales message, a reminder message, or an action message. Examples include ads on telephones, garbage cans, blimps, and grocery carts.

QUESTIONS

1. Why is Yellow Pages advertising described as "directional"?

2. Outdoor advertising is described as "quick impact." What does that mean? How do you design effective messages for this medium?

3. Since his freshman year in college, Phil Dawson, an advertising major, has waited on tables at Alfredo's, a small family-operated restaurant featuring excellent food and an intimate atmosphere. The owner has been approached by a Yellow Pages representative to run a display ad. He asks Phil for advice on whether a display would help, and if so, what the ad should look like. What should Phil recommend?

4. You are constantly exposed to poster advertising all over your campus. If you had authority over all poster advertising, what would you do to improve the effectiveness of poster advertising on campus?

5. There is some extraordinary outdoor billboard technology under development that will allow advertising images to be projected onto the board space. The same technology could also provide public information (in addition to the advertising) from each board location. The creative possibilities of computer-controlled projection are obvious, but what about the ability to convert each location into a special message board? What sort of services could key locations provide that would contribute to public service? Do you feel that such ideas would improve public opinion toward outdoor billboards?

6. One of the most logical opportunities for new advertising methods is to expand the communication options found inside stores. What are some store-level activities that could be used in (a) supermarkets and (b) department stores?

SUGGESTED CLASS PROJECT

Test the following research hypothesis about directory advertising by either surveying advertisers, customers, or both.

- Hypothesis 1: Larger ads produce more sales than smaller ads.

- Hypothesis 2: Ads later in the alphabet create more sales.

- Hypothesis 3: Ads with some color produce more sales.

FURTHER READINGS

The Big Outdoor (New York: The Institute of Outdoor Advertising).

A Creative Guide to Outdoor Advertising (New York: The Institute of Outdoor Advertising).

FLETCHER, ALAN D., *Yellow Pages Advertising* (Chesterfield, MO: American Association of Yellow Pages Publishers, 1986).

HENDERSON, SALLY, AND ROBERT LANDAU, *Billboard Art* (San Francisco: Chronicle Books, 1981).

"Multiple Directories: A Publisher's Point of View," *Update*, Summer 1986, pp. 2–3.

"Yellow Pages Co-op Advertising: The $2 Billion Advertisers Bonanza," *Update*, Summer 1986, pp. 4–5.

$\mathcal{V}$IDEO $\mathcal{C}$ASE

Cadillac Style

The Balloonist's Prayer

The winds have welcomed you with softness.
The sun has blessed you with his warm hands.
You have flown so high, and so well,
that God has joined you in your laughter
and set you gently back again
into the loving arms of Mother Earth.

Everyone loves hot-air balloons, and that includes bottom-line corporate advertising executives who understand the balloon's nearly unparalleled ability to generate publicity and draw crowds. Corporate giants like the Cadillac Motor Car Division of General Motors, Disney, Coca-Cola, and Kodak as well as small companies like Herring Gas in Naches, Mississippi, Houser Asphalt Company in Dayton, Ohio, and Mr. Rubbish, a garbage hauler in Ann Arbor, Michigan fly balloons emblazoned with their corporate messages to create open-air spectacles featuring their companies as the stars.

"There's no better way to touch people around the country than with hot-air balloons," said Larry P. Anderson, manager of dealer marketing for Cadillac. Tucker Comstock, president of Cameron Balloons, a custom-balloon manufacturer based in Ann Arbor, agrees. "Balloons make large companies real for people. They turn cold corporate identities into joyful, personal experiences."

Cadillac's commitment to hot-air ballooning began in 1989. Today, the 70-foot-high Cadillac balloon, equipped with a rattan, birch, and suede basket that carries three, appears in 18 major balloon and corporate events as well as 35 dealer promotions nationwide. These events, including the Albuquerque International Balloon Fiesta and the Colorado Springs Balloon Classic, draw 3 million on-site spectators. National, regional, and local media coverage spreads Cadillac's corporate image to an additional 45 million potential buyers. The reward for Cadillac has been a sixfold return on investment, based on these events generating 60 incremental vehicle sales. The current value of the program exceeds $1 million.

A cornerstone of Cadillac's program is dealer-based participation. For a fee of $700 a day, the Cadillac hot-air balloon can either be tethered or launched from a dealership. To maximize the promotional impact, dealers issue press releases, inviting the media and public to attend the ballooning event and enjoy no-cost balloon flights. The program has been so popular that dealer demand now exceeds balloon availability and has created an army of devoted followers. Daniel Jobe, a Cadillac dealer from Greenbelt, Maryland, is one. "Please put me down for our balloon event every year," said Jobe.

Print collateral pieces bolster the program's impact. In 1993 alone 500,000 calendars, postcards, balloon race brochures, travel and tourism brochures, and major event publications were distributed to spread the impact of the various ballooning events.

Why is ballooning such a successful promotional technique? Because people love balloons and because balloons create thousands of impressions as they fly over a community. Indeed, the late Malcolm Forbes, arguably the ultimate capitalist and a hot-air balloon aficionado, believed that the cost of a corporate balloon is returned 100 times in its publicity value.

Sources: Cadillac Hot-Air Balloon/Cold-Air Balloon Programs: Sponsorship Impact, 1993; Cadillac Hot-Air Balloon Program, 1993 Promotional Materials; Telephone interview with Larry P. Anderson, manager dealer marketing, Cadillac Motor Car Division, General Motors Corporation, March 4, 1993; Telephone interview with Tucker Comstock, president Cameron Balloons, March 3, 1993.

Questions

1. How effective are hot-air balloons as brand-reminder advertising?

2. In your opinion, is the promotional impact of the corporate hot-air balloon greatest on the local, regional, or national level?

3. Why are local dealership tie-ins so crucial to the success of the Cadillac program?

Lands' End: Advertising with a Direction

Over the past 30 years Lands' End has become one of the most successful direct merchants of "cut-and-sewn" products in the United States. Customers can use Lands' End catalogs to order traditionally styled recreational and informal clothing for men, women, and children, shoes, accessories, and soft luggage without leaving their homes (see Exhibit A). The company's success stems in part from its policy of supplying quality merchandise at reasonable prices, backed by excellent customer service. However, customers might never have heard of Lands' End had it not been for an aggressive—and effective—advertising campaign.

Lands' End was founded in 1963 by former copywriter Gary Comer. The company was started in a basement along the river in Chicago's old tannery district. Comer and his staff were all sailors and initially the company supplied sailboat hardware and equipment by mail. Early catalogs included a clothing section to complement other products. Incidentally, the misplaced apostrophe in the company's logo is explained rather simply—it was a typo in the first printed piece, and it was too expensive to reprint and correct it.

In 1976 Lands' End decided to focus its efforts on selling "soft goods"—clothing and soft luggage. By 1979

Exhibit A

the company had moved to Dodgeville, Wisconsin, expanded the clothing offerings in its catalog, and began recruiting personnel experienced in the area of fabrics and clothing manufacturing. The company had been a leader in the integration of consumer advertising techniques with mail-order practices. By 1980 Lands' End was offering its line of quality cut-and-sewn clothing and luggage to about 400,000 customers, and sales were growing at better than 50 percent annually.

Despite this success, Comer remained convinced that his company had not realized its full potential. He consulted consumer-media specialist Richard C. Anderson, who recommended an ambitious, 5-year consumer-advertising plan that would focus on building a national reputation for quality, value, and service. The strategy ultimately called for placing Lands' End ads in the medium best suited to the targeted audience of upscale, professional people Comer's philosophy attracted—consumer magazines such as *New York*, *Smithsonian*, and *Travel and Leisure*. Exhibit B is the first ad ever run by Lands' End. The ads were full-page, black and white, with simple artwork (no photography) and detailed descriptive copy. Black-and-white ads were both cost-efficient and distinctive, and they typified the company philosophy of substance over flash. Ads included an address and a toll-free number that consumers could use to order a free catalog.

By 1981 Lands' End had begun its national advertising campaign to describe its business philosophy and expand its reputation for quality, value, and service. The campaign introduced the phrase "direct merchant" to illustrate the company's approach to its business.

This long-range image-building approach was a major departure from conventional mail-order advertising, which measured success by such short-term results as cost per inquiry and revenue per ad. Direct-mail advertising traditionally is relegated to small spaces in the back of books or the mail-order section of magazines where a coupon is offered for a catalog request. Lands' End advertising is more like product advertising. It always takes up an entire page and focuses on the company image and reputation.

The campaign proved so successful that it was extended beyond the "5-year mark" right through to the present. As indicated by Exhibit C, the style of the campaign is essentially unchanged. Note the consistency of

Exhibit B

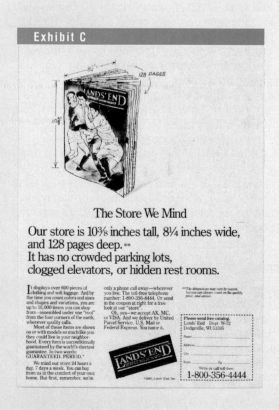

Exhibit C

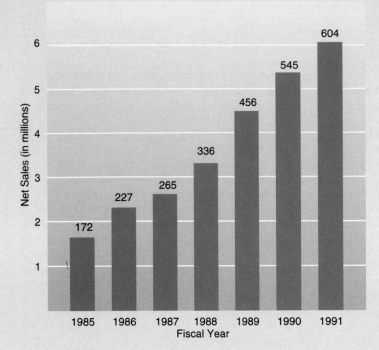

6

5

4

Net Sales (in millions)

3

2

1

604

545

456

336

265

227

172

1985   1986   1987   1988   1989   1990   1991

Fiscal Year

Exhibit D

Lands' End sales growth 1985 to 1991.

style in this ad compared with Exhibit B. How effective has the campaign been in recent years? Net income for the fiscal year ended January 31, 1991 was $14.7 million on net sales of $604 million, about 70 times what they were before the campaign was initiated in 1980. Exhibit D lists the company's sales growth since 1985.

In order to establish a relationship with its customers, Lands' End encloses a get-acquainted piece in catalogs sent to first-time customers. Exhibit E is an example of a Dodgeville piece that is enclosed in catalogs, which details the company's history and sets forward the Lands' End philosophy of quality, value, and service. The underlying message of the advertising is that the Lands' End people wouldn't sell anything they wouldn't wear themselves. Exhibit F is an example of a recent catalog. Exhibit G lists the Lands' End business principles Comer established from the very beginning, which became the foundation for the company's marketing philosophy.

The Lands' End Market

Recent market research has revealed a great deal of information about the 5.5 million Lands' End customers spread across the United States (a smaller number reside in Canada or overseas). Relatively larger concentrations live in metropolitan areas, in the major lake regions, and along the coastlines. Research has found that nearly nine out of ten customers have some level of college education. In comparison, this is only true for about 35 percent of the U.S. population. Lands'

End customers are five times more likely than the general population to have some level of postgraduate education. High education is reflected in the occupations of Lands' End customers. A high percentage are in professional and managerial positions, and many of the women are employed outside the home. Lands' End consumers fall primarily within the 25- to 54-year-old age group, with the largest portion between 35 to 44 years of age.

As a result of their professional and educational achievements, Lands' End customers are relatively affluent. Over two-thirds of Lands' End households have annual incomes above $35,000. Lands' End customers also tend to be participants and are involved in a broad range of personal interests. They tend to travel far more than the average American both for pleasure and business. They participate in a wide variety of active sports and differentiate themselves most from the general population by their interest in tennis, sailing, skiing, and gardening.

In order to appeal to these consumers, Lands' End has primarily relied on print advertising, particularly ads in upscale magazines. The company rents lists to look for potential customers. In addition, it includes subscription cards in catalogs for referrals of new customers. Lands' End was a well-kept secret for a long time, but it is now an outstanding example of how a well-managed company that produces quality goods can use a creative advertising approach to create a success story.

Courtesy of Lands' End.

Exhibit E

Exhibit F

Exhibit G

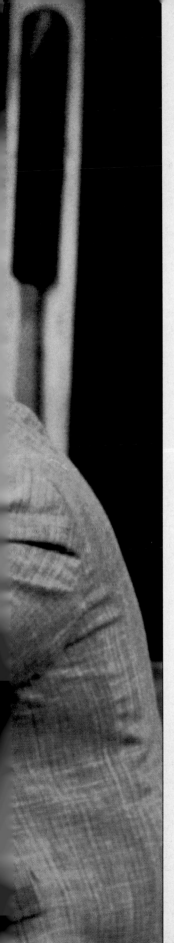

$\mathscr{S}$ALES PROMOTION

18

CHAPTER OBJECTIVES

When you have completed this chapter, you should be able to:

- Distinguish between sales promotion and advertising

- Explain how promotion and advertising work together within the marketing mix

- List several types of promotions, both for consumers and for resellers

- Understand why advertisers are spending increasing sums of money on sales promotion

- Explain the advantages and disadvantages of sales promotion as compared to advertising

CHEERS FOREVER

Cheers ended its epic run on NBC May 20, 1993, but not without one last call. NBC and *Cheers* producer Paramount Communications teamed up that night to offer the most massive merchandising event in television history.

To commemorate the end of the long-running series, Paramount and NBC offered viewers a one-time only opportunity to buy a piece of television history: a *Cheers* commemorative T-shirt that carried a "*Cheers* Last Call" logo. Paramount and NBC jointly designed the logo.

The project, however, faced several serious hurdles because of its potential massive response. NBC executives projected that the *Cheers* finale would deliver more than a 50 share (which it did) of all television homes and possibly as many as 100 million viewers, making it the second-highest rated show, right behind the season finale of CBS's *M*A*S*H* in 1983, which delivered 122 million viewers. The problem they faced was whether to insert a promotional spot in the episode, fearing that pitching the one-time-only product during the show would generate millions of orders, far more than their inbound telemarketing bureaus could process. "A spot placed during the height of an emotional event like that could generate tremendous volume," said an executive close to the project. "If millions of people go off-hook all at once, only tens of thousands actually get through and that would be under an ideal scenario using a combination of telephone services," another telemarketing executive said. Even the Home Shopping Network, which boasts the largest inbound telephone call capacity, can only process 15,000 calls during any given minute.

The NBC/Paramount dilemma suggests there are limitations on the ability to use mass television programming to market products instantaneously to consumers. Indeed, when CBS and MCA/Universal teamed up to offer *Northern Exposure* viewers a chance to buy sweatshirts featuring a logo of the CBS series, they were overwhelmed by the initial response, which was only in the multithousands. MCA/Universal was unable to process all the calls that night. In January 1991, Pepsi-Cola Company, at the last minute, scrapped a plan to run a spot in Super Bowl XXV with an 800-number call-in promotion, fearing it would overwhelm phone lines during the height of the Persian Gulf War.

NBC and Paramount considered two other options: creating a network of local phone operations or possibly offering the promotion only in a few select markets. They chose the latter. At least some fans have a *Cheers* remembrance.[1]

Most companies would like to have the problem NBC/Paramount faced. Imagine expecting sales of a product to be so high that taking orders fast enough was your major concern. Needless to say, not all sales-promotion programs produce this kind of result. Yet, there is substantial evidence that the promotional efforts of many businesses have moved away from advertising to sales promotion.

Advertising agencies, already faced with higher client expectations and cost problems (see Chapter 4), have been hit by reductions of 30 to 40 percent in media budgets by their major clients. Agencies initially reacted to this trend by arguing that advertising was a far more effective communication device than sales promotion. Some still believe this is true. Others have come to realize that sales promotion is here to stay, and they are learning how to incorporate it into the advertising campaign. Yet there is still a great deal of confusion about the definition of sales promotion, its role in marketing, and how it should interact with advertising.

---

[1] Adapted from Joe Mendese, "NBC Orders Up Massive Promo for 'Cheers' Finale," *Advertising Age* (April 19, 1993):3, 41.

$\mathcal{D}$EFINING SALES PROMOTION

sales promotion Those marketing activities that add value to the product for a limited period of time to stimulate consumer purchasing and dealer effectiveness.

The evolution of **sales promotion** has also changed the way experts define the practice. At one point, the official definition of sales promotion proposed by the American Marketing Association (AMA) was: "Marketing activities, other than personal selling, advertising, and publicity, that stimulate consumer purchasing and dealer effectiveness, such as displays, shows, exhibitions, demonstrations, and various nonrecurrent selling efforts not in the ordinary routine."[2]

In 1988 the AMA offered a new definition: "Sales promotion is media and nonmedia marketing pressure applied for a predetermined, limited period of time in order to stimulate trial, increase consumer demand, or improve product quality."[3] The Council of Sales Promotion Agencies offers a somewhat broader perspective: "Sales promotion is a marketing discipline that utilizes a variety of incentive techniques to structure sales-related programs targeted to consumers, trade, and/or sales levels that generate a specific, measurable action or response for a product or service."[4] All these definitions present sales promotion as a set of techniques that prompts members of the target audience to take action—preferably immediate action.

Principle

Sales promotion offers an extra incentive for consumers to take action.

We can refine the definitions by examining what sales promotion does today. Sales promotion offers an "extra incentive" for consumers to act. Although this extra incentive is usually in the form of a price reduction, it may be additional amounts of the product, cash, prizes, premiums, and so on. Furthermore, sales promotions usually include specified limits, such as an expiration date or a limited quantity of the merchandise. Finally, sales promotion has three somewhat different goals, which relate to its three target audiences: (1) to increase immediate *customer* sales, (2) to increase support among the marketer's *sales force*, and (3) to gain the support of *intermediaries* (resellers) in marketing the product.

$\mathcal{T}$HE SIZE OF SALES PROMOTION

Determining the actual size of the sales promotion industry is difficult; estimates vary according to which agency or research firm collects the data. For example, according to the *1992 Promotion Industry Expenditure Report*, revenues generated by promotional marketing services companies in 14 industry sectors reached $60.2 billion in 1992. The $60.2 billion figure pertains to consumer promotion, not trade spending, which would account for another $116.8 billion. The combined figures would bring total promotional spending to $177.0 billion for 1992. (See Table 18.1.) Current trends suggest that more dollars are now spent on sales promotion than on advertising (roughly 75 percent versus 25 percent, per Figure 18.1).[5] Sales promotion is growing at an annual rate of 8 percent. Finally, with the growth of sales promotion has come the growth of organizations supporting sales promotion. Virtually all major advertising agencies have

---

[2]American Marketing Association, *Marketing Definitions: A Glossary of Marketing Terms* (Chicago, 1960):20.
[3]Russ Brown, "Sales Promotion," *Marketing & Media Decisions* (February 1990):74.
[4]"Shaping the Future of Sales Promotion," *Council of Sales Promotion Agencies* (1990):3.
[5]Kenneth Wylie, "Integration to the Wave in Recharged $816.6 Million Industry; Newly Formed Gage and Alcove Tops on Their Specialties," *Advertising Age* (May 17, 1993):S–1.

Premium Incentives	$17,700,000
P-of-P Displays	15,700,000
Couponing	7,030,000
Specialty Advertising	5,220,000
Promotional Licensing	4,400,000
Sponsored Events	3,200,000
Specialty Printing	2,600,000
Fulfillment	2,200,000
Meas./Evaluation	728,000
Promotion Agencies	523,000
Telepromotions	435,000
Merchandising Services	238,000
Product Sampling	175,900
In-Store Advertising	116,800
TOTAL	$60,266,700

Source: "Still Climbing," PROMO (July 1993):128.

acquired a sales promotion subsidiary or have brought sales promotion in-house. Table 18.2 lists the top independent sales promotion agencies of 1992.

REASONS FOR THE GROWTH OF SALES PROMOTION

The statistics presented thus far pose one question: Why are companies spending more and more money on sales promotion? The chief reasons are the pressure for short-term profits, the accountability factor, economic factors, changes in the marketplace, and the increasing power of retailers.

Short-Term Solutions. Most U.S. companies have a drive for immediate profits and progress, which sales promotion satisfies. Vincent Sottasanti, president and CEO of the consulting firm Comart-KLP, states: "There's pressure on the brand manager and senior management as well for short-term profits as well as long-term goals."[6] Others agree that product managers are under pressure to generate quarterly sales increases. Because advertising's benefits are often apparent

---

[6]"Sales Promotion: What's Ahead?" *Advertising Age* (May 8, 1989):38.

Figure 18.1

The percentage spent
on consumer and trade
promotion compared to
advertising media.

*(Source: "Still Climbing," Promo
Magazine's 1994 SourceBook, July
1993, p. 128.)*

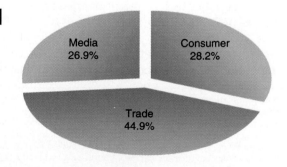

Media 26.9%   Consumer 28.2%   Trade 44.9%

Table 18.2

Table 18.2 Top Agencies by U.S. Sales Promotion Revenue

Rankings*			Agency, headquarters	U.S. sales promotion			Total U.S. revenue			Leading service by % of revenue	
All	PM	PS		1992	1991	% chg.	1992	1991	%		
1	–	1	**Gage Marketing Group,** Minneapolis	$67,106	$59,820	12.2	$67,106	$59,820	12.2	Fulfillment	43
2	1	–	**Alcone Sims O'Brien,** Irvine, Calif.	48,803	41,708	17.0	48,803	41,709	17.0	Strategic planning/concept development	40
3	–	2	**Lintas:Marketing Communications,** Warren, Mich.	36,411	34,459	5.7	76,376	60,526	26.2	NA	NA
4	–	3	**DCI Marketing,**** Milwaukee	35,400	36,929	-4.1	59,000	61,548	-4.1	Merchandising	60
5	2	–	**D.L. Blair,** Garden City, N.Y.	33,606	33,323	0.8	33,606	33,323	0.8	Concept development	32
6	3	–	**Marketing Corp. of America,** Westport, Conn.	31,042	27,134	14.4	31,042	27,134	14.4	Consulting	30
7	–	4	**Clarion Marketing & Communications,** Greenwich, Conn.	27,479	26,809	2.5	27,479	26,809	2.5	Direct marketing	20
8	4	–	**Ross Roy Group,** Bloomfield Hills, Mich.	27,074	25,384	6.7	81,400	80,600	1.0	Strategic planning	26
9	5	–	**Comart,** New York	25,659	28,056	-8.5	25,659	28,056	-8.5	Direct marketing	14
10	6	–	**Frankel & Co.,** Chicago	25,221	22,130	14.0	25,221	22,130	14.0	Strategic planning	50
11	7	–	**Wunderman Cato Johnson,** New York	20,725	23,926	-13.4	65,623	60,083	9.2	Strategic planning	50
12	8	5	**Ryan Partnership,** Westport, Conn.	18,959	14,699	29.0	18,959	14,699	29.0	Concept development	23
13	–	–	**Marden-Kane,** Mahasset, N.Y.	18,000	18,000	0.0	18,000	18,000	0.0	Sweepstakes/games/contests	40
14	–	6	**Schmidt-Cannon International,** City of Industry, Calif.	17,200	16,900	1.8	17,200	16,900	1.8	Premiums/incentives	50
15	9	–	**Flair Communications Agency,** Chicago	15,312	15,185	0.8	15,312	15,185	0.8	Strategic planning/concept development	30
16	10	–	**IMPACT,** Chicago	14,250	11,700	21.8	14,250	11,700	21.8	Strategic planning/concept development	60
17	–	7	**MarketSource,**** Cranbury, N.J.	13,500	12,375	9.1	30,000	27,500	9.1	Direct marketing	55
18	11	–	**QLM Associates,** Princeton, N.J.	12,545	12,184	3.0	12,545	12,184	3.0	Concept development	37
19	–	8	**Stratmar Systems,** Port Chester, N.Y.	1,000	14,000	-21.4	11,000	14,000	-21.4	Sampling	60
20	12	–	**Columbian Advertising,** Chicago	10,760	9,658	11.4	10,760	9,658	11.4	Strategic planning/direct marketing	40
21	13	–	**Communications Diversified,** New York	9,200	8,900	3.4	9,200	8,900	3.4	Graphics/collateral	23
22	14	–	**Einson Freeman,** Paramus, N.J.	9,029	7,032	28.4	9,029	7,032	28.4	Concept development	20
23	15	–	**Feldman Associates,** Chicago	8,500	7,200	18.1	8,500	7,200	18.1	Consulting	30
24	–	9	**Merchandising Workshop,** New York	8,000	9,500	-15.8	8,000	9,500	-15.8	Graphics/collateral	55
25	16	–	**Guild Group,** Pleasantville, N.Y.	7,951	6,833	16.4	7,951	6,833	16.4	Concept development	34

Notes: Dollars are in thousands.
Source: Reprinted with permission from Kenneth Wylie, "Sales Promotion," Advertising Age (May 17, 1993):S–1. Copyright, Crain Communications, Inc., 1993.

only in the long term, companies are investing more money in sales promotion, which generates immediate results.

Need for Accountability. Another reason for the growth is the accountability of sales promotion techniques. It is relatively easy to determine whether a given sales promotion strategy accomplished its stated objectives. Moreover, this assessment can be done rather quickly. Providing accountability is critical at a time when marketers want to know exactly what they are getting for their promotional dollars.

Economic Factors. Advertisers also cite economic reasons for the shift. Media costs have escalated to the point where alternatives must be thoroughly explored. The cost of mass-media advertising increased approximately 4 percent in 1991, compared to sales promotion cost increases of only 2 percent. But as the networks have been raising their prices, their share of prime-time television viewing has been dropping (to approximately 70 percent in 1988 from 92 percent in 1979). Advertisers therefore are exploring fresh new media forms that cost less and produce immediate, tangible results, and sales promotion is able to produce the desired results.

Consumer Behavior. Other reasons for the move toward sales promotion reflect changes in the marketplace. For instance, shoppers today are better educated, more selective, and less loyal to brand names than in the past. In addition, many new markets are developing because of demographic shifts. The affluent "gray" market, the "new man," the "yuppie," and the working woman are all markets that appear responsive to the benefits of sales promotion. The use of sales promotion targeted to the "mature" market is discussed in the Concepts and Applications Box.

From the consumer's perspective, sales promotion reduces the *risk* associated with purchase because promotions typically offer the consumer "more for less." This attitude was reinforced during the recession of the 1970s, when people were desperately looking for opportunities to save. That economic downturn introduced many consumers to the benefits of sales promotion, and they apparently enjoyed the experience.

Lack of New-Product Categories. Although we are constantly bombarded with the terms *new* and *improved*, very few entirely new product categories have emerged since World War II. Today's marketplace is characterized by mature product categories and considerable consumer experience and knowledge. In most industries, the battle is for market share rather than general product growth. In many instances advertising remains the best tool for launching new products, especially when the need for brand awareness is important. However, sales promotion is often the most effective strategy for increasing share and volume for an existing product.

The Pricing Cycle. Retail pricing has also been influential in creating opportunities for the increased use of sales promotion, particularly in the highly volatile supermarket environment. Prices soared during the inflationary 1970s as the result of increased costs of labor, raw materials, and manufacturing. This situation led to the growth of low-priced private-label brands and the emergence of generic products. Having adjusted to these lower-priced goods, consumers have

Promoting to the Mature Market

When Kraft General Foods wanted to find a way to perk up Sanka coffee sales, all it had to do was take a long look at the mature market. "Sanka is a venerable old trademark that had always been positioned for a mainstream audience," says Carolyn Lo Galbo, Maxwell House Category manager. "But when we looked into it, we learned that significant volume was coming from a more mature market."

In a planning effort lasting 18 months, the company repositioned Sanka with a new marketing program that pinpoints seniors. Instead of relying solely on FSIs, or *free-standing inserts*, promotional efforts now focus on targeted media: coupons tipped into *Modern Maturity* magazine and also delivered by direct mail via Carol Wright Plus, the new name for Donnelley Marketing's 14 million 50-plus household database. The transformation eventually will encompass new easy-open packaging with larger print that avoids hard to read drop-out type.

Marketers do not have to go for an all-out product repositioning as did Sanka, but promotions targeted to the over-50 market can help boost sales. Nabisco recently ran several programs that generated exposure and promotional opportunities in 1,400 of the nation's 15,000 senior centers. The Senior Network (TSN), based in Stamford, Connecticut, coordinated the effort. The group maintains "informational wallboards" in senior centers; one promotion offered a free nutrition chart, refrigerator magnet, and coupons for Fleischmann's margarine, Egg Beaters, and Nabisco's Shredded Wheat cereal to seniors who filled out business reply cards they found on the wallboards.

A new TSN continuity program called "Golden Gifts" is currently being launched. It encourages center members to collect product proofs of purchase and redeem them for items that benefit the center, such as big-screen televisions and recreational equipment. Participants include brands from Kellogg's, Quaker Oats, Bristol-Myers, Nabisco, Kraft General Foods, Polaroid, Bausch & Lomb, and Ocean Spray. "Golden Gifts plays off the center members' community spirit by offering a way of earning gifts or equipment and at the same time generating unit sales for participating brands," says Frederick Adler, TSN president.

Natural Nectar Corporation of Santa Monica, California, reported an excellent response to the prime-time sampling of its Fi-Bar snack bar. The effort, which was part of the company's first foray into mature marketing, taught it a valuable lesson: Next time, literature with Fi-Bar samples will tell consumers where to find the snack bars. "We didn't sample a huge quantity, but our numbers are up globally and we think the activity was due to our campaign in *Modern Maturity*," notes marketing director Rick Persley. "The mature market is a vital group, they're not sitting in rocking chairs," says Ray Lewis of Larry Tucker Inc., which maintains a list of 17.5 million households of adults 50 to 65 years old.

Adapted from Glenn Heitsmith, "Heading for the New Age Frontier," Promo (November 1992):10, 22–23.

---

come to expect constant short-term price reductions such as coupons, sales, and price promotions.

The Power of the Retailer. The final reason for the growth of sales promotion is the increasing power of the modern retailer. Dominant players, such as Safeway, Wal-Mart, K Mart, Toys 'R' Us, and Home Depot, demand a variety of promotional incentives before allowing products into their stores. Obtaining desirable shelf location requires special in-store merchandising support. Procter & Gamble, for example, estimates that 25 percent of sales time and approximately 30 percent of brand-management time are spent in designing, implementing, and overseeing promotions.[7]

---

[7] Robert D. Buzzell, John A. Quelch, and Walter J. Salmon, "The Costly Bargain of Sales Promotion," *Harvard Business Review* (March–April 1990):141.

PEANUTS *reprinted by permission of UFS, Inc.*

THE ROLE OF SALES PROMOTION IN MARKETING

As explained in Chapter 3, sales promotion is just one element of the marketing communication mix available to the marketer, the other three being personal selling, advertising, and public relations. Because of its unique characteristics, however, the various sales promotion techniques we just discussed can accomplish certain communication goals that the other elements cannot.

For example, research suggests that there are certain things that sales promotion can and cannot do. Promotion alone cannot create an image for a brand. It cannot compensate for low levels or lack of advertising. It cannot do much to change negative attitudes toward a product, overcome product problems, or reverse a declining sales trend. But promotion can help introduce a new product as well as build a brand over time by reinforcing advertising images and messages, by generating positive brand experiences among buyers in many places along the purchase continuum, by creating an affinity between brands and buyers, and by providing new channels for reaching audience segments.

Promotion can offer consumers an immediate inducement to buy a product, often by the simple step of making the product more valuable. Promotion can cause consumers who know nothing about your product to try it, and it can persuade them to buy again.[8]

---

[8]J. Brian Robinson, "Promotion is a New Way to Make Brand Contact With Buyers," *The Marketing News* (April 12, 1993):2, 16.

Sales promotion should be incorporated into the company's strategic marketing planning, along with advertising, personal selling, and public relations. This means establishing sales promotion goals and selecting appropriate strategies. A separate budget should be set up for sales promotion. Finally, management should evaluate the sales promotion performance.

Although all these elements are important, setting promotional objectives is particularly important. Our definition of sales promotion implied three broad objectives:

1. To stimulate demand by industrial users or household consumers
2. To improve the marketing performance of resellers
3. To supplement and coordinate advertising, personal selling, and public relations activities

The more specific objectives of sales promotion are quite similar to those of advertising. For example, in order to *get customers to try a new product*, companies such as Del Monte, Ralph Lauren, Wilkinson Sword, and VLI's Today sponge distribute over 500,000 free samples in Daytona Beach each spring break. To *encourage increased spending during the holiday season*, Kraft food products and Hasbro toys participated in a joint promotion through a nationally distributed free-standing newspaper insert that included cents-off coupons and rebates on toys. To *encourage present customers to use the product more often* in France, Orangina sales rocketed when the tangerine-flavored soft drink tied in with a fast-food chain to offer music-related premiums to consumers who ordered the drink.

Thus, sales promotion has become an important element in the strategy of many marketers. Like advertising, it is not right for everyone, however, and it will be effective only if it is carefully managed.

THE RELATIONSHIP BETWEEN SALES PROMOTION AND ADVERTISING

As we mentioned earlier, advertising and sales promotion are two of the elements that make up the promotional mix. These two elements have a number of similarities and often work together toward a common goal, but they also differ in many ways.

DIFFERENCES AND SIMILARITIES

Differences. The major differences between advertising and sales promotion concern their methods of appeal and the value they add to the sale of the product or service. Whereas advertising is interested in creating an image and will take the time to do so, sales promotion is interested in creating immediate action, preferably a sale. In order to accomplish this immediate goal, sales promotion relies heavily on rational appeals, whereas advertising relies on emotional appeals to promote the product's image. Advertising also tends to add intangible value to the good or service and makes a moderate contribution to profitability. In contrast, sales promotion adds tangible value to the good or service and contributes greatly to profitability (see Table 18.3).

Table 18.3

The Differences Between
Advertising and Sales Promotion

Advertising	Sales Promotion
■ Creates an image over time	■ Creates immediate action
■ Relies on emotional appeals	■ Relies on rational appeals
■ Adds intangible value to the product or service	■ Adds tangible value to the product or service
■ Contributes moderately to profitability	■ Contributes greatly to profitability

Similarities. Advertising and sales promotion also have much in common. According to Leonard Lodish, an international expert on sales promotion, the two share the same roles: to increase the number of customers and to increase the use of the product by current customers. Both tasks attempt to change audience perceptions about the product or service, and both attempt to make people do something.[9] Of course, the specific techniques used to accomplish these tasks differ.

INTRODUCING A NEW PRODUCT

One area in which advertising and promotion work well together is the introduction of new products and services. Suppose we are introducing a new corn chip named Corn Crunchies. Our first challenge is to create awareness of this product. This is the real strength of advertising. However, sometimes advertising should be combined with an appropriate sales promotion device calling attention to the advertising and the brand name. Possibilities are colorful point-of-purchase displays, a reduced introductory price, and a special tie-in with a well-known chip dip company.

Creating awareness will only take the product so far, however. Corn Crunchies must also be perceived as offering some clear benefit compared to the competitors to convince consumers to purchase it. Advertising promotes this perception through informational and transformational executions. Recall from Chapter 8, informational advertising provides meaningful facts to the consumer when needed, whereas transformational advertising moves the consumer emotionally to a point of greater acceptance. Sales promotion enhances the message by offering coupons as part of the ad (known as an *overlay* ad), mailing free samples of Corn Crunchies to households, and conducting a contest in conjunction with the product introduction during the July 4th holiday. Ad 18.1 for Rubbermaid food containers is an example of an overlay ad. If we have successfully implemented this *pull strategy*, consumers will be convinced of the value of Corn Crunchies and go to their supermarkets and demand that the product be stocked. By asking for it, they will *pull* it through the channel of distribution.

Unfortunately, creating awareness and desire means nothing unless the product is available where the consumer thinks it should be. Somehow resellers (the trade) must be convinced that the product will move off the shelves before they will stock it. Therefore, a *push promotional strategy* is used to convince members of the distribution network to carry and market Corn Crunchies. We literally *push* the product through the channel. This is accomplished through two

[9]Leonard M. Lodish, *The Advertising and Promotion Challenge* (New York: Oxford University Press, 1986):18.

Rubbermaid Servin' Saver™ Food Containers.
For use at home or anywhere. This summer, keep
your picnic fresh and flavorful, neat and nice.
A container and serving dish all in one! See-thru
and seal-tight, they snap closed easily, lift open
quickly with handy tab. Perfect!

Picnic perfect.

Don't you wish everything
was made like

Rubbermaid ®

c 1986 by Rubbermaid Incorporated,
Wooster, Ohio 44691

Ad 18.1

Advertisers often offer
coupons as part of the
ad to enhance the sales
promotion message.

*(Courtesy of Rubbermaid
Incorporated)*

devices, *trade advertising* and *trade sales promotion*. Trade advertising directed at
wholesalers and retailers can be effective in providing resellers with important
information. In addition, trade sales promotion techniques, especially price discounts, point-of-purchase displays, and advertising allowances, help to gain
shelf space.

In reality, most marketers use some combination of push and pull strategies.
Using one to the exclusion of the other would usually prove risky, given the need
to appeal to both customers—reseller and consumer.

After the initial purchase we want the customer to repeat purchase, and we
also want retailers to allocate more shelf space to Corn Crunchies. This means
that advertising copy is changed to remind customers about the positive experience they had with the product, and sales promotion is used to reinforce their
loyalty with coupons, rebates, and other rewards. Retailers will be rewarded as

well, with a predictable customer who will not only buy the product being promoted but will also purchase other products while in the store.

CAN SALES PROMOTION BUILD BRANDS?

For several years now there has been a heated debate between the advertising industry and the sales promotion industry concerning brand building. Advertisers claim that the strength of advertising is creating and maintaining brand image and that sales promotion negates all their hard work by diverting the emphasis from the brand to the price. The result is a brand-insensitive consumer. Critics of sales promotion cite the price-cutting strategies followed by Coke and Pepsi as an example of two brands that are now interchangeable in the minds of many consumers. On any given weekend, especially holiday weekends, Coke and Pepsi product displays are located on end-of-the-aisle caps or island displays featuring per-case prices as low as $4 and six-pack prices as low as $1.29, down from the regular price of $5.50 and $2.69, respectively. Procter & Gamble's division manager of advertising and sales promotion, V. O. "Bud" Hamilton, describes the situation as follows: "Too many marketers no longer adhere to the fundamental premise of brand building, which is that franchises aren't built by cutting price but rather by offering superior quality at a reasonable price and clearly communicating that value to consumers. . . . The price-cutting patterns begun in the early 1970s continue today, fostering a short-term orientation that has caused long-term brand building to suffer."[10] Critics point to a general decline in consumer brand loyalty as just one negative consequence caused by sales promotion.

Experts in sales promotion respond to this criticism in two ways. First, they argue that the claim that sales promotion destroys brand image is greatly exaggerated. They refer to many cereal brands, rental car companies, airlines, and hotels that have used a variety of well-planned sales promotion strategies to enhance their brand image. Hertz, for example, uses price promotions regularly, yet they have increased sales and market share both during and after these promotions. Second, they acknowledge that *continuous* promotion—particularly continuous price promotion—does not always work. They point to situations in which an entire advertising/promotion budget has been committed to a single promotion technique, causing the brand to self-destruct. Sears's predictable price reductions are a classic example of a company that destroyed its brand name through poor promotion planning,. Conversely, continuous sales promotion can and does work if it is part of a well-analyzed and well-executed strategy. Furthermore, such promotion works most efficiently when it is part of a well-integrated advertising/promotion plan.

Finally, the criticism that sales promotion destroys brand loyalty appears to be exaggerated. In a 17-year tracking survey of brand equity conducted by HPD Group, the results show that loyalty to top brands has been steady since 1987.[11] Besides, notes Michael Schrage, "traditional advertising no longer has the responsibility of maintaining brand equity. Product value is no longer created through advertising imagery, it is determined by the price/performance relationship.[12]

---

[10]Scott Hume, "Rallying to Brands' Rescue," *Advertising Age* (August 13, 1990):3.
[11]Scott Hume, "Brand Loyalty Steady," *Advertising Age* (March 2, 1992):19.
[12]Michael Schrage, "Reinventing the Wheel," *Adweek* (April 6, 1993):23.

TYPES OF SALES PROMOTION

Principle

Consumer sales promotion is most effective if the product or service is presold by advertising.

Sales promotion strategies are divided into three primary types: end-user or consumer, reseller or trade, and salesforce strategies. The first two have direct implications for advertising and will be discussed in some detail. Salesforce sales promotions are simply activities directed at the firm's salespeople to motivate them to strive to increase their sales levels. These activities are classified in two ways. The first set of activities includes programs that better prepare salespeople to do their jobs, such as sales manuals, training programs, and sales presentations, as well as supportive materials like films, slides, videos, and other visual aids. The second set of activities is concerned with promotional efforts or incentives that will motivate salespeople to work harder. Contests dominate this category.

CONSUMER SALES PROMOTION

Consumer sales promotions are directed at the ultimate user of the good or service. They are intended to "presell" consumers so that when people go into a store they will look for a particular brand. Most often, consumer sales promotions are the responsibility of the product manager, along with the advertising campaign planner, the advertising department, or a sales promotion agency or advertising agency.

The primary strengths of consumer sales promotions are their variety and flexibility. There are a large number of techniques that can be combined to meet almost any objective of the sales promotion planner. This flexibility means that sales promotion can be employed by all kinds of businesses. Figure 18.2 depicts the relative use of the primary sales promotion techniques, comparing 1991 with 1993.

price deal A temporary reduction in the price of a product.

Price Deals. A temporary reduction in the price of a product is called a **price deal**. Price deals are commonly used to encourage trial of a new product, to persuade existing users to buy more or at a different time, or to convince new users to try an established product. They are effective only if price is an important factor in brand choice or if consumers are not brand loyal.

There are two principal types of consumer price deals: cents-off deals and price-pack deals. A *cents-off deal* is a reduction in the normal price charged for a good or service (for example, "was $1,000, now $500," or "50 percent off"). Cents-off deals can be announced at the point of sale or through mass or direct advertising. Point-of-sale announcements include the package itself and signs near the product or elsewhere in the store. Advertising includes sales flyers, newspaper ads, and broadcast ads. Both types of cents-off deals can be initiated by the manufacturer, the wholesaler, or the retailer. (See Ad 18.2.)

Price-pack deals provide the consumer with something extra through the package itself. There are two types of pack deals: bonus packs and banded packs. *Bonus packs* contain additional amounts of the product free when the standard size is purchased at the regular price. For example, Purina Dog Food may offer 25 percent more dog food in the bag. Often this technique is used to introduce a new large-size package of the product. When one or more units of a product are sold at a reduced price compared to the regular single-unit price, a

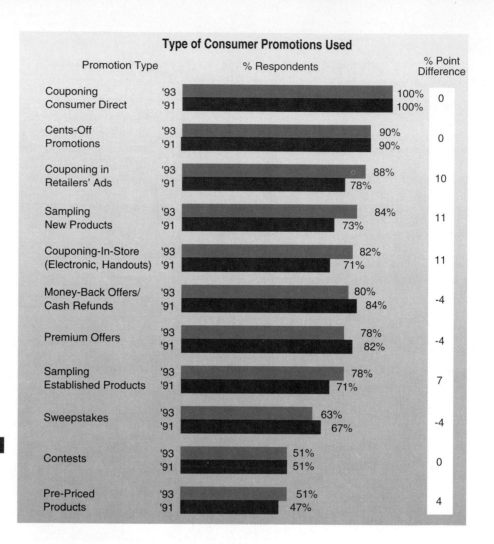

Type of Consumer Promotions Used

Promotion Type		% Respondents	% Point Difference
Couponing Consumer Direct	'93	100%	0
	'91	100%	
Cents-Off Promotions	'93	90%	0
	'91	90%	
Couponing in Retailers' Ads	'93	88%	10
	'91	78%	
Sampling New Products	'93	84%	11
	'91	73%	
Couponing-In-Store (Electronic, Handouts)	'93	82%	11
	'91	71%	
Money-Back Offers/ Cash Refunds	'93	80%	-4
	'91	84%	
Premium Offers	'93	78%	-4
	'91	82%	
Sampling Established Products	'93	78%	7
	'91	71%	
Sweepstakes	'93	63%	-4
	'91	67%	
Contests	'93	51%	0
	'91	51%	
Pre-Priced Products	'93	51%	4
	'91	47%	

Figure 18.2

Type of consumer promotions used.

(Source: Donnelley Marketing's 16th Annual Survey of Promotional Practices)

banded pack is being offered. Sometimes the products are physically banded together. The Pillsbury Company has been banding three cans of their biscuits together for many years. Bar soap, such as Dial, often is offered this way. In most cases the products are simply offered as two-for, three-for, five-for, and so on.

Coupons. Legal certificates offered by manufacturers and retailers that grant specified savings on selected products when presented for redemption at the point of purchase are called **coupons**. *Manufacturer-sponsored coupons* can be redeemed at any outlet distributing the product. *Retailer-sponsored coupons* can only be redeemed at the specified retail outlet. The primary advantage of the coupon is that it allows the advertiser to lower prices without relying on cooperation from the retailer.

There are several disadvantages associated with coupons, however. Over 91 percent of consumer product marketers used coupons in 1992, but the redemption rate was only 2.3 percent for those delivered through FSIs and 4 to 6 percent for those delivered through direct mail. Depending on the product category, between 60 to 90 percent of coupons are delivered through free-standing inserts. Insert fees (the fees newspapers charge for inserting FSIs) are increasing dra-

coupons Legal certificates offered by manufacturers and retailers that grant specified savings on selected products when presented for redemption at the point of purchase.

matically, making coupon distribution very expensive. To limit their liability, manufacturers are reducing the time between distribution and expiration. The average coupon distributed during 1992 had a duration of 3.9 months, compared with 4.4 months in 1991. Another problem is misredemption (accidentally or intentionally misredeeming coupons) and, finally, fraud (counterfeit coupons).[13]

Manufacturer-sponsored coupons can be distributed directly (direct mail, door-to-door), through media (newspaper/magazine ads, free-standing inserts), in or on the package itself, or through the retailer (co-op advertising). Manufacturers also pay retailers a fee for handling their coupons. Ad 18.3 is an example of a typical coupon ad.

In 1991, 314 billion coupons were distributed in the United States, and 7.5 billion were redeemed. This was a 4.5 percent increase over 1990. Projections for 1992 are for a 10 percent increase, with redemptions exceeding 8 billion. Coupon face value averaged 57 cents, or 5 cents higher than 1990. Up to 77 percent of U.S. households use coupons to some degree, many of them saving as

---

[13]Scott Hume, "Coupon Use Jumps 10% as Distribution Soars," *Advertising Age* (October 5, 1992):3.

much as $1,000 a year.[14] According to a 1993 study conducted by the Food Marketing Institute, coupon usage does vary:

- Shoppers who live in the East and Midwest are most likely to use coupons.
- One-person households are the most infrequent users of coupons.
- The most avid coupon users are those with a high school education or less and those in the $15,000 to $25,000 annual income bracket.
- Only 32 percent of shoppers under age 24 use coupons.[15]

contests Sales promotion activities that require participants to compete for a prize on the basis of some skill or ability.

sweepstakes Sales promotion activities that require participants to submit their names to be included in a drawing or other type of chance selection.

game A type of sweepstake that requires the player to return to play several times.

Contests and Sweepstakes. The popularity of contests and sweepstakes grew dramatically during the 1980s. These strategies create excitement by promising "something for nothing" and offering impressive prizes. **Contests** require participants to compete for a prize or prizes on the basis of some sort of skill or ability. **Sweepstakes** require only that participants submit their names to be included in a drawing or other chance selection. A **game** is a type of sweepstake. It differs from a one-shot drawing-type of sweepstake in that the time frame is much longer. A continuity is established, requiring customers to return several

---

[14]Kerry Smith, "Cents-Off Currency: The Case for Chaos," *Promo* (April 1992):29–32.
[15]Bob Gatty, "Consumers Using Fewer Coupons," *Promo* (June 1993):85.

times to acquire additional pieces (such as bingo-type games) or to improve their chances of winning.

A good contest or sweepstakes generates a high degree of consumer involvement, which can revive lagging sales, help obtain on-floor displays, provide merchandising excitement for dealers and salespeople, give vitality and a theme to advertising, and create interest in a low-interest product. Contests are viewed favorably by advertising designers because the copy tends to write itself as long as it is supported by background enthusiasm and excitement.

Conversely, contests and sweepstakes also have the potential for tremendous disasters. Two recent examples come to mind. The more serious occurred in 1992, when Anheuser-Busch acknowledged its "Bud Summer Games" sweepstake had been launched with an accidental printing of a "very small" number of winning second-place tickets beyond the number originally planned. The contest originally called for 500 winning second-place tickets out of 60 million printed in magazines and free-standing inserts. Winning numbers could claim a Kawasaki jet ski or $4,000. To correct the error, Anheuser-Busch announced it would double to 1,000 the number of $4,000 cash/jet ski prizes it would give away, at an additional cost of $2 million. It also announced a random drawing that would be held among the additional winners for the prizes that Anheuser-Busch added after the mishap occurred. As for the winning second-place entries in the original contest, the winners received prizes based on whether their entries had the proper "verification symbols." The symbols did not appear on the accidentally printed winning entries.[16] The second snafu took place when New York City trash collectors discovered approximately 2,000 Publishers Clearing House sweepstakes envelopes with entry forms strewn along the railroad tracks in the borough of Queens. The dumping incident prompted the company to set up a new facility for opening envelopes and removing entry forms. In addition, a full-time Publishers Clearing House employee now supervises all work done by outside contractors.[17]

refund An offer by the marketer to return a certain amount of money to the consumer who purchases the product.

Refunds and Rebates. Simply stated, a **refund** is an offer by the marketer to return a certain amount of money to the consumer who purchases the product. Most refunds encourage product purchase by creating a deadline. The details of the refund offer are generally distributed through print media or direct mail. General information may be delivered through broadcast media. Refunds are attractive because they stimulate sales without the high cost and waste associated with coupons. The key to success is to make the refund as uncomplicated and unrestrictive as possible. The refund may take the form of a cash *rebate* plus a low-value coupon for the same product or other company products, a high-value coupon alone, or a coupon good toward the brand purchased plus several other brands in the manufacturer's line.

In a 1992 survey, 85 percent of the respondents would rather use a coupon valued at $1 than send in for a refund worth $2. Furthermore, 40 percent of U.S. consumers had taken the time to mail in a refund over the past year, compared to more than 70 percent who regularly use coupons.[18]

premium A tangible reward received for performing a particular act, such as purchasing a product or visiting the point of purchase.

Premium Offers. A **premium** is a tangible reward received for performing a particular act, usually purchasing a product or visiting the point of purchase. The

---

[16]Ira Teinowitz, "Anheuser-Busch to Polish 'Bud Summer Games' After Ticket Fiasco," *Advertising Age* (May 25, 1992):4.
[17]Glenn Heitsmith, "Prosecutors Eye 'No Purchase' Claims," *Promo* (March 1993):1.
[18]Glenn Heitsmith, "Rebates are Getting a Bad Rap," *Promo* (March 1993):10, 42.

Table 18.4

Incentives by the Billions

The Incentive Field at a Glance (in $ billions)	
Trade Incentives	
Merchandise	$6.6
Travel	2.7
Consumer Premiums	6.7
Business Gifts	1.8
Total promotion	$17,729,419,000

1992 Top 20 Incentive Users by Industry (in $ millions)	
Retailers	$2,928
Food Industry	1,995
Wholesalers and Distributors	1,793
Toiletries and Cosmetics	1,250
Misc. Services	1,170
Auto Parts, Tires, Accessories	1,024
Misc. Manufacturers	981
Insurance	913
Electronics, Radio, TV	588
Autos and Trucks	531
Building Materials	440
Publishers, Printers, Broadcasters	328
Heating and Air Conditioning	325
Office Equipment	325
Petroleum Products	299
Beer, Ale, and Softdrinks	292
Detergents and Cleansers	284
Feed, Fertilizer, and Farm Supplies	242
Farm Equipment	241
Electric Appliances	138

Source: Incentive Magazine (December 1992); Glenn Heitsmith, "Building Brand Image the Premium Way," Promo (May 1993):81.

toy in Cracker Jacks, glassware in a box of detergent, and a transistor radio given for taking a real estate tour are examples of premiums. Premiums are usually free. If not, the charge tends to be quite low.

As indicated in Table 18.4, over $17 billion were spent on all premiums in 1992, with $6.7 billion going to consumer premiums.

Direct Premiums There are two general types of premiums: direct and mail. *Direct premiums* award the incentive immediately, at the time of purchase. There are four variations of direct premiums:

1. Store premiums: given to customers at the retail site
2. In-packs: inserted in the package at the factory
3. On-packs: placed on the outside of the package at the factory
4. Container premiums: the package is the premium

Mail Premiums In contrast, *mail premiums* require the customer to take some action before receiving the premium. The original mail premium is called a *self-liquidator*. Self-liquidators usually require that some proof of purchase and payment be mailed in before receiving the premium. The amount of payment is sufficient to cover the cost of the item, handling, mailing, packaging, and taxes, if any. The food industry is the largest user of self-liquidating premiums. Country Pride Fresh Chicken, for example, offers an apron in exchange for the proof-of-purchase of their product (see Ad 18.4). The *coupon plan* or *continuity-coupon plan* is the second type of mail premium. It requires the customer to save coupons or special labels attached to the product that can be redeemed for merchandise. This plan has been used by cigarette and diaper manufacturers. The final type of mail premium is the *free-in-the-mail* premium. In this case the customer mails in a purchase request and proof of purchase to the advertiser. For example, Procter & Gamble offered a discount on a down comforter premium with proof of purchase of White Cloud toilet paper.

One advantage of premiums is their ability to enhance an advertising campaign or a brand image. The best examples of this strategy are those brands or companies that are symbolized by characters such as the Campbell Soup Kids, Charlie the Tuna, Tony the Tiger, Cap'n Crunch, Ronald McDonald, and the Pillsbury Doughboy.

Specialty Advertising. Advertising specialties are similar to premiums, except that the consumer does not have to purchase anything in order to receive the specialty item. These items normally have a promotional message printed on them somewhere. Although specialties are often given away as year-end gifts (the calendar hanging in the kitchen), they can be used throughout the year in particular sales situations. For example, some specialties, including pens, pencils, and organizers, are ideal for desktops. Other items work well because they are attention-grabbing novelties. Balloons, fans, litter bags, and tote bags fall into this category. The ideal specialty item is something that is kept out in the open where a great number of people can see it, such as a calendar or penholder dis-

---

Ad 18.4

Self-liquidating premiums require the consumer to mail in proof-of-purchase before receiving the premium.

(Courtesy of Country Pride Chicken)

Specialty items can be effective memory devices if they are useful and reasonably well made.

(Teri Stratford)

playing the company's name. Most notably, the cost of specialty advertising is often quite high, especially in comparison to the actual value derived. A specialty silkscreened baseball hat may cost as much as $11.00.

The 15,000-plus specialty items that are manufactured by companies are used for a variety of marketing purposes: thanking customers for patronage, reinforcing established products or services, generating sales leads. Specialty advertising has numerous advantages, but it also has some disadvantages.

Some people question the value of specialty advertising. A study sponsored by Specialty Advertising Association of Greater New York, however, suggests the contrary. Consider this: (1) 83 percent of consumers use such products; (2) 94 percent appreciate receiving them; (3) 94 percent have a positive attitude toward the advertiser.[19]

continuity program A program that requires the consumer to continue purchasing the product or service in order to receive a reward.

Continuity Programs. A **continuity program** requires the consumer to continue purchasing the product in order to receive the benefit or reward. The purpose of any type of continuity program is to tie consumers to the organization by rewarding them for their loyalty. Typically, the higher the purchase level, the greater the benefits. In the 1950s and 1960s the popular type of continuity program was trading stamps. Today continuity programs are synonymous with the word "frequent." Frequent-flier clubs sponsored by airlines are the model of a modern continuity program. They offer a variety of rewards, including seat upgrades, free tickets, and premiums based on the number of frequent-flier miles accumulated. Continuity programs work in very competitive situations where the consumer has difficulty perceiving real differences between brands. For example, in a joint continuity program American Airlines offered College Savings Bank's College Sure certificate of deposit (CD) as a premium for the airline's A Advantage frequent-flier members. The CD, designed to help parents save for their children's college educations, has a lower price (about $16,400 per unit, rather than $18,000) and higher yield (a minimum interest rate of 5 percent) than the bank's standard CDs (4 percent).[20]

sampling An offer that allows the customer to use or experience the product or service free of charge or for a very small fee.

Consumer Sampling. Allowing the consumer to experience the product or service free of charge or for a small fee is called **sampling**. It is a very effective strat-

[19]"Consumers Notice Specialty Items," *Promo* (June 1992):74.
[20]Alison Fahey and Bradley Johnson, "Frequent Shopper Programs Ripen," *Advertising Age* (August 6, 1990):21.

egy for introducing a new or modified product or for dislodging an entrenched market leader. To be successful, the product sampled must virtually sell itself on the basis of a certain uniqueness and ability to create a strong positive impact with minimal trial experience.

Samples can be distributed to consumers in several ways. The most common method is through the mail. An alternative is to hire companies specializing in door-to-door distribution. Advertisers can design ads with coupons for free samples, place samples in special packages, or distribute samples at special in-store displays. Ad 18.5 for Sampling Corporation of America suggests how targeted a sampling program can be.

Quaker Oats provides an interesting example of product sampling. The program involved their new Quaker Oat Cups shelf-stable oatmeal cereal. In Chicago, sample crews took to the streets during the morning rush hours handing out free Quaker Oat Cups to workers outside office buildings and near train stations. Because the product was already premixed with water, workers could then zap Quaker Oat Cups in the office microwave to enjoy a hot oatmeal breakfast.[21]

In general, retailers and manufacturers maintain that sampling can boost sales volume as much as five to ten times during a product demonstration and 10 to 15 percent thereafter. Sampling is generally most effective when reinforced on the spot with product coupons. Most consumers like sampling because they do not lose any money if they do not like the product.[22]

Although all of these consumer sales promotion techniques can be effective alone, they can also be combined to create a tremendous impact. The Nestlé Foods Corporation did just this with the material shown in Ad 18.6. The company positioned three of its products—Raisinets®, Goobers®, and Crunch™— as the "Home Video Candy" in a promotion where consumers could redeem a

[21]Glenn Heitsmith, "Try It, You'll Like It," *Promo* (September 1992):6.
[22]*The Wall Street Journal* (August 28, 1986):19.

Ad 18.5

This ad is targeted at companies who might want to sample to school children.

(Courtesy of Sampling Corporation of America)

Your Apples* Can Reach Kids Where They Do The Most Good – IN SCHOOL!

TEEN CO-OPS — 5MM April & 5MM September, non-duplicating, gender specific

ELEMENTARY SCHOOL CO-OP — 7 MM October, household income 25M or greater

1993 CUSTOM PROGRAMS — Reach up to 16MM age 6-12, 14MM teens — through schools

*Your apples might be cereal, candy, shampoo, or gym shoes! Give our proven vehicles a chance to produce tasty results for your brand! Call us today — we'll polish one up for you.

CALL **708/296-7032**
SAMPLING CORPORATION OF AMERICA

TARGETED IN-SCHOOL SCA COUPONING/SAMPLING PROGRAMS

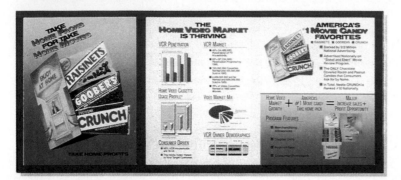

mail-in certificate with any VCR movie rental receipt along with proof-of-purchase and receive $2 cash rebate. The certificate was available in free-standing inserts and at point-of-purchase displays, and the three candy products were packaged in a take-home pack. The promotion was developed by Saxton Communications Group, New York.

RESELLER (TRADE) SALES PROMOTION

Resellers, or intermediaries, are the 1.3 million retailers and 338,000 wholesalers who distribute the products made by manufacturers to other resellers and ultimate users. The manufacturer usually is certain the product is acceptable only if resellers are willing to carry and *push* it. Sales promotion is used to bring resellers to that point of conviction.

Reseller sales promotions are intended to accomplish four overall goals:

1. Stimulate in-store merchandising or other trade support (for example, feature pricing, superior store location, and/or shelf space)

2. Manipulate levels of inventory held by wholesalers and retailers

3. Expand product distribution to new areas of the country or new classes of trade

4. Create a high level of excitement about the product among those responsible for its sale

The ultimate gauge of a successful reseller promotion is whether sales increase among ultimate users.

The actual size/worth of trade promotions is difficult to accurately determine. Although this category represented nearly 45 percent of total promotional spending, this varies by industry and size of business. Moreover, there are millions (or perhaps billions) of trade dollars that are difficult to trace. There does appear to be a shift, however, away from trade promotion toward consumer promotions.

A great many promotional devices that are designed to motivate resellers to engage in certain sales activities are available to the manufacturer. The major ones are discussed in the following paragraphs.

point-of-purchase display (P-O-P) A display designed by the manufacturer and distributed to retailers in order to promote a particular brand or line of products.

Point-of-Purchase Displays. A **point-of-purchase display (P-O-P)** is designed by the manufacturer and distributed to retailers in order to promote a particular brand or group of products. Although the forms vary by industry, P-O-P can include special racks, display cartons, banners, signs, price cards, and mechanical product dispensers. Point of purchase is the only advertising that occurs when all the elements of the sale—the consumer, the money, and the product—come together at the same time. As we move toward a self-service retail environment in which fewer and fewer customers expect help from sales clerks, the role of point of purchase will continue to increase. According to the Point of Purchase Advertising Institute (POPAI), 66 percent of purchase decisions are made in the store rather than before entering the store.[23]

Principle

Point of purchase brings all the elements of the sale together: the consumer, the product, and the money.

Point of purchase is a big-business effort ($15 billion in 1991) that must be well though out if it is to be successful.[24] Advertisers must consider not only whether P-O-P is appealing to the end user but also whether it will be used by the reseller. Retailers will use a P-O-P only if they are convinced that it will generate greater sales.

A P-O-P should be coordinated with the theme used in advertisements. This not only acts as a type of repetition, it also creates a last-minute association between the campaign and the place of decision.

Dealer Contests and Sweepstakes. As in the case of consumer sales promotion, contests and sweepstakes can be developed to motivate resellers. Contests are far more common, primarily because contest prizes are usually associated with the sale of the sponsor's product. A sales quota is set, for example, and the company or individual who exceeds the quota by the largest percentage wins the contest.

The need to create the desired amount of excitement and motivation has forced designers to develop spectacular contests with very impressive prizes. It is also important to offer the right incentive. According to a survey sponsored by *Business & Incentive Strategies* magazine, 46 percent of women and 51 percent of men would opt for cold cash, followed by merchandise worth $1,000 or more, and travel.[25] Frequent contests quickly lose their excitement, however. Contests are effective only if they take place periodically. If conducted properly, contests can provide short-term benefits and can improve the relationship between the manufacturer and the reseller.

Trade Shows and Exhibits. Many industries present and sell their merchandise at trade shows and exhibits that allow demonstrating the product, providing information, answering questions, comparing competing brands, and writing orders. In turn, trade shows permit manufacturers to gather a great deal of information about their competition. In an environment where all the companies are attempting to give a clear picture of their products to potential customers, competitors can easily compare quality, features, prices, and technology.

Because of the tremendous importance of trade shows, companies spend a

---

[23]Cyndee Miller, "P.O.P. Gains Followers as 'Era of Retailing' Dawns," *Marketing News* (May 14, 1990):2.
[24]"Growth in P-O-P Spending Slows," *Promo* (May 1992):16.
[25]"Our Favorite Incentives," *Adweek* (October 19, 1992):20.

Jennifer Edwards, Account Coordinator, Wolf Blumberg Krody, Cincinnati

As an account coordinator for the Procter & Gamble Company, Jennifer Edwards is responsible for coordinating the details of promotional and advertising projects for P&G's Coin Vend Laundry Brands and Old Spice's Athlete of the Month promotion. In addition, Edwards is involved in several internal committees within WBK.

8:15–9:00 A.M.   I begin my day with a quick ride over the Ohio River into the city of Cincinnati for another busy day of work. Dressed in my best suit, I'm a bit nervous about the new business pitch I've been asked to participate in. The five-minute ride leaves me plenty of time to get situated at my desk with my cup of coffee and my day planner before the telephone starts to ring. I always check my voice mail for any urgent messages that may need my immediate attention and spend the next few minutes returning calls and writing reminder notes.

9:00–9:30 A.M.   Meeting with the account supervisor for the Coin Vend and Old Spice brands to go over our plans for the day. Last-minute details for the business pitch are finalized and the plan is ready.

9:30–10:00 A.M.   With briefcases in hand, the time spent on the way over to P&G is used to update each other on any new information affecting our projects or changes in any plans that need to be accounted for.

10:00–11:00 A.M.   Two members from P&G's public relations department and two team members from the Old Spice Brand are present for the presentation. Our goal here today is to convince the brand to renew our contract for the Old Spice Athlete of the Month contract and to present several new ideas and improvements for next year's program. The presentation is concluded by answering questions and explaining in further detail the changes we want to implement.

11:00–12:00 P.M.   On the way back to the office, we spend the time reflecting on the presentation and decide it went as well as expected. Our next steps will include drafting a conference report to inform WBK management of the details of the presentation and waiting to hear from Old Spice next week. Several messages and deliveries are waiting for me at my desk and the next half hour is spent returning phone calls and opening the packages. I have been waiting for two of the packages that are part of a quality control check for a direct-marketing project I am heading up. Immediately, I inspect the contents of the packages. Everything looks in place and I notify the mail house that all is intact and to continue ahead with the program.

12:00–1:00 P.M.   The account supervisor and I discuss details for another meeting we have with P&G Coin Vend over lunch at a nearby deli. We discuss key elements of the meeting and go over a weekly status report that we furnish for the client. I am reminded

great deal of money each year (approximately $8 billion) planning and staging them. Trade shows generated over $70 billion in sales in 1992.[26] For some companies, this expense represents most of their promotional expenditure.

Trade Incentives. There is an alternative for instances when a contest is not

---

[26] "The Power of Trade Shows," *The Trade Show Bureau* (1993):2.

that I will be presenting one of the projects I have been working on and we go over key issues that need to be addressed. We enjoy the remainder of our lunch, taking special care to avoid spilling on our clothes. There's nothing more embarrassing than showing up at a meeting with food stains on your shirt!

1:00–2:00 P.M. Back to the office for a couple of hours of organizing and monitoring progress on several projects. It isn't uncommon to have 10 or 20 different deadlines join on at the same time. The most important thing to remember is to keep extremely organized and on top of the situation for every project in order to meet your goals. I spend a half hour writing job updates and filling out paper work to expedite my projects. The sooner I can get the materials in to the art director's hands, the more time they will have to work on my project. I stop at the Coin Vend art director's desk for several minutes to give her more detail on a couple of projects and allow her to ask any questions she has for me.

2:00–3:00 P.M. It's already 2:00 and I realize that I have to make media calls for the Athlete of the Year promotion before the next meeting. I only have to make 15 more calls to the Seattle market before the next phase of the promotion begins. I'll start that tomorrow.

3:00–3:30 P.M. Time to leave for P&G once again. This is a weekly meeting we have with the Coin Vend Brand to discuss the status of projects in progress.

3:30–5:15 P.M. Our meeting is a long one. This has been an extremely busy quarter for us and it takes quite a while to update our client on the progress of all the projects. The project I presented was well received and they agreed with many of the issues I pointed out to them. We decided on an execution that best suits his needs and the needs of his consumers.

5:15–5:30 P.M. There is still a lot to be done and we realize the next couple of days will have to be spent concentrating on the execution of our projects. In addition, more projects were assigned and we divide them up between the two of us, making sure to schedule it into our planners.

5:30–6:45 P.M. When I returned back to the office, there was a message on my voice mail regarding a direct-marketing project I am working on. The client needs several materials by tomorrow at noon in Minnesota. I work frantically to draft the materials, make the appropriate copies, and prepare the package for Federal Express A.M. delivery. With that mini-crisis taken care of, I can now prepare to go home.

6:45–7:00 P.M. Another busy day over. I clear off my desk, making sure to lock all my files and secure all sensitive information. I fill out my end-of-day paperwork and make a few notes in my planner for the next day.

7:00–7:15 P.M. On my drive back across the river, I make more mental notes for tomorrow. Suddenly I smile to myself as I realize just how successful today really was and the part I played in it!

appropriate or the goal may be to gain extra shelf space or to increase use of promotional material rather than to increase sales. In such cases trade incentives for accomplishing certain tasks are offered to the reseller by the marketer. The only requirement is that the reseller demonstrate in some way that the object was displayed. For example, a retailer might send the manufacturer a photograph of the display he or she promised to use. Incentive programs are very common when attempting to introduce a new product into a market, gain shelf space, or get retailers to stock more of a product. For example, a manufacturer may offer a substantial prize of cash or merchandise to a retailer who orders a certain amount of product or a certain product. Most incentive programs are customized for each reseller and each situation. However, there are two types of trade incentive programs that are somewhat standard—push money and dealer loaders.

push money (spiffs) A monetary bonus paid to a salesperson based on units sold over a period of time.

Push Money Push-money, or *spiffs,* is a monetary bonus paid to a salesperson based on units sold over a period of time. For example, a manufacturer of air conditioners might offer a $50 bonus for the sale of model EJ1, $75 for model EJ19, and $100 for model EX3 between April 1 and October 1. At the end of that period each salesperson sends in evidence of total sales to the manufacturer and receives a check for the appropriate amount.

dealer loader A premium given to a retailer by a manufacturer for buying a certain quantity of product.

Dealer Loader A **dealer loader** is a premium (comparable to a consumer premium) that is given to a retailer by a manufacturer for buying a certain amount of a product. The two most common types of dealer loaders are *buying loaders* and *display loaders.* Buying loaders award gifts for buying a certain order size. Budweiser offered store managers a free trip to the Super Bowl if they sold a certain amount of beer in a specified period of time before the event. Display loaders award the display to the retailer after it has been taken apart. For example, Dr Pepper built a store display for the July 4th holiday, which included a gas grill, picnic table, basket, and so forth. The store manager was awarded these items after the promotion ended. Both techniques can be effective in getting sufficient amounts of a new product into retail outlets or in getting a point-of-purchase display into a store. The underlying motivation for both arrangements is to sell large amounts of the product in a short period of time.

trade deals An arrangement in which the retailer agrees to give the manufacturer's product a special promotional effort in return for product discounts, goods, or cash.

Trade Deals. **Trade-deals** are the most important reseller sales promotion technique. A retailer is "on deal" when he or she agrees to give the manufacturer's product a special promotional effort that it would not normally receive. These promotional efforts can take the form of special displays, extra purchases, superior store locations, or greater promotion in general. In return, retailers sometimes receive special allowances, discounts, goods, or cash.

No one knows exactly how much money is spent on trade deals; experts estimate approximately $8 billion to $12 billion annually.[27] In some industries, such as grocery products, electronics, computers, and automobiles, trade deals are expected. A manufacturer would find it impossible to compete in these industries without offering trade discounts. In fact, the requirement to "deal" has become so prevalent that many advertisers fear it is now more important in determining which products receive the greatest promotion than either the value of the product or the expertise of the manufacturer. In the grocery field, for example, approximately 60 percent of all manufacturers' sales are accompanied by a trade deal averaging about 12 percent of the asking price.[28] The requirement to deal has been a point of contention between manufacturers and retailers for many years. As indicated in the Issues and Controversies box, some manufacturers are trying to stop.

[27]Kevin T. Higgins, "Sales Promotion Spending Closing in on Advertising," *Marketing News* (July 4, 1986):8.
[28]Keith M. Jones, "Held Hostage by the Trade?" *Advertising Age* (April 27, 1987):18.

P&G Won't Deal

Quietly but forcefully, Procter & Gamble has declared war on "the deal"—and the supermarket industry doesn't like it one bit. The weapon is a pricing strategy that takes direct aim at forward-buying, diversion, and other practices that over the long run reward retailers more for purchasing wisely than for selling many of the items they carry.

At issue is nothing less than the reversal of a decade-long trend that has transformed the manufacturer-sponsored trade allowance into a standard requirement by retailers operating in an environment of intense competition, high-debt loads, and low-profit margins.

Retailers call Procter & Gamble's strategy *everyday low pricing.* This decision systematically lowers the price P&G charges for the goods it sells to retailers and keeps prices low to avoid what many manufacturers consider excessive charges for trade-based promotions that either fall short or never take place.

Retailers hate the new policy. They argue that it not only wipes out their ability to forward-buy and divert, which they see as legitimate activities, it also takes away their flexibility to promote. To retailers the manufacturer appears to be saying it's okay if the manufacturer's product isn't promoted as long as it is on the shelf every day of the week. The retailer says "All right, I'll leave it on the shelf, and if it gathers too much dust I'll just throw it out. I'll even drop the price, but look what's going to happen: A dollar-per-case cost reduction comes out to less than 10 cents per unit, so on an 89-cent item I may be able to go as low as 86 or 85 cents."

Those who take issue with that scenario point out that since virtually every product is sold on deal today, retailers couldn't perform on every allowance even if they wanted to—which they don't—and yet they demand the money anyway. "Retailers must begin to realize the implications of the strong-arm tactics they use," commented John Cioffi, director of sales administration for Bristol-Myers. "Increased trade dollars without incremental volume depletes brand resources," Cioffi notes. "The misconception (among retailers) is that there's unlimited money on the street and that it's up to the retailers to be the best in the market at getting it. The fact is, the more you move your resources into trade, the more you deplete your ability to use them in other ways."

Industry experts report that discontent is turning into alarm in retail circles as brokers, wholesalers, and chain-store executives discover just how comprehensive and calculated the new P&G strategy is. They know that P&G has the strength, the expertise, the marketing depth, and the knowledge of where it stands in its markets—and that other big companies don't. They know that others are watching and waiting, and that no company can afford to alienate its customers for long. The only way we'll know it's working is if P&G keeps on doing it.

Adapted from "P&G Declares War on Trade Deals," *Promo* (March 1992):1, 26.

Buying Allowances There are two general types of trade deals. The first is referred to as *buying allowances* and includes situations in which a manufacturer pays a reseller a set amount of money for purchasing a certain amount of the product during a specified time period. All the retailer has to do is meet the purchase requirements. The payment may be given in the form of a check from the manufacturer or a reduction in the face value of an invoice.

Advertising Allowances The second category of trade deals includes advertising and display allowances. An *advertising allowance* is a common technique employed primarily in the consumer-products area in which the manufacturer pays the wholesaler or retailer a certain amount of money for advertising the manufacturer's product. This allowance can be a flat dollar amount or it can be a percentage of gross purchases during a specified time period. *Cooperative advertising* involves a contractual arrangement between the manufacturer and the resellers whereby the manufacturer agrees to pay a part or all of the adver-

tising expenses incurred by the resellers (as examined in Chapters 3 and 4). A *display allowance* involves a direct payment of cash or goods to the retailer if the retailer agrees to set up the display as specified. The manufacturer requires the retailer to sign a certificate of agreement before being paid.

Ultimately, the willingness of retailers to carry and support a manufacturer's brands depends on both direct incentives offered to the retailers along with the promotions offered to consumers. The latter suggests that the brand is adequately supported by the manufacturer and ensures the product will prove profitable to the retailer. Ad 18.7 shows an example of a program that the General Mills salesperson would present to supermarket managers.

THE FUTURE OF SALES PROMOTION

It should be obvious by now that sales promotion is a very diverse area. Trying to become an expert on all aspects of sales promotion may be unrealistic, and special skills in certain areas may be best learned on the job.

Certainly, when we talk about integrated marketing communication, sales promotion skills remain the most difficult for advertisers to learn. Of course, this difficulty may be due partly to the historical division in the creative philosophies between the two. As long as advertisers feel that sales promotion is denigrating the brand and stealing dollars from them, cooperation and synergy are unlikely.

Experts predict that sales promotion will experience the following trends in the mid-1990s:[29]

- More targeted promotions
- Increased co-op or "account-specific" tie-ins
- Greater use of hi-tech P-O-P and direct mail
- Consumer loyalty will continue to be built via consumer databases
- Continuing concern over price versus value added
- Expansion of frequency (loyal user) plans
- Longer-term planning (with flexibility)
- More group promotions and tie-ins

It is apparent that sales promotion will continue to grow as a promotional alternative. Whether it will diminish the importance of advertising is still debatable, but certainly the varieties and styles of sales promotion are changing the world of advertising.

---

[29]Russ Bowman, "Sales Promotion," *Marketing & Media Decisions* (July, 1990):21.

SUMMARY

- Sales promotion offers an "extra incentive" to take action. It gives the product or service additional value.

- Sales promotion is growing rapidly for many reasons. It offers the manager short-term solutions; the extent to which sales promotion has achieved objectives can be assessed; sales promotion is less expensive than advertising; it speaks to the current needs of the consumer to receive more value from products; and it responds to the new power acquired by modern retailers.

- Sales promotion has three broad roles: to stimulate demand by users or household consumers; to improve the marketing performance of resellers; and to supplement and coordinate advertising, personal selling, and public relations activities. In turn, sales promotion can move the consumer to purchase.

- Sales promotions directed at consumers include price deals, coupons, contests and sweepstakes, refunds, premiums, specialty advertising, continuity programs, and sampling.

- Reseller sales promotion includes point-of-purchase displays, contests and sweepstakes, trade shows, trade premiums, and trade deals.

QUESTIONS

1 What is sales promotion? What are the broad goals of sales promotion in terms of its three target audiences, and how do these goals differ from those of advertising? How are they the same? Discuss when sales promotion and advertising should be used together.

2 One agency executive was quoted as saying the following: "Advertising is on its way out. All consumers want is a deal. Sales promotion is the place to be." What do you think this executive meant? Do you agree or disagree?

3 You have just been named product manager for

Bright White, a new laundry detergent that will be introduced to the market within the next 6 months. What type of sales promotion strategy would work best for this product? What types of advertising would enhance this strategy?

4 The chapter discussion says that sales promotion has made significant strides in marketing investment at the expense of advertising. Many companies show more confidence in direct sales stimulation. Why has this happened? Try to identify which explanations fit in each of these categories: (a) changes in advertising, (b) changes in consumer needs/wants, and (c) changes in marketing strategy. Does some change in any of these signal a shift back to more advertising emphasis?

5 Tom Jackson's promotional strategy professor is covering some sales promotion methods, explaining that, in selecting the consumer sales promotion, planners must know the brand situation and objectives *before techniques* are chosen; some ways are for increased product usage, and some are for getting new consumers to try the product. "Which methods belong with which objective and why?" the professor asks. How should Tom answer this question?

6 Janice Wilcox is a brand manager for a very new line of eye cosmetics. She is about to present her planning strategy to division management. Janice knows her company has been successful in using sales promotion plans lately, but she has strong misgivings about following the company trend. "This new line must create a consumer brand franchise—and promotion isn't the best way to do that," she thinks to herself. What is a weakness of sales promotion in "brand franchising"? Should Janice propose no promotion or is there a reasonable compromise for her to consider?

7 Jambo Product's promotion manager, Sean Devlin, is calculating the cost of a proposed consumer coupon drop for March. The media cost (FSI) and production charges are $125,000. The distribution will be 4 million coupons with an expected redemption of 5 percent. The coupon value is 50 cents, and Devlin has estimated the handling and compensation (store) to be 8 cents per redeemed coupon. Based on these estimates, what will be the cost to Devlin's budget?

$\mathscr{S}$UGGESTED CLASS PROJECTS

1 Observe your local newspaper and identify a retailer who is engaging in co-op advertising. Interview the store manager and determine the specific arrangements that exist between the advertiser and the retailer. What is the attitude of the retailer toward this arrangement? Write a two-page report.

2 Select a print ad for a national marketer. Redesign the ad, including at least two types of consumer sales promotion techniques. Show both before version and after version to five people. Assess whether the second version has increased their intention to buy.

$\mathscr{F}$URTHER READINGS

BABAKUS, EMIN, PETER TAT, and WILLIAM CUNNINGHAM, "Coupon Redemption: A Motivational Perspective," *Journal of Consumer Marketing* (Spring 1988):40.

FITZGERALD, KEN, "Ad Support Builds for Tools," *Advertising Age* (August 28, 1989):20.

HALEY, DOUGLAS F., "Industry Promotion and Advertising Trends: Why Are They Important?" *Journal of Advertising Research* (December 1987–January 1988):RC–6.

HUME, SCOTT, "Premiums & Promotions: After Buying-Binge, What?" *Advertising Age* (September 12, 1988):S1–S5.

LODISH, LEONARD M., *The Advertising and Promotion Challenge* (New York: Oxford University Press, 1986).

McCANN, THOMAS, "Promotions Will Gain More Clout in the '90s," *Marketing News* (November 6, 1989):4, 24.

QUELCH, JOHN A., *Sales Promotion Management* (Englewood Cliffs, NJ: Prentice Hall, Inc., 1989).

VIDEO CASE

Telemarketing and Sales Promotion

Lens Express, a Deerfield Beach, Florida, marketer of contact lenses, had created an advertising presence through television and magazine ads that features Lynda Carter, television's "Wonder Woman." However, compared to its competitors, its use of advertising is relatively limited. Instead, the company relies on telemarketing, generated through toll-free telephone numbers. After viewing an ad, interested consumers call the number and set into motion Lens Express's telemarketing response. Customers needing a prescription are referred to a local doctor. Otherwise calls are handled by a telephone representative who takes orders and tells customers about special sales promotions entitling them to use the services of an eye-care professional.

An increasing number of companies are using the phone to sell everything from cruises to mufflers to municipal bonds to health insurance with the result that the value of goods and services sold via telemarketing skyrocketed from $56 billion in 1983 to $300 billion in 1992. The number of telemarketers also increased from 175,000 in 1983 to more than 5 million in 1994.

In the case of Lens Express, contact between the telemarketer and the customer was generated by the customer. In other cases, the company calls first, a technique many people consider intrusive. Despite the annoyance level these calls sometimes generate, they also generate a return that makes the effort worthwhile. "While a segment of people complain about telemarketing, it's still supereffective," explains Robert Blattberg, a marketing professor at Northwestern's business school. You only need a 1 percent to 2 percent success rate for telemarketing to be effective."

Another company that has used telemarketing successfully in sales promotion is Olan Mills Inc., the largest portrait photography firm in the United States. "We got to be number one because we never gave up on telemarketing," said co-owner Olan Mills, II who hires 7,000 telemarketers to operate the phones in search of business and only 1,500 photographers. The company started telemarketing in 1952 as a way of spreading business throughout the year, instead of seeing customers only at Christmas. Co-owner Charles George Mills explains: "Back in 1952 Dad had this idea to get on the phone and sell a package of three sittings for $3, taken over a 12-month period. Invariably, customers arriving for the sec-

ond or third sitting would buy additional photos, increasing the cash flow throughout the year." Although it now costs $15, the same sales promotion package is used today. As a direct result of its telemarketing efforts, Olan Mills's sales have grown 8 to 10 percent a year over the past five years compared to half that amount for its competitors.

Often, telemarketing is most effective when used in conjunction with other media, including direct mail. Telemarketing consultant Bernie Goldberg explains: "Your relationship to the customer is the key to everything. If you announce your program in a letter to customers and set the relationship, the phone call is easy. The best offer will have a yes/no response."

Despite its success as a sales promotion tool, telemarketing has an image problem with consumers who consider telemarketers uninvited dinner guests. Many people are also concerned about unscrupulous behavior. A case in point: Telemarketers working for long-distance carriers, including U.S. Sprint, offered consumers special sales promotions if they agreed to switch phone companies. Although most of the switches were handled correctly, some switches were made without customer approval; no written authorization was needed to process the change. Sprint realized what was happening only when consumer complaints began pouring in. Since then it uses a variety of safeguards, including random confirmation calls to customers who have switched.

Sprint is not alone in realizing that its image is on the line with every call. Although the potential to close sales is there, the potential to turn people off is also present—a realization that has convinced many companies that telemarketing's success is linked to the skill and professionalism of those delivering the message.

Sources: Martin Everett, "Your Job Is On the (Phone) Line," *Sales & Marketing Management* (May 1993):66–71; John Greenwald, "Sorry, Right Number," *Time* (September 13, 1993):66; Linda J. Neff, "Six Myths About Telemarketing," *Sales & Marketing Management* (October 1992):108–111; Roger Peterson, "Uninvited Dinner Guests," *Newsweek* (March 23, 1992):18; Ernan Roman, "More for Your Money," *Inc.* (September 1992):113–116; Aimee L. Stern, "Telemarketing Polishes Its Image," *Sales & Marketing Management* (June 1991):107–110; William M. Stern, "We Got On the Phone," *Forbes* (March 1, 1993):94–95.

Questions

1. Why is telemarketing an effective sales promotion tool?

2. Why is telemarketing most effective when used in conjunction with other media?

3. What can companies do to overcome telemarketing's image problem?

PUBLIC RELATIONS

CHAPTER OBJECTIVES

When you have completed this chapter, you should be able to:

- Understand what public relations is, how it differs from advertising, and what its advantages are

- Explain how public relations, advertising, and other marketing communications can work together to achieve greater benefit for an organization

- Identify the areas in which public relations operates and some of the activities performed in those areas

- Understand the value and importance of measuring the results of public relations efforts

ALL THE RIGHT MOVES, BABY!

The call came at 2:00 a.m. in the predawn dark of Monday, June 14. A drowsy Cathy Dial, Pepsi-Cola Company's director of consumer relations, picked up the phone at home. It was the company's after-hours consumer hot line: A woman from the Cleveland area had called. She said she had found a hypodermic syringe in a can of Diet Pepsi. Ms. Dial called the woman back. She repeated her claim. It was the first such report from outside the Seattle area, where Pepsi and the Food & Drug Administration were already investigating two similar claims; the first was made June 9.

A little later, closer to normal wake-up time, Ms. Dial called Pepsi's public relations and regulatory affairs people with the bad news. It was just the beginning of what became a national public relations nightmare for Pepsi, one that threatened lasting damage to one of the most successful brands in marketing.

By 9:30 a.m. Monday there was another claim. Then another. Before the day was over, Ms. Dial and her two dozen Pepsi-Cola consumer relations representatives, who typically field mundane questions about calories and the like, had received eight calls. News reports from the Seattle claims had intensified on Sunday, after the FDA had issued a five-state alert advising consumers to inspect Diet Pepsi before drinking it. So Rebecca Madeira, Pepsi's vice-president for public affairs, was already huddling with her crisis team early Monday, in response to the Seattle situation.

But if the varying locations of the claims meant Pepsi had a national media crisis on its hands, they also confirmed what the company believed all along. There was no manufacturing crisis. "Eight cases that day, all over the country. We just said nope, that does not make sense," Ms. Madeira noted.

With those conclusions reached, Craig Weatherup, president/CEO of Pepsi-Cola North America, and his colleagues decided upon the strategy Pepsi would follow, a strategy that would make the handling of the crisis a case study of success. Pepsi would fight the media crisis with media. Pepsi would not recall any products. That night, FDA commissioner David Kessler called Mr. Weatherup at home. Dr. Kessler agreed with Weatherup, there was no need for a product recall. "We knew there was something at work here that had little or nothing to do with the production of the product or the package it was in," agreed Weatherup.

The company's next steps were clear, Ms. Madeira says: "If you're going to conduct your trial in the media, you've got to do it with the tools they're used to working with." That meant making Mr. Weatherup available for interviews and constantly furnishing news media with visuals and anything else that would show the bottling process was absolutely safe.

On Tuesday, Pepsi and a long-time vendor, Robert Chang Productions, rushed to produce the first of four video news releases that would be distributed by satellite to any station that wanted to use the footage. The files showed scenes of the production process, verifying the virtual impossibility that tampering could take place before the product reached the stores. Medialink, a New York public relations company, distributed the video release just several hours later. It estimates the footage was ultimately seen by 187 million viewers on 403 stations. That night, Mr. Weatherup appeared on ABC's *Nightline* with Dr. Kessler. It was the CEO's first network television appearance.

On Wednesday the marketer got its big break, thanks to an alert Pepsi manager in Colorado. On a visit to a retailer where a syringe reportedly had been found, he noticed the store surveillance camera. He asked to see the tape from the previous day, and there it was: A clear picture of a woman shopper putting something into an open Diet Pepsi can, then calling the sales clerk's attention to the "found" object. Three more people were arrested for making false claims. In the end, the scares were proven to be a series of hoaxes.

The one thing Pepsi knew it wanted to do was formally close the issue. To do so, the company ran a national newspaper ad on June 19 to June 21 declaring: "Pepsi is pleased to announce . . . nothing." On the Fourth of July weekend, Pepsi mounted a massive coupon promotion celebrating its "freedom."[1]

A Video Case called Pepsi's Public Relations Challenge follows this chapter. The video and our study of it provide a more detailed look into the classic role of public relations.

THE CHALLENGE OF PUBLIC RELATIONS

The goodwill of the public is the greatest asset any organization can have. A public that is well informed and holds a positive attitude toward the organization is critical to its survival. If Pepsi had been wrong about the faith it had in its manufacturing process, the consequences may have been disastrous. Instead, they carefully researched the problem and designed a public relations strategy that was both well thought out and decisive. Furthermore, following the integrated approach we have seen underlining much of this text, Pepsi employed sales promotion and advertising as a complement to its public relations efforts. In this chapter we will examine public relations, how it is implemented, and how it fits in with advertising.

The art of public relations is very old. Historians tell us that Caesar and Alexander had their publicists. Kings and emperors staged special events to enhance their images. Counselors, heralds, bards, and even court artists sometimes assumed the functions we will later ascribe to public relations. Edward L. Bernays, considered the father of public relations, was the first to call himself a public relations counsel. In 1923, he wrote the first book on the subject, *Crystallizing Public Opinion,* and he taught the first college course on public relations at New York University. Despite this lengthy tradition, however, there is confusion about the nature of public relations.

public relations A management function enabling organizations to achieve effective relationships with their various audiences through an understanding of audience opinions, attitudes, and values.

Although there is no universally accepted definition of **public relations**, the First World Assembly of Public Relations Associations in Mexico City offered the following definition in 1978: "The art and social science of analyzing trends, predicting their consequences, counseling organizational leaders, and implementing planned programs of action which will serve both the organization and the public interest." A much simpler definition is offered by Dilenschneider and Forrestal in the *Public Relations Handbook:* "Public relations is the use of information to influence public opinion."[2]

Both definitions treat public relations as a management function that is prac-

[1]Marcy Magiera, "The Pepsi Crisis: What Went Right?" *Advertising Age* (July 19, 1993):14-15; Gary Levin, "Where Was PR Community in Pepsi Crisis? Nowhere," *Advertising Age* (July 19, 1993):14; Marcy Magiera, "Pepsi Weathers Tampering Hoaxes," *Advertising Age* (June 21, 1993):1,46; Laura Zinn, "The Right Moves, Baby," *Business Week* (July 5, 1993):30-31.
[2]Robert L. Dilenschneider and Dan J. Forrestal, *Public Relations Handbook,* 3rd rev. ed. (Chicago, Illinois: The Dartnell Corporation, 1987):5.

ticed by companies, governments, trade and professional associations, nonprofit organizations, the travel and tourism industry, the educational system, labor unions, politicians, organized sports, and media. Its audiences (publics) may be external (customers, the news media, the investment community, the general public, the government) and also internal (stockholders, employees).

Public relations is a growing industry. It is estimated that the public relations industry employs 145,000 people and that its billings are increasing by 18 to 20 percent annually.[3] Virtually every city in the United States contains at least one public relations practitioner serving clients of every size and interest. Annual fees paid by these clients range from a few hundred dollars to several million. Table 19.1 lists the 50 largest public relations firms and their annual fees. In addition, many companies, such as Texas Instruments, have their own in-house public relations departments and do not contract with public relations agencies. Others, such as Exxon, consult with agencies only about specific activities.

Public relations, advertising, and sales promotion together present the marketing communication strategy of an organization. What a company's advertising says, how it says it, and what medium it uses have a direct bearing on the company's public relations strategy and vice versa. Thus advertising agencies need to understand what public relations is and how it works with advertising to benefit both public relations and advertising. Furthermore, advertising strategists, especially copywriters and media specialists, often play a major role in the design and placement of public relations messages in mass media. Accordingly, this chapter attempts both to provide an overview of public relations and to show its direct applications to advertising.

Before we enter into this discussion, however, we must distinguish advertising from public relations.

COMPARING PUBLIC RELATIONS AND ADVERTISING

Developing strategies, designing ads, preparing written messages, and buying time or space for their exposure are the primary concerns of advertising people. If we believe in an integrated approach to mass communication, advertising and public relations should be complementary. Unfortunately, in many companies they often remain a separate function. Partly this is due to tradition and partly due to differences in functions. With respect to the former, public relations has historically been physically separated from advertising. This separation has been a result of the nature of the work performed by public relations as well as the people working in public relations. Public relations has often been viewed as a luxury that received little respect from the rest of the organization. Since public relations is not considered a direct profit generator and has difficulty verifying its accomplishments, individuals working in advertising are reluctant to incorporate public relations into their planning. Conversely, individuals working in public relations are often unwilling to work with others outside their field. Public relations people are typically trained as writers, with little background in marketing or advertising.

As noted, public relations and advertising also differ in how certain tasks are

---

[3]Public Relations Society of America, *Careers in Public Relations* (1990):1.

Table 19.1 The 25 Largest U.S. Public Relations Firms and Their Annual Fees

	1992 Net Fees	Employees	% Change from 1991
1. Burson-Marsteller (A)	$203,683,000	2,071	+1.93
2. Shandwick	166,100,000	1,857	−3.93
3. Hill and Knowlton (A)	149,100,000	1,577	−14.0
4. Omnicom PR Network (A)	65,569,433	987	+2.5
5. Edelman Public Relations Worldwide	59,614,538	684	+13.3
6. Fleishman-Hillard	58,651,100	638	+12.3
7. Ketchum Public Relations (A)	45,600,000	396	+9.1
8. The Rowland Co. (A)	44,000,000	490	−8.3
9. Ogilvy Adams & Rinehart (A)	36,124,000	338	−36.5
10. Manning, Selvage & Lee (A)	31,424,000	320	+3.6
11. GCI Group (A)	28,095,400	356	−1.0
12. Ruder Finn	27,076,769	271	−4.1
13. Robinson, Lake, Lerer & Montgomery/Bozell PR* (A)	21,200,000	145	+3.0
14. Cohn & Wolfe (A)	14,200,000	118	−0.85
15. Sawyer Miller Group*	11,700,000	100	+23.0
16. Financial Relations Board	10,263,134	126	+16.4
17. Gibbs & Soell	8,831,752	92	+11.9
18. Powell Tate	8,800,469	61	Founded 1991
19. Earle Palmer Brown PR (A)	7,497,785	65	+31.1
20. The Kamber Group	7,438,013	85	−11.6
21. The Jefferson Group	7,383,421	55	+50.2
22. Stoorza, Ziegaus & Metzger	7,084,004	106	+31.8
23. Cunningham Communication	7,002,817	68	+36.2
24. E. Bruce Harrison Co.	6,826,949	54	+0.3
25. Morgen-Walke Assocs.	5,530,535	51	+50.5

* Robinson, Lake, Lerer & Montgomery and Sawyer Miller merged April 1, 1993. Bozell, Jacobs, Kenyon & Eckhardt is the parent company. (A) means ad agency related.

performed. Specifically, they differ in the way they employ the media, the level of control they have over message delivery, and their perceived credibility.

MEDIA APPROACH

To begin with, public relations practitioners have a different approach to the media than do advertisers. Whenever possible, they avoid purchasing time or space to communicate messages. Instead, they seek to persuade media "gatekeepers" to carry their information. These gatekeepers include writers, producers, editors, talk show coordinators, and newscasters. This type of public relations is labeled **publicity** and is characterized as cost-free because there are no direct media costs. There are indirect costs, however, such as production expenses and getting the cooperation of the gatekeepers.

Even when public relations uses paid-for media, the nature of the message tends to be general with little or no attempt to sell a brand or product line. The goal is to change the attitudes of the public in favor of the sponsoring organization. This type of advertising is referred to as **corporate or institutional advertising.**

publicity Cost-free public relations that relates messages through gatekeepers.

corporate/institutional advertising Advertising used to create a favorable public attitude toward the sponsoring organization.

Shelli Manning, Associate Account Executive, Public Relations Department, Marketing Resources of America, Inc.

Shelli is responsible for project management and writing for Caterpillar, Inc. Truck Engine Division. She also handles special writing projects and media relations for Navistar International Transportation Corporation and the Board of Public Utilities.

8:00 A.M.   It's always nice to see Ro, the receptionist, first thing in the morning. She wasn't able to say good morning, but she waved. There is a lot of paperwork in my chair, after just returning from vacation. Nothing too urgent—a notice of a project update meeting at 2 P.M., a request from my boss to close some jobs that have been completed, edits on a news release I wrote, follow-up on an assignment, and a request from accounting to assign a job number to an item on an invoice.

8:15 A.M.   Only three messages on voice mail. Looked at my Daytimer to remind myself of priorities. I have a small amount of media follow-up to do, and I need to continue the research and writing of builder testimonials for the Board of Public Utilities. Copy is due to the client on Thursday. I'm also scheduled to attend a Public Relations Society of America/ Kansas City Chapter luncheon at 11:30

A.M. And, before I forget, go and get coffee!

8:30 A.M.   Met quickly with my boss to go over the activities for the day and the rest of the week. She gave me some information from Caterpillar on a database program we're devising for them. I passed the information on to the manager of direct-marketing services and followed up with her on progress.

9:00 A.M.   The most urgent item to attend to was a voice-mail message from Toromont Power, a Caterpillar dealer in Canada. We manage a reorder service for materials on a customer satisfaction program called "The Race For #1." They sent a check in September but haven't received their materials yet and think they may have forgotten to enclose the order form. I found nothing in my file, so I checked with accounting. They received the check and it has been deposited. I then had Toromont fax their order and sent a request to our production manager to fill this order, plus another one I just received in the mail today.

9:30 A.M.   Dealt with everything that was on my chair, passed on a layout that arrived on

An example of corporate advertising used to counter bad publicity is Denny's Restaurants' response to the debacle that surrounded the organization in 1993. For several months there were reports that Denny's was engaged in a pattern of racial discrimination, including requiring cover charges and prepayment of meals from minorities. On May 24, 1993, a lawsuit was filed by six African-American Secret Service agents, who claimed they were denied equal service at Denny's in Annapolis, Maryland, because of deliberately slow service. In response, Denny's aired a 60-second spot nationwide that featured Caucasian, African-American, Hispanic, and Asian employees of Denny's, who indicated how much they cared about *all* their customers. A print campaign followed using the same creative approach.[4] More on corporate advertising will be discussed in detail later in the chapter.

The American Association of Retired Persons (AARP), the nation's largest

---

[4]Chuck Hawkins, "Denny's: The Stain That Isn't Coming Out, " *Business Week* (June 28, 1993):98-99.

	my desk for approval, and did media follow-up. We sent out a local news release for National/Auto Truckstops, Inc., and have not yet received coverage, but it's in line to run at all the publications.
10:15 A.M.	Got my time sheet from last week in order, approved, and sent through the system.
10:30 A.M.	Tried to contact two of the people on my list for BPU testimonials, but they weren't available. The hardest part about this project is getting in touch with the contacts.
10:45 A.M.	Went through other mail and read a couple of FYIs.
11:00 A.M.	Drive to PRSA luncheon at the Embassy Suites on the Plaza, approximately 30 minutes away.
11:30 A.M.	It's too bad it was such a small group today. The speaker was wonderful. AMC Entertainment International, Inc. president David Seal shared his insights on global communications and how we, as public relations professionals, can prepare and position ourselves for successful foreign relations.
1:15 P.M.	Drive back. It really is a beautiful day.
1:45 P.M.	Informed by account service that the project update meeting will take place later than 2 P.M.
2:00 P.M.	Our AE, who is in Peoria, Illinois, with the client today, called to check in.
2:15 P.M.	The project we met about is a guidebook

	we are designing and assembling for 300 Caterpillar dealers. I am the project manager. It was a very informative and productive meeting. Direction was given to the creative department, a few new ideas and suggestions were thrown out, and a revised production schedule is required by the traffic department.
3:00 P.M.	Stopped by the main conference room to view an in-house display of different account projects the agency has completed in the past year. My team's display looks excellent!
3:15 P.M.	Was able to get in touch with only one of the contacts for the BPU testimonials. He has not yet obtained approval to proceed from his public affairs department.
3:30 P.M.	Sent out the local news release I edited earlier today.
4:30 P.M.	Got an update from the manager of direct-marketing services that our vendor has almost completed coding the database system for Caterpillar and we should see something by tomorrow.
4:45 P.M.	Determine priorities and make a list for tomorrow, which I am so looking forward to. It's my birthday!
5:00 P.M.	Quick check-in with my boss.
5:15 P.M.	Looking forward to a short, five minute drive home to see the cats, finish unpacking, and decided if I want to watch the NAFTA debate or just read about it tomorrow.

organization of people aged 50 and older, engages in both publicity and corporate advertising. The AARP has recently attempted to develop a national program to reduce health-care costs without sacrificing the quality of the care. Part of this program involves educating older consumers about these issues. To reach this large audience the AARP advertises its program—that is, it creates print advertisements and purchases space in newspapers to carry the ads. This special type of corporate advertising tends to be targeted and delivers a pointed message. It is labeled **advocacy advertising**. The organization also persuades television talk shows to invite AARP spokespersons to appear and encourages radio call-in programs to air the association's views of the issues.

advocacy advertising A type of corporate advertising that involves creating advertisements and purchasing space to deliver a specific, targeted message.

CONTROL

Amount of control is the second inherent difference between advertising and public relations. In the case of publicity, the public relations strategist is at the mercy of the media representative. There is no guarantee that all or even part of the story will appear. In fact, there is the real risk that the story may be rewritten or reorganized so that it no longer means what the strategist intended. In contrast, advertising is paid for, so there are many checks to ensure that the message is accurate and appears when scheduled.

The difficulty in measuring the results of public relations is another problem. It may take months or even years to change public opinion. In addition, it is hard to measure accurately the components that reflect public opinion.

CREDIBILITY

Public relations efforts that are successful do offer a credibility not usually associated with advertising, however. For example, a two-minute story delivered by Tom Brokaw on the *NBC Evening News* about an Eli Lilly Drugs medical breakthrough is far more credible than a print ad sponsored by Eli Lilly.

Consumers assume that the media are trustworthy and that they wouldn't deliver a story that was not true. Adding to this credibility is the amount of information provided by the media. A feature story on General Electric that appears in *Forbes* magazine may be 6 to 8 pages long, compared to a print ad containing 100 words of copy. Being able to tell a more complete and objective story about a company or product is something advertising cannot do.

Ultimately, the difference between advertising and public relations is that public relations takes a longer, broader view of the importance of reputation as a competitive asset. Although advertising must also be cognizant of a client's reputation, the focus is on reaching brand-related communication goals within a much shorter time frame. However, with the emphasis on integrated marketing communication, the separation between advertising and public relations is beginning to diminish.

THE COMPONENTS OF PUBLIC RELATIONS

As noted, the emerging partnership of public relations and advertising is moving rapidly toward a focused interaction with all individuals who are in a position to influence the fortunes of an organization. Public relations must increasingly become a management discipline, like advertising, involved in the earliest stages of corporate strategy. As mentioned, every company has a corporate image, although sometimes not quite by design. Managing a public relations image begins with a plan. The plan should complement your marketing and advertising strategies so you communicate with one clear voice. Public relations should align the organization's interests with the public interest so that both are served. These public interests are expressed as public opinions.

MEASURING PUBLIC OPINION

publics Those groups or individuals who are involved with an organization, including customers, employees, competitors, and government regulators.

Traditionally in public relations, the term **public** has been used to describe any group who has some involvement with an organization, including customers, employees, competitors, and government regulators. The public relations strategist researches the answers to two primary questions. First, which publics are

public opinion People's beliefs, based on their conceptions or evaluations of something rather than on fact.

most important to my organization, now and in the future? Second, what do these publics think? In identifying important publics, public relations follows the same process as advertising does in identifying a target market, which is simply the group of people or institutions we wish to receive our message (see Chapter 7). Determining what these publics think, however, is often quite challenging. **Public opinion**, the label used to denote what people think, is defined as "a belief, based not necessarily on fact but on the *conception* or *evaluation* of an event, person, institution, or product."[5]

The power of public opinion cannot be denied. It created the dictatorial influence of Adolf Hitler, made a hero of John F. Kennedy and a villain of Gary Hart, and has prompted countries to go to war. However, as many celebrities, politicians, and major corporations have found, public opinion is very fickle because of its fragile base in perceptions. Such perceptions are difficult to control, and often the public keys in on cues that are either negative or easily misinterpreted. Hot words and phrases, such as "abortion," "taxes," "alleged misuse of power," and "equal rights," can be taken out of context or overshadow the real message. Physical appearance, mannerisms, or one poorly handled event can influence public opinion.

Despite the critical need to understand public opinion, there is still no one system of measurement of the "climate of public opinion." Polls only measure public opinion on a particular issue at a given time. Different people maintain different values; likewise, a person's values can change over time. Clients of public relations agencies may rely on the research capabilities of the firm to evaluate public opinion, but they are more likely to rely on professional pollsters such as Louis Harris, George Gallup, and the Opinion Research Corporation.

One renowned expert on measuring public opinion is Daniel Yankelovich. In his recent book *Coming to Public Judgment,* he contends that public opinion evolves through seven stages, and unless one knows an opinion's stage of development on an issue, poll numbers will usually mislead. Furthermore, public opinion on any issue develops slowly over time—at least ten years for a complex issue. The seven stages follow:

Stage 1: Dawning awareness. Here people become aware of an issue or some aspect of it. At this stage most people remain largely unaware of the more specific issues and may express strong but unsettled opinions on the problem.

Stage 2: Greater urgency. People now acquire a sense of real urgency about the issue, with the dominant sentiment being "Do something!" Real "consciousness raising" has occurred.

Stage 3: Discovering the choices. In the third stage the public begins to focus on alternatives for dealing with issues. The timing of Stage 3 varies by issue. For some issues, choices become clear almost immediately, but for most issues they do not. This stage begins the process of converting the public's free-floating concern about the need to do something into proposals for action.

Stage 4: Wishful thinking. This is where the public's resistance to facing trade-offs kicks in. Most of the time on most issues, the public raises a barricade of wish-

[5]Doug Newsom, Alan Scott, and Judy Van Slyke Turk, *This Is PR: The Realities of Public Relations,* 4th ed. (Belmont, CA: Wadsworth Publishing Co., 1989):99.

ful thinking that must be overcome before people come to grips with issues realistically. To make sacrifices ungrudgingly, people must understand why these sacrifices are needed, and they must have some say in the types, forms, and conditions of sacrifices they are asked to make.

Stage 5: *Weighing the choices.* Here the public weighs the pros and cons of alternatives for dealing with the issue. In practice Stages 4 and 5 overlap, with people thinking through how they feel at the same time that they continue to resist coming to grips with the hard choices.

Stage 6: *Taking a stand intellectually.* This works in conjunction with Stage 7.

Stage 7: *Making a responsible judgment morally and emotionally.* As the stages of resolution, these last two can be considered together. People are quicker to accept change in their minds than in their hearts. Intellectual resolution requires people to clarify fuzzy thinking, reconcile inconsistencies, consider relevant facts and new realities, and grasp the full consequences of choices. Emotional resolution requires people to confront their own ambivalent feelings, adjust to unwelcome realities, and overcome an urge to procrastinate.[6] (see Ad 19.1)

We can illustrate Yankelovich's seven-stage process with a look at the current health-care debate and its hopeful resolution. The process will begin when the public learns that more than waste and greed are involved in driving costs higher (Stage 1). People's sense of urgency will grow less panicky and more tightly concentrated on controlling and reducing costs (Stage 2). Voters will focus particularly on choices entailing a larger role for government (Stage 3). Resistance will grow as people learn more about the options and the extent to which each involves higher costs and less choice for the individual. Resistance will focus particularly on options requiring employees to pay more, limits on technology, rationing of health care, and any efforts that otherwise restrict choice and access (Stage 4). If the debate genuinely engages the voters, then the public, in Stage 5, should be ready to consider the merits of proposals concerning some degree of federal regulation of costs, extending coverage to those who lack it, or curtailing heroic measures applied to those who are dying. A few choices may even make their way to Stage 6. If the national debate is productive, Americans will support, at least intellectually, proposals for drastically reducing the incentives for malpractice lawyers to drive up settlement costs. It is unlikely that Americans can reach Stage 7, the public judgment stage, on a vexing issue in a short time.

$\mathcal{P}$UBLIC RELATIONS TECHNIQUES

The arsenal of tools available to the public relations practitioner is vast and diverse. One way of organizing the available material is to divide it into two categories: controlled media and uncontrolled media. Controlled media include house ads, public service announcements, corporate (institutional) advertising, in-house publications, and visual presentations. These techniques are paid for by

---

[6]Daniel Yankelovich, "How Public Opinion Really Works," *Fortune* (October 5, 1992):102-108.

Ad 19.1

This ad appeals to a person who has reached the sixth and seventh stages of public opinion on the issue of the environment.

(Courtesy of Good Housekeeping, a publication of Hearst Magazines, a division of the Hearst Corporation.)

the sponsoring organizations. In turn, the organization maintains total control over how and when the message is delivered. The two exceptions to the paid-for criteria are house ads and public service announcements. Uncontrolled public relations media include the press release, the press conference, and crisis management.

PUBLIC RELATIONS IMPLEMENTED THROUGH CONTROLLED MEDIA

House Ads. A house ad is an ad that is prepared by the organization for use in its own publication or a publication over which it has some control. Consequently, no money changes hands, even though a particular organization may use some sort of billing mechanism. For instance, a local television station may run a house ad announcing its new fall programming.

Public service announcements. **PSAs** are announcements designed by charitable and civic organizations and broadcast on television or radio or placed in print media free of charge. The United Way, the American Heart Association, and the local arts council all rely on public service announcements. These ads are prepared just like commercials, and in many instances ad agencies donate their expertise to the design of PSAs.

The Advertising Council is a private nonprofit organization that conducts public service advertising campaigns in the public interest. The Advertising Council follows a prescribed procedure in evaluating and producing PSA campaigns (see Figure 19.1). Essentially, all public service announcements appearing on network television have been produced by the Advertising Council.

Unfortunately, networks and publishers have been so inundated with requests to run public service announcements that many are never aired or are run during very low viewing times or printed at the end of magazines. This severe competition has forced nonprofit organizations to do a better job design-

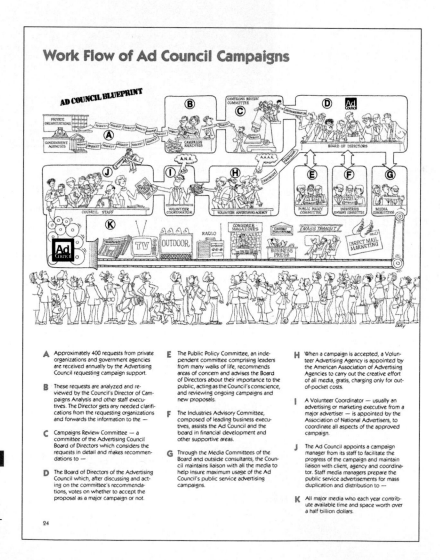

Figure 19.1

The organization of the Advertising Council.

Source: The Advertising Council Report to the American People, 1988-1989.

A Approximately 400 requests from private organizations and government agencies are received annually by the Advertising Council requesting campaign support.

B These requests are analyzed and reviewed by the Council's Director of Campaigns Analysis and other staff executives. The Director gets any needed clarifications from the requesting organizations and forwards the information to the —

C Campaigns Review Committee — a committee of the Advertising Council Board of Directors which considers the requests in detail and makes recommendations to —

D The Board of Directors of the Advertising Council which, after discussing and acting on the committee's recommendations, votes on whether to accept the proposal as a major campaign or not.

E The Public Policy Committee, an independent committee comprising leaders from many walks of life, recommends areas of concern and advises the Board of Directors about their importance to the public, acting as the Council's conscience, and reviewing ongoing campaigns and new proposals.

F The Industries Advisory Committee, composed of leading business executives, assists the Ad Council and the board in financial development and other supportive areas.

G Through the Media Committees of the Board and outside consultants, the Council maintains liaison with all the media to help insure maximum usage of the Ad Council's public service advertising campaigns.

H When a campaign is accepted, a Volunteer Advertising Agency is appointed by the American Association of Advertising Agencies to carry out the creative effort of all media, gratis, charging only for out-of-pocket costs.

I A Volunteer Coordinator — usually an advertising or marketing executive from a major advertiser — is appointed by the Association of National Advertisers, to coordinate all aspects of the approved campaign.

J The Ad Council appoints a campaign manager from its staff to facilitate the progress of the campaign and maintain liaison with client, agency and coordinator. Staff media managers prepare the public service advertisements for mass duplication and distribution to —

K All major media who each year contribute available time and space worth over a half billion dollars.

Public Service Announcements or Paid Ads?

Critics charge that the line between public service and corporate promotion is becoming blurred and that some cause-oriented spots are actually commercials in disguise. "The lines are being blurred by for-profit organizations who are trying to profit from nonprofits, wrapping themselves in the cloak of 'public service' for corporate benefit," said Don Schultz, professor at Northwestern University's Medill School of Journalism.

In October 1990, for example, McDonald's planned to sponsor a 30-minute public service television special, "Stay in School," to be aired in February 1991, produced in association with the National Basketball Association, NBC, Turner Network Television, and Nickelodeon. The special was to be run in donated network television time and include spots for the nonprofit Ronald McDonald Children's Charities. The question that results from such sponsorship is whether marketers are pushing cause marketing into ethical gray areas in their search for effective nontraditional marketing tools.

Dan Langdon, senior vice president at the Advertising Council, presents the issue this way: "Is there self-interest on the part of McDonald's? If you looked at [Ronald McDonald Children's Charities] without the 'McDonald' attached, sure, it's legitimate public service advertising. But does the company accrue benefit from this program? Sure." In response, McDonald's Children's Charities counter that it is not their intention to advertise McDonald's but to fund worthwhile projects that help the children.

McDonald's is not the only company to come under fire. Quaker Oats was refused air time by some broadcasters for including its public service announcements for the American Medical Association, starring Wilford Brimley, as part of the company's media plan for Quaker oatmeal. Philip Morris was criticized for funding the National Archives' celebration of the Bill of Rights bicentennial when critics charged that the campaign was "an attempt to subvert the ban on broadcast cigarette advertising."

Nike's "Don't be Stupid, Stay in School" campaign, Anheuser-Busch's "Know When to Say When" promotion—are these public service announcements or commercials in disguise? Advertisers are being approached more frequently by nonprofit organizations to sponsor cause-oriented programming, and they are getting more equal billing for doing so. When does such cause-related marketing become suspect?

According to Phil Schuman, vice president-associate creative director at Burson-Marstellar in New York, "a cause-marketing effort needs to be appropriate and tasteful—and viewed as legitimate—or run the risk of backfiring. The public will reject any form of disguised commercial." There is also the very real danger of negative backlash if the sponsoring organization overtly acts in the interest of making a profit.

The arguments are strong on both sides. Critics maintain that the growth in paid public service announcements may eliminate opportunities for some organizations that can't afford to advertise and don't have access to the Nikes and Quakers of the world. Furthermore, they feel that overexposure will lead to consumer apathy to charitable organizations in general. In contrast, those who favor such paid announcements argue that nonprofit organizations are eager for visibility and funding and that buying television time gives them more control over their message.

Source: Adapted from Julie Liesse, "Line Between Public Service, Paid Ads Blurs," *Advertising Age* (October 8, 1990):26.

---

ing PSAs or to run them as paid-for commercials. For a more in-depth look into public service announcements, see the box entitled "Public Service Announcements or Paid Ads?"

Corporate (Institutional) Advertising. As we mentioned earlier, corporate advertising is designed and paid for by the organization to enhance or charge the image of the firm. There is no attempt to sell a particular product. This type of advertising sometimes takes the form of position statements directed at the public. Companies seeking public support for corporate policies and programs have begun to invest more in this type of advertising, called *advocacy advertising.* For example, during the breakup of AT&T in the early 1980s, the Pacific Telesis Group had a negative image with the financial community, which viewed the firm as a high-risk investment. Among its other problems, Pacific Telesis had the lowest earning record of the seven Regional Bell Holding Companies that began operation independently on January 1, 1984. In preparation for the AT&T divestiture, however, Pacific Telesis embarked on a strategic plan to turn the firm around. Convinced that the strength of the plan, combined with the company's vastly improved financial condition, would more than compensate for poor earnings in the past, the company believed that all that remained to be accomplished was to communicate these changes to the financial community. Pacific Telesis did this through institutional advertising. The first print ad laid out the whole story—from the company's financial health, to its marketing strategy, to the strength of its top management team.[7]

corporate identity advertising
A type of advertising used by firms to establish their reputation or increase awareness.

Corporate identity advertising is another type of advertising used by firms that want to enhance or maintain their reputation among specific audiences or to establish a level of awareness of the company's name and nature of its business. Johnson & Johnson (see Ad 19.2) targeted their Healthy Start institutional campaign at pregnant women in an attempt to position itself as a concerned company. Companies that have changed their names, such as Nissan (formerly Datsun) and Exxon (formed from Esso, Humble Oil, and Standard Oil of New Jersey), have also employed corporate identity advertising.

A Case Study: Dun & Bradstreet. A classic example of what a well-planned public relations program can do for an organization involves the firm of Dun & Bradstreet (D&B). Research indicated that D&B's world leadership in providing credit information to businesses dominated the business market's perception of the company. As a result, many businesses were unaware of D&B's other informational capabilities. To promote D&B's publishing, marketing, and business information services, D&B and its agency aimed a public relations program at present and potential customers, government economists, the financial community, and the media. They created a flow of business information to promote the company's other "brand names," including Moody's Investor Service and A. C. Nielsen Research. News releases, regional economic forecasts, and a spokesperson program (using a media-trained chief economist) secured extensive media coverage in the United States, Canada, Great Britain, and West Germany. Major stories emphasizing D&B's leadership role in the business information industry appeared in *Fortune, The New York Times,* and *The Wall Street Journal.* The media coverage reached an estimated 890 million readers during the program's first year, and calls to D&B's economic analysis department for business information increased by 280 percent.

IN-HOUSE PUBLICATIONS

There is an almost endless list of publications provided by organizations to their employees and other publics. Examples are pamphlets, booklets, annual reports, books, bulletins, newsletters, inserts and enclosures, position papers, and information racks. In-house publications differ from house ads in that the latter are not distributed in-house. Rather, house ads are carried by a medium owned by

---

[7]William R. Brittingham, "How a Brand New $16 Billion Company Assesses Its Communication Needs," *Sixth Annual ARF Business Advertising Research Conference* (Advertising Research Foundation: Grand Hyatt Hotel, New York City, October 4, 1984).

Johnson & Johnson
"Healthy Start"

From the moment you become pregnant, everything you do to your body,

you do to your baby.

If you smoke...

your baby

smokes.

If you drink...

your baby

drinks.

If you do drugs...

your baby

does drugs.

And if you don't see a doctor

early and often

neither does your baby.

Johnson & Johnson brings you this message because it's never

too early to give your baby a healthy start.

Ad 19.2

This ad is targeted at pregnant women as an act of concern by Johnson & Johnson.

(Courtesy of Johnson & Johnson)

the organization that conveys information outside the organization. For example, NBC might broadcast a commercial about a new television program or *Sports Illustrated* might run an ad about its Swimsuit edition. An example of an in-house publication is the free booklet Corning Fiberglass Insulation offers on home insulation "do's and don'ts" as an integral part of its promotion effort, which is highlighted in its advertising campaign. A company's financial report, especially the annual report, may be the single most important document the company distributes. Millions of dollars are spent on the editing and design of annual reports.

SPEAKERS, PHOTOGRAPHS, AND FILMS

Maintaining visual contact with the various publics is a big part of public relations. Many companies have a speakers' bureau of articulate people who are

DUN & BRADSTREET REDEPLOYS THE RICHES

In a flurry of acquisition and divestiture, Dun & Bradstreet has sold five companies and bought 33. It still has cash for more. To whatever it buys, the company brings the technological muscle that makes it a leader in the business of business information. ■ *by Stuart Gannes*

WITH HIS deep-throated Nixonian baritone, Charles W. Moritz, chairman and chief executive of Dun & Bradstreet, likes to note the importance of tradition at the 144-year-old company. Yet he is changing the face of the business information giant. In a mere 18 months, Dun & Bradstreet has sold its TV broadcasting and book-publishing properties, while investing $1.8 billion in a breathtaking 33 acquisitions and dozens of internal development projects. The company is debt-free and has $650 million in cash and marketable securities in the till. Deciding how to invest that money is the biggest challenge Dun & Bradstreet faces.

Moritz won't say where or when his next move will come, but his strategy is clear. He has devised a two-pronged expansion plan to make Dun & Bradstreet the world's leading provider of what he calls "products and services that help business people do their job." First, he is sinking the proceeds from divestitures into high-growth acquisitions in the U.S. and Europe. Second, he is spending millions to squeeze more profits out of a private treasure trove of facts and figures—databases, in computer lingo. Dun & Bradstreet Credit Services, for example, tracks the credit history of seven million businesses. Donnelley Marketing, the company's direct mail operation, keeps current addresses and other data on 75 million U.S. households. Through computer technology Dun & Bradstreet is transforming these proprietary databases into a stream of new information products tailored to the varying needs of millions of disparate customers.

Moritz is moving at a time of intense interest in the "information industry." The exact nature of this industry is frustratingly fuzzy. Until recently it was the domain of traditional media companies: magazine, newspaper, and book publishers, and TV and radio broadcasters. Now the definition is expanding to include the business of selling computer-generated data and data services that massage the information. Scores of companies have claimed turf in the information industry. They range from data network operators to telephone service providers to banks. GE Information Services, a division of General Electric, says it is an information industry leader because it operates the world's largest private telecommunications network. AT&T and its seven offspring all see themselves as information industry powerhouses. Claiming to be a player, Citicorp says, "Information about money has become almost as important as money itself." Publishers and broadcasters also insist they can grab pieces of the market for computerized data.

Yet security analysts regard Dun & Bradstreet and other compilers of business statistics like Dow Jones (owner of the *Wall Street Journal*) and McGraw-Hill (owner of Standard & Poor's) as the purest, most attractive information industry plays. Beginning a decade ago, these companies created records, partly to control internal costs. They have since realized that widespread use of remote terminals and personal computers equipped to receive data from mainframes has created a vast new market for electronically generated information.

Dun & Bradstreet's profits have been superb. They're down for the last four quarters, but that's mainly because nonrecurring gains on the sale of properties had pumped up profits the year before. Dun & Bradstreet's three main operating divisions—business information services, publishing, and marketing services—all chalked up record operating revenue and income last year. And the company ranked 23rd in return on shareholders' equity in FORTUNE's directory of the 500 largest U.S. service corporations; over the past ten years, return on equity has averaged more than 25%.

Wall Street investment firms widely recommend the stock, even though it recently hit a record high and is selling at more than 20 times earnings. "If somebody wanted to take over Dun & Bradstreet he might have to pay 40 times earnings, and it might still be a good deal," says Victoria A. Butcher, who follows the company for the New York brokerage firm of F. Eberstadt & Co.

Chairman Moritz, 49, and President Robert E. Weissman, 44, took over in January. "They are very different individuals, and each is making a major contribution," says Harvard economics professor John R. Meyer, a Dun & Bradstreet director since 1961. Moritz, who has a marketing background, began his career as an account executive at Reuben H. Donnelley, acquired by Dun & Bradstreet in 1961 and now the largest publisher of Yellow Pages other than the telephone companies. "I've always been conscious of the needs of the customer," he says. "When people come to me with a new business proposal, I tell them, 'Put it in

Joyce "the Voice" Gordon records messages in a New York studio for DunsVoice, an automated service customers phone for credit information.

Reprinted through the courtesy of the Editors of FORTUNE.
© 1985 TIME INC.

terms a customer can relate to.'" Weissman, who is chief operating officer, is an admitted "techie." He hacks away at the personal computer in his office, compiling private databases on everything from jokes and Christmas card addresses to a shopping list of compact audio disks.

In 1983 Moritz, Weissman, and ten senior managers drafted a 28-page corporate strategy statement that laid out Dun & Bradstreet's new policy on acquisitions and internal development. Moritz carries a copy in his briefcase at all times. Although he won't let outsiders see the document, Moritz says, "The word 'customer' is the most frequent word in there." The statement was approved by his predecessor, Harrington Drake, in late 1983. The effects soon rippled through the Dun & Bradstreet empire. In January 1984 the company sold Funk & Wagnalls, a publisher whose reference books retail in supermarkets. Dun & Bradstreet says Funk & Wagnalls failed to meet objectives for profitability and growth. Four days later the company completed the sale of Corinthian Broadcasting Corp., which owns six TV stations, to Dallas-based A.H. Belo for $606 million. The problem there wasn't lack of profits or growth. With 1983 earnings of $47.2 million on revenues of $100.6 million, says Moritz, "Corinthian was a hell of a good business, but we saw it was going to require a whole set of management skills that we weren't really that good at."

Dun & Bradstreet has done plenty to offset the divestitures. It made 23 acquisitions in 1984, and ten this year. The best known are Datastream, a British investment analysis firm, and the U.S. division of Britain's Thomas Cook travel agency. Others include market research and insurance services companies, specialty software developers, six more publishers of Yellow Pages, and technical magazines. Many are cash-hungry businesses growing 30% to 50% annually.

INTERNAL DEVELOPMENT projects got an infusion of $140 million. The databases range from Credit Services and Donnelley Marketing to Moody's Investors Service, which publishes corporate financial profiles, and Official Airline Guides, which sells up-to-date airline schedules to travel agents and companies. Research expenditures, mostly on computer software to manipulate these data, increased more than 30% last year. "We've been able to take an existing database, reformat it, spin it around, and develop a whole slew of new products for our customers," explains Moritz. Ten years ago, Dun & Bradstreet credit reports were as uniform as Model T Fords. Today they challenge Heinz for variety.

Dun & Bradstreet can tailor products to specific customers. The company can electronically comb the credit information database and generate reports on individual companies or industry groups. Topics range from a firm's bill payment history to the number of contracts it has with federal agencies. "Gillette's razors help it sell more blades," says James E. Rutter, an executive vice president who runs Dun & Bradstreet Credit Services. "Our software is the conduit for more data."

Take, for instance, Donnelley Marketing. Its database of consumers—gleaned from census tracts, telephone listings, auto registrations, and other public sources—grew out of its direct mail business, which distributes grocery coupons to households. Moritz explains how he thought about expanding the business: "As long as we viewed this as a mailing list, we were putting blinders on. We asked what would happen if we said, 'This is

---

Dun & Bradstreet's public relations campaign resulted in widespread publicity for the company's varied informational services, as illustrated in this edition of *Fortune*.

(Courtesy of Doremus Porter Novelli.)

made available to talk about topics at the public's request. Apple Computer, Harvard University, and the Children's Hospital in Houston, Texas, all have speakers' bureaus.

Pictures of people, products, places, and events may all be desired by some publics. It is important for an organization that receives such requests to maintain a picture file and make sure these photographs are accurate, in good condition, and delivered promptly. Even the permissions for ads in this book were provided because they present the advertisers in a positive light. Companies seldom give permission for ads that are to be criticized.

Films, especially videotapes, have become a major public relations tool for a great many companies. At $1,000 to $2,000 per minute, these videos are not cheap. However, for a company like Cunard Cruise Line, mailing videotapes that show the beauty of a newly developed Caribbean paradise to 10,000 travel agents is a worthwhile investment.

DISPLAYS, EXHIBITS, AND STAGED EVENTS

There is no clear distinction between displays, exhibits, and staged events, though display is thought of as the simplest technique of the three. A picture of a new store being built and a presentation of a company's product line at a regional fair are examples of displays. Exhibits tend to be larger, may have moving parts, sounds, or video, and are usually manned by a company representative. Booth exhibits are very important at trade shows, where many companies take orders for a majority of their annual sales. Parade floats, museum exhibits, and historic exhibits are other common types.

There are various kinds of staged events, such as open houses and plant tours. However, the use of more elaborate staged events has seen the most growth. Corporate sponsorship of various sporting events has evolved as a favorite public relations tactic.

For example, *Sports Illustrated* magazine has developed an elaborate events strategy in order to attract new advertisers. The centerpiece of that strategy is the Sports Festival, a 70,000-square-foot exhibition that tours Time-Warner's six Six Flags theme parks during the summers, spending ten days at each park. The exhibition will include interactive games allowing participants to slam dunk a basketball or simulate a race against Carl Lewis. Eventually, 15,000-square-foot versions will start touring college campuses and shopping malls.[8]

PUBLIC RELATIONS IMPLEMENTED THROUGH UNCONTROLLED MEDIA

As we mentioned earlier, there are instances when an organization has no direct control over how the media will report on corporate activities. Sometimes the company will initiate the publicity and even provide pertinent information to be used by the media. In other cases the media will report a news event (good or bad) without guidance from the company. In order for either scenario to turn out favorably for the company, it is necessary for the public relations practitioner to become an expert at *press relations*.

The relationship between the public relations person and the media representative is tenuous at best and often adversarial. The reporter is motivated by the public's right to know, and the public relations practitioner's loyalty is to the client or company. A successful relationship between public relations and media is built on a reputation for honesty, accuracy, and professionalism. Once this reputation is tarnished or lost, the public relations person cannot function

news release Primary medium used to deliver public relations messages to the media.

The News Release. The **news release,** or press release, is the primary medium used to deliver public relations messages to the various media editors and reporters. It must be written differently for each medium, accommodating space and time limitations. The more carefully the news release is planned and written, the better the chance it has of being accepted and published as written. Being a good writer is considered a prerequisite for going into public relations. The news release is the primary reflection of this skill. Note the tight and simple writing style in the news release from Plumbing-Heating-Cooling Information Bureau, the official spokesperson for that industry.

press conference A public gathering of media people for the purpose of establishing a company's position or making a statement.

The Press Conference. One of the riskiest public relations activities is the **press conference.** Although some companies, such as Polaroid and Chrysler Motors, have been very successful in introducing new products through press conferences, there have been many disasters. For example, in the fall of 1990 Victor Kiam, president of Remington Razors and owner of the New England Patriots football team, called a press conference concerning the allegations against his players over the improper treatment of a female reporter in the locker room.

---

[8]Scott Donaton, "Playing Hardball: 'SI' Rethinks Strategy," *Advertising Age* (March 15, 1993):3, 54.

An example of a news release. The language is concise and simple.

Protesters were refusing to buy Remington products, and questions raised by reporters and answers given by Kiam had serious repercussions on the sale of his razors.

Companies worry about various issues when planning a press conference. Will the press show up? Will they ask the right questions? Will they ask questions the company cannot or will not answer? One way to avoid some of these problems is to design an effective press kit. A press kit, normally in a folder form, provides all the important background information to members of the press either before they arrive or when they arrive at the press conference. The risk in offering press kits is that they give reporters all the necessary information so that the press conference itself becomes unnecessary.

Crisis Management. The 1980s and 1990s seemed to be two decades of corporate disasters. Insider trading scandals, oil spills, plane crashes, and management improprieties made it difficult *not* to characterize American business as corrupt and poorly managed. This image is due in part to our efficient mass communication system and in part to the media's desire to publish sensational news. Handling bad news is the responsibility of public relations. The pubic relations strategist must anticipate the possibility of a crisis and establish a mechanism for dealing with it and ensuring that it will not happen again. Johnson & Johnson demonstrated the correct way to handle a crisis when in 1982 an unknown person) contaminated dozens of Tylenol capsules with cyanide, causing the death of eight people and a loss of $100 million in recalled packages for Johnson &

Press conferences are high risk activities, but can pay-off in a big way if managed correctly.

Johnson. In 1986 a second poisoning incident forced J&J to withdraw all Tylenol capsules from the market at a loss of $150 million. The company abandoned the capsule form of medication and consequently had to redesign its production facilities. It also ran a series of ads informing the consumer of these changes, gave away free packages of the new product, and endeared the consumer through its honesty and quick action.

In contrast, Jack-in-the-Box restaurants may never recover from the public relations disaster they created in 1993. The tragedy began with a $2.69 "Kid's Meal." On January 11, Michael Nole, 2, happily tore into the dinnertime cheeseburger bought for him at the Jack-in-the-Box restaurant on South 56th Street in Tacoma, Washington. The next night, the boy was admitted to Children's Hospital & Medical Center in Seattle. Ten days later, Michael died of kidney and heart failure. Soon reports came in that over 300 people had been stricken with the same *E. coli* bacteria responsible for Michael's death. Most victims had eaten recently at Jack-in-the-Box outlets in Idaho, Nevada, and Washington. Others apparently got sick after contact with restaurant customers.

The company's 12-person crisis team, working from a plan devised in the mid-1980s, quickly scrapped nearly 20,000 pounds of hamburger patties prepared at meat plants where the bacteria was suspected of originating. It also changed meat suppliers, installed a toll-free number to field consumer complaints, and instructed employees to turn up the cooking heat to kill the deadly germ. But it took nearly a week for the company to admit publicly its responsibility for the poisonings. Even then, the admission seemed half-hearted. At a Seattle news conference, Jack-in-the-Box president Robert J. Nugent attempted to deflect blame—first criticizing state health authorities for not telling his company about new cooking regulations, then pointing a finger at Vos Companies, which supplied the meat. Sales dropped off 20 percent the first week.[9]

Sometimes a company handles a crisis poorly at the onset and makes good

[9]Ronald Grover, "Boxed in a Jack in the Box," *Business Week* (February 5, 1993):40.

decisions later. This is what happened to Sears, Roebuck and Co. in 1992 when a scandal emerged in response to several of its automotive service departments. Apparently several stores were engaging in a variety of illegal activities, including charging for work not performed, charging for parts not replaced, and installing used parts. Sears's initial response was to deny the allegations. When it became clear that the reports were true, Sears changed its position and accepted responsibility.

Sometimes, in the case of natural disasters, prevention is not possible. However, there are instances when a carefully planned strategy is appropriate. When Hurricane Andrew struck Louisiana and Florida in 1992, businesses had a choice as to how they would respond to this terrible disaster. Some supermarkets decided to take advantage of people in crisis by charging exorbitant prices for food, batteries, bottled water, and so forth. Insurance companies also hurt their reputations by their slow response in adjustments and payments. Conversely, several companies did the right thing:

- AT&T provided 200 coinless public phones and donated to shelters 2,000 TeleTickets usable for free local and long-distance calls.
- American Express pledged $100,000 and relief supplies to the American Red Cross Disaster Relief Fund.
- Campbell Soup shipped approximately 5,000 cases of food to southern Florida. Another 5,000 cases were sent to Lafayette, Louisiana.
- Coors shipped 80,000 quarts of drinking water to both states.
- Toyota Motor Sales USA donated $250,000 to the Red Cross.
- Ford Motor Company provided more than $800,000 in cash contributions and goods and services to the relief efforts, including more than 100 vehicles for use by nonprofit organizations in both states.[10]

$\mathcal{N}$ONCOMMERCIAL ADVERTISING

Thus far we have discussed public relations advertising employed by corporations and organizations that are motivated to increase profits or create a positive company image. This is not the only type of public relations. **Noncommercial advertising** is advertising that is sponsored by business or organizations that are not motivated by the maximization of profits. The emphasis in this type of advertising is on changing attitudes or behaviors relative to some idea or cause. This is not to say that these organizations operate cost-free or are staffed by all volunteers. There are often pleas for donations in order to keep the organization going, but acquiring money is not the ultimate goal. Noncommercial advertising is typically sponsored by nonprofit organizations.

noncommercial advertising
Advertising that is sponsored by an organization to promote a cause rather than to maximize profits.

NONPROFIT ORGANIZATIONS

Placing an organization in the nonprofit category is not simple. Although the Red Cross and the Salvation Army are clearly considered nonprofit, organizations such as the U.S. Postal Service are not as easy to classify. Ultimately, the only

---

[10]"Marketers Come to Aid of Victims," *Advertising Age* (August 31, 1992):38.

important classification dimension is a legal one. Section 501 of the Revenue Code grants tax-exempt status to 23 categories of organizations. Thirty-nine percent of these are covered under Section 501(c)(3), which includes charitable, religious, scientific, and educational institutions. Section 501(c)(4) of the tax code includes civic leagues; Section 501(c)(6) covers business leagues; and Section 501(c)(7) includes social clubs.

The government's rationale for giving these organizations special status is twofold. First, the concept of "public goods" argues that nonprofit organizations provide services, such as health care, education, and basic research, that would not be provided were it not for the tax subsidy. Second, nonprofit organizations provide "quality assurance" in that they furnish services in areas in which consumers are ordinarily ill-equipped to judge quality, such as health care and education.

In their book *Strategic Marketing for Nonprofit Organizations,* Philip Kotler and Alan Andreasen contend that all advertising sponsored by nonprofit organizations falls into one of six categories:

1. Political advertising (local, state, federal)

2. Social-cause advertising (Drug-Free America, Planned Parenthood)

3. Charitable advertising (Red Cross, United Way)

4. Government advertising (parks and recreation departments, U.S. Armed Forces)

5. Private nonprofit advertising (colleges, universities, symphonies, museums)

6. Association advertising (American Dental Association, The American Bankers Association)[11]

Each of these six categories reflects a slightly different approach toward advertising. Political advertising, for example, has reached a very high level of sophistication and is guided by in-depth research and highly creative minds. On the topic of research, see the Issues and Controversies box for an example of how the American Cancer Society conducts its campaign.

Conversely, charitable and private organizations have limited funding and expertise and rely heavily on outside assistance and public service announcements. An example of nonprofit advertising is the TV spot Dave Thomas, founder of Wendy's and an adopted child himself, did for the Adopt-A-Child organization.

EVALUATING PUBLIC RELATIONS

Measuring the effectiveness of public relations has been a problem, which is a major reason that public relations has not been accepted as an efficient and effective approach to behavior change. We need better standards for gauging the effectiveness of public relations efforts.

Evaluating public relations differs in several ways from evaluating advertising. One major difference relates to the lack of control public relations practi-

---

[11]Philip Kotler and Alan R. Andreasen, *Strategic Marketing for Nonprofit Organizations,* 3rd ed. (Englewood Cliffs, NJ: Prentice Hall, 1987):544-545.

Cancer Society Tests the Waters

The American Cancer Society is considering its first paid advertising campaign to deliver a blunt anti-smoking message and directly criticize tobacco companies. The burning question, however, is whether any magazines would run it.

Many magazines are addicted to tobacco advertising and would likely be reluctant to run controversial ads that bite the hand that feeds them, even if the ads are paid for. Last year, the tobacco industry spent $264 million on magazine advertising, accounting for 4 percent of all magazine revenue, according to Publishers Information Bureau.

So, for the first time in its 80-year history, the American Cancer Society has commissioned a study to ascertain whether magazines, as well as television, billboards, and radio, would accept blunt anti-smoking ads. The reaction thus far has been what publishers politely characterize as "cautious." The society hasn't created actual ads, as yet. In the survey, a magazine is asked by mail or telephone about specific sentences that could be included in a final campaign and whether a publisher is concerned "that tobacco companies might cancel their advertising as a result of your magazine running an anti-smoking ad." An example of a proposed ad includes the following statements: "If you don't smoke, don't start," or "According to the Surgeon General, tobacco is more addictive than crack and cocaine," or "More Americans die each year from illness related to smoking than from heroin, crack, homicide, car accidents, fires, and AIDS put together."

The tobacco industry itself is fuming over the possible assault from the American Cancer Society. "We don't encourage underage smoking," says a spokesperson from Philip Morris USA. The company has an ad campaign of its own with the slogan "It's the Law," referring to the fact that individuals have to be at least 18 years old to buy a pack of smokes. And the Washington-based Tobacco Institute says it offers free guides to parents on how to "discourage youth smoking."

The anti-smoking campaign is one of several under consideration. The American Cancer Society, which collected $350 million in donations in 1992, is planning a campaign to educate women in the nation's inner cities about free mammograms to detect breast cancer. The organization launched a modest test campaign with a budget not exceeding $30,000 in Philadelphia. The campaign will coincide with free public service announcements in a city with a similar-size population. This dual approach let the American Cancer Society gauge whether free or paid advertising is more effective.

The organization is also polling its contributors and volunteers to determine whether these individuals want even a portion of the money they contribute to go toward advertising. Why paid advertising in the first place? The space for so-called public service announcements has gotten increasingly crowded and that has frustrated the American Cancer Society.

Adapted from Kevin Goldman, "Cancer Society Runs Ad Ideas Past Media," *The Wall Street Journal* (December 16, 1992):B3.

---

tioners exercise over whether their message appears in the media and what it will look like if it does appear. Advertisers at least know the exact nature of their messages and the schedule of exposure to target audiences. Public relations practitioners must devote significant effort just to identifying and tracking the output of a campaign.

Public relations measurement may be divided into two categories: *process evaluation* (what goes out) and *outcome evaluation* (effect on the audience).

PROCESS EVALUATION

process evaluation Measuring the effectiveness of media and nonmedia efforts to get the desired message out to the target audience.

Process evaluation examines the success of the public relations program in getting the message out to the target audiences. It focuses on media and nonmedia approaches with such questions as:

Ad 19.3

Companies such as Burrelle's, which provide evaluation services, are very important to public relations.

(Courtesy of Burrelle's Press Clipping Service)

■ How many placements did we get? (see Ad 19.3.) For example, how many articles were published? How many times did our spokesperson appear on talk shows? How much airplay did our public service announcements receive?

■ Has there been a change in audience knowledge, attitudes, or reported behavior (as measured in the pre- and posttracking)?

■ Can we associate actual behavior change (for example, product trial, repeat purchase, voting, or joining) with the public relations effort?

Outcome Evaluation. There are several difficulties in evaluating the outcome of public relations efforts. As with advertising, it is hard to assess the public rela-

Concepts & APPLICATIONS

Does Public Relations Make a Difference?

Results and measurement are two of the hottest buzz words in public relations today. The current emphasis by senior management and shareholders on quarterly earnings as the main measurement of success has accelerated the pressure on public relations to contribute directly to the bottom line through marketing. Historically, this type of public relations was known as publicity and promotion, and success was measured by the amount of news clips the public relations professional generated or simply the number of people who attended a special event.

Evaluating more broad-based public relations calls for more sophisticated research, too. There is a variety of research techniques that can be used to develop and evaluate a company's public relations program and its contribution to the bottom line. The right mix of research can help determine audience receptivity to the message, their information needs, their concerns that relate to the company and its products, and ultimately whether or not the communication effort is having the desire effect. Public opinion surveys, focus groups, and secondary data research are some of the ways to collect information and evaluate an organization's communications efforts. They give the practitioner statistical validation for programs.

Public opinion surveys should be conducted by a firm that specializes in providing such a service. A research expert will help develop the questionnaire, identify potential respondents, administer the survey, and provide an analysis and interpretation. The company should work closely with the research firm and give as much information as possible about company objectives and how the information will be used. Results are useful when first developing a public relations program, launching new products, or making business decisions around public policy issues.

Focus groups are a qualitative research method in which a group of individuals representing a company's target audience is recruited for a guided discussion. The information gathered in focus groups is not quantifiable—it cannot be applied or projected to the whole target audience—but it often yields a vast amount of information about how effective a communication strategy might be or how receptive an audience might be to a specific public relations effort.

Numerous studies (secondary research) are being done around the country and the world. The results of many of these studies are available through on-line databases such as Lexis/Nexis. This is a much less costly way to get quantifiable data to use in public relations planning. However, the information generally will not be specific to a secondary situation. So a thorough evaluation of the data, as they relate to the company's information needs, is necessary to make the data of real value.

Adapted from Jeffrey Julin, "Counting New Clips to Primary Research," *A&M Review* (April 1993):32-33.

tions contribution within a larger marketing communications mix. In fact, because public relations programs have smaller budgets and, presumably, more modest effects, results are even more difficult to isolate and measure than they are for advertising. In addition, unless the program is directly aimed at changing a specific audience behavior, such as product purchase, "success" is ambiguous and hard to ascertain. This is also true of "image" campaigns, such as corporate communications or community relations. How do you determine whether a public relations campaign has changed popular attitudes toward a product or an organization? And even if a positive change in awareness and attitudes is achieved, it is difficult to know whether these changes will lead to desired behaviors, such as receptivity to salespeople, donations, or a purchase. See the Concepts and Applications box for further discussion of the measurement problem in public relations.

Despite the problems associated with evaluating public relations, there is little doubt that carefully planned public relations works. The key here is to move public relations into the realm of professional management. Major public relations firms leave nothing to chance. They carefully identify target markets, establish appropriate objectives, and design and implement public relations strategies that are equivalent to the best advertising strategies. It is under these conditions that public relations complements advertising and vice versa.

$\mathscr{S}$UMMARY

- Public relations is a management function practiced by companies, governments, trade and professional associations, and nonprofit institutions.

- Advertising and public relations are separate activities, but the two work best when they are integrated.

- Both advertising and public relations use a number of different media. Public relations practitioners often have less control over their messages than do advertisers.

- Public relations activities can be performed by a department within a large organization or by a public relations agency.

- Public relations techniques can be divided into controlled media and uncontrolled media.

- Corporate advertising is implemented by organizations to enhance or change the firm's image.

- Managing crises is the responsibility of public relations.

- Public relations is similar to advertising in that it must be evaluated, although its direct effects on the audience are difficult to establish.

$\mathscr{Q}$UESTIONS

1 How does public relations differ from advertising? Does public relations offer advantages not available through advertising? Explain.

2 Define the concept of public opinion. Why is it so important to the success of public relations?

3 Dynacon Industries is a major supplier of packaging containers for industrial and food-service companies. Its research labs have developed a foam-polymer container with revolutionary environmental characteristics. The public relations department learns the trade and consumer press is unwilling to give the product the coverage the company needs. Public relations proposes that paid space (news and trade magazines) be used. The message will feature product background and the story about the environmental implications. Public relations argues that half the media and creative costs should be shared from the advertising budget. If you were in charge of these budgets, what would you recommend?

4 The chapter makes clear that prescription drug companies are supposed to be forbidden by law to advertise directly to consumers. However, Upjohn has run a campaign on hair-loss on commercial television. Similarly, CIBA-GEIGY has promoted an oral medication as an alternative to gallbladder surgery in daily newspaper ads. Is this considered legal because it is public relations (despite using paid space and time)? What difference should it make whether the consumer is reached through advertising or public relations?

5 Wendy Johnson and Phil Draper are having a friendly career disagreement before class. Wendy claims that she is not interested in advertising because she dislikes the "crass-commercialism" of promoting products and services that many people don't need. Phil counters by saying that public relations is doing the same thing by "selling ideas and images," and its motives are usually just as economic as advertising. If you overheard this discussion would you take Wendy's or Phil's side? Could you offer advice on ethical considerations of both careers?

6 Suppose your fraternity, sorority, or other campus group was planning a special weekend event on campus to raise public support and funds for a local charity. This will cost your organization time and money. Although contributions at the event will be some measure of the effectiveness of your public relations program, what other things could you do to evaluate the public relations activities?

$\mathscr{S}$UGGESTED CLASS PROJECT

Locate library materials on two organizational crises, one whose outcome was positive and the other negative. Evaluate why these outcomes resulted.

$\mathscr{F}$URTHER READINGS

CAMINITI, SUSAN, "The Payoff from a Good Reputation," *Fortune* (February 10, 1992):74-77.

CANTOR, BILL, *Inside Public Relations: Experts in Action* (New York: Longman, 1984).

HWANG, SUEIN L., "Linking Products to Breast-Cancer Fight Helps Form Bond with Their Customers," *The Wall Street Journal* (September 21, 1993): B-1.

KLIPPER, MICHAEL, *Getting Your Message Out: How to Get, Use, and Survive Radio and TV Air Time* (Englewood Cliffs, NJ: Prentice Hall, 1984).

LOVELL, RONALD, *Inside Public Relations* (Boston: Allyn & Bacon, 1982).

NAGER, NORMAN R., AND RICHARD H. TRUITT, *Strategic Public Relations Counseling* (New York: Longman, 1987).

SCOTT, WILLIAM G., "The Management of Crises and Tribulations," *Journal of Management Inquiry*, 2, no. 2 (June 1993):184-189.

WALSH, FRANK, *Public Relations Writer in the Computer Age* (Englewood Cliffs, NJ: Prentice Hall, 1985).

Pepsi's Public Relations Challenge

Advertising Age called Pepsi's handling of its 1993 product tampering scare a "a textbook case of how to come through a public relations crisis." Although in retrospect, this was certainly true, Pepsi executives had no way of knowing, in the midst of the crisis, that their approach was working. Clouding their vision were public relations critics who second-guessed Pepsi.

The crisis began on June 10 and 11 when two Seattle residents reported finding syringes in cans of Diet Pepsi. Although alarmed, Pepsi executives considered the reports local issues. Pepsi's attitude changed when a third incident was reported in New Orleans two days later. Soon, more than 50 people scattered across 24 states reported finding syringes and hypodermic needles in Pepsi cans. These reports had the potential to destroy public confidence in the purity of Pepsi products just at the peak soft-drink sales season.

Pepsi formed a crisis-management team. Its mission was to get the company through the crisis while protecting the public health. After assuring himself that it was virtually impossible to insert a syringe in a can of Pepsi before it was filled, Craig Weatherup, CEO of Pepsi-Cola North America, took to the airways to calm public fears. Appearing on ABC's *Nightline,* he stated, "The can is probably the most tamper-proof package of any food or beverage product in this country. . . ."

Appealing to logic was an important element in Weatherup's public relations approach. Appearing on a succession of news programs, he explained that 1,600 cans a minute travel down the conveyor belt in each of Pepsi's 140 bottling plants. The conveyer flips the open cans upside down immediately before filling and turns them rightside up just as the soda is poured. Seconds later the cans are sealed.

Though Weatherup's approach was convincing, his alliance with Food & Drug Administration commissioner David Kessler was a stroke of public relations genius. After quickly becoming convinced that Pepsi's production process was virtually tamper-proof, Kessler appeared with Weatherup on *Nightline.* Their united front convinced many consumers that there was no danger. Tom Pirko, a beverage-industry consultant, is one of many who believed that consumers would probably not have had this feeling if Weatherup appeared alone.

"There was no question that [Kessler] was the dominant influence in terms of the public believing [Pepsi] and cauterizing the whole thing," he explained.

On other fronts, Pepsi's public relations machine was at work calming public fears. On Tuesday, June 15, it beamed via satellite to news organizations throughout the world video footage demonstrating the safety of the canning process. After the Federal Bureau of Investigation arrested four people for making false tampering claims on June 17 and Kessler declared that there was no evidence of nationwide tampering, Pepsi ran an ad in newspapers throughout the country thanking consumers for their support. Created by BBDO Worldwide, the ad stated, "As America now knows, those stories about Diet Pepsi were a hoax. Plain and simple, not true. Hundreds of investigations have found no evidence to support a single claim."

By the time the crisis ended, 20 people were charged with making false tampering claims. Although it risked financial ruin had it mishandled the crisis, Pepsi emerged in the glow of positive public opinion and with no significant decline in sales. Consumers who believed that Pepsi did everything it could to protect the public health responded with sympathy. "People are cheering for Pepsi," explained Doug Hall, president of Richard Saunders Inc., a market research company. They believed that Pepsi had been the victim of hoaxes and copycats and that Pepsi had earned their support.

Giangola put the public relations ordeal in perspective when he stated, "It was never a production problem. There were never any injuries. There was never any health risk. And yet our product is put on trial, unjustifiably so, for an entire week. Pepsi was on trial, and we didn't do anything wrong. The reality is our cans were on network television with a needle next to them for a 72-hour period. That's an indelible image, and that's what we're trying to erase."

Sources: Marcy Magiera, "Pepsi Weathers Tampering Hoaxes," *Advertising Age* (June 21, 1993):1, 46; Michael J. McCarthy, Pepsi Faces Problem in Trying to Contain Syringe Scare," *The Wall Street Journal* (June 17, 1993):B1, B8; Laura Zinn, "The Right Moves, Baby," *Business Week* (July 5, 1993):30-31.

Questions

1. Why was Craig Weatherup's televised alliance with David Kessler so important to Pepsi's public relations success?

2. Why was it important to mount a public relations campaign on many fronts including newspaper and television ads and public appearances by senior executives?

3. Does the crisis-management aspect of public relations require split-second decision making? Provide examples from this case.

THE ADVERTISING CAMPAIGN

CHAPTER OBJECTIVES

When you have completed this chapter, you should be able to:

- Understand the role of the situation analysis in identifying key problems to be solved by the advertising

- Understand how the basic strategy decisions are developed for an advertising campaign

- Analyze how the message strategy solves the key problem

- Explain how the media plan relates to advertising objectives and message needs

- Explain how the effectiveness of an advertising campaign is evaluated

ORLANDO, FLORIDA: PROMOTING THE MAGIC VACATION

Orlando, Florida, home of Walt Disney World, Universal Studios, Sea World of Florida, and a number of other major attractions, is perceived worldwide as a top leisure destination. This should make the marketing communication program for the Orlando/Orange County Convention and Visitors Bureau Inc. an easy sell. But even in paradise, there are still promotional challenges. For one thing, there is still room for growth in the number of visitors who can be served, particularly in off seasons.

There are some other strategic problems, too. As one of the largest bureaus in the country with a budget of approximately $14 million and 1,285 member organizations—ranging from the largest attractions like Walt Disney World and Universal Studios, to small suppliers like the person who works out-of-home preparing gift packs—it has to serve a varied set of member needs.

The bureau also has a diverse group of stakeholders—members, local community leaders, its visitors, convention planners and delegates, and the travel industry—also all with varying needs. And to reach all of these different audiences the bureau has an extensive marketing communications program that involves advertising, public relations, promotions, direct marketing, trade shows, and a variety of communication tools.

Disney began the development of tourism-related activities that resulted in an explosion in visitors and the formation of the bureau in 1984. The bureau's concerns now extend beyond the Magic Kingdom, and its membership represents much more than just Disney. Both the bureau's ten-year-old slogan, *Orlando—Go for the Magic*, and its primary promotion, the *Orlando Magicard*™ allude, however, to Disney magic and its impact on the area.

The bureau's mission, according to its annual report, is to "promote the area worldwide as a premier leisure and business destination and to provide industry leadership for the community." In other words, the bureau represents every facet of the Orlando travel experience, from attractions to hotels to shopping and dining. Its mission in the mid-1990s is to bring all the convention and tourism businesses together to make things happen for the entire area.

As the bureau reflects on its mission as part of its tenth-year anniversary in 1994, one of its more difficult decisions is whether to change its slogan and other references to the "magic," and, if so, to determine in what new directions the convention and tourist association should move.[1]

This chapter will use the Orlando tourism effort as an extended case study in campaign planning. It will explain how all the pieces of this complex marketing communication program are managed under the umbrella theme of *Orlando—Go for the Magic*. It will end with a discussion of new directions for the bureau.

THE STRUCTURE OF A CAMPAIGN PLAN

In Chapter 7 we talked about the use of military metaphors for advertising planning. The *campaign* is another military term adopted by the advertising

---

[1]Special thanks to Danny Radcliff and Bob Moquin, North American Tourism Division, Orlando/Orange County Convention and Visitors Bureau.

advertising campaign
A comprehensive advertising plan for a series of different but related ads that appear in different media across a specified time period.

industry. An **advertising campaign** is a comprehensive advertising plan for a series of different but related ads that appear in different media across a specified time period. The campaign is designed strategically to meet a set of objectives and to solve some critical problem. It is a short-term plan that usually runs for a year or less.

Many of the advertisements you see are "single-shot" ads. However, much of the advertising national advertisers use is developed as a campaign that extends across time, different audiences and stakeholders, and different advertising vehicles and marketing communication opportunities. A campaign may focus on one specific product attribute or one audience, or it may cover all the attributes and reach all the audiences.

A campaign plan summarizes the marketplace situation and the strategies and tactics for the primary areas of creative and media, as well as the other marketing communication areas of sales promotion, direct marketing, and public relations. The campaign plan is presented to the client in a formal business presentation. It is also summarized in a written document called a *plans book*.

The Orlando Bureau incorporates all its planning into an annual marketing plan that focuses primarily on its marketing communications efforts. An annual publication called *Marketing Resource Book* summarizes the marketing plan for members. It details all of its advertising, promotion, and public relations plans.

SITUATION ANALYSIS

SWOT analysis   A study of the Strengths, Weaknesses, Opportunities, and Threats that will impact upon the successful promotion of the product, the service, or the company.

The first section of most campaign plans is a *situation analysis* that summarizes all the relevant information available about the product, the company, the competitive environment, the industry, and the consumers. Sometimes called a *business review*, this information is obtained using primary and secondary research techniques.

One approach to managing the information compiled in this process is the use of a **SWOT analysis**, which stands for Strengths, Weaknesses, Opportunities, and Threats. During the situation analysis, you are compiling all the information you can about the brand and its competitive situation, marketplace factors such as the health of the category, and the behavior of consumers relative to this brand. In order to make sense of what you find, some planners recast this information in terms of *internal factors*—strengths that lead to opportunities— and *external factors*—weaknesses that make the brand vulnerable to threats from outside. We will describe the basic sections of a situation analysis here, using the Orlando plan, and we will conclude with a section on the type of information that might be included by a client, here the bureau, in its SWOT analysis.

The Orlando Bureau. We will begin with a background review for this case which illustrates the type of information in a situation analysis. The Orlando/ Orange County Convention and Visitors Bureau, which was founded in 1984, is a community-supported organization charged with marketing the Orlando destination worldwide. With a staff of over 100 full-time employees, the bureau maintains offices in Orlando, Chicago, and Washington, DC. It also has representatives in five overseas locations: London, Brussels, Frankfurt, Tokyo, Seoul. An office in Coral Gables serves the Latin American market.

Once a small rural town known for sunshine and acres of surrounding citrus groves, Orlando today is recognized around the world for its world-class attractions; it is also known as a sophisticated center for meetings and conventions. Orlando plays host to more than 13 million visitors each year. Although

Disney was the force behind the development of a major tourism industry in Orange County in the 1970s, other attractions, such as Cypress Gardens, were founded in central Florida in the 1940s. Thus, the tourism industry has been an important industry for 60 years.

A membership organization, the bureau's members represent every facet of the Orlando travel experience. The bureau's primary function is, first, to book conventions and, second, to manage the exchange of information and business leads to and from members. Its publications are supported totally by advertising purchased by members. The bureau doesn't make a final sale other than in signing up conventions; in general it makes arrangements and then passes the information on to members who follow through on the business. In that sense, it is a facilitating service.

The Orlando Market. The bureau's business is divided into two basic groups—tourists and conventioneers. The tourists come by train, air, and car; the conventioneers primarily arrive by air. The tourists usually plan their own trips or use an auto club or travel agent; conventioneers generally use a travel agent or meeting planner.

Passenger traffic at Orlando International Airport is increasing every year; for example, it increased 15 percent in 1992 and 12 percent in 1993. At the same time, air traffic nationally increased by only 3.7 percent. Because of this growth, the airport is planning an expansion that will triple present capacity.

The Orlando area hosts over 10,000 meetings annually; combined with the number of visitors to trade shows, the area brings in an estimated 1.4 million delegates to the area per year, resulting in an economic impact of over $1 billion. Meetings may be corporate—many big companies hold annual sales meetings at vacation destinations like Orlando—or noncorporate, a group that includes associations and their meetings and conventions. Some meetings combine both.

The majority of the meetings are noncorporate, accounting for 53 percent of

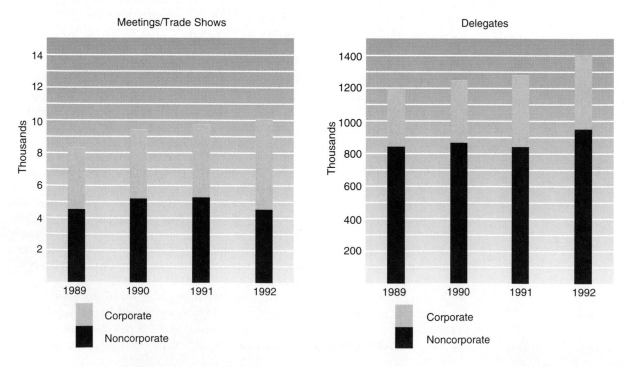

the total meetings and 67 percent of the total delegates. The greatest growth area, however, has been corporate meetings. The total average group size of Orlando's meeting business was 133 delegates, with noncorporate meetings averaging 168 delegates versus 93 for corporate meetings. As Figure 20.1 illustrates, the number of meetings as well as the delegate count have been increasing steadily since 1989.

In terms of expenditures, delegates average $152 per day; association expenditures are $16; and exhibitor expenditures are $80. Of the delegate expenditures, 51 percent goes to lodging, 22.3 percent to food, 8.1 percent to retail, and the remaining 18.6 percent is miscellaneous.

The seasonality patterns for meetings are different from those of the more general occupancy rates with January, February, October, and November being the key months; attendance is highest in January and lowest in June, July, and December. The highest number of corporate meetings was hosted in February, while the highest level of noncorporate meetings was experienced in October.

Consumer Review. Consumers buy vacations just like they buy other products—they search for information, they shop around, they compare costs and features. Particularly in periods of economic downturns, they are value conscious. Destinations that cater to travelers by offering high value and quality will prosper not only in the difficult times but also in the years that follow.

In terms of the information search for travelers and vacationers, the bureau's surveys show that the majority of people who request information do come to Orlando within three years of receiving the bureau's information packet, and key decisions about what to do and where to stay are usually made before visitors leave home. Generally, the travel decision is a joint family decision, although the female head of household usually collects the travel information.

In terms of business visitors, the decision is much more complex and involves intermediaries such as conference planners and travel agents. The visitor, in other words, is often only indirectly involved in the actual decision about where to go. The convention planner, who recommends such decisions, is often working many years in advance of the conference.

In terms of an average visitor profile, the bureau characterizes its visitors as 42 years old, with an income of $40,000 plus, having three people in the party (28 percent traveling with children), staying four to five days, and likely to return to the area within another three years. The average delegate expenditures are $623 per day, and the average leisure traveler spends $75 a day. Table 20.1 gives the demographics of visitors to Orlando.

Table 20.2 summarizes the characteristics of air and auto visitors in 1992. Note that the air visitors generally spent more, however, the auto visitors brought more people and stayed longer; they also drove in more from neighboring states—although the visitors from Ontario made the longest commute. New York is the state that supplied the most visitors when the two lists are combined. The differences in expenditures probably reflect the fact that a higher proportion of air visitors are either business travelers attending conferences or international visitors; the family driving to Orlando on a vacation is likely to be more cost conscious. The percentage of repeat visitors is around 85 percent for both groups, which is a good indication of the level of customer satisfaction associated with an Orlando visit.

Seasonality affects visits to Orlando as illustrated in Figure 20.2. The occupancy rates are at their highest in February, March, and April and then again in June and July. The early winter months of November, December, and January are

Table 20.1

Demographics of Orlando Visitors
from North America

Consumer Profile		Visitors to Orlando (%)
Sex	Male	53
	Female	47
Age	Under 25 yrs	10
	25–44 yrs	49
	45–54 yrs	18
	Over 55 yrs	23
Income		
	Under $20,000/yr	7
	20,000–35,000	21
	35,001–50,000	29
	Over $50,000/yr	43
Marital Status		
	Married	68
	Single	32
Geographic Distribution		
	New England	6
	Mid Atlantic	20
	South Atlantic	29
	South Central	13
	W. South Central	14
	E. North Central	9
	W. North Central	3
	Mountain	6
	Pacific	9

Source: 1992 Orlando Perspective, Orlando/Orange County Convention & Visitors Bureau, Inc., Research Dept.

Table 20.2

Descriptive Data: Area Visitors,
1992

	Air Visitors	Auto Visitors
Average expenditures/party/trip	$1,440.32	$1,167.84
Average number/party	2.62	3.00
Average expenditures/person/trip	$548.63	$393.09
Average number of nights	4.92	6.5
Average expenditures/person/day	$112.29	$60.60
Average expenditures/party/day	$293.92	$180.08
Percent of repeat visitors	87	88
Used travel agent for making some arrangements	59	9
Used services of an auto club for planning the trip	13	21
Used advance reservations for paid lodging	85	63
Used a package plan on the trip	28	11
Used a rental car for the trip	66	N/A
Origins of Visitors from North America	NY, NJ, CA, MA, PA, IL, TX, OH, MI, VA	GA, NY, NC, OH, PA, SC, MI, TX, ONT, TN

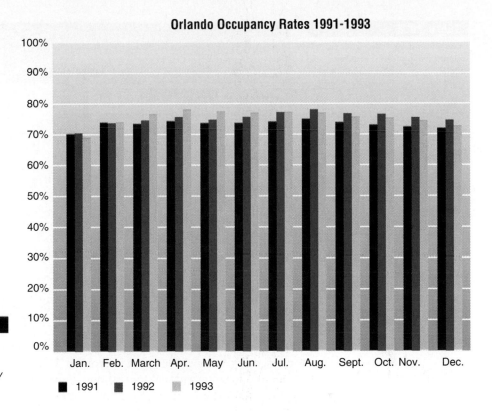

Orlando Occupancy Rates 1991-1993

Figure 20.2

Orlando occupancy rates, 1991–1993.

(Courtesy of Orlando/Orange County Convention & Visitors Bureau, Inc.)

■ 1991 ■ 1992 ▨ 1993

low, as are the late summer and fall months of August, September, and October. Figure 20.2 also illustrates the impact of the 1991 recession and the Gulf War, which were periods when occupancy dropped dramatically. As you can see, the trend is on the increase as the economic conditions in the United States slowly turn around.

Competitive Review. The competition in the tourism and convention industry is intense. There is always a trade-off between … "new" areas, with all their appeal to exploration, and the older well-regarded attractions, with their glamour and tradition. Orlando is lucky to have both. However, a number of new attractions, as well as well-loved older places in other parts of Florida—and outside the state—compete both for vacationers and conventioneers. In Orange County a new theme attraction—Florida Splendid China—opened in 1993. That same year Disney revealed its long-range plan for tapping into the growing consumer sports craze with a new sports park attraction. Disney is also working on plans for Celebration, a mixed-use model city development with offices, housing, schools, and commercial areas. Given such activities, Orlando's share of the Florida visitors market has continued to increase. In 1985, Orlando drew 24 percent of the visitors, and that number increased to 33 percent in the 1990s.

Worldwide, new and established destinations pursue the same consumer whom Orlando has long regarded as its loyal customer. Such challenges were reflected in hotel occupancies, rates, and resort tax collections, which alternately dropped or increased only slightly throughout 1993. Such events as The World Cup of Golf and Mickey Mouse's 65th birthday (1993) and World Cup Soccer (1994) kept Orange County competitive for both international and American tourists.

Table 20.3

International Tourism: Orlando Gained Position and Market Share

1991 Total U.S. Overseas Visitors	Rank	1992 Total U.S. Overseas Visitors
New York City (23.9%)	1	New York City (22.1%)
Los Angeles (19.9%)	2	Los Angeles (17.2%)
San Francisco (15.7%)	3	**Orlando (16.5%)**
Oahu/Honolulu (14.9%)	4	Miami (15.7%)
Miami (14.7%)	5	San Francisco (13.3%)
Orlando (13.8%)	6	Oahu/Honolulu (12.3%)
Washington, DC (7.6%)	7	Washington, DC (7.9%)
Las Vegas (7.5%)	8	Las Vegas (7.2%)
Boston (5.2%)	9	Boston (5.2%)
Chicago (5.0%)	10	Chicago (5.0%)

Orlando, however, has been continuing to grow even in these intensely competitive times. It was announced in 1993, for example, that the Orlando area moved from the sixth most popular U.S. destination in 1991 among overseas travelers to the third most popular by the end of 1992. Table 20.3 illustrates this change and shows the other important U.S. destinations that compete with Orlando for international tourists and conventions.

At the local level, an interesting aspect of the competitive situation is that neighboring Osceola County also has its own bureau. The Osceola Bureau is an agency of the government rather than a nonprofit membership organization, and it competes locally for tourism business, particularly for lodging.

SWOT ANALYSIS

The concluding section of the situation analysis is where the significance of the research is analyzed. Some plans include a section called "Problems and Opportunities"; others call it a SWOT analysis and look at the plan's Strengths, Weaknesses, Opportunities, and Threats. The strengths-and-weaknesses discussion compares the product or brand with the competition, and the opportunities-and-threats discussion analyzes the brand's situation in the marketplace. These sections serve as a transition that leads directly into the key strategic decisions that will form the foundation of the campaign plan.

As one member of the Orlando Convention and Visitors Bureau has observed, the tourism industry is "the engine that pulls the regional economy." Consequently, tourism has the support of most of the major businesses in the Orange County area. This, of course, is a major *strength* of the program.

Threats are external factors that impact upon a marketing communication program. Even though tourism is a healthy industry, it has gone through some belt-tightening, particularly during the economic downturn of the early 1990s, which continues to be a *threat*. The effects of the recession are still being felt by many members and promotion budgets, including the bureau's budget, have been flat. As the 1993 *Marketing Resource Book* explained, "The years of exponential growth in funding and programs are at a standstill."

The perception of crime in Florida, particularly by international visitors, is a new *threat* to the tourism industry and it even affects such stable areas as Orlando. Competition for the tourist and convention business is also intensifying, as more new attractions entice people who might otherwise make repeat trips to Orlando; this is another type of *threat*.

An important *opportunity* was the hosting of the World Cup Soccer matches in June and July of 1994. This provided an opportunity to increase the visibility of Orlando internationally, as well as increase business during that period.

Although Orlando is a leading tourist and convention destination, which is a strength, it still has room to grow, which is where you find *opportunities*. There is still excess inventory—rooms unfilled in hotels, tables unfilled in restaurants, and so on—in most categories of business, which is both a problem and an opportunity. As the bureau's resource book for its members explains, "So long as we're not #1 we still face challenges—and opportunities." On a more tangible level, the bureau sees a gap between supply and demand at its members' hotels, attractions, transportation companies, restaurants, and retail outlets. As the resource book explains:

> That gap remains both a shortfall and a windfall. A shortfall because unused capacity represents lost sales—lost dollars for our community. And a windfall because that unused capacity is our opportunity, our challenge to find resources and develop strategies that will sell our travel product while serving the community at large.

Opportunities are built on strengths. Orlando has a good record of repeat business, with a return rate of 85 percent. As every marketer knows, the best customer is your own satisfied customer; therefore, an *opportunity* exists to extend this customer base. Likewise, the U.S. and Canadian leisure traveler represents 67 percent of Orlando's business, and that opens up an opportunity for diversification by increasing business from Latin American markets and from overseas, as well as from business travelers. The seasonality patterns of the vacation traveler tend to be opposite those of the business visitor, and that creates an opportunity to even out the business cycles by increasing business traveler visits.

Finally, Orlando's historical strength lies with the success of Walt Disney World, yet the area's growth also lies with newer attractions that extend the appeal, as well as the number of days spent in the area. Disney with its plans for a new sports park and its new city called Celebration also brings more growth opportunity to the area.

From all of these strengths and opportunities, the Orlando Bureau identified four key challenge areas for the 1994 campaign year:

1. Compete effectively for leisure travel with limited resources and increased competition.

2. Avoid downturn in visitation from nonsoccer fans as a result of hosting World Cup Soccer.

3. Increase visitation among first-time and repeat visitors.

4. Implement convenient methods for distributing information on Orlando to consumers.

CAMPAIGN STRATEGY

After the situation analysis and the SWOT analysis, most advertising campaign plans focus on the key strategic decisions that will guide the campaign. These decisions were discussed in detail in Chapter 7; they include such activities as specifying the objectives, targeting the audience, identifying the competitive advantage, and locating the best position for the product or brand. They are fundamental decisions that are relevant for all areas of marketing-communication planning, from the creative plan to the media, sales promotion, and public relations plans.

OBJECTIVES

The objectives for the bureau's marketing communication program focus on increasing demand and maintaining its important relationships with members, the travel trade, and its previous customers. Specifically, the objectives are to:

- Meet consumers' demand for value or perceived value, as in the Magicard™ promotion.
- Generate demand for its destination information.
- Maintain its traditionally strong ties to its travel trade partners to increase convention business and international visits.
- Encourage its members to support bureau programs and advertise in its publications to reach key targets.

TARGETING

For an association like the bureau, targeting involves reaching both trade (travel agents, tour operators, convention planners) and consumer audiences, using both push and pull strategies. In general, the targeting strategy focuses on the visitor because in nine out of ten instances the destination decision is made by the visitor. Therefore, a consumer orientation drives much of the bureau's marketing strategy. This varies, however, with type of traveler; Canadian and international travelers are more likely to work with travel agents and tour operators than are U.S.-based visitors, so the Canadian and international markets are targeted more through the trade, using push strategies. Consumers are addressed more directly in the U.S. markets, using pull strategies.

The primary external target audience, particularly for the U.S. market, is the potential consumer visitor who makes up 80 percent of the Orlando business. While the demographics of the visitor base are known (as shown in Table 20.1 on p. 650) the important person in the demand for information tends to be the female head of household.

However, there are other important external audiences in addition to consumers, such as convention planners and delegates and the trade. They are particularly important because many of the opportunities for new business lie with increased convention business, as well as with more recommendations from travel agents and more tour arrangements for international travel visits.

The bureau is particularly interested, for example, in customers who stay longer or spend more, or both—people like international leisure travelers. To increase convention business, the bureau would also like to focus on meeting planners on both sides of the Atlantic.

Because the bureau is an association rather than a government department, members serve as an important internal target audience, and much of the bureau's programming is in support of its members. Because of the important role tourism plays in the economic health of the area, another important external target audience is the local community.

Table 20.4

North American Tourism: 1994
Promotional Target Markets

Region	United States Market	Rating
East		
New England	Boston	Primary
Middle Atlantic	Washington, D.C.	Primary
Midwest		
East Central	Chicago	Primary
	Cleveland	Primary
West Central	St. Louis	Secondary
South		
Southeast	Atlanta	Primary
Southwest	Dallas	Primary
	Houston	Secondary
West		
Pacific	Los Angeles	Primary

Region	Canada Market	Rating
Province		
Ontario	Toronto	Primary

GEOGRAPHICAL STRATEGIES

Given the costs and complexity of developing new geographical markets and the current restricted resources, it has been in the mutual interests of bureau members and staff to concentrate efforts in established source markets, while also targeting key secondary cities. The local area is important because 30 percent of the visitors are from within the state; another 22 percent are international visitors. In terms of numbers, 8.9 million are from the United States, 2.9 million are from overseas, and 1 million are from Canada. In comparison, another 1.4 million are convention delegates.

Most of the visitors, however, are from other areas in North America. In terms of cities, Atlanta is the number-one market for visitors who drive to Orlando, and New York City is the number-one market for visitors who fly. In terms of regions, the highest concentration comes from the South Atlantic region (Delaware, Washington, D.C., Georgia, Maryland, North Carolina, South Carolina, Virginia, and West Virginia), followed by the Mid-Atlantic region (New Jersey, New York, and Pennsylvania), and the East North Central (Indiana, Illinois, Michigan, Ohio, and Wisconsin). The bureau's efforts will focus on these areas, as can be seen in Table 20.4, which identifies key target markets for promotional strategies.

POSITIONING

Orlando's position in the travel market is built on its perception worldwide as a premier leisure and business destination. One aspect of its position, however, has been inextricably linked with Walt Disney World, its most important founding member. On one hand, people in the community acknowledge the contributions Disney has made to tourism in Orange County; at the same time there are people who want the community and the bureau to move beyond the Disney angle in its focuses and services. There are people who resent being "in the shadow of the ears," and this sets up an interesting positioning problem for the bureau.

The connection has been reflected in the past in the *Orlando—Go for the Magic* slogan with its subtle reference to Disney's *Magic Kingdom*. Orlando, of course, has many more attractions and services to offer in addition to Disney; however, Disney World still remains the area's biggest draw. To take advantage of both positions, the magic reference has been used more recently to express the feeling people have of a "magic experience" when visiting the Orlando area, not just as a pointer to the Magic Kingdom.

A new slogan is under development that will further broaden this position by appealing to a wider range of ages and interests. Think through this strategic problem as if you were marketing communication director for the bureau. What position would you recommend for its marketing communication program?

CONVENTION SALES

In terms of its convention program, the bureau booked over $1 billion in convention business in 1993, which was the fifth consecutive year at that level. Particularly targeted were the Northeast U.S. and Western Europe corporate markets. Satellite offices in Washington, D.C. and Chicago work directly with various associations headquartered in those cities to plan their meetings.

The bureau also continued a successful team-selling program with the Orange County Convention Center staff. The groups booked for 1993 at the center had an attendance of 857,000 and an economic impact of $918 million. The center is slated to grow to 1.1 million square feet by 1998. With Phase III and Phase IV of its construction program underway, convention planners are now booking conventions, particularly larger conventions, for the center into the year 2019.

In addition, the convention sales staff is also making greater efforts to support in-hotel conferences by making *value* a key selling point to price-sensitive and date-flexible groups. Such efforts take advantage of Orlando's ever-growing hotel capacity. The convention sales team also now routinely prospects for amateur and professional sporting events, such as the World Golf Cup and the World Cup Soccer matches.

Convention sales takes its *Hot Dates! Great Rates!* campaign road show to targeted corporate meeting planners in major U.S. cities. Such selling efforts generated more than 2,000 leads in 1993. Nearly two-thirds of the leads were for groups requiring 300 or fewer rooms. These smaller meetings remain the backbone of Orlando's meeting business.

After meetings are booked in Orlando, the convention services department contacts the meeting planner directly to begin the service process. This department *generates service leads and coordinates site inspections*, giving bureau members direct contact with the meeting planner. It is through these leads and site inspections that actual service business is directed to bureau members. The following are the Orlando publications and services provided to convention planners and bureau members:

- *Professional Meeting Planners Guide*: A key resource manual used by association and corporate meeting planners across the country and internationally.

- *Official Visitors Guide*: Convention delegates like to enjoy free time in Orlando, which is why this guide should be an important consideration in members' advertising plans. (See p. 661 for a description of the guide.)

- *Advertising Co-op Guide*: A 16-page annual insert and reply card that appears in eight major publications with a combined circulation of 364,000. Insertion dates coincide with industry shows and special editorial features.

- *Convention Calendar*: Published every January and July, this bureau publication lists hundreds of meetings and conventions scheduled to meet in Orlando. Bureau members receive exclusive information on the businesses that have booked in the area, which in turn helps them reach potential clients directly.

- **Newsletter Sponsorships:** Advertising in quarterly specialized publications for both the corporate and associate planner.

- **Information Cart:** For conventions at the Orange County Convention/Civic Center, the bureau operates a mobile information center, providing information and reservations at area restaurants as well as offering a complete brochure rack.

- **Sales Blitzes:** Sales blitzes to Atlanta, Chicago, Tallahassee, and Washington, D.C., give members an opportunity to call on clients directly.

MARKETING COMMUNICATION ACTIVITIES

A campaign is a complex communication program that is tightly interwoven with all of an organization's marketing efforts. This total communication program reaches all stakeholders, all audiences, and all publics with the same promotional theme. Message variations related to that theme speak to the interests of the different audiences. For the Orlando bureau, the two-pronged message focuses on the fun of tourism and the quality of a convention experience in the Orlando area.

CREATIVE THEME

A campaign is a series of ads built around one central theme. The various ads are designed to be different in order to speak to different audiences or address different copy points. The campaign theme, then, must be a strong concept that can hold all these diverse efforts together. When Pepsi, for example, created the classic "Pepsi generation" theme, a new position and an entirely new type of lifestyle advertising was created. That theme continues to be expressed in subsequent campaigns through the years even though the specific campaigns change. (See opening story in Chapter 13).

GET THE FEELING—IT'S MAGIC!

Orlando's magic begins the moment you arrive. Thrill to the excitement at Walt Disney World, Sea World and Universal Studios. Watch it come to life at Busch Gardens, Gatorland and Kennedy Space Center. Dance 'til dawn in the magic at Church Street Station. Plus, dine, golf and shop day and night!

GET IN TOUCH—SAVE TIME AND MONEY!

Whether business or pleasure, start your visit at the Official Visitor Information Center. Located on International Drive, we're ready to help with maps, brochures, directions and discounted attraction tickets.

GET YOUR ORLANDO MAGICARD™—IT'S FREE!

CALL TOLL-FREE
1-800-527-4352

The ORLANDO MAGICARD is absolutely FREE and lets members SAVE HUNDREDS on accommodations, attractions, dining, shopping and transportation.

Call now for your ORLANDO MAGICARD *plus* Orlando's OFFICIAL VISITORS GUIDE...everything you'll need for a memorable, magical, money-saving visit.

ORLANDO/ORANGE COUNTY CONVENTION & VISITORS BUREAU, INC.
8445 International Drive, Suite 152, Orlando, FL 32819

ORLANDO MAGICARD™ is a promotional program of the Orlando/Orange County Convention & Visitors Bureau, Inc. See Magicard brochure for complete details and restrictions.

CVB-806/SA10-2200

A strong umbrella theme holds the various ads together and creates the synergy that comes from using different messages for different audiences in different media that are still linked to some central image or position. Synergy is important because it intensifies the impact, but that impact is created by repetition. In order for a message to be repeated, it has to be interesting. Maintaining interest is the reason variation is built into a campaign.

Continuity devices, such as the Jolly Green Giant and the Pillsbury Doughboy, are also used in campaign planning to create the link from ad to ad. Slogans are another important type of continuity devise. Such phrases as "Reach Out and Touch Someone" (AT&T), "It's the Real Thing" (Coke), and "Let the Good Times Roll" (Kawasaki) are corporate slogans that serve like a "battle cry." A good slogan generates its own excitement but, more importantly, it is highly memorable and can be used in a variety of different situations.

The Magic Theme. The Orlando logo and the *Go for the Magic* theme have been used throughout all bureau communication for ten years. The theme has been supported in recent years by the promotion of an Orlando area discount card, called the Orlando Magicard™ (see Ad 20.1). Fantasy graphics depicting a montage of activities and attractions reinforce the theme visually. This easily recognized artwork is used in bureau ads placed in media all over the world.

While the slogan and theme appear in all communications, the program has to be adapted for various audiences as it moves toward a truly integrated marketing communication effort. The graphic image and hot colors, for example, have not been used consistently across all of the bureau's publications because of the different objectives of various publications. For example, in convention circles the audience is generally more conservative in its appeal, so this fantasy approach may not be as appropriate.

Achieving an integrated program may be easier as the new creative theme comes on line. The assignment was given to a local agency, Gouchenhour Advertising, and the bureau and the agency spent 15 months in 1992 and 1993 exploring this new direction. The goal: to come up with a slogan and position that are broader than the old ones and speak to more of the members and their services. With 1,285 members and a powerful board, arriving at agreement on such a change is a major challenge. The bureau's tenth anniversary in 1994 was celebrated with the unveiling of the new slogan. Once again, think through this creative challenge as if you were on the advertising team for the bureau. Brainstorm and develop a list of possible slogans that would reinforce a broader position.

The biggest problem in achieving an IMC plan is coordinating all the communication planning, particularly for those efforts handled by members (rather than from inside the bureau's office) that focus on the members' individual services and message strategies. In other words, as a bureau staff member explained, "Execution is always in the hands of a hundred different people—our members—and everyone is a captain."

Following is a review of the bureau's activities in the areas of advertising, member relations, consumer publications and direct mail, trade direct mail and promotions, public relations, and international advertising and promotion.

ADVERTISING MEDIA

Other association-sponsored advertisements promote consumer information or the trade information packages. Advertising is also run in support of special promotions like the Magicard™ discount card. The media planning and buying is handled by a freelance media planner, who has been working with the bureau for many years.

Consumer Advertising. Greater awareness of the area is achieved by creating a special Orlando identification through a unique Orlando advertising look, as Ad 20.1 shows. These ads, which offer tourism information or promote the Magicard™, run in the following North American publications:

- U.S. magazines: *AAA Today, Modern Bride, Rand McNally, Southern Living, Ladies Home Journal, Better Homes & Gardens, National Geographic Traveler, USA Weekend Magazine, Good Housekeeping, Parenting, Sunset Magazine, AAA Home & Away, Atlanta Magazine, Florida Vacation Guide*

- U.S. newspapers: *USA Today, Midwest Newspapers* inserts, *Southeastern Tourism* newspaper inserts, *Miami Herald, St. Petersburg Times, Ft. Lauderdale Sun Sentinel*

- Canadian magazines: *Chatelaine, Maclean's, Canadian Travel Press Weekly, L'Actualite, Leisureways, Travelweek,* and *Westworld*

- Canadian newspapers: *Montreal Gazette, Ontario Star, Toronto Star, Toronto Sun, Hamilton Ontario Spectator*

The consumer advertising plan also attempts to create awareness through traditional, but very cost-effective, co-op advertising in which a number of members' ads are grouped together. The 1993 plan contained 15 such ventures, each of which allowed member participants to reach target audiences at greatly reduced rates. The media in which this co-op advertising runs are selected based on ability to reach the traveling public and generate demand for information from the primary requester, the female head of household. Also, it's important, given the image of the area, that these ads be placed in quality publications. Sometimes the co-op advertising is built around a theme, as in a honeymoon ad. The magazines used in the co-op ad schedule for 1993 include:

January: *Adventure Road, Mature Outlook*

February: *Bride's*

March: *Endless Vacations, Midwest Living, Southeastern Tourism* newspaper inserts (10), *Woman's Day*

April: *Travel & Leisure, Travel Holiday, USA Today*

May: *Better Homes & Gardens*

September: *Midwest Living, New Choices, Travel & Leisure, Travel Holiday, USA Today*

October: *Reader's Digest*–Canada, *Modern Maturity*

November: *Toronto Star*–Canada

Here is how the bureau's co-op advertising program works: In *USA Today*, for example, the bureau will negotiate a full-page, four-color buy. The bureau is able to negotiate a good rate with the publication because of the size of the space and, in some cases, the frequency of the insertions. That rate is then passed on to members. The publication will follow up with sales calls directly to members and the members make their own arrangements. In other words, the bureau does the deal; the publication does the sale; and the member does the advertising and gets access to publications that it could not afford individually.

Trade Advertising. In addition to consumer advertising, the bureau also maintains a program of trade advertising directed at the travel industry. Ad 20.2 is an example of one that addresses the travel industry. The following is the schedule for 1993 showing the other publications used in this program:

January: *Recommend, Travel Agent*

February: *Agent Canada, Recommend, Tour & Travel News, Travel Age*

March: *Travel Weekly*

April: *Canadian Travel Press Weekly*

October: *Canadian Traveler*

November: *Agent Canada, Canadian Travel Press Weekly*

Electronic Media. During 1993 the bureau also made a major transition from print to electronic media, particularly for its trade advertising. Advertising messages can be embedded in the central reservation systems used by airlines and travel agents worldwide through an automated information system named World Travel File. Announcements on that system linking travel agents world-

Ad 20.2

An ad for the travel industry continues the Magic theme.

(Courtesy of Orlando/Orange County Convention & Visitors Bureau, Inc.)

wide can be purchased monthly. When a travel agent's computer is turned on in the morning, an ad message comes up immediately as the system comes on line. Then when a travel agent looks up a hotel, for example, a line can appear on the bottom of the screen that tells the agent how to get more information about the hotel and related services. The agent can then exit the reservation system and access the World Travel directory that contains this database of basic information plus the advertising and promotional messages.

DIRECT-RESPONSE MESSAGES

As mentioned in the preceding discussion, the number of consumers contacting the bureau for tourism or convention information annually is more than 500,000. Approximately a third of these contacts come through the bureau's 800 number. These people receive a variety of publications in addition to member brochures as part of the *consumer mailing package*. Consumers requesting information will receive:

- *Official Visitors Guide*: The key element in the bureau's information arsenal, the visitors guide is printed twice a year and lists attractions, dining, sightseeing, shopping, as well as information on climate, history, and tips on how best to experience Orlando. These guides are must-have planning tools for Orlando-bound travelers and their agents. Over 1 million are printed each year.

- *Accommodations Guide*: Also printed twice a year, the accommodations guide features the lodging choices available to Orlando visitors. It also provides information on transportation. At least 500,000 are printed each year.

- *Attraction Guide*: Comprehensive, categorical directories of area attractions are given along with maps pinpointing key locations, price guidelines, and descriptive information. Approximately 3 million are printed annually.

Another important resource is the *brochure mailing service*. Members are encouraged to provide their brochures to the bureau, which will then distribute them to the more than 500,000 consumers who contact the bureau each year for information. These information packages are custom designed for qualified and high-potential prospects.

MEMBER RELATIONS

The bureau is an association of more than 1,285 members. One of its functions is to get as many of these people and companies together as possible to talk about the future of the Orlando area and how it can best be promoted. As part of that effort, the bureau sponsors a number of events including monthly luncheons and mixers that serve as after-hour mini trade shows, providing an opportunity for members to meet members. In addition to the more social side of these meetings, they also provide an opportunity to present programs on such topics as international tourism and convention sales and marketing.

Since information is the heart of the service the bureau provides to its members, publications serve a very important function. The bureau publishes a *Monthly Membership Newsletter*, which details bureau activities, events, and marketing opportunities. The bureau also circulates business leads in two forms: (1) *Weekly Leads* is a weekly newsletter than includes opportunities to solicit upcoming meetings and conventions and to participate in cooperative advertising, promotions, publicity, and familiarization trips offered to the travel industry. It is published every Friday and can run from 10 to 40 pages. (2) *Faxtips*, an overnight fax service to hotels, provides business leads every working day. This daily information service reinforces Orlando's reputation for responsiveness by allowing participating hotels to respond to customer inquiries in less than 24 hours from the time of initial contact with the bureau.

A key publication for members is the *Marketing Resource Book*, which is published annually and describes the marketing plan for the year. It outlines all the tie-in promotions, special events, and co-op advertising opportunities in three primary areas: North American tourism, international tourism, and convention sales. It includes schedules for each area as well as a master calendar.

The *brochure mailing service*, described earlier, is not only a resource for consumers, it is also a service for members that saves them much trouble and money. This service lets members reach qualified consumers before they leave home. Other services include distribution of members' brochures at the Official Visitor Information Center, listings in bureau publications and directories, Orlando decals for on-site display and slicks of the official Orlando logo to use on member literature, names of newcomers relocating to the Orlando area, and monthly member orientation meetings for new and established members.

CONSUMER PROMOTIONS

To reach consumers, the bureau encourages its members to participate in the exposure-rich activities and programs that its promotions department creates. Coupled with publicity and advertising, promotions such as the Orlando Magicard™ generate exposure for Orlando and participating members in those competitive consumer markets where the travel decision begins. These promotions generate millions of dollars worth of exposure.

Alliances and partnerships with consumer product or media companies are also useful to the bureau because they extend the bureau's promotion reach. Such companies as Coca-Cola, Pizza Hut, Borden, McDonald's, NBA Basketball, Major League Baseball, Tropicana, Safeway, and numerous radio and television stations have all been tie-in partners on various promotions. Orlando messages, for example, have appeared on over 100 million Tropicana Juice containers and 56 million newspaper advertising inserts. More than 750,000 consumers entered the Tropicana sweepstakes, and 160,000 of these consumers submitted proof-of-purchase labels for an Orlando Magicard™. Ad 20.3 shows how one tie-in promotion, a sweepstakes between Nabisco and the bureau, was advertised.

ORLANDO MAGICARD™

The Magicard™ has been mentioned previously, but let's talk about how this highly successful promotion works. Its objective is to add value and convenience to value-conscious visitors. Whenever possible, the bureau incorporates the Magicard™ in its activities and promotions, believing it addresses the interests of consumers who remain cautious in a still uncertain economy. Over 2 million cards have been sent to value-conscious consumers (Ad 20.4).

The promotion started when the economy slowed in early 1991 and the Gulf War heated up. It is a way to position Orlando as an affordable vacation.

The membership offers discounts in their directory listings to visitors carrying the card. For example, visitors to Sea World get $3.00 off per person for up to six people, a savings of $15 to $18. The total distribution of the Magicard™ increased by more than 50 percent in 1993 for a total distribution of almost 2 million, and 110 member companies participate in its discount offerings.

TRADE ACTIVITIES

The bureau also offers support to the trade through sales literature, trade shows, sales missions, and familiarization trips—all designed to help sell Orlando. The following publications help with trade promotions:

Tour Travel Official Reference Manual Widely used by travel agents, wholesalers, and tour operators, the *Official Tour & Travel Reference Manual* contains comprehensive information of critical importance to the travel trade booking business. All sectors of the tourism industry, including hotels, attractions, restaurants, and transportation companies, are profiled in detail. More than 100,000 are printed annually.

Travel & Tour Newsletter Members can talk directly to key travel agents through the *Tour & Travel Newsletter*. Exclusive full-page sponsorship in the quarterly newsletter delivers a highly targeted national readership among retail, wholesale, and other trade partners. Bureau surveys reveal that virtually all respondents circulate the newsletter throughout their office, greatly extending readership beyond the 17,000 circulation base.

The newsletter also contains articles on "What's New in Orlando," including stories on new programs and current issues affecting area tourism.

Trade Shows. Bureau staff and members attend 40 to 50 trade shows in the United States and internationally to display information about the Orlando area as a meeting and vacation destination. Trade shows allow bureau staff to meet face to face with clients and get a feel for the pulse and climate of future bookings. The bureau also hosted the March 1993 convention of the American Society of Association Executives, which brings hundreds of convention and meeting decision makers, and the National Tour Association conference in 1995.

Bureau Trade Missions. Bureau missions to key markets, also called *sales blitzes*, bring members and agents together for one-on-one exchanges at seminars, breakfasts, and luncheons. Round table discussions also enhance understanding—and sales—of Orlando's enormously diverse leisure product. Both exhibitors and travel professionals profit from these missions, preferring this informal format to traditional tabletop sales presentations.

Familiarization Trips. The bureau also targets top-producing travel agents and other industry representatives for on-site trips to Orlando that make them better Orlando salespeople. Part social, part business, these trips showcase the fun that Orlando has to offer the travel agents' customers.

PUBLIC RELATIONS

Most of the bureau's activities involve public relations programming in one way or another through publications, publicity, or special event planning. One activity of interest is media relations, which involves working with the press, providing press members with information when they request it, and attempting to get positive coverage in their publications. The bureau's in-house public relations department is particularly good at placing stories about Orlando or getting Orlando mentioned in stories on bigger topics such as Florida tourism in general, as the story shown here (Figure 20.3) from a Canadian publication, *Maclean's*, illustrates. The public relations department works with both domestic as well as international publications. In addition to media relations, the public relations department has also produced a video on the Orlando area that, among other uses, is used at trade shows and in convention recruiting.

Public relations works with trade and consumer editors worldwide to inform them about "what is new in Orlando" and other top-of-mind topics such as visitor safety and special events. For important conventions, the public relations department will host visiting journalists and set up their itineraries. The department also works closely with local media to communicate information on the industry and other issues important to the local community and its economy. In addition, it handles the bureau's annual report.

In 1993, because of the increase in tourist assaults in Florida, the focus of the bureau's communication program moved from an aggressive marketing stance to one reflecting more of a public relations orientation. The bureau has met the issue of tourist shootings head-on with an information campaign directed to journalists plus programs emphasizing increased law enforcement patrols and local member crime initiatives.

Figure 20.3

The Public Relations Department of the Orlando Convention and Visitors Bureau works hard to get mentions of Orlando and its attractions in articles for tourists.

(Courtesy of Orlando/Orange County Convention & Visitors Bureau, Inc.,)

Within the image:

COVER

MY CANADA INCLUDES FLORIDA...

Millions of winter-weary Canadians flock to the sun

T he seat backs and tray tables are in their original upright positions. All seat belts have been securely fastened; all carry-on luggage has been safely stowed. The jet taxis down the runway, waits its turn, and then, with a stirring roar—the escape signal for a planeload of pent-up Canadians—lifts off into the chalky winter skies. On board, the passengers—some already in brightly colored polo shirts or sweat suits—stare down at the shrinking city below, the tiny cars moving indifferently through the gray-white streets, the surrounding snow soiled as oil rags. And then it is gone, the roads and buildings buried beneath puffy clouds, and the passengers settle back. It will not be long now: a few hours, a couple of drinks, maybe a movie, soothers or pocket video games for the kids. The next time the plane touches earth, it will enter a land of palms and pastels and sun-bathed parking lots, of Donald and Mickey, key lime pies, bare-butt postcards, white shoes and blue rinse, shuffleboard and golf and great sandy beaches strewn with baking bodies and sweet with suntan oil.

Florida.

It is a national mantra, a mental bumper sticker: *My Canada Includes Florida.* And not only Florida but the Caribbean, Mexico, Venezuela, Arizona (page 43), Texas, Southern California, Hawaii (page 42)—any place where the air is warm, the drinks are cool and the only shovelling is to build sand castles. Millions flee to the southern sun each winter, delighting Canadian travel companies and distant tourism officials and returning with the obligatory conch shells, straw hats and tan lines. And tour operators say that, while the recession has driven people to seek the best possible travel deals, the exodus has continued unabated. "Once it was thought of as a luxury, but now it's becoming more of an annual rite," says Bryan Wolfenden, spokesman for Canadian Holidays, a Toronto-based charter company. "We've often had customers say, 'So much for the new car, when's the next flight to Honolulu?' "

For Canadians, Florida is by far the hot spot of choice. Nearly 2.4 million of them flocked to the Sunshine State in 1991—compared with 638,000 to all Caribbean islands combined—and about 600,000 snowbirds stayed in Florida for up to six months. More than half fly, while the rest barrel down interstates 95 or 75, some steering recreational vehicles or pulling trailers to a place where the food is familiar, the water is safe and the flamingos are real. French-speakers tend to congregate on the Atlantic Coast, English-speakers on the Gulf Coast, and both enjoy newspapers and TV and radio news programs geared directly to them. All are drawn to the inland city of Orlando, the onetime orange-and-grapefruit centre that is now home to Disney World and other theme parks.

Florida is a democratic destination. The Canadians, who include Prime Minister Brian Mulroney, Liberal Leader Jean Chrétien and other prominent politicians, range from the mega-wealthy to the budget-bound, from solid families to spring break singles. "There's a little piece of Florida for every Canadian," boasts Ellis Webber, director of Canadian marketing for the Florida division of tourism. Canadians, meanwhile, leave a sizable piece of Canada behind: more than $2 billion in tourist dollars annually.

Of course, every sun spot has its clouds. Canadian critics contend that the country's leaders set a bad example by spending their travel dollars on foreign sand. And some visitors maintain that, far from paradise, Florida is a state of crime, congestion, drugs, endless shopping malls and a blight of billboards advertising everything from gasoline to gator wrestling. But such complaints are lost on Florida's Canadian faithful—on residents of a northern nation who view a bit of southern exposure as a basic birthright. "Why am I here?" says Dennis Maurice, a 47-year-old sales representative from Collingwood, Ont., lounging at a beachside bar in ritzy Longboat Key. "I'm sitting by the beach, relaxing with a beer after a game of tennis. How can it get any better than this?"

BOB LEVIN

INTERNATIONAL PROGRAM

Offices in London, Brussels, Frankfurt, Tokyo, Seoul, and Latin America (through the Coral Gables international office) have given Orlando a presence around the world. Orlando ranks sixth among U.S. destinations for hosting international visitors to the United States. Only New York, Los Angeles, San Francisco, Miami, and Honolulu surpass this destination.

Orlando International Airport (OIA) is ranked the thirteenth busiest—and fastest growing—international gateway into the United States. OIA processes more than 2.5 million international passengers a year.

Orlando's major international visitors are from the United Kingdom, Germany, Brazil, Argentina, France, and Spain. It ranks third in popularity with all Western European visitors, fourth with Central American and Far Eastern visitors, and fifth with Australian visitors.

Orlando's overseas visitors stay an average of 18 days in the United States and visit an average of two states during their trip. Their average party size of 2.1 spends over $2,088 per trip.

International Advertising. The international media schedule reaches consumers and trade partners in selected international markets including the United Kingdom, Germany, Latin America, Korea, and Japan. The ads shown here (Ad 20.5) are from Mexico's *Turistampa* and Japan's *Travel Journal.* The following

Ad 20.5

Orlando is an international destination for tourists, as well as convention delegates. In order to maintain its presence in international markets, the bureau maintains an advertising program in key countries. These two ads are Spanish and Japanese versions of the Magic theme.

(Courtesy of Orlando/Orange County Convention & Visitors Bureau, Inc.)

consumer advertising media schedule illustrates the breadth of this program:

January: *Daily Telegraph* (United Kingdom), *Global* (Germany), *Travel Journal* (Japan)

February: *Travel Weekly* (United Kingdom), *America Live*/Bunte/Bild, *Funk*, *Geo Mundo* (Latin America), *World Tour* (Korea)

March: *AB Road Travel Directory* (Japan)

April: *Reader's Digest* (Mexico)

September: *Daily Telegraph* (United Kingdom), *Discover North America* (United Kingdom)

October: *Discover America* (United Kingdom)

November: *America Live/Radio Times/TV Times* (United Kingdom), *Daily Telegraph* (United Kingdom)

International Co-op Advertising. As with the domestic co-op program, there are also opportunities for members to participate in international media at negotiated rates. The annual advertising schedule makes it possible for bureau members to reach the international traveler and travel industry in important international markets at significant savings. International co-op ads are used to provide visibility for a number of different attractions and services that can be combined in one promotional effort.

The primary markets for international co-op advertising include the United

Kingdom, Germany, Latin America, Korea, and Japan. Special advertising sections are focused on major trade shows such as World Travel Mart in London, COTAL in Panama, and ITB in Berlin. The 1993 trade advertising schedule included:

January: *Travel Journal* (Japan), *Florida International Travel Planner* (Worldwide)

February: *Travel Weekly* (United Kingdom), *America Live/Reiseboro Bulletin* (Germany), *Turistampa* (Mexico)

March: *Reiseboro Bulletin* (Germany), *Boletin Touristico* (Mexico), *Travel Management* (Japan), *Korean Tourism News* (Korea)

April: *Tour Times* (Korea)

May: *Travel Weekly* (United Kingdom), *Travel Trade Gazette* (United Kingdom), *FVW International* (Germany)

June: *Selling Long Haul* (United Kingdom), *Brasiltouris Jornal* (Brazil), *Contact USA* (Worldwide), *Travel Management* (Japan)

September: *Al Dia* (Latin America), *Reiseboro Bulletin* (Germany)

October: *Brasiltouris Jornal* (Brazil), *Turistampa* (Mexico)

November: *Travel Trade Gazette* (United Kingdom), *FVW International* (Germany), *Travel Times* (Japan)

Members are also offered opportunities to participate in co-op advertising for the trade. These special sections are featured in the following publications: *COTAL* (Latin America), *GeoMundo* (Latin America), *Travel Times* (Japan), *Reiseboro Bulletin* (Germany), *Travel Weekly* (United Kingdom).

Consumer Promotion Program. The international tourism department is dedicated to maximizing Orlando's position as a leading destination for international leisure travelers. To do so, it provides *The Official International Area Guide,* where bureau members can speak to consumers in Spanish, Portuguese, French, Italian, German, Korean, Japanese, French-Canadian, and English by advertising in the bureau's international area guide. Total circulation is 450,000 with distribution in the same markets as the reference manual but aimed at consumers. Members can place an ad in nine different languages. It's easy for members because the bureau does all the translation.

Trade Promotions. Members also have the opportunity to participate in other special promotions for the international travel market.

Official Tour & Travel Reference Manual. This definitive reference manual about the Orlando area is distributed through a variety of channels including the U.S. Travel and Tourism Agency and Visit USA, as well as at 49 international trade shows, four bureau trade missions, and to approximately 50 familiarization tours that visit Orlando annually. Additionally, the bureau's six international offices distribute the manual to key members of the travel trade and in response to the bureau's international travel trade advertising schedule.

International Trade Missions and Sales Blitzes. The cities visited have included Hannover, Berlin, and Leipzig in Germany; Maracaibo, Balencia, and Caracas in Venezuela; Paris and Lyon in France; and Osaka, Nagoya, Tokyo, and

Urayasu in Japan. The missions are designed to be all inclusive, which means they include air fare, hotel accommodations, and ground transfers. Participation is limited and notification is made via the bureau's weekly business leads. The bureau's missions involve the cooperation and support of Delta Airlines in Germany and France, Aeropostal in Venezuela, and All Nippon Airways in Japan.

A TOTAL COMMUNICATION PROGRAM

The Orlando/Orange County Convention and Visitors Bureau operates a total communication program that involves a variety of different marketing communication areas, target audiences, media, and messages. It is a complex and challenging program for a dynamic growth industry and area. It operates with a sophisticated marketing plan that provides direction for all these communication activities.

How do you measure the success of such a broad marketing communication program? In addition to the data already provided on convention bookings and increased business they represent, there are also other indicators of the bureau's effectiveness. In 1993, the nearly 200 convention assistants earned an average of 4.87 on a five-point scale in surveys of all groups using bureau personnel. The convention services sales team fielded 3,500 requests for information resulting in 2,425 leads for member business. The multilingual Visitor Information Center welcomed some 375,000 travelers and answered the phone calls of another 105,000 visitors who wanted information. In a survey, 88 percent of the Visitor Center visitors said they were "very satisfied." The publications' staff numbers are staggering: 1.1 million visitors guides, 3.1 million accommodation guides, 800,000 Magicards™, and so on.

In a sense, the bureau is a victim of its own success—it faces a nearly chronic shortage of materials. The demand for information has grown exponentially. But the real measure of the program's success is *brand equity*. Orlando has been successful at cultivating such equity, which entails high levels of both name recognition and customer loyalty, because of its successful marketing communication programs.

SUMMARY:

- The situation analysis includes primary and secondary research findings about the organization, its product, the competition, the marketplace, and consumers.

- The SWOT analysis summarizes the situation in terms of key strengths, weaknesses, opportunities, and threats.

- The strategy section of a campaign plan identifies the key problems to be solved and the advertising objectives that will accomplish those tasks,

the target audience, the competitive advantage, and the position.

- The creative plan includes a theme, or creative concept, and variations, or executions, for different media, situations, audiences, and times of the year.

- The media plan includes media objectives, media selection, geographic strategies, timing schedules, and a budget.

QUESTIONS

1. The advertising trade press, including *Advertising Age* and *Adweek*, usually carries articles about new campaigns. Find such an article and outline the key planning decisions behind the campaign discussed in the article. What's missing? What more do you need to know to have a comprehensive outline of the campaign?

2. Summarize and critique the Orlando Convention and Visitors Bureau's targeting efforts. Where do the most important opportunities lie for increased business?

3. The Magicard™ promotion has been highly successful. Come up with an idea for a new promotion that can be used as the focal point either of the bureau's tenth anniversary celebration or of its Year 2000 campaign.

4. The research director for the bureau has asked you to come up with some ideas on how to evaluate the impact of the bureau's marketing communication program. Develop a list of research activities that you would recommend to document the effectiveness of this program.

SUGGESTED CLASS PROJECTS

1. Interview a local advertiser about a local campaign and write a report on how and why it was developed, its strategy, its creative theme, its media plan, and its evaluation.

2. Develop a research proposal in outline form for a program that you would recommend to evaluate the effectiveness of the most current campaign for Pepsi, Coca-Cola, Burger King, Wendy's, or McDonald's.

3. The bureau's advertising is primarily print, although it has done some tie-in promotion commercials with sponsors. Let's assume the bureau has funds to begin using television advertising for its Magicard™ promotion. Develop a scrip

and storyboard for a 30-second commercial that you believe would effectively translate the information in Ad 20.1 to a video format.

4. You have been hired by the bureau to come up with proposals for its new position and theme. Remember the objective is to broaden the appeal. What would you recommend in terms of a new position statement and slogan?

5. You have been asked by the bureau to study its total communication program and develop a plan to move it into a more integrated marketing communication program. What needs to be done? What are the key recommendations you would propose to make this an IMC campaign?

# FURTHER READINGS

AAKER, DAVID A., and JOHN G. MYERS, *Advertising Management*, 3rd ed. (Englewood Cliffs, NJ: Prentice Hall, 1987).

HEIBING, ROMAN G., and SCOTT W. COOPER, *How to Write a Successful Marketing Plan* (Lincolnwood, IL: NTC Business Books, 1990).

SCHULTZ, DON E., *Strategic Advertising Campaigns*, 4th ed. (Chicago: Crain Books, 1995).

TAYLOR, JAMES W., *How to Develop a Successful Advertising Plan* (Lincolnwood, IL: NTC Business Books, 1993).

$\mathscr{E}$VALUATIVE RESEARCH

CHAPTER OBJECTIVES

When you have completed this chapter, you should be able to:

- Explain why advertisers devote time and money to evaluative research

- Distinguish between evaluative and diagnostic research

- Identify the eight major evaluative research methods and what each one claims to test

- Evaluate the strengths and weaknesses of various forms of testing

- Understand the concerns surrounding the issues of validity and reliability

WHY CAN'T CANNES AGREE?

Every year the International Advertising Film Festival (also known as the Cannes festival) attracts more than 3,700 entries from all over the world. Because it confers the most prestigious awards in all of advertising, and because it is held in Cannes, on the French Riviera, it also attracts many of advertising's creative stars.

The 23 Cannes judges are leaders of major international advertising agencies. As a panel, they narrow the entries to a short list, then select winners in each product category through lengthy, sometimes acrimonious debate. The top commercial in each category receives a "Gold Lion." The Grand Prix, the "best of show," is advertising's most coveted award.

Although the Cannes Festival is the world's top advertising competition, it is punctuated by disagreement. The judges disagree with one another. The attendees disagree with the judges' decisions; sometimes they even throw vegetables at the screen. For weeks after the festival the advertising trade press prints caustic comments from critics who didn't like the way the contest turned out.

The Cannes festival is not atypical. A judge of the One Show—a U.S.-based event similar to the Cannes festival—had this to say about the entries:

> It was like going through thousands of garbage cans looking for something to eat.
>
> Judging is always painful. But this year, it made you sick to your stomach.
>
> There was little, if any, movement creativity. With a few minor exceptions, the work was a bad imitation of what has gone before.
>
> The same old ground, the same old foot-prints. You read this stuff, watched this stuff, hour after hour, day after day, and you got mad.
>
> It was insulting. A horrendous waste of money.[1]

Disagreements among creative directors are matched by disagreements between agencies and their clients. Agencies insist that their work merits at least an A+. Typically, clients are not so sure. They want the most effective advertising they can get. Maybe some other approach would work better. Maybe the agency's recommendation will not work at all.

Faced with such conflicts of opinion, many advertisers turn to evaluative research. Here, the term **evaluative research** means research used to make final go/no-go decisions about finished or nearly finished ads, as distinguished from the *strategic research* described in Chapter 6, which is used to test strategies and different versions of a concept or approach. Advertisers who use evaluative research hope that it will provide a valid measure of effectiveness, and that it will eliminate the risks and conflicts inevitable when decisions are based on judgment alone.

The stakes are high. By the time an average 30-second commercial is ready

evaluative research Research intended to measure the effectiveness of finished or nearly finished advertisements.

---

[1]Dan Wieden, "Blue Penciling a Year of Creative," *Adweek* (June 10, 1991): 12.
[2]*Adweek* (August 13, 1993):7.

for national television, it has cost about $200,000.[2] If it is run nationally, its sponsor invests several million dollars in air time. Furthermore, careers are on the line. Brand managers and advertising managers are rewarded for successes and punished for failures. Among the agency creatives, the reel or the portfolio—a collection of advertisements "authored" by an individual writer, art director, or producer—is both the key to salary increases and the passport to professional respect.

Ideally, the results of evaluative research would be available before large sums of money have been invested in finished work. Failing that, advertisers want a test that predicts effectiveness before millions of media dollars have been spent in purchasing space or time. Test results may even be useful after an advertisement has been placed. Sales may fall, or they may not increase as rapidly as expected. Is the advertising at fault? Would sales be better if the advertising were "working harder"? Advertisers may feel a need to test their advertising anywhere along the line.

EVALUATIVE RESEARCH SUPPLIERS AND METHODS

Evaluative research suppliers are listed in the American Marketing Association's *International Directory of Marketing Research Companies and Services*, which we described in Chapter 6. Most major advertisers have a favorite supplier and a favorite research method; a few use proprietary methods of their own (methods that have been developed by, and are used exclusively by, one advertiser). Some of the best-known evaluative research suppliers are listed in Table 21.1

This list is not exhaustive. Many other research companies offer some form of copy testing, including qualitative, in-depth interviews, and focus groups. The question is: Which (if any) of the evaluative research methods really work?

Although every supplier is in some way unique, all use copy-testing methods that fall into eight major categories: (1) memory tests, (2) persuasion tests,

Table 21.1

Suppliers of Evaluative Research

Supplier	Medium	Methods
ASI Market Research, Inc. New York, NY	Television, print	Recall Persuasion
Bruzzone Research Co. Alameda, CA	Television	Recognition
Burke Marketing Research Cincinnati, OH	Television, print	Recall; Persuasion; In-market sales
Communications Workshop, Inc. Chicago, IL	Television, print, radio	Communications test
Diagnostic Research, Inc.	Television, print, radio	Communications test
Gallup and Robinson, Inc. Princeton, NJ	Television, print	Recall; Persuasion
Information Resources, Inc. Chicago, IL	Television	In-market sales
Starch INRA Hooper, Inc. Mamaroneck, NY	Print	Recognition

(3) direct-response counts, (4) communication tests, (5) focus groups, (6) physiological tests, (7) frame-by-frame tests, and (8) in-market tests. Of these eight types, memory, persuasion, communication, and focus groups are the most widely employed.

MEMORY TESTS

Memory tests are based on the assumption that an advertisement leaves a mental "residue" with the person who has been exposed to it. One way to measure an advertisement's effectiveness, therefore, is to contact consumers and find out what they remember about it. Memory tests fall into two major groups: *recall tests* and *recognition tests*.

RECALL TESTS

The supplier most commonly associated with day-after recall (DAR) tests is Burke Marketing Services. Gallup and Robinson's In-View Service is another recall test designed to show which ads best capture and hold attention. In a traditional **recall test** a finished commercial is run on network television within a regular prime-time program. The next evening, interviewers in three or four cities make thousands of random phone calls until they have contacted about 200 people who were watching the program at the exact time the commercial appeared. The interviewer then asks a series of questions:

recall test A test that evaluates the memorability of an advertisement by contacting members of the advertisement's audience and asking them what they remember about it.

- Do you remember seeing a commercial for any charcoal briquettes?
- (If no) Do you remember seeing a commercial for Kingsford charcoal briquettes? (Memory prompt)
- (If yes to either of the above) What did the commercial say about the product? What did the commercial show? What did the commercial look like? What ideas were brought out?

The first type of question is called *unaided recall* because the particular brand is not mentioned. The second question is an example of *aided recall*, where the specific brand name is mentioned. The answers to the third set of questions are written down verbatim. The nature of these questions is important. Interviewers do not ask, "Please tell me about all the commercials you remember seeing on television last night" or "Please tell me about any charcoal briquette commercials you remember." The test requires that the respondent link a specific brand name, or at least a specific product category, to a specific commercial. If the commercial fails to establish a tight connection between the brand name and the selling message, the commercial will not get a high recall score.

The traditional recall test has many variations. In one variation interviewers prerecruit people to watch a specified program and recontact only those respondents the following day. This method saves research costs and eliminates the need to make thousands of phone calls to find 200 viewers who happen to have been watching the program on which the test commercial appeared. Another method exposes respondents to commercials in a theater setting. The respondents are then telephoned at home 24 or 72 hours later. In a third variation respondents are prerecruited to watch a program telecast on local cable television. The latter two methods are popular because, unlike recall tests that employ network television, they can be used to test rough executions.

Analyzing Test Results. Recall test results are analyzed by examining the verbatim responses (verbatims) to determine how many viewers remembered something specific about the ad. If an answer indicates that the viewer was merely guessing, or remembering other advertising, that viewer is not counted toward the recall score. Furthermore, even though some recall test verbatims are surprisingly detailed, many are so sketchy that it is hard to be sure the respondent was remembering a specific ad. Here are your typical verbatims. Which prove recall of the specific commercial being tested?

1. The guy was in his backyard, I think, and he was using them. I'm not really sure about that. The guy was using them in his grill.

2. I think they grilled a steak. I just remember it was Kingsford. They were grilling a steak.

3. They showed the bag of charcoal. It was fast lighting. I think it said it burned evenly.

4. I remember numerous grills in the commercial.

5. I remember, I think it was the one with big letters, with reference to the professionals, what the professionals use. I thought it was a pretty good advertising scheme. Amateur chefs like to think they're professionals. It was mostly the big letters. I remember a guy with a chef's hat on, smiling real big. I think the guy had dark hair. It was sort of a quick, not a subliminal thing but everything flashed real quick, the big letters, sort of a rapid fire approach. Just all I remember was that line, what the pros use.

Typically, anywhere from zero to 60 to 70 percent of viewers are able to prove recall. The average recall score for a 30-second commercial across a range of product categories is about 20 percent. In other words, about one in five of those who view a commercial can recall something about it the following day.[3]

Print Ad Recall Tests. When recall tests are used to evaluate magazine advertisements, respondents who have read the magazine go through a deck of cards containing brand names. If the respondent says, "Yes, I remember having seen an advertisement for that brand," the interviewer asks the respondent to describe everything he or she can remember about the ad. As in a television recall test, answers are taken down verbatim and studied later to determine how many respondents remembered the specific advertisement being tested.

Assessing Recall Tests. Recall tests have several advantages over other memory methods. First, they have been around for a long time, almost since the beginning of national advertising. Advertisers are accustomed to using them—for some advertisers, they have become part of the corporate culture, an ingrained tradition.

Second, because recall tests have been so popular, research companies that conduct them have accumulated *norms*—records of results that serve the same

---

[3]David W. Stewart and David H. Furse, *Effective Television Advertising* (Lexington, MA: DC Heath & Co., 1986).

purpose as batting averages. Norms allow the advertiser to tell whether a particular advertisement is above or below the average for either the brand or its product category. Without norms the advertiser would not know whether a score of 23, for example, is good or bad. Like students, commercials are graded with reference to others in the category being tested.

reliability A characteristic that describes a test that yields essentially the same results when the same advertisement is tested time after time.

Reliability A third advantage of recall tests is **reliability**. In this context, the term *reliable* means that the commercial gets essentially the same score every time it is tested. Reliability is important because, like all tests scores, recall test scores incorporate a certain amount of random measurement error. Measurement errors are due to differences among interviewers and among the programs or magazines that carry the advertisement, as well as a host of other factors that vary from time to time. When the amount of measurement error is high, as it is in some of the more qualitative methods of evaluating advertisements, scores vary from test to test—a high score this time, a low score the next time, a medium score the time after. When results are inconsistent, the test obviously is not dependable.

Although recall tests are not perfectly reliable, they are more reliable than most tests. That fact alone helps to explain why they remain popular with advertisers.

validity The ability of a test to measure what it is intended to measure.

Validity Reliability is only one measure of the value of a copy test. An advertiser who uses a recall score is assuming that the score reflects the ad's ability to sell the product. At first glance, it might seem obvious that the most effective advertisements would make the most indelible impressions. Yet everyone can remember advertisements for brands they never use, and everyone uses some brands without being able to remember any advertising for them. The real question is whether there is a strong positive relationship between the ad's overall score and some later assessment of its sales effectiveness.

The technical term for what we are discussing is **validity**. When an advertiser uses a recall test, the advertiser is assuming that the recall score is a valid indication of the advertisement's sales effectiveness. Many researchers and most of advertising's creative leaders believe that this assumption is incorrect. Here is what one well-known researcher said about the validity of day-after recall tests:

> We know that recall data are inherently weak. We know that the theory on which recall data are based is shaky. We know that the evidence for the validity of recall is—to be charitable—checkered. We may not know the answer to the longest playing controversy in all of marketing research, but we know what the answer is not—and it's not recall.[4]

Cost Recall tests are not inexpensive. On the average, television recall tests cost from $9,000 to $17,000 per commercial; and print recall tests cost from $7,000 to $13,000 per ad. These costs limit the number of advertisements that an advertiser can afford to test.

Recall Tests and Decision Making. If recall tests are costly and if their validity is unknown (to say the least), why do so many advertisers use them? One rea-

---

[4]Lawrence D. Gibson, "If The Question Is Copy Testing, The Answer Is Not Recall," *Journal of Advertising Research* 23 (1983):39–46.

LIFESTYLES

Foreign and Domestic Car Owners

A nationwide study on car ownership revealed some basic data about the population of car owners. The study found that 72 percent of Americans owned domestic cars only, 19 percent possessed foreign cars only, and just 9 percent owned both types of cars at the same time. What do the personal opinions, activities, purchasing styles, media habits, and background characteristics of these people tell us about the differences between foreign and domestic car owners?

Research reveals quite a few surprises about the foreign car owner. This person is apt to be female, under 35, and either single or divorced. Not only has she graduated from college, but she has most likely attended graduate school as well. Most probably, she lives in a large metropolitan area in the Pacific region. She sees herself as a career woman and works full time in a professional or managerial position, earning a pretty good salary. Two out of three of these women earn at least $30,000 a year, and one out of two has an income over $40,000. Being more affluent than the typical domestic car owner does not mean that she necessarily feels content with her salary. However, she does assume that in the future she will probably be more financially comfortable than she is at present. In fact, she has a pretty positive outlook on life in general and is convinced that her greatest achievements are yet to come.

The foreign car owner's buying style is not a cautious one. She will be the first to buy that new electronic product, perhaps even on a whim, although she is far more careful about buying major items. She would by no means restrict either small or large purchases to American-made products. She has no compunctions about using a bank credit card; unlike the domestic car owner, she doesn't feel she should necessarily pay cash for her purchases.

This woman is willing to take calculated risks in the investment realm. High interest rates are considerably more appealing to her than is the sheer safety of an investment. She relishes the speed of the sports car, but she is neither a wild driver nor a wild purchaser. On the contrary, she is a thorough shopper, searching for the best price. She is also far more concientious about using her seat belt than is the domestic car buyer. Although she will probably have mufflers, shock absorbers, and spark plugs changed at a specialty shop, she's not adverse to doing some of this work herself.

She is generally more liberal than the American car buyer. For instance, she thinks television advertising for contraceptive products is quite desirable, and she is in favor of legalized abortion. Moreover, she does not agree with the domestic car owner that the government should exercise more control over television content. As you might predict, the foreign car owner is not a believer that a woman's place is in the home. She is all for the woman's liberation movement.

Not surprisingly, the foreign car owner likes to travel and to see foreign places, and she travels more frequently than do domestic car owners. Television is not her primary mode of entertainment, but she does like to watch rented movies on her VCR. She enjoys all types of music, with the exception of country-western. Active sports, such as cycling and swimming, appeal to her, and she is likely to attend exercise classes or work out at a health club. No matter what her chronological age, she has a youthful, adventurous, and optimistic outlook.

Exercise
1. Knowing what you do about foreign car owners, which of the two version of the Peugeot ad in Ad 21.1 do you think would be more effective? Why?
2. If you were marketing auto parts or auto services, how would you tailor your advertising specifically to female foreign-car owners? How would you evaluate its effectiveness?

Source: Adapted from DDB Needham Worldwide, *A Lifestyle Profile of Foreign and Domestic Car Owners* (July 1989).

Principle

In spite of much research, the relationship between day-after recall scores and sales effectiveness is still unknown.

son is that recall is a relatively reliable measure of *something*, and many advertisers believe—despite evidence to the contrary—that recall must be related to effectiveness. It just seems logical that a well-remembered advertisement will, on average, be more effective than an advertisement that leaves little impression in the viewer's mind.

But the most fundamental reason that advertisers use recall tests is that test scores help them make decisions. As we noted earlier, the decision to run or not to run an advertisement affects the careers of everyone involved and triggers the expenditure of very large marketing resources. Aware of the consequences, and beset on all sides by doubts and conflicting opinions, decision makers need something to help them justify the decisions they make. In so tense a setting, a recall test—or any other test that has been approved by corporate tradition—can play a decisive role even when no one is really sure that the test predicts sales effects.

RECOGNITION TESTS

Another way to measure memory is to show the advertisement to people and ask them if they remember having seen it. The latter kind of test is generally called a **recognition test**. Like recall tests, recognition tests were first used to evaluate print advertising. One of the earliest, and still one of the most popular recognition tests, is named after its inventor, Daniel Starch. Ad 21.1 is an example of a test the Starch Advertisement Readership Service conducted to test two different approaches to automobile advertising.

The Starch Test. The Starch test can test only print ads that have already run. After verifying that the respondent at least looked through the magazine being studied, the interviewer proceeds page by page, asking whether the respondent remembers having seen or read each ad.

In the magazine used in the interview, each ad is assigned an item number and is broken down into component parts (such as illustration, headline, logo, or main body of print) that are identified by codes. Figure 21.1 shows the various components as they are measured by the Starch test. If the respondent says he or she remembers having seen a specific ad in that particular issue, the interviewer then asks a prescribed series of questions to determine exactly how much of the ad the respondent saw or read. The Starch procedure produces three scores:

1. *Noted:* The percentage of respondents who say they noticed the ad when they looked through the magazine on some previous occasion.

2. *Associated:* The percentage of respondents who said they noticed a part of the ad that contains the advertiser's name or logo.

3. *Read Most:* The percentage of respondents who reported reading 50 percent or more of the ad copy.

Assessing the Starch Test. Compared with a recall test, the Starch test has some valuable advantages. First, because the questions are easier, the Starch interview proceeds more rapidly. A faster interview allows more advertisements to be tested, which in turn lowers the cost per advertisement. Starch tests cost $600 per ad, much less than the cost of recall tests. Lower cost implies a better investment of the advertiser's research resources.

Norms Like recall tests, the Starch test has been in use for many years, and the research supplier has accumulated norms that help interpret individual test scores. The Starch test's norms now include many different product categories. This specificity makes interpretation more precise.

Reliability The Starch procedure is very reliable. Repeated evaluations have shown that Starch scores are remarkably consistent. In fact, in the print medium Starch tests are substantially more reliable than are recall tests.

Validity In experiments on the Starch method some respondents have claimed recognition of unpublished advertisements they could not possibly have seen. These false claims show that claimed recognition is not a perfectly valid measure of memory and that something else is probably at work.

Subsequent investigations have suggested that when a Starch respondent says, "Yes, I looked at that ad when I went through the magazine," he or she is really saying, "Ads like that usually attract my attention." When the Starch respondent says, "I didn't look at that ad," he or she is saying. "I usually ignore that kind of advertising." If that interpretation is correct, a Starch score actually represents a kind of consumer vote on whether that advertisement is worth more than a passing glance.[5] Given that the ability to attract and hold attention is a quality most advertisers want in their advertising, the Starch procedure is probably well worth its relatively modest cost.

The Bruzzone Test. A television analogue of the Starch test is offered by the Bruzzone Research Company (BRC). The Bruzzone test is conducted through the mail. Consumers receive questionnaires that show scenes from television

---

[5]Herbert K. Krugman, "Point Of View: Limits Of Attention To Advertising," *Journal of Advertising Research* 38 (1988):47–50.

Figure 21.1

An example of a Starch test of a well-known ad.

(Courtesy of Starch INRA Hooper and IBM.)

commercials along with the scripts, but minus the brand names (see Figure 21.2). The questionnaire asks whether they remember having seen each commercial before. If the answer is "yes," the respondents are asked to identify the brand and to rate the commercial on the basis of a short checklist of adjectives. This procedure produces a recognition score for each commercial, along with a brief assessment of how many respondents liked it and how many thought it said something relevant to their needs.

The Bruzzone test has many of the same advantages as the Starch test. The

Please look over these pictures and words from a TV commercial and answer the questions on the right.

(Boy #1) What's this stuff?

(Boy #2) Some cereal. Supposed to be good for you.

(Boy #1) Did you try it?

(Boy #2) I'm not going to try it. You try it.

(Boy #1) I'm not going to try it.

(Boy #2) Let's get Mikey.

(Boy #1) Yeah.

(Boy #2) He won't eat it. He hates everything.

He likes it!
Hey, Mikey!

(Announcer) When you bring brand name home, * don't tell the kids it's one of those nutritional cereals you've been trying to get them to eat. You're the only one who has to know.

Do you remember seeing this commercial on TV?

6-1 ☐ Yes   -2 ☐ No   -3 ☐ Not sure-I may have

How interested are you in what this commercial is trying to tell you or show you about the product?

7-1 ☐ Very interested   -2 ☐ Somewhat interested   -3 ☐ Not interested

How does it make you _feel_ about the product?

8-1 ☐ It's good -2 ☐ It's OK -3 ☐ It's bad -4 ☐ Not sure

Please check any of the following if you feel they describe this commercial.

9-1 ☐ Amusing	10-1 ☐ Familiar	11-1 ☐ Pointless
-2 ☐ Appealing	-2 ☐ Fast moving	-2 ☐ Seen a lot
-3 ☐ Believable	-3 ☐ Gentle	-3 ☐ Sensitive
-4 ☐ Clever	-4 ☐ Imaginative	-4 ☐ Silly
-5 ☐ Confusing	-5 ☐ Informative	-5 ☐ True to life
-6 ☐ Convincing	-6 ☐ Irritating	-6 ☐ Warm
-7 ☐ Dull	-7 ☐ Lively	-7 ☐ Well done
-8 ☐ Easy to forget	-8 ☐ Original	-8 ☐ Worn out
-9 ☐ Effective	-9 ☐ Phony	-9 ☐ Worth remembering

Thinking about the commercial as a whole would you say you:

12-1 ☐ Liked it a lot   -4 ☐ Disliked it somewhat
-2 ☐ Liked it somewhat   -5 ☐ Disliked it a lot
-3 ☐ Felt neutral about it

* We have blocked out the name. Do you remember which brand was being advertised?   Does anyone in your household use this type of product?

13-1 ☐ Life   14-1 ☐ Regularly
-2 ☐ Total   -2 ☐ Occasionally
-3 ☐ Special K   -3 ☐ Seldom or never
-4 ☐ Don't know

Figure 21.2 **Bruzzone Test Questionnaire.** (Courtesy of Bruzzone Research Company.)

scores it produces are quite reliable. Compared with other television copy-testing methods, it is relatively inexpensive—about $1,450 per ad. The research supplier also has accumulated norms that help the advertiser interpret scores. The Bruzzone test also shares the Starch test's principle drawback, however: It cannot be used until after all the costs of final production and placement in the media have already been incurred.

$\mathscr{P}$ERSUASION TESTS

persuasion test A test that evaluates the effectiveness of an advertisement by measuring whether the ad affects consumers' intentions to buy a brand.

The basic format for a **persuasion test**, or attitude-change test, is this: Consumers are first asked how likely they are to buy a specific brand. They they are exposed to an advertisement for that brand. After exposure, they are again asked about what they intend to purchase. Results are analyzed to determine whether intention to buy has increased as a result of exposure to the advertisement.

TYPES OF PERSUASION TESTS

Research companies that conduct persuasion tests often invite consumers to a theater to see a "preview of a new television show." They use this pretense because they do not want respondents to pay undue attention to advertising before coming to the testing session and because they want to minimize artificial attention to the commercials once the testing session has begun.

Before the audience members see the program, they fill out a questionnaire that asks about their preferences for various brands. They then watch a television program, complete with commercials, after which they answer questions concerning their reactions to the entertainment. They then respond to the brand-preference questions again.

At the beginning of the session most members of the audience believe that their major task will be to evaluate the entertainment. Before the session is over, however, most respondents have figured out that the commercials are the object of the test. Although some respondents react negatively when they realize their cooperation has been secured through false pretenses, most go along with the instructions and evaluate the different ads.

Like recall tests, persuasion tests come in several different versions. In one variation, respondents are telephoned at home and requested to watch a program at a certain time. During the course of the recruitment interview they are asked about their brand preferences. After the program has been telecast, they are recontacted and asked about their brand preferences again. Another method exposes respondents to commercials only, without program material. The procedure is basically the same in all such variations: pretest-exposure-retest, with a comparison of purchasing intentions before and after exposure to the advertisement.

ASSESSING PERSUASION TESTS

Audience Composition. The validity of a persuasion test depends in part on whether participants in the experiment constitute a good sample of the prospects the advertiser is trying to reach. A dog-food advertiser, for example, would not be interested in responses from people who do not own dogs. That requirement creates a problem because, unless the audience has been specially recruited to contain only dog owners, many of the responses in a typical persuasion test audience will come from people who are not really interested in the product.

Audience composition becomes especially important when the target audience is relatively small. Denture wearers, heavy users of pain relievers, and potential buyers of luxury automobiles will be tiny minorities of the audience in any normal persuasion test. Yet their reactions are the only reactions the advertiser really wants.

To control costs, persuasion test suppliers usually evaluate five or six commercials in different product categories during the same testing session. This means that even if the audience has been recruited to match the requirements of one product category—dog food, for example—it will not match the requirements of the other commercials being tested. An audience of dog owners will not necessarily be denture wearers, heavy users of pain relievers, and potential buyers of expensive European cars.

Because perfectly appropriate samples are so difficult to get, advertisers are tempted to ignore audience composition and to take findings from the entire group, regardless of how many respondents are really potential buyers. An understandable decision, but to anyone concerned with validity, wrong.

The Environment. Because respondents are in a strange environment and because they may feel that they themselves are being tested, they are likely to be more alert, attentive, and critical than they would be at home. These characteristics of the theater environment may produce artificially high levels of attention and may exaggerate rational, as distinguished from emotional, response.

Brand Familiarity. When the advertisement being tested is for a well-known brand, the amount of change created by one exposure to one commercial is almost always very small. Small changes tend to be unreliable. The advertiser cannot tell whether small differences among commercials are real or due to some random combination of factors that accidentally affected the results.

The small size and consequent unreliability of persuasion test scores for well-known brands is an important limitation. Advertisers of well-known brands are heavy users of persuasion testing. Yet the better known the brand, the less dependable the results.

Cost. Persuasion tests are unusually expensive. A typical persuasion test costs between $11,000 and $15,000, and if special efforts to recruit a hard-to-find sample are required, the cost can go much higher. One justification for this large expenditure is that persuasion test suppliers typically provide recall scores and attitude scores, along with persuasion scores, when reporting their findings. Another even more important justification is that persuasion is what advertisements are all about. Because an unpersuasive advertisement is nearly worthless, even a rough indication of persuasive power is evidence that the message will have its intended effect.

Protest. Naturally, creative directors do not like persuasion tests any more than they like recall tests. When, for example, the Carnation company decided to compensate its agencies through a formula based in part on persuasion test scores, creative directors predicted dire consequences. One said, "It's the end of creativity, the end of anything meaningful or right in the advertising business if this isn't laughed out of the business quickly." Another said, "I think it's insane. There's going to be a lot more commercials that are good for [research companies] and less that are good with the consumer."[6]

Research executives have been less vehement. Although audience composition, the environment, and brand familiarity pose serious threats to persuasion test validity, evidence has shown that, when persuasion tests are competently conducted, scores are positively related to sales effectiveness—especially for advertisements that have something new and important to say about the brand.[7]

Despite all the arguments against persuasion tests, advertisers continue to use them for the same basic reason they continue to use recall tests: The tests help them make difficult and important decisions. Advertisers reason that even though the tests may not be perfect, they provide some objective information. When conflicting arguments intrude from every side, some objective information is a lot more reassuring than none at all.

Principle

For well-known brands the change produced by one exposure to one advertisement may be too small to measure accurately.

---

[6]Marcy Magiera, "Admen Question Carnation Plan," *Advertising Age* (March 13, 1989):4.
[7]Anthony J. Adams and Margaret Hendersen Blair, "Persuasive Advertising and Sales Accountability: Past Experience and Forward Validation," Advertising Research Foundation 35th Annual Conference, New York City, April 1989.

DIRECT-RESPONSE COUNTS

direct-response counts
Evaluative tests that count the number of viewers or readers who request more information or who purchase the product.

Some television commercials request direct response via an 800 number. Some print ads request direct response via an 800 number, a coupon, or an offer embedded in the body copy. Responses to these requests provide direct measures of effectiveness. Instead of depending on memory or persuasion or some other indirect and possibly misleading indication of effectiveness, the advertiser simply counts the number of viewers or readers who request more information or buy the product. **Direct-response counts** are sometimes called *inquiry tests*. This name is not quite accurate, however, because increasingly the counts are of actual sales rather than inquiries.

In some cases, direct-response advertisements are split run—the advertisements being tested are bound into alternate copies of newspapers or magazines. Because each advertisement has its own code on the reply coupon or its own box number in the return address, the advertiser can tell exactly which ad produced the best results. Compared with recall tests and persuasion tests, few reliability or validity problems plague this type of evaluative research.

Of course, direct-response counts cannot be used to test all advertisements. Most ads are intended to encourage purchase at a retail outlet—an automobile showroom, a supermarket, or a department store, for example. When the product is distributed through retail outlets, the direct connection between ad and purchase is lost, and no one can tell which purchaser responded to which, if any, of the advertiser's ads. The box entitled "Television's Longest-Running Spot" takes a closer look at how direct-response evaluation saved one ad.

COMMUNICATION TESTS

The communication test described in Chapter 6 is sometimes used for final evaluation as well as for diagnostic research. Advertisers who are not convinced that recognition, recall, or persuasion are adequate measures of an ad's effectiveness, and who can't rely on direct-response counts, may settle for answers to the three basic communication questions: Did the ad deliver the message it was intended to deliver? Did the ad deliver any messages it was *not* intended to deliver? How did the representatives of the target audience react to the message, the characters, the situation, and the tone? Although the answers to these questions are a far cry from definitive measures of sales effectiveness, they obviously are important. Because these answers are important and because communication tests are relatively inexpensive, some major advertisers have decided that communication tests are about the best evaluation tests they can get.

Memory test scores, persuasion test scores, and direct-response counts are final grades that can be quickly interpreted as good, bad, or indifferent, pass or fail. In contrast, communication tests do not give single scores, but rather patterns of findings, which require detailed analysis and interpretation of con-

Television's Longest-Running Spot

Because direct-response counts provide an exact measure of an ad's effectiveness, they can keep a very effective advertisement in circulation long after the ad might ordinarily be judged to have worn out.

A good example of an extremely long-running direct-response television advertisement is a commercial for "150 Music Masterpieces," first aired in 1968. It made a profit for 15 years for the client, Vista Marketing, and its agency, Wunderman, Ricotta & Kline, grossing $25 million and garnering 2.5 million orders of the five-record sets of abbreviated musical themes. (The average direct-marketing album commercial sells a half million sets.) The commercial cost only $5,000 to produce.

In "150 Musical Masterpieces" actor John Williams says, "I'm sure you recognize this lovely melody, 'A Stranger in Paradise,' but did you know the original theme is from the 'Polovetsian Dance No. 2' by Borodin? Ah, it's a priceless introduction to the classics that will enrich every home." Directed at fans of Lawrence Welk, Roy Rogers and Dale Evans, and Jackie Gleason, the 2-minute commercial remained relatively unchanged over the years, with the exception of the tagline announcing the price. Originally offered at $5.95, by the mid-1980s the albums sold for $12.95 and the tapes for $14.95. John William's part of the taping took only 3 to 4 hours, for which the late actor received residuals for the next 15 years, amounting to between $250,000 and $500,000.

The history of this commercial has become a case study in the use of direct marketing. In the New York market it first ran about 150 times a week for 2 years. Spot time was bought in all major markets. After the fifth year, research revealed that the commercial was no longer receiving the kind of response it had been getting, so it was shelved for a few months. Direct-response evaluation indicated, however, that there were certain times of the day and stations that still worked well for the ad, and so it was brought back into

The late John Williams: His commercial lives on.

particular spots and advertised on such shows as the syndicated *Merv Griffin Show* and other programs that appealed to older women, such as daytime game shows.

Had this commercial been an advertisement intended to encourage retail purchases, it probably would have been judged "worn-out" after its first few months. Because Vista had an exact record of the ad's effectiveness, however, it stayed on the air and continued to work. This case raises an interesting question: How many commercials that have not had the advantage of direct-response evaluation have been discarded while they were still in the prime of life?

Source: Adapted from Maria Fisher, "TV's Longest-Running Spot: 15 Years and Still Selling," *Adweek* (May 16, 1983):20.

sumers' reactions to the advertisement. This quality is both a disadvantage and an advantage. On the one hand, it increases the unreliability caused by subjective interpretation. On the other hand, it provides richer, more detailed information about how consumers reacted to the ad.

FOCUS GROUPS

Some advertisers use focus groups to make final go/no-go decisions about television commercials and print ads. This practice is popular because—compared with memory tests, persuasion tests, and even communication tests—focus groups can provide quicker feedback and can be less expensive.

However, this practice has an important downside: When used to make final go/no-go decisions, focus groups are notoriously unreliable. Because so much can happen in the course of a group discussion, different groups of respondents and different moderators often produce dramatically different evaluations.

When focus groups are used to gather background information, as described in Chapter 6, respondents' reactions are treated as clues to be weighed and evaluated, accepted or rejected, in the context of information from many other sources. But when focus groups are used as juries, respondents' reactions are liable to be taken literally, and accepted at face value. When that happens, the fate of an expensive creative product is determined by a complex set of semi-accidental happenings. Advertisers who use focus groups to make final go/no-go decisions are placing far too much weight on extremely unreliable results.

PHYSIOLOGICAL TESTS

All of the methods discussed thus far require consumers to make verbal responses: Do you remember seeing a commercial for a detergent? As you were looking at the commercial, what thoughts or ideas went through your mind? Which brand do you intend to buy? The value of those questions depends on the respondents' ability to observe their own reactions and to report those responses accurately.

physiological tests Tests that measure emotional reactions to advertisements by monitoring reactions such as pupil dilation and heart rate.

Aware of the shortcomings of verbal response, investigators have tried to use **physiological tests** to evaluate emotional reactions to ads. They reasoned that physiological measurements might pick up responses that the person was unable or unwilling to report. Some physiological measurements that have been tried are:

- *Heart rate:* The heart speeds up during an emotional response.
- *Pupil dilation:* The pupil of the eye dilates when a person sees something especially interesting.
- *Galvanic skin response:* Emotional reactions produce measurable changes in the electrical conductivity of the skin.
- *Electroencephalographic (EEG) response:* Electrical activity in the brain changes as the brain processes information.

Principle

Many physiological tests are so sensitive to outside influences that their test-retest reliability is unacceptably low.

ASSESSING PHYSIOLOGICAL TESTS

Despite their apparent advantages, physiological measurements have not yet come into general use. Validity has been a problem because physiological reac-

Physiological tests measure emotional responses to advertising.

(Tim Davis/Photo Researchers)

tions are often caused by minor changes in the testing environment, changes in a commercial's brightness or color, or even random thoughts. Such instability leads to questions about what is being measured and to inconsistent findings when the same ad is tested more than once.

The Test Environment. Most physiological tests require that respondents report to a laboratory, a setting that is hardly conducive to natural responses. Also, many of the tests require that respondents be attached to unfamiliar laboratory instruments, sometimes for extended periods of time. These requirements reduce the representativeness of samples because many consumers cannot be persuaded to submit to such unusual and possibly threatening procedures. They also reduce the representativeness of the environment in which the advertisement is shown.

Furthermore, no one is entirely sure how to interpret any of the physiological reactions. A change in emotional response may mean that the consumer likes the advertisement or the product. Then again, it may mean that the consumer is irritated or upset by something in the advertisement or by something in the testing situation itself. Researchers have had a hard time deciding what bearing any of that might have on the advertisement's intended effect.

Because physiological measurements show so much theoretical promise, investigators have gone back to them again and again. However, every attempt to put them into commercial practice has run aground on the reliability and validity difficulties just described. As a result, although physiological tests continue to attract intermittent attention and interest, they are not now a major factor in evaluative research.

Some Things I Think I Know About Studying Television Commercials
John S. Coulson

John Coulson is a former vice president in charge of research at the Leo Burnett agency and a partner in Communication Workshop, Inc., a creative and marketing research company that specializes in developing and evaluating new products and corporate communications. In both capacities he has evaluated numerous televisions commercials. The following observations are based on his research experiences.

1. No single set of measurements will serve to evaluate all commercials. A commercial is a very complex communication with many different goals. It is part of a total advertising program that is part of a total marketing program. Studying it out of context can produce highly irrelevant information.
2. A key element in the results of a commercial test is the type of people among whom the commercial is being studied. Some people are more receptive to a particular brand's advertising than are others. For example, product and brand users are generally more receptive to a message about that brand than are nonusers. Trier-rejecters show even less interest and acceptance. Generally women are more accepting than men, older adults are more accepting than younger adults, and children are more accepting than adults.
3. The most basic rule for achieving a successful commercial is that its viewers be able to identify the product and brand being advertised. Occasionally a competitive brand is misidentified as the advertiser. To be sure that the brand is correctly identified, it must be an integral part of the story line of the commercial rather than an element that is out of synch with the rest of the commercial.
4. The commercial's ability to create brand or product recall is largely independent of its effect on the viewer's attitudes toward the brand or product. Recall is a measure of how well the commercial is communicating its message. It is related to the commercial's *efficiency* rather than to the *effectiveness* of its communication.
5. One effective commercial format is to provide news that is relevant and important to viewers. Information about a product can be news to the public for a long time, particularly if it can be given a fresh twist. Advertisers frequently feel that news is stale long before the public does.
6. When the objective of the commercial is to provide news, the news should be seen as important and relevant to the way the consumer uses the product, it should be believable, and it should be unique to the brand being advertised. Otherwise the commercial will be less effective.
7. The measurement of believability is tricky. If there is no news in the commercial, it tends to be rated as believable. Also, the believability of the mes-

FRAME-BY-FRAME TESTS

frame-by-frame test Tests that evaluate consumers' reactions to the individual scenes that unfold in the course of a television commercial.

A great deal goes on while a television commercial unfolds. Even though the commercial may be very brief, it is always made up of separate parts. As those episodes progress, viewers' responses to the commercial change as well.

Researchers have attempted to track those changes in several different ways. In one form of **frame-by-frame test**, viewers turn a dial or press numbers on an electronic keypad to indicate their moment-to-moment reactions to what they are seeing on the screen. That procedure produces a "trace"—a continuous record of ups and downs. When the trace is correlated with the commercial frame by frame, it provides a record of which parts of the commercial increased

Courtesy of John S. Coulson

8. A basic problem of advertising with the goal of providing news is trying to cover too many ideas. It is more than twice as difficult to deliver two ideas as it is to deliver one, and the attempt to deliver three or four ideas almost always produces a jumble that is quickly forgotten.

9. An attractive spokesperson who is appropriate for the product or brand attracts attention and makes the message more believable and compelling.

10. Viewers are wary about the use of celebrity spokespeople in advertising. If the spokespeople are not appropriate to the commercial, viewers do not believe them and reject the message.

11. In addition to informative commercials, another widely used approach to television advertising is a mood or emotional commercial designed to create greater awareness of, and favorable reaction to, the product or the brand. Many commercials successfully combine the two approaches.

12. When a commercial is delivering news of real interest to its viewers, liking the commercial or empathizing with its situation is generally not critical to its effectiveness. Instead, clarity and simplicity are important. For mood commercials, on the other hand, likability and empathy are far more important than clarity and simplicity.

sage in the commercial is not always important to the commercial's success. If the product is relatively low priced, consumers might purchase it just to test the claim that they found difficult to believe in the commercial.

13. Appropriate music can enhance the mood of a commercial. Music can make a commercial more memorable and improve consumer attitudes toward the product.

attention (or liking of whatever is being measured) and which parts reduced it.

One of the best-known frame-by-frame tests is VIEWFACTS' PEAC test, in which respondents in a minitheater setting press buttons on hand-held keypads to indicate how much they like or dislike what they are seeing on a television screen. The test commercial is embedded in a series of commercials, and respondents indicate their reactions to each one. As respondents are reacting, a computer collects and averages the responses and translates them into a continuous trace line keyed to the commercial's scenes.

After respondents give their initial reactions, they use their keypads to answer a set of questions that resemble those asked in a communication test. The computer collects the answers and tabulates them for discussion later on.

In the second half of a PEAC session the computer superimposes the response line over the test commercial on the screen (see Figure 21.3). An inter-

Figure 21.3

The PEAC test.
(Courtesy of VIEWFACTS.)

viewer stops the commercial at key turning points and asks the audience members why their evaluations went up or down. Toward the end of the sessions the interviewer reviews the communication questions and asks the respondents to explain why they reacted the way they did.

Thus the PEAC test combines the advantages of moment-to-moment response with an opportunity to ask and discuss questions about the respondents' reactions. Although the PEAC test is relatively expensive, this combination provides useful diagnostic information that cannot be accumulated in any other way.

In another form of frame-by-frame test viewers wear tiny electrodes that measure the electrical conductivity of the skin. As various parts of the commercial provoke an emotional reaction, electrical conductivity changes, producing an "emotional response" trace line. Unlike the PEAC test, which produces a voluntary measure of liking, electrical conductivity tests measure involuntary, emotional reactions. Although this method is still in the early stages of development, it shows considerable promise. It combines the advantages of frame-by-frame analysis with the advantages of involuntary emotional response.

ASSESSING FRAME-BY-FRAME TESTS

Frame-by-frame tests can be useful because they provide some guidance as to how the commercial might be improved. When a commercial gets a low recall score or a low persuasion score, no one can really be sure what will bring that score up. In contrast, because the trace line in frame-by-frame tests goes up in response to some scenes and down in response to others, it provides direct clues as to which parts of the commercial need further work.

As usual, reliability and validity are difficult to establish. Traces can be unstable from person to person and from group to group, especially when physiological measures are involved. Furthermore, the relationship between the trace's form or level and the advertisement's ultimate effect is uncertain. Even when the trace can be shown to be reliable, the question remains: Exactly what is the trace a reliable measurement of?

Nevertheless, frame-by-frame tests bring something to advertising research that other methods do not. They provide an opportunity to look inside a commercial, and they offer clues as to what scenes produce what kind of response. Because that is such a valuable advantage, the PEAC test and its direct competitors are becoming more widely used.

$\mathcal{I}$N-MARKET TESTS

in-market tests Tests that measure the effectiveness of advertisements by measuring actual sales results in the marketplace.

In-market tests evaluate advertisements by measuring their influence on sales. In view of all the problems discussed thus far, a sales-impact measurement might appear to be the only measurement that an advertiser should accept. However, the practical difficulties of conducting in-market tests are so great that full-scale in-market tests are seldom attempted in evaluating individual ads.

One problem is that sales are produced by a tightly interwoven net of factors, including economic conditions, competitive strategies, and all of the marketing activities in which the advertiser is engaged. Within that complicated set of interrelationships the effect of any single advertisement is extremely difficult to detect. Even with the benefit of a carefully designed, large-scale (and therefore costly and time-consuming) experiment, the effect of a single advertisement may be entirely lost.

Another reason that in-market tests are not popular is that by the time sales figures become available, most of the important investments have already been made: The advertisement has been produced, and media costs have all been incurred. For purposes of evaluating an advertisement, in-market test results become available very late in the game.

SIMULATED TEST MARKETS

simulated test market Research procedure in which respondents are exposed to advertisements and then permitted to shop for the advertised products in an artificial environment where records are kept of their purchases.

Some of those problems can be avoided by using **simulated test markets**. In a simulated test market the research company conducting the test exposes respondents to advertising and then asks them to choose among competing brands. Later the researchers contact respondents who have used the advertiser's brand to ask if they would purchase the same brand again. The two numbers produced by that pair of interviews are *trial*—the proportion of respondents who chose to try the brand after seeing an advertisement for it—and *repeat*—the proportion of respondents who, having tried the product, chose to purchase the same brand again.

Despite the artificiality of simulated test markets, research companies have developed trial-and-repeat formulas that have proved to be remarkably accurate predictors of later in-market success. One of the reasons for this accuracy is that the trial-and-repeat numbers are much closer to what happens in the real marketplace than are the numbers provided by memory or *persuasion* tests.

In a simulated test market, however, the advertisement's effect is combined with the effects of packaging and pricing, and of course with reactions to the product itself. Therefore, although simulated test markets can predict the success of a marketing program as a whole, they cannot give more than a rough indication of the advertisement's independent influence on sales.

In principle, this problem could be solved by conducting multiple simulated test markets in which only the advertisements were varied and everything else remained the same. This solution runs into the problem of cost. The cost of conducting a single simulated test market runs from $50,000 to $75,000. The cost of conducting multiple experiments is higher than most advertisers believe they can afford.

SINGLE-SOURCE DATA

In another major substitute for a full in-market test, the research company conducting the test arranges to control the television signal received by the households in a community. The company divides the households into equivalent matched groups. It then sends advertisements to one group of households but not to the other and collects exact records of what every household purchases. Because advertising is the only variable being manipulated here, the method permits an unambiguous reading of cause and effect. The data collected in this way are known as *single-source data* because exposure records and purchasing records come from the same source.

Principle

The most realistic tests of an advertisement's effectiveness are too expensive for routine use.

Single-source data can produce exceptionally dependable results. Real advertisements are used, and they are received under natural conditions in the home. The resulting purchases are real purchases made by real consumers for their own use. The method is very expensive, however—$200,000 to $300,000 per test. Furthermore, the method usually requires more than 6 months to produce usable results. It is therefore not acceptable for routine testing of individual ads.

IMPLICATIONS OF EVALUATIVE RESEARCH

In evaluative copy testing, the advertiser must make trade-offs. In-market tests, which come closest to duplicating the most important features of the natural environment, are too expensive and too time-consuming to be used on a regular basis. Tests that are fast and affordable have so many obvious flaws. Added to all that, creative "experts" within the company and—especially—within the advertising agency fight all kinds of evaluative research at every step. Faced with such problems, advertisers must either depend on unaided judgment, which may be less reliable and less valid than even the least reliable and least valid research, or supplement judgment with research findings that, although far from perfect, are likely to be better than no help at all.

In this dilemma the advertiser joins the government official, the military leader, the business executive, the economist, the physician, and the educator. When decisions are difficult, important, and controversial, research cannot tell the decision maker what to do. However, it can provide guidance, and when that guidance is used reasonably, decisions generally turn out better than they would have if based on intuition alone.

The same principles apply to selection and purchase of advertising media. Whereas research can be a valuable guide, decisions as to how much to spend—and when, where, and how to allocate those funds—always include an element of hard data and an element of hunch.

$\mathscr{S}$UMMARY

- Creative experts disagree with one another, and agencies disagree with their clients. Faced with these conflicts of opinion, advertisers often resort to evaluative research in the hope that it will provide a reliable and valid prediction of an advertisement's sales effectiveness.

- The major evaluative research methods fall into eight major groups: (1) memory tests, (2) persuasion tests, (3) direct-response counts, (4) communication tests, (5) focus groups, (6) physiological tests, (7) frame-by-frame tests, and (8) in-market tests.

- Although memory tests have a long history in advertising research, no one knows whether they predict sales. Many creative leaders and many research leaders believe that they do not.

- Persuasion tests are relatively good predictors of effectiveness when the ad has something new and interesting to say. However, when brands are well known, and when all messages are similar, persuasion findings may be largely due to chance.

- Direct-response counts show exactly how many consumers responded to each ad. Although this method is highly accurate, it can be used only with advertisements that request a direct response. It cannot be used with television commercials or print ads intended to encourage purchases at retail stores.

- Communication tests do not produce simple pass-fail results. Rather, they provide a detailed analysis of consumers' subjective reactions to the advertisements being tested. This quality makes them less useful for go/no-go decisions but more useful for understanding how the advertisement works.

- Focus groups are the least reliable of the major evaluative research methods. Advertisers who use them for this purpose are leaving too much to chance.

- Although physiological tests show considerable theoretical promise, low reliability and high cost have excluded them from routine use in evaluative research.

- Frame-by-frame tests allow advertisers to examine viewers' reactions as a television commercial unfolds. Because they link reactions to specific scenes, frame-by-frame tests provide especially useful clues as to how a commercial may be improved.

- When properly conducted, in-market tests are the most valid of all types of evaluative research. However, they are so expensive and so time consuming that they are not practical options for testing individual ads.

- Each evaluative method has its own unique pattern of costs, assets, and liabilities. In the end, advertisers must make trade-offs in deciding which method or methods to use. Advertisers make this decision in the same way they make any other business decision: They ask themselves, "which alternative, including unaided judgment, provides the most benefit, given its cost?"

$\mathscr{Q}$UESTIONS

1. Make a list of the assets and liabilities of each of the copy-testing methods reviewed in this chapter. Considering this list, if you were an advertiser with a $100 million advertising budget, which method would you use? Why? Would your answer change if you had a $1 million budget? In what way?

2. Suppose you are in charge of advertising a student production of a Broadway play and that an advertising class has developed several quite dif-

ferent ads. How would you decide which ad to use? How would you know whether you made the right choice?

3 The problems an advertiser encounters in trying to evaluate an individual advertisement resemble the problems a college administrator encounters in trying to evaluate an individual college course. In what ways are the two sets of problems similar? In what ways are they different?

4 Professor Fletcher is illustrating research principles by describing a case in which he was involved. A marketer of men's cologne was testing its advertisement for recognition. Ten sample groups of men aged 25 to 40 were tested, and the recognition scores for each sample were in the 25 to 35 percent range. Fletcher tells the class that the data were clearly reliable but very likely invalid. Then he asks the class two questions: Why must a result be reliable in order to be valid? Why was the cologne testing probably invalid? What would your answers be?

5 One of the methods used for testing television commercial impact is the theater test. Approximately 100 people are invited to view television programs being considered by the networks, and the commercials are embedded in the programs. Prior to the viewing, the audience is asked to select products that they would like to receive if they were a door-prize winner. After the viewings (and drawings), the audience repeats its choices. The tested products (and competing brands) are on the selection lists. What dimension of consumer effect is being tested in this way? Is this a valid method of testing for this effect?

6 The chapter discusses one weakness of physiological testing by pointing out that results from these experiments are very hard to interpret for eventual sales effectiveness. A number of researchers claim the same sort of weakness affects many recall and attitude procedures used in copy testing. Why would these very popular tests be criticized this way? What is the best way to measure the persuasion of an advertising message?

7 Through advanced technology (UPC scanning), research companies are able to speed up results from fields tests on advertising effectiveness. Although companies do not have to wait several months for results, many are still fearful of real-life field testing. In part, this fear explains the continued popularity of simulated test market studies. What is this fear about? What serious validity threat to test marketing can be relieved by a market simulation?

*S*UGGESTED CLASS PROJECT

Following the description of the Starch test in this chapter, test recognition of five advertisements from a recent edition of the college newspaper. What do the *noted, associated,* and *read most associated* scores tell about the advertisements' effectiveness?

*F*URTHER READINGS

CLANCY, KEVIN J., AND LYMAN E. OSTLUND, "Commercial Effectiveness Measures," *Journal of Advertising Research 16*, (1976):29–34.

FLETCHER, ALAN D., AND THOMAS A. BOWERS, *Fundamentals of Advertising Research*, 3rd ed. (Belmont, CA: Wadsworth Publishing Co., 1988).

KALWANI, MANOHAR U., AND ALVIN J. SILK, "On the Reliability and Predictive Validity of Purchase Intention Measures," *Marketing Science* 1, (1980):243–86.

STEWART, DAVID W., "Measures, Methods, and Models in Advertising Research," *Journal of Advertising Research* 29, (1989):54–60.

STEWART, DAVID W., AND DAVID H. FURSE, *Effective Television Advertising* (Lexington, MA: D.C. Heath and Co., 1986).

WALKER, DAVID, AND MICHAEL F. VON GONTEN, "Explaining Related Recall Outcomes: New Answers from a Better Model," *Journal of Advertising Research* 29 (1989):11–21.

YOUNG SHIRLEY, "Copy Testing Without Magic Numbers," *Journal of Advertising Research* 12 (1972):3–12.

"Perfect" Navy by Cover Girl

The women's fragrance category accounts for over $2 billion and has experienced annual growth rates of approximately 4 percent. Unlike traditional consumer products, however, the women's fragrance category has hundreds of competitors, many with fractional shares. The category is, extremely fragmented and is further segmented by "mass versus class" channels of distribution. Approximately half of the women's fragrances are sold through broad (mass) distribution channels, such as drug and mass merchandisers. The remaining products are sold through higher priced, more exclusive (class) locations, such as department and specialty stores.

Cover Girl developed the Navy fragrance for introduction in Spring of 1990. The product was designed for mass-distribution outlets. In such a highly fragmented category full of brands with short life expectancies, strong initial success is considered critical for long-term success. Cover Girl's ultimate goal for advertising was to achieve sales and share for Navy among the top ten brands in mass distribution within 3 years. The objective of the resulting "Perfect" campaign for Navy was to communicate strongly a highly desirable brand personality. Cover Girl also established objectives related to awareness, trial, purchase intent, and brand image/personality. The specific image/personality goal was to create an "aspiration" brand image that would establish Navy as a clean, classic fragrance, with a personality that would be stylish, smart, sexy, and confident—"perfect" for any occasion.

Because Cover Girl wanted women to consider Navy appropriate for all-day, year-round usage, the main promise for the new campaign was "You always feel perfect in Navy."

Demographically, Navy's target audience was identified as women 18 to 34 years of age who are regular users of fragrance, who currently include mass-market brands among their "wardrobe" of personal fragrances, and for whom fashion is an important consideration. Navy's introductory media spending amounted to approximately 7.5 percent of the total media expenditures in the women's fragrance category. Media vehicles included a 30-second television commercial and four-color, full-page magazine ads with scent strips.

Navy's initial success surpassed the objectives. After 3 months of introductory advertising, the brand's share of unit volume established it as the number two mass-distributed brand in the category, trailing the number one brand by only a narrow margin. It ranked third in terms of dollar sales, behind two well-established major brands. Consumer awareness of Navy's advertising immediately following the launch of the campaign was in the same range as the strongest brands in the category, whose campaigns had run for several years. Further consumer tracking study data indicated that Navy easily exceeded all of its awareness, trial, purchase intent, and attitudinal objectives. Among the brand's target group, Navy's purchase intent scores ranked second in the category, and its advertising ranked first in terms of recall. Cover Girl also reported that the advertising successfully communicated its brand image objectives, as consumers characterized the product as "stylish, confident, and sexy," a scent that can be worn at any time.

NEW YORK

Source: Courtesy of Lotas Minard Patton McIver, Inc.

Questions

1 With the shortened product life cycles common in the women's fragrance category, why do you think it is essential for brands to establish strong rapid trial and awareness during their introductory periods?

2 Manufacturers of women's fragrances have successfully positioned their products as similar to apparel styles. Fragrances, like clothes, should be unique, ever-changing, and always up-to-date. How has this success heightened new product competition, shortened product life cycles, and increased product development and advertising costs?

3 What problems and difficulties described in this chapter apply to evaluating the effectiveness of the "Perfect" Navy campaign? Which measures of this campaign's effect might be unreliable? Which might be invalid?

Cancer Treatment Centers of America

After having watched has mother die from what he felt was ineffective treatment of her cancer, Richard Stephenson, with the help of a group of investors, bought the failing Zion Community Hospital in 1975, which had a specialty program in cancer treatment. He gathered together a professional staff with the objective of finding better and more successful ways of treating cancer and founded Cancer Treatment Centers, a chain of hospitals specializing in the treatment of many forms of cancer. This is the story of how that hospital built itself into an internationally recognized cancer specialty operation, drawing its patients from across the nation and outside the country through a combination of a comprehensive team approach to cancer treatment and a level of service within the hospital unmatched by any.

The initial hospital building had a 95-bed capacity. When the private investors bought the property, they agreed with the community to set aside 25 percent of the beds to maintain community service. Because a specialization in cancer had been his dream, Mr. Stephenson (currently Chairman of the Board) set about to staff the cancer unit with the best physicians, laboratory technicians, radiologists, surgeons, and chemotherapy professionals he could find. From the beginning, the hospital practiced a team approach, involving the patient in all of the meetings at which potential treatments were discussed and determined. Family members were encouraged to remain with the patient and even to participate in the decision. The three classic approaches to treating cancer—surgery, radiation therapy, and chemotherapy—were supplemented with nutrition programs, psychological counseling, and attentive and personal nursing care. The ratio of staff to patients is six to one, nearly twice that of the typical hospital.

As the average daily census (ADC) began to grow in the hospital, the management observed that many of the patients who were attracted to the hospital were unusually well-read about their disease, they understood it better than did patients of other disease, and they responded better to the natural-food diet that was part of the hospital's regimen. Early marketing efforts involved distributing pamphlets to health-food stores around the country. The pamphlets were developed in-house and were distributed by marketing staff members or by agents retained to call on health-food stores.

As word of mouth grew, it was observed that an increasing number of patients had been referred by chiropractors. Because many chiropractors use X-rays in their work, a special campaign thanking chiropractors for their early detection of cancer and encouraging them to refer patients to the Zion hospital was initiated. This campaign was advertised in chiropractor journals and

via direct mail, personal contact, and specialized follow-ups.

These early marketing efforts saw rapid and dramatic results. In 1985 the ADC of cancer patients in the hospital was five. The next year this number had jumped to 11. With increasing direct marketing, the ADC rose to 22 in 1987 and by 1990 it was 45.

Advertising was begun in 1986 and is done in-house by a freelance creative and design team. Media management has been assigned to CPM, Incorporated, of Chicago. One of the first advertisements developed, "Relentless" (see Exhibit A) was developed in-house and ran in such publications as *Prevention* and other smaller magazines aimed primarily at a health-conscious public. Almost from the beginning any advertising was reviewed by a focus group of patients then at the hospital. Although the "relentless" copy rang true ("Cancer can be relentless, so can we"), it seemed to lack the warmth and personal testimonials that were part of the experience of so many patients as they returned to the hospital for check ups. This finding was consistent in repeated focus groups.

In 1988 the hospital began using stories of patients

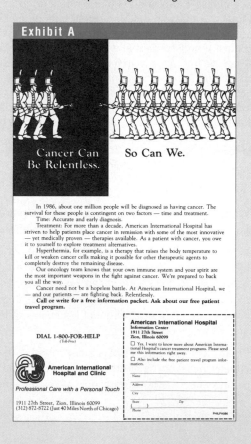

Exhibit A

Exhibit B

"CANCER IS NOT INVINCIBLE. I KNOW."

Just as every treatment at the Cancer Treatment Centers of America hospitals is carefully reviewed by a board of medical, professional, and ethical experts (the hospital was one of the pioneers in the use of ethicists on its review board), so too all the advertising is reviewed by the medical staff and by attorneys. This ensures that every statement can be verified and that none of the copy is inadvertently missing.

As the creative, media placement, and media buying were further refined by experts in the field, the response rate to the advertising continued to grow and at a more efficient rate. Exhibit C indicates the number of responses to the advertising over the years 1987 through 1990. The rate of response went from nearly 3000 in 1989 to 13,000 in 1990, more than doubling between 1989 and 1990, with a budget increase of 60 percent. Efficiency continued to climb each month.

With units in Zion, Illinois, and Tulsa, Oklahoma, Cancer Treatment Centers of America (the name adopted for national marketing in 1990) now plans to open additional units around the country at a rate of roughly one per year. Local, regional, and national marketing efforts will be used to support this extension of service.

Locally, newspaper, outdoor, local television, and staff media appearances have been used, especially to advertise the Tulsa unit. Regional marketing has consisted of advertising in regional editions of *Parade, USA Weekend, People, TV Guide, National Geographic,* among other publications. Television advertising is concentrated in cities within 600 to 700 miles of Tulsa or Chicago. National marketing includes insertions in *Prevention, American Health, Health,* and *Coping.* Cable television is used sparingly, including Discovery Channel, Prevue Channel, Lifetime, and Turner Broadcasting System. Each medium or publication has its own 800 number so that responses can be tracked precisely by city, day, and hour. As the number of hospitals expands, Cancer Treatment Centers will continue to refine its marketing with focus-group research on creative plans, statistical analysis or response rates, demographic analysis of responding patients, and by testing new ways to reach cancer victims in smaller areas.

Source: Courtesy of Cancer Treatment Centers of America.

who had been treated. The results indicated that the personal style added to the warmth and drawing power of the campaign. Exhibit B is an example of the personal style of these ads. By 1990 additional focus groups within the hospital and results from advertising placed in various print media showed that one of the most successful ads ever run was the story of Flossie Dishong. Flossie's story was also made into an unscripted television commercial, with Flossie talking about her favorable experience at Cancer Treatment Centers of America. The making of this commercial set the pattern for future commercials. Although it might take 8 hours of shooting to get 60 seconds of material, the effort produced very believable advertising.

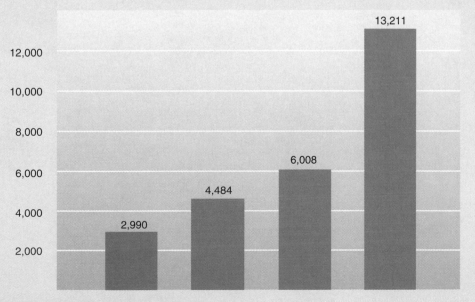

Exhibit C

Increasing response to advertising.

- 2,990
- 4,484
- 6,008
- 13,211

$\mathscr{B}$USINESS-TO-BUSINESS AND RETAIL ADVERTISING

CHAPTER OBJECTIVES

When you have completed this chapter, you should be able to:

- Explain business-to-business advertising objectives

- List the different markets in the business arena and the various media used in business advertising

- Understand how local retail advertising differs from national brand advertising

- Understand how cooperative advertising works

701

$\mathscr{R}$ETAILING IN THE FUTURE

Navigating through the supermarket of the future will be like visiting a Disney World of marketing. Grab a shopping cart and head for Aisle 1, where the LED cart handle is telling you Tide is on special. As you stroll down the aisle, a three-dimensional Bounty ad dangling from a light fixture catches your eye, but what clinches the sale is a 50-cents-off coupon dispensed from a machine attached to the shelf. In the aural background the store's own radio station plays, and you hear the adult-contemporary version of Nirvana's *Smells Like Teen Spirit* segue into an ad for Coca-Cola.

At the checkout counter, Headline News is on the monitor. A Snickers commercial flickers on the screen and you match one from an adjacent rack. As you pull out your debit card to pay the bill, the cash register electronically makes note of your purchases and sends the information to the supermarket's database. Two weeks later a letter arrives—with more coupons—welcoming you to the frequent deli-meat buyer club.

This scenario may smack of science fiction, but it's no futurist's fantasy. Much of the technology already exists and is in stores, and it will be rolled out nationally over the next few years thanks to companies like Actmedia, an in-store promotion and advertising firm, and Turner Broadcasting Systems. For the battle over consumer dollars increasingly is taking place in the supermarkets, drugstores, and mass merchandisers. "The store is the only place where the product, the advertiser's message, and the consumer all come together in one place," notes David Walthall, president of Heritage Media Corporation.

Fueling this rapid growth of in-store expenditures is the explosion of new products and the continuing splintering of the mass market. In 1976, the average supermarket carried 9,000 products; today it has more than 30,000. "Now there's such a plethora of products, so many messages, so much clutter, that mass messages don't work so well anymore," said Ross Blair, senior vice president of Information Resources, a marketing information firm. "It's much more cost-effective to target in-store than nationally. And it is this marketing dynamic that will drive much more micromarketing and geodemographic clustering—targeting consumers by lifestyle, income and education."

The advent of the marketing tools and the growing importance of the in-store environment opens up "sizable opportunities to coordinate the advertiser's message," said Blair. For too long manufacturers have not linked the brand advertising and promotional programs they run. "Promotions may boast short-term sales, but promotions will just become an escalation war—a Cold War—because competitors can cut prices too," Blair added. "But if you have image-building with the promotion, you can lock consumers in for the long term." Actmedia experts agree that advertising and promotional strategies need to be integrated more seamlessly.[1]

As indicated in the introductory discussion, dramatic changes are taking place with a number of retailers. In turn, advertising will also have to adjust, both in content and delivery. This chapter deals with two special types of advertising—business-to-business and retail—that are not known for producing great advertising. In fact, words such as "dull" and "uninspiring" typically describe ads found in these two categories. Such labels are unfair, however, given the limitations and special circumstances with which both types of advertising must cope.

---

[1]Adapted from Lorne Manly, "Selling in the Stores of the Future," *Adweek* (January 20, 1992):12–13.

These factors, as well as the special adjustments necessary to create effective business-to-business and retail advertising, will be discussed in this chapter.

 BUSINESS-TO-BUSINESS ADVERTISING

business-to-business advertising Advertising directed at people who buy or specify products for business use.

Business-to-business advertising is directed at people in business who buy or specify products for business use. As Figure 22.1 shows, these people work in a variety of business areas, such as commercial enterprises (retailing and manufacturing), government agencies (federal, state, and local), and nonprofit institutions (universities and hospitals), and purchase many different types of products. Although personal selling is the most common method of communicating with business buyers, business advertising is used to create product awareness, enhance the firm's reputation, and support salespeople and other

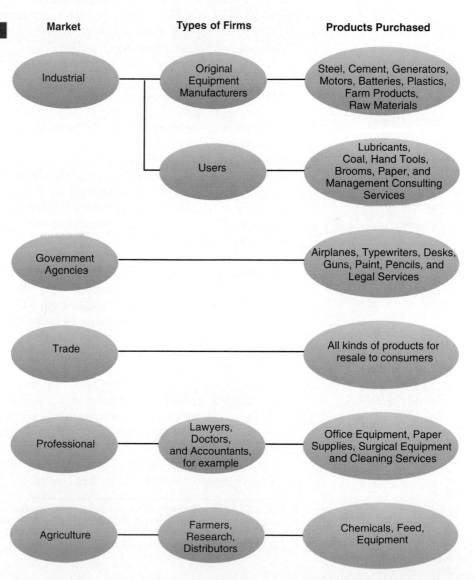

channel members. A purchaser in the business market, just as a consumer, "gathers information about alternatives, processes this information, learns about available products, determines which alternatives match the perceived needs most closely, and carries through by making a purchase."[2]

In the business arena, however, many people can be involved in the purchasing decision—people from different functional areas, such as marketing, manufacturing, or purchasing, who have varying information needs. For example, when a purchasing decision might result in a product change, such as altering the product's materials or packaging, marketing interest centers on product salability; manufacturing interest centers on production costs. Thus business advertising is also used to (1) reach the various influencers involved and (2) communicate the different information needs.

TYPES OF BUSINESS-TO-BUSINESS ADVERTISING

Information needs also depend on the type of business market the business advertiser is trying to reach. The business arena is comprised of five very distinct markets, each of which tends to purchase products and services quite differently. These markets are most frequently referred to as the *industrial, government, trade, professional,* and *agricultural* markets.

Industrial Advertising. Original equipment manufacturers (OEMs), such as IBM and General Motors, purchase industrial goods and/or services that either become a part of the final product or facilitate the operation of their businesses. Information needs, then, depend on the reason for the purchase of the product. **Industrial advertising** is directed at such businesses. *Business Week, Auto World,* and *Fortune* may all be used for industrial advertising. For example, when General Motors purchases tires from Goodyear, information needs focus on whether the purchase will contribute to a quality finished product. When Goodyear purchases packaging material to ship the tires it manufacturers, information needs focus on prompt, predictable delivery. Ad 22.1 for IBM stresses the technical advantages of the company's products to potential business users.

Government Advertising. The largest purchasers of industrial goods in the United States are federal, state, and local governments. These government units purchase virtually every kind of good—from $15 hammers to multimillion-dollar Polaris missiles. Such goods may be advertised in *Federal Computer Week, Commerce Business Daily,* or *Defense News.* Interestingly, however, you seldom see advertisements targeted directly to government agencies. Perhaps this is because government agencies normally use advertising to notify potential suppliers that they are in the process of taking bids. Supplier reputation, however, plays an important role in the selection decision. Because government buyers are responsible to, and influenced by, numerous interest groups that specify, legislate, evaluate, and use the goods and services that governments purchase, corporate image advertising is one way of influencing the government market.[3] Such interest groups include Congress, the Office of Management and Budget, and external watchdogs, such as the Consumer Union.

industrial advertising
Advertising directed at businesses that buy products to incorporate into other products or to facilitate the operation of their businesses.

---

[2]Edward F. Fern and James R. Brown, "The Industrial/Consumer Marketing Dichotomy: A Case of Insufficient Justification," *Journal of Marketing,* 48 (Spring 1984):68—77.
[3]"Selling to the Government Market: Local, State, and Federal," *Government Products News* (Cleveland, OH: Government Product News, 1977).

Open systems.

Everyone agrees they're good, but not always from the same point of view.

The idea of open systems—that computers should easily share things and basically behave like friends—is what everybody is aiming for.

Still, you hear lots of definitions for open systems, from many points of view. So, on the subject of openness, IBM remains open.

Instead of insisting that one operating system, like UNIX,® is more open than another, we're for anything that gets your existing and future systems working together. So to us, each customer's open system will be different, and unless your pockets are incredibly deep, you'll begin with the systems you already have.

An ideal open system begins with a plan tailored for your business needs, and IBM can help you with it, probably better than anyone. Our stake in open systems goes far beyond hardware, operating systems and all the standards we support. It includes the *services* you'll need to make everything work.

Call us and we'll listen to your business needs first, then we'll get into computer solutions, present and future. After that, we'll build a plan for opening things up, and of course we'll work with other vendors—that's what open systems are about.

At Republic National Bank of New York, for

example, we built an open system that's improving customer service. Based on the IBM RISC System/6000,® it works in close partnership with their DEC,® Tandem® and IBM mainframes, on a network that includes both TCP/IP and SNA protocols. And along with IBM banking software (customized by one of our Business Partners), it runs a wide variety of off-the-shelf UNIX applications. And we not only helped integrate the whole system, we provide ongoing service.

We're open to helping you, too. To learn more, call us at 1 800 IBM 6676, ext. 730.

IBM

Ad 22.1

This IBM ad is typical of an industrial appeal, using a great deal of technical information.

(Courtesy of International Business Machines Corporation)

trade advertising Advertising used to influence resellers, wholesalers, and retailers.

professional advertising Advertising directed at people such as lawyers, doctors, and accountants.

agricultural advertising Advertising directed at large and small farmers.

Trade Advertising. **Trade advertising** is used to persuade resellers, wholesalers, and retailers in the consumer market to stock the products of the manufacturer. *Chain Store Age, Florist's Review,* and *Pizza and Pasta* are examples of trade publications. Because resellers purchase products for resale to ultimate consumers, they want information on the profit margins they can expect to receive, the product's major selling points, and what the producer is doing in the way of consumer advertising and other promotional support activities. Ad 22.2 for Kellogg's is a public relations ad targeted at wholesalers and retailers who carry Kellogg's products.

Professional Advertising. **Professional advertising** is directed at a diverse group of mostly white-collar people such as lawyers, accountants, management consultants, doctors, teachers, funeral directors, and marketing research specialists. Advertisers interested in attracting professionals advertise in publications such as the *Music Educator Journal* or *Advertising Age.* Information needs depend on both the advertiser's product and the desired audience.

Agricultural Advertising. **Agricultural advertising** promotes a variety of products and services, such as animal-health products, seeds, farm machinery and equipment, crop dusting, and fertilizer. Large and small farmers alike want to know how industrial products can assist them in the growing, raising, or production of agricultural commodities. They turn to publications such as *California Farmer* or *Trees and Turf* for such assistance.

BUSINESS VERSUS CONSUMER MARKETING

There are several inherent characteristics that differentiate business marketing from consumer marketing, including the market concentration, decision makers, strategy, and purchasing objectives. As a result, the process of creating business-to-business advertising, as well as the expertise of the people involved, differs from that involved in consumer marketing. For example, in Ad 22.3, ITT Hartford is directing its appeal to benefits managers in large companies.

Market Concentration. The market for a typical business good is relatively small compared to the market for a consumer good. In some cases, particularly where an original equipment manufacturer (OEM) is concerned, the market may even be geographically concentrated. For example, the auto industry is located primarily in Detroit, the steel industry in Pennsylvania and Illinois, and the furniture industry in North Carolina. These concentrations have direct ramifications for media selection and the ability to target media. For example, businesses selling special computer hardware and software used in stock-and-bond purchases can run their ads in media concentrated in cities, such as New York and Chicago, or zone editions of magazines that reach these markets.

In addition to geographic concentration, businesses can be grouped according to the *Standard Industrial Classification (SIC) System.* The U.S. government established the SIC system in order to group organizations on the basis of major activity or major product or service provided. It enables the federal government

to publish the number of establishments, number of employees, and sales volume for each group, designated by a commercial code. Geographic breakdowns are also provided where possible. The SIC system classifies more than 4 million manufacturers into ten major categories that are each subdivided into more specific groups. For example, food SIC is 20, meat products is 201, and canned food is 2032. The SIC system permits an advertiser to find the SIC codes of its customers and then obtain SIC-coded lists that also include publication usages by SIC classifications. This publication usage information allows the advertiser to select media that will reach the businesses in a certain SIC.

Decision Makers. In general, those involved in making decisions for businesses are professionals who utilize rational criteria when comparing choices. Many times these professionals possess technical knowledge and expertise about the products and services being advertised. Moreover, it isn't uncommon for as many as 15 to 20 people to be involved in a particular purchase decision. Unfortunately, little is known about the inner workings of the decision process or the people involved. Dillard B. Tinsley, a professor of marketing at Stephen F. Austin State University, suggests that we must understand a firm's organizational culture before we know how decisions are made at that firm. Organizational culture includes the stories and anecdotes employees tell about

Eric Isherwood, Account Manager, The Schutte Group, Buffalo

As an account manager within the Business-to-Business Division of the Schutte Group, Eric has the responsibility of assisting management of the Rich Products account. Rich Products is a privately held food service manufacturer, which also has a Consumer/Retail Division that is handled by a different account staff at The Schutte Group. The account covers divisions in Canada and internationally. His responsibilities range from the day-to-day account administration of work in progress to long-term planning and pursuing new business opportunities.

8:15 A.M. I arrive at the office, after a short drive, to begin my day. My first priority is to check my agency voice mail and my client's voice mail to see what items may need immediate attention. Make notes concerning the day's activity and check my Daytimer for any appointments. Fire up my computer and grab a cup of joe.

8:30 A.M. Meet with the group (senior account manager and the group vice president) to update each other on ongoing projects and address any concerns we may have.

9:00 A.M. Time to get in the car and head across the border to consult with Rich's Canadian Division. We are working with Rich Canada to complete an ad series highlighting winners of a recipe contest that was held in Toronto recently. This continuity campaign began with solicitation of recipes from food service industry professionals and culminates with previewing the winning recipes in trade publications throughout Canada. The winning recipes were recreated by a food stylist in a photo studio and shot for use in the ads. Due to the client's travel schedule, he was unable to attend the shoot and will be given the opportunity to review the photography for the first time this morning. We will also review the copy that has been written for the ads.

10:30 A.M. Return to the agency and complete all the administrative details that pertain to this morning's meeting. Client has approved the photography and requested several revisions to the copy. We will proceed to mechanicals at this point and any additional revisions will be made on these. Our film date is fast approaching, so we need to get final approval for these ads in less than three days.

11:00 A.M. Client scheduled a meeting to discuss the details of revising their 68-page product catalog and the budget associated with its production. We have a good deal to discuss, so we will work through lunch and order in.

1:30 P.M. Combined proofs have arrived for a 22-page brochure that we have been working on. They look great except for some minor tweaks, which the creative director, the production manager, and I have indicated. The films will be completed with these changes and sent counter to counter from Buffalo to Chicago, where our printer is located for this particular job. The schedule is extremely tight for pro-

their company, how they feel about their competitors, and how they feel about being (for example) the industry leader, as well as company procedures, policies, rules, job descriptions, and other formalized guidelines for employee activities.[4]

According to a study sponsored by the newspaper *Australia Post,* there are four types of business decision makers: (1) *information seekers* (25 percent), who are very receptive to both advertising and sales representatives; (2) *hesitants* (19 percent), who are concerned about the quality of both the advertising and the sales representatives; (3) *innovators* (31 percent), who are particularly positive toward advertising efforts, but negative toward sales representatives; and (4)

[4]Dillard B. Tinsley, "Understanding Business Customers Means Learning About Its Culture," *Marketing News* (March 14, 1988):5, 15.

viding finished materials to the client for their national business meeting in two weeks. Arrangements have been made for the production manager and the client to attend the press run so they can approve color on press and avoid any further delays.

3:00 P.M.   Meeting with the creative director to discuss an ad that is being produced for Rich Canada. We have taken an existing ad from the U.S. Division and had it translated into French for use in a publication in Quebec. We intend to use the same four-color unit from the existing film and make a black plate change for the new copy. The translation runs considerably longer than the copy in English. Therefore, a determination must be made on how to keep the typeface at a legible size. After reviewing various options, the creative director advised that the headline be moved and the copy wrapped more tightly around the visual to allow it to be readable and not interfere with the visual design. The layout will be revised on the computer and sent to the client for approval.

3:45 P.M.   Review mail and return phone calls, as the messages have piled up during my meeting.

4:15 P.M.   Product cutting at Research and Development in the test kitchen. Client is interested in introducing a product-line extension and has asked the agency to take part in the qualitative analysis of the product and "put their two cents in." Our clients place a great deal of trust in us to deliver a varied amount of marketing insight and this goes far beyond the mere advertising support of a product. This also helps us to develop our marketing programs because we have been included in the project from its inception and understand the reasoning for its introduction.

5:15 P.M.   Meeting with client and his packaging and legal departments to review final mechanicals for packaging the agency was asked to develop. Due to new regulations in labeling, there was a strict mandate on what information had to be provided and even specifics involving typefaces and sizes. Therefore, we wanted to review the materials carefully and discuss with everyone involved the specific details to ensure there was no confusion. The vendor for this packaging had an incredible lead time for production, so the client was thankful to finally have finished materials in hand.

6:00 P.M.   Return to the office and document the meeting while it's still fresh in my mind.

6:15 P.M.   Final check of voice mail and quick review of Daytimer to see what tomorrow will bring. Write reminder notes and make a record of the time I spent on each job today. Gotta run, my girlfriend and I are taking the dog for a walk and the Bills are on Monday Night Football at Rich Stadium. Can't miss another road to the Super Bowl—and a win this time!

doubters (25 percent), who are negative toward both the advertising and sales representatives.[5] Advertisers may create separate messages and media strategies to reach each of these diverse groups.

Strategic Orientation. Unlike the typical consumer who makes decisions based on partial information and irrational criteria, businesses tend to be guided by a specific strategy. This strategy eliminates much of the autonomy available in other kinds of decision making. Factors such as cost pressures, measures of advertising effectiveness, the agency-client partnership, company-customer linkages, and distribution may dictate what a business must do regardless of the

---

[5]Tony Rambaut, "Getting Through to Business Consumers," *Direct Marketing* (March 1989):78–81.

advertising message. Therefore, advertisers must understand the components of a business's strategy and adjust their own strategies accordingly.[6]

One major adjustment is simply accepting the time frame of a typical business strategy. Buying decisions, as well as advertising decisions, are often made by committees and are influenced by others within the organization. This process can take days, weeks, or months. Furthermore, creative efforts and media buys may no longer be valid when approval is finally given. Each of the other functional areas may also have its own timetable. The product-development people will not be willing to introduce the product until test results have achieved certain scores; finance won't fund the effort until certain conditions prevail; and the marketing director will closely monitor the chosen market segment, looking for strategic opportunities that signal a successful product launch.

Purchasing Objectives. As you can see in the Mazda advertisement, (Ad 22.4), purchasing objectives in the business market for the most part center on rational, pragmatic considerations such as price, service, quality, and assurance of supply. The Mazda ad assures business purchasers that the company offers a "complete business portfolio," an affirmation it backs up with detailed data about the various resources it employs.

1. **Price**   Buyers in the business arena are more concerned than ordinary consumers are with the cost of owning and using a product. Most notably, the large volume of a particular product purchased, or the high

---

[6]Richard A. Kozak, "Business-to-Business Ad Trends," *Marketing News* (March 19, 1990):32.

per-unit cost, means that businesses spend thousands or millions of dollars with each purchase decision. In evaluating price, therefore, businesses consider a variety of factors that generate or minimize costs, such as: What amount of scrap or waste will result from the use of the material? What will the cost of processing the material be? How much power will the machine consume?

2. **Services** Business buyers require multiple services, such as technical assistance, availability of spare parts, repair capability, and training information. Thus the technical contributions of suppliers are highly valued wherever equipment, materials, or parts are in use.

3. **Quality** Organizational customers search for quality levels that are consistent with specifications. Thus they are reluctant to pay for extra quality or to compromise specifications for a reduced price. The crucial factor is uniformity or consistency in product quality that will guarantee uniformity in end products, reduce the need for costly inspections and testing of incoming shipments, and ensure a smooth blending with the production process.

4. **Assurance of Supply** Interruptions in the flow of parts and materials can shut down the production process, resulting in costly delays and lost sales. To guard against interruptions in supply, business firms rely on a supplier's established reputation for delivery.

BUSINESS-TO-BUSINESS ADVERTISING OBJECTIVES

The average cost of an industrial sales call is $227.27.[7] Business-to-business advertising enables a business marketer to reach a large portion of the market at a lower cost. For example, according to one study, the *adjusted* cost per thousand for ads by Minolta, IBM, and Toshiba in the same issue of *Time* magazine ran from $49.71 to $51.78.[8]

Although business advertising is an economical means of reaching large numbers of buyers, it is primarily used to assist and support the selling function. Thus business advertising objectives center on creating company awareness, increasing overall selling efficiency, and supporting distributors and resellers.

Creating Company Awareness. Effectively planned business advertising assists the industrial salesperson by increasing customer awareness of, and interest in, the supplier's product. When buyers are aware of a company's reputation, products, and record in the industry, salespeople are more effective.

Increasing Overall Selling Efficiency. Salespeople most often deal with purchasing agents or buyers and are frequently unaware of people within a firm who are in a position to exert influence on a purchasing decision. Such influencers could be engineers who design the product, production experts who manufacture the product, or financial people who maintain cost controls. These influencers, however, do read trade magazines and general business publications, and they can be reached through advertising. By responding to these ads, unknown influencers often identify themselves, making it possible for salespeople to con-

---

[7]"Median Cost Per Call by Industry, 1989-92," *Sales & Marketing Management* (June 28, 1993):65.
[8]Joan Treistman, "Where the Reader's Eye Roams," *Business Marketing* (April 1984):101–118.

tact them. Such advertising, therefore, generates leads for the salesforce. Furthermore, for some producers, particularly those of industrial supplies, advertising may be the only way of reaching broad groups of buyers efficiently.

Supporting Channel Members. Business advertising frequently provides an economical and efficient supplement to personal selling by providing information to distributors and resellers as well as to end users. It can reassure intermediaries that the end users are aware of the company's products. At the same time, it can answer the most common resellers' questions, such as what profit they can expect on a product and what the producer is doing in the way of consumer advertising and other promotional support. Rarely can a salesforce be deployed to reach all potential distributors and resellers often enough to satisfy all of these information needs.

CREATING BUSINESS-TO-BUSINESS ADS

As in consumer advertising, the best business-to-business ads are relevant, understandable, and strike an emotion in the prospective client. There are, however, adjustments that must be made in light of the differences discussed earlier. According to Steve Penchina, creative director of Penchina, Selkowitz of New York, effective business-to-business ads must establish an emotional connection between the product and the prospective client and the ad should sell to people, not to companies. The classic Xerox Leonardo da Vinci ad is an example (see Ad 22.5). Penchina is bothered by boring or ridiculous visuals, trite taglines, and irrelevant or insulting metaphors.[9] Another expert, Sandra Tenney, posits that

[9]Patricia Winters, "Business-to-Business: Trite Is Blight," *Advertising Age* (August 28, 1989):48.

Ad 22.5

This Xerox ad uses a series of subheadings to attract and hold the reader's interest.

(Courtesy of Xerox Corporation; Lamb & Hall, Inc., photography.)

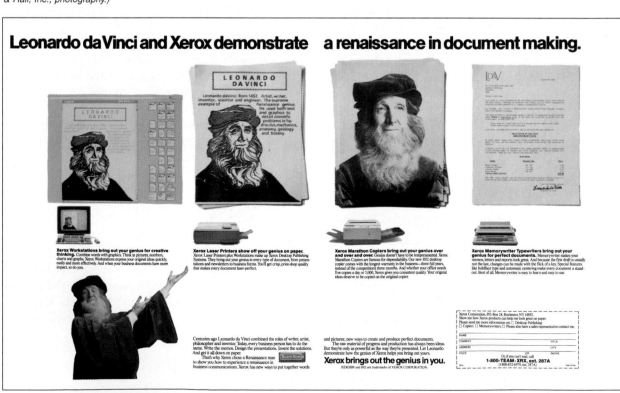

the two keys to successful business-to-business advertising are headlines and art. "Headlines should demonstrate specific benefits in language readers understand. Excellent photography and clear illustrations increase readership while strengthening headlines or elaborating on them," she notes.[10] Finally, John Graham, president of John R. Graham, a public relations/advertising agency, provides three guidelines for business-to-business advertising: (1) Make it easy for the prospect to respond or to pursue further information; (2) send reprints of ads with a personal letter to current customers and prospects explaining why you are advertising and where your ads will appear; and (3) combine advertising with media stories and a newsletter and mail these to prospects.[11]

BUSINESS-TO-BUSINESS ADVERTISING MEDIA

Although some business advertisers use traditional consumer media, most rely on general business or trade publications, industrial directories, direct marketing, or some combination thereof.

GENERAL BUSINESS AND TRADE PUBLICATIONS

horizontal publications
Publications directed to people who hold similar jobs in different companies across different industries.

vertical publications
Publications directed to people who hold different positions in the same industries.

General business and trade publications are classified as either horizontal or vertical. **Horizontal publications** are directed to people who hold similar jobs in different companies across different industries. For example, *Purchasing* is a specialized business publication that is targeted to people across industries who are responsible for a specific task or function. The magazines read by accountants or computer programmers are other examples of horizontal publications.

In contrast, **vertical publications**, such as *Iron Age* and *Steel*, are targeted toward people who hold different positions in the same industries. Some general business publications, such as *Fortune, Business Week,* and *The Wall Street Journal,* tend to be read by business professionals across all industries because of the general business news and editorials they provide. Advertisers select publications on the basis of whom they want to reach and what their goals are. Other specialized business publications, such as *Iron Age* and *Steel,* however, are targeted to people in a specific industry and are therefore classified as vertical publications.

DIRECTORY ADVERTISING

Every state has an industrial directory, and there are also a number of private ones. One of the most popular industrial directories is the New York-based *Thomas Register.* The *Register* consists of 19 volumes that contain 60,000 pages of 50,000 product headings and listings from 123,000 industrial companies selling everything from heavy machine tools to copper tubing to orchestra pits.

DIRECT MARKETING

In addition to trade magazines and general business publications, business advertisers use various other vehicles, such as direct mail, catalogs, and data

---

[10]Sandra M. Tenney, "For Good Business Ads, Apply Some Simple Rules," *Marketing News* (March 14, 1988):12.
[11]John R. Graham, "Business-to-Business Ads Can Work," *Marketing News* (March 13, 1989):7.

data sheets Advertising that provides detailed technical information.

sheets, to reach their markets. Business advertisers often use direct mail to prepare the groundwork for subsequent sales calls. Catalogs and **data sheets** support the selling function by providing technical data about the product as well as supplementary information concerning price and availability.

Direct mail emerged as a primary medium for several business-to-business advertisers during the last decade. Thanks to the evolution of computer software, direct mail can be designed in a manner that personalizes the message to specific customers, includes highly technical information, and provides top-notch photography and designs. Long copy, illustrations, diagrams, or any other device can be carried through direct mail. In addition, dramatic improvements in the accuracy of mailing lists have reduced the waste historically associated with direct mail. Direct mail has the capacity to sell the product, provide sales leads, or lay the groundwork for subsequent sales calls.

CONSUMER MEDIA

Consumer media, despite their wasted circulation, can sometimes be very effective owing to the lack of competition from other business advertisers. Because the message exposure occurs away from the office, it also encounters less competition from the receiver's other business needs. Although consumer media are also an excellent means of reaching a market where market coverage is limited geographically, they are still not used much. According to a survey sponsored by the Business/Professional Advertising Association, consumer publications received about 3 percent of the total dollar amount spent on business-to-business advertising, and spot radio and spot television each picked up only 1 percent, whereas network television accounted for under 1 percent.[12] Sometimes, as in the case of Velux (Ad 22.6), businesses advertise in consumer magazines (such as *Better Homes and Gardens*) in hopes of influencing consumers to ask for specific brands when they go to a business.

In addition to the use of traditional consumer media, there has been a tremendous growth in business television programming that is targeted at both businesspeople and consumers who are interested in business-related topics. For example, FNN not only produces its own business shows, it also provides the syndicated business shows *This Morning's Business* and *First Business*. Introduced in 1989, CNBC was conceived with the consumer in mind, and its programming focuses more on personal finances and health.[13]

RECENT TRENDS IN MEDIA SERVICES

Today there are more media choices available to the business-to-business advertiser than ever before. Consequently, media that can offer advertisers a competitive advantage in reaching their customers will be quite appealing. In some instances an existing medium has developed a unique service unmatched by its competitors. For example, *Business Week* offers a Federal Express service so subscribers can get their issues on Friday instead of waiting for the Monday mail. New media have also emerged. Responding to the desire of readers to receive financial news sooner, *Financial World* in conjunction with UPI and State News Service put out *The Latest News,* an hourly newspaper distributed free between

---

[12]Andrew Jaffe, "The Big Guys Get Serious," *Adweek Special Report* (May 23, 1988):B.M.6.
[13]Debra Goldman, "Is More News Good News?" *Adweek* (May 21, 1990):B.M.29.

WHY THE COST OF ADDING ON IS SENDING PEOPLE THROUGH THE ROOF.

It doesn't have to cost an arm and a leg to find the extra room you need in your home. Send in this coupon or call 1-800-283-2831 for our free Hidden Spaces brochure, and we'll show you exactly how easy and economical it is with VELUX® products. One look at all the possibilities and you'll wonder why you didn't go through the roof sooner.

VELUX®

The World Leader in Roof Windows and Skylights

©1992 VELUX GROUP @VELUX is a registered trademark.

Send this coupon for our free Hidden Spaces brochure.

Name:

Address:

City:

State: Zip: Phone:

Mail to: VELUX- AMERICA INC.
Dept. M, P.O. Box 3001
Greenwood, SC 29648-5001

Ad 22.6

Although this ad runs in a consumer magazine, its purpose is to influence consumers to ask for the advertiser's brand of windows when remodeling.

(Courtesy of Velux-America, Inc.)

2:30 and 7:30 P.M. on Pan Am's East Coast shuttle.[14] Of course the role of inter-active media technology on business-to-business media still is evolving. Clearly, businesses that are far more comfortable with computers will accept interactive alternatives much faster than will individual consumers.

The videocassette industry has also entered the fray as a reliable business-to-business medium. Videocassettes can be sent to customers requesting product information or a product demonstration. They can also be mailed unsolicited as an exciting selling tool. Entire catalogs can be put on video, called video logs. This is affordable owing to the development of disposable videocassettes that have a life of 10 to 12 plays and cost just pennies to produce.

DOES BUSINESS ADVERTISING SELL?

Although few business marketers today rely exclusively on their sales forces to reach potential buyers, many people have questioned the effectiveness of business advertising. However, in 1987 the Advertising Research Foundation (ARF) and the Association of Business Publishers (ABP) undertook to study the link between business advertising and industrial product sales and profits. The researchers monitored product sales and the level and frequency of their advertising schedules for a period of 1 year. To ensure that the study's findings could be applied to a wide range of industries and products, three very different products were monitored: a portable safety device that sold for less than $10, a commercial transportation component package that sold for around $10,000, and highly specialized laboratory equipment priced between $5,000 and $10,000. Despite the diversity in price, product life, purchase complexity, and distribution channels, the study found that, for all three products:

- Business-to-business advertising created more sales than would have occurred without advertising.
- Increased advertising frequency resulted in increased product sales.
- It paid to advertise to both dealers and end users when the product was sold through dealers.
- Increased advertising frequency increased sales leads and generated higher profits.
- It took 4 to 6 months to see the results of the advertising program.
- The use of color in the advertising made a dramatic difference.
- The advertising campaign was effective long after the campaign had ended.
- Advertising favorably affected purchasers' awareness of, and attitudes toward, industrial products.[15]

As indicated by the tongue-in-cheek memo found in the Concepts and Applications box, business-to-business advertising has a reputation for poor advertising planning and execution. The future of business-to-business, however, is dependent upon how well it adapts to the following trends:

- More accountability and efficiency in marketing communications programs are being required of business-to-business marketers.

---

[14]"Faster Than a Speeding Bullet," *Adweek* (May 21, 1990):B.M.7.
[15]"From a Reporter to a Source: A New Survey of Selling Costs," *Sales & Marketing Management* (February 16, 1987):12.

To: H.C. Smith, COO, MaxiTech Industries
From: Bob Frapples, A&SP director, MaxiTech Industries
Subj: Creative strategy and implementation: 1991 Piezodichometer ad campaign

I heartily appreciate this timely opportunity to update you and other members of the executive committee on the status of the new ad campaign scheduled for launch this month in your favorite electronics publication. Here at the marketing communications department, we remain ever vigilant keeping MaxiTech Industries at the forefront of high technology.

Some concerns had been raised about the advertising some committee members thought we were almost going to run to support the introduction of our new Piezodichometer technology. Please allow me to take this opportunity to explain what caused those unfortunate misconceptions and to assure you that the campaign's creative strategy and implementation are now on track.

Our revised creative strategy hews to the product's mission statement as you've written it: "Because MaxiTech is the acknowledged leader in many areas of advanced electronics, our piezodichometer technology cannot be beaten."

It has a real ring to it, H. C.!

I sincerely regret, however, that we could not use those inspiring words as the headline of our first insertion. Blowing up the photo of the executive committee dressed in overalls, standing alongside the piezodichometer assembly line, leaves little room for a long headline along with body copy and the 2-inch-high MaxiTech intertwined MT logo—even on as much as a whole half-page of space. That's why, with your indulgence, we shortened the headline to: "The best from the best." We are pleased that you approve of the change.

Furthermore, I do not think that the agency's departure will impair our creative product. Ad agencies have been known to forget who pays the bills and resign in fits of unbusinesslike pique.

No one in this department supported the agency's creative recommendation. We heartily concur that their headline, "How you'll achieve six-sigma reliability in half the time," fails to convey the spirit and excitement of MaxiTech leadership and the reputation behind the name.

And showing a microphoto closeup of the defects our machine catches that other technologies skip, as the agency insisted, may please our R&D department, but again it fails to reflect MaxiTech dedication and teamwork, as you averred.

I am also pleased to report that our in-house copy editor has suggested few, if any, changes to the spirited body copy you were so kind to offer us. Here's how it will read when the first ad breaks in April and when the campaign concludes with a third ad in October:

"Welcome to MaxiTech class.

"Perspicacious engineers who specify MaxiTech join an elite fraternity of discerning experts elevated to the summit of professionalism, soaring above the commonplace on the wings of MaxiTech technological virtuosity.

"Our latest innovation does not surprise them. For they know innovation is MaxiTech Industries' middle name. All our renowned dedication, experience, commitment, and integrity infuse our new line of advanced MT Piezodichometers.

"We could boast about their ability to give you six-sigma reliability in half the time. Or wax poetic about beta test results far exceeding alternative technologies' best performances.

"But we know what is most important to the MaxiTech fraternity: standing tall in the pantheon of MaxiTech customers, sharing our total quality commitment to excellence, and a nobility of devotion mere numbers cannot portray."

Yes H. C., it is riveting copy. It is unfortunate that the agency foolishly insisted that engineers who don't already endorse MaxiTech won't feel the warmth of your heartfelt testimony. Had it been done properly, their research surely would have reflected MaxiTech's universal fame.

Rest assured that we are now busily seeking a new ad agency to handle our collateral. I've asked six contenders to work up complete speculative creative. I'll take the initiative and select—subject to your approval, of course—the shop whose work comes closest to your creative genius.

Source: Bob Donath, "Secret Memo Yields Ad Campaign Insights," *Marketing News* (April 15, 1991):15.

- Since advertising efficiency is not easy to measure, ad programs and staff, seen as marginal expenses in many business-to-business companies, are being pared down or eliminated.

- Business-to-business marketing itself is becoming more people-oriented, with the best television and print ads addressing a product's solution to human problems.[16]

Clearly the crunch has come. With scaled-down in-house marketing departments and more outsourcing of the various functions, the role of advertising is going to change. Business-to-business marketing is like trying to move a battleship; consumer marketing is like turning a corner. Change will not come easy, but it must come.

RETAIL ADVERTISING

Most discussions of advertising focus on commercials that run on the Super Bowl, full-page ads in *Time* magazine, and copy strategies used by companies like Procter & Gamble. Often overlooked is **retail advertising**, which is used by local merchants to sell their products and services directly to consumers and which accounts for nearly half of all the money spent on advertising.

Just as advertising is part of the marketing mix for nationally promoted products and services, it also plays an important role in the marketing or merchandising mix for retailers. Therefore, to understand retail advertising, it is first necessary to see how it differs from national advertising.

RETAIL ADVERTISING VERSUS NATIONAL ADVERTISING

Retail advertising is often called *local advertising* because the target market is frequently local in nature. However, institutions that may advertise locally, such as banks, financial services, and real estate organizations, are not considered part of the retail trade by the Bureau of the Census. Moreover, some retailers, such as Sears and J. C. Penney, advertise nationally. Thus when we talk about retail advertising, we are referring to advertising disseminated by retail institutions. Although retailers try to create a local presence, a great deal of retail advertising is standardized across regions of the country or even nationally. Retail advertising is designed to perform several universal functions: selling a variety of products, encouraging store traffic, delivering sales promotion messages, and creating and communicating a store image or "personality."

Retail advertising differs from national advertising in various ways. First, retail advertising, whether sponsored by a national chain or a local retailer, is targeted at people living in the local community. Such advertising is customized to match the needs, wants, culture, and idiosyncrasies of these people. In comparison, national advertisers must deliver a standardized message that often deals with generalities that do not address the needs of individuals. Second, national advertising supports the brand(s) of the sponsor, whereas retail advertising may promote several different brands or even competing brands. The retailer's loyalty gravitates to whichever brand is selling best. Retail advertising also has an

---

[16]Lynn G. Coleman, "The Crunch Has Come," *The Marketing News* (March 4, 1991):1, 16.

inherent urgency. Everything about the ad pushes the consumer toward a behavior, typically visiting the store. Consequently, the retail ad includes price information, conditions of sales, color, sizes, and so on. National advertising is more concerned with image and attitude change. As a result, there tends to be less copy and fewer specifics. The third difference is that retail advertising is customized, to some extent, to reflect the local store. Usually it includes basic information such as the store's name, address, telephone number, hours open for business, and so forth.

To build and maintain store traffic, a retailer must meet four objectives: build store *awareness,* create consumer *understanding* of items or services offered, *convince* consumers that the store's items and services are high-quality or economical, and create *consumer desire* to shop at this particular store. In addition, most retailers use advertising to help attract new customers, build store loyalty, increase the amount of the average sale, maintain inventory balance by moving out overstocks and outdated merchandise, and help counter seasonal lows.

With a few exceptions, retail advertising is less sophisticated and more utilitarian than national advertising. There are several reasons for this. First, retail advertising is more *short-term* than national advertising. Most retail ads deal with price and run for only a few days, whereas a national ad may be used for months or years.

In addition, retailers can't justify high production costs for advertising. National advertisers can easily justify spending $5,000 to produce a newspaper ad when they are paying $200,000 to run it in 100 large markets. A local retailer who places an ad in the local newspaper might have a media cost of only $400, making it difficult to justify spending $5,000 on production.

Most retailers have little formal training in advertising and therefore are often uncomfortable making professional advertising decisions. Consequently they rely on their media sales representatives to design and produce their ads. Most media advertising departments turn out several dozen ads a day, rather than working on one ad for several days as ad agencies do. Also, print media generally use *clip art* rather than custom art. Clip art services provide books of copyright-free pieces of art, which can be clipped and used as the advertiser sees fit. The ads work, but they are generally less "creative" than national brand advertising.

COOPERATIVE ADVERTISING

cooperative advertising A form of advertising in which the manufacturer reimburses the retailer for part or all of the advertising expenditures.

One way retailers can compensate for their smaller budgets and limited expertise is to take advantage of **cooperative advertising**, in which the manufacturer reimburses the retailer for part or all of the advertising expenses. Most manufacturers (or franchisers) have some type of ongoing promotional program that provides retailers with advertising support in the form of money and advertising materials. Funds for cooperative advertising are available subject to certain guidelines and are generally based on a percentage of sales to the retailer. Ad 22.7 is an example of co-op advertising.

Co-op funds, which are sometimes referred to as *ad allowances,* are no longer just "a little something extra" from the manufacturer. Ad allowances have become so widespread, in fact, that most retailers won't even consider taking on a new brand, especially one in a heavily advertised category, without receiving some support. (This was also discussed in Chapter 18.)

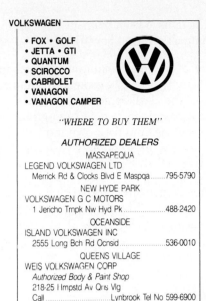

VOLKSWAGEN

- FOX • GOLF
- JETTA • GTI
- QUANTUM
- SCIROCCO
- CABRIOLET
- VANAGON
- VANAGON CAMPER

"WHERE TO BUY THEM"

AUTHORIZED DEALERS

MASSAPEQUA
LEGEND VOLKSWAGEN LTD
   Merrick Rd & Clocks Blvd E Maspqa........795-5790
NEW HYDE PARK
VOLKSWAGEN G C MOTORS
   1 Jericho Trnpk Nw Hyd Pk.................488-2420
OCEANSIDE
ISLAND VOLKSWAGEN INC
   2555 Long Bch Rd Ocnsid................536-0010
QUEENS VILLAGE
WEIS VOLKSWAGEN CORP
   Authorized Body & Paint Shop
   218-25 I Impstd Av Qns Vlg
   Call..................Lynbrook Tel No 599-6900

"Ad money," as it is also called, generally comes to retailers in one of three ways. An ad allowance is an amount that can change from month to month for each unit of purchase. The higher the amount, the more the retailer is expected to do. With an *accrual fund* the manufacturer automatically "accrues," or sets aside, a certain percentage of a retailer's purchases that the retailer may use for advertising at any time within a specified period.

Vendor support programs are developed by retailers themselves. Large drug and discount chains, for example, will periodically schedule a special advertising supplement. Their suppliers are offered an opportunity to "buy" space in this supplement. Suppliers are generally promised that no competing brands will be included.

tear sheet The pages from a newspaper on which an ad appears.

To receive co-op money retailers must send the manufacturer a **tear sheet**, which is proof that the ad ran, and an invoice showing the cost of the advertising. For broadcast ads, stations will provide the retailer with a letter, or *affidavit*, stating when the ad ran.

dealer tag Time left at the end of a broadcast advertisement that permits identification of the local store.

Manufacturers also make artwork available, which can be used for preparing catalogs and other print ads. Some manufacturers also provide a **dealer tag**, in which the store is mentioned at the end of a radio or television ad. Also available are window banners, bill inserts, and special direct-mail pieces, such as four-color supplements that carry the store's name and address.

The Robinson-Patman Act prohibits a manufacturer from offering one retailer a price or promotion incentive that will give that retailer an advantage over competitors in the same trading area. This restriction becomes especially delicate in food and pharmaceutical retailing, where almost all advertising is price advertising.

TRENDS IN RETAILING

The good old days of the mom-and-pop retailers who knew all their customers personally and who could count on their continued loyalty are gone. During the last 40 years there have been dramatic changes in retailing, many of which have had a direct impact on retail advertising.

Location. One of the most significant changes in retailing has been the relocation of retail activity from city centers to suburbs. With the growth of the suburbs has come the development of shopping centers and malls. Merchants located in these complexes benefit from group promotions for the entire shopping center as well as from their own individual advertising.

The importance of location is discussed further in the Concepts and Applications box.

Consolidation. Ownership consolidation, especially among department stores and specialty chains, has brought mass merchandising to many stores that formerly operated on a smaller scale. This consolidation of power among fewer retailers has changed the nature of the relationship between manufacturers and retailers. Retailers now dictate terms of sale, delivery dates, and product specifications.

Wal-Mart for example, has so much clout that Procter & Gamble has placed some 70 employees near Wal-Mart's Arkansas headquarters to quickly service the account.[17]

Consolidation has also given retailers a much greater interest in mass advertising. For example, Pier 1 Imports, a once-small specialty retailer, now spends $40 million annually on billable media (see Ad 22.8). Retailers such as Wal-Mart have also been able to dictate the creative strategy of many manufacturers. In addition, they have created tremendous growth in the use of different media, such as free-standing inserts, in lieu of traditional newspaper space.

Nonstore Retailing. Nonstore retailing is when the exchange between the manufacturer/retailer and the consumer takes place outside the traditional retail store. In the case of Mary Kay Cosmetics and Lands' End, the companies produce the product and sell it through door-to-door and catalog selling, respectively. Lillian Vernon, in contrast, purchases products from a variety of manufacturers and sells the products through its catalog. Nonstore retailing has grown in popularity for a variety of reasons. Most notably, the time-conscious consumer is no longer inclined to spend hours shopping for goods and services. Simultaneously, the quality and selection of the merchandise sold through nonstore retailing has greatly improved. Warranties and guarantees remove the risk associated with purchasing unseen merchandise. Finally, improvements of mailing lists have better matched the marketer with potential customers. The use of nonstore retailing has shifted a great deal of retail advertising toward direct marketing and direct mail.

Demographics. Several demographic changes in our society have a bearing on retail advertising. These changes include time compression, the aging of the population, geomarketing, and market fragmentation.

For families in which both spouses work, time is a valuable commodity. As a result, creative avenues must be found to reach consumers with messages that are short and sweet.

The population is made up of more elderly people, who are knowledgable

---

[17]Wendy Zellner, "Clout: More and More, Retail Giants Rule the Marketplace," *Business Week* (December 21, 1992):66–71.

Concepts & APPLICATIONS

Location, Location, Location!

A time-honored real estate adage is emerging as one of the most important keys to retail success: Location, location, location! Fast-changing consumer habits, population trends, retail management strategies, and real estate values are fueling the focus on location, with make-or-break ramifications for retailers. Forty years ago, the location question was more easily solved: You would do a survey of how many people walked or drove by a certain location each day, and that's where you would build your store. Today, far more complex factors must be considered, such as long-term population patterns, demographics, and the location of a direct competitor. Given wide duplication of merchandise, price, and retail format, the store with the best location wins.

Although change is constant in retailing, observers agree the rate of change in the retail industry has increased dramatically in the past few years. "We're overstored across the United States, and the pace of change has accelerated in recent years. Locations have become critical to survival," says Carl Steidtman, chief economist with Management Horizons, Price Waterhouse's retail management consultancy.

Some of the savviest location experts in recent years have been T.J. Maxx Stores and Toys 'R' Us, retail industry experts say. Both retailers put the majority of their new locations in fast-growing areas where the population closely matches their customer base. Others, including F. W. Woolworth and Montgomery Ward, have been adept at relocating their stores.

Woolworth closed many of its older, downtown locations, making way for tonier buildings (a downtown Chicago Woolworth closed to make way for the Hyatt Regency Suites hotel). The retailer, in turn, opened Woolworth Express outlets in fast-paced shopping centers and some new downtown locations.

But the undisputed winner in the locations derby is Wal-Mart Stores, whose strategy of being the first mass merchandiser to locate in small and rural markets caused it to catapult to the number-one retailer in 1990, knocking Sears, Roebuck & Co. to the number-three position behind K mart Corp. The leader didn't land in those locations by accident. Industry watchers who knew founder Sam Walton say he was one of the first retailers to focus on site selection. Wal-Mart's planners used to fly over potential store locations in Sam's private turbo-prop airplane, looking at proximity to highways, major traffic routes, and other retailers. Based on what they saw, they negotiated cheap leases in expanding populations with other businesses nearby to help draw customers. While Wal-Mart was perfecting the science of strategic locations, regional mall-based department stores such as Sears waited for customer traffic to come in. Instead, the opposite happened. Wal-Mart drew retailers such as Home Depot and Toys 'R' Us to its sites and traffic began drifting away from those older, regional shopping malls.

Adapted from Kate Fitzgerald, "All Roads Lead to...," *Advertising Age* (February 1, 1993):S-1.

and adept at shopping and have definite opinions on the value of brand names and the relationship between price and quality. Advertising copy must facilitate such comparisons.

In targeting consumers, a retailer's first concern is geography: Where do my customers live? How far will they drive to come to my store? The next concern is consumer taste. *Geomarketing* is a phenomenon geared to the increasing diversity in tastes and preferences. Retailers are attempting to develop offers that appeal to consumers in different parts of the country as well as in different neighborhoods in the same suburb. For example, H.E.B. Supermarkets operates its stores in both central and south Texas. In San Antonio, the stores located in Mexican-American neighborhoods carry a very different merchandise assortment than do those located in neighborhoods dominated by upscale apartments

Ad 22.8

Pier 1 Imports' use of quality, four-color photography and catchy headlines shows how a retailer can create a positive image.

(Courtesy of Pier 1 Imports)

and condominiums. In contrast, national advertising targeting is more concerned with other factors such as age, income, education, and lifestyle.

Markets will continue to decrease in size as competitors segment them according to values, lifestyles, demographics, geographics, and product benefits. Advertising strategies must place greater emphasis on developing the appropriate image to match the consumer's lifestyle and less emphasis on price promotions. Ultimately, consumers want to be assured that the quality of value, service, and price are all there.

Product Specialization. Many retailers have begun to specialize in merchandising products, such as electronics, running shoes, tennis equipment, baked potatoes, toys, and the like. The largest of these retail specialists are referred to as *superstores.* Examples include HQ Office Supplies, Sportmart, Home Base, and Circuit City. The idea behind the superstore is fairly simple: Provide customers with the ultimate assortment in a product category—say, hardware—and they will come. In these cases retail advertising has become more like manufacturer advertising in that fewer products are high-lighted and the emphasis is on image rather than a quick sale. Benetton, a clothing company that specializes in Italian sportswear, is an example of this type of retailing. Its ads often feature founder Luciano Benetton touting two or three of his new designs. Originality, quality, and image are always emphasized over price. However, as will become apparent in the discussion that follows, price copy is still prevalent because of growing competition in retailing and an uncertain economy.

Price Advertising. In recent years retail advertising has focused on price—more specifically on sale or discounted prices. Many retailers now use any reason they can find to have a sale (Presidents' Day, Tax Time, Over-stocked). There are also EOM (end-of-month) sales and even hourly sales (Ayre's 14-Hour Sales, K mart's Midnight Madness Sale). This trend has led to retailers' complaints about the disappearance of consumer loyalty as people move from store to store searching for the best price.

As strange as it may seem, the items that retailers advertise at reduced prices are often not the ones they really want to sell. In order to offer a reduced price, retailers generally have to sacrifice part of their profit on each of these products. Sometimes stores even offer items for less than they paid for them merely to attract customers to the store. These items are called **loss leaders**.

TYPES OF RETAIL ADVERTISING

Despite the great diversity in retailing, the nature of the advertising employed can be placed in one of two categories: product or institutional. *Product* advertising presents specific merchandise for sale and urges customers to come to the store immediately to buy it. This form of advertising helps to create and maintain the store's reputation through its merchandise. Product advertising centers around themes relating to merchandise that is new, exclusive, and of superior quality and designs (called *nonpromotional* advertising), as well as around themes relating to complete assortments and merchandise events (called *assortment* advertising). Sales announcements, special promotions, and other immediate-purpose ads are other forms of product advertising. When the sale price dominates the ad, it is called *promotional* or *sales* advertising. When sales items are interspersed with regular-priced items in the ad, it is referred to as *semipromotional* advertising.

Institutional retail advertising sells the store as an enjoyable place to shop. Through institutional advertising, the store helps to establish its image as a leader in fashion, price, and wide merchandise selection, as well as superior service, or quality, or whatever image the store chooses to cultivate.

$\mathcal{R}$ETAIL ADVERTISING: CREATIVITY, MEDIA, AND RESEARCH

CREATING THE RETAIL AD

The primary difference between national and retail ad copy is the emphasis retail advertising places on *prices* and *store name*. Store image should be as important to a retailer as brand image is to a manufacturer. In order to build store traffic, ads are designed either to emphasize a reduced price on a popular item or to promote the store image by focusing on such things as unusual or varied merchandise, friendly clerks, or prestige brands.

Image or Price. For retail operations that sell products and services where there is little product differentiation, such as gasoline, banking, and car rentals, a positive, distinctive image is a valuable asset. The retailer can only convey this image through advertising. Pier 1 Imports, for example, has maintained a very positive image through its high-quality print ads, as Ad 22.8 shows.

Price also can be a factor in establishing a store's image. Most discount stores signal their type of merchandise with large, bold prices. Several specialty retailers emphasize price by offering coupons in much of their print advertising. Featuring prices doesn't necessarily apply only to ads that give the store a bargain or a discount image, however. Price can help the consumer comparison-shop without visiting the store. Many customers appreciate this basic information.

Executing Retail Ads. Because the main objective of retail ads is to attract customers, store location (or telephone number, if advertising a service) is essential. For merchandise that is infrequently purchased, such as cars, furniture, wallpaper, and hearing aids, the ad should include a map or mention a geographical reference point (for example, three blocks north of the state capitol building) in addition to the regular street address.

A creative mistake some retailers make is wanting to be the star or key spokesperson in their advertising. This is especially noticeable in broadcast commercials, where a presenter needs acting talent or training. Although hiring the acting superstars of advertising is beyond the budgets of most retailers, competent and affordable actors abound in most cities. In fact, local celebrities typically have greater attention-getting potential than does imported talent.

Small- and medium-size retailers often save money by using stock artwork. All daily newspapers subscribe to clip art services that provide a wide range of photographs and line drawings. Add 22.9 is an example of stock artwork.

Larger retailers generally have their art custom-designed, which gives all of their ads a similar look and helps confer a distinctive image. Retailers have also found ways to make their television production more efficient by using a "donut" format in which the opening and closing sections are the same, whereas the middle changes to focus on different merchandise.

The recent trend in shopping center advertising is to produce a slick four-color "magazine" that carries editorial material, such as recipes, a calendar of local events, and other topics of local interest, in addition to ads for the retail stores in the shopping center. Centers interested in projecting a status image to upscale consumers make the greatest use of this magazine concept.

Who Does the Creative Work? Most retail advertising is created and produced by one or a combination of the following: in-house staff, media, ad agencies, and freelancers. The larger the retail operation, the more likely it is to have an in-house advertising staff. An in-house agency can guarantee a consistent look and can react on short notice. One disadvantage of the in-house agency is lack of creativity, as many good creative people prefer working for a multiclient agency where the work is more diversified and the pay is often higher.

All local media create and produce ads for retailers. With the exception of television, most provide this service free. The medium- and larger-size newspapers and stations often have people whose only job is to write and produce ads.

Although some professional retail ads are created by agencies, this is the most costly way to produce ads. Also, because agencies work for many different clients, they cannot always respond as quickly as an in-house agency can. Mary Joan Glynn, former marketing vice president at Bloomingdale's, who became the managing director of BBDO Merchants Group, claims that no agency is prepared to handle the large number of day-to-day copy changes that are characteristic of major retail advertising. She says that what an agency can best do for a retailer is develop an image or position that can then "be set and implemented in-house for newspapers with the agency handling the electronic media."[18]

Freelancers often provide a good compromise between an in-house staff and an ad agency. They generally charge a lower hourly rate than do ad agencies because they work out of their homes, and therefore have minimal overhead.

BUYING AND SELLING LOCAL MEDIA

Perhaps the most rapidly changing area in retail advertising is the buying and selling of local media time and space. On the buying side, retailers are becoming more sophisticated about media as they are being forced to work with tighter budgets, are getting more advertising help and advice from their suppliers, are being exposed to more media ideas at association workshops and seminars, and are being educated by a growing number of media salespeople.

At the same time, local media competition has significantly increased. Nearly all major markets now have, in addition to network affiliates, at least one local independent plus a public television station (which now solicits underwriting, a type of soft-sell advertising). These stations, along with local advertising that is now being sold by the national cable networks, have created many more television opportunities for the retailer. Most of the top 50 markets have at least one local magazine offering retailers high-quality four-color ads to reach the

Retail stores often advertise which credit cards are accepted.

(Mike Mazzaschi/Stock, Boston.)

---

[18]"Retail Report," *Television/Radio Age* (September 29. 1986):59.

upscale consumer. Examples are *Los Angeles Magazine, Southwest,* and *Palm Springs Life.*

The increase in competition for the retailers' advertising dollar has resulted in a different type of selling. Salespeople increasingly emphasize advertising and promotion ideas rather than just rate cards and circulation figures. Unfortunately, many retailers still buy advertising strictly on price or number of spots. Some retailers don't realize that five spots during morning-drive time on the market's leading radio station can sometimes reach more people than can 50 spots that run between 2:00 A.M. and 4:00 A.M.

Retail Media Strategy. Unlike national advertisers, retailers generally prefer reach over frequency. A retailer with a "1/3 Off All Women's Casual Shoes" ad doesn't have to tell this more than once or twice to women interested in saving money on a pair of casual shoes. In contrast, a national advertiser with an image campaign like Coke continually needs to remind soft drink users that "Coke is it."

Because retailers can choose from many local media, they must be careful not to buy a lot of wasted circulation (see Chapter 9). Take, for example, an ordinary bakery in an area of dominant interest (ADI) like Des Moines, Iowa, that has approximately 380,000 households and 24 other bakeries. Over 80 percent of this bakery's business could come from within a 3-mile radius that contains only 6 percent of the ADI's households. If this bakery uses television advertising that covers the total ADI, the bakery will be wasting over 90 percent of its advertising dollars. Successful retailers use media that minimize waste. Direct mail, which is narrowly targeted, is now the second-largest advertising medium used by retailers. Also, many newspapers can zone the delivery of advertising circulars and inserts, offering geographical targeting to neighborhoods, counties, or even zip codes.

MEDIA ALTERNATIVES

Retailers may choose from the entire arsenal of media alternatives. Both local and national retailers may use an identical media mix to reach a particular local target market. In general, however, local retailers are interested only in local media and stay clear of media that reach an audience beyond their immediate markets. There are several media that are more relevant to retailers.

Newspapers. Newspapers have always made up the bulk of the retailer's advertising, probably because the local nature of newspapers fits the retailer's desire for geographic coverage, prestige, and immediacy. In addition, newspapers are a participative medium that people read in part for the advertising. In fact, many people use newspapers as a shopping guide. Also, retailers can gain some measure of audience selectivity by advertising in specific sections of the paper, such as the sports, society, and financial pages.

Most retailers that advertise regularly make *space contracts* with the newspaper. In the contract the retailer agrees to use a certain amount of space over the year and pay a certain amount per line, which is lower than the paper's open rate for the same space. The lower rate is simply a quantity discount.

In addition to special rates, newspapers have developed several other products or services to remain competitive. Many newspapers will provide retail advertisers with their zip/postal code circulation reports, which identify the cir-

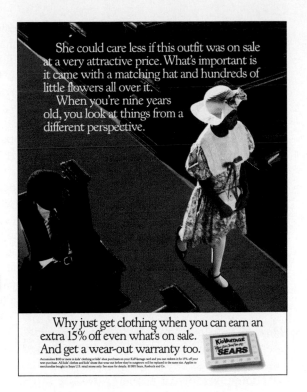

She could care less if this outfit was on sale at a very attractive price. What's important is it came with a matching hat and hundreds of little flowers all over it.
When you're nine years old, you look at things from a different perspective.

Why just get clothing when you can earn an extra 15% off even what's on sale. And get a wear-out warranty too.

Accumulate $100 or more in kids' clothing or kids' shoe purchases on your KidVantage card and you can redeem it for 15% off your next purchase. All kids' clothes and kids' shoes that wear out before they're outgrown will be replaced in the same size. Applies to merchandise bought in Sears U.S. retail stores only. See store for details. © 1993 Sears, Roebuck and Co.

Ad 22.10

Sears tends to place many of its ads in magazines such as *Readers' Digest* and *Better Homes and Gardens.*

(Courtesy of Sears)

culation level for that newspaper in the various zip codes. This information, combined with zone editions of the paper (certain versions of the paper go to certain counties, cities, and so on), greatly reduces the wasted circulation often associated with large newspapers. Special advertising sections, such as preprints, can be inserted in these various papers. Specialty-type papers, such as shoppers, have also emerged.

Shoppers and Preprints Free-distribution newspapers (shoppers) that are dropped off at millions of suburban homes once or twice each week are becoming increasingly popular advertising outlets for retailers. More than 3,000 such papers are published in the United States, such as *Center Island Pennysavers,* distributed in Long Island, New York.[19]

Preprints are advertising circulars furnished by a retailer for distribution as a *free-standing insert* in newspapers. In recent years preprinted inserts have also become popular with retailers striving for greater market coverage. For example, preprints account for 81 percent of Wal-Mart's advertising budgets.[20]

Magazines. Many magazines have regional or metropolitan editions. They enable local retailers to buy exposure to the audience within their trading area only. Sears, K mart, and J. C. Penney advertise in monthlies targeted to particular audience segments and in weeklies to accommodate short-term sales patterns. Grocery retailers use magazines primarily for institutional or image ads.

Ad 22.10 for Sears appeared in magazines such as *Better Homes & Gardens* and *Readers Digest.*

---

[19]"Free-Distribution Shoppers Are Posing Serious Threat to Daily Newspapers," *The Wall Street Journal* (June 19, 1984):31.
[20]Susan Caminiti, "What Ails Retailing," *Fortune* (January 30, 1989):61–62.

Broadcast Media. Local retailers advertise on television and radio as well, but broadcast media are used primarily to supplement newspaper advertising. Both offer important advantages over print media. Radio has a relatively low cost and a high degree of geographic and audience selectivity. It also provides high flexibility in spot scheduling, and this flexibility carries over into creativity. Radio will help retail advertisers write the ads, provide live hookups from the store or any other location, and is able to take advantage of last-minute events. For example, a station in Colorado Springs helped a hardware store sell hundreds of snow shovels when an unexpected storm dumped 7 inches of snow one April morning.

Many of the same advantages are found in local television. The cost of television is higher, however, as is the creative expertise needed to produce satisfactory commercials. Television stations will produce commercials for a fee. The expense problem has been reduced somewhat by the advent of cable television with its ability to show a retail commercial in the local market only. Cable also offers the retailer the kind of selectivity that network television cannot. Undoubtedly, as more and more homes are hooked up to cable, retailers will view television as an affordable, effective media alternative.

Directories. Telephone directories (the Yellow Pages) are important advertising media for retailers. In the Yellow Pages the retailer pays for an alphabetical listing (and a larger display ad, if desired) within a business category. The overwhelming majority of retailers advertise in the Yellow Pages (refer to Chapter 17). The advantages are widespread customer usage and long life (1 year or more). The disadvantages included limited flexibility and long lead times for new ads. Retailers who don't get their ads to the Yellow Pages in time (for example, a camera-ready ad must often be mailed by May or June for the September directory) will have to wait an entire year.

Direct Response. Direct response is a medium retailers use extensively to communicate their product offerings to a select group of consumers. In direct-response advertising, the retailer creates its own advertisement and distributes it directly to consumers either through the mail or through the personal distribution of circulars, handbills, and other printed matter. Although direct-response advertising is expensive in terms of cost per thousand, it is actually the most selective medium because the ads are read only by people the retailer selects. It is also a personal form of advertising and extremely flexible. Direct-response advertising can include pictures, letters, records, pencils, coins, coupons, premiums, samples, and any other gifts the retailer chooses.

RETAIL MARKET RESEARCH

Information about the local market is becoming more and more valuable to retailers. Although retail stores that belong to a national chain often receive research findings from their parent company, most independent retailers must depend on the media and their suppliers for local marketing research information. Many commercial research companies like Simmons and PRIZM provide information on the top markets.

One of the most valuable, yet inexpensive, types of research a retailer can conduct is to identify its customers. This can be done by analyzing charge-card files or by sponsoring a contest or sweepstakes. Businesses that issue their own charge cards report that two-thirds of their sales come from their charge-card customers. Smart retailers send up to a dozen direct-mail pieces to these customers each year in addition to their regular advertising. Sweepstakes use an entry form that asks for customer name, address, age, income, or whatever information is desired.

Retailers can also conduct focus groups to help determine their store's image. These are best if arranged and conducted by an outside, trained research service. To help test ad copy, one furniture retailer had a direct-mail piece made up for a mattress sale and sent it to a limited number of households. When he found it had a relatively good response, he then placed the same copy and artwork in a newspaper ad.

Just as most retailers can't justify spending large sums on ad production, neither can they for marketing research. Retailers have direct consumer contact and can quickly determine which ads work. That's one advantage they have over national advertisers.

$\mathcal{S}$UMMARY

- Business-to-business advertising is used to influence demand and is directed at people in the business arena who buy or specify products for business use. Its objectives include creating company awareness, increasing selling efficiency, and supporting channel members.

- Compared to the consumer market, the market for business goods is relatively limited, decision making tends to be shared by a group of people, and purchasing decisions center around price, services, product quality, and assurance of supply.

- Business-to-business media consists of general business and trade publications, directories, direct mail, catalogs, data sheets, and consumer media.

- Compared to national advertising, retail advertising is less concerned with brand awareness and more concerned with attracting customers.

- Retail advertising uses various media alternatives, from shoppers and preprinted inserts to television and radio.

- Identifying customers is one of the most valuable kinds of research a retailer can conduct.

$\mathcal{Q}$UESTIONS

1 You are developing an ad to reach chemists in the oil industry. Would you place this ad in a general business magazine or in a trade publication? Why?

2 How does retail advertising differ from national advertising?

3 Think of a restaurant in your community. What types of people does it target? Would you recommend that its advertising focus on price or image? What is (or should be) its image? Which media should it use?

4 Biogen Corporation's corporate mission is to become a leading company in genetic research and development for health industries. Privately held at time of incorporation, it has decided to go public and have its stock traded. How would corporate advertising assist Biogen in its mission? What audience targets should be priorities for its communication programs? Should it develop more than one campaign?

5 Although personal selling is a vital marketing tool for industrial (business-to-business) compa-

nies, advertising also has a significant role in many marketing situations. What if a limited budget means expanding one at the sacrifice of the other, however? Suppose you were making a decision for a company that is beginning a marketing effort for a new set of products; you'll need approximately six new salespeople. If an advertising campaign to introduce the firm would mean hiring four salespeople instead of six, is the advertising worth it? Explain the strengths and weaknesses of this idea.

6 Tom and Wendi Promise have just purchased a frozen-yogurt franchise. They found a good lease in a neighborhood shopping center, but the cost of franchising, leasing, and other charges have left them very little for advertising. With limited dollars, Tom and Wendi can only afford one of the following options: (a) Yellow Pages display ad, (b) a series of advertisements in the area's weekly "shopper" newspaper, (c) advertising in the area's college newspaper (the campus is six blocks from the store). Which of these opportunities will best help Tom and Wendi get the awareness they need?

7 Abby Wilson, the advertising manager for a campus newspaper (published four times per week) is discussing ways to increase advertising revenues with her sales staff. She asks opinions on using sales time to promote a co-op program to interest campus-area businesses. One salesperson says the retailers won't be bothered with all the "paperwork." Another explains that newspaper reps really have to understand co-op to sell it, and that none of Wilson's staff has experience. Would you be persuaded that promoting cooperative advertising is more trouble than it is worth?

*S*UGGESTED CLASS PROJECT

Select a print ad directed to a business-to-business consumer. Think about how this ad should be converted into a television commercial. Indicate examples of when this broadcast ad would be aired.

*F*URTHER READINGS

BEISEL, JOHN L., *Contemporary Retailing* (New York: Macmillan, 1987).

BERMAN, BARRY, AND JOEL R. EVANS, *Retail Management: A Strategic Approach,* 3rd ed. (New York: Macmillan, 1986).

BOLEN, WILLIAM H., *Contemporary Retailing,* 3rd ed. (Englewood Cliffs, NJ: Prentice Hall, 1988).

DIAMOND, JAY, AND GERALD PINTEL, *Retailing Today* (Englewood Cliffs, NJ: Prentice Hall, 1988).

FERN, EDWARD F., AND JAMES R. BROWN, "The Industrial/Consumer Marketing Dichotomy: A Case of Insufficient Justification," *Journal of Marketing,* 48 (Spring 1984):68–77.

HALL, S. ROLAND, *Retail Advertising and Selling* (New York: Garland Publications, 1985).

MAHEN, PHILIP W., *Business-to-Business Marketing* (Boston: Allyn & Bacon, 1991).

MASON, J. BARRY, AND MORRIS L. MAYER, *Modern Retailing: Theory and Practice,* 4th ed. (Plano, TX: Business Publications, Inc., 1987).

STERN, L. W., ADEL I. EL-ANSARY, AND JAMES R. BROWN, *Management in Marketing Channels* (Englewood Cliffs, NJ: Prentice Hall, 1992).

Price Chopper: "Best Foods/Best Price"

As the largest grocery retailer in the Kansas City area Price Chopper continually faced increasing competition from both new and existing retail grocery operations. As the volume leader, Price Chopper stood to lose the most in terms of market share, particularly because the Kansas City area was experiencing no significant population growth.

To combat this increased competition, Noble & Associates, Price Chopper's advertising agency, recommended a new creative strategy for its client in 1989. The principle campaign objective was to maintain Price Chopper's share of market leadership while fighting off the increased competition from new and existing retail grocery competitors in the Kansas City market. The creative strategy itself offered shoppers the dual benefits of low price and high quality. Thus, it positioned Price Chopper as the retail grocery that sold the best and the freshest perishable foods.

Price Chopper and Nobel & Associates summarized the consumer benefits of this creative strategy as follows: Price Chopper brings consumers the best and the freshest food at the best price. All effective creative strategies include "support" statements that justify the consumer benefit and, thus, enhance its credibility. The support for Price Chopper's consumer benefit include the following: 1) Price Chopper buys and makes the best food in Kansas City; 2) Price Chopper buys more food than any other retail grocery operation in Kansas City; 3) Price Chopper's large volume purchasing results in the lowest prices in Kansas City; and 4) Price Chopper's large volume purchasing and high turnover results in the freshest food.

Price Chopper primarily targeted women between the ages of 18 and 54 and identified men between 18 and 54 as a secondary target. This is a fairly traditional retail grocery target audience because women still represent the most common grocery shoppers. The target audiences were further defined as men and women who are concerned about both good value and good quality. Noble & Associates also knew from syndicated data that Price Chopper held the largest share of voice in the Kansas City Area of Dominant Influence (ADI). Specifically, this put Price Chopper in the best position to create or modify consumer's perceptions.

Within the first year of the campaign's introduction in October 1989, Price Chopper's market share had increased by 5 points to 36 percent, more than double the share increase experienced in the prior year. This was achieved during a period of flat population growth in the Kansas City area and less than a 1 percent increase in all-commodity grocery sales volume (ACV) and no new Price Chopper store openings.

Research results indicated that consumer recall of the campaign tagline "Best Food/Best Price" was 80 percent among Price Chopper customers and 43 percent among total Kansas City residents. Research conducted just 2 months after the campaign started indicated that the "Jammin Nanas" spot successfully communicated the overall message of "Price Chopper sells more quality fruit at a lower price than any other store.

Source: Courtesy of Noble & Associates.

Questions

1. Typically grocery retailers emphasize either food price or food quality in their advertising. Explain what additional demographic factors besides age and sex should be included in a grocery retailer's target audience definition for a price-based advertising strategy and for a food quality-based advertising strategy.

2. Explain why it would be difficult for a smaller grocery retailer in the Kansas City market to successfully employ a "Best Food/Best Price" advertising strategy.

3. Based on your existing knowledge of traditional retail grocery advertising, what general characteristics in addition to those discussed above make "Jammin Nanas" different from the bulk of existing grocery advertising?

$\mathcal{I}$NTERNATIONAL ADVERTISING

CHAPTER OBJECTIVES

When you have completed this chapter, you should be able to:

- Distinguish among local, regional, international, or global brands

- Explain how international advertising is created and executed

- Understand how international agencies are organized

- List the special problems that international advertisers face

- Watch with greater understanding the growth of global advertising

GOOD IDEAS KNOW NO BOUNDARIES

Switzerland is the fourteenth largest advertising market in the world and the eighth largest market in Europe. It is a small country (population 6.9 million) with a reputation for a stable currency and a solid banking system expected to run as surely and predictably as a Swiss watch.

This is the story of Hans Rudolph Jost, owner and managing director of the Quadri Agency for Communications, Zurich, who proved Switzerland could break out of a pattern and think big.

In 1991–92, the Swiss economy began to feel the effects of the European recession. Export markets for its horological products, pharmaceuticals, and precision machinery were down. The recession reduced tourism, a major source of business for Switzerland. By the fall of 1992, Jost began to sense the agency and his clients were dispirited, even discouraged. The agency needed something to get excited about, to generate vitality for itself. But, thought Jost, the best way to get the agency staff more upbeat was to find ways to get clients excited and optimistic. How could the agency do that if the whole continental economy is in the doldrums? Perhaps the problem was attitude. The attitude of people in Switzerland affected the attitude of client management, which in turn affected the agency.

So, searching for the heart of the problem, Jost tried to think what would get Switzerland revitalized in outlook and spirit. No small task. But worth the attempt.

Jost initiated the Vitalizer Project. This small 17-person agency began a process that got the attention of the top levels of business and government. The centerpiece was a dinner, to which the agency invited the leaders of business, industry, banking, publishing, the arts, and government. More than 350 dignitaries came to hear speeches by leaders of government, business, and the arts and to share ideas.

Making vitality the keynote of one evening was still not the whole idea. Vitality became the mission of the agency. To clients, the Quadri Agency promised to bring vitality not just to ideas or ads or even campaigns. Each member of the agency was asked to write a statement explaining how he or she would bring vitality to the agency. An all-day meeting developed the mission statement and a commitment to vitalizing all relationships.

Jost also decided that the Vitalizer Project required philosophical underpinnings, so he carved a month out of his schedule and wrote a book on bringing vitality to business. The book was a minor sensation and the media made the book a feature story upon publication.

The project caused Jost to reorganize the agency, adopt a new logo, move from a traditional Swiss building that had once been a dairy to nontraditional new surroundings overlooking Lake Zurich, and to focus the agency and client energies on bringing vitality to every activity. With its outlook and dedication, the agency won three of the next four accounts for which it was asked to present. The story proves that good ideas are the heart of the agency business worldwide.

EVOLUTION OF INTERNATIONAL MARKETING

Since Wendell Willkie coined the phrase "One World" in his 1940 presidential campaign, the distance between the concept and the reality has narrowed. The

Table 23.1   Top 25 Global Marketers in 1992 (figures in millions)

Advertiser	Headquarters	Worldwide Spending	U.S. Spending	Non-U.S. Spending	% Non-U.S.
1 Procter & Gamble	Cincinnati, OH	$4,009.2	$2,165.6	$1,843.6	46.0
2 Philip Morris Cos.	New York, NY	2,702.4	2,024.1	678.3	25.1
3 Unilever	Rotterdam/London	2,563.8	672.8	1,891.0	73.8
4 Nestlé SA	Vevey, Switzerland	1,935.0	733.4	1,201.6	62.1
5 Ford Motor Co.	Dearborn, MI	1,361.1	794.5	566.6	41.6
6 Toyota Motor Corp.	Toyota City, Japan	1,239.2	648.9	509.3	47.6
7 PepsiCo	Purchase, NY	1,215.3	928.6	286.7	23.6
8 McDonald's Corp.	Oak Brook, IL	994.5	743.6	250.9	25.2
9 Kellogg Co.	Battle Creek, MI	977.5	630.3	347.2	35.5
10 Sony Corp.	Tokyo, Japan	904.3	507.9	396.4	43.8
11 Fiat SpA	Turin, Italy	868.3	0.2	868.1	100.0
12 Coca-Cola	Atlanta, GA	798.8	392.0	406.8	50.9
13 PSA Peugeot-Citroen SA	Paris, France	791.3	0.0	791.3	100.0
14 Matsushita Electrical Industries Co.	Osaka, Japan	775.2	304.2	471.0	60.8
15 General Motors Corp.	Detroit, MI	756.5	623.2	133.4	17.6
16 Volkswagen AG	Wolfsburg, Germany	754.0	59.5	694.4	92.1
17 Nissan Motor Co.	Tokyo, Japan	749.2	370.7	378.5	50.5
18 Mars, Inc.	McLean, VA	743.4	320.4	423.0	56.9
19 Colgate-Palmolive Co.	New York, NY	709.6	315.5	394.1	55.5
20 Honda Motor Co.	Tokyo, Japan	705.4	349.1	356.3	50.5
21 Renault SA	Paris, France	593.1	0.0	593.1	100.0
22 Mazda Motor Corp.	Hiroshima, Japan	497.3	215.4	281.9	56.7
23 Ferrero SpA	Perugia, Italy	472.9	7.3	465.5	98.4
24 Philips NV	Eindhoven, Netherlands	456.9	161.5	295.4	64.7
25 Henkel Group	Dusseldorf, Germany	438.8	0.0	438.8	100.0
		$28,012.9	$12,968.7	$15,044.2	53.7

Source: Reprinted with permission from Advertising Age (December 13, 1993):I-11. Copyright Crain Communications, Inc., 1993.

local brand A brand that is marketed in one specific country.

regional brand A brand that is available throughout a regional trading bloc.

international brand A brand or product that is available in most parts of the world.

international advertising Advertising designed to promote the same product in a number of countries.

top 25 worldwide marketers spent approximately 54 percent of their advertising dollars outside the United States in 1992, up from 45 percent in 1989. Ten of those marketers were headquartered in the United States. Six were from Japan and no other nation had more than two. Table 23.1 lists the top 25 international advertisers of 1992. The subject of this chapter is the evolution of advertising from the home country to a foreign country to regional blocs to a worldwide audience. Included in this discussion are the tools of international management, the means of organizing for international advertising, creating and planning international advertising campaigns, and special problems in the field.

In most countries, markets are composed of local, regional, and international brands. A **local brand** is one marketed in a single country. A **regional brand** is one marketed throughout a region, for example, North America or Europe. An **international brand** is available virtually everywhere in the world. This chapter deals with regional and international brands, products, and services, and with the advertising that supports them.

International advertising is a relatively recent development within international commerce. It did not appear in any organized manner until the late nineteenth century. Ancient records in Egypt, Persia, Greece, and Rome refer to metals, spices, fabrics, gemstones, and other materials of value that were exchanged over great distances. Except for tribute or taxes, this commercial intercourse was based on the trading of goods from one region to another.

By the Middle Ages, Holland was trading tulip bulbs internationally in exchange for various products and services. English, French, Spanish, and Dutch companies procured spices, tea, and silk in the Orient for European consumers. This was not considered marketing as we define it, however, because the old trading companies were not developing products for the European market, nor were producers in Turkey, China, the Philippines, and Indonesia seeking to stimulate demand for their goods in Europe.

Marketing emerged when the emphasis changed from importing products (tea, spices, silk, gold, and silver) to exporting products. Advertising was used to introduce, explain, and sell the benefits of a product—especially a branded product—in markets outside the home country. The current patterns of international expansion emerged largely in the twentieth century. Understanding these trading patterns helps us appreciate both how they operated in the past and some of the restrictions that custom and history have imposed on them through the years.

HOME-COUNTRY PRODUCTION

Figure 23.1 illustrates the development of products from companies such as S. C. Johnson, Nestlé, and Stanley Tools outside the home market. It starts with a product that begins to reach the saturation point in its home market and cannot grow faster than the population. At this point, management seeks to recapture the sales gains of the growth period. This can be accomplished in one of two ways. The company can introduce new products in its home market, or it can expand into foreign markets. International expansion traditionally has involved the following steps:

- Production of goods in the home country.
- Export of goods to another country and appointment of an importer or a local distributor.
- Transfer of management from home-country export manager to on-site management.
- Local manufacture of the imported products and of new products for the product line; acquisition of companies in the local market, wherever that is, to expand the products offered; or acquisition of another company anywhere in the world whose products can be added to the company's offerings.
- Coordinated regional manufacturing, marketing, and advertising.
- Coordinated global marketing with sourcing from the most cost-efficient factories or suppliers.

This progression in the development of regional trading blocs and then in global marketing and advertising is far smoother in text than reality. Wars, currency fluctuations, product shortages, and restriction of capital movement (such as in the United States in the late 1960s) all affect planning. These factors make up what is known as **political risk**.

It is not the saturation of home-country market alone that causes companies to move products outside home markets. After World War II, market research

political risk Risk due to uncertainty in a nations political climate. While political risk is outside the area of marketing and advertising, its effects can seriously and drastically alter company plans.

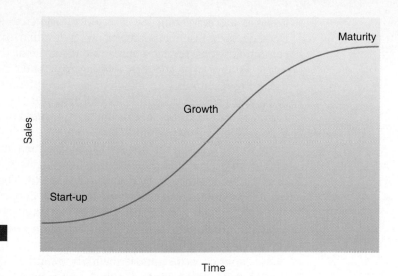

was used to evaluate market potential; merger and acquisitions put companies into new national markets and added products to company lines whose potential could be exploited in neighboring countries, and companies moved into other markets to preempt development by competitors. By studying the historical sequence, we can get a better understanding of the growth and intensity of international marketing and advertising.

EXPORT

Exporting a product requires a means of inserting this product into the distribution system of another country. The exporter typically appoints a distributor or an importer who assumes responsibility for marketing and advertising in the new country.

As volume grows, the complexity of product sizes, product lines, pricing, and local adaptation increases. The exporter might send an employee to work with the importer to handle details, to verify that promised activities are being carried out, and to solve communication problems. This employee serves as a facilitator between the exporter and the importer. Some companies prefer to appoint a local distributor who knows the language and the distribution system and can, therefore, handle customers and the government better than a foreigner could.

The Japanese, for example, followed this route in their export drive after World War II. Although they set up their own companies in some major countries, they relied heavily on local, particularly U.S., ad agencies, which built relationships with Japanese managements and learned Japanese business customs. For example, McCann-Erickson serves Canon in Europe and Asia. FCB Publicis works for Mazda Motors in North America and five other nations. Grey Advertising handles Sony in eight markets, while Young & Rubicam handles the advertiser in 13. Saatchi & Saatchi handles Toyota in North America and 15 other countries. The agency has a senior executive at Toyota headquarters to coordinate international advertising whose advertising budget for Toyota is said to be more than $150 million worldwide.

The large Japanese agencies typically have not been given global assignments to extend their services for clients outside the home islands, but Japanese agencies are emulating Western global agencies. Kouichi Segawa, director of Dentsu's overseas operations planning division, has said, "Our concept of a communications service company outside Japan is a little different from the usual pattern of a Western-style agency (and) could include sports events, designing restaurants or showrooms, space planning, corporate identity, packaging and product design."[1] Both Dentsu and Hakuhodo, the leading Japanese agencies, are examining opportunities to expand or to establish joint ventures in Europe, North America, and Latin America.

Exporting is still the first step in international marketing. In 1989, for example, Lands' End tested the European and Japanese markets by shipping directly from its home office in Dodgeville, Wisconsin. The company generated orders by placing small space advertising in English in both Japan and Europe, encouraging Americans to order their products by fax. By 1993, Lands' End had opened a distribution center in the United Kingdom and was hiring staff in Japan to expand marketing there.

As airlines move outside their home market, they are in effect exporting a service. American Airlines' "Smiles" campaign ran in Europe, basically changing only the language. See Ad 23.1.

TRANSFER OF MANAGEMENT

As the product or product line grows in export markets, it receives greater attention from the exporter. This process may involve sending someone from management to work in the importer's organization or to supervise the importer from an office in the importing country. At this point, the company still considers itself a domestic producer, exporting products to other markets. As long as this is true, the transferred employee must secure approval of plans, obtain funds for operations, and defend sales forecasts to a company management that is primarily concerned with its domestic market.

NATIONALIZATION

As the local importer-distributor grows with the imported line, the exporter may want greater control over the product or a larger share of the profits. As a result, the exporting company may buy back the rights contracted to the importer or set up assembly (or even manufacturing) facilities in the importing country. The result is the transfer of management and manufacturing to what was the importing country. The resourceful transferee will seek means of increasing sales and profits. At this point, key marketing decisions focus on acquiring or introducing products especially for the local market. For example, Japanese car makers now are developing cars specifically for the United States from design studios in California to be built in their "transplants" in America. Ford's new "world car," named the Mondeo, was developed primarily in Europe for adaptation and manufacture in plants in the United States, Latin America, and Asia.

REGIONALIZATION

As the exporter's operations become nationalized in one of the regional blocs, the company establishes an international regional management center and transfers

---

[1]David Kilburn, "Dentsu Expanding to Mideast, Europe," *Advertising Age* (September 7, 1992):4.

The American Way to America.

Ett leende kostar så lite...

ChicagoExpressen till Amerika.

Millas de sonrisas.

El servicio sin escalas de American a los Estados Unidos.

Tout un voyage sous le signe du sourire.

Laissez-nous vous accompagner en Amérique.

responsibilities for day-to-day management from the home country to the regional office. The regions are the major trading areas: Europe, Latin America, Asia-Pacific, and North America. Numerous American companies followed this pattern after World War II: exporting, establishing local subsidiaries, and acquiring local companies. Corporations such as ITT, S. C. Johnson, Procter & Gamble, and IBM all had European management centers by the 1960s, and most major companies have management centers now for Latin America, usually directed from Miami, and the Asia-Pacific region, directed from Hong Kong, Singapore, Sydney, or Tokyo. When a company is regionalized, it may still focus on its domestic market, but international considerations become more important. In the 1980s, Ford Motor Company lost money on North American automobile operations but was profitable and growing in Europe, which sustained the whole organization.

$\mathscr{T}$HE GLOBAL PERSPECTIVE

global perspective A corporate philosophy that directs products and advertising toward a worldwide rather than a local or regional market.

After a company has established regional operations with a management structure in Europe, Latin America, and the Pacific, if it is still managing its North American operations as well as the regional activities from North America, it faces the ultimate decision: Should it establish a world corporate headquarters? That is, should North American and global operations be separated and a new global headquarters created? Once this decision has been made, a truly **global perspective** will emerge, one not tied to any geographic area. Change to such an international or global management structure has been made by companies such as Unilever and Shell (both of which have twin world headquarters in the United Kingdom and the Netherlands), Arthur Andersen, IBM, Nestlé, and Interpublic. The achievement of a global perspective requires internationalizing the management group. As long as management is drawn exclusively from one country, a global perspective is difficult to achieve in a manufacturing company—or in an advertising agency.

As mentioned earlier, virtually every product category can be divided into local (or national), regional (trading bloc), and international brands. *Inter-national brands* are those that are marketed in two or more of the four major regional market blocs: North America, Latin America, Europe, and Asia-Pacific. (China is becoming a major part of the Asia-Pacific bloc.) Tables 23.2a, b, and c list the top agencies in the Latin American, European, and Asia-Pacific blocs. The fifth bloc, Eastern Europe, has changed substantially since 1989 and is increasingly participating in European commerce. Although the Eastern European bloc will exist as a trading region for years, the Western-most countries in this group seem likely to be subsumed into the European bloc, while Russia and the Asian republics of the former Soviet Union may coalesce into a smaller fifth bloc. Note the Peugeot ad that ran in 1993 in Russia, Ukraine, and the Baltic States (Ad 23.2). The sixth bloc—Africa, the Middle East, and Southern Asia—is so much smaller economically than the others that it is usually attached to Europe or Asia-Pacific in the way in which it is managed as a regional bloc.

global brand A brand that has the same name, same design, and same creative strategy everywhere in the world.

GLOBAL BRANDS

Table 23.2a

Who's on Top in Latin America

Rank	Agency	1992 Lat. Am. gross income by equity	% change from 1991	1992 Lat. Am. billings by equity	1992 GAAP gross income
1	McCann-Erickson Worldwide	$108,912	27.8	$726,072	$108,912
2	Lintas:Worldwide	70,164	−14.6	467,990	69,710
3	J. Walter Thompson Co.	61,895	26.5	376,920	56,894
4	Young & Rubicam	50,584	58.2	289,959	50,557
5	Ogilvy & Mather Worldwide	50,335	47.8	293,720	48,099
6	Leo Burnett Co.	45,137	39.9	307,412	46,130
7	BBDO Worldwide	33,705	59.6	155,638	42,352
8	Grey Advertising	29,022	42.7	174,385	27,845
9	Duailibi, Petit, Zaragoza	28,000	−29.0	106,830	28,000
10	Foote, Cone & Belding Communications	24,810	31.4	165,187	28,492

Figures are in thousands. GAAP = Generally Accepted Accounting Principles: Equity less than 50% excluded; if an agency owns 50% or more equity, 100% of gross income included. Agency omitted because it lacks an office outside the home country is Salles/Interamericana de Publicidade.
Source: Reprinted with permission from Advertising Age (May 17, 1993): I-22. Copyright, Crain Communications, Inc., 1993.

Table 23.2b

Who's on Top in Asia/Pacific

Rank	Agency	1992 Asia/Pacific gross income by equity	% change from 1991	1992 Asia/Pacific billings by equity	1992 GAAP gross income
1	Dentsu	$1,283,432	−4.4	$9,668,350	$1,285,012
2	Hakuhodo	578,288	0.7	4,548,365	579,967
3	Daiko	175,901	0.9	1,330,860	175,901
4	Asatsu	153,815	8.9	1,102,920	153,815
5	Dai-ichi Kikaku	123,700	−5.5	892,381	125,779
6	McCann-Erickson Worldwide	115,504	8.2	770,411	170,254
7	I&S Corp.	107,412	2.5	854,447	107,412
8	Dentsu, Young & Rubicam Partnerships	105,968	6.2	735,983	107,320
9	J. Walter Thompson Co.	104,088	26.2	695,131	105,485
10	Chell Communications	103,330	4.1	377,983	104,561
11	Backer Spielvogel Bates	103,215	6.6	685,780	106,697
12	Leo Burnett Co.	83,672	6.2	557,831	81,582
13	Ogilvy & Mather Worldwide	72,842	−10.4	506,235	63,032
14	Foote, Cone & Belding Communications	57,579	6.4	357,970	53,969
15	Lintas:Worldwide	56,424	12.4	376,338	60,549

Figures are in thousands. GAAP = Generally Accepted Accounting Principles: Equity less than 50% excluded; if any agency owns 50% or more equity, 100% of gross income included. Agencies omitted because they lack an office outside their home country include Tokyu Agency, Tokyo; Yomiko Advertising, Tokyo; Asahi Advertising, Tokyo; Man Nen Sha, Osaka, Japan; Nikkeisha Inc., Tokyo.
Source: Reprinted with permission from Advertising Age (May 17, 1993):I-22. Copyright, Crain Communications, Inc., 1993.

Table 23.2c

Who's on Top in Europe

Rank	Agency	1992 European gross income by equity	% change from 1991	1992 European billings by equity	1992 GAAP gross income
1	Euro RSCG	$775,494	–2.6	$5,355,014	$775,494
2	Publicis FCB	560,437	12.6	3,746,425	557,727
3	McCann-Erickson Worldwide	417,995	13.0	2,788,028	418,429
4	Young & Rubicam	372,220	–2.6	2,563,193	412,546
5	Backer Spielvogel Bates Worldwide	339,515	18.1	2,270,738	366,288
6	Saatchi & Saatchi Advertising Worldwide	335,823	7.8	2,336,228	340,827
7	Ogilvy & Mather Worldwide	323,967	0.7	2,336,687	312,694
8	Lintas:Worldwide	323,854	4.5	2,160,111	322,242
9	J. Walter Thompson Co.	321,796	7.1	2,314,833	311,719
10	Grey Advertising	312,171	13.3	2,109,466	335,383
11	DDB Needham Worldwide	296,673	18.2	2,125,447	293,521
12	BBDO Worldwide	263,378	13.5	1,835,829	346,186
13	D'Arcy Masius Benton & Bowles	251,597	8.1	1,916,220	254,149
14	BDDP Worldwide	213,931	6.5	1,294,010	213,931
15	Leo Burnett Co.	173,278	13.7	1,155,242	173,766
16	Lowe Group	167,279	31.6	1,115,262	171,134
17	N W Ayer	96,485	35.9	686,419	109,602
18	TBWA	95,512	9.4	690,055	107,974
19	FCA Group	76,258	13.3	571,913	78,472
20	Armando Testa Group	73,303	12.2	559,597	69,424

Figures are in thousands. GAAP = Generally Accepted Accounting Principles: Equity less than 50% excluded; if an agency owns 50% or more equity, 100% of gross income included.
Source Reprinted with permission from Advertising Age (May 17, 1993):I-22. Copyright, Crain Communications, Inc., 1993.

in the world. The product that is almost always used as an example of a global brand is Coca-Cola. The global definition breaks down slightly, however, because Classic Coke appears only in the United States and a few other markets. Elsewhere Coke is Coke, and it is marketed virtually the same way everywhere.

Other global brands are emerging as well: Revlon, IBM, Apple, Marlboro, Xerox (including Rank Xerox and Fuji Xerox), Avis, Hertz, Chanel, Gillette, BMW, Mercedes-Benz, products from Pepsi-Cola Foods, McDonald's, Rolex, Toyota, Nissan, Ford, and Henkel all have global brands in their product lines, or their company name is considered a global trademark. The controversy arises not so much over the concept of a global brand, as defined, but how and whether it will be realized.

Principle

Ideas are global; products or services that embody those ideas might not be.

THE GLOBAL DEBATE AND ADVERTISING AGENCIES

The global controversy was ignited by an article in the May/June 1983 issue of *Harvard Business Review* by Theodore Levitt, professor of business administra-

tion and marketing at Harvard Business School. In his article, Levitt argued that companies should operate as if there were only one global market. He stated that differences among nations and cultures were not only diminishing but should be ignored altogether because people throughout the world are motivated by the same desires and wants. Furthermore, Levitt argued, businesses will be more efficient if they plan for a global market. In other words, we should see the world market as one.

The London-based Saatchi & Saatchi company adopted this philosophy in a bid to become the first global advertising agency. In 1984 the agency ran a two-page ad in both *The New York Times* and the *Times* of London with the headline, "The Opportunity for World Brands." This ad applied Levitt's global proposition to advertising and to the service to be expected of global agencies.

Under the subheading, "Impact on Agency Structure," Saatchi & Saatchi stated in its ad:

What are the implications of these trends for the advertising industry?…

Most observers believe that the trend to pan-regional or global marketing will have a marked impact on the structure of advertising agencies…because world brands require world agencies.

A HANDFUL OF WORLDWIDE AGENCY NETWORKS WILL HANDLE THE BULK OF $140 BILLION IN WORLD ADVERTISING EXPENDITURE FOR MAJOR MULTINATIONALS.[2]

Other agencies tried to incorporate the global concept as well. A typical response was that of Grey Advertising, which took the position "Global Vision with Local Touch." As one of Grey's presentations in 1986 states:

Every idea needs a champion and Global Vision with Local Touch needs several at both the client company and its agencies.…The role of these Grey champions is to:

■ Provide the global vision

■ Look for the positive signals that point to global applications

■ Ward off the NIH (not invented here) factor and develop mutual trust and respect with local client managers

■ Employ all of Grey's tools, knowledge, and considerable resources to achieve global application.[3]

Philip Kotler, marketing professor at Northwestern University, disagreed with Levitt's philosophy. According to Kotler, Levitt misinterpreted the overseas

---

[2]Courtesy of Saatchi & Saatchi.
[3]Courtesy of Grey Advertising.

success of Coca-Cola, PepsiCo, and McDonald's. "Their success," he argued, "is based on variation, not offering the same product everywhere."[4]

Eight years later, in 1992, Levitt remained committed to his position, "I haven't backed away from the theory of globalization. It's a big mistake for advertisers to think that everything is becoming narrow. The challenge is to effectively come up with ways to communicate the same message to a homogenized audience all over the world."[5]

The focus of this section is perspective. Levitt and Kotler are theorizing; neither is totally correct. Global advertising is restricted by language, regulation, and lack of global media. The direction toward global is inescapable. Will true global advertising ever be achieved? Probably not. At least probably not soon. Ideas are global. Management thinking is increasingly global. The challenge in advertising is the careful and sophisticated use of Kotler's "variations" nationally or regionally to a basic Levitt-style global plan.

$\mathcal{E}$AST AND WEST—WILL THEY EVER MEET?

The epic events of 1989 in the communist bloc produced waves of changes and reactions, especially in Europe. In his book *The New Realities*, published in 1989, Peter Drucker predicted that the market economy would prevail. The impact of the changes and the difficulties Western companies encountered attempting to enter Eastern Europe were unforeseen, however.

In 1990, unemployment in Poland, which went "cold turkey" into a market economy, reached 25 percent in six months. Advertising virtually stopped, and the few advertising agencies that existed went bankrupt or cut back severely. Consumer marketing froze. By 1993, the Polish electorate halted the radical market reforms by electing officials with prior Communist background leanings, who promised a "softer landing."

In Hungary, the most market-oriented country of the Eastern bloc, Western companies jostled for position. A few joint ventures or acquisitions were approved, most notably the U.S. General Electric acquisition of control of Osram, an electrical manufacturing company already exporting to Europe and the United States but in need of capital and technology. In this case, the government could approve the transaction. But what of other entities?

In Budapest, as elsewhere in former communist economies, advertising agencies and other firms seeking partners were confronted with a new problem: There was no basic law of private property. Even after the revolution, this law was still being drafted, starting with definitions for such concepts as property, rights of shareholders, even profits—concepts out of use for 40 years. Even more cumbersome was one aspect of the process of privatization, electing management. The existing managers, sometimes Communist functionaries, could not negotiate deals with Western companies for which they had a "right" to sign until the workers voted, and voting was delayed until the laws were codified. One international agency network was preparing to sign an agreement with a Budapest agency only to be told the workers had thrown the management out.

---

[4]"Colleague Says Levitt Wrong," *Advertising Age* (June 25, 1984): 50.
[5]Kevin Goldman, "Professor Levitt Stands by Global Ad Theory," *The Wall Street Journal* (October 13, 1992):B7.

In October 1990, East Germany solved its problem by merging with West Germany. Czechoslovakia followed a path similar to Hungary but split into its two parts in 1992. Romania and Bulgaria progressed very slowly, the latter having voted the renamed Communist Party into power. By 1993, most of the global agencies had offices or working arrangements with agencies in the former Eastern bloc. Retail shelves now are filled with global and regional brands.

Russia, anxious for showcase deals, negotiated through government agencies but relaxed currency regulations or laws to sign Fiat, General Motors, Coca-Cola, Pizza Hut, and McDonald's. Young & Rubicam, BBDO, McCann-Erickson, and other global agencies made various arrangements to open offices in Moscow, either alone or in partnership with state entities.

As the Eastern bloc shed the stifling weight of a planned economy, abolishing regulations and freeing businesses to compete, the opposite trend appeared in the Common Market and North America. New regulations were proposed, more restrictions were written into law, and draft provisions for a unified Common Market after 1992 alarmed the advertising industry. These concerns came to a head at the International Advertising Association (IAA) world convention in Hamburg, Germany, in June 1990. Philip Geier of Interpublic challenged the attendees by stating that no organization adequately represented the three segments of the industry—the advertisers, the media, and the agencies. The IAA, under the leadership of its director-general, Norman Vale, former Grey Advertising executive, successfully pulled the warring or disaffected elements together by convincing the parties that the IAA was best suited for the task. They then began a coordinated effort to maintain more freedom and individual rights in consumer markets, in Europe and elsewhere.[6]

From this start, the IAA developed an advertising campaign that has been run in virtually every country in the world. A benchmark research project was conducted for the IAA by Gallup International in 22 countries in Europe, Asia-Pacific, Africa, and Latin America. Some 22,000 respondents were asked to agree or disagree with eight statements. The IAA cited four answers to its members:

1. *Advertising has an important role to play in the health of a modern economy.*

   Agreement with this statement was high with 75 percent among Western Europeans, 76 percent in Asia-Pacific, and 71 percent in the Baltic republics. Bulgaria and South Africa (82 percent) plus Uruguay (81 percent) were in exceptionally high agreement. Egypt was the only country to disagree, with 77 percent of the population overall and 32 percent disagreeing completely. Majorities clustered around the midpoint in the United Kingdom (62 percent), Finland (59 percent), Japan 56 percent), and New Zealand (50 percent).

2. *If a product is legal to sell, it should also be legal to advertise.*

   In all countries, majorities in excess of 65 percent agreed. Estonia (91 percent) and Bulgaria (88 percent) exhibited the highest level of agreement. Countries where a third or more of the population agreed completely were Switzerland (32 percent), Estonia (47 percent), South Africa (55 percent), Latvia (38 percent), Bulgaria (55 percent), Finland (34 percent), Turkey (32 percent), Australia (32 percent), and Uruguay (38 percent).

---

[6]*International Advertising Association Perspectives* (November 20, 1990).

3. *Advertising helps improve the quality of goods and services by causing companies to compete more directly with one another.*

Approximately 70 percent of respondents agree with this statement, with the highest level of agreement from Bulgaria (87 percent), South Africa (84 percent), Uruguay (80 percent), Australia, New Zealand, and Finland (78 percent).

4. *Without advertising, newspapers and magazines would be more costly or unavailable in such a wide variety.*

Overall, there was overwhelming agreement in all countries. Most noticeably, agreement was particularly strong (more than 80 percent) in the United Kingdom. The Netherlands, Luxembourg, Switzerland, Germany, Finland, Japan, Australia, New Zealand, and Uruguay were also in agreement. The newly democratized countries of Central and Eastern Europe, although in agreement with this statement (ranging from 51 percent to 76 percent), were in less agreement than the other countries. This lower awareness of advertising's contribution to print media could be attributed to government control of media and lack of advertising in these countries before the fall of communism.[7]

Gallup found widely differing opinions on a fifth statement: "If advertising were banned tomorrow, I would miss it." As Figure 23.2 shows, 79 percent disagreed with that statement in Egypt, and would not miss advertising, while 78

Figure 23.2

Global attitudes toward advertising.

Note: Percentages do not necessarily total 100% due to non-response or answer of "Don't know."
Source: Gallup International

[7]IAA Hotline Bulletin (October 11, 1993).

Responses to the statement, "If advertising were banned tommorrow, I would miss it."

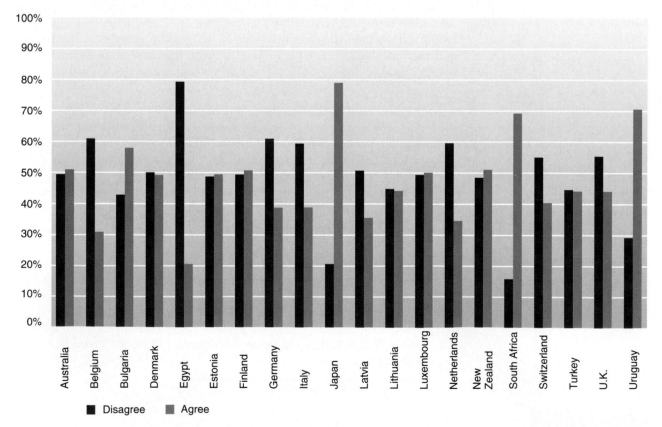

percent in Japan, 71 percent in Uruguay, and 68 percent in South Africa said they would miss advertising.

Michael Reinarz, director of visual communications at Nestlé, explains the dichotomy between the breakdown of the restrictive communist system in the Eastern countries and the increase in legislative control and censorship in the West:

> For both the West and the East it is the loss of power to the people. Once people are informed—have tasted freedom and can choose freely their religion, political party, newspaper, TV channel, supermarket, or spaghetti brand—that freedom cannot be taken away. And if people have the choice and therefore the power, one must "sell" them a specific ideology, religion, newspaper, TV channel, supermarket, or spaghetti brand. This means politicians, religious leaders, media owners, distributors, and manufacturers all have to do "marketing."[8]

Consequently, Reinarz states, competition is the key to any successful economic system. A free-market economy not only is preferable, it is mandatory. His solution to the growing changes in Eastern and Western thought is simple: "All goods and services which are legally in the marketplace should enjoy the same freedom of commercial speech. Now that the Eastern countries have begun to acknowledge this philosophy, we must make sure that the West does not forget it."

$\mathcal{T}$OOLS OF INTERNATIONAL MANAGEMENT

As soon as a second country is added to a company's operations, management practices begin to change. Experience has shown that regardless of the company's form or style of management, internationalization requires new management disciplines or tools. These tools include one language (usually English), one control mechanism (the budget), and one strategic plan (the marketing strategy).

LINGUA FRANCA

It is not difficult to understand why English would be the language of choice. Because the expansion of international marketing was accomplished chiefly by American companies within the Common Market, language was not an issue. To succeed within the company, and sometimes even to be hired, a person needed a working knowledge of English.

The American companies brought with them standardized forms of accounting, law, and banking. As a result, local lawyers, accountants, and bankers found it necessary to speak English in order to serve international clients and to have a hope of securing business from local companies owned or operated by Americans.

Language also affects the creation of the advertising itself. English normally requires the least space in printed material or air time. The range of words (esti-

---

[8]Michel Reinarz, "Will the West Liberate Itself After the East?" *IAA Perspectives* (August 24, 1990).

Concepts & APPLICATIONS

International Pet Talk

LONDON—When advertising across Europe, any copywriters worth their weight in pencils know that language is not to be ignored. Now one marketing consultant has set out to help the pet-food industry clear some of the Continent's lesser-known linguistic hurdles.

What a faux paw it would be to think dogs in Italy say "woof-woof," as they do in Britain. Instead "bau-bau" is the term of choice. Austrian dogs say "wuff-wuff," while Norwegian dogs bark "vov-vov." Romanian dogs, among the more original, let loose with "ham-ham." And so it goes, from country to country.

The cacophony extends to cats as well, with Belgian felines uttering "miaou" if they are Flemish but "miauw" if they live with French speakers. In a rare linguistic convergence, cats in Finland, Germany, Hungary, Portugal, Romania, most of Spain, and other countries all say "miau." But cats in Spain's Catalonia region go their own way, preferring "meu-meu."

To help advertisers through this pet-sized Tower of Babel, Frederick Marsh, an international marketing consultant, surveyed pet-food ads to compile a glossary of terms used to represent sounds made by cats and dogs. The results have surprised some people in the industry.

"I thought all dogs' barking sounded the same," says Kloskk Kaye, the account manager at ad agency BSB Dorland for Pedigree Chum dog food, a brand owned by Mars, Inc. Then again Ms. Kaye adds, "In our ads, we don't have dogs barking. We have breeders talking about the dogs."

Indeed, in television ads, dogs and cats usually speak in their own lingua franca, limiting the need for translation. But Mr. Marsh says his information can be useful. "If you have an ad for dog food, whether its in the trade press or television, if you write it wrong, no one knows what you're talking about," he says. "It has to be in the right language of the country."

Nonsense, says Nestlé, maker of Friskies pet food. All dogs in Europe speak with a deep British "ruff-ruff," says a Nestlé spokesperson.

Moreover, he adds, the important thing is proper portrayal of people-pet relationships—especially in Britain. Nestlé's surveys find over half of all Britons have a portrait of their pet in the living room. One-fifth say they wouldn't go on holiday if they had to "leave Fido or Tiddles in a kennel or cattery." Only 6 percent would part with their pet for $1 million.

Janet Guyon, *The Wall Street Journal* (December 1, 1993):B1.

---

mated at over 900,000) and the ease with which English adopts words from other languages make it more exact and more economical than other languages. This creates a major problem when the space for copy is laid out for English and one-third more space is needed for French or Spanish.

Headlines in any language often involve a play on words, themes that are relevant to one country, or slang. The images called to mind in the originating language are distorted or poorly communicated in another. Unintentional meanings, slang, and national styles must be removed from the advertising unless the meaning or intent can be recreated in other languages. For this reason, international campaigns are not translated, they are rewritten by a copywriter into a second language.

Every international advertiser has an example of how a word translated into another language produced a disaster. An example is Coca-Cola's use of "Coke adds life" in China. The Chinese translation reportedly came out "Coke brings your ancestors back from the dead." On the same note, translations of languages into English have the same problems. From a Japanese hotel: "You are invited to take advantage of the chambermaid." From a Bangkok dry cleaners: "Drop your trousers here for best results."[9] In an ad for a Rome laundry: "Ladies, leave your

---

[9]Courtesy of Hood, Light & Geise Advertising, Spring 1990 Newsletter:1.

clothes here and spend the afternoon having a good time." And from a Moscow weekly: "There will be a Moscow Exhibition of Arts by 15,000 Soviet Republic painters. These were executed over the past two years."[10]

Some languages simply do not have words equivalent to English expressions. Computer words and advertising terms are almost universally of English derivation. The French since 1539 have had legislation to keep their language "pure" and now have a government agency to prevent words, especially English words, from corrupting the French language. *Marketing* and *weekend*, unacceptable to the French government agency, are translated literally as "study of the market" or in another attempt "pertaining to trade," and "end of the week," respectively. Neither captures the essence of the English word. As if to prove how difficult it is to dislodge the most appropriate word, the French functionary who announced the preceding equivalents for "marketing" and "weekend" was pressed at the news conference why the agency head was not present. Without thinking, he replied "Monsieur is gone for *le weekend*."

Bilingual Copywriting. Experience has shown that the only reasonable solution to language problems is to employ bilingual copywriters who understand the full meaning of the English text and can capture the essence of the message in the second language. It takes a brave and trusting international creative director to approve copy he or she doesn't understand but is assured is right. A back translation into English is always a good idea, but it never conveys a cultural interpretation.

The language problem is intensified in bilingual countries such as Canada or Belgium, and even more in Switzerland which has three main languages, or in China which has more than 20 dialects. Multiple back translations can produce sharply different messages in English, even if they have the desired strategic focus in the language used.

BUDGET CONTROL

The budget has become almost another language—in this instance, one of control. Centralized companies distribute budget responsibility to branch operations. As a result, techniques of forecasting, currency fluctuation, hedging against swings in exchange rates, and monitoring improved, especially with the development of advanced computer techniques. Companies have refined budget steps, standardized budget philosophies, and now tie performance to achievement. Local managements negotiate final budgets.

STRATEGIC PLAN

The strategic plan is prepared in conjunction with the budget. Basically, the plan outlines the marketing strategy, whereas the budget allocates the funds. If one is changed, the other must change as well. This principle is especially important in international management. Two major models of assessing how to advertise in foreign cultures have developed, one market oriented, the other culture oriented.

The Market-Analysis Model. This model is based on data and observation from several countries. It recognizes the existence of local, regional, and international brands in almost every product category. The two major variables are the share of market of brands within a category and the size of the category.

---

[10]Mike Shoup, "Ah, Translation," *Chicago Tribune Travel Section* (May 12, 1991):14.

Fabian Lazovski, Creative Director, Camara Comunicacion Publicitaria, Montevideo

8:50 A.M. Each day of work always starts the same, tuning the car's radio on the way to the agency. I listen to the national and international news while I review the jobs for the week and the problems to resolve in the near future.

9:00 A.M. Before going to the meeting room, I stop at my office and see all the work and the best terms of delivery.

9:30 A.M. Our first meeting of the day is with each area's directors. While having breakfast together, we analyze the jobs that are finished, the ones that we are working with, and the future ones. The agenda for the week is now ready, allowing for some margin for error.

10:30 A.M. I reorganize my department according to what was arranged at the board meeting. Everything is taken into account, the jobs to create and the terms for suppliers. Immediately, I ask the receptionist for the calls and distribute the work among the creatives. Today is a trainee's second day. So I not only do my daily work but explain to the trainee the characteristics of the agency clients, its image, structure, and later I can explain the marketing and communication objectives.

11:30 A.M. Creatives are working very hard. I go from one side of the table to the other, hearing ideas and pointing out other paths. Tomorrow is essential to present a commercial of the New Financial Plan of Consorcio del Uruguay, another for Paddock's winter collection, three press notices promoting tourist programs for Jorge Martinez & Asociados. Furthermore, for the day after tomorrow, the account executive should have the multimedia promotion for Devoto Supermarkets. Today is like every other one. With less hours than are really needed and with more work than yesterday, but less than tomorrow. I do not complain. I enjoy it. I love what I do and with whom I work.

12:00 noon Before having lunch, I get in touch with the media director, art director, and account executive. This afternoon is the presentation of the Federal Express Annual Multimedia so we have to complete the latest details. Federal Express's general manager, together with the Latin America manager, are coming to the agency. We decided that only the media director and I will guide that meeting. The attention will be centered on two persons: He will display the global media strategy while I will do the same with the creative pieces.

12:15 P.M. I make two personal phone calls. Work is not the only thing in life, although some days it is a great part of it. I also receive the call from Video Production. I arrange the appointment with them early in the afternoon. I can't waste time; the budget was approved by the client so the commercial should be ready as soon as possible. Furthermore, shooting is one of the

For example, the brand's percentage share of the category market might vary substantially in four countries:

	Country A	Country B	Country C	Country D
Global Brands	25%	30%	50%	20%
Regional Brands	60	30	10	55
Local Brands	15	40	40	25

According to this example, Country C looks very valuable for the global

things I enjoy most in my work. I sit next to the film director and won't get up until he does the same.

12:30 P.M. I have lunch with two agency friends. A delicious barbecue in a warm place near the agency. Luckily, or unfortunately, also during lunch I am a creative: During all our lunch the "work" topic was present even with the dessert.

2:00 P.M. I return to work at approximately 2 P.M. Over coffee, I discuss the morning's work with the creatives. The Paddock commercial presents a good communication tone but it lacks the creative step that attracts the public. I launch an idea. The press notices are ready; I do not have to make any corrections and I believe they are going to be O.K. The same with the 7 percent promotion of Devoto Supermarkets. Now there is a jingle left to be done. It must be the leitmotiv of the advertising.

4:30 P.M. I redistribute the work and take advantage of the time to create a new commercial for Consorcio del Uruguay before the meeting at 5 P.M. Every time I start thinking about something new for this client, the same thing happens: Our communication is really different from our competitors and brings profitable results. I know that this client is a leader in the market but he can't stop thinking that the only axiom of his company is selling, selling, and selling.
I know what to do to sell the "Effective Plan." I have a direct and rational plan in mind. I prefer to find other ways and leave this for tomorrow. Now I have a meeting with the media director and

account executive; in a few minutes the national and regional managers from Federal Express are coming. I review what to say and how I am going to do it; I check the folders and press notice roughly and I notice that they are practically originals. I love this campaign, they are really two. I am going to present two different options in the same communication skeleton.

5:00 P.M. They have just arrived, what punctuality! We greet each other, chat for a few minutes before we start with the dealing. While I am listening, I think of how am I going to present the campaigns. I have my favorite but I will try to be as objective as possible. Both of them fit very well with Federal Express's interests.

6:00 P.M. It is my time. When the sun hides and the moon rises. I begin with the television commercials, they laugh, they like them. I continue with press, finish with broadcast, and I do an analysis of the pieces. They have it very clearly, I am feeling a deep emotion. Today, as every day, when I have to make a presentation, when I see the client's face, I feel a deep emotion.

7:50 P.M. The night comes. They have gone. The media director, the account executive, and I are in the agency's office. We cannot go without saying something about the presentation. In this moment, words are worthless. Faces express everything. And not only because of what happened today, but also because tomorrow is going to be another day. Different but touching.

brand. Considering the size of the market changes the picture, however. Assume that the category market in the four countries is as follows:

	Country A	Country B	Country C	Country D
Category Units	200,000	100,000	50,000	300,000
Global Brands	25%	30%	50%	20%
Global Market Size	50,000	30,000	25,000	60,000

When the market-analysis model is used, Country C actually is much less important. Half of this smaller market is already in global brands. Country D not only is a larger global brand market but also is a much larger total market. A headquarters marketing manager must look not only at share but also at market size, growth rates, and opportunities for growth through new products or increased expenditures.

For example, cola-flavored soft drinks are not nearly as dominant in Germany as they are in the United States. To generate sales in Germany, therefore, a soft-drink company would have to develop orange and lemon-lime entries. McDonald's serves beer in Germany, wine in France, a local fruit-flavored shake in Singapore and Malaysia, and even a Portuguese sausage in Hawaii, in addition to the traditional Big Macs, fish sandwiches, and French fries in order to cater to local tastes.

Such "variations" to the uniform global-brand strategy are adjusted by market, by season, and by company. Wise global companies employ a flexible global strategy and allow management to test new local brands. They realize that almost every successful global or multinational brand started as a local brand somewhere. In contrast, in 1990, after extensive research and development, Gillette launched the Sensor razor virtually worldwide without first establishing it in one country. The product was so successful that Gillette had difficulty fulfilling early demand.

The largest advertising agencies have benefited from the increasing volume of global planning. In the 13 years from 1976 to 1989, the market share of the multinational agencies rose from 14 percent to 30 percent of worldwide billings, as advertisers aligned brand advertising with the same agencies across Europe, Asia, and North America.[11] By 1992, top ten agency networks' combined share of global ad spending had risen to more than 48 percent.[12] See Table 23.3 for the largest global advertising agencies.

The Culture-Oriented Model. The second model of international advertising emphasizes the cultural differences among peoples and nations. This school of thought recognizes that people worldwide share certain needs, but it also stresses the fact that these needs are met differently in different cultures.

Although the same emotions are basic to all humanity, the degree to which these emotions are expressed publicly varies from culture to culture. The camaraderie typical in an Australian business office would be unthinkable in Japan. The informal, first-name basis relationships common in North America are frowned upon in Germany, where coworkers often do not use first names. In Japan, the gulf between management and staff is submerged in uniforms and group dynamics but is actually wider than in most western nations. Likewise, the ways in which we categorize information and the values we attach to people, places, and things depend on the settling in which we were raised.

High-Context versus Low-Context Cultures How do cultural differences relate to advertising? According to the high-context/low-context theory, although the *function* of advertising is the same throughout the world, the *expression* of its message varies in different cultural settings.[13] The major distinction is between *high-context cultures*, in which the meaning of a message can be understood only within a specific context, and *low-context cultures*, in which the mes-

---

[11]*The Economist* (June 9, 1990).
[12]"The Global Decade of Alignment," *Advertising Age* (September 20, 1993):1–10.
[13]The high-context/low-context distinction is adapted from two books by Edward T. Hall, *The Silent Language* (New York: Doubleday, 1973); and *Beyond Culture* (New York: Doubleday, 1977).

Table 23.3

World's Top 20 Advertising Organizations
(ranked by worldwide equity gross income)

Rank 1992	Rank 1991	Advertising organizations, headquarters	U.S.-based agency brands included	Worldwide gross income 1992	1991	% chg	Worldwide capitalized volume 1992	1991	% chg
1	1	WPP Group, London	**Ogilvy & Mather Worldwide;** Cole & Weber; Ogilvy & Mather Direct; Ogilvy & Mather Yellow Pages: A Eicoff & Co.; **J. Walter Thompson Co.;** Brouillard Communications; J. Walter Thompson Direct; Thompson Healthcare; Thompson Recruitment Advertising; **Scall, McCabe, Sieves;** Fallon McElligott; Morton Goldberg Associates; **Martin Agency;** Stennch Group	$2,813.5	$2,661.8	5.7	$18,954.9	$17,915.8	5.8
2	2	Interpublic Group of Cos., New York	**Lintas:Worldwide;** Dailey & Associates; Fahlgren Martin GS&B Lintas. Lintas:MGI; Lintas:Marketing Communications, Long, Haymes & Carr. **Lowe Group;** Lowe & Partners; Lowe Direct; LCF&L; **McCann-Erickson Worldwide;** McCann Direct; McCann Healthcare	1,989.2	1,835.9	8.4	13,342.8	12,333.0	8.2
3	3	Omnicom Group, New York	**BBDO Worldwide;** Baxter, Gunan & Mazzer; Frank J. Corbett Inc.; Doremus & Co.; Lavey/Wolff/Swift; **DDB Needham Worldwide;** Bernard Hodes Group, Kallir, Philips, Ross; **(shared shops):** Rainoldi, Kerzner & Radcliff; Rapp Collins Marcoa; Alcone Sims O'Brien; Harrison, Star, Wiener & Bertler **(other independent units):** TBWA Advertising; Goodby, Berlin & Silverstein; Altschiller Reitzfield	1,806.7	1,687.3	7.1	13,225.9	12,040.6	9.8
4	4	Saatchi & Saatchi Co., London	**Saatchi & Saatchi Advertising Worldwide;** Conill Advertising, Cliff Freeman & Partners; Klemtner Advertising; Rumnill-Hoyt Team One **Backer Spielvogel Bates Worldwide;** AC&R Advertising; Kobs & Draft **CME KHBB**	1,696.5	1,651.0	2.8	11.575.4	11,513.2	0.5
5	5	Dentsu Inc., Tokyo	Dentsu Corp. of America	1,387.6	1,451.0	–4.4	10,477.3	10,680.1	–1.9
6	6	Young & Rubicam, New York	Young & Rubicam; Chapman Direct; Creswell Munsell Fultz & Zirbel Muldoon Agency; Sudler & Hennessey; Wunderman Cato Johnson Worldwide	1,072.3	1,057.1	1.4	7,879.0	7,840.1	0.5
7	7	Euro RSCG, Neuilly, France	Robert A. Becker Inc.; Cohn & Wells; Comart-KLP; Lally McFarland & Pantello. Messner Vetere Berger McNamee Schmetterer/Euro RSCG Tatham Euro RSCG	951.2	999.0	–4.8	6,887.6	6,953.0	–0.9
8	8	Grey Advertising, New York	Grey Advertising; Beaumont-Bennett Group Font & Vaamonde Gross Townsend Frank Hoffman; Grey Direct International	735.4	673.2	9.2	4,915.9	4,530.5	8.5
9	10	Foote, Cone & Belding Communications, Chicago	Foote, Cone & Belding Communications, FCB Direct/U S IMPACT Krupp Taylor U.S.A; Vicom/FCB; Wahlstrom & Co.	682.7	619.5	10.2	5,197.8	4,803.6	8.2
10	9	Hakuhodo, Tokyo	Hakuhodo America Advertising	661.1	655.6	0.8	5,077.9	4,877.1	4.1
11	11	Leo Burnett Co., Chicago	Leo Burnett Co.	643.8	576.6	11.7	4,304.3	3,890.6	10.6
12	13	Publicis-FCB Communications, Paris	Publicis Inc.	590.1	505.8	16.7	3,821.6	3,376.7	13.2
13	12	D'Arcy Masius Benton & Bowles, New York	D'Arcy Masius Benton & Bowles; Clanon Marketing Communications; Medicus Intercon International	558.4	534.6	4.5	4,700.7	4,509.3	4.2
14	14	BDDP Worldwide, Paris	McCracken Grooks Communications; Wells Rich Greene BDDP	293.0	277.0	5.8	1,999.2	1,871.1	6.8
15	15	Bozell, Jacobs, Kenyon & Eckhardt, New York	Bozell; Poppe Tyson; Temerlin McClain	231.0	221.0	4.5	1,805.0	1,660.0	8.7
16	16	Tokyo Agency, Tokyo	NA	179.4	176.9	1.4	1,593.7	1,482.4	7.5
17	18	Daiko Advertising, Osaka, Japan	NA	175.9	174.3	0.9	1,330.9	1,278.1	4.1
18	17	N W Ayer, New York	N W Ayer; Ayer Direct	175.0	174.6	0.2	1,581.5	1,386.7	14.0
19	20	Asatsu, Tokyo	Asatsu America	165.9	149.3	11.1	1,245.9	1,130.6	10.2
20	19	Dai-ichi Kikaku, Tokyo	Kresser Craig/D.I.K.	151.4	159.9	–5.3	1,102.7	1,113.1	–0.9

Source: Reprinted with permission from Advertising Age (April 14, 1993);12. Copyright, Crain Communications, Inc.., 1993.

sage can be understood as an independent entity. The following is a list of cultures from high to low context, with Japanese being the highest-context culture: Japanese, Chinese, Arabic, Greek, Spanish, Italian, English, French, North American, Scandinavian, and German.

As mentioned earlier, an issue that cannot be overlooked in international advertising involves language concerns. The differences between Japanese and English are instructive. English is a low-context language. English words have very clearly defined meanings that are not highly dependent on the words surrounding them. In Japanese, however, a word can have multiple meanings. Listeners or readers will not understand the exact meaning of a word unless they clearly understand the preceding or following sentences, that is, the context in which the word is used.

Advertising messages constructed by writers from high-context cultures might be difficult to understand in low-context cultures because they do not get right to the point. In contrast, messages constructed by writers from low-context cultures may be difficult to understand in high-context cultures because they omit essential contextual detail.

In discussing the Japanese way of advertising, Takashi Michioka, president of DYR, joint-venture agency of Young & Rubicam and Dentsu, put it this way:

> In Japan, differentiation among products does not consist of explaining with words the points of difference among competing products as in America. Differentiation is achieved by bringing out the people appearing in the commercial—the way they talk, the music, the scenery—rather than emphasizing the unique features and dissimilarities of the product itself.

ORGANIZATION OF INTERNATIONAL ADVERTISING AGENCIES

THE SCOPE OF INTERNATIONAL ADVERTISING

Zenith Media Worldwide tabulates world advertising spending, converted to U.S. dollars. Table 23.4 lists the top 20 countries in expenditures in 1980, 1991, and 1994. Although the United States still dominates world advertising spending, advertising growth rates outside the United States, reinforced by a weaker dollar since 1985, have outstripped U.S. growth.

Most international advertisers can be analyzed according to the model presented in Figure 23.3. Most companies fall on the axis from similar products and centralized managements (quadrant 1) to different or localized products and decentralized managements (quadrant 3). There are exceptions, however. For example, McDonald's products are largely standardized, and its international management is decentralized (quadrant 2). Nestlé allows some local autonomy but markets a large number of products (quadrant 4). Each company develops its own policy to guide its application of resources in regional or global marketing.

Agencies have to develop techniques to service brands that are marketed around the world. Some agencies exercise tight control, others allow more local

Table 23.4

Top 20 Countries by Advertising Expenditure (US$ million at current prices)

		1980		1991		1994
1	United States	35,501.0	United States	81,492.0	United States	87,888.0
2	Japan	12,930.7	Japan	31,981.3	Japan	37,089.9
3	Germany	6,670.6	Germany	14,154.3	Germany	16,489.3
4	United Kingdom	4,607.5	United Kingdom	13,507.7	United Kingdom	16,398.5
5	Canada	2,637.1	France	8,701.5	Italy	9,562.3
6	France	2,364.4	Spain	7,868.7	France	9,508.1
7	Netherlands	1,539.3	Italy	7,508.5	Spain	8,838.0
8	Australia	1,315.4	Canada	6,492.1	Canada	7,836.3
9	Switzerland	1,212.7	Australia	3,662.8	South Korea	5,600.6
10	Italy	1,003.5	South Korea	3,176.8	Australia	3,855.1
11	Spain	799.6	Netherlands	2,384.9	Turkey	3,171.4
12	Sweden	552.8	Switzerland	2,254.5	Taiwan	3,146.5
13	Belguim	481.0	Taiwan	2,038.3	Netherlands	2,534.6
14	Denmark	446.4	Sweden	1,694.6	Switzerland	2,487.4
15	Austria	400.6	Belgium	1,353.9	Mexico	2,144.3
16	Taiwan	351.7	Mexico	1,203.0	Sweden	1,807.2
17	Norway	337.5	Denmark	1,098.3	Venezuela	1,624.7
18	Finland	336.3	Finland	1,031.7	Belgium	1,619.3
19	South Korea	329.0	Austria	1,006.5	Colombia	1,465.9
20	Puerto Rico	180.4	Hong Kong	972.8	Hong Kong	1,442.6

Source: Zenith Media Worldwide

autonomy. All of these techniques fall into three groups: tight central international control, centralized resources with moderate control, and matching the client.

Henkel, a large German manufacturer of household and cleaning products, provides an example of how centralized management with similar products works. Henkel's international strategy was designed to accomplish three goals: to eliminate duplication of effort among its national companies, to provide central direction for new products, and to achieve efficiency in advertising production and impact. It included these steps:

Figure 23.3

The product management axis.

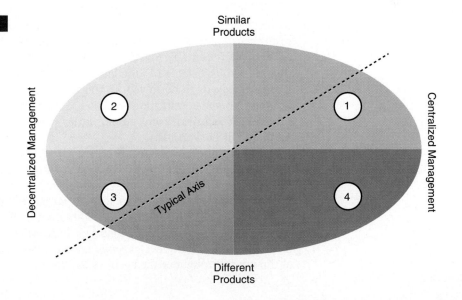

- Identifying the need to be fulfilled or the function of a product.
- Determining the commonality of that need or its benefit in Europe or a larger area.
- Assigning that specific need or benefit to one product with one brand name.
- Assigning that brand to one brand manager and one advertising agency to develop and market.
- Not allowing the benefit, the name, or the creative campaign of that brand to be used by any other brand in the company.

TIGHT CENTRAL INTERNATIONAL CONTROL

McCann-Erickson, a subsidiary of Interpublic Group, relies on tight central international control. Among its clients, McCann-Erickson handles Coca-Cola. The Leo Burnett Company uses an very similar system, especially for Marlboro cigarettes. (See Table 23.5 for a listing of the top 25 agency brands, based on billings under a single agency name.)

CENTRALIZED RESOURCES WITH MODERATE CONTROL

Agencies such as BBDO Worldwide, Grey Advertising, and DDB Needham centralize their resources for clients but allow their agencies local autonomy in creatively executing centrally planned strategies.

MATCHING THE CLIENT

Matching the client must be part of any international support system for a client. Companies with few international clients can easily offer each one personalized services. Those with more clients must decide whether each client will receive tailored service or whether some features will be standardized to establish a pattern of service.

What is emerging in international marketing is a flexible system, responsive to local or national needs, tailored to client needs, a melding of centralized resources deployed to match client requirements.

The more centralized the client, the more likely the agency is to have a headquarters group assigned to the client with a tactical team ready to fly anywhere a problem needs to be solved. In the future, international agencies increasingly will base this team outside the United States and will have multiple centers of service. McCann-Erickson, among others, uses tactical teams to support local national offices worldwide.

In analyzing how clients work, the J. Walter Thompson agency, a unit of WPP Group PLC, identified three strata of support for international campaigns: exchange, encouragement, and enforcement. At the first level, the agency office at client headquarters (the lead agency) *exchanges* information, advertising campaigns, and material with its other international offices. At the next level, agency management more actively *encourages* local offices to follow the international direction. At the third level, agency management is asked to *enforce* international direction throughout the agency's network.

Table 23.5   World's Top 25 Agency Brands

Rank	Agency	Worldwide gross income			Worldwide capitalized volume		
		1992	1991	% chg	1992	1991	% chg
1	Dentsu Inc.	$1,356.2	$1,415.8	−4.2	$10,281.3	$10,440.2	−1.5
2	McCann-Erickson Worldwide	922.3	825.8	11.7	6,151.1	5,522.4	11.4
3	Euro RSCG	876.7	945.1	−7.2	6,338.6	6,559.4	−3.4
4	Young & Rubicam	822.7	824.4	−0.2	6,186.5	6,282.4	−1.5
5	J. Walter Thompson Co.	774.8	689.6	12.4	5,419.3	4,798.9	12.9
6	Saatchi & Saatchi Advertising	685.6	665.6	3.0	4,682.1	4,487.4	4.3
7	BBDO Worldwide	681.5	643.4	5.9	4,899.9	4,444.0	10.3
8	Hakuhodo	661.1	655.6	0.8	5,077.9	4,877.1	4.1
9	Leo Burnett Co.	643.8	576.6	11.7	4,304.3	3,890.6	10.6
10	Ogilvy & Mather Worldwide	642.3	618.1	3.9	4,471.2	4,290.8	4.2
11	Lintas:Worldwide	611.8	596.0	2.6	4,091.2	3,982.9	2.7
12	Grey Advertising	611.0	557.5	9.6	4,085.0	3,759.0	8.7
13	DDB Needham Worldwide	605.4	585.2	3.4	4,565.4	4,306.9	6.0
14	Publicis-FCB Communications	590.1	505.8	16.7	3,821.6	3,376.7	13.2
15	Backer Spielvogel Bates Worldwide	578.8	534.8	8.2	3,873.8	3,584.8	8.1
16	D'Arcy Massius Benton & Bowles	446.7	425.6	5.0	3,871.5	3,714.7	4.2
17	Foote, Cone & Belding Communications	320.5	299.1	7.2	2,833.7	2,661.9	6.5
18	BDDP Worldwide	293.0	277.0	5.8	1,999.2	1,871.1	6.8
19	Tokyu Agency	179.4	176.9	1.4	1,593.7	1,482.4	7.5
20	Daiko Advertising	175.9	174.3	0.9	1,330.9	1,278.1	4.1
21	N W Ayer	166.7	166.1	0.4	1,525.6	1,329.7	14.7
22	Asatsu	165.9	149.3	11.1	1,245.9	1,130.6	10.2
23	Bozell	163.3	89.7	82.1	1,230.0	1,176.0	4.6
24	TBWA Advertisng	158.7	146.2	8.5	1,122.2	1,010.5	11.1
25	CME KHBB	157.1	165.5	−5.1	1,141.3	1,196.9	−4.6

Notes: Figures are in millions of U.S. dollars. The worldwide brand includes an agency's U.S. branded proportics (minus its U.S. branded specialty chops) and the international network that is not related to those specialty shops omitted in the U.S. (See page 20 of methodology on branding agencies)

Source: Reprinted with permission from Advertisng Age (April 14, 1993):8. Copyright, Crain Communications, Inc., 1993.

CREATING AND PLANNING INTERNATIONAL ADVERTISING CAMPAIGNS

Principle

Every sale is local, although the persuasion that led to the sale might have been part of an international campaign. The plan will fail if the individual buyer is not motivated or cannot find a way to take action.

According to an old axiom, "All business is local." This proverb should be modified to read "Almost all *transactions* are local." Although advertising campaigns can be created for worldwide exposure, the advertising is intended to persuade a reader or listener to do something (buy, vote, phone, order). That something is a transaction that is usually completed at home, near home, or usually in the same country if by direct mail. Even this will change as multinational direct-mail campaigns will be possible in a unified common market. How are these cam-

French Agency Chooses Pay Cut Over Layoffs

PARIS—Publicis Conseil resorted to an unusually democratic method to deal with an anticipated shrinkage in 1993 revenues: It asked employees to vote for layoffs or lower salaries.

Anticipating a revenue slump partly due to France's new media law, the agency held a referendum on whether it should cut salaries to avoid laying off 25 to 40 staffers. The plan won overwhelming approval, with a 221–81 vote for salary cuts. There were 14 blank ballots, and another 49 staffers didn't vote for other reasons.

Publicis president, Maurice Levy, who came up with the referendum idea and favored salary cuts, said the vote was bittersweet.

"On the one hand, it shows that the feeling of sol- idarity, the [staff's] identification with the agency and one another is very strong at Publicis," Mr. Levy said. "But it is painful to have to ask one's collaborators to make this kind of decision."

The media law contributing to the revenue decline went into effect in March 1993; it bans agencies' 15 percent commission on media budgets and otherwise restricts their income. According to French industry insiders, it could lower agency revenues by as much as 20 percent this year and force them to cut staff levels by 17 percent.

Source: Reprinted with permission from *Advertising Age* (May 24 1993):8. Copyright, Crain Communications, Inc., 1993.

paigns, which can have near-global application, created? For international advertising campaigns, the two basic starting points are: (1) success in one country; or (2) a centrally conceived strategy, a need, a new product, or a directive.

EXPANDING A NATIONAL SUCCESS

In the first case, a successful advertising campaign, conceived for national application, is modified for use in other countries. The acclaimed Avis campaign, "We try harder," began in the United States and spread extensively. Wrigley, Marlboro, IBM, Waterman Pen, Seiko Watches, Philips Shavers, Procter & Gamble, Ford, Hasbro, and many other companies have taken successful campaigns from one country and transplanted them around the world. A strong musical theme, especially typical of McDonald's, makes the transfer even smoother because music is an international language.

CENTRALLY CONCEIVED CAMPAIGNS

The second form, a centrally conceived campaign, was pioneered by Coca-Cola and is now used increasingly in global strategies. Although the concept is simple, the application is difficult. A work team, task force, or action group (the names vary) is assembled from around the world. Usually a basic strategy is presented. The strategy is debated, modified if necessary, and accepted (or imposed) as the foundation for the campaign. Some circumstances require that a strategy be imposed even if a few countries object. Primarily, cost is a factor. If the same photography and artwork can be used universally, this can save the $10,000 or more each local variation might cost. Or, if leakage across borders is foreseen, international management may insist on the same approach. Colgate, among others, faced this problem before its red dentifrice package and typography were standardized when distributors in Asia bought shipments from the United States or Europe, depending upon currency rates and shipping dates. A variety of packages for the same product is confusing to the consumer.

A variation on this procedure occurs when a promising new product is being developed. The team is assembled and might begin its work by developing a common global strategy.

Once the strategy is developed, the members of the team responsible for creative execution go to work. In the case of one Coke campaign, the multinational group was sequestered until a campaign emerged. In other cases, the team may return to its home country, develop one or more approaches or prototype campaigns. reassemble in a matter of weeks, review all the work, and decide on one or two executions to develop into a full campaign. Such a campaign would include television, radio, newspaper, magazine, cinema and outdoor advertising, and collateral extensions (brochures, mailings, counter cards, in-store posters, handouts, take-one folders, or whatever is appropriate). The team can stay together to finish the work, or it can ask the writer or developer of the campaign to finish or supervise the completion of the entire project.

In order to communicate their positions clearly and cope with rapidly changing conditions, several major advertisers gather their agencies for strategy sessions. McDonald's does this every year in August or September to announce the forthcoming year's plans. Eastman Kodak called its agencies together in early 1990 to discuss needs to economize and "get more bang for the buck." Nestlé convened its five major agencies—J. Walter Thompson, Ogilvy & Mather, McCann-Erickson, Lintas: Worldwide, and Publicis-FCB— to discuss agency alignments by product group, how a more market-driven and consumer-driven Nestlé is responding to change. Barry Day, Lintas' assistant to the CEO and an attendee, said "I believe agencies have to match the client organization. They must mold to (the client) philosophy and respond in kind."[14]

VARIATIONS ON CENTRAL CAMPAIGNS

Variations of the centrally conceived campaign do exist. For example, Rank Xerox may handle its European creative development by asking the European offices of Young & Rubicam to develop a campaign for a specific product—telecopiers, copiers, or whatever. The office that develops the approved campaign would be designated the "lead agency." That agency office would then develop all the necessary pattern elements of the campaign and the relationship of the various elements to one another, shoot the photography or supervise the artwork, and prepare a standards manual for use in other countries. This manual would include examples of layouts, patterns for television (especially the treatment of the logo or the product), and design standards for all elements. Individual offices could either order the elements from the lead agency or produce them locally if this were less expensive. Because photography, artwork, television production, and color printing are very costly, performing all of these in one location and then overprinting typography or rerecording the voice track in the

---

[14]Laurel Wentz, *Advertising Age* (September 10, 1990):87.

local language saves money. But advertisers must be careful to look local. In Ad. 23.3, note how Pioneer subtly changed its U.S. ad to run in French Canada.

McDonald's Coca-Cola, and others record basic music for campaigns and make various sound tracks available for local use. This work is not necessarily done in the home country. Superb sound studios and musicians are available, for example, in Spain, where costs are significantly lower than in the United States.

LOCAL APPLICATION AND APPROVAL

Beyond central approval is local application and approval. Every ad in every country cannot come back to regional and world headquarters for approval. Local application is simplified when common material originates from a central source. Within a campaign framework, most companies allow a degree of local autonomy. Some companies want to approve only *pattern ads* (usually the two or three ads that introduce the campaign) and commercials and allow local approval of succeeding executions. Others want to approve only television commercials and allow local freedom for other media. In any case, free-flowing communication is necessary. Senior officers travel, review work, and bring with them the best of what is being done in other countries. Seminars, workshops, and annual conventions all serve to disseminate campaign strategies, maintain the

Ad 23.3

In order to look local and use basically the same layout—in case a reader saw both versions—Pioneer Hi-Bred changed the contents of the attaché case. The English version ran in the United States; the French version in French-speaking Quebec and Ontario, Canada.

(Courtesy of Pioneer Hi-Bred and Meyocks Benkstein Associates.)

PIONEER DAYS.
IT'S A BUSINESS TRIP.

From February 7-12 growers across the country will be going on a business trip. A trip that saves them 5% on all Pioneer® brand products, with purchases counting toward Pioneer Quantity Savings as well. We call this business trip Pioneer Days. Come harvest time, you'll call it a smart business investment.

PIONEER.
BRAND·PRODUCTS

PIONEER® brand products are sold subject to the terms and conditions of sale which are part of the labeling and sale documents.
®Registered trademark of Pioneer Hi-Bred International, Inc., Des Moines, Iowa, U.S.A.

SAVE 5% - FEBRUARY 7-12, 1994

LES JOURNÉES PIONEER:
DES DÉPLACEMENTS D'AFFAIRES

Du 21 au 26 février, partout au pays, les agriculteurs effectueront de nombreux déplacements d'affaires. À la suite de ces déplacements, ils économiseront 6 % à l'achat de produits de marque Pioneer® et leurs achats compteront pour les économies sur quantité de Pioneer. Ces déplacements d'affaires, on appelle ça les journées Pioneer. Et lors de la récolte, vous appellerez ça un investissement d'affaires judicieux.

PRODUITS DE MARQUE
PIONEER.

Toutes les ventes sont sujettes aux modalités qui apparaissent sur les étiquettes et les documents commerciaux. ® Marque déposée dont l'usager autorisé est Pioneer Hi-Bred Limitée, Chatham (Ontario) N7M 5L1.

ÉCONOMISEZ 6 % — DU 21 AU 26 FÉVRIER 1994

campaign's thrust, and stimulate development of new ideas. Today, companies must balance the globalization of concepts and strategy with the localization of application.

The evolution in this globalization/localization process was brilliantly described by Stanley Bendelac, president of Backer Spielvogel Bates-Europe at the IAA Latin American Advertising Congress in Caracas, Venezuela, in 1993. Bendelac started with the basic split.

But analyzed the steps that have occurred:

1. Globalization

2. Localization

3. Concentration of market share among fewer companies

4. Specialization in business
    By geography
    By category
    By channels of distribution

5. Harmonization within the global companies
    By product line
    By name
    By formula
    By price

6. Adaptation of harmonized brands
    To local tastes
    To local customs
    To local sizes and containers

7. Centralization
    Of management
    Of production

8. Devolution of defined authority for execution

9. Coordination of plans, budgets, and strategies

10. Innovation in meeting local needs, customs, or market niches

As companies learn to move faster and give national managers more latitude for innovation, Step 10 feeds back to Step 1 as a successful local product is adopted by a global company as a global brand. Oil of Olay, a successful product acquired by Procter & Gamble in the United States, moved from a national to a global brand in fewer than five years. P&G took a campaign for Pantene shampoo with vitamins developed by its agency in Taiwan to Latin America, changing the commercial only to accommodate regional hair types; sales for the already distributed product soared.

HOW WELL DOES ADVERTISING CROSS BORDERS?

One of the most interesting studies on this question was conducted in 1990 by Alice, a French advertising agency, and IPSOS, a French research group. "Rather than measuring what is acceptable in all markets (and lowering creative standards), we have taken the most competitive advertising in each local market and found out how competitive it remains in the other markets."[15] Top commercials from France, Germany, Holland, Italy, Spain, and the United Kingdom were judged by 100 consumers in each of those countries. Each commercial was adapted into each of the six languages. At the end of each commercial, an explanation or further translation appeared. The conclusions of this research were:

1. *Local nationality characteristics dominate in a market.* The most competitive commercials in each market, those that garnered the strongest responses, are from local commercials.

2. *There exist genuine national advertising cultures.* Local creation and production recognize these local cultures. What makes a commercial strong in its home market also makes understanding difficult outside the local market.

3. *A basic creative approach explains the capacity of some commercials to cross frontiers.* The key determinates of commercials both "liked" and "convincing" were the strength of their emotional appeal, the quality of their entertainment value, and the simplicity of the human situations they portray.

As the report states in its final page, "decentralized advertising appears to be the most competitive approach because of the importance of national cultures [however] globalization is possible but in the most extreme way, benefiting [from] the strongest ideas. Supra-national can only be creative."

SELECTING MEDIA FOR INTERNATIONAL CAMPAIGNS

As we have seen, advertising practitioners can debate the applications of global theories to their profession, but one fact is inescapable: Global media do not currently exist. Television can transmit the Olympics around the globe, but no one network controls this global transmission. Therefore, an advertiser seeking global exposure would have to deal with different networks in different countries. Satellite transmission now places programs with advertising into many European homes, but its availability is not universal because of the "footprint" (coverage area of the satellite), the technical limitations, and the regulations on transmission by the various governments. As other satellites have been launched, they beam signals to more than one country in Europe, the Asian subcontinent, North America, and the Pacific, but they will be regional, not global.

For example, as a series of events seized the world's attention in the late 1980s, Cable News Network (CNN) became the medium for the exchange of news for most of the world. Advertisers were quick to see this network as a means of reaching influential consumers even before CNN was available in homes. The 1991 Gulf War heightened CNN's recognition and increased its influence. By 1993, it was a nearly global electronic medium, reaching 141 million households in more than 100 countries. However, its coverage was in English, a language understood by less than 20 percent of the world's population. CNN has competition from the BBC and from MTV, now available in many satellite transmissions. Music is a more universal language than English, even though the language of pop culture is English. (See Figure 23.4 for data on satellite viewership.)

---

[15]"Europe: Can Creative Advertising Cross Frontiers?" Alice and IPSOS, 1990.

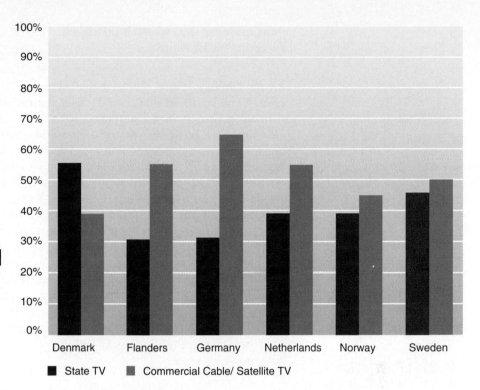

Figure 23.4

European viewers prefer satellite and cable.

(Source: Pan European Television Audience Research. Reprinted with permission from Advertising Age International *(April 19, 1993):I-4. Copyright, Crain Communications, Inc., 1993.)*

Global campaigns are becoming more and more common and successful. At a rate of seven or eight per month, new global campaigns are being launched. Levi Strauss & Co. racked up record sales in 1991 on the strength of a campaign pitched, unchanged, to Europeans, Latin Americans, and Australians. To handle this surge, advertising agencies have had to find ways to execute concepts globally. Of the 40 largest agencies in the United States and Britain, 39 have global networks compared to fewer than one-third in 1987.[16]

EXECUTION OF INTERNATIONAL CAMPAIGNS

Media planning for an international campaign does follow the same principles used for reaching a national target audience. The execution, however, is more complex.

International campaigns are not always centrally funded. The global corporation has operating companies locally registered in most major countries. Advertising might have to be funded through these local entities for maximum tax benefits or to meet local laws of origination. Therefore, the media planner might only be able to establish the media definition of the target audience, lay down a media strategy, and set the criteria for selecting media. Greater latitude is allowed in media application than in creative variation. For example, a media campaign in the southern hemisphere, especially for consumer goods and seasonal items, requires major changes from a northern hemisphere campaign. In the southern hemisphere, summer, Christmas, and back-to-school campaigns are all compressed from November through January. National media directors

---

[16]Ken Wells, "Global Ad Campaigns, After Many Missteps, Finally Pay Dividends," *The Wall Street Journal* (August 27, 1992):A1.

must examine local research on audience characteristics and use judgment in executing media strategies.

Media Choices. Once the basic global media strategy and plan have been created and approved, the central media planner will look for regional or multinational media. If magazines are part of the plan, advertising space in *Time, Newsweek, The Economist, Reader's Digest*, and other magazines with international editions may be bought. With the exception of *Reader's Digest*, these publications are available in English only. The *International Herald Tribune* and *The Wall Street Journal* are published simultaneously in a number of major cities using satellite technology. See Table 23.6 for a listing of global media circulation. Magazines published by international airlines for their passengers are another option. Multinational satellites, such as British Satellite Broadcasting in Europe and Star in Hong Kong, provide opportunities to place the same message before a target audience at the same time across national boundaries. If the audience is targeted for a consumer product, local planning and purchase are required. This is accomplished in one of two ways: through an international advertising agency (or international consortium of agencies) or an international media-buying service. If these two methods are not used, the media executive must execute the plan through a multitude of local, national, or regional media-buying services or advertising agencies.

International Advertising Agencies If the campaign is being handled by one of the international advertising agencies, the senior media officer in the office that works for client headquarters will be in charge. He or she will supervise the efforts of that agency's offices in cities around the world in executing the media plan. Media orders will be placed locally, with copies sent to the coordinating agency office for review and compilation. In other cases, the plan will be reviewed centrally and placement will be handled locally without reporting to headquarters.

International networks of independent agencies have been formed to provide their members with global reach and to prevent the loss of clients to the international corporate agencies. Examples include Affiliated Advertising Agencies International, Advertising and Marketing International Network, and International Federation of Advertising Agencies. Similar groups are forming in regional blocs, such as the National Advertising Agency Network in the United States and the Association for European Marketing, Advertising, and Public Relations in Europe. These groups provide multinational media buying for their clients.

International Media-Buying Services The other primary option of media placement is to use international media-buying services. These services usually work for smaller international companies that do not have well-developed agency relationships in each country in which they operate. Regional media-buying services, such as Carat of France, are gaining great strength in Europe.

International Production The Wace Group PLC, the world's largest producers of color separations used in printing, provides advertisers and media with a

Table 23.6 International Global Media (distribution by circulation and household reach)

	Total Distribution 1993	North America	Central/South America	Europe	Middle East Africa	Asia/ Pacific	Australia New Zealand
DAILIES							
Financial Times, London	290,124	26,942	1,172	252,029	2,861	6,848	272
International Herald Tribune, Neuilly, France	195,075	8,988	1,489	134,118	6,438	43,624	418
USA Today, Arlington, VA	2,064,808	1,996,952	—	47,811	—	20,045	—
The Wall Street Journal, New York	1,994,863	1,894,248	—	57,505	—	43,110	—
WEEKLIES							
Business Week, New York	1,013,602	896,139	18,296	63,048	—	36,119	—
The Economist, London	534,122	236,665	9,115	219,985	14,238	42,061	12,058
The Guardian Weekly, Manchester, England	105,910	42,149	1,376	48,558	2,779	2,142	8,906
Newsweek, New York	3,845,000	3,100,000	70,000	285,000	55,000	225,000	110,000
Paris Match, Paris	187,033	30,594	1,610	132,656	21,495	678	—
Time, New York	5,510,000	4,350,000	95,000	560,000	85,000	270,000	150,000
MONTHLIES							
Cosmopolitan, New York	5,812,085	2,705,224	517,343	1,728,434	151,862	393,000	316,222
Esquire, New York	1,174,558	713,960	—	110,598	—	350,000	—
Good Housekeepng, New York	5,657,739	5,012,159	199,361	446,219	—	—	—
Harper's Bazaar, New York	1,028,198	715,680	76,354	155,164	—	81,000	—
National Geographic, Washington, DC	9,560,741	8,164,959	97,599	841,945	68,369	145,588	242,281
Reader's Digest, Pleasantville, NY	27,925,000	17,965,000	1,157,000	6,680,000	400,000	1,080,000	643,000
Redbook, New York	3,941,694	3,367,778	—	433,916	—	—	140,000
Runner's World, Emmaus, PA	512,000	430,000	—	70,000	12,000	—	—
Scientific American, New York	626,157	518,847	7,944	73,100	1,801	8,700	15,765
The WorldPaper, Boston	1,230,000	3,000	298,300	560,000	10,000	359,000	—
OTHER PRINT							
Fortune, New York	870,000	740,000	10,000	65,000	—	55,000	—
TV							
BBC World Service TV, London	19,500,000	6,500,000	—	1,800,000	—	11,200,000	—
CNN, Atlanta	141,300,000	68,000,000	1,300,000	60,000,000	4,000,000	8,000,000	—
Cartoon Network, Atlanta	24,000,000	9,000,000	1,000,000	14,000,000	—	—	—
MTV: Music Television, New York	154,100,000	58,300,000	26,000,000	58,300,000	—	11,500,000	—
TNT, Atlanta	75,983,000	59,983,000	2,000,000	14,000,000	—	—	—

Source: Reprinted with permission from Advertising Age International (February 21, 1994): I-11. Copyright, Crain Communications, Inc., 1994.

satellite-linked network of printing facilities. This will allow for global print advertising transmission in the same way satellites have made multinational television commercials possible in most parts of the world.[17]

---

[17]Scott Hume, *Advertising Age* (September 17, 1990):30.

SPECIAL INTERNATIONAL CONSIDERATIONS

International advertising has a worldly glamour about it—extensive travel, cultural opportunities, exotic places and cuisines, and the excitement of spending a weekend half a world away from home. It is also tough work, with long days, jet lag, insomnia, and dysentery. The business itself has some peculiar problems. We already discussed the problems that language creates. Other concerns relate to laws, customs, time, inertia, resistance, rejection, and politics.

International advertisers do not fear actual laws; they fear not knowing those laws. For example, a marketer cannot advertise on television to children under 12 in Sweden or Germany, cannot advertise a restaurant chain in France, and cannot advertise at all on Sunday in Austria. Until recently, a model wearing lingerie could not be shown on television in the United States. In contrast, nudity is acceptable in France. In Malaysia jeans are considered to be Western and decadent, and are prohibited. A commercial can be aired in Australia only if it is shot with an Australian crew. A contest or promotion might be successful in one country and illegal in another.

CUSTOMS

Customs can be even stronger than laws. When advertising to children age 12 and over was approved in Germany, local custom was so strong that companies risked customer revolt by continuing to advertise. In many countries naming a competitor is considered bad form.

Customs are often more subtle and, therefore, easier to violate than laws. Quoting an obscure writer or poet would be risky in the United States, whose citizens would not respond to the unknown author. In Japan, the audience would respect the advertiser for using the name or become embarrassed at not knowing a name they were expected to recognize. Thus, in the United States the audience might be turned off, whereas in Japan consumers might search for the meaning in the message. In one case, the communication might be terminated, and in the other case, reinforced.

TIME

Time is the enemy in international advertising. Everything takes longer. The New York business day overlaps for only three hours with the business day in London, for two hours with most of Europe, and for one hour with Greece. Normal New York business hours do not overlap at all with Japan, Hong Kong, the Middle East, or Australia. Overnight parcel service is dependable to most of Europe, if the planes are able to take off and land. For these reasons, telecopy transmission is now the mode for international communication. Facsimile or "fax" numbers have become as universal as telephone numbers on stationery and business cards in international companies. No matter what the activity, it always seems to take longer in another country, even if that second country is the United States.

Time is an enemy in other ways. France and Spain virtually close down in August for vacation. National holidays are also a problem. U.S. corporations average 14 to 15 paid legal holidays a year. The number escalates to over 20 in

Europe (with over 30 in Italy). Some countries have patron saints for industry sectors. For example, Spain should be avoided on St. Barbara's Day. St. Barbara is the patron saint of advertising and artillery.

INERTIA, RESISTANCE, REJECTION, AND POLITICS

Inertia, resistance, rejection, and politics are sometimes lumped together as "not invented here" situations. Advertising is a medium for change, and change may frighten people. Every new campaign is a change. A highly successful campaign from one country might or might not be successful in another country. (Experience suggests the success rate in moving a winning campaign to another country is about 60 percent.) Creative directors often resist advertising that arrives from a distant headquarters rather than advertising created within the local agency. This resistance is partially the result of a very real problem in local offices of international agencies: an inability to develop a good creative team or a strong creative reputation when most of the advertising emanating from the office originates elsewhere. Government approval of television commercials can also be difficult to secure in some countries. Standards may seem to be applied more strictly to international than to national products.

Flat rejection or rejection by delay or lack of support must be anticipated with every global strategy and global campaign. Typical responses may be, "We do not do it that way here," or "You do not understand how different we are in this country," or "We tried that once and it did not work." The best solution is to test a locally produced version of the advertising against an original ad both based on the global pattern advertising. As mentioned, the global strategy usually wins 60 percent of the time. If the locally produced advertising of the global strategy wins, the victory must be decisive or the costs of the variation may not be affordable. Or, a new campaign may have been found. These are times that try the will and the tact of global advertising managers. Global companies must remain flexible enough always to adopt a new winner if it emerges. This is the case with the Wrigley Spearmint campaign that used the no-smoking symbol. The U.S. campaign has been adapted for use in Hong Kong and Singapore in Chinese. (See Ad. 23.4.)

Overcoming Inertia and Resistance At times the resistance and rejection are political. These may be the result of office politics or an extension of international politics. Trying to sell a U.S. campaign in a foreign country, for example, can be difficult if relations between the two nations are strained. Being politic in the diplomatic sense of the word is the only practical way to overcome local resistance. International advertising involves the forging of consensus. This cannot be accomplished by mail. Successful international companies have frequent regional and world conferences, maintain a constant flow of communication, transfer executives, and keep their executives well informed through travel, videotapes, teleconferences, and consultation. They have learned that few actions are as flattering as asking for advice. When local managements are asked to comment on a developing strategy or campaign, their involvement often turns into support.

Another proven axiom is always go to a problem, do not bring it to headquarters. Solutions worked out in the country that has the problem are seldom what either party anticipated and are frequently better than either could have

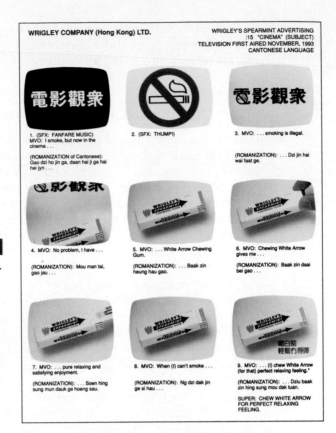

hoped. The adrenalin that precedes an "international confrontation" can often be directed to very positive solutions.

Despite its complexities and difficulties, international advertising is growing and will continue to grow in an increasingly interconnected world economy. Two of the largest agency groups are British-owned Saatchi & Saatchi and WPP, and one of the largest single agencies is Japanese (Dentsu), indicating that international advertising is no longer under American control. Students in the United States need to understand how international advertising works if they wish to succeed in this ever-changing industry. In fact, the United States is the only major country that still distinguishes between business and international business. Most of the Western world has made the transition.

SUMMARY

- International business and trade now account for more than 10 percent of domestic production in almost every industrialized country and the percentage is growing.

- Another way to look at this is that more than 10 percent of the products and services in the industrialized countries are either very similar

(localized versions) or the same everywhere

- The communication of the benefits and characteristics of products and services are much the same; as the world's various regional blocs have become more homogenized, consumers in these regions are becoming more similar in taste and outlook.

- Advertising provides a valuable function and the dominant structure for providing advertising is the advertising agency, whose importance on a global stage is increasing.
- An understanding of the origin, role, and func- tion of advertising as the commercial voice of the global marketplace will help students understand better the currents of world trade and international marketing.

SUGGESTED CLASS PROJECT

To demonstrate the problems of language in adver- tising, divide the class into teams of five or six. Each team should choose a print advertisement it believes would have universal appeal. Take the headline and one paragraph of body copy to a language professor or someone who is proficient in a language other than English. See if you can do this for up to five dif- ferent languages. Next take that translation to anoth- er professor or native language speaker of the same language and ask for a back translation into English. Compare and report on whether the concept traveled easily or with difficulty.

QUESTIONS

1. What are the differences among a local, regional, and international brand?
2. When did marketing emerge in international trade?
3. What pattern did Japanese companies follow in introducing their products in new markets?
4. Why would an exporter of goods nationalize its operations in another country?
5. Give three examples of global brands.
6. What belief does Professor Levitt hold? Which agency adopted his theory?
7. What are the tools of international management?
8. Is English a high-context or low-context lan- guage?
9. Name some impediments to international adver- tising.

FURTHER READINGS

AXTELL, ROGER E., *The Do's and Taboos of International Trade* (New York: John Wiley & Sons, Inc., 1994).

Global Management, 1994 (London: Sterling Publishing Group, PLC, 1994).

DeMOOIJ, MARIEKE K. , *Advertising Worldwide* (London: Prentice Hall International, 1991).

WELLS, WILLIAM D., "What's Global; What's Not," published by DDB Needham Worldwide.

Golden Arches in Moscow

Attempts by U.S. firms to break into international markets are littered with horror stories of translational gaffes and unintentional cultural slurs. When Perdue Chicken attempted to translate its famous tagline "It takes a tough man to make a tender chicken" into Spanish for Hispanic markets, the phrase was literally translated as "It takes a sexually aroused man to make a chick excited." Similarly, Anheuser-Busch's "King of Beers" Budweiser slogan ended up as "Queen of Beers" in Spanish.

Such examples are all too common as companies attempt to master the marketing strategies necessary not only to overcome language barriers but to address cultural differences. Some of the hard-won lessons of international advertising and marketing include the hiring of local marketing and advertising staff to develop and implement the plans to achieve the broader business objectives defined by the corporate parent. Consequently, if domestic sacred cows, such as long-used advertising taglines or positionings, are inappropriate for use in foreign countries, they should not be considered unless budgetary considerations mandate it.

Despite the promise of multinational, mega-merger agencies resulting from the acquisition frenzy of the 1980s, few domestic campaigns have translated into truly international efforts to date. Only very simple graphic images for fashion and other intangibly based product benefits have succeeded in developing international appeal, such as the "United Colors of Benetton" campaign.

Given these obstacles, when McDonald's secured the rights to open its first restaurant in the Soviet Union after decades of negotiations, it was committed to doing it right. With competition escalating and domestic fast-food sales flattening, the international market represents one of the most promising areas for revenue expansion in the industry. So, when McDonald's began planning its largest restaurant for Pushkin Square in Moscow, it devoted a great deal of time to studying the culture, hiring and training local staff, and procuring local sources of ingredients. In some cases, when the quality of local ingredients was below McDonald's standards, arrangements were made to contract-produce an adequate supply of ingredients exclusively for McDonald's use.

Although state-run restaurants in the Soviet Union were famous for bad food and service, their prices were extremely low. Without state subsidization, McDonald's recognized that a typical meal at the Golden Arches would require a princely fee from Soviet citizens. Consequently, they focused on the other critical elements of successful fast-food operations: quality and service. Thoroughly screened Soviet youths were hired and trained to be courteous to all patrons, a novelty in Moscow restaurants. With over 700 seats, the Moscow Golden Arches location would be among the first to offer fast food with consistent quality and friendly service.

To date, McDonald's sales in Moscow have exceeded expectations, with Muscovites continuing to endure lengthy waits for a chance to dine on a Big Mac and fries and to sample capitalist enterprise at close range. Despite 400 percent increases in food prices, sales have scarcely been affected. In fact, waiting in line at McDonald's has become the premiere people-watching spot in Moscow, with youths emulating western fashions seen in fashion magazines from Europe and the United States.

Source: ABC News, *Prime Time Live* (January 24, 1990).

Questions

1 Traditionally, international marketers identify current cultural norms and attempt to mimic them in the presentation of their product or service in other countries. Why did McDonald's choose to deviate from the existing cultural norms for restaurant service in Moscow?

2 What characteristics common to Soviet shopping practices actually offer advantages for McDonald's over its domestic operations?

3 The basic elements of food-service success are quality, service, cleanliness and value. Without state subsidies, McDonald's could not address the value component via meal prices as effectively as state-run restaurants. Why was the company still able to create a high perceived value among Soviet consumers?

Repepping Diet Dr. Pepper

Between 1987 and 1991, Diet Dr. Pepper's share of the carbonated soft drink market declined about 3 percent, while other diet soft drinks grew more than 30 percent. In a final attempt to salvage the brand, Diet Dr. Pepper and Young & Rubicam—Diet Dr. Pepper's advertising agency—relaunched it with a new formulation, new packaging, and new advertising.

In addition to its small and declining share, Diet Dr. Pepper faced four marketing obstacles: Because Diet Dr. Pepper was not sold "on deal" as often as its direct competitors, it was priced considerably higher on an average cents-per-ounce basis. It had poor distribution in vending machines and soda fountains—traditional trial-inducing channels. Most of its volume came through Coca-Cola and Pepsi bottlers, who understandably paid less attention to Diet Dr. Pepper than to their own brands, and would see any significant progress as a competitive threat. Furthermore, Coke and Pepsi were out-advertising Dr. Pepper about ten to one.

In the face of these formidable obstacles, Diet Dr. Pepper launched its 1991 campaign with the following ambitious objectives: (1) Increase Diet Dr. Pepper sales by 7 per cent—the projected growth rate of the diet soft drink category. (2) Heighten advertising awareness levels. (3) Generate trial from all soft drink users, particularly diet soft-drink users. (4) Convince consumers that new Diet Dr. Pepper "tastes more like regular Dr. Pepper." (5) Encourage repeat usage among those who try the reformulated product.

The creative strategy was, simply, "the new Diet Dr. Pepper tastes more like regular Dr. Pepper." The initial execution of this strategy was a series of three startling 15-second television commercials in which a "Diet Dr. Pepper vending machine" crashed through a living room ceiling. In the first of these spots, a woman sitting in her living room reading the newspaper says to her husband, "It says here there's a new Diet Dr. Pepper that tastes more like regular Dr. Pepper." He says, "No kidding." She says, "I wonder when it will get here?" At this point, the vending machine crashes through the ceiling, and the announcer (voice over) says, "New Diet Dr. Pepper. There's no stopping the taste." This fanciful introduction was intended to generate awareness and trial.

In the second spot, the same husband says, "They're right! New Diet Dr. Pepper does taste more like regular Dr. Pepper." The wife says, "So let's have another," whereupon the vending machine crashes into the scene again. This spot was intended to reinforce the

"new taste" proposition. In the third spot, a downstairs neighbor who has heard the crash calls to ask, "What was that?" The wife says, "Diet Dr. Pepper. It tastes more like regular Dr. Pepper." The neighbor asks, "Can I try one?" and the vending machine crashes through to her floor. This spot was intended to encourage repeat usage and expanded trial. Whenever possible pairs of these spots were shown at the beginning and end of commercial pods or at the beginning and end of program segments to reinforce the connections between them.

"Bottler-driven" marketing programs supplemented the television portion of the campaign. These programs included a distribution allowance to retailers who agreed to add new package types to their stock, a bonus pack—15 cans instead of the usual 12—to encourage trial, and coupons good for a price reduction on another Diet Dr. Pepper purchase.

In spite of the marketing obstacles described above, Diet Dr. Pepper achieved its 1991 reintroduction objectives. Gallonage and case sales increased more than 100 percent. Advertising awareness grew from 0.8 percent in 1990 to 7.0 per cent in the last quarter of 1991. Diet Dr. Pepper gained new users, more than half of whom said they had tried the reformulated product because it tastes more like regular Dr. Pepper. Among triers of the new Diet Dr. Pepper, more than nine out of ten purchased it more than once.

Having met its reintroduction objectives, Diet Dr. Pepper's challenge for 1992 was to continue its sales momentum in a marketplace characterized by both category-specific and franchise-specific problems. The principle category-specific problem was that category growth had slowed dramatically. Consumers were not switching to diet soft drinks as rapidly as before. The franchise-specific problems were hold-overs from 1991. Despite the doubling of its business, Diet. Dr. Pepper still had a smaller than 1 percent share of the carbonated soft drink market. Because it was not sold as often "on deal," Diet Dr. Pepper was still priced considerably higher than Coca-Cola and Pepsi-Cola products. Diet Dr. Pepper still had channel problems—inadequate distribution at soda fountains and vending machines. Diet Dr. Pepper was still being distributed via the Coca-Cola and Pepsi-Cola bottler networks, where it received relatively low priority and retail support. In advertising and promotion, it was still being vastly outspent.

The campaign objectives for 1992 were: (1) Continue to increase sales by one and one-half times

CLIENT: DR PEPPER
PRODUCT: DIET DR PEPPER
TITLE: "PHONE CALL"

LENGTH: 15 SECONDS
COMM. NO.: DPYS 1030
DATE: APRIL 1991

SFX: PHONE RINGING

This is Thelma downstairs. What was that?

WOMAN: Diet Dr Pepper. Tastes more like regular Dr Pepper.

VOICE ON PHONE: Really. Can I try one?
WOMAN: I'll send George down.

SFX: FLOOR BREAKING

V/O and SUPER: There's no stopping the taste.

projected growth of the diet soft drink category. (2) Grow the Diet Dr. Pepper franchise so that Diet Dr. Pepper is the number one diet non-cola. (3) Position Diet Dr. Pepper as a mainstream brand while maintaining its unique and distinctive "reason for being." (4) Continue to generate trial and repeat usage among likely prospects and current Dr. Pepper users.

The creative strategy—that Diet Dr. Pepper now tastes more like regular Dr. Pepper—continued, as did the crashing Diet Dr. Pepper vending machine. However, the machine now crashed into additional environments—an office-building stairwell, a china shop, a busy city intersection, and a desert movie, for example. As in 1991, these executions included the tagline, "there's no stopping the taste."

To attain increased visibility, the media strategy incorporated highly visible major sporting events such as sponsorships of the National Football League Championship Games, National Basketball Association Championships, the NFL/NBC Game of the Month, and the National and American Baseball Leagues' Championship Series. The media strategy also incorporated such prime-time specials as David Letterman's

10th Anniversary and celebrity interviews by Barbara Walters. To provide continuity, Young & Rubicam purchased time on syndicated and network television programs throughout the soft-drink selling season.

In the fourth quarter of 1991, a "Peel a Pepper" promotion gave consumers a chance to win a free two-liter bottle of Dr. Pepper by peeling back specially marked bottles of Dr. Pepper products. In the first quarter of 1992, a three-phase mailing to key retailers and beverage bottlers described the "little known bigness" of Dr. Pepper in the marketplace, and a "Hover Over Hawaii" Sweepstakes boosted sales in supermarkets. In the second quarter, a "Pepper Pay Day" promotion gave consumers a chance to win Dr. Pepper soft drinks and Pay Day candy bars in convenience stores.

As a result of this integrated marketing communication program, Diet Dr. Pepper's case sales grew more than 18 percent in 1992, making Diet Dr. Pepper the best selling and fastest-growing diet soft drink in America. In brand personality surveys, more than 80 percent of respondents rated Diet Dr. Pepper as "popular," and more than 90 percent rated it "distinctive" and "unique."

Diet Dr. Pepper's successful relaunch—and its advertising and marketing problems and strategies—continued the following year. By 1993, Diet Dr. Pepper had become a strong and viable player in the carbonated soft drink category. However, in addition to the price, distribution, and share-of-advertising handicaps it had faced in 1991 and 1992, Diet Dr. Pepper now faced a lingering economic recession that encouraged consumers to purchase private label soft drinks and to pay increased attention to the relative prices of national brands. Diet Dr. Pepper also faced increasing competition from "New Age" beverages (natural sodas, flavored waters, and sparking juices) that were claiming a growing "share-of-thirst."

The objectives of the 1993 campaign, called "The taste you've been looking for," were: (1) Continue to increase sales by one and one-half times the growth of the diet soft drink category. (2) Strengthen and solidify Diet Dr. Pepper's newly attained position as the nation's number one diet noncola. (3) Communicate key brand personality characteristics—fun, clever, entertaining, and unique. (4) Increase use of Diet Dr. Pepper in general but specifically among males and among older segments of the target audience—segments that were keys to future growth.

Although the main creative strategy—that Diet Dr. Pepper tastes more like regular Dr. Pepper—continued, the crashing vending machine executions did not. Now, the television advertising placed Diet Dr. Pepper in a variety of realistic but fanciful settings—a law school lecture hall, a desert gas station, a championship golf course, a water rescue, and so on. In each setting, characters (or, in two executions, voice-over choruses) seized opportunities to underline the campaign's main idea: "Diet Dr. Pepper does taste more like regular Dr. Pepper."

As in previous years, the broadcast media strategy included highly visible events: National Football League Championship Games, the national Country Music Awards, American and National Baseball League Championship Series and the NBC/NFL Game of the Month. It also included prime-time network, cable, and syndicated television programs favored by the target group; and local radio and television spots.

New sales promotions reinforced the broadcast advertising. In the first quarter, an "American Traveler Game" gave consumers a chance to win a year's worth of free travel by peeling labels off specially marked two-liter bottles. In the second quarter, "Pepper Pick Up" gave consumers a chance to win a Chevrolet Pickup truck and other prizes by discovering prize descriptions written inside the bottoms of specially marked Diet Dr. Pepper cans. In the third quarter, "Peel-a Pepper" gave

consumers a chance to win two-liter bottles of Diet Dr. Pepper by peeling back specially marked Diet Dr. Pepper products. Bottlers supported these promotions with point-of-purchase materials, radio tags, and 10-second TV tags.

In 1993, Diet Dr. Pepper's sales grew more than 8 percent, exceeding both the average growth of the diet soft drink category and the growth of sparkling waters. In a test of "Lift," one of the advertisements in the "taste you've been looking for" campaign, more than two-thirds of the respondents rated the commercial "fun," "clever," and "entertaining." "Lift," and the "taste you've been looking for" campaign of which it was a part, received the American Marketing Association's "Gold Effie"—the association's top effectiveness award.

When a brand is in decline, one alternative is to discontinue it. In this case, a reformulated product—backed by new packaging, new promotion, and award-winning advertising—revived a franchise that could have been in its last days.

Questions for Discussion

1. Given Diet Dr. Pepper's advertising and marketing situation in 1991, what arguments would favor salvaging the brand? What arguments would favor discontinuing it?

2. Given Diet Dr. Pepper's advertising and marketing situation in 1991, and given a decision to salvage the brand, what advertising and marketing measures—other than those taken—would have been available?

3. What do you think of the "crashing vending machine" idea? Can you think of an alternative that would have been just as effective? Explain.

4. Diet Dr. Pepper discontinued a successful creative execution—the crashing vending machine—after that execution had run its course. How can an advertiser determine when to discontinue an execution that has worked well?

5. Throughout its relaunch, Diet Dr. Pepper faced both "category-specific" and "franchise-specific" problems. Think of another brand, described in a previous chapter, that faced those two kinds of problems. How were those problems. overcome? In what ways are the two cases similar? In what ways are they different?

6. Trace and criticize the evolution of Diet Dr. Pepper's media strategy.

7. Diet Dr. Pepper's relaunch provides an example of a successful integrated marketing communication campaign. In addition to advertising, what were that campaign's primary elements? What other elements might have been used?

CAREERS IN ADVERTISING

The American Association of Advertising Agencies publishes a brochure entitled "Go For It: A Guide to Careers in Advertising," which provides detailed job descriptions and advice for pursuing a career in advertising. The material found in this appendix provides a more in-depth look at agency positions, their requirements and career opportunities, as well as helpful information on preparing a résumé and for a job interview.

JOBS IN AN ADVERTISING AGENCY

As you have seen in these chapters, agencies handle a broad range of tasks requiring people with experience and ability in overall management as well as specialized fields. In a small agency, one person may wear several hats, such as media planner and buyer, whereas at a large agency some people will tend to specialize, such as a network television buyer. In all agencies, however, the jobs usually fall into five categories:

- Account management
- Creative
- Media
- Market research
- Support services and administration

ACCOUNT MANAGEMENT

At an agency, the client and its business are usually called "the account." One advertiser may offer many products or services and ask separate agencies to handle each one. Another may use a single agency to handle several products or services. No matter what the particular situation, the account management department is where the resources of the agency and the needs of the client connect.

The account manager oversees the advertising business that has been assigned to the agency and is ultimately responsible for the quality of service the client receives. The account manager serves as the client's representative at the agency and the agency's representative at the client's organization. It is his or her job to get the client its money's worth—to get the best possible work from the agency for the client—but at a profitable return for the agency. This means knowing how to handle people at the agency so that they give the client their best effort without spending more time than the income from the client's business justifies.

The effective account manager develops a thorough knowledge of the client's business, the consumer, the marketplace, and all aspects of advertising, including creative, media, research, and commercial production. As team leader and strategist, the account person must communicate the client's needs clearly to the agency team, plan effectively to maximize staff time and energy, and present the agency's recommendations candidly to the client. He or she must also know all about the agency: who are the most qualified people in each department and how to get their attention when it is needed.

The account manager must also know all about the client, enthusiastically learning every aspect of the client's business—ideally, from product development through the entire marketing operation—well enough to command the client's respect when presenting the agency's recommendations. In the final analysis, the account person must be able to foster productive communication between client and agency staffs, identify common goals, and make sure that the final product is profitable and effective for the client and the agency.

ENTRY-LEVEL POSITIONS

Assistant Account Executive (Manager) The typical assistant account executive reports directly to an account executive and has a wide range of responsibilities. Some common duties include reporting client billing and forecasting agency income, analyzing competitive activity and consumer trends, writing conference reports from meetings, and coordinating creative, media, research, and production projects.

Successful candidates have strong general business skills, the ability to write and spell effectively, demonstrated leadership experience, a capability for statistical analysis, and developed organizational skills. In addition, it is important to be able to work well under pressure, handle a variety of tasks simultaneously, and coordinate the work and energy of diverse types of people, as well as to have creative sensibility and an intense interest in advertising and marketing.

Candidates for this position should have a bachelor's degree and, in some cases, a master of business administration. A degree in advertising or marketing is not a prerequisite. Within the agency business, agency account management and media departments hire the greatest number of entry-level candidates. Some of the large agencies offer entry-level training programs in account management.

Career Opportunities An entry-level position in account management usually leads to account executive and then to more senior positions, with responsibility for more than one account and for the work of several account executives. Ultimately, account management can assume broader office and corporate positions. Currently the largest percentage of top agency management positions are filled from the ranks of the account management department.

CREATIVE

The creative department of an advertising agency is responsible for developing the ideas, images, and words that make up commercials and ads. Although many people contribute to the process, the invention and production of advertising is mainly the responsibility of copywriters and art directors.

When a copywriter and art director are assigned to an account, they must learn about the product or service to be advertised, marketing strategy, consumer or potential consumer, media to be used, advertising by competitors, production budget, and the client personnel (such as brand managers) with whom the agency deals. The research, account management, and media departments provide basic information on all these topics. However, the creative people will most likely want to gain first-hand experience with the client's product.

After the creative people assimilate as much information as possible, they agree on a general direction. The art director and copywriter work as a team trying out ideas first on each other, on the creative director, and on the other agency groups working on the account. These executions are reviewed by senior members of the agency (including legal counsel), sometimes called the review board, to evaluate whether they match the goals of the marketing and advertising strategy.

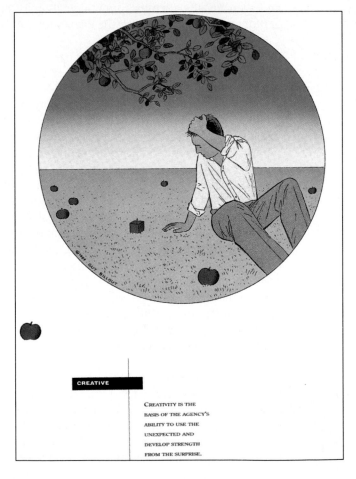

CREATIVE

CREATIVITY IS THE
BASIS OF THE AGENCY'S
ABILITY TO USE THE
UNEXPECTED AND
DEVELOP STRENGTH
FROM THE SURPRISE.

The reviewed creative executions are presented to the client for approval. Once the client approves, the art director and copywriter work with print and broadcast production people to produce the final version of the advertisement. Magazines and newspapers require camera-ready copy. To prepare such print advertisements, agencies rely on outside services, from photographers to type-setters. Agency specialists in print production oversee this contracted work. Television stations require videotape; radio stations must have audio tape. Broadcast commercials often involve a large cast of outside specialists. Agency producers oversee the completion of television and radio commercials. They hire directors, production studios with film crews, and actors. In addition, produc-ers administer the budget, work with composers and musicians, and participate in the review and editing of the rough film or videotape into the final version.

ENTRY-LEVEL POSITIONS

Junior Copywriter A junior copywriter assists one or more copywriters in edit-ing and proofreading ad copy, writing body copy for established print cam-paigns, and developing merchandising and sales promotion materials. With proven ability and experience, assignments might include generating ideas for product or company names and writing dialog for television commercials and scripts for radio ads.

A successful candidate not only has outstanding skills in writing but has a "love affair" with words and symbols and their use in communication. Interest in a wide range of subjects and an insatiable sense of curiosity are assets. Candidates should have some knowledge of marketing and how words and visu-als have been used in advertising.

Agencies expect job candidates to demonstrate their talent by showing port-folios of previous creative work, seminal ideas, and "rough" designs of potential campaigns, even if they were done in the classroom or on your own. Although a bachelor's degree is not required, most agencies look for candidates with proven intellectual ability and emotional maturity. Degrees in English, journal-ism, or advertising and marketing can be helpful. Opportunities for candidates who have no writing experience are limited. Some of the largest agencies offer entry-level training programs in copywriting.

Junior or Assistant Art Director The junior art director assists one or more art directors in preparing paste-ups, rough lettering, and layouts for print ads and television storyboards, developing visual concepts and designs, and overseeing photo sessions and the filming of television commercials.

A successful candidate will have strong visual concept skills and good basic drawing and design ability. Although an assistant art director must be capable of handling day-to-day lettering and matting tasks, agencies are also interested in identifying candidates with visual imagination and an interest in applying that ability to marketing and advertising problems.

Agencies expect candidates to show portfolios displaying their basic draw-ing skills and roughs of ideas for potential advertising campaigns. Although a bachelor's degree is not required, most agencies look for candidates with at least a two-year degree from an art or design school. Entry-level opportunities are very limited for candidates with only some related business experience, such as in a retail advertising department.

Career Opportunities An entry-level position as junior copywriter leads to copywriter. An entry-level position as a junior art director leads to art director. In these more senior positions, each is given more responsibility and freedom in developing the visual and copy ideas for campaigns and may work on more than one account or on accounts that make special demands.

The position of art director or copywriter can lead to creative supervisor, the professional responsible for the work of a group of copywriters or art directors. More senior positions usually include creative group head, responsible for supervising teams of art directors and copywriters as well as production functions; creative director, responsible for all creative work produced by the agency for either all clients or a group of clients; and chief or executive creative director, responsible for overall creative work in a division, region, or company-wide. Senior creative people are important to the overall management of an agency. Many of them reach top agency management positions.

$\mathcal{M}$EDIA

Even the most innovative and highly creative advertising in the world can fail if it is presented to the wrong audience or if it is presented at the wrong time or in the wrong place. The media department of an advertising agency is responsible for placing advertising where it will reach the right people in the right place and do so in a cost-effective way.

To bring advertising messages to the public, agencies must use a carrier, called a medium of communication or simply a medium. The four most commonly used media are television, radio, magazines, and newspapers. Some other media include billboards, posters, printed bulletins, and even skywriting.

Planning and buying media at an advertising agency is exciting and challenging because ways of communicating are constantly changing and becoming more complex. Such technological advances as cable television or videotext make an impact on what media are available for advertising and how viewership is calculated. A recent increase in the number of specialty publications enables more precise targeting of consumers. Today, more than ever, agencies and clients are recognizing the importance of creative and innovative media planning and buying.

When working on a particular advertising campaign, the media planners discuss, with the client and other agency people, the goals of the marketing strategy as well as a description of the potential consumer. As planners, they think about the kinds of media the target group might read, listen to, or watch. They compare the content, image, and format of each medium with the nature of the product or service, its image, and the goals of the advertising campaign. In discussions with the creative department and account team, planners suggest which media can be used most effectively to reach the target audience.

The media department is responsible for developing a plan that answers the question: How can the greatest number of people in the target group be reached often enough to have the advertising message seen and remembered—and at the lowest possible cost? Once the media plan has been developed, presented to the client, and approved, the department's media buyers start negotiating for space and time. Buyers purchase space in which to display their messages in print media. They buy time in the broadcast media.

Buyers must not only find and reserve available space and time, but also negotiate the best price. Will a station offer a lower price if more time slots are bought? Will prime time be discounted if the buyer is willing to purchase, in addition, some less desirable time in the morning or late at night? Buyers who have outstanding negotiating skills are valuable assets to any agency's media department.

After the space and time have been purchased, the department must monitor the media to make sure that the advertising actually appeared, in the proper form and at the proper time as it was ordered. If a discrepancy occurs, the department negotiates an adjustment to the billing or accepts a credit for additional time or space.

ENTRY-LEVEL POSITIONS

Assistant Media Planner The typical assistant media planner reports to a media planner and gathers and studies information about people's viewing and reading habits, evaluates editorial content and programming of various media vehicles, calculates reach and frequency for specific target groups and campaigns, learns all there is to know about the media in general (magazines, newspapers, radio, television) and about media vehicles in particular (*Time, The Wall Street Journal*), and becomes thoroughly familiar with media data banks and information sources.

Accomplishing these tasks requires the ability to find and analyze data, apply computer skills, ask innovative questions, and interpret or explain findings with attention to quantitative and qualitative considerations. In short, a planner must gain knowledge of what information is important and where to find it. By assisting in gathering statistics to support a variety of plans, he or she eventually becomes familiar with broader characteristics and trends in all media.

Assistant Media Buyer The typical assistant media buyer reports directly to a media buyer and knows when and where space and time are available for purchase, reconciles agency media orders with what actually appears, calculates rates, usage, and budget, learns buying terminology and operating procedures, develops skills in negotiation and communication with media sales representatives, and becomes familiar with the media market. Accomplishing these tasks requires ease at working with numbers and budgets, outstanding communication skills, and the ability to work under pressure. Skills in negotiation and sales are especially advantageous.

Successful candidates have strong general business skills: the ability to write and speak effectively, developed organizational skills, aptitude for working with numbers and statistics, and basic computer skills. In addition, other important attributes are working well under pressure, maintaining priorities while handling a variety of tasks simultaneously, the ability and desire to interact with a wide range of personalities at the agency, the client, and within the media industry, an intense curiosity and interest in all types of media and their role in the marketing process, and understanding of sales and negotiation concepts (leverage, timing, and positioning), and a winning personal attitude.

Candidates should have a bachelor's degree. A degree in advertising or marketing is not a prerequisite. In most agencies, the media department, along with account management, hires the greatest number of entry-level candidates. Most larger agencies offer entry-level training programs in media.

The organization of a media department varies with the size of the agency.

In large agencies, a person may specialize by medium, whereas in small and medium-sized agencies each person may handle all media. The media function is headed by a media director, who usually reports to the highest level of management.

Career Opportunities An entry-level position as an assistant media planner usually leads to media planner, the person responsible for developing a media plan. An entry-level position as an assistant media buyer usually leads to media buyer, responsible for negotiating time and space. It is common for the planner and buyer to develop expertise in specific media categories, such as magazine or network or spot television. In a small agency, the two jobs may be combined.

The next step is supervisory. The media planning supervisor coordinates the work of planners and presents recommendations to the account group and client. The broadcast buying supervisor oversees buying operations.

With greater knowledge and experience, media people advance to any of several positions—associate media director, manager of media research, network supervisor, director of spot broadcast, groups media director, director of programming and negotiations, and media director. Many agencies have top media people represented in senior management and as members of their boards of directors.

$\mathcal{M}$ARKET RESEARCH

The basic role of the market research department in an advertising agency is to understand the wants, desires, thoughts, concerns, motivating forces, and ideas of the consumer. By researching secondary information, conducting focus groups or one-on-one interviews, testing people's reactions to new advertising copy, tracking sales volume, or studying buying trends, the advertising agency researcher becomes an expert on consumer behavior.

Most researchers are assigned to specific accounts and work as advisors to the account, creative, and media people. They help develop, refine, and evaluate potential strategies and are called on to react to possible creative approaches based on their understanding of the consumer. This might be done with the creative team during the process or with account managers as evaluators of creative alternatives.

Some agencies also employ researchers who specialize in specific areas of quantitative or qualitative research. Consumer trends and lifestyle research are two ares in which most large agencies maintain continuing studies. Findings from these specialized studies tend to have an impact on all agency clients as well as on the process of creating advertising. In addition, the research department oversees projects that are subcontracted to "out-of-house" research firms. A typical example is surveys of shoppers at malls. The agency researchers design the questionnaire and interpret results, but a private firm conducts the interviews and summarizes the data so the researcher can write a report on the survey.

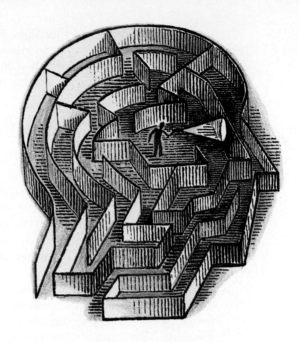

ENTRY-LEVEL POSITIONS

Assistant Research Executive. The typical assistant reports directly to a research executive. Duties usually include compiling data from secondary resources, following the progress of research projects, assisting in the development of primary research tools, and learning to analyze facts and numbers, interpreting and explaining what these really mean.

Successful candidates have strong quantitative skills and the aptitude for analyzing and interpreting qualitative as well as quantitative data. Computer literacy is also advantageous. In addition, candidates should be able to write and speak effectively, work well under pressure, and organize work priorities. They should have an interest in forecasting trends and patterns and a fascination with human behavior and motivation.

A bachelor's degree is the minimum requirement, but it is not unusual to find people who have master's or doctorate degrees employed in agency research departments. Although a specific major is not a prerequisite, many employers are attracted to candidates whose coursework is related to research. Some academic disciplines fitting this category are sociology, psychology, marketing, marketing research, economics, journalism, quantitative methods, anthropology, and mass communications.

Entry-level positions in agency research departments are relatively rare, especially in medium- and small-sized agencies. Candidates who have only bachelor's or master's degrees and no experience might find some opportunities at the largest agencies or at research firms.

Career Opportunities An entry-level position as an assistant research executive usually leads to a supervisory position with responsibility for managing research on individual accounts or brands overseeing the work of assistant research executives. During this stage a person might identify a personal interest in a specific research area and seek to specialize. The next step is management of a specialized research function or responsibility for all research on more than one account. Ultimately, a research person may have the opportunity to move into more general corporate management or marketing functions.

Support Services

Like any well-run business, the advertising agency must maintain a full complement of people who handle accounting, personnel, clerical, and office services. In addition, agency traffic managers make sure than, once started, an ad or commercial moves smoothly through the agency, additions and corrections are obtained, and the whole job arrives at the publication or the broadcast station on time.

Cost controllers monitor agency costs, making sure that work stays within budget or that everyone is aware of, and approves, any needed changes in the budget. Other agency employees may include lawyers, librarians, and certain specialists. For example, agencies with big food or packaged-goods accounts sometimes keep nutritionists and home economists on staff. Those with health products or medical accounts may employ physicians. Such diversity is one more aspect that makes agency work such a fascinating and rewarding career choice.

Preparing for a Career in Advertising

Breaking into advertising is not easy. Most jobs require a college degree. Internships and related work experience can be helpful. Retail selling experience is also excellent preparation. In addition to all this, however, getting a job in an advertising agency requires determination for two reasons. First, there are few job openings, and second, a lot of other bright people, like yourself, want those jobs, too. This year alone many agencies will receive thousands of inquiries for entry-level opportunities. Of this number, a very large agency might hire only 30. In short, there are many more people interested in working at agencies than there are openings. Nothing guarantees a job with an agency, but there are seven basic steps you should consider.

1. EDUCATE YOURSELF ABOUT THE BUSINESS

Find out as much as possible about the advertising business, what an agency does, and the career area or department in which you would like to work. Read every bit of relevant material you can find—articles, books, and such trade journals as *Advertising Age, Mediaweek,* and *Adweek.*

Talk to people. Track down any contacts or friends you have in the business. Sit down with your college instructors and career counselors. Make inquiries at such professional organizations as the American Association of Advertising Agencies, Advertising Women of New York, the American Advertising Foundations, or your local advertising club. Find out about seminars and attend them. One source of information can lead you to ten others. The more you know about your chosen area, the better you can present yourself as a first-rate candidate.

2. TARGET YOUR PROSPECTS

Decide what factors are important to you about a company and evaluate prospective employers on that basis. Make use of the *Standard Directory of Advertising Agencies,* popularly known as the "Agency Red Book." It is available at most libraries and lists all the agencies worldwide. It gives names and titles of key people, size of the agency (in dollar billings, number of offices, and total personnel), the agency's accounts, and a breakdown of the media in which the agency invests its client' money.

Read the trade press to learn more about specific agencies you want to target. For example, *Advertising Age* prints a special issue each year that provides profiles of individual agency business activity during the previous 12 months. It also selects an "agency of the year" and publishes an in-depth description.

3. DEVELOP A STRATEGY

With all the competition for jobs in advertising, you must develop your own "unique selling proposition" to communicate your own unique qualities. It is not enough that you are interested in advertising, or that you made dean's list eight times, or that you wrote for the school newspaper. So did most of your competition. You have to connect what you have done in the past, in a unique way, to what you will do for the agency in the future. Developing a strategy gets your commitment, imagination, and analytical thinking out in the limelight. It is the key to making you stand out from other candidates.

4. CREATE A GOOD RÉSUMÉ

The primary purpose of a résumé is to get you an interview. Used correctly, it can open doors. Used incorrectly, it slams them shut. A good résumé connects your experience to your job goal. Support your candidacy by highlighting relevant skills, such as writing, speaking, managing, and so on. Include any activities, jobs, or internships directly related to advertising. Did you sell space for the school's newspaper? Were you yearbook editor? Or stage manager for the college theater group? Add less related activities only if they are outstanding. Be selective. Your résumé is a selling tool, not a life history. Keep it neat, clear, precise, and all on one page. Try to make it unique and interesting but not gimmicky.

5. TAKE PAINS WITH EACH COVER LETTER

A cover letter works hand in hand with your résumé. Together they create a first impression of you. Your cover letter should work as a connecting tool between you and the agency you are writing to. Don't let it read like a form letter. Instead, include real knowledge of the agency, its clients, its work, and its position in the industry. Tell the agency why you are interested in them and why you think you'd be right for them. Then make sure that you are prepared to discuss in your interview whatever you say in the cover letter. Remember, you are being judged on communicative skill. Watch spelling, grammar, and typing. Most importantly, be clear, crisp, and brief.

6. ASSEMBLE A PORTFOLIO

To help you get a job in an agency creative department, you must prepare a portfolio that shows your thinking and imagination. If you are an aspiring art director, this clearly has to include ample demonstration of your design ability and graphic sense. If you want to be a copywriter, visuals are less critical than is demonstration of your writing ability and marketing sense.

In either case, show your very best work. If you have not had any experience, pick some currently running campaigns, determine their objectives, and interpret them in your own way. It doesn't matter if your "ads" are not professional. Your prospective employer wants to see fresh concepts and new ideas that prove you have potential. Then keep making changes to improve your portfolio. For more specific suggestions, see Maxine Paetro's book on building portfolios, entitled *How to Put Your Book Together and Get a Job in Advertising*.

7. PREPARE FOR YOUR INTERVIEW

At most agencies, an invitation to be interviewed reflects more than casual interest in a candidate. If you have made it this far, you're at least in the quarterfinals. And if you've done your homework, you should have nothing to worry about.

Before the interview, organize your thinking. Review your résumé and the cover letter you sent the agency. Decide what key selling points you should communicate about yourself. Think how you can best do this. Review the information you have about the agency. Be aware of its current campaigns and any fast-breaking developments. Commenting on these can help you make an immediate connection with the interviewer.

Be ready to discuss your point of view on advertising in general and your area of interest in particular. Be articulate. Be self-confident and enthusiastic, but relax and do it naturally. Don't try to recite everything you know. Selectivity shows you are thinking.

Remember, someone is interested enough in your background to invest 30 minutes or more in you. That person wants you to succeed.

Source: Courtesy of The American Association of Advertising Agencies.

GLOSSARY

A

Account management (p. 135) The function within an advertising agency that maintains liaison with the client, supervises day-to-day work and development of recommendations and plans.

Account planner (p. 218) The person responsible for the creation, implementation, and modification of the strategy on which creative work is based.

Adese (p. 448) Formula writing that uses clichés, generalities, stock phrases, and superlatives.

Advertiser (p. 16) The individual or organization that initiates the advertising process.

Advertising (p. 11) Paid nonpersonal communication from an identified sponsor using mass media to persuade or influence an audience.

Advertising campaign (p. 647) A comprehensive advertising plan for a series of different but related ads that appear in different media across a specified time period.

Advertising plan (p. 246) A plan that proposes strategies for targeting the audience, presenting the advertising message, and implementing media.

Advocacy advertising (p. 623) A type of corporate advertising that involves creating advertisements and purchasing space to deliver a specific, targeted message.

Affiliate (p. 363) A station that is contracted with a national network to carry network-originated programming during part of its schedule.

Agricultural advertising (p. 705) Advertising directed at large and small farmers.

Allocations (p. 404) Division or proportions of advertising dollars among the various media.

Animatic (p. 502) A preliminary version of a commercial with the storyboard frames recorded on videotape along with a rough sound track.

Animation (p. 498) A type of recording medium in which objects are sketched and then filmed one frame at a time.

Answer print (p. 506) The final finished version of the commercial with the audio and video recorded together.

Aperture (p. 297) The ideal moment for exposing consumers to an advertising message.

Appeal (p. 280) Something that moves people.

Arranger (p. 502) The person who orchestrates the music, arranging it for the various instruments, voices, and scenes.

Art (p. 457) The visual elements in an ad, including illustrations, photos, type, logos and signatures, and the layout.

Art director (p. 446) The person who is primarily responsible for the visual image of the advertisment.

Attitude (p. 188) A learned predisposition that we hold toward an object, person, or ideal.

B

Benefits (p. 260) Statements about what the product can do for the user.

Body copy (p. 460) The text of the message.

Brag-and-boast copy (p. 448) Advertising text that is written from the company's point of view to extol its virtues and accomplishments.

Brainstorming (p. 429) A creative-thinking technique using free association in a group environment to stimulate inspiration.

Brand equity (p. 284) The use of a respected brand name to add value to a product.

Brand image (p. 283) The mental image that reflects the way a brand is perceived, including all the identification elements, the product personality, and the emotions and associations evoked in the mind of the consumer.

Branding (p. 98) The process of creating an identity for a product using a distinctive name or symbol.

Brand loyalty (p. 279) Existing positive opinions held by consumers about the product or service.

Broadsheet (p. 332) A newspaper with a size of eight columns wide and 22 inches deep.

Broadsheets (p. 541) Large brochures that unfold like a map.

Business strategic plan (p. 239) An overriding business plan that deals with the broadest decisions made by the organization.

Business-to-business advertising (p. 703) Advertising directed at people who buy or specify products for business use.

Business unit (p. 133) A cluster of related products or services that functions as if it were a company within a larger corporation.

C

Cable television (p. 364) A form of subscription television in which the signals are carried to households by a cable.

Car cards (p. 574) Small advertisements that are mounted in racks inside a vehicle.

Carry-over effect (p. 308) A measure of residual effect (awareness or recall) of the advertising message some time after the advertising period has ended.

Cease-and-desist order (p. 73) A legal order requiring the advertiser to stop its unlawful practices.

Channel of distribution (p. 100) People and organizations involved in moving products from producers to consumers.

Circulation (p. 334) A measure of the number of copies sold.

Claim (p. 259) A statement about the product's performance.

Classified advertising (p. 339) Commercial message arranged in the newspaper according to the interests of readers.

Claymation (p. 498) A technique that uses figures sculpted from clay and filmed one frame at a time.

Cliché (p. 424) A trite expression, an overused idea.

Cognitive dissonance (p. 183) A tendency to justify the discrepancy between what a person receives relative to what he or she expected to receive.

Color separation (p. 479) The process of splitting a color image into four images recorded on negatives; each negative represents one of the four process colors.

Commission (p. 145) A form of payment in which an agent or agency receives a certain percentage (historically 15 percent) of media charges.

Composer (p. 502) The person who writes the music.

Comprehensive (p. 470) A layout that looks as much like the final printed ad as possible.

Consent decree (p. 73) An order given by the FTC and signed by an advertiser, agreeing to stop running a deceptive ad.

Consumers (p. 163) People who buy or use products.

Contests (p. 600) Sales promotion activities that require participants to compete for a prize on the basis of some skill or ability.

Continuity (p. 308) The strategy and tactics used to schedule advertising over the time span of the advertising campaign.

Continuity program (p. 604) A program that requires the consumer to continue purchasing the product or service in order to receive a reward.

Convergent thinking (p. 427) Thinking that uses logic to arrive at the "right" answer.

Conviction (p. 280) A particularly strong belief that has been anchored firmly in the attitude structure.

Cooperative advertising (p. 101) A form of advertising in which the manufacturer reimburses the retailer for part or all of the retailer's advertising expenditures.

Copy (p. 457) The written elements in an ad, including headlines, underlines and overlines, subheads, body copy, captions, slogans, and taglines.

Copywriter (p. 446) The person who writes the text for an ad.

Corporate identity advertising (p. 630) A type of advertising used by firms to establish their reputation or increase awareness.

Corporate/institutional advertising (p. 621) Advertising used to create a favorable public attitude toward the sponsoring organization.

Corrective advertising (p. 74) A remedy required by the FTC in which an advertiser who produced misleading messages is required to issue factual information to offset these messages.

Cost per rating (CPR) (p. 314) A method of comparing media vehicles by relating the cost of the message unit to the audience rating.

Cost per thousand (CPM) (p. 314) The cost of exposing each 1,000 members of the target audience to the advertising message.

Cost trends (p. 402) A history of changes in the average unit (per message) prices for each medium that is used in cost forecasting.

Coupons (p. 598) Legal certificates offered by manufacturers and retailers that grant specified savings on selected products when presented for redemption at the point of purchase.

CPM trends (p. 403) Longitudinal (long-term) history of average cost-per-thousand tendencies of advertising media that is used to assist in forecasting future CPM levels.

Crawl (p. 497) Computer-generated letters that move across the bottom of the screen.

Creative concept (p. 421) A "big idea" that is original and dramatizes the selling point.

Creative platform (p. 258) A document that outlines the message strategy decisions behind an individual ad.

Cultural and social influences (p. 167) The forces that other people exert on your behavior.

Culture (p. 167) The complex whole of tangible items, intangible concepts, and social behaviors that define a group of people or a way of life.

Cut (p. 498) An abrupt transition from one shot to another.

Cutouts (p. 566) Irregularly shaped extensions added to the top, bottom, or sides of standard outdoor boards.

Databases (p. 522) Lists of consumers with information that helps target and segment those who are highly likely to be in the market for a certain product.

Data sheets (p. 714) Advertising that provides detailed technical information.

Dealer loader (p. 610) A premium given to a retailer by a manufacturer for buying a certain quantity of product.

Dealer tag (p. 719) Time left at the end of a broadcast advertisement that permits identification of the local store.

Demography (p. 173) The study of social and economic factors that influence human behavior.

Diagnostic research (p. 223) Research used to identify the best approach from among a set of alternatives.

Directional advertising (p. 555) Advertising that directs the buyer to the store where the product or service is available.

Direct marketing (p. 523) A type of marketing that uses media to contact a prospect directly and elicit a response without the intervention of a retailer or personal sales.

Director (p. 502) The person in charge of the actual filming or taping of the commercial.

Direct-response advertising (p. 529) A type of marketing communication that achieves an action-oriented objective as a result of the advertising message.

Direct-response counts (p. 686) Evaluation

tests that count the number of viewers or readers who request more information or who purchase the product.

Discretionary income (p. 178) The money available for spending after taxes and necessities are covered.

Display advertising (p. 339) Sponsored messages that can be of any size and location within the newspaper, with the exception of the editorial page.

Display copy (p. 460) Type set in larger sizes that is used to attract the reader's attention.

Divergent thinking (p. 427) Thinking that uses free association to uncover all possible alternatives.

Drama (p. 438) A story built around characters in a situation.

Dubbing (p. 506) The process of making duplicate copies of a videotape.

E

Early feedback (p. 223) Preliminary reactions to alternative creative strategies.

Editor (p. 502) The person who assembles the best shots to create scenes and who synchronizes the audio track with the images.

Effective frequency (p. 313) A recent concept in planning that determines a range (minimum and maximum) of repeat exposure for a message.

Evaluative research (p. 674) Research intended to measure the effectiveness of finished or nearly finished advertisements.

Exchange (p. 87) The process whereby two or more parties give up a desired resource to one another.

Execution (p. 422) The form taken by the finished advertisement.

Experiments (p. 224) A research method that manipulates a set of variables to test hypotheses.

Exploratory research (p. 210) Informal intelligence gathering, backgrounding.

Extensions (p. 566) Embellishments to painted

billboards that expand the scale and break away from the standard rectangle limitations.

Exterior transit advertising (p. 574) Advertising posters that are mounted on the sides, rear, and top of vehicles.

F

Family (p. 171) Two or more people who are related by blood, marriage, or adoption and live in the same household.

Feature analysis (p. 252) A comparison of your product's features against the features of competing products.

Federal Communications Commission (FCC) (p. 77) A federal agency that regulates broadcast media and has the power to eliminate messages, including ads, that are deceptive or in poor taste.

Federal Trade Commission (FTC) (p. 66) A federal agency responsible for interpreting deceptive advertising and regulating unfair methods of competition.

Fee (p. 148) A mode of payment in which an agency charges a client on the basis of the agency's hourly rates.

Film (p. 497) A strip of celluloid with a series of still images, called frames.

Flighting (p. 308) An advertising scheduling pattern characterized by a period of intensified activity called a flight, followed by a period of no advertising, called a hiatus.

Focal point (p. 472) The first element in a layout that the eye sees.

Focus group (p. 210) A group interview that tries to stimulate people to talk candidly about some topics or products.

Font (p. 475) A complete set of letters in one size and face.

Food and Drug Administration (FDA) (p. 77) A federal regulatory agency that oversees package labeling and ingredient listings for food and drugs.

Frame-by-frame tests (p. 690) Tests that evaluate consumers' reactions to the individual scenes that unfold in the course of a television commercial.

Free association (p. 426) An exercise in which you describe everything that comes into your mind when you think of a word or an image.

Freelance artists (p. 459) Independent artists who work on individual assignments for an agency or advertiser.

Free-standing insert advertisements (p. 340) Preprinted advertisements that are placed loosely within the newspaper.

Frequency (p. 311) The number of times an audience has an opportunity to be exposed to a media vehicle or vehicles in a specified time span; also, (p. 384). The number of radio waves produced by a transmitter in 1 second.

Function plans (p. 239) Plans that relate to specific business functions.

Game (p. 600) A type of sweepstakes that requires the player to return to play several times.

Global brand (p. 740) A brand that has the same name, same design, and same creative strategy everywhere in the world.

Global perspective (p. 740) A corporate philosophy that directs products and advertising toward a worldwide rather than a local or regional market.

Gross impressions (p. 309) The sum of the audiences of all the media vehicles used within a designated time span.

Gross rating points (GRP) (p. 310) The sum of the total exposure potential of a series of media vehicles expressed as a percentage of the audience population.

Gütenberg diagonal (p. 471) A visual path that flows from the upper left corner to the lower right.

Halftones (p. 477) Images with a continuous range of shades from light to dark.

Hard sell (p. 438) A rational, informational message that emphasizes a strong argument, and calls for action.

Headline (p. 460) The title of an ad; it is set in large type to get the reader's attention.

Hierarchy of effects (p. 248) A set of consumer responses that moves from the least serious, involved, or complex up through the most serious, involved, or complex.

High-involvement decision process (p. 193) Decisions that require an involved purchase process with information search and product comparison.

Holography (p. 570) A technique that produces a projected three-dimensional image.

Horizontal publications (p. 713) Publications directed to people who hold similar jobs in different companies across different industries.

Household (p. 171) All those people who occupy one living unit, whether or not they are related.

Impact (p. 424) The effect that a message has on the audience.

Indicia (p. 575) The postage label printed by a postage meter.

Industrial advertising (p. 704) Advertising directed at businesses that buy products to incorporate into other products or to facilitate the operation of their businesses.

Infomercial (p. 514) A long commercial that provides extensive product information.

Informational advertising (p. 276) Advertising that presents a large amount of information about the product.

In-house agency (p. 20) An advertising department on the advertiser's staff that handles most, if not all, of the functions of an outside agency.

In-market tests (p. 693) Tests that measure the effectiveness of advertisements by measuring actual sales results in the marketplace.

In register (p. 458) A precise matching of colors in images.

Integrated marketing communications (p. 37) The concept or philosophy of marketing that stresses bringing together all the variables of the marketing mix, all the media, all the actions with which a company reaches its publics, and integrating the company's strategy and programs.

Interconnects (p. 366) A special cable technology that allows local advertisers to run their commercials in small geographical areas through the interconnection of a number of cable systems.

Interior transit advertising (p. 574) Advertising on posters that are mounted inside vehicles such as buses, subway cars, and taxis.

Interlock (p. 506) A version of the commercial with the audio and video timed together, although the two are still recorded separately.

International advertising (p. 735) Advertising designed to promote the same product in different countries and cultures.

International brand (p. 735) A brand or product that is available in most parts of the world.

Involvement (p. 276) The intensity of the consumer's interest in a product.

Italic (p. 476) A type variation that uses letters that slant to the right.

Jingles (p. 282) Commercials with a message that is presented musically.

Justified (p. 477) A form of typeset copy in which the edges of the lines in a column of type are forced to align by adding space between words in the line.

Key frame (p. 500) A single frame of a commercial that summarizes the heart of the message.

Key visual (p. 282) A dominant image around which the commercial's message is planned.

Kinetic boards (p. 571) Outdoor advertising that uses moving elements.

Kiosks (p. 565) Multisided bulletin board structures designed for public posting of messages.

Layout (p. 467) A drawing that shows where all the elements in the ad are to be positioned.

Lecture (p. 438) Instruction delivered verbally to present knowledge and facts.

Lifestyle (p. 171) The pattern of living that reflects how people allocate their time, energy, and money.

Line art (p. 477) Art in which all elements are solid with no intermediate shades or tones.

Local brand (p. 735) A brand that is marketed in one specific country.

Logo (p. 283) Logotype; a distinctive mark that identifies the product, company, or brand.

Loss leader (p. 723) Product advertised at or below cost in order to build store traffic.

Low-involvement decision process (p. 193) Decisions that require limited deliberation; sometimes purchases are even made on impulse.

Makegoods (p. 410) Compensation given by the media to advertisers in the form of additional message units that are commonly used in situations involving production errors by the media and preemption of the advertiser's programming.

Market (p. 90) An area of the country, a group of people, or the overall demand for a product.

Marketing (p. 87) Business activities that direct the exchange of goods and services between producers and consumers.

Marketing plan (p. 241) Document that proposes strategies for employing the various elements of the marketing mix to achieve marketing objectives.

Marketing research (p. 210) Research that investigates all the elements of the marketing mix.

Market research (p. 210) Research that gathers information about specific markets.

Mechanicals (keylines) (p. 471) A finished pasteup, with every element perfectly positioned, that is photographed to make printing plates for offset printing.

Media (p. 21) The channels of communication used by advertisers.

Media-buying service (p. 132) A company that offers to buy media directly for advertisers and performs basically only this service.

Media planning (p. 297) A decision process leading to the use of advertising time and space to assist in the achievement of marketing objectives.

Merging (p. 530) The process of combining two or more lists of prospects.

Mixing (p. 513) Combining different tracks of music, voices, and sound effects to create the final ad.

Motive (p. 156) An unobservable inner force that stimulates and compels a behavioral response.

Needs (p. 187) Basic forces that motivate you to do or to want something.

Network radio (p. 385) A group of local affiliates providing simultaneous programming via connection to one or more of the national networks through AT&T telephone wires.

Newsprint (p. 457) An inexpensive, tough paper with a rough surface, used for printing newspapers.

News release (p. 633) Primary medium used to deliver public relations messages to the media.

Noncommercial advertising (p. 636) Advertising that is sponsored by an organization to promote a cause rather than to maximize profits.

Nontraditional delivery (p. 349) Delivery of magazines to readers through such methods as door hangers or newspapers.

Norms (p. 167) Simple rules for behavior that are established by cultures.

Open pricing (p. 407) A method of media pricing in which prices are negotiated on a contract-by-contract basis for each unit of media space or time.

Optical center (p. 473) A point slightly above the mathematical center of a page.

Original (p. 423) One of a kind; unusual and unexpected.

Out-of-home advertising (p. 563) Advertising that embraces all advertising that is displayed outside the home—from billboards, to blimps, to in-store aisle displays.

Participations (p. 372) An arrangement in which a television advertiser buys commercial time from a network.

Perceived value (p. 280) The value that a customer or buyer intrinsically or subjectively attaches to a brand or service. It is the image or personality that differentiates one product from a virtually identical competitor.

Percent-of-sales method (p. 256) A technique for computing the budget level that is based on the relationship between cost of advertising and total sales.

Perception (p. 182) The process by which we receive information through our five senses and acknowledge and assign meaning to this information.

Perceptual map (p. 253) A map that shows where consumers locate various products in the category in terms of several important features.

Personality (p. 188) Relatively long-lasting personal qualities that allow us to cope with and respond to the world around us.

Persuasion test (p. 683) A test that evaluates the effectiveness of an advertisement by measuring whether the ad affects consumers' intentions to buy a specific brand.

Photoboard (p. 502) A type of rough commercial, similar to an animatic except that the frames are actual photos instead of sketches.

Physiological tests (p. 688) Tests that measure emotional reactions to advertisements by monitoring reactions such as pupil dilation and heart rate.

Pica (p. 477) A unit of type measurement used to measure width and depth of columns; there are 12 points in a pica and 6 picas in an inch.

Point (p. 476) A unit used to measure the height of type; there are 72 points in an inch.

Point-of-purchase display (P-O-P) (p. 607) A display designed by the manufacturer and distributed to retailers in order to promote a particular brand or line of products.

Political risks (p. 736) Risks due to uncertainty in a nation's political climate. While political risk is outside the area of marketing and advertising its effects can seriously and drastically alter company plans.

Population (p. 224) Everyone included in a designated group.

Positioning (p. 253) The way in which a product is perceived in the marketplace by consumers.

Preferred positions (p. 407) Sections or pages of magazine and newspaper issues that are in high demand by advertisers because they have a special appeal to the target audience.

Premium (p. 601) A tangible reward received for performing a particular act, such as purchasing a product or visiting the point of purchase.

Press conference (p. 633) A public gathering of media people for the purpose of establishing a company's position or making a statement.

Price deal (p. 597) A temporary reduction in the price of a product.

Primary research (p. 213) Information that is collected from original sources.

Process colors (p. 479) Four basic inks—magenta, cyan, yellow, and black—that are mixed to produce a full range of colors found in four-color printing.

Process evaluation (p. 635) Measuring the effectiveness of media and nonmedia efforts to get the desired message out to the target audience.

Producer (p. 502) The person who supervises and coordinates all of the elements that go into the creation of a television commercial.

Professional advertising (p. 705) Advertising directed at people such as lawyers, doctors, and accountants.

Profile (p. 252) A composite description of a target audience employing personality and lifestyle characteristics.

Program preemptions (p. 410) Interruptions in local or network programming caused by special events.

Promotion (p. 105) That element in the marketing mix that communicates the key marketing messages to target audiences. Also called marketing communication.

Promotion mix (p. 105) The combination of personal selling, advertising, sales promotion, and public relations to produce a coordinated message structure.

Psychographics (p. 182) All the psychological variables that combine to shape our inner selves, including activities, interests, opinions, needs, values, attitudes, personality traits, decision processes, and buying behavior.

Publicity (p. 621) Cost-free public relations that relates messages through gatekeepers.

Public opinion (p. 625) People's beliefs, based on their conceptions or evaluations of something rather than on fact.

Public relations (p. 619) A management function enabling organizations to achieve effective relationships with their various audiences through an understanding of audience opinions, attitudes, and values.

Publics (p. 624) Those groups or individuals who are involved with an organization, including customers, employees, competitors, and government regulators.

Public service announcement (PSA) (p. 628) A type of public relations advertising that deals with public welfare issues and is typically run free of charge.

Puffery (p. 49) Advertising or other sales representation that praises the item to be sold using subjective opinions, superlatives, and similar mechanisms that are not based on specific fact.

Pulsing (p. 308) An advertising scheduling pattern in which time and space are scheduled on a continuous but uneven basis, lower levels are followed by bursts or peak periods of intensified activity.

Purging (p. 530) The process of deleting repeated names when two or more lists are combined.

Push money (p. 610) (*spiffs*) A monetary bonus paid to a salesperson based on units sold over a period of time.

Qualitative data (p. 217) Research that seeks to understand how and why people think and behave as they do.

Quantitative data (p. 217) Research that uses statistics to describe consumers.

Reach (p. 310) The percentage of different homes or people exposed to a media vehicle or vehicles at least once during a specific period of time. It is the percentage of unduplicated audience.

Reason why (p. 261) A statement that explains why the feature will benefit the user.

Recall (p. 282) The ability to remember specific information content.

Recall test (p. 676) A test that evaluates the memorability of an advertisement by contacting members of the advertisement's audience and asking them what they remember about it.

Recognition (p. 282) An ability to remember having seen something before.

Recognition test (p. 680) A test that evaluates the memorability of an advertisement by contacting members of the audience, showing them the ad, and asking if they remember it.

Reference group (p. 170) A group of people that a person uses as a guide for behavior in specific situations.

Refund (p. 601) An offer by the marketer to return a certain amount of money to the consumer who purchases the product.

Regional brand (p. 735) A brand that is available throughout a regional trading bloc.

Release prints (p. 506) Duplicate copies of a commercial that are ready for distribution.

Relevance (p. 422) That quality of an advertising message that makes it important to the audience.

Reliability (p. 675) A characteristic that describes a test that yields essentially the same results when the same advertisement is tested time after time.

Retail advertising (p. 717) A type of advertising used by local merchants who sell directly to consumers.

Rough cut (p. 506) A preliminary rough edited version of the commercial.

Rushes (p. 504) Rough versions of the commercial assembled from unedited footage.

Sales promotion (p. 587) Those marketing activities that add value to the product for a limited period of time to stimulate consumer purchasing and dealer effectiveness.

Sample (p. 224) A selection of people who are identified as representative of the larger population.

Sampling (p. 604) An offer that allows the customer to use or experience the product or service free of charge or for a very small fee.

Sans serif (p. 476) A typeface that does not have the serif detail.

Script (p. 500) A written version of a radio or television commercial.

Secondary research (p. 212) Information that has been compiled and published.

Selective distortion (p. 183) The interpretation of information in a way that is consistent with the person's existing opinions.

Selective exposure (p. 183) The ability to process only certain information and avoid other stimuli.

Selective perception (p. 183) The process of screening out information that does not interest us and retaining information that does.

Selective retention (p. 183) The process of remembering only a small portion of what a person is exposed to.

Selling premises (p. 259) The sales logic behind an advertising message.

Semicomp (p. 470) A layout drawn to size that depicts the art and display type; body copy is simply ruled in.

Serif (p. 476) A typeface with a finishing stroke on the main strokes of the letters.

Set (p. 496) A constructed setting where the action in a commercial takes place.

Share of voice (p. 305) The percentage of advertising messages in a medium by one brand among all messages for that product or service.

Signals (p. 384) A series of electrical impulses that compose radio and television broadcasting.

Signature (p. 283) The name of the company or product written in a distinctive type style.

Simulated test market (p. 693) Research procedure in which respondents are exposed to advertisements and then permitted to shop for the advertised products in an artificial environment where records are kept of their purchases.

Slice of life (p. 440) A problem-solution message built around some common, everyday situation.

Slogans (p. 282) Frequently repeated phrases that provide continuity to an advertising campaign.

Social class (p. 169) A way to categorize people on the basis of their values, attitudes, lifestyles, and behavior.

Societal marketing concept (p. 78) A concept that requires balancing the company, consumer, and public interest.

Soft sell (p. 438) An emotional message that uses mood, ambiguity, and suspense to create a response based on feelings and attitudes.

Sound effects (SFX) (p. 511) Lifelike imitations of sounds.

Spectaculars (p. 570) Billboards with unusual lighting effects.

Sponsorship (p. 372) An arrangement in which the advertiser produces both a television program and the accompanying commercials.

Spot announcements (p. 373) Ads shown during the breaks between programs.

Spot radio advertising (p. 387) A form of advertising in which an ad is placed with an individual station rather than through a network.

Stereotyping (p. 52) Presenting a group of people in an unvarying pattern that lacks individuality and often reflects popular misconceptions.

Stop motion (p. 498) A technique in which inanimate objects are filmed one frame at a time, creating the illusion of movement.

Storyboard (p. 501) A series of frames sketched to illustrate how the story line will develop.

Strategy formulation (p. 241) Specifies how the business expects to reach stated objectives.

Subliminal message (p. 61) A message transmitted below the threshold of normal perception so that the receiver is not consciously aware of having viewed it.

Superimpose (p. 283) A television technique where one image is added to another that is already on the screen.

Supplements (p. 340) Syndicated or local full-color advertising inserts that appear in newspapers throughout the week.

Survey research (p. 224) Research using structured interview forms that ask large numbers of people exactly the same questions.

Sweepstakes (p. 600) Sales promotion activities that require participants to submit their names to be included in a drawing or other type of chance selection.

SWOT analysis (p. 647) A study of the Strengths, Weaknesses, Opportunities, and Threats that will impact upon the successful promotion of the product, the service, or the company.

Synchronize (p. 504) Matching the audio to the video in a commercial.

Syndication (p. 369) Television or radio shows that are reruns or original programs purchased by local stations to fill in during open hours.

Tabloid (p. 332) A newspaper with a page size five to six columns wide and 14 inches deep.

Taglines (p. 282) Clever phrases used at the end of an advertisement to summarize the ad's message.

Talent (p. 496) People who appear in television commercials.

Target audience (p. 249) People who can be reached with a certain advertising medium and a particular message.

Task-objective method (p. 256) A budgeting method that builds a budget by asking what it will cost to achieve the stated objectives.

Tear sheet (p. 719) The pages from a newspaper on which an ad appears.

Telemarketing (p. 547) A type of marketing that uses the telephone to make a personal sales contact.

Television market (p. 379) An unduplicated geographical area to which a county is assigned on the basis of the highest share of the viewing of television stations.

Testimonial (p. 440) An advertising format in which a spokesperson describes a positive personal experience with the product.

Thumbnail sketches (p. 468) Small preliminary sketches of various layout ideas.

Tip-ins (p. 483) Preprinted ads that are provided by the advertiser to be glued into the binding of a magazine.

Trade advertising (p. 705) Advertising used to influence resellers, wholesalers, and retailers.

Trade deals (p. 610) An arrangement in which the retailer agrees to give the manufacturer's product a special promotional effort in return for product discounts, goods, or cash.

Trademark (p. 285) Sign or design, often with distinctive lettering, that symbolizes the brand.

Traditional delivery (p. 349) Delivery of magazines to readers through newsstands or home delivery.

Trailers (p. 574) Advertisements that precede the feature film in a movie theater.

Transformation advertising (p. 286) Image advertising that changes the experience of buying and using a product.

Unique selling proposition (p. 262) A benefit statement about a feature that is both unique to the product and important to the user.

Validity (p. 678) The ability of a test to measure what it is intended to measure.

Value and Lifestyle Systems (VALS) (p. 190) Classification systems that categorize people by values for the purpose of predicting effective advertising strategies.

Values (p. 167) The source for norms, which are not tied to specific objects or behaviors.

Vampire creativity (p. 282) An advertising problem in which an ad is so creative or entertaining that it overwhelms the product.

Vendors (p. 21) Institutions that provide certain expertise that advertisers and agencies cannot perform.

Verbatims (p. 224) Spontaneous comments by people who are being surveyed.

Vernacular (p. 509) Language that reflects the speech patterns of a particular group of people.

Vertical publications (p. 713) Publications directed to people who hold different positions in the same industries.

Videotape (p. 498) A type of recording medium that electronically records sound and images simultaneously.

Voice-over (p. 496) A technique used in commercials in which an off-camera announcer talks about the on-camera scene.

Weighted audience values (p. 405) Numerical values assigned to different audience characteristics that help advertisers assign priorities when devising media plans.

J. Walter Thompson agency (JWT), 28–29, 250–51, 756, 759

for children, 326
collectibles advertised in, 350
consumer, 347–48, 403
and CPM, 314
disadvantages of, 353–55
measuring readership of, 350–51
readers of, 349
for retail advertising, 727
structure of, 346–49
total advertising spending for, 328–29
Magnuson-Moss Warranty/FTC
    Improvement Act (1975), 68, 77
Maidenform ad campaign, 53–55
Mailing lists, 541–42
    and databases, 530–31
    merging and purging of, 530, 542
    and privacy, 532
Mail order catalogs, as interactive media,
    415
Mail Preference Service (MPS), Direct
    Marketing Association, 532
Mail premiums, 603
Makegoods, 410
Male image, 162
Malone, John, 364
Management, in advertising agency, 125–26
Management Horizons, 721
Management supervisor, 137
Manning, Shelli, 622–23
Manufacturers, as advertisers, 17
Map of the marketplace, 253
Map recall method, 572
Margeotes, Fertitta & Weise, 149
Marineland, 570–71
Mark, Marky, 162
Market(s), 90
    business-to-business (industrial), 90
    consumer, 90
    as homogeneous vs. heterogeneous, 244
    institutional, 92
    reseller, 92
Market Analysis and Information Database,
    Inc., 212
Market-analysis model, in international
    strategic plan, 749–52
Market coverage, 103
Market economy, and Eastern Europe,
    744–45, 747
Marketing, 86–90
    4Ps of, 93–94, 95
        place, 100–101, 103
        pricing, 103–5
        product, 94–100
        promotion, 105–7
    and interactive media, 414–16
    international, 734–40
    niche, 38
    sales promotion in, 592–93
    for state of Oklahoma, 291
Marketing budget, advertising in, 255–56
Marketing communication, 14, 89, 94, 105
    and budget, 256

integrated, 37–38, 117–22, 291, 659
    in Orlando advertising campaign, 657–69
Marketing concept, 92–93
Marketing mix, 14, 94
    and advertising, 107–8
Marketing objective, 219–20, 242
    for milk, 223
Marketing plan, 87, 88, 89, 239, 241–45
Marketing research, 210
    See also Research
Marketing Resources of America, 127
Marketing role of advertising, 14
Marketing services, 140–42
Marketing sources, 298–99
Marketing strategies, 244
Market research, 210
    career opportunities in, 780–82
    See also Research
Market segment, 243
Market segmentation, 164–65, 166
    by Copper Mountain Resort, 230–31
    in mailing list, 541–42
    See also Consumer behavior; Targeting
        and target audience
Marlboro cigarettes:
    billboard for, 569, 570
    as global, 742
    and international advertising, 756, 758
    and women, 253
Marlboro Man, 8, 9, 35, 285, 436
Mars, Inc., 748
Mary Kay Cosmetics, 720
M*A*S*H, finale of, 586
Maslow, Abraham, 187
Massachusetts Institute of Technology,
    Media Laboratory at, 344
Mass marketing, age of, 25
Master Card, 292–93, 490
Mat, 481–82
Mat service, 458
Mature market, sales promotion for, 590,
    591
MaxiMarketing, 530
Maxwell House Division of General Foods,
    216
Maybelline, 413, 469
Mayflower Moving trucks, 572
Mayner, John, 32–33
Maytag washing machines, 286
Mazda Motors of America, Inc., 710
MCA/Universal, 586
MCI Communications, 538
Meals:
    trends in, 201
    See also Foods
Measurement:
    of audience, 309–10
        magazine, 350–51
        newspaper, 336–38
        out-of-home viewing, 573
        radio, 387–88
        television, 374–77

of direct-market response, 523, 549, 687
of public opinion, 624–25
of public relations success, 640
of social trends, 199, 200
Mechanicals, 471
Media, 21
    for direct-response advertising, 537–47
    gate-keepers in, 621
    innovative, 575–76
    interactive, 516–17 (see also Interactive
        media)
    for international campaigns, 762, 764,
        765
    in Orlando campaign, 659–61
    and retail advertising, 725–28
Media, broadcast, See Broadcast media;
    Radio; Television
Media, print, See Magazines; Newspapers;
    Print media
Media brokers, 25
Media buyer, 141
Media buying, 140–42, 397–99
    maintaining plan performance, 410–11
    and media opportunities, 399–401
    and media pricing, 401–3
    media vehicle selection and negotiation,
        403–5, 407–8
Media-buying services, 132–33
    international, 764
Media characteristics, 300
Media clutter, 316
    See also Clutter
Media content:
    and media buying, 399
    product compatibility of, 315
    and TV future, 514
Media department, 140–42
    career opportunities in, 142, 778–80
Media Drop In Productions, 516
Medialink, 618
Mediamark Research, Inc. (MRI), 213, 351
Media plan, 317–20
    monitoring performance against, 410–11
Media planners, 141
    and creative team, 296
    and media buying, 397
Media planning, 140–42, 297
    aperture concept, 297, 317–18
    information sources and analysis,
        298–300
    media selection, 309–16
    setting objectives, 300–305
    staging media plan, 317–20
    strategy development, 305–9
Media price formats (rate cards), 402–3
Media prices, 401–3
    negotiating of, 398, 407
Media relations, in Orlando campaign, 665
Media sources, 299–300
Media vehicle:
    monitoring performance of, 399
    negotiating over, 407

Media vehicle: *(Cont.)*
    selection of, 398, 403–5
Medical agencies, 129
Medicus Intercom, 129
Member relations, and Orlando advertising
    campaign, 662
Memory, and locking power, 281–82
Memory tests, 676
    recall, 676–80
    recognition, 680–83
Mennen Skin Bracer, 491
Mental imagery, of radio, 388–89
Meranus, Arthur, 515
Mercedes-Benz, 742
Merck, 466
Meredith Corporation, 408
Mergers, in cable industry, 364
Merging of databases, 530
Message characteristics, 299
Message design, 436
    hard and soft sell, 437–38
    lectures and drama, 438–39
    for movie advertising, 575
    for outdoor advertisements, 567–69
    for transit advertising, 574
    See also Design
Message development research, 221–23
Message format, for direct mail, 539
Message strategies, 259, 435–39
    for radio, 508–9
    for television, 492–95
Message tone, 442
Metaphors, 429–30
Michelob, 54
Michioka, Takashi, 754
Microsoft, 241
Midwest Express Airlines, 253, 255, 260
"Mikey" commercial (Life cereal), 7, 683
Miller, Pepper, 181
Miller beer, and women, 253
Miller Lite beer, 37, 244, 494
Mills, Charles George, 615
Minitel, 562
Minority agencies, 129
Minority groups:
    in advertisements, 55–56
    as consumers, 179–80
    cosmetics for minority women, 413
    and Denny's public-relations campaign,
        622
    targeting of, 129–30
Mirimax Films, 301
Missed closings, 410–11
Mitchum, Robert, 12
Mixer, 504
Mixing, 513
Modern advertising, 27–37
Modern Maturity magazine, 591
Mondale, Walter, 491
Montgomery Ward, 721
Montgomery Ward catalog, 524, 542
Mood, media-created, 315

Mood commercials, 691
Moore, Charlotte, 456
Moore, Mary, 456
Moore, Timothy, 64
Morris, Eugene, 181
Morris the Cat, 35
Morrow, Rob, 490
Moss, Kate, 162, 487
Mothers Against Drunk Driving (MADD),
    13, 17, 566
Motivation, 186–87
Motive, 186
Movie advertising, 575–76
Movies, targeting audiences for, 301
Mr. Goodwrench, 285–86
MRI service, 351
MTV, 221, 400, 442, 516, 547, 762
Multiculturalism, and cosmetic companies,
    413
Multipoint distribution systems (MDS), 366
Murdoch, Rupert, 365
Music:
    in radio commercials, 390, 508, 510–11
    in television commercials, 691
Mustang, 471, 472

N

Namelab, 285
Names, research into, 285
NAPA auto parts, 438
Narrative style, 463
NASA, 554
National Advertising Agency Network, 764
National Advertising Bureau (NAB), 338
National Advertising Division (NAD),
    Council of Better Business Bureaus,
    Inc., 59, 79–80
National Advertising Review Board (NARB),
    80
National Advertising Review Council, 79
National Association of Attorneys General,
    67
National Basketball Association, 629
National Broadcasting Company (NBC), 33,
    361, 371, 376, 586, 629
National consumer advertising, 12–13
National Dairy Board, 317, 318, 319, 320
National display advertising, 340
National Geographic, children's version of,
    326
Nationalization of exported goods, 738
National Soft Drink Association, 212
Natural Nectar Corporation, 591
Nature Valley Granola Bars and Bites, 519
Navy fragrance by Cover Girl, 697
NBC (National Broadcasting Company), 33,
    361, 371, 376, 586, 629
Needham Harper Worldwide, 150
Need recognition, 194
Needs, 186-88, 189

and timing of radio ad, 508
Negative option, 524
Negotiation, by media buyer, 398, 407–8
Nelson, Bruce, 393
Nelson, Willie, 516
Nestlé Foods Corporation, 605–6, 740, 748,
    754, 759
Netolicky, Marie, 409
Network radio, 383–85
Network scheduling, 361
Network television:
    decreased viewing share of, 590
    unwired, 361
    wired, 361
Neutrogena Shampoo, 261
New England Patriots, and allegations by
    female reporter, 633–34
New-product categories, and sales promo-
    tion, 590
Newspapers, 330
    advantages of, 341–42
    advertising in, 338–41, 457–59
        for large-size women's clothing, 393
    and audiotext, 345
    and children, 326
    disadvantages of, 342–44
    future of, 344
    measuring audience of, 336–38
    readers of, 335–36
    for retail advertising, 726–27
    structure, 330–35
    total advertising spending for, 328–29
Newsprint, 457
News release, 633, 634
Newsweek, 354
Newsweek Interactive, 527
New York Homeless Coalition, 437
New York Times, The, 344
Niche marketing, 38
Nickelodeon, 629
Nickelodeon magazine, 326
Nielsen, A. C., 30
Nielsen indexes, 375
    See also A.C. Nielsen Company
Nielsen Market Research, 573
Nielsen Media Research, 376
Nike, Inc.:
    vs. adidas, 2
    and African-American community, 130
    and benefits of exercise, 124
    classic ads from, 6
    "Hubble Telescope" radio ad by, 508
    image advertising of, 8
    Michael Jordan for, 438
    and product life cycle, 97
    stay-in-school campaign of, 629
    women's campaign by, 450, 456, 459,
        460, 461, 462, 464
Nintendo, 530–31
Nissan Motor Corporation, 154, 630, 742
Noble & Asociados, 129
Noble & Associates, 731

Citizens Consumer Council, 65
Virtual reality, 416
Visa card, 292–93
Vista Marketing, 687
Visualization, 470
Visualization skills, 431
Visual path, 471
Visuals, 445
  key, 282
  new importance of, 457
  and radio, 389–90, 507
Vitalizer Project, Quadri Agency, 734
Voice, 510
Voice-over, 496
Voice Powered Technology, 515
Volkswagen, 541, 719
Volvo, 372, 439
Von Furstenberg, Diane, 551

Wacc Group PLC, 764–65
Wagner, Anita, 393
Walker, Kent, 366
Wallas, Graham, 427
Wall Street Journal, The, 330, 345, 463, 764
Wal-Mart Stores, 100, 720, 721, 727
Walt Disney Company, 285, 575
Walt Disney World, 646, 653, 655-56
Walthall, David, 702
Walton, Sam, 721
Wanamaker, John, 25-26
War Advertising Council (WAC), 31
Warner Bros., 301
Warner-Lambert Co., 238
Warner-Lambert v. FTC, 74–76
Warranties, in "Advertising Principles," 48
Washington Post, 345
Waste coverage, 381
Waterman Pen, 758
Weathashade division of the Gale Group, 214–16

Weatherup, Craig, 420, 429, 618, 643
"We" copy, 448
Weiden & Kennedy agency, 124, 450, 456
Weighted audience values, 405
Weisinberger, Charlotte, 341
Wendy's, 56, 491, 494
Western International Media Corporation, 133
Westwood One, 384
Wheeler-Lea Amendment (1938), 30, 66, 68
White, Gordon, 432
White, Hooper, 495
White, Vanna, 372
White space, 472
Wilde, Don, 510
Wilke, Jerry G., 86
Wilkinson, 111
Williams, John, 687, 689
Willkie, Wendell, 734
Wired network television, 361
Women:
  in advertisements, 52–55
  and advertising agencies, 131–32
  advertising copy for, 456
  of color, 413
  divorced with children, 177
  as foreign car owners, 679
  large-size clothing for, 393
  magazines for, 353
  Marlboro and Miller for, 253
  Nike ads for, 460, 464
  and products for men, 162
  and razor blades, 176
  young mothers, 222
Wood, Kimba, 76
Woolworth, F. W., 721
Work plan, 435
World War II, 31, 34
WPP Group, 17, 768
Wrangler, 265, 516
Wrigley, William, Jr., 238
Wrigley's Chewing Gum, 236, 238, 239

analogy in ad of, 426, 430
as global, 758, 767, 768
problem-solution message of, 440
Wunderman, Ricotta & Kline, 687
Wyden, Ron, 69
Wyeth-Ayerst Labs, 466

Xerox Corporation:
  "Brother Dominic" ads for, 36, 37
  as global, 742
  Leonardo da Vinci ad of, 712
  slogan of, 285

Yankelovich, Daniel, 625–26
Yeager, Chuck, 188, 190, 438
Yellow Pages advertising, 13, 555–61, 728
"You" copy, 447–48
Young, James Webb, 426
Young, John Orr, 30
Young & Rubicam, 17, 30, 37
  creative viewpoint of, 138, 139
  and Dr. Pepper, 771, 772
  and DYR, 754
  and Idaho Potatoes ad, 254
  and IMC, 119
  originality as aim of, 272
  research department of, 216
  in Russia, 745
  and Sony, 737

Zapping, 268, 514, 515
Zenith Media Worldwide, 754
ZIP edition, 349
Zipping, 268
Zwief, Jennifer, 342–43